D0685871

CANADIAN ORGANIZATIONAL BEHAVIOUR

SIXTH EDITION

Steven L. McShane
University of Western Australia

McGraw-Hill Ryerson

Toronto Montreal Boston Burr Ridge, IL Dubuque, IA Madison, WI New York
San Francisco St. Louis Bangkok Bogotá Caracas Kuala Lumpur Lisbon London
Madrid Mexico City Milan New Delhi Santiago Seoul Singapore Sydney Taipei

The McGraw·Hill Companies

 McGraw-Hill
Ryerson

CANADIAN ORGANIZATIONAL BEHAVIOUR
Sixth Edition

ISBN: 0-07-087694-0

1 2 3 4 5 6 7 8 9 10   QPD   0 9 8 7 6

Publisher: Nicole Lukach
Sponsoring Editor: Kim Brewster
Developmental Editor: Lori McLellan
Photo Research: Karen Becker
Manager, Editorial Services: Kelly Dickson
Senior Supervising Editor: Margaret Henderson
Copy Editor: Erin Moore
Senior Production Coordinator: Paula Brown
Composition: Heather Brunton/ArtPlus Limited
Cover Design: Greg Devitt
Cover Image: Daryl Benson/Masterfile
Printer: Quebecor Printing Dubuque

Library and Archives Canada Cataloguing in Publication

McShane, Steven Lattimore
    Canadian organizational behaviour / Steven L. McShane. — 6th ed.

Includes bibliographical references and index.
ISBN 0-07-087694-0

    1. Organizational behavior—Canada.   I. Title.

HD58.7.M32 2006   658.3   C2005-907782-4

Dedicated with love and devotion to Donna,
and to our wonderful daughters,
Bryton and Madison

Steven L. McShane

Steven L. McShane is Professor of Management in the Graduate School of Management at the University of Western Australia (UWA). He is also an Honourary Professor at Universiti Tunku Abdul Rahman (UTAR) in Malaysia. Steve previously taught in the business faculties at Simon Fraser University and Queen's University in Canada. He is a past president of the Administrative Sciences Association of Canada.

Steve earned his PhD from Michigan State University, a Master of Industrial Relations from the University of Toronto, and an undergraduate degree from Queen's University in Kingston. He receives high teaching ratings from MBA and doctoral students in Perth, Australia, Singapore, and other cities where UWA offers its programs. Steve is also a popular visiting speaker, having given more than 40 talks over the past two years to faculty and students at universities around the world.

Along with writing *Canadian Organizational Behaviour*, Steve and Professor Mary Anne Von Glinow co-author *Organizational Behavior: Emerging Realities for the Workplace Revolution*, Third Edition (2005), McGraw-Hill's highly successful American adaptation of this text, as well as their brief edition, *Organizational Behavior: Essentials* (2006). Steve is also a co-author with Professor Tony Travaglione of *Organisational Behaviour on the Pacific Rim, Enhanced Edition* (2005), which, in its first three years, matched the popularity of the incumbent best-selling OB book in Australia and New Zealand. Steve has published several dozen articles and conference papers on the socialization of new employees, gender bias in job evaluation, wrongful dismissal, media bias in business magazines, and other diverse issues.

Along with teaching and writing, Steve enjoys spending his leisure time swimming, body board surfing, canoeing, skiing, and travelling with his wife and two daughters.

BRIEF CONTENTS

CONTENTS

CHAPTER SEVEN

Work-Related Stress and Stress Management   186

PART THREE

Team Processes

CHAPTER EIGHT

Decision Making and Creativity   214

CHAPTER NINE

Foundations of Team Dynamics   244

CHAPTER TEN

Developing High-Performance Teams   270

CHAPTER THIRTEEN

Conflict and Negotiation in the Workplace   356

CHAPTER FOURTEEN

Leadership in Organizational Settings   382

Welcome to a new era of organizational behaviour! Virtual teams are replacing committees. Values and self-leadership are replacing command-and-control supervision. Knowledge is replacing infrastructure. Companies are looking for employees with emotional intelligence, not just technical smarts. Globalization has become the mantra of corporate survival. Co-workers aren't down the hall; they're at the other end of an Internet connection located somewhere else on the planet.

Canadian Organizational Behaviour, Sixth Edition is written in the context of these emerging workplace realities. This edition explains how emotions guide employee motivation, attitudes, and decisions; how values have become the new resource to shape workplace behaviour; how a person's social identity relates to team dynamics, stereotyping, and organizational culture; and how appreciative inquiry has become one of the most important strategies in organizational change. This book also presents the new reality that organizational behaviour is not just for managers; it is relevant and useful to anyone who works in and around organizations.

CANADIAN AND GLOBAL ORIENTATION

Canadian Organizational Behaviour, Sixth Edition is written by a Canadian for Canadians. It includes several Canadian cases, makes solid use of Canadian scholarship, and is filled with Canadian examples of organizational behaviour in practice. For example, you will read about team dynamics at Lighthouse Publishing in Bridgewater, Nova Scotia; the foundations of corporate culture at Cirque du Soleil in Montreal; rewards, empowerment, and other applied performance practices at WestJet in Calgary; and the creative dynamics of employees at Vancouver-based game developer Radical Entertainment.

Love it or hate it, globalization is part of the emerging reality of organizations. So, along with its Canadian focus, *Canadian Organizational Behaviour*, Sixth Edition introduces globalization in the opening chapter and highlights global issues throughout the book. To further emphasize the emerging reality of globalization, every chapter has one or more *GLOBAL Connections*, a highlighted feature that links OB concepts to organizational incidents in diverse countries. For example, *GLOBAL Connections* features describe how young people in Japan are dramatically altering the traditional employment relationship by becoming "freeters," how a German advertising and Web design firm is gaining attention by adopting a no-nonsense "back to work" corporate culture, how employees in Argentina are saving their jobs by taking over the businesses abandoned by their employers, and how executives are learning to lead the "ubuntu" way in Africa.

LINKING THEORY WITH REALITY

Every chapter of *Canadian Organizational Behaviour*, Sixth Edition, is filled with real-life examples to make OB concepts more meaningful and reflect the relevance and excitement of this field. For example, you will read how Vancouver City Savings Credit Union has become one of Canada's most successful financial institutions by ensuring that its staff experience plenty of positive emotions every day; how Toronto-based Celestica Inc. remains competitive through high-performance teams and lean manufacturing practices; how W. L. Gore & Associates remains nimble through an organizational structure that has no bosses; and how corporate leaders are turning to blogs to communicate more personally with employees and customers.

These real-life stories appear in many forms. Every chapter of *Canadian Organizational Behaviour*, Sixth Edition is filled with photo captions and in-text anecdotes about work life in this new millennium. Each chapter also includes *Connections*, a special feature that "connects" OB concepts with real organizational incidents. Case studies in each chapter and video case studies related to various topics in this book also connect OB concepts to the emerging workplace realities. These stories provide representation across Canada and around the planet. Moreover, they cover a wide range of industries—from software to government—and from small businesses to the *Financial Post 500*.

ORGANIZATIONAL BEHAVIOUR KNOWLEDGE FOR EVERYONE

Another distinctive feature of *Canadian Organizational Behaviour*, Sixth Edition is that it is written for everyone in organizations, not just "managers." The philosophy of this book is that everyone who works in and around organizations needs to understand and make use of organizational behaviour knowledge. The new reality is that people throughout the organization—systems analysts, production employees, accounting professionals—are assuming more responsibilities as companies remove layers of management and give the rest of us more autonomy over our work. This book helps everyone make sense of organizational behaviour, and provides the tools to work more effectively in the workplace.

CONTEMPORARY THEORY FOUNDATION

Canadian Organizational Behaviour, Sixth Edition has a solid foundation of contemporary and classic research and writing. You can see this in the references. Each chapter is based on dozens of articles, books, and other sources. The most recent literature receives thorough coverage, resulting in what we believe is the most up-to-date organizational behaviour textbook available. These references also reveal that we reach out to information systems, marketing, and other disciplines for new ideas. At the same time, this textbook is written for students, not the scholars whose work is cited. So, while this book provides new knowledge and its practical implications, you won't find detailed summaries of specific research studies. Also, this textbook rarely names specific researchers and their university affiliations; instead, it focuses on organizational behaviour knowledge rather than "who's who" in the field.

Canadian Organizational Behaviour was the first textbook to discuss workplace emotions, social identity theory, appreciative inquiry, virtual teams, future search events, Schwartz's values model, the employee-customer-profit chain model, learning orientation, workaholism, and several other groundbreaking topics. This edition is particularly innovative and contemporary with the latest knowledge on four-drive theory, resilience, communication blogs and wikis, separating socio-emotional conflict from constructive conflict, Goleman's emotional intelligence model, and the automaticity and emotionality of the perceptual process.

CONTINUOUS DEVELOPMENT

Canadian Organizational Behaviour is not a "Canadianized" adaptation of an American book. Although I also co-author *Organizational Behavior* in the United States and internationally (now in its successful third edition) and *Organisational Behaviour on the Pacific Rim* (entering its second edition), all three books update each other in a virtuous cycle of continuous development. *Canadian Organizational Behaviour*, Sixth Edition updates information from the third U.S. edition, and the next Pacific Rim edition will update this book.

This is apparently the only business textbook anywhere that practices continuous development because it is the only book where the lead author actively writes in all three regions. This global approach to textbook development ensures that *Canadian Organizational Behaviour* offers Canadians the latest organizational behaviour concepts, issues, and examples at the time of publication. The next section highlights the results of this continuous development process.

CHANGES TO THE SIXTH EDITION

Canadian Organizational Behaviour, Sixth Edition has benefited from reviews by more than 100 organizational behaviour scholars and teachers in several countries over the past three years. Chapter structure changes in the previous (fifth) edition proved very popular with instructors here in Canada and in other countries, so this sixth edition largely keeps the previous organization of chapters. In addition to substantially updated examples throughout the book, most of the improvements to this edition are in the new topics noted below:

- *Chapter 1: Introduction to the Field of Organizational Behaviour*—This chapter includes updated knowledge on the bottom-line benefits of organizational behaviour, more emphasis on work/life balance, a revised section on virtual work, and further emphasis on values and corporate social responsibility.

- *Chapter 2: Individual Behaviour, Values, and Personality*—This chapter introduces students to the emerging concept of employee engagement, and links this concept to the MARS model of individual behaviour and performance. The section on personal values is also updated with more details about different forms of values congruence. The section on Canadian vs. American values is significantly updated.

- *Chapter 3: Perception and Learning in Organizations*—This chapter reflects current thinking about selective attention, organization, and interpretation as automatic unconscious emotional (rather than logical/mechanical) processes. It also writes about categorical thinking as part of the perceptual process, updates the highly popular concept of social identity theory, provides new details about when self-fulfilling prophecy is more (or less) likely to occur, and further highlights the importance of the learning orientation concept in experiential learning.

■ *Chapter 4: Workplace Emotions and Attitudes*—*Canadian Organizational Behaviour* was the first OB textbook (in 1998) to fully discuss workplace emotions, and this chapter continues to keep students up-to-date on how emotions drive attitudes, decisions, and behaviour in the workplace. For instance, this chapter notes how we "listen in" on our emotions when figuring out our attitudes. It also addresses the situation where emotions and cognitions (logical thinking) conflict with each other. This chapter also introduces Goleman's revised model of emotional intelligence, identifies shared values as a factor in organizational commitment, and discusses psychological contracts across cultures and generations.

■ *Chapter 5: Motivation in the Workplace*—Recognizing that needs hierarchy models lack research support, *Canadian Organizational Behaviour* was the first OB textbook (in 2004) to introduce four-drive theory as an alternative model to understand the dynamics of needs and drives in organizational settings. This chapter further explains how that model works, and identifies its implications for practice in the workplace. This chapter also explains the ongoing relevance of Maslow's ideas, and further emphasizes the role of procedural justice in organizational justice.

■ *Chapter 6: Applied Performance Practices*—This chapter has relatively minor changes. The chapter is somewhat shorter in this edition by condensing the section on rewards. The chapter also refines some of the details about scientific management and updates details about self-leadership in practice.

■ *Chapter 7: Work-Related Stress and Stress Management*—This chapter updates information about individual differences in the stress experience, including the important concept of resilience. It also provides new details about psychological harassment and work hours in Canada as a stressor.

■ *Chapter 8: Decision Making and Creativity*—This chapter is moved slightly from the previous edition and transfers information about team decision making over to Chapter 10. The chapter further compares the rational choice paradigm against human imperfections of decision making. It identifies three ways that emotions affect the evaluation of alternatives. This chapter also introduces new evidence about escalation of commitment, intuition in decision making, and how people evaluate opportunities.

■ *Chapter 9: Foundations of Team Dynamics*—This chapter more explicitly explains why organizations rely on teams. It also offers new information about Belbin's team roles model as well as team composition and diversity.

■ *Chapter 10: Developing High-Performance Teams*—This chapter further refines our knowledge of self-directed work teams and sociotechnical systems theory. It also updates the section on team trust. This chapter also incorporates writing on team decision making, including new knowledge about groupthink and brainstorming.

■ *Chapter 11: Communicating in Teams and Organizations*—Along with updating information about email and instant messaging, *Canadian Organizational Behaviour*, Sixth Edition is apparently the first to discuss the role of blogs and wikis in corporate communication. This chapter also provides new information about media richness and the organizational grapevine.

■ *Chapter 12: Power and Influence in the Workplace*—This chapter updates our knowledge of power and influence derived from social networks. It also introduces three contingencies to consider when applying various influence tactics.

■ *Chapter 13: Conflict and Negotiation in the Workplace*—This chapter offers new information about the relationship between constructive (task-related) conflict and socioemotional conflict, and identifies ways to minimize the latter while engaging in the former. It also summarizes current thinking about how to minimize conflict through communication and understanding, including talking circles.

■ *Chapter 14: Leadership in Organizational Settings*—This chapter updates information about leadership substitutes, the implicit leadership perspective, and gender differences in leadership. It also provides further evidence separating charismatic from transformational leadership.

■ *Chapter 15: Organizational Structure*—This chapter updates information about coordination mechanisms, the optimal level of decentralization, and problems with matrix structures. The section on contingencies of organizational design was also re-organized to emphasize the external environment as a central contingency.

■ *Chapter 16: Organizational Culture*—This chapter sharpens the focus on the advantages and limitations of strong organizational cultures. This chapter also adds in information about organizational socialization processes, including stages of socialization, realistic job previews, and socialization agents.

■ *Chapter 17: Organizational Change*—This chapter provides additional information about creating an urgency to change and diffusing change from a pilot project. The chapter ends the book with an outline of four strategies for personal change and development in organizations.

SUPPORTING THE LEARNING PROCESS

The changes described above refer only to the text material. *Canadian Organizational Behaviour*, Sixth Edition also has improved technology supplements, cases, videos, team exercises, and self-assessments.

Chapter Cases and Additional Cases   Every chapter includes at least one short case that challenges students to diagnose issues and apply ideas from that chapter. Several comprehensive cases also appear at the end of the book. Several cases are new to this book and are written by Canadian instructors from St. John to Vancouver. Others, such as Arctic Mining Consultants, are classics that have withstood the test of time.

Video Cases   *Canadian Organizational Behaviour*, Sixth Edition provides a full complement of video cases to liven up the classroom experience. Many are from the Canadian Broadcasting Corporation, such as VanCity's CEO returning to the frontlines, workplace loyalty, drum room team building, and scenario planning. Other excellent video programs, from sources such as PBS, NBC, and independent production companies, look at stress in Japan, workplace emotions at Pike Place Fish Market, charismatic CEOs, and business ethics at Wal-Mart.

Team Exercises and Self-Assessments   Experiential exercises and self-assessments represent an important part of the active learning process. *Canadian Organizational Behaviour*, Sixth Edition facilitates that process by offering one or two team exercises in every chapter. Many of these learning activities, such as Where in the World are We? (Chapter 8) and the Cross-Cultural Communication Game (Chapter 11), are not available in other organizational behaviour textbooks. This edition also has nearly three dozen self-assessments in the book or on the student Online Learning Centre (OLC). Self-assessments personalize the meaning of several organizational behaviour concepts, such as workaholism, self-leadership, empathy, stress, creative disposition, and tolerance of change.

Student Online Learning Centre   *Canadian Organizational Behaviour* first introduced Web-based support for students in 1995, and continues that tradition with a comprehensive and user-friendly Online Learning Centre. The site includes practice questions in a format similar to those found in the test bank, links to relevant external Web sites, and other valuable resources for students such as:

- Chapter outlines and objectives
- Chapter summaries
- Online quizzing
- Video streaming and full video listing and questions by part
- Links to relevant external Web sites
- Link to OB Online
- Link to PowerWeb
- Searchable glossary

Online Student Study Guide   NEW! An online Study Guide is now offered for packaging with this edition. This interactive product includes key study aids, summaries, and self-testing modules.

OB Online is our OB online experience. Through the wonders of the latest Web technology, students can:

- Choose exercises from a list of topics
- Run activities and self-assessments geared toward groups and teams, individual differences, international organizational behaviour, and motivation and empowerment
- Launch into "Business Around the World" to find an outstanding resource for researching and exploring Organizational Behaviour Online

PowerWeb is dynamic, easy to use, and available for packaging with this textbook. It provides supplemental content that is course based and saves time. PowerWeb is the first online supplement to offer students access to the following:

- Course-specific current articles refereed by content experts
- Course-specific, real-time, and daily news
- Weekly course updates
- Interactive exercises and assessment tools
- Student study tips, Web research tips, and exercises
- Refereed and updated research links
- Access to the Northernlight.com's Special Collection of journals and articles

Indexes, Margin Notes, and Glossary   While minimizing unnecessary jargon, *Canadian Organizational Behaviour* assists the learning process by highlighting key terms in bold and providing brief definitions in the margin. These definitions are also presented in an alphabetical glossary at the end of the text. We have also developed a comprehensive index of content, names, and organizations described in this book.

INSTRUCTOR SUPPORT MATERIALS

Canadian Organizational Behaviour, Sixth Edition includes a variety of supplemental materials to help instructors prepare and present the material in this textbook more effectively.

Instructor Online Learning Centre   Along with the Student OLC (see above), *Canadian Organizational Behaviour* includes a password-protected Web site for instructors. The site offers

- Downloadable supplements: Microsoft® PowerPoint® Presentations, Instructor's Manual, and a databank of figures to create your own presentations
- Video streaming and full video listing and questions/answers by chapter
- Link to OB Online
- Link to PowerWeb
- Online updates to chapter topics
- PageOut
- Sample syllabi
- Links to OB news
- Updates and other resources

Canadian Organizational Behaviour was apparently the first OB textbook (in 1995) to introduce a complete set of PowerPoint® Presentation files. This resource is now more sophisticated than ever. Each PowerPoint® file has more than 18 slides relating to the chapter, all of which display one or more photographs from the textbook.

Instructor's Resource CD-ROM   This CD-ROM includes

Instructor's Resource Manual   Steve McShane co-authored the *Instructor's Resource Manual* with Claude Dupuis of Athabasca University to ensure that it represents the textbook's content and supports instructor needs. Each chapter includes the learning objectives, glossary of key terms, a chapter synopsis, complete lecture outline with thumbnail images of corresponding PowerPoint® slides, and solutions to the end-of-chapter discussion questions. It also includes teaching notes for the chapter case(s), team exercises, and self-assessments. Many chapters include supplemental lecture notes and suggested videos. *The Instructor's Resource Manual* also includes teaching notes for the end-of-text cases.

Test Bank and Computerized Test Bank   The *Test Bank* manual includes more than 2,400 multiple choice, true/false, and essay questions, most written by Steve McShane. Each question identifies the relevant page reference and difficulty level. The entire *Test Bank* manual is also available in an updated computerized version. Instructors receive special software that lets them design their own examinations from the test bank questions. It also lets instructors edit test items and add their own questions to the test bank.

Integrator   This pioneering instructional resource from McGraw-Hill Ryerson is your road map to all the other elements of your text's support package. Keyed to the chapters and topics of your McGraw-Hill Ryerson textbook, the integrator ties together all of the elements in your resource package, guiding you to where you'll find corresponding coverage in each of the related support package components!

Team Learning Assistant (TLA)   TLA is an interactive online resource that monitors team members' participation in a peer review. The program is designed to maximize the team learning experience and to save professors and students valuable time. (Available as an optional package.)

eInstruction's Classroom Performance System (CPS)   Bring interactivity into the classroom or lecture hall. CPS is a student response system using wireless connectivity. It gives instructors and students immediate feedback from the entire class. The response pads are remotes that are easy to use and engage students. CPS allows you to

- increase student preparation, interactivity, and active learning so you can receive immediate feedback and know what students understand.
- administer quizzes and tests, and provide immediate grading.
- create lecture questions in multiple choice, true/false, and subjective.
- evaluate classroom attendance, activity, and grading for your course as a whole. All results and scores can easily be imported into Excel and can be used with various classroom management systems.

CPS-ready content is available for use with *Canadian Organizational Behaviour*, Sixth Edition. Please contact your iLearning Sales Specialist for more information on how you can integrate CPS into your OB classroom.

Manager's Hot Seat   In today's workplace, managers are confronted daily with issues such as diversity, working in teams, and the virtual workplace. The Manager's Hot Seat is an interactive DVD (available for packaging) that allows students to watch as 15 real managers apply their years of experience to confront these issues.

Create a custom course Website with **PageOut**, free with every McGraw-Hill Ryerson textbook.

To learn more, contact your McGraw-Hill Ryerson publisher's representative or visit www.mhhe.com/solutions

PageOut   Visit www.mhhe.com/pageout to create a Web page for your course using our resources. PageOut is the McGraw-Hill Ryerson Web site development centre. This Web page-generation software is free to adopters and is designed to help faculty create an online course, complete with assignments, quizzes, links to relevant Web sites, and more—all in a matter of minutes.

www.blackboard.com

WebCT/Blackboard   In addition, content cartridges are available for the course management systems WebCT and Blackboard. These platforms provide instructors with user-friendly, flexible teaching tools. Please contact your local McGraw-Hill Ryerson iLearning Sales Specialist for details.

Superior Service   Service takes on a whole new meaning with McGraw-Hill Ryerson and *Canadian Organizational Behaviour*, Sixth Edition. More than just bringing you the textbook, we have consistently raised the bar in terms of innovation and educational research—both in management, and in education in general. These investments in learning and the education community have helped us to understand the needs of students and educators across the country, and allowed us to foster the growth of truly innovative, integrated learning.

INTEGRATED LEARNING

Your Integrated Learning Sales Specialist is a McGraw-Hill Ryerson representative who has the experience, product knowledge, training, and support to help you assess and integrate any of our products, technology, and services into your course for optimum teaching and learning performance. Whether it's using our test bank software, helping your students improve their grades, or putting your entire course online, your iLearning Sales Specialist is there to help you do it. Contact your local iLearning Sales Specialist today to learn how to maximize all of McGraw-Hill Ryerson's resources!

iLearning Services Program   McGraw-Hill Ryerson offers a unique iServices package designed for Canadian faculty. Our mission is to equip providers of higher education with superior tools and resources required for excellence in teaching. For additional information, visit http://www.mcgrawhill.ca/higher education/iservices/.

TEACHING, TECHNOLOGY & LEARNING CONFERENCE SERIES

The educational environment has changed tremendously in recent years, and McGraw-Hill Ryerson continues to be committed to helping you acquire the skills you need to succeed in this new milieu. Our innovative Teaching, Technology & Learning Conference Series brings faculty together from across Canada with 3M Teaching Excellence award winners to share teaching and learning best practices in a collaborative and stimulating environment. Pre-conference workshops on general topics, such as teaching large classes and technology integration, will also be offered. We will also work with you at your own institution to customize workshops that best suit the needs of your faculty at your institution.

ACKNOWLEDGMENTS

Canadian Organizational Behaviour, Sixth Edition symbolizes the power of team-work. More correctly, it symbolizes the power of a *virtual team* because I wrote this book from Perth, Australia with editorial and production support from people located in several places throughout Canada.

Superb virtual teams require equally superb team members, and we were fortunate to have this in our favour. Sponsoring Editor Kim Brewster led the way with unwavering support, while solving the behind-the-scenes challenges that made everyone's lives much easier. Lori McLellan (Developmental Editor) demonstrated amazingly cool coordination skills as Steve pushed the deadline limits so students have the latest OB knowledge. The keen copy editing skills of Erin Moore made *Canadian Organizational Behaviour*, Sixth Edition incredibly error free. Margaret Henderson, our Senior Supervising Editor, met the challenge of a tight production schedule. Thanks also to Kelly Dickson, Manager of Editorial Services and Design, for her ongoing support and to Karen Becker for finding the many photos that Steve had identified for this book. Thanks to you all. This has been an exceptional team effort!

As was mentioned earlier, more than 100 instructors around the world reviewed parts or all of *Canadian Organizational Behaviour*, Sixth Edition or its regional editions over the past three years. Their compliments were energizing, and their suggestions significantly improved the final product. Among others, the following people from Canadian colleges and universities deserve recognition for providing the most recent feedback for improvements specifically for *Canadian Organizational Behaviour*, Sixth Edition through preliminary, chapter and full manuscript reviews, as well as participation in focus groups:

Celeste Brotheridge, *University of Regina*
Wayne Cadence, *Northern Alberta Institute of Technology*
Jin Nam Choi, *McGill University*
Debby Cleveland, *British Columbia Institute of Technology*
Robert Dabous, *Cambrian College*
Wenlu Feng, *Centennial College*
Hugh Gunz, *University of Toronto*
Anne Harper, *Humber Institute of Technology & Advanced Learning*
Jean Helms Mills, *Saint Mary's University*
Kate Hoye, *University of Waterloo*
Diane Jurkowski, *York University*
Stefane Kabene, *University of Western Ontario*
Sue Kieswetter, *Conestoga College*
R.L. Kirby, *Carleton University*
Raymond Lee, *University of Manitoba*
Don Miskiman, *Malaspina University-College*
Carol Riggs, *Seneca College*
Geoffrey Smith, *University of Guelph*
Debra Warren, *Centennial College*
Brian Worth, *Georgian College*

I would also like to extend sincere thanks to the exceptional efforts of Claude Dupuis, Athabasca University, who co-authored the Instructor's Resource Manual and is authoring the first edition of the new online Student Study Guide. Claude's enthusiasm and expertise in organizational behaviour teaching really comes through in his work on this project.

I would also like to extend my sincerest thanks to the many instructors in Canada and abroad who contributed cases and exercises to this edition of *Canadian Organizational Behaviour*:

Alicia Boisnier, *SUNY at Buffalo*

James Buchkowsky, *Saskatchewan Institute of Applied Science & Technology*

Sharon Card, (formerly at) *Saskatchewan Institute of Applied Science & Technology*

Jeewon Cho, *SUNY at Buffalo*

Cathy Fitzgerald, *Okanagan College*

Mary Gander, *Winona State University*

Beth Gilbert, *University of New Brunswick, Saint John*

Swee C. Goh, *University of Ottawa*

Cheryl Harvey, *Wilfrid Laurier University*

Lisa Ho, *Prada Shoes, Singapore*

Theresa Kline, *University of Calgary*

Rosemary Maellaro, *University of Dallas*

Fiona McQuarrie, *University College of the Fraser Valley*

Susan Meredith, *Selkirk College*

Jean Helms Mills, *Saint Mary's University*

Kim Morouney, *Wilfrid Laurier University*

Joseph C. Santora, *Essex County College & TST, Inc.*

Peter Seidl, *British Columbia Institute of Technology*

William Todorovic, *Purdue University*

Lisa V. Williams, *SUNY at Buffalo*

Along with the reviewers, contributors, and editorial team, I would like to extend special thanks to my students for sharing their learning experiences and assisting with the development of the three organizational behaviour textbooks in Canada, the United States, and the Pacific Rim. I am also very grateful to my colleagues at the Graduate School of Management who teach organizational behaviour, including (in alphabetical order): Gail Broady, Renu Burr, Ron Cacioppe, Stacy Chappell, Nick Forster, Catherine Jordan, Sandra Kiffin-Petersen, Chris Perryer, David Plowman, Chris Taylor, and Barb Wood. These wonderful people listen patiently to my ideas, diplomatically correct my wayward thoughts, and share their experiences using the American or Pacific Rim editions of this book in Perth (Australia), Jakarta (Indonesia), Manila (Philippines), and Singapore.

Finally, I am forever indebted to my wife, Donna McClement, and to our wonderful daughters Bryton and Madison. Their love and support give special meaning to my life.

·1·

INTRODUCTION TO THE FIELD OF ORGANIZATIONAL BEHAVIOUR

LEARNING OBJECTIVES

AFTER READING THIS CHAPTER, YOU SHOULD BE ABLE TO:

- Define organizational behaviour and give three reasons for studying this field of inquiry.

- Discuss how globalization influences organizational behaviour.

- Summarize the apparent benefits and challenges of telecommuting.

- Identify changes in the workforce in recent years.

- Describe employability and contingent work.

- Explain why values have gained importance in organizations.

- Define corporate social responsibility and argue for or against its application in organizations.

- Identify the five anchors on which organizational behaviour is based.

- Diagram an organization from an open systems view.

- Define knowledge management and intellectual capital.

- Identify specific ways that organizations acquire and share knowledge.

About a dozen years ago, Dofasco suffered huge losses as low-cost imported steel entered the Canadian market. "We started to see globalization as a factor," recalls Don Pether, Dofasco's CEO who was then a metallurgist. To avoid bankruptcy, the Hamilton, Ontario, steelmaker slashed its workforce, restated and communicated the company's core values, and refocused the business around the continuous innovation of high-value products. Dofasco's brightest employees travelled around the world to discover best practices elsewhere, which resulted in several radical recommendations: introduce a more flexible team-based manufacturing process, flatten the organizational structure, and replace Dofasco's much-loved paternalistic culture of entitlement with a performance culture in which employees focus on earnings.

Today, Dofasco stands out as a role model of innovation, customer service, and profitability in the North American steel industry. "We need to add value for our customers, not just provide product," explains Dofasco's general manager of Manufacturing Services. "In order to add value, we need to engage our employees, make sure they understand our goals and strategies, and empower them to execute them."

Dofasco engages employees in several ways. Employees share equally in profit-sharing bonuses representing as much as 20 percent of their annual pay. The company invests heavily in training, ranging from award-winning literacy and computer skills programs to team-based problem solving. Dofasco is also one of the best places to work in Canada, and has

Dofasco has leveraged the power of organizational behaviour to become one of the most successful and respected companies in the global steel industry and among companies in Canada. *Courtesy of Dofasco*

won top awards for its wellness program and exceptional social activities (including Canada's largest Christmas party). And in spite of being in a "smokestack" industry, Dofasco is one of only 13 Canadian companies to receive top honours for sustainability by the Dow Jones Sustainability World Index.

Dofasco also encourages innovation through self-directed work teams. For example, one cross-functional team recently introduced an innovative ultra-light steel into General Motors' production process in only three months. Another innovation support strategy at Dofasco is sharing knowledge through communities of practice, which are groups of specialists who exchange new information on specific technical topics through seminars and electronic media. "The most important thing here is the interaction between people," says Vitor Chupil, who coordinates Dofasco's eight communities of practice. "It's what they can learn from each other and we can learn from them that matters."[1]

www.dofasco.com

Dofasco has become a powerhouse in the steel industry, but its real power comes from applying organizational behaviour theories and practices. More than ever, organizations are relying on organizational behaviour knowledge to remain competitive. For example, Dofasco executives re-examined their core values to anchor decisions and actions. They introduced several motivation and training activities to support "employee engagement." Self-directed work teams and organizational learning practices have made Dofasco more innovative and responsive than most other firms in Canada. These and many other organizational behaviour concepts and practices make a difference in the organization's success and employee well-being.

This book is about people working in organizations. Its main objective is to help you understand behaviour in organizations and to work more effectively in organizational settings. While organizational behaviour knowledge is often presented for "managers," this book takes a broader and more realistic view that organizational behaviour ideas are relevant and useful to anyone who works in and around organizations. In this chapter, we introduce you to the field of organizational behaviour, outline the main reasons why you should know more about it, highlight some of the trends influencing the study of organizational behaviour, describe the anchors supporting the study of organizations, and introduce the concept that organizations are knowledge and learning systems.

■ THE FIELD OF ORGANIZATIONAL BEHAVIOUR

organizational behaviour (OB)
The study of what people think, feel, and do in and around organizations.

Organizational behaviour (OB) is the study of what people think, feel, and do in and around organizations. OB researchers systematically study individual, team, and organizational-level characteristics that influence behaviour within work settings. By saying that organizational behaviour is a field of study, we mean that OB experts have been accumulating a distinct knowledge about behaviour within organizations—a knowledge base that is the foundation of this book.

By most estimates, OB emerged as a distinct field around the 1940s.[2] However, its origins can be traced much further back in time. The Greek philosopher Plato wrote about the essence of leadership. The writings of Chinese philosopher Confucius in 500 BC are beginning to influence contemporary thinking about ethics and leadership. In 1776, Adam Smith advocated a new form of organizational structure based on the division of labour. One hundred years later, German sociologist Max Weber wrote about rational organizations and initiated discussion of charismatic leadership. Soon after, Frederick Winslow Taylor introduced the systematic use of goal setting and rewards to motivate employees. In the 1920s, Elton Mayo and his colleagues discovered the importance of formal and informal group dynamics in the workplace, resulting in a dramatic shift towards the "human relations" school of thought. OB has been around for a long time; it just wasn't organized into a unified discipline until after World War II.

WHAT ARE ORGANIZATIONS?

Organizations have existed for as long as people have worked together. Massive temples dating back to 3500 BC were constructed through the organized actions of many people. Craftspeople and merchants in ancient Rome formed guilds, complete with elected managers. And more than 1,000 years ago, Chinese factories were producing 125,000 tonnes of iron a year.[3] We have equally impressive examples of contemporary organizations, ranging from Wal-Mart, the world's largest and most successful retailer, to the giant oil sands projects around Fort McMurray, Alberta. "A company is one of humanity's most amazing inventions," says Steven Jobs, CEO of Apple Computer and Pixar Animation Studios. "It's totally abstract. Sure, you have to build something with bricks and mortar to put the people in, but basically a company is this abstract construct we've invented, and it's incredibly powerful."[4]

organizations
Groups of people who work interdependently toward some purpose.

So, what are these powerful constructs that we call **organizations**? They are groups of people who work interdependently toward some purpose.[5] Organizations are not buildings or other physical structures. Rather, they consist of people who interact with each other to achieve a set of goals. Employees have structured patterns of interaction, meaning that they expect each other to complete certain tasks in a coordinated way—in an *organized* way.

Organizations have a purpose, whether it's producing oil from oil sands or selling books on the Internet. Some OB experts are skeptical about the relevance of goals in a definition of organizations.[6] They argue that an organization's mission statement may be different from its true goals. Also, they question the assumption that all organizational members believe in the same goals. These points may be true, but imagine an organization without goals: it would consist of a mass of people wandering around aimlessly without any sense of direction. Overall, organizations likely have a collective sense of purpose, even though this purpose is not fully understood or agreed upon.

WHY STUDY ORGANIZATIONAL BEHAVIOUR?

Organizational behaviour seems to get more respect from people who have been in the workforce a while than from students who are just beginning their careers. Many of us specialize in accounting, marketing, information systems, and other fields with corresponding job titles, so it's understandable that students focus on these career paths. After all, who ever heard of a career path leading to a "vice-president of OB" or a "chief OB officer"? Even if organizational behaviour doesn't have its own job title, most people eventually come to realize that this field is a potential gold mine of valuable knowledge. The fact is, everyone in the workforce needs to understand, predict, and influence behaviour (both their own and that of others) in organizational settings (see Exhibit 1.1). Marketing students learn marketing concepts and computer science students learn about circuitry and software code. But everyone benefits from organizational behaviour knowledge to address the people issues when trying to apply marketing, computer science, and other fields of knowledge.

Understanding, predicting, and influencing Each one of us has an inherent need to understand and predict the world in which we live.[7] Since much of our time is spent working in or around organizations, OB theories are particularly helpful in satisfying this innate drive to make sense of the workplace. OB theories also give us the opportunity to question and rebuild our personal mental models that have developed through observation and experience.

While understanding and predicting are important, most of us need to influence the organization in various ways. Whether you are trying to introduce a new marketing strategy, encourage staff to adopt new information technology, or negotiate more flexible work arrangements with your boss, you'll find that OB concepts play an important role in performing your job and working more effectively within organizations. This practical side of organizational behaviour is, according to some experts, a critical feature of the best OB theories.[8]

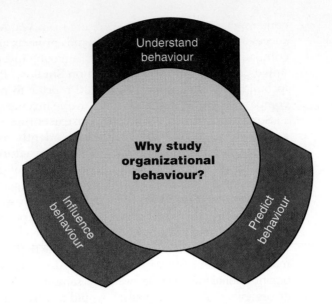

Organizational behaviour is for everyone   This book takes the view that organizational behaviour knowledge is for everyone—not just managers. We all need to understand organizational behaviour and to master the practices that influence organizational events. That's why you won't find very much emphasis in this book on "management." Yes, organizations will continue to have managers, but their roles have changed. More important, the rest of us are now expected to manage ourselves, particularly as companies remove layers of management and delegate more responsibilities. In the words of one forward-thinking organizational behaviour writer many years ago: Everyone is a manager.[9]

OB and the bottom line   So far, our answer to the question "Why study OB?" has focused on how OB knowledge benefits you as an individual. But organizational behaviour knowledge is just as important for the organization's financial health. According to one estimate, Canadian, American, and European firms that apply performance-based rewards, employee communication, work/life balance, and other OB practices have three times the level of financial success as companies where these practices are absent. Another study concluded that companies that earn "the best place to work" awards (such as Dofasco) have significantly higher financial and long-term stock market performance. Essentially, these firms leverage the power of OB practices, which translate into more favourable employee attitudes, decisions, and performance. These findings are not new to Warren Buffett and other financial gurus who consider the organization's leadership and quality of employees as two of the best predictors of the firm's financial potential.[10]

■ ORGANIZATIONAL BEHAVIOUR TRENDS

There has never been a better time to learn about organizational behaviour. The pace of change is accelerating, and most of the transformation is occurring in the workplace. Let's take a brief tour through five trends in the workplace: globalization, the changing workforce, evolving employment relationships, virtual work, and workplace values and ethics.

GLOBALIZATION

globalization
When an organization extends its activities to other parts of the world, actively participates in other markets, and competes against organizations located in other countries.

In 1978, after working as an engineer at Ford of Canada and other companies, Klaus Woerner established Automation Tooling Systems (ATS), a small business with four employees to make special-purpose machines for automated production operations. Today, with its headquarters in Cambridge, Ontario, ATS is a global powerhouse employing 4,000 people at 26 facilities on three continents. ATS might not be a household name to most Canadians, but the company is the world's leading designer and producer of sophisticated automated manufacturing equipment, as well as an emerging leader in solar energy cells. This global presence gives ATS a unique competitive advantage—the ability to leverage the benefits of global innovation while serving customers locally on their own turf. "You must live with your customers in [their] plants worldwide," explains an ATS executive in Germany. "That is the philosophy of ATS."[11]

The ATS story is a rich example of the phenomenal globalization of business over the past few decades. **Globalization** refers to economic, social, and cultural connectivity with people in other parts of the world. ATS and other organizations globalize when they actively participate in other countries and cultures. While organizations have operated across borders for centuries, the degree of globalization today is unprecedented because information technology and transportation systems allow a much more intense level of connectivity and interdependence around the planet.[12]

Experts continue to debate whether globalization improves the financial and social development of poorer nations, but at least this issue has made executives more aware of the ethics of serving communities, not just shareholders. Meanwhile, globalization has provided ATS and other firms with new markets and resources as well as a broader net to attract valuable knowledge and skills.[13]

But globalization is also criticized for increasing competitive pressures and market volatility, both of which nearly put Dofasco out of business a decade ago. Globalization is also linked to "offshoring"—outsourcing work to lower-wage countries. Collectively, these events potentially reduce job security, increase work intensification, and demand more work flexibility from employees. Thus, globalization might partly explain why many of us now work longer hours, have heavier workloads, and experience more work–family conflict than at any time in recent decades.[14]

While continuing to debate its merits, globalization is now well entrenched, so the real issue is how corporate leaders and employees alike can lead and work effectively in this emerging reality.[15] OB researchers are turning their attention to this topic, such as determining

Global Cultural Intelligence at Four Seasons Hotels and Resorts

Four Seasons Hotels and Resorts is the leading global name in luxury accommodation. From one modest motor inn in 1961, the Toronto-based company now manages over 60 hotels and resorts in 29 countries, with 20 more in development around the world. Four Seasons' expansion, particularly over the past decade, has required global organizational behaviour practices as well as leaders with global cultural intelligence. Antoine Corinthios, Four Seasons president for Europe, Middle East, and Africa, is such an example of this global cultural intelligence. "When I speak the language of the environment I am in, I start to think in the language I am in and adapt to that culture," explains Corinthios, who was raised in Cairo and joined Four Seasons two decades ago as a manager in Montreal. "If you are going global, you cannot be one way."[16] *Courtesy of Four Seasons*
www.fourseasons.com

how well OB theories and practices work across cultures. Project GLOBE, for instance, is a large consortium of OB experts studying leadership and organizational practices across dozens of countries. Globalization also has important implications for how we learn about organizational behaviour. The best performing companies may be in Finland, Brazil, or Singapore, not just in Calgary or Toronto. That's why this book presents numerous examples from around the planet. We want you to learn from the best, no matter where their headquarters are located.

THE CHANGING WORKFORCE

Walk into almost any branch of HSBC Bank Canada and you might think you have entered a United Nations building. Over 40 percent of Vancouver-based financial institution's employees are visible minorities from dozens of cultural backgrounds. "Diversity is core to our business," says Sarah Morgan-Silvester, an executive vice-president at HSBC Bank Canada. "It really is part of our corporate strategy, and it's reflected in our brand." HSBC Bank is a reflection of Canada as a multicultural society that embraces diversity. Indeed, if Canada has a global "brand" image, it is as a country that has pioneered and leveraged the benefits of multiculturalism. It is a valued policy that almost all Canadians believe should be preserved and enhanced.[17]

Exhibit 1.2 identifies the primary and secondary dimensions of workforce diversity. The primary categories—gender, ethnicity, age, race, sexual orientation, and mental/physical qualities—represent personal characteristics that influence an individual's socialization and social identity. The secondary dimensions are those features that we learn or have some control over throughout our lives, such as education, marital status, religion, and work experience. The Canadian workforce has become more diverse along many of these primary and secondary dimensions, particularly in terms of race/ethnicity, gender, and generation (age/work experience).

Racial/ethnic diversity The percentage of Canadian residents identified as members of a visible minority jumped from less than 5 percent in 1981 to over 13 percent in 2001. By 2017, over 20 percent of all Canadians will be in a visible minority category, over two-thirds of whom will be immigrants to Canada. This increasing cultural diversity is most apparent in Toronto and Vancouver where nearly 40 percent of residents are currently in a visible minority group, rising to more than 50 percent by 2017.[18]

Women in the workforce Women now account for nearly half of the paid workforce in Canada, compared to just 20 percent a few decades ago. Gender-based shifts continue to occur within many occupations. For example, women represent the majority of students in Canadian medical schools, compared with only 11 percent in the mid-1960s.[19]

Generational diversity Another noticeable change is the values and expectations of people in various generational cohorts.[20] Several writers suggest that *baby boomers*—people born between 1946 and 1964—tend to expect and desire more job security (at least, at this stage in their lives), and seem more intent on improving their economic and social status. In contrast, *Generation-X* employees—those born between 1965 and 1979—are typically less loyal to one organization and, in return, expect less job security. Instead, they are motivated more by workplace flexibility, the opportunity to learn (particularly new technology), and working in an

■ **EXHIBIT 1.2**

Primary and secondary dimensions
of workforce diversity

■ Primary dimension

■ Secondary dimension

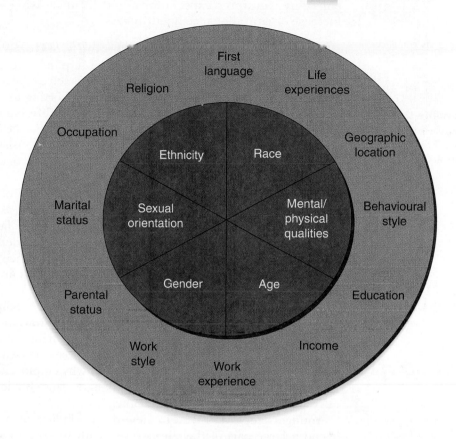

Sources: Adapted from M. Loden, *Implementing Diversity*, (Chicago: Irwin, 1996); S. Bradford, "Fourteen Dimensions of Diversity: Understanding and Appreciating Differences in the Workplace," in J. W. Pfeiffer (Ed.) 1996 Annual: Volume 2 *Consulting* (San Diego: Pfeiffer and Associates, 1996), pp. 9–17.

egalitarian and "fun" organization. Meanwhile, some observers suggest that *Generation-Y* employees (those born after 1979) are noticeably self-confident, optimistic, multi-tasking, and independent than even Gen-X co-workers. These statements certainly don't apply to everyone in each cohort, but they do reflect the fact that each generation brings a different set of values and expectations.

Diversity presents both opportunities and challenges in organizations.[21] In some circumstances and to some degree, diversity can become a competitive advantage by improving decision making and team performance on complex tasks. For many businesses, a diverse workforce is also valuable to provide better customer service in a diverse society. At the same time, workforce diversity presents new challenges, such as conflict, miscommunication, and discrimination in organizations and society.[22] We will explore these diversity issues more closely under various topics throughout this book, such as stereotyping, team dynamics, and conflict management.

EVOLVING EMPLOYMENT RELATIONSHIPS

Globalization and the evolving workforce have fuelled two contrasting changes in relationships between employers and employees: (1) aligning the workplace with emerging workforce expectations, and (2) increasing workforce flexibility to increase organizational competitiveness.

Aligning the workplace with emerging workforce expectations   When 1,000 Canadians were asked to identify the "top indicators of success in your own career," they had a number of great choices, such as salary level, challenging job, level of responsibility, and loyalty of people reporting to them. But none of these options were at the top of the list. Instead, **work/life balance**—the minimization of conflict between work and nonwork demands—was the number one indicator of career success, far ahead of the alternatives. This is consistent with another recent study reporting that work/life balance is the number one priority for Canadians when considering a new job offer.[23]

Work/life balance was seldom mentioned a couple of decades ago, probably because employees at the time viewed work/life balance as a luxury that they must earn through hard work.[24] But with more two-income families and the expectations among Gen-X/Gen-Y employees of a better lifestyle, it is a "must-have" condition in the employment relationship. Work/life balance is so important that, as Connections 1.1 describes, younger Canadian lawyers are willing to change jobs and sacrifice income to achieve this balance.

Along with providing greater work/life balance, companies are adjusting to emerging workforce expectations of a more egalitarian workplace by reducing hierarchy and replacing command-and-control management with facilitating and teacher-oriented leaders. Gen-X/Gen-Y employees also want to work in companies that make a difference, which may explain why employers are paying more attention to serving the community rather than just shareholders, a trend that we'll discuss in more detail later in this chapter.

Younger employees tend to view the workplace as a community where they spend a large part of their lives (even with work/life balance), so many expect opportunities for more social fulfillment and fun. Again, several companies are making this shift in the employment relationship. For instance, Radical Entertainment's spacious workplace in Vancouver features a huge "leisure zone" with a massive kitchen stocked with free food, comfy sofas near a real fireplace, and plenty of games facilities. The video game developer even has a 150-square-metre (1,600-square foot) log cabin in the middle of the office where Radical's 250 staff can watch big screen TV or hold conferences.[25]

Increasing workforce flexibility   While companies are aligning employment practices with emerging workforce expectations, they are also demanding more flexibility from employees to remain responsive to globalization and other sources of turbulence. This increased flexibility partly occurs through **employability**, in which employees are expected to manage their own careers by anticipating future organizational needs and developing new competencies that match those needs.[26] From this perspective, organizations are customers, and employees keep their jobs by continuously developing new competencies for the future and performing a variety of work activities over time. Furthermore, employability shifts the burden of this adaptability to employees rather than employers, although the latter are expected to offer the resources and opportunities to assist in the process. "I think

work/life balance
The minimization of conflict between work and nonwork demands.

employability
An employment relationship in which people are expected to continually develop their skills to remain employed.

Attracting Talent Through Work/Life Balance

At first, the judge couldn't believe Dominic Naud's reason to seek postponement of a court date for one of his cases. Naud's wife had just given birth to their first child, so Naud was going to take the three-month paternity leave offered by the Montreal law firm where he works, Nicholl Paskell-Mede. "He [the judge] was really surprised that a male lawyer would leave his profession to take care of his baby," Naud recalls.

Although still fairly rare, particularly among Canadian lawyers, paternity leave and other activities that improve work/life balance are quickly gaining in popularity. Generation-X employees in particular are demanding better work arrangements to suit their lifestyle. "The younger lawyers coming out of school are less workaholic than their older counterparts," says Sharon Druker, a lawyer at Gowling Lafleur Henderson in Montreal.

Druker, who works about 50 hours on clients' work plus several more hours each week on soliciting new business, says that achieving a balance is difficult. "It's a struggle for any working parent to balance work and family," she says. "And there are some professions that are more demanding than others, law being one of them." Linda Pieterson agrees. "It's very difficult for anyone in corporate law to try to leave at five," says Pieterson, a partner at Toronto-based law firm McCarthy Tétrault. She adds that working 9 to 5 would be considered part-time in private legal practice.

Maybe so, but Canadian lawyers increasingly expect a more balanced work schedule, and are willing to change jobs to find that balance. A recent survey of over 1,400 associates and partners in 100 Canadian law firms reported the two most important reasons for choosing to work for another firm were to work in an environment more supportive of their family and personal commitments, and to have more control over their work schedule. The study also found that both female and male lawyers at Canadian firms with a supportive work/life balance culture intended to stay with the firm

Dominic Naud (left) and Jennifer DeLeskie (right) enjoy work/life balance at the Montreal law firm that Mindy Paskell-Mede (centre) and John Nicholl established a decade ago.
Phil Carpenter, The Gazette (Montreal)

over twice as long as lawyers at firms that do not support work/life balance.

Achieving better work/life balance was one of the reasons why Mindy Paskell-Mede and John Nicholl left a large Montreal law firm a decade ago to establish Nicholl Paskell-Mede, where Dominic Naud and two dozen other lawyers now work. "We didn't want to work ridiculous hours," Paskell-Mede recalls. "We wanted to spend time with our families." So, they decided to set billable hours at 1,450 hours rather than the minimum 1,800 hours at other firms. Nicholl Paskell-Mede lawyers earn less money, but they gain better personal fulfillment and reduce the risk of burnout.

Sources: V. Galt, "Professionals Demanding a Work/Life Balance—and Backing It Up," *Globe & Mail*, March 17, 2005, p. B1; Catalyst Canada, *Beyond a Reasonable Doubt: Building the Business Case for Flexibility.* (Toronto: Catalyst, April 2005); S. Whittaker, "Lawyers Want Lives Back," *The Gazette* (Montreal), April 11, 2005, p. B1; S. Whittaker, "Law Firm Sets Workload Precedent," *The Gazette* (Montreal), May 9, 2005, p. B4.

---

contingent work
Any job in which the individual does not have an explicit or implicit contract for long-term employment, or one in which the minimum hours of work can vary in a nonsystematic way.

people are starting to understand the concept of lifetime employability rather than lifetime employment," says Rich Hartnett, global staffing director at aerospace manufacturer Boeing. "It's a good idea to stay current with what's out there and take personal responsibility for our own employability."[27]

Contingent work   Along with employability, companies are making more use of **contingent work** to increase workforce flexibility. Contingent work includes any job in which the individual does not have an explicit or implicit contract for long-term employment, or one in which the minimum hours of work can vary in a nonsystematic way. This employment relationship includes anyone with temporary or seasonal employment, freelance contractors (sometimes called "free agents"), and temporary staffing agency workers.[28]

Statistics Canada estimates that 12 percent of the work force has "nonpermanent" employment. The growth of contingent work is evident when we look at statistics on temporary employment (the most common form of contingent work). In 1989, 14 percent of 25- to 64-year old employees hired within the previous two years held temporary jobs; today 21 percent recently hired employees in Canada are in temporary employment. For 17- to 25-year-olds with less than two years seniority, the percentage in temporary jobs has jumped from 11 percent in 1989 to 32 percent today.[29]

Contingent work allows companies to reduce costs by more closely matching employment levels and competencies with product or service demands. It is also the preferred employment relationship for "free agents" with high-demand skills and who enjoy a variety of interesting assignments. At the same time, research suggests that contingent workers potentially have higher accident rates as well as lower performance and loyalty. However, these outcomes depend on the type of contingent workers (e.g., "free agent" contractors vs. new hires on temporary status) as well as whether contingent workers are separated from, or interact regularly with, permanent staff. Another concern is that permanent employees feel injustice against their employer if contingent workers are treated as second-class citizens.[30]

VIRTUAL WORK

Up to a point, Karen Dunn Kelley follows a familiar routine as a mother and busy executive. She puts her school-aged children on the bus, feeds breakfast to her 19-month-old before handing him off to a nanny, and then heads off to the office. But Kelley's daily commute is different from most; it's just a short walk from her house to the office over her garage. Furthermore, Kelley is an executive with Houston-based AIM Management Group, yet the home office where she oversees 40 staff and US$75 billion in assets is located in Pittsburgh.[31]

virtual work
Employees use information technology to perform their jobs away from the traditional physical workplace.

Karen Dunn Kelley's daily routine is an example of **virtual work**, whereby employees use information technology to perform their jobs away from the traditional physical workplace. Kelly's virtual work, called *teleworking* or *telecommuting*, involves working at home rather than commuting to the office. Virtual work also includes employees connected to the office while on the road or at clients' offices. By most estimates, less than 10 percent of Canadian employees engage in telework, whereas nearly 20 percent of Americans work at home at least one day each month. The low Canadian figure is unusual considering that nearly half of Canadian employees say they would be lured to another job if they could work at home one day each week.[32]

According to some research, virtual work potentially reduces employee stress by offering better work/life balance and dramatically reducing time lost through commuting to the office. Under some circumstances, it also increases productivity and job satisfaction. Nortel Networks reports that 71 percent of its U.K. staff feels more empowered through virtual work arrangements. Others point out that virtual work reduces the cost of office space, and improves the environment through less pollution and traffic congestion.[33]

In spite of these benefits, virtual workers face a number of real or potential challenges.[34] Family relations may suffer rather than improve if employees lack sufficient space and resources for a home office. Some virtual workers complain of lack of recognition, although virtual work does not seem to undermine career progression or performance ratings. Loneliness is another common complaint, particularly among virtual workers who rarely visit the office.

Along with some degree of technological savvy, virtual workers need to be self-motivated, organized, and have sufficient fulfillment of social needs elsewhere in their lives. They also work better in organizations that evaluate employees by their performance outcomes rather than "face time." "The reason why there isn't more uptake into telework is there's a cultural barrier there," said Lorenzo Mele, transportation coordinator at the city of Markham, Ontario. "If a manager is managing by attendance as opposed to performance, productivity and other measures, then clearly something like telework could never fit into the way they do business."[35]

Virtual teams   Another variation of virtual work occurs in **virtual teams**—cross-functional groups that operate across space, time, and organizational boundaries with members who communicate mainly through information technology.[36] Virtual teams exist when some members telework, but also when team members are located on company premises, but at different sites around the country or world. Teams have varying degrees of virtualness, depending on how often and how many team members interact face-to-face or at a distance. There is currently a flurry of research activity studying the types of work best suited to virtual teams and the conditions that improve and hinder their effectiveness. As with telework, some people are also better suited than others to virtual team dynamics. Chapter 10 will examine these virtual team issues in detail.

virtual teams
Teams whose members operate across space, time, and organizational boundaries and are linked through information technologies to achieve organizational tasks.

values
Stable, long-lasting beliefs about what is important in a variety of situations.

Values-Based Leadership at Dubai's Department of Economic Development

The senior management team at the Department of Economic Development (DED) in the Emirate of Dubai recently devoted several months to identifying the agency's core values: accountability, teamwork, and continuous improvement. Each of these three values is anchored with specific behaviour descriptions to ensure that employees and other stakeholders understand their meaning. DED also organized a series of workshops (shown in photo) in which employees participated in a "Values Mystery" exercise to help them recognize values-consistent behaviours. To develop a values-based organization, DED will also use these three values to evaluate employee performance, assess employee competencies, and identify management potential.[39]
Courtesy of Dubai Department of Economic Development
feed.dubainews.net

WORKPLACE VALUES AND ETHICS

Search through most annual reports and you'll soon discover that corporate leaders view values as the *sine qua non* of organizational excellence. For example, as described in the opening story to this chapter, senior management at Dofasco re-examined and then extensively communicated the company's core values before embarking on the steelmaker's dramatic transformation. Values have also become important anchors for transforming government departments in Canada and other countries.[37]

Values represent stable, long-lasting beliefs about what is important in a variety of situations that guide our decisions and actions. They are evaluative standards that help define what is right or wrong, or good or bad, in the world. Values dictate our priorities, our preferences, and our desires. They influence our motivation and decisions. "Ninety-nine percent of what we say is about values," advises Anita Roddick, founder of the Body Shop.[38] Although leaders refer to the core values of their companies, values really exist only within individuals, which we call *personal values*. However, groups of people might hold the same or similar values, so we tend to ascribe these *shared values* to the team, department, organization, profession, or entire society.

Importance of values in the workplace   Values have been studied in organizational behaviour research for a long time, but they have only recently become a popular topic in corporate boardrooms. One reason is that leaders are looking for better ways to guide employee decisions and behaviour. As we learned earlier in this chapter, today's increasingly educated and independent workforce resents the traditional "command-and-control" supervision, so values represent a way to keep employees' decisions and actions aligned with corporate goals. Values represent the unseen magnet that pulls employees in the same direction. They foster a common bond and help to ensure that everyone in the organization—regardless of job or rank—has aligned goals.[40]

A second reason for the recent interest in values is that globalization has raised our awareness of and sensitivity to differences in values across cultures. Organizations face the challenge of ensuring consistent decisions and actions around the world even though their employees may have diverse cultural values. Reinforcing a common set of core values isn't easy, because some of these values may conflict with individual and societal values.[41]

The third reason why values have gained prominence is that organizations are under increasing pressure to engage in ethical practices and corporate social responsibility. **Ethics** refers to the study of moral principles or values that determine whether actions are right or wrong and outcomes are good or bad. We rely on our ethical values to determine "the right thing to do." Ethical behaviour is driven by the moral principles we use to make decisions. These moral principles represent fundamental values. Unfortunately, a lot of people give executives low grades on their ethics report cards these days, so ethics and values will continue to be an important topic in OB teaching.[42]

Corporate social responsibility   Over 30 years ago, economist Milton Friedman pronounced that "there is one and only one social responsibility of business—to use its resources and engage in activities designed to increase its profits." Friedman is a respected scholar, but this argument was not one of his more popular—or accurate—statements. Today, any business that follows Friedman's advice will face considerable trouble in the marketplace. Indeed, only 20 percent of Canadians agree with Friedman, whereas more than 70 percent believe that business executives have a responsibility to take into account the impact their decisions have on employees, local communities, and the country. In other words, Canadians expect organizations in this country to engage in corporate social responsibility.[43]

Corporate social responsibility (CSR) refers to an organization's moral obligation toward all of its **stakeholders**. Stakeholders are the shareholders, customers, suppliers, governments, and any other groups with a vested interest in the organization.[44] As part of corporate social responsibility, many companies have adopted the triple bottom line philosophy. This means that they try to support or "earn positive returns" in the economic, social, and environmental spheres of sustainability. Firms that adopt the triple bottom line aim to survive and be profitable in the marketplace (economic), but they also intend to maintain or improve conditions for society (social) as well as the physical environment.[45]

More than ever, companies in Canada and elsewhere are coming under scrutiny for their CSR practices. Shareholders, job applicants, current employees, and suppliers are increasingly deciding whether to associate with an organization based on how well it applies virtuous values. "People increasingly prefer to work for or do business with what is deemed to be a socially responsible company," says Nick Wright, London-based head of corporate responsibility at investment bank UBS Warburg.[46]

ethics
The study of moral principles or values that determine whether actions are right or wrong and outcomes are good or bad.

corporate social responsibility (CSR)
An organization's moral obligation toward its stakeholders.

stakeholders
Shareholders, customers, suppliers, governments, and any other groups with a vested interest in the organization.

CSR is Part of Bridges Transitions' DNA

Corporate social responsibility (CSR) is part of the corporate DNA at Bridges Transitions. The Kelowna, B.C., online career exploration and planning company actively serves the community with fundraising and other projects to improve society and the environment. "We have a fun(d) committee that meets monthly whose purpose is not only to plan team-building events, but also to have those team-building events focus on both fun for staff and also provide a benefit to the community," explains Bridges vice-president Norm Thompson. On Earth Day, for instance, (shown in this photo) nearly 80 Bridges employees and friends planted 2,000 ponderosa pine seedlings in an area burned by the devastating Okanagan mountain fire a couple of years earlier. Bridges Transitions has also twice won Kelowna's Run for the Cure "corporate spirit" award as the company raising the most money for breast cancer research.[50]

Courtesy of Bridges Transitions Inc.

www.bridges.com

Most executives surveyed around the world agree that corporate social responsibility is vital to any company's profitability, yet few of them publicly report their social responsibility practices. One exception is Vancouver City Savings Credit Union (VanCity). The Vancouver-based financial institution retains an independent, external social auditor to report on the inclusivity, embeddedness, and continuous improvement of its social and environmental performance. The auditor considers how well VanCity genuinely engages its stakeholders, integrates corporate social responsibility into all its operations and policymaking, and applies what it learns to improve future performance on the triple bottom line. "If companies take a chance, and take their corporate strategy in a new direction—one that respects people, the environment, and the bottom line—they will profit in ways they never dreamed of," advises VanCity CEO Dave Mowat.[47]

■ THE FIVE ANCHORS OF ORGANIZATIONAL BEHAVIOUR

Globalization, the changing workforce, evolving employment relationships, virtual work, and workplace values and ethics are just a few of the trends that we will explore in this textbook. To understand these and other topics, the field of organizational behaviour relies on a set of basic beliefs or knowledge structures (see Exhibit 1.3). These conceptual anchors represent the way that OB researchers think about organizations and how they should be studied. Let's look at each of these five beliefs that anchor the study of organizational behaviour.

THE MULTIDISCIPLINARY ANCHOR

Organizational behaviour is anchored around the idea that the field should develop from knowledge in other disciplines, not just from its own isolated research base. Some OB experts have recently argued that the field suffers from a "trade deficit"—importing far more knowledge from other disciplines than it is exporting to other disciplines. While this is a possible concern, organizational behaviour has thrived through its diversity of knowledge from other disciplines.[48]

The upper part of Exhibit 1.4 (on page 17) identifies the traditional disciplines from which organizational behaviour knowledge has developed. For instance, sociologists have contributed to our knowledge of team dynamics, organizational socialization, organizational power, and other aspects of the social system. The field of psychology has aided our understanding to most issues relating to individual and interpersonal behaviour. Recently, even the field of neuroscience has contributed new ideas about human drives and behaviour.[49]

■ **EXHIBIT 1.3**

Five conceptual anchors of
organizational behaviour

The bottom part of Exhibit 1.4 identifies some of the emerging fields from which organizational behaviour knowledge is acquired. The communications field helps us to understand the dynamics of knowledge management, electronic mail, corporate culture, and employee socialization. Information systems scholars are exploring the effects of information technology on team dynamics, decision making, and knowledge management. Marketing scholars have enhanced our understanding of job satisfaction and customer service, knowledge management, and creativity. Women's studies scholars are studying perceptual biases and power relations between men and women in organizations.

THE SYSTEMATIC RESEARCH ANCHOR

A second anchor for organizational behaviour researchers is their belief in the value of studying organizations through systematic research methods. Traditionally, scholars have relied on the **scientific method** by forming research questions, systematically collecting data, and testing hypotheses against those data. This approach relies mainly on quantitative data (numeric information) and statistical procedures to test hypotheses. The idea behind the scientific method is to minimize personal biases and distortions about organizational events.

More recently, OB scholars have also adopted qualitative methods and, in particular, **grounded theory** to understand the workplace. Grounded theory is a process of developing a theory through the constant interplay between data gathering and the development of theoretical concepts. Through observation, interviews, and other forms of data collection, researchers form concepts and theories. But as they return to gather more information each time, they also test the concepts and theory created up to that point in the research study.[51] Appendix A at the end of this book provides an overview of research design and methods commonly found in organizational behaviour studies.

scientific method
A set of principles and procedures that help researchers to systematically understand previously unexplained events and conditions.

grounded theory
A process adopted in most qualitative research of developing knowledge through the constant interplay of data collection, analysis, and theory development.

■ **EXHIBIT 1.4**

Multidisciplinary anchor of organizational behaviour

Discipline	Relevant OB topics
Traditional Disciplines	
Psychology	Drives, perception, attitudes, personality, job stress, emotions, leadership
Sociology	Team dynamics, roles, socialization, communication patterns, organizational power, organizational structure
Anthropology	Corporate culture, organizational rituals, cross-cultural dynamics, organizational adaptation
Political science	Intergroup conflict, coalition formation, organizational power and politics, decision making, organizational environments
Economics	Decision making, negotiation, organizational power
Industrial engineering	Job design, productivity, work measurement
Emerging Disciplines	
Communications	Knowledge management, electronic mail, corporate culture, employee socialization
Information systems	Team dynamics, decision making, knowledge management
Marketing	Knowledge management, creativity, decision making
Women's studies	Organizational power, perceptions

THE CONTINGENCY ANCHOR

"It depends" is a phrase that **OB** scholars often use to answer a question about the best solution to an organizational problem. The statement may seem evasive, yet it reflects an important way of understanding and predicting organizational events, called the **contingency approach**. This anchor states that a particular action may have different consequences in different situations. In other words, no single solution is best in all circumstances.[52]

The contingency anchor explains why OB experts tend to be skeptical about sure-fire recommendations that are so common in the media and consulting literature. While the ideal situation is to identify universal theories—where the concepts and practices have equal success in every situation—the reality is that there are usually too many exceptions to make these "one best way" theories useful. Even when a theory seems to work everywhere, OB scholars remain doubtful; an exception is somewhere around the corner. For example, in Chapter 14 we will learn that leaders should use one style (e.g., participation) in some situations and another style (e.g., direction) in other situations. Thus, when faced with a particular problem or opportunity, we need to understand and diagnose the situation and select the strategy most appropriate *under those conditions*.[53]

Although contingency-oriented theories are necessary in most areas of organizational behaviour, we should also be wary about carrying this anchor to an extreme. Some contingency models add more confusion than value over universal ones. Consequently, we need to balance the sensitivity of contingency factors with the simplicity of universal theories.

contingency approach
The idea that a particular action may have different consequences in different situations.

■ **EXHIBIT 1.5**

Three levels of analysis in
organizational behaviour

THE MULTIPLE LEVELS OF ANALYSIS ANCHOR

This textbook divides organizational behaviour topics into three levels of analysis: individual, team, and organization (see Exhibit 1.5). The individual level includes the characteristics and behaviours of employees as well as the thought processes that are attributed to them, such as motivation, perceptions, personalities, attitudes, and values. The team level of analysis looks at the way people interact. This includes team dynamics, decisions, power, influence, conflict, and leadership. At the organizational level, we focus on how people structure their working relationships and on how organizations interact with their environments.

Although an OB topic is typically pegged into one level of analysis, it usually relates to multiple levels.[54] For instance, communication is located in this book as a team (interpersonal) process, but we also recognize that it includes individual and organizational processes. Therefore, you should try to think about each OB topic at the individual, team, and organizational levels, not just at one of these levels.

THE OPEN SYSTEMS ANCHOR

Hewlett-Packard may have lots of buildings and equipment, but former HP CEO Carly Fiorina says that a leader's job is to nurture something that is alive. "I think that a company is a living system," says Fiorina. "It is an organism, it is operating in other living systems, and a leader has to think about the company as a living, breathing system."[55] Carly Fiorina is describing the fifth anchor of organizational behaviour—the view that organizations are **open systems**.

open systems

Organizations that take their sustenance from the environment and, in turn, affect that environment through their output.

Organizations are open systems because they take their sustenance from the environment and, in turn, affect that environment through their output. A company's survival and success depend on how well employees sense environmental changes and alter their patterns of behaviour to fit those emerging conditions.[56] In contrast, a closed system has all the resources needed to survive without dependence on the external environment. Organizations are never completely closed systems, but monopolies operating in stable environments come close because they can ignore stakeholders for a fairly long time without adverse consequences.

As Exhibit 1.6 illustrates, organizations acquire resources from the external environment, including raw materials, employees, financial resources, information, and equipment. Inside the organization are numerous subsystems, such as processes (communication and reward systems), task activities (production, marketing), and social dynamics (informal groups, power dynamics). With the aid of technology (such as equipment, work methods, and information), these subsystems transform

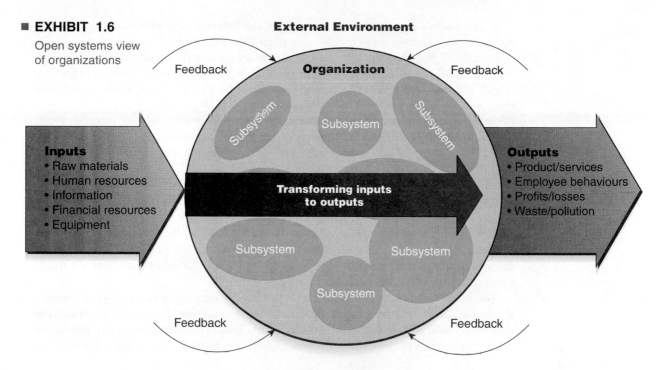

■ EXHIBIT 1.6

Open systems view
of organizations

inputs into various outputs. Some outputs (e.g., products and services) may be valued by the external environment, whereas other outputs (e.g., employee layoffs, pollution) have adverse effects. The organization receives feedback from the external environment regarding the value of its outputs and the availability of future inputs. This process is cyclical and, ideally, self-sustaining, so that the organization may continue to survive and prosper.

External environment and stakeholders   It is almost a cliché to say that most organizations today operate in more dynamic, fast-paced environments than they did a few decades ago. To illustrate how fast organizations are changing, consider this: In the 1920s, companies stayed on the S&P 500 stock exchange list an average of 67 years. Today, the average company life cycle on the S&P 500 is about 12 years. In other words, your grandparents could work for the same organization all of their lives, whereas you will likely outlive two or three companies.[57] Similarly, the most valued companies in Canada today—such as Research in Motion, Radical Entertainment, and Automation Tooling Systems—were either junior start-ups or nonexistent 20 years ago. And unless these firms anticipate and adapt to continual change, few of them will be around 20 years from now.

As open systems, successful organizations monitor their environments and have the ability to change their outputs and transformational processes in order to maintain a close fit with the evolving external conditions.[58] At the same time, this dynamic capability must not be accelerated to the point where it depletes the organization's resources or gets too far ahead of market demand, which has happened at Nortel, 360Networks, JDS Uniphase, and other Canadian firms. The point here is that organizations need to adapt to changing environments, but not so much that they overspend their resources or overshoot stakeholder needs.

Stakeholders represent a central part of the internal and external environment. As mentioned earlier, these include any person or entity with a vested interest in the organization. Stakeholders influence the firm's access to inputs and ability to discharge outputs. And unless they pay attention to the needs of all stakeholders, organizational leaders may find their business in trouble. For instance, leaders may put their organization at risk if they pay attention only to shareholders and ignore the broader corporate social responsibility.[59] We see this stakeholder misalignment when job applicants avoid companies that ignore corporate social responsibility and when organizations fail to treat their employees and suppliers with respect.

Systems as interdependent parts   The open systems anchor states that organizations consist of many internal subsystems that need to be continuously aligned with each other. As companies grow, they develop more and more complex subsystems that must coordinate with each other in the process of transforming inputs to outputs.[60] These interdependencies can easily become so complex that a minor event in one subsystem may amplify into serious unintended consequences elsewhere in the organization.

The open systems anchor is an important way of viewing organizations. However, it has traditionally focused on physical resources that enter the organization and are processed into physical goods (outputs). This was representative of the industrial economy but not of the "new economy," where the most valued input is knowledge.

■ KNOWLEDGE MANAGEMENT

knowledge management
Any structured activity that improves an organization's capacity to acquire, share, and use knowledge in ways that improve its survival and success.

Knowledge management is any structured activity that improves an organization's capacity to acquire, share, and use knowledge in ways that improve its survival and success.[61] The knowledge that resides in an organization is called its **intellectual capital**, which is the sum of everything that an organization knows that gives it competitive advantage—including its human capital, structural capital, and relationship capital.[62]

- *Human capital*—This is the knowledge that employees possess and generate, including their skills, experience, and creativity.
- *Structural capital*—This is the knowledge captured and retained in an organization's systems and structures. It is the knowledge that remains after all the human capital has gone home.
- *Relationship capital*—This is the value derived from an organization's relationships with customers, suppliers, and other external stakeholders who provide added value for the organization. For example, this includes customer loyalty as well as mutual trust between the organization and its suppliers.

intellectual capital
The sum of an organization's human capital, structural capital, and relationship capital.

KNOWLEDGE MANAGEMENT PROCESSES

Intellectual capital represents the stock of knowledge held by an organization. This stock of knowledge is so important that some companies try to measure its value.[63] But knowledge management is much more than the organization's stock of knowledge. It is a *process* that develops an organization's capacity to acquire, share, and use knowledge more effectively. This process is often called *organizational learning* because companies must continuously learn about their various environments in order to survive and succeed through adaptation.[64] The "capacity" to acquire, share, and use knowledge means that companies have established systems, structures, and organizational values that support the knowledge management process. Let's look more closely at some of the strategies companies use to acquire, share, and use knowledge.

Knowledge acquisition   Knowledge acquisition includes the process of extracting information and ideas from its environment as well as through insight. One of the fastest and most powerful ways to acquire knowledge is by hiring individuals or acquiring entire companies. Knowledge also enters the organization when employees learn from external sources, such as discovering new resources from suppliers or becoming aware of new trends from clients. A third knowledge acquisition strategy is through experimentation. Companies receive knowledge through insight as a result of research and other creative processes.[65]

One of the main concerns about knowledge acquisition is that organizations must have enough **absorptive capacity** to acquire the knowledge. *Absorptive capacity* refers to the ability to recognize the value of new information, assimilate it, and apply it to commercial ends. The capacity to acquire new knowledge depends on the company's existing store of knowledge. Without basic knowledge of wireless technology, for example, employees would have difficulty understanding and acquiring new information from a technical seminar on this field. Similarly, it would be difficult to recognize new opportunities with a client if you didn't have the benefit of past experience with this client. The main point here is that acquiring new knowledge from the environment requires an absorptive capacity, which depends on the organization's existing foundation of knowledge. This absorptive capacity is so important that it affects how quickly organizations and entire societies can grow and prosper.[66]

Knowledge sharing   Many organizations are reasonably good at acquiring knowledge, but they waste this resource by not effectively disseminating it. As several executives have lamented: "I wish we knew what we know."[67] Valuable ideas sit idly—rather like unused inventory—or remain hidden as "silos of knowledge" throughout the organization. Many organizations improve knowledge sharing by creating digital repositories of knowledge—computer intranets in which employees document and store new knowledge as it becomes available. While somewhat useful, these electronic storage systems can be expensive to maintain; they also overlook the fact that a lot of knowledge is difficult to document.[68]

An alternative strategy for knowledge sharing is to give employees more opportunities for informal online or face-to-face communication. Dofasco, described at the beginning of this chapter, supports informal knowledge sharing **communities of practice**. These are informal groups bound together by shared expertise and passion for a particular activity or interest.[69] Another Canadian pioneer in communities of practice is Clarica Life Insurance Company. Realizing that its agents possess valuable knowledge that is often isolated from other agents, the Waterloo, Ontario-based firm created a process whereby the knowledge can be actively shared with others. This includes both a formal computer network as well as opportunities for informal dialogue among agents.[70]

Knowledge use   Acquiring and sharing knowledge are wasted exercises unless knowledge is effectively put to use. To do this, employees must realize that the knowledge is available and that they have enough freedom to apply it. This requires a culture that supports experiential learning, which we will describe in Chapter 3.

absorptive capacity
The ability to recognize the value of new information, assimilate it, and apply it to commercial ends.

communities of practice
Informal groups bound together by shared expertise and passion for a particular activity or interest.

Ontario Power Generation Captures Knowledge
The lights might not go out, but Ontario Power Generation (OPG) could face an expensive and somewhat risky period of corporate amnesia. Over the next five years, the Crown corporation that manages Ontario's electricity supply is about to lose one-quarter of its 11,000 employees due to retirement, many of them senior engineers and managers with valuable knowledge locked inside their heads. "Somebody with intellectual capital walking out the door could cause a team of 20 or 30 people to spend several weeks trying to re-study a particular piece of technology to come up with a solution," says John Murphy, OPG's executive vice-president of human resources. Fortunately, OPG is minimizing the amount of corporate memory loss by introducing several practices that capture knowledge. It introduced an online knowledge portal to document and store information. Younger employees are being groomed now for future leadership roles, and some are encouraged to develop skills for two or more future jobs so the Crown corporation can fill sudden knowledge gaps.[75]
Courtesy of Ontario Power Generation
www.opg.com

ORGANIZATIONAL MEMORY

A few years ago, Evercare decided to move its headquarters and manufacturing from Flint, Michigan, to Waynesboro, Georgia. The move nearly killed the manufacturer of Lint Pic-up and other household cleaning products because none of Evercare's production employees wanted to leave Flint. So, when the company's executives arrived in Georgia to set up production, they struggled to rebuild the company's manufacturing and distribution systems from scratch. "Nothing was documented," recalls an Evercare executive. "All of the knowledge, all of the practices were built in people's heads."[71]

Evercare's experience is a reminder that intellectual capital can be lost as quickly as it is acquired.[72] Corporate leaders need to recognize that they are the keepers of an **organizational memory**. This unusual metaphor refers to the storage and preservation of intellectual capital. It includes information that employees possess as well as knowledge embedded in the organization's systems and structures. It includes documents, objects, and anything else that provides meaningful information about how the organization should operate.

How do organizations retain intellectual capital? One way is by keeping good employees. "Our assets walk up and down the stairs every day," says Ian Wilkinson, founder of Radical Entertainment in Vancouver. "If we keep smart, motivated people, we can do everything."[73] As we noted earlier in this chapter, Radical Entertainment and other progressive companies are keeping smart, motivated staff by adapting their employment practices to become more compatible with emerging workforce expectations, including work/life balance, egalitarian hierarchy, and a workspace that generates more fun. A second organizational memory strategy is to systematically transfer knowledge before employees leave. This occurs when new recruits apprentice with skilled employees, thereby acquiring knowledge that is not documented. A third strategy is to transfer knowledge into structural capital. This includes bringing out hidden knowledge, organizing it, and putting it in a form that can be available to others.

Before leaving the topic of organizational memory and knowledge management, you should know that successful companies also unlearn. Sometimes it is appropriate for organizations to selectively forget certain knowledge.[74] This means that they should cast off the routines and patterns of behaviour that are no longer appropriate. Employees need to rethink their perceptions, such as how they should interact with customers and which is the "best way" to perform a task. As we shall discover in Chapter 17, unlearning is essential for organizational change.

organizational memory
The storage and preservation of intellectual capital.

■ THE JOURNEY BEGINS

This chapter gives you some background about the field of organizational behaviour. But it's only the beginning of our journey. Throughout this book, we will challenge you to learn new ways of thinking about how people work in and around organizations. We begin this process in Chapter 2 by presenting a basic model of individual behaviour, then introducing over the next five chapters various stable and mercurial characteristics of individuals that relate to elements of the individual behaviour model. Next, this book moves to the team level of analysis. We examine a model of team effectiveness and specific features of high-performance teams. We also look at decision making and creativity, communication, power and politics, conflict and negotiation, and leadership in team settings. Finally, we shift our focus to the organizational level of analysis, where the topics of organizational structure, organizational culture, and organizational change are examined in detail.

CHAPTER SUMMARY

Organizational behaviour is the study of what people think, feel, and do in and around organizations. Organizations are groups of people who work interdependently toward some purpose. OB concepts help us to predict and understand organizational events, adopt more accurate theories of reality, and influence organizational events. This field of knowledge also improves the organization's financial health.

There are several trends in organizational behaviour. Globalization requires corporate decision makers to be sensitive to cultural differences. Another trend is increasing racial/ethnic and generational diversity as well as increasing percentage of women in the Canadian workforce. Employment relations are also evolving as companies adapt workplace practices to support emerging workforce expectations, while also demanding more flexibility through employability and contingent work.

A fourth trend, virtual work, occurs when employees use information technology to perform their jobs away from the traditional physical workplace. Virtual work includes teleworking as well as virtual teams—cross-functional groups that operate across space, time, and organizational boundaries with members who communicate mainly through information technology. Values and ethics represent the fifth trend. In particular, companies are learning to apply values in a global environment, and they are under pressure to abide by ethical values and higher standards of corporate social responsibility.

Organizational behaviour scholars rely on a set of basic beliefs to study organizations. These anchors include beliefs that OB knowledge should be multidisciplinary and based on systematic research, that organizational events usually have contingencies, that organizational behaviour can be viewed from three levels of analysis (individual, team, and organization), and that organizations are open systems.

The open systems anchor suggests that organizations have interdependent parts that work together to continually monitor and transact with the external environment. They acquire resources from the environment, transform them through technology, and return outputs to the environment. The external environment consists of the natural and social conditions outside the organization. External environments are generally highly turbulent today, so organizations must become adaptable and responsive.

Knowledge management develops an organization's capacity to acquire, share, and use knowledge in ways that improve its survival and success. Intellectual capital is knowledge that resides in an organization, including its human capital, structural capital, and relationship capital. Organizations acquire knowledge through various practices, including individual learning and experimentation. Knowledge sharing occurs mainly through various forms of communication, including communities of practice. Knowledge use occurs when employees realize that the knowledge is available and that they have enough freedom to apply it. Organizational memory refers to the storage and preservation of intellectual capital.

KEY TERMS

absorptive capacity, p. 21

communities of practice, p. 21

contingency approach, p. 17

contingent work, p. 11

corporate social responsibility (CSR), p. 14

employability, p. 10

ethics, p. 14

globalization, p. 7

grounded theory, p. 16

intellectual capital, p. 20

knowledge management, p. 20

open systems, p. 18

organizational behaviour (OB), p. 4

organizational memory, p. 22

organizations, p. 5

scientific method, p. 16

stakeholders, p. 14

values, p. 13

virtual work, p. 12

virtual teams, p. 13

work/life balance, p. 10

DISCUSSION QUESTIONS

1. A friend suggests that organizational behaviour courses are useful only to people who will enter management careers. Discuss the accuracy of your friend's statement.

2. Look through the list of chapters in this textbook and discuss how globalization could influence each organizational behaviour topic.

3. Corporate social responsibility is one of the hottest issues in corporate boardrooms these days, partly because it is becoming increasingly important to employees and other stakeholders. In your opinion, why have stakeholders given CSR more attention recently? Does abiding by CSR standards potentially cause companies to have conflicting objectives with some stakeholders in some situations?

4. "Organizational theories should follow the contingency approach." Comment on the accuracy of this statement.

5. A number of years ago, employees in Calgary's water distribution unit were put into teams and encouraged to find ways to improve efficiency. The teams boldly crossed departmental boundaries and areas of management discretion in search of problems. Employees working in other parts of the city began to complain about these intrusions. Moreover, when some team ideas were implemented, the city managers discovered that a dollar saved in the water distribution unit may have cost the organization two dollars in higher costs elsewhere. Use the open systems anchor to explain what happened here.

6. After hearing a seminar on knowledge management, a mining company executive argues that this perspective ignores the fact that mining companies could not rely on knowledge alone to stay in business. They also need physical capital (such as digging and ore processing equipment) and land (where the minerals are located). In fact, these two may be more important than what employees carry around in their heads. Discuss the merits of the mining executive's comments.

7. At a recent seminar on information technology, you heard a consultant say that over 30 percent of Canadian and U.S. companies use software to manage documents and exchange information, whereas firms in Europe are just beginning to adopt this technology. Based on this, the consultant concluded that "knowledge management in Europe is at its beginning stages." In other words, few firms in Europe practice knowledge management. Comment on this consultant's statement.

8. BusNews Ltd. is the leading stock market and business news service. Over the past two years, BusNews has experienced increased competition from other news providers. These competitors have brought in Internet and other emerging computer technologies to link customers with information more quickly. There is little knowledge within BusNews about how to use these computer technologies. Based on the knowledge acquisition processes for knowledge management, explain how BusNews might gain the intellectual capital necessary to become more competitive in this respect.

C A S E   S T U D Y   1.1

ANCOL LTD.

Paul Simard was delighted when Ancol Ltd. offered him the job of manager at its Jonquiere, Quebec, plant. Simard was happy enough managing a small metal stamping plant with another company, but the headhunter's invitation to apply for the plant manager job at one of Canada's leading metal fabrication companies was irresistible. Although the Jonquiere plant was the smallest of Ancol's 15 operations across Canada, the plant manager position was a valuable first step in a promising career.

One of Simard's first observations at Ancol's Jonquiere plant was that relations between employees and management were strained. Taking a page from a recent executive seminar that he attended on building trust in the workplace, Simard ordered the removal of all time clocks from the plant. Instead, the plant would assume that employees had put in their full shift. This symbolic gesture, he believed, would establish a new level of credibility and strengthen relations between management and employees at the site.

Initially, the 250 production employees at the Jonquiere plant appreciated their new freedom. They felt respected and saw this gesture as a sign of positive change from the new plant manager. Two months later, however, problems started to appear. A few people began showing up late, leaving early, or taking extended lunch breaks. Although this represented only about 5 percent of the employees, others found the situation unfair. Moreover, the increased absenteeism levels were beginning to have a noticeable effect on plant productivity. The problem had to be managed.

Simard asked supervisors to observe and record when the employees came or went and to discuss attendance problems with those abusing their privileges. But the supervisors had no previous experience with keeping attendance and many lacked the necessary interpersonal skills to discuss the matter with subordinates. Employees resented the reprimands, so relations with supervisors deteriorated. The additional responsibility of keeping track of attendance also made it difficult for supervisors to complete their other responsibilities. After just a few months, Ancol found it necessary to add another supervisor position and reduce the number of employees assigned to each supervisor.

But the problems did not end there. Without time clocks, the payroll department could not deduct pay for the amount of time that employees were late. Instead, a letter of reprimand was placed in the employee's personnel file. However, this required yet more time and additional skills from the supervisors. Employees did not want these letters to become part of their permanent record, so they filed grievances with their labour union. The number of grievances doubled over six months, which required even more time for both union officials and supervisors to handle these disputes.

Nine months after removing the time clocks, Paul Simard met with union officials, who agreed that it would be better to put the time clocks back in. Employee-management relations had deteriorated below the level when Simard had started. Supervisors were burnt out from overwork. Productivity had dropped due to poorer attendance records and increased administrative workloads.

A couple of months after the time clocks were put back in place, Simard attended an operations meeting at Ancol's headquarters in Toronto. During lunch, Simard described the time clock incident to Liam Jackson, Ancol's plant manager in Northern B.C. Jackson looked surprised, then chuckled. He explained that the previous B.C. plant manager had done something like that with similar consequences six or seven years ago. The manager had left some time ago, but Jackson heard about the B.C. time clock from a supervisor during his retirement party two months ago.

"I guess it's not quite like lightning striking the same place twice," said Simard to Jackson. "But it sure feels like it."

Discussion Questions

1. Use the open systems model to explain what happened when Ancol removed the time clocks.

2. What changes should occur to minimize the likelihood of these problems in the future?

© Copyright 2000 Steven L. McShane. This case is based on actual events, but names and some facts have been changed to provide a fuller case discussion.

TEAM EXERCISE   1.2

HUMAN CHECKERS

Purpose   This exercise is designed to help students understand the importance and application of organizational behaviour concepts.

Materials   None, but the instructor has more information about the team's task.

Instructions

■ *Step 1:* Form teams with six students. If possible, each team should have a private location where team members can plan and practice the required task without being observed or heard by other teams.

■ *Step 2:* All teams will receive special instructions in class about the team's assigned task. All teams have the same task and will have the same amount of time to plan and practice the task. At the end of this planning and practice, each team will be timed while completing the task in class. The team that completes the task in the least time wins.

■ *Step 3:* No special materials are required or allowed for this exercise. Although the task is not described here, students should learn the following rules for planning and implementing the task:

Rule #1: You cannot use any written form of communication or any props to assist in the planning or implementation of this task.

Rule #2: You may speak to other students in your team at any time during the planning and implementation of this task.

Rule #3: When performing the task, you must move only in the direction of your assigned destination. In other words, you can only move forward, not backward.

Rule #4: When performing the task, you can move forward to the next space, but only if it is vacant (see Exhibit 1).

Rule #5: When performing the task, you can move forward two spaces, if that space is vacant. In other words, you can move around a student who is one space in front of you to the next space if that space is vacant (see Exhibit 2).

Exhibit 1   **Exhibit 2**

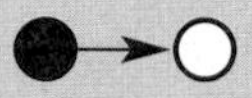

■ *Step 4:* When all teams have completed their task, the class will discuss the implications of this exercise for organizational behaviour.

Discussion Questions

1. Identify organizational behaviour concepts that the team applied to complete this task.

2. What personal theories of people and work teams were applied to complete this task?

3. What organizational behaviour problems occurred and what actions were (or should have been) taken to solve them?

W E B   E X E R C I S E   1.3

DIAGNOSING ORGANIZATIONAL STAKEHOLDERS

Purpose   This exercise is designed to help you understand how stakeholders influence organizations as part of the open systems anchor.

Materials   Students need to select a Canadian (or foreign) company and, prior to class, retrieve and analyze publicly available information over the past year or two about that company. This may include annual reports, which are usually found on the Web sites of publicly-traded companies. Where possible, students should also scan full-text newspaper and magazine databases for articles published over the previous year about the company.

Instructions   The instructor may have students work alone or in groups for this activity. Students will select a Canadian (or foreign) company and will investigate the relevance and influence of various stakeholder groups on the organization. Stakeholders will be identified from annual reports, newspaper articles, Web site statements, and other available sources. Stakeholders should be rank ordered in terms of their perceived importance to the organization.

Students should be prepared to present or discuss their organization's rank ordering of stakeholders, including evidence for this rank ordering.

Discussion Questions

1. What are the main reasons why certain stakeholders are more important than others for this organization?

2. Based on your knowledge of the organization's environmental situation, is this rank order of stakeholders in the organization's best interest, or should other stakeholders be given higher priority?

3. What societal groups, if any, are not mentioned as stakeholders by the organization? Does this lack of reference to these unmentioned groups make sense?

IT ALL MAKES SENSE?

Purpose   This exercise is designed to help you understand how organizational behaviour knowledge can help you to understand life in organizations.

Instructions   (Note: This activity may be done as a self-assessment or as a team activity.) Read each of the statements below and circle whether each statement is true or false, in your opinion. The class will consider the answers to each question and discuss the implications for studying organizational behaviour.

Due to the nature of this activity, the instructor will provide information about the most appropriate answer. The scoring key is *not* found in Appendix B.

1.	True	False	A happy worker is a productive worker.
2.	True	False	Decision makers tend to continue supporting a course of action even though information suggests that the decision is ineffective.
3.	True	False	Organizations are more effective when they prevent conflict among employees.
4.	True	False	It is better to negotiate alone than as a team.
5.	True	False	Companies are more effective when they have a strong corporate culture.
6.	True	False	Employees perform better without stress.
7.	True	False	Effective organizational change always begins by pinpointing the source of its current problems.
8.	True	False	Female leaders involve employees in decisions to a greater degree than do male leaders.
9.	True	False	People in Japan value group harmony and duty to the group (high collectivism) more than do Canadians (low collectivism).
10.	True	False	The best decisions are made without emotion.
11.	True	False	If employees feel they are paid unfairly, then nothing other than changing their pay will reduce their feelings of injustice.

Copyright © 2003 Steven L. McShane

TELEWORK DISPOSITION ASSESSMENT

Go to the Online Learning Centre to complete this interactive self-assessment.

Purpose   This exercise is designed to help you assess the extent to which you possess the personal characteristics most suitable for telecommuting.

Instructions   This instrument asks you to indicate the degree to which you agree or disagree with each of the statements provided. You need to be honest with yourself to obtain a reasonable estimate of your telework disposition. The results provide a rough indication of how well you would adapt to telework. Please keep in mind that this scale only considers your personal characteristics. Other factors, such as organizational, family, and technological systems support must also be taken into account.

Copyright © 2003 Steven L. McShane

Online Learning Centre with POWERWEB

After studying the preceding material, be sure to check out our Online Learning Centre at

www.mcgrawhill.ca/college/mcshane

for more in-depth information and interactivities that correspond to this chapter.

Case 1   GLOBAL GIANT

Wal-Mart has grown from a single Arkansas store in the 1960s into the largest company in the world. But with such a ruthless focus on prices and productivity, Wal-Mart is now experiencing numerous ethical problems, including a massive class-action suit alleging that the retailer favours men over women in promotion to store management. Critics also charge that Wal-Mart's low wage policy forces employees to rely on public services. Wal-Mart argues that most of its employees are college students or senior citizens working to supplement their incomes. A third complaint is that Wal-Mart's manufacturing operations are rolling back wages and benefits, whereas Wal-Mart claims that it is monitoring its suppliers and raising working standards.

Discussion Questions

1. Identify the ethical and corporate social responsibility concerns that various groups are raising against Wal-Mart in this video program.

2. If you were the CEO of Wal-Mart, how would you address each of these concerns? What effect, if any, would your actions have on the company's competitiveness in the marketplace?

Case 2   BALANCING WORK AND LIFE

Work/life balance is the hottest topic among human resource executives these days, and for good reason. Most Canadians have a serious lack of balance, which is costing employers plenty. Companies have introduced several practices to minimize the damage to time-stressed staff, such as fitness programs, career breaks, daycare centres, flex-time, job sharing, telework, and so on. But a major Canadian study has reported that Canadians are still stressed. University of Guelph professor Peter Hausdorf says that part of the problem is that employers don't want to deal with the main cause of poor work/life balance: workload. Carleton University professor Linda Duxbury asks how companies can afford *not* to help employees maintain a work/life balance. This CBC video program investigates these and other issues regarding work/life balance among Canadian employees.

Discussion Questions

1. Explain how companies that encourage work-life balance might be more successful than those pushing more hours of work out of their staff.

2. Looking through other chapters in this book, identify topics that might explain why work/life balance is linked to employee performance and workplace productivity.

·2·

INDIVIDUAL BEHAVIOUR, VALUES, AND PERSONALITY

LEARNING OBJECTIVES

AFTER READING THIS CHAPTER, YOU SHOULD BE ABLE TO:

■ Diagram the MARS model.

■ Describe three types of ways to match individual competencies to job requirements.

■ Identify five types of individual behaviour in organizations.

■ Define values and explain why values congruence is important.

■ Define five main values that vary across cultures.

■ List three ethical principles.

■ Explain how moral intensity, ethical sensitivity, and the situation influence ethical behaviour.

■ Identify the "Big Five" personality dimensions.

■ Summarize the personality concepts behind the Myers-Briggs Type Indicator.

■ Explain how personality relates to Holland's model of vocational choice.

A recent report by the Auditor General of British Columbia on the status of the province's public service didn't dwell on employee attitudes. Instead, it focused on "employee engagement" as one of the four cornerstones of service quality. B.C. government employees scored below the national average, prompting the report to give a blunt warning: "With employees who are only moderately engaged, government is not likely receiving the best performance possible from its staff."

The British Columbia government and dozens of other organizations across Canada have made employee engagement a key part of their business strategy. Although its definition varies from one source to the next, employee engagement generally refers to how much employees identify with and are emotionally committed to their work, are cognitively focused on that work, and possess the ability and resources to do so. Employee engagement has become big business among consulting firms because research indicates that companies with an engaged workforce have significantly higher productivity, customer satisfaction, and profits, as well as lower accident rates and employee turnover.

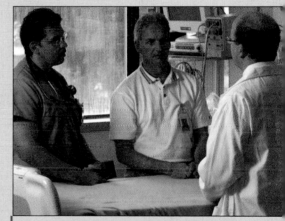

The Fraser Valley Health Authority and many other Canadian organizations are making employee engagement the cornerstone of their organizational effectiveness strategy. *Courtesy of Fraser Health Authority*

This evidence was enough to convince the Fraser Valley Authority (FVA) to make employee engagement a cornerstone of its organizational effectiveness strategy. "By measuring and improving employee engagement, our goal is to improve the quality of the working environment and of the services we provide," explains an executive at FVA, which oversees public health care facilities in eastern Vancouver and the Fraser Valley. Vancouver Coastal Health is following the same path. The agency responsible for public health care elsewhere in Vancouver even has a "vice-president of employee engagement" responsible for human resource practices.

Other Canadian business leaders should take notice as employee engagement gains popularity. Two separate studies estimated that only 20 to 25 percent of the Canadian workforce is fully engaged, 60 to 65 percent is somewhat engaged, and 15 to 20 percent is actively disengaged or "checked out" from their work. Pfizer Canada is identified as one of the firms with a large percentage of fully engaged employees. "We strive to create a positive and proactive culture for all of our employees," explains Pfizer Canada president Jean-Michel Halfon. "It is one of the reasons why people join Pfizer Canada and stay with the organization."[1] ■

www.fraserhealth.ca

The groundswell of interest in **employee engagement** makes a great deal of sense when we realize that this concept includes most of the drivers of individual behaviour and performance. It refers to employees' emotional and cognitive (rational) motivation, the ability to perform the job, a clear understanding of the organization's vision and their specific role in that vision, and a belief that they have been given the resources to get their job done. This chapter begins by presenting the MARS model, which outlines these four drivers of individual behaviour and results. Next, this chapter briefly looks at the six main types of individual behaviour in the workplace.

The latter half of this chapter looks at values and personality, two deeply-held characteristics of people that influence their attitudes, motivation, and behaviour in the workplace. The section on values describes Schwartz's model of personal values, issues relating to values congruence, the dynamics of cross-cultural values, and key features of ethical values in the workplace. The section on personality introduces the five-factor model of personality, the Myers-Briggs Type Indicator, and other personality characteristics that are often discussed in organizational behaviour research.

■ MARS MODEL OF INDIVIDUAL BEHAVIOUR AND RESULTS

Why do individuals behave the way they do and perform well or poorly in the workplace? This question has been the Holy Grail of much research in organizational behaviour, and it is the focus of the next six chapters in this book. We begin the journey by presenting a basic model of individual behaviour and results (called the MARS model) and outlining the main types of behaviour in organizational settings. Then, we set out to examine the main individual difference topics underlying the MARS model, beginning with two of the most stable influences: values and personality.

The MARS model, illustrated in Exhibit 2.1, is a useful starting point to understanding the drivers of individual behaviour and results. The model highlights the four factors that directly influence an employee's voluntary behaviour and resulting performance—motivation, ability, role perceptions, and situational factors, or the acronym "MARS."[2] The MARS model shows that these four factors have a combined effect on individual performance. If any factor weakens, employee performance will decrease. For example, enthusiastic salespeople (motivation) who understand their job duties (role perceptions) and have sufficient resources (situational factors) will not perform their jobs as well if they lack sufficient knowledge and sales skill (ability). Look back at the opening story and you will see that employee engagement captures all four MARS drivers of individual behaviour and results. No wonder employee engagement has become such a popular concept among practitioners!

Exhibit 2.1 also shows that the four factors in the MARS model are influenced by several other individual variables that we will discuss over the next few chapters. Personality and values are the most stable characteristics,[3] so we look at them later in this chapter. Emotions, attitudes, and stress are much more fluid characteristics, whereas individual perceptions and learning usually lie somewhere between. Each of these factors relates to the MARS model in various ways. For example, personal values affect an employee's motivation through emotions and tend to shape role perceptions through the perceptual process. Learning influences ability, role perceptions, and motivation, as we shall learn in Chapter 3. Before

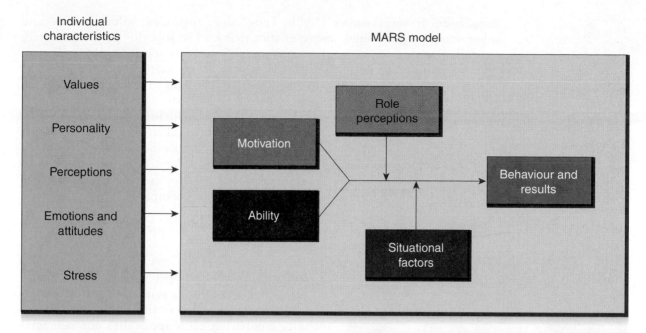

Individual characteristics

MARS model

examining these individual characteristics, let's briefly introduce the four elements
of the MARS model, followed by an overview of the different types of individual
behaviour in the workplace.

EMPLOYEE MOTIVATION

motivation
The forces within a
person that affect
his or her direction,
intensity, and persist-
ence of voluntary
behaviour.

Motivation represents the forces within a person that affect his or her direction,
intensity, and persistence of voluntary behaviour.[4] *Direction* refers to the fact that
motivation is goal-oriented, not random. People are motivated to arrive at work
on time, finish a project a few hours early, or aim for many other targets. *Intensity*
is the amount of effort allocated to the goal. For example, two employees might be
motivated to finish their project a few hours early (direction), but only one of
them puts forth enough effort (intensity) to achieve this goal. Finally, motivation
involves varying levels of *persistence*, that is, continuing the effort for a certain
amount of time. Employees sustain their effort until they reach their goal or give
up beforehand. Chapter 5 looks more closely at the conceptual foundations of
employee motivation, and Chapter 6 considers some applied motivation practices.

ABILITY

ability
Both the natural
aptitudes and learned
capabilities required
to successfully
complete a task.

Employee abilities also make a difference in behaviour and task performance.
Ability includes both the natural aptitudes and learned capabilities required to
successfully complete a task. *Aptitudes* are the natural talents that help employees
learn specific tasks more quickly and perform them better. For example, some
people have a more natural ability than others to manipulate small objects with
their fingers (called finger dexterity). There are many different physical and mental
aptitudes, and our ability to acquire skills is affected by these aptitudes. *Learned
capabilities* refer to the skills and knowledge that you have actually acquired. This
includes the physical and mental skills you possess as well as the knowledge you
acquire and store for later use.

Employee competencies   Skills, knowledge, aptitudes, values, drives, and other underlying personal characteristics that lead to superior performance are typically bunched together into the concept of **competencies**. Competencies are relevant to an entire job group rather just than to specific jobs. For instance, Canada's RBC Financial Group recently determined that to thrive in a turbulent, globalized world, it would require leaders who have strong competencies in (1) shaping the future, (2) driving to succeed, (3) leading with integrity, and (4) leading continuous change in reinvention. Ericsson, the Swedish telecommunications giant, has identified several competencies that apply across most jobs, such as teamwork, communications, and cultural awareness.[5] Most large organizations spend a lot of money identifying key competencies, but some competencies are described too broadly to guide hiring and training people. Also, companies wrongly assume that everyone should have the same set of competencies, whereas the truth seems to be that people with another combination of competencies may be equally effective.[6]

competencies
The abilities, values, personality traits, and other characteristics of people that lead to superior performance.

Person–job matching   There are three approaches to matching individual competencies with job requirements. One strategy is to select applicants whose existing competencies best fit the required tasks. This includes comparing each applicant's competencies with the requirements of the job or work unit. A second approach is to provide training so employees develop required skills and knowledge. The third way to match people with job requirements is to redesign the job so employees are given tasks only within their capabilities. AT&T's customer service operations in Dallas took this approach when they realized that many employees were overwhelmed by the increasing variety of products (cable, Internet, HDTV, home theatre, etc.) "Our employees just said 'Help! This is way too complex, we're trained on three things and we need help!'" recalls an AT&T executive. The company's solution was to redesign jobs so that employees could begin with one area of product knowledge, such as video cable, then progress to a second knowledge area when the first product has been mastered.[7]

Developing RAT Competencies

Joel McIsaac (shown in photo) and several other skilled tradespeople are dangling from ropes for a week to develop skills as remote access technicians (known as RATs) at Remote Access Technology Inc. in Dartmouth, Nova Scotia. Remote Access sends its RAT teams to oil rigs, refineries, power generating stations, pulp and paper plants, and other sites where people must gain access to extreme heights or depths. The company has plenty of business in Canada and the United States, but finding people with the right competencies is a challenge. In addition to being skilled electricians, painters, or blasters, RATs require exceptional strength, agility, and a comfort with heights to work in these demanding conditions.[9]

E. Wynne, Halifax Herald

www.rat.ca

ROLE PERCEPTIONS

The opening vignette for this chapter stated that a large percentage of employees in Canada are only moderately (or not at all) engaged in their work. One of the reasons for this disconnected situation, according to a recent survey of 3,000 Canadian employees, is that while most understand their organization's business goals, only 39 percent know what to do in their own jobs to achieve those business goals.[8] In other words, employee engagement and job performance are undermined by inaccurate or ambiguous *role perceptions*. Employees have accurate role perceptions when they understand the specific tasks assigned to them, the relative importance of those tasks, and the preferred behaviours to accomplish those tasks. The most basic way to improve these role perceptions is for staff to receive a clear job description and ongoing coaching. Employees also clarify their role perceptions as they work together over time and receive frequent and meaningful performance feedback.

SITUATIONAL FACTORS

With high levels of motivation and ability, along with clear role perceptions, people will perform well only if the situation also supports their task goals. Situational factors include conditions beyond the employee's immediate control that constrain or facilitate his or her behaviour and performance.[10] Some situational characteristics—such as consumer preferences and economic conditions—originate from the external environment and, consequently, are beyond the employee's and organization's control. However, some situational factors—such as time, people, budget, and physical work facilities—are controlled by others in the organization. Corporate leaders need to arrange these conditions carefully so employees can achieve their performance potential.

Motivation, ability, role perceptions, and situational factors affect all conscious workplace behaviours and their performance outcomes. The next section outlines the five categories of behaviour in organizational settings.

■ TYPES OF INDIVIDUAL BEHAVIOUR IN ORGANIZATIONS

People engage in many different types of behaviour in organizational settings. Exhibit 2.2 highlights the five types of behaviour discussed most often in the organizational behaviour literature: task performance, organizational citizenship, counterproductive work behaviours, joining and staying with the organization, and work attendance.

TASK PERFORMANCE

task performance
Goal-directed activities that are under that individual's control.

Task performance refers to goal-directed behaviours under the individual's control that support organizational objectives. Task performance behaviours transform raw materials into goods and services or support and maintain the technical activities.[11] For example, foreign exchange traders at TD Waterhouse make decisions and take actions to exchange currencies. Employees in most jobs have more than one performance dimension. Foreign exchange traders must be able to identify profitable trades, work cooperatively with clients and co-workers in a stressful environment, assist in training new staff, and work on special telecommunications equipment without error. Some of these performance dimensions are more important than others, but only by considering all of them can we fully evaluate an employee's contribution to the organization.

EXHIBITING ORGANIZATIONAL CITIZENSHIP

One of the defining characteristics of engaged employees is that they perform beyond standard task performance standards or expectations. "When employees become engaged, they develop a stronger conscientiousness about what they can

■ EXHIBIT 2.2

Types of work-related behaviour

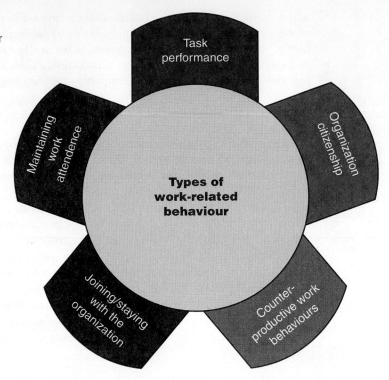

do," explains Bill Erikson, vice chairman of consulting firm Kenexa. "They will go the extra step, or maybe even the extra mile, to support the interest of the organization." In short, engaged employees practise **organizational citizenship**. They help others without selfish intent, are actively involved in organizational activities, avoid unnecessary conflicts, perform tasks beyond normal role requirements, and gracefully tolerate impositions. Several factors described throughout this book explain why some employees are good organizational citizens and others are not. Later in this chapter, for example, we learn that people with a conscientiousness personality trait have higher organizational citizenship.[12]

organizational citizenship
Behaviours that extend beyond the employee's normal job duties.

COUNTERPRODUCTIVE WORK BEHAVIOURS

According to Canadian research, managers rely not just on task performance and organizational citizenship behaviours to evaluate employee performance. Some also pay attention to **counterproductive work behaviours (CWBs)**. CWBs are voluntary behaviours that have the potential to directly or indirectly harm the organization. These CWBs can be organized into five categories: abuse of others (e.g., insults and nasty comments), threats (threatening harm), work avoidance (e.g., tardiness), work sabotage (doing work incorrectly), and overt acts (theft). Counterproductive work behaviours are not minor concerns. One recent study found that units of a fast-food restaurant chain with higher CWBs had a significantly worse performance, whereas organizational citizenship had a relatively minor benefit. Counterproductive behaviours will be discussed throughout this book, such as when discussing organizational justice (Chapter 5), workplace stress (Chapter 7), and organizational politics (Chapter 12).[13]

counterproductive work behaviours (CWBs)
Potentially harmful voluntary behaviours enacted on an organization's property or employees.

Organizational Citizenship at Moncton's Delta Beauséjour Hotel

Organizational citizenship is a way of doing business for employees at the Delta Beauséjour Hotel in Moncton, New Brunswick. A front desk agent briefly skipped home to lend her own guitar to a group of hotel guests who were having an in-room sing-along. The hotel chef called a regular guest to ask if there was any "comfort food" he could prepare to make the time away from home less impersonal. And seeing a guest who was clearly feeling low, a housekeeping attendant set aside her own tasks to share an uplifting chat. Martin Leclerc, Delta Beauséjour's general manager, says these moments of organizational citizenship are representative of an engaged workforce: "Having a workplace where staff go above and beyond is really about creating engagement—letting them see that they can make a difference, and that we want and will allow them to do that." *Courtesy of Moncton Delta Beauséjour Hotel*
www4.deltahotels.com

JOINING AND STAYING WITH THE ORGANIZATION

Task performance, organizational citizenship, and the lack of counterproductive work behaviours are obviously important, but if qualified people don't join and stay with the organization, none of these performance-related behaviours would occur. Attracting and retaining talented people is particularly important as worries about skills shortages heat up. For instance, almost all of the industry associations in western Canada expect moderate to severe labour shortages in some occupations over the next five years. In the United States, NASA projects that U.S. colleges will graduate less than 200,000 engineering and science students to replace 2 million baby boomers who retire from these jobs between 1998 and 2008.[14]

The war for talent includes keeping the best people, not just hiring them. As we learned in Chapter 1, much of an organization's intellectual capital is the knowledge employees carry around in their heads. Long-service staff members, in particular, have valuable information about work processes, corporate values, and customer needs. Very little of this is documented anywhere. Thus, knowledge management involves keeping valuable employees with the organization. "At 5 p.m., 95 percent of our assets walk out the door," says an executive at SAS Institute, a leading statistics software firm. "We have to have an environment that makes them want to walk back in the door the next morning." The problem is that many employees don't return the next morning. Nearly half of the 3,000 Canadian employees recently surveyed say they would change companies if offered a comparable job.[15]

job satisfaction
A person's evaluation of his or her job and work context.

Why do people quit their jobs? Traditionally, OB experts have identified low job satisfaction as the main cause of turnover. **Job satisfaction** is a person's evaluation of his or her job and work context (see Chapter 4). Employees become dissatisfied with their employment relationship, which motivates them to search for and join another organization with better conditions. While job dissatisfaction builds over time and eventually affects turnover, the most recent opinion is that specific "shock events" need to be considered.[16] These shock events, such as the boss's unfair decision or a conflict episode with a co-worker, create strong emotions that trigger employees to think about and search for alternative employment.

MAINTAINING WORK ATTENDANCE

Along with attracting and retaining employees, organizations need everyone to show up for work at scheduled times. Statistics Canada reports that more than 750,000 employees—about 7 percent of the full-time workforce—are absent from work due to illness or personal reasons at some time during any given week. This rate is higher than most other OECD countries and is up from 5.5 percent a decade ago.[17] Situational factors—such as a snowstorm or car breakdown—explain some work absences. Motivation is another factor. Employees who experience job dissatisfaction or work-related stress are more likely to be absent or late for work because taking time off is a way to withdraw temporarily from stressful or dissatisfying conditions. Absenteeism is also higher in organizations with generous sick leave because this benefit limits the negative financial impact of taking time away from work.[18]

The MARS model and the five types of individual behaviour and results provide a foundation for the ideas presented over the next few chapters. For the remainder of this chapter, we will look at two of the most stable individual differences: values and personality.

■ VALUES IN THE WORKPLACE

Astral Media has come a long way since its humble beginnings 40 years ago as a photo-finishing store. Today, the Montreal-based company touches everyone's lives through pay TV, specialty television, radio, and outdoor advertising. Astral executives claim that these achievements are partly due to the company's four clearly stated and consistently executed core values. "Throughout the evolution of Astral, I am convinced that our emphasis on the principles of performance, integrity, commitment and respect has been a key element of our success," explains Astral Media CEO Ian Greenberg. "These intangible corporate values are the Astral stamp."[19]

Several bestselling management books conclude that Astral Media and other successful companies have a deeply entrenched and long-lasting set of core values.[20] To emulate this success, executives have been keen to identify, communicate, and align a set of core values in their own firms. **Values** are stable, long-lasting beliefs that guide our preferences for outcomes or courses of action in a variety of situations.[21] They are perceptions about what is good or bad, right or wrong. Values tells us what we "ought" to do. They serve as a moral compass that directs our motivation and, potentially, our decisions and actions. Values partly define who we are as individuals and as members of groups with similar values.

People arrange values into a hierarchy of preferences, called a *value system*. Some individuals value new challenges more than they value conformity. Others value generosity more than frugality. Each person's unique value system is developed and reinforced through socialization from parents, religious institutions, friends, personal experiences, and the society in which he or she lives. As such, a person's hierarchy of values is stable and long lasting. For example, one study found that value systems of a sample of adolescents were remarkably similar 20 years later as adults.[22]

Notice that our description of values has focused on individuals, whereas Astral Media's CEO described values as though they belong to the organization. In reality, values exist only within individuals, which we call *personal values*. However, groups of people might hold the same or similar values, so we tend to ascribe these shared values to the team, department, organization, profession, or entire society. The values shared by people throughout an organization (*organizational values*) will receive fuller discussion in Chapter 16 because they are a key part of corporate culture. The values shared across a society (*cultural values*) will receive attention later in this chapter.

values

Stable, long-lasting beliefs about what is important in a variety of situations.

espoused values

Values that we say we use and think we use.

enacted values

Values we rely on to guide our decisions and actions.

Before discussing workplace values in more detail, we need to distinguish between espoused and enacted values.[23] **Espoused values** represent the values that we say we use and, in many cases, think we use. Corporate leaders might say they value environmentalism, creativity, and politeness, whether or not they really do value these things in practice. Values are socially desirable, so people create a positive public image by claiming to believe in values that others expect them to embrace. Also, corporate values are usually considered espoused values because, although leaders might abide by them, we don't know whether lower level employees share this commitment. **Enacted values**, on the other hand, represent the values we actually rely on to guide our decisions and actions. These values-in-use are apparent by watching people in action. Just as we judge an individual's personality by behavioural tendencies, so too do we judge enacted values by behavioural tendencies.

TYPES OF VALUES

Values come in many forms, and experts on this topic have devoted considerable attention to organizing them into coherent groups. The model in Exhibit 2.3, developed and tested by social psychologist Shalom Schwartz, has become the most widely studied and generally accepted model today.[24] Schwartz reduced dozens of personal values into these 10 broader domains of values and further organized these domains around two bipolar dimensions.

Along the left side of the horizontal dimension in Schwartz's model is *openness to change*, which represents the extent to which a person is motivated to pursue innovative ways. Openness to change includes the value domains of self-direction (independent thought and action) and stimulation (excitement and challenge). *Conservation*, the opposite end of Schwartz's horizontal dimension, is the extent to which a person is motivated to preserve the status quo. Conservation includes the value clusters of conformity (adherence to social norms and expectations), security (safety and stability), and tradition (moderation and preservation of the status quo).

The vertical dimension in Schwartz's model ranges from self-enhancement to self-transcendence. *Self-enhancement*—how much a person is motivated by self-interest—includes the values of achievement (pursuit of personal success) and power (dominance over others). The opposite of self-enhancement is *self-transcendence*, which refers to the motivation to promote the welfare of others and nature. Self-transcendence includes the values of benevolence (concern for others in one's life) and universalism (concern for the welfare of all people and nature).

VALUES AND INDIVIDUAL BEHAVIOUR

Personal values guide our decisions and actions, but this connection isn't as direct as it sounds. Our habitual behaviour tends to be consistent with our values, but our everyday conscious decisions and actions apply our values much less consistently. The main reason for the "disconnect" between personal values and individual behaviour is that values are abstract concepts that sound good in theory but are less easily followed in practice. A lot of people say that benevolence is an important value to them, yet they don't think about being benevolent in many situations. Benevolence becomes a "truism" that gets lost in translation in everyday activities.

Benevolence and other values do influence decisions and behaviour if three conditions are met.[25] First, a specific value affects our behaviour when something makes us mindful (consciously aware) of that value. Co-workers tend to treat each other

■ **EXHIBIT 2.3**

Schwartz's values circumplex

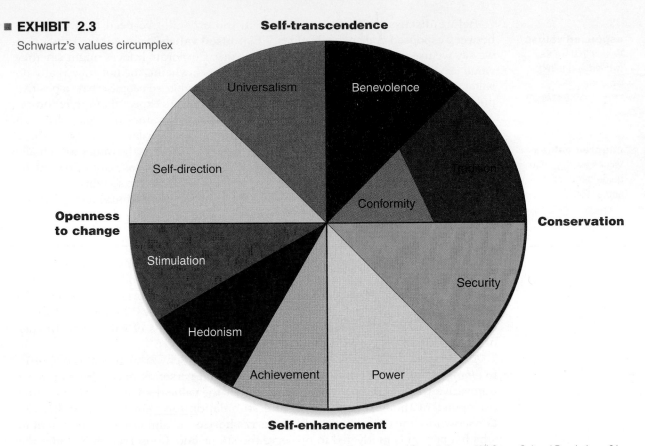

Source: S. H. Schwartz and G. Sagie, "Value Consensus and Importance: A Cross-national Study," *Journal of Cross-Cultural Psychology*, 31 (July 2000), pp. 465–97; S. H. Schwartz, "Universals in the Content and Structure of Values: Theoretical Advances and Empirical Tests in 20 Countries," *Advances in Experimental Social Psychology*, 25 (1992), pp. 1–65.

with much more respect and consideration immediately after a senior executive gives a speech on the virtues of benevolence in the workplace. The speech makes employees temporarily mindful of this value, so they think about it in their behaviour towards others. Second, even if a particular value is important and we are mindful of it, we still need to have logical reasons in our head for applying that value. In other words, we tend to apply our values only when we can think of specific reasons for doing so. For example, you will be more motivated to switch your vacation time with a co-worker who needs that time off if you are mindful of your value of benevolence and you can think of good reasons why it's good to be benevolent.

The third condition that improves the linkage between our values and behaviour is the situation. Work environments shape our behaviour, at least in the short term, so they necessarily encourage or discourage values-consistent behaviour. The fact is, our jobs sometimes require us to act in ways that are inconsistent with our personal values. This incongruence between our personal values and work requirements can also have a powerful effect on employee attitudes and other behaviours, as we'll see next.

VALUES CONGRUENCE

A few years ago, Copenhagen Business School professor Peter Pruzan held a seminar on workplace values with executives at a large European-based multinational manufacturing company. Working in teams, the executives developed a list of their five most important personal values. The personal values list included honesty, love, beauty, peace of mind, and happiness (most of which fall under the categories of universalism and benevolence in Exhibit 2.3). In the afternoon, the teams developed a list of the enacted (not espoused) values of their company. The company values list included success, efficiency, power, competitiveness, and productivity (most of which are represented by achievement and power in Exhibit 2.3). In other words, the organization's values were almost completely opposite to the executives' personal values. After an embarrassing silence, the CEO briefly spoke, announcing that he would consider resigning. He said that he had actively constructed a monster, a corporate Frankenstein![26]

The CEO of the European firm didn't resign, but he and his executive team did act quickly to improve **values congruence** in the organization. Values congruence refers to the similarity of value systems between two entities. In the example of the European manufacturer, the organization's value system was incongruent with the value systems of its managers (called *person-organization values congruence*). Research indicates that this form of incongruence is common. Three out of four managers surveyed in one study said their company's values conflict to some extent with their own ethical values. A recent major survey of MBA students in Canada, the U.S., and the U.K. revealed that half of them anticipate (and have experienced) making business decisions that conflict with their personal values.[27]

Person-organization values incongruence has a number of undesirable consequences, including higher stress and turnover as well as lower organizational citizenship, loyalty, and job satisfaction. "We've found that the higher the disconnect between one's values and those of the organization, the higher the potential for burnout," says Jayne Hayden, manager of the Career Resource Centre at the University of Waterloo. Values are guideposts, so incongruence also reduces the chance that employees will make decisions compatible with the organization's values.[28]

Does this mean that the most successful organizations perfectly align employee values with the organization's values? Not at all! While a comfortable degree of values congruence is necessary for the reasons just noted, organizations also benefit from some level of values incongruence. Employees with diverse values offer different perspectives, which often leads to better decision making (see Chapter 8). Moreover, too much congruence can create a "corporate cult" that potentially undermines creativity, organizational flexibility, and business ethics (see Chapter 16).[29]

Other types of values congruence   A second type of values congruence refers to how closely the values apparent in our actions (enacted values) are consistent with what we say we believe in (espoused values). This *espoused-enacted values congruence* is especially important for people in leadership positions because any obvious gap between espoused and enacted values undermines their perceived integrity, a critical feature of effective leaders (see Chapter 14).[30] Even for nonmanagement staff, espoused-enacted values congruence affects how much co-workers can trust them, which has implications for team dynamics.

A third type of values congruence refers to the compatibility of an organization's dominant values with the prevailing values of the community or society in which it conducts business.[31] For example, an organization originating from one country that tries to impose its value system on stakeholders located in another culture may experience higher employee turnover and have more difficult relations with the communities in which the company operates. SC Johnson was aware of this

values congruence
A situation wherein two or more entities have similar value systems.

need for values congruence for its Australian business. The American household products firm is "a family company with family values." But Australians generally like to separate their work from their personal lives, so SC Johnson's solution tweaked its values somewhat. "You can't sell that family company idea in Australia, so we position it as family values with work/life balance," explains an SC Johnson executive.[32] Let's look more closely at cross-cultural values.

■ VALUES ACROSS CULTURES

Anyone who has worked long enough in other countries will know that values differ across cultures. Some cultures value group decisions, whereas others think that the leader should take charge. Meetings in Germany usually start on time, whereas they might be half an hour late in Brazil without much concern. We need to understand differences in cultural values to avoid unnecessary conflicts and misunderstandings between people from different countries. That's why, as GLOBAL Connections 2.1 describes, American employees at Hyundai's new manufacturing facility in Montgomery, Alabama, are learning about Korean values, and why Hyundai executives are adapting their Korean business practices to be more compatible with American culture.

INDIVIDUALISM AND COLLECTIVISM

individualism
The extent to which a person values independence and personal uniqueness.

Let's start by looking at the two most commonly mentioned cross-cultural values, individualism and collectivism. **Individualism** is the extent to which we value independence and personal uniqueness. Highly individualist people value personal freedom, self-sufficiency, control over their own lives, and appreciation of the unique qualities that distinguish them from others. This value relates most closely to the self-direction dimension shown earlier in Exhibit 2.3. **Collectivism** is the extent to which we value our duty to groups to which we belong, and to group harmony. Highly collectivist people define themselves by their group membership and value harmonious relationships within those groups.[33] Collectivism is located within the conservation range of values (security, tradition, conformity) in Exhibit 2.3.

collectivism
The extent to which people value duty to groups to which they belong, and to group harmony.

You might think from these definitions that individualism and collectivism are opposites. Until recently, many scholars thought so, too, but the two concepts are actually unrelated, according to research studies.[34] Some people and cultures have both high individualism and high collectivism, for example.

How individualistic and collectivistic are Canadians? Exhibit 2.4 shows that Canadians with European heritage are relatively more individualistic than people in most other countries. Only people in some South American countries (such as Chile and Peru) are apparently more individualistic. Exhibit 2.4 also shows that European Canadians are relatively low in collectivism, whereas people in Italy, Taiwan, Peru, Zimbabwe, and most other countries have higher collectivism.

One notable observation in Exhibit 2.4 is that people in Japan are less collectivist than most cultures. This is a stark contrast to statements in many cross-cultural books that Japan is one of the most collectivist countries on the planet! The problem was that a major study more than 20 years ago identified Japan as collectivist, but it measured collectivism in a way that bears little resemblance to how the concept is usually defined.[35] Subsequent studies have reported that Japan is relatively low on the collectivist scale (as Exhibit 2.4 reveals), but these persistent results have been slow to replace the old views on this matter.

South Korean Culture Meets North American Values

Residents of Montgomery, Alabama, are taking a lot more interest in Korean culture these days. That's because the Korean automobile giant Hyundai Motor Co. is building its first American manufacturing plant in the area. Montgomery City Library has ordered more books and tapes on Korean culture and language. Auburn University is oversubscribed for its luncheons on Korean and business etiquette.

Hyundai is also helping people to learn about Korean values. Every American employee hired completes a 16-hour course in Korean culture. American executives at Hyundai have already been immersed in Korean and Hyundai values with a week-long trip to Ulsan, South Korea. The education includes eating Korean food, learning about Korean history, and touring Hyundai's main manufacturing operations in Ulsan (where almost half of the 1 million residents work for the Korean automaker).

Hyundai's American executives also say they are adjusting their practices in Ulsan to fit American culture. However, Hyundai's reflection of Korea's high power distance culture—which reveres hierarchy and power of executives—may be difficult to leave behind. Hyundai's swankiest office in Montgomery is reserved for Hyundai Chairman Chung Mong-Koo when he occasionally visits. They even fly over his exclusive limousine before his arrival. When a Korean-born Hyundai executive was asked if he had met Chairman Chung during one of his visits to Montgomery, he quickly replied: "He is too high. I could not personally speak with him."

Hyundai Motor Co. says its business practices in South Korea (shown in photo) will be adapted at its new plant in Alabama to more closely suit American values.
Cho Sung-Su/Corbis

Jim Crate, foreign editor for Detroit-based *Automotive News*, says Montgomery residents will likely see Hyundai's practices clash with American values in a variety of ways. "It's a very Korean company," Crate says. "They will have to evolve in coming to America."

Sources: K. M. Dugan, "Hyundai Workers Meld Into Area's Cultural Mix," *Montgomery Advertiser*, August 15, 2004; B. Clanton, "It's A Job to Fill 1,600 Jobs," *Montgomery Advertiser*, August 19, 2003, p. B8; B. Clanton, "At Home with Hyundai: Part 2— Culture Shock," *Montgomery Advertiser*, June 2, 2003; B. Clanton, "Execs Sop up Korean Culture," *Montgomery Advertiser*, April 14, 2003 p. A1; B. Clanton, "Hyundai Plant Ignites Interest," *Montgomery Advertiser*, September 17, 2002; T. Kleffman, "Company Faces Culture Clash," *Montgomery Advertiser*, April 3, 2002.
www.hyundai-motor.com

POWER DISTANCE

power distance

The extent to which people accept unequal distribution of power in a society.

A third cross-cultural value that will be mentioned frequently in this book is **power distance**. Power distance is the extent that people accept unequal distribution of power in a society.[36] Those with high power distance accept and value unequal power. They value obedience to authority and are comfortable receiving commands from their superiors without consultation or debate. High power distance individuals also prefer resolving differences or contradict their boss indirectly through formal procedures rather than directly. People in Malaysia, the Philippines, and Venezuela tend to have a high power distance value.

In contrast, people with low power distance expect relatively equal power sharing. They view the relationship with their boss as one of interdependence, not dependence; that is, they believe their boss is also dependent on them, so they expect power sharing and consultation before decisions affecting them are made. Those with low

■ EXHIBIT 2.4

Individualism and collectivism in selected countries

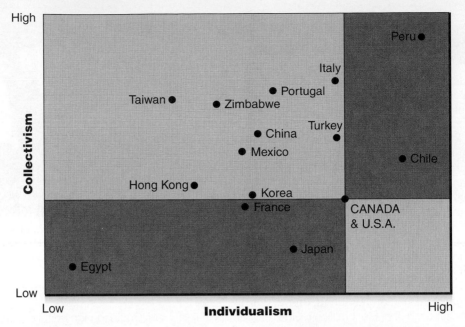

Source: Based on information in D. Oyserman, H. M. Coon, and M. Kemmelmeier, "Rethinking Individualism and Collectivism: Evaluation of Theoretical Assumptions and Meta-Analyses," *Psychological Bulletin*, 128 (2002), pp. 3–72. The countries shown here represent only a sample of those in Oyserman's meta-analysis. *Note:* The United States includes studies from both the U.S. and Canada and refers only to people with European heritage in those countries.

power distance readily approach and contradict their boss. Power distance is lowest among people in Australia and Israel. Canadians generally have a moderately low power distance.

OTHER CROSS-CULTURAL VALUES

Cross-cultural researchers have investigated many other values, but the only other two that we will mention are uncertainty avoidance and achievement-nurturing orientation. **Uncertainty avoidance** is the degree to which people tolerate ambiguity (low uncertainty avoidance) or feel threatened by ambiguity and uncertainty (high uncertainty avoidance). Employees with high uncertainty avoidance value structured situations where rules of conduct and decision making are clearly documented. They usually prefer direct rather than indirect or ambiguous communications. People in Japan and Greece tend to have high uncertainty avoidance, whereas very low uncertainty avoidance scores have been reported in past studies for people in Singapore and Jamaica. Canadians tend to have moderate levels of uncertainty avoidance.

Achievement-nurturing orientation reflects a competitive versus cooperative view of relations with other people.[37] People with a high achievement orientation value assertiveness, competitiveness, and materialism. They appreciate people who are tough and favour the acquisition of money and material goods. In contrast, people in nurturing-oriented cultures emphasize relationships and the well-being of others. They focus on human interaction and caring rather than competition and personal success. People in the Netherlands and Sweden score very low on achievement orientation (i.e., they have a high nurturing orientation), whereas people in Japan tend to have high scores on this cultural value. Canadians score somewhere around the middle of the pack compared with other countries.

uncertainty avoidance

The degree to which people tolerate ambiguity or feel threatened by ambiguity and uncertainty.

achievement-nurturing orientation

A competitive versus cooperative view of relations with other people.

Before leaving this topic, we need to acknowledge two concerns about the cross-cultural values information provided here.[38] First, the statements about how high or low people in various countries score on power distance, uncertainty avoidance, and achievement-nurturing orientation are based on a survey of IBM employees worldwide more than a quarter century ago. Over 100,000 IBM staff in dozens of countries completed that survey, but it is possible that these IBM employees do not represent the general population. There is also evidence that values have changed quite a bit in some countries since then. A second concern is the assumption that everyone in a society has similar cultural values. This may be true in a few countries, but not in culturally diverse societies such as Canada. Indeed, one major cultural analysis divided Canadians into 13 fairly distinct groups in terms of their social values. By assigning certain values to an entire society, we are engaging in a form of stereotyping that limits our ability to understand the more complex reality of that society.

CANADIAN VS. AMERICAN VALUES

Wal-Mart entered this country a dozen years ago and has since become Canada's largest retailer, but the American firm stumbled over Canada's cultural values along the way. The effusive American-style greeters seem a little too phony to Canadians, and the Wal-Mart cheer that employees must repeat every morning is considered a bit too cult-like. More recently, Wal-Mart discovered that Canadians have a tendency to join labour unions, something that the Bentonville, Arkansas, retailer is having trouble recognizing.[39]

Do Canadians have different values than their American cousins? Wal-Mart Canada executives would probably agree they differ, and that's also the conclusion of ongoing research by Michael Adams and his group at Environics Research in Toronto. "Canadians may like Americans, speak the same language, and consume more of their fast food and popular culture, but we embrace a different hierarchy of values," writes Adams.[40] Not only do Canadians and Americans have a different hierarchy of values, the differences have increased over the past decade or more. As another Canadian scholar recently emphasized, the 49th parallel border is more than just an imaginary geographic division; it is a symbol of the widening ideological divide in North America.[41]

The most striking difference is that Canadians question authority and value autonomy from these institutions, whereas Americans have a relatively high deference to authority. Religious opinions and practices provide one indicator of this distinction. Canadians are almost half as likely as Americans to be associated with a religious institution and are less likely to believe that these institutions should influence public policy. Canadians are also more than twice as likely as Americans to believe that organizations work better without a single leader. Another telling difference is in responses to the statement: "The father of the family must be the master in his own house." The percentage of Canadians agreeing with this statement has plummeted from 42 percent in the early 1980s to 26 percent in 1992 and just 18 percent today. In contrast, 49 percent of Americans agree or strongly agree with this statement today, a slight *increase* from 42 percent in 1992.[42]

Along with differences in authority-autonomy, Canadians have significantly higher tolerance or moral permissiveness than do Americans. Canadians are more accepting of a cultural mosaic rather than a homogeneous melting pot, of unmarried couples as parents, and (at least more than Americans) same-sex marriage. A third distinction is that Canadians are somewhat more collectivist and egalitarian than are Americans. Surveys indicate that Canadians are more willing to allow collective rights over individual rights, are less accepting of large wealth differences within society, and throw more support behind the notion of teaching children the need to care for others.[43]

The information above might lead you to think that Americans and Canadians are worlds apart when it comes to values. They aren't! Although most experts agree that cultural differences exist, some suggest these differences are relatively small when we compare Canadian values to those in, say, China or Brazil. Another revealing observation is that the United States and Canada seem to consist of four cultural groups: the Southern U.S., Northern U.S., Anglophone (English-speaking) Canada, and Francophone (French-speaking) Canada. The Southern U.S. is largely inhabited by people with the most conservative, hawkish, and deeply religious values of the four groups. Francophone Canadians, the second cluster, hold the most tolerant or morally permissive values. This leaves Anglophone Canadians and Americans residing in the northern U.S. Research suggests that these two groups have very similar cultural values.[44]

Nunavut's Legislative Assembly Reflects Inuit Values

Walk into the Legislative Assembly of Nunavut, Canada's newest territory, and you will soon realize that Inuit culture is quite different from the Western values embedded in *Robert's Rules of Order*. Politicians aren't grouped into political parties sitting across from each other. Indeed, there are no political parties, just 19 members seated in a circle. The lack of partisanship is representative of Inuit culture. "The one thing that reflects the Inuit culture the most is the consensus system of government," explains John Amagoalik, who chaired the Nunavut Implementation Commission. Low power distance and high collectivism are also found in many other First Nations cultures in Canada, as well as in organizations founded by people with First Nations heritage.[48]

CP/Kevin Frayer

www.assembly.nu.ca

Francophone and First Nations values   The idea that Canada has two cultural clusters—Anglophones and Francophones—is not new. In fact, the oldest form of Canadian cultural diversity has been the so-called "two solitudes" between these two groups. At one time, Francophones were more religious, traditional, and deferent to authority, compared with Anglophones. Now, the opposite is almost true. Francophones have lower scores than Anglophones on respect for patriarchal authority, and they tend to have more tolerant or morally permissive opinions regarding marriage, sexual activity, and nonmarried parenthood.[45] There is also evidence that the cultural values of Anglophone and Francophone Canadians are converging to some extent. One study reported that Anglophone and Francophone Canadian public sector male managers had similar degrees of individualism and collectivism. Another study found that the two groups held similar values regarding environmentalism.[46]

Canada's cultural diversity is further evident in the values of First Nations people and their organizations. Organizations with First Nations founders and leaders tend to have a strong collectivist value, low power distance, low uncertainty avoidance, and a relatively nurturing rather than achievement orientation. These values are evident from consensus-oriented decision making (low power distance), focus more on the group than individuals (high collectivism), fewer rules and procedures (low uncertainty avoidance), and emphasis on the holistic well-being of employees and community (nurturing more than achievement orientation).[47]

Canada's cultural diversity extends beyond Anglophone, Francophone, and First Nations peoples to the incredible variety of new Canadians who were raised elsewhere in the world.[49] Collectively, this information reinforces the fact that Canadians hold value systems that to some extent vary with each other and with people from other societies. These values guide our decisions and actions, and distinguish us from people in other cultures. Values also represent the foundation of ethical decisions and conduct, which we read about next.

■ ETHICAL VALUES AND BEHAVIOUR

When the Business Council of British Columbia recently asked employers to list the most important characteristics they look for in new hires, the top factor wasn't performance standards, customer service, or common sense. Although these characteristics were important, the most important characteristic in almost every job group was honesty/ethics.[50] **Ethics** refers to the study of moral principles or values that determine whether actions are right or wrong and outcomes are good or bad. People rely on their ethical values to determine "the right thing to do."

Canada is recognized around the world for its high ethical standards—it ranks fifth lowest on the global corruption index, for example—yet it has its share of scandals involving unethical corporate behaviour. A small sample of alleged wrongdoing (many of these cases are still in court or being investigated) include accounting fraud at Nortel and Livent, corporate espionage at WestJet, fraudulent financing at CIBC, misleading statements about nonexistent product developments at VisuaLabs, and misuse of company funds at Hollinger. Even WorldCom, the largest accounting fraud in U.S. history, was instigated by Bernie Ebbers, who was born and raised in Edmonton.[51]

ethics
The study of moral principles or values that determine whether actions are right or wrong and outcomes are good or bad.

THREE ETHICAL PRINCIPLES

To better understand the ethical dilemmas facing organizations, we need to consider three distinct types of ethical principles: utilitarianism, individual rights, and distributive justice.[52] While you might prefer one principle more than the others based on your personal values, all three should be actively considered to put important ethical issues to the test.

- *Utilitarianism*—**Utilitarianism** advises us to seek the greatest good for the greatest number of people. In other words, we should choose the option providing the highest degree of satisfaction to those affected. This is sometimes known as a consequential principle because it focuses on the consequences of our actions, not on how we achieve those consequences. One problem with utilitarianism is that it is almost impossible to evaluate the benefits or costs of many decisions, particularly when many stakeholders have wide-ranging needs and values. Another problem is that most of us are uncomfortable engaging in behaviours that seem, well, unethical, to attain results that are ethical.

- *Individual rights*—The **individual rights principle** reflects the belief that everyone has entitlements that let them act in a certain way. Some of the most widely cited rights are freedom of movement, physical security, freedom of speech, fair trial, and freedom from torture. The individual rights principle includes more than legal rights; it also includes human rights that everyone is granted as a moral norm of society. For example, access to education and knowledge isn't a

utilitarianism
The moral principle stating that decision makers should seek the greatest good for the greatest number of people when choosing among alternatives.

individual rights principle
The moral principle stating that every person is entitled to legal and human rights.

legal requirement everywhere, but most of us believe that it is a human right. One problem with individual rights is that certain individual rights may conflict with others. The shareholders' right to be informed about corporate activities may ultimately conflict with an executive's right to privacy, for example.

■ *Distributive justice*—The **distributive justice principle** suggests that people who are similar in relevant ways should receive similar benefits and burdens; those who are dissimilar should receive different benefits and burdens in proportion to their dissimilarity. For example, we expect that two employees who contribute equally in their work should receive similar rewards, whereas those who make a lesser contribution should receive less. A variation of this principle says that inequalities are acceptable where they benefit the least well off in society. Thus, employees in risky jobs should be paid more if this benefits others who are less well off. One problem with the distributive justice principle is that it is difficult to agree on who is "similar" and what factors are "relevant." Most of us agree that race and gender should not be relevant when distributing paycheques. But should rewards be determined purely by an employee's performance, or should effort, seniority, and other factors also be taken into account?

MORAL INTENSITY, ETHICAL SENSITIVITY, AND SITUATIONAL INFLUENCES

Along with ethical principles and their underlying values, we need to consider three other factors that influence ethical conduct in the workplace: the moral intensity of the issue, the individual's ethical sensitivity, and situational factors.

Moral intensity is the degree to which an issue demands the application of ethical principles. Decisions with high moral intensity are more important, so the decision maker needs to more carefully apply ethical principles to resolve it. Stealing from your employer is usually considered high on moral intensity, whereas borrowing a company pen for personal use is much lower on the scale. To determine the moral intensity of an issue, we tend to consider the six factors shown in Exhibit 2.5. Keep in mind that this list represents the factors people naturally think about; some of them might not be considered morally acceptable when formally making ethical decisions.[53]

Even if an issue has high moral intensity, some employees might not recognize its ethical importance because they have low ethical sensitivity. **Ethical sensitivity** is a personal characteristic that enables people to recognize the presence and determine the relative importance of an ethical issue.[54] Ethically sensitive people are not necessarily more ethical. Rather, they are more likely to recognize whether an issue requires ethical consideration; that is, they can more accurately estimate the moral intensity of the issue. Ethically sensitive people tend to have higher empathy. They also have more information about the specific situation. For example, accountants would be more ethically sensitive regarding the appropriateness of specific accounting procedures than would someone who has not received training in this profession.

The third important factor explaining why good people do bad things is the situation in which the unethical conduct occurs. A few recent surveys have reported that employees regularly experience corporate pressure that leads to selling beyond the customers' needs, lying to the client, or making unrealistic promises. Other surveys have found that most employees believe they experience so much pressure that it compromises their ethical conduct. For instance, nearly two-thirds of the managers in one academic study stated that pressure from top management causes people further down in hierarchy to compromise their beliefs, whereas 90 percent

---

distributive justice principle
The moral principle stating that people who are similar should be rewarded similarly, and those dissimilar should be rewarded differently.

moral intensity
The degree to which an issue demands the application of ethical principles.

ethical sensitivity
A personal characteristic that enables people to recognize the presence and determine the relative importance of an ethical issue.

■ **EXHIBIT 2.5**   Factors influencing perceived moral intensity

Moral Intensity Factor	Moral Intensity Question	Moral Intensity is Higher When...
Magnitude of consequences	How much harm or benefit will occur to others as a result of this action?	...the harm or benefit is larger
Social consequences	How many other people agree that this action is ethically good or bad?	...many people agree
Probability of effect	(a) What is the chance that this action will actually occur? (b) What is the chance that this action will actually cause good or bad consequences?	...the probability is higher
Temporal immediacy	How long after the action will the consequences occur?	...the time delay is shorter
Proximity	How socially, culturally, psychologically, and/or physically close to me are the people affected by to this decision?	...those affected are close rather than distant
Concentration of effect	(a) How many people are affected by this action? (b) Are the people affected by this action easily identifiable as a group?	...many people are affected ...easily identifiable as a group

NOTE: These are factors people tend to ask themselves when determining the moral intensity of an issue. Whether some of these questions should be relevant is itself an ethical question

Source: T. J. Jones, "Ethical Decision Making by Individuals in Organizations: An Issue Contingent Model," *Academy of Management Review* 16 (1991), pp. 366–95.

of top management disagreed with this statement.[55] The point here is not to justify unethical conduct. Rather, we need to recognize the situational factors that influence wrongdoing so that organizations can correct these problems in the future.

SUPPORTING ETHICAL BEHAVIOUR

Most large and medium-size organizations in Canada and several other countries have developed and communicated ethical codes of conduct. These statements establish the organization's ethical standards and signal to employees that the company takes ethical conduct seriously. However, written ethics codes alone won't prevent wrongdoing in the workplace.[56] As Connections 2.2 reveals, it's easy for ethics strategies to get tangled up or undermined by other factors, with the result that the organization's ethical standards may not improve at all.

To supplement ethics codes, many firms provide ethics training. For instance, following a series of scandals in the United States, CIBC introduced a new ethics program that includes online training for all staff on legal issues and advanced ethics training for those involved in complex transactions. The bank will also add an ethics hotline where employees can report ethical irregularities. In addition to receiving mandatory ethics training, civil servants in the Canadian government are urged to consult ethics officers regarding specific dilemmas.[57]

Potholes Along the Road to a More Ethical Workplace

Canadian businesses and governments are scrambling to install ethics programs, but ethics experts warn that it is a long journey from posting an ethics code to actually having employees follow it. For instance, the Nova Scotia government has ethics codes in most departments, ranging from social work to libraries. It even has a checklist for employees to determine whether an outside activity contravenes the government's ethics code. In spite of these initiatives, Nova Scotia's civil servants might not try to reduce unethical conduct among co-workers. In a recent survey, more than half said they fear reprisal if they report any ethical problems.

The Royal Bank of Canada (RBC) has been at the forefront of ethics testing and training for more than 20 years. As part of RBC's strategy to ensure ethical conduct, every employee must complete an online ethics test every two years. The electronic role-play presents a series of scenarios that require ethical judgment, and the results are reviewed by senior management to ensure that employees understand RBC's code of conduct. However, some employees and managers think the exercise is a waste of time. "People were annoyed that they had to do them," says a former RBC employee. "A lot of the account managers thought it was stupid."

Their solution: they asked co-workers who performed well on the test to complete the online test in their place. "I would just knock these things out," says the former RBC employee, referring to the number of ethics tests he completed for other RBC staff.

Nortel is making ethics a priority after its former CEO and nearly a dozen senior executives were fired for using illegal accounting practices. The unethical conduct occurred because the executives stood to earn sizeable bonuses from an incentive plan— which Nortel now describes as "deceitful"—if they could create a paper profit each quarter. So, it was with considerable pride that Nortel recently announced the appointment of a new chief ethics officer to help clean up the high-tech company's image and ethical practices. The high-profile executive will earn a $375,000 base salary as well as an annual bonus worth $225,000. Some experts were stunned by the remuneration package. Nortel's new ethics watchdog will be tied to the same or similar incentive scheme that motivated the former executives to engage in unethical accounting practices!

Sources: L. Bogomolny, "Good Housekeeping," *Canadian Business*, 77 (March 1, 2004), pp. 87–88; D. Jackson, "Too Scared to Blow Whistle," *Chronicle-Herald* (Halifax), August 6, 2004; S. Brearton, "Corporate Social Responsibility: 2nd Annual Ranking," *The Globe & Mail*, February 25, 2005, p. 42.

Aside from these programs and practices, one of the strongest influences on the moral fibre of an organization is the ethical conduct and vigilance of its leaders.[58] As we will learn in Chapter 14, effective leaders have integrity in the eyes of followers. By the same token, leaders must demonstrate authentic ethical conduct to be effective. Their espoused values must be consistent with their enacted values. By acting with the highest standards of moral conduct, leaders not only gain support and trust from followers, they also role model the ethical standards that employees are more likely to follow.

■ PERSONALITY IN ORGANIZATIONS

Ethical, cultural, and personal values are relatively stable characteristics, so they are an important influence on individual behaviour. Another individual characteristic that has long-term stability is personality. In fact, there is considerable evidence that values and personality traits are interrelated and reinforce each other.[59] Personality refers to the relatively stable pattern of behaviours and consistent internal states that explain a person's behavioural tendencies. Personality has both internal and external elements. External traits are the observable behaviours that we rely on to identify someone's personality. For example, we can see that a person is extroverted by the way he or she interacts with other people. The internal states represent the thoughts, values, and genetic characteristics that we infer from the observable behaviours. Experts continue to debate the extent to which personality is genetically coded through evolution or shaped from childhood and other early life experiences.[60]

We say that personality explains behavioural tendencies because individuals' actions are not perfectly consistent with their personality profile in every situation. Personality traits are less evident in situations where social norms, reward systems, and other conditions constrain our behaviour.[61] For example, talkative people remain relatively quiet in a library where "no talking" rules are explicit and strictly enforced.

PERSONALITY AND ORGANIZATIONAL BEHAVIOUR

Brigitte Catellier's final hurdle to become vice-president of legal affairs at Montreal-based Astral Media Inc wasn't quite what she might have anticipated. For seven hours, Catellier sat through eight aptitude, preferences, and personality tests, some of which asked unusual questions such as whether she would prefer to be an astronaut or an acrobat. "I was told very directly there are two candidates and you are both doing the same tests," says Catellier, who was later offered the job. Astral decided a few years ago to include psychological tests in the hiring process, including instruments that measure personality traits such as dominance and tolerance. "This helps us not make mistakes, and we have made mistakes from time to time in the past," says Astral's vice-president of human resources, referring to people hired in the past whose personalities didn't fit the company or job requirements.[62]

Astral Media is among the growing number of Canadian firms that have introduced psychological testing in the hiring process. While aptitude tests have been used regularly for decades, personality tests have had a rocky experience in the selection process. At one time, scholars often explained employee behaviour in terms of personality traits and companies regularly administered personality tests to job applicants. This changed in the 1960s when researchers reported that the relationship between personality and job performance is very weak.[63] They cited problems with measuring personality traits and explained that the connection between personality and performance exists only under very narrowly defined conditions. Companies stopped using personality tests due to concerns that these tests might unfairly discriminate against visible minorities and other identifiable groups.

Over the past decade, personality has regained some of its credibility in organizational settings.[64] Recent studies have reported that certain personality traits predict certain work-related behaviours, stress reactions, and emotions fairly well under certain conditions. Experts have reintroduced the idea that effective leaders have identifiable traits and that personality explains some of a person's positive attitudes and life happiness. Personality traits also seem to help people find the jobs that best suit their needs.[65] Personality is a remote concept, so it isn't the best predictor of most jobs, but it is increasingly clear that some personality traits are relevant. Some of the most relevant personality traits for job performance and well-being are found in the Big Five personality dimensions.

THE "BIG FIVE" PERSONALITY DIMENSIONS

Since the days of Plato, scholars have been trying to develop lists of personality traits. About 100 years ago, a few personality experts tried to catalogue and condense the many personality traits that had been described over the years. They found thousands of words in *Roget's Thesaurus* and *Webster's Dictionary* that represented personality traits. They aggregated these words into 171 clusters, then further shrunk them down to five abstract personality dimensions. Using more sophisticated techniques, recent investigations identified the same five dimensions—known as the **"Big Five" personality dimensions**.[66] These five dimensions, represented by the handy acronym CANOE, are outlined in Exhibit 2.6 and described below:

- *Conscientiousness*—Conscientiousness refers to people who are careful, dependable, and self-disciplined. Some scholars argue that this dimension also includes the will to achieve. People with low conscientiousness tend to be careless, less thorough, more disorganized, and irresponsible.
- *Agreeableness*—This includes the traits of being courteous, good-natured, empathic, and caring. Some scholars prefer the label of "friendly compliance" for this dimension, with its opposite being "hostile noncompliance." People with low agreeableness tend to be uncooperative, short-tempered, and irritable.
- *Neuroticism*—Neuroticism characterizes people with high levels of anxiety, hostility, depression, and self-consciousness. In contrast, people with low neuroticism (high emotional stability) are poised, secure, and calm.
- *Openness to experience*—This dimension is the most complex and has the least agreement among scholars. It generally refers to the extent to which people are sensitive, flexible, creative, and curious. Those who score low on this dimension tend to be more resistant to change, less open to new ideas, and more fixed in their ways.
- *Extroversion*—**Extroversion** characterizes people who are outgoing, talkative, sociable, and assertive. The opposite is **introversion**, which refers to those who are quiet, shy, and cautious. Introverts do not necessarily lack social skills. Rather, they are more inclined to direct their interests to ideas than to social events. Introverts feel quite comfortable being alone, whereas extroverts do not.

"Big Five" personality dimensions
The five abstract dimensions representing most personality traits: conscientiousness, agreeableness, neuroticism, openness to experience, and extroversion (CANOE).

extroversion
A "Big Five" personality dimension that characterizes people who are outgoing, talkative, sociable, and assertive.

introversion
A "Big Five" personality dimension that characterizes people who are territorial and solitary.

■ **EXHIBIT 2.6**   "Big Five" personality dimensions

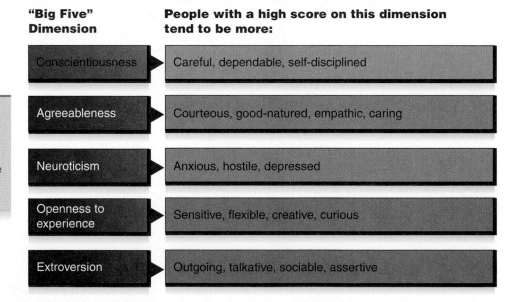

"Big Five" Dimension	People with a high score on this dimension tend to be more:
Conscientiousness	Careful, dependable, self-disciplined
Agreeableness	Courteous, good-natured, empathic, caring
Neuroticism	Anxious, hostile, depressed
Openness to experience	Sensitive, flexible, creative, curious
Extroversion	Outgoing, talkative, sociable, assertive

These five personality dimensions affect work-related behaviour and job performance to varying degrees.[67] People with high emotional stability tend to work better than others in high-stressor situations. Those with high agreeableness tend to handle customer relations and conflict-based situations more effectively. However, conscientiousness has taken centre stage as the most valuable personality trait for predicting job performance in almost every job group. Conscientious employees set higher personal goals for themselves, are more motivated, and have higher performance expectations than do employees with low levels of conscientiousness. High-conscientiousness employees tend to have higher levels of organizational citizenship and work better in workplaces that give employees more freedom than in traditional "command and control" workplaces. Employees with high conscientiousness, as well as agreeableness and emotional stability, also tend to provide better customer service.

MYERS-BRIGGS TYPE INDICATOR

Myers-Briggs Type Indicator (MBTI)

A personality test that measures each of the traits in Jung's model.

More than half a century ago, the mother and daughter team of Katherine Briggs and Isabel Briggs-Myers developed the **Myers-Briggs Type Indicator (MBTI)**, a personality inventory designed to identify individuals' basic preferences for perceiving and processing information. The MBTI builds on the personality theory proposed in the 1920s by Swiss psychiatrist Carl Jung that identifies the way people prefer to perceive their environment as well as obtain and process information. Jung suggested that everyone is either extroverted or introverted in orientation and has particular preferences for perceiving (sensing or intuition) and judging or deciding on action (thinking or feeling). The MBTI is designed to measure these as well as a fourth dimension relating to how people orient themselves to the outer world (judging versus perceiving).[68] Extroversion and introversion were discussed earlier, so let's examine the other dimensions:

- ◼ *Sensing/intuition*—Some people like collecting information through their five senses. Sensing types use an organized structure to acquire factual and preferably quantitative details. In contrast, intuitive people collect information nonsystematically. They rely more on subjective evidence as well as their intuition and sheer inspiration. Sensers are capable of synthesizing large amounts of seemingly random information to form quick conclusions.
- ◼ *Thinking/feeling*—Thinking types rely on rational cause-effect logic and the scientific method (see Chapter 1) to make decisions. They weigh the evidence objectively and unemotionally. Feeling types, on the other hand, consider how their choices affect others. They weigh the options against their personal values more than rational logic.
- ◼ *Judging/perceiving*—Some people prefer order and structure in their relationship with the outer world. These judging types enjoy the control of decision making and want to resolve problems quickly. In contrast, perceiving types are more flexible. They like to spontaneously adapt to events as they unfold and want to keep their options open.

The MBTI questionnaire combines the four pairs of traits into 16 distinct types. For example, ESTJ is one of the most common types for managers, meaning that they are extroverted, sensing, thinking, and judging types. Each of the 16 types has its strengths and weaknesses. ENTJs are considered natural leaders, ISFJs have a high sense of duty, and so on. These types indicate people's preferences, not the way they necessarily behave all of the time.

Effectiveness of the MBTI   Is the MBTI useful in organizations? Many business leaders think so. The MBTI is one of the most widely used personality tests in work settings and is equally popular for career counselling and executive coaching.[69] Still, evidence regarding the effectiveness of the MBTI and Jung's psychological types is mixed.[70] The MBTI does a reasonably good job of measuring Jung's psychological types. The MBTI predicts preferences for information processing in decision making and preferences for particular occupations. However, other evidence is less supportive regarding the MBTI's ability to predict job performance. Overall, the MBTI seems to improve self-awareness for career development and mutual understanding, but it probably should not be used in selecting job applicants.

OTHER PERSONALITY TRAITS

The Big Five personality dimensions and the MBTI don't capture every personality trait. We will discuss a few others where they fit specific topics in later chapters, such as positive and negative affectivity (Chapter 4), Type A and Type B behaviour patterns (Chapter 7), and Machiavellianism (Chapter 12). Two other personality traits that you should know are locus of control and self-monitoring.

locus of control

A personality trait referring to the extent to which people believe events are within their control.

Locus of control   **Locus of control** refers to a generalized belief about the amount of control people have over their own lives. Individuals who feel that they are very much in charge of their own destiny have an internal locus of control; those who think that events in their life are due mainly to fate/luck or powerful others have an external locus of control. Locus of control is a generalized belief, so people with an external locus can feel in control in familiar situations (such as opening a door or serving a customer). However, their underlying locus of control would be apparent in new situations in which control over events is uncertain. Compared with a external locus of control, people with a moderately strong internal locus of control tend to perform better in most employment situations, are more successful in their careers, earn more money, and are better suited for leadership positions. Internals are also more satisfied with their jobs, cope better in stressful situations, and are more motivated by performance-based reward systems.[71]

self-monitoring

A personality trait referring to an individual's level of sensitivity and ability to adapt to situational cues.

Self-monitoring   **Self-monitoring** refers to an individual's level of sensitivity to the expressive behaviour of others and the ability to adapt appropriately to these situational cues. High self-monitors can adjust their behaviour quite easily, whereas low self-monitors are more likely to reveal their emotions, so predicting their behaviour from one situation to the next is relatively easy.[72] The self-monitoring personality trait has been identified as a significant factor in many organizational activities. Employees who are high self-monitors tend to be better at social networking, interpersonal conversations, and leading people. They are also more likely than low self-monitors to be promoted within the organization and to receive better jobs elsewhere.[73]

PERSONALITY AND VOCATIONAL CHOICE

Self-monitoring, locus of control, conscientiousness, and the many other personality traits help us to understand individual behaviour in organizations. One fairly successful application of personality is in the area of vocational choice. Vocational choice is not just about matching your skills with job requirements. It is a complex alignment of personality, values, and competencies with the requirements of work and characteristics of the work environment. You might be very talented at a particular job, but your personality and values must also be aligned with what the job offers.

John Holland, a career development scholar, was an early proponent of this notion that career success depends on the degree of congruence between the person and his or her work environment.[74] Holland argued that people can be classified into different types relating to their personality and that they seek out and are more satisfied in work environments that are congruent with their particular profile. Thus, congruence refers to the extent to which someone has the same or similar personality type as the environment in which he or she is working. Some research has found that high congruence leads to better performance, satisfaction, and length of time in that career, but other studies are less supportive of the model.[75]

Finding a Career that Fits the Personality

While working as a Navy diver, Dan Porzio prepared for his next career in financial planning. But he was far from happy in his new field, so he took a job selling cellular telephones. Still unhappy, Porzio moved into the investment industry, where he worked for three years. During that time, he visited a career counsellor and discovered why he lacked interest in his work. "I thought those other jobs were ones that I wanted to do but I found out I was doing things that didn't jive with my character," Porzio explains. With that knowledge in hand, Porzio found a job that fit his personality as captain of the Annabelle Lee Riverboat in Richmond, Virginia (shown in photo).[76]

C. Blanchard, Richmond Times-Dispatch

Holland's six types   Holland's theory classifies both individual personalities and work environments into six categories: realistic, investigative, artistic, social, enterprising, and conventional. Exhibit 2.7 defines these types of people and work environments and suggests sample occupations representing those environments. Few people fall squarely into only one of Holland's classifications. Instead, Holland refers to a person's degree of *differentiation*; that is, the extent to which the individual fits into one or several types. A highly differentiated person is aligned with a single category, whereas most people fit into two or more categories.

Since most people fit into more than one personality type, Holland developed a model shaped like a hexagon with each personality type around the points of the model. Consistency refers to the extent that a person is aligned with similar types, which are next to each other in the hexagon, whereas dissimilar types are opposite. For instance, the enterprising and social types are next to each other in Holland's model, so individuals with both enterprising and social personalities have high consistency.

Practical implications of Holland's theory   Holland's vocational fit model is the basis of much career counselling today. Still, some aspects of the model don't seem to work. Holland's personality types represent only some of the Big Five personality dimensions, even though other dimensions should be relevant to vocational fit.[77] Also, research has found that some "opposing" categories of Holland's hexagon are not really opposite to each other. There are also doubts about whether Holland's model can be generalized to other cultures. Aside from these concerns, Holland's model seems to explain individual attitudes and behaviour to some extent.[78]

Personality and values lay some of the foundation for our understanding of individual behaviour in organizations. However, people are, of course, also influenced by the environments in which they live and work. These environments are perceived and learned, the two topics presented in the next chapter.

■ **EXHIBIT 2.7**   Holland's six types of personality and work environment

Holland type	Personality traits	Work environment characteristics	Sample occupations
Realistic	Practical, shy, materialistic, stable	Work with hands, machines, or tools; focus on tangible results	Assembly worker; dry cleaner, mechanical engineer
Investigative	Analytic, introverted, reserved, curious, precise, independent	Work involves discovering, collecting, and analyzing; solving problems	Biologist, dentist, systems analyst
Artistic	Creative, impulsive, idealistic, intuitive, emotional	Work involves creation of new products or ideas, typically in an unstructured setting	Journalist, architect, advertising executive
Social	Sociable, outgoing, conscientious, need for affiliation	Work involves serving or helping others; working in teams	Social worker, nurse, teacher, counsellor
Enterprising	Confident, assertive, energetic, need for power	Work involves leading others; achieving goals through others in a results-oriented setting	Salesperson, stockbroker, politician
Conventional	Dependable, disciplined, orderly, practical, efficient	Work involves systematic manipulation of data or information	Accountant, banker, administrator

Sources: Based on information in D.H. Montross, Z.B. Leibowitz, and C.J. Shinkman, *Real People, Real Jobs* (Palo Alto, CA: Davies-Black, 1995); J.H. Greenhaus, *Career Management* (Chicago, Ill.: Dryden, 1987).

CHAPTER SUMMARY

Individual behaviour is influenced by motivation, ability, role perceptions, and situational factors (MARS). Motivation consists of internal forces that affect the direction, intensity, and persistence of a person's voluntary choice of behaviour. Ability includes both the natural aptitudes and learned capabilities required to successfully complete a task. Role perceptions are a person's beliefs about what behaviours are appropriate or necessary in a particular situation. Situational factors are environmental conditions that constrain or facilitate employee behaviour and performance. Collectively, these four factors are included in the concept of employee engagement.

The five main types of workplace behaviour are task performance, organizational citizenship, counterproductive work behaviours, joining and staying with the organization, and work attendance.

Values are stable, evaluative beliefs that guide our preferences for outcomes or courses of action in a variety of situations. They influence our decisions and interpretation of what is ethical. People arrange values into a hierarchy of preferences, called a value system. Espoused values—values that we say we use and think we use—are different from enacted values, which are values evident from our actions. Shalom Schwartz grouped the dozens of individual values described by scholars over the years into 10 broader domains, which are further reduced to four quadrants of a circle.

Values are abstract concepts that are not easily followed in practice. A personal value influences our decisions and actions when (1) something makes us mindful of that value, (2) we can think of specific reasons for applying the value in that situation, and (3) the work environment supports behaviours consistent with the value. Values congruence refers to the similarity of value systems between two entities. Person-organization values incongruence has a number of undesirable consequences, but some incongruence is also desirable. Espoused–enacted values incongruence is contrary to effective leadership and undermines trust.

Five values that differ across cultures are individualism, collectivism, power distance, uncertainty avoidance, and achievement-nurturing orientation. As a whole, Canadians have low collectivism, high individualism, moderately low power distance, moderate uncertainty avoidance, and moderate achievement-nurturing orientation. Canadian and American values differ in three ways: (1) Canadians question authority and value autonomy from these institutions, whereas Americans have a relatively high deference to authority, (2) Canadians have significantly higher tolerance or moral permissiveness than do Americans, and (3) Canadians are somewhat more collectivist and egalitarian than are Americans. However, Canada has several subcultures, including somewhat different values among Anglophone, Francophone, First Nations, and new Canadians.

Three values that guide ethical conduct are utilitarianism, individual rights, and distributive justice. Three factors that influence ethical conduct are the extent that an issue demands ethical principles (moral intensity), the person's ethical sensitivity to the presence and importance of an ethical dilemma, and situational factors that cause people to deviate from their moral values. Companies improve ethical conduct through a code of ethics, ethics training, ethics officers, and the conduct of corporate leaders.

Personality refers to the relatively stable pattern of behaviours and consistent internal states that explain a person's behavioural tendencies. Personality is shaped by both heredity and environmental factors. Most personality traits are represented within the Big Five personality dimensions (CANOE): conscientiousness, agreeableness, neuroticism, openness to experience, and extroversion. Conscientiousness is a relatively strong predictor of job performance.

The Myers-Briggs Type Indicator measures how people prefer to focus their attention, collect information, process and evaluate information, and orient themselves to the outer world. Another popular personality trait in organizational behaviour is locus of control, which is a generalized belief about the amount of control people have over their own lives. Another trait, called self-monitoring, refers to an individual's level of sensitivity and ability to adapt to situational cues. Holland developed a model of vocational choice that defines six personalities and their corresponding work environments.

KEY TERMS

ability, p. 33

achievement-nurturing orientation, p. 44

"Big Five" personality dimensions, p. 52

collectivism, p. 42

competencies, p. 34

counterproductive work behaviours (CWBs), p. 36

distributive justice principle, p. 48

employee engagement, p. 32

enacted values, p. 39

espoused values, p. 39

ethical sensitivity, p. 48

ethics, p. 47

extroversion, p. 52

individualism, p. 42

individual rights principle, p. 47

introversion, p. 52

job satisfaction, p. 37

locus of control, p. 54

moral intensity, p. 48

motivation, p. 33

Myers-Briggs Type Indicator (MBTI), p. 53

organizational citizenship, p. 36

power distance, p. 43

self-monitoring, p. 54

task performance, p. 35

uncertainty avoidance, p. 44

utilitarianism, p. 47

values, p. 38

values congruence, p. 41

DISCUSSION QUESTIONS

1. An insurance company has high levels of absenteeism among the office staff. The head of office administration argues that employees are misusing the company's sick leave benefits. However, some of the mostly female staff members have explained that family responsibilities interfere with work. Using the MARS model, as well as your knowledge of absenteeism behaviour, discuss some of the possible reasons for absenteeism here and how it might be reduced.

2. Most large organizations spend a lot of money identifying the key competencies for superior work performance. What are the potential benefits and pitfalls associated with identifying competencies? Are there alternatives to selecting employees rather than by identifying their competencies?

3. Executives at a major Canadian insurance firm devoted several days to a values identification seminar in which they developed a list of six core values to drive the company forward. All employees attended sessions in which they learned about these values. In spite of this effort and ongoing communication regarding the six values, the executive team concluded two years later that employees were often making decisions and engaging in behaviours that were inconsistent with these values. Provide three possible explanations why employees have not enacted the values espoused by top management at this company.

4. This chapter discussed the concept of values congruence in the context of an employee's personal values with the organization's values. But values congruence also relates to the juxtaposition of other pairs of value systems. Explain how values congruence is relevant with respect to organizational versus professional values.

5. People in a particular South American country have high power distance and high collectivism. What does this mean, and what are the implications of this information when you (a senior executive) visit employees working for your company in that country?

6. This chapter states that Canadians and Americans differ from each other in three significant ways. Describe these three values-based differences and provide specific examples of how those differences are evident.

7. "All decisions are ethical decisions." Comment on this statement, particularly by referring to the concepts of moral intensity and ethical sensitivity.

8. Look over the four pairs of psychological types in the Myers-Briggs Type Indicator and identify the personality type (i.e., four letters) that would be best for a student in this course. Would this type be appropriate for students in other fields of study (e.g., biology, fine arts)?

CASE STUDY 2.1

PUSHING PAPER CAN BE FUN

A large American city government was putting on a number of seminars for managers of various departments throughout the city. At one of these sessions, the topic discussed was motivation—how we can get public servants motivated to do a good job. The plight of a police captain became the central focus of the discussion:

> I've got a real problem with my officers. They come on the force as young, inexperienced rookies, and we send them out on the street, either in cars or on a beat. They seem to like the contact they have with the public, the action involved in crime prevention, and the apprehension of criminals. They also like helping people out at fires, accidents, and other emergencies.
>
> The problem occurs when they get back to the station. They hate to do the paperwork, and because they dislike it, the job is frequently put off or done inadequately. This lack of attention hurts us later on when we get to court. We need clear, factual reports. They must be highly detailed and unambiguous. As soon as one part of a report is shown to be inadequate or incorrect, the rest of the report is suspect. Poor reporting probably causes us to lose more cases than any other factor.
>
> I just don't know how to motivate them to do a better job. We're in a budget crunch and I have absolutely no financial rewards at my disposal. In fact, we'll probably have to lay some people off in the near future. It's hard for me to make the job interesting and challenging because it isn't—it's boring, routine paperwork, and there isn't much you can do about it.
>
> Finally, I can't say to them that their promotions will hinge on the excellence of their paper-

work. First of all, they know it's not true. If their performance is adequate, most are more likely to get promoted just by staying on the force a certain number of years than for some specific outstanding act. Second, they were trained to do the job they do out in the streets, not to fill out forms. All through their career it is the arrests and interventions that get noticed.

> Some people have suggested a number of things, like using conviction records as a performance criterion. However, we know that's not fair—too many other things are involved. Bad paperwork increases the chance that you lose in court, but good paperwork doesn't necessarily mean you'll win. We tried setting up team competitions based upon the excellence of the reports, but the officers caught on to that pretty quickly. No one was getting any type of reward for winning the competition, and they figured why should they bust a gut when there was no payoff.
>
> I just don't know what to do.

Discussion Questions

1. What performance problems is the captain trying to correct?

2. Use the MARS model of individual behaviour and performance to diagnose the possible causes of the unacceptable behaviour.

3. Has the captain considered all possible solutions to the problem? If not, what else might be done?

Source: T. R. Mitchell and J. R. Larson, Jr., *People in Organizations*, 3rd ed. (New York: McGraw-Hill, 1987), p. 184. Used with permission.

T E A M   E X E R C I S E   2.2

COMPARING CULTURAL VALUES

Purpose   This exercise is designed to help you determine the extent that students hold similar assumptions about the values that dominate in other countries.

Instructions   The names in the left column represent labels that a major consulting project identified with business people in a particular country, based on its national culture and values. These names appear in alphabetical order. In the right column are the names of countries, also in alphabetical order, corresponding to the labels in the left column.

■ *Step 1:* Working alone, students will connect the labels with the countries by relying on your perceptions of these countries. Each label is associated with only one country, so each label will be connected to only one country, and vice versa. Draw a line to connect the pairs, or put the label number beside the country name.

■ *Step 2:* The instructor will form teams of four or five members. Members of each team will compare their results and try to reach consensus on a common set of connecting pairs.

■ *Step 3:* Teams or the instructor will post the results for all to see the extent that students hold common opinions about business people in other cultures. Class discussion can then consider the reasons why the results are so similar or different, as well as the implications of these results for working in a global work environment.

Values Labels and Country Names	
Country Label (alphabetical)	**Country Name (alphabetical)**
1. Affable Humanists	Australia
2. Ancient Modernizers	Brazil
3. Commercial Catalysts	Canada
4. Conceptual Strategists	China
5. Efficient Manufacturers	France
6. Ethical Statesmen	Germany
7. Informal Egalitarians	India
8. Modernizing Traditionalists	Netherlands
9. Optimistic Entrepreneurs	New Zealand
10. Quality Perfectionists	Singapore
11. Rugged Individualists	Taiwan
12. Serving Merchants	United Kingdom
13. Tolerant Traders	United States

Source: Based on R. Rosen, P. Digh, M. Singer, and C. Phillips, *Global Literacies* (New York: Simon & Schuster, 2000).

TEAM EXERCISE 2.3

ETHICS DILEMMA VIGNETTES

Purpose This exercise is designed to make you aware of the ethical dilemmas people face in various business situations, as well as the competing principles and values that operate in these situations.

Instructions The instructor will form teams of four or five students. Team members will read each case below and discuss the extent to which the company's action in each case was ethical. Teams should be prepared to justify their evaluation using ethics principles and perceived moral intensity of each incident.

Case One

An employee who worked in Toronto for a major food retailer wrote a Weblog (blog) and, in one of his writings, complained that his boss wouldn't let him go home when he felt sick and that his district manager refused to promote him because of his dreadlocks. His blog named the employer, but the employee didn't use his real name. Although all blogs are on the Inernet, the employee claims that his was low profile and that it didn't show up when doing a Google search of his name of the company. Still, the employer somehow discovered the blog, figured out the employee's real name, and fired him for "speaking ill-will of the company in a public domain."

Case Two

Computer printer manufacturers usually sell printers at a low margin cost and generate much more income from subsequent sales of the high-margin ink cartridges required for each printer. One global printer manufacturer now designs its printers so they only work with ink cartridges made in the same region. For example, ink cartridges purchased in Canada will not work for the same printer model sold in Europe. This "region coding" of ink cartridges does not improve performance. Rather, this action prevents consumers and grey marketers from buying the product at a lower price in another region. The company says this action allows it to maintain stable prices within a region rather than continually changing prices due to currency fluctuations.

Case Three

For the past few years, the design department of a small (40-employee) company has been using a particular software program, but the three employees who use the software have been complaining for more than a year that the software is out of date and is slowing down their performance. The department agreed to switch to a competing software program, costing several thousand dollars. However, the next version won't be released for six months and buying the current version will not allow much discount toward the next version. The company has put in advanced orders for the next version. Meanwhile, one employee was able to get a copy of the current version of the software from a friend in the industry. The company has allowed the three employees to use this current version of the software even though they did not pay for it.

SELF-ASSESSMENT EXERCISE 2.4

IDENTIFYING YOUR SELF-MONITORING PERSONALITY

Purpose This self-assessment is designed to help you estimate your level of self-monitoring personality.

Instructions The statements in this scale refer to personal characteristics than might or might not be characteristic of you. Mark the box indicating the extent that the statement is true or false

as a characteristic of you. Then use the scoring key in Appendix B of this book to calculate your results. This exercise is completed alone so students assess themselves honestly without concerns of social comparison. However, class discussion will focus on the relevance of self-monitoring personality in organizations.

SELF-MONITORING SCALE						
Indicate the degree to which you think the following statements are true or false.	**Very False** ▼	**Somewhat False** ▼	**Slightly More False than True** ▼	**Slightly More True than False** ▼	**Somewhat True** ▼	**Very True** ▼
1. In social situations, I have the ability to alter my behaviour if I feel that something else is called for.	☐	☐	☐	☐	☐	☐
2. I am often able to read people's true emotions correctly through their eyes.	☐	☐	☐	☐	☐	☐
3. I have the ability to control the way I come across to people, depending on the impression I wish to give them.	☐	☐	☐	☐	☐	☐
4. In conversations, I am sensitive to even the slightest change in the facial expression of the person I'm conversing with.	☐	☐	☐	☐	☐	☐
5. My powers of intuition are quite good when it comes to understanding others' emotions and motives.	☐	☐	☐	☐	☐	☐
6. I can usually tell when others consider a joke in bad taste, even though they may laugh convincingly.	☐	☐	☐	☐	☐	☐
7. When I feel that the image I am portraying isn't working, I can readily change it to something that does.	☐	☐	☐	☐	☐	☐
8. I can usually tell when I've said something inappropriate by reading the listener's eyes.	☐	☐	☐	☐	☐	☐
9. I have trouble changing my behaviour to suit different people and different situations.	☐	☐	☐	☐	☐	☐
10. I have found that I can adjust my behaviour to meet the requirements of any situation I find myself in.	☐	☐	☐	☐	☐	☐
11. If someone is lying to me, I usually know it at once from that person's manner of expression.	☐	☐	☐	☐	☐	☐
12. Even when it might be to my advantage, I have difficulty putting up a good front.	☐	☐	☐	☐	☐	☐
13. Once I know what the situation calls for, it's easy for me to regulate my actions accordingly.	☐	☐	☐	☐	☐	☐

Source: R. D. Lennox and R. N. Wolfe, "Revision of the Self-Monitoring Scale," *Journal of Personality and Social Psychology*, 46 (June 1984), pp. 1348–64. The response categories in this scale have been altered slightly due to limitations with the original scale responses.

S E L F - A S S E S S M E N T   E X E R C I S E   2.5

IDENTIFYING YOUR DOMINANT VALUES

Go to the Online Learning Centre to complete this interactive self-assessment.

Purpose This self-assessment is designed to help you identify your dominant values in Schwartz's values model.

Instructions This instrument consists of numerous words and phrases, and you are asked to indicate whether each word or phrase is highly opposed or highly similar to your personal values, or some point in between these two extremes. When you have finished answering all items, the results will indicate your values on Schwartz's 10 value groups described in this chapter.

SELF-ASSESSMENT EXERCISE   2.6

INDIVIDUALISM–COLLECTIVISM SCALE

Go to the Online Learning Centre to complete this interactive self-assessment.

Purpose   This self-assessment is designed to help you identify your level of individualism and collectivism.

Instructions   This scale consists of several statements, and you are asked to indicate how well each statement describes you. Read each statement in this self-assessment and select the response that best indicates how the statement describes you. You need to be honest with yourself to receive a reasonable estimate of your level of individualism and collectivism.

SELF-ASSESSMENT EXERCISE   2.7

IDENTIFYING YOUR LOCUS OF CONTROL

Go to the Online Learning Centre to complete this interactive self-assessment.

Purpose   This self-assessment is designed to help you estimate the extent to which you have an internal or external locus of control personality.

Instructions   This instrument asks you to indicate the degree to which you agree or disagree with each of the statements provided. You need to be honest with yourself to obtain a reasonable estimate of your locus of control. The results show your relative position in the internal-external locus continuum and the general meaning of this score.

SELF-ASSESSMENT EXERCISE   2.8

MATCHING HOLLAND'S CAREER TYPES

Go to the Online Learning Centre to complete this interactive self-assessment.

Purpose   This self-assessment is designed to help you understand Holland's career types.

Instructions   Holland's theory identifies six different types of work environments and occupations in which people work. Few jobs fit purely in one category, but all have a dominant type. Your task is to state the Holland type that you believe best fits each of the occupations presented in the instrument. While completing this self-assessment, you can open your book to the exhibit describing Holland's six types.

 **Online Learning Centre with POWERWEB**   After studying the preceding material, be sure to check out our Online Learning Centre at

www.mcgrawhill.ca/college/mcshane

for more in-depth information and interactivities that correspond to this chapter.

·3·

PERCEPTION AND LEARNING IN ORGANIZATIONS

LEARNING OBJECTIVES

AFTER READING THIS CHAPTER, YOU SHOULD BE ABLE TO:

- Outline the perceptual process.

- Explain how we perceive ourselves and others through social identity.

- Outline the reasons why stereotyping occurs and describe ways to minimize its adverse effects.

- Describe the attribution process and two attribution errors.

- Summarize the self-fulfilling prophecy process.

- Explain how empathy and the Johari Window can help improve our perceptions.

- Define learning and explain how it affects individual behaviour.

- Describe the A-B-C model of behaviour modification and the four contingencies of reinforcement.

- Describe the three features of social learning theory.

- Summarize the four components of Kolb's experiential learning model.

With full schedules of executive meetings and visits to suppliers and clients, CEOs of large firms can easily lose touch with reality inside their own organization. That's why VIA Rail CEO Paul Coté makes a habit of strolling around VIA's Montreal maintenance centre to mingle with front-line employees. The head of Canada's national passenger train service also hops on board VIA's trains to chat with customers and staff. This front-line experience provides him with a clearer perception of what's really going on. "That's how you get to know the business; you can't do that from your office," Coté explains.

Delta Hotels president John Pye recently took a more hands-on approach by actually performing several front-line jobs for an entire week. The role switch was filmed by the CBC television program *Venture* as a Canadian version of the British series *Back to the Floor*. Pye accepted the challenge, which included cleaning rooms, handling baggage, and preparing banquets, because he wanted to get a reality check. "Part of the objective is for me to work with the people in the hotel for two or three days to appreciate what they go through on a day-to-day basis," says Pye, who began his career as a bellman at Delta Vancouver. "I've already got a list of five or six things that I want to look into."

At Domino's Pizza, sending the CEO back to the front lines isn't good enough. The Ann Arbor, Michigan, company has developed a weeklong Pizza Prep School where its administrative and management staff receive 20 hours of classroom instruction in operating a pizza store along with 24 hours of hands-on experience. This arrangement gives everyone a better understanding of how their decisions affect the company's retail outlets.

Vancouver-based rubbish removal company 1-800-GOT-JUNK? follows a similar practice. Every new hire in the company's 130 franchises spends an entire week on a junk removal truck to understand better how the business works. "How can you possibly [have empathy] with someone out in the field unless you've been on the truck yourself?" asks Brian Scudamore, CEO of the company recently voted the best place to work in British Columbia.[1] ∎

www.viarail.ca

VIA Rail CEO Paul Coté keeps his perceptions in focus by wandering around the maintenance centre and hopping on the trains to meet staff and customers. *CP Photo/Ryan Remiorz*

Working in front-line jobs and keeping in close contact with staff and customers is recognized increasingly as a powerful way for executives to improve their perceptions of the world around them and to learn about the consequences of their actions. **Perception** is the process of receiving information about and making sense of the world around us. It entails deciding which information to notice, how to categorize this information, and how to interpret it within the framework of our existing knowledge. This chapter begins by describing the perceptual process, that is, the dynamics of selecting, organizing, and interpreting external stimuli. Social identity theory, which has become a leading perceptual theory in organizational behaviour, is then introduced, followed by a description of stereotyping, including ways of minimizing stereotype biases in the workplace. Next, we look at attribution, self-fulfilling prophecy, and other perceptual issues, followed by an overview of empathy and Johari Window as general strategies to minimize perceptual problems.

The opening vignette also refers to the topic of learning because executives working on the front lines learn about what employees and customers experience every day. Indeed, it is difficult to discuss perceptions without also referring to the knowledge and skills learned from those perceptions. That's why perceptions and learning are combined in this chapter. The latter part of this chapter introduces the concept of learning as well as the related concepts of tacit and explicit knowledge. We then look at three perspectives of learning: behaviour modification, social learning theory, and experiential learning.

perception
The process of selecting, organizing, and interpreting information in order to make sense of the world around us.

■ THE PERCEPTUAL PROCESS

The Greek philosopher Plato wrote long ago that we see reality only as shadows reflected on the rough wall of a cave.[2] In other words, reality is filtered through an imperfect perceptual process. This imperfect process, which is illustrated in Exhibit 3.1, begins when environmental stimuli are received through our senses. Most stimuli are screened out; the rest are organized and interpreted. The resulting perceptions influence our conscious emotions and behaviour toward those objects, people, and events.[3]

SELECTIVE ATTENTION

Our five senses are constantly bombarded with stimuli. Some things are noticed, but most are screened out. A nurse working in postoperative care might ignore the smell of recently disinfected instruments or the sound of co-workers talking nearby. Yet a small flashing red light on the nurse station console is immediately noticed because it signals that a patient's vital signs are failing. This process of attending to some information received by our senses and ignoring other information is called **selective attention**. Selective attention is influenced by two sets of factors: (1) characteristics of the person or object being perceived and (2) characteristics of the individual doing the perceiving.[4]

selective attention
The process of filtering information received by our senses.

Characteristics of the object   Some things stand out more than others because of their size, intensity, motion, repetition, and novelty. The red light on the nurse station console receives attention because it is bright (intensity), flashing (motion), and a rare event (novelty). As for people, we would notice two employees

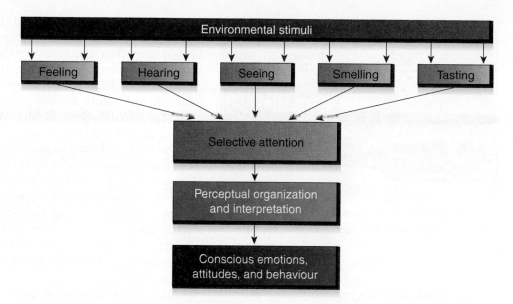

having a heated debate if co-workers normally don't raise their voices (novelty and intensity). Notice that selective attention is also influenced by the context in which the target is perceived. You might be aware that a client has a German accent if the meeting takes place in Halifax, but not if the conversation took place in Germany, particularly if you had been living there for some time. On the contrary, it would be your accent that would be noticed!

Characteristics of the perceiver   Characteristics of the perceiver play an important role in selection attention, much of it without our awareness.[5] When information is received through the senses, our brain quickly and unconsciously assesses whether it is relevant or irrelevant to us. Emotional markers (worry, happiness, anger) are attached to the relevant information based on this rapid evaluation, and these emotionally tagged bits of stimuli compete for our conscious attention.

Although selective attention is largely unconscious, to some extent selective attention is consciously redirected through our anticipation of future events.[6] For instance, a particular email from a colleague is more likely to get noticed from the daily bombardment of messages if you expect to receive that email than if the email isn't expected. Unfortunately, expectations also delay our awareness of unexpected information. If we focus on what competitors are doing with their products and sales, we might not pay attention to increasing employee turnover or slipping production schedules in our organization. If we form a theory too early regarding a particular customer trend, we might not notice information indicating a different trend. In other words, our expectations and cognitive attention toward one issue tend to reduce our sensitivity to information about other issues. The solution here is to keep an open mind and take in as much information as possible without forming theories too early.

PERCEPTUAL ORGANIZATION AND INTERPRETATION

People make sense of information even before they become aware of it. This sense making partly includes **categorical thinking**—the mostly unconscious process of organizing people and objects into preconceived categories that are stored in our

categorical thinking

The mostly unconscious process of organizing people and objects into preconceived categories that are stored in our long-term memory.

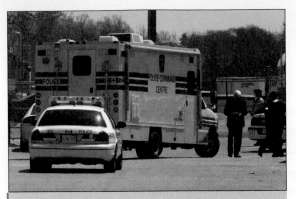

**Detective Theories Increase Risk of
Overlooking Good Evidence**

Good detective work involves more than forming a
good theory about the crime. It also involves not
forming a theory too early in the investigation. "When
you get a theory, it can put blinders on to what really
happened," explains Ottawa-Carleton police detective
Roch Lachance about a homicide with few leads or
suspects. Toronto Police Sgt. Jim Muscat has similar
advice: "Investigators must keep an open mind,
and not get hung up on any tunnel vision or any
one specific area of this kind of an investigation,"
he said when asked by reporters about motives for
a young girl's abduction. Theories make sense of
disparate pieces of information, but they also cause
detectives to perceptually ignore evidence that
seems irrelevant or contrary to the theory.[11]

CP Photo/Saul Porto

long-term memory.[7] Categorical thinking relies on a variety of automatic perceptual grouping principles. Things are often grouped together based on their similarity or proximity to others. If you notice that a group of people includes several professors, for instance, then you will likely assume that the others in that group are also university faculty. Another form of perceptual grouping is based on the need for cognitive closure, such as filling in missing information about what happened at a meeting that you did not attend (e.g., who was there, where it was held). A third form of grouping occurs when we think we see trends in otherwise ambiguous information. Several research studies have found that people have a natural tendency to see patterns that really are random events, such as presumed winning streaks among sports stars or in gambling.[8]

Making sense also involves interpreting incoming information, and this happens just as quickly as the brain selects and organizes that information. The emotional markers that the brain attaches to incoming stimuli are essentially quick judgments about whether those stimuli are good or bad for us. To give you an idea about how quickly and systematically this unconscious perceptual process occurs, consider the following study:[9] Eight observers were shown video clips of university instructors teaching an undergraduate class, then rated the instructors on several personal characteristics (optimistic, likeable, anxious, active, etc.). The observers did not know the instructors and completed their ratings independently, yet they agreed with each other on many characteristics. Equally important, these ratings matched the ratings completed by students who actually attended the entire class.

These results may be interesting, but the extraordinary discovery is that the observers formed their perceptions based on just six seconds of video—three segments of two seconds each selected randomly across the one-hour class! Furthermore, the video didn't have any sound. In spite of these very thin slices of information, the observers developed similar perceptions of the instructor, and those perceptions were comparable to the perceptions formed by students attending the entire class. Other studies have reported parallel results using two 15-second video segments of high school teachers, courtroom judges, and physicians. Collectively, these "thin slices" studies reveal that selective attention as well as perceptual organization and interpretation operate very quickly and to a large extent without our awareness.

mental models
The broad worldviews or "theories in-use" that people rely on to guide their perceptions and behaviours.

Mental models   To achieve our goals with some degree of predictability and sanity, we need to have road maps of the complex environments in which we live. These road maps, called **mental models**, are internal representations of the external world.[10] They consist of broad worldviews or templates of the mind that provide enough stability and predictability to guide our preferences and behaviours. For example, most of us have a mental model about attending a college or university lecture or seminar. We have a set of assumptions and expectations about how people arrive, arrange themselves in the room, ask and answer questions, and so forth. We can create a mental image of what a class would look like in progress.

We rely on mental models to make sense of our environment through perceptual grouping; they fill in the missing pieces, including the causal connection among events. Yet, mental models may also blind us from seeing that world in different ways. For example, accounting professionals tend to see corporate problems in terms of accounting solutions, whereas marketing professionals see the same problems from a marketing perspective. Mental models also block our recognition of new opportunities. How do we change mental models? It's a tough challenge. After all, we developed models from several years of experience and reinforcement. The most important way to minimize the perceptual problems with mental models is to constantly question them. We need to ask ourselves about the assumptions we make. Working with people from diverse backgrounds is another way to break out of existing mental models. Colleagues from different cultures and areas of expertise tend to have different mental models, so working with them makes your assumptions more obvious.

> **social identity theory**
>
> A theory stating that much learning occurs by observing others and then modelling the behaviours that lead to favourable outcomes and avoiding the behaviours that lead to punishing consequences.

■ SOCIAL IDENTITY THEORY

The perceptual process is an interesting combination of our self-perceptions and perceptions of others. Increasingly, experts are discovering that how we perceive the world depends on how we define ourselves. This connection between self-perception and perception of others is explained through social identity theory.[12] According to **social identity theory**, people maintain a social identity by defining themselves in terms of the groups to which they belong and have an emotional attachment. For instance, someone might have a social identity as a Canadian, a graduate of the University of New Brunswick, and an employee at CIBC World Markets (see Exhibit 3.2). Everyone engages in this social categorization process because it helps to make sense of where we fit within the social world.

■ EXHIBIT 3.2

Self-perception and social perception through social identity

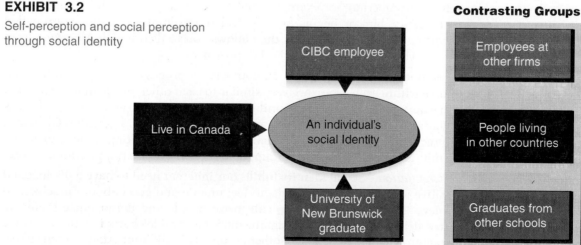

Along with a social identity, people have a personal identity—characteristics that make them unique and distinct from people in any particular group. For instance, an unusual achievement that distinguishes you from other people typically becomes a personal identity characteristic. Personal identity refers to something about you as an individual without reference to a larger group. Social identity, on the other hand, defines you in terms of characteristics of the group. By perceiving yourself as a CIBC employee, you are assigning characteristics to yourself that you believe are also characteristics of CIBC employees in general.

Social identity is a complex combination of many memberships arranged in a hierarchy of importance. One factor determining this importance is how obvious our membership is in the group. We tend to define ourselves by our gender, race, age, and other observable characteristics because other people easily identify our membership in those groups. It is difficult to ignore your gender in a class where most other students are the opposite gender, for example. In that context, gender tends to become a stronger defining feature of your social identity than in social settings where there are many people of the same gender.

Along with our demographic characteristics, group status is typically an important influence on our social identity. Most of us want to have a positive self-image, so we identify with groups that have higher status or respect. Medical doctors usually define themselves in terms of their profession because of its high status, whereas people in low-status jobs tend to define themselves in terms of non-job groups. Some people define themselves in terms of where they work because their employer has a favourable reputation in the community; other people never mention where they work if the firm has a poor reputation in the community.[13]

PERCEIVING OTHERS THROUGH SOCIAL IDENTITY

Social identity theory explains more than just how we develop self-perceptions. It also explains the dynamics of *social perception*—how we perceive others.[14] This social perception is influenced by three activities in the process of forming and maintaining our social identity: categorization, homogenization, and differentiation.

- *Categorization*—Social identity is a comparative process, which begins by categorizing people into distinct groups. By viewing someone (including yourself) as an Albertan, for example, you remove that person's individuality and, instead, see him or her as prototypical representative of the group called Albertans. This categorization then allows you to distinguish Albertans from people who live in Ontario and other provinces.

- *Homogenization*—To simplify the comparison process, we tend to think that people within each group are very similar to each other. For instance, we think Albertans collectively have similar attitudes and characteristics, whereas Ontarians collectively have their own unique brand of characteristics. Of course, we recognize that every individual is unique, but thinking about our social identity and of people in other groups tends to homogenize people within groups.

- *Differentiation*—Social identity fulfills our inherent need to have a distinct and positive identity, in other words, to feel unique and good about ourselves. To achieve this, we do more than categorize people and homogenize them; we also differentiate groups by assigning more favourable characteristics to people in our groups than to people in other groups. This differentiation is often subtle. Even by constructing favourable images of our own social identity groups, we implicitly form less favourable images of people belonging to other social categories. However, when other groups compete or conflict with our groups, the "good guy–bad guy" contrast becomes much stronger. Under these conditions, the negative image of opponents preserves our self-image against the threatening outsiders.[15]

To summarize, the social identity process explains how we perceive ourselves and other people. We partly identify ourselves in terms of our membership in social groups. This comparison process includes categorizing people into groups, forming a homogeneous image of people within those groups, and differentiating groups by assigning more favourable features to our own groups than to other groups. This perceptual process makes our social world easier to understand and fulfills an innate need to feel unique and positive about ourselves. This social identity process is also the basis for stereotyping people in organizational settings, which we discuss next.

■ STEREOTYPING IN ORGANIZATIONAL SETTINGS

stereotyping

The process of assigning traits to people based on their membership in a social category.

Stereotyping is an extension of social identity theory and a product of our natural process of organizing information.[16] The first step in stereotyping occurs when we develop social categories and assign traits that are difficult to observe. For instance, students might form a stereotype that professors are both intelligent and absentminded. Personal experiences shape stereotypes to some extent, but stereotypes are mainly provided to us through cultural upbringing and media images (e.g., movie characters).

The second step in stereotyping involves assigning people to one or more social categories based on easily observable information about them, such as their gender, appearance, or physical location. Observable features allow us to assign people to a social group quickly and without much investigation. The third step consists of assigning the stereotyped group's cluster of traits to people identified as members of that group. For example, we tend to think that professors are absentminded because people often include this trait in their stereotype of professors.

WHY STEREOTYPING OCCURS

Stereotyping occurs for three reasons.[17] First, stereotyping relies on categorical thinking which, as we learned earlier, is a natural process to simplify our understanding of the world. We depend on categorical thinking and stereotyping because it is impossible to recall all of the unique characteristics of every person we meet. Second, we have an innate need to understand and anticipate how others will behave. We don't have much information when first meeting someone, so we rely heavily on stereotypes to fill in the missing pieces. As you might expect, people with a stronger need for this cognitive closure have a higher tendency to stereotype others.

The third reason why stereotyping occurs is that it enhances our self-perception and social identity. Recall from social identity theory that we tend to emphasize the positive aspects of the groups to which we belong, which implicitly or explicitly generates less favourable views of people in contrasting groups. This explains why we are particularly motivated to use negative stereotypes toward people who hurt our self-esteem.[18]

PROBLEMS WITH STEREOTYPING

Stereotypes tend to have some inaccuracies, some overestimation or underestimation of real differences, and some degree of accuracy.[19] Still, they cause numerous problems in the workplace that need to be minimized. One problem is that stereotypes do not accurately describe every person in that social category. For instance, the widespread "bean counter" stereotype of accountants collectively views people in this profession as "single-mindedly preoccupied with precision and form, methodical and conservative, and a boring joyless character."[20] Although this may be true of some accountants, it is certainly not characteristic of all—or even most—people in this profession. One unfortunate consequence of these negative stereotypes is that they discourage people from entering the profession. As Connections 3.1 describes, the "geek" or "nerd" stereotype of engineers and scientists is partly responsible for the low percentage of women in these occupations. Notice how the individual's social identity plays an important role in deciding whether to enter these professions.

Another problem with stereotyping is that it lays the foundation for discriminatory behaviour. According to Statistics Canada, 64 percent of visible minorities in Canada say they feel or experience discrimination in the workplace.[21] To a large extent, these people experience *unintentional (systemic) discrimination*, whereby decision makers rely on stereotypes to establish notions of the "ideal" person in specific roles. A person who doesn't fit the ideal is likely to receive a less favourable evaluation. This is increasingly apparent in age discrimination claims. Recruiters say they aren't biased against older job applicants, yet older workers have a much more difficult time gaining employment even though research indicates they are well qualified.

A more overt form of discrimination is **prejudice**, which refers to unfounded negative emotions and attitudes toward people belonging to a particular stereotyped group.[22] Overt prejudice is less apparent today than a few decades ago, but it still exists. Quebec's Human Rights Tribunal was recently shocked to discover that one of Canada's largest vegetable farms prevented black employees from eating in the regular cafeteria. Instead, they were relegated to a "blacks only" eating area that lacked heat, running water, proper toilets, and refrigeration. A study of forestry work on Vancouver Island revealed that qualified women are often denied employment in traditionally male jobs specifically because of their gender. One example of this prejudice occurred at a pulp and paper plant in Port Alice, B.C., where women were explicitly told that they could apply only for clerical jobs, not the higher-paying production jobs. The mill maintained this policy until female applicants recently complained and won their case at the B.C. Labour Relations Board.[23]

MINIMIZING STEREOTYPING BIAS

If stereotyping is such a problem, shouldn't we try to avoid this process altogether? Unfortunately, it's not that simple. Most scholars agree that categorical thinking (including stereotyping) is an automatic and unconscious process. Intensive training can minimize stereotype activation to some extent, but for the most part the process is hardwired in our brain cells.[24] Also remember that stereotyping helps us in several valuable (although fallible) ways described earlier: minimizing mental effort, filling in missing information, and supporting our social identity. The good news is that while it is very difficult to prevent the *activation* of stereotypes, we can

prejudice
The unfounded negative emotions and attitudes toward people belonging to a particular stereotyped group.

Social Identity and Gender in Engineering

Women make up 59 percent of university graduates in Canada, but only about 20 percent of graduates in engineering programs. "Women are still in the minority here," says Azar Mouzari, a fourth year student of electrical engineering at the University of Ottawa. "You can feel it. When I went into a class of 40 or 50, there were only three or four women." The problem is even more acute in computer science. At the University of Waterloo, for instance, the percentage of female applicants in computer science has declined from 33 percent in the 1980s to just 13 percent today.

One problem is that the stereotype of engineers and computer scientists doesn't fit the self-images that most women want for themselves. "It's the unappealing image of the computer science geek" that keeps women away from these programs, complains Sandy Graham, a computer science lecturer at the University of Waterloo. Graham and instructors at other universities have set up special programs where female high school students can discover that these unattractive images are not representative of work or people in these fields.

Women are also discouraged by others from entering engineering and computer science because of traditional stereotypes. Edna Lee grew up in Vancouver with aspirations of becoming a chemical engineer, but her parents had other ideas. "My parents said that a woman would not be able to get very far as an engineer," recalls Edna, who has since become a chartered accountant. "They thought that engineering was more a 'male' job."

Monique Frize, an engineering professor at both Carleton University and University of Ottawa, says the discrimination against women in engineering is more subtle today than a few decades ago, but it's still there. "Some professors still feel women don't belong," Frize says. "Engineering is still a pretty macho world." Frize also notes that engineering professors seem to make more eye contract with men than woman in class, are more likely to call male students by their first names, and call on male more than female students to answer the difficult questions.

University of Ottawa student Azar Mouzari, shown here with Dean Tyseer Aboulnasr, and other women are underrepresented in engineering programs partly because the stereotype of engineers doesn't fit the self-images most women want for themselves. *Lynn Ball, The Ottawa Citizen*

Another problem is that women tend to perceive themselves as less capable in engineering programs, even though men and women actually perform equally well. This lack of self-confidence causes female engineers to blame themselves for any poor grades, which increases their likelihood of leaving the program. "Guys that aren't doing well will blame the prof, or the book, or the class that sucks," says University of Calgary engineering student Justyna Krzysiak. "Girls tend to blame themselves more. They'll say 'I'm just not smart enough to be an engineer,' or, 'this isn't really for me.'"

Sources: D. Rucker, "Barrier Breakers," *Oilweek*, April 2, 2001, p. 30ff; H. Sokoloff, "'Geek' Culture Turns Women Off Computer Studies: Report," *National Post*, March 19, 2002, p. A1; R. Ross, "System Favours the Few, the Male," *Toronto Star*, May 20, 2002, p. E1; M. Orton, "'You Feel Very Isolated'," *Ottawa Citizen*, July 25, 2002; P. Shih, "Breaking Down Barriers," *Jasmine Magazine*, Premiere Issue (2003); D. Butler, "An 'Amazing Revolution,'" *Ottawa Citizen*, February 9, 2004, p. A1; C. Teasdale, "Booting Up Girls' Interest in Computer Science," *Imperial Oil Review* no. 2 (2004), pp. 26–30
www.swe.org

minimize the application of stereotypic information. In other words, we can avoid using our stereotypes in our decisions and actions toward other people. Three strategies for minimizing the application of stereotyping are diversity awareness training, meaningful interaction, and decision-making accountability.

Diversity awareness training   Diversity awareness training tries to minimize discrimination by dispelling myths about people from various cultural and demographic groups and by identifying the organizational benefits of diversity and the problems with stereotyping. Some sessions rely on role playing and other exercises to help employees discover the subtle, yet pervasive effects of stereotyping in their decision making and behaviour.[25] Diversity training does not correct deep-rooted prejudice; it probably doesn't even change stereotypes in tolerant people. What diversity training can potentially do, however, is to increase our sensitivity to equality and motivate us to block inaccurate perceptions arising from ingrained stereotypes.

Meaningful interaction   The more meaningful interaction we have with someone, the less we rely on stereotypes to understand that person.[26] This statement, which describes the **contact hypothesis**, sounds simple enough, but in reality it works only under specific conditions. Participants must have close and frequent interaction working toward a shared goal where they need to rely on each other (i.e., cooperate rather than compete with each other). Everyone should have equal status in that context and should be engaged in a meaningful task. An hour-long social gathering between executives and front-line employees does not satisfy these conditions. On the other hand, having executives work in front-line jobs, which we described at the beginning of this chapter, does seem to represent meaningful interaction. By working in front-line jobs, these executives have equal status with other staff, cooperate toward a common goal, and have close and frequent interaction with front-line employees.

Decision-making accountability   A third way to minimize the biasing effects of stereotyping is to hold employees accountable for their decisions.[27] This accountability encourages more active information processing and, consequently, motivates decision makers to suppress stereotypic perceptions in favour of more precise and logical information. In contrast, less concern about accountability allows decision makers to engage in more passive information processing, which includes more reliance on discriminatory stereotypes.

Overall, social identity theory and stereotyping are central activities in the perceptual process, most of which occurs automatically and unconsciously. Without our awareness, our brain identifies and organizes the incoming information around preconceived categories and assigns emotional markers representing an initial reaction to whether the information is good, bad, or irrelevant. It may be difficult to prevent this categorization and activation of stereotypes, but we can consciously control the application of stereotypes in decision making and behaviour. Now, let's look at another perceptual activity, called attribution.

■ ATTRIBUTION THEORY

Earlier, in Connections 3.1, some female engineering students said they blame themselves for poor performance in school, whereas male students tend to blame external causes. This process of assigning credit or blame to yourself (internal) or the situation (external) is called the **attribution process**.[28] Internal factors originate from within a person, such as the individual's ability or motivation. We make an internal attribution by believing that an employee performs the job poorly

contact hypothesis
The theory that as individuals interact with one another they rely less on stereotypes about each other.

attribution process
The perceptual process of deciding whether an observed behaviour or event is caused largely by internal or by external factors.

because he or she lacks the necessary competencies or motivation. External factors originate from the environment, such as lack of resources, other people, or just luck. An external attribution would occur if we believe that the employee performs the job poorly because he or she doesn't receive sufficient resources to do the task.

People rely on the three attribution rules shown in Exhibit 3.3 to determine whether someone's behaviour mainly has an internal or external attribution. Internal attributions are made when the observed individual behaved this way in the past (high consistency), behaves like this toward other people or in different situations (low distinctiveness), and other people do not behave this way in similar situations (low consensus). On the other hand, an external attribution is made when there is low consistency, high distinctiveness, and high consensus.

Here's an example that will help to clarify the three attribution rules. Suppose that an employee is making poor-quality products one day on a particular machine. We would probably conclude that there is something wrong with the machine (an external attribution) if the employee has made good-quality products on this machine in the past (low consistency), the employee makes good-quality products on other machines (high distinctiveness), and other employees have recently had quality problems on this machine (high consensus). We would make an internal attribution, on the other hand, if the employee usually makes poor-quality products on this machine (high consistency), other employees produce

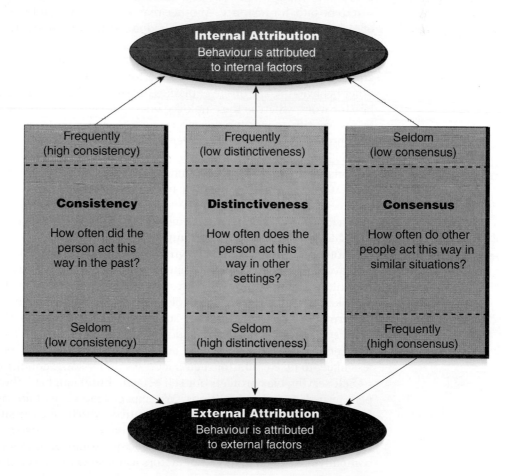

■ **EXHIBIT 3.3**

Rules of attribution

good-quality products on this machine (low consensus), and the employee also makes poor-quality products on other machines (low distinctiveness).[29]

Attributions are an essential part of our perceptual world because they link together the various pieces of that world in cause-effect relationships. As a result, our decisions and actions are influenced by our prior attributions.[30] Students who make internal attributions about their poor performance are more likely to drop out of their programs. Our satisfaction with work accomplishments is influenced to a large degree by whether we take credit for those accomplishments or attribute the success to external causes. Whether employees support or resist organizational change initiatives depends on whether they believe management introduced those changes due to external pressures or their personal motives.

ATTRIBUTION ERRORS

fundamental attribution error
The tendency to attribute the behaviour of other people more to internal than to external factors.

People are far from perfect when making attributions. One bias, called **fundamental attribution error**, refers to our tendency to see the person rather than the situation as the main cause of that person's behaviour.[31] If an employee is late for work, observers are more likely to conclude that the person is lazy than to realize that external factors may have caused this behaviour. One reason why fundamental attribution error occurs is that observers can't easily see the external factors that constrain the person's behaviour. We didn't see the traffic jam that caused the person to be late, for instance. Another reason is that we tend to believe in the power of the person; we assume that individuals can overcome situational constraints more than they really can.

Fundamental attribution error can lead to disagreement over how much employees should be held responsible for their poor performance, lateness, and other behaviours. The observer blames the employee's lack of motivation for arriving late for work, whereas the employee does not feel responsible because the lateness is due to traffic congestion or other factors beyond his or her control. While fairly common in Canada, this disagreement is less common in Asian cultures because people in those cultures are less likely to have fundamental attribution error.[32] The reason for this East-West difference is that Asians are taught from an early age to pay attention to the context in interpersonal relations and to see everything connected in a holistic way. Westerners, on the other hand, learn about the importance and independence of the individual; the person and situation are separate from each other, not seamlessly connected.

self-serving bias
A perceptual error whereby people tend to attribute their favourable outcomes to internal factors and their failures to external factors.

Another attribution error, known as **self-serving bias**, is the tendency to attribute our favourable outcomes to internal factors and our failures to external factors. Simply put, we take credit for our successes and blame others or the situation for our mistakes. In one study, 90 percent of the employees who received lower than-expected performance ratings blamed their supervisor, the organization, the appraisal system, or other external causes. Only a handful blamed themselves for the unexpected results. Self-serving bias seems to occur across cultures, although women are somewhat less likely to take credit for their successes under some conditions.[33]

Self-serving bias protects our self-esteem, but it can have the opposite effect for people in leadership positions. We expect leaders to take ownership of their failures, so we have less respect for executives who blame the situation rather than take personal responsibility. Still, self-serving bias is consistently found in annual reports; executives mainly refer to their personal qualities as reasons for the company's gains and to external factors as reasons for the company's losses.[34]

■ SELF-FULFILLING PROPHECY

self-fulfilling prophecy

Occurs when our expectations about another person cause that person to act in a way that is consistent with those expectations.

Cocoplans is recognized throughout the Philippines as a top-performing insurance company with excellent customer service. This success is due, in part, to the way Cocoplan executives perceive their sales staff. "At Cocoplans, we treat sales people as our internal customers, while plan holders are our external customers," explains Cocoplans president Caesar T. Michelena. "It's a self-fulfilling prophecy. If you believe that they will not last, your behaviour towards them will show it .... You get what you expect."[35]

Executives at Cocoplans rely on **self-fulfilling prophecy** to improve employee performance and well-being. Self-fulfilling prophecy occurs when our expectations about another person cause that person to act in a way that is consistent with those expectations. In other words, our perceptions can influence reality. Exhibit 3.4 illustrates the four steps in the self-fulfilling prophecy process using the example of a supervisor and subordinate.[36]

1. *Expectations formed*—The supervisor forms expectations about the employee's future behaviour and performance. These expectations are sometimes inaccurate, because first impressions are usually formed from limited information.

2. *Behaviour toward the employee*—The supervisor's expectations influence his or her treatment of employees. Specifically, high-expectancy employees (those expected to do well) receive more emotional support through nonverbal cues (e.g., more smiling and eye contact), more frequent and valuable feedback and reinforcement, more challenging goals, better training, and more opportunities to demonstrate their performance.

3. *Effects on the employee*—The supervisor's behaviours have two effects on the employee. First, through better training and more practice opportunities, a high-expectancy employee learns more skills and knowledge than a low expectancy employee. Second, the employee becomes more self-confident, which results in higher motivation and willingness to set more challenging goals.[37]

■ **EXHIBIT 3.4**

The self-fulfilling prophecy cycle

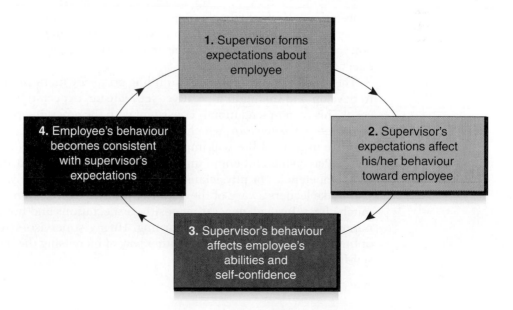

4. *Employee behaviour and performance*—With higher motivation and better skills, high-expectancy employees are more likely to demonstrate desired behaviours and better performance. The supervisor notices this, which supports his or her original perception.

There are plenty of examples of self-fulfilling prophecies in work and school settings.[38] Research has found that women score lower on math tests when people around them convey a negative stereotype of women regarding math tests. Women perform better on these tests when they are not exposed to this negative self-fulfilling prophecy. Another study reported that the performance of Israeli Defence Force trainees was influenced by their instructor's expectations regarding the trainee's potential in the program. Self-fulfilling prophecy was at work here because the instructors' expectations were based on a list provided by researchers showing which recruits had high and low potential, even though the researchers had actually listed these trainees randomly.

CONTINGENCIES OF SELF-FULFILLING PROPHECY

Self-fulfilling prophecies are more powerful under some conditions than others.[39] Managers' expectations have a stronger effect on employee behaviour at the beginning of the relationship (i.e., when employees are first hired) than after they have known each other for some time. Self-fulfilling prophecy is also more powerful when several people have these expectations toward an individual than when the expectations are perceived by just one person. In other words, we might be able to ignore one person's doubts about our potential, but not the collective doubts of several people.

A third factor is the individual's past achievements. Both positive and negative self-fulfilling prophecies have a stronger effect on people with a history of low achievement than of those with high achievement. High achievers are less affected by negative expectations because they can draw on the strength of their successful past experiences. Low achievers don't have these past successes to support their self-esteem, so they give up more easily when they sense their boss's low expectations. Fortunately, the opposite is also true: low achievers respond more favourably than high achievers to positive self-fulfilling prophecy. Low achievers don't receive this positive encouragement very often, so it probably has a strong effect on their motivation to excel.[40]

The main lesson from the self-fulfilling prophecy literature is that leaders need to develop and maintain a positive, yet realistic, expectation toward all employees.[41] This recommendation is consistent with the emerging philosophy of *positive organizational behaviour*, which suggests that focusing on the positive rather than negative aspects of life will improve organizational success and individual well-being. Perceiving and communicating hope is so important that it is one of the key competencies of physicians and surgeons. Unfortunately, training programs that make leaders aware of the power of positive expectations don't seem to have much effect. Instead, generating positive expectations and hope depend on a corporate culture of support and learning. Hiring supervisors who are inherently optimistic toward their staff is another way of increasing the incidence of positive self-fulfilling prophecies.

■ OTHER PERCEPTUAL ERRORS

Self-fulfilling prophecy, attribution, and stereotyping are processes that both assist and interfere with the perceptual process. Four other well-known perceptual biases in organizational settings are primacy effect, recency effect, halo effect, and projection bias.

PRIMACY EFFECT

primacy effect
A perceptual error in which we quickly form an opinion of people based on the first information we receive about them.

First impressions are lasting impressions. This well-known saying isn't a cliché; it's a well-researched observation known as the **primacy effect**. The primacy effect refers to our tendency to quickly form an opinion of people based on the first information we receive about them.[42] This rapid perceptual organization and interpretation occurs because we need to make sense of the world around us. The problem is that first impressions—particularly negative first impressions—are difficult to change. After categorizing someone, we tend to select subsequent information that supports our first impression and screen out information that opposes that impression. Negative impressions tend to "stick" more than positive impressions because negative characteristics are more easily attributed to the person, whereas positive characteristics are often attributed to the situation.

RECENCY EFFECT

recency effect
A perceptual error in which the most recent information dominates one's perception of others.

The **recency effect** occurs when the most recent information dominates our perceptions.[43] This effect is most common when making an evaluation involving complex information, particularly among people with limited experience. For instance, auditors must digest large volumes of information in their judgments about financial documents, and the most recent information received prior to the decision tends to get weighted more heavily than information received at the beginning of the audit. Similarly, when supervisors evaluate the performance of employees over the previous year, the most recent performance information dominates the evaluation because it is the most easily recalled. Some employees are well aware of the recency effect and use it to their advantage by getting their best work on the manager's desk just before the performance appraisal is conducted.

DILBERT reprinted by permission of United Feature Syndicate, Inc.

HALO EFFECT

halo effect
A perceptual error whereby our general impression of a person, usually based on one prominent characteristic, colours the perception of other characteristics of that person.

Halo effect occurs when our general impression of a person, usually based on one prominent characteristic, colours our perception of other characteristics of that person.[44] If a supervisor who values punctuality notices that an employee is sometimes late for work, the supervisor might form a negative image of the employee and evaluate that person's other traits unfavourably as well. Generally, one trait important to the perceiver forms a general impression, and this impression becomes the basis for judgments about other traits. Halo effect is most likely to occur when concrete information about the perceived target is missing or we are not sufficiently motivated to search for it. Instead, we use our general impression of the person to fill in the missing information.

PROJECTION BIAS

projection bias
A perceptual error in which an individual believes that other people have the same beliefs and behaviours that he/she does.

Projection bias occurs when we believe other people have the same beliefs and behaviours that we do.[45] If you are eager for a promotion, you might think that others in your position are similarly motivated. If you are thinking of quitting your job, you start to believe that other people are also thinking of quitting. Projection bias is also a defence mechanism to protect our self-esteem. If we break a work rule, projection bias justifies this infraction by claiming that "everyone does it." We feel more comfortable with the thought that our negative traits exist in others, so we believe that others also have these traits.

■ IMPROVING PERCEPTIONS

We can't bypass the perceptual process, but we should make every attempt to minimize perceptual biases and distortions. Earlier, we learned about diversity awareness, meaningful interaction, and accountability practices to minimize the adverse effects of biased stereotypes. Two other broad perceptual improvement practices are developing empathy and improving self-awareness.

IMPROVING PERCEPTIONS THROUGH EMPATHY

empathy
A person's ability to understand and be sensitive to the feelings, thoughts, and situations of others.

Empathy refers to a person's understanding of and sensitivity to the feelings, thoughts, and situation of others. Empathy has both a cognitive (thinking) and emotional component.[46] The cognitive component, which is sometimes called perspective taking, represents a cognitive awareness of another person's situational and individual circumstances. The emotional component of empathy refers to experiencing the feelings of the other person. You have empathy when actively visualizing the other person's situation (perspective taking), and feeling that person's emotions in that situation. Empathizing with others improves our sensitivity to external causes of another person's performance and behaviour, thereby reducing fundamental attribution error. A supervisor who imagines what it's like to be a single mother, for example, would become more sensitive to the external causes of lateness and other events among these employees.

Our empathy towards others improves through feedback, such as from a supervisor, co-worker, or coach. Pratt & Whitney Canada president Alain Bellemare recalls how his first supervisor gave him valuable feedback in the fine art of empathy. "He was phenomenal in coaching me, in how to talk to people and how to be sensitive to

Architects Improve Empathy in Customers' Wheelchairs

Barbara Fabiani doesn't normally have any trouble opening doors. But on this day, Fabiani and other architects discovered that opening a door while being confined to a wheelchair presents unique challenges. "Well, that only took forever," joked Fabiani after finally getting through the doorway. Fabiani and her colleagues spent an afternoon at Gaylord Hospital in New Haven, Connecticut, pretending to have disabilities so they could develop a better appreciation of the physical barriers facing people with disabilities. Some participants were outfitted with arm slings and soft leg braces to simulate inability to use a leg and an arm. Several were blindfolded so they could see what it's like to live without sight. "Now, they have some sympathy and understanding of what people with these disabilities have to go through," says one of the organizers of the event.[51]
Michael McAndrews, Hartford Courant

their situation," Bellemare recalls. Executive coaches also provide empathy-related feedback by attending meetings and later debrief executives regarding how well they demonstrated empathy toward others in the meeting.[47] Another way to improve empathy is to literally walk in the other person's shoes. The opening story to this chapter described how several executives are following this practice by working in front-line jobs once in a while. The more you personally experience the environment in which other people live and work, the better you will understand and be sensitive to their needs and expectations.

KNOW YOURSELF: APPLYING THE JOHARI WINDOW

Knowing yourself—becoming more aware of your values, beliefs, and prejudices—is a powerful way to improve your perceptions.[48] Let's say that you had an unpleasant experience with lawyers and developed negative emotions toward people in this profession. Being sensitive to these emotions should enable you to regulate your behaviour more effectively when working with legal professionals. Moreover, if co-workers are aware of your antipathy to lawyers, they are more likely to understand your actions and help you to be objective in the future.

The **Johari Window** is a popular model for understanding how co-workers can increase their mutual understanding.[49] Developed by Joseph Luft and Harry Ingram (hence the name Johari), this model divides information about you into four "windows"—open, blind, hidden, and unknown—based on whether your own values, beliefs, and experiences are known to you and to others (see Exhibit 3.5). The *open area* includes information about you that is known both to you and to others. For example, both you and your co-workers may be aware that you don't like to be near people who smoke cigarettes. The *blind area* refers to information that is known to others but not to you. For example, your colleagues might notice that you are self-conscious and awkward when meeting the company CEO, but you are unaware of this fact. Information known to you but unknown to others is found in the *hidden area*. We all have personal secrets about our likes, dislikes, and personal experiences. Finally, the *unknown area* includes your values, beliefs, and experiences that aren't known to you or others.

The main objective of the Johari Window is to increase the size of the open area so that both you and colleagues are aware of your perceptual limitations. This is partly accomplished by reducing the hidden area through *disclosure*—informing others of your beliefs, feelings, and experiences that may influence the work relationship.[50] The open area also increases through *feedback* from others about your behaviours. This information helps you to reduce your blind area, because co-workers often see things in you that you do not see. Finally, the combination of disclosure and feedback occasionally produces revelations about information in the unknown area.

Johari Window
The model of personal and interpersonal understanding that encourages disclosure and feedback to increase the open area and reduce the blind, hidden, and unknown areas of oneself.

■ **EXHIBIT 3.5**
Johari Window

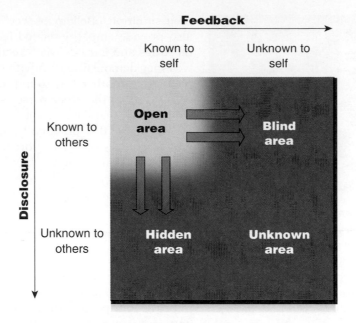

The Johari Window applies to some diversity awareness and meaningful contact activities that we described earlier. By learning about cultural differences and communicating more with people from different backgrounds, we gain a better understanding of their behaviour. Engaging in open dialogue with co-workers also applies the Johari Window. As we communicate with others, we naturally tend to disclose more information about ourselves and eventually feel comfortable providing candid feedback to them.

The perceptual process represents the filter through which information passes from the external environment to our brain. As such, it is really the beginning of the learning process, which we discuss next.

■ LEARNING IN ORGANIZATIONS

What do employees at Wipro Technologies appreciate most about working at the Indian software giant? Financial rewards and challenging work are certainly on the list, but one of the top benefits is learning. "Wipro provides great learning opportunities," says CEO Vivek Paul. "The core of how employees think about us and value us revolves around training. It simply isn't something we can back off from."[52]

learning
A relatively permanent change in behaviour that occurs as a result of a person's interaction with the environment.

Learning is a relatively permanent change in behaviour (or behaviour tendency) that occurs as a result of a person's interaction with the environment. Learning occurs when the learner behaves differently. For example, we can see that you have "learned" computer skills when you operate the keyboard and windows more quickly than before. Learning occurs when interaction with the environment leads to behaviour change. This means that we learn through our senses, such as through study, observation, and experience.

Learning influences individual behaviour and performance through three elements of the MARS model (see Chapter 2). First, people acquire skills and knowledge through learning opportunities, which gives them the competencies to perform tasks more effectively. Second, learning clarifies role perceptions.

Employees develop a better understanding of their tasks and relative importance of work activities. Third, learning occurs through feedback, which motivates employees when they see that they are accomplishing the task.

LEARNING EXPLICIT AND TACIT KNOWLEDGE

When employees learn, they acquire both explicit and tacit knowledge. Explicit knowledge is organized and can be communicated from one person to another. The information you receive in a lecture is mainly explicit knowledge because the instructor packages and consciously transfers it to you. Explicit knowledge can be written down and given to others.

However, explicit knowledge is really only the tip of the knowledge iceberg. Most of what we know is **tacit knowledge**.[53] You have probably said to someone: "I can't tell you how to do this, but I can show you." Tacit knowledge is not documented; rather, it is action-oriented and known below the level of consciousness. Some writers suggest that tacit knowledge also includes the organization's culture and a team's implicit norms. People know these values and rules exist, but they are difficult to describe and document. Tacit knowledge is acquired through observation and direct experience. For example, airline pilots learn to operate commercial jets more by watching experts and practising on flight simulators than through lectures. They acquire tacit knowledge by directly experiencing the complex interaction of behaviour with the machine's response.

The rest of this chapter introduces three perspectives of learning tacit and explicit knowledge: reinforcement, social learning, and direct experience. Each perspective offers a different angle for understanding the dynamics of learning.

tacit knowledge
Knowledge embedded in our actions and ways of thinking, and transmitted only through observation and experience.

■ BEHAVIOUR MODIFICATION: LEARNING THROUGH REINFORCEMENT

behaviour modification
A theory that explains learning in terms of the antecedents and consequences of behaviour.

One of the oldest perspectives on learning, called **behaviour modification** (also known as *operant conditioning* and *reinforcement theory*), takes the rather extreme view that learning is completely dependent on the environment. Behaviour modification does not question the notion that thinking is part of the learning process, but it views human thoughts as unimportant intermediate stages between behaviour and the environment. The environment teaches us to alter our behaviours so that we maximize positive consequences and minimize adverse consequences.[54]

A-B-Cs OF BEHAVIOUR MODIFICATION

The central objective of behaviour modification is to change behaviour (B) by managing its antecedents (A) and consequences (C). This process is nicely illustrated in the A-B-C model of behaviour modification, shown in Exhibit 3.6.[55] *Antecedents* are events preceding the behaviour, informing employees that certain behaviours will have particular consequences. An antecedent may be a sound from your computer signalling that an email has arrived or a request from your supervisor to complete a specific task by tomorrow. These antecedents let employees know that a particular action will produce specific consequences. Notice that antecedents do not cause behaviours. The computer sound doesn't cause us to open our email. Rather, the sound is a cue telling us that certain consequences are likely to occur if we engage in certain behaviours.

■ **EXHIBIT 3.6**   Primary and secondary dimensions of workforce diversity

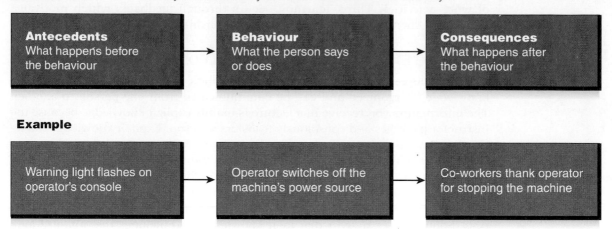

Sources: Adapted from T. K. Connellan, *How to Improve Human Performance*, (New York: Harper & Row, 1978), pg. 50; F. Luthans and R. Kreitner, *Organizational Behavior Modification and Beyond*, (Glenview, IL: Scott, Foresman, 1985), pp. 85–88.

Although antecedents are important, behaviour modification mainly focuses on the *consequences* of behaviour. Consequences are events following a particular behaviour that influence its future occurrence. Generally speaking, people tend to repeat behaviours that are followed by pleasant consequences and are less likely to repeat behaviours that are followed by unpleasant consequences or no consequences at all.

CONTINGENCIES OF REINFORCEMENT

Behaviour modification identifies four types of consequences that strengthen, maintain, or weaken behaviour. These consequences, collectively known as the *contingencies of reinforcement*, include positive reinforcement, punishment, negative reinforcement, and extinction.[56]

■ *Positive reinforcement*—**Positive reinforcement** occurs when the introduction of a consequence increases or maintains the frequency or future probability of a specific behaviour. Receiving a bonus after successfully completing an important project is considered positive reinforcement because it typically increases the probability that you use those behaviours in the future.

■ *Punishment*—**Punishment** occurs when a consequence decreases the frequency or future probability of a behaviour. This consequence typically involves introducing something that employees try to avoid. For instance, most of us would consider a demotion or being ostracized by our co-workers as forms of punishment.[57]

■ *Negative reinforcement*—**Negative reinforcement** occurs when the removal or avoidance of a consequence increases or maintains the frequency or future probability of a specific behaviour. Supervisors apply negative reinforcement when they stop criticizing employees whose substandard performance has improved. When the criticism is withheld, employees are more likely to repeat behaviours that improved their performance. Notice that negative reinforcement is not punishment. It actually reinforces behaviour by removing punishment.

---

positive reinforcement
Occurs when the introduction of a consequence increases or maintains the frequency or future probability of a behaviour.

punishment
Occurs when a consequence decreases the frequency or future probability of a behaviour.

negative reinforcement
Occurs when the removal or avoidance of a consequence increases or maintains the frequency or future probability of a behaviour.

extinction
Occurs when the
target behaviour
decreases because
no consequence
follows it.

■ *Extinction*—**Extinction** occurs when the target behaviour decreases because no consequence follows it. In this respect, extinction is a do-nothing strategy. Generally, behaviour that is no longer reinforced tends to disappear; it becomes extinct. For instance, research suggests that when managers stop congratulating employees for their good performance, that performance tends to decline.[58]

Which contingency of reinforcement should we use in the learning process? In most situations, positive reinforcement should follow desired behaviours and extinction (do nothing) should follow undesirable behaviours. This approach is preferred because punishment and negative reinforcement generate negative emotions and attitudes toward the punisher (e.g., supervisor) and organization. However, some form of punishment (dismissal, suspension, demotion, etc.) may be necessary for extreme behaviours, such as deliberately hurting a co-worker or stealing inventory. Indeed, research suggests that, under certain conditions, punishment maintains a sense of equity.[59]

SCHEDULES OF REINFORCEMENT

Along with the types of reinforcement, the frequency and timing of those reinforcers also influence employee behaviours.[60] These reinforcement schedules can be continuous or intermittent, fixed or variable. The most effective reinforcement schedule for learning new tasks is *continuous reinforcement*—providing positive reinforcement after every occurrence of the desired behaviour. Employees learn desired behaviours quickly and, when the reinforcer is removed, extinction also occurs very quickly.

The other schedules of reinforcement are intermittent. Most people get paid with a *fixed interval schedule* because they receive their reinforcement (paycheque) after a fixed period of time. A *variable interval schedule* is common for promotions. Employees are promoted after a variable amount of time. If you are given the rest of the day off after completing a fixed amount of work (e.g., serving a specific number of customers), then you would have experienced a *fixed ratio schedule*—reinforcement after a fixed number of behaviours or accomplishments.

Finally, companies often use a *variable ratio schedule* in which employee behaviour is reinforced after a variable number of times. Salespeople experience variable ratio reinforcement because they make a successful sale (the reinforcer) after a varying number of client calls. They might make four unsuccessful calls before receiving an order on the fifth one, then make 10 more calls before receiving the next order, and so on. The variable ratio schedule is a low-cost way to reinforce behaviour because employees are rewarded infrequently. It is also highly resistant to extinction. Suppose your boss walks into your office at varying times of the day. Chances are that you would work consistently better throughout the day than if your boss visits at exactly 11 a.m. every day. If your boss doesn't walk into your office at all on a particular day, you would still expect a visit right up to the end of the day if previous visits were random.

BEHAVIOUR MODIFICATION IN PRACTICE

Everyone practises behaviour modification in one form or another. We thank people for a job well done, are silent when displeased, and sometimes try to punish those who go against our wishes. Behaviour modification also occurs in various formal programs to reduce absenteeism, encourage safe work behaviours, and improve task performance. GLOBAL Connections 3.2 describes how behaviour

Reinforcing Lagging and Leading Indicators of Workplace Safety

For many years, companies have had workplace safety programs that reward employees for accident-free milestones. At Dragon Cement's plant in Thomaston, Maine, for example, employees earn gift certificates for every three months that there is no lost-time injury at the facility. The certificates start at $25 per person and grow by $5 each quarter. The Thomaston plant recently achieved six years without an accident, so the quarterly certificate has become quite valuable.

The problem with rewarding accident-free milestones and similar "lagging indicators" is that they really reinforce accident reporting avoidance. There are reported cases where employees with broken arms or other injuries requiring rehabilitation have shown up for work because they didn't want to be held responsible for losing everyone's cherished safety bonus.

To avoid these unintended behaviours, companies are now focusing ways to reinforce safe work behaviours as "leading indicators." For instance, ExxonMobil's Fawley refinery in the U.K. introduced a "Behave Safely Challenge" program in which supervisors rewarded employees and contractors on the spot when they exhibited good safety behaviour or intervened to improve the safe behaviour of co-workers. The company also introduced a system in which co-workers observe each other's safety behaviours.

Lionore Australia also relies on employees to reinforce the safe work behaviour of co-workers on the job. But the Australian subsidiary of the Toronto-based mining company discovered that the success of this peer reinforcement system depended on how tactfully employees communicated their observations to the people around them. With this in mind, Lionore Australia launched a training program in which actors re-enacted real workplace incidents involving effective and ineffec-

Employees at ExxonMobil's Fawley refinery in the U.K. receive various types of reinforcement for safe work behaviours and outcomes.
Photo by Ian Jackson. Courtesy of Exxon Mobil

tive communication about safety violations. The humorous, yet realistic role-plays provided behaviour modelling for employees so they learn how to approach colleagues whose behaviour is unsafe.

Sources: "Dragon Cement Marks Two Years, No Lost-time Injury," *Cement Americas*, January 1, 2002; ExxonMobil, *UK and Ireland Corporate Citizenship*, Unpublished brochure, August 2004; "All Safety is a Stage," *SafetyWA*, August 2004, pp. 1, 8; W. Atkinson, "Safety Incentive Programs: What Works?" *Occupational Hazards*, August 11, 2004; "Dragon's Concrete Division Passes 6-Year Mark Without a Lost-time Injury," Dragon Products Company news release, December 6, 2004.
www.exxonmobil.com

modification practices aimed at workplace safety have shifted their focus from reinforcing the lack of accidents to reinforcing safety behaviours. The latter is more consistent with behaviour modification theory because it focuses on behaviours within the employee's control. Also notice how some of these safety reinforcement programs use lottery-type rewards. Lotteries are popular in behaviour modification because they provide a variable ratio schedule of reinforcement.

While behaviour modification can be effective, it has several limitations.[61] One problem is "reward inflation," in which the reinforcer is eventually considered an entitlement. For this reason, most behaviour modification programs must run infrequently and for short durations. A second problem is that some people revolt against the lottery-style variable ratio schedule because they consider gambling unethical. Third, behaviour modification's radical "behaviourist" philosophy (that human thinking processes are unimportant) has lost favour because it is now evident that people can learn through mental processes, such as observing others and thinking logically about possible consequences.[62] Thus, without throwing away the principles of behaviour modification, most learning experts today also embrace the concepts of social learning theory.

■ SOCIAL LEARNING THEORY: LEARNING BY OBSERVING

social learning theory
A theory stating that much learning occurs by observing others and then modelling the behaviours that lead to favourable outcomes and avoiding the behaviours that lead to punishing consequences.

Social learning theory states that much learning occurs by observing others and then modelling the behaviours that lead to favourable outcomes and avoiding behaviours that lead to punishing consequences.[63] Three related features of social learning theory are behaviour modelling, learning behaviour consequences, and self-reinforcement.

BEHAVIOUR MODELLING

People learn by observing the behaviours of a role model on the critical task, remembering the important elements of the observed behaviours, and then practising those behaviours.[64] Behaviour modelling works best when the model is respected and the model's actions are followed by favourable consequences. For instance, recently hired college graduates learn better by watching a previously hired college graduate who successfully performs the task.

Behaviour modelling is a valuable form of learning for two reasons. First, tacit knowledge and skills are mainly acquired from others through observation. The adage that a picture is worth a thousand words applies here. It is difficult to document or verbally explain every detail on how a master baker kneads dough. Instead, this information is more effectively learned by observing the baker's actions and the consequences of those actions. Second, employees tend to have a higher belief that they can perform the work after seeing someone else perform the task. This effect is particularly strong when observers identify with the model, such as someone who is similar with respect to age, experience, and gender. For instance, students are more confident about taking a challenging course when they are mentored by students similar to them who have just completed that course.

LEARNING BEHAVIOUR CONSEQUENCES

A second element of social learning theory says that we learn the consequences of behaviour through logic and observation, not just through direct experience. People logically anticipate desirable consequences after completing a task well and undesirable consequences (punishment or extinction) after performing the job poorly. It just makes sense to expect these outcomes, until we learn otherwise. We also learn behavioural consequences by observing the experiences of other people. This process, known as *vicarious learning*, occurs all the time in organizational settings. You might notice how co-workers mock another employee who dresses formally at work. By observing this incident, you learn about the group's preference for wearing casual attire. You might see how another worker serves customers better by keeping a list of their names, which teaches you to do the same. In each case, you have learned vicariously, not through your own experience.[65]

SELF-REINFORCEMENT

Self-reinforcement, the third element of social learning theory, occurs whenever an employee has control over a reinforcer but doesn't "take" it until completing a self-set goal.[66] For example, you might be thinking about having a snack after you finish reading the rest of this chapter—and not before! You could take a break right now, but you don't use this privilege until you have achieved your goal of reading the chapter. Raiding the refrigerator is a form of self-induced positive reinforcement. Self-reinforcement can take many forms, such as taking a short walk, watching a movie, or simply congratulating yourself for completing the task. Self-reinforcement has become increasingly important because employees are given more control over their working lives and are less dependent on supervisors to dole out positive reinforcement and punishment.

■ LEARNING THROUGH EXPERIENCE

Mandy Chooi is about to attend a meeting with a lower level manager who has botched a new assignment. She is also supposed to make a strategy presentation to her boss in three hours, but the telephone won't stop ringing and she is deluged with email. It's a stressful situation. Fortunately, the challenges facing the Motorola human resources executive from Beijing on this particular day are not real. Chooi is sitting in a simulation to develop and test her leadership skills. "It was hard. A lot harder than I had expected," she says. "It's surprising how realistic and demanding it is."[67]

Many organizations are shifting their learning strategy away from the classroom and toward a more experiential approach. Classrooms transfer explicit knowledge that has been documented, but most tacit knowledge and skills are acquired through experience as well as observation. Experiential learning has been conceptualized in many ways, but one of the most enduring perspectives is Kolb's experiential learning model, shown in Exhibit 3.7. This model illustrates experiential learning as a cyclical four-stage process.[68]

■ EXHIBIT 3.7

Kolb's experiential learning model

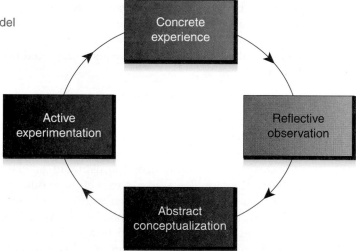

Sources: Based on information in J.E. Sharp, "Applying Kolb Learning Style Theory in the Communication Classroom," *Business Communication Quarterly,* 60 (June 1997), pp. 129–134; D.A. Kolb, *Experiential Learning* (Englewood Cliffs, NJ: Prentice-Hall, 1984).

Experiential Learning for HUSAR

Physicians Jonathan Sherbino and Ivy Chong (far right) prepare to amputate the leg of Wesley Bagshaw who is pinned by a fallen beam in this collapsed building. "If we don't do this, you're going to die," says Sherbino in response to Bagshaw's anguished protests. Fortunately for Bagshaw, the bone saw cuts through a pig's leg rather than his own. The entire incident was a mock disaster to help train Toronto's Heavy Urban Search And Rescue (HUSAR) team. For four hours, HUSAR crews located the victims with dogs and search equipment at this Toronto Fire Services special operations training centre site, secured the structure, treated Bagshaw and 15 other "victims," and extricated them to a mock hospital at Centennial College. In all, over 300 HUSAR and Greater Toronto medical professionals were involved. "People from the hospitals love these exercises because they get to try out all the ideas they have and no one is (adversely) affected," explains one of the event's organizers. "It was definitely a lot more realistic than anything we've done in the past."[69]
Michael Stuparyk, Toronto Star
www.toronto.ca/ems

Concrete experience involves sensory and emotional engagement in some activity. It is followed by *reflective observation*, which involves listening, watching, recording, and elaborating on the experience. The next stage in the learning cycle is *abstract conceptualization*. This is the stage in which we develop concepts and integrate our observations into logically sound theories. The fourth stage, *active experimentation*, occurs when we test our previous experience, reflection, and conceptualization in a particular context. People tend to prefer and operate better in some stages than in others due to their unique competencies and personality. Still, experiential learning requires all four stages in proper balance.

EXPERIENTIAL LEARNING IN PRACTICE

learning orientation
The extent to which an organization or individual supports knowledge management, particularly opportunities to acquire knowledge through experience and experimentation.

Learning through experience works best in organizations with a strong **learning orientation**—they value learning opportunities and, in particular, the generation of new knowledge while employees perform their jobs. If an employee initially fails to perform a task, then the experience might still be a valuable learning opportunity. In other words, organizations encourage employees to appreciate the process of individual and team learning, not just the performance results.

Organizations achieve a learning orientation culture by rewarding experimentation and recognizing mistakes as a natural part of the learning process. They encourage employees to take reasonable risks to ultimately discover new and better ways of doing things. Without a learning orientation, mistakes are hidden and problems are more likely to escalate or re-emerge later. It's not surprising, then, that one of the most frequently mentioned lessons from the best performing manufacturers is to expect mistakes. "[Mistakes] are a source of learning and will improve operations in the long run," explains an executive at Lockheed Martin. "[They] foster the concept that no question is dumb, no idea too wild, and no task or activity is irrelevant."[70]

action learning
A variety of experiential learning activities in which employees are involved in a "real, complex, and stressful problem," usually in teams, with immediate relevance to the company.

Action learning   One application of workplace experiential learning that has received considerable interest, particularly in Europe, is **action learning**. Action learning occurs when employees, usually in teams, investigate and apply solutions to a situation that is both real and complex, with immediate relevance to the company.[71] In other words, the task becomes the source of learning. Kolb's experiential learning model presented earlier is usually identified as the main template for action learning. Action learning requires concrete experience with a real organizational problem or opportunity, followed by "learning meetings" in which participants reflect on their observations about that problem or opportunity. Then, they develop and test a strategy to solve the problem or realize the opportunity. The process also encourages plenty of reflection so the experience becomes a learning process.

Action learning is one of the main vehicles for leadership development at GE, Nokia, Samsung, and Boeing, yet it is relatively rare in Canadian organizations. One exception is TD Bank Financial Group, where several hundred managers have entered a leadership program based on action learning principles. Participants identify a workplace issue "of some substance" as well as specific leadership competencies they expect to improve when addressing that workplace issue. Action learning is considered one of the best ways to develop leadership competencies.[72] It involves both tacit and explicit learning, forces employees to diagnose new situations, and makes them rethink current work practices. At the same time, the results of action learning potentially add value to the organization in terms of a better work process or service. "Action learning has become the primary vehicle for generating creative ideas and building business success at Heineken," says the chairman of the executive board at the European brewery.[73]

This chapter has introduced you to two fundamental activities in human behaviour in the workplace: perceptions and learning. These activities involve receiving information from the environment, organizing it, and acting on it as a learning process. Our knowledge about perceptions and learning in the workplace lays the foundation for the next chapter, which looks at workplace emotions and attitudes.

CHAPTER SUMMARY

Perception involves selecting, organizing, and interpreting information to make sense of the world around us. Selective attention is influenced by characteristics of the person or object being perceived (i.e., their size, intensity, motion, repetition, and novelty), and characteristics of the person doing the perceiving. Perceptual organization engages categorical thinking—the mostly unconscious process of organizing people and objects into preconceived categories that are stored in our long-term memory. To a large extent, our perceptual interpretation of incoming information also occurs before we are consciously aware of it. Mental models—broad worldviews or templates of the mind—also help us to make sense of incoming stimuli.

The social identity process explains how we perceive ourselves and other people. We partly identify ourselves in terms of our membership in social groups. This comparison process includes categorizing people into groups, forming a homogeneous image of people within those groups, and differentiating groups by assigning more favourable features to our own groups than to other groups.

Stereotyping is a derivative of the social identity theory, in which people assign traits to others based on their membership in a social category. Stereotyping economizes mental effort, fills in missing information, and enhances our self-perception and social identity. However, it also lays the foundation for prejudice and systemic discrimination. It is very difficult to prevent the activation of stereotyping, but we can minimize the application of stereotypic information in our decisions and actions. Three strategies to minimize the influence of stereotypes are diversity awareness training, meaningful interaction, and decision-making accountability.

The attribution process involves deciding whether the behaviour or event is largely due to the situation (external attributions) or personal characteristics (internal attributions). Attributions are decided by perceptions of the consistency, distinctiveness, and consensus of the behaviour. This process helps us to link together the various pieces of our world in cause-effect relationships, but it is also subject to attribution errors, including fundamental attribution error and self-serving bias.

Self-fulfilling prophecy occurs when our expectations about another person cause that person to act in a way that is consistent with those expectations. Essentially, our expectations affect our behaviour toward the target person, which then affects the employee's opportunities and attitudes, which then influences his or her behaviour. Self-fulfilling prophecies tend to be stronger at the beginning of the relations (such as when employees first join the department), when several people hold the expectations toward the employee, and when the employee has a history of low achievement.

Four other perceptual errors commonly noted in organizations are primacy effect, recency effect, halo effect, and projection bias. We can minimize these and other perceptual problems through empathy and becoming more aware of our values, beliefs, and prejudices (Johari Window).

Learning is a relatively permanent change in behaviour (or behaviour tendency) that occurs as a result of a person's interaction with the environment. Learning influences individual behaviour and performance through ability, role perceptions, and motivation. Some learning results in explicit knowledge, which can be verbally transferred between people. But much of what we learn is tacit knowledge, which is embedded in our actions without conscious awareness.

The behaviour modification perspective of learning states that behaviour change occurs by altering its antecedents and consequences. Antecedents are environmental stimuli that provoke (not necessarily cause) behaviour. Consequences are events following behaviour that influence its future occurrence. Consequences include positive reinforcement, punishment, negative reinforcement, and extinction. The schedules of reinforcement also influence behaviour.

Social learning theory states that much learning occurs by observing others and then modelling those behaviours that seem to lead to favourable outcomes and avoiding behaviours that lead to punishing consequences. It also recognizes that we often engage in self-reinforcement. Behaviour modelling is effective because it transfers tacit knowledge and enhances the observer's confidence in performing the task.

Many companies now use experiential learning because employees do not acquire tacit knowledge through formal classroom instruction. Kolb's experiential learning model is a cyclical four-stage process that includes concrete experience, reflective observation, abstract conceptualization, and active experimentation. Action learning is experiential learning in which employees investigate and act on significant organizational issues.

KEY TERMS

action learning, p. 90

attribution process, p. 74

behaviour modification, p. 83

categorical thinking, p. 67

contact hypothesis, p. 74

empathy, p. 80

extinction, p. 85

fundamental attribution error, p. 76

halo effect, p. 80

Johari Window, p. 81

learning, p. 82

learning orientation, p. 90

mental models, p. 68

negative reinforcement, p. 84

perception, p. 66

positive reinforcement, p. 84

prejudice, p. 72

primacy effect, p. 79

projection bias, p. 80

punishment, p. 84

recency effect, p. 79

selective attention, p. 66

self-fulfilling prophecy, p. 77

self-reinforcement, p. 88

self-serving bias, p. 76

social identity theory, p. 69

social learning theory, p. 87

stereotyping, p. 71

tacit knowledge, p. 83

DISCUSSION QUESTIONS

1. You are part of a task force to increase worker responsiveness to emergencies on the production floor. Identify four factors that should be considered when installing a device that will get every employee's attention when there is an emergency.

2. What mental models do you have about attending a college or university lecture? Are these mental models helpful? Could any of these mental models hold you back from achieving the full benefit of the lecture?

3. Contrast "personal" and "social" identity. Do you define yourself in terms of the university or college you attend? Why or why not? What implications does your response have for the future of your university or college?

4. During a diversity management session, a manager suggests that stereotypes are a necessary part of working with others. "I have to make assumptions about what's in the other person's head, and stereotypes help me do that," she explains. "It's better to rely on stereotypes than to enter a working relationship with someone from another culture without

any idea of what they believe in!" Discuss the merits of and problems with the manager's statement.

5. At the end of an NHL hockey game the coach of the losing team was asked to explain his team's defeat. "I dunno," he begins, "we've done well in this rink over the past few years. Our busy schedule over the past two weeks has pushed the guys too hard, I guess. They're worn out. You probably noticed that we also got some bad breaks on penalties tonight. We should have done well here, but things just went against us." Use attribution theory to explain the coach's perceptions of the team's loss.

6. Describe how a manager or coach could use the process of self-fulfilling prophecy to enhance an individual's performance.

7. Describe a situation in which you used behaviour modification to influence someone's behaviour. What specifically did you do? What was the result?

8. Why are organizations moving toward the use of experiential approaches to learning? What conditions are required for success?

CASE STUDY 3.1

NUPATH FOODS LTD.

James Ornath read the latest sales figures with a great deal of satisfaction. The vice-president of marketing at Nupath Foods Ltd. was pleased to see that the marketing campaign to improve sagging sales of Prowess cat food was working. Sales volume of the product had increased 20 percent in the past quarter compared with the previous year, and market share was up.

The improved sales of Prowess could be credited to Denise Roberge, the brand manager responsible for cat foods at Nupath. Roberge had joined Nupath less than two years ago as an assistant brand manager after leaving a similar job at a consumer products firm. She was one of the few women in marketing management at Nupath and had a promising career with the company. Ornath was pleased with Roberge's work and tried to let her know this in the annual performance reviews. He now had an excellent opportunity to reward her by offering the recently vacated position of market research coordinator. Although technically only a lateral transfer with a modest salary increase, the marketing research coordinator job would give Roberge broader experience in some high-profile work, which would enhance her career with Nupath. Few people were aware that Ornath's own career had been boosted by working as marketing research coordinator at Nupath several years before.

Denise Roberge had also seen the latest sales figures on Prowess cat food and was expecting Ornath's call to meet with her that morning. Ornath began the conversation by briefly mentioning the favourable sales figures, and then explained that he wanted Roberge to take the marketing research coordinator job. Roberge was shocked by the news. She enjoyed brand management and particularly the challenge involved with controlling a product that directly affected the company's profitability. Marketing research coordinator was a technical support position—a "backroom" job—far removed from the company's bottom-line activities. Marketing research was not the route to top management in most organizations, Roberge thought. She had been sidelined.

After a long silence, Roberge managed a weak "Thank you, Mr. Ornath." She was too bewildered to protest. She wanted to collect her thoughts and reflect on what she had done wrong. Also, she did not know her boss well enough to be openly critical. Ornath recognized Roberge's surprise, which he naturally assumed was her positive response to

hearing of this wonderful career opportunity. He, too, had been delighted several years earlier about his temporary transfer to marketing research to round out his marketing experience. "This move will be good for both you and Nupath," said Ornath as he escorted Roberge from his office.

Roberge had several tasks to complete that afternoon, but was able to consider the day's events that evening. She was one of the top women in brand management at Nupath and feared that she was being sidelined because the company didn't want women in top management. Her previous employer had made it quite clear that women "couldn't take the heat" in marketing management and tended to place women in technical support positions after a brief term in lower brand management jobs. Obviously Nupath was following the same game plan. Ornath's comments that the coordinator job would be good for her was just a nice way of saying that Roberge couldn't go any further in brand management at Nupath. Roberge was now faced with the difficult decision of confronting Ornath and trying to change Nupath's sexist practices or submitting her resignation.

Discussion Questions

1. What symptom(s) exist in this case to suggest that something has gone wrong?

2. What caused these symptoms?

3. What actions should the organization take to correct these problems?

Copyright © Steven L. McShane.

C L A S S   E X E R C I S E   3.2

THE LEARNING EXERCISE

Purpose This exercise is designed to help you understand how the contingencies of reinforcement in behaviour modification affect learning.

Materials Any objects normally available in a classroom will be acceptable for this activity.

Instructions The instructor will ask for three volunteers, who are then briefed outside the classroom. The instructor will spend a few minutes briefing the remaining students in the class about their duties. Then, one of the three volunteers will

enter the room to participate in the exercise. When completed, the second volunteer enters the room and participates in the exercise. When completed, the third volunteer enters the class and participates in the exercise.

For students to gain the full benefit of this exercise, no other information will be provided here. However, your instructor will have more details at the beginning of this fun activity.

Copyright © Steven L. McShane.

TEAM EXERCISE   3.3

WHO AM I?

Purpose   This exercise is designed to help you understand the elements and implications of social identity theory.

Materials   None.

Instructions

■ *Step 1:* Working alone (no discussion with other students), use the space provided below or a piece of paper to write down 12 words or phrases that answer the question "Who am I?" Write your words or phrases describing you as they come to mind; don't worry about their logical order here. Please be sure to fill in all 12 spaces.

■ *Step 2:* Circle the "S" beside the items that define you in terms of your social identity, such as your demographics and formal or informal membership in a social group or institution (school, company, religious group). Circle the "P" beside the items that define you in terms of your personal identity; that is, unique personality, values, or experiences that are not connected to any particular social group. Next, underline one or more items that you believe will still be a strong characteristic of you 10 years from now.

■ *Step 3:* Form small groups. If you have a team project for this course, your project team would work well for this exercise. Compare your list

Phrases that describe you   **Circle S or P**

1. I AM _____   S   P

2. I AM _____   S   P

3. I AM _____   S   P

4. I AM _____   S   P

5. I AM _____   S   P

6. I AM _____   S   P

7. I AM _____   S   P

8. I AM _____   S   P

9. I AM _____   S   P

10. I AM _____   S   P

11. I AM _____   S   P

12. I AM _____   S   P

with the lists that others in your group wrote about themselves. Discuss the following questions in your group and prepare notes for class discussion and possible presentation of these questions:

1. Among members of this team, what was the typical percentage of items representing the person's social versus personal identity? Did some team members have many more or less social identity items compared to other team members? Why do you think these large or small differences in emphasis on social or personal identity occurred?

2. What characteristics did people in your group underline as being the most stable (i.e., remaining the same 10 years from now)? Were these underlined items mostly social or personal identity features? How similar or different were the underlined items among team members?

3. What do these lists say about the dynamics of your group as a team (whether or not your group for this activity is actually involved in a class project for this course)?

Sources: M. H. Kuhn and T. S. McPartland, "An Empirical Investigation of Self-Attitudes," *American Sociological Review*, 19 (February 1954), pp. 68–76; C. Lay and M. Verkuyten, "Ethnic Identity and Its Relation to Personal Self-Esteem: A Comparison of Canadian-Born and Foreign-Born Chinese Adolescents," *Journal of Social Psychology*, 139 (1999), pp. 288–99; S. L. Grace and K. L. Cramer, "The Elusive Nature of Self-Measurement: the Self-Construal Scale versus the Twenty Statements Test," *Journal of Social Psychology*, 143 (2003), pp. 649–68.

WEB EXERCISE 3.4

ANALYZING CORPORATE ANNUAL REPORTS

Purpose This exercise is designed to help you diagnose evidence of stereotyping and corporate role models that minimize stereotyping in corporate annual reports.

Materials Students need to complete their research for this activity prior to class, including selecting a publicly traded Canadian company and downloading the past four or more years of its fully illustrated annual reports. (The instructor may allow students to study non-Canadian companies.)

Instructions The instructor may have students work alone or in groups for this activity. Students will select a Canadian company that is publicly traded and makes its annual reports available on the company Web site. Ideally, annual reports for at least the past four years should be available, and these reports should be presented in the final illustrated format (typically PDF replicas of the original hard copy report).

Students will closely examine images in the selected company's recent annual reports in terms of how women, visible minorities, and older employees and clients are presented. Specifically, students should be prepared to discuss and provide details in class regarding:

1. The percentage of images showing (i.e., visual representation of) women, visible minorities, and older workers and clients. Students should also be sensitive to the size and placement of these images on the page and throughout the annual report.

2. The roles in which women, visible minorities, and older workers and clients are depicted. For example, are women shown more in traditional or non-traditional occupations and nonwork roles in these annual reports?

3. If several years of annual reports are available, pick one that is a decade or more old and compare its visual representation of and role depiction of women, visible minorities, and older employees and clients.

If possible, pick one of the most blatantly stereotypic illustrations you can find in these annual reports to show in class, either as a hard copy printout or as a computer projection.

SELF-ASSESSMENT EXERCISE   **3.5**

ASSESSING YOUR PERSONAL NEED FOR STRUCTURE

Purpose   This self-assessment is designed to help you estimate your personal need for perceptual structure.

Instructions   Read each of the statements below and decide how much you agree with each according to your attitudes, beliefs, and experiences. Then use the scoring key in Appendix B of this book to calculate your results. It is important for you to realize that there are no "right" or "wrong" answers to these questions. This self-assessment is completed alone so that students rate themselves honestly without concerns of social comparison. However, class discussion will focus on the meaning of need for structure in terms of how we engage differently in the perceptual process at work and in other settings.

PERSONAL NEED FOR STRUCTURE SCALE						
To what extent do you agree or disagree with each of these statements about yourself?	Strongly Agree ▼	Moderately Agree ▼	Slightly Agree ▼	Slightly Disagree ▼	Moderately Disagree ▼	Strongly Disagree ▼
1. It upsets me to go into a situation without knowing what I can expect from it.	☐	☐	☐	☑	☐	☐
2. I'm not bothered by things that interrupt my daily routine.	☐	☑	☐	☐	☐	☐
3. I enjoy being spontaneous.	☐	☐	☑	☐	☐	☐
4. I find that a well-ordered life with regular hours makes my life tedious.	☐	☑	☐	☐	☐	☐
5. I find that a consistent routine enables me to enjoy life more.	☐	☐	☐	☐	☑	☐
6. I enjoy having a clear and structured mode of life.	☐	☐	☐	☑	☐	☐
7. I like to have a place for everything and everything in its place.	☐	☐	☐	☐	☑	☐
8. I don't like situations that are uncertain.	☐	☐	☐	☑	☐	☐
9. I hate to change my plans at the last minute.	☐	☐	☐	☐	☑	☐
10. I hate to be with people who are unpredictable.	☐	☐	☑	☐	☐	☐
11. I enjoy the exhilaration of being in unpredictable situations.	☐	☐	☑	☐	☐	☐
12. I become uncomfortable when the rules in a situation are not clear.	☐	☐	☐	☑	☐	☐

Source: M. M. Thompson, M. E. Naccarato, and K. E. Parker, "Assessing Cognitive Need: the Development of the Personal Need for Structure and the Personal Fear of Invalidity Scales," Paper presented at the Annual meeting of the Canadian Psychological Association, Halifax, Nova Scotia (1989).

4 + 2 + 3 + 2 + 3 + 2 + 4 + 3 + 4 + 3 + 2 + 3 = 35

SELF-ASSESSMENT EXERCISE | 3.6

ASSESSING YOUR PERSPECTIVE-TAKING (COGNITIVE EMPATHY)

Go to the Online Learning Centre to complete this interactive self-assessment.

Purpose This exercise is designed to help you understand and estimate your propensity for perspective taking, which represents the cognitive (thinking) aspect of empathy.

Instructions This instrument asks you to indicate the degree to which each of the statements presented does or does not describe you very well. You need to be honest with yourself to obtain a reasonable estimate of your level of perspective taking. The results show your relative position in the internal-external locus continuum and the general meaning of this score.

SELF-ASSESSMENT EXERCISE | 3.7

ASSESSING YOUR EMOTIONAL EMPATHY

Go to the Online Learning Centre to complete this interactive self-assessment.

Purpose This exercise is designed to help you understand and estimate your propensity for emotional empathy.

Instructions This instrument asks you to indicate the degree to which each of the statements presented does or does not describe you very well. You need to be honest with yourself to obtain a reasonable estimate of your level of perspective taking. The results show your relative position in the internal-external locus continuum and the general meaning of this score.

·4·

WORKPLACE EMOTIONS AND ATTITUDES

LEARNING OBJECTIVES

AFTER READING THIS CHAPTER, YOU SHOULD BE ABLE TO:

- Define emotions and identify the two dimensions around which emotions are organized.

- Explain how cognitions and emotions influence attitudes and behaviour.

- Identify the conditions that require and the problems associated with emotional labour.

- Describe the four dimensions of emotional intelligence.

- Summarize the effects of job dissatisfaction in terms of the exit-voice-loyalty-neglect model.

- Discuss the relationships between job satisfaction and performance as well as job satisfaction and customer satisfaction.

- Compare the effects of affective and continuance commitment on employee behaviour.

- Describe five strategies to increase organizational commitment.

- Contrast transactional and relational psychological contracts.

Corporate five-year business plan presentations are often boring affairs, but not at Vancouver City Savings Credit Union (VanCity). Employees at the financial institution recently received a video with executives dressed up as famous movies characters to depict VanCity's five business pillars. "I was dressed like Morpheus," recalls VanCity executive Donna Wilson, who played a scene from *The Matrix* by offering viewers either the red pill or blue pill to accept VanCity's new objectives. "Even though I was in the form of *The Matrix*, I was talking the language of a very important part of our five-year plan."

VanCity goes beyond the ordinary to maintain employee satisfaction and loyalty. Along with producing offbeat videos, the company hosts awards nights, family picnics, and an annual costume gala attended by over 1,000 staff. Fully paid benefits, tuition reimbursement, flexible schedules, profit sharing, and meditation and lactation rooms at head office add to the positive work experience.

Employee loyalty is further strengthened by the company's stellar reputation in the community, its high ethical standards, and a culture that gives employees lots of freedom to perform their jobs and encourages active involvement in company decisions. "It's a dynamic environment and you get a sense of accomplishment," says Robert Nenadic, VanCity's team leader for network services.

Based on these and other features, VanCity receives awards every year as one of the best places

CEO Dave Mowat and happy employees celebrate the announcement that VanCity is the best place to work in Canada. *Glen Baglo/Vancouver Sun*

to work in Canada. The company boasts over 10,000 job applications each year and a turnover rate far below the industry average. For instance, when asked if she thought about working somewhere else, VanCity accounts manager Laura Victoria quickly replied: "No, they'd have to push me out. It's worth every minute of it here."

Why does VanCity place such importance on the positive emotions and attitudes? The answer is that it's ethically the right thing to do and is good for business. "Treating our employees well is central to our business case," explains VanCity CEO Dave Mowat. "Business depends on the employees who love their work. That's integral to what we do."[1] ■

www.vancity.com

Workplace emotions and attitudes are receiving a lot more attention these days at VanCity and in many other organizations across Canada. That's because emotions and attitudes can make a huge difference in individual behaviour and well-being, as well as in the organization's performance and customer satisfaction. Over the past decade, the field of organizational behaviour has experienced a sea change in thinking about workplace emotions, so this chapter begins by introducing the concept and explaining why researchers are so eager to discover how emotions influence attitudes and behaviour.

Next, we consider the dynamics of emotional labour, including the conditions requiring emotional labour. This is followed by the popular topic of emotional intelligence, in which we examine the components of emotional intelligence and ways of improving this ability. The specific work attitudes of job satisfaction and organizational commitment are then discussed, including their association with various employee behaviours and work performance. Organizational commitment is strongly influenced by the psychological contract, so the final section of this chapter looks briefly at this topic.

■ EMOTIONS IN THE WORKPLACE

emotions

Psychological and physiological episodes experienced toward an object, person, or event that create a state of readiness.

Emotions have a profound effect on almost everything we do in the workplace. This is a strong statement, and one that you would rarely find a decade ago in organizational behaviour research or textbooks. For most of its history, the field of OB assumed that a person's thoughts and actions are governed primarily by conscious reasoning (called cognitions). Yet, groundbreaking neuroscience discoveries have revealed that our perceptions, decisions, and behaviour are influenced by both cognition and emotion, and that the latter often has the greater influence. By ignoring emotionality, many theories have overlooked a large piece of the puzzle about human behaviour in the workplace. Today, OB scholars and their colleagues in marketing, economics, and many other social sciences, are catching up by making emotions a key part of their research and theories.[2]

"Biosensors. The whole company knows instantly when I'm displeased."

So, what are emotions? **Emotions** are physiological, behavioural, and psychological episodes experienced toward an object, person, or event that create a state of readiness.[3] There are four key elements of this definition. First, emotions are brief events or "episodes." Your irritation with a customer, for instance, would typically subside within a few minutes. Second, emotions are directed toward someone or something. We experience joy, fear, anger, and other emotional episodes toward tasks, customers, public speeches we present, a software program we are using, and so on. This contrasts with *moods*, which are less intense emotional states that are not directed toward anything in particular.[4]

Third, emotions are experiences. They represent changes in a person's physiological conditions, such as blood pressure, heart rate, and perspiration, as well as changes in behaviour, such as facial expression, voice tone, and eye movement. These emotional reactions are involuntary and often occur without our awareness.

When aware of these responses, we also develop feelings (worry, fear, boredom) that further mark the emotional experience. The experience of emotion also relates to the fourth element, namely, that emotions put people in a state of readiness. When we get worried, for example, our heart rate and blood pressure increase to make our body better prepared to engage in fight or flight. Emotions are also communications to our conscious selves. Some emotions (e.g., anger, surprise, fear) are particularly strong "triggers" that interrupt our train of thought, demand our attention, and generate the motivation to take action. They make us aware of events that may affect our survival and well-being.[5]

TYPES OF EMOTIONS

Emotions come in many forms, and experts have generally organized them around two or three dimensions. The most widely recognized arrangement is the Circumplex Model of Emotions shown in Exhibit 4.1, which organizes emotions on the basis of their pleasantness and activation (the extent that the emotion produces alertness and motivation to act).[6] Fear, for example, is an unpleasant experience (i.e., we try to avoid conditions that generate fear) and has high activation (i.e., it motivates us to act). Emotions on the opposite side of the circle have the opposite effect. As we see in Exhibit 4.1, calm is the opposite to fear; it is a pleasant experience that produces very little activation in us.

■ **EXHIBIT 4.1**

Circumplex model of emotions

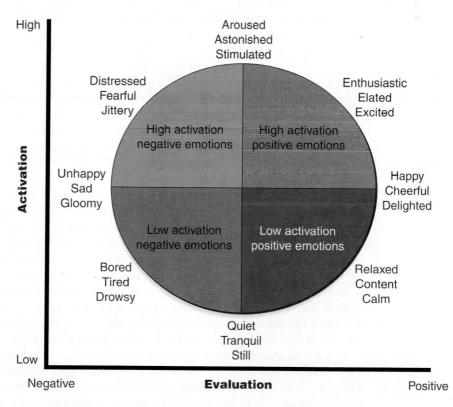

Sources: Adapted from J. Larson, E. Diener, and R. E. Lucas, "Emotion: Models, Measures, and Differences," in R. G. Lord, R. J. Klimoski, & R. Kanfer (Eds.) *Emotions in the Workplace* (San Francisco: Jossey-Bass, 2002), pp. 64–113; J. A. Russell, "Core Affect and the Psychological Construction of Emotion." *Psychological Review* 110, no. 1 (2003), pp. 145–172.

EMOTIONS, ATTITUDES, AND BEHAVIOUR

attitudes
The cluster of beliefs, assessed feelings, and behavioural intentions toward an object.

Emotions influence our thoughts and behaviour, but to explain this effect we first need to know about attitudes. **Attitudes** represent the cluster of beliefs, assessed feelings, and behavioural intentions toward a person, object, or event (called an *attitude object*).[7] Attitudes are *judgments*, whereas emotions are *experiences*. In other words, attitudes involve conscious logical reasoning, whereas emotions operate as events, often without our awareness. We also experience most emotions briefly, whereas our attitude toward someone or something is more stable over time.

Attitudes include three components—beliefs, feelings, and behavioural intentions—and we'll look at each of them using attitude toward mergers as an illustration:

- *Beliefs*—These are your established perceptions about the attitude object—what you believe to be true. For example, you might believe that mergers reduce job security for employees in the merged firms. Or you might believe that mergers increase the company's competitiveness in this era of globalization. These beliefs are perceived facts that you acquire from past experience and other forms of learning.
- *Feelings*—Feelings represent your positive or negative evaluations of the attitude object. Some people think mergers are good; others think they are bad. Your like or dislike of mergers represents your assessed feelings toward the attitude object.
- *Behavioural intentions*—These represent your motivation to engage in a particular behaviour with respect to the attitude object. You might plan to quit rather than stay with the company during the merger. Alternatively, you might intend to email the company CEO to say that this merger was a good decision.

Traditional cognitive model of attitudes   Until recently, attitude experts assumed that these three attitude components are connected to each other and to behaviour only through the cognitive (logical reasoning) process shown on the left side of Exhibit 4.2. Let's look at the left side of the model more closely. First, our beliefs about mergers are formed from various learning experiences, such as reading about the effects of mergers in other organizations or personally experiencing them in the past.

Next, beliefs about mergers shape our feelings toward them. Suppose you are quite certain that mergers improve the organization's competitiveness (positive outcome with high probability) and sometimes reduce job security (negative outcome with medium probability) for employees in the merged organization. Overall, you might have a somewhat positive attitude toward mergers if your feelings about corporate competitiveness are stronger than your feelings about reduced job security. The probability of those outcomes also weighs their effect on your feelings.

In the third step of the model, feelings directly influence behavioural intentions.[8] However, two people with the same feelings might have different behavioural intentions based on their past experience and personality. Some employees with negative feelings toward mergers may intend to quit, whereas others might want to complain about the decision. People choose the behavioural intention that they think will work best or make them feel most comfortable.

In the final step, behavioural intentions are better than feelings or beliefs at predicting a person's behaviour because they are specific to that behaviour. Even so, behavioural intentions might not predict behaviour very well because intentions represent only the motivation to act, whereas behaviour is also caused by the other three factors in the MARS model—ability, role perceptions, and situational factors. You might plan to send an email to management complaining about the announced merger, but never get around to this task due to a heavy workload and family obligations.

■ **EXHIBIT 4.2**

Model of emotions, attitudes, and behaviour

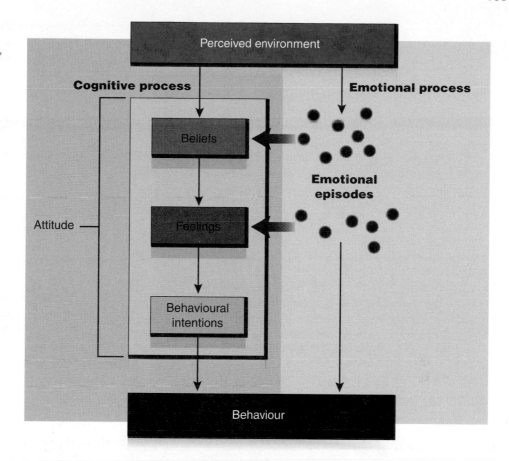

How emotions influence attitudes and behaviour   The cognitive model has dominated attitude research for decades, yet we now know that it only partially describes what really happens.[9] According to neuroscience research, incoming information from our senses is routed to the emotional centre as well as the cognitive (logical reasoning) centre of our brain.[10] We have already described the logical reasoning process, depicted on the left side of Exhibit 4.2. The right side of Exhibit 4.2 offers a simple depiction of how emotions influence our attitudes and behaviour.

The emotional side of attitude formation begins with the dynamics of the perceptual process, particularly perceptual interpretation, described in Chapter 3. When receiving incoming sensory information, we automatically form emotions regarding that information before consciously thinking about it.[11] More specifically, the emotional centre quickly and imprecisely evaluates whether the incoming sensory information supports or threatens our innate drives, then attaches emotional markers to the information. These are not calculated feelings; they are automatic and unconscious emotional responses based on very thin slices of sensory information.

Returning to our previous example, you might experience excitement, worry, nervousness, or happiness upon learning that your company intends to merge with a competitor. The large dots on the right side of Exhibit 4.2 illustrate these multiple emotional episodes triggered by the merger announcement, subsequent thinking about the merger, discussion with co-workers about the merger, and so on. These emotions are transmitted to the logical reasoning process, where they swirl around and ultimately shape our conscious feelings toward the attitude object.[12] Thus, while consciously evaluating the merger—that is, logically figuring out whether it is a good or bad thing– your emotions have already formed an opinion that then sways your thoughts. If you experience excitement, delight, comfort, and other positive emotions whenever you think about or discuss the merger, then these positive emotional episodes will lean your logical reasoning toward positive feelings regarding the merger.[13]

Emotions operate automatically and unconsciously most of the time, but research tells us that the logical reasoning process actually "listens in" on the person's emotions and uses this information when translating beliefs into feelings.[14] When thinking about whether the announced merger is good or bad, we try to sense our emotional reactions to the event, then use this emotional awareness as factual information in our logical evaluation. In some cases, the perceived emotions change the value of some beliefs or the probability that they are true. If you sense that you are worried and nervous about the merger, then your logical analysis might pay more attention to your belief about job insecurity and put less weight on your belief that mergers increase the organization's competitiveness.

You can see how emotions affect workplace attitudes. When performing our jobs or interacting with co-workers, we experience a variety of emotions that shape our longer term feelings toward the company, our boss, the job itself, and so on. The more we experience positive emotions, the more we form positive attitudes toward the targets of those emotions. Furthermore, we pay attention to our positive emotions to the extent that they offset negative workplace experiences. The opening story to this chapter described how Vancouver City Savings Credit Union injects more fun at work so employees experience plenty of positive emotional episodes each day. Connections 4.1 looks at other means by which organizations have created positive emotions. In each case, the idea is to generate emotional episodes that result in favourable judgments about the organization.

When cognitions and emotions conflict   The influence of both logical reasoning and emotions on attitudes is most apparent when they disagree with each other. Everyone occasionally experiences this mental tug-of-war, sensing that something isn't right even though they can't think of any logical reason to be concerned. This conflicting experience indicates that our logical analysis of the situation (left side of Exhibit 4.2) can't identify reasons to support the automatic emotional reaction (right side of Exhibit 4.2).[15] Should we pay attention to our emotional response or our logical analysis? This question is not easy to answer because, as we just learned, the emotional and rational processes interact with each other so closely. However, some studies indicate that while executives tend to make quick decisions based on their gut feelings (emotional response), the best decisions tend to occur when executives spend time logically evaluating the situation.[16] Thus, we should pay attention to both the cognitive and emotional side of the attitude model, and hope they agree with each other most of the time!

One last observation about the attitude model in Exhibit 4.2 relates to the arrow directly from the emotional episodes to behaviour. This indicates that people have direct behavioural reactions to their emotions. Even low intensity emotions automatically change your facial expressions. High intensity emotions can have a more powerful effect, which is apparent when an upset employee bangs their fist on the desk or an overjoyed colleague embraces someone nearby. These actions are not carefully thought out. They are fairly automatic emotional responses that serve as coping mechanisms in that situation.[17]

Creating Positive Emotions in the Workplace

Web design can be hard work, but that doesn't stop employees at redengine from enjoying themselves on the job. "Humour is a big thing for our company," says Max Frank, redengine's director of product marketing. Along with friendly practical jokes, the Edmonton-based company's 16 staff members keep upbeat by holding foosball tourneys, playing with big yellow exercise balls, and traversing the hallways on a silver scooter or red bike. "We try to implement fun in everything we do," Frank explains.

Fun at work? It sounds like an oxymoron. But in order to attract and keep valuable talent, companies are finding creative ways to generate positive emotions in the workplace. At Alias, the Toronto company whose software is used in *Star Wars* and *Lord of the Rings*, employees enjoy summer deck parties, free family movie screenings, and a games room. Employees at Lighthouse Publishing in Bridgewater, Nova Scotia, have weekly barbeques in summer and massage sessions every month. Lynn Hennigar, president of the award-winning publisher, acknowledges that her four dozen staff have few opportunities for promotion, "so we've tried to find other ways to keep people happy."

Baycrest Centre for Geriatric Care in Toronto turned up the fun meter by introducing the Fish! philosophy. The concept started at Pike Place Fish Market in Seattle. Fishmongers turned a money-losing, morale-draining business into a world-famous attraction by deciding to have fun at work—largely by tossing fish around and joking with customers. Baycrest employees are now applying the four FISH! principles to their workplace: play, make their day, be there, and choose your attitude. "FISH! fits with our values and our client focus and addresses needs identified in the Employee Engagement Survey," explains Baycrest executive Pat Howard.

Michael Worry and Geoff White like to bring some Canadian humour to San Jose, California, where their engineering design firm, Nuvation, was founded a decade ago. Along with enjoying office Nerf gunfights, robot combat tournaments, movie nights, and wine tours, Nuvation's 30 staff share the office with a life-size fibreglass blue and orange Canadian moose. "We like to take

Staff at the Baycrest Centre in Toronto are enjoying a new wave of positive emotions by adopting the FISH! Philosophy. *Courtesy of Baycrest Centre for Geriatric Care*

the moose out to our parties," says Worry, a University of Waterloo graduate. "We take it down the stairs in our office and strap it in the back of a pick-up truck and drive around the highways here. People get a kick out of that." The moose is also mascot for Digital Moose Lounge, a social club for Canadians working in Silicon Valley.

These fun and games may seem silly, but some corporate leaders are deadly serious about their value. "It's pretty simple," explains Nathan Rudyk, president of market2world communications in Almonte, Ontario. "If you want to make the most money, you must attract the best people. To get the best people, you must be the most fun."

Sources: F. Piccolo, "Brownie Points," *Atlantic Business Magazine*, 15, no. 5 (Oct-Nov 2004); R. Deruyter, "Firm's Goals are Business Success and Having Fun," *Kitchener-Waterloo Record*, 30 October 2004, p. F1; J. Leeder, "Who Knew Work was So Much Fun?" *Edmonton Journal*, 1 April 2004, p. A2; R. W. Yerema, *Canada's Top 100 Employers, 2004* (Toronto: MediaCorp Canada, 2004), p. 21; "FISH! Program Makes Waves at Terraces of Baycrest and Wagman Centre," *At the Centre* (Baycrest Centre newsletter), January 2004, pp. 1–2; J. Elliott, "All Work and No Play can Chase Workers Away," *Edmonton Journal*, February 28, 2000, p. A5.
www.baycrest.org

cognitive dissonance

Occurs when people perceive an inconsistency between their beliefs, feelings, and behaviour.

Cognitive dissonance Emotions and attitudes usually lead to behaviour, but the opposite sometimes occurs through the process of **cognitive dissonance**.[18] Cognitive dissonance occurs when we perceive an inconsistency between our beliefs, feelings, and behaviour. This inconsistency creates an uncomfortable feeling that motivates to change one or more of these elements. Behaviour is usually the most difficult element to change, particularly when it is known to everyone, was done voluntarily, and can't be undone. Thus, we usually change our beliefs and feelings to reduce the inconsistency.

Emotions and personality   Our coverage of the dynamics of workplace emotions wouldn't be complete unless we mentioned that emotions are also partly determined by a person's personality, not just workplace experiences.[19] Some people experience positive emotions as a natural trait. These people are generally extroverted—outgoing, talkative, sociable, and assertive (see Chapter 2). In contrast, some people have a personality with a tendency to experience more negative emotions. Positive and negative emotional traits affect a person's attendance, turnover, and long-term work attitudes. For example, several studies— including a recent analysis of employees at Transport Canada—have found that people with a negative emotional trait have lower levels of job satisfaction. Another Canadian study reported that employees with a negative emotional trait experience higher levels of job burnout.[20] While these positive and negative personality traits have some effect, other research concludes that the actual situation in which people work has a noticeably stronger influence on their attitudes and behaviour.[21]

■ MANAGING EMOTIONS AT WORK

The Elbow Room Café is packed and noisy on this Saturday morning. A customer at the Vancouver restaurant half shouts across the room for more coffee. A passing waiter scoffs: "You want more coffee, get it yourself!" The customer only laughs. Another diner complains loudly that he and his party are running late and need their food. This time, restaurant manager Patrick Savoie speaks up: "If you're in a hurry, you should have gone to McDonald's." The diner and his companions chuckle.

To the uninitiated, the Elbow Room Café is an emotional basket case, full of irate guests and the rudest staff on Canada's West Coast. But it's all a performance— a place where guests can enjoy good food and play out their emotions about dreadful customer service. "It's almost like coming to a theatre," says Savoie, who spends much of his time inventing new ways to insult the clientele.[22]

Whether giving the most insulting service at Elbow Room Café or the friendliest service at Vancouver City Savings Credit Union, employees are usually expected to manage their emotions in the workplace. **Emotional labour** refers to the effort, planning, and control needed to express organizationally desired emotions during interpersonal transactions.[23] When interacting with co-workers, customers, suppliers, and others, employees are expected to abide by *display rules*. These rules are norms requiring employees to display certain emotions and withhold others.

emotional labour
The effort, planning, and control needed to express organizationally desired emotions during interpersonal transactions.

CONDITIONS REQUIRING EMOTIONAL LABOUR

Air Canada employees need to smile more often. That's the advice of Air Canada chief executive Robert Milton in a letter urging staff to win back the hearts of passengers. "In everyday life, you make your consumer decisions based on where you receive the best overall value and, in the case of a tie, we all do the same thing—

we go to where the people are the nicest," says Milton. Over at The Beer Store's call centre in London, Ontario, staff are also encouraged to "smile" through their voices. "Our thing is, 'let them hear you smile,'" says the head of the Beer Store's call centre.[24]

Air Canada, The Beer Store, and every other organization in Canada expect employees to engage in some level of emotional labour. Emotional labour is higher in jobs requiring a variety of emotions (e.g., anger as well as joy) and more intense emotions (e.g., showing delight rather than smiling weakly), as well as where interaction with clients is frequent and for longer durations. Emotional labour also increases when employees must precisely rather than casually abide by the display rules. For instance, "Smile: we are on stage" is one of the most important rules at the Ritz-Carlton in San Francisco, so employees must always engage in this form of emotional labour.[25]

Emotional display norms across cultures

How much we are expected to hide or reveal our true emotions in public depends to some extent on the culture in which we live. Cultural values in some countries — particularly Ethiopia, Korea, Japan, and Austria—expect people to display a neutral emotional demeanour. In the workplace and other public settings, employees try to subdue their emotional expression and minimize physical contact with others. Even voice intonation tends to be monotonic. In other countries— notably Kuwait, Egypt, Spain, and Russia—cultural values allow or encourage open display of one's true emotions. People are expected to be transparent in revealing their thoughts and feelings, dramatic in their conversational tones, and animated in their use of nonverbal behaviours to get their message across. These cultural variations in emotional display can be quite noticeable. One survey reported that 83 percent of

Localizing Emotional Display Rules at Four Seasons Hotels

As one of the world's leading operators of luxury hotels, Toronto-based Four Seasons Hotels and Resorts trains employees and audits hotel performance to ensure that guests consistently experience the highest standards of service quality. Yet Four Seasons also adapts its legendary service to the local culture. "McDonald's is the same all over. We do not want to be that way; we are not a cookie cutter company," says Four Seasons executive David Crowl. One of the most obvious forms of localization is in the way Four Seasons staff are allowed to display emotions that reflect their own culture. "What changes [from one country to the next] is that people do it with their own style, grace, and personality," explains Antoine Corinthios, president of Four Seasons' operations in Europe, Middle East, and Africa. "In some cultures you add the strong local temperament. For example, an Italian concierge has his own style and flair. In Turkey or Egypt you experience different hospitality."[26]

Courtesy of Four Seasons

www.fourseasons.com

Japanese believe it is inappropriate to get emotional in a business context, compared with 40 percent of Americans, 34 percent of French, and only 29 percent of Italians. In other words, Italians are more likely to accept or tolerate people who display their true emotions at work, whereas this would be considered rude or embarrassing in Japan.[27]

EMOTIONAL DISSONANCE

Emotional labour can be challenging for most of us because it is difficult to conceal true emotions and to display the emotions required by the job. The main problem is that joy, sadness, worry and other emotions automatically activate a complex set of facial muscles that are difficult to prevent, and equally difficult to fake. Our true emotions tend to reveal themselves as subtle gestures, usually without our awareness. Meanwhile, pretending to be cheerful or concerned is difficult because several specific facial muscles and body positions must be coordinated. More often than not, observers see when we are faking and sense that we feel a different emotion.[28]

emotional dissonance
The conflict between required and true emotions.

Along with the challenges of hiding and displaying emotions, emotional labour often creates a conflict between required and true emotions, called **emotional dissonance**. The larger the conflict between the required and true emotions, the more employees tend to experience stress, job burnout, and psychological separation from self (i.e., *work alienation*).[29] These negative outcomes of emotional dissonance occur when engaging in *surface acting*—modifying behaviour to be consistent with required emotions but continuing to hold different internal feelings. *Deep acting*, on the other hand, involves changing true emotions to match the required emotions. Rather than feeling irritated by a particular customer, you might view the difficult person as an opportunity to test your sales skills. This change in perspective can potentially generate more positive emotions next time you meet that difficult customer, which produces friendlier displays of emotion.[30]

Along with teaching employees how to apply deep acting, companies minimize emotional dissonance by hiring people with a natural tendency to display desired emotions. For example, when CiCi's Pizza opens new stores, it looks for job applicants with a "happy, cheery" attitude. The American restaurant franchise believes that it is easier to teach new skills than attitudes. "We hire for attitude and train for skill," says one of CiCi's franchisees.[31] In some respects, this also means that CiCi's and other companies look for people with well-developed emotional intelligence, which we discuss next.

EMOTIONAL INTELLIGENCE

Each year, the U.S. Air Force hires about 400 recruiters, and each year up to 100 of them are fired for failing to sign up enough people for the service. Selecting and training 100 new recruiters costs US$3 million, not to mention the hidden costs of their poor performance. So the Air Force decided to test its 1,200 recruiters on how well they manage their emotions and the emotions of others. The test indicated that the top recruiters were better at asserting their feelings and thoughts, empathizing with others, feeling happy in life, and being aware of their emotions in a particular situation. The next year, the Air Force selected new recruiters partly on their results on this test. The result: Only eight recruiters got fired or quit a year later.[32]

emotional intelligence (EI)

The ability to perceive and express emotion, assimilate emotion and thought, understand and reason with emotion, and regulate emotion in oneself and others.

To select the best recruiters, the U.S. Air Force considers more than the cognitive intelligence of job applicants; it also looks at their **emotional intelligence (EI)**. EI is the ability to perceive and express emotion, assimilate emotion in thought, understand and reason with emotion, and regulate emotion in oneself and others.[33] In other words, EI represents a set of competencies that allow us to perceive, understand, and regulate emotions in ourselves and in others. Exhibit 4.3 illustrates the most recent EI model. According to this model, EI can be organized into four dimensions representing the recognition of emotions in ourselves and in others, as well as the regulation of emotions in ourselves and in others. Each dimension consists of a set of emotional competencies that people must possess to fulfill that dimension of emotional intelligence.[34]

- *Self-awareness*—Self-awareness refers to having a deep understanding of one's own emotions as well as strengths, weaknesses, values, and motives. Self-aware people are better able to eavesdrop on their emotional responses to specific situations and to use this awareness as conscious information.[35]

- *Self-management*—This represents how well we control or redirect our internal states, impulses, and resources. It includes keeping disruptive impulses in check, displaying honesty and integrity, being flexible in times of change, maintaining the drive to perform well and seize opportunities, and remaining optimistic even after failure. Self-management involves an inner conversation that guides our behaviour.

■ **EXHIBIT 4.3** Emotional intelligence competencies model

	Self **(personal competence)**	**Other** **(social competence)**
Recognition of emotions	**Self-awareness** • Emotional self-awareness • Accurate self-assessment • Self-confidence	**Social awareness** • Empathy • Organizational awareness • Service
Regulation of emotions	**Self-management** • Emotional self-control • Transparency • Adaptability • Achievement • Initiative • Optimism	**Relationship management** • Inspirational leadership • Influence • Developing others • Change catalyst • Conflict management • Building bonds • Teamwork and collaboration

Sources: D. Goleman, R. Boyatzis, and A. McKee, *Primal Leadership* (Boston: Harvard Business School Press, 2002), Chapter 3; D. Goleman, "An EI-Based Theory of Performance," in C. Cherniss and D. Goleman, (Eds.), *The Emotionally Intelligent Workplace* (San Francisco: Jossey-Bass, 2001), p. 28.

■ *Social awareness*—Social awareness is mainly about empathy—having understanding and sensitivity to the feelings, thoughts, and situation of others (see Chapter 3). This includes understanding another person's situation, experiencing the other person's emotions, and knowing their needs even though unstated. Social awareness extends beyond empathy to include being organizationally aware, such as sensing office politics and understanding social networks.

■ *Relationship management*—This dimension of EI refers to managing other people's emotions. It is linked to a wide variety of practices, such as inspiring others, influencing people's beliefs and feelings, developing others' capabilities, managing change, resolving conflict, cultivating relationships, and supporting teamwork and collaboration.

These four dimensions of emotional intelligence form a hierarchy.[36] Self-awareness is the lowest level of EI because it does not require the other dimensions; instead it is a prerequisite for the other three dimensions. Self-management and social awareness are necessarily above self-awareness in the EI hierarchy. You can't manage your own emotions (self-management) if you aren't good at knowing your own emotions (self-awareness). Relationship management is the highest level of EI because it requires all three other dimensions. In other words, we require a high degree of emotional intelligence to master relationship management because this set of competencies requires sufficiently high levels of self-awareness, self-management, and social awareness.

EI has its roots in the social intelligence literature introduced more than 80 years ago, but scholars mainly focused since then on cognitive intelligence (IQ). Now, the U.S. Air Force and others are realizing that EI is an important set of competencies in the performance of most jobs. As we described in Chapter 2, people perform better when their aptitudes—including general intelligence—match the job requirements. But most jobs also involve social interaction, so employees also need emotional intelligence to work effectively in social settings. The evidence so far indicates that people with high EI are better at interpersonal relations, perform better in jobs requiring emotional labour, and are more successful in many aspects of job interviews. Teams whose members have high emotional intelligence initially perform better than teams with low EI.[37]

Improving emotional intelligence   Emotional intelligence is related to several personality traits, but it can also be learned to some extent. Endpoint Research, a Canadian firm specializing in pharmaceutical and biotechnology clinical trials, has put all 65 of its employees through the EI assessment so they can develop their weak areas. Methodist Hospitals of Dallas has also introduced emotional intelligence training to its management group, with the CEO front-and-centre participating in the program. One recent study reported that business students scored higher on emotional intelligence after taking an undergraduate interpersonal skills course.[38] These training programs improve EI to some extent, but the most effective approach is through personal coaching, plenty of practice, and frequent feedback. Emotional intelligence also increases with age; it is part of the process called maturity. Overall, emotional

Improving Emotional Intelligence at ANZ Bank

Executives at ANZ Banking Group learned that they were above average on financial and operational activities, but needed improvement with values and social competencies. So, with the guidance of McKinsey & Company, the Australian financial institution introduced a training program in which thousands of ANZ managers learned about emotional intelligence and how to apply these competencies to create "caring, connected relationships between employees at ANZ, as well as the bank's millions of customers," explains an ANZ executive. "This transformation is an ongoing journey, which realizes the importance of engaging employees on both an emotional and intellectual level."[44] *Courtesy of ANZ Banking Group*
www.anz.com

intelligence offers considerable potential, but we also have a lot to learn about its measurement and effects on people in the workplace.[39]

So far, this chapter has laid out the model of emotions and attitudes, but we also need to understand specific workplace attitudes. The next two sections of this chapter look at two of the most widely studied attitudes: job satisfaction and organizational commitment.

■ JOB SATISFACTION

Job satisfaction, which is probably the most studied attitude in organizational behaviour, represents a person's evaluation of his or her job and work context.[40] It is an *appraisal* of the perceived job characteristics, work environment, and emotional experiences at work. Satisfied employees have a favourable evaluation of their job, based on their observations and emotional experiences. Job satisfaction is really a collection of attitudes about different aspects of the job and work context. You might like your co-workers but be less satisfied with workload, for instance.

How satisfied are Canadians at work? Pollsters are focusing more on employee engagement than job satisfaction these days, but the most recent surveys indicate that between 80 and 90 percent of Canadians are moderately or very satisfied overall with their jobs.

job satisfaction
A person's attitude regarding his or her job and work content.

This is similar to satisfaction levels a decade ago. Global survey results, including those shown in Exhibit 4.4, indicate that Canadian job satisfaction levels are, on average, higher than in most other countries. Only employees in Denmark, the United States, and a few other countries have higher job satisfaction than Canadians, according to several of these multi-country surveys.[41]

Do these surveys mean that we have high job satisfaction? Well, maybe, but probably not as high as these statistics suggest. The problem is that surveys often use a single direct question, such as "How satisfied are you with your job?" Many dissatisfied employees are reluctant to reveal their feelings in a direct question because this is tantamount to admitting that they made a poor job choice and are not enjoying life. One indication that the overall satisfaction ratings are inflated is that nearly half of all of Canadians say they would abandon their employer if offered a comparable job elsewhere! Another indication is that employees rate almost all aspects of the job lower than their overall satisfaction.[42] We also need to keep in mind that cultural values make it difficult to compare job satisfaction across countries.[43] People in China, Korea, and Japan tend to subdue their emotions in public, so they probably avoid extreme survey ratings such as "very satisfied."

■ **EXHIBIT 4.4**   Job satisfaction across cultures

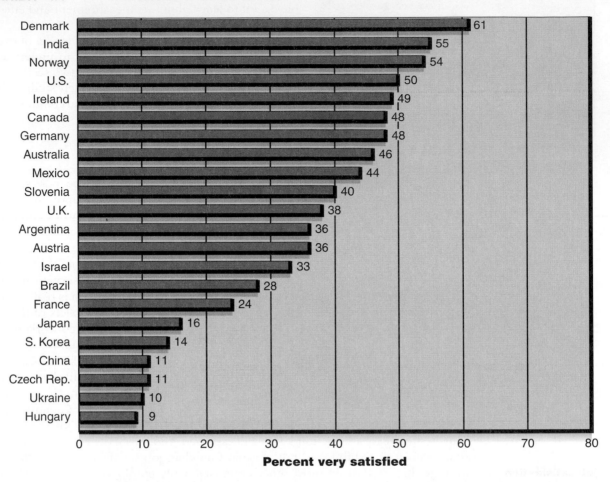

Sources: Based on Ipsos-Reid survey of 9,300 employees in 39 countries in middle of year 2000. See "Ipsos-Reid Global Poll Finds Major Differences in Employee Satisfaction Around the World," Ipsos-Reid News Release, January 8, 2001. A sample of 22 countries across the range are shown here, including all of the top scoring countries.

JOB SATISFACTION AND WORK BEHAVIOUR

Annette Verschuren, president of The Home Depot Canada, pays a lot of attention to job satisfaction. "I can tell you within two seconds of entering a store whether morale is good," says Verschuren. The main reason for her interest is that job satisfaction is a key driver to corporate success. "With an unhappy workforce you have nothing and you will never be great," Verschuren warns.[45]

Home Depot Canada, Fours Seasons Hotels and Resorts, Telus Corp, and a flock of other Canadian firms are paying a lot more attention to job satisfaction these days. In some firms, such as VanCity, executive bonuses depend partly on employee satisfaction ratings. The reason for this attention is simple: Job satisfaction affects many of the individual behaviours introduced in Chapter 2. A useful template to organize and understand the consequences of job dissatisfaction is the **exit-voice-loyalty-neglect (EVLN)** model. As the name suggests, the EVLN model identifies four ways that employees respond to dissatisfaction:[46]

exit-voice-loyalty-neglect (EVLN) model

The four ways, as indicated in the name, employees respond to job dissatisfaction.

- *Exit*—Exit refers to leaving the organization, transferring to another work unit, or at least trying to make these exits. Employee turnover is a well-established outcome of job dissatisfaction, particularly for employees with better job opportunities elsewhere. Exit usually follows specific "shock events," such as when your boss treats you unfairly.[47] These shock events generate strong emotions that energize employees to think about and search for alternative employment.

- *Voice*—Voice refers to any attempt to change, rather than escape from, the dissatisfying situation. Voice can be a constructive response, such as recommending ways for management to improve the situation, Or, it can be more confrontational, such as by filing formal grievances.[48] In the extreme, some employees might engage in counterproductive behaviours to get attention and force changes in the organization. Thus, voice might be more correctly viewed as either constructive or destructive.

- *Loyalty*—Loyalty has been described in different ways, but the most widely held view is that "loyalists" are employees who respond to dissatisfaction by patiently waiting—some say they "suffer in silence"—for the problem to work itself out or get resolved by others.[49]

- *Neglect*—Neglect includes reducing work effort, paying less attention to quality, and increasing absenteeism and lateness. It is generally considered a passive activity that has negative consequences for the organization.

Which of the four EVLN alternatives do employees use? It depends on the person and situation. One determining factor is the availability of alternative employment. With poor job prospects, employees are less likely to use the exit option. Those who identify with the organization are also more likely to use voice rather than exit. People with a high conscientiousness personality are less likely to engage in neglect and more likely to engage in voice. Some experts suggest that employees differ in their EVLN behaviour depending on whether they have high or low collectivism. Finally, past experience influences our choice of action. Employees who were unsuccessful with voice in the past are more likely to engage in exit or neglect when experiencing job dissatisfaction in the future.[50]

JOB SATISFACTION AND PERFORMANCE

One of the oldest beliefs in the business world is that "a happy worker is a productive worker." Is this statement true? Organizational behaviour scholars have waffled on this question for the past century. In the 1980s, they concluded that job satisfaction has a weak or negligible association with task performance.[51] Now, the evidence suggests that the popular saying may be correct after all. Citing problems with the earlier studies, a groundbreaking analysis recently concluded that there is a *moderate* relationship between job satisfaction and job performance. In other words, happy workers really are more productive workers *to some extent*.[52]

Even with a moderate association between job satisfaction and performance, there are a few underlying reasons why the relationship isn't even stronger.[53] One argument is that general attitudes (such as job satisfaction) don't predict specific behaviours very well. As we learned with the EVLN model, job dissatisfaction can lead to a variety of outcomes rather than lower job performance (neglect). Some employees continue to work productively while they complain (voice), look for another job (exit), or patiently wait for the problem to be fixed (loyalty).

A second explanation is that job performance leads to job satisfaction (rather than vice versa), but only when performance is linked to valued rewards. Higher performers receive more rewards and, consequently, are more satisfied than low-performing employees who receive fewer rewards. The connection between job satisfaction and performance isn't stronger because many organizations do not reward good performance. The third explanation is that job satisfaction might influence employee motivation, but this has little influence on performance in jobs where employees have little control over their job output (such as assembly line work). This point explains why the job satisfaction–performance relationship is strongest in complex jobs, where employees have more freedom to perform their work or to slack off.

JOB SATISFACTION AND CUSTOMER SATISFACTION

Along with the job satisfaction–performance relationship, corporate leaders are making strong statements that happy employees produce happy customers. "We demand more of our employees, but we do our best to assure they are happy," says an executive at Toronto-based Four Seasons Hotels and Resorts. "Employees who are happy provide better service." Virgin Group founder Richard Branson agrees. "It just seems common sense to me that if you start with a happy, well-motivated workforce, you're much more likely to have happy customers," says Branson.[54]

Fortunately, research generally agrees that job satisfaction has a positive effect on customer satisfaction.[55] There are two main reasons for this relationship. First, employees are usually in a more positive mood when they feel satisfied with their job and working conditions. Employees who are in a good mood tend to display friendliness and positive emotions more naturally and frequently, which puts customers in a better mood. Second, satisfied employees are less likely to quit their jobs, so they have better knowledge and skills to serve clients. Lower turnover also gives customers the same employees to serve them, so there is more consistent service. There is some evidence that customers build their loyalty to specific employees, not to the organization, so keeping employee turnover low tends to build customer loyalty.[56]

Before leaving this topic, it's worth mentioning that job satisfaction does more than improve work behaviours and customer satisfaction. Job satisfaction is also an ethical issue that influences the organization's reputation in the community. People spend a large portion of their time working in organizations, and many societies now expect companies to provide work environments that are safe and enjoyable. Indeed, many Canadians closely monitor ratings of the best companies to work for, an indication that employee satisfaction is a virtue worth considerable goodwill to employers. This virtue is apparent when an organization has low job satisfaction. The company tries to hide this fact and, when morale problems become public, corporate leaders are usually quick to improve the situation.

■ ORGANIZATIONAL COMMITMENT

During the mid-1800s, Samuel Cunard founded Cunard Lines, the greatest steamship line ever to cover the Atlantic Ocean. The energetic Nova Scotian was able to make ship transportation dependable and safe, long before it was thought possible, by having the best ships, officers, and crew. He insisted on safety before profits and, by listening to his technical experts, was able to introduce the latest innovations.

continuance commitment
A bond felt by an employee that motivates him or her to stay only because leaving would be costly.

organizational (affective) commitment
The employee's emotional attachment to, identification with, and involvement in a particular organization.

Above all, Cunard had the quaint notion that if you picked people well, paid them well, and treated them well, they would return the favour with loyalty and pride.[57]

Over 150 years later, Samuel Cunard's assumptions about organizational commitment still hold true. **Organizational (affective) commitment** refers to the employee's emotional attachment to, identification with, and involvement in a particular organization.[58] This definition refers specifically to *affective commitment* because it refers to the individual's feelings of loyalty toward the organization. However, affective commitment can also refer to loyalty toward co-workers, customers, or a profession. We will concentrate mainly on the employee's overall commitment to the organization.

Along with affective commitment, employees have varying levels of **continuance commitment**.[59] Continuance commitment occurs when employees believe it is in their own personal interest to remain with the organization. In other words, this form of commitment is a calculative rather than emotional attachment to the organization. For example, some employees who do not particularly identify with the organization where they work but feel bound to remain there because it would be too costly to quit, possibly because they would lose a large bonus by leaving early or because they are well-established in the community where they work. Continuance commitment is this motivation to stay because of the high cost of leaving.[60]

Wal-Mart Canada Staff Show Their Loyalty
Wal-Mart Canada may be getting some bad press recently for apparent wage discrimination, gender bias, and attempts to avoid unionization, but that hasn't dampened the loyalty of some employees. "Everything about this company is great," exclaims Judy Wemyss, who joined Wal-Mart as a part-time sales associate in Mississauga, Ontario, nearly a decade ago and worked her way up to become a full-time department manager. The dedicated Wal-Mart staffer has even made a few trips to Arkansas to visit Wal-Mart's global headquarters and attend its annual meetings, where she and a co-worker built up a collection of Wal-Mart pins. This photo shows a Wal-Mart greeter in Calgary wearing several of these pins.[63] *CP Photo/Todd Korol*
www.walmart.ca

CONSEQUENCES OF ORGANIZATIONAL COMMITMENT

Corporate leaders have good reason to pay close attention to employee loyalty because it can be a significant competitive advantage. Employees with high levels of affective commitment are less likely to quit their jobs and be absent from work. Organizational commitment also improves customer satisfaction because long-tenure employees have better knowledge of work practices, and clients like to do business with the same employees. Employees with high affective commitment also have higher work motivation and organizational citizenship, as well as somewhat higher job performance.[61]

However, employees can have too much affective commitment. One concern is that organizational loyalty results in low turnover, which limits the organization's opportunity to hire new employees with new knowledge and fresh ideas. Another concern is that loyalty results in conformity, which can undermine creativity and ethical conduct. For instance, a former executive at Arthur Andersen claims that one reason for the accounting firm's downfall was that it created a cult-like level of employee loyalty where no one questioned or second-guessed top management's decisions.[62]

Consequences of continuance commitment
Creating too much affective commitment is probably much less of a problem in Canadian organizations

compared with concerns about company practices that increase continuance commitment. Many firms tie employees financially to the organization through low-cost loans, stock options, deferred bonuses, and other "golden handcuffs." For instance, when CIBC took over Merrill Lynch's Canadian retail brokerage business, Merrill's top financial advisors received retention bonuses worth up to one year's pay if they stayed long enough with the merged company.[64] Continuance commitment might also be higher in one-company towns throughout Canada because there are few alternative employers, employees may have difficulty selling their home to work elsewhere, and people don't want to give up the spacious lifestyle in these small communities.

All of these financial, employment, and personal factors reduce turnover, but they also increase continuance commitment, not affective commitment. Research suggests that employees with high levels of continuance commitment have lower performance ratings and are less likely to engage in organizational citizenship behaviours! Furthermore, unionized employees with high continuance commitment are more likely to use formal grievances, whereas employees with high affective commitment engage in more constructive problem solving when employee–employer relations sour.[65] Although some level of financial connection may be necessary, employers should not confuse continuance commitment with employee loyalty. Employers still need to win employees' hearts (affective commitment) beyond tying them financially to the organization (continuance commitment).

BUILDING ORGANIZATIONAL COMMITMENT

There are almost as many ways to build organizational loyalty as topics in this textbook, but the following list is most prominent in the literature.

- *Justice and support*—Affective commitment is higher in organizations that fulfill their obligations to employees and abide by humanitarian values, such as fairness, courtesy, forgiveness, and moral integrity. These values relate to the concept of organizational justice that we discuss in the next chapter. Similarly, organizations that support employee well-being tend to cultivate higher levels of loyalty in return.[66]
- *Shared values*—The definition of affective commitment refers to a person's identification with the organization, and that identification is highest when employees believe their values are congruent with the organization's dominant values. Also, employees experience more comfort and predictability when they agree with the values underlying corporate decisions. This comfort increases their motivation to stay with the organization.[67]
- *Trust*—**Trust** is a psychological state comprising the intention to accept vulnerability based upon positive expectations of the intent or behaviour of another person.[68] Trust means putting faith in the other person or group. It is also a reciprocal activity: To receive trust, you must demonstrate trust. Employees identify with and feel obliged to work for an organization only when they trust its leaders. This explains why layoffs are one of the greatest blows to employee loyalty—by reducing job security, company's reduce the trust employees have in their employer and the employment relationship.[69]
- *Organizational comprehension*—Affective commitment is a person's identification with the company, so it makes sense that this attitude is strengthened when employees understand the company, including its past, present, and future. Thus, loyalty tends to increase with open and rapid communication to and from corporate leaders, as well as with opportunities to interact with co-workers across the organization.[70]

trust
A psychological state comprising the intention to accept vulnerability based upon positive expectations of the intent or behaviour of another person.

■ *Employee involvement*—Employee involvement increases affective commitment by strengthening the employee's social identity with the organization. Employees feel that they are part of the organization when they make decisions that guide the organization's future. For example, one Canadian study reported higher levels of affective commitment in workplaces with moderate levels of employee involvement.[71] Employee involvement also builds loyalty because giving this power is a demonstration of the company's trust in its employees.

Look closely at some of the recommendations above and you will see that one of the key influences on organizational commitment is the employment relationship. In particular, affective commitment is sensitive to how well the organization fulfills the psychological contract, which we look at in the last section of this chapter.

■ PSYCHOLOGICAL CONTRACTS

Employees at the Toyota Canada manufacturing plant in Cambridge, Ontario, were shocked when the company began imposing overtime. Overtime was previously voluntary, but Toyota maintains that everyone checked a small box on the application form indicating that they would work overtime if required to do so. With huge demand for Toyota vehicles, the company needed almost two additional hours from each employee most days. Employees were so incensed with the imposed overtime that some created a Web site to protest the change, while others complained to the Ontario government's employment standards office. Ultimately, the government sided with employees.[72]

Toyota Canada employees experienced the shock of having their psychological contract violated. This isn't unusual. According to one university study, 24 percent of employees are "chronically" angry at work, mostly because they feel their employer violated basic promises and didn't fulfill the psychological contract.[73]

psychological contract

The individual's beliefs about the terms and conditions of a reciprocal exchange agreement between that person and another party.

The **psychological contract** refers to the individual's beliefs about the terms and conditions of a reciprocal exchange agreement between that person and another party. This is inherently perceptual, so one person's understanding of the psychological contract may differ from the other party's understanding. In employment relationships, psychological contracts consist of beliefs about what the employee is entitled to receive and is obliged to offer the employer in return.[74] For example, Toyota Canada employees believed that their psychological contract included the right to refuse overtime, whereas the employer says its employment forms include the right to impose overtime.

TYPES OF PSYCHOLOGICAL CONTRACTS

Psychological contracts vary in many ways.[75] One of the most fundamental differences is the extent to which they are transactional or relational. As Exhibit 4.5 indicates, *transactional contracts* are primarily short-term economic exchanges. Responsibilities are well defined around a fairly narrow set of obligations that do not change over the life of the contract. People hired in temporary positions and as consultants tend to have transactional contracts. To some extent, new employees also form transactional contracts until they develop a sense of continuity with the organization.

Relational contracts, on the other hand, are rather like marriages; they are long-term attachments that encompass a broad array of subjective mutual obligations. Employees with a relational psychological contract are more willing to contribute their time and effort without expecting the organization to pay back this debt in

■ **EXHIBIT 4.5**   Types of psychological contracts in employment

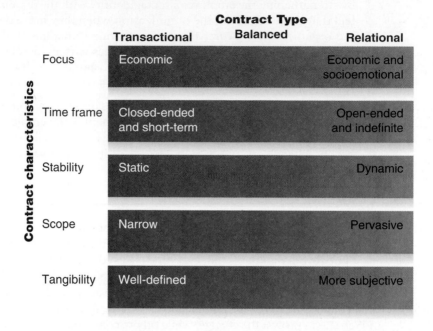

Sources: Based on information in D. M. Rousseau and J. M. Parks, "The Contracts of Individuals and Organizations," *Research in Organizational Behavior* 15 (1993), pp. 1–43; D. M. Rousseau, *Psychological Contracts in Organizations* (Thousand Oaks, CA: Sage, 1995).

the short term. Relational contracts are also dynamic, meaning that the parties tolerate and expect that mutual obligations are not necessarily balanced in the short run. Not surprisingly, organizational citizenship behaviours are more likely to prevail under relational than transactional contracts. Permanent employees are more likely to believe they have a relational contract.

PSYCHOLOGICAL CONTRACTS ACROSS CULTURES AND GENERATIONS

Psychological contracts are influenced by the social contexts in which the contracting process occurs.[76] In other words, they vary across cultures and groups of employees based on their unique cultures and cohort experiences. For instance, employees in Canada expect some involvement in company decisions (i.e., they have low power distance), whereas employees in Taiwan and Mexico are more willing to accept arbitrary orders from their supervisors (i.e., they have high power distance).

Psychological contracts also seem to vary across generations of employees. A few decades ago, many Canadians (at least, those in white collar jobs) could expect secure jobs with steady promotions through the hierarchy. They often devoted their entire lives to the same company, put in regular hours, and rarely thought about changing employers. Some older Canadians still hold on to these expectations, whereas fewer people under 30 years old make these conditions part of their psychological contract because they have never experienced that degree of employment stability.

Japan's Freeters Bring a New Psychological Contract to the Workplace

Tatsuhiro Nakayama scoffs at the 'live-to-work' philosophy that his parents embraced. "I don't feel like working and I don't have any problems with it," says the 26-year-old who lives in Tokyo with financial support from his parents when not earning money in odd jobs. Nakayama is one of more than 2 million "freeters" in Japan, double the number a decade ago. Freeters are young people, including university graduates, who scrape by with low-paying part-time jobs.

The original explanation for the burgeoning freeter population is that Japan's struggling economy prevented young people from entering meaningful jobs. However, recent surveys indicate that a large portion of freeters don't try to find permanent jobs, don't worry at all about long-term careers, and think job-hopping is a badge of honour. Instead, they prefer a psychological contract with employers that is short-term, transactional, and flexible—just the opposite to what their parents expected in an employment relationship.

"Living as a freeter, I get more freedom and I like that," says Mika Onodera, a 28-year-old bakery employee in Tokyo. Onodera, who shares an apartment with her sister, is on her fifth job in as many years. "Although I cut back on my spending, I have enough money to go out with friends and live comfortably."

Worried that a generation of freeters will undermine Japan's already fragile economy, several government departments have developed a counterattack, including funds for more school counsellors and a program to teach elementary school pupils the importance of full-time employment. Another government program provides financial aid to companies who hire freeters so they can "test-drive" a permanent job.

More than 2 million young Japanese have become "freeters," casual workers with an equally casual psychological contract that emphasizes personal freedom over loyalty.
© AP Photo/Koji Sasahara

The government's test-drive program seems to be having some effect. "You can't tell much about a job just by reading the description in a classified ad," says Hidenobu Kawai, a 23-year-old freeter who accepted employment through the government program with Yoshida Taro Co., a trading house in Tokyo. "After I actually started working, I realized the job suited me."

Sources: "Officials Worry as Younger Japanese Embrace 'Freeting,'" *Taipei Times*, June 4, 2003, p. 12; C. Fujioka, "Idle Young Adults Threaten Japan's Workforce," *Reuters News*, February 28, 2005; "Ministry Scheme Lets You Test-drive a Job," *Yomiuri Shimbun* (Tokyo), April 22, 2005.
www.mhlw.go.jp/english/

In Japan, meanwhile, the shift toward employability is much more recent and has produced some rather startling changes in the psychological contract expectations of many young Japanese. As GLOBAL Connections 4.2 describes, new employment relationships and economic turbulence have given rise to a large cohort of "freeters"—young people who hop from one job to the next, usually with a distinctly transactional psychological contract. In a country where loyalty has been the gold standard of employee expectations for decades, the opposing psychological contract expectations of freeters has motivated the Japanese government to introduce various schemes that will change their views on the employment relationship.

Psychological contracts are changing, as is the entire field of organizational behaviour, by embracing new knowledge about emotions in the workplace. Emotional brain centres, emotional labour, emotional intelligence, and other topics in this chapter were unheard of 10 or 15 years ago. Now, they are essential reading to improve our grasp of the complex dynamics of employee attitudes and behaviour. You will see several references to emotions-related concepts throughout this book, including the next chapter on employee motivation.

CHAPTER SUMMARY

Emotions are physiological, behavioural, and psychological episodes experienced toward an object, person, or event that create a state of readiness. Emotions are typically organized into a bipolar circle (circumplex) based on their pleasantness and activation. Emotions differ from attitudes, which represent the cluster of beliefs, feelings, and behavioural intentions toward a person, object, or event. Beliefs are a person's established perceptions about the attitude object. Feelings are positive or negative evaluations of the attitude object. Behavioural intentions represent a motivation to engage in a particular behaviour with respect to the target.

Attitudes have traditionally been described as a process in which we logically calculate our feelings toward the attitude object based on an analysis of our beliefs. Thus, beliefs predict feelings, which predict behavioural intentions, which predict behaviour. But this traditional perspective overlooks the role of emotions, which have an important influence on attitudes and behaviour. Emotions typically form before we think through situations, so they influence this rational attitude formation process. This dual process is apparent when we internally experience a conflict between what logically seems good or bad and what we emotionally feel is good or bad in a situation. Emotions also affect behaviour directly.

Behaviour sometimes influences our subsequent attitudes through cognitive dissonance. People also have personality traits which affect their emotions and attitudes.

Emotional labour refers to the effort, planning, and control needed to express organizationally desired emotions during interpersonal transactions. This is more common in jobs requiring a variety of emotions and more intense emotions, as well as where interaction with clients is frequent and for longer durations. The extent to which we are expected to hide or reveal our true emotions in public depends to some extent on the culture in which we live.

Emotional labour can be challenging for most of us because it is difficult to conceal true emotions and to display the emotions required by the job. It also creates emotional dissonance when required and true emotions are incompatible with each other. Deep acting can minimize this dissonance, as can the practice of hiring people with well-developed emotional intelligence.

Emotional intelligence is the ability to perceive and express emotion, assimilate emotion in thought, understand and reason with emotion, and regulate emotion in oneself and others. This concept includes four components arranged in a hierarchy: self-awareness, self-management, social awareness, and relationship management. Emotional intelligence can be learned to some extent, particularly through personal coaching.

Job satisfaction represents a person's evaluation of his or her job and work context. Although surveys indicate Canadians are highly satisfied with their jobs, these results may be somewhat inflated by the use of single-item questions and cultural differences. The exit-voice-loyalty-neglect model outlines four possible consequences of job dissatisfaction. Job satisfaction has a moderate relationship with job performance and with customer satisfaction. Job satisfaction is also a moral obligation in many societies.

Affective organizational commitment (loyalty) refers to the employee's emotional attachment to, identification with, and involvement in a particular organization. This contrasts with continuance commitment, which is a calculative bond with the organization. Affective commitment improves motivation and organizational citizenship, and somewhat higher job performance, whereas continuance commitment is associated with lower performance and organizational citizenship. Companies build loyalty through justice and support, shared values, trust, organizational comprehension, and employee involvement.

The psychological contract refers to the individual's beliefs about the terms and conditions of a reciprocal exchange agreement between that person and another party. Transactional psychological contracts are primarily short-term economic exchanges, whereas relational contracts are long-term attachments that encompass a broad array of subjective mutual obligations. Psychological contracts seem to vary across cultures as well as across generations of employees.

KEY TERMS

attitudes, p. 102

cognitive dissonance, p. 105

continuance commitment, p. 115

emotional dissonance, p. 108

emotional intelligence (EI), p. 109

emotional labour, p. 106

emotions, p. 100

exit-voice-loyalty-neglect (EVLN) model, p. 112

job satisfaction, p. 111

organizational (affective) commitment, p. 115

psychological contract, p. 117

trust, p. 116

DISCUSSION QUESTIONS

1. After a few months on the job, Susan has experienced several emotional episodes ranging from frustration to joy about the work she has been assigned. Explain how these emotions affect Susan's level of job satisfaction with the work itself.

2. A recent study reported that college and university instructors are frequently required to engage in emotional labour. Identify the situations in which emotional labour is required for this job. In your opinion, is emotional labour more troublesome for college and university instructors or for telephone operators working at a 911 emergency service?

3. "Emotional intelligence is more important than cognitive intelligence in influencing an individual's success." Do you agree or disagree with this statement? Support your perspective.

4. Describe a time when you effectively managed someone's emotions. What happened? What was the result?

5. The latest employee satisfaction survey in your organization indicates that employees are unhappy with some aspects of the organization. However, management tends to pay attention to the single-item question asking employees to indicate their overall satisfaction with the job. The results of this item indicate that 86 percent of staff members are very or somewhat satisfied, so management concludes that the other results refer to issues that are probably not important to employees. Explain why management's interpretation of these results may be inaccurate.

6. "Happy employees create happy customers." Explain why this statement might be true, and identify conditions in which it might not be true.

7. What factors influence an employee's organizational loyalty?

8. This chapter argues that psychological contracts vary across cultures and generations. Identify some of the psychological contract expectations around which younger and older employees differ in Canada.

C A S E   S T U D Y   4.1

DIANA'S DISAPPOINTMENT: THE PROMOTION STUMBLING BLOCK

By Rosemary Maellaro, University of Dallas.

Diana Gillen had an uneasy feeling of apprehension as she arrived at the Cobb Street Grille corporate offices. Today she was meeting with her supervisor, Julie Spencer, and regional director, Tom Miner, to learn the outcome of her promotion interview for the district manager position. Diana had been employed by this casual dining restaurant chain for 12 years and had worked her way up from waitress to general manager. Based on her track record, she was the obvious choice for the promotion; and her friends assured her that the interview process was merely a formality. Diana was still anxious, though, and feared that the news might not be positive. She knew she was more than qualified for the job, but that didn't guarantee anything these days.

Nine months ago, when Diana interviewed for the last district manager opening, she thought her selection for the job was inevitable. She was shocked when that didn't happen. Diana was so upset about not getting promoted then that she initially decided not to apply for the current opening. She eventually changed her mind—after all, the company had just named her *Restaurant Manager of the Year* and entrusted her with managing their flagship location. Diana thought her chances had to be really good this time.

A multi-unit management position was a desirable move up for any general manager and was a goal to which Diana had aspired since she began working in the industry. When she had not been promoted the last time, Julie, her supervisor, explained that her people skills needed to improve. But Diana knew that explanation had little to do with why she hadn't gotten the job—the real reason was corporate politics. She heard that the person they hired was some super star from the outside—a district manager from another restaurant company who supposedly had strong multi-unit management experience and a proven track record of developing restaurant managers. Despite what she was told, she was convinced that Tom, her regional manager, had been unduly pressured to hire this person, who had been referred by the CEO.

The decision to hire the outsider may have impressed the CEO, but it enraged Diana. With her successful track record as a store manager for the Cobb Street Grille, she was much more capable, in her opinion, of overseeing multiple units than someone who was new to the operation. Besides, district managers had always been promoted internally among the store managers and she was unofficially designated as the next one to move up to a district position. Tom had hired the outside candidate as a political manoeuvre to put himself in a good light with management, even though it meant overlooking a loyal employee like her in the process. Diana had no patience with people who made business decisions for the wrong reasons. She worked very hard to avoid politics—and it especially irritated her when the political actions of others negatively impacted on her.

Diana was ready to be a district manager nine months ago, and thought she was even more qualified today—provided the decision was based on performance. She ran a tight ship, managing her restaurant completely by the book. She meticulously adhered to policies and procedures and rigorously controlled expenses. Her sales were growing, in spite of new competition in the market, and she received relatively few customer complaints. The only number that was a little out of line was the higher turnover among her staff.

Diana was not too concerned about the increasing number of terminations, however; there was a perfectly logical explanation for this. It was because she had high standards—for herself and her employees. Any employee who delivered less than 110 percent at all times would be better off finding a job somewhere else. Diana didn't think she should bend the rules for anyone, for whatever reason. A few months ago, for example, she had to fire three otherwise good employees who decided to try a new customer service tactic—a so-called innovation they dreamed up—rather than complying with the established process. As the general manager, it was her responsibility to make sure that the restaurant was managed strictly in accordance with the operations manual and she could not allow deviations. This by-the-book approach to managing had served her well for many years. It got her promoted in the past and she was not about to jinx that now. Losing a few employees now and then—particularly those who had difficulty following the rules—was simply the cost of doing business.

During a recent store visit, Julie suggested that Diana might try creating a friendlier work environment because she seemed aloof and interacted with employees somewhat mechanically. Julie even told her that she overheard employees refer to Diana as the "Ice Maiden" behind her back. Diana was surprised that Julie brought this up because her boss rarely criticized her. They had an unspoken agreement: since Diana was so technically competent and always met her financial targets, Julie didn't need to give her much input. Diana was happy to be left alone to run her restaurant without needless advice.

At any rate, Diana rarely paid attention to what employees said about her. She wasn't about to let something as childish as a silly name cause her to modify a successful management strategy. What's more, even though she had recently lost more than the average number of employees due to "personality differences" or "miscommunications" over her directives, her superiors did not seem to mind when she consistently delivered strong bottom line results every month.

As she waited in the conference room for the others, Diana worried that she was not going to get this promotion. Julie had sounded different in the voicemail message she left to inform her about this meeting, but Diana couldn't put her finger on exactly what it was. She would be very angry if she was passed over again and wondered what excuse they would have this time. Then her mind wandered to how her employees would respond to her if she did not get the promotion. They all knew how much she wanted the job and she cringed at how embarrassed she would be if she didn't get it. Her eyes began to mist over at the sheer thought of having to face them if she was not promoted today.

Julie and Tom entered the room then and the meeting was under way. They told Diana, as kindly as they could, that she would not be promoted at this time; one of her colleagues would become the new district manager. She was incredulous. The individual who got promoted had only been with the company three years—and Diana had trained her! She tried to comprehend how this happened, but it did not make sense. Before any further explanation could be offered, she burst into tears and left the room. As she tried in vain to regain her composure, Diana was overcome with crushing disappointment.

Discussion Questions

1. Within the framework of the emotional intelligence domains of *self-awareness*, *self-management*, *social awareness*, and *relationship management*, discuss the various factors that might have led to Diana's failure to be promoted.

2. What competencies does Diana need to develop to be promotable in the future? What can the company do to support her developmental efforts?

CLASS EXERCISE **4.2**

STEM-AND-PROBE INTERVIEW ACTIVITY

Purpose   To help students experience the effects of emotional experiences on behaviour.

Materials   None

Instructions   This simple, yet powerful, exercise consists of students conducting and receiving a detailed stem-and-probe interview with other students in the class. Each student will have an opportunity to interview and be interviewed. However, to increase the variation and novelty of this experience, the student conducting the first interview should NOT be interviewed by the student who was just interviewed. Instead, the instructor should either form groups of four students (two pairs) at the beginning of this exercise, or have two pairs of students swap after the first round. Each of the two sets of interviews should take 10–15 minutes and use a stem-and-probe interview method. The stem-and-probe method, as well as the topic of the interview, are described next.

Stem-and-probe interviewing: This interview method attempts to receive more detail from the interviewee than typically occurs in semi-structured or structured interviews. The main interview question, called the "stem" is followed by a series of probing questions that encourages the interviewee to provide more details relating to a particular incident or situation. The stem question for this exercise is stated later in this description. There are several "probes" that the interviewee can use to elicit more

detail, and the best probe depends on the circumstances, such as what information has already been provided. Some common probe questions include: "Tell me more about that"; "What did you do next?"; "Could you explain that further, please?"; "What else can you remember about that event?" Notice that each of these probes is open-ended, not closed ended questions such as "Is there anything else you want to tell me" in which a simple "Yes" or "No" is possible. Stem-and-probe interviewing also improves when the interviewer engages in active listening and isn't afraid of silence—giving the interviewee time to think and motivating them to fill in the silence with new information.

Interview Topic: In both sets of interviews, the "stem" question is:

> *"Describe two or three things you did this past week that made someone else feel better."*

Through this interview process, the interviewer's task is to receive as much information as possible (that the interviewee is willing to divulge) about the details of these two or three things that the interviewee did over the past week.

Following the two sets of interviews (where each student has interviewed and been interviewed once), the class will discuss the emotional and attitudinal dynamics of this activity.

TEAM EXERCISE **4.3**

RANKING JOBS ON THEIR EMOTIONAL LABOUR

Purpose This exercise is designed to help you understand the jobs in which people tend to experience higher or lower degrees of emotional labour.

Instructions

- *Step 1:* Individually rank order the extent to which the jobs listed below require emotional labour. In other words, assign a "1" to the job you believe requires the most effort, planning, and control to express organizationally desired emotions during interpersonal transactions. Assign a "10" to the job you believe requires the least amount of emotional labour. Mark your rankings in column 1.

- *Step 2:* The instructor will form teams of four or five members and each team will rank order the items based on consensus (not simply averaging the individual rankings). These results are placed in column 2.

- *Step 3:* The instructor will provide expert ranking information. This information should be written in column 3. Then, students calculate the differences in columns 4 and 5.

- *Step 4:* The class will compare the results and discuss the features of jobs with high emotional labour.

OCCUPATIONAL EMOTIONAL LABOUR SCORING SHEET					
Occupation	(1) Individual Ranking	(2) Team Ranking	(3) Expert Ranking	(4) Absolute Difference of 1 and 3	(5) Absolute Difference of 2 and 3
Bartender					
Cashier					
Dental hygienist					
Insurance adjuster					
Lawyer					
Librarian					
Postal clerk					
Registered nurse					
Social worker					
Television announcer					
			TOTAL		

(The lower the score, the better.)   Your score   Team score

SELF-ASSESSMENT EXERCISE   4.4

SCHOOL COMMITMENT SCALE

Purpose   This self-assessment is designed to help you understand the concept of organizational commitment and to assess your commitment to the college or university you are currently attending.

Overview   The concept of commitment is as relevant to students enrolled in college or university courses as it is to employees working in various organizations. This self-assessment adapts a popular organizational commitment instrument so it refers to your commitment as a student to the school where you are attending this program.

Instructions   Read each of the statements below and circle the response that best fits your personal belief. Then use the scoring key in Appendix B of this book to calculate your results. This self-assessment is completed alone so that students rate themselves honestly without concerns of social comparison. However, class discussion will focus on the meaning of the different types of organizational commitment and how well this scale applies to the commitment of students toward the college or university they are attending.

SCHOOL COMMITMENT SCALE							
To what extent do you agree or disagree with each of these statements.	Strongly Agree ▼	Moderately Agree ▼	Slightly Agree ▼	Neutral ▼	Slightly Disagree ▼	Moderately Disagree ▼	Strongly Disagree ▼
1. I would be very happy to complete the rest of my education at this school.	☐	☐	☐	☐	☐	☐	☐
2. One of the difficulties of leaving this school is that there are few alternatives.	☐	☐	☐	☐	☐	☐	☐
3. I really feel as if this school's problems are my own.	☐	☐	☐	☐	☐	☐	☐
4. Right now, staying enrolled at this school is a matter of necessity as much as desire.	☐	☐	☐	☐	☐	☐	☐
5. I do not feel a strong sense of belonging to this school.	☐	☐	☐	☐	☐	☐	☐
6. It would be very hard for me to leave this school right now even if I wanted to.	☐	☐	☐	☐	☐	☐	☐
7. I do not feel emotionally attached to this school.	☐	☐	☐	☐	☐	☐	☐
8. Too much of my life would be disrupted if I decided to move to a different school now.	☐	☐	☐	☐	☐	☐	☐
9. I do not feel like part of the "family" at this school.	☐	☐	☐	☐	☐	☐	☐
10. I feel that I have too few options to consider leaving this school.	☐	☐	☐	☐	☐	☐	☐

SCHOOL COMMITMENT SCALE (continued)							
To what extent do you agree or disagree with each of these statements.	Strongly Agree ▼	Moderately Agree ▼	Slightly Agree ▼	Neutral ▼	Slightly Disagree ▼	Moderately Disagree ▼	Strongly Disagree ▼
11. This school has a great deal of personal meaning for me.	☐	☐	☐	☐	☐	☐	☐
12. If I had not already put so much of myself into this school, I might consider completing my education elsewhere.	☐	☐	☐	☐	☐	☐	☐

Source: Adapted from: J. P. Meyer, N. J. Allen, and C. A. Smith, "Commitment to organizations and occupations: Extension and test of a three-component model," *Journal of Applied Psychology*, 78 (1993), pp. 538–551.

S E L F - A S S E S S M E N T   E X E R C I S E   4.5

DISPOSITIONAL MOOD SCALE

Go to the Online Learning Centre to complete this interactive self-assessment.

Purpose This self-assessment is designed to help you understand mood states or personality traits of emotions and to assess your own mood or emotion personality.

Instructions This self-assessment consists of several words representing various emotions that you might have experienced. For each word pre-sented, indicate the extent to which you have felt this way generally across all situations **over the past six months**. You need to be honest with yourself to receive a reasonable estimate of your mood state or personality trait on these scales. The results provide an estimate of your level on two emotional personality scales. This instrument is widely used in research, but it is only an esti-mate. You should not assume that the results are accurate without a more complete assessment by a trained professional.

After studying the preceding material, be sure to check out our Online Learning Centre at
www.mcgrawhill.ca/college/mcshane
for more in-depth information and interactivities that correspond to this chapter.

·5·

MOTIVATION IN THE WORKPLACE

LEARNING OBJECTIVES

AFTER READING THIS CHAPTER, YOU SHOULD BE ABLE TO:

■ State three reasons why motivating employees has become more challenging in recent years.

■ Explain why Maslow's needs hierarchy theory is not as good a model of employee motivation than is popularly believed.

■ Describe four-drive theory and explain how these drives influence motivation and behaviour.

■ Summarize McClelland's learned needs theory, including the three needs he studied.

■ Discuss the practical implications of motivation theories about needs and drives.

■ Diagram the expectancy theory model and discuss its practical implications for motivating employees.

■ Describe the characteristics of effective goal setting and feedback.

■ Summarize the equity theory model, including how people try to reduce feelings of inequity.

■ Identify the factors that influence procedural justice, as well as the consequences of procedural justice.

Not long ago, an employee at one of Fairmont's (formerly CP Hotels) Canadian resorts saw a car with a flat tire at the side of the road, so he pulled over to offer assistance. The Fairmont employee soon realized that the car's occupants were guests at the resort, so he changed the flat tire himself and escorted the guests back to the resort. The employee's exceptional service might have gone unnoticed, except Fairmont has a program, called BravoGrams, that encourages employees and customers to recognize and praise employees who go beyond the call of duty. The employee who changed the guest's flat tire received a BravoGram from the grateful guests and he became eligible for prizes later in the year.

Fairmont Hotels and other Canadian firms are returning to good old-fashioned praise and recognition to motivate staff. Stock options can evaporate and incentive plans often backfire, whereas a few words of appreciation almost always create a warm glow of satisfaction and a renewed energy. In a recent survey of 100 executives across Canada, one-third identified lack of recognition as having the most negative effect on employee morale. Over half of these executives recommended various forms of recognition to improve morale and motivation.

The challenge is to "catch" employees doing good deeds, so Fairmont and other firms rely on customers and employees as partners in the motivation process. ScotiaBank, for example, has a Web-based peer-to-peer recognition process, called Scotia Applause. Employees at the Canadian financial institution document incidents in which co-workers demonstrated one or more of the program's principles: integrity, respect, commitment, insight, and spirit. Recognized employees receive certificates and accumulate points that can be redeemed for merchandise.

Fairmont Hotels (shown in photo) and other Canadian firms are returning to good old-fashioned praise and recognition to motivate staff. *Courtesy of Four Seasons*

The Abbotsford office of the British Columbia government's Food Safety and Quality Branch took a different approach to peer recognition. The branch posted a large "Appreciation Tree" in the front office and surrounded it with photos of staff members. Branch employees added leaves to the tree that identified specific co-workers and what they specifically did that was valued. Over time, the Appreciation Tree was filled with leaves recognizing the contributions that employees made to the branch's success.[1] ■

www.fairmont.com

motivation

The forces within a person that affect his or her direction, intensity, and persistence of voluntary behaviour.

BravoGrams at Fairmont Hotels, Scotia Applause at ScotiaBank, and Appreciation Trees at the B.C. Government are designed to maintain and improve employee motivation. **Motivation** refers to the forces within a person that affect the direction, intensity, and persistence of voluntary behaviour.[2] Motivated employees are willing to exert a particular level of effort (intensity), for a certain amount of time (persistence), toward a particular goal (direction). Motivation is one of the four essential drivers of individual behaviour and performance (see the MARS model in Chapter 2) and, consequently, is an integral component of employee engagement. An engaged workforce is an important predictor of the organization's competitiveness, so it's easy to see why employee motivation is continuously on the minds of corporate leaders.

The quest for a motivated and engaged workforce has not been easy, however. Most employers—92 percent of them, according to one major survey—say that motivating employees has become more challenging. Three factors seem to be responsible for this increasing challenge. First, globalization, information technology, corporate restructuring, and other changes have dramatically altered the employment relationship. These changes potentially undermine the levels of trust and commitment necessary to energize employees beyond minimum standards. Perhaps this explains why nearly one-fifth of the Canadian workforce is disengaged—retired on the job.[3]

Second, in decades past, companies typically relied on armies of supervisors to closely monitor employee behaviour and performance. Even if commitment and trust were low, employees performed their jobs with the boss watching them closely. But most companies thinned out their supervisory ranks when they flattened the organizational structure to reduce costs. Supervisors now have many more employees, so they can't possibly keep a watchful eye out for laggards. This is just as well because today's educated workforce resents the old "command-and-control" approach to performance management. Most people enjoy the feeling of being motivated, but this requires the right conditions, so employers need to search for more contemporary ways to motivate staff.

The third challenge is that a new generation of employees has brought different expectations to the workplace. A few years ago, various writers disparaged Generation-X and Generation-Y employees as slackers, cynics, whiners, and malcontents. Now, we know that the problem wasn't their lack of motivational potential; it was that employers didn't know how to motivate them! It seems that many companies still haven't figured this out: according to one report, more than 40 percent of employees aged 25 to 34 sometimes or frequently feel demotivated compared to 30 percent of 35- to 44-year-olds and just 18 percent of 45- to 54-year-olds.[4]

In this chapter, we begin the process of understanding and facilitating employee motivation by looking at the core theories of motivation in organizational settings. The chapter begins by describing Maslow's needs hierarchy theory and explaining why this incredibly popular theory as well as other needs hierarchy models are neither valid nor useful. We then turn to four-drives theory and McClelland's learned needs theory, both of which offer more promise. After discussing these needs-based theories, we turn our attention to a rational decision model of employee motivation, called expectancy theory. The third section of this chapter covers the key elements of goal setting and feedback, including the topics of multisource feedback and executive coaching. In the final section, we look at organizational justice, including the dimensions and dynamics of equity theory and procedural justice.

■ NEEDS, DRIVES, AND EMPLOYEE MOTIVATION

needs
Deficiencies that energize or trigger behaviours to satisfy those needs.

Motivation begins with individual needs and their underlying drives. In spite of some confusion in the literature regarding "needs" and "drives," we will define **needs** as deficiencies that energize or trigger behaviours to satisfy those needs. Unfulfilled needs create a tension that makes us want to find ways to reduce or satisfy those needs. The stronger your needs, the more motivated you are to satisfy them. Conversely, a satisfied need does not motivate. **Drives** are instinctive or innate tendencies to seek certain goals or maintain internal stability. Drives are hardwired in the brain—everyone has the same drives—and they most likely exist to help the species survive.[5] Needs are typically produced by drives, but they may also be strengthened through learning (reinforcement) and social forces such as culture and childhood upbringing. We'll discuss needs and drives later in this section, after describing Maslow and other needs hierarchy theories.

drives
Instinctive or innate tendencies to seek certain goals or maintain internal stability.

MASLOW'S NEEDS HIERARCHY THEORY

More people have probably heard about **Maslow's needs hierarchy theory** than any other concept in organizational behaviour. Developed by psychologist Abraham Maslow in the 1940s, the model has been applied in almost every human pursuit, from marketing products to rehabilitating prison inmates. This incredible popularity is rather odd, considering that most research has reported little or no support for the theory. According to his later journal entries, even Maslow was amazed that people had accepted his theory wholeheartedly as gospel truth without any critique. Normally, a theory that fails to live up to its predictions is laid to rest. However, Maslow's model is described here because of its significant historic value.

Maslow's needs hierarchy theory
A motivation theory of needs arranged in a hierarchy, whereby people are motivated to fulfill a higher need as a lower one becomes gratified.

The needs hierarchy model emerged out of Maslow's concern that scholars had splintered needs and drives into dozens of categories, each studied in isolation using nontypical subjects (usually animals or people with severe psychological dysfunctions).[6] He argued that isolating narrowly-defined needs and drives was inappropriate because human behaviour is typically initiated by more than one of these needs or drives with varying degrees of influence on that behaviour. While most scholars at the time focused on drive deprivation (particularly hunger), Maslow suggested that need gratification is just as important and that higher level needs (such as status) are influenced by social dynamics and culture, not just instincts. Maslow's call for a more holistic, humanistic, and positive approach to human motivation research was a significant shift in thinking which largely remains with us today.

Maslow's needs hierarchy theory takes a holistic approach by condensing the long list of needs into a hierarchy of five basic categories.[7] As Exhibit 5.1 illustrates, physiological needs (need for food, air, water, shelter, etc.) are at the bottom of the hierarchy. Next are safety needs—the need for a secure and stable environment and the absence of pain, threat, or illness. Belongingness includes the need for love, affection, and interaction with other people. Esteem includes self-esteem through personal achievement as well as social esteem through recognition and respect from others. At the top of the hierarchy is **self-actualization**, which represents the need for self-fulfillment—a sense that the person's potential has been realized. In addition to these five, Maslow describes the need to know and need for aesthetic beauty as two needs that do not fit within the hierarchy.

self-actualization
The need for self-fulfillment in reaching one's potential.

Maslow says that we are motivated simultaneously by several needs, but the strongest source is the lowest unsatisfied need at the time. As the person satisfies a

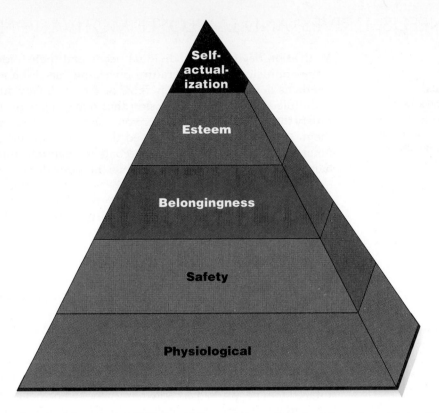

Sources: Based on information in A.H. Maslow, "A Theory of Human Motivation," *Psychological Review 50*, (1943), pp. 370–96.

lower level need, the next higher need in the hierarchy becomes the primary motivator and remains so even if never satisfied. Physiological needs are initially the most important and people are motivated to satisfy them first. As they become gratified, safety needs emerge as the strongest motivator. As safety needs are satisfied, belongingness needs become most important, and so forth. The exception to this need fulfillment process is self-actualization; as people experience self-actualization, they desire more rather than less of this need. Thus, while the bottom four groups are *deficiency needs* because they become activated when unfulfilled, self-actualization is known as a *growth need* because it continues to develop even when fulfilled.

Evaluating needs hierarchy theory   As mentioned already, Maslow's needs hierarchy theory has not received much scientific support.[8] Researchers have found that needs do not cluster neatly around the hierarchy's five categories. Also, gratification of one need level does not necessarily lead to increased motivation to satisfy the next higher need level. Some people can be very hungry and yet strive to fulfill their social needs; others can self-actualize while working in a risky environment. The theory also assumes that need priorities shift over months or years, whereas the importance of a particular need likely changes more quickly with the situation.

In spite of the flaws of needs hierarchy theory, Maslow shifted research away from studies of narrowly defined needs and drives and raised awareness of the importance of social and cultural factors, not just hunger-like instincts. But Maslow's most important contribution is his work on self-actualization, which he considered far more important than the needs hierarchy model.[9] Throughout his career, Maslow emphasized that people are naturally motivated to reach their potential (once lower needs are fulfilled), and that organizations and societies need to be structured to help people continue and develop this motivation. Maslow called for more "enlightened management" to provide meaningful work and freedom, rather than tedious work with oppressive bureaucratic controls, so employees can experience self-actualization and fulfill their other needs.[10]

What's wrong with needs hierarchy models?   Maslow's theory is not the only attempt to map employee needs onto a hierarchy. The most comprehensive of the alternative models is **ERG theory**, which re-organizes Maslow's five groups into three—existence, relatedness, and growth.[11] Unlike Maslow's theory, which only explained how people progress up the hierarchy, ERG theory also describes how people regress down the hierarchy when they fail to fulfill higher needs. ERG theory seems to explain human motivation somewhat better than Maslow's needs hierarchy, but that's mainly because it is easier to cluster human needs around ERG's three categories than Maslow's five categories. Otherwise, the research findings are fairly clear that ERG theory only marginally improves our understanding of human needs.[12]

Why have Maslow's needs hierarchy, ERG theory, and other needs hierarchies largely failed to explain the dynamics of employee needs? The most glaring explanation is that people don't fit into a single universal needs hierarchy. We can think of acquaintances who seem addicted to social status even though they haven't fulfilled all of their lower needs, or who consider personal development and growth an ongoing priority over social relations. There is increasing evidence that needs hierarchies are unique, not universal, because a person's needs are strongly influenced by his or her social identity and values.[13] People with a strong social identity tend to emphasize social needs, whereas those with a strong personal identity focus more on their self-actualization needs.

Values also influence a person's unique needs hierarchy.[14] If your fundamental values lean toward stimulation and self-direction, you probably pay more attention to self-actualization needs. If power and achievement are at the top of your value system, then status needs might be stronger most of the time. This connection between values and needs suggests that a needs hierarchy is unique to each person and can change over time, just as values change over a lifetime. In summary, we seem to have a personal and somewhat flexible needs hierarchy, not one that is hardwired in human nature, as needs hierarchy theories assume.

FOUR-DRIVE THEORY

Motivation experts have mostly abandoned needs hierarchy theories, but not the notion that needs and drives are relevant. On the contrary, recent discoveries in neuroscience have prompted experts to reconsider a more coherent and integrated approach to innate drives. Building on recent research on innate drives, emotions, and social intelligence, Harvard Business School professors Paul Lawrence and Nitin Nohria have proposed **four-drive theory** to explain human motivation.[15] This model is both holistic (it pulls together the many drives and needs) and humanistic (it considers human thought and social influences rather than just instinct). These were two conditions that Maslow felt were essential for a solid theory of human motivation.

ERG theory
A motivation theory of three needs arranged in a hierarchy, in which people progress to the next higher need when a lower one is fulfilled, and regress to a lower need if unable to fulfill a higher one.

four-drive theory
A motivation theory based on the innate drives to acquire, bond, learn, and defend that incorporates both emotions and rationality.

Four fundamental drives   Four-drive theory organizes drives into four categories: the drives to acquire, bond, learn, and defend. These drives are innate and universal, meaning that they are hardwired in our brains through evolution and are found in everyone. They are also independent of each other, so one drive is neither dependent on nor inherently inferior or superior to another drive. Four-drive theory also states that these four drives are a complete set—there are no other fundamental drives excluded from the model. Another key feature is that three of the four drives are "proactive," meaning that we regularly try to fulfill them. Thus, any notion of fulfilling drives is temporary, at best.

- *Drive to acquire*—This is the drive to seek, take, control, and retain objects and personal experiences. The drive to acquire extends beyond basic food and water; it includes the need for relative status and recognition in society. Thus, it is the foundation of competition and the basis of our need for esteem. Four-drive theory states that the drive to acquire is insatiable because the purpose of human motivation is to achieve a higher position than others, not just to fulfill one's physiological needs.

- *Drive to bond*—This is the drive to form social relationships and develop mutual caring commitments with others. It also explains why people form social identities by aligning their self-image with various social groups (see Chapter 3). Research indicates that people invest considerable time and effort forming and maintaining relationships without any special circumstances or ulterior motives.[16] Moreover, people fairly consistently experience negative emotions when relationships are dissolved, such as when the business shuts down or co-workers are laid off. The drive to bond motivates people to cooperate and, consequently, is a fundamental ingredient in the success of organizations and the development of societies.

- *Drive to learn*—This is the drive to satisfy one's curiosity, to know and understand ourselves and the environment around us. When observing something that is inconsistent with or beyond our current knowledge, we experience a tension that motivates us to close that information gap. In fact, studies at McGill University in the 1950s revealed that people who are removed from any novel information will crave even boring information (outdated stock reports)![17] The drive to learn fulfills our need for personal and social identity (see Chapter 3) and is related to the higher order needs of growth and self-actualization described earlier.

- *Drive to defend*—This is the drive to protect ourselves physically and socially. Probably the first drive to develop, it creates a "fight-or-flight" response in the face of personal danger. The drive to defend goes beyond protecting our physical self. It includes defending our relationships, our acquisitions, and our belief systems. The drive to defend is always reactive—it is triggered by threat. In contrast, the other three drives are always proactive—we actively seek to improve our acquisitions, relationships, and knowledge.

How drives influence employee motivation   Four-drive theory explains how drives translate into employee choices and effort in two steps: (1) by relating how the four drives fit into the "dual processes" of emotionality and rationality that was described in previous chapters, and (2) by explaining how and why people are usually consciously motivated rather than guided instinctively by the four drives.

Dofasco Events Fulfill the Drive to Bond

According to four-drive theory, social interaction gives employees an opportunity to fulfill their drive to bond and for performance-oriented companies to prevent too much competitive behaviour. Dofasco, the Hamilton-based steelmaker, solidly follows this advice by hosting Canada's largest Christmas party, a mammoth Canada Day celebration, and numerous smaller social gatherings at other times. At the Christmas event, over 30,000 Dofasco employees and their families pour into the Copps Coliseum in Hamilton to mingle with friends, skate around the enormous Christmas tree at centre ice, receive gifts, and shake hands with the top brass who greet them at the front door. "It reinforces a very direct connection with our community and their families," says Dofasco spokesperson Bill Gair. Carl Morrison, who has worked at Dofasco for a few decades, agrees: "It keeps everybody bonded together."[21]

Courtesy of Dofasco

www.dofasco.ca

For the first part of the explanation, you might recall from previous chapters that our perceptions of the external world are routed to two parts of the brain—the emotional centre and the rational centre.[18] The emotional centre, which operates faster than the rational centre, makes a "quick and dirty" evaluation and attaches emotional markers (fear, contentment, excitement, etc.) to the information. The emotional markers are transmitted (usually unconsciously) to the rational centre of the brain where they influence the rational process of analysing the information against our memory and logical analysis. Our motivation to act is therefore a result of rational thinking influenced by these emotional markers.[19]

The four drives fit into this tango of emotionality and rationality by determining which emotional markers, if any, are attached to the perceived information. For example, suppose that your department has just received a new computer program that you are eager to try out (the eagerness emotion is triggered by your drive to learn). However, your boss says that you are too inexperienced to use the new system yet, which makes you somewhat angry (the anger is triggered by your drive to defend against the insult about your inexperience). Both the curiosity about the software program and your anger from the boss's beliefs about your experience demand your attention and energize you to act. The key point here is that the four innate drives determine which emotions to trigger in each situation.

The second part of four-drive theory, which is illustrated in Exhibit 5.2, states that drives generate independent and usually competing signals that require our attention in most situations.[20] So, when we perceive a situation, chances are that two or more drives generate emotional markers that compete with each other. For example, suppose you learn that your boss has been promoted and an outsider has been hired to fill that role. Research has found that this sort of event usually triggers both the drive to defend and the drive to know—you are worried about how the new manager will affect your work and also curious about what the new boss looks and acts like.

Competing emotional signals usually get raised to the level of our consciousness. When aware of this internal conflict, we rely on a built-in skill set to resolve these dilemmas. These skills take into account social norms, past experience, and personal values. The result is goal-directed decision and effort that fits within the constraints of cultural and moral expectations. In other words, our conscious analysis of competing demands from the four drives generates needs that energize us to act in ways acceptable to society and our own moral compass.

■ **EXHIBIT 5.2**   Four-drive theory of motivation

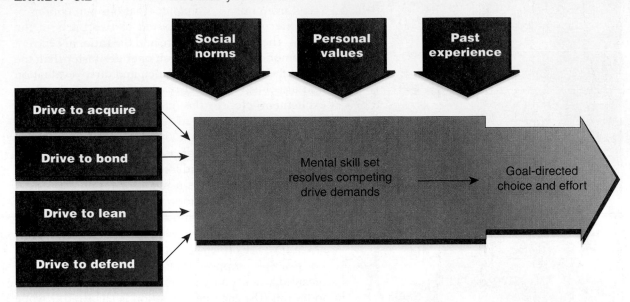

Sources: Based on information in P.R. Lawrence and N. Nohria, *Driven: How Human Nature Shapes Our Choices* (San Francisco: Jossey-Bass, 2002).

Evaluating four-drive theory   Four-drive theory potentially offers a rich explanation for employee motivation. It avoids the assumption found in needs hierarchy theories that everyone has the same needs hierarchy. Instead, it explains how our needs are based on innate drives, how emotions are generated from those drives in the context of a specific situation, and how personal experience and cultural values influence the intensity, persistence, and direction of effort. Four-drive theory also provides a much clearer understanding about the role of emotional intelligence in employee motivation and behaviour (see Chapter 4). Employees with high emotional intelligence are more sensitive to competing demands from the four drives, are better able to avoid impulsive behaviour from those drives, and can judge the best way to act to fulfill those drive demands in a social context.

Four-drive theory is based on some fairly solid evidence regarding the existence and dynamics of the four innate drives and of the interaction of emotions and cognitions (logical thinking) in employee behaviour. However, the overall model is quite new and requires much more work to clarify the role of skill sets in forming goal-directed choice and effort. The theory also ignores the fact that the needs can be strengthened through learning. Four-drive theory likely accommodates the notion of learned needs, but it does not explain them. Fortunately, other motivational researchers, notably David McClelland, have provided some clarification about learned needs, which we examine next.

THEORY OF LEARNED NEEDS

At the beginning of this chapter, we learned that needs typically originate from drives—your need for social interaction with co-workers is usually created out of the innate drive to bond, for instance. But needs can also be strengthened through reinforcement, including through childhood learning, parental styles, and social norms. Psychologist David McClelland popularized the idea of learned needs years ago through his research on three learned needs: achievement, power, and affiliation.

need for achievement (nAch)

A learned need in which people want to accomplish reasonably challenging goals through their own efforts, like being successful in competitive situations, and desire unambiguous feedback regarding their success.

■ *Need for Achievement (nAch)*—People with a strong **need for achievement (nAch)** want to accomplish reasonably challenging goals through their own effort. They prefer working alone rather than in teams and they choose tasks with a moderate degree of risk (i.e., neither too easy nor impossible to complete). High nAch people also desire unambiguous feedback and recognition for their success. Money is a weak motivator, except when it provides feedback and recognition.[22] In contrast, employees with a low nAch perform their work better when money is used as an incentive. Successful entrepreneurs tend to have a high nAch, possibly because they establish challenging goals for themselves and thrive on competition.[23]

need for affiliation (nAff)

A learned need in which people seek approval from others, conform to their wishes and expectations, and avoid conflict and confrontation.

■ *Need for Affiliation (nAff)*—**A need for affiliation (nAff)** refers to a desire to seek approval from others, conform to their wishes and expectations, and avoid conflict and confrontation. People with a strong nAff try to project a favourable image of themselves. They tend to actively support others and try to smooth out workplace conflicts. High nAff employees generally work well in coordinating roles to mediate conflicts, and in sales positions where the main task is cultivating long-term relations. However, they tend to be less effective at allocating scarce resources and making other decisions that potentially generate conflict. People in decision-making positions must have a relatively low need for affiliation so that their choices and actions are not biased by a personal need for approval.[24]

need for power (nPow)

A learned need in which people want to control their environment, including people and material resources, to benefit either themselves (personalized power) or others (socialized power).

■ *Need for Power (nPow)*—People with a high **need for power (nPow)** want to exercise control over others and are concerned about maintaining their leadership position. They frequently rely on persuasive communication, make more suggestions in meetings, and tend to publicly evaluate situations more frequently. McClelland pointed out that there are two types of nPow. Those who enjoy their power for its own sake, use it to advance personal interests, and wear their power as a status symbol have *personalized power*. Others mainly have a high need for *socialized power* because they desire power as a means to help others.[25] McClelland argues that effective leaders should have a high need for socialized rather than personalized power. They have a high degree of altruism and social responsibility and are concerned about the consequences of their own actions on others.

Learning needs McClelland argued that achievement, affiliation, and power needs can be strengthened through learning, so he developed training programs for this purpose. In his achievement motivation program, trainees write achievement-oriented stories and practise achievement-oriented behaviours in business games. They also complete a detailed achievement plan for the next two years and form a reference group with other trainees to maintain their newfound achievement motive style.[26] These programs seem to work. Participants attending a need for achievement course in India subsequently started more businesses, had greater community involvement, invested more in expanding their businesses, and employed twice as many people as nonparticipants. Research on similar achievement-motive courses for North American small-business owners reported dramatic increases in the profitability of the participants' businesses.

PRACTICAL IMPLICATIONS OF NEEDS/DRIVE-BASED THEORIES

We can take away a few practical recommendations based on four-drive theory, learned needs theory, and Maslow's research on self-actualization. Lawrence and Nohria devote an entire chapter describing the following piece of advice from four-drive theory: ensure that individual jobs and workplaces provide a balanced opportunity to fulfill the drive to acquire, bond, learn, and defend.[27] There are really two key recommendations here. The first one is that everyone in the workplace needs to regularly fulfill all four drives. This is in sharp contrast to the ill-fated needs hierarchy theories, which suggested that employees are motivated mainly by one need at a time. Four-drive theory says that each of us continuously seeks fulfillment of our innate drives. Thus, the best workplaces for motivation and morale provide sufficient rewards, learning opportunities, social interaction, and so forth for all employees.

The second recommendation from four-drive theory is that these four drives must be kept in "balance"; that is, organizations should avoid too much or too little opportunity to fulfill each drive. The reason for this advice is that the four drives counterbalance each other. Companies that help employees fulfill one drive but not the others will face long-term problems. An organization that energizes the drive to acquire without the drive to bond may eventually suffer from organizational politics and dysfunctional conflict. Change and novelty in the workplace will aid the drive to learn, but too much of it will trigger the drive to defend to such an extent that employees become territorial and resistant to change. Creating a workplace that supports the drive to bond can, at extreme levels, undermine the diversity and constructive debate required for effective decision making.

Another recommendation from the needs/drives-based theories is to offer employees a choice of rewards rather than give everyone the same specific reward. Although we possess the same drives and require their ongoing fulfillment, people differ in their needs at any given time. Due to their unique values system and social learning, some employees generally have a strong need to achieve whereas others are motivated more by social factors. A narrow application of this recommendation is to let employees choose their own rewards from catalogues, as Telus Corporation and other Canadian firms have done. At a broader level, employees need to have career choices and diverse opportunities to discover and experience their potential. One of the enduring recommendations from Maslow's work on self-actualization is that employees must have sufficient freedom to discover their potential. It cannot be assumed or dictated by management.

Recognition Worth More than Money at EnCana
Executives at EnCana Corporation had launched a recognition program called "High Five" in which employees and managers were encouraged to recommend any deserving colleague for a high-five card, which is redeemable for $5. The token amount was intended to symbolize their value as an employee and to provide a small financial incentive. But rather than cashing in their cards for money, many employees at the Calgary-based energy company displayed the cards in their offices. The visible symbol of recognition was apparently worth more to many people than the cash value of the card.[28] *Courtesy of EnCana*
www.encana.com

■ EXPECTANCY THEORY OF MOTIVATION

expectancy theory

A motivation theory based on the idea that work effort is directed toward behaviours that people believe will lead to desired outcomes.

The theories described so far mainly explain what motivates employees. But how do these drives and needs translate into specific effort and behaviour? One of the best theories to answer this question is expectancy theory of motivation. **Expectancy theory** is based on the idea that work effort is directed toward behaviours that people believe will lead to desired outcomes.[29] Through experience, we develop expectations about whether we can achieve various levels of job performance. We also develop expectations about whether job performance and work behaviours lead to particular outcomes. Finally, we naturally direct our effort toward outcomes that help us fulfill our needs.

EXPECTANCY THEORY MODEL

The expectancy theory model is presented in Exhibit 5.3. The key variable of interest in expectancy theory is *effort*—the individual's actual exertion of energy. An individual's effort level depends on three factors: effort-to-performance (E-to-P) expectancy, performance-to-outcome (P-to-O) expectancy, and outcome valences (V). Employee motivation is influenced by all three components of the expectancy theory model. If any component weakens, motivation weakens.

E-to-P expectancy   The *effort-to-performance (E-to-P)* expectancy is the individual's perception that his or her effort will result in a particular level of performance. Expectancy is defined as a probability, and therefore ranges from 0.0 to 1.0. In some situations, employees may believe that they can unquestionably accomplish the task (a probability of 1.0). In other situations, they expect that even their highest level of effort will not result in the desired performance level (a probability of 0.0). For instance, unless you are an expert skier, you probably aren't motivated to try some of the black diamond ski runs at Whistler. The reason is a very low E-to-P expectancy. Even your best effort won't get you down the hill feet first! In most cases, the E-to-P expectancy falls somewhere between these two extremes.

■ EXHIBIT 5.3

Expectancy theory of motivation

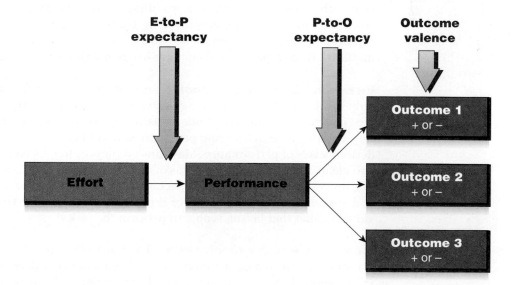

P-to-O expectancy   The *performance-to-outcome (P-to-O) expectancy* is the perceived probability that a specific behaviour or performance level will lead to specific outcomes. This probability is developed from previous learning. For example, students learn from experience that skipping class either ruins their chance of a good grade or has no effect at all. In extreme cases, employees may believe that accomplishing a particular task (performance) will definitely result in a particular outcome (a probability of 1.0), or they may believe that this outcome will have no effect on successful performance (a probability of 0.0). More often, the P-to-O expectancy falls somewhere between these two extremes.

One important issue in P-to-O expectancies is which outcomes we think about. We certainly don't evaluate the P-to-O expectancy for every possible outcome; there are too many of them. Instead, we think only about outcomes of interest to us at the time. One day, your motivation to complete a task may be fuelled mainly by the likelihood of getting off work early to meet friends. Other times, your motivation to complete the same task may be based more on the P-to-O expectancy of a promotion or pay increase. The main point is that your motivation depends on the probability that a behaviour or job performance level will result in outcomes that you think about.

valence
The anticipated satisfaction or dissatisfaction that an individual feels toward an outcome.

Outcome valences   The third element in expectancy theory is the **valence** of each outcome that you consider. Valence refers to the anticipated satisfaction or dissatisfaction that an individual feels toward an outcome. It ranges from negative to positive. (The actual range doesn't matter; it may be from -1 to $+1$, or from -100 to $+100$.) An outcome valence represents a person's anticipated satisfaction with the outcome.[30] Outcomes have a positive valence when they are consistent with our values and satisfy our needs; they have a negative valence when they oppose our values and inhibit need fulfillment. If you have a strong need for social interaction, for example, you would value group activities and other events that help to fulfill that need. Outcomes that move you further away from fulfilling your social need—such as working alone from home—will have a strong negative valence.

EXPECTANCY THEORY IN PRACTICE

One of the appealing characteristics of expectancy theory is that it provides clear guidelines for increasing employee motivation by altering the person's E-to-P expectancies, P-to-O expectancies, and/or outcome valences.[31] Several practical implications of expectancy theory are listed in Exhibit 5.4 and described below.

Increasing E-to-P expectancies   E-to-P expectancies are influenced by the individual's belief that he or she can successfully complete the task. Some companies increase this can-do attitude by assuring employees that they have the necessary competencies, clear role perceptions, and necessary resources to reach the desired levels of performance. Matching employees to jobs based on their abilities and clearly communicating the tasks required for the job is an important part of this process. Similarly, E-to-P expectancies are learned, so behavioural modelling and supportive feedback (positive reinforcement) typically strengthen the individual's belief that he/she is able to perform the task.[32]

Increasing P-to-O expectancies   The most obvious ways to improve P-to-O expectancies are to measure employee performance accurately and distribute more valued rewards to those with higher job performance. Unfortunately, many organ-

■ **EXHIBIT 5.4**   Practical implications of expectancy

Expectancy Theory Component	Objective	Applications
E→ P expectancies	To increase the belief that employees are capable of performing the job successfully	• Select people with the required skills. • Provide required training and clarify job requirements. • Provide sufficient time and resources. • Assign simpler or fewer tasks until employees can master them. • Provide examples of similar employees who have successfully performed the task. • Provide coaching to employees who lack self-confidence.
P→ O expectancies	To increase the belief that good performance will result in certain (valued) outcomes	• Measure job performance accurately. • Clearly explain the outcomes that will result from successful performance. • Describe how the employee's rewards were based on past performance. • Provide examples of other employees whose good performance has resulted in higher rewards.
Outcome valences	To increase the expected value of outcomes resulting from desired performance	• Distribute rewards that employees value. • Individualize rewards. • Minimize the presence of countervalent outcomes.

izations have difficulty putting this straightforward idea into practice. Some executives are reluctant to withhold rewards for poor performance because they don't want to experience conflict with employees. Others don't measure employee performance very well. For instance, a recent study reported that less than half of the 6,000 Canadian and American employees surveyed said they know how to increase their base pay or cash bonuses. In other words, most employees and managers have a generally low P-to-O expectancy regarding their paycheques.[33] Chapter 6 looks at reasons why rewards aren't connected to job performance.

P-to-O expectancies are perceptions, so employees should believe that higher performance will result in higher rewards. Having a performance-based reward system is important, but this fact must be communicated. When rewards are distributed, employees should understand how their rewards have been based on past performance. More generally, companies need to regularly communicate the existence of a performance-based reward system through examples, anecdotes, and public ceremonies.

Increasing outcome valences   Performance outcomes influence work effort only when those outcomes are valued by employees. This brings us back to what we learned from the needs/drives-based theories of motivation, namely, that companies should develop more individualized reward systems so that employees who perform well are offered a choice of rewards. Expectancy theory also emphasizes the need to discover and neutralize countervalent outcomes. These are performance outcomes that have negative valences, thereby reducing the effectiveness of existing reward systems. For example, peer pressure may cause some employees to perform their jobs at the minimum standard even though formal rewards and the job itself would otherwise motivate them to perform at higher levels.

DOES EXPECTANCY THEORY FIT REALITY?

Expectancy theory remains one of the better theories for predicting work effort and motivation. In particular, it plays a valuable role by detailing a person's thinking process when translating the competing demands of the four drives into specific effort. Expectancy theory has been applied to a wide variety of studies, such as predicting student motivation to participate in teaching evaluations, using a decision support system, leaving the organization, and engaging in organizational citizenship behaviours.[34] Research also indicates that expectancy theory predicts employee motivation in different cultures.[35]

One limitation is that expectancy theory seems to ignore the central role of emotion in employee effort and behaviour.[36] As we learned earlier in this and previous chapters, emotions serve an adaptive function that demand our attention and energize us to take action. The valence element of expectancy theory captures some of this emotional process, but only peripherally. Thus, theorists probably need to redesign the expectancy theory model in light of new information about the importance of emotions in motivation and behaviour.

■ GOAL SETTING AND FEEDBACK

Walk into almost any call centre in Canada—whether its Dell Computer's new centre in Edmonton or eBay's customer contact centre in Vancouver—and you will notice that work activities are dominated by goal setting and plenty of feedback. Call centre performance is judged on several metrics such as average time to answer the call, length of time per call, and abandon rates (customers who hang up before the call is handled by a customer service representative). Some call centres have large electronic boards showing how many customers are waiting, the average time they have been waiting, and the average time before someone talks to them. Employees sometimes receive feedback on their computer, such as the average length of time for each call at their workstation. Meanwhile, supervisors spend an average of 52 percent of their time monitoring customer calls—usually six per month per employee—and regularly coaching employees based on those observations.[37]

goal setting
The process of motivating employees and clarifying their role perceptions by establishing performance objectives.

Call centres across Canada rely on goal setting and feedback to motivate employees and achieve superior performance.[38] **Goal setting** is the process of motivating employees and clarifying their role perceptions by establishing performance objectives. It potentially improves employee performance in two ways: (1) by stretching the intensity and persistence of effort and (2) by giving employees clearer role perceptions so that their effort is channelled toward behaviours that will improve work performance.

CHARACTERISTICS OF EFFECTIVE GOALS

Goal setting is more complex than simply telling someone to "do your best." Instead, it requires six conditions to maximize task effort and performance: specific goals, relevant goals, challenging goals, goal commitment, participation in goal formation (sometimes), and goal feedback.[39]

Goal Setting and Feedback at Inco's Copper Cliff Smelter

Inco Ltd. has a secret weapon to make it a highly efficient and competitive mining operation. The company has rolled out a front-line planning and scheduling system at its Copper Cliff smelter in Sudbury, Ontario, in which the daily, weekly, and monthly goals for production and maintenance are established and clearly communicated every day. The plans are posted in advance in a highly visible location so employees have clear goals and expectations. Timing is so important in these operations that any variances in the plan can result in substantial productivity losses. So, each day, any breakdowns or setbacks that upset the work goals are reported and discussed. These feedback sessions are valuable because employees are encouraged to comment on ways to improve the longer term plan, thereby developing better goals. "We're trying to get the key people who actually do the work to get directly involved in the planning process," explains Adam MacMillan, an Inco engineer involved in the scheduling process.[45] *Courtesy of Inco Ltd.*

www.inco.com

- *Specific goals*—Employees put more effort into a task when they work toward specific goals rather than "do your best" targets.[40] Specific goals have measurable levels of change over a specific and relatively short time frame, such as "reduce scrap rate by 7 percent over the next six months." Specific goals communicate more precise performance expectations, so employees can direct their effort more efficiently and reliably.

- *Relevant goals*—Goals must also be relevant to the individual's job and within his or her control. For example, a goal to reduce waste materials would have little value if employees don't have much control over waste in the production process.

- *Challenging goals*—Challenging goals (rather than easy ones) cause people to raise the intensity and persistence of their work effort and to think through information more actively. They also fulfill a person's achievement or growth needs when the goal is achieved. General Electric, Goldman Sachs, and many other organizations emphasize stretch goals. These goals don't just stretch your abilities and motivation; they are goals that you don't know how to reach, so you need to be creative to achieve them.[41]

- *Goal commitment*—Although goals should be challenging, employees also need to be committed to accomplishing goals. Thus, we need to find an optimal level of goal difficulty where the goals are challenging, yet employees are still motivated to achieve them.[42] This is the same as the E-to-P expectancy that we learned about in the section on expectancy theory. The lower the E-to-P expectancy that the goal can be accomplished, the less committed (motivated) the employee is to the goal.

- *Goal participation (sometimes)*—Goal setting is usually (but not always) more effective when employees participate in setting goals.[43] Employees identify more with goals they are involved in setting than goals assigned by a supervisor. In fact, today's workforce increasingly expects to be involved in goal setting and other decisions that affect them. Participation may also improve goal quality, because employees have valuable information and knowledge that may not be known to managers who normally develop these goals alone. Thus, participation ensures that employees buy into the goals and have the competencies and resources necessary to accomplish them.

feedback
Any information that people receive about the consequences of their behaviour.

- *Goal feedback*—Feedback is another necessary condition for effective goal setting.[44] **Feedback** is any information that people receive about the consequences of their behaviour. Feedback lets us know whether we have achieved the goal or are properly directing our effort toward it. Feedback is also an essential ingredient in motivation because our growth needs can't be satisfied unless we receive information on goal accomplishment. Feedback is so central to goal setting that we will look more closely at it next.

CHARACTERISTICS OF EFFECTIVE FEEDBACK

Feedback is a key ingredient in goal setting and employee performance. It communicates what behaviours are appropriate or necessary in a particular situation (i.e., clarifies role perceptions) and improves ability by frequently providing information to correct performance problems. Information that identifies a gap between the actual and ideal performance is known as *corrective feedback*, because it raises awareness of performance errors and identifies ways to correct those errors.

A third benefit is that, under some conditions, feedback motivates employees. This is particularly true when feedback is positive, such as the peer-to-peer recognition activities described in the opening vignette to this chapter. These recognition programs communicate feedback as rewards, so they have the double benefit of informing employees about their performance and fulfilling their needs. Corrective feedback can also be motivating when employees have a strong "can-do" attitude toward the task and a learning orientation. For these people, less-than-ideal performance feedback motivates them to improve rather than to deny or reject the feedback.[46]

Many of the characteristics of effective goal setting also apply to effective feedback (see Exhibit 5.5). First, feedback should be *specific*. The information provided should be connected to the details of the goal, rather than subjective and general phrases such as "your sales are going well." Second, feedback must be *relevant*; it must relate to the individual's behaviour rather than to conditions beyond the individual's control. This ensures that the feedback is not distorted by situational factors. Third, feedback should be timely; it should be available as soon as possible after the behaviour or results. Timeliness helps employees see a clear association between their behaviour and its consequences.

■ **EXHIBIT 5.5**   Characteristics of effective feedback

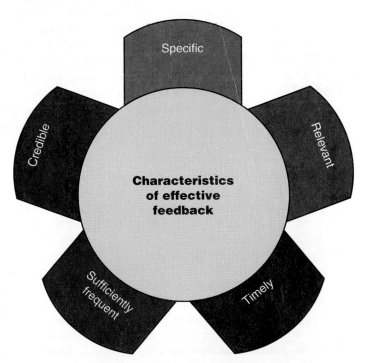

Fourth, feedback should be *sufficiently frequent*. How frequent is "sufficiently"? The answer depends on at least two things. One consideration is the employee's knowledge and experience with the task. Feedback is a form of reinforcement, so employees working on new tasks should receive more frequent corrective feedback because they require more behaviour guidance and reinforcement (see Chapter 3). Employees who are repeating familiar tasks can receive less frequent feedback. The second factor is how long it takes to complete the task. Feedback is necessarily less frequent in jobs with a long cycle time (e.g., executives and scientists) than in jobs with a short cycle time (e.g., grocery store cashiers). The final characteristic of effective feedback is that it should be *credible*. Employees are more likely to accept feedback (particularly corrective feedback) from trustworthy and credible sources.

SOURCES OF FEEDBACK

Feedback can originate from nonsocial or social sources. Nonsocial sources provide feedback without someone communicating that information. The opening paragraph to this section mentioned that call centres have various forms of nonsocial feedback, such as electronic displays showing how many callers are waiting and the average time they have been waiting.[47] Some professionals have "executive dashboards" on their computer screens that display the latest measures of sales, inventory, and other indicators of corporate success. The job itself can be a nonsocial source of feedback. Many employees see the results of their work effort while making a product or providing a service where good and poor performance is fairly obvious.

Social sources of feedback include supervisors, clients, co-workers, and anyone else who communicates information about the employee's behaviour or results. Supervisors in some call centres meet with each employee a few times each month to review monitored calls and discuss ways to improve those events. In most other organizations, employees receive formal feedback maybe once or twice each year, but informal feedback occurs more often. Customer surveys have become a popular form of feedback for teams of employees, such as everyone who works at a bank branch.

Multisource (360-degree) feedback   Telus Corporation, Radical Entertainment, and many other Canadian firms try to improve the quality of performance feedback by introducing a process called **multisource (360-degree) feedback**. As the name implies, multisource feedback is information about an employee's performance collected from a full circle of people, including subordinates, peers, supervisors, and customers. Nearly half of Canada's largest firms use multisource feedback, typically for managers rather than for nonmanagement employees. Most plans (87 percent) also give employees complete freedom to choose who will rate them.[48]

Research suggests that multisource feedback tends to provide more complete and accurate information than feedback from a supervisor alone. It is particularly useful when the supervisor is unable to observe the employee's behaviour or performance throughout the year. Lower level employees also feel a greater sense of fairness and open communication when they are able to provide upward feedback about their boss's performance.[49]

However, as Connections 5.1 reveals, multisource feedback also creates challenges. Having several people review so many other people can be expensive and time-consuming. With multiple opinions, the 360-degree process can also produce ambiguous and conflicting feedback, so employees may require guidance to interpret

multisource (360-degree) feedback
Performance feedback received from a full circle of people around an employee.

The Perils of Multisource Feedback

Karim Mamdani devoted a lot of time to shoring up financial controls during his first year as corporate controller at Toronto-based University Health Network. He thought department managers also saw the need for these changes, until he received his first 360-degree performance evaluation. "I thought we were all on the same page until the 360 revealed that one department head found my approach overly bureaucratic," Mamdani recalls. This feedback was valuable because he redoubled his effort to understand concerns among departmental managers and to explain the controls more carefully.

Mamdani's experience with 360-degree feedback turned out well, but others say there is a dark side to multisource feedback. One concern is that the feedback must be anonymous; otherwise the evaluations that people write could affect their future in the organization. "[360-degree feedback] is very sensitive information that, if put in the wrong hands, could be career making or breaking," acknowledges Sofia Theodorou, director of organizational development at Rogers Communications. To maintain confidentiality, the Canadian cable company relies on a consulting firm to operate the 360-degree process.

A Concordia University study of more than 100 Canadian firms revealed that time consumption is the biggest complaint with the 360-degree process. Upper-level managers, in particular, receive numerous invitations from lower level staff to complete feedback forms. One Canadian manager was said to have received more than 3,000 feedback requests! The survey found that the politics of multisource feedback is another issue. "Some raters abuse the system and used it to stab colleagues," warned one manager who may have been burned by the process.

Multisource feedback is also a challenge for those with weak egos. "Initially you do take it personally," admits Russell Huerta, a senior accounts manager at software maker Autodesk. "[360-degree feedback] is meant to be constructive, but you have to internally battle that." Huerta manages his emotional reaction to the feedback by pretending the advice is about someone else, then learning how to improve his own behaviour from that information. "It's almost an out-of-body experience, to take your mind and your emotions out of it," he recommends.

Sources: P. Kamen, "The Way That You Use It," *CMA Management*, April 2003, pp. 10–12; M. Debrayen and S. Brutus, "Learning from Other's 360-Degree Experiences," *Canadian HR Reporter*, February 10, 2003, pp. 18–19; S. Watkins, "Ever Wanted to Review the Boss?" *Investor's Business Daily*, August 10, 2001, p. A1.

---

the results. A third concern is that peers may provide inflated rather than accurate feedback to avoid conflicts over the forthcoming year. A final concern is that critical feedback from many people can create stronger emotional reaction than if the critical judgment originates from just one person (your boss).[50]

executive coaching

A helping relationship using behavioural methods to assist clients in identifying and achieving goals for their professional performance and personal satisfaction.

Executive coaching Another rapidly growing practice involving feedback and motivation is **executive coaching**, which uses a wide variety of behavioural methods to assist clients in identifying and achieving goals for their performance and well-being. Executive coaching is usually conducted by an external consultant and is essentially one-on-one "just-in-time" personal development using feedback and other techniques. Coaches do not provide answers to the employee's problems. Rather, they are "thought partners" who offer more accurate feedback, open dialogue, and constructive encouragement to improve the client's performance and personal well-being.

The evidence so far is that executives who work with an executive coach perform better than those who do not. Coaching comes in many forms, so this positive result should be treated cautiously. Still, executive coaching is spreading throughout Canadian organizations, including Aventis Pasteur, Providence Health Care, B.C. Hydro, and Nisbett Burns. Many participants are also quick to praise executive coaching. "I was better at my job and more efficient instantly," says Michael Nott, a manager at financial services company Great Pacific Management in Vancouver. "At the end of one year, I couldn't believe the improvement."[51]

Choosing feedback sources   With so many sources of feedback—executive coaching, multisource feedback, executive dashboards, customer surveys, equipment gauges, nonverbal communication from your boss, and so on—which one works best under which conditions? The preferred feedback source depends on the purpose of the information. To learn about their progress toward goal accomplishment, employees usually prefer nonsocial feedback sources, such as computer printouts or feedback directly from the job. This is because information from nonsocial sources is considered more accurate than information from social sources. Corrective feedback from nonsocial sources is also less damaging to self-esteem. This is probably just as well because social sources tend to delay negative information, leave some of it out, and distort the bad news in a positive way.[52] When employees want to improve their self-image, they seek out positive feedback from social sources. It feels better to have co-workers say that you are performing the job well than to discover this from a computer printout.

EVALUATING GOAL SETTING AND FEEDBACK

A recent survey of organizational behaviour researchers identified goal setting as one of the top OB theories in terms of validity and usefulness.[53] This high score is not surprising given the impressive research support and wide application of this concept in a variety of settings. In partnership with goal setting, feedback also has an excellent reputation for improving employee motivation and performance.

Nevertheless, both goal setting and feedback have a few limitations.[54] One problem is that combining goals with monetary incentives motivates many employees to set up easy rather than difficult goals. In some cases, employees have negotiated goals with their supervisor that have already been completed! Another limitation is that goal setting potentially focuses employees on a narrow subset of measurable performance indicators while ignoring aspects of job performance that are difficult to measure. The saying, "What gets measured, gets done" applies here. A third problem is that setting performance goals is effective in established jobs, but seems to interfere with the learning process in new, complex jobs. Thus, we need to be careful not to apply goal setting where an intense learning process is occurring.

■ ORGANIZATIONAL JUSTICE

Taiwan has legislation guaranteeing gender equality in the workplace, but over half of the 4,000 working women recently surveyed in that country say men get paid more for doing the same work. "It's unfair," says Hsieh Hsuen-Hui, a senior trade specialist at an export company in Taipei. "Monthly salaries that male colleagues receive are about NT$10,000 (Cdn$400) higher than what I get, even though we are doing the same job." Hsieh's boss believes that men should be paid higher wages since they are more flexible when it comes to overseas business travel. Some employers openly say they pay men more because they have a greater need for income as the breadwinners. But Hsieh and other women claim that neither reason justifies the significant pay differences. "We have tried to express our dissatisfaction, but our boss says those are the rules of the game and anyone who doesn't agree can just leave," says Hsieh.[55]

Most corporate leaders know that treating employees fairly is both morally correct and good for employee motivation, loyalty, and well-being. Yet, the feelings of injustice that Hsieh Hsuen-Hui describes are regular occurrences in a variety of situations. To minimize these incidents, we need to first understand that there are two forms of organizational justice: distributive justice and procedural justice.[56] **Distributive justice** refers to perceived fairness in the outcomes we receive relative to our contributions and the outcomes and contributions of others. **Procedural justice**, on the other hand, refers to fairness of the procedures used to decide the distribution of resources. Hsieh Hsuen-Hui felt distributive injustice because male colleagues were paid significantly more than she was, even though their contribution to the organization was comparable. Hsieh also experienced procedural injustice because of the way her boss responded to her concerns.

DISTRIBUTIVE JUSTICE AND EQUITY THEORY

The first thing we usually think about and experience in situations of injustice is distributive injustice—the belief (and its emotional response) that the distribution of pay and other outcomes is unfair. What is considered "fair" varies with each person and situation. We apply an *equality principle* when we believe that everyone in the group should receive the same outcomes. Companies apply this principle when allocating some employee benefits and parking spaces, for example. The *need principle* is applied when we believe that those with the greatest need should receive more outcomes than others with less need. As mentioned in the story above, some Taiwanese employers use the need principle to justify paying men more than women; they say men need the higher pay as family bread winners. Hsieh Hsuen-Hui applied the *equity principle* by inferring that people should be paid in proportion to their contribution. The equity principle is the most common distributive justice rule in organizational settings, so let's look at it in more detail.

Elements of equity theory   To explain how the equity principle operates in our heads, OB scholars developed **equity theory**, which says that employees determine feelings of equity by comparing their own outcome/input ratio to the outcome/input ratio of some other person.[57] The outcome/input ratio is the value of the outcomes you receive divided by the value of inputs you provide in the exchange relationship. Hsieh Hsuen-Hui probably included her level of responsibility, effort, and performance as inputs. Other inputs might include skills, experience, status, and amount of time worked. Outcomes are the things employees receive from the organization in exchange for the inputs. In the case involving Hsieh Hsuen-Hui, the main outcome is the paycheque. Some other outcomes might be promotions, recognition, or an office with a window.

Equity theory states that we compare our outcome/input ratio with a comparison other.[58] In our earlier example, Hsieh Hsuen-Hui compared herself with her male colleagues in similar positions. However, the comparison other may be another person, group of people, or even yourself in the past. It may be someone in the same job, another job, or another organization. Chief executives have no direct comparison within the firm, so they tend to compare themselves with their counterparts in other organizations. Some research suggests that employees frequently collect information on several referents to form a "generalized" comparison other.[59] For the most part, however, the comparison other varies from one person to the next and is not easily identifiable.

Equity evaluation   We form an equity evaluation after determining our own outcome/input ratio and comparing this with the comparison other's ratio. Let's con-

---

distributive justice
The perceived fairness in outcomes we receive relative to our contributions and the outcomes and contributions of others.

procedural justice
The fairness of the procedures used to decide the distributions of resources.

equity theory
Theory that explains how people develop perceptions of fairness in the distribution and exchange of resources.

■ **EXHIBIT 5.6**   Equity theory model

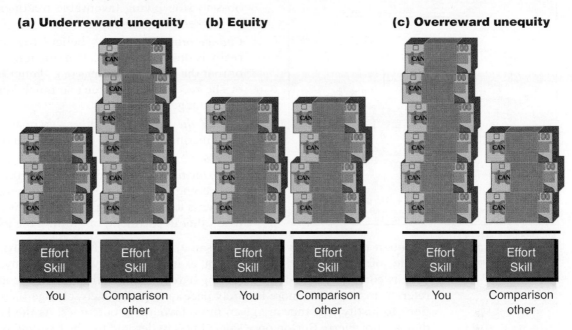

(a) Underreward unequity   (b) Equity   (c) Overreward unequity

sider the experience of Hsieh Hsuen-Hui again. Hsieh feels underreward inequity because her male counterparts receive higher outcomes (pay) for inputs that are, at best, comparable to what she contributes. Exhibit 5.6 (a) illustrates this condition.

In the equity condition, Hsieh would believe that her outcome/input ratio is similar to the ratio of male colleagues. Specifically, if she believes that she provides the same inputs as the male senior trade specialists, then she would feel equity if both men and women received the same pay and other outcomes (see Exhibit 5.6 (b)). If the male senior trade specialists claim they make a greater contribution because they have more flexibility, then they would have feelings of equity only if they receive proportionally more pay than Hsieh and other female trade specialists. It is also possible that some male trade specialists experience overreward inequity (Exhibit 5.6 (c)). They would feel that their jobs have the same value as Hsieh's job, yet they earn more money. However, overreward inequity isn't as common as underreward inequity.

Correcting inequity feelings   We experience an emotional tension with perceived inequities, and, when sufficiently strong, the tension motivates us to reduce the inequities. But what are we motivated to do to reduce this tension? Research has identified several reactions that people have to inequity. Some actions are reasonable, whereas others are dysfunctional; some are illegal, such as theft and sabotage. Here are the main ways that people correct inequity feelings when they are underrewarded compared to a co-worker (comparison other):[60]

■ *Reduce our inputs*—perform at a lower level, give fewer helpful suggestions, engage in less organizational citizenship behaviour
■ *Increase our outcomes*—ask for a pay increase, make unauthorized use of company resources
■ *Increase comparison other's inputs*—subtly ask the better off co-worker to do a larger share of the work to justify his/her higher pay or other outcomes

"O.K., if you can't see your way to giving me a pay raise, how about giving Parkerson a pay cut?"

■ *Reduce comparison other's outcomes*—ask the boss to stop giving favourable treatment to the co-worker (see cartoon)

■ *Change our perceptions*—believe the co-worker really is doing more (e.g., working longer hours), or that the higher outcomes (e.g., better office) he or she receives really aren't so much better than what you get

■ *Change the comparison other*—compare yourself to someone else closer to your situation (job duties, pay scale)

■ *Leave the field*—avoid thinking about the inequity by keeping away from the office where the co-worker is located, taking more sick leave, moving to another department, or quitting the job

Although the categories remain the same, people who feel overreward inequity would, of course, act differently. For example, overrewarded employees don't usually correct this tension by working harder. Instead, they might encourage the referent to work at a more leisurely pace or, equally likely, change their perceptions to justify why they are given more favourable outcomes. As the late Canadian author Pierre Burton once said: "I was underpaid for the first half of my life. I don't mind being overpaid for the second half."[61]

equity sensitivity
A person's outcome/input preferences and reaction to various outcome/input ratios.

Individual differences: equity sensitivity   Thus far, we have described equity theory as though everyone has the same feelings of inequity in a particular situation. The reality, however, is that people vary in their **equity sensitivity**, that is, their outcome/input preferences and reaction to various outcome/input ratios.[62] At one end of the equity sensitivity continuum are the "benevolents"—people who are tolerant of situations where they are underrewarded. They might still prefer equal outcome/input ratios, but they don't mind if others receive more than they do for the same inputs. In the middle are people who fit the standard equity theory model. These "equity sensitives" want their outcome/input ratio to be equal to the outcome/input ratio of the comparison other. Equity sensitives feel increasing inequity as the ratios become different. At the other end are the "entitleds." These people feel more comfortable in situations where they receive proportionately more than others. They might accept having the same outcome/input ratio as others, but they would prefer receiving more than others performing the same work.[63]

Evaluating equity theory   Equity theory is widely studied and quite successful at predicting various situations involving feelings of workplace injustice, such as major baseball league salary disputes and remuneration of British CEOs.[64] Feelings of inequity are regular occurrences in every workplace. Some tensions are minor and temporary misunderstandings of the situation; others produce emotions or worse, major theft and sabotage of company resources. Feelings of inequity are based on the moral principle of distributive justice (see Chapter 2), so companies that act unfairly toward their employees also face the charge of unethical conduct. GLOBAL Connections 5.2 describes a popular movement in the U.K. where employees (and shareholders) publicly berate "fat cat" CEOs for being paid much more than they are worth when compared to the paycheques of their staff. These

Protesting Unfair "Fat Cat" Pay in the U.K.

Cats have become an increasingly common sight at corporate annual general meetings throughout the United Kingdom. More precisely, dozens of people have been dressing up as "fat cats" in business suits as a way of protesting the generous paycheques of British executives. Labour unions are behind many of these antics, but institutional investors and private shareholders are also expressing their feelings of unfairness by voting against executive remuneration.

Over half of GlaxoSmithKline's shareholders opposed a Cdn$45-million golden parachute that chief executive Jean-Pierre Garnier would be paid if fired from the pharmaceutical giant. A larger percentage of shareholders also opposed or abstained from voting for overly generous pay packages for executives at advertising group WPP and engineering group BAE Systems.

Critics say there is plenty of reason for the theatrics and shareholder unrest against executive pay. Piers Morgan was ousted as editor of the *Daily Mirror* after the British tabloid lost 800,000 readers and faced an embarrassing incident of fake photos of Iraqi prisoner abuse while under Morgan's watch. In spite of these failings, Morgan was sent out the door with Cdn$4 million to buy out the remaining two years of his contract. Sir Phillip Watts didn't suffer too badly, either, with his Cdn$2.3-million farewell handshake from Shell. Under Watts' command, the Anglo-Dutch oil giant admitted overstating its gas and oil reserves by more than 20 percent.

Employees and commuters were also miffed recently when Network Rail bosses gave themselves healthy

British protesters express their anger over unfair executive pay by dressing as "fat cats" in business suits outside the company's annual general meetings. © *Simon Clark*

bonuses soon after hundreds of staff were laid off. The publicly owned rail company's chief executive and deputy officer each received a bonus of over Cdn $200,000. "It is hard to understand how Network Rail bosses can sack 650 experienced managers last year to save costs and justify six figure bonuses for themselves six months later," complains a spokesperson for the union representing the company's office staff.

Sources: K. Walker, "Rail Fat Cats Scandal," *The Express* (London), June 3, 2004, p. 10; H. Jones, "Fat Cats Rewarded for Failure," *The Express* (London), August 28, 2004, pp. 48–49; W. Wallace, "British Shareholders Battle 'American-Style' Exec Pay," *Los Angeles Times*, June 2, 2003, p. 5; "Handfuls of Protesters Decrying 'Fat Cat' Paycheques," *Canadian Press*, May 25, 2003; "Heads, They Win," *The Guardian*, May 9, 2003.

exhibitions aren't just appealing to the logic of inequity; they are publicly leveraging the moral argument against overpaid chief executives.

In spite of its research support, equity theory has a few limitations. One concern is that the theory isn't sufficiently specific to predict employee motivation and behaviour. It doesn't indicate which inputs or outcomes are most valuable, and it doesn't identify the comparison other against which the outcome/input ratio is evaluated. These vague and highly flexible elements may explain why OB scholars think equity theory is highly valid but only moderately useful.[65]

A second problem is that equity theory incorrectly assumes people are individualistic, rational, and selfish. In reality, people are social creatures who define themselves as members of various group memberships (see social identity theory in Chapter 3). They share goals with other members of these groups and commit themselves to the norms of their groups. A third limitation is that recent studies have found that equity theory accounts for only some of our feelings of fairness or justice in the workplace. Experts now say that procedural justice, which we look at next, is at least as important as distributive justice.

PROCEDURAL JUSTICE

For many years, OB researchers believed that distributive justice was more important than procedural justice in explaining employee motivation, attitudes, and behaviour. This belief was based on the assumption that people are driven mainly by self-interest, so they try to maximize their personal outcomes. Today, we know that people seek justice for its own sake, not just as a means to improve their paycheque. Thus, procedural justice seems to be as important as (some experts say more important than) distributive justice in explaining employee attitudes, motivation, and behaviour.[66]

Structural rules of justice   Procedural justice is influenced by both structural rules and social rules (see Exhibit 5.7).[67] Structural rules represent the policies and practices that decision makers should follow. The most frequently identified structural rule in procedural justice research is people's belief that they should have a "voice" in the decision process.[68] Voice allows employees to convey what they believe are relevant facts and views to the decision maker. Voice also provides a "value-expressive" function; employees tend to feel better after having an opportunity to speak their mind. Other structural rules are that the decision maker is unbiased, relies on complete and accurate information, applies existing policies consistently, has listened to all sides of the dispute, and allows the decision to be appealed to a higher authority.[69]

■ **EXHIBIT 5.7**   Components of organizational justice

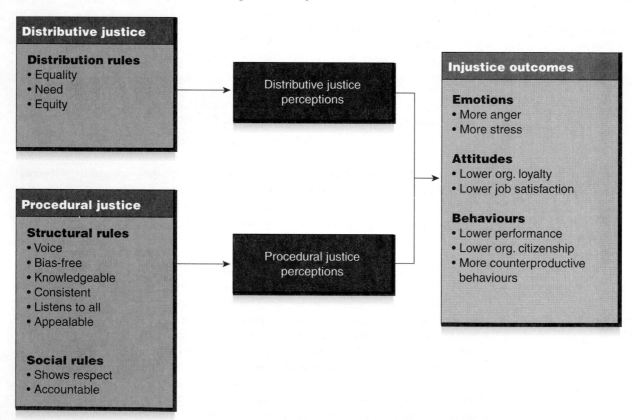

Social rules of justice Along with structural rules, procedural justice is influenced by social rules, that is, how well the decision maker treats employees during the process. The two key social rules are respect and accountability. Employees feel greater procedural justice when they are treated with respect. For instance, one Canadian study found that nonwhite nurses who experienced racism tended to file grievances only after experiencing disrespectful treatment in their attempt to resolve the racist situation. Similarly, another study found that employees with repetitive strain injuries were more likely to file workers' compensation claims after experiencing disrespectful behaviour from management. According to another recent Canadian study, employees have stronger feelings of injustice when the manager has a reputation of treating people unfairly most of the time.[70]

The other social rule that has attracted attention is accountability. People believe that they are entitled to explanations about decisions, particularly when the results have potentially negative consequences for them. For instance, suppose a co-worker receives a better office than you do (distributive injustice). Chances are, you will feel less injustice after hearing the decision maker's explanation for that decision.

Consequences of procedural injustice Procedural justice has a strong influence on a person's emotions and motivation. Employees tend to experience anger toward the source of the injustice, which generates various response behaviours that scholars categorize as either withdrawal or aggression.[71] Notice how these response behaviours are similar to the fight-or-flight responses described earlier in the chapter regarding situations that activate our drive to defend. Withdrawal behaviours might include avoiding those who acted unjustly or being less willing to comply with their future requests. For instance, employees who believe their boss relies on an unfair decision process may be less likely to "walk the extra mile" in the future and might complete any assigned work only at a minimal standard.

Aggressive responses to procedural injustice include several counterproductive work behaviours, such as sabotage, theft, conflict, and acts of violence.[72] However, most employees who experience injustice respond with milder forms of retaliation, such as showing indignation and denouncing the decision maker's competence. Research suggests that being treated unfairly undermines our self-esteem and social status, particularly when others see that we have been unjustly treated. Consequently, employees retaliate to restore their self-esteem and reinstate their status and power in the relationship with the perpetrator of the injustice. Employees also engage in these counterproductive behaviours to educate the decision maker, thereby minimizing the chance of future injustices.[73]

ORGANIZATIONAL JUSTICE IN PRACTICE

One of the clearest lessons from equity theory is that we need to continually treat people fairly in the distribution of organizational rewards. Unfortunately, this is perhaps one of life's greatest challenges because most of us seem to have unique opinions about the value of inputs and outcomes. Decision makers need to carefully understand these dynamics along with the distribution rules—equity, equality, or need—that the organization wants to apply. From the procedural justice literature, we can see that justice also depends on whether or not employees believe the decision-making process follows a fair set of rules and that they are personally treated fairly in that process.

In spite of the many challenges of creating justice in the workplace, managers can improve their procedural fairness through training programs. In one study, supervisors participated in role-play exercises to develop several procedural justice practices in the disciplinary process, such as maintaining the employee's privacy, giving employees some control over the process, avoiding arbitrariness, and exhibiting a supportive demeanour. Judges subsequently rated supervisors who received the procedural justice training as behaving more fairly than supervisors who did not receive the training. In another study, managers received procedural justice training through lectures, case studies, role playing, and discussion. Three months later, subordinates of the trained managers had significantly higher organizational citizenship behaviours than the subordinates of managers who did not receive procedural justice training.[74] Overall, it seems that justice can be improved in the workplace.

CHAPTER SUMMARY

Motivation refers to the forces within a person that affect his or her direction, intensity, and persistence of voluntary behaviour in the workplace. Motivation has become more challenging because of an increasingly turbulent work environment, the removal of direct supervision as a motivational instrument, and the lack of understanding about what motivates the new generations of people entering the workforce.

Maslow's needs hierarchy groups needs into a hierarchy of five levels and states that the lowest needs are initially most important, but higher needs become more important as the lower ones are satisfied. Although very popular, the theory lacks research support, as does ERG theory, which attempted to overcome some of the limitations in Maslow's needs hierarchy. Both models assume that everyone has the same hierarchy, whereas the emerging evidence suggests that needs hierarchies vary from one person to the next based on their social identity and personal values.

Four-drive theory states that everyone has four innate drives—the drive to acquire, bond, learn, and defend. These drives create emotional markers that motivate us. The drives generate competing emotions, however, so we consciously reconcile these competing impulses through a skill set that considers social norms, past experience, and personal values. Four-drive theory offers considerable potential for understanding employee motivation, but it still requires clarification and research to understand how people translate competing emotions into motivated behaviour.

McClelland's learned needs theory argues that needs can be strengthened through learning. The three needs studied in this respect have been need for achievement, need for power, and need for affiliation.

The practical implication of needs/drives-based motivation theories is that corporate leaders need to ensure that everyone in the workplace is able to regularly fulfill all four drives, that organizations should avoid too much or too little opportunity to fulfill each drive, and that employees should be offered a choice of rewards rather than given the same reward as everyone else.

Expectancy theory states that work effort is determined by the perception that effort will result in a particular level of performance (E-to-P expectancy), the perception that a specific behaviour or performance level will lead to specific outcomes (P-to-O expectancy), and the valences that the person feels for those outcomes. The E-to-P expectancy increases by improving the employee's ability and confidence to perform the job. The P-to-O expectancy increases by measuring performance accurately, distributing higher rewards to better performers, and showing employees that rewards are performance-based. Outcome valences increase by finding out what employees want and using these resources as rewards.

Goal setting is the process of motivating employees and clarifying their role perceptions by establishing performance objectives. Goals are more effective when they are specific, relevant, and challenging; have employee commitment; and are accompanied by meaningful feedback. Participative goal setting is important in some situations. Effective feedback is specific, relevant, timely, credible, and sufficiently frequent (which depends on the length of the task cycle and the employee's knowledge/experience with the task). Two increasingly popular forms of feedback are multisource (360-degree) assessment and executive coaching. Feedback from nonsocial sources is also beneficial.

Organizational justice consists of distributive justice (perceived fairness in the outcomes we receive relative to our contributions and the outcomes and contributions of others) and procedural justice (fairness of the procedures used to decide the distribution of resources). Equity theory, which considers the most common principle applied in distributive justice, has four elements: outcome/input ratio, comparison other, equity evaluation, and consequences of inequity. The theory also explains what people are motivated to do when they feel inequitably treated. Equity sensitivity is a personal characteristics that explains why people react differently to varying degrees of inequity.

Procedural justice is influenced by both structural rules and social rules. Structural rules represent the policies and practices that decision makers should follow; the most frequently identified is giving employees "voice" in the decision process. Social rules refer to standards of interpersonal conduct between employees and decision makers; they are best observed by showing respect and providing accountability for decisions. Procedural justice is as important as distributive justice, and it influences organizational commitment, trust, and various withdrawal and aggression behaviours.

KEY TERMS

distributive justice, p. 148

drives, p. 131

equity sensitivity, p. 150

equity theory, p. 148

ERG theory, p. 133

executive coaching, p. 146

expectancy theory, p. 139

feedback, p. 143

four-drive theory, p. 133

goal setting, p. 142

Maslow's needs hierarchy theory, p. 131

motivation, p. 130

multisource (360-degree) feedback, p. 145

need for achievement (nAch), p. 137

need for affiliation (nAff), p. 137

need for power (nPow), p. 137

needs, p. 131

procedural justice, p. 148

self-actualization, p. 131

valence, p. 140

DISCUSSION QUESTIONS

1. This chapter begins by suggesting that motivating employees has become more challenging in recent years, partly because younger employees (Generation-X and Generation-Y) have different expectations than baby boomers. How do you think these younger and older generation groups differ in their expectations? Generally speaking, what would motivate a typical Generation-Y (under 25 years old) at work more than a typical baby boomer (over 45 years old)?

2. Four-drive theory is conceptually different from the Maslow's needs hierarchy (as well as ERG theory) in several ways. Describe these differences. At the same time, needs are typically based on drives, so the four drives should parallel the seven needs that Maslow identified (five in the hierarchy and two additional needs). Map Maslow's needs onto the four drives in four-drive theory.

3. Use all three components of expectancy theory to explain why some employees are motivated to show up for work during a snowstorm whereas others make no effort to leave their home.

4. What are the limitations of expectancy theory in predicting an individual's work effort and behaviour?

5. Using your knowledge of the characteristics of effective goals, establish two meaningful goals related to your performance in this class.

6. When do employees prefer feedback from nonsocial rather than social sources? Explain why nonsocial sources are preferred under these conditions.

7. Several service representatives are upset that the newly hired representative with no previous experience will be paid $3,000 a year above the usual starting salary in the pay range. The department manager explained that the new hire would not accept the entry-level rate, so the company raised the offer by $3,000. All five reps currently earn salaries near the top of the scale ($15,000 higher than the new recruit), although they all started at the minimum starting salary a few years earlier. Use equity theory to explain why the five service representatives feel inequity in this situation.

8. Organizational injustice can occur in the classroom as well as in the workplace. Identify classroom situations in which you experienced feelings of injustice. What can instructors do to maintain an environment that fosters both distributive and procedural justice?

CASE STUDY 5.1

NO FAIR PAY IN *THIS* PLACE

By Susan Meredith, Selkirk College.

It was my degree in business administration that Mr. James admired when he hired me to manage his western satellite office in B.C. The focus of my work was planning and problem solving with the occasional crisis intervention. I was also responsible for supervising several employees, including our public relations rep, Dan Donaldson. Dan's job was to write the press releases and schedule all the public appointments and appearances for Mr. James while he was in town. Dan had a double degree in journalism and political science. I often wondered if his education had prepared him for the office politics that would become so much a part of our lives while working for Mr. James at the other end of the country from Toronto where our head office was located.

I was never really sure why the head office was in Toronto as no product was produced and virtually no service rendered from Toronto yet it was the heart of the organization. On the other hand, the front lines of the job were here in B.C. where the client base was centred, yet our work was treated as insignificant. Was it because we didn't generate any revenue? We certainly felt that our customer base was obvious proof that our work was critical to the organization. So important in fact that without us to represent the firm regionally, there would be no customer contact at all, therefore no business—period.

One day during an unusual but welcomed pause from the incessant demands of the telephone, fax, and walk-in traffic, Dan and I were complaining about our jobs. We started comparing them with Helen's, our one colleague at head office. What was it she did, anyway? We wondered what our days would be like without the heavy load of unhappy clients and their urgent demands and especially without the stress. While we both knew that without these complaining customers neither of us would have a job, there were some days when that really didn't seem like a bad thing.

It was just prior to one of Mr. James' hectic but brief cross-country check ups that this unexpected lull happened. In the process of confirming the schedule with Dan we began to discuss our "comparison other"—the horrible head office honcho,

Helen. Inevitably we found ourselves speculating in a not very complimentary way about Helen's interpersonal skills, or rather, lack of them. Dan wanted to know if I knew how much Helen was making.

No, how could I? This had always been a forbidden topic of discussion. At the time of hiring, Mr. James made a point of emphatically instructing each new person not to discuss their salary with any other employees. The justification had always been that we wouldn't want to upset the others, would we?

While I was responsible for submitting everyone's time sheets, in the eight months I'd been with Mr. James I had never dared ask anyone anything about their salaries. Yet, to my surprise I didn't hesitate telling Dan that I was earning $30,000 a year, which was pretty disappointing since I had 20 years of customer relations and supervisory experience. Plus with my recent honours degree in business I had been hoping to make more than before I spent four hard years in university.

Dan couldn't believe I was only making $30,000. He had just assumed I was making the same as Horrible Helen who had virtually no customer contact, no one to supervise, no university education, and no seniority. Dan swore he knew for certain Helen was making $40,000 in only 10 months instead of my 12. That worked out to an annual salary of $48,000. I was getting really upset—really fast!

Dan and I hashed this about until the boss came in. I had to decide if I believed Dan and if so what was I going to do. I chose to wait and seek proof one way or the other. Not an easy task in this secrecy shrouded environment. As it turned out Dan would be going to Toronto when the boss was returning next week. Feeling responsible for bringing up the whole upsetting subject, Dan promised to find and send me a copy of Helen's contract.

By the time I saw the contract for myself I had worked myself into quite a dither. I stewed and fretted and when I couldn't stand it anymore I scheduled a meeting with the boss during his next monthly check up session. I was determined that I would convince him of my superior performance, academic achievements, work experience, and interpersonal skills.

When the day came, I was ready. I was so ready that I barely waited for Mr. James to get seated before I began. However, I'd barely gotten started when Mr. James quietly agreed. He agreed so readily that I didn't have to finish my arguments. I didn't have to persuade him of anything. Stunned I stopped, searching for something nice to say, and that's when he said in his quiet air of dismissal— "Nobody said it was fair, but that's what staff earn in Toronto and that's what you are worth out here." All he was interested in was how I had found out about Helen's salary.

That was the end of the discussion. There was no validation. No explanation and no satisfaction. Mr. James apparently couldn't care less how I felt. He certainly ignored me and as far as I was concerned that meant he ignored his investment in me. I knew I'd never work as hard for him as I had in the past. For that matter I didn't want to work for him at all.

I'm embarrassed to say my attitude took a serious nosedive and my work habits did too. Within weeks my output matched my salary—about $18,000 a year less than what I had been doing previously. I had a really hard time taking any calls from Helen. I wanted to scream at her and she didn't even know. It wasn't just the money, either. If Mr. James had said anything about my dedication, my hard work, the reputation building I had accomplished—anything at all, I might have been able to get over the injustice. Since none of that happened, I left before my next evaluation. Still he said nothing.

Discussion Questions

1. What are some of the elements that contributed to this employee's feelings of inequality?

2. Why was the Toronto worker considered a "comparison other" but not the co-worker in B.C?

3. How was the inequity solved?

4. What other factors may have contributed to the job dissatisfaction experienced by these two employees?

T E A M   E X E R C I S E   5.2

NEEDS PRIORITY EXERCISE

Purpose   This class exercise is designed to help you understand the characteristics and contingencies of employee needs in the workplace

Instructions

■ *Step 1:* The table below lists in alphabetical order 14 characteristics of the job or work environment. Working alone, use the far left column to rank order these characteristics in terms of how important they are to you personally. Write in "1" beside the most important characteristic, "2" for the second most important, and so on through to "14" for the least important characteristic on this list.

■ *Step 2:* In the second column, rank order these characteristics in the order that you think human resource managers believe are important for their employees.

■ *Step 3:* Your instructor will provide results of a recent large-scale survey of employees. When these results are presented, identify the reasons for any noticeable differences. Relate these differences to your understanding of the emerging view of employee needs and drives in work settings.

Importance to YOU	What HR Managers Believe are Important to Employees	
————	————	Autonomy and independence
————	————	Benefits (health care, dental, etc.)
————	————	Career development opportunities
————	————	Communication between employees and senior mgt
————	————	Compensation/pay
————	————	Feeling safe in the work environment
————	————	Flexibility to balance work/life issues
————	————	Job security
————	————	Job specific training
————	————	Management recognition of employee job performance
————	————	Opportunities to use skills/abilities
————	————	Organization's commitment to professional development
————	————	Relationship with immediate supervisor
————	————	The work itself

SELF-ASSESSMENT EXERCISE   5.3

MEASURING YOUR EQUITY SENSITIVITY

Purpose This self-assessment is designed to help you estimate your level of equity sensitivity.

Instructions Read each of the statements below and circle the response that you believe best reflects your position regarding each statement. Then use the scoring key in Appendix B to calcu-

late your results. This exercise is completed alone so students assess themselves honestly without concerns of social comparison. However, class discussion will focus on equity theory and the effect of equity sensitivity on perceptions of fairness in the workplace.

EQUITY PREFERENCE QUESTIONNAIRE

To what extent do you agree or disagree that...	Strongly Agree ▼	Agree ▼	Neutral ▼	Disagree ▼	Strongly Disagree ▼
1. I prefer to do as little as possible at work while getting as much as I can from my employer.	1	2	3	4	5
2. I am most satisfied at work when I have to do as little as possible.	1	2	3	4	5
3. When I am at my job, I think of ways to get out of work.	1	2	3	4	5
4. If I could get away with it, I would try to work just a little bit slower than the boss expects.	1	2	3	4	5
5. It is really satisfying to me when I can get something for nothing at work.	1	2	3	4	5

To what extent do you agree or disagree that...	Strongly Agree ▼	Agree ▼	Neutral ▼	Disagree ▼	Strongly Disagree ▼
6. It is the smart employee who gets as much as he/she can while giving as little as possible in return.	1	2	3	4	5
7. Employees who are more concerned about what they can get from their employer rather than what they can give to their employer are the wisest.	1	2	3	4	5
8. When I have completed my task for the day, I help out other employees who have yet to complete their tasks.	1	2	3	4	5
9. Even if I receive low wages and poor benefits from my employer, I would still try to do my best at my job.	1	2	3	4	5
10. If I had to work hard all day at my job, I would probably quit.	1	2	3	4	5
11. I feel obligated to do more than I am paid to do at work.	1	2	3	4	5
12. At work, my greatest concern is whether or not I am doing the best job I can.	1	2	3	4	5
13. A job which requires me to be busy during the day is better than a job which allows me a lot of loafing.	1	2	3	4	5
14. At work, I feel uneasy when there is little work for me to do.	1	2	3	4	5
15. I would become very dissatisfied with my job if I had little or no work to do.	1	2	3	4	5
16. All other things being equal, it is better to have a job with a lot of duties and responsibilities than one with few duties and responsibilities.	1	2	3	4	5

Source: K.S. Sauleya and A.G. Bedeian "Equity Sensitivity: Construction of a Measure and Examination of its Psychometric Properties," *Journal of Management*, 26 (September 2000), pp. 885–910.

SELF-ASSESSMENT EXERCISE **5.4**

MEASURING YOUR GROWTH NEED STRENGTH

Go to the Online Learning Centre to complete this interactive self-assessment.

Purpose This self-assessment is designed to help you estimate your level of growth need strength.

Instructions People differ in the kind of jobs they would most like to hold. This self-assessment gives you a chance to say just what it is about a job that is most important to you. Please indicate which of the two jobs you personally would prefer if you had to make a choice between them. In answering each question, assume that everything else about the jobs is the same. Pay attention only to the characteristics actually listed.

Source: Adapted from the Job Diagnostic Survey, developed by J. R. Hackman and G. R. Oldham. The authors have released any copyright ownership of this scale (see J. R. Hackman and G. Oldham, *Work Redesign* (Reading, MA: Addison-Wesley, 1980), p. 275).

·6·

APPLIED PERFORMANCE
PRACTICES

LEARNING OBJECTIVES

AFTER READING THIS CHAPTER, YOU SHOULD BE ABLE TO:

- Discuss the advantages and disadvantages of the four reward objectives.

- Identify two team- and four organizational-level performance-based rewards.

- Describe five ways to improve reward effectiveness.

- Discuss the advantages and disadvantages of job specialization.

- Diagram the job characteristics model of job design.

- Identify three strategies to improve employee motivation through job design.

- Define empowerment and identify strategies to support empowerment.

- Describe the five elements of self-leadership.

A few years ago, a maintenance employee stormed into the offices of Clive Beddoe, demanding to know why the WestJet co-founder and CEO squandered some of the company's money on a catered barbecue for WestJet's managers at his fishing lodge the previous weekend. The employee was humbled when Beddoe explained that he paid for the party out of his own pocket. "He's like a watchdog, and he hates inequities," says Beddoe of the maintenance employee. "That's the spirit of WestJet."

The spirit of WestJet started a little over a decade ago by Beddoe and three fellow entrepreneurs who were fed up with high fares and dour service on Canada's airlines. Today, the Calgary-based company is the country's second most respected corporation and second largest airline, as well as one of the top North American airlines for on-time performance and customer service.

While many factors explain WestJet's success, the most prominent are the applied performance practices that have created a highly efficient and motivated workforce. First, WestJet carefully selects people who are self-motivated, which allows it to operate at a lower cost with fewer supervisors. Second, WestJet employees (called WestJetters) perform a variety of tasks. For example, flight attendants double as reservation agents and pilots sometimes help clean up the cabin between flights. "I go back and clean and help with the guests," says one WestJet pilot. "It's almost standard operating procedure at WestJet."

Third, WestJetters have considerable autonomy to serve customers more effectively. When a Regina woman developed a sinus infection during her WestJet flight to Edmonton, the ground crew accompanied her and her two young children to hospital, paid for their accommodation in a hotel while staying in an adjourning room, and flew one of the customer's friends

WestJet's success is driven by employees who are rewarded and empowered to serve customers effectively and efficiently.
Courtesy of WestJet

to Edmonton the same night. None of these actions required management approval. "We empower our people to do whatever it takes to satisfy a customer in their best judgment," explains WestJet corporate sales manager Judy Goodman. "Whatever they think is appropriate, they are free to do."

Fourth, WestJet has an ownership culture through profit sharing and employee share ownership. Every employee receives up to 20 percent of the company's profit margin, prorated to their base salary. WestJet also has a generous arrangement in which it matches every dollar employees invest in company stock up to 20 percent of salary. Over 80 percent of WestJetters own company shares. "We've got employees who own the company, whose interests are directly aligned with the interests of the company," says WestJet chief financial officer Sandy Campbell.[1] ■
www.westjet.com

The opening story highlights the importance of rewards, job design, empowerment, and self-leadership in WestJet's success. This chapter looks at each of these applied performance practices. The chapter begins with an overview of financial reward practices, including the different types of rewards and how to implement rewards effectively. Next, we look at the dynamics of job design, including specific job design strategies to motivate employees. We then consider the elements of empowerment as well as conditions that support empowerment. The final part of this chapter explains how employees manage their own performance through self-leadership.

▪ FINANCIAL REWARD PRACTICES

Financial rewards are probably the oldest—and certainly the most fundamental—applied performance practice in organizational settings. At the most basic level, financial rewards represent a form of exchange; employees provide their labour, skill, and knowledge in return for money and benefits from the organization. From this perspective, money and related rewards align employee goals with organizational goals.

However, financial rewards do much more than pay employees back for their contributions to organizational objectives. One study reported that pay has multiple meanings to Canadian managers. It is a symbol of success, a reinforcer and motivator, a reflection of one's performance, and a source of reduced anxiety. With so many different purposes, it is little wonder that people rank pay and benefits as two of the most important features in the employment relationship.[2]

The value and meaning of money also varies considerably from one person to the next. One large-scale survey revealed that men in almost all of the 43 countries studied attach more importance or value to money than do women. This result is consistent with public opinion polls reporting that money has a higher priority for men than for women, particularly as a symbol of power and status.[3] Cultural values also seem to influence the meaning and value of money. People in countries with a long-term orientation and high power distance (such as China and Japan) tend to have a high respect and priority for money, whereas people in countries with a strong egalitarian culture (such as Australia, New Zealand, and Scandinavian countries) are discouraged from openly talking about money or displaying their personal wealth.[4]

Financial rewards come in many forms, which can be organized into the four specific objectives identified in Exhibit 6.1: membership and seniority, job status, competencies, and performance.

MEMBERSHIP- AND SENIORITY-BASED REWARDS

Membership- and seniority-based rewards (sometimes called "pay for pulse") represent the largest part of most paycheques. Some employee benefits, such as health care, remain the same for everyone, whereas others increase with seniority. For instance, Canadian fashion guru Peter Nygard recently handed out $10,000 cheques to each of his 107 longest-serving Winnipeg employees.[5] These rewards tend to attract job applicants (particularly those who desire predictable income), reduce stress, and may reduce turnover. However, they do not directly motivate job performance; on the contrary, they discourage poor performers from seeking out work better suited to their abilities. Instead, the good performers are lured to better-paying jobs. Some of these rewards are also golden handcuffs which, as we learned in Chapter 4, can potentially weaken job performance by creating continuance commitment.

■ **EXHIBIT 6.1**   Reward objectives, advantages, and disadvantages

Reward objective	Sample Rewards	Advantages	Disadvantages

Membership/seniority	• Fixed pay
	• Most employee benefits
	• Paid time off
		• May attract applicants
		• Minimizes stress
		  of insecurity
		• Reduces turnover
			• Doesn't directly
			  motivate performance
			• May discourage poor
			  performers from leaving
			• Golden handcuffs may
			  undermine performance

Job status	• Promotion-based
	  pay increase
	• Status-based benefits
		• Tries to maintain
		  internal equity
		• Minimizes pay
		  discrimination
		• Motivates employees to
		  compete for promotions
			• Encourages hierarchy,
			  which may increase
			  costs and reduce
			  responsiveness
			• Reinforces status differences
			• Motivates job competition
			  and exaggerated job worth

Competencies	• Pay increase based
	  on competency
	• Skill-based pay
		• Improves workforce
		  flexibility
		• Tends to improve quality
		• Consistent with
		  employability
			• Subjective measurement
			  of competencies
			• Skill-based pay plans
			  are expensive

Task performance	• Commissions
	• Merit pay
	• Gainsharing
	• Profit sharing
	• Stock options
		• Motivates task performance
		• Attracts performance-
		  oriented applicants
		• Organizational rewards
		  create an ownership culture
		• Pay variability may avoid
		  layoffs during downturns
			• May weaken job content
			  motivation
			• May distance reward
			  giver from receiver
			• May discourage creativity
			• Tends to address symptoms,
			  not underlying causes
			  of behaviour

JOB STATUS-BASED REWARDS

Almost every organization rewards employees to some extent based on the status or worth of the jobs they occupy. According to one estimate, 73 percent of Canadian firms use **job evaluation** methods to estimate job worth. Most job evaluation methods give higher value to jobs that require more skill and effort, have more responsibility, and have more difficult working conditions.[6] Aside from receiving higher pay, employees with more valued jobs sometimes receive larger offices, company-paid vehicles, and access to exclusive dining rooms.

Job status-based rewards maintain feelings of equity (that people in higher valued jobs should get higher pay) and motivate employees to compete for promotions. However, at a time when companies are trying to be more cost efficient and responsive to the external environment, job status-based rewards potentially do the opposite by encouraging bureaucratic hierarchy. These rewards also reinforce a status mentality, whereas Gen-X/Gen-Y employees expect a more egalitarian workplace. Furthermore, status-based pay potentially motivates employees to compete with each other for higher status jobs and to raise the value of their own jobs by exaggerating job duties and hoarding resources.[7]

job evaluation
Systematically evaluating the worth of jobs within an organization by measuring their required skill, effort, responsibility, and working conditions. Job evaluation results create a hierarchy of job worth.

COMPETENCY-BASED REWARDS

Over the past decade, many firms have shifted from job status to competency-based rewards. For instance, Syracuse University in upstate New York replaced its 20-pay-grade hierarchy with just seven wider pay bands. Employees now receive pay increases within each pay band partly based on how well they have acquired new knowledge and skills.[8] Skill-based pay is a variation of competency-based rewards in which employees are rewarded for the number of skill modules mastered and, consequently, on the number of jobs they can perform.

Competency-based rewards improve workforce flexibility by motivating employees to learn a variety of skills and thereby perform a variety of jobs. Product or service quality tends to improve because employees with multiple skills are more likely to understand the work process and know how to improve it. Competency-based rewards are also consistent with employability because they reward employees who continuously learn skills that will keep them employed. One potential problem is that measuring competencies can be subjective, particularly where they are personality traits or personal values. Skill-based pay systems measure specific skills, so they are usually more objective and accurate. However, they are expensive because employees spend more time learning new tasks.[9]

PERFORMANCE-BASED REWARDS

Performance-based rewards have existed since Babylonian days in the 20th century BC, but their popularity has increased dramatically over the past couple of decades.[10] Some of the most popular individual, team, and organizational performance-based rewards are described next.

Individual rewards   Many employees receive individual bonuses or awards for accomplishing a specific task or performance goal. Real estate agents and other salespeople typically earn commissions, in which their pay increases with sales volume. Piece-rate systems reward employees based on the number of units produced.

Team rewards   Organizations are shifting their focus from individuals to teams and, consequently, employees are finding a larger part of their total paycheque based on team performance. For the past 40 years, Wal-Mart has been awarding bonuses determined by sales at the store where employees work. Brokerage firms increasingly award bonuses based on team rather than individual performance.[11]

Rather than calculating bonuses from sales or performance, **gainsharing plans** award bonuses based on cost savings and productivity improvement. For instance, over two-thirds of mining companies in Canada have a gainsharing bonus system, typically where mining teams share the cost savings of extracting more ore at lower cost. With considerable caution, American hospitals have introduced gainsharing programs where surgeons and other medical staff share cost reductions in surgery and patient care.[12] Gainsharing plans tend to improve team dynamics, knowledge sharing, and pay satisfaction. They also create a reasonably strong link between effort and performance because much of the cost reduction and labour efficiency is within the team's control.

Organizational rewards   WestJet Airlines, described at the beginning of this chapter, relies on two organizational-level rewards to motivate employees: profit sharing and employee stock ownership. More than half of Canada's fastest growing

gainsharing plan
A reward system that rewards team members for reducing costs and increasing labour efficiency in their work process.

profit-sharing plans
A reward system that pays bonuses to employees based on the previous year's level of corporate profits.

employee stock ownership plans (ESOPs)
A reward system that encourages employees to buy shares of the company.

March Networks Launches Employee Stock Options

These employees at March Networks are celebrating the company's public stock offering in Toronto and London, UK. The smiles are not just a result of the $55 million of working capital the public launch generated for the Ottawa-based digital surveillance systems firm. These employees also have stock options, and by going public, they hope to see the value of those options rise and reward them handsomely in the future. Sir Terry Matthews, who founded March Networks (as well as Mitel, Newbridge, and other Canadian technology companies), is a strong believer in employee stock options because they create an ownership culture.[17]
Chris Mikula, The Ottawa Citizen
www.marchnetworks.com

companies also apply one or both of these organizational rewards. **Profit-sharing plans** pay bonuses based on the previous year's level of corporate profits. **Employee stock ownership plans (ESOPs)** encourage employees to buy company shares, usually at a discounted price (WestJet pays 50 percent of the cost up to an annual limit based on the employee's salary). Employees are subsequently rewarded through dividends and market appreciation of those shares. One concern occurs where ESOPs become the company's pension plan. If the company goes bankrupt, employees lose both their jobs and a large portion of their retirement nest egg.[13]

A third organizational-level reward, called **stock options**, give employees the right to purchase company stock at a future date at a predetermined price. For example, Telus Corp. in Burnaby, B.C., granted 100 stock options to each of its employees at a purchase price of $34.88 with vesting in two years. This means that Telus employees can purchase the shares two years later from the company at $34.88 and sell them at a profit if the stock exchange price is above that amount. If the market price is below $34.88, employees can wait up to eight years to purchase the stock at $34.88, or let the offer lapse at no cost to them.[14]

A fourth organizational-level reward strategy, called **balanced scorecard**, is a performance measurement system that rewards people (typically executives) for improving performance on a composite of financial, customer, and internal processes, as well as employee factors. The better the measurement improvements, the larger the bonus awarded. For instance, Nova Scotia Power developed an executive-level scorecard that calculates improvements in internal costs, customer loyalty, earnings, and employee commitment.[15]

How effective are organizational-level rewards? ESOPs, stock options, and balanced scorecards tend to create an "ownership culture" in which employees feel aligned with the organization's success. Balanced scorecards have the added benefit of aligning rewards to several specific measures of organizational performance. Profit sharing tends to create less ownership culture, but it has the advantage of automatically adjusting employee compensation with the firm's prosperity, thereby reducing the need for layoffs or negotiated pay reductions during recessions.[16]

The main problem with ESOPS, stock options, and profit sharing (less so with balanced scorecards) is that employees often perceive a weak connection between individual effort and corporate profits or the value of company shares. Even in small firms, the company's stock price or profitability is influenced by economic conditions, competition, and other factors beyond the employee's immediate control. This low individual performance-to-outcome expectancy weakens employee motivation.

stock options
A reward system that gives employees the right to purchase company shares at a future date at a predetermined price.

balanced scorecard
A reward system that pays bonuses to executives for improved measurements on a composite of financial, customer, internal process, and employee factors.

IMPROVING REWARD EFFECTIVENESS

Performance-based rewards have come under attack over the years for discouraging creativity, distancing management from employees, distracting employees from the meaningfulness of the work itself, and being quick fixes that ignore the true causes of poor performance. While these issues have kernels of truth under specific circumstances, they do not necessarily mean that we should abandon performance-based pay. On the contrary, the top performing companies around the world are more likely to have performance-based rewards.[18] Reward systems do motivate most employees, but only under the right conditions. Here are some of the more important strategies to improve reward effectiveness.

Link rewards to performance   Behaviour modification theory (Chapter 3) and expectancy theory (Chapter 5) both recommend that employees with better performance should be rewarded more than those with poorer performance. Unfortunately, this simple principle seems to be unusually difficult to apply. According to a recent major survey, only 27 percent of Canadian employees say there is a clear link between their job performance and pay. Another Canadian study found that managers put different weights on task performance, organizational citizenship, and counterproductive work behaviours, resulting in inconsistent performance evaluations. A third study discovered that management's performance evaluations of 5,000 customer service employees in a U.S. telecommunications company were uncorrelated with the performance ratings that customers gave those employees.[19]

How can we improve the pay–performance linkage? Inconsistencies and bias can be minimized by introducing gainsharing, ESOPs, and other plans that use objective performance measures. Where subjective measures of performance are necessary, companies should rely on multiple sources of information, such as 360-degree feedback. Companies also need to apply rewards soon after the performance occurs, and in a large enough dose (such as a bonus rather than pay increase) so employees experience positive emotions when they receive the reward.[20]

Ensure that rewards are relevant   Companies need to align rewards with performance within the employee's control. The more employees see a "line of sight" between their daily actions and the reward, the more they are motivated to improve performance. Wal-Mart applies this principle by rewarding bonuses to top executives based on the company's overall performance, whereas front-line employees earn bonuses based on the sales volume of the store where they work. Reward systems also need to correct for situational factors. Salespeople in one region may have higher sales because the economy is stronger there than elsewhere, so sales bonuses need to be adjusted for these economic factors.

Use team rewards for interdependent jobs   Team rewards should be used rather than individual rewards when employees work in highly interdependent jobs because it is difficult to measure individual performance in these situations. Team rewards also encourage cooperation, which is more important when work is highly interdependent. A third benefit of team rewards is that they tend to support employee preferences for team-based work. On the other hand, employees (particularly the most productive employees) in Canada and many other low-collectivism cultures prefer rewards based on their individual performance rather than team performance.[21]

Ensure that rewards are valued   It seems obvious that rewards work best when they are valued. Yet companies sometimes make false assumptions about what employees want, with unfortunate consequences. The solution, of course, is to ask employees what they value. Campbell Soup did this a few years ago at its Canadian distribution centres. Executives thought the employees would ask for more money in a special team reward program. Instead, distribution staff said the most valued reward was a leather jacket with the Campbell Soup logo on the back.[22]

Watch out for unintended consequences   Performance-based reward systems sometimes have an unexpected—and undesirable—effect on employee behaviours. Consider the pizza company that decided to reward its drivers for on-time delivery. The plan got more hot pizzas to customers on time, but it also increased the accident rates of its drivers because the incentive motivated them to drive recklessly.[23] Connections 6.1 describes a few other examples where reward systems had unintended consequences. The solution here is to carefully think through the consequences of rewards and, where possible, test incentives in a pilot project before applying them across the organization.

Financial rewards come in many forms and, as was mentioned at the outset of this section, influence employees in complex ways. But money isn't the only thing that motivates people to join an organization and perform effectively. "The reward of doing a job well is in having done the job," says Richard Currie, who built Loblaws into one of the top 10 mass retailing companies in the world and is currently Chancellor of the University of New Brunswick. "The money is a by-product."[24] In other words, companies motivate employees mainly by designing interesting and challenging jobs, which we discuss next.

■ JOB DESIGN PRACTICES

job design
The process of assigning tasks to a job, including the interdependency of those tasks with other jobs.

How do you build a better job? That question has challenged organizational behaviour experts as well as psychologists, engineers, and economists for a few centuries. Some jobs have very few tasks and usually require very little skill. Other jobs are immensely complex and require years of experience and learning to master them. From one extreme to the other, jobs have different effects on work efficiency and employee motivation. The challenge, at least from the organization's perspective, is to find the right combination so work is performed efficiently but employees are motivated and engaged.[25] This challenge requires careful **job design**—the process of assigning tasks to a job, including the interdependency of those tasks with other jobs. A job is a set of tasks performed by one person. To understand this issue more fully, let's begin by describing early job design efforts aimed at increasing work efficiency through job specialization.

JOB DESIGN AND WORK EFFICIENCY

job specialization
The result of division of labour in which each job includes a subset of the tasks required to complete the product or service.

Using a pair of tweezers, an employee at Medtronic's assembly line in Minneapolis, Minnesota, loads 275 feedthroughs—tiny needlelike components for pacemakers and neurostimulators—onto a slotted storage block. She fills a block in about 15 minutes, then places the completed block on a shelf, and loads the next block.[26] The Medtronics employee works in a job with a high degree of **job specialization**. Job specialization occurs when the work required to build a pacemaker—or any other product or service—is subdivided into separate jobs assigned to different people.

When Rewards Go Wrong

There is an old saying that "what gets rewarded, gets done." But what companies reward isn't always what they had intended for employees to do. Here are a few dramatic examples:

- Reeling from record losses, Nortel's board of directors offered CEO Frank Dunn and his executive team a lucrative "return-to-profitability" bonus. Within a year, Canada's flagship technology company was miraculously making money again. When Nortel's board heaped on a second bonus along with stock to Dunn and his team, the company's profits soared. Dunn and several Nortel executives each received millions in bonuses in one year, while Dunn personally saw huge appreciation of his 1.1 million shares of Nortel stock. Unfortunately, the bonus plan didn't motivate Nortel's executives to improve profitability; it motivated them to apply dodgy accounting practices so the company appeared highly profitable. When the world discovered that most of Nortel's profitability was an accounting fabrication, Nortel's stock collapsed and the board fired Dunn along with nearly a dozen top executives.
- Integrated steel companies often rewarded managers for increased labour efficiency. The lower the labour hours required to produce a tonne of steel, the larger the manager's bonus. Unfortunately, steel firms usually didn't count the work of outside contractors in the formula, so the reward system motivated managers to hire expensive contractors in the production process. By employing more contractors, the cost of production actually increased, not decreased.

- Toyota rewards its dealerships based on customer satisfaction surveys, not just car sales. What Toyota discovered, however, is that this motivates dealers to increase satisfaction scores, not customer satisfaction. One Toyota dealership received high ratings because it offered free detailing to every customer who returned a "very satisfied" survey. The dealership even had a special copy of the survey showing clients which boxes to check off. This increased customer ratings, but not customer satisfaction.
- Donnelly Mirrors (now part of Canada's Magna International empire) introduced a gainsharing plan that motivated employees to reduce labour but not material costs. Employees at the automobile parts manufacturer knew they worked faster with sharp grinding wheels, so they replaced the expensive diamond wheels more often. This action reduced labour costs, thereby giving employees the gainsharing bonus. However, the labour savings were easily offset by much higher costs for diamond grinding wheels.

Sources: T. Hamilton, "Driving from a Profit to a Loss," *Toronto Star*, January 13, 2005, p. D01; S. Maich, "How Greed Took Down Nortel," *National Post*, April 29, 2004, p. FP1; D. Ebner, "Nortel Brass Get Millions More in Bonuses," *The Globe & Mail*, February 4, 2004, p. B3; A. Holeck, "Griffith, Ind., Native Takes Over as Steel Plant Manager," *Northwest Indiana Times*, May 25, 2003,; F. F. Reichheld, *The Loyalty Effect* (Boston, MA: Harvard University Press, 1996), p. 236; D. R. Spitzer, "Power Rewards: Rewards that Really Motivate," *Management Review*, May 1996, pp. 45–50.

Each resulting job includes a narrow subset of tasks, usually completed in a short "cycle time." Cycle time is the time required to complete the task before starting over with a new work unit. For the Medtronics employee, the cycle time for loading each feedthrough is a few seconds.

The economic benefits of dividing work into specialized jobs have been described and applied for at least two millenia. More than 2,300 years ago, the Chinese philosopher Mencius and Greek philosopher Plato noted that division of labour improves work efficiency. In 1436 AD, the waterways of Venice became an assembly line loading 10 galleons in just six hours. More than 200 years ago, economist Adam Smith described a small factory where 10 pin makers collectively produced as many as 48,000 pins per day because they performed specialized tasks, such as straightening, cutting, sharpening, grinding, and whitening the pins. In contrast, Smith explained that if these 10 people worked alone, they would collectively produce no more than 200 pins per day.[27]

One reason why job specialization potentially increases work efficiency is that employees have fewer tasks to juggle and therefore spend less time changing activities.

They also require fewer physical and mental skills to accomplish the assigned work, so less time and resources are needed for training. A third reason is that employees practise their tasks more frequently with shorter work cycles, so jobs are mastered quickly. A fourth reason why work efficiency increases is that employees with specific aptitudes or skills can be matched more precisely to the jobs for which they are best suited.[28]

Scientific management   One of the strongest advocates of job specialization was Frederick Winslow Taylor, an American industrial engineer who introduced the principles of **scientific management** in the early 1900s.[29] Scientific management consists of a toolkit of activities. Some of these activities—training, goal setting, and work incentives—are common today but were rare until Taylor popularized them. However, scientific management is mainly associated with high levels of job specialization and standardization of tasks to achieve maximum efficiency.

According to Taylor, the most effective companies have detailed procedures and work practices developed by engineers, enforced by supervisors, and executed by employees. Even the supervisor's tasks should be divided: one person manages operational efficiency, another manages inspection, and another is the disciplinarian. Taylor and other industrial engineers demonstrated that scientific management significantly improves work efficiency. No doubt, some of the increased productivity can be credited to the training, goal setting, and work incentives, but job specialization quickly became popular in its own right.

Frederick Taylor and his contemporaries focused on how job specialization reduces labour "waste" by improving the mechanical efficiency of work (i.e., matching skills, faster learning, less switch-over time). Yet, they didn't seem to notice how this extreme job specialization has an adverse effect on employee attitudes and motivation. Some jobs—such as loading feedthroughs at Medtronics— are so specialized that they quickly become tedious, trivial, and socially isolating. Employee turnover and absenteeism tends to be higher in specialized jobs with very short time cycles. Companies sometimes have to pay higher wages to attract job applicants to this dissatisfying, narrowly defined work.[30]

Job specialization often reduces work quality because employees see only a small part of the process. As one observer of an automobile assembly line work reports: "Often [employees] did not know how their jobs related to the total picture. Not knowing, there was no incentive to strive for quality—what did quality even mean as it related to a bracket whose function you did not understand?"[31]

Equally important, Taylor's reliance on job specialization to improve employee performance ignores the motivational potential of jobs. As jobs become specialized, the work tends to become easier to perform but less motivating. As jobs become more complex, work motivation increases but the ability to master the job decreases. Maximum job performance occurs somewhere between these two extremes, where most people can eventually perform the job tasks efficiently, yet the work is interesting.

JOB DESIGN AND WORK MOTIVATION

Industrial engineers may have overlooked the motivational effect of job characteristics, but it is now the central focus of many job design changes. Organizational behaviour scholar Frederick Herzberg is credited with shifting the spotlight when he introduced **motivator-hygiene theory** in the 1950s.[32] Motivator-hygiene theory proposes that employees experience job satisfaction when they fulfill growth and esteem needs (called *motivators*), and they experience dissatisfaction when they

---

scientific management

Involves systematically partitioning work into its smallest elements and standardizing tasks to achieve maximum efficiency.

---

motivator–hygiene theory

Herzberg's theory stating that employees are primarily motivated by growth and esteem needs, not by lower-level needs.

job characteristics model

A job design model that relates the motivational properties of jobs to specific personal and organizational consequences of those properties.

skill variety

The extent to which employees must use different skills and talents to perform tasks within their job.

have poor working conditions, job security, and other factors related to lower order needs (called *hygienes*). Herzberg argued that only characteristics of the job itself motivate employees, whereas the hygiene factors merely prevent dissatisfaction. It might seem rather obvious to us today that the job itself is a source of motivation, but it was radical thinking when Herzberg proposed the idea.

Motivator-hygiene theory didn't find much research support, but Herzberg's ideas generated new thinking about the motivational potential of the job itself.[33] Out of subsequent research emerged the **job characteristics model**, shown in Exhibit 6.2. The job characteristics model identifies five core job dimensions that produce three psychological states. Employees who experience these psychological states tend to have higher levels of internal work motivation (motivation from the work itself), job satisfaction (particularly satisfaction with the work itself), and work effectiveness.[34]

Core job characteristics   The job characteristics model identifies five core job characteristics. Under the right conditions, employees are more motivated and satisfied when jobs have higher levels of these characteristics.

- *Skill variety*—**Skill variety** refers to the use of different skills and talents to complete a variety of work activities. For example, sales clerks who normally only serve customers might be assigned the additional duties of stocking inventory and changing storefront displays.

■ **EXHIBIT 6.2**

The job characteristics model

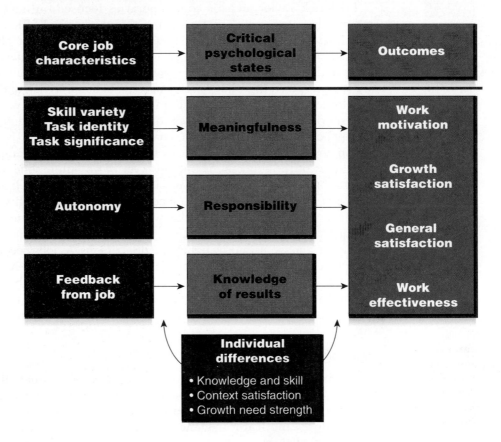

Source: J. R. Hackman and G. Oldham, *Work Redesign* (Reading, MA: Addison-Wesley, 1980), p. 90. Used with permission.

task identity
The degree to which a job requires completion of a whole or an identifiable piece of work.

- *Task identity*—**Task identity** is the degree to which a job requires completion of a whole or identifiable piece of work, such as assembling an entire computer modem rather than just soldering in the circuitry.
- *Task significance*—**Task significance** is the degree to which the job affects the organization and/or larger society. For instance, Medtronics hosts special sessions where patients give testimonials to remind staff of their task significance. "We have patients who come in who would be dead if it wasn't for us," says a Medtronic production supervisor. Little wonder that 86 percent of Medtronic employees say their work has special meaning and 94 percent feel pride in what they accomplish.[35]

task significance
The degree to which the job has a substantial impact on the organization and/or larger society.

- *Autonomy*—Jobs with high levels of **autonomy** provide freedom, independence, and discretion in scheduling the work and determining the procedures to be used to complete the work. In autonomous jobs, employees make their own decisions rather than relying on detailed instructions from supervisors or procedure manuals.
- *Job feedback*—Job feedback is the degree to which employees can tell how well they are doing based on direct sensory information from the job itself. Airline pilots can tell how well they land their aircraft and road crews can see how well they have prepared the road bed and laid the asphalt.

autonomy
The degree to which a job gives employees the freedom, independence, and discretion to schedule their work and determine the procedures used in completing it.

Critical psychological states   The five core job characteristics affect employee motivation and satisfaction through three critical psychological states shown earlier in Exhibit 6.2. One of these psychological states is *experienced meaningfulness*—the belief that one's work is worthwhile or important. Skill variety, task identity, and task significance directly contribute to the job's meaningfulness. If the job has high levels of all three characteristics, employees are likely to feel that their job is highly meaningful. Meaningfulness drops as the job loses one or more of these characteristics.

Work motivation and performance increase when employees feel personally accountable for the outcomes of their efforts. Autonomy directly contributes to this feeling of *experienced responsibility*. Employees must be assigned control of their work environment to feel responsible for their successes and failures. The third critical psychological state is *knowledge of results*. Employees want information about the consequences of their work effort. Knowledge of results can originate from co-workers, supervisors, or clients. However, job design focuses on knowledge of results from the work itself.

Individual differences   Job design doesn't increase work motivation for everyone in every situation. Employees must have the required skills and knowledge to master the more challenging work. Otherwise, job design tends to increase stress and reduce job performance. The original model also suggests that increasing the motivational potential of jobs will not motivate employees who are dissatisfied with their work context (e.g., working conditions, job security) or who have a low growth need strength. However, research findings have been mixed, suggesting that employees might be motivated by job design no matter how they feel about their job context or how high or low they score on growth need strength.[36]

JOB DESIGN PRACTICES THAT MOTIVATE

Three main strategies can increase the motivational potential of jobs: job rotation, job enlargement, and job enrichment. This section also identifies several ways to implement job enrichment.

Alberici Constructors Job Motivates

In the language of organizational behaviour experts, Francesca Ottoni has a job with a high motivational potential score. Every day brings a new challenge requiring a variety of skills for the director of business development for Alberici Constructors Ltd. in Hamilton, Ontario. "You're working on new projects and you're working in different industries," Ottoni explains enthusiastically. "One day you're at an automotive client's, one day you're at a hospital, the next day you're at a school." The job also allows Ottoni to be involved from beginning to end on projects that clearly benefit the client and society. One recent example is the University of Waterloo's School of Architecture building, in which she managed the construction process and worked closely with the architect to transform the century-old converted silk mill in Galt into an attractive and functional university building. "We're really proud of this facility," says Ottoni of the architecture school building. "It turned out to be a beautiful project."[37] *Tomasz Adamski*
www.hhca.ca/hhgca/alberici-constructors.html

job rotation
The practice of moving employees from one job to another.

Job rotation   **Job rotation** is the practice of moving employees from one job to another. At Baxter Corp.'s dialysis solution plant in Alliston, Ontario, for example, employees on the hemodialysis product line rotate several times each day through the three assembly-line positions as well as two non-assembly jobs (forklift operator and warehouse loader).[38] The medical products company and other organizations introduce job rotation for three reasons. First, it minimizes health risks from repetitive strain and heavy lifting because employees use different muscles and physical positions in the various jobs. Second, it makes the workforce multiskilled so they can fill in for each other when sick or on vacation. A third benefit of job rotation is that it potentially reduces the boredom of highly repetitive jobs. On Baxter's hemodialysis product line, the warehouse and forklift jobs are more intellectually stimulating, so working on these tasks breaks the tedium of the repetitive assembly line jobs.

job enlargement
Increasing the number of tasks employees perform within their job.

Job enlargement   **Job enlargement** adds tasks to an existing job. This might involve combining two or more complete jobs into one, or just adding one or two more tasks to an existing job. Either way, skill variety increases because there are more tasks to perform. Video journalists represent a clear example of an enlarged job. As Exhibit 6.3 illustrates, a traditional news team consists of a camera operator, a sound

■ EXHIBIT 6.3

Job enlargement of video journalists

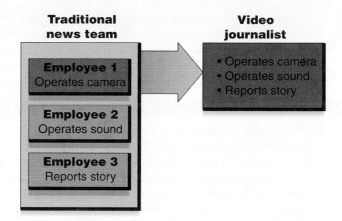

and lighting specialist, and the journalist who writes and presents or narrates the story. One video journalist performs all of these tasks.

The Canadian Broadcasting Corporation introduced video journalists several years ago at CBET (Windsor, Ontario, affiliate of CBC), and several other news organizations are now following CBC's lead. "Correspondents would do well to learn how to shoot and edit . . . and smart shooters and editors will learn how to write and track," CNN executives wrote in a memo to employees when the news network introduced video journalist jobs a few years ago. "CNN will always value exceptional ability, [but] the more multi-talented a news gatherer, the more opportunity the News Group will provide that person."[39]

Job enlargement significantly improves work efficiency and flexibility. However, research suggests that simply giving employees more tasks won't affect motivation, performance, or job satisfaction. Instead, these benefits result only when skill variety is combined with more autonomy and job knowledge.[40] In other words, employees are motivated when they perform a variety of tasks and have the freedom and knowledge to structure their work to achieve the highest satisfaction and performance. These job characteristics are at the heart of job enrichment.

Job enrichment   **Job enrichment** occurs when employees are given more responsibility for scheduling, coordinating, and planning their own work.[41] Generally, people in enriched jobs experience higher job satisfaction and work motivation, along with lower absenteeism and turnover. Productivity is also higher when task identity and job feedback are improved. Product and service quality tend to improve because job enrichment increases the jobholder's felt responsibility and sense of ownership over the product or service.[42]

One way to increase job enrichment is by combining highly interdependent tasks into one job. This *natural grouping* approach is reflected in the video journalist job. As we noted earlier, video journalist is an enlarged job, but it is also an example of job enrichment because video journalism naturally groups tasks together to complete an entire product (i.e., a news clip). By forming natural work units, jobholders have stronger feelings of responsibility for an identifiable body of work. They feel a sense of ownership and, therefore, tend to increase job quality. Forming natural work units increases task identity and task significance because employees perform a complete product or service and can more readily see how their work affects others.

A second job enrichment strategy, called *establishing client relationships*, involves putting employees in direct contact with their clients rather than using the supervisor as a go-between. By being directly responsible for specific clients, employees have more

job enrichment

Employees are given more responsibility for scheduling, coordinating, and planning their own work.

information and can make decisions affecting those clients.[43] Establishing client relationships also increases task significance because employees see a line-of-sight connection between their work and consequences for customers. This was apparent among medical secretaries at a large regional hospital in Sweden after the hospital reduced its workforce by 10 percent and gave the secretaries expanded job duties. Although these employees experienced more stress from the higher workloads, some of them also felt more motivated and satisfied because they now had direct interaction with patients through shared receptionist duties. "Before, I never saw a patient; now they have a face," says one medical secretary. "I feel I have been useful when I go home. I'm tired, but at the same time I feel satisfied and pleased with myself; you feel someone needs you."[44]

Forming natural task groups and establishing client relationships are common ways to enrich jobs, but the heart of the job enrichment philosophy is to give employees more autonomy over their work. This basic idea is at the core of one of the most widely mentioned—and often misunderstood—practices, known as empowerment.

■ EMPOWERMENT PRACTICES

When Clive Beddoe co-founded WestJet Airlines, he wanted to create an organization where employees had the freedom to serve customers rather than follow strict rules. Beddoe explains that most other airlines in the world have a military mindset. "You see it even in their flight uniforms and the autocratic way their companies behave," Beddoe points out. "Manuals and polices have to be followed exactly and, while that's necessary in the cockpit, it's not the best way when it comes to customer service." Beddoe emphasizes that WestJet is the opposite. "Here, we empower our employees and encourage them to be free-thinking and to do whatever it takes in whatever way they feel it's appropriate to solve customer problems."[45]

WestJet creates a work environment that makes employees feel empowered. **Empowerment** is a term that has been loosely tossed around in corporate circles and has been the subject of considerable debate among academics. However, the most widely accepted definition is that empowerment is a psychological concept represented by four dimensions: self-determination, meaning, competence, and impact of the individual's role in the organization. Empowerment consists of all four dimensions. If any dimension weakens, the employee's sense of empowerment will weaken.[46]

empowerment
A psychological concept in which people experience more self-determination, meaning, competence, and impact regarding their role in the organization.

- *Self-determination*—Empowered employees feel that they have freedom, independence, and discretion over their work activities.
- *Meaning*—Employees who feel empowered care about their work and believe that what they do is important.
- *Competence*—Empowered people are confident about their ability to perform the work well and have a capacity to grow with new challenges.
- *Impact*—Empowered employees view themselves as active participants in the organization; that is, their decisions and actions have an influence on the company's success.

From this definition, you can see that empowerment is not a personality trait, although personality might influence the extent to which someone feels empowered. People also experience degrees of empowerment, which can vary from one work environment to the next. One company that sets the standard for extreme empowerment is Semco Corporation, SA. GLOBAL Connections 6.2 describes how the Brazilian conglomerate has become world famous for giving employees complete freedom, even if their actions overrule managers and company owner Ricardo Semler.

The Empowerment of Semco

Most executives like to say they empower their workforce, but few come close to the work arrangements at Semco Corporation, SA. "Can an organization let people do what they want, when they want and how they want?" asks Ricardo Semler, who took over his father's marine pump business in São Paulo, Brazil, 20 years ago. The answer appears to be "yes." Today, Semco pushes the limits of empowerment at its dozen businesses—high-tech mixing equipment, inventory control, environmental resources management, to name a few—with 3,000 employees and $160 million revenue.

Organized into small groups of six to 10 people, Semco employees choose their objectives every six months, hire their co-workers, work out their budgets, set their own salaries, decide when to come to work, and even elect their own bosses. Semco factory workers have chosen future factory sites management didn't like, and commissioned an artist to paint the entire plant like a canvas.

The success of Semco's approach to empowerment was recently demonstrated when Carrefour, the French supermarket chain, hired Semco to take inventory at its 42 Brazilian hypermarkets on June 30. The assignment required 1,000 workers in 20 cities on the same day, a major challenge for any firm. Unfortunately, June 30 also turned out to be the day that Brazil played in the World Cup soccer finals. If Brazil won the game (which it did), employers could count on losing 40 percent of their employees to street celebrations. Semco managers asked employees to figure out among themselves how to work out this dilemma, which they did. Semco completed the task on time. In fact, Brazil's second largest supermarket chain asked Semco a week later to take inventory because the competitor hired for the job didn't have enough staff show up to count inventory during the World Cup final.

Ricardo Semler, shown here with staff in hammocks at head office, has taken empowerment to the extreme at Brazilian conglomerate, Semco Corporation.
Photo courtesy of Semco

Semco may have radical empowerment, but Semler says that the company is "only 50 or 60 percent where we'd like to be." Semler believes that replacing head office with several satellite offices around São Paulo would give employees even more opportunity for empowerment. "If you don't even know where people are, you can't possibly keep an eye on them," Semler explains. "All that's left to judge on is performance."

Sources: "Ricardo Semler Set Them Free," *CIO Insight*, April 2004, p. 30; S. Caulkin, "Who's in Charge Here?" *The Observer*, April 27, 2003, p. 9; S. Moss, "Portrait 'Idleness is Good'," *The Guardian*, April 17, 2003, p. 8; D. Gardner, "A Boss Who's Crazy About His Workers," *Sunday Herald* (Scotland), April 13, 2003, p. 6; R. Semler, *The Seven-Day Weekend* (Century: London, 2003).

SUPPORTING EMPOWERMENT

Chances are that you have heard corporate leaders say they are "empowering" the workforce. What these executives really mean is that they are changing the work environment to support empowerment.[47] Numerous individual, job design, and organizational or work context factors support empowerment. At the individual level, employees must possess the necessary competencies to be able to perform the work as well as handle the additional decision-making requirements. While other individual factors have been proposed (e.g., locus of control), they do not seem to have any real effect on whether employees feel empowered.[48]

Job characteristics clearly influence the dynamics of empowerment.[49] To generate beliefs about self-determination, employees must work in jobs with a high degree of autonomy with minimal bureaucratic control. To maintain a sense of meaningfulness, jobs must have high levels of task identity and task significance. And to maintain a sense of self-confidence, jobs must provide sufficient feedback.

Several organizational and work context factors also influence empowerment. Employees experience more empowerment in organizations where information and other resources are easily accessible. Empowerment also requires a learning orientation culture. In other words, empowerment flourishes in organizations that appreciate the value of the employee learning and that accept reasonable mistakes as a natural part of the learning process. Furthermore, empowerment requires corporate leaders who trust employees and are willing to take the risks that empowerment creates. "Executives must give up control and trust the power of talent," advises Ricardo Semler, head of Semco Corporation in Sao Paulo, Brazil.[50]

With the right individuals, job characteristics, and organizational environment, empowerment can have a noticeable effect on motivation and performance. For instance, a study of Canadian bank employees concluded that empowerment improved customer service and tended to reduce conflict between employees and their supervisors. A study of Canadian nurses reported that empowerment is associated with higher trust in management, which ultimately influences job satisfaction, belief and acceptance of organizational goals and values, and effective organizational commitment.[51] Empowerment also tends to increase personal initiative because employees identify with and assume more psychological ownership of their work.

■ SELF-LEADERSHIP PRACTICES

self-leadership
The process of influencing oneself to establish the self-direction and self-motivation needed to perform a task.

WestJet has been mentioned several times throughout this chapter because the Calgary-based airline illustrates how to improve employee performance through rewards, job design, and empowerment practices. The company also symbolizes another increasingly important applied performance practice, called **self-leadership**. "What occurred to me," says WestJet CEO Clive Beddoe, "is we had to overcome the inherent difficulty of trying to manage people and to hone the process into one where people wanted to manage themselves."[52]

Self-leadership refers to the process of influencing oneself to establish the self-direction and self-motivation needed to perform a task.[53] This concept includes a toolkit of behavioural activities borrowed from social learning theory and goal setting. It also includes constructive thought processes that have been extensively studied in sports psychology. Overall, self-leadership takes the view that individuals mostly regulate their own actions through these behavioural and cognitive (thought) activities.

Although we are in the early stages of understanding the dynamics of self-leadership, Exhibit 6.4 identifies the five main elements of this process. These elements, which generally follow each other in a sequence, are personal goal setting, constructive thought patterns, designing natural rewards, self-monitoring, and self-reinforcement.[54]

PERSONAL GOAL SETTING

The first step in self-leadership is to set goals for your own work effort. This applies the ideas we learned in Chapter 5 on goal setting, such as identifying goals that are specific, relevant, and challenging. The main difference is that self-leadership involves setting goals alone, rather than having them assigned by or jointly decided with a supervisor. Research suggests that employees are more focused and perform better when they set their own goals, particularly in combination with other self-leadership practices.[55]

■ **EXHIBIT 6.4**   Elements of self-leadership

CONSTRUCTIVE THOUGHT PATTERNS

Before beginning a task and while performing it, employees should engage in positive (constructive) thoughts about that work and its accomplishment. In particular, employees are more motivated and better prepared to accomplish a task after they have engaged in positive self-talk and mental imagery.

Positive self-talk   Do you ever talk to yourself? Most of us do, according to a major study of Canadian university students.[56] **Self-talk** refers to any situation in which we talk to ourselves about our own thoughts or actions. Some of this internal communication assists the decision-making process, such as weighing the advantages of a particular choice. Self-leadership is mostly interested in evaluative self-talk, in which you evaluate your capabilities and accomplishments.

The problem is that most evaluative self-talk is negative; we criticize much more than encourage or congratulate ourselves. Negative self-talk undermines our confidence and potential to perform a particular task. In contrast, positive self-talk creates a "can-do" belief and thereby increases motivation by raising our effort-to-performance expectancy. We often hear that professional athletes "psyche" themselves up before an important event. They tell themselves that they can achieve their goal and that they have practised enough to reach that goal. They are motivating themselves through self-talk.

> **self-talk**
>
> Talking to ourselves about our own thoughts or actions for the purpose of increasing our self-confidence and navigating through decisions in a future event.

Mental imagery   You've probably heard the phrase "I'll cross that bridge when I come to it!" Self-leadership takes the opposite view. It suggests that we need to mentally practise a task and imagine successfully performing it beforehand. This process, known as **mental imagery**, has two parts. One part involves mentally practising the task, anticipating obstacles to goal accomplishment, and working out solutions to those obstacles before they occur. By mentally walking through the activities required to accomplish the task, we begin to see problems that may occur. We can then imagine what responses would be best for each contingency.[57]

While one part of mental imagery helps us to anticipate things that could go wrong, the other part involves visualizing successful completion of the task. We imagine the experience of completing the task and the positive results that follow. Everyone daydreams and fantasizes about being in a successful situation. You might imagine yourself being promoted to your boss's job, receiving a prestigious award, or taking time off work. This visualization increases goal commitment and motivates us to complete the task effectively.

> **mental imagery**
>
> Mentally practising a task and visualizing its successful completion.

DESIGNING NATURAL REWARDS

Self-leadership recognizes that employees actively craft their jobs. To varying degrees, they can alter tasks and work relationships to make the work more motivating.[58] One way to build natural rewards into the job is to alter the way a task is accomplished. People often have enough discretion in their jobs to make slight changes to suit their needs and preferences. For instance, you might try out a new software program to design an idea, rather than sketch the image with pencil. By using the new software, you are adding challenge to a task that may have otherwise been mundane.

SELF-MONITORING

Self-monitoring is the process of keeping track of one's progress toward a goal. In the section on job design, we learned that feedback from the job itself communicates whether we are accomplishing the task successfully. Self-monitoring includes the notion of consciously checking naturally occurring feedback at regular intervals. It also includes designing artificial feedback where natural feedback does not occur. Salespeople might arrange to receive monthly reports on sales levels in their territory. Production staff might have gauges or computer feedback systems installed so they can see how many errors are made on the production line. Research suggests that people who have control over the timing of performance feedback perform their tasks better than those with feedback assigned by others.[59]

SELF-REINFORCEMENT

Self-leadership includes the social learning theory concept of self-reinforcement. Self-reinforcement occurs whenever an employee has control over a reinforcer but doesn't "take" the reinforcer until completing a self-set goal.[60] A common example is taking a break after reaching a predetermined stage of your work. The work break is a self-induced form of positive reinforcement. Self-reinforcement also occurs when you decide to do a more enjoyable task after completing a task that you dislike. For example, after slogging through a difficult report, you might decide to spend time doing a more pleasant task, such as catching up on industry news by scanning Web sites.

SELF-LEADERSHIP IN PRACTICE

Self-leadership is shaping up to be a valuable applied performance practice in organizational settings. A respectable body of research shows consistent support for most elements of self-leadership. Self-set goals and self-monitoring increased the frequency of wearing safety equipment among employees in a mining operation. Airline employees who received constructive thought training experienced better mental performance, enthusiasm, and job satisfaction than co-workers who did not receive this training. Mental imagery helped supervisors and process engineers in an Ontario pulp and paper mill to transfer what they learned in an interpersonal communication skills class back to the job.[61] Studies also indicate that self-set goals and constructive thought processes improve individual performance in swimming, tennis, ice skating, soccer, and other sports. Indeed, studies show that almost all Olympic athletes rely on mental rehearsal and positive self-talk to achieve their performance goals.[62]

Self-leadership behaviours are more frequently found in people with specific personality characteristics, notably conscientiousness and extroversion.[63] However, one of the benefits of self-leadership is that it can be learned. Training programs have helped

Self-leadership at Bristol Group

From its beginnings a quarter century ago in St. John's Newfoundland, Bristol Group has grown to become the largest and most successful marketing communications company in Atlantic Canada. The innovative firm created the breathtaking images for Newfoundland and Labrador Tourism, the elegant marketing for Toyota in Atlantic Canada, the summer scenes billboards for Atlantic Superstore, and many other portfolios throughout the region. All of this requires incredibly talented and motivated employees. According to Bristol Group co-founder Rick Emberley, the key ingredient in this mixture is to hire people who practise self-leadership. "Hire self-motivated, independent-thinking people who don't require constant supervision on the front end, and who don't require constant back-slapping on the back end."[64]

Photo courtesy of Bristol Group

www.bristolgroup.ca

employees to improve their self-leadership skills. Organizations can also encourage self-leadership by providing sufficient autonomy and establishing rewards that reinforce self-leadership behaviours. Employees are also more likely to engage in self-monitoring in companies that emphasize continuous measurement of performance. Overall, self-leadership promises to be an important concept and practice for improving employee motivation and performance.

Self-leadership, job design, empowerment, and rewards are valuable approaches to improving employee performance. However, performance is also affected by work-related stress. As we learn in the next chapter, too much stress is causing numerous problems with employee performance and well-being, but there are also ways to combat this epidemic.

CHAPTER SUMMARY

Money and other financial rewards are a fundamental part of the employment relationship, but their value and meaning varies from one person to the next. Organizations reward employees for their membership and seniority, job status, competencies, and performance. Membership-based rewards may attract job applicants and seniority-based rewards reduce turnover, but these reward objectives tend to discourage turnover among those with the lowest performance. Rewards based on job status try to maintain internal equity and motivate employees to compete for promotions. However, they tend to encourage bureaucratic hierarchy, support status differences, and motivate employees to compete and hoard resources. Competency-based rewards are becoming increasingly popular because they improve workforce flexibility and are consistent with the emerging idea of employability. However, they tend to be subjectively measured and can result in higher costs as employees spend more time learning new skills.

Awards/bonuses, commissions, and other individual performance-based rewards have existed for centuries and are widely used. Many companies are shifting to team-based rewards such as gainsharing plans and to organizational rewards such as employee stock ownership plans (ESOPs), stock options, profit sharing, and balanced scorecards. ESOPs and stock options create an ownership culture, but employees often perceive a weak connection between individual performance and the organizational reward.

Financial rewards have a number of limitations, but reward effectiveness can be improved in several ways. Organizational leaders should ensure that rewards are linked to work performance, rewards are aligned with performance within the employee's control, team rewards are used where jobs are interdependent, rewards are valued by employees, and rewards have no unintended consequences.

Job design refers to the process of assigning tasks to a job, including the interdependency of those tasks with other jobs. Job specialization subdivides work into separate jobs for different people. This increases work efficiency because employees master the tasks quickly, spend less time changing tasks, require less training, and can be matched more closely with the jobs best suited to their skills. However, job specialization may reduce work motivation, create mental health problems, lower product or service quality, and increase costs through discontentment, absenteeism, and turnover.

Contemporary job design strategies reverse job specialization through job rotation, job enlargement, and job enrichment. The job characteristics model is a template for job redesign that specifies core job dimensions, psychological states, and individual differences. Organizations introduce job rotation to reduce job boredom, develop a more flexible workforce, and reduce the incidence of repetitive strain injuries. Two ways to enrich jobs are clustering tasks into natural groups and establishing client relationships.

Empowerment is a psychological concept represented by four dimensions: self-determination, meaning, competence, and impact regarding the individual's role in the organization. Individual characteristics seem to have a minor influence on empowerment. Job design is a major influence, particularly autonomy, task identity, task significance, and job feedback. Empowerment is also supported at the organizational level through a learning orientation culture, sufficient information and resources, and corporate leaders who trust employees.

Self-leadership is the process of influencing oneself to establish the self-direction and self-motivation needed to perform a task. This includes personal goal setting, constructive thought patterns, designing natural rewards, self-monitoring, and self-reinforcement.

Constructive thought patterns include self-talk and mental imagery. Self-talk refers to any situation in which a person talks to himself or herself about his or her own thoughts or actions. Mental imagery involves mentally practising a task and imagining successfully performing it beforehand.

KEY TERMS

autonomy, p. 171

balanced scorecard, p. 165

employee stock ownership plans (ESOPs), p. 164

empowerment, p. 174

gainsharing plan, p. 164

job characteristics model, p. 170

job design, p. 167

job enlargement, p. 172

job enrichment, p. 173

job evaluation, p. 163

job rotation, p. 172

job specialization, p. 167

mental imagery, p. 177

motivator-hygiene theory, p. 169

profit-sharing plans, p. 164

scientific management, p. 169

self-leadership, p. 176

self-talk, p. 177

skill variety, p. 170

stock options, p. 165

task identity, p. 171

task significance, p. 171

DISCUSSION QUESTIONS

1. As a consultant, you have been asked to recommend either a gainsharing plan or a profit-sharing plan for employees who work in the four regional distribution and warehousing facilities of a large retail organization. Which reward system would you recommend? Explain your answer.

2. You are a member of a team responsible for developing performance measures for your college or university department or faculty unit based on the balanced scorecard approach. Identify one performance measurement for each of the following factors: financial, customer satisfaction, internal processes, and employee performance.

3. Okanagan Tire Corporation redesigned its production facilities around a team-based system. However, the company president believes that employees will not be motivated unless they receive incentives based on their individual performance. Give three explanations why Okanagan Tire should introduce team-based rather than individual rewards in this setting.

4. What can organizations do to increase the effectiveness of financial rewards?

5. Most of us have watched pizzas being made while waiting in a pizzeria. What level of job specialization do you usually notice in these operations? Why does this high or low level of specialization exist? If some pizzerias have different levels of specialization than others, identify the contingencies that might explain these differences.

6. Can a manager or supervisor "empower" an employee? Discuss fully.

7. Describe a time when you practised self-leadership to successfully perform a task. With reference to each step in the self-leadership process, describe what you did to achieve this success.

8. Can self-leadership replace formal leadership in an organizational setting?

CASE STUDY 6.1

THE REGENCY GRAND HOTEL

By Lisa Ho, under the supervision of Steven L. McShane.

The Regency Grand Hotel is a five-star hotel in Bangkok, Thailand. The hotel was established 15 years ago by a local consortium of investors and has been operated by a Thai general manager throughout this time. The hotel is one of Bangkok's most famous hotels and its 700 employees enjoy the prestige of being associated with the hotel. The hotel provides good employee benefits, above market rate salary, and job security.

In addition, a good year-end bonus amounting to four months' salary is rewarded to employees regardless of the hotel's overall performance during the year.

Recently, the Regency was sold to a large American hotel chain that was very keen to expand its operations into Thailand. When the acquisition was announced, the general manager decided to take early retirement when the hotel changed ownership. The American hotel chain kept all the Regency employees, although a few were transferred to other positions. John Becker, an American with 10 years of management experience with the hotel chain, was appointed as the new general manager of Regency Grand Hotel. Becker was selected as the new general manager because of his previous successes in integrating newly acquired hotels in the United States. In most of the previous acquisitions, Becker took over operations with poor profitability and low morale.

Becker is a strong believer in empowerment. He expects employees to go beyond guidelines/standards to consider guest needs on a case-to-case basis. That is, employees must be guest-oriented at all times as so to provide excellent customer service. From his U.S. experience, Becker has found that empowerment increases employee motivation, performance, and job satisfaction, all of which contribute to the hotel's profitability and customer service ratings. Soon after becoming general manager of Regency Grand, Becker introduced the practice of empowerment so as to replicate the successes that he had achieved back home.

The Regency Grand Hotel has been very profitable since it opened 15 years ago. The employees have always worked according to management's instructions. Their responsibility was to ensure that the instructions from their managers were carried out diligently and conscientiously. Innovation and creativity were discouraged under the previous management. Indeed, employees were punished for their mistakes and discouraged from trying out ideas that had not been approved by management. As a result, employees were afraid to be innovative and to take risks.

Becker met with Regency's managers and department heads to explain that empowerment would be introduced in the hotel. He told them that employees must be empowered with decision-making authority so that they can use their initiative, creativity, and judgment to satisfy guest needs or handle problems effectively and efficiently. However, he stressed that the more complex issues and decisions were to be referred to superiors, who were to coach and assist rather than provide direct orders. Furthermore, Becker stressed that mistakes were allowed as long as the same ones were not repeated. He advised his managers and department heads not to discuss minor issues/problems or decisions with him. Nevertheless, he told them that they are to discuss important/major issues and decisions with him. He concluded the meeting by asking for feedback. Several managers and department heads told him that they liked the idea and would support it, while others simply nodded their heads. Becker was pleased with the response, and was eager to have his plan implemented.

In the past, the Regency had emphasized administrative control, resulting in many bureaucratic procedures throughout the organization. For example, the front counter employees needed to seek approval from their manager before they could upgrade guests to another category of room. The front counter manager would then have to write and submit a report to the general manager justifying the upgrade. Soon after his meeting with managers, Becker reduced the number of bureaucratic rules at the Regency and allocated more decision-making authority to front-line employees. This action upset those who previously had decision-making power over these issues. As a result, several of these employees left the hotel.

Becker also began spending a large portion of his time observing and interacting with the employees at the front desk, lobby, restaurants, and various departments. This direct interaction with Becker helped many employees understand what he wanted and expected of them. However, the employees had much difficulty trying to distinguish between a major and minor issue/decision. More often than not, supervisors would reverse employee decisions by stating that they were major issues requiring management approval. Employees who displayed initiative and made good decisions in satisfying the needs of the guests rarely received any positive feedback from their supervisors. Eventually, most of these employees lost confidence in making decisions, and reverted back to relying on their superiors for decision making.

Not long after the implementation of the practice of empowerment, Becker realized that his subordinates were consulting him more frequently than before. Most of them came to him with minor issues and decisions. He had to spend most of his time attending to his subordinates. Soon he began to feel highly frustrated and exhausted, and very often would tell his secretary that "unless the hotel is on fire, don't let anyone disturb me."

Becker thought that the practice of empowerment would benefit the overall performance of the hotel. However, contrary to his expectation, the business and overall performance of the hotel began to deteriorate. The number of complaints from guests had been increasing. In the past, the hotel had minimal guest complaints. Now there has been a significant number of formal written complaints every month. Many other guests voiced their dissatisfaction verbally to hotel employees. The number of mistakes made by employees had been on an increase. Becker was very upset when he realized that two of the local newspapers and an overseas newspaper had published negative feedback on the hotel in terms of service standards. He was most distressed when an international travel magazine had voted the hotel as "one of Asia's nightmare hotels."

The stress levels of the employees were continuously mounting since the introduction of the practice of empowerment. Absenteeism due to illness was increasing at an alarming rate. In addition, the employee turnover rate had reached an all-time high. The good working relationships that were established under the old management had been severely strained. The employees were no longer united and supportive of each other. They were quick to "point fingers" at or to "back stab" one another when mistakes were made and when problems occurred.

Discussion Questions

1. Identify the symptoms indicating that problems exist in this case.

2. Diagnose the problems in this case using organizational behaviour concepts.

3. Recommend solutions that overcome or minimize the problems and symptoms in this case.

Note: This case is based on true events, but the industry and names have been changed.

TEAM EXERCISE 6.2

IS STUDENT WORK ENRICHED?

Purpose This exercise is designed to help you learn how to measure the motivational potential of jobs and evaluate the extent that jobs should be further enriched.

Instructions Being a student is like a job in several ways. You have tasks to perform and someone (such as your instructor) oversees your work. Although few people want to be students most of their lives (the pay rate is too low!), it may be interesting to determine how enriched your job is as a student.

■ *Step 1:* Students are placed into teams (preferably four or five people).

■ *Step 2:* Working alone, each student completes both sets of measures in this exercise. Then, using the guidelines below, they individually calculate the score for the five core job characteristics as well as the overall motivating potential score for the job.

■ *Step 3:* Members of each team compare their individual results. The group should identify differences of opinion for each core job characteristic. They should also note which core job characteristics have the lowest scores and recommend how these scores could be increased.

■ *Step 4:* The entire class will now meet to discuss the results of the exercise. The instructor may ask some teams to present their comparisons and recommendations for a particular core job characteristic.

JOB DIAGNOSTIC SURVEY

Circle the number on the right that best describes student work.	Very Little ▼			Moderately ▼			Very Much ▼
1. To what extent does student work permit you to decide on your own how to go about doing the work?	1	2	3	4	5	6	7
2. To what extent does student work involve doing a whole or identifiable piece of work, rather than a small portion of the overall work process?	1	2	3	4	5	6	7
3. To what extent does student work require you to do many different things, using a variety of your skills/talents?	1	2	3	4	5	6	7
4. To what extent are the results of your work as a student likely to significantly affect the lives and well-being of other people (e.g., within your school, your family, society)?	1	2	3	4	5	6	7
5. To what extent does working on student activities provide information about your performance?	1	2	3	4	5	6	7

Circle the number on the right that best describes student work.	Very Inaccurate ▼			Uncertain ▼			Very Accurate ▼
6. Being a student requires me to use a number of complex and high-level skills	1	2	3	4	5	6	7
7. Student work is arranged so that I do NOT have the chance to do an entire piece of work from beginning to end.	7	6	5	4	3	2	1
8. Doing the work required of students provides many chances for me to figure out how well I am doing.	1	2	3	4	5	6	7
9. The work students must do is quite simple and repetitive.	7	6	5	4	3	2	1
10. The work of a student is one where a lot of other people can be affected by how well the work gets done.	1	2	3	4	5	6	7
11. Student work denies me any chance to use my personal initiative or judgment in carrying out the work.	7	6	5	4	3	2	1
12. Student work provides me the chance to completely finish the pieces of work I begin.	1	2	3	4	5	6	7
13. Doing student work by itself provides very few clues about whether or not I am performing well.	7	6	5	4	3	2	1
14. As a student, I have considerable opportunity for independence and freedom in how I do the work.	1	2	3	4	5	6	7
15. The work I perform as a student is NOT very significant or important in the broader scheme of things.	7	6	5	4	3	2	1

Adapted from the Job Diagnostic Survey, developed by J. R. Hackman and G. R. Oldham. The authors have released any copyright ownership of this scale (see J. R. Hackman and G. Oldham, *Work Redesign* (Reading, MA: Addison-Wesley, 1980), p. 275).

CALCULATING THE MOTIVATING POTENTIAL SCORE

Scoring Core Job Characteristics: Use the following set of calculations to estimate the motivating potential score for the job of being a student. Use your answers from the Job Diagnostic Survey that you completed above.

Skill Variety (SV) $\dfrac{\text{Question } 3 + 6 + 9}{3}$ = _____   *Autonomy* $\dfrac{\text{Question } 1 + 11 + 14}{3}$ = _____

Task Identity (TI) $\dfrac{\text{Question } 2 + 7 + 12}{3}$ = _____   *Job Feedback* $\dfrac{\text{Question } 5 + 8 + 13}{3}$ = _____

Task Significance (TS) $\dfrac{\text{Question } 4 + 10 + 15}{3}$ = _____

Calculating Motivating Potential Score (MPS): Use the following formula and the results above to calculate the motivating potential score. Notice that skill variety, task identity, and task significance are averaged before being multiplied by the score for autonomy and job feedback.

$$\left(\frac{SV + TI + TS}{3} \right) \times \text{Autonomy} \times \text{Job Feedback}$$

$$\left(\frac{\_ + \_ + \_}{3} \right) + \_\_ + \_\_ = \_\_\_\_$$

SELF-ASSESSMENT EXERCISE 6.3

WHAT IS YOUR ATTITUDE TOWARD MONEY?

Purpose This exercise is designed to help you understand the types of attitudes toward money and assess your attitude toward money.

Instructions Read each of the statements below and circle the response that you believe best reflects your position regarding each statement. Then use the scoring key in Appendix B to calculate your results. This exercise is completed alone so students assess themselves honestly without concerns of social comparison. However, class discussion will focus on the meaning of money, including the dimensions measured here and other aspects of money that may have an influence on behaviour in the workplace.

MONEY ATTITUDE SCALE					
To what extent do you agree or disagree that. . .	Strongly Agree ▼	Agree ▼	Neutral ▼	Disagree ▼	Strongly Disagree ▼
1. I sometimes purchase things because I know they will impress other people.	5	4	3	2	1
2. I regularly put money aside for the future.	5	4	3	2	1
3. I tend to get worried about decisions involving money.	5	4	3	2	1
4. I believe that financial wealth is one of the most important signs of a person's success.	5	4	3	2	1
5. I keep a close watch on how much money I have.	5	4	3	2	1
6. I feel nervous when I don't have enough money.	5	4	3	2	1

MONEY ATTITUDE SCALE (continued)					
To what extent do you agree or disagree that. . .	Strongly Agree ▼	Agree ▼	Neutral ▼	Disagree ▼	Strongly Disagree ▼
7. I tend to show more respect to people who are wealthier than I am.	5	4	3	2	1
8. I follow a careful financial budget.	5	4	3	2	1
9. I worry about being financially secure.	5	4	3	2	1
10. I sometimes boast about my financial wealth or how much money I make.	5	4	3	2	1
11. I keep track of my investments and financial wealth.	5	4	3	2	1
12. I usually say "I can't afford it," even when I can afford something.	5	4	3	2	1

Sources: Adapted from J.A. Roberts and C.J. Sepulveda, "Demographics and Money Attitudes: A Test of Yamauchi and Templer's (1982) Money Attitude Scale in Mexico," *Personality and Individual Differences*, 27 (July 1999), pp. 19–35; K. Yamauchi and D. Templer, "The Development of a Money Attitudes Scale," *Journal of Personality Assessment*, 46 (1982), pp. 522–28.

SELF-ASSESSMENT EXERCISE   6.4

ASSESSING YOUR SELF-LEADERSHIP

Go to the Online Learning Centre to complete this interactive self-assessment.

Purpose This exercise is designed to help you understand self-leadership concepts and assess your self-leadership tendencies.

Instructions Indicate the extent to which each statement in this instrument describes you very well or does not describe you at all. Complete each item honestly to get the best estimate of your score on each self-leadership dimension.

SELF-ASSESSMENT EXERCISE   6.5

STUDENT EMPOWERMENT SCALE

Go to the Online Learning Centre to complete this interactive self-assessment.

Purpose This exercise is designed to help you understand the dimensions of empowerment and assess your level of empowerment as a student.

Instructions Empowerment is a concept that applies to people in a variety of situations. This instrument is specifically adapted to your position as a student at this college or university. Indicate the extent to which you agree or disagree with each statement in this instrument, then request the results, which provide an overall score as well as scores on each of the four dimensions of empowerment. Complete each item honestly to get the best estimate of your level of empowerment.

After studying the preceding material, be sure to check out our Online Learning Centre at
www.mcgrawhill.ca/college/mcshane
for more in-depth information and interactivities that correspond to this chapter.

·7·

WORK-RELATED STRESS
AND STRESS MANAGEMENT

LEARNING OBJECTIVES

AFTER READING THIS CHAPTER, YOU SHOULD BE ABLE TO:

■ Define stress and describe the stress experience.

■ Outline the stress process from stressors to consequences.

■ Identify the different types of stressors in the workplace.

■ Explain why a stressor might produce different stress levels in two people.

■ Discuss the physiological, psychological, and behavioural effects of stress.

■ Identify five ways to manage workplace stress.

Nick Salaysay admits that he doesn't leave his work behind when on holidays. "I have a BlackBerry, so I check my email a lot when I'm supposed to be on vacation," says the corporate lawyer in Calgary. Salaysay also routinely works 10-hour days. "If I'm closing a big deal out of town, sometimes I'll work from 8 in the morning until 11 at night," he says. "You work until the deal is closed."

At least Nick Salaysay goes on vacation. Brian Rose is entitled to three weeks off each year, but says he hasn't used any of it for almost a decade. The Halifax Chamber of Commerce sales and marketing director did spend two days at a cottage six years ago, but that wouldn't count as holiday time. "I brought everyone with me [from work]," Rose recalls. "I had more meetings at the cottage than I do in the office!"

Across the country, Canadians are working longer hours, mixing work with leisure, taking less vacation time and, as a result, experiencing more stress and health problems. A report from the Canadian government's Public Health Agency estimates that 58 percent of employees experience high levels of role overload. Another study revealed that Canadians are more likely than Americans or people in all 15 European countries surveyed to feel that they work at "high speed all the time." Canadians are also less likely than people in most other developed countries to use up their annual vacation entitlement. And like Nick Salaysay, many Canadians remain connected to the office even when they are on vacation. For example, nearly one-quarter of Canadian chief financial officers say they contact their office every day while on holidays.

Calgary lawyer Nick Salaysay and many other Canadians work long days and continue working during vacations. Research indicates that this work intensification lifestyle is stressful.
Calgary Herald/Mikael Kjellstrom

Ericsson Canada executives were concerned that their employees were working long hours and not taking much time off to recover, so they took steps to correct the problem. The Montreal-based telecommunications firm now requires everyone to take at least two weeks of vacation each year, including at least one full week at a time. Virgin Mobile has taken the mandatory vacation time one step further at its Toronto office. Employees are banned from calling a co-worker or boss while on vacation (although the occasional email is allowed). "We encourage people to work hard while they're at work, but we also make sure they make time for really relaxing," says Nathan Rosenberg, Virgin Canada's chief marketing officer.[1] ■

www.phac-aspc.gc.ca

Working longer hours and devoting less time to leisure are partly responsible for record levels of work-related stress among Canadians in recent years. A Canadian Mental Health Association survey found that over half of Canadians feel really stressed a few times each week, with 9 percent of them feeling this way all of the time. According to Statistics Canada, 26 percent of Canadians admit to suffering from stress quite a lot. The Conference Board of Canada revealed that stress levels among Canadians have nearly doubled over the past decade. Another study, sponsored by the Canadian Heart and Stroke Foundation, reported that almost one-third of employees regularly have difficulty coping with the demands of their jobs.[2]

Of course, stress isn't just a Canadian affliction. According to a Gallup poll, 80 percent of Americans feel too much stress on the job; nearly half indicate that they need help coping with it. Approximately one in every four employees in the United Kingdom feels "very or extremely stressed," and this condition has become the top cause of absenteeism there. Over half of call centre staff in India feel so stressed by the tough working conditions that they end up quitting. The Japanese government, which tracks work-related stress every five years, has found that the percentage of Japanese employees who feel "strong worry, anxiety or stress at work or in daily working life" has increased from 51 percent in 1982 to almost two-thirds of the population today.[3]

In this chapter, we look at the dynamics of work-related stress and how to manage it. The chapter begins by describing the stress experience. Next, the causes and consequences of stress are examined, along with the factors that cause some people to experience stress when others do not. The final section of this chapter looks at ways to manage work-related stress from either an organizational or individual perspective.

■ WHAT IS STRESS?

stress

An individual's adaptive response to a situation that is perceived as challenging or threatening to the person's well-being.

Stress is an adaptive response to a situation that is perceived as challenging or threatening to the person's well-being.[4] The stress response is a complex emotion that produces physiological changes to prepare us for "fight or flight"—to defend the threat or flee from it. Specifically, our heart rate increases, muscles tighten, breathing speeds up, and perspiration increases. Our body also moves more blood to the brain, releases adrenaline and other hormones, fuels the system by releasing more glucose and fatty acids, activates systems that sharpen our senses, and conserves resources by shutting down our immune system.

We often hear about stress as a negative consequence of modern living. People are stressed from overwork, job insecurity, information overload, and the increasing pace of life. These events produce *distress*—the degree of physiological, psychological, and behavioural deviation from healthy functioning. There is also a positive side of stress, called *eustress*, which refers to the healthy, positive, constructive outcome of stressful events and the stress response. Eustress is the stress experience in moderation, enough to activate and motivate people so that they can achieve goals, change their environments, and succeed in life's challenges. In other words, we need some stress to survive.[5] However, most research focuses on distress, because it is a significant concern in organizational settings. Employees frequently experience enough stress to hurt their job performance and increase their risk of mental and physical health problems. Consequently, our discussion will focus more on distress than on eustress.

■ **EXHIBIT 7.1**

Selye's general
adaptation syndrome

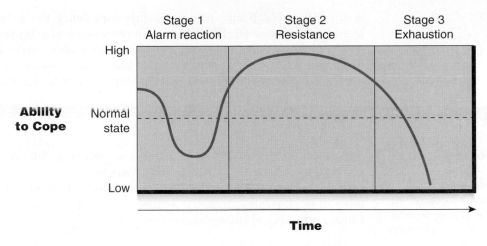

Sources: Adapted from H. Selye, *The Stress of Life* (New York: McGraw-Hill, 1956).

GENERAL ADAPTATION SYNDROME

The stress experience was first documented 50 years ago by Dr. Hans Selye, the Montreal-based pioneer in stress research.[6] Selye determined that people have a fairly consistent physiological response to stressful situations. This response, called the **general adaptation syndrome**, provides an automatic defence system to help us cope with environmental demands. Exhibit 7.1 illustrates the three stages of the general adaptation syndrome: alarm, resistance, and exhaustion. The curved line in this exhibit shows the individual's energy and ability to cope with the stressful situation.

Alarm reaction   The alarm reaction stage occurs when a threat or challenge activates the physiological stress responses that we noted earlier, such as increased respiration rate, blood pressure, heartbeat, and muscle tension. The individual's energy level and coping effectiveness decrease in response to the initial shock. In extreme situations, this shock can result in incapacity or death because the body is unable to generate enough energy quickly enough. Most of the time, the alarm reaction alerts the person to the environmental condition and prepares the body for the resistance stage.

Resistance   The person's ability to cope with the environmental demand rises above the normal state during the resistance stage because the body activates various biochemical, psychological, and behavioural mechanisms. For example, we have a higher than normal level of adrenaline and glucose during this stage, which give us more energy to overcome or remove the source of stress. At the same time, the body shuts down the immune system to focus energy on the source of the stress. This explains why people are more likely to catch a cold or other illness when they experience prolonged stress.

Exhaustion   People have a limited resistance capacity and, if the source of stress persists, they will eventually move into the exhaustion stage. In most work situations, the general adaptation syndrome process ends long before total exhaustion. Employees resolve tense situations before the destructive consequences of stress become manifest, or they withdraw from the stressful situation, rebuild their survival capabilities, and return later to the stressful environment with renewed

**general
adaptation
syndrome**
A model of the stress
experience, consisting of three stages:
alarm reaction, resistance, and exhaustion.

energy. However, people who frequently experience the general adaptation syndrome have increased risk of long-term physiological and psychological damage.[7]

The general adaptation syndrome describes the stress experience, but this is only part of the picture. To effectively manage work-related stress, we must understand its causes and consequences as well as individual differences in the stress experience.

■ STRESSORS: THE CAUSES OF STRESS

stressors
The causes of stress, including any environmental conditions that place a physical or emotional demand on the person.

Stressors, the causes of stress, include any environmental conditions that place a physical or emotional demand on the person.[8] There are numerous stressors in organizational settings and other life activities. Exhibit 7.2 lists the four main types of work-related stressors: interpersonal, role-related, task control, organizational and physical environment stressors.

INTERPERSONAL STRESSORS

Among the four types of stressors, interpersonal stressors seem to be the most pervasive in the workplace. The trend toward teamwork generates interpersonal stressors because employees must interact more with co-workers. Organizational politics, which we'll discuss in Chapter 12, is another interpersonal stressor. Bad bosses can also be quite stressful. For instance, one study discovered that female healthcare assistants experienced much higher blood pressure when working with an inef-

■ **EXHIBIT 7.2**

Causes and consequences of stress

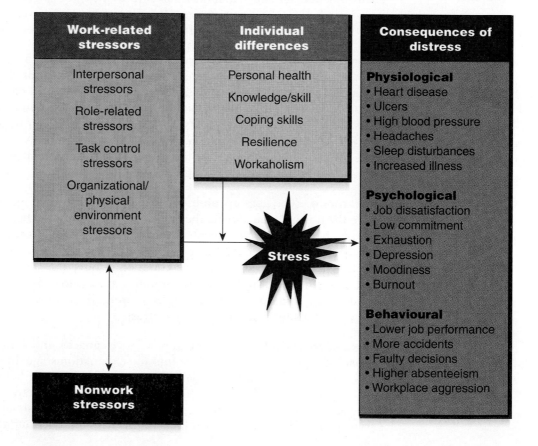

fective rather than effective supervisor. Over a sustained period, the higher blood pressure would increase the risk of stroke by 38 percent![9] Two other interpersonal stressors are workplace violence and harassment, which are discussed next.

Workplace violence   Workplace violence immediately brings to mind the United States, where 900 employees are murdered on the job each year and 2 million others experience lesser forms of physical violence. While these figures are troubling, the International Labour Organization (ILO) reports that Canadian employees are more at risk than Americans and people in most other developed countries with respect to workplace assault and sexual harassment. Another ILO study reported that over 60 percent of healthcare staff in Bulgaria, Australia, South Africa, and Portugal had experienced at least one incident of physical or psychological violence in the previous year.[10]

Victims of workplace violence experience severe stress symptoms. Those who observe the violence also tend to experience stress. After a serious workplace incident, counsellors assist many employees, not just the direct victims. Even employees who have not directly experienced or observed violence may show signs of stress if they work in jobs that expose them to a higher incidence of violence.

Psychological and sexual harassment   A family therapist at the Children's Aid Society of Cape Breton-Victoria had a history of anxiety attacks, which worsened after his new supervisor became irritated and critical of his recordkeeping. The supervisor eventually called a meeting in which he accused the employee of unprofessional practice. With another supervisor and union representative watching, the supervisor repeatedly demanded that the employee provide a date when the records would be caught up; the employee kept replying that the supervisor should give *him* a date. The argument got more heated and almost became violent as the two moved aggressively closer to each other. Abruptly, the employee left the meeting, saying "You may intimidate a lot of these young people around here, but you don't intimidate me!" Too shaken to get any work done, the employee went home, where his wife immediately sent him to the doctor to address his anxiety attack. The employee was suspended for a week, but then went on stress leave for several months.[11]

The Nova Scotia Court of Appeal recently concluded that the supervisor's behaviour was aggressive, his complaints were personal attacks, and the meeting was intended to embarrass and debase the employee. In other words, the supervisor engaged in **psychological harassment**. Psychological harassment includes repeated and hostile or unwanted conduct, verbal comments, actions or gestures, which affect an employee's dignity or psychological or physical integrity and that result in a harmful work environment for the employee. This covers a broad landscape of behaviours, from threats and bullying to subtle yet persistent forms of incivility.[12]

Psychological harassment has become such a problem that some European governments explicitly prohibit it in the workplace. The Quebec government, which recently passed the first workplace anti-harassment legislation in North America, received over 2,500 complaints in the first year alone! A massive survey of nearly 10,000 people in Quebec also revealed that 20 percent had been subjected to physical violence, intimidation, or unwelcome behaviour of a sexual nature at work over the previous 12 months. Furthermore, the comprehensive study of work and nonwork stressors concluded that workplace harassment had one of the strongest effects on psychological distress. Consistent with these findings, the Nova Scotia Court of Appeal concluded that the family therapist at the Children's Aid Society of Cape Breton experienced "traumatic" stress from the harassment dished out by his supervisor.[13]

psychological harassment
Repeated and hostile or unwanted conduct, verbal comments, actions or gestures, which affect an employee's dignity or integrity and result in a harmful work environment for the employee.

Burnaby Fire Captains Feel the Heat of Alleged Harassment

As one of the City of Burnaby's first three female firefighters, Boni Prokopetz faced more than her share of stressful experiences. On her first day of work in 1993, Prokopetz was shocked when co-workers gave her a copy of *Playgirl* magazine as "reading material." Her first performance review includes a written statement (still in her personnel file) from her supervisor that "she's not hard on the eyes." The supervisor also made several public comments over several years about her physique. Prokopetz also endured having co-workers watching pornographic movies in the fire hall, placing pornographic magazines on her bunk, and editing a recorded telephone conversation with a co-worker so it sounded sexually suggestive. Copies of the falsified "Bonigate" tape were circulated for several years and recently turned into a skit at a firefighter's retirement party.

The sexual and psychological harassment escalated in October 2003 when Prokopetz was promoted to captain in the fire prevention unit. Several people were upset with the promotion because they thought it should go to another firefighter even though he lacked the necessary qualifications. Prokopetz says that her direct supervisor rarely spoke to her after the promotion, communicating mainly with sticky notes. Some fire crews stopped calling her to investigate fire deaths or submitting reports to her. Someone drew a sexually explicit cartoon of Prokopetz with the fire chief, copies of which were circulated and posted at most fire halls. She also says the fire

Boni Prokopetz (shown in photo) had numerous stressful experiences over the past decade as a firefighter with the City of Burnaby. *Peter Battistoni/Vancouver Sun*

prevention unit chief would insult her in front of co-workers. Union leaders were notified of these and earlier problems, but apparently took no corrective action.

In January 2004, the Burnaby fire chief allegedly grabbed and tried to kiss Prokopetz in the parking lot. A few weeks later, the unit chief told both Prokopetz and a co-worker that they would no longer be given much real

---

sexual harassment

Unwelcome conduct of a sexual nature that detrimentally affects the work environment or leads to adverse job-related consequences for its victims.

Sexual harassment is a variation of harassment in which a person's employment or job performance is conditional on unwanted sexual relations (called *quid pro quo*), and/or the person experiences sexual conduct from others (such as posting pornographic material) that unreasonably interferes with work performance or creates an intimidating, hostile, or offensive working environment (called *hostile work environment*). One study points out that men tend to have a narrower interpretation than do women over what constitutes hostile work environment, so they sometimes engage in this form of sexual harassment without being aware of their transgressions.[14] Another issue is that sexual harassment sometimes escalates into psychological harassment after the alleged victim complains of the sexual wrongdoing. Connections 7.1 describes a recent example of this. What began as an internal complaint of sexual harassment by a female firefighter at the City of Burnaby allegedly developed into various forms of psychological harassment involving two male co-workers who supported her allegations.

Psychological and sexual harassment are stressful experiences that undermine employee well-being and performance. To minimize these interpersonal stressors, management and union leaders at British Columbia Rapid Transit Co. (which operates Van-

work. Prokopetz filed a complaint with the city and went on paid stress leave while the city hired an independent lawyer to investigate her charges. The report was submitted in May 2004 but never released, and the city said it needed more time to study the issue. By July 2004, fed up with the process, Prokopetz filed a formal complaint of sexual harassment and discrimination with the British Columbia Human Rights Tribunal. Soon after, the City of Burnaby asked the tribunal to drop the case because Prokopetz didn't file her complaint within the required six months of the harassment events. (The tribunal later rejected the city's argument.)

Two male Burnaby fire captains, Perry Talkkari and Garry Wilson, also filed claims of harassment in September 2004 against the city of Burnaby and the union. Talkkari worked with Prokopetz in her new job and helped train her when no one else was apparently willing to do so. However, Talkkari says his supervisor reprimanded him when "caught" providing this training. When he and Prokopetz were told that they would be stripped of real duties, Talkkari took stress leave until June 2004. When he returned, Talkkari says that he was almost completely ostracized from co-workers because he had agreed to support Prokopetz's claims. "I walk in the room, and they walk out the other door."

Meanwhile Wilson says the workplace became "poisonous" after co-workers learned that he intended to support Prokopetz's sexual harassment claims. Wilson says the union president warned him that his career would be scuttled unless he stayed out of the issue; the assistant fire chief allegedly gave him a similar warning a couple of months later.

Several other stressful events occurred leading up to the human rights tribunal hearings. However, Prokopetz was able to return to work in January 2005 as a fire prevention captain with a different supervisor and in a situation that didn't require contact with people identified in her complaint. In March 2005, a few weeks before the scheduled human rights hearing, Prokopetz reached a settlement with the City of Burnaby, and Talkkari and Wilson withdrew their complaints. The City of Burnaby has introduced sessions to make firefighters more sensitive to gender issues in the workplace.

Sources: CBC Radio, B.C. Almanac, Interview with Burnaby city manager Bob Moncur, September 1, 2004 (rtsp://media.cbc.ca/clips/Vancouver/rm-audio/bc_moncur_040901.rm); "Fire Captain Refuses Back-to-Work Order," *Vancouver Sun*, September 4, 2004; M. McQuillan, "City Won't React," *Burnaby News-Leader*, September 10, 2004; M. McQuillan, "New Complaints Levelled at Fire Department," *Burnaby NewsLeader*, September 17, 2004; J. Armstrong, "Female Firefighter Fuels a Firestorm," *The Globe & Mail*, September 18, 2004, p. A1; British Columbia Human Rights Tribunal, *Prokopetz v. City of Burnaby and others*, 2004 BCHRT 282 (December 14); "B.C. Firefighter Who Alleged Harassment Returning to Work," *CBC News*, January 7, 2005; British Columbia Human Rights Tribunal, *Talkkari v. City of Burnaby and others*, 2005 BCHRT 68 (February 9); British Columbia Human Rights Tribunal, *Wilson v. City of Burnaby and others*, 2005 BCHRT 69 (February 9); "Human Rights Victory for Firefighter Whistleblowers," *CBC News*, February 11, 2005; J. MacLellan, "City and Prokopetz Reach a Settlement," *Burnaby Now*, March 28, 2005.

couver's Skytrain system) developed a policy and program a decade ago to create a more respectful workplace. Past behaviour is the best predictor of future behaviour, so companies should carefully screen applicants in terms of past incidents. Multisource feedback is another valuable tool to let employees know that co-workers and direct reports find their behaviour intimidating or sexually inappropriate. Along with these practices, companies need to develop a grievance, mediation, or other conflict resolution process that employees trust when they become victims of workplace harassment.[15]

ROLE-RELATED STRESSORS

Role-related stressors include conditions where employees have difficulty understanding, reconciling, or performing the various roles in their lives. Three types of role-related stressors are role conflict, role ambiguity, and work overload. **Role conflict** refers to the degree of incongruity or incompatibility of expectations associated with the person's role. Some people experience stress when they have two roles that conflict with each other. For example, various Canadian studies have recently reported this inter-role conflict among human service workers and

role conflict
Conflict that occurs when people face competing demands.

healthcare providers, where workloads and bureaucratic procedures interfered with their ability to serve clients or patients.[16] Role conflict also occurs when an employee's personal values are incompatible with the organization's values, a topic that was detailed in Chapter 2.

role ambiguity
Uncertainty about job duties, performance expectations, level of authority, and other job conditions.

Role ambiguity refers to the lack of clarity and predictability of the outcomes of one's behaviour. Role ambiguity produces unclear role perceptions, which has a direct effect on job performance. It is also a source of stress in a variety of situations, such as joining the organization or working in a new joint venture, because people are uncertain about task and social expectations.[17]

Work overload   A half-century ago, social scientists predicted that technology would allow employees to enjoy a 15-hour work week at full pay by 2030. So far, it hasn't turned out that way. As depicted in the opening story to this chapter, Canadians experience considerable *work overload*—working more hours and more intensely during those hours than they can reasonably cope. Although official paid work hours are lower than a century ago, they have moved consistently upward in recent years. Nearly one-quarter of Canadian employees work more than 50 hours per week, compared with only 10 percent a decade ago. Equally significant, Canadians are working more *unofficial* hours. Surveys indicate that 81 percent of Canadians accept business calls at home, 65 percent check their work email after hours, and 59 percent check their work voice-mail after hours.[18]

Some writers suggest that the rising workload is caused by globalization and its demands for more work efficiency. Culture is another factor. Working long hours is still considered a badge of honour in some organizations, as well as in many countries, such as Japan. In that country, 20 percent of male Japanese employees chalk up more than 80 hours of overtime each month. The Japanese government is actively discouraging this work overload because of dramatic increases in *karoshi*—death from overwork. Karoshi occurs because long work hours cause an unhealthy lifestyle, such as smoking, poor eating habits, lack of physical exercise, and sleeplessness. This results in weight gain which, along with stressful working conditions, damages the cardiovascular system and leads to strokes and heart attacks.[19]

TASK-CONTROL STRESSORS

As a private driver for an executive in Jakarta, Eddy knows that traffic jams are a way of life in Indonesia's largest city. "Jakarta is traffic congestion," he complains. "All of the streets in the city are crowded with vehicles. It is impossible to avoid this distressing fact every day." Eddy's boss complains when traffic jams make him late for appointments, which makes matters even more stressful. "Even watching soccer on TV or talking to my wife doesn't get rid of my stress. It's driving me mad."[20]

Eddy and many other people experience stress due to a lack of task control. Along with driving through congested traffic, low task control occurs where the employee's work is paced by a machine, the job involves monitoring equipment, or the work schedule is controlled by someone else. For instance, significantly higher stress was reported among employees after "lean production" practices were introduced because these practices reduced employee control over the work process. Many people also experience stress because computers, cellphones, and other technologies control their time and intrude on their private lives. A Statistics Canada study of 12,000 Canadians reported that employees in production, sales, and service jobs have higher psychological stress because of their lack of work control.[21]

The extent to which low task control is a stressor increases with the burden of responsibility the employee must carry. Assembly line workers have low task control, but their stress can also be fairly low if their level of responsibility is also low. In contrast, sports coaches are under immense pressure to win games (high responsibility), yet have little control over what happens on the playing field (low task control). Similarly, Eddy (the Jakarta driver) is under pressure to get his employer to a particular destination on time (high responsibility), yet he has little control over traffic congestion (low task control).

ORGANIZATIONAL AND PHYSICAL ENVIRONMENT STRESSORS

Organizational and physical environment stressors come in many forms. Downsizing (reducing the number of employees) is extremely stressful to those who lose their jobs. However, layoff survivors also experience stress because of the reduced job security, chaos of change, additional workloads, and guilt of having a job as others lose theirs. For example, employees in Finland who survived a major downsizing took twice as much sick leave than they did before the downsizing.[22]

Some stressors are found in the physical work environment, such as excessive noise, poor lighting, and safety hazards. People working in dangerous work environments also tend to experience higher stress levels. This is powerfully illustrated in GLOBAL Connections 7.2, which describes the stressful experiences of medical staff at Prince of Wales Hospital in Hong Kong during the SARS crisis. Notice how the stress of working with an unknown disease is amplified by other stressors, including the uncomfortable clothing, aggressive patients, and work–family conflict.

WORK–NONWORK STRESSORS

The stress model shown earlier in Exhibit 7.2 has a two-way arrow, indicating that stressors from work spill over into nonwork and vice-versa.[23] There are three types of work–nonwork stressors: time-based, strain-based, and role-based conflict.

Time-based conflict Time-based conflict refers to the challenge of balancing the time demanded by work with family and other nonwork activities. Time-based conflict relates back to the work overload stressor described earlier. As Canadians work longer hours (and more intensely during those hours), they have little time or energy left for themselves and their family. Inflexible work schedules, business travel, and rotating shift schedules also take a heavy toll because they reduce the ability to effectively juggle work and nonwork.[24] Time-based conflict is usually more acute for women than for men because housework and childcare continue to fall more on their shoulders as a "second shift" in most dual-career families.

Strain-based conflict Strain-based conflict occurs when stress from one domain spills over to the other. Relationship problems, financial difficulties, and loss of a loved one usually top the list of nonwork stressors. New responsibilities, such as marriage, birth of a child, and a mortgage, are also stressful to most of us. Stress at work also spills over to an employee's personal life and often becomes the foundation of stressful relations with family and friends. In support of this, one study found that fathers who experience stress at work engage in dysfunctional parenting behaviours, which then lead to their children's behaviour problems in school.[25]

The Stress of SARS

Hong Kong physician Tom Buckley has faced many challenges, including treating victims of a devastating fire in 1996 and the bird flu outbreak in 1997. But neither of those events compared to the stress that Buckley and his colleagues experienced during the recent outbreak of atypical pneumonia, known as severe acute respiratory syndrome (SARS). "Having been through those two events, I thought it was probably impossible that there would be anything that would ever match them for stress and anxiety, but this SARS outbreak has put those into the background very much," says Buckley, who formed the SARS unit at Hong Kong's Prince of Wales Hospital and now leads the intensive care unit at Princess Margaret Hospital in Toronto.

In less than five months, SARS infected 8,000 people worldwide and took the lives of more than 800 of them. The early weeks of the outbreak, centred around Hong Kong and mainland China, were particularly terrifying because no one knew how the virus spread or what medical interventions would work. Staff felt anxiety regarding their personal safety, particularly when colleagues became infected or they experienced high risk incidents. Prince of Wales nurse Joanna Pong recalls one incident in which an elderly SARS patient suffering from dementia lowered her mask and coughed hard at Pong. "It was a scary feeling," says Pong, who fortunately did not catch the disease.

Intensive care units were filled quickly beyond capacity with SARS patients. Nurses were exhausted by overwork and the challenges of wearing uncomfortable body suits, disposable surgical gowns, goggles, gloves, and tight-fitting masks throughout their shift. "Working with a mask on all day is incredibly exhausting," says Prince of Wales nurse Josephine Chung Yuen-man. "Some of my colleagues have lost a lot of weight due to all the stress."

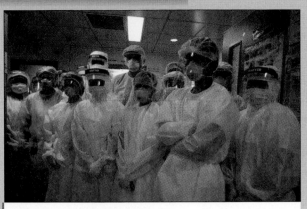

These medical professionals at Prince of Wales Hospital in Hong Kong were on the front-line treating patients with the SARS virus, which claimed over 800 lives and created high stress levels among nurses and doctors. *AP Photo/ Vincent Yu*

For many medical staff, however, the greatest stress of the SARS epidemic was the isolation from loved ones. "I feel terribly lonely and cut off from other people," lamented Eric Wong, a Prince of Wales Hospital nurse in the SARS ward who spent most of his free time in the nursing quarters. "But I fear getting infected and spreading the virus on." During the epidemic, Wong avoided seeing friends and delayed his flight to New Zealand, where his wife and children live.

Sources: H. Luk, "Hong Kong's SARS-Stressed Nurses Describe Pressure, Isolation," *Associated Press*, May 22, 2003, p. 4; K. Bradsher, "SARS Takes High Toll on Nurses," *International Herald Tribune*, May 10, 2003, p. 1; N. Law, "Behind the Mask: Josephine Chung Yuen-Man," *South China Morning Post* (Hong Kong), May 1, 2003, p. 5; N. Fraser, "Devoted to Care, Despite their Fear," *South China Morning Post* (Hong Kong), April 20, 2003, p. 4.

Role behaviour conflict   A third work–nonwork stressor, called role behaviour conflict, occurs when people are expected to act quite differently at work than in nonwork roles. For instance, people who act logically and impersonally at work have difficulty switching to a more compassionate behavioural style in their personal lives. Thus, stress occurs in this adjustment from one role to the other.[26]

STRESS AND OCCUPATIONS

Several studies have attempted to identify which jobs have more stressors than others.[27] These lists are not in complete agreement, but Exhibit 7.3 identifies a representative sample of jobs and their relative level of stressors. We need to view

■ **EXHIBIT 7.3** Stressors in occupations

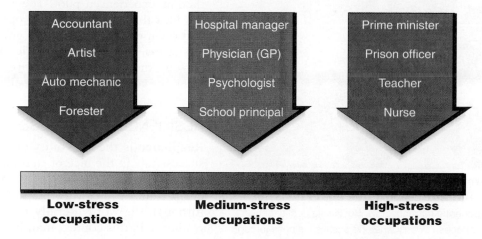

this information with some caution, however. One problem with rating occupations in terms of their stress levels is that a particular occupation may have considerably different tasks and job environments across organizations and societies. A nurse's job may be less stressful in a small-town medical clinic, for instance, than in the emergency room of a large city hospital.

Another important point to remember when looking at Exhibit 7.3 is that a major stressor to one person may be less significant to another. Thus, not everyone in so-called high-stress occupations actually experience more stress than people in other occupations. High-stress jobs have more stressors, but people don't experience more stress if they are carefully selected and trained for this type of work. The next section discusses individual differences in stress.

■ INDIVIDUAL DIFFERENCES IN STRESS

As indicated earlier in Exhibit 7.2, individual characteristics moderate the effect of stressors on the stress experience. Two people may be exposed to the same stressful conditions, such as having too many deadlines, yet one experiences much more stress than the other person due to a variety of personal factors.

One reason why people exhibit different stress outcomes is that they have different threshold levels of resistance to the stressor. Younger employees generally experience fewer and less severe stress symptoms than older employees because they have a larger store of energy to cope with high stress levels. Exercise and healthy lifestyles (including work-free holidays) are discussed later in this chapter as ways to manage stress because these activities rebuild this store of energy. A second reason for different stress outcomes is that people use different coping strategies, some of which are more effective than others. Research suggests that employees who try to ignore or deny the existence of a stressor suffer more in the long run than those who try to find ways to weaken the stressor and seek social support.[28]

The third reason why some people experience less stress than others in the same situation is that they have different beliefs about the threat and their ability to withstand it. This explanation really has two parts. The first part refers to the notion that people with more knowledge and skill usually feel more confident about successfully managing or overcoming the threat. For instance, someone who flies a plane

Stress-free at Finster Honey Farms
Working around honeybees is a heart-thumping experience for most of us. But Hakija Pehlic (shown here) doesn't worry when he pushes his nose through a layer of European honeybees to better determine the type of honey produced on a honeycomb frame. Pehlic, a beekeeper at Finster Honey Farms in Schuyler, New York, doesn't experience much stress in this situation because he is trained to know when it's safe to smell the honey and how to avoid getting stung. Most of the time, says Pehlic, honeybees are gentle insects that won't bother you. Maybe so, but you probably shouldn't try this at home.[34] *Heather Ainsworth, Observer-Dispatch (Utica, NY)*

for the first time tends to experience much more stress than an experienced pilot. The second part refers to the idea that people who are optimistic, confident, and often experience positive emotions tend to feel less stress.[29] This characteristic extends beyond the person's knowledge and skill; it refers to an important emerging concept, known as resilience.

RESILIENCE AND STRESS

Resilience is the capability of individuals to cope successfully in the face of significant change, adversity, or risk. Everyone has some resiliency; it occurs every time we pull through stressful experiences. Although the word literally means to "leap back," resilience in this context mainly refers to withstanding adversity rather than recovering from it. While everyone needs to recuperate to some extent following a stressful experience, people with high resilience are better able to maintain an equilibrium and, consequently, have lost little ground in the first place. In fact, some writers believe that resilience moves people to a higher plateau after the adversity.[30]

Experts have looked at the characteristics of resilience from different perspectives. One perspective is that resilient people have personality traits that generate more optimism, confidence, and positive emotions. These traits include high extroversion, low neuroticism, internal locus of control, high tolerance of change, and high self-esteem.[31]

resilience
The capability of individuals to cope successfully in the face of significant change, adversity, or risk.

A second perspective is that resilience involves specific competencies and behaviours to respond and adapt more effectively to stressors. Research indicates that resilient people have higher emotional intelligence and good problem-solving skills. They also apply productive coping strategies, such as analyzing the sources of stress and finding ways to neutralize these problems. In contrast, people with low resilience tend to avoid or deny the existence of stressors.[32]

The third perspective is that resilience is an inner force that motivates us to move forward. This emerging view is connected to the concept of self-actualization that psychologist Abraham Maslow popularized and made his life's work a half-century ago (see Chapter 5). It is also connected to recent OB writing on workplace spirituality, which investigates a person's inner strength and how it nurtures and is nurtured by the workplace. Resilience as an inner force has some empirical support. Research has found that resilience is stronger when people have a sense of purpose and are in touch with their personal values.[33]

workaholic
A person who is highly involved in work, feels compelled to work, and has a low enjoyment of work.

WORKAHOLISM AND STRESS

While resilience helps people to withstand stress, another personal characteristic—workaholism—attracts more stressors and weakens the capacity to cope with them. The classic **workaholic** (also called "work addict") is highly involved in work, feels compelled or driven to work because of inner pressures, and has a low enjoyment of work. He or she is compulsive and preoccupied with work, often to the exclusion and detriment of personal health, intimate relationships, and family. Work addicts are typically hard-driving, competitive individuals who tend to be impatient, lose their temper, and interrupt others during conversations.[35] These latter characteristics are collectively known as a **Type A behaviour pattern**.

According to a recent Statistics Canada study, 27 percent of adult Canadians (about the same percentage for men and women) say they are workaholics. Using a more comprehensive measure of workaholism, a study of York University MBA alumni reported that 16 percent are classic work addicts. The study also found that an additional 19 percent are enthusiastic workaholics and 14 percent are work enthusiasts.[36] Enthusiastic workaholics have high levels of all three components—high work involvement, drive to succeed, and work enjoyment. Work enthusiasts have high work involvement and work enjoyment, but low drive to succeed.

Workaholism is relevant to our discussion of stress because classic work addicts are more prone to job stress and burnout. They also have significantly higher scores on depression, anxiety, and anger than do non-workaholics, as well as lower job and career satisfaction. Furthermore, work addicts of both sexes report more health complaints.[37]

■ CONSEQUENCES OF DISTRESS

The previous sections on workplace stressors and individual differences in stress have made some reference to the various outcomes of the stress experience. These stress consequences are typically grouped into three categories: physiological, psychological, and behavioural.

PHYSIOLOGICAL CONSEQUENCES

Stress takes its toll on the human body.[38] The stress response shuts down the immune system, which makes us more vulnerable to virus and bacterial infection. Many people experience tension headaches due to stress. Others get muscle pain and related back problems. These physiological ailments are attributed to muscle contractions that occur when people are exposed to stressors.

Cardiovascular disease is one of the most disturbing effects of stress in modern society. Strokes and heart attacks were rare a century ago but are now one of the leading causes of death among Canadian adults. Various investigations, including a recent global study led by researchers at McMaster University, have found that stress is a significant cause of heart attacks.[39]

PSYCHOLOGICAL CONSEQUENCES

Stress produces various psychological consequences, including job dissatisfaction, moodiness, depression, and lower organizational commitment.[40] Emotional fatigue is another psychological consequence of stress and is related to job burnout.

Job burnout   **Job burnout** refers to the process of emotional exhaustion, cynicism, and reduced feelings of personal accomplishment resulting from prolonged exposure to stress.[41] It is a complex process that includes the dynamics of stress, coping strategies, and stress consequences. Burnout is caused by excessive demands made on people who serve or frequently interact with others. In other words, burnout

Type A behaviour pattern
A behaviour pattern associated with people having premature heart disease; Type A people tend to be impatient, lose their tempers easily, talk rapidly, and interrupt others.

job burnout
The process of emotional exhaustion, depersonalization, and reduced personal accomplishment resulting from prolonged exposure to stress.

■ **EXHIBIT 7.4**

The job burnout
process

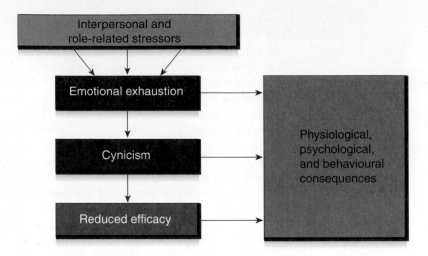

is mainly due to interpersonal and role-related stressors, and is most common in helping occupations (e.g., nurses, teachers, police officers).

Exhibit 7.4 diagrams the relationship among the three components of job burnout. *Emotional exhaustion*, the first stage, is characterized by a lack of energy, tiredness, and a feeling that one's emotional resources are depleted. Emotional exhaustion is sometimes called compassion fatigue because the employee no longer feels able to give as much support and care to clients.

Cynicism (also called *depersonalization*) follows emotional exhaustion. It is identified by an indifferent attitude toward work and the treatment of others as objects rather than people. At this stage, employees become emotionally detached from clients and cynical about the organization. This detachment is to the point of callousness, far beyond the normal level in helping occupations. Cynicism is also apparent when employees strictly follow rules and regulations rather than try to understand the client's needs and search for a mutually acceptable solution.

Reduced professional efficacy (also called *reduced personal accomplishment*), the final component of job burnout, refers to feelings of diminished confidence in the ability to perform the job well. In these situations, employees develop a sense of learned helplessness as they no longer believe that their efforts make a difference.

BEHAVIOURAL CONSEQUENCES

Moderate levels of stress focus our attention and concentrate resources where they are most needed. But when stress becomes distress, job performance falls, memory becomes impaired, workplace accidents are more frequent, and decisions are less effective.[42] You have probably experienced this in an exam or emergency work situation. You forget important information, make mistakes, and otherwise "draw a blank" under intense pressure.

Overstressed employees also tend to have higher levels of absenteeism. One reason is that stress makes people susceptible to viruses and bacterial infections. The other reason is that absenteeism is a coping mechanism. At a basic level, we react to stress through "fight or flight." Absenteeism is a form of flight—temporarily withdrawing from the stressful situation so that we have an opportunity to re-energize. Companies may try to minimize absenteeism, but it sometimes helps employees avoid the exhaustion stage of the stress experience.[43]

Workplace aggression Workplace aggression is more than the serious interpersonal stressor described earlier. It is also an increasingly worrisome behavioural consequence of stress. Aggression represents the fight (instead of flight) reaction to stress. In its mildest form, employees engage in verbal harassment. They "fly off the handle" and are less likely to empathize with co-workers. Like most forms of workplace behaviour, co-worker aggression is caused by both the person and the situation. While certain individuals are more likely to be aggressive, their behaviour is also usually a consequence of extreme stress to some extent.[44] In particular, employees are more likely to engage in aggressive behaviour if they believe they have been treated unfairly, experience other forms of frustration beyond their personal control, and work in physical environments that are stressful (e.g., hot, noisy).

MANAGING WORK-RELATED STRESS

After returning from maternity leave, Susanne Zorn-Smith was handed a job as financial services manager at a busy, understaffed branch in eastern Ontario. The Bank of Montreal employee was ill-qualified for the job, but refusal meant a pay cut. In addition, the bank insisted that she complete ongoing coursework for the job. Zorn-Smith's performance reviews describe her as hardworking, conscientious, loyal, well-liked, and full of initiative. Consistent with this record, she tried to keep up by working long hours, often returning to the bank until after midnight after feeding her three children and putting them to bed. She complained to management as her stress grew worse and her marriage began to suffer, but the bank did not correct the workload or understaffing. After two years, Zorn-Smith simply stopped functioning. She was diagnosed with job burnout.[45]

Susanne Zorn-Smith slowly recovered from her stressful experience, and the Bank of Montreal now uses this incident as a case study to train managers. It not only reveals the serious consequences of work-related stress, but also how companies need to pay attention to workplace stressors. The solution is for both employers and employees to discover the toolkit of effective stress management strategies identified in Exhibit 7.5, and to determine which ones are best for the situation.[46]

REMOVE THE STRESSOR

From the categories in Exhibit 7.5, some writers argue that the only way companies can effectively manage stress is by removing the stressors that cause unnecessary strain and job burnout. Other stress management strategies may keep employees "stress-fit," but they don't solve the fundamental causes of stress.

Removing the stressor usually begins by identifying areas of high stress and determining its main causes. Ericsson Canada, which was described at the beginning of this chapter, conducts this diagnosis through an annual survey that includes a stress index. Executives at the telecommunications company use the index to identify departments where stress problems may be developing. "We look at those scores and if there appears to be a problem in a particular group, we put in action plans to try and remedy and improve the work situation that may be causing the stress," explains Ericsson Canada vice-president Peter Buddo.[47]

An important, but very difficult, approach to stress reduction is changing the corporate culture to support a work/life balance rather than dysfunctional worka-

■ **EXHIBIT 7.5**

Stress management
strategies

holism. Another strategy is to give employees more control over their work and work environment. Role-related stressors can be minimized by selecting and assigning employees to positions that match their competencies. Noise and safety risks are stressful, so improving these conditions would also go a long way to minimizing stress in the workplace. Workplace harassment can be minimized by carefully selecting employees and having clear guidelines of behaviour and feedback to those who violate those standards.[48]

Employees can also take an active role in removing stressors. If stress is caused by ambiguous role expectations, for example, employees might seek out more information from others to clarify these expectations. If a particular piece of work is too challenging, they might break it into smaller sets of tasks so that the overall project is less threatening or wearing. To some extent, employees can also minimize workplace harassment by learning to identify early warning signs of aggression in customers and co-workers and by developing interpersonal skills that dissipate aggression.

Work/life balance initiatives   In a variety of ways, companies can help employees experience a better balance between their work and personal lives. Five of the most common work/life balance initiatives are flexible work time, job sharing, teleworking, personal leave, and childcare support.

■ *Flexible work time*—Some firms are flexible on the hours, days, and amount of time employees work. For example, flexible and part-time work schedules have become so popular at PricewaterhouseCoopers that the accounting firm now has an online program for employees to schedule them.[49]

■ *Job sharing*—Job sharing splits a career position between two people so they experience less time-based stress between work and family. They typically work different parts of the week with some overlapping work time in the weekly schedule to coordinate activities. Although traditionally aimed at non-management positions, job sharing is also starting to occur in executive jobs.[50]

■ *Teleworking*—Chapter 1 described how an increasing number of employees are teleworking. This reduces the time and stress of commuting to work and makes it easier to fulfill family obligations, such as temporarily leaving the home office to pick the kids up from school. Research suggests that teleworkers experience a healthier work/life balance.[51] However, teleworking may increase stress for those who crave social interaction and who lack the space and privacy necessary to work at home.

■ *Personal leave*—Employers with strong work/life values offer extended maternity, paternity, and personal leaves to care for a new family member or take advantage of a personal experience. Governments across Canada offer paid maternity leave, and some firms extend or top-up this paid time off. Increasingly, employees require personal leave to care for elderly parents who need assistance.

■ *Childcare support*—On-site childcare centres have existed since World War II, when women worked in war factories. In 1964, Toronto's Riverdale Hospital became one of the first organizations during the post-war era to have a childcare centre. Today, childcare facilities are found at L'Oreal Canada in Montreal, the City of Mississauga, New Brunswick's South-East Regional Health Authority, and at many other Canadian organizations.[52] Childcare support reduces stress because employees are less rushed to drop off children and less worried during the day about how well they are doing.

Given the high levels of work/life conflict that we read about earlier, you would think that organizations are encouraging employees to apply these initiatives. The reality, according to some critics, is that while these practices are available, employees either feel guilty about using them or are discouraged from using them. To ensure that employees actually develop a work/life balance, the top 500 managers at accounting firm RSM McGladrey, Inc., receive annual 360-degree reviews in which peers, subordinates, and managers rate how well the executive respects and encourages "balance of work and personal life priorities" among employees.[53]

Singing the Stress Away

When employees at Liggett-Stashower Inc. need a short break from the daily stresses of work, they retreat to one of three theme rooms specially designed for creativity and respite. Staff at the Cleveland advertising firm can enter the bowling room and knock down a few pins. Or they might try out the Zen room, which serves as a quiet, relaxing place to think. Behind the third door is a karaoke room where frustrated employees can belt out tunes. "The higher the stress level, the more singing there is going on," says Kristen Flynn, a Liggett-Stashower art director.[54] *Courtesy of Liggett-Stashower*

www.liggett.com

WITHDRAW FROM THE STRESSOR

Removing the stressor may be the ideal solution, but it is often not feasible. An alternative strategy is to permanently or temporarily remove employees from the stressor. Permanent withdrawal occurs when employees are transferred to jobs that better fit their competencies and values.

Temporary withdrawal strategies Temporarily withdrawing from stressors is the most frequent way that employees manage stress. SOLCORP, a major software provider, recently moved to a new head office in downtown Toronto where employees can recharge

Controlling Stress through Exercise
Chris Beaton's job at the Ford Credit call centre in Edmonton is quite stressful, particularly when dealing with difficult people in arrears. Fortunately, Beaton can take a stress break and build up his stamina at the company's well-equipped fitness centre. "It's a bit of escapism," admits Beaton, shown here with co-workers Anne Desrochers (left) and Marie-Josee Fortier. "You come in, relax, and get away from work for awhile," Beaton explains. "When you come back in the afternoon, you've burned off a bit of tension—you're not as pent up as you were when you first came down. *Ian Jackson, Edmonton Journal*
www.fordcredit.ca

their energy in a Zen garden and relaxation room. Lighthouse Publishing in Bridgewater, N.S., offers employees massage sessions every month. At TeleTech's call centre in Orillia, Ontario, employees can retreat to a cyber café near the cafeteria, which features a soothing tropical desert island mural that employees painted.[55]

Days off and vacations represent somewhat longer temporary withdrawals from stressful conditions. One study of a police and emergency response services department in Western Canada found that this leisure time significantly improved the employees' ability to cope with work-related stress. A few Canadian firms, including McDonald's of Canada, accounting firm KPMG, and law firm McCarthy Tetrault, offer paid sabbaticals to long-service employees.[56]

CHANGE STRESS PERCEPTIONS

Earlier, we learned that employees often experience different levels of stress in the same situation because they have different levels of self-confidence and optimism. Consequently, corporate leaders need to look at ways for employees to strengthen their confidence and self-esteem so that job challenges are not perceived as threatening. Self-leadership practices seem to help here. For example, positive self-talk can boost self-confidence. A study of newly hired accountants reported that personal goal setting and self-reinforcement can also reduce the stress that people experience when they enter new work settings.[57] Humour can also improve optimism and create positive emotions by taking some psychological weight off the situation.

CONTROL THE CONSEQUENCES OF STRESS

Coping with workplace stress also involves controlling its consequences. For this reason, many Canadian companies have fitness centres where employees can keep in shape. Research indicates that physical exercise reduces the physiological consequences of stress by helping employees moderate their breathing and heart rate, muscle tension, and stomach acidity.[58]

Another way to control the physiological consequences of stress is through relaxation and meditation. For instance, employees at pharmaceutical company AstraZeneca practise a form of meditation called Qi Gong during department meetings and coffee breaks. Research has found that Qi and other forms of meditation reduce anxiety, reduce blood pressure and muscle tension, and moderate breathing and heart rate.[59]

Along with fitness and relaxation/meditation, many firms have shifted to the broader approach of wellness programs. These programs educate and support employees in better nutrition and fitness, regular sleep, and other good health habits. For example, the Town of Richmond Hill, Ontario, has a comprehensive wellness program for employees that includes health risk assessment reviews, awareness sessions, special health clinics, and fitness club membership subsidies.[60]

employee assistance programs (EAPs)
Counselling services that help employees overcome personal or organizational stressors and adopt more effective coping mechanisms.

Many large employers offer **employee assistance programs (EAPs)**—counselling services that help employees overcome personal or organizational stressors and adopt more effective coping mechanisms. Most EAPs are "broadbrush" programs that assist employees on any work or personal problems. Family problems often represent the largest percentage of EAP referrals, although this varies with industry and location. For instance, Canada's major banks provide post-trauma stress counselling for employees after a robbery. EAPs can be one of the most effective stress management interventions where the counselling helps employees to understand the stressors, acquire stress management skills, and practise those stress management skills.[61]

RECEIVE SOCIAL SUPPORT

Social support from co-workers, supervisors, family members, friends, and others is generally regarded as one of the more effective stress management practices. Social support refers to the person's interpersonal transactions with others and involves providing either emotional or informational support to buffer the stress experience. Seeking social support is called a "tend and befriend" response to stress, and research suggests that women often follow this route rather than the "fight-or-flight" alternative that was mentioned earlier in this chapter.[62]

Social support reduces stress in at least three ways.[63] First, employees improve their perception that they are valued and worthy. This, in turn, increases resilience because they have higher self-esteem and confidence to cope with the stressor. Second, social support provides information to help employees interpret, comprehend, and possibly remove the stressor. For instance, social support might reduce a new employee's stress because co-workers describe ways to handle difficult customers. Finally, emotional support from others can directly help to buffer the stress experience. This last point reflects the idea that "misery loves company." People seek out and benefit from the emotional support of others when they face threatening situations.[64]

Social support is an important way to cope with stress that everyone can practise by maintaining friendships. This includes helping others when they need a little support from the stressors of life. Organizations can facilitate social support by providing opportunities for social interaction among employees as well as their families. People in leadership roles also need to practise a supportive leadership style when employees work under stressful conditions and need this social support. Mentoring relationships with more senior employees may also help junior employees cope with organizational stressors.

CHAPTER SUMMARY

Stress is an adaptive response to a situation that is perceived as challenging or threatening to the person's well-being. Distress represents high stress levels that have negative consequences, whereas eustress represents the moderately low stress levels needed to activate people. The stress experience, called the *general adaptation syndrome*, involves moving through three stages: alarm reaction, resistance, and exhaustion. The stress model shows that stress is caused by stressors, but the effect of these stressors on stress is moderated by individual characteristics.

Stressors are the causes of stress and include any environmental conditions that place a physical or emotional demand on the person. Stressors are found in the physical work environment, the employee's various life roles, interpersonal relations, and organizational activities and conditions. Conflicts between work and nonwork obligations are a frequent source of employee stress.

Two people exposed to the same stressor may experience different stress levels because they have different threshold stress levels, use different coping strategies, or have different beliefs about the threat and their ability to withstand it. People experience less stress when they have high resilience—the capability of individuals to cope successfully in the face of significant change, adversity, or risk. Classic workaholics (work addicts)—those who are highly involved in work, feel compelled or driven to work because of inner pressures, and have a low enjoyment of work—tend to experience more stress.

Intense or prolonged stress can cause physiological symptoms, such as cardiovascular disease headaches, and muscle pain. Psychologically, stress reduces job satisfaction and organizational commitment, and increases moodiness, depression, and job burnout. Job burnout refers to the process of emotional exhaustion, cynicism, and reduced efficacy resulting from prolonged exposure to stress. It is mainly due to interpersonal and role-related stressors and is most common in helping occupations. Behavioural symptoms of stress include lower job performance, poorer decisions, more workplace accidents, higher absenteeism, and more workplace aggression.

Many interventions are available to manage work-related stress. Some directly remove unnecessary stressors or remove employees from the stressful environment. Others help employees alter their interpretation of the environment so that it is not viewed as a serious stressor. Wellness programs encourage employees to build better physical defences against stress experiences. Social support provides emotional, informational, and material resource support to buffer the stress experience.

KEY TERMS

employee assistance programs (EAPs), p. 205

general adaptation syndrome, p. 189

job burnout, p. 199

psychological harassment, p. 191

resilience, p. 198

role ambiguity, p. 194

role conflict, p. 193

sexual harassment, p. 192

stress, p. 188

stressors, p. 190

Type A behaviour pattern, p. 199

workaholic, p. 198

DISCUSSION QUESTIONS

1. Several Web sites, including www.unitedmedia.com/comics/dilbert/ and www.cartoonwork.com, use humour to describe problems that people experience at work. Scan through these and other Web sites and determine what types of work-related stressors are described.

2. Is being a full-time college or university student a stressful role? Why or why not? Contrast your response with other students' perspectives.

3. Two recent college graduates join the same major newspaper as journalists. Both work long hours and have tight deadlines to complete their stories. They are under constant pressure to scout out new leads and be the first to report new controversies. One journalist is increasingly fatigued and despondent and has taken several days of sick leave. The other is getting the work done and seems to enjoy the challenges. Use your knowledge of stress to explain why these two journalists are reacting differently to their jobs.

4. Resilience is an individual characteristic that plays an important role in moderating the effect of stressors. Suppose that you have been put in charge of a task force in a large government department to ensure that employees are highly resilient. What would you and your task force do to accomplish this objective?

5. If you were asked to identify people who are classic workaholics (work addicts), what would you look for?

6. A friend says that he is burned out by his job. What questions might you ask this friend to determine whether he is really experiencing job burnout?

7. What should organizations do to reduce employee stress? What is the responsibility of an employee to manage stress effectively? How might fitness programs help employees working in stressful situations?

8. A senior official of a labour union stated: "All stress management does is help people cope with poor management. [Employers] should really be into stress reduction." Discuss the accuracy of this statement.

CASE STUDY 7.1

JIM BLACK: SALES REPRESENTATIVE

Jim Black impatiently drummed the steering wheel and puffed a cigarette as his car moved slowly northbound along the Don Valley Parkway. Traffic congestion was normal in the late afternoon, but it seemed much heavier today. In any event, it was another irritation that was going to make him late for his next appointment.

As a sales representative at Noram Canada Ltd., Jim could not afford to keep clients waiting. Sales of compressed oxygen and other gases were slower during this prolonged recession. Other compressed gas suppliers were eager to grab new accounts and it was becoming more common for clients to switch from one supplier to another. Jim pressed his half-finished cigarette against the ash tray and accelerated the car into another lane.

Buyers of compressed gases knew that the market was in their favour and many were demanding price discounts and shorter delivery times. Earlier in the week, for example, one of Jim's more demanding customers telephoned for another shipment of liquid oxygen to be delivered the next morning. To meet the deadline, Jim had to complete an expedited delivery form and then personally convince the shipping group to make the delivery in the morning rather than later in the day. Jim disliked making expedited delivery requests, even though this was becoming increasingly common among the reps, because it often delayed shipment of Noram's product to other clients. Discounts were even more troublesome because they reduced his commission and, except for very large orders, were frowned upon by Noram management.

Meanwhile, at Noram Canada's headquarters in nearby Brampton, Ontario senior managers were putting more pressure on sales reps to produce. They complained that the reps weren't aggressive enough and area supervisors were told to monitor each sales rep's monthly numbers more closely. Jim fumbled for another cigarette as the traffic stopped momentarily.

Two months ago, the area sales supervisor had "a little chat" (as he called it) with Jim about the stagnant sales in his district and loss of a client to the competition. It wasn't exactly a threat of being fired—other reps also received these chats—but Jim felt nervous about his work and began having sleepless nights. He began making more calls to potential clients, but was only able to find this time by completing administrative paperwork in the evenings. The evening work wasn't helping relations with his family.

To make matters worse, Noram's parent company in New York announced that it planned to sell the Canadian operations. Jim had heard rumours that a competitor was going to purchase the firm, mainly to expand its operations through Noram's Western Canadian sales force and production facilities. The competitor was well established in Ontario and probably wouldn't need a larger sales force here, so Jim's job would be in jeopardy if the acquisition took place. Jim felt another headache coming on as he stared at the endless line of red tail lights slithering along the highway ahead.

Even if Jim kept his job, any promotion into management would be a long way off if the competitor acquired Noram Canada. Jim had no particular desire to become a manager, but his wife was eager for him to receive a promotion because it would involve less travel and provide a more stable salary (less dependent on monthly sales). Business travel was a nuisance, particularly for out-of-town appointments, but Jim felt less comfortable with the idea of sitting behind a desk all day.

The loud honk of another car startled Jim as he swerved into the exit lane at Eglinton Avenue. A few minutes later, he arrived at the client's parking lot. Jim rummaged through his brief case for some pills to relieve the headache. He heaved a deep sigh as he glanced at his watch. Jim was 15 minutes late for the appointment.

Discussion Questions

1. What stress symptoms is Jim experiencing?

2. What stressors can you identify in this case?

3. What should Jim do to minimize his stress?

Copyright © Steven L. McShane.

T E A M   E X E R C I S E   7.2

STAGE FRIGHT!

Purpose   This exercise is designed to help you diagnose a common stressful situation and determine how stress management practices apply to this situation.

Background   Stage fright—including the fear of public speaking—is one of the most stressful experiences many people have in everyday life. According to some estimates, nearly three-quarters of us frequently get stage fright, even when speaking or acting in front of a small audience. Stage fright is an excellent topic for this team activity on stress management because the psychological and physiological symptoms of stage fright are really symptoms of stress. In other words, stage fright is the stress experience in a specific context involving a public audience. Based on the personal experiences of team members, your team is asked to identify the symptoms of stage fright and to determine specific stress management activities that effectively combat stage fright.

Instructions

■ *Step 1:* Students are organized into teams, typically four to six students per team. Ideally, each team should have one or more people who acknowledge that they have experienced stage fright.

■ *Step 2:* Each team's first task is to identify the symptoms of stage fright. The best way to organize these symptoms is to look at the three categories of stress outcomes described in the textbook: physiological, psychological, and behavioral. The specific stage fright symptoms may be different from the stress outcomes described in the textbook, but the three broad categories would be relevant. Teams should be prepared to identify several symptoms and to present one or two specific examples of stage fright symptoms based on personal experiences of team members. (Please remember that individual students are not required to describe their experiences to the entire class.)

■ *Step 3:* Each team's second task is to identify specific strategies people could or have applied to minimize stage fright. The five categories of stress management presented in the textbook will likely provide a useful template in which to organize the specific stage fright management activities. Each team should document several strategies to minimize stage fright and be able to present one or two specific examples to illustrate some of these strategies.

■ *Step 4:* The class will congregate to hear each team's analysis of symptoms and solutions to stage fright. This information will then be compared to the stress experience and stress management practices, respectively.

S E L F - A S S E S S M E N T   E X E R C I S E   7.3

CONNOR-DAVIDSON RESILIENCE SCALE (CD-RISC)

Purpose   This self-assessment is designed to help you estimate your personal level of resilience.

Instructions   Please check the box indicating the extent that each statement is true for you **over the past month**. Then use the scoring key in Appendix B of this book to calculate your results.

It is important for you to realize that there are no "right" or "wrong" answers to these questions. This self-assessment is completed alone so that you can use this instrument honestly without concerns of social comparison. However, class discussion will focus on the meaning of resilience and how it relates to workplace stress.

CONNOR-DAVIDSON RESILIENCE SCALE (CD-RISC)					
To what extent are these statements true about you over the past month?	Not at all true	Rarely true	Sometimes true	Often true	True nearly all of the time
1. I am able to adapt to change.	☐	☐	☐	☐	☐
2. I have close and secure relationships.	☐	☐	☐	☐	☐
3. I take pride in my achievements.	☐	☐	☐	☐	☐
4. I work to attain my goals.	☐	☐	☐	☐	☐
5. I feel in control of my life.	☐	☐	☐	☐	☐
6. I have a strong sense of purpose.	☐	☐	☐	☐	☐
7. I see the humorous side of things.	☐	☐	☐	☐	☐
8. Things happen for a reason.	☐	☐	☐	☐	☐
9. I have to act on a hunch.	☐	☐	☐	☐	☐
10. I can handle unpleasant feelings.	☐	☐	☐	☐	☐
11. Sometimes fate or God can help.	☐	☐	☐	☐	☐
12. I can deal with whatever comes my way.	☐	☐	☐	☐	☐
13. Past success gives me confidence for new challenges.	☐	☐	☐	☐	☐
14. Coping with stress strengthens me.	☐	☐	☐	☐	☐
15. I like challenges.	☐	☐	☐	☐	☐
16. I can make unpopular or difficult decisions.	☐	☐	☐	☐	☐
17. I think of myself as a strong person.	☐	☐	☐	☐	☐
18. When things look hopeless, I don't give up.	☐	☐	☐	☐	☐
19. I give my best effort, no matter what.	☐	☐	☐	☐	☐
20. I can achieve my goals.	☐	☐	☐	☐	☐
21. I am not easily discouraged by failure.	☐	☐	☐	☐	☐
22. I tend to bounce back after a hardship or illness.	☐	☐	☐	☐	☐
23. I know where to turn to for help.	☐	☐	☐	☐	☐
24. Under pressure, I focus and think clearly.	☐	☐	☐	☐	☐
25. I prefer to take the lead in problem solving.	☐	☐	☐	☐	☐

Source: K. M. Connor and J. R. T. Davidson, "Development of a New Resilience Scale: The Connor-Davidson Resilience Scale (CD-RISC)," *Depression and Anxiety* 18, no. 2 (2003), pp. 76–82.

S E L F - A S S E S S M E N T   E X E R C I S E   **7.4**

WORK ADDICTION RISK TEST

Go to the Online Learning Centre to complete this interactive self-assessment.

Purpose This self-assessment is designed to help you identify the extent to which you are a workaholic.

Instructions This instrument presents several statements, and asks you to indicate the extent to which each statement is true of your work habits. You need to be honest with yourself for a reasonable estimate of your level of workaholism.

SELF-ASSESSMENT EXERCISE   7.5

PERCEIVED STRESS SCALE

Go to the Online Learning Centre to complete this interactive self-assessment.

Purpose   This self-assessment is designed to help you estimate your perceived general level of stress.

Instructions   The items in this scale ask you about your feelings and thoughts during the last month. In each case, please indicate how often you felt or thought a certain way. You need to be honest with yourself for a reasonable estimate of your general level of stress.

SELF-ASSESSMENT EXERCISE   7.6

STRESS COPING PREFERENCE SCALE

Go to the Online Learning Centreto complete this interactive self-assessment.

Purpose   This self-assessment is designed to help you identify the type of coping strategy you prefer to use in stressful situations.

Instructions   This scale lists a variety of things you might do when faced with a stressful situation. You are asked how often you tend to react in these ways. You need to be honest with yourself for a reasonable estimate of your preferred coping strategy.

Case 1   VANCITY SWITCHEROO

Dave Mowat has worked in many aspects of banking prior to his current job as CEO of Vancouver City Savings Credit Union (VanCity). But in this CBC video program Mowat moves to the financial institution's true frontlines, where he has never worked before. Meanwhile, Lisa Paille is relinquishing her front desk position at a VanCity suburban branch to fill Dave Mowat's job. This program takes us through the next three days as Paille adjusts to making tough decisions and Mowat tries out various frontline jobs, from mailroom and maintenance to call centre and branch services.

Discussion Questions

1. What evidence suggests that Dave Mowat and Lisa Paille improved their perceptions of and empathy for the other's job through this switcheroo experience?

2. Both Dave Mowat and Lisa Paille experienced plenty of learning during this short switcheroo event. What type of learning occurred and how effective was this learning?

Case 2   PIKE PLACE FISH MARKET

Fifteen years ago, Pike Place Fish Market in Seattle had unhappy employees and was in financial trouble. Rather than close shop, owner John Yokoyama sought help from consultant Jim Bergquist to improve his leadership and energize the workforce. Rather than continuing to rule as a tyrant, Yokoyama learned how to actively involve employees in the business. Soon, staff felt more empowered and gained more enjoyment from their work. They also began to actively have fun at work, including setting goals as a game, throwing fish to each other as sport, and pretending they are "world famous." Today, thanks to these and other strategies described in this video case, Pike Place *is* world famous. The little shop has become a tourist attraction and customers from California to New York call in orders.

Discussion Questions

1. Based on the model of emotions and attitudes in Chapter 4, explain how the changes at Pike Place Fish Market improved job satisfaction and reduced turnover. How did these attitude changes affect customer satisfaction?

2. Goal setting is discussed as an important activity at Pike Place. Evaluate the effectiveness of this goal-setting process in the context of the characteristics of effective goals described in Chapter 5 of this textbook.

3. How is coaching applied at Pike Place, and how does this coaching influence employee performance?

Case 3   MONEY & ETHICS

Is business ethics an oxymoron? Although stock manipulation and other forms of business fraud have occurred for hundreds of years, Barbara Toffler, an ethics professor and former ethics consultant at Arthur Andersen, believes that business can be more ethical. Still, she acknowledges that being ethical isn't easy. Most executives know right from wrong, yet they make unethical decisions when the financial rewards and pressure to perform are high enough. This video program documents Toffler's experience at Arthur Andersen, where greed overwhelmed ethical values. It also tells the story of grocer Stew Leonard, Sr., who was jailed for tax fraud just two years after being featured in an ethics video.

Discussion Questions

1. Identify the various strategies described in this video program to encourage ethical conduct and discourage or punish wrongdoing. Explain why each of these practices is, or is not, effective.

2. Use the expectancy theory of motivation model, discussed in Chapter 5, to explain why people engage in unethical behavior even though they know it is wrong.

Case 4   EMPLOYEE LOYALTY

Not so long ago, companies offered secure employment. In return, workers showed their loyalty by remaining with one company for most of their careers. Not any more! This CBC video program illustrates how dramatically times have changed. Joel Baglole received an internship at the *Toronto Star* and later was offered a full-time job. Baglole happily accepted the position, but quit six weeks later when the prestigious *Wall Street Journal* offered him a job. Baglole explains why he has no obligation to be loyal to the *Toronto Star*, whereas *Toronto Star* publisher John Honderich believes that loyalty is important and should be expected. This program also examines ways that the *Toronto Star* and other companies try to increase employee loyalty.

Discussion Questions

1. Which, if any, of the five strategies to build organizational commitment would be effective in this situation involving Joel Baglole?

2. Explain how Joel Baglole's psychological contract is influenced by organizational loyalty in this situation.

Case 5   STRESS IN JAPAN (FROM THE SPEED TRAP)

Stress from overwork has become an epidemic in Japan. This video program consists of two segments that illustrate the degree to which some Japanese employees are overworked, as well as the consequences of their overwork. The first segment follows a typical day of a Japanese manager, from his two-hour morning commute to his late night working hours. The program also shows how he is under constant pressure to improve efficiency, and experiences a heavy burden and responsibility to do better. The second segment describes how *karoshi*— death from overwork—took the life of 23-year-old Yoshika. It reconstructs Yoshiko's work life as a graphic artist up to the time when she died suddenly on the job due to a brain hemorrhage.

Discussion Questions

1. Identify the various sources of stress (i.e., stressors) that the Japanese manager in the first segment likely experiences each day. Does he do anything to try to manage his stress?

2. What conditions led up to the karoshi death of Yoshika? Are these conditions commonly found in the country where you live?

·8·

DECISION MAKING AND CREATIVITY

LEARNING OBJECTIVES

AFTER READING THIS CHAPTER, YOU SHOULD BE ABLE TO:

■ Explain why people have difficulty identifying problems and opportunities.

■ Contrast the rational choice paradigm with how people actually evaluate and choose alternatives.

■ Describe three ways that emotions influence the selection of alternatives.

■ Outline how intuition operates.

■ Describe four causes of escalation of commitment.

■ Describe four benefits of employee involvement in decision making.

■ Identify four contingencies that affect the optimal level of employee involvement.

■ Outline the four steps in the creative process.

■ Describe the characteristics of employees and the workplace that support creativity.

What does a swarm of robot bees sound like? Cory Hawthorne tried to figure that out by listening to dozens of sounds and loops. Suddenly, eureka! The sound effects specialist at Vancouver-based Radical Entertainment found the right combination when he mixed his humming through a kazoo with the noise of operating an electric beard trimmer across the surface of his bathtub. The robot bees now had a menacing audio effect in the electronic game that Hawthorne was working on, *The Simpsons: Hit and Run*.

Radical depends on Cory Hawthorne and its other 230 employees to have plenty of "eureka!" moments in order to succeed in the competitive video game marketplace. "Hit games are made by people who have the freedom and support to put unconventional ideas in motion," explains Radical founder and CEO, Ian Wilkinson. "So, we give our employees the autonomy to drive real change, whatever their role in the company. No other games developer offers this level of creative freedom."

Danielle Michael, Radical's vice-president of business development, echoes Wilkinson's view that the best decisions in this fast-paced industry come from employee involvement and autonomy: "People are hugely empowered to be creative, to go beyond the call of duty to come up with great ideas and to actually implement them," says Michael.

To help guide employee decision making, posters hung throughout Radical's headquarters state the company's succinct values, including "Take risks, always learn." Wilkinson takes these

Radical Entertainment founder Ian Wilkinson (third from right) meets with employees every week to reinforce the Vancouver-based games developer's emphasis on creative decision making and employee involvement. *Ron Sangha*

values seriously. He lunches with a half-dozen employees each week (as shown in the photo), encouraging them to apply the company's values in their everyday decisions.

Creative ideas are also cross-pollinated through Radical's monthly "game fair" day, in which teams show off their products and make presentations to other teams in the organization. "I don't want to be hearing what other companies are doing," Wilkinson advises staff. "I want to do innovative stuff and have some people say we're crazy."[1] ■

www.radical.ca

decision making
A conscious process of making choices among one or more alternatives with the intention of moving toward some desired state of affairs.

Employees at Radical Entertainment make thousands of strategic and creative decisions that keep the electronic games developer at the forefront of innovation. **Decision making** is a conscious process of making choices among one or more alternatives with the intention of moving toward some desired state of affairs.[2] This chapter begins by outlining the rational choice paradigm of decision making. Then, we examine this perspective more critically by recognizing how people identify problems and opportunities, choose among alternatives, and evaluate the success of their decisions differently from the rational model. Bounded rationality, escalation of commitment, and intuition are three of the more prominent topics in this section. Next, we explore the role of employee involvement in decision making, including the benefits of involvement and the factors that determine the optimal level of involvement. The final section of this chapter examines the factors that support creativity in decision making, including characteristics of creative people, work environments that support creativity, and creativity activities.

■ RATIONAL CHOICE PARADIGM OF DECISION MAKING

How do people make decisions in organizations? For most of written history, philosophers, economists, and most scholars in Western societies have stated or assumed that people should—and typically do—make decisions based on pure logic or rationality. This rational choice paradigm began 2,500 years ago when Plato and his contemporaries in ancient Greece raised logical debate and reasoning to a fine art. A few centuries later, Greek and Roman Stoics insisted that one should always "follow where reason leads" rather than fall victim to passion and emotions. Over 500 years ago, several European philosophers emphasized that the ability to make logical decisions is one of the most important accomplishments of human beings. By the 1900s, social scientists and mathematicians had developed elegant rational choice models and formulae that are now embedded in operations research and other decision sciences.[3]

Exhibit 8.1 illustrates the rational choice process.[4] The first step is to identify the problem or recognize an opportunity. A problem is a deviation between the current and the desired situation—the gap between "what is" and "what ought to be." This deviation is a symptom of more fundamental root causes that need to be corrected.[5] An opportunity is a deviation between current expectations and a potentially better situation that was not previously expected. In other words, decision makers realize that some decisions may produce results beyond current goals or expectations.

The second step involves deciding how to process the decision.[6] One issue is whether the decision maker has enough information or needs to involve others in the process. Another issue is whether the decision is programmed or nonprogrammed. *Programmed decisions* follow standard operating procedures; they have been resolved in the past, so the optimal solution has already been identified and documented. In contrast, *nonprogrammed* decisions require all steps in the decision model because the problems are new, complex, or ill-defined. The third step is to develop a list of possible solutions. This usually begins by searching for ready-made solutions, such as practices that have worked well on similar problems. If an acceptable solution cannot be found, then decision makers design a custom-made solution or modify an existing one.

■ **EXHIBIT 8.1**

Rational choice decision-
making process

The fourth step is to choose from among the alternatives. The rational choice paradigm assumes that people naturally select the alternative with the highest *subjective expected utility*.[7] Subjective expected utility refers to how much the selected alternative benefits or satisfies the decision maker. Figuring out the alternative with the highest utility (total value or happiness) involves identifying all the outcomes that would occur if the alternative is selected and estimating the amount of satisfaction the person would feel from each of those outcomes. This is incredibly complex, but rational choice assumes that everyone does this calculation without any problem. The fifth step is to implement the selected alternative. This is followed by the sixth step, evaluating whether the gap has narrowed between "what is" and "what ought to be." Ideally, this information should come from systematic benchmarks, so that relevant feedback is objective and easily observed.

PROBLEMS WITH THE RATIONAL CHOICE PARADIGM

The rational choice paradigm seems so logical, yet it is rarely practised in reality. One reason is that the model assumes people are efficient and logical information processing machines. But as the next few pages will reveal, people have difficulty recognizing problems; they cannot (or will not) simultaneously process the huge volume of information needed to identify the best solution; and they have difficulty recognizing when their choices have failed. The second reason why the rational model doesn't fit reality is that it focuses on logical thinking and completely ignores the fact that emotions also influence—perhaps even dominate—the decision-making process. As we shall discover in this chapter, emotions both support and interfere with our quest to make better decisions.[8] With these points in mind, let's look again at each step of decision making, but with more detail about what really happens.

■ IDENTIFYING PROBLEMS AND OPPORTUNITIES

When Albert Einstein was asked how he would save the world in one hour, he replied that he would spend the first 55 minutes defining the problem and the last five minutes solving it.[9] Problem identification, the first step in decision making, is arguably the most important step. But problems and opportunities do not appear on our desks as well-labelled objects. Instead, decision makers translate information into evidence that something is wrong or that an opportunity is available.

To some extent, this discovery process occurs through conscious evaluation of the facts and persuasive arguments by other people. But what is becoming increasingly apparent is that a fair amount of problem recognition actually occurs during the mostly unconscious processes of perceptual selective attention and attitude formation (described in Chapters 3 and 4, respectively).[10] Specifically, we evaluate information as soon as we perceive it by attaching emotional markers (anger, caution, delight, etc.) to that information. The emotional markers are then sent to the rational centre where they influence the slower logical analysis of the situation. The result is that both the emotional markers and the logical analysis determine whether you perceive something as a problem, opportunity, or irrelevant.

Let's say that a worried-looking colleague tells you that the company's salesperson in Atlantic Canada just quit. You might immediately become worried or frustrated because your emotional brain centre quickly assigned these emotional markers to the news about the salesperson quitting. Meanwhile, the rational part of your brain works through this information, recalling from memory related knowledge that the former salesperson's performance had been mediocre and that an excellent salesperson at another company wants to join your firm in that region. What initially felt like a problem was really an opportunity based on your rational analysis of the situation. The initial emotions of worry or frustration might have been wrong in this situation, but sometimes your emotions provide a good indicator of problems or opportunities. Later, we'll see how emotions can be valuable allies in the quest to identify problems and choose the best solution.

PROBLEMS WITH PROBLEM IDENTIFICATION

Several problems occur in problem identification.[11] One concern is that employees, clients, and other stakeholders with vested interests try to influence the decision maker's perceptions of problems or opportunities. This persuasion "frames" the decision maker's view of the situation, which short-circuits a full assessment of the problem or opportunity. A second biasing effect is that under some conditions people block out negative information as a coping mechanism. Their brain refuses to see information that threatens self-esteem. A third perceptual challenge is that mental models blind people from seeing opportunities that deviate from the status quo. If an idea doesn't fit the existing mental model of how things should work, then the idea is dismissed as unworkable or undesirable. Connections 8.1 describes how narrow mental models are the source of several famous missed or near-missed opportunities.

A fourth barrier to effective problem identification is that decision makers often exhibit faulty diagnostic skills.[12] One diagnostic flaw is that leaders are expected to be decisive, and this decisive image motivates them to zero in on a problem without sufficiently analyzing the facts. Another diagnostic skill flaw is the tendency to define problems in terms of their solutions. Someone who says "The problem is that we need more control over our suppliers" has fallen into this trap.

Famous Missed Opportunities

Mental models create road maps that guide our decisions. Unfortunately, these maps also potentially block our ability to see emerging problems and opportunities. Here are a few famous examples:

Nia Vardalos's comedy screenplay about her Greek-Canadian family in Winnipeg was rejected by Hollywood literary agents and studios, yet it eventually became the top-grossing independent film in history and was nominated for an Oscar. *CP/Everett Collection*

- Nia Vardalos wrote a comedy screenplay based on incidents involving her Greek-Canadian family in Winnipeg. Unfortunately, none of Hollywood's literary agents were interested. "They all said it's not good; it's not funny," said Vardalos, who honed her writing and acting skills at the Second City comedy group in Toronto and Chicago before moving to Los Angeles. Undeterred, Vardalos turned the script into a successful one-woman show. None of Hollywood's talent agents accepted her invitation to see the show, but when actors Rita Wilson and Tom Hanks watched her skits, they immediately supported her on making a movie. Even with Hanks on board, Hollywood studios rejected the script. HBO agreed to provide a paltry US$2.5 million "as a favour" to Hanks. With a budget of only $5 million, *My Big Fat Greek Wedding* became one of the top five films of 2002 and the highest grossing independent film of all time. The screenplay that no one in Hollywood wanted was also nominated for an Oscar.

- Graphical user interfaces, mice, windows, pull-down menus, laser printing, distributed computing, and ethernet technologies weren't invented by Apple, Microsoft, or IBM. These essential elements of contemporary personal computing originated in the 1970s from researchers at Xerox PARC. Unfortunately, Xerox executives were so focused on their photocopier business that they didn't bother to patent most of these inventions. Xerox has successfully applied some of its laser technology, but the lost value of Xerox PARC's other computing discoveries is much larger than the entire photocopier industry today.

- When the World Wide Web burst onto the cyberspace scene in the early 1990s, Bill Gates wondered what all the fuss was about. Even as late as 1996, the Microsoft founder lampooned investors for their love-in with companies that made Internet products. However, Gates eventually realized the error in his mental model of computing. Making up for lost time, Microsoft bought Hotmail and other Web-savvy companies, and added Internet support to its Windows operating system.

- The best television commercial in history (as rated by *Advertising Age*) almost never saw the light of day. The Apple Macintosh "Why 1984 won't be like 1984" clip features a female athlete hurling a sledgehammer at a giant TV screen of an Orwellian Big Brother, liberating thousands of subjugated followers. Apple initially rejected the ad agency's (Chiat-Day) now-memorable phrase in an Apple II newspaper ad, but agreed to use this theme to launch the Macintosh computer during the 1984 Superbowl. The Macintosh team and sales force were ecstatic with rough cuts of the ad, but every outside director on Apple's board despised it. One remarked that it was the worst commercial of all time; another insisted that Apple immediately change its ad agency. Based on the board's reaction, Apple CEO John Sculley asked Chiat-Day to cancel the Superbowl ad space. Fortunately, the agency claimed it could only sell off some of the time, so Apple had to show the commercial. The single 60-second ad shown during the Superbowl had such a huge effect that it was featured on evening news over the next several days. A month later, Apple's board members applauded the Macintosh team for a successful launch and apologized for their misjudgment of the 1984 commercial.

Sources: T. Abate, "Meet Bill Gates, Stand-Up Comic," *San Francisco Examiner*, March 13, 1996, p. D1; O. Port, "Xerox Won't Duplicate Past Errors," *Business Week*, September 29, 1997, p. 98; B. Campbell and M. Conron, "Xerox Ready to Hit Another Home Run," *Ottawa Citizen*, June 28, 1999; P. Nason, "A Big Fat Hollywood Success Story," *United Press International*, December 12, 2002; M. McCarthy, "Top 20 in 20 Years: Apple Computer—1984," *Adweek Online*, www.adweek.com/adweek/creative/top20_20years/index.jsp (accessed January 16, 2003); A. Hertzfeld, "1984," www.folklore.org (accessed July 31, 2005).

© 1998 Randy Glasbergen.

"My team has created a very innovative solution, but we're still looking for a problem to go with it."

Randy Glasbergen.
Used with permission.

Notice that this statement focuses on a solution (controlling suppliers), whereas proper diagnosis would determine the cause of symptoms before jumping to solutions. This tendency is consistent with evidence that people form preferences for alternatives as soon as they are identified, rather than after understanding the problem.[13]

Defining a problem in terms of a preferred solution occurs because it gives decision makers a sense of comforting clarity in an ambiguous situation. It also occurs because people rely on a preferred set of actions that have worked well in the past. Some executives are known for cutting the workforce whenever they face problems; others introduce a new customer service program as their favourite solution to a variety of problems. The point here is that decision makers tend to look at problems from the perspective of the ready-made solutions that worked for them in the past.

IDENTIFYING PROBLEMS AND OPPORTUNITIES MORE EFFECTIVELY

Recognizing problems and opportunities will always be a challenge, but the process can be improved through awareness of these perceptual and diagnostic limitations. By recognizing how mental models restrict a person's understanding of the world, decision makers learn to openly consider other perspectives of reality. Perceptual and diagnostic weaknesses can also be minimized by discussing the situation with colleagues. Decision makers discover blind spots in problem identification by hearing how others perceive certain information and diagnose problems. Leaders require considerable will power to resist the temptation to look decisive when a more thoughtful examination of the situation should occur. Opportunities also become apparent when outsiders explore this information from their different mental models.

■ EVALUATING AND CHOOSING ALTERNATIVES

According to the rational choice model of decision making, people rely on logic to evaluate and choose alternatives. This process assumes that decision makers have well-articulated and agreed-on organizational goals, that they efficiently and simultaneously process facts about all alternatives and the consequences of those alternatives, and that they choose the alternative with the highest payoff.

Nobel Prize–winning organizational scholar Herbert Simon questioned these assumptions half a century ago. He argued that people engage in **bounded rationality** because they process limited and imperfect information and rarely select the best choice.[14] Simon and other OB experts demonstrated that how people evaluate and choose alternatives differs from the rational choice paradigm in several ways, as illustrated in Exhibit 8.2. These differences are so significant that even economists have shifted from rational choice to bounded rationality assumptions in their theories. Let's look at these differences in terms of goals, information processing, and maximization.

bounded rationality
Processing limited and imperfect information and satisficing rather than maximizing when choosing among alternatives.

■ **EXHIBIT 8.2**

Rational choice assumptions versus organizational behaviour findings about choosing alternatives

Rational choice paradigm assumptions	Observations from organizational behaviour
Goals are clear, compatible, and agreed upon.	Goals are ambiguous, in conflict, and lack full support.
Decision makers can calculate all alternatives and their outcomes.	Decision makers have limited information-processing abilities.
Decision makers evaluate all alternatives simultaneously.	Decision makers evaluate alternatives sequentially.
Decision makers use absolute standards to evaluate alternatives.	Decision makers evaluate alternatives against an implicit favourite.
Decision makers use factual information to choose alternatives.	Decision makers process perceptually distorted information.
Decision makers choose the alternative with the highest payoff.	Decision makers choose the alternative that is good enough.

PROBLEMS WITH GOALS

We need clear goals to choose the best solution. Goals identify "what ought to be" and, therefore, provide a standard against which each alternative is evaluated. The reality, however, is that organizational goals are often ambiguous or in conflict with each other. For instance, one survey found that 25 percent of managers and employees felt decisions are delayed because of difficulty agreeing on what they want the decision to achieve.[15]

PROBLEMS WITH INFORMATION PROCESSING

People do not make perfectly rational decisions because they don't process information very well. One problem is that decision makers can't possibly think through all of the alternatives and the outcomes of those alternatives. Consequently, they look at only a few alternatives and only some of the main outcomes of those alternatives.[16] For example, there may be dozens of computer brands to choose from and dozens of features to consider, yet people typically evaluate only a few brands and a few features.

A related problem is that decision makers typically look at alternatives sequentially rather than all at the same time. As a new alternative comes along, it is immediately compared to an **implicit favourite**. An implicit favourite is an alternative

implicit favourite
The decision maker's preferred alternative against which all other choices are judged.

that the decision maker prefers and is used as a comparison against which other choices are judged. There are two problems with this sequential implicit favourite process. First, as was mentioned earlier, we form preferences as soon as alternatives are identified without conscious evaluation and with very limited information. As a result, our implicit favourite might not be the best choice. Second, people unconsciously try to make their implicit favourite come out the winner by distorting information and changing the importance of decision criteria.[17] This effect was observed in a recent study of Canadian auditing students. Students who decided that the company in a case study had significant financial problems distorted the available information to make those problems appear worse. Students who felt the financial problems were not significant enough to report in a formal audit minimized any reference to the negative information in their case reports.[18]

PROBLEMS WITH MAXIMIZATION

satisficing
Selecting a solution that is satisfactory, or "good enough" rather than optimal or "the best."

Decision makers tend to select the alternative that is acceptable or "good enough," rather than the one with the highest payoff (i.e., the highest subjective expected utility). In other words, they engage in **satisficing** rather than maximizing. Satisficing occurs because it isn't possible to identify every alternative, and information about available alternatives is imperfect or ambiguous. Satisficing also occurs because, as mentioned already, decision makers tend to evaluate alternatives sequentially, not all at the same time. They evaluate each alternative against the implicit favourite and eventually select an option that is good enough to satisfy their needs or preferences.[19]

EVALUATING OPPORTUNITIES

Opportunities are just as important as problems, but what happens when an opportunity is "discovered" is quite different from the process of problem solving. According to a recent study of decision failures, decision makers do not evaluate several alternatives when they find an opportunity; after all, the opportunity is the solution, so why look for others! An opportunity is usually experienced as an exciting and rare revelation, so decision makers tend to have an emotional attachment to the opportunity. Unfortunately, this emotional preference generates a motivation to apply the opportunity and short-circuit any detailed evaluation of it.[20]

EMOTIONS AND MAKING CHOICES

Herbert Simon and others who studied this topic demonstrated that people do not evaluate alternatives nearly as well as is assumed by the rational choice paradigm. However, they neglected to mention another glaring weakness with rational choice—it completely ignores the effect of emotions in human decision making. Just as both the rational and emotional brain centres alert us to problems, these processes also influence our choice of alternatives.

The rapidly growing emotions literature identifies three ways that emotions affect the evaluation of alternatives. First, the emotional marker process described earlier in this chapter as well as in previous chapters (Chapters 3 through 5) determines our preferences for each alternative. Basically, our brain very quickly attaches specific emotions to information about each alternative, just as it does for information about problems or opportunities. Our logical thinking connects existing knowledge in our memory to new information and transmits this connected knowledge to the emotional centre where emotions are attached to that logical information. Ultimately, emotions, not rational logic, energize us to make the preferred choice. (People with damaged emotional brain centres have difficulty making choices.)

Second, moods and specific emotions influence the process of evaluating alternatives. For instance, we pay more attention to details when in a negative mood, possibly because a negative mood signals that there is something wrong that requires attention. When in a positive mood, on the other hand, we pay less attention to details by relying on a more programmed decision routine. Regarding specific emotions, decision makers rely on stereotypes and other shortcuts to speed up the choice process when they experience anger. They also tend to be more optimistic about the success of risky alternatives whereas fearful decision makers are less optimistic.[21]

Third, people "listen in" on their emotions to provide guidance when making choices.[22] Most emotional experiences remain below the radar screen of awareness, but sufficiently intense emotions are picked up consciously and figured into our decision. Suppose that you need to choose among a few advertising firms for a new product. You would logically consider several factors, such as previous experience, the agency's resources, and so on. But you would probably also pay attention to your gut feeling about each agency. If you feel good about a particular advertising firm, that feeling tends to get weighted into the decision. These gut feelings are given more weight by some people than others (see the Myers-Briggs Type Indicator in Chapter 2) and under different circumstances.[23] But all of us listen in on our emotions to some degree. This "emotions-as-information" phenomenon ties directly into our next topic, intuition.

INTUITION AND MAKING CHOICES

Greg McDonald felt uneasy about a suspicious-looking crack in the rock face, so the veteran Potash Corp. of Saskatchewan miner warned a co-worker to stay away from the area. "There was no indication there was anything wrong—just a little crack," McDonald recalled. A few minutes later, the ceiling in that mine shaft 1,000 metres underground caved in. Fortunately, the co-worker heeded McDonald's advice. "If he had been there, he would be dead," McDonald said in an interview following a near-sleepless night after the incident.[24]

intuition
The ability to know when a problem or opportunity exists and select the best course of action without conscious reasoning.

The gut instinct that helped Greg McDonald save his co-worker's life is known as **intuition**—the ability to know when a problem or opportunity exists and to select the best course of action without conscious reasoning.[25] Intuition is both an emotional experience and a rapid unconscious analytic process. As was mentioned in the previous section, the gut feelings we experience are emotional signals that have enough intensity to make us consciously aware of them. These signals warn us of impending danger, such as an unsafe mine wall, or motivate us to take advantage of an opportunity. Some intuition also directs us to preferred choices relative to other alternatives in that situation.

While all gut feelings are emotional signals, not all emotional signals are intuition. The key distinction is that intuition involves rapidly comparing what we see or otherwise sense with deeply held patterns learned through experience.[26] These templates represent tacit knowledge that has been implicitly acquired over time. When a template fits or doesn't fit the current situation, emotions are produced that motivate us to act. Intuition also relies on mental models, internal representations of the external world that allow us to anticipate future events from current observations. Greg McDonald's years of experience produced mental templates of unsafe rock faces that matched what he saw on that fateful day. Studies have also found that chess masters receive emotional signals when they sense an opportunity through quick observation of a chessboard. They can't immediately explain why they see a favourable move on the chessboard—they just feel it.

As mentioned, some emotional signals (gut feelings) are not intuition because they are not based on well-grounded templates or mental models. Instead, they occur when we compare the current situation to our templates and mental models of distant circumstances, which may or may not be relevant. Thus, whether the emotions we experience in a situation represent intuition or not depends largely on our level of experience in that situation.

So far, intuition has been described as an emotional experience (gut feeling) and a process of pattern matching in which we compare the current situation with well-established templates and mental models. Intuition also relies on *action scripts*—preprogrammed routines for responding to pattern matches or mismatches.[27] Action scripts allow us to act quickly by identifying the preferred course of action without consciously evaluating the alternatives. These action scripts are generic, so we need to consciously adapt them to the specific situation.

MAKING CHOICES MORE EFFECTIVELY

It is very difficult to get around the human limitations of making choices, but a few strategies may help. One important discovery is that decisions tend to have a higher failure rate when leaders are decisive rather than contemplative about the available options. Of course, problems also arise when decisions take too long, but research indicates that a lack of logical analysis is a greater concern. By systematically evaluating alternatives, decision makers minimize the implicit favourite and satisficing problems that occur when relying on general subjective judgments. Intuition still figures into this analysis, but so does careful consideration of relevant information.[28]

Another issue is how to minimize the adverse effects of emotions on the decision process. The first recommendation here is that we need to be constantly aware that decisions are influenced by both rational and emotional processes. With this awareness, some decision makers deliberately revisit important issues so that they look at the information in different moods and have allowed their initial emotions to subside. Others practice **scenario planning**, in which they anticipate emergencies long before they occur, so that alternative courses of action are evaluated without the pressure and emotions that occur during real emergencies.[29]

scenario planning
A systematic process of thinking about alternative futures, and what the organization should do to anticipate and react to those environments.

■ EVALUATING DECISION OUTCOMES

postdecisional justification
Justifying choices by unconsciously inflating the quality of the selected option and deflating the quality of the discarded options.

Contrary to the rational choice paradigm, decision makers aren't completely honest with themselves when evaluating the effectiveness of their decisions. One concern is that after making a choice, decision makers tend to support their choice by forgetting or downplaying the negative features of the selected alternative and emphasizing its positive features. This perceptual distortion, known as **postdecisional justification**, results from the need to maintain our self-esteem.[30] Postdecisional justification gives people an excessively optimistic evaluation of their decisions, but only until they receive very clear and undeniable information to the contrary. Unfortunately, it also inflates the decision maker's initial evaluation of the decision, so reality often comes as a painful shock when objective feedback is finally received.

ESCALATION OF COMMITMENT

escalation of commitment

The tendency to repeat an apparently bad decision or allocate more resources to a failing course of action.

A second problem when evaluating decision outcomes is **escalation of commitment**— the tendency to repeat an apparently bad decision or allocate more resources to a failing course of action.[31] There are plenty of escalation examples, including the Darlington nuclear power plant in Ontario, a subway extension project in Tokyo, and development of the Concorde supersonic airliner. (Some people still refer to escalation of commitment as the "Concorde fallacy.") One of the most dramatic recent examples is Scotland's recently opened parliament building. The project began in 1997 with an estimated cost of Cdn$110 million and completion by 2001. Instead, thanks to several escalation factors and other decision debacles, the building opened in 2004 at a cost exceeding Cdn$1 billion.[32]

Causes of escalating commitment   Why are people led deeper and deeper into failing projects? There are several reasons, including self-justification, prospect theory effect, perceptual blinders, and closing costs.

- *Self-justification*—Individuals are motivated to maintain their course of action when they have a high need to justify their decision. This self-justification is particularly evident when decision makers are personally identified with the project and have staked their reputations to some extent on the project's success.[33] This is likely the main reason why a former premier of British Columbia continued the PacifiCat ferry project (see photo) long after others would have cancelled the project.

- *Prospect theory effect*—You would think that people dislike losing $50 just as much as they like receiving $50, but that isn't true for most of us. We actually dislike losing a particular amount more than we like gaining the same amount. We also take fewer risks to receive gains and take more risks to avoid losses. This effect, called **prospect theory**, is a second explanation for escalation of commitment. Stopping a project is a certain loss, which is more painful to most people than the uncertainty of success associated with continuing to fund the project. Given the choice, decision makers choose the less painful option.[34]

prospect theory

An effect in which losing a particular amount is more disliked than gaining the same amount.

- *Perceptual blinders*—Escalation of commitment sometimes occurs because decision makers do not see the problems soon enough. They unconsciously screen out or explain away negative information to protect self-esteem. Serious problems initially look like random errors along the trend line to success. Even when they see that something is wrong, the information is sufficiently ambiguous that it can be misinterpreted or justified.

- *Closing costs*—Even when a project's success is in doubt, decision makers will persist because the costs of ending the project are high or unknown. Terminating a major project may involve large financial penalties, a bad public image, or personal political costs. This effect was apparent when a former premier of Ontario was asked why he didn't shut down the Darlington nuclear plant project. "I don't think anybody can look at a situation with . . . $7 billion in the ground and just cavalierly write it off," he replied.[35] The project eventually escalated to over $11 billion and is partly responsible for Ontario's high energy costs today.

These four conditions make escalation of commitment look selfish or foolhardy. Usually it is, but there are exceptions. Recent studies suggest that throwing more money into a failing project is sometimes a logical attempt to further understand an ambiguous situation. This strategy is essentially a variation of testing unknown waters. By

B.C. Ferries Escalates Commitment

In 1994, British Columbia Ferry Services (B.C. Ferries) decided to design and build three catamaran-style ferries for its route between the City of Vancouver and Vancouver Island. The premier of British Columbia, who championed these "PacifiCats," promised that they would travel faster than conventional ferries and cost $210 million "right down to the toilet paper." Instead, costs ballooned to nearly $500 million. The ferries were also plagued with maintenance problems, burned much more fuel than traditional ferries, took longer to turn around at the dock, and created such a large wake that they were slowed to nearly the speed of the current fleet to avoid damaging the shoreline. Five years later, with the PacifiCat project still supported by the premier, the B.C. auditor-general slammed the project, saying that government pressure had forced the B.C. Ferries board to endorse the project. When the B.C. premier was replaced (for other reasons), the new premier almost immediately cancelled the project. B.C. Ferries was privatized under the next government. The three fast ferries were sold at auction in 2003 for a total of $20 million. As a final irony, the company that bought them had offered $210 million in 1999, but the B.C. government had rejected the earlier offer.[36] *Ric Ernst/Vancouver Province*

adding more resources, the decision maker gains new information about the effectiveness of these funds, which provides more feedback about the project's future success. This strategy is particularly common where the project has high closing costs.[37]

EVALUATING DECISION OUTCOMES MORE EFFECTIVELY

One of the most effective ways to minimize escalation of commitment and postdecisional justification is to separate decision choosers from decision evaluators. This minimizes the self-justification effect because the person responsible for evaluating the decision is not connected to the original decision. A second strategy is to publicly establish a preset level at which the decision is abandoned or reevaluated. This is similar to a stop-loss order in the stock market, whereby the stock is sold if it falls below a certain price. The problem with this solution is that conditions are often so complex that it is difficult to identify an appropriate point to abandon a project.[38]

Finally, projects might have less risk of escalation if several people are involved. Co-workers continuously monitor each other and might notice problems sooner than someone working alone on the project. Employee involvement offers these and other benefits to the decision-making process, as we learn next.

■ EMPLOYEE INVOLVEMENT IN DECISION MAKING

employee involvement
The degree to which employees influence how their work is organized and carried out.

In this world of rapid change and increasing complexity, leaders rarely have enough information to make the best decision alone. Whether this information is about reducing costs or improving the customer experience, employee involvement can potentially solve problems or realize opportunities more effectively. **Employee Involvement** (also called *participative management*) refers to the degree to which employees influence how their work is organized and carried out.[39] At the lowest level, participation involves asking employees for information. They do not make recommendations and might not even know what the problem is about. At a moderate level of involvement, employees are told about the problem and provide recommendations to the decision maker. At the highest level of involvement, the entire decision-making process is handed over to employees. They identify the problem, choose the best alternative, and implement their choice.

Every organization has some form and various levels of employee involvement. Each year, a cross-section of employees at MAC Closures in Waterloo, Quebec and Oakville, Ontario, participate in a two-day retreat to draft the company's strategic plan for the following year. At Zenon Environmental Inc., employees decide on corporate changes affecting them through the firm's "Employee Parliament." At Calgary-based WestJet, a nonmanagement employee sits on the airline's board of director. And at Radical Entertainment, described in the opening vignette for this chapter, employees provide ongoing suggestions to CEO Ian Wilkinson and other executives through weekly luncheons.[40] GLOBAL Connections 8.2 provides a particularly dramatic example of high involvement, where employees in several Argentinean companies have completely taken over day-to-day decisions after the original owners abandoned their debt-ridden companies.

BENEFITS OF EMPLOYEE INVOLVEMENT

For the past half-century, organizational behaviour scholars have advised that employee involvement potentially improves decision-making quality and commitment.[41] Involving employees potentially improves decision quality by recognizing problems more quickly and defining them more accurately. Employees are, in many respects, the sensors of the organization's environment. When the organization's activities misalign with customer expectations, employees are usually the first to know. Employee involvement ensures that everyone in the organization is quickly alerted to these problems.[42]

Employee involvement can also potentially improve the number and quality of solutions generated. In a well-managed meeting, team members create synergy by pooling their knowledge to form new alternatives. In other words, several people working together can potentially generate more and better solutions than the same people working alone. A third benefit is that employee involvement often improves the likelihood of choosing the best alternative. This occurs because the decision is reviewed by people with diverse perspectives and a broader representation of values.[43]

Along with improving decision quality, employee involvement tends to strengthen employee commitment to the decision. Rather than viewing themselves as agents of someone else's decision, staff members feel personally responsible for its success. Employee involvement also increases perceptions of fairness because workers participate in the allocation of resources and rewards in the project. Consequently, employees are more motivated to implement the decision and are less likely to resist changes resulting from the decision. As one respected scholar recently wrote:

High Involvement Saves Argentine Companies

Empire Pizzeria's owners abandoned the business when they racked up huge debts, including overdue salaries and four years of back rent. Bankruptcy would have created severe hardship for the company's 30 employees because the shop is located in Buenos Aires, Argentina, a country with 22-percent unemployment and one of the worst recessions in 100 years. So, employees applied a unique solution: they formed a cooperative and took over the business. "If we were not running the business, we would be out on the street," explains an Empire waiter. "Most of us are over 50 and no employer wants someone our age." The company is now settling past debts and prospering in spite of difficult times.

Over 10,000 employees at more than 160 businesses throughout Argentina are experimenting with self-management through cooperatives that operate businesses abandoned by the original owners. Most of the employee-operated businesses are manufacturing concerns, such as a tractor factory in Córdoba and a tile and ceramics plant in Patagonia. Some of them are struggling, while others are booming since employees took over.

IMPA aluminum factory is one of the success stories. Forty workers took over the factory in 1998 and, for almost one year, scraped by on five pesos a day (equivalent to Cdn$2.10). Four years later, IMPA employed 172 people, each earning $350 a month. IMPA and most other cooperatives are run by administrative councils elected by employees. Wages, future employment levels, and other important business issues are discussed at monthly meetings. Employee enthusiasm is easily apparent. "Everybody is a partner here," says Guillermo Robledo, IMPA's elected plant manager. "That's our strength, the commitment we feel to something that is our own."

One challenge is that longstanding suppliers and customers have been reluctant to work with companies run by low-level employees. "It was difficult to get started because even though the company had a reputation,

Empire Pizzeria in Buenos Aires, Argentina, is a symbol of how employees (including from left Jose Gonzalez and Jose Lazarte) have successfully taken over a business that the original owners abandoned under weight of debt. *AP Photo/Natacha Pisarenko*

people did not believe that we workers were capable of managing things," explains an employee at a cooperative that prints art books, posters, and calendars. "We had to show that the high level of quality was still intact and that the only thing missing was a few executives in the front office."

Sources: L. Rohter, "Workers in Argentina Take Over Abandoned Factories," *New York Times*, July 8, 2003; P. Moser, "In Crisis-Torn Argentina, Workers Rescue their Factories," *Agence France Presse*, May 17, 2003; C. Fagan, "In Argentine Crisis, Workers become Entrepreneurs to Survive," *Associated Press*, December 8, 2002; M. Valente, "Argentina: Workers' Cooperatives Revive Bankrupt Companies," *Inter Press Service*, November 29, 2002.

www.globalexchange.org/campaigns/wto/ 771.html

"The new organizational realities are that top-down decision making is not sufficiently responsive to the dynamic organizational environment. Employees must be actively involved in decisions—or completely take over many decisions."[44]

CONTINGENCIES OF EMPLOYEE INVOLVEMENT

If employee involvement is so wonderful, why don't companies leave all decisions to employees further down the hierarchy? The answer is that the optimal level of employee involvement depends on the situation. The employee involvement model shown in Exhibit 8.3 indicates that the best level of employee involvement depends

■ **EXHIBIT 8.3**

Model of employee
involvement in
decision making

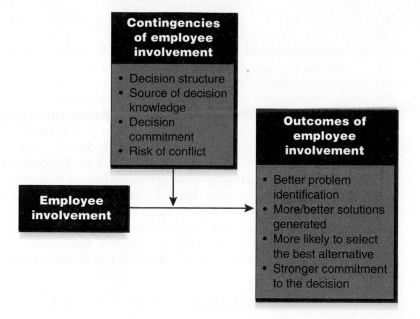

on the decision structure, source of decision knowledge, decision commitment,
and risk of conflict in the decision process.

■ *Decision structure*—At the beginning of this chapter, we learned that some
decisions are programmed, whereas others are nonprogrammed. Programmed decisions are less likely to need employee involvement because the
solutions are already worked out from past experience. In other words, the
benefits of employee involvement increase with the novelty and complexity of
the problem or opportunity.

■ *Source of decision knowledge*—Subordinates should be involved in some level
of decision making when the leader lacks sufficient knowledge and subordinates have additional information to improve decision quality. In many cases,
employees are closer to customers and production activities, so they often
know where the company can save money, improve product or service quality,
and realize opportunities. This is particularly true for complex decisions
where employees are more likely to possess relevant information.[45]

■ *Decision commitment*—Participation tends to improve employee commitment
to the decision. If employees are unlikely to accept a decision made without
their involvement, then some level of participation is usually necessary.

■ *Risk of conflict*—Two types of conflict undermine the benefits of employee
involvement. First, if employee goals and norms conflict with the organization's goals, then only a low level of employee involvement is advisable. Second, the degree of involvement depends on whether employees will reach
agreement on the preferred solution. If conflict is likely, then high involvement
(i.e., where employees make the decision alone) would be difficult to achieve.

Employee involvement is an important component of the decision-making process.
To make the best decisions, we need to involve people who have the most valuable
information and who will increase commitment to implement the decision. Another
important component of decision making is creativity, which we discuss next.

■ CREATIVITY

Parcel delivery might seem like a routine business, but that's not the way the folks at Yamato Transport Company see it. The Japanese company was the first to deliver customers' ski equipment to resorts and homes. To keep better track of shipments, customers receive the mobile telephone numbers of Yamato's delivery personnel, not just distribution centres. One local branch office recently started testing the use of lockers at train stations around Japan for pickup and delivery locations, notifying customers by email of the delivery times.[46]

Yamato Transport is successful in Japan's fiercely competitive delivery service industry because it relies on creativity for innovative new services. **Creativity** is the development of original ideas that make a socially recognized contribution.[47] Although there are unique conditions for creativity that we discuss over the next few pages, it is really part of the decision-making process described earlier in the chapter. We rely on creativity to find problems, identify alternatives, and implement solutions. Creativity is not something saved for special occasions. It is an integral part of decision making.

> **creativity**
> The development of original ideas that make a socially recognized contribution.

THE CREATIVE PROCESS MODEL

One of the earliest and most influential models of creativity is shown in Exhibit 8.4.[48] The first stage is preparation—the person's or group's effort to acquire knowledge and skills regarding the problem or opportunity. Preparation involves developing a clear understanding of what you are trying to achieve through a novel solution, then actively studying information seemingly related to the topic.

The second stage, called incubation, is the stage of reflective thought. We put the problem aside, but our mind is still working on it in the background.[49] The important condition here is to maintain a low-level awareness by frequently revisiting the problem. Incubation does not mean that you forget about the problem or issue. Incubation assists **divergent thinking**—reframing the problem in a unique way and generating different approaches to the issue. This contrasts with convergent thinking—calculating the conventionally accepted "right answer" to a logical problem. Divergent thinking breaks us away from existing mental models so we can apply concepts or processes from completely different areas of life. Consider the following classic example: Years ago, the experimental bulbs in Thomas Edison's lab kept falling off their fixtures until a technician wondered whether the threaded caps that screwed down tightly on kerosene bottles would work on light bulbs. They did, and the design remains to this day.[50]

> **divergent thinking**
> Involves reframing a problem in a unique way and generating different approaches to the issue.

Insight, the third stage of creativity, refers to the experience of suddenly becoming aware of a unique idea.[51] Insight is often visually depicted as a light bulb, but a better image would be a brief flash of light or perhaps a flickering candle because these bits of inspiration are fleeting and can be quickly lost if not documented. For this reason, many creative people keep a journal or notebook nearby at all times, so that they can jot down these ideas before they disappear. Also, these flickering ideas don't keep a particular schedule; they might come to you at any time of day

> **■ EXHIBIT 8.4**
>
> The creative process model

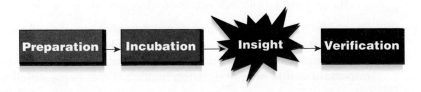

or night. Insights are merely rough ideas. Their usefulness still requires verification through conscious evaluation and experimentation. Thus, although verification is labelled the final stage of creativity, it is really the beginning of a long process of experimentation and further creativity.

CREATIVE PEOPLE AND WORK ENVIRONMENTS

Radical Entertainment, which was introduced at the beginning of this chapter, has an impressive list of successful electronic games, including *The Simpsons: Road Rage, Crash Tag Team Racing,* and *The Incredible Hulk.* The company achieves this success by finding creative people and putting them in an environment that encourages creative ideas. In other words, Radical's executives know that creativity is a function of both the person and the situation.

Characteristics of creative people Everyone is creative, but some people seem to be more creative than others. Four of the main features of creative people are intelligence, persistence, subject-matter knowledge and experience, and inventive thinking style. First, creative people have above-average intelligence to synthesize information, analyze ideas, and apply their ideas.[52] Like the fictional sleuth Sherlock Holmes, creative people recognize the significance of small bits of information and are able to connect them in ways that no one else could imagine. Then, they have the capacity to evaluate the potential usefulness of their ideas.

Persistence is the second feature of creative people. The fact is that innovations derive more from trial and error than from intelligence and experience. Persistence drives creative people to continue developing and testing after others have given up. In other words, people who develop more creative products and services are those who develop more ideas that don't work. Thomas Edison emphasized this point in his famous statement that genius is 1 percent inspiration and 99 percent perspiration. Edison and his staff discovered hundreds of ways not to build a light bulb before they got it right! This persistence is based on a high need for achievement and moderate or high degree of self-confidence.[53]

A third feature of creative people is that they possess sufficient knowledge and experience on the subject.[54] Creativity experts explain that discovering new ideas requires knowledge of the fundamentals. For example, 1960's rock group The Beatles produced most of their songs only after they had played together for several years. They developed extensive experience singing and adapting the music of other people before their creative talents soared.

Although knowledge and experience may be important in one sense, they can also undermine creativity because people develop mental models that lead to "mindless behaviour," whereby they stop ques-

Creativity in Motion

Mike Lazaridis faced plenty of industry doubters when he first proposed the idea of a handheld wireless communication device more than a dozen years ago. Then the company that he and Jim Balsillie founded, Research in Motion (RIM), worked through numerous failures before getting closer to Lazaridis' vision. "Mike is one of the most tenacious people I've ever met," says a former Ericsson executive. "[He] keeps grinding towards his goal until he gets there. There were eight or nine failures before BlackBerry. He took lots of at-bats before he hit his home run." Through this persistence, RIM has become a leader in wireless communication.[55]

CP/Kitchener-Waterloo Record/Rick Koza

www.rim.net

tioning their assumptions.[56] This explains why some corporate leaders like to hire people from other industries and areas of expertise. For instance, Geoffrey Ballard, founder of Ballard Power Systems in Vancouver, B.C., hired a chemist to develop a better battery. When the chemist protested that he didn't know anything about batteries, Ballard replied: "That's fine. I don't want someone who knows batteries. They know what won't work."[57] Ballard explained that he wanted to hire people who would question and investigate what experts stopped questioning.

The fourth characteristic of creative people is that they have an inventive thinking style. Creative types are divergent thinkers and risk takers. They are not bothered about making mistakes or working with ambiguous information. They take a broad view of problems, don't like to abide by rules or status, and are unconcerned about social approval of their actions.[58]

Organizational conditions supporting creativity   Hiring creative people is only part of the creativity equation. Organizations also need to maintain a work environment that supports the creative process for everyone.[59] One of the most important conditions is that the organization has a learning orientation; that is, leaders recognize that employees make reasonable mistakes as part of the creative process. "Every time you fail, you learn something new," says Yves Doucet, CEO of Les Enterprises DOVICO in Moncton, New Brunswick. "When you see someone who has been successful, it's a series of failures that brought them there."[60]

Motivation from the job itself is another important condition for creativity.[61] Employees tend to be more creative when they believe their work has a substantial impact on the organization and/or larger society (i.e., task significance) and when they have the freedom to pursue novel ideas without bureaucratic delays (i.e., autonomy). This emphasis on autonomy is apparent at Radical Entertainment, the Vancouver-based electronic games maker described at the beginning of this chapter. Creativity is about changing things, and change is possible only when employees have the authority to experiment. More generally, jobs encourage creativity when they are challenging and aligned with the employee's competencies.

Along with supporting a learning orientation and intrinsically motivating jobs, companies foster creativity through open communication and sufficient resources. They provide a reasonable level of job security, which explains why creativity suffers during times of downsizing and corporate restructuring.[62] To some degree, creativity also improves with support from leaders and co-workers. One recent Canadian study reported that effective product champions provide enthusiastic support for new ideas. Other studies suggest that co-worker support can improve creativity in some situations, whereas competition among co-workers improves creativity in other situations.[63] Similarly, it isn't clear how much pressure should be exerted on employees to produce creative ideas. Extreme time pressures are well-known creativity inhibitors, but lack of pressure doesn't seem to produce the highest creativity, either.

ACTIVITIES THAT ENCOURAGE CREATIVITY

Along with hiring creative people and giving them a supportive work environment, organizations have introduced numerous activities that attempt to crank up the creative potential. One set of activities encourages employees to redefine the problem. This occurs when we revisit old projects that have been set aside. After a few months of neglect, these projects might be seen in new ways.[64] Another strategy involves asking people unfamiliar with the issue (preferably with different expertise) to explore the problem with you. You would state the objectives and give some facts, then let the other person ask questions to further understand the situation. By verbalizing the problem, listening to questions, and hearing what others think, you are more likely to form new perspectives on the issue.[65]

A second set of creativity activities, known as *associative play*, range from art classes to impromptu storytelling. Wedgwood, the Irish tableware company, brought together its overseas executives in a workshop where they tore up magazines, pasted up pictures, and selected music that represented what they thought the Wedgwood brand should become. Employees at Telus Corp., the Burnaby, B.C.-based telecommunications provider, worked with an improvisational theatre troupe to act out goofy roles as machines, animals, and other characters. "A necessity for organizations is to empower people to take risks," explains Jay Ono, who led the corporate improv program at Telus.[66]

Another associative play activity, called *morphological analysis*, involves listing different dimensions of a system and the elements of each dimension, then looking at each combination. This encourages people to carefully examine combinations that initially seem nonsensical. Tyson Foods, the world's largest poultry producer, applied this activity to identify new ways to serve chicken for lunch. The marketing and research team assigned to this task focused on three categories: occasion, packaging, and taste. Next, the team worked through numerous combinations of items in the three categories. This created unusual ideas, such as cheese chicken pasta (taste) in pizza boxes (packaging) for concessions at baseball games (occasion). Later, the team looked more closely at the feasibility of these combinations and sent them to customer focus groups for further testing.[67]

A third set of activities that encourages creativity in organizations is known as *cross-pollination*.[68] As described in the opening story to this chapter, Radical Entertainment practises cross-pollination through its monthly "game fair" day, in which teams show off their products and make presentations to other teams in the organization. IDEO, the California-based product design company, has a similar effect by mixing together employees from different past projects so they share new knowledge with each other.

Cross-pollination highlights the fact that creativity rarely occurs alone. Some creative people may be individualistic, but most creative ideas are generated through teams and informal social interaction. This probably explains why Jonathon Ive, the award-winning designer of Apple Computer products, always refers to his team's creativity rather than anything that he alone might have thought up. "The only time you'll hear [Jonathan Ive] use the word 'I' is when he's naming some of the products he helped make famous: iMac, iBook, iPod," says one writer.[69] The next chapter introduces the main concepts in team effectiveness. Then, in Chapter 10, we learn about high-performance teams, including ways to improve team decision making and creativity.

CHAPTER SUMMARY

Decision making is a conscious process of making choices among one or more alternatives with the intention of moving toward some desired state of affairs. The rational choice paradigm of decision making includes identifying problems and opportunities, choosing the best decision style, developing alternative solutions, choosing the best solution, implementing the selected alternative, and evaluating decision outcomes.

Persuasion by stakeholders, perceptual biases, and poor diagnostic skills affect our ability to identify problems and opportunities. We can minimize these challenges by being aware of the human limitations and discussing the situation with colleagues.

Evaluating and choosing alternatives is often challenging because organizational goals are ambiguous or in conflict, human information processing is incomplete and subjective, and people tend to satisfice rather than maximize. Decision makers also short-circuit the evaluation process when faced with an opportunity rather than a problem. Emotions shape our preferences for alternatives and the process we follow to evaluate alternatives. We also listen in to our emotions for guidance when making decisions. This latter activity relates to intuition—the ability to know when a problem or opportunity exists and to select the best course of action without conscious reasoning. Intuition is both an emotional experience and a rapid unconscious analytic process that involves both pattern matching and action scripts.

People generally make better choices by systematically evaluating alternatives. Scenario planning can help to make future decisions without the pressure and emotions that occur during real emergencies.

Postdecisional justification and escalation of commitment make it difficult to accurately evaluate decision outcomes. Escalation is mainly caused by self-justification, the prospect theory effect, perceptual blinders, and closing costs. These problems are minimized by separating decision choosers from decision evaluators, establishing a preset level at which the decision is abandoned or reevaluated, relying on more systematic and clear feedback about the project's success, and involving several people in decision making.

Employee involvement (or participation) refers to the degree that employees influence how their work is organized and carried out. The level of participation may range from an employee providing specific information to management without knowing the problem or issue, to complete involvement in all phases of the decision process. Employee involvement may lead to higher decision quality and commitment, but several contingencies need to be considered, including the decision structure, source of decision knowledge, decision commitment, and risk of conflict.

Creativity is the development of original ideas that make a socially recognized contribution. The four creativity stages are preparation, incubation, insight, and verification. Incubation assists divergent thinking, which involves reframing the problem in a unique way and generating different approaches to the issue.

Four of the main features of creative people are intelligence, persistence, subject-matter knowledge and experience, and inventive thinking style. Creativity is also strengthened for everyone when the work environment supports a learning orientation, the job has high intrinsic motivation, the organization provides a reasonable level of job security, and project leaders provide appropriate goals, time pressure, and resources. Three types of activities that encourage creativity are redefining the problem, associative play, and cross-pollination.

KEY TERMS

bounded rationality, p. 220

creativity, p. 230

decision making, p. 216

divergent thinking, p. 230

employee involvement, p. 227

escalation of commitment, p. 225

implicit favourite, p. 221

intuition, p. 223

postdecisional justification, p. 224

prospect theory, p. 225

satisficing, p. 222

scenario planning, p. 224

DISCUSSION QUESTIONS

1. A management consultant is hired by a manufacturing firm to determine the best site for its next production facility. The consultant has had several meetings with the company's senior executives regarding the factors to consider when making the recommendation. Discuss the decision-making problems that might prevent the consultant from choosing the best site location.

2. You have been asked to personally recommend a new travel agency to handle all airfare, accommodation, and related travel needs for your organization of 500 staff. One of your colleagues, who is responsible for the company's economic planning, suggests that the best travel agent could be selected mathematically by inputting the relevant factors for

each agency and the weight (importance) of each factor. What decision-making approach is your colleague recommending? Is this recommendation a good idea in this situation? Why or why not?

3. Intuition is both an emotional experience and an unconscious analytic process. One problem, however, is that not all emotions signalling that there is a problem or opportunity represent intuition. Explain how we would know if our "gut feelings" are intuition or not, and if not intuition, suggest what might be causing them.

4. A developer received financial backing for a new business financial centre along a derelict section of the waterfront, a few miles from the current downtown area of a large European city. The idea

was to build several high-rise structures, attract large tenants to those sites, and have the city extend transportation systems out to the new centre. Over the next decade, the developer believed that others would build in the area, thereby attracting the regional or national offices of many financial institutions. Interest from potential tenants was much lower than initially predicted and the city did not build transportation systems as quickly as expected. Still, the builder proceeded with the original plans. Only after financial support was curtailed did the developer reconsider the project. Using your knowledge of escalation of commitment, discuss three possible reasons why the developer was motivated to continue with the project.

5. Ancient Book Company has a problem with new book projects. Even when others are aware that a book is far behind schedule and may engender little public interest, sponsoring editors are reluctant to terminate contracts with authors whom they have signed. The result is that editors invest more

time with these projects than on more fruitful projects. As a form of escalation of commitment, describe two methods that Ancient Book Company can use to minimize this problem.

6. Employee involvement applies just as well to the classroom as to the office or factory floor. Explain how student involvement in classroom decisions typically made by the instructor alone might improve decision quality. What potential problems may occur in this process?

7. Think of a time when you experienced the creative process. Maybe you woke up with a brilliant (but usually sketchy and incomplete) idea, or you solved a baffling problem while doing something else. Describe this incident to your class and explain how the experience followed the creative process.

8. Two characteristics of creative people are that they have relevant experience and are persistent in their quest. Does this mean that people with the most experience and the highest need for achievement are the most creative? Explain your answer.

CASE STUDY 8.1

EMPLOYEE INVOLVEMENT CASES

Case 1: The Sugar Substitute Research Decision

You are the head of research and development (R&D) for a major Canadian beer company. While working on a new beer product, one of the scientists in your unit seems to have tentatively identified a new chemical compound that has few calories but tastes closer to sugar than current sugar substitutes. The company has no foreseeable need for this product, but it could be patented and licensed to manufacturers in the food industry.

The sugar substitute discovery is in its preliminary stages and would require considerable time and resources before it would be commercially viable. This means that it would necessarily take some resources away from other projects in the lab. The sugar substitute project is beyond your technical expertise, but some of the R&D lab researchers are familiar with that field of chemistry. As with most forms of research, it is difficult to determine the amount of research required to further identify and perfect the sugar substitute. You do not know how much demand is expected for this product. Your

department has a decision process for funding projects that are behind schedule. However, there are no rules or precedents about funding projects that would be licensed but not used by the organization.

The company's R&D budget is limited and other scientists in your work group have recently complained that they require more resources and financial support to get their projects completed. Some of these other R&D projects hold promise for future beer sales. You believe most researchers in the R&D unit are committed to ensuring that the company's interests are achieved.

Case 2: Coast Guard Cutter Decision Problem

You are the captain of a 72-metre Coast Guard cutter, with a crew of 16, including officers. Your mission is general at-sea search and rescue. At 2:00 this morning, while en route to your home port after a routine 28-day patrol, you received word from the nearest Coast Guard station that a small plane had crashed 100 kilometres offshore. You obtained all the available information concerning the location of the crash, informed your crew of the mission, and set a new course at maximum speed for the scene to commence a search for survivors and wreckage.

You have now been searching for 20 hours. Your search operation has been increasingly impaired by rough seas, and there is evidence of a severe storm building. The atmospherics associated with the deteriorating weather have made communications with the Coast Guard station impossible. A decision must be made shortly about whether to abandon the search and place your vessel on a course that would ride out the storm (thereby protecting the vessel and your crew, but relegating any possible survivors to almost certain death from exposure) or to continue a potentially futile search and the risks it would entail.

Before losing communications, you received an update weather advisory concerning the severity and duration of the storm. Although your crew members are extremely conscientious about their responsibility, you believe that they would be divided on the decision of leaving or staying.

Discussion Questions (for both cases)

1. To what extent should your subordinates be involved in this decision? Select one of the following levels of involvement:

   - *No involvement*: You make the decision alone without any participation from subordinates.

   - *Low involvement*: You ask one or more subordinates for information relating to the problem, but you don't ask for their recommendations and might not mention the problem to them.

   - *Medium involvement*: You describe the problem to one or more subordinates (alone or in a meeting) and ask for any relevant information as well as their recommendations on the issue. However, you make the final decision, which might or might not reflect their advice.

   - *High involvement*: You describe the problem to subordinates. They discuss the matter, identify a solution without your involvement (unless they invite your ideas), and implement that solution. You have agreed to support their decision.

2. What factors led you to choose this level of employee involvement rather than the others?

3. What problems might occur if less or more involvement occurred in this case (where possible)?

Sources: The Sugar Substitute Research Decision is written by Steven L. McShane, copyright © 2002. The Coast Guard Cutter case is adapted from V. H. Vroom and A. G. Jago, *The New Leadership: Managing Participation in Organizations* (Englewood Cliffs, N.J.: Prentice Hall, 1988). Copyright © 1987 V. H. Vroom and A. G. Jago. Used with permission of the authors.

CLASS EXERCISE   8.2

FOR WHAT IT'S WORTH

Purpose   This exercise is designed to help you understand the issues involved with making perfectly rational decisions.

Materials   The instructor will either bring to class or show a computer image of three products. Students will need their social insurance number (a driver's licence or other piece of identity with several numbers can substitute).

Instructions

- *Step 1:* The instructor will show the three products (or image of the products) to the class and describe each product so students are sufficiently informed of their features and functions. The instructor will NOT provide any information about the price paid or market value of these products.

- *Step 2:* Working alone, each student will write down at the top of the calculation sheet (Exhibit 1) the last two digits of his/her social insurance number (or driver's licence or other identification if a SIN is not available). Each student will also write down in the left column of Exhibit 1 the name of each product shown by the instructor. Then, each student will circle "Yes" or "No" in

Exhibit 1 for each product, indicating whether he/she would be willing to pay the dollar equivalent of the two-digit number for each product if looking to purchase such a product.

■ *Step 3:* In the right-hand column of the calculation sheet (Exhibit 1), students (still working alone) will write down the maximum dollar value they would be willing to pay for each product if they were looking to purchase such a product.

■ *Step 4:* After completing their calculations alone, students will be organized into four or five groups as specified by the instructor. Group size is unimportant, but the instructor's criterion for organizing teams is very important and must be followed. Each team will calculate the average price that students within that group were willing to pay for each product. The team will also calculate the percentage of people within the group who indicated "Yes" (willing to purchase at the stated price) for each product.

■ *Step 5:* Each team will report its three average maximum willingness-to-pay prices as well as percentage of students in the team who indicated "Yes" for each product. The instructor will outline a concept relevant to rational decision making and how that concept relates to this exercise.

■ **EXHIBIT 1**   For what it's worth calculation sheet

Two-digit number: _____ _____

Product name (Write in product names below)	Willing to pay two-digit number price for this product? (Circle your answer)	Maximum willingness to pay for this product
_____	NO YES	$ ____ ____ ____:00
_____	NO YES	$ ____ ____ ____:00
_____	NO YES	$ ____ ____ ____:00

Source: Based on information in D. Ariely, G. Loewenstein, and D. Prelec, "'Inherent Arbitrariness': Stable Demand Curves Without Stable Preferences," *Quarterly Journal of Economics*, February 2003, pp. 73–105.

TEAM EXERCISE 8.3

WHERE IN THE WORLD ARE WE?

Purpose This exercise is designed to help you understand the potential advantages of involving others in decisions rather than making decisions alone.

Materials Students require an unmarked copy of the map of Canada with grid marks (Exhibit 2). Students are not allowed to look at any other maps or use any other materials. The instructor will provide a list of communities located somewhere on Exhibit 2. The instructor will also provide copies of the answer sheet after students have individually and in teams estimated the locations of communities.

Instructions

■ *Step 1:* Write down in Exhibit 1 the list of communities identified by your instructor. Then, working alone, estimate the location in Exhibit 2 of these communities, all of which are in Canada. For example, mark a small "1" in Exhibit 2 on the spot where you believe the first community is located. Mark a small "2" where you think the second community is located, and so on. Please be sure to number each location clearly and with numbers small enough to fit within one grid space.

■ *Step 2:* The instructor will organize students into approximately equal sized teams (typically five or six people per team). Working with your team members, reach a consensus on the location of each community listed in Exhibit 1. The instructor might provide teams with a separate copy of this map, or each member can identify the team's numbers using a different coloured pen on their individual maps. The team's decision for each location should occur by consensus, not voting or averaging.

■ *Step 3:* The instructor will provide or display an answer sheet, showing the correct locations of the communities. Using this answer sheet, stu-dents will count the minimum number of grid squares between the location they individually marked and the true location of each community. Write the number of grid squares in the second column of Exhibit 1, then add up the total. Next, count the minimum number of grid squares between the location the team marked and the true location of each community. Write the number of grid squares in the third column of Exhibit 1, then add up the total.

■ *Step 4:* The instructor will ask for information about the totals and the class will discuss the implication of these results for employee involvement and decision making.

■ **EXHIBIT 1**   Canadian communities and calculation sheet

Number	Community	Individual distance in grid units from the true location	Team distance in grid units from the true location
1			
2			
3			
4			
5			
6			
7			
8			
		Total:	Total:

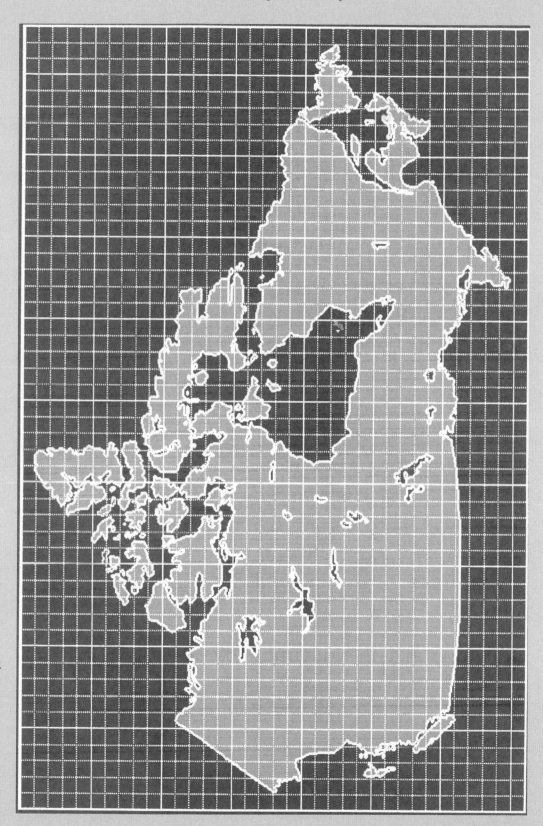

■ EXHIBIT 2 Map of Canada

T E A M   E X E R C I S E   8.4

WINTER SURVIVAL EXERCISE

Purpose This exercise is designed to help you understand the potential advantages of involving others in decisions rather than making decisions alone.

Instructions

■ *Step 1:* Read the "Situation" at right. Then, working alone, rank order the 12 items shown in the chart below according to their importance to your survival. In the "Individual Ranking" column, indicate the most important item with "1," going through to "12" for the least important. Keep in mind the reasons why each item is or is not important.

■ *Step 2:* The instructor will divide the class into small teams (four to six people). Each team will rank order the items in the second column. Team rankings should be based on consensus, not simply averaging the individual rankings.

■ *Step 3:* When the teams have completed their rankings, the instructor will provide the expert's ranking, which can be entered in the third column.

■ *Step 4:* Each student will compute the absolute difference (i.e., ignore minus signs) between the individual ranking and the expert's ranking. Record this information in column four, and sum the absolute values at the bottom of column four.

■ *Step 5:* In column five, record the absolute difference between the team's ranking and the expert's ranking, and sum these absolute scores at the bottom. A class discussion will follow regarding the implications of these results for employee involvement and decision making.

Situation You have just crash-landed somewhere in the woods of southern Manitoba or possibly northern Minnesota. It is 11:32 a.m. in mid-January. The small plane in which you were travelling crashed on a small lake. The pilot and co-pilot were killed. Shortly after the crash, the plane sank completely into the lake with the pilot's and co-pilot's bodies inside. Everyone else on the flight escaped to land dry and without serious injury.

The crash came suddenly before the pilot had time to radio for help or inform anyone of your position. Since your pilot was trying to avoid the storm, you know the plane was considerably off course. The pilot announced shortly before the crash that you were 72 kilometres northwest of a small town that is the nearest known habitation.

You are in a wilderness area made up of thick woods broken by many lakes and rivers. The snow depth varies from above the ankles in windswept areas to more than knee-deep where it has drifted. The last weather report indicated that the temperature would reach minus 15 degrees Celsius in the daytime and minus 26 degrees at night. There are plenty of dead wood and twigs in the area around the lake. You and the other surviving passengers are dressed in winter clothing appropriate for city wear—suits, pantsuits, street shoes, and overcoats. While escaping from the plane, your group salvaged the 12 items listed in the tally sheet opposite. You may assume that the number of persons in the group is the same as the number in your group, and that you have agreed to stay together.

WINTER SURVIVAL TALLY SHEET					
Items	Step 1 Your individual ranking	Step 2 Your team's ranking	Step 3 Survival expert's ranking	Step 4 Difference between steps 1 and 3	Step 5 Difference between steps 2 and 3
Ball of steel wool					
Newspapers					
Compass					
Hand axe					
Cigarette lighter					
45-calibre pistol					
Section air map					
Canvas					
Shirt and pants					
Can of shortening					
Whiskey					
Chocolate bars					
			Total		
				Your score	Team score

(The lower the score, the better)

Source: Adapted from "Winter Survival" in D. Johnson and F. Johnson, *Joining Together*, 3rd ed. (Englewood Cliffs, N.J.: Prentice Hall, 1984).

C L A S S   E X E R C I S E   8.5

CREATIVITY BRAINBUSTERS

Purpose This exercise is designed to help students understand the dynamics of creativity and team problem solving.

Instructions This exercise may be completed alone or in teams of three or four people. If teams are formed, students who already know the solutions to one or more of these problems should identify themselves and serve as silent observers. When finished (or, more likely, time is up), the instructor will review the solutions and discuss the implications of this exercise. In particular, be prepared to discuss what you needed to solve these puzzles and what may have prevented you from solving them more quickly (or at all).

1. Double Circle Problem

Draw two circles, one inside the other, with a single line and with neither circle touching the other (as shown below). In other words, you must draw both of these circles without lifting your pen (or other writing instrument).

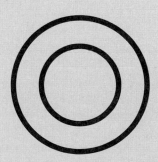

2. Nine Dot Problem

Below are nine dots. Without lifting your pencil, draw no more than four straight lines that pass through all nine dots.

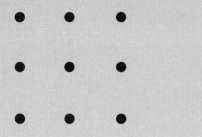

3. Nine Dot Problem Revisited

Referring to the nine dot exhibit above, describe how, without lifting your pencil, you could pass a pencil line through all dots with three (3) or fewer straight lines.

4. Word Search

In the following line of letters, cross out five letters so that the remaining letters, without altering their sequence, spell a familiar English word.

CFRIVEELATETITEVRSE

5. Burning Ropes

You have two pieces of rope of unequal lengths and a box of matches. In spite of their different lengths, each piece of rope takes one hour to burn; however, parts of each rope burn at unequal speeds. For example, the first half of one piece might burn in 10 minutes. Use these materials to determine accurately when 45 minutes has elapsed.

SELF-ASSESSMENT EXERCISE   8.6

MEASURING YOUR CREATIVE PERSONALITY

Purpose   This self-assessment is designed to help you measure the extent to which you have a creative personality.

Instructions   Listed below is an adjective checklist with 30 words that may or may not describe you. Put a mark in the box beside the words that you think accurately describe you. Please DO NOT mark the boxes for words that do not describe you. When finished, you can score the test using the scoring key in Appendix B. This exercise is completed alone so students assess themselves without concerns of social comparison. However, class discussion will focus on how this scale might be applied in organizations, and the limitations of measuring creativity in work settings.

ADJECTIVE CHECKLIST					
Affected	☐	Honest	☐	Reflective	☐
Capable	☐	Humorous	☐	Resourceful	☐
Cautious	☐	Individualistic	☐	Self-confident	☐
Clever	☐	Informal	☐	Sexy	☐
Commonplace	☐	Insightful	☐	Sincere	☐
Confident	☐	Intelligent	☐	Snobbish	☐
Conservative	☐	Inventive	☐	Submissive	☐
Conventional	☐	Mannerly	☐	Suspicious	☐
Dissatisfied	☐	Narrow interests	☐	Unconventional	☐
Egotistical	☐	Original	☐	Wide interests	☐

Source: Adapted from and based on information in H. G. Gough and A. B. Heilbrun, Jr., *The Adjective Check List Manual* (Palo Alto, CA: Consulting Psychologists Press, 1965).

TESTING YOUR CREATIVE BENCH STRENGTH

Go to the Online Learning Centre to complete this interactive self-assessment.

This self-assessment takes the form of a self-scoring quiz. It consists of 12 questions that require divergent thinking to identify the correct answers. For each question, type in your answer in the space provided. When finished, look at the correct answer for each question, along with the explanation for that answer.

DECISION-MAKING STYLE INVENTORY

Go to the Online Learning Centre to complete this interactive self-assessment.

People have different styles of decision making that are reflected in how they identify problems or opportunities and make choices. This self-assessment estimates your decision-making style through a series of statements describing how individuals go about making important decisions. Please indicate whether you agree or disagree with each statement. Answer each item as truthfully as possible so that you get an accurate estimate of your decision-making style. This exercise is completed alone so students assess themselves honestly without concerns of social comparison. However, class discussion will focus on the decision-making style that people prefer in organizational settings.

After studying the preceding material, be sure to check out our Online Learning Centre at

www.mcgrawhill.ca/college/mcshane

for more in-depth information and interactivities that correspond to this chapter.

Online
LearningCentre
with POWERWEB

·9·

FOUNDATIONS OF TEAM DYNAMICS

LEARNING OBJECTIVES

AFTER READING THIS CHAPTER, YOU SHOULD BE ABLE TO:

- Define teams.

- Explain why employees belong to informal groups.

- Outline the model of team effectiveness.

- Identify six organizational and team environmental elements that influence team effectiveness.

- Explain the influence of team task, composition, and size on team effectiveness.

- Describe the five stages of team development.

- Identify three factors that shape team norms.

- List six factors that influence team cohesiveness.

- Discuss the limitations of teams.

- Explain how companies minimize social loafing.

After circling for 15 minutes above the dark August thunderstorm, the captain and co-pilot of Air France flight 358 landed at Toronto's Pearson International Airport. The plane touched down at normal speed, but too far along to stop within the remaining length of runway. Passengers reported that the Airbus 340 plane swerved soon after touchdown, possibly causing the engine to hit the ground and catch fire. The plane continued 200 metres beyond the runway, crashing in a wooded ravine. All 309 passengers and crew escaped alive just before flames and black smoke engulfed the cabin.

Behind the headlines, daily announcements, and passenger recollections of the Air France crash is a powerful illustration of how teams play a vital role in complex organizational activities. With a few exceptions, passengers praised Air France's cabin crew and pilots for collectively directing everyone off the plane within two minutes. The crew deliberately kept two exit doors closed due to external fires, redirecting panicking passengers to the alternative routes. The cabin crew was "very, very organized," recalls one passenger. "They immediately opened the side of the plane where they couldn't see any flames and then they told us to jump." The Pearson airport emergency crews also acted quickly, arriving within one minute to extinguish the blaze and assist passengers injured during evacuation.

Events surrounding and following the Air France crash at Toronto's Pearson International Airport illustrate the importance of teams in complex organizational activities. *CP Photo/Frank Gunn*

Several hospitals were alerted within minutes of the crash, kicking into action procedures that emergency teams regularly practice. On-duty medical staff from several specialties immediately took their emergency roles; off-duty staff raced to their hospital to also assist injured passengers. "I cannot say enough about the exceptional service provided and the teamwork demonstrated by the staff," announced the CEO of William Osler Health Centre, which received more than a dozen injured Air France passengers.

Within hours of flight 358's ill-fated landing, Canada's Transportation Safety Board (TSB) assigned Real Levasseur to lead the team investigating the crash. Levasseur and other TSB staff quickly identified three dozen experts from across Canada and other countries to join the team. "The team will be addressing all aspects of [the crash], including the operation of the airplane, the operation of the airport and right down to including the crash, fire and rescue, which seems to have been very well handled," explains Don Enns, a member of the Air France crash investigation team.[1] ∎
www.tsb.gc.ca

The Air France crash at Pearson International Airport in Toronto reveals in a variety of ways how team dynamics are critical to organizations. Organizations ultimately consist of individuals, but corporate leaders are discovering that people working alone usually lack sufficient knowledge or capacity to achieve organizational objectives. That's why Bay Street and Wall Street brokerage firms have shifted toward team-based work to better satisfy more complex client needs. SANS Fibres, the South African manufacturer of synthetic fibre and polyester polymers, relies on the team approach to eliminate waste, maximize manufacturing flow, minimize inventories, and meet customer requirements. International Steel Group's (ISG) Cleveland plant rose from the ashes of bankruptcy and quickly became profitable in part because it formed teams where employees share duties and help others across departments. "It wasn't the traditional one job for one person," says ISG executive John Mang III. "It was a team."[2]

teams
Groups of two or more people who interact and influence each other, are mutually accountable for achieving common objectives, and perceive themselves as a social entity within an organization.

Teams are groups of two or more people who interact and influence each other, are mutually accountable for achieving common goals associated with organizational objectives, and perceive themselves as a social entity within an organization.[3] All teams exist to fulfill some purpose, such as assembling a product, providing a service, designing a new manufacturing facility, or making an important decision. Team members are held together by their interdependence and need for collaboration to achieve common goals. All teams require some form of communication so members can coordinate and share common objectives. Team members also influence each other, although some members are more influential than others regarding the team's goals and activities.

All teams are **groups** because they consist of people with a unifying relationship. But not all groups are teams; some groups are just people assembled together without any necessary interdependence or organizationally focused objective. For example, the friends you meet for lunch wouldn't be called a team because they have little or no task interdependence (each person could just as easily eat lunch alone) and no organizational purpose beyond their social interaction. Although the terms "group" and "team" are used interchangeably, "teams" has largely replaced "groups" in the business language.[4]

groups
Two or more people with a unifying relationship.

This chapter looks at the complex conditions that make teams more or less effective in organizational settings. This chapter begins by explaining why people join informal groups and why organizations rely on teams. Most of the chapter examines each part of this model, including team and organizational environment, team design, and the team processes of development, norms, roles, and cohesiveness.

■ TYPES OF TEAMS AND INFORMAL GROUPS

There are many types of teams and other groups in organizational settings. Exhibit 9.1 categorizes groups in terms of their permanence (teams versus informal groups) and formality in the organization. Permanent work teams are responsible for a specific set of tasks or work processes in the organization. For instance, the Pearson International Airport fire crews that put out the Air France blaze are relatively permanent teams because they work together for an indefinite time. In contrast, the Transportation Safety Board team responsible for investigating the Air France crash is a temporary team, usually called a *task force*, because it is organized for a limited time (in this case a few months) to complete a specific task.

Along with formal work teams, organizations consist of *informal groups*. Informal groups are not initiated by the organization and usually do not perform organiza-

■ **EXHIBIT 9.1**

Types of teams and groups

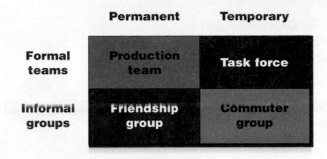

tional goals (thus they are "informal"). Instead, they exist primarily for the benefit of their members. Some informal groups, such as the group you meet for lunch, exist primarily to satisfy the drive to bond. These groups are relatively permanent because they are held together by lasting friendships and by the structure of formal teams.

WHY PEOPLE BELONG TO INFORMAL GROUPS

Why do people belong to informal groups? One reason is that they fulfill the innate drive to bond. Indeed, some experts suggest that group formation is hard-wired through evolutionary development of the human species.[5] People invest considerable time and effort forming and maintaining relationships without any special circumstances or ulterior motives. Second, social identity theory says that we define ourselves by our group affiliations. We are therefore motivated to belong to work teams or informal groups that are viewed favourably by others. We are also motivated to become members of groups that are similar to ourselves because this reinforces our social identity.[6]

A third reason why people join informal groups is that these groups accomplish tasks that cannot be achieved by individuals working alone. For example, employees will sometimes form a group to oppose organizational changes because they have more power when banded together than complaining separately. A fourth explanation for informal groups is that in stressful situations we are comforted by the mere presence of other people and are therefore motivated to be near them. When passengers fled from the burning Air France jet in Toronto, they likely congregated near each other after getting far enough away from the danger. Similarly, employees tend to mingle more often when hearing rumours that the company might be sold.[7]

WHY RELY ON TEAMS?

Teams have become an important element in most organizations. In fact, a survey of human resource professionals recently concluded: "Teams are now an integral part of workplace management." Why all the fuss about teams? The answer to this question has a long history, dating back to research on British coal mining in the 1940s and the Japanese economic miracle of the 1970s.[8] These early studies revealed that under the right conditions, teams make better decisions, develop better products and services, and create a more energized workforce compared with employees working alone.[9] These explanations partly explain the Ontario government's recent initiative to form "Family Health Teams" throughout the province. As Connections 9.1 describes, these teams are expected to operate more effectively than when professions work independently, although some physicians are resisting this team structure.

Ontario Government Introduces Collaborative Family Health Teams

The Ontario government believes that the chronic shortage of family doctors in the province and the large number of people visiting emergency rooms as a replacement for doctor's offices can be corrected through teamwork. The province has set aside funding for family health teams (FHTs) to serve communities that lack sufficient medical support through the traditional single physician model. More than 50 FHTs were set up in the first year. Some operate 24 hours per day and most have three or more physicians.

Unlike traditional family doctors' offices, FHTs are multidisciplinary clinics in which physicians work closely and collaboratively with nurses, nurse-practitioners, and other health professionals such as social workers, therapists, pharmacists, and dieticians. The government predicts that by sharing more duties with other team members, physicians will be able to see more patients.

A recent Canadian survey reported that 97 percent of health care managers, 95 percent of pharmacists and nurses, and 87 percent of the public preferred a team approach to health care. However, the report also found that 69 percent of Canadian doctors value teams, suggesting more resistance from people in this profession. Ken Babey, lead physician at a family health network in Mount Forest, Ontario, explains that physicians resist the team approach because they worry it will require more effort without the expected benefits. "Doctors are concerned implementing (collaborative care) will mean more work and higher costs," says Babey. "They want to see the evidence such models will work, so there is a basic level of mistrust."

The Ontario government hopes to ease the shortage of family doctors through the introduction of multidisciplinary family health teams. *CP/Phototake*

However, several physicians who have already shifted towards the family health team model believe their colleagues will eventually embrace multidisciplinary teamwork. "The biggest hurdle for physicians, really, is to get out of the status quo," suggests Eric Paquette, a physician at the White Pine Family Health Network in Timmins, Ontario. "Once we've done that, we're quite open now to working in different ways."

Sources: M. Borsellino, "Doctors Cooler on Collaborative Care than Others," *Medical Post* 39, June 10, 2003; K. Pole, "Teamwork Key to Successful Health Reform," *Medical Post* 40, December 14, 2004, p. 35; M. Sylvain, "Ont. Family Health Teams on Fast Track," *Medical Post* 41, February 8, 2005; R. Ferguson, "Family Health Teams Prescribed as New Health Fix," *Toronto Star*, April 23, 2005, p. F03. **www.health.gov.on.ca**

As a form of employee involvement, teams are generally more successful than individuals working alone at identifying problems, developing alternatives, and choosing from those alternatives. For instance, the Transportation Safety Board team investigating the Air France crash consists of experts from various disciplines who collectively would discover much more about the incident than an individual working alone. Similarly, team members can quickly share information and coordinate tasks, whereas these processes are slower and prone to more errors in traditional departments led by supervisors. Teams typically provide superior customer service because they provide more breadth of knowledge and expertise to customers than individual "stars" can offer.

In many situations, individuals are potentially more energized or engaged when working in teams. People have a drive to bond and are motivated to fulfill the goals of groups to which they belong. For instance, one Canadian study reported that employees had a stronger sense of belongingness when they worked in teams rather than alone.[10] Another consideration is that people potentially have higher motivation completing complex tasks in a team because the effort-to-performance expectancy would be much lower if performing the entire task alone.

■ A MODEL OF TEAM EFFECTIVENESS

You might have noticed that we hedged our glorification of teams by saying that they are "potentially" better than individuals "under the right conditions." The reason for this cautious writing is that many organizations have introduced team structures that have become spectacular failures. Why are some teams effective while others fail? This question has challenged organizational researchers for some time and, as you might expect, numerous models of team effectiveness have been proposed over the years.[11]

Let's begin by clarifying the meaning of **team effectiveness**. Team effectiveness refers to how the team affects the organization, individual team members, and the team's existence.[12] First, most teams exist to serve some purpose relating to the organization or other system in which the group operates. As described in the opening story to this chapter, the Canadian Transportation Safety Board investigation team members are responsible for looking for all possible causes of the Air France crash. Some informal groups also have task-oriented (although not organizationally mandated) goals, such as sharing information in an informal community of practice.

Second, team effectiveness relies on the satisfaction and well-being of its members. People join groups to fulfill their personal needs, so effectiveness is partly measured by this need fulfillment. Finally, team effectiveness includes the team's viability— its ability to survive. It must be able to maintain the commitment of its members, particularly during the turbulence of the team's development. Without this commitment, people leave and the team will fall apart. It must also secure sufficient resources and find a benevolent environment in which to operate.

Exhibit 9.2 presents the model of team effectiveness that we will examine closely over the rest of this chapter. We begin by looking at elements of the team's and organization's environment that influence team design, processes, and outcomes.

■ **EXHIBIT 9.2**

Model of team effectiveness

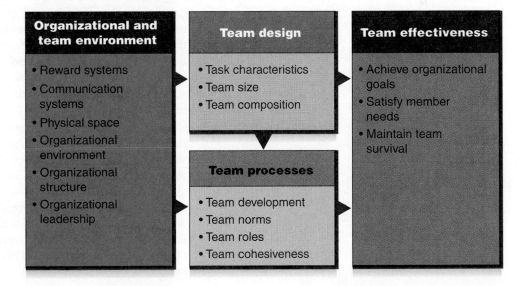

■ ORGANIZATIONAL AND TEAM ENVIRONMENT

Our discussion of team effectiveness logically begins with the contextual factors that influence the team's design, processes, and outcomes.[13] There are many elements in the organizational and team environment that influence team effectiveness. Six of the most important elements are reward systems, communication systems, physical space, organizational environment, organizational structure, and organizational leadership.

■ *Reward systems*—Team members tend to work together more effectively when they are at least partly rewarded for team performance.[14] This doesn't mean that everyone on the team should receive the same amount of pay based on the team's performance. On the contrary, rewards tend to work better in Canada and other Western societies when individual pay is based on a combination of individual and team performance.

■ *Communications systems*—A poorly designed communication system can starve a team of valuable information and feedback, or it may swamp it with information overload. As we will learn in the next chapter, communication systems are particularly important when team members are geographically dispersed.

■ *Physical space*—The layout of an office or manufacturing facility does more than improve communication among team members. It also shapes employee perceptions about being together as a team and influences the team's ability to accomplish tasks. Employees at Celestica's manufacturing facility in Toronto arranged their work stations into a U-shaped production system to allow closer interaction with each other and make it easier to help each other when bottlenecks occur. Toyota puts everyone involved in product design in a large room (called an obeya) so they have a sense of being a team and can communicate more quickly and effectively.[15]

■ *Organizational environment*—Team success depends on the company's external environment. If the organization cannot secure resources, for instance, the team cannot fulfill its performance targets. Similarly, high demand for the team's output creates feelings of success, which motivates team members to stay with the team. A competitive environment can motivate employees to work together more closely.

■ *Organizational structure*—Many teams fail because the organizational structure does not support them. Teams work better when there are few layers of management and teams are given autonomy and responsibility for their work. This structure encourages interaction with team members rather than with supervisors. Teams also flourish when employees are organized around work processes rather than specialized skills. This structure increases interaction among team members.[16]

Obeya Builds Team Dynamics

As with most automakers, Toyota relies on engineers, design stylists, suppliers, assembly workers, and marketing people to help design new vehicles (including the cars built in Toyota's Canadian plant, shown here). To speed up the design process, Toyota moves these experts out of their departments and into one big room as a team. About the size of a basketball court, the "obeya" (Japanese for "big room") arrangement has cut Toyota's product development time and costs by 25 and 50 percent, respectively. "The reason obeya works so well is that it's all about immediate face-to-face human contact," explains Atsushi Niimi, president of Toyota Motor Manufacturing North America. Max Gillard, who oversees Toyota's obeya in Melbourne, Australia, adds that everyone in the obeya can hear conversations between a few people, which encourages others to join the discussion. "There is a hubbub," says Gillard. "You can go there and feel the excitement of the place. It is not like an office environment where people sit quietly tapping away at their computers."[17]
Courtesy of Toyota Canada

■ *Organizational leadership*—Teams require ongoing support from senior executives to align rewards, organizational structure, communication systems, and other elements of team context. They also require team leaders or facilitators who provide coaching and support. Team leaders are also enablers, meaning that they ensure teams have the authority to solve their own problems and resources to accomplish their tasks.[18] Leaders also maintain a value system that supports team performance more than individual success.

■ TEAM DESIGN FEATURES

There are several elements to consider when designing an effective team. Three of the main design elements are task characteristics, team size, and team composition. As we saw earlier in the team effectiveness model (Exhibit 9.2), these design features influence team effectiveness directly as well as indirectly through team processes, described later.

TASK CHARACTERISTICS

More than a decade ago, Varian Australia introduced continuous improvement process (CIP) teams to assist productivity improvement. A recent evaluation found that while CIP teams reduced the product development cycle by up to 50 percent, most fell apart after a few years. One of the main problems, the company discovered, was that many CIP teams ran out of ways to improve productivity. Others gave up because they were assigned projects beyond their capability.[19]

Varian Australia and other companies have discovered that whether teams flourish or fail is partly determined by their assigned tasks or goals. However, the effect of the team's task on team effectiveness is somewhat complex. Teams tend to be more effective when they work on well-structured tasks because the clear structure makes it easier to coordinate work among several people. At the same time, some research indicates that teams flourish more on complex tasks because the complexity motivates them to work together as a team.[20] The difficulty here is that while task structure and task complexity aren't opposites, it can be difficult to find complex work that is well structured.

task interdependence
The degree to which a task requires employees to share common inputs or outcomes, or to interact in the process of executing their work.

Task interdependence   **Task interdependence** is a critically important task characteristic because it relates to the definition of teams (i.e., that they interact and influence each other and are mutually accountable). Task interdependence exists when team members must share common inputs to their individual tasks, need to interact in the process of executing their work, or receive outcomes (such as rewards) that are partly determined by the performance of others.[21] The higher the level of task interdependence, the greater the need for teams rather than individuals working alone.

Teams are well suited to highly interdependent tasks because people coordinate better when working together than separately. Employees tend to be motivated and more satisfied working on teams when their tasks are highly interdependent. However, this motivation and satisfaction occurs only when team members have the same job goals, such as serving the same clients or collectively assembling the same product. In contrast, frustration is more likely to occur when each team member has unique goals (such as serving different clients) but must depend on other team members (high task interdependence) to achieve those unique goals.[22]

■ **EXHIBIT 9.3**

Levels of task interdependence

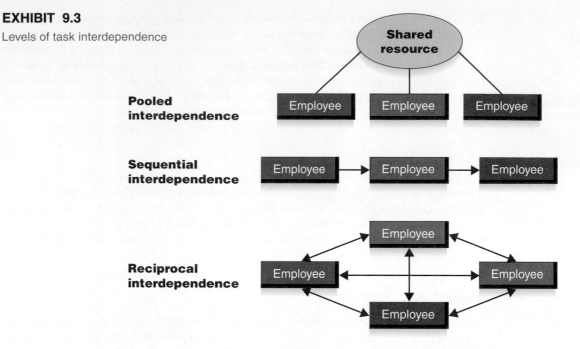

The solution here is to ensure that task interdependence is highest when team members also share the same goals and to minimize task interdependence when employees work toward different goals.

Exhibit 9.3 illustrates three levels of task interdependence.[23] Pooled interdependence is the lowest level of interdependence (other than independence), in which individuals operate independently except for reliance on a common resource or authority. Employees share a common payroll, cafeteria, and other organizational resources. In most cases, they can work well alone rather than in teams if pooled interdependence is the highest relationship among them.

Sequential interdependence occurs where the output of one person becomes the direct input for another person or unit. This interdependent linkage is found in most assembly lines. Although employees in the production line process usually work alone, they are sufficiently interdependent that Toyota and other companies create teams around these processes. Reciprocal interdependence represents the highest level of interdependence, in which work output is exchanged back and forth among individuals. Employees with reciprocal interdependence should almost always be organized into teams to facilitate coordination in their interwoven relationship.

TEAM SIZE

Semco SA is a conglomerate of a dozen businesses operating out of São Paulo, Brazil. Semco tries to keep work units within each business to fewer than 200 employees, which CEO Ricardo Semler reckons is as big as an organization can get without excessive controls. But within each work unit, employees directly interact with between six and ten co-workers. "The maximum anyone is able to regularly deal with is a half dozen people," suggests Semler.[24]

Team size is an important concern at Semco. Some writers claim that team size should be no more than 10 people, making Semco's limit well within those guidelines.

Bioware Picks Team Players

Each year, developers release nearly 3,000 electronic games and only a small fraction of them ever recover their costs. Bioware Corp., the Edmonton-based electronic games developer has handily beat those odds with successful products such as *Jade Empire*, *Neverwinter Nights*, and *Star Wars: Knights of the Old Republic*. Bioware's secret is to spend time hiring talented people such as programmer Sophie Smith (shown in photo) with the right fit for Bioware's team-based culture. Job applicants participate in several interviews and meet up to 30 Bioware employees and managers. Staff are looking for applicants who love electronic games and have the right skill set, but also can collaborate with others. "We look carefully for signs that may indicate the person is not a team player," says Ray Muzyka, who shares the CEO role with Greg Zeschuk.[30]

Shaughn Butts/Edmonton Journal

www.bioware.com

Optimal team size depends on several factors, however, such as the number of people required to complete the work and the amount of coordination needed to work together. The general rule is that teams should be large enough to provide the necessary competencies and perspectives to perform the work, yet small enough to maintain efficient coordination and meaningful involvement of each member.[25]

Larger teams are typically less effective because members consume more time and effort coordinating their roles and resolving differences. For instance, some of the continuous improvement process teams at Varian Australia (described earlier) suffered because they had more than a dozen members, making it difficult to reach agreement on ideas. In these larger teams, individuals have less opportunity to participate and, consequently, are less likely to feel that they are contributing to the team's success. Larger work units tend to break into informal subgroups around common interests and work activities, leading members to form stronger commitments to their subgroup than to the larger team.

TEAM COMPOSITION

When Hewlett-Packard Co. (H-P) hires new talent, it doesn't just look for technical skills and knowledge. The high-tech computer manufacturer looks for job applicants who fit into a team environment. "It's important for candidates to prove to us that they can work well with others," explains business-development manager Bill Avey. "We're looking for people who value the different perspectives that each individual brings to a team." Avey describes how H-P recruiters will ask applicants to recall a time they worked in a group to solve a problem. "Successful candidates tend to show how they got differences out in the open and reached a resolution as a team," says Avey.[26]

Hewlett-Packard has a strong team orientation, so it carefully selects people with the necessary motivation and competencies for teamwork. Teams require members who are motivated to remain team members. In particular, they must be motivated to work together rather than alone, abide by the team's rules of conduct, and buy in to the team's goals. Employees with a strong collectivist orientation—those who value group goals more than their own personal goals—tend to perform better in work teams.[27] Effective team members also possess valuable skills and knowledge for the team's objectives, and are able to work well with others. Notably, research suggests that high-performing team members demonstrate more cooperative behaviour toward others and generally have more emotional intelligence.[28]

homogeneous teams

Teams that include members with common technical expertise, demographics (age, gender), ethnicity, experiences, or values.

Team diversity   Another important dimension of team composition is the diversity of team members.[29] **Homogeneous teams** include members with common technical expertise, demographics (age, sex), ethnicity, experiences, or values, whereas

heterogeneous teams

Teams that include members with diverse personal characteristics and backgrounds.

heterogeneous teams have members with diverse personal characteristics and backgrounds. Some forms of diversity are apparent on the surface, such as differences in sex and race. Deep-level diversity, on the other hand, refers to differences in the personalities, values, attitudes, and other psychological characteristics of team members. Surface-level diversity is apparent as soon as the team forms, whereas deep-level diversity emerges over time as team members discover each other's values and beliefs.[31]

Should teams be homogeneous or heterogeneous? Both have advantages and disadvantages, and their relative effectiveness depends on the situation.[32] Heterogeneous teams experience more conflict and take longer to develop. They are susceptible to "faultlines"—hypothetical dividing lines that may split a team into subgroups along gender, ethnic, professional, or other dimensions. Teams with strong faultlines—such as where team members fall into two or more distinct demographic groups—have a higher risk of dysfunctional conflict and other behaviours that undermine team effectiveness. Under these circumstances, leaders need to restructure the work to minimize interaction among these subgroups.[33] In contrast, members of homogeneous teams experience higher satisfaction, less conflict, and better interpersonal relations. Consequently, homogeneous teams tend to be more effective on tasks requiring a high degree of cooperation and coordination, such as emergency response teams.

Although heterogeneous teams experience more conflict, they are generally more effective than homogeneous teams in executive groups and in other situations involving complex problems requiring innovative solutions. One reason is that people from different backgrounds see a problem or opportunity from different perspectives. A second reason is that they usually have a broader knowledge base. For example, the team investigating the Air France crash (described in the opening story) is necessarily composed of people who have deep knowledge in several fields, ranging from combustible materials to weather systems. Without these heterogeneous characteristics, the team would be much less effective in its assigned task.

A third reason why heterogeneous teams are generally more effective than homogeneous teams is that the diversity provides representation to the team's constituents, such as other departments or clients from similarly diverse backgrounds. When a team represents various professions or departments, those constituents are more likely to accept and support the team's decisions and actions.

■ TEAM PROCESSES

We've looked at two sets of elements in the team effectiveness model so far: (1) organizational and team environment and (2) team design. Over the next few pages, we will learn about the third set of team effectiveness elements, collectively known as team processes. These processes—team development, norms, roles, and cohesiveness—are influenced by both team design and organizational and team environment factors.

TEAM DEVELOPMENT

A few years ago, the National Transportation Safety Board (NTSB) in the United States studied the circumstances under which airplane cockpit crews were most likely to have accidents and related problems. What they discovered was startling: 73 percent of all incidents took place on the crew's first day, and 44 percent occurred on the crew's very first flight together. This isn't an isolated example. NASA studied fatigue of pilots after returning from multiple-day trips. Fatigued pilots made more errors in the NASA flight simulator, as one would expect. But the NASA researchers didn't expect the discovery that fatigued crews who had worked together made fewer errors than did rested crews who had not yet flown together.[34]

The NTSB and NASA studies reveal that team members must resolve several issues and pass through several stages of development before emerging as an effective work unit. They must get to know each other, understand their respective roles, discover appropriate and inappropriate behaviours, and learn how to coordinate their work or social activities. The longer that team members work together, the better they develop common mental models, mutual understanding, and effective performance routines to complete the work. For this reason, Budd Canada resisted union demands for a new work schedule that would create new work teams. "Even though the individual level of skills could be good, people who work together as a team regularly are always slightly ahead of a team that is put together on an ad hoc basis," explains Budd Canada executive Winston Wong.[35]

The five-stage model of team development, shown in Exhibit 9.4, provides a general outline of how teams evolve by forming, storming, norming, performing, and eventually adjourning.[36] The model shows teams progressing from one stage to the next in an orderly fashion, but the dashed lines illustrate that they might also fall back to an earlier stage of development as new members join or other conditions disrupt the team's maturity.

1. *Forming*—The first stage of team development is a period of testing and orientation in which members learn about each other and evaluate the benefits and costs of continued membership. People tend to be polite during this stage and will defer to the existing authority of a formal or informal leader who must provide an initial set of rules and structures for interaction. Members try to find out what is expected of them and how they will fit into the team.

2. *Storming*—The storming stage is marked by interpersonal conflict as members become more proactive and compete for various team roles. Coalitions may form to influence the team's goals and means of goal attainment. Members try to

■ **EXHIBIT 9.4**

Stages of team development

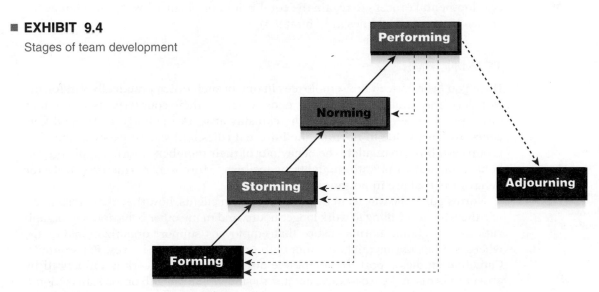

establish norms of appropriate behaviour and performance standards. This is a tenuous stage in the team's development, particularly when the leader is autocratic and lacks the necessary conflict-management skills.

3. *Norming*—During the norming stage, the team develops its first real sense of cohesion as roles are established and a consensus forms around group objectives. Members have developed relatively similar mental models, so they have common expectations and assumptions about how the team's goals should be accomplished. They have developed a common team-based mental model that allows them to interact more efficiently so they can move into the next stage, performing.[37]

4. *Performing*—The team becomes more task-oriented in the performing stage. Team members have learned to coordinate and resolve conflicts more efficiently. Further coordination improvements must occasionally be addressed, but the greater emphasis is on task accomplishment. In high-performance teams, members are highly cooperative, have a high level of trust in each other, are committed to group objectives, and identify with the team. There is a climate of mutual support in which team members feel comfortable about taking risks, making errors, or asking for help.[38]

5. *Adjourning*—Most work teams and informal groups eventually end. Task forces disband when their project is completed. Informal work groups may reach this stage when several members leave the organization or are reassigned elsewhere. Some teams adjourn as a result of layoffs or plant shutdowns. Whatever the cause of team adjournment, members shift their attention away from task orientation to a socioemotional focus as they realize that their relationship is ending.

The team development model is a useful framework for thinking about how teams develop. Indeed, a recent Canadian study suggests that it fits nicely with student recollections of their team development experiences.[39] Still, Tuckman's model is not a perfect representation of the dynamics of team development. The model does not explicitly show that some teams remain in a particular stage longer than others, and that team development is a continuous process. As membership changes and new conditions emerge, teams cycle back to earlier stages in the developmental process to regain the equilibrium or balance lost by the change (as shown by the dashed lines in Exhibit 9.4).

TEAM NORMS

Have you ever noticed how employees in one branch office practically run for the exit door the minute the workday ends, whereas their counterparts in another office seem to be competing for who can stay at work the longest? These differences are partly due to **norms**—the informal rules and shared expectations that groups establish to regulate the behaviour of their members. Norms apply only to behaviour, not to private thoughts or feelings. Moreover, norms exist only for behaviours that are important to the team.[40]

Norms guide the way team members deal with clients, how they share resources, whether they are willing to work longer hours, and many other behaviours in organizational life. Some norms ensure that employees support organizational goals, whereas other norms might conflict with organizational objectives. For example, Canadian studies report that employee absenteeism from work is influenced by absence norms in the workplace, not just the individual's health or job satisfaction.[41]

norms

The informal rules and expectations that groups establish to regulate the behaviour of their members.

Conformity to team norms   Everyone has experienced peer pressure at one time or another. Co-workers grimace if we are late for a meeting or make sarcastic comments if we don't have our part of the project completed on time. In more extreme situations, team members may try to enforce norms by temporarily ostracizing deviant co-workers or threatening to terminate their membership. This heavy-handed peer pressure isn't as rare as you might think. One survey revealed that 20 percent of employees have been pressured by their colleagues to slack off at work. Half the time, the peer pressure occurred because colleagues didn't want to look like poor performers against their more productive co-workers.[42]

Team Huddles Reinforce Norms
One of the first and last tasks of the day at The Container Store is for staff to gather for the "huddle." At The Container Store outlet in White Plains, New York, floor leader Scott Buhler (shown in photo) starts the morning huddle by declaring the day's sales target. Then he asks the group about the store's vision and today's product tip. "We always highlight a product or do a quiz to make sure employees are familiar with new products," Buhler says. The Container Store institutionalized huddle sessions to educate employees, create a team environment, and reinforce norms that the company wants to instill in employees. "The spirit was to keep people on the same page," explains Garrett Boone, co-founder and chairman of the Dallas-based seller of customized storage products. *H. Darr Beiser, USA Today*
www.containerstore.com

Norms are also directly reinforced through praise from high-status members, more access to valued resources, or other rewards available to the team. But team members often conform to prevailing norms without direct reinforcement or punishment because they identify with the team and want to align their behaviour with its values. The more tightly the person's social identity is connected to the group, the more the individual is motivated to avoid negative sanctions from that group.[43] This effect is particularly strong in new members because they are uncertain of their status and want to demonstrate their membership in the team. GLOBAL Connections 9.2 provides an extreme example of the consequences of team norms and conformity in organizational settings.

How team norms develop   Norms develop as soon as teams form because people need to anticipate or predict how others will act. Even subtle events during the team's formation, such as how team members initially greet each other and where they sit in the first meetings, can initiate norms that are later difficult to change. At first, most norms are fuzzy, such as "team members should communicate frequently with each other." Over time, norms tend to become more specific, such as "check and reply to your email daily."[44]

Norms form as team members discover behaviours that help them function more effectively (such as the need to respond quickly to email). In particular, a critical event in the team's history can trigger formation of a norm or sharpen a previously vague one. As an example, if a co-worker slipped on metal scraps and seriously injured herself, team members might develop a strong norm to keep the work area clean. Along with the effect of initial experiences and critical events, a third influence on team norms is the past experiences and values that members bring to the team. If most people who join a new team value work/life balance, then norms are likely to develop that discourage long hours and work overload.[45]

Elite New Zealand Prison Team's "Culture of Obedience"

Members of a special emergency response team congregated at dawn for a covert mission. The 16 handpicked and specially trained members based at Paparua Prison, New Zealand, were supposed to reduce prison violence, prevent drugs from entering prisons, and improve prisoner compliance. But the mission on this day was different. The response team was hunting for an escapee—a rooster belonging to a member of the response team that had escaped to a neighbouring farm.

This is just one of the bizarre incidents about the special unit, dubbed the "Goon Squad" by adversaries. The team worked independently of the prison officers and had its own distinctive black uniforms. Unfortunately, a government report also concluded that the team developed a distinctive set of norms, some of which violated Corrections Department policies.

A government investigation and subsequent court case heard claims that the team falsified time sheets, juggled the work roster for personal gain, used department vehicles for personal use, used unnecessary intimidation on inmates, consumed alcohol on duty, acted inappropriately in public, and hunted wayward roosters on company time.

The special unit also conducted missions in the outside community even though its mandate was restricted to the prison. "Our focus moved to a policeman's role, which we should not have been doing," admits one former member.

None of the members complained during the unit's existence because of "a culture of obedience." For example, when one member refused to go to a party, others in the unit allegedly went to his home, restrained him, hit him over the head with an axe handle, handcuffed him, and dragged him along to the party.

"The most chilling thing about the team was an apparent fear of authority among members, leading to a culture of obedience and silence," says an executive member of the Howard League for Penal Reform. "In effect, they became a law unto themselves."

Sources: Y. Martin, "'Goon Squad' Vote Today," *The Press (Christchurch),* September 10, 2003; Y. Martin, "The Goon Squad—The Fallout Continues," *The Press (Christchurch),* August 16, 2003, p. 15; Y. Martin, "Goon Squad," *The Press (Christchurch),* June 9, 2001, p. 2; "'Goon Squad' Prison Staff Disciplined," *New Zealand Press Association,* May 23, 2001; Y. Martin, "Crack Prison Team Members Guilty of Serious Misconduct," *The Press (Christchurch),* May 24, 2001, p. 1.
www.howardleague.co.nz

Preventing and changing dysfunctional team norms   Team norms often become deeply anchored, so the best way to avoid norms that undermine organizational success or employee well-being is to establish desirable norms when the team is first formed. As mentioned above, norms form from the values that people bring to the team, so one strategy is to select people with appropriate values. If organizational leaders want their teams to have strong safety norms, then they should hire people who already value safety.

Another strategy is to clearly state desirable norms as soon as the team is created. For instance, when Four Seasons Hotels & Resorts opens a new hotel, it forms a 35-person task force of respected staff from other Four Seasons hotels to get the new hotel up and running. Their mandate also includes helping to "Four Seasonize" the new staff by watching for behaviours and decisions that are inconsistent with the Four Seasons way of doing things. "The task force helps establish norms [in the new hotel]," explains a manager at the Toronto-based company.[46]

Of course, most teams are not just starting up, so how can norms change in older teams? One way is for the leader to explicitly discuss the counterproductive norm with team members using persuasive communication tactics. For example, the surgical team of a small Ontario hospital had developed a norm of arriving late for operations. Patients and other hospital staff often waited 30 minutes or more for the team to arrive. The hospital CEO eventually spoke to the surgical team about their lateness and, through moral suasion, convinced team members to arrive for operating room procedures no more than five minutes late for their appointments.[47]

Team-based reward systems can sometimes weaken counterproductive norms. Unfortunately, the pressure to conform to the counterproductive norm is sometimes stronger than the financial incentive. This problem occurred in the classic story of a pajama factory where employees were paid under a piece rate system. Some individuals in the group were able to process up to 100 units per hour and thereby earn more money, but they all chose to abide by the group norm of 50 units per hour. Only after the team was disbanded did the strong performers working alone increase their performance to 100 units per hour.[48]

Finally, a dysfunctional norm may be so deeply ingrained that the best strategy is to disband the group and replace it with people having more favourable norms. Companies should seize the opportunity to introduce performance-oriented norms when the new team is formed, and select members who will bring desirable norms to the group.

TEAM ROLES

role
A set of behaviours that people are expected to perform because they hold certain positions in a team and organization.

Every work team and informal group has various roles necessary to coordinate the team's task and maintain the team's functioning. A **role** is a set of behaviours that people are expected to perform because they hold certain positions in a team and organization.[49] Some roles help the team achieve its goals; other roles maintain relationships so the team survives and team members fulfill their needs. Some team roles are formally assigned to specific people. For example, team leaders are usually expected to initiate discussion, ensure that everyone has an opportunity to present their views, and help the team reach agreement on the issues discussed. But team members often take on various roles informally based on their personality, values, and expertise. These role preferences are usually worked out during the storming stage of team development. However, in a dynamic environment, team members often need to assume various roles temporarily as the need arises.[50]

Various team role theories have been proposed over the years, but Meredith Belbin's team role theory is the most popular.[51] The model identifies nine team roles (see Exhibit 9.5) that are related to specific personality characteristics. People have a natural preference for one role or another, although they can adjust to a secondary role. Belbin's model emphasizes that all nine roles must be engaged for optimal team performance. Moreover, certain team roles should dominate over others at various stages of the team's project or activities. For example, shapers and coordinators are key figures when the team is identifying its needs, whereas completers and implementers are most important during the follow-through stage of the team's project.

How accurate is Belbin's team roles model? The evidence is mixed.[52] Research indicates that teams do require a balance of roles, and that people do tend to prefer one type of role. However, Belbin's nine roles typically boil down to six or seven roles in empirical studies. For example, the implementer and completer roles are the same or too similar to distinguish from each other. Scholars have also criticized how Belbin's roles are measured, which creates difficulty in determining the accuracy of the model. Overall, teams do have a variety of roles that must be fulfilled for team effectiveness, but we are still trying to figure out what these roles are and how to measure them.

TEAM COHESIVENESS

team cohesiveness
The degree of attraction people feel toward the team and their motivation to remain members.

Team cohesiveness—the degree of attraction people feel toward the team and their motivation to remain members—is considered an important factor in a team's success.[53] Employees feel cohesiveness when they believe the team will

EXHIBIT 9.5   Belbin's team roles

Role label	Role description
Plant	Creative, imaginative, unorthodox. Solves difficult problems.
Coordinator	Mature, confident, a good chairperson. Clarifies goals, promotes decision-making, delegates well.
Monitor evaluator	Sober, strategic, and discerning. Sees all options. Judges accurately.
Implementer	Disciplined, reliable, conservative, and efficient. Turns ideas into practical actions.
Completer finisher	Painstaking, conscientious, anxious. Searches out errors and omissions. Delivers on time.
Resource investigator	Extrovert, enthusiastic, communicative. Explores opportunities. Develops contacts.
Shaper	Challenging, dynamic, thrives on pressure. The drive and courage to overcome obstacles.
Team worker	Co-operative, mild, perceptive, and diplomatic. Listens, builds, averts friction.
Specialist	Single-minded, self-starting, dedicated. Provides knowledge and skills in rare supply.

Sources: R. M. Belbin, *Team Roles At Work* (Oxford, UK: Butterworth-Heinemann, 1993); www.belbin.com.

help them achieve their personal goals, fulfill their need for affiliation or status, or provide social support during times of crisis or trouble. Cohesiveness is an emotional experience, not just a calculation of whether to stay or leave the team. It exists when team members make the team part of their social identity. Cohesiveness is the glue or *esprit de corps* that holds the group together and ensures that its members fulfill their obligations.

Influences on team cohesiveness   Several factors influence team cohesiveness: member similarity, team size, member interaction, difficult entry, team success, and external competition or challenges. For the most part, these factors reflect the individual's social identity with the group and beliefs about how team membership will fulfill personal needs.[54] Several of these factors are related to our earlier discussion about why people join informal groups and how teams develop. Specifically, teams become more cohesive as they reach higher stages of development and are more attractive to potential members.

- *Member similarity*—Earlier in this chapter we learned that highly diverse teams potentially create faultlines that can lead to factious subgroups and higher turnover among team members. Other research has found that people with similar values have a higher attraction to each other. Collectively, these findings suggest that homogeneous teams are more cohesive than heterogeneous teams. However, not all forms of diversity reduce cohesion. For example, teams consisting of people from different job groups seem to gel together just as well as teams of people from the same job.[55]
- *Team size*—Smaller teams tend to be more cohesive than larger teams because it is easier for a few people to agree on goals and coordinate work activities. The smallest teams aren't always the most cohesive, however. Small teams are

less cohesive when they lack enough members to perform the required tasks. Thus, team cohesiveness is potentially greatest when teams are as small as possible, yet large enough to accomplish the required tasks.

■ *Member interaction*—Teams tend to be more cohesive when team members interact with each other fairly regularly. This occurs when team members perform highly interdependent tasks and work in the same physical area.

■ *Somewhat difficult entry*—Teams tend to be more cohesive when entry to the team is restricted. The more elite the team, the more prestige it confers on its members, and the more they tend to value their membership in the unit. Existing team members are also more willing to welcome and support new members after they have "passed the test," possibly because they have shared the same entry experience. This raises the issue of how difficult the initiation for entry into the team should be. Research suggests that severe initiations can potentially lead to humiliation and psychological distance from the group, even for those who successfully endure the initiation.[56]

■ *Team success*—Cohesion is both emotional and instrumental, with the latter referring to the notion that people feel more cohesion to teams that fulfill their goals. Consequently, cohesion increases with the team's level of success.[57] Furthermore, individuals are more likely to attach their social identity to successful teams than to those with a string of failures. Team leaders can increase cohesiveness by regularly communicating and celebrating the team's successes. Notice that this can create a spiral effect. Successful teams are more cohesive and, under certain conditions, increased cohesiveness increases the team's success.

■ *External competition and challenges*—Team cohesiveness tends to increase when members face external competition or a valued objective that is challenging. This might include a threat from an external competitor or friendly competition from other teams. These conditions tend to increase cohesiveness because employees value the team's ability to overcome the threat or competition if they can't solve the problem individually. They also value their membership as a form of social support. We need to be careful about the degree of external threat, however. Evidence suggests that teams seem to be less effective when external threats are severe. Although cohesiveness tends to increase, external threats are stressful and cause teams to make less effective decisions under these conditions.[58]

Consequences of team cohesiveness   Every team must have some minimal level of cohesiveness to maintain its existence. People who belong to high-cohesion teams are motivated to maintain their membership and to help the team perform effectively.

Lighthouse Publishing's Team Cohesion

The staff at Lighthouse Publishing in Bridgewater, Nova Scotia, are a highly cohesive group that successfully keeps its much larger competitors off-guard. "Lighthouse staff members [have] kept us independent in the face of stiff competition and corporate takeovers," says Lighthouse president Lynn Hennigar. Its weekly newspaper, the *Bridgewater Bulletin*, is regularly judged as best in class for Atlantic Canada and the top of its class across Canada in 2002. In all, the company received more than two dozen awards in 2004. Lighthouse's mostly female staff often demonstrate their cohesion when faced with new challenges. For instance, the team performed above any reasonable expectations when the press broke down, which threatened to delay getting the paper out on time. On another occasion, when putting together an interactive CD-ROM promoting Nova Scotia tourism, Lighthouse staff displayed skills that Hennigar admits she didn't even know about. "Lighthouse succeeds because of its multi-talented, highly-dedicated team of employees," says Hennigar. "It's a team that embraces change."[59]

Courtesy of Atlantic Business Magazine and Lighthouse Publishing. Photo by Robert Hirtle

www.lighthouse.ns.ca

Compared to low-cohesion teams, high-cohesion team members spend more time together, share information more frequently, and are more satisfied with each other. They provide each other with better social support in stressful situations.[60]

Members of high-cohesion teams are generally more sensitive to each other's needs and develop better interpersonal relationships, thereby reducing dysfunctional conflict. When conflict does arise, members tend to resolve these differences swiftly and effectively. For example, one Canadian study reported that cohesive recreational ice hockey teams engaged in more constructive conflict—that is, team members tried to resolve their differences cooperatively—whereas less cohesive teams engaged in more combative conflict.[61]

With better cooperation and more conformity to norms, high-cohesion teams usually perform better than low-cohesion teams. However, the relationship is a little more complex. Exhibit 9.6 illustrates how the effect of cohesiveness on team performance depends on the extent that team norms are consistent with organizational goals. Cohesive teams will likely have lower task performance when norms conflict with organizational objectives, because cohesiveness motivates employees to perform at a level more consistent with group norms.[62]

■ THE TROUBLE WITH TEAMS

As we explained near the beginning of this chapter, organizational leaders are placing a lot more emphasis on teams these days. While this chapter has outlined the benefits of teams, the reality is that teams aren't always needed.[63] Sometimes, a quick and decisive action by one person is more appropriate. Some tasks are also performed just as easily by one person as by a group. "The now fashionable team in which everybody works with everybody on everything from the beginning rapidly is becoming a disappointment," warns management guru Peter Drucker.[64]

A second problem is that teams take time to develop and maintain. Scholars refer to these hidden costs as **process losses**—resources (including time and energy) expended toward team development and maintenance rather than the task.[65] It is much more efficient for an individual to work out an issue alone than to

process losses
Resources (including time and energy) expended toward team development and maintenance rather than the task.

■ **EXHIBIT 9.6**

Effect of team cohesiveness on task performance

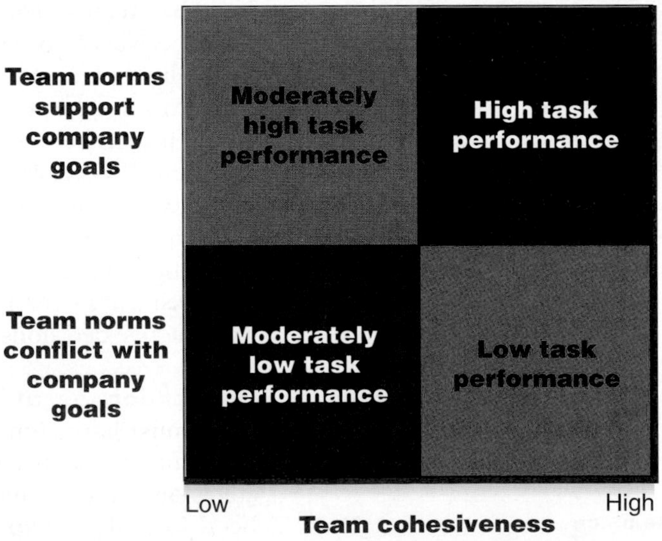

Team norms support company goals — Moderately high task performance | High task performance

Team norms conflict with company goals — Moderately low task performance | Low task performance

Low ← Team cohesiveness → High

resolve differences of opinion with other people. The process loss problem becomes apparent when adding new people to the team. The group has to recycle through the team development process to bring everyone up to speed. The software industry even has a name for this. "Brooks's law" says that adding more people to a late software project only makes it later. Researchers point out that the cost of process losses may be offset by the benefits of teams. Unfortunately, few companies conduct a cost-benefit analysis of their team activities.[66]

A third problem is that teams require the right environment to flourish. Many companies forget this point by putting people in teams without changing anything else. As we noted earlier, teams require appropriate rewards, communication systems, team leadership, and other conditions. Without these, the shift to a team structure could be a waste of time. At the same time, critics suggest that changing these environmental conditions to improve teamwork could result in higher costs than benefits for the overall organization.[67]

SOCIAL LOAFING

social loafing

A situation in which people exert less effort (and usually perform at a lower level) when working in groups than when working alone.

Perhaps the best-known limitation of teams is the risk of productivity loss due to **social loafing**. Social loafing occurs when people exert less effort (and usually perform at a lower level) when working in groups than when working alone.[68] A few scholars question whether social loafing is common, but students can certainly report many instances of this problem in their team projects!

Social loafing is most likely to occur in large teams where individual output is difficult to identify. This particularly includes situations in which team members work alone toward a common output pool (i.e., they have low task interdependence). Under these conditions, employees aren't as worried that their performance will be noticed. Social loafing is less likely to occur when the task is interesting, because individuals have a higher intrinsic motivation to perform their duties. It is less common when the group's objective is important, possibly because individuals experience more pressure from other team members to perform well. Finally, social loafing occurs less frequently among members with a strong collectivist value, because they value group membership and believe in working toward group objectives.[69]

How to minimize social loafing   By understanding the causes of social loafing, we can identify ways to minimize this problem. Some of the strategies listed below reduce social loafing by making each member's performance more visible. Others increase each member's motivation to perform his or her tasks within the group.[70]

- *Form smaller teams*—Splitting the team into smaller groups reduces social loafing because each person's performance becomes more noticeable and important for team performance. A smaller group also potentially increases cohesiveness, so that would-be shirkers feel a greater obligation to perform fully for their team.
- *Specialize tasks*—Each person's contribution is easier to see when each team member performs a different work activity. For example, rather than pooling their effort for all incoming customer inquiries, each customer service representative might be assigned a particular type of client.
- *Measure individual performance*—Social loafing is minimized when each member's contribution is measured. Of course, individual performance is difficult to measure in some team activities, such as problem-solving projects in which the team's performance depends on one person discovering the best answer.

- *Increase job enrichment*—Social loafing is minimized when team members are assigned more motivating jobs, such as requiring more skill variety or having direct contact with clients. More generally, social loafing is less common among employees with high job satisfaction.
- *Select motivated employees*—Social loafing can be minimized by carefully selecting job applicants who are motivated by the task and have a collectivist value orientation. Those with a collectivist value are motivated to work harder for the team because they value their membership in the group.

This chapter has laid the foundation for our understanding of team dynamics. To build an effective team requires time, the right combination of team members, and the right environment. We will apply these ingredients of environment and team processes in the next chapter, which looks at high-performance teams, including self-directed teams and virtual teams.

CHAPTER SUMMARY

Teams are groups of two or more people who interact and influence each other, are mutually accountable for achieving common objectives, and perceive themselves as a social entity within an organization. All teams are groups, because they consist of people with a unifying relationship; not all groups are teams, because some groups do not have purposive interaction.

Groups can be categorized in terms of their permanence and formality in the organization. Informal groups exist primarily for the benefit of their members rather than for the organization. Teams have become popular because they tend to make better decisions, support the knowledge management process, and provide superior customer service. In many situations, employees are potentially more energized and engaged working in teams rather than alone.

Team effectiveness includes the group's ability to survive, achieve its system-based objectives, and fulfill the needs of its members. The model of team effectiveness considers the team and organizational environment, team design, and team processes. The team or organizational environment influences team effectiveness directly, as well as through team design and team processes. Six elements in the organizational and team environment that influence team effectiveness are reward systems, communication systems, physical space, organizational environment, organizational structure, and organizational leadership.

Three team design elements are task characteristics, team size, and team composition. Teams tend to be more effective when they work on well-structured or complex tasks. The need for teamwork increases with task interdependence. Teams should be large enough to perform the work, yet small enough for efficient coordination and meaningful involvement. Effective teams are composed of people with the competencies and motivation to perform tasks in a team environment. Heterogeneous teams operate best on complex projects and problems requiring innovative solutions.

Teams develop through the stages of forming, storming, norming, performing, and eventually adjourning. Teams develop norms to regulate and guide member behaviour. These norms may be influenced by initial experiences, critical events, and the values and experiences that team members bring to the group. Team members also have roles—a set of behaviours they are expected to perform because they hold certain positions in a team and organization.

Cohesiveness is the degree of attraction people feel toward the team and their motivation to remain members. Cohesiveness increases with member similarity, smaller team size, higher degree of interaction, somewhat difficult entry, team success, and external challenges. Teams need some level of cohesiveness to survive, but high-cohesive units have higher task performance only when their norms do not conflict with organizational objectives.

Teams are not always beneficial or necessary. Moreover, they have hidden costs, known as process losses, and require particular environments to flourish. Teams often fail because they are not set up in supportive environments. Social loafing is another potential problem with teams. This is the tendency for individuals to perform at a lower level when working in groups than when alone. Social loafing can be minimized by making each member's performance more visible and increasing each member's motivation to perform his or her tasks within the group.

KEY TERMS

groups, p. 246

heterogeneous teams, p. 254

homogeneous teams, p. 253

norms, p. 256

process losses, p. 262

role, p. 259

social loafing, p. 263

task interdependence, p. 251

team cohesiveness, p. 259

team effectiveness, p. 249

teams, p. 246

DISCUSSION QUESTIONS

1. Informal groups exist in almost every form of social organization. What types of informal groups exist in your classroom? Why are students motivated to belong to these informal groups?

2. You have been asked to lead a complex software project over the next year that requires the full-time involvement of approximately 100 people with diverse skills and backgrounds. Using your knowledge of team size, how can you develop an effective team under these conditions?

3. You have been put in charge of a cross-functional task force that will develop enhanced Internet banking services for retail customers. The team includes representatives from marketing, information services, customer service, and accounting, all of whom will move to the same location at headquarters for three months. Describe the behaviours you might observe during each stage of the team's development.

4. You have just been transferred from the Regina office to the Saskatoon office of your company, a national sales organization of electrical products for developers and contractors. In Regina, team members regularly called customers after a sale to ask whether the products arrived on time and whether they are satisfied. But when you moved to the Saskatoon office, no one seemed to make these follow-up calls. A recently hired co-worker explained that other co-workers discouraged her from making those calls. Later, another co-worker suggested that your follow-up calls were making everyone else look lazy. Give three possible reasons why the norms in Saskatoon might be different from those in the Regina office, even though the customers, products, sales commissions, and other characteristics of the workplace are almost identical.

5. An employee at a brokerage firm recently made the following comment about his team, using a baseball metaphor: "Our team has a great bunch of people. But just like a baseball team, some people need to hit the home run, whereas others have to play catcher. Some need to be coaches and others have to be experts at fixing the equipment every day. The problem with our team is that we don't have people in some of these other jobs. As a result, our team isn't performing as well as it should." What team dynamics topic is this person mainly referring to, and what is he saying about his team in the context of that topic?

6. You have been assigned to a class project with five other students, none of whom you have met before. To what extent would team cohesiveness improve your team's performance on this project? What actions would you recommend to build team cohesiveness among student team members in this situation?

7. This chapter described the employees at Lighthouse Publishing as a highly cohesive group. From the description provided, what factors contribute to this cohesion?

8. Management guru Peter Drucker recently stated: "The now-fashionable team in which everybody works with everybody on everything from the beginning rapidly is becoming a disappointment." Discuss three problems associated with teams.

CASE STUDY 9.1

TREETOP FOREST PRODUCTS

Treetop Forest Products Ltd. is a sawmill operation in British Columbia that is owned by a major forest products company, but operates independently of headquarters. It was built 30 years ago, and completely updated with new machinery five years ago. Treetop receives raw logs from the area for cutting and planing into building-grade lumber, mostly 2-by-4 and 2-by-6 pieces of standard lengths. Higher grade logs leave Treetop's sawmill department in finished form and are sent directly to the packaging department. The remaining 40 percent of sawmill output are cuts from lower grade logs, requiring further work by the planing department.

Treetop has one general manager, 16 supervisors and support staff, and 180 unionized employees. The unionized employees are paid an hourly rate specified in the collective agreement, whereas management and support staff are paid a monthly salary. The mill is divided into six operating departments: boom, sawmill, planer, packaging, shipping, and maintenance. The sawmill, boom, and packaging departments operate a morning shift starting at 6 a.m. and an afternoon shift starting at 2 p.m. Employees in these departments rotate shifts every two weeks. The planer and shipping departments operate only morning shifts. Maintenance employees work the night shift (starting at 10 p.m.).

Each department, except for packaging, has a supervisor on every work shift. The planer supervisor is responsible for the packaging department on the morning shift, and the sawmill supervisor is responsible for the packaging department on the afternoon shift. However, the packaging operation is housed in a separate building from the other departments, so supervisors seldom visit the packaging department. This is particularly true for the afternoon shift, because the sawmill supervisor is the furthest distance from the packaging building.

Packaging Quality

Ninety percent of Treetop's product is sold on the international market through Westboard Co., a large marketing agency. Westboard represents all forest products mills owned by Treetop's parent company as well as several other clients in the region. Because

there are numerous mills selling a relatively undifferentiated product, the market for building-grade lumber is very price competitive. However, some differentiation does occur in product packaging and presentation. Buyers will look closely at the packaging when deciding whether to buy from Treetop or another mill.

To encourage its clients to package their products better, Westboard sponsors a monthly package quality award. The marketing agency samples and rates its clients' packages daily, and the sawmill with the highest score at the end of the month is awarded a plaque. Package quality is a combination of how the lumber is piled (e.g., defects turned in), where the bands and dunnage are placed, how neatly the stencil and seal are applied, the stencil's accuracy, and how neatly and tightly the plastic wrap is attached.

Treetop Forest Products won Westboard's packaging quality award several times over the past few years, and received high ratings in the months that it didn't win. However, the mill's ratings have started to decline over the past couple of years, and several clients have complained about the appearance of the finished product. A few large customers switched to competitors' lumber, saying that the decision was based on the substandard appearance of Treetop's packaging when it arrived in their lumber yard.

Bottleneck in Packaging

The planing and sawmilling departments have significantly increased productivity over the past couple of years. The sawmill operation recently set a new productivity record on a single day. The planer operation has increased productivity to the point where last year it reduced operations to just one (rather than two) shifts per day. These productivity improvements are due to better operator training, fewer machine breakdowns, and better selection of raw logs. (Sawmill cuts from high-quality logs usually do not require planing work.)

Productivity levels in the boom, shipping, and maintenance departments have remained constant. However, the packaging department has recorded decreasing productivity over the past couple of years, with the result that a large backlog of finished product is typically stockpiled outside the packaging building. The morning shift of the packaging department is unable to keep up with the combined production of the sawmill and planer departments, so the unpackaged output is left for the afternoon shift. Unfortunately, the afternoon shift packages even less product than the morning shift, so the backlog continues to build. The backlog adds to Treetop's inventory costs and increases the risk of damaged stock.

Treetop has added Saturday overtime shifts as well as extra hours before and after the regular shifts for the packaging department employees to process this backlog. Last month, the packaging department employed 10 percent of the work force but accounted for 85 percent of the overtime. This is frustrating to Treetop's management, because time and motion studies recently confirmed that the packaging department is capable of processing all of the daily sawmill and planer production without overtime. Moreover, with employees earning one and a half or two times their regular pay on overtime, Treetop's cost competitiveness suffers.

Employees and supervisors at Treetop are aware that people in the packaging department tend to extend lunch by 10 minutes and coffee breaks by five minutes. They also typically leave work a few minutes before the end of shift. This abuse has worsened recently, particularly on the afternoon shift. Employees who are temporarily assigned to the packaging department also seem to participate in this time loss pattern after a few days. Although they are punctual and productive in other departments, these temporary employees soon adopt the packaging crew's informal schedule when assigned to that department.

Discussion Questions

1. Based on your knowledge of team dynamics, explain why the packaging department is less productive than are other teams at Treetop.

2. How should Treetop change the nonproductive norms that exist in the packaging group?

3. What structural and other changes would you recommend that may improve this situation in the long term?

TEAM EXERCISE   9.2

TEAM TOWER POWER

Purpose   This exercise is designed to help you understand team roles, team development, and other issues in the development and maintenance of effective teams.

Materials   The instructor will provide enough Lego pieces or similar materials for each team to complete the assigned task. All teams should have identical (or very similar) amount and type of pieces. The instructor will need a measuring tape and stopwatch. Students may use writing materials during the design stage (Stage 2 below). The instructor will distribute a "Team Objectives Sheet" and "Tower Specifications Effectiveness Sheet" to all teams.

Instructions

■ *Step 1:* The instructor will divide the class into teams. Depending on class size and space available, teams may have between four to seven members, but all teams should be approximately equal size.

■ *Step 2:* Each team is given 20 minutes to design a tower that uses only the materials provided, is freestanding, and provides an optimal return on investment. Team members may wish to draw their tower on paper or flip chart to assist the tower's design. Teams are free to practise building their tower during this stage. Preferably, teams are assigned to their own rooms so the design can be created privately. During this stage, each team will complete the Team Objectives Sheet distributed by the instructor. This sheet requires the Tower Specifications Effectiveness Sheet, also distributed by the instructor.

■ *Step 3:* Each team will show the instructor that it has completed its Team Objectives Sheet. Then, with all teams in the same room, the instructor will announce the start of the construction phase. The time elapsed for construction will be closely monitored and the instructor will occasionally call out time elapsed (particularly if there is no clock in the room).

■ *Step 4:* Each team will advise the instructor as soon as it has completed its tower. The team will write down the time elapsed that the instructor has determined. It may be asked to assist the instructor by counting the number of blocks used and height of the tower. This information is also written on the Team Objectives Sheet. Then, the team calculates its profit.

■ *Step 5:* After presenting the results, the class will discuss the team dynamics elements that contribute to team effectiveness. Team members will discuss their strategy, division of labour (team roles), expertise within the team, and other elements of team dynamics.

Source: Several published and online sources describe variations of this exercise, but there is no known origin to this activity.

SELF-ASSESSMENT EXERCISE   9.3

TEAM ROLES PREFERENCES SCALE

Purpose   This self-assessment is designed to help you identify your preferred roles in meetings and similar team activities.

Instructions   Read each of the statements below and circle the response that you believe best reflects your position regarding each statement.

Then use the scoring key in Appendix B to calculate your results for each team role. This exercise is completed alone so students assess themselves honestly without concerns of social comparison. However, class discussion will focus on the roles that people assume in team settings. This scale only assesses a few team roles.

TEAM ROLES PREFERENCES SCALE

Circle the number that best reflects your position regarding each of these statements.	Does not describe me at all ▼	Does not describe me very well ▼	Describes me somewhat ▼	Describes me well ▼	Describes me very well ▼
1. I usually take responsibility for getting the team to agree on what the meeting should accomplish.	1	2	3	4	5
2. I tend to summarize to other team members what the team has accomplished so far.	1	2	3	4	5
3. I'm usually the person who helps other team members overcome their disagreements.	1	2	3	4	5
4. I try to ensure that everyone gets heard on issues.	1	2	3	4	5
5. I'm usually the person who helps the team determine how to organize the discussion.	1	2	3	4	5
6. I praise other team members for their ideas more than others do in the meetings.	1	2	3	4	5
7. People tend to rely on me to keep track of what has been said in meetings.	1	2	3	4	5
8. The team typically counts on me to prevent debates from getting out of hand.	1	2	3	4	5
9. I tend to say things that make the group feel optimistic about its accomplishments.	1	2	3	4	5
10. Team members usually count on me to give everyone a chance to speak.	1	2	3	4	5
11. In most meetings, I am less likely than others to "put down" the ideas of team mates.	1	2	3	4	5
12. I actively help team mates to resolve their differences in meetings.	1	2	3	4	5
13. I actively encourage quiet team members to describe their ideas on each issue.	1	2	3	4	5
14. People tend to rely on me to clarify the purpose of the meeting.	1	2	3	4	5
15. I like to be the person who takes notes or minutes of the meeting.	1	2	3	4	5

·10·

DEVELOPING HIGH-PERFORMANCE TEAMS

LEARNING OBJECTIVES

AFTER READING THIS CHAPTER, YOU SHOULD BE ABLE TO:

■ Identify the characteristics of self-directed work teams (SDWTs).

■ Describe the four conditions in sociotechnical systems theory that support SDWTs.

■ Summarize three challenges to SDWTs.

■ Explain why virtual teams have become more common in organizations.

■ Describe the role of communication systems, task structure, team size, and team composition in virtual team effectiveness.

■ Summarize the three foundations of trust in teams.

■ Identify five problems facing teams when making decisions.

■ Describe the five structures for team decision making.

■ Discuss the potential benefits and limitations of brainstorming.

■ Outline the four types of team building.

From the day it was spun off from IBM 10 years ago, Celestica Inc. has been under intense pressure to reduce costs. The Toronto-based manufacturer of circuit boards and other electronic equipment for Dell, IBM, Hewlett-Packard, and many others has moved some work to low-wage countries, but it has also remained competitive by relying on high-performance teams and lean manufacturing practices.

A few years ago, Celestica began the process of transforming its traditional assembly lines into team-based units. Using sociotechnical systems principles, teams mapped out work processes and identified key factors that they could control to improve efficiency and quality. Now, Celestica is further pushing development of self-directed teams through lean manufacturing initiatives. "It's about moving away from complex IT types of systems so everyone can be involved in making improvements," explains Rob Hemmant, Celestica's global lean architect.

Shown in this photo with Hemmant (third from right) are employees from the rework cell in Toronto— the team responsible for repairing rejected parts from other cells (team units) for reintroduction into the manufacturing process. The rework team participated in a four-day kaizen blitz, during which they completely re-organized their physical space and workflow to remove wasteful activities and resources.

These rework team members at Celestica's manufacturing facility in Toronto completely redesigned the cell's work process, reflecting their company's movement toward self-directed work teams. *Don Golding*

"We implemented a U-shaped cell from incoming repair material to outgoing products," says rework team member Muhammad Khan (fourth from left). Khan adds that the blitz cut space, time, and distance, resulting in an impressive 86-percent reduction in lead times. These kaizen blitzes are so successful that Celestica runs an average of three of them every week at various sites around the world.

Along with improving efficiency, kaizen blitzes and their underlying lean manufacturing principles push teams to become more autonomous and self-sufficient. For instance, the rework team in Toronto previously had to get approval from an engineering group before repairing certain circuit boards; now, team members decide among themselves whether the boards should be repaired.

"People are starting to get involved and you can see the culture is starting to change," points out cell engineer Chris Barlosky (second from left at back in this photo). "The [kaizen] events are designed to empower operators so they can run the cell on their own. There's more ownership for the tools, machines and processes and they're eager to see improvements."[1] ■

www.celestica.com

271

elestica Inc. has succeeded in an extremely tough business partly by depending on high-performance teams to complete work more efficiently and with higher quality than traditional assembly line approaches. Numerous organizations in Canada—Dofasco, Pratt & Whitney Canada, and Canadian Mental Health Association, to name a few—have also benefited from the efficiency of these work arrangements. This chapter extends our discussion of teams by focusing on high-performance teams, including self-directed work teams, virtual teams, effective decision making in teams, and team building strategies.

The chapter starts by introducing the features of self-directed work teams as well as the elements of sociotechnical systems theory, upon which these high-performance teams are based. Next, we look at the increasing popularity of virtual teams and summarize current research on how to ensure that these virtual teams are effective. We also look at the important topic of trust in virtual teams and other groups. This chapter then focuses on effective decision making in teams, including challenges and strategies to minimize problems with effective team decision making. The last section of this chapter looks at various team-building strategies.

■ SELF-DIRECTED WORK TEAMS

Surrounded by tall prairie grass, Harley-Davidson's new assembly plant near Kansas City, Missouri, exemplifies the philosophy of a high-involvement organization. There are no supervisors. Instead, natural work teams of eight to 15 employees make most day-to-day decisions through consensus. An umbrella group, representing teams and management, makes plantwide decisions. "There is more pressure on employees here because they must learn to do what supervisors did," admits Karl Eberle, vice-president and general manager of Harley-Davidson's Kansas City operations. Still, Harley-Davidson is taking employee involvement far beyond the traditional workplace. "There's a lot of work being done to empower the work force," says Eberle. "But there are very few examples of where they've taken the work force to run the factory. And that's what we've done."[2]

self-directed work teams (SDWTs)
Cross-functional work groups organized around work processes that complete an entire piece of work requiring several interdependent tasks, and that have substantial autonomy over the execution of those tasks.

Harley-Davidson and many other organizations have adopted a form of work structure that relies on **self-directed work teams (SDWTs)**. Surveys estimate that somewhere between one-third and two-thirds of the medium and large organizations in the United States use SDWT structures for part of their operations. Statistics Canada reports that less than 10 percent of Canadian firms have SDWTs; it isn't clear why SDWTs are less common in Canada.[3]

SDWTs complete an entire piece of work requiring several interdependent tasks and have substantial autonomy over the execution of these tasks. These teams vary somewhat from one firm to the next, but they generally have the features listed in Exhibit 10.1.[4] First, SDWTs complete an entire piece of work, whether it's a product, a service, or part of a larger product or service. For instance, rework team members at Celestica are responsible for the entire process. Second, the team—not supervisors—assigns tasks that individual team members perform. In other words, the team plans, organizes, and controls work activities with little or no direct involvement of a higher status supervisor.

Third, SDWTs control most work inputs, flow, and output. This occurs at Celestica, where team members might work directly with suppliers on the input side and with customers on the output side. Fourth, SDWTs are responsible for correcting work flow problems as they occur. In other words, the teams maintain

■ **EXHIBIT 10.1**

Features of
self-directed
work teams

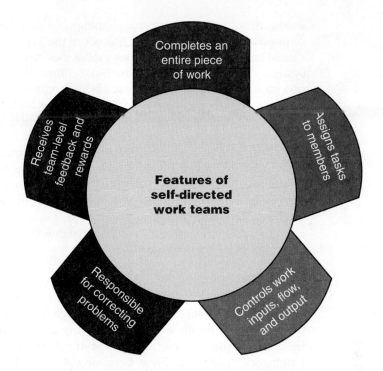

their own quality and logistical control. The lean manufacturing philosophy tends to encourage this feature because teams are expected to continuously improve quality and efficiency in their cells through regular discussion and the occasional kaizen blitz.[5] Fifth, SDWTs receive team-level feedback and rewards. This recognizes and reinforces the fact that the team—not individuals—is responsible for the work, although team members may also receive individual feedback and rewards.

You may have noticed from this description that members of SDWTs have enriched and enlarged jobs. The team's work includes all the tasks required to make an entire product or provide the service. The team is also mostly responsible for scheduling, coordinating, and planning these tasks.[6] Self-directed work teams were initially designed around production processes. However, they are also found in administrative and service activities, banking services, city government administration, and customer assistance teams in courier services. These service tasks are well suited to self-directed work teams when employees have interdependent tasks and decisions require the knowledge and experience of several people.[7]

SOCIOTECHNICAL SYSTEMS THEORY AND SDWTs

sociotechnical systems (STS) theory

A theory stating that effective work sites have joint optimization of their social and technological systems, and that teams should have sufficient autonomy to control key variances in the work process.

How do companies create successful self-directed work teams? To answer this question, we need to look at **sociotechnical systems (STS) theory**, which is the main source of current SDWT practices. STS theory was introduced during the 1940s at Britain's Tavistock Institute, where researchers had been studying the effects of technology on coal mining in the United Kingdom.[8]

The Tavistock researchers observed that the new coal mining technology (called the "long wall" method) led to lower, not higher, job performance. They analyzed the causes of this problem and established the idea that organizations need "joint optimization" between the social and technical systems of the work unit. In other words, they need to introduce technology in a way that creates the best structure for semi-autonomous work teams. Moreover, the Tavistock group concluded that teams should be sufficiently autonomous so that they can control the main "variances" in the system. This means that the team must control the factors with the greatest impact on quality, quantity, and the cost of the product or service. From this overview of STS, we can identify four main conditions for high-performance SDWTs.[9]

SDWTs are a primary work unit   STS theory suggests that self-directed teams work best when they are a primary work unit; in other words, they are responsible for making an entire product, providing a service, or otherwise completing an entire work process. By making an entire product or service, the team is sufficiently independent that it can make adjustments without interfering, or having interference from, other work units. At the same time, the primary work unit ensures that employees perform interdependent subtasks within their team so they have a sense of cohesiveness by working toward a common goal.[10]

SDWTs have sufficient autonomy   STS theory says that an SDWT must have sufficient autonomy to manage the work process. The team should be able to organize and coordinate work among its members to respond more quickly and effectively to its environment. This autonomy also motivates team members through feelings of empowerment, which is apparent in the self-directed teams at The Patchwork Traditional Food Company. As GLOBAL Connections 10.1 describes, teams at the gourmet food maker in northern Wales decide their own work schedules, production and post-production activities, and are involved in product development.

SDWTs control key variances   STS theory says that high-performance SDWTs have control over "key variances." These variances represent the disturbances or interruptions in the work process that affect the quality or performance of the product or service. For instance, the mixture of ingredients would be a key variance for employees in food processing because the mixture is within the team's control and it influences the quality of the final product. In contrast, applying STS offers little advantage when the primary causes of good or poor performance are mainly due to technology, supplies, or other factors beyond the team's control.

joint optimization
The balance that is struck between social and technical systems to maximize an operation's effectiveness

SDWTs operate under joint optimization   Perhaps the most crucial feature of STS theory is **joint optimization**—the notion that the work process needs to balance the social and technical subsystems.[11] In particular, the technological system should be implemented in a way that encourages or facilitates team dynamics, job enrichment, and meaningful feedback. This idea of joint optimization was quite radical in the 1940s, a time when many thought that technology dictated how employees should be organized. In many cases, the technology resulted in people working alone with little opportunity to directly coordinate their work or share knowledge and ideas. Sociotechnical systems theory, on the other hand, says that companies can and must introduce technology so that it supports a semi-autonomous, team-based structure.

APPLYING STS THEORY AND SELF-DIRECTED WORK TEAMS

If Statistics Canada correctly estimates that less than 10 percent of Canadian firms use self-directed work teams in any way, then most Canadian businesses are missing out on a potentially huge opportunity to become more competitive. Numerous studies

Self-Directed Work Teams à la carte in Wales

Twenty years ago, Margaret Carter started selling pâté and other gourmet food products to local pubs as a way to support herself and her children following her divorce. Today, her Welsh company, the Patchwork Traditional Food Company, is a bustling operation whose 35 employees manufacture gourmet foods for clients throughout the United Kingdom and continental Europe.

Carter says that the company's two ingredients for success are making its products by hand in small batches and relying on self-directed work teams. "We've had the self-directed teams for about 15 years, and the idea is that nobody has titles and staff are empowered to make their own decisions," she says. The production team calls itself the Motley Crew; the postproduction team is known as the Musketeers.

Once each week, team members gather for a 59:59 meeting (which lasts no more than 59 minutes and 59 seconds) to discuss problems during the previous week and goals for the forthcoming week. Each team decides its own production schedules and work patterns, is able to recruit collectively, and is involved in everything from the design of new packaging to product development. Team members become multiskilled and eventually get rotated into the roles of team leader and communication officer.

Each team also has a daily "huddle" meeting. "In the morning everybody arrives in their various teams and the first thing they do is have something called a huddle," Carter explains. "So for 10 minutes everybody discusses the workload for the day and the issues that have arisen from the previous day." To maintain a team focus and to

Patchwork Traditional Food Company, the Welsh maker of pâté and other gourmet foods, relies on high-performance, self-directed work teams. *Courtesy of Patchwork Traditional Food Company*

remove any status differences, staff conduct their morning huddle away from individual desks. "They stand in a circle away from their desks so there is no control issue," says Carter, who now spends much of her time speaking to other businesses about implementing work teams.

Sources: D. Jones, "Food Firm Expands Creating 20 Jobs," *Daily Post* (Liverpool, UK) May 29, 2003, p. 23; D. Devine, "Recipe For Making Things Happen," *Western Mail (Wales)*, July 10, 2002, p. 9; www.patchwork-pate.co.uk.
www.crc-wmc.org.uk/patchwork.asp

have found that, with a few important caveats to consider, self-directed work teams make a difference. As we read at the beginning of this chapter, Celestica Inc. has significantly improved productivity through lean manufacturing and self-directed work teams. "What I like about the STS process is that the change has been driven by the employees—those responsible for execution—as opposed to management dictating how it's going to be," says a Celestica employee about the company's transition to self-directed teams.[12]

A decade ago, Canon Inc. introduced self-directed teams at all 29 of its Japanese plants. The camera and copier company claims that a team of a half-dozen people can now produce as much as 30 people in the old assembly line system. One study found that car dealership service garages that organize employees into self-directed teams were significantly more profitable than service garages where employees work without a team structure. Another reported that both short and long-term measures of customer satisfaction increased after street cleaning employees in a German city were organized into SDWTs.[13]

STS theory provides some guidance for designing self-directed work teams, but it doesn't provide enough detail regarding the optimal alignment of the social and technical system. Volvo's Uddevalla manufacturing plant in Sweden is a case in point.[14] Opened in 1988 as a model of sociotechnical design, the Uddevalla plant replaced the traditional assembly line with fixed workstations at which teams of approximately 20 employees assemble and install components in an unfinished automobile chassis. The work structure created a strong team orientation, but productivity was among the lowest in the automobile industry. (Producing a car at Uddevalla took 50 hours versus 25 hours at a traditional Volvo plant and 13 hours at a Toyota plant.)

The Uddevalla plant was shut down in 1993 and re-opened two years later. The plant still makes use of highly skilled teams, but they are organized around a more traditional assembly line process (similar to Toyota's production system). Some writers argue that organizational politics and poor market demand closed the Uddevalla experiment prematurely. However, Federal Signal recently had a very similar experience in its truck assembly plant in the United States. It seems that both Volvo and Federal Signal failed to identify the best alignment of the social and technical subsystems.

CHALLENGES TO SELF-DIRECTED WORK TEAMS

Along with determining the best combination of social and technical subsystems, corporate leaders need to recognize and overcome at least three potential barriers to self-directed work teams: cross-cultural issues, management resistance, and employee and labour union resistance.

Cross-cultural issues   SDWTs are difficult to implement in high power distance cultures.[15] Employees in these cultures are more comfortable when supervisors give them directions, whereas low power distance employees value their involvement in decisions. One study reported that employees in Mexico (which has a high power distance culture) expect managers to make decisions affecting their work, whereas SDWTs emphasize self-initiative and individual responsibility within teams. Some writers also suggest that SDWTs are more difficult to implement in cultures with low collectivism because employees are less comfortable collaborating and working interdependently with co-workers.[16]

Management resistance   Poet Robert Frost once wrote, "The brain is a wonderful organ; it starts working the moment you get up in the morning and does not stop until you get into the office." Frost's humour highlights the fact that many organizations expect employees to park their brains at the door. Consistent with this view, studies report that supervisors and higher level managers are often the main source of resistance to the transition to self-directed work teams. Their main worry is losing power when employees gain power through empowered teams. Some managers are concerned that their jobs will lose value, whereas others believe that they will not have any jobs at all.[17]

Self-directed teams operate best when supervisors shift from "hands-on" controllers to "hands off" facilitators, but many supervisors have difficulty changing their style. This was one of the biggest stumbling blocks to self-directed work teams at a TRW auto parts plant. Many supervisors kept slipping back into their command-and-control supervisory style. As one TRW employee explains: "One of the toughest things for some of them was to shift from being a boss to a coach, moving from saying, 'I know what's good for you' to 'How can I help you?'"

Adjusting to Self-Directed Work Teams

When Standard Motor Products (SMP) introduced self-directed work teams at its Edwardsville, Kansas, plant, supervisors had a tough challenge replacing their command-and-control management style with something closer to a mentor or facilitator. "It wasn't easy for managers who were raised in the top-down authority model," recalls Darrel Ray, the nationally recognized consultant who worked with the auto parts company during the transition. "It is far easier to be a tyrant than it is to be a psychologist or a teacher," explains distribution manager Don Wakefield. Steve Domann was one of the managers who had difficulty adjusting. "I thought about quitting when the changes were announced," says Domann, who now oversees plant work teams as a team developer. "Some of the old management team couldn't conform to the team, but I'm glad I did."[23] *Courtesy of Standard Motor Products*
www.smpcorp.com

Research suggests that supervisors are less likely to resist self-directed work teams when they have personally worked in a high involvement workplace and receive considerable training in their new facilitation role.[18]

Employee and labour union resistance   Employees sometimes oppose SDWTs because they require new skills or appear to require more work. Many feel uncomfortable as they explore their new roles, and they may be worried that they lack the skills to adapt to the new work requirements. For instance, professional surveyors at a Swedish company reported increased stress when their company introduced customer-focused self-directed teams.[19]

Labour unions supported the early experiments in sociotechnical change in Europe and India, but some unions in North America have reservations about SDWTs.[20] One concern is that teams improve productivity at the price of higher stress levels among employees, which is sometimes true. Another worry is that SDWTs require more flexibility by reversing work rules and removing job categories that unions have negotiated over the years. Labour union leaders are therefore concerned that regaining these hard-fought union member rights will be a difficult battle.

In spite of these challenges, self-directed work teams offer enormous potential for organizations when they are implemented under the right conditions, as specified by sociotechnical systems theory. Meanwhile, information technologies and knowledge work have enabled virtual teams to gain popularity. The next section examines this new breed of team, including strategies to create high-performance virtual teams.

■ VIRTUAL TEAMS

virtual teams
Teams whose members operate across space, time, and organizational boundaries and are linked through information technologies to achieve organizational tasks.

Denis Chamberland admits that he had trouble recognizing most of his colleagues when he worked at Accenture. That's because Chamberland was chief legal counsel in Toronto for the global consulting firm, whereas his boss and co-workers operated out of London, Chicago, and other far-flung locations. "There were many people who I worked with for years and never actually met. In many cases, I never even talked to them on the phone," says Chamberland, who is now a partner at Toronto law firm Aird & Berlis LLP.[21]

Denis Chamberland has had plenty of experience with the growing trend toward **virtual teams**. Virtual teams are teams whose members operate across space, time, and organizational boundaries and are linked through information technologies to achieve organizational tasks.[22] As with all teams, virtual teams are groups of two or more people who interact and influence each other, are mutually accountable for achieving common goals associated with organizational objectives, and perceive themselves as a social entity within an organization. However, virtual teams differ from traditional teams in two ways: (1) they are not usually co-located (work in the same physical area), and (2) due to their lack of co-location, members of virtual teams depend primarily on information technologies rather than face-to-face interaction to communicate and coordinate their work effort.

WHY COMPANIES FORM VIRTUAL TEAMS

Virtual teams are one of the most significant developments in organizations over the past decade. "Virtual teams are now a reality," says Frank Waltmann, head of learning at pharmaceuticals company Novartis. One reason for their popularity is that Internet, intranets, instant messaging, virtual whiteboards, and other products have made it easier than in the past to communicate with and coordinate people at a distance.[24]

The shift from production-based to knowledge-based work has also made virtual teamwork feasible. Information technologies allow people to exchange knowledge work, such as software code, product development plans, and ideas for strategic decisions. In contrast, relying on virtual teams for production work, in which people develop physical objects, is still very difficult (although not completely impossible).

Information technologies and knowledge-based work make virtual teams possible, but two other factors—knowledge management and globalization—make them increasingly necessary. Virtual teams represent a natural part of the knowledge management process because they allow and encourage employees to share and use knowledge where geography limits more direct forms of collaboration. Similarly, virtual teamwork crosses organizational boundaries to tap expertise wherever it exists. For instance, the Sable Island Offshore Energy Project off the Nova Scotia coast relied on virtual teams of engineers from several consortium companies in Canada, the United Kingdom, and the United States. By using an intranet portal, these teams were able to tap the knowledge of people in several companies, thereby cutting development time in half.[25]

Globalization represents the other reason why virtual teams are increasingly necessary. As we described in Chapter 1, globalization has become the new reality in many organizations. Companies are opening businesses overseas, forming tight alliances with companies located elsewhere, and serving customers who want global support. These global conditions require a correspondingly global response in the form of virtual teams that coordinate these operations.[26]

DESIGNING HIGH-PERFORMANCE VIRTUAL TEAMS

As with all teams, high-performance virtual teams are affected by the elements of the team effectiveness model in Chapter 9. Exhibit 10.2 outlines the key design issues for virtual teams that we discuss over the next couple of pages.

Virtual team environment   Reward systems, communication systems, organizational environment, organizational structure, and leadership influence the effectiveness of all teams, including virtual teams. Communication systems are particularly important because, unlike conventional teams, virtual teams cannot rely on face-to-face meetings whenever they wish. As we will learn in the next chapter, face-to-face communication transfers the highest volume and complexity of information and offers the timeliest feedback. In contrast, email, telephone, and other information technologies fall far behind in their ability to exchange

■ **EXHIBIT 10.2**   Designing high-performance virtual teams

Team Design Element	Special Virtual Team Requirements
Team environment	• Virtual teams need several communication channels available to offset lack of face-to-face communication
Team tasks	• Virtual teams operate better with structured rather than complex and ambiguous tasks
Team size and composition	• Virtual teams usually require a smaller team size than conventional teams • Virtual team members must have skills in communicating through information technology and ability to process multiple threads of conversation • Virtual team members are more likely than conventional team members to require cross-cultural awareness and knowledge
Team processes	• Virtual team development and cohesiveness require some face-to-face interaction, particularly when forming the team

information. "Having a four- to five-hour discussion is hard to do by phone, especially where you need to read body language," says an executive at accounting giant PricewaterhouseCoopers. Even videoconferencing, which seems similar to face-to-face meetings, actually communicates much less than we realize.[27]

To become a high-performance virtual team, the organization needs to provide a variety of communication media so that virtual team members have the freedom to creatively combine these media to match the task demands.[28] For instance, virtual team members might rely on email to coordinate routine tasks but quickly switch to videoconferences and electronic whiteboards when emergencies arise. The lack of face-to-face communication isn't all bad news for virtual teams. Working through email or intranet systems can minimize status differences related to language skills. Team members whose first language is not English may be overwhelmed into silence in face-to-face meetings but have time to craft persuasive messages in cyberspace.

Virtual team tasks   Experts suggest that virtual teams operate best with structured tasks requiring only moderate levels of task interdependence.[29] Consider the task structure of client service engineers at BakBone Software. Each day, BakBone engineers in San Diego pick up customer support problems passed on from colleagues in Maryland and England. At the end of the workday, they pass some of these projects on to BakBone co-workers in Tokyo. The assignments sent on to Tokyo must be stated clearly because overseas co-workers can't ask questions in the middle of San Diego's night.

BakBone's virtual team works well with these structured tasks, whereas the lack of co-location makes it difficult for them to consult and communicate on complex and ambiguous tasks. "You don't have the time for open-ended conversation [in a virtual team]," admits BakBone engineer Roger Rodriguez. "You can't informally brainstorm with someone."[30] Generally, complex and ambiguous tasks should be assigned to co-located teams. Similarly, virtual teams should work on tasks requiring moderate levels of interdependence among team members. High levels of interdependence require more intense communication, so they are better assigned to co-located teams.

Virtual team size and composition   The problems of team size that we learned about in the previous chapter are amplified in virtual teams due to the limits of information technologies. In other words, virtual teams need to be smaller than comparable co-located teams to develop as quickly and coordinate as effectively. The team composition issues covered in Chapter 9 apply to virtual teams, with the added requirement that virtual team members need additional communication skills. They need to be sensitive to emotional reactions to emails and listen to more subtle nonverbal signals in teleconferences. "On a call, I use subtle listening," explains Karim Ladak at Procter & Gamble in Toronto, whose virtual team members live in at least six other cities around the world. "I listen for a quiver or a pause. And even then I know that I can very quickly miss something," admits Ladak.[31]

Virtual teams often span across cultures, so team members must also be aware of cross-cultural issues. For example, one study reported that virtual teams of American and Belgian college students were easily confused by differing conventions in the use of commas versus decimal points in numbers (e.g., $2.953 million versus $2,953 million). They also experienced cultural differences in socializing. The American students were willing to engage in social communication after they completed the assignment, whereas the Belgian students were more interested in developing a relationship with their partners before beginning work on the project.[32]

Team processes   Team development and cohesiveness are particular concerns for virtual teams because they lack the face-to-face interaction that supports these processes. For example, one recent university study found that face-to-face teams communicate better than virtual teams during the early stages of a project; only after gaining experience did virtual teams share information as openly as face-to-face teams. Other studies have reported that employees who work at a distance (such as through telework) from other team members tend to feel less connected with their team.[33] There is no "virtual" solution to this dilemma. As Connections 10.2 describes, companies try to ensure that virtual team members have good skills for communicating across distances. They also encourage virtual team members to meet face to face, particularly when the team is formed.

■ TEAM TRUST

trust
A psychological state comprising the intention to accept vulnerability based upon positive expectations of the intent or behaviour of another person.

Any relationship—including the relationship among virtual team members—depends on a certain degree of trust between the parties.[34] **Trust** is a psychological state comprising the intention to accept vulnerability based on positive expectations of the intent or behaviour of another person. A high level of trust occurs when others affect you in situations where you are at risk, but you believe they will not harm you.

Trust has been discussed as both beliefs and conscious feelings about the relationship and other party. In other words, a person both logically evaluates the situation as trustworthy and feels that it is trustworthy.[35] Trust can also be understood in terms of the foundation of that trust. From this perspective, people trust others based on three foundations: calculus, knowledge, and identification (see Exhibit 10.3).

■   *Calculus-based trust*—This minimal level of trust refers to an expected consistency of behaviour based on deterrence. Each party believes that the other will deliver on its promises because punishments will be administered if they fail.[36] For example, most employees have at least calculus-based trust because co-workers could get fired if they attempt to undermine another employee's work effort.

Adjusting to a New (Virtual) Reality

Working on a virtual team is pretty much a given at IBM, says Susan Turner, IBM Canada's director of diversity and workplace programs. "It's a global company working in 170 countries in the world. Just that alone would dictate that we do work with people we've never met face to face and may never meet," she points out. That observation extends to many other organizations. According to one estimate, over 60 percent of professionals are members of a virtual team at some point during the year. "We are in a world today where we cannot assume that the only way to build relationships is in a face-to-face environment," Taylor explains.

To deal with this new reality, IBM and other firms are trying to determine how to make virtual teams work as effectively as face-to-face teams. One solution, ironically, is to have virtual team members meet face to face once in a while. "Virtual teams cannot completely displace the need for human contact," suggests Ron Babin, an associate partner at the Toronto office of consulting firm Accenture Canada.

For instance, when staff from Shell Canada and IBM Canada formed a virtual team to build an electronic customer-access system for Shell, they began with an "all hands" face-to-face gathering to assist the team development process. The two firms also made a rule that the dispersed team members should have face-to-face contact at least once every six weeks throughout the project. Without this, "after about five or six weeks we found some of that communication would start to break down," says Sharon Hartung, the IBM co-manager for the project.

Canadian organizations increasingly rely on virtual teams, but some are also learning to jump-start those teams with face-to-face meetings.
© Royalty-Free/Corbis

Sources: S. Prashad, "Building Trust Tricky for 'Virtual' Teams," *The Toronto Star*, October 23, 2003, p. K06; G. Buckler, "Staking One for the Team," *Computing Canada*, October 22, 2004, pp. 16–17; K. Marron, "Close Encounters of the Faceless Kind," *The Globe & Mail*, February 9, 2005, p. C1. **www.ibm.com/ca**

- *Knowledge-based trust*—Knowledge-based trust is grounded on the other party's predictability. The more we understand others and can predict what they will do in the future, the more we trust them, up to a moderate level. For instance, employees are more willing to trust leaders who "walk the talk" because their actions are aligned with their words. Even if we don't agree with the leader, this consistency generates some level of trust. Knowledge-based trust also relates to confidence in the other person's ability or competence. People trust others based on their known or perceived expertise, such as when they trust a physician.[37]

- *Identification-based trust*—This third foundation of trust is based on mutual understanding and an emotional bond between the parties. Identification occurs when one party thinks like, feels like, and responds like the other party. High-performance teams exhibit this level of trust because they share the same values and mental models. Identification-based trust is connected to the concept of social identity; the more you define yourself in terms of membership in the team, the more trust you have in that team.[38]

■ **EXHIBIT 10.3**
Three foundations
of trust in teams

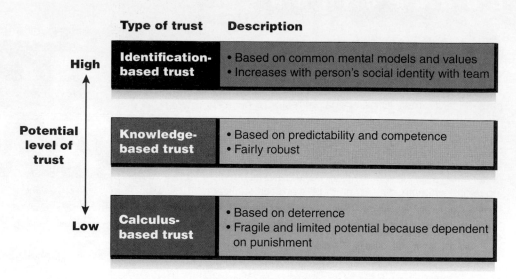

	Type of trust	Description
High	**Identification-based trust**	• Based on common mental models and values • Increases with person's social identity with team
Potential level of trust	**Knowledge-based trust**	• Based on predictability and competence • Fairly robust
Low	**Calculus-based trust**	• Based on deterrence • Fragile and limited potential because dependent on punishment

These three foundations of trust can be arranged in a hierarchy. Calculus-based trust offers the lowest potential level of trust and is easily broken by a violation of expectations. Generally, calculus-based trust alone cannot sustain a team's relationship, because it relies on deterrence. Relationships don't become very strong when based only on the threat of punishment if one party fails to deliver its promises. Knowledge-based trust offers a higher potential level of trust and is more stable because it develops over time. Suppose that another member of your virtual team submitted documentation to you on schedule in the past, but it arrived late this time. Knowledge-based trust might be dented, but not broken, in this incident. Through knowledge-based trust, you "know" that the late delivery is probably an exception because it deviates from the co-worker's past actions.

Identification-based trust is potentially the strongest and most robust of all three. The individual's self-image (social identity) is based partly on membership in the team and he/she believes their values highly overlap, so any transgressions by other team members are quickly forgiven. People are more reluctant to acknowledge a violation of this high-level trust because it strikes at the heart of their self-image.

INDIVIDUAL DIFFERENCES IN TRUST

Along with these three foundations of trust, the level of trust depends on a person's general propensity to trust.[39] Some people are inherently more willing than others to trust in a given situation. When joining a new work team, you might initially have very high trust in your new teammates, whereas another new team member might only feel a moderate level of trust. This difference is due to each individual's personality, values, and socialization experiences. Our willingness to trust others also varies with the emotions experienced at the moment. In particular, we trust people more when experiencing pleasant emotions than when angry, even when those emotions aren't connected with the other person.

DYNAMICS OF TRUST IN TEAMS

A common misconception is that team members build trust from a low level when they first join the team. Yet, studies suggest that people typically join a virtual or conventional team with a moderate or high level—not a low level—of trust in their new co-workers. The main explanation for the initially high trust (called *swift trust*) in organizational settings is that people usually believe their teammates are reasonably competent (knowledge-based trust) and they tend to develop some degree of social identity with the team (identification-based trust). Even when working with strangers, most of us display some level of trust, if only because it supports our self-impression of being a nice person.[40]

However, trust is fragile in new relationships because it is based on assumptions rather than well-established experience. Consequently, recent studies of virtual teams report that trust tends to decrease rather than increase over time. In other words, new team members experience trust violations, which pushes their trust to a lower level. Employees who join the team with identification-based trust tend to drop back to knowledge-based or perhaps calculus-based trust. Declining trust is particularly challenging in virtual teams because research identifies communication among team members as an important condition for sustaining trust. Equally important, employees become less forgiving and less cooperative toward others as their level of trust decreases, which undermines team and organizational effectiveness.[41]

■ TEAM DECISION MAKING

Self-directed work teams, virtual teams, and practically all other groups are involved to some degree in making decisions. Under certain conditions, teams are more effective than individuals at identifying problems, choosing alternatives, and evaluating their decisions. To leverage these benefits, however, we first need to understand the constraints on effective team decision making. Then, we look at specific team structures that try to overcome these constraints.

CONSTRAINTS ON TEAM DECISION MAKING

Anyone who has spent enough time in the workplace can rhyme off several ways in which teams stumble in decision making. The five most common problems are time constraints, evaluation apprehension, pressure to conform, groupthink, and group polarization.

Time constraints   There's a saying that "committees keep minutes and waste hours." This reflects the fact that teams take longer than individuals to make decisions.[42] Unlike individuals, teams require extra time to organize, coordinate, and socialize. The larger the group, the more time required to make a decision. Team members need time to learn about each other and build rapport. They need to manage an imperfect communication process so that there is sufficient understanding of each other's ideas. They also need to coordinate roles and rules of order within the decision process.

Another time-related constraint found in most team structures is that only one person can speak at a time.[43] This problem, known as **production blocking**, undermines idea generation in several ways. First, team members need to listen in on the conversation to find an opportune time to speak up, and this monitoring makes it difficult for them to concentrate on their own ideas. Second, ideas are fleeting, so the longer they wait to speak up, the more likely these flickering ideas will die out. Third, team members might remember their fleeting thoughts by concentrating on them, but this causes them to pay less attention to the conversation. By ignoring what others are saying, team members miss other potentially good ideas as well as the opportunity to convey their ideas to others in the group.

production blocking
A time constraint in team decision making due to the procedural requirement that only one person may speak at a time.

evaluation apprehension
When individuals are reluctant to mention ideas that seem silly because they believe (often correctly) that other team members are silently evaluating them.

groupthink
The tendency of highly cohesive groups to value consensus at the price of decision quality.

group polarization
The tendency of teams to make more extreme decisions than individuals working alone.

Evaluation apprehension   Individuals are reluctant to mention ideas that seem silly because they believe (often correctly) that other team members are silently evaluating them.[44] This **evaluation apprehension** is based on the individual's desire to create a favourable self-presentation and need to protect self-esteem. It is most common in meetings attended by people with different levels of status or expertise, or when members formally evaluate each other's performance throughout the year (as in 360-degree feedback). Creative ideas often sound bizarre or illogical when presented, so evaluation apprehension tends to discourage employees from mentioning them in front of co-workers.

Pressure to conform   Recall from the previous chapter that cohesiveness leads individual members to conform to the team's norms. This control keeps the group organized around common goals, but it may also cause team members to suppress their dissenting opinions, particularly when a strong team norm is related to the issue. When someone does state a point of view that violates the majority opinion, other members might punish the violator or try to persuade him or her that the opinion is incorrect. Conformity can also be subtle. To some extent, we depend on the opinions that others hold to validate our own views. If co-workers don't agree with us, then we begin to question our own opinions even without overt peer pressure.

Groupthink   One team decision-making problem that most people have heard about is **groupthink**— the tendency of highly cohesive groups to value consensus at the price of decision quality.[45] Groupthink goes beyond the problem of conformity by focusing on how decisions go awry when team members try to maintain harmony. This desire for harmony exists as a group norm and is most apparent when team members have a strong social identity with the group. Along with a desire for harmony, groupthink supposedly occurs when the team is isolated from outsiders, the team leader is opinionated (rather than impartial), the team is under stress due to an external threat, the team has experienced recent failures or other decision-making problems, and the team lacks clear guidance from corporate policies or procedures.

Although the word "groupthink" is now part of everyday language, the concept gets mixed reviews among OB experts because some of the above-mentioned groupthink characteristics actually improve rather than undermine the team decision-making process in some situations.[46] Although the groupthink concept as a whole doesn't stand up to testing, some parts are still valid concerns. For example, groupthink characteristics cause teams to be highly confident in their decisions. Yet, one recent Canadian study reported that highly confident teams are less attentive in decision making than moderately confident teams. This is consistent with previous evidence that overconfident executive groups make sloppy decisions because they are complacent and have a false sense of invulnerability.[47]

Group polarization   **Group polarization** refers to the tendency of teams to make more extreme decisions than individuals working alone.[48] Suppose that a group of people meets to decide on the future of a new product. Individual team members might come to the meeting with various degrees of support or opposition to the product's future. Yet, by the end of the meeting, chances are that the team will agree on a more extreme solution than the average person had when the meeting began.

There are three reasons why group polarization occurs (see Exhibit 10.4). First, team members become comfortable with more extreme positions when they realize that co-workers also generally support the same position. Second, persuasive arguments

■ **EXHIBIT 10.4**

The group
polarization process

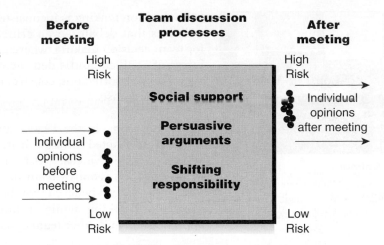

favouring the dominant position convince doubtful members and help form a consensus around the extreme option. Finally, individuals feel less personally responsible for the decision consequences because the decision is made by the team. Social support, persuasion, and shifting responsibility explain why teams make extreme decisions, but they also make *riskier* decisions due to the natural tendency to take higher risks when facing certain losses. Even when they don't face losses, teams might become victims of the "gambler's fallacy"—thinking that they can beat the odds. Thus, team members are more likely to favour the high-risk than the low-risk option.[49]

TEAM STRUCTURES TO IMPROVE CREATIVITY AND DECISION MAKING

The constraints on team decision making are potentially serious, but several solutions also emerge from these bad-news studies. Team members need to be confident in their decision making, but not so confident that they collectively feel invulnerable. This calls for team norms that encourage critical thinking as well as team membership that maintains sufficient diversity. Team leaders and other powerful members can sway the rest of the group, so checks and balances need to be in place to avoid the adverse effects of this power. Another practice is to maintain an optimal team size. The group should be large enough that members possess the collective knowledge to resolve the problem, yet small enough that the team doesn't consume too much time or restrict individual input.

Team structures also help to minimize the problems described over the previous few pages. Five team structures potentially improve creativity and decision making in team settings: constructive conflict, brainstorming, electronic brainstorming, Delphi method, and nominal group technique.

**constructive
conflict**

Any situation
where people
debate their different
opinions about an
issue in a way that
keeps the conflict
focused on the task
rather than on people.

Constructive conflict   Constructive conflict occurs when team members debate their different perceptions about an issue in a way that keeps the conflict focused on the task rather than people. This conflict is called "constructive" because participants pay attention to facts and logic and avoid statements that generate emotional conflict. The main advantage of this debate is that it presents different points of view, which encourages everyone to re-examine their assumptions and logic.

One problem with constructive conflict is that it is difficult to apply; healthy debate can slide into personal attacks. Also, the effect of constructive conflict on

NASA Encourages Debate

The ill-fated flight of the space shuttle Columbia was a wake-up call for how NASA's mission management team makes decisions. The Columbia accident investigation team concluded that concerns raised by engineers were either deflected or watered down because the mission management team appeared to be "immersed in a culture of invincibility" and hierarchical authority discouraged constructive debate. If top decision makers had more fully considered the extent of damage during takeoff, they might have been able to save Columbia's seven crew members. To foster more open communications and constructive debate, the mission management team's assigned seating rectangular table has been replaced by a C-shaped arrangement where people sit wherever they want (shown in photo). None of the 24 members stands out above the others in the new set-up. Around the walls of the room are pearls of wisdom reminding everyone of the pitfalls of team decision making. "People in groups tend to agree on courses of action which, as individuals, they know are stupid," warns one poster.[54] *Courtesy of Johnson Space Center* **www.nasa.gov/home/index.html**

team decision making is inconsistent. Some research indicates that debate—even criticism—can be good for team decision making, whereas others say that all forms of conflict can be detrimental to teams. Until this issue gets sorted out, constructive conflict should be used cautiously.[50]

Brainstorming In the 1950s, advertising executive Alex Osborn wanted to find a better way for teams to generate creative ideas.[51] Osborn's solution, called **brainstorming**, requires team members to abide by four rules. Osborn believed that these rules encourage divergent thinking while minimizing evaluation apprehension and other team dynamics problems.

■ *Speak freely*—Brainstorming welcomes wild and wacky ideas because these become the seeds of divergent thinking in the creative process. Crazy suggestions are sometimes crazy only because they break out of the mould set by existing mental models.

■ *Don't criticize*—Team members are more likely to contribute wild and wacky ideas if no one tries to mock or criticize them. Thus, a distinctive rule in brainstorming is that no one is allowed to criticize any ideas that are presented.

■ *Provide as many ideas as possible*—Brainstorming is based on the idea that quantity breeds quality. In other words, teams generate better ideas when they generate many ideas. This relates to the belief that divergent thinking occurs after traditional ideas have been exhausted. Therefore, the group should think of as many possible solutions as they can and go well beyond the traditional solutions to a problem.

■ *Build on the ideas of others*—Team members are encouraged to "piggyback" or "hitchhike," that is, combine and improve on the ideas already presented. Building on existing ideas encourages the synergy of team processes that was mentioned earlier in this chapter as a benefit of employee involvement.

brainstorming
A freewheeling, face-to-face meeting where team members generate as many ideas as possible, piggyback on the ideas of others, and avoid evaluating anyone's ideas during the idea-generation stage.

Brainstorming is a well-known team structure for encouraging creative ideas. Yet, for several years, researchers concluded that this practice is ineffective. Lab studies found that brainstorming groups generate fewer ideas, largely because production blocking and evaluation apprehension still interfere with team dynamics.[52] However, these conclusions contrast with more recent real world evidence that highly creative firms such as IDEO, the California product design firm, thrive on brainstorming.

There seems to be a few explanations why the lab studies differ from real world evidence.[53] First, the lab studies measured the number of ideas generated, whereas brainstorming seems to provide more creative ideas, which is the main reason why companies use brainstorming. Evaluation apprehension may be a problem for students brainstorming in lab experiments, but it is less of a problem in high-performing teams that trust each other and embrace a learning orientation culture. The lab studies also overlooked the fact that brainstorming participants interact and participate directly, thereby increasing decision acceptance and team cohesiveness.

Brainstorming sessions also provide valuable nonverbal communication that spreads enthusiasm which, in turn, provides a more creative climate. Clients are sometimes involved in brainstorming sessions, so these positive emotions may produce higher customer satisfaction than if people are working alone on the product. Overall, while brainstorming might not always be the best team structure, it seems to be more valuable than some of the earlier research studies indicated.

Electronic brainstorming   **Electronic brainstorming** tries to minimize many of the problems described earlier with face-to-face brainstorming by having people generate and share ideas through computers. A facilitator begins the process by posting a question. Participants then enter their answers or ideas on their computer terminal. Soon after, everyone's ideas are posted anonymously and randomly on the computer screens or at the front of the room. Participants eventually vote electronically on the ideas presented. Face-to-face discussion usually follows the electronic brainstorming process.

Research indicates that electronic brainstorming generates more ideas than traditional brainstorming and more creative ideas than traditional interacting teams. Participants also tend to be more satisfied, motivated, and confident in the decision-making exercise than in other team structures.[55] One reason for these favourable outcomes is that electronic brainstorming significantly reduces production blocking. Participants are able to document their ideas as soon as they pop into their heads, rather than wait their turn to communicate.[56] The process also supports creative synergy because participants can easily develop new ideas from those generated by other people. Electronic brainstorming also minimizes the problem of evaluation apprehension because ideas are posted anonymously. "The equipment allows them to throw some crazy ideas out without people knowing they are the author of it," explains a civil servant who organized a brainstorming session among Ontario government cabinet ministers.[57]

Despite these numerous advantages, electronic brainstorming is not widely used by corporate leaders. One possible reason is that it might be too structured and technology-bound for some executives. Furthermore, some decision makers may feel threatened by the honesty of statements generated through this process and by their limited ability to control the discussion. A third explanation is that electronic brainstorming may work best for certain types of decisions, but not for others. For example, electronic brainstorming may be less effective than face-to-face meetings where effective decision making is less important than social bonding and emotional interaction.[58] Overall, electronic brainstorming can significantly improve decision making under the right conditions, but more research is required to identify those conditions.

Delphi method   The **Delphi method** was developed by the RAND think tank in the 1950s and has regained attention over the past decade. Delphi systematically pools the collective knowledge of experts on a particular subject to make decisions, predict the future, or identify opposing views (called dissensus).[59] There are a few variations, but most Delphi groups have the following features. They do not meet face to face; in fact, participants are often located in different parts of the world and may not know each other's identity. As with electronic brainstorming, Delphi participants do not know who "owns" the ideas submitted. Typically, Delphi group members submit possible

---

electronic brainstorming
Using special computer software, participants share ideas while minimizing the team dynamics problems inherent in traditional brainstorming sessions.

Delphi method
A structured team decision-making process of systematically pooling the collective knowledge of experts on a particular subject to make decisions, predict the future, or identify opposing views.

solutions or comments regarding an issue to the central convener, although computer technology is turning this stage into an automatic compilation process. The compiled results are returned to the panel for a second round of comments. This process may be repeated a few more times until consensus or dissensus emerges.

nominal group technique

A structured team decision-making process whereby team members independently write down ideas, describe and clarify them to the group, and then independently rank or vote on them.

Nominal group technique Nominal group technique is a variation of traditional brainstorming that tries to combine individual efficiencies with team dynamics.[60] The method is called nominal because participants form a group in name only during two stages of decision making. This process, shown in Exhibit 10.5, first involves the individual, then the group, and finally the individual again. After the problem is described, team members silently and independently write down as many solutions as they can. During the group stage, participants describe their solutions to the other team members, usually in a round-robin format. As with brainstorming, there is no criticism or debate, although members are encouraged to ask for clarification of the ideas presented. In the final stage, participants silently and independently rank order or vote on each proposed solution.

Nominal group technique tends to generate a higher number and better quality ideas compared with traditional interacting and possibly brainstorming groups.[61] Due to its high degree of structure, nominal group technique usually maintains a high task orientation and relatively low potential for conflict within the team. However, team cohesiveness is generally lower in nominal decisions because the structure minimizes social interaction. Production blocking and evaluation apprehension still occur to some extent.

■ TEAM BUILDING

team building

Any formal activity intended to improve the development and functioning of a team.

Before Milton Elementary School in Milton, Delaware, opened its doors for the first time, school principal Sheila Baumgardner took her new teaching and support staff to Arlington Echo Outdoor Education Center in Millersville, Maryland, for three days of **team building**. "The idea behind that is to develop teamwork skills since I'm bringing teachers together from buildings all over the district," Baumgardner explains. Along with walking in the woods and sharing meals together, staff spent time developing school support programs. "Our main purpose is to develop teamwork skills—camaraderie—to facilitate communication once the school year begins," she says.[62]

■ **EXHIBIT 10.5**   Nominal group technique

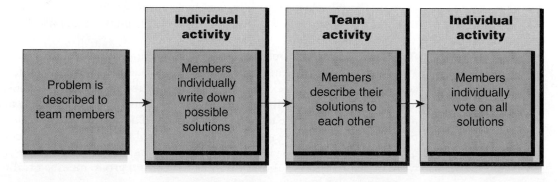

Volunteerism: The New Team-Building

Across Canada, companies are turning to a team-building activity that also helps the community: volunteering. PricewaterhouseCoopers Calgary supports volunteering with paid time off, including 10 staff who recently spent a day building homes with Habitat for Humanity. "It's a good way to work together on a team with people you may not usually be with in the same firm," says a PricewaterhouseCoopers team member. A team-building committee at Bridges Transitions Inc. in Kelowna, B.C., plans fun events that provide a benefit to the community. Nurse Ann Hayward (centre in this photo) chairs a committee at Toronto's Hospital for Sick Children, which coordinates and raises funds for a medical team to spend a week assisting local staff at hospitals in a developing nation. Recently, two dozen Sick Kids staff spent their vacation time working at the Nepal Medical College and Teaching Hospital in Kathmandu. "You make lifelong connections" with the local people, says Catherine Hogan, who travelled with Hayward and others to Nepal. "It was also wonderful to get to know your colleagues. These are the people you see everyday, but you don't really get to know them [until these trips]."[67] *Paul Irish/Toronto Star*

www.sickkids.ca

Sheila Baumgardner knows that speeding up the team development process requires one of the many forms of team building—any formal activity intended to improve the development and functioning of a work team.[63] Some team-building activities also reshape team norms and strengthen cohesiveness. Team building is sometimes applied to newly established teams, such as Milton Elementary School, because team members are at the earliest stages of team development. However, it is more common among existing teams that have regressed to earlier stages of team development. Team building is therefore most appropriate when the team experiences high membership turnover or members have lost focus of their respective roles and team objectives.

TYPES OF TEAM BUILDING

There are four main types of team building: goal setting, role definition, interpersonal processes, and problem solving.[64]

■ *Goal setting*—Some team-building interventions clarify the team's performance goals, increase the team's motivation to accomplish these goals, and establish a mechanism for systematic feedback on the team's goal performance. This is very similar to individual goal setting described in Chapter 5, except that the goals are applied to teams.

■ *Role definition*—Clarifying role definitions is often associated with goal setting team building. Role definition team building involves clarifying and reconstructing each member's perceptions of their role as well as the role expectations they have of other team members. Various interventions may be applied, ranging from open discussion to structured analysis of the work process. Role definition encompasses the emerging concept of team mental models. Recall from Chapter 3 that mental models are internal representations of the external world. Research studies indicate that team processes and performance depend on how well teammates share common mental models about how they should work together.[65] Team-building activities help team members to clarify and form a more unified perspective of their team mental models.

■ *Interpersonal processes*—This category of team building covers a broad territory. Conflict management fits under this heading, both as a symptom to identify the team's underlying weaknesses and as an ongoing interpersonal process that team members learn to continuously manage constructively. Early team-building interventions relied on direct confrontation sessions to give the sources of conflict an airing. This can work with professional facilitation, but experts warn that open **dialogue** is not always the most effective way to solve team conflicts.[66] Another interpersonal process is building (or rebuilding) trust among team members.

dialogue

A process of conversation among team members in which they learn about each other's mental models and assumptions, and eventually form a common model for thinking within the team.

Popular interventions such as wilderness team activities, paintball wars, and obstacle course challenges are typically offered to build trust. "If two colleagues hold the rope for you while you're climbing 10 metres up, that is truly team building," explains Jan Antwerpes, a partner in a German communications consulting firm. "It also shows your colleagues that you care for them."[68]

■ *Problem solving*—This type of team building focuses on decision making, including the issues mentioned earlier in this chapter and the decision-making process described in Chapter 8. To improve their problem-solving skills, some teams participate in simulation games that require team decisions in hypothetical situations.

IS TEAM BUILDING EFFECTIVE?

Are team-building interventions effective? Is the money well spent? So far, the answer is an equivocal "maybe." Studies suggest that some team-building activities are successful, but just as many fail to build high-performance teams.[69] One problem is that corporate leaders assume team-building activities are general solutions to general team problems. No one bothers to diagnose the team's specific needs (e.g., problem solving, interpersonal processes) because the team-building intervention is assumed to be a broad-brush solution. Instead, effective team building should begin with a sound diagnosis of the team's health, then select team-building interventions that address weaknesses.[70]

Another problem is that corporate leaders tend to view team building as a one-shot medical inoculation that every team should receive when it is formed. In truth, team building is an ongoing process, not a three-day jumpstart. Some experts suggest, for example, that wilderness experiences often fail because they rarely include follow-up consultation to ensure that team learning is transferred back to the workplace.[71]

Finally, we must remember that team building occurs on the job, not just on an obstacle course or in a national park. Organizations should encourage team members to reflect on their work experiences and to experiment with just-in-time learning for team development. This dialogue requires open communication, so employees can clarify expectations, coordinate work activities, and build common mental models of working together. The next chapter looks at the dynamics of communicating in teams and organizations.

CHAPTER SUMMARY

Self-directed work teams (SDWTs) complete an entire piece of work requiring several interdependent tasks and have substantial autonomy over the execution of these tasks. Sociotechnical systems (STS) theory identifies four main conditions for high-performance SDWTs. SDWTs must be a primary work unit, have sufficient autonomy, have control over key variances, and operate under joint optimization.

STS theory has been widely supported since its origins in the 1950s. However, it is not very helpful at identifying the optimal alignment of the social and

technical system. SDWTs also face cross-cultural issues, management resistance, and labour union and employee resistance.

Virtual teams are teams whose members operate across space, time, and organizational boundaries and are linked through information technologies to achieve organizational tasks. Unlike conventional teams, virtual team members are not co-located, so they are more dependent on information technologies rather than face-to-face interaction. Virtual teams are becoming more popular because information technology and knowledge-based work makes it easier to collaborate from a distance. Virtual teams are becoming increasingly necessary because they represent a natural part of the knowledge management process. Moreover, as companies globalize, they must rely more on virtual teams than co-located teams to coordinate operations at distant sites.

Several elements in the team effectiveness model stand out as important issues for virtual teams. High performance virtual teams require a variety of communication media, and virtual team members need to creatively combine these media to match the task demands. Virtual teams operate better with structured rather than complex and ambiguous tasks. They usually cannot maintain as large a team as is possible in conventional teams. Members of virtual teams require special skills in communication systems and should be aware of cross-cultural issues. Virtual team members should also meet face to face, particularly when the team forms, to assist team development and cohesiveness.

Trust is important in team dynamics, particularly in virtual teams. Trust is a psychological state comprising the intention to accept vulnerability based on positive expectations of the intent or behaviour of another person. The minimum level of trust is calculus-based trust, which is based on deterrence. Teams cannot survive with this level of trust. Knowledge-based trust is a higher level of trust and is grounded on the other party's predictability. The highest level of trust, called identification-based trust, is based on mutual understanding and emotional bond between the parties. Most employees join a team with a fairly high level of trust, which tends to decline over time.

Team decisions are impeded by time constraints, evaluation apprehension, conformity to peer pressure, groupthink, and group polarization. Production blocking—where only one person typically speaks at a time—is a form of time constraint on teams. Evaluation apprehension occurs when employees believe that others are silently evaluating them, so they avoid stating seemingly silly ideas. Conformity keeps team members aligned with team goals, but it also tends to suppress dissenting opinions. Groupthink is the tendency of highly cohesive groups to value consensus at the price of decision quality. Group polarization refers to the tendency of teams to make more extreme decisions than individuals working alone.

To minimize decision-making problems, teams should be moderately (not highly) confident, ensure that the team leader does not dominate, maintain an optimal team size, and ensure that team norms support critical thinking. Five team structures that potentially improve team decision making are constructive conflict, brainstorming, electronic brainstorming, Delphi method, and nominal group technique. Constructive conflict occurs when team members debate their different perceptions about an issue in a way that keeps the conflict focused on the task rather than people. Brainstorming requires team members to speak freely, avoid criticism, provide as many ideas as possible, and build on the ideas of others. Electronic brainstorming uses computer software to share ideas while minimizing team dynamics problems. Delphi method systematically pools the collective knowledge of experts on a particular subject without face-to-face meetings. In nominal group technique, participants write down ideas alone, describe these ideas in a group, then silently vote on these ideas.

Team building is any formal activity intended to improve the development and functioning of a work team. Four team-building strategies are goal setting, role definition, interpersonal processes, and problem solving. Some team-building events succeed, but companies often fail to consider the contingencies of team building.

KEY TERMS

brainstorming, p. 286

constructive conflict, p. 285

Delphi method, p. 287

dialogue, p. 289

electronic brainstorming, p. 287

evaluation apprehension, p. 284

group polarization, p. 284

groupthink, p. 284

joint optimization, p. 274

nominal group technique, p. 288

production blocking, p. 283

self-directed work teams (SDWTs), p. 272

sociotechnical systems (STS) theory, p. 273

team building, p. 288

trust, p. 280

virtual teams, p. 277

DISCUSSION QUESTIONS

1. How do self-directed work teams differ from conventional teams?

2. Advanced Telecom Ltd. has successfully introduced self-directed work teams at its operations throughout Canada. The company now wants to introduce SDWTs at its plants in Thailand and Mexico. What potential cross-cultural challenges might Advanced Telecom experience as it introduces SDWTs in these high power distance countries?

3. A chicken processing company wants to build a processing plant designed around sociotechnical systems principles. In a traditional chicken processing plant, employees work in separate departments—cleaning and cutting, cooking, packaging, and warehousing. The cooking and packaging processes are controlled by separate workstations in the traditional plant. How would the company change this operation according to sociotechnical systems design?

4. What can organizations do to reduce management resistance to self-directed work teams?

5. Suppose the instructor for this course assigned you to a project team consisting of three other students who are currently taking similar courses in Ireland, India, and Brazil. All students speak English and have similar expertise of the topic. Use your knowledge of virtual teams to discuss the problems that your team might face, compared with a team of local students who can meet face to face.

6. What can virtual teams do to sustain trust among team members?

7. Some Canadian firms have turned to volunteering as a form of team building, whereby a group of employees spends a day working together on a community project, often outside their expertise. In what ways might volunteering be an effective team-building activity?

8. Bangalore Technologies wants to use brainstorming with its employees and customers to identify new uses for its technology. Advise Bangalore's president about the potential benefits of brainstorming, as well as its potential limitations.

CASE STUDY 10.1

THE SHIPPING INDUSTRY ACCOUNTING TEAM

For the past five years, I have been working at McKay, Sanderson, and Smith Associates, a mid-sized accounting firm in Halifax that specializes in commercial accounting and audits. My particular speciality is accounting practices for shipping companies, ranging from small fishing fleets to a couple of the big firms with ships on the St. Lawrence Seaway.

About 18 months ago, McKay, Sanderson, and Smith Associates became part of a large merger involving two other accounting firms across Canada. These firms have offices in Montreal, Ottawa, Toronto, Calgary, and Vancouver. Although the other two accounting firms were much larger than McKay, all three firms agreed to avoid centralizing the business around one office in Toronto. Instead, the new firm—called Goldberg, Choo, and McKay Associates—would rely on teams across the country to "leverage the synergies of our collective knowledge" (an often-cited statement from the managing partner soon after the merger).

The merger affected me a year ago when my boss (a senior partner and vice-president of the merger

firm) announced that I would be working more closely with three people from the other two firms to become the new shipping industry accounting team. The other "team members" were Rochelle in Montreal, Thomas in Toronto, and Brad in Vancouver. I had met Rochelle briefly at a meeting in Montreal during the merger, but have never met Thomas or Brad, although knew that they were shipping accounting professionals at the other firms.

Initially, the shipping "team" activities involved emailing each other about new contracts and prospective clients. Later, we were asked to submit joint monthly reports on accounting statements and issues. Normally, I submitted my own monthly reports that summarize activities involving my own clients. Coordinating the monthly report with three other people took much more time, particularly since different accounting documentation procedures across the three firms were still being resolved. It took numerous emails and a few telephone calls to work out a reasonable monthly report style.

During this aggravating process, it became apparent—to me at least—that this "teams" business was costing me more time than it was worth. Moreover, Brad in Vancouver didn't have a clue as to how to communicate with the rest of us. He rarely replied to emails. Instead, he often used the telephone voice-mail system, which resulted in lots of telephone tag. Brad arrives at work at 9 a.m. in Vancouver (and is often late!), which is early afternoon in Halifax. I work from 8 a.m. to 4 p.m., a flexible arrangement so I can chauffeur my kids after school to sports and music lessons. So Brad and I have a window of less than three hours to share information.

The biggest nuisance with the shipping specialist accounting team started two weeks ago when the firm asked the four of us to develop a new strategy for attracting more shipping firm business. This new strategic plan is a messy business. Somehow, we have to share our thoughts on various approaches, agree on a new plan, and write a unified submission to the managing partner. Already, the project is taking most of my time just writing and responding to emails, and talking in conference calls (which none of us did much before the team formed).

Thomas and Rochelle have already had two or three "misunderstandings" via email about their different perspectives on delicate matters in the strategic plan. The worst of these disagreements required all of us to resolve through a conference call. Except for the most basic matters, it seems that we can't understand each other, let alone agree on key issues. I have come to the conclusion that I would never want Brad to work in my Halifax office (thank goodness, he's on the other side of the country). While Rochelle and I seem to agree on most points, the overall team can't form a common vision or strategy. I don't know how Rochelle, Thomas, or Brad feel, but I would be quite happy to work somewhere that did not require any of these long-distance team headaches.

Discussion Questions

1. What type of team was formed here? Was it necessary, in your opinion?
2. Use the team effectiveness model in Chapter 9 and related information in this chapter to identify the strengths and weaknesses of this team's environment, design, and processes.
3. Assuming that these four people must continue to work as a team, recommend ways to improve the team's effectiveness.

TEAM EXERCISE 10.2

EGG DROP EXERCISE

Purpose This exercise is designed to help you understand the dynamics of high-performance teams.

Materials The instructor will provide various raw materials with which to complete this task. The instructor will also distribute a cost sheet to each team, and will post the rules for managers and workers. Rule violations will attract penalties that increase the cost of production.

Team Task The team's task is to design and build a protective device that will allow a raw egg (provided by the instructor) to be dropped from a great height without breaking. The team wins if its egg does not break using the lowest priced device.

Instructions

- *Step 1:* The instructor will divide the class into teams, with approximately six people on each team. Team members will divide into groups of "managers" and "workers." The team can have as many people as they think is needed for managers and workers as long as all team members are assigned to one of these roles. Please note from the cost sheet that managers and workers represent a cost to your project's budget.

- *Step 2:* Within the time allotted by the instructor, each team's managers will design the device to protect the egg. Workers and managers will then purchase supplies from the store, and workers will then build the egg protection device. Team members should read the rules carefully to avoid penalty costs.

Source: This exercise, which is widely available in many forms, does not seem to have any known origins.

THE TEAM PLAYER INVENTORY

By Theresa Kline, University of Calgary.

Purpose This exercise is designed to help you estimate the extent to which you are positively predisposed to work in teams.

Instructions Read each of the statements below and circle the response that you believe best indicates the extent to which you agree or disagree with that statement. Then use the scoring key in Appendix B to calculate your results for each scale. This exercise is completed alone so students assess themselves honestly without concerns of social comparison. However, class discussion will focus on the characteristics of individuals who are more or less compatible with working in self-directed work teams.

THE TEAM PLAYER INVENTORY					
To what extent to do you agree or disagree that...?	Completely disagree ▼	Disagree somewhat ▼	Neither agree nor disagree ▼	Agree somewhat ▼	Completely agree ▼
1. I enjoy working on team projects.	☐	☐	☐	☐	☐
2. Team project work easily allows others not to "pull their weight."	☐	☐	☐	☐	☐
3. Work that is done as a team is better than the work done individually.	☐	☐	☐	☐	☐
4. I do my best work alone rather than in a team.	☐	☐	☐	☐	☐
5. Team work is overrated in terms of the actual results produced.	☐	☐	☐	☐	☐
6. Working in a team gets me to think more creatively.	☐	☐	☐	☐	☐
7. Teams are used too often when individual work would be more effective.	☐	☐	☐	☐	☐
8. My own work is enhanced when I am in a team situation.	☐	☐	☐	☐	☐
9. My experiences working in team situations have been primarily negative.	☐	☐	☐	☐	☐
10. More solutions or ideas are generated when working in a team situation than when working alone.	☐	☐	☐	☐	☐

Source: T. J. B. Kline, "The Team Player Inventory: Reliability and Validity of a Measure of Predisposition Towards Organizational Team Working Environments," *Journal for Specialists in Group Work*, 24 (1999), pp. 102–12.

PROPENSITY TO TRUST SCALE

Go to the Online Learning Centre to complete this interactive self-assessment.

Trust is a psychological state comprising the intention to accept vulnerability based on positive expectations of the intent or behaviour of another person. While trust varies from one situation to the next, some people have a higher or lower propensity to trust. In other words, some people are highly trusting of others, even when first meeting them, whereas others have difficulty trusting anyone, even over a long time. This self-assessment provides an estimate of your propensity to trust. Indicate your preferred response to each statement, being honest with yourself for each item. This self-assessment is completed alone, although class discussion will focus on the meaning of propensity to trust, why it varies from one person to the next, and how it affects teamwork.

·11·

COMMUNICATING IN TEAMS AND ORGANIZATIONS

LEARNING OBJECTIVES

AFTER READING THIS CHAPTER, YOU SHOULD BE ABLE TO:

- Explain the importance of communication and diagram the communication process.

- Describe problems with communicating through electronic mail.

- Identify two ways in which nonverbal communication differs from verbal communication.

- Identify two conditions requiring a channel with high media richness.

- Identify four common communication barriers.

- Discuss the degree to which men and women communicate differently.

- Outline the key elements of active listening.

- Summarize four communication strategies in organizational hierarchies.

H aving a conversation with 90,000 employees in 48 countries is a monumental challenge for any chief executive. Yet Intel CEO Paul Otinelli meets this challenge by writing his own weblog. Blogs (as weblogs are commonly called) are online journals or diaries. Otinelli writes personal musings in his blog every few weeks, including thoughts on Intel's future and successes of its competitors. His blog also includes a forum where employees can add their views. "The Blog does 'top-down' one step better," wrote an Intel employee on Otinelli's blog forum. "It's almost like a subordinate brown bag luncheon with the top dog."

Few Canadian executives do blogging, even though some of the world's top blog evangelists live in this country. "[Blogging] is a fantastically effective listening device," says Tim Bray, the Vancouver-based director of Web technologies at Sun Microsystems. "There's an immediacy of interaction you can get with your audience through blogging that's hard to get any other way, except by face-to-face communication."

Jeremy Wright, another Canadian evangelist, sees blogging as the next great platform for employee communication. For example, the St. Stephen, N.B., entrepreneur set up employee blogs at Mitsubishi after the Japanese automaker realized that employees weren't reading the expensive company magazine. "The company wanted a live two-way employee communication device," Wright explains. "If you transmit your message [such as through newsletters], people will ignore it. If you create a different medium that is engaging [such as blogs], people will engage."

Tim Bray, the Vancouver, B.C.-based director of Web technologies at Sun Microsystems, says that blogs have a lot to offer as a communication medium in organizations.
Ian Smith/Vancouver Sun

Corporate and employee blogs may be a promising form of communication, but many firms have difficulty accepting the increased transparency created by blogging. An employee at the Nunavut Tourism agency had her employment terminated after posting photos on her personal blog showing abandoned machinery and rusted cans lying on the snowy tundra outside Iqaluit. She thought they represented beautiful photography, but her employer felt they hurt tourism. A Starbucks supervisor in Toronto complained on his blog that his boss refused to let him go home when sick. The rant didn't actually name the boss, and the supervisor used a pseudonym, but Starbucks discovered the blogger's identity and fired him.

In spite of these incidents, Tim Bray reckons that the rewards of corporate blogs easily outweigh the risks. "[Blogging is] a morale booster in the company, and I believe it helps our position in the market," concludes Bray, who co-invented the emerging language for Web pages (XML and RSS).[1] ■
http://ca.sun.com/en/

I t's almost a cliché to say that information technologies have transformed communication in organizations. Yet we may still be at the beginning of this revolution. Wire cables and telephones introduced a century ago are giving way to email, instant messaging, weblogs, and podcasting. Each of these inventions creates fascinating changes in how people interact with each other in the workplace. **Communication** refers to the process by which information is transmitted and *understood* between two or more people. The word "understood" is emphasized because transmitting the sender's intended meaning is the essence of good communication. Intel, Sun Microsystems, and other large organizations require innovative strategies to keep communication pathways open. Smaller businesses may have fewer structural bottlenecks, but they, too, can suffer from subtle communication barriers.

communication
The process by which information is transmitted and understood between two or more people.

Effective communication is vital to all organizations because it coordinates employees, fulfills employee needs, supports knowledge management, and improves decision making.[2] First, the ability to exchange information is an essential part of the coordination process, allowing employees to develop common mental models that synchronize their work. Second, communication is the glue that holds people together. It helps people satisfy their drive to bond and, as part of the dynamics of social support, eases work-related stress.

Communication is also a key driver in knowledge management. It brings knowledge into the organization and distributes it to employees who require that information. As such, it minimizes the "silos of knowledge" problem that undermines an organization's potential. Fourth, communication influences the quality of decision making. Individuals rarely have enough information alone to make decisions on the complex matters facing businesses today. Instead, problem solvers require information from co-workers, subordinates, and anyone else with relevant knowledge.

By improving decision making, knowledge management, employee needs, and coordination, workplace communication has a significant effect on organizational performance.[3] One report estimates that a company's market value increases by over 7 percent when it improves its "communications integrity." Another identifies the leader's communication skills as an important influence on company performance. Communication is also a key ingredient in employee satisfaction and loyalty.

This chapter begins by presenting a model of the communication process and discussing several communication barriers. Next, the different types of communication channels, including computer-mediated communication, are described, followed by factors to consider when choosing a communication medium. This chapter then presents some options for communicating in organizational hierarchies and describes the pervasive organizational grapevine. The latter part of the chapter examines cross-cultural and gender differences in communication and outlines strategies to improve interpersonal communication.

■ A MODEL OF COMMUNICATION

The communication model presented in Exhibit 11.1 provides a useful "conduit" metaphor for thinking about the communication process.[4] According to this model, communication flows through channels between the sender and receiver. The sender forms a message and encodes it into words, gestures, voice intonations, and other symbols or signs. Next, the encoded message is transmitted to the intended receiver through one or more communication channels (media). The

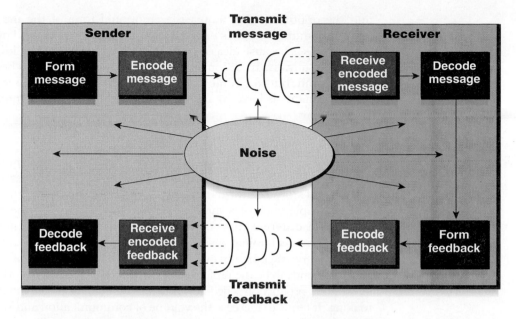

■ **EXHIBIT 11.1**

The communication process model

receiver senses the incoming message and decodes it into something meaningful. Ideally, the decoded meaning is what the sender had intended.

In most situations, the sender looks for evidence that the other person received and understood the transmitted message. This feedback may be a formal acknowledgment, such as "Yes, I know what you mean," or indirect evidence from the receiver's subsequent actions. Notice that feedback repeats the communication process. Intended feedback is encoded, transmitted, received, and decoded from the receiver to the sender of the original message.

This model recognizes that communication is not a free-flowing conduit. Rather, the transmission of meaning from one person to another is hampered by noise—the psychological, social, and structural barriers that distort and obscure the sender's intended message. If any part of the communication process is distorted or broken, the sender and receiver will not have a common understanding of the message.

■ COMMUNICATION CHANNELS

A critical part of the communication model is the channel or medium through which information is transmitted. There are two main types of channels: verbal and nonverbal. Verbal communication includes any oral or written means of transmitting meaning through words. Nonverbal communication, which we discuss later, is any part of communication that does not use words.

VERBAL COMMUNICATION

Different forms of verbal communication should be used in different situations. Face-to-face interaction is usually better than written methods for transmitting emotions and persuading the receiver. This is because nonverbal cues accompany oral communications, such as voice intonations and use of silence. Furthermore, face-to-face interaction provides the sender with immediate feedback from the receiver and the opportunity to adjust the emotional tone of the message accordingly. Written communication is more appropriate for recording and presenting technical details. This is because ideas are easier to follow when written down than when communicated aurally. Traditionally, written communication has been slow to develop and transmit, but electronic mail, weblogs, and other computer-mediated communication channels have significantly improved written communication efficiency.

ELECTRONIC COMMUNICATION

Electronic mail (email) is revolutionizing the way we communicate in organizational settings. It's easy to understand its popularity. Messages are quickly formed, edited, and stored. Information can be appended and transmitted to many people with a simple click of a mouse. Email is asynchronous (messages are sent and received at different times), so there is no need to coordinate a communication session. This technology also allows fairly random access of information; you can select any message in any order and skip to different parts of a message.

Email tends to be the preferred medium for coordinating work (e.g., confirming a co-worker's production schedule) and for sending well-defined information for decision making. It tends to increase the volume of communication and significantly alter the flow of that information within groups and throughout the organization.[5] Specifically, it reduces some face-to-face and telephone communication but increases the flow of information to higher levels in the organization. Some social and organizational status differences still exist with email, but they are less apparent than in face-to-face communication. Email also reduces many selective attention biases because it hides our age, race, weight, and other features that are observable in face-to-face meetings.

Problems with email   In spite of the wonders of email, anyone who has used this communication medium knows that it also creates several problems. Consider the following incident: A DigitalEve Toronto team member sent a Russian-speaking member an email saying that her latest Web design work was awesome. The Russian colleague immediately shot back a reply to her Canadian counterpart, slamming the team for its harsh evaluation of her work and lack of respect. Subsequent email volleys escalated the anger and hurt feelings. Another Russian colleague soon discovered the cause of the problem. The Russian team member's language translator had translated "awesome" as "awful."[6]

The email problem at DigitalEve Toronto was more than a faulty language translator. It reveals that email is a poor medium for communicating emotions. People rely on facial expressions and other nonverbal cues to interpret the emotional meaning of words, and email lacks these symbols. Communicators instead use language and symbols to transmit emotional meaning through email, but these are often more ambiguous. In a face-to-face situation, the Russian team member would have immediately noticed that the "awful" evaluation of her work didn't match the Canadian's positive facial expression. Email aficionados try to clarify the emotional tone of their messages by inserting graphic faces called emoticons, or "smileys." PriceWaterhouseCoopers takes another approach. The accounting firm has a rule for virtual team members: "Assume positive intent of your team mates."[7]

The incident at DigitalEve Toronto also illustrates a second problem, namely that email is an impersonal medium that seems to reduce our politeness and respect for others. This is mostly evident through the increased frequency of **flaming**—the act of sending an emotionally charged message to others. Email often lacks diplomacy

flaming
The act of sending an emotionally charged electronic mail message to others.

because people can post email messages before their emotions subside, whereas emotions usually cool down by the time someone sends a traditional memo or letter. Email is also so impersonal that employees often write things that they would never say in person. Fortunately, the number of flaming incidents in virtual teams decreases as the team develops and when explicit norms and rules of communication are established.[8]

A third problem with email is that it is an inefficient medium for communicating in ambiguous, complex, and novel situations. The communicating parties lack mutual mental models under these circumstances, so rapid and frequent two-way communication is needed to form mutual understanding. "I've stopped using email volleys where you just keep going back and forth and back and forth and nothing is going in the right direction," says Kevin Scott, who is responsible for the supply planning and trading group at the Irving Oil refinery in Saint John, N.B. Now, he talks with his colleague in person when the issue is complicated. "I find I'm coming up with much better outcomes and a much better understanding of an issue."[9] This same reasoning is used to ban email once in a while at some companies. GLOBAL Connections 11.1 describes how Liverpool City Council and other British organizations believe that some things are better discussed in person than in cyberspace.

A fourth difficulty with email is that it contributes to information overload. Many email users are overwhelmed by hundreds of messages each week, many of which are either unnecessary or irrelevant to the receiver. This occurs because emails can be easily created and copied to thousands of people through group mailbox systems. Email overload may eventually decrease as people become more familiar with it, but count on fairly large email inboxes for the foreseeable future.

Other electronic communication   IBM executives weren't surprised when a survey indicated that IBM employees rated co-workers as one of the two most credible or useful sources of information. What did surprise IBM executives was that the other equally credible and important source of information was IBM's intranet. Intranets, extranets, Blackberry wireless emailing, instant messaging, blogging, podcasting, and other forms of computer-mediated communication are fuelling the hyperfast world of corporate information sharing.[10]

Employees at IBM, Sun Microsystems, and some other companies now use *instant messaging* (IM) almost as much as email to transmit information quickly with co-workers. IM is more efficient than email because messages are brief (usually just a sentence or two with acronyms and sound-alike letters for words) and appear on the receiver's screen as soon as they are sent. IM also creates real-time communities of practice as employees form clustered conversations around specific fields of expertise. However, as a Canadian study recently noted, IM requires a large enough group of participating users. Another advantage of IM, also noted in the Canadian study, is that since each discussion group is streamed through a separate window, IM users frequently carry on several discrete conversations at the same time. "No matter how good you are on the phone, the best you can do is carry on two conversations at once," says one New York City broker. "With IM, I can have six going at once . . . That allows me to get my job done and serve clients better."[11]

As described in the opening story to this chapter, blogs are vehicles for executives to communicate with employees more personally, and they allow employees to give feedback regarding the executives' comments. Sun Microsystems and a few other firms support employee blogs because they empower staff to share information both internally and externally, and let co-workers know more about each other. Blogs also allow firms to archive discussions, something that is less easily

British Organizations Ban Email to Rediscover the Art of Conversation

For the past 800 years, citizens in the port city of Liverpool, England, have relied on face-to-face communication to conduct trade and resolve their differences. But leaders at Liverpool City Council are concerned that email is becoming a threat to the noble practice of dialogue among its employees. "We'd seen a doubling in internal emails and found a lot of emails were unnecessary," says David Henshaw, chief executive of Liverpool City Council. "A lot of the stuff could be dealt with over the phone, or by getting up and walking to the person next to you."

To battle email overload, Henshaw has asked his employees to avoid using this medium of communication on Wednesdays. So far, Henshaw's own email flow has dropped from 250 per day to just 25 on that day. Not everyone is convinced the ban will last for long. "In business the pressure is on," says Leicestershire Chamber of Commerce chief executive Martin Traynor. "If people email you in the morning, by lunch they're asking why you haven't emailed back."

Perhaps so, but Liverpool City Council is not alone in its quest for more old-fashioned face-to-face conversation. Nestle Rowntree executives asked staff to hit the email "send" button less often on Fridays to "reduce needless information flow across the organization." Camelot, the British lottery operator, also discouraged emails on the last day of the workweek. "We needed to make staff more aware of other forms of communication," explained a Camelot spokesperson.

Phones 4U CEO John Caudwell became so fed up with the time wasted with email that he has banned his

Liverpool City Council has banned email one day a week so employees rediscover the benefits of face-to-face communication. *P. Noble/AP Files*

2,500 employees from emailing each other at all. Email is allowed only sparingly when communicating with customers who insist on using it. "The quality and efficiency of communication have increased in one fell swoop," says Caudwell. "Things are getting done and people aren't tied to their personal computers."

Sources: R. Steiner and M. Chittenden, "Office Workers Told to Take an E-mail Holiday," *Sunday Times (London)*, March 4, 2001, p. 8; O. Burkeman, "Post Modern," *The Guardian (London)*, June 20, 2001; "Does E-Mail Really Help Us Get The Message?" *Leicester Mercury*, August 31, 2002; D. J. Horgan, "You've Got Conversation," *CIO Magazine*, October 15, 2002; M. Greenwood, "I Have Banned Emails…They are the Cancer of Modern Business," *The Mirror (London)*, September 19, 2003, p. 11. **www.liverpool.gov.uk**

---

done in instant messaging. Podcasting is quickly becoming another way to communicate. Although primarily aimed at the public, podcasts—radio-like programs formatted for digital music players and computer music software—are starting to appear as messages from executives to employees and customers alike.[12]

NONVERBAL COMMUNICATION

Idle chit-chat is difficult for those working on the cutting line at the Maple Leaf meat processing plant in Brandon, Manitoba. Employees wear earmuffs to block out the deafening noise of machinery, so they convey information through hand gestures and other forms of nonverbal communication. *Nonverbal communication* includes facial gestures, voice intonation, physical distance, and even silence. This communication channel is necessary where physical distance or noise prevents effective verbal exchanges and the need for immediate feedback precludes written communication. But even in quiet face-to-face meetings, most information is communicated nonverbally. Rather like a parallel conversation, nonverbal cues signal subtle information to both parties, such as reinforcing their interest in the verbal conversation or demonstrating their relative status in the relationship.[13]

Nonverbal communication differs from verbal communication in a couple of ways. First, it is less rule-bound than verbal communication. We receive a lot of formal training on how to understand spoken words, but very little on understanding the nonverbal signals that accompany those words. Consequently, nonverbal cues are generally more ambiguous and susceptible to misinterpretation. At the same time, many facial expressions (such as smiling) are hardwired and universal, thereby providing the only reliable means of communicating across cultures. This point is powerfully illustrated in GLOBAL Connections 11.2. To overcome language and physical noise barriers, the quick-thinking leader of a coalition forces unit during the Iraq war relied on nonverbal communication to communicate its friendly intentions, thereby narrowly avoiding a potentially deadly incident.

The other difference between verbal and nonverbal communication is that the former is typically conscious, whereas most nonverbal communication is automatic and unconscious. We normally plan the words we say or write, but we rarely plan every blink, smile, or other gesture during a conversation. Indeed, as we just mentioned, many of these facial expressions communicate the same meaning across cultures because they are hardwired unconscious or preconscious responses to human emotions.[14] For example, pleasant emotions cause the brain centre to widen the mouth, whereas negative emotions produce constricted facial expressions (squinting eyes, pursed lips, etc.).

Emotional contagion   One of the most fascinating effects of emotions on nonverbal communication is the phenomenon called **emotional contagion**, which is the automatic process of "catching" or sharing another person's emotions by mimicking that person's facial expressions and other nonverbal behaviour. Consider what happens when you see a co-worker accidentally bang his or her head against a filing cabinet. Chances are, you wince and put your hand on your own head as if you had hit the cabinet. Similarly, while listening to someone describe a positive event, you tend to smile and exhibit other emotional displays of happiness. While some of our nonverbal communication is planned, emotional contagion represents unconscious behaviour—we automatically mimic and synchronize our nonverbal behaviours with other people.[15]

Emotional contagion serves three purposes. First, mimicry provides continuous feedback, communicating that we understand and empathize with the sender. To consider the significance of this, imagine employees remaining expressionless after watching a co-worker bang his or her head! The lack of parallel behaviour conveys a lack of understanding or caring. Second, mimicking the nonverbal behaviours of other people seems to be a way of receiving emotional meaning from those people. If a co-worker is angry with a client, your tendency to frown and show anger while listening helps you share that emotion more fully. In other words, we receive meaning by expressing the sender's emotions as well as by listening to the sender's words.

Last, emotional contagion is associated with the drive to bond that was described in Chapter 5. Social solidarity is built out of each member's awareness of a collective sentiment. Through nonverbal expressions of emotional contagion, people see others share the same emotions that we feel. This strengthens team cohesiveness by providing evidence of member similarity.[16]

emotional contagion

The automatic and unconscious tendency to mimic and synchronize one's own nonverbal behaviours with those of other people.

Nonverbal Gestures Help Crowd Control During Iraq War

The southern Iraqi city of Najaf is home to one of Islam's holiest sites, the Ali Mosque. The site is believed to be the final resting place of Ali, son-in-law of the prophet Mohammed. It is also home to Grand Ayatollah Ali Hussein Sistani, one of the most revered Shiites in the Muslim world and a potential supporter of U.S. efforts to introduce a more moderate government in Iraq.

One week before Saddam Hussein's regime was overthrown, Sistani sent word that he wanted to meet with senior officers of the American forces. Fearing assassination, he also asked for soldiers to secure his compound, located along the Golden Road near the mosque. But when 130 soldiers from the 101st Airborne's 2nd Battalion, 327th Infantry and their gun trucks turned onto the Golden Road to provide security, hundreds of Iraqis in the area started to get angry. Clerics tried to explain to the crowd why the Americans were approaching, but they were drowned out. The crowd assumed the Americans would try to enter and possibly attack the sacred mosque.

The chanting got louder as the quickly growing crowd approached the soldiers. Anticipating a potentially deadly situation, Lieutenant Colonel Christopher Hughes, the battalion's commander, picked up a loudspeaker and called out the unit's nickname: "No Slack Soldiers!" Then he commanded: "All No Slack Soldiers, take a knee." According

to journalists witnessing this incident, every soldier almost immediately knelt down on one knee. Hughes then called out: "All No Slack Soldiers, point your weapons at the ground." Again, the soldiers complied.

With the crowd still chanting in anger, Hughes spoke through the loudspeaker a third time: "All No Slack Soldiers, smile," he commanded. "Smile guys, everybody smile." And in this intensely difficult situation, the kneeling troops showed the friendliest smile they could muster toward the crowd.

Eyewitnesses say that these nonverbal gestures started to work; some people in the crowd smiled back at the Americans and stopped chanting. But insurgents in the crowd (apparently Hussein supporters planted to misinform the crowd), continued to yell. So Hughes spoke one more time: "All vehicles, all No Slack Soldiers, calmly stand up and withdraw from this situation," he said. "We'll go so the people understand we are not trying to hurt him. C'mon, Bravo, back off. Smile and wave and back off." And with that, the soldiers walked backwards 100 yards, then turned around and returned to their compound.

Sources: W. Allison, "March to Mosque Provokes Worst Fears," *St. Petersburg Times* (Florida) April 4, 2003, p. 1A; "All Things Considered," *National Public Radio (NPR)*, April 4, 2003; R. Chilcote, "Iraqis Mistakenly Believe Soldiers have their Sights on a Sacred Landmark," *CNN*, April 4, 2003.

▪ CHOOSING THE BEST COMMUNICATION CHANNELS

Employees perform better if they can quickly determine the best communication channels for the situation and are flexible enough to use different methods, as the occasion requires. But which communication channels are most appropriate? We partly answered this question in our evaluation of the different communication channels. However, two additional contingencies worth noting are media richness and symbolic meaning.

MEDIA RICHNESS

Soon after Ernst & Young encouraged its employees around the globe to form virtual teams, the accounting firm realized that email and voice mail weren't sufficient for these groups. "Try coming to an agreement on the verbiage of a legal contract with a team of lawyers and engineers representing multiple interests using only the telephone and email," quips John Whyte, Ernst & Young's chief information officer. Now, employees discuss complex issues through special software that provides a virtual whiteboard on the computer screen along with instant messaging. It's not quite as good as face-to-face meetings, but much better than the previous patchwork of email and telephone calls.[17]

Ernst & Young discovered that some issues require more media richness than email and telephone messages can offer. **Media richness** refers to the medium's *data-carrying capacity*—the volume and variety of information that can be transmitted during a specific time.[18] Face-to-face meetings have the highest data-carrying capacity because the sender simultaneously uses multiple communication channels (verbal and nonverbal), the receiver can provide immediate feedback, and the information exchange can be customized to suit the situation. Instant messaging (IM) is somewhat lower in the hierarchy, and email is further below IM. Financial reports and other impersonal documents represent the leanest media because they allow only one form of data transmission (e.g., written), the sender does not receive timely feedback from the receiver, and the information exchange is standardized for everyone.

Exhibit 11.2 shows that rich media are better than lean media when the communication situation is nonroutine and ambiguous. In nonroutine situations (such as an unexpected and unusual emergency), the sender and receiver have little common experience, so they need to transmit a large volume of information with immediate feedback. Lean media work well in routine situations because the sender and receiver have common expectations through shared mental models. Ambiguous situations (such as Ernst & Young's complex contract development) also require rich media because the parties must share large amounts of information with immediate feedback to resolve multiple and conflicting interpretations of their observations and experiences.[19]

What happens when we choose the wrong level of media richness for the situation? When the situation is routine or clear, using a rich medium—such as holding a special meeting—would seem like a waste of time. On the other hand, if a unique and ambiguous issue is handled through email or another lean medium, then issues take longer to resolve and misunderstandings are more likely to occur. This is the problem that employees at Ernst & Young experienced.

■ **EXHIBIT 11.2**

Media richness hierarchy

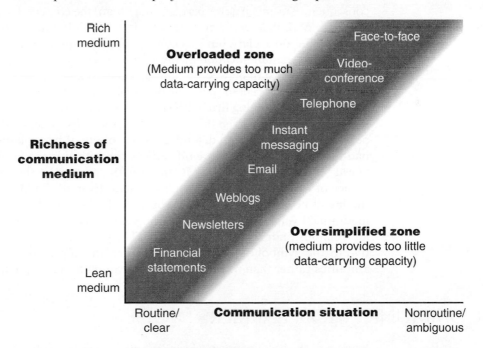

Sources: Based on R. Lengel and R. Daft, "The Selection of Communication Media as an Executive Skill," *Academy of Management Executive* 2, no. 3 (August 1988), p. 226; R.L. Daft and R.H. Lengel, "Information Richness: A New Approach to Managerial Behavior and Organization Design," *Research in Organizational Behavior*, 1984, p. 199.

Research studying traditional channels (face-to-face, written memos, etc.) generally supports the media richness proposition—that rich media are better than lean media when the situation is nonroutine and/or ambiguous. But the evidence is mixed when emerging information technologies are studied. One reason for this inconsistency is that we need to take into account the communicator's previous experience with email, IM, and other means of communication that do not exist naturally. People who have plenty of experience with a particular communication medium can "push" the amount of media richness normally possible through that information channel. Experienced Blackberry users, for instance, can whip through messages in a flash, whereas new users struggle to type email notes and organize incoming messages. Experience is less relevant with traditional media because they are learned early in life and, indeed, may be hardwired in our evolutionary development.[20]

A second contingency is the communicator's previous experience with the receiver. The more two or more people share common mental models, the less information exchange is required to communicate new meaning. People who know each other have similar "codebooks," so the sender can communicate with fewer words or other symbols and doesn't need to check as closely that the message has been understood. Without this common codebook, the sender needs to add in more redundancy (such as saying the same thing in two different ways) and requires more efficient feedback to ensure that the receiver understood the message.

SYMBOLIC MEANING OF THE MEDIUM

"The medium is the message."[21] This famous phrase by the late Canadian communications guru Marshall McLuhan means that the channel of communication has social consequences as much as (or perhaps more than) the content that passes through that medium. McLuhan was referring mainly to the influence of television and other "new media" on society, but this concept applies equally well to how the symbolic meaning of a communication medium influences our interpretation of the message and the relationship between sender and receiver.

The following recent incident will help to illustrate this principle: Nearly 700 British employees at consulting firm KPMG were recently given layoff notices by email. The message would have been the same whether sent by email or stated by the boss in person. Moreover, KPMG defended its use of email by explaining that employees had asked to receive their layoff notices through this medium. Still, the outside world swiftly condemned KPMG, not for the content of the message, but for the choice of medium through which it was sent. Even the KPMG executives who sent the layoff notices were hesitant to use email when employees first suggested this medium. "I was horrified about telling staff via email as I knew it would make us look callous," admitted one executive.[22] The point here is that we need to be sensitive to the symbolic meaning of the communication medium to ensure that it amplifies rather than misinterprets the meaning found in the message content.

■ COMMUNICATION BARRIERS (NOISE)

In spite of the best intentions of sender and receiver to communicate, several barriers inhibit the effective exchange of information. As author George Bernard Shaw wrote, "The greatest problem with communication is the illusion that it has been accomplished." Four pervasive communication barriers (called "noise" earlier in Exhibit 11.1) are perceptions, filtering, language, and information overload. Later, we will also investigate cross-cultural and gender communication barriers.

PERCEPTIONS

The perceptual process determines what messages we select or screen out, as well as how the selected information is organized and interpreted. This can be a significant source of noise in the communication process if the sender and receiver have different perceptual frames and mental models. For instance, corporate leaders are watched closely by employees, and the most inane words or gestures are interpreted with great meaning even though they occurred without intention.

FILTERING

Some messages are filtered or stopped altogether on their way up or down the organizational hierarchy. Filtering may involve deleting or delaying negative information or using less harsh words so that events sound more favourable.[23] Employees and supervisors usually filter communication to create a good impression of themselves to superiors. Filtering is most common where the organization rewards employees who communicate mainly positive information and among employees with strong career mobility aspirations.

jargon
The technical language and acronyms as well as recognized words with specialized meanings in specific organizations or groups.

LANGUAGE

Words and gestures carry no inherent meaning, so the sender must ensure the receiver understands these symbols and signs. In reality, lack of mutual understanding is a common reason why messages are distorted. Two potential language barriers are jargon and ambiguity.

Jargon "Our company has experienced a paradigm shift that will empower employees to leverage the company's core competencies and, moving forward, capture the low hanging fruit." If that line sounds like something your boss might utter, then welcome to the world of corporate jargon! **Jargon** consists of technical language and acronyms as well as recognized words with specialized meaning in specific organizations or social groups. Some jargon potentially makes communication more efficient when both sender and receiver understand this specialized language. Jargon also maintains an organization's culture and symbolizes an employee's identity in a group, because people feel more connected by common language.[24]

However, jargon becomes a barrier to effective communication when the receiver lacks the jargon dictionary used by the sender. Another problem occurs when people spew out gibberish jargon (such as the statement above) even though it adds no value to the conversation. In fact, one recent survey found that people react negatively to unnecessary jargon, which is probably contrary to the sender's intention to look "cool" using the latest buzzwords.[25]

"That's my commendation for deciphering all the sales talk when we needed to upgrade the computer."

Ambiguity   Most languages—and certainly the English language—include some degree of ambiguity because the sender and receiver interpret the same word or phrase differently. If a co-worker says "Would you like to check the figures again?" the employee may be politely *telling* you to double-check the figures. But this message is sufficiently ambiguous that you may think the co-worker is merely *asking* if you want to do this. The result is a failure to communicate.

However, ambiguity is also used deliberately in work settings.[26] Corporate leaders rely on metaphors and other vague language to describe ill-defined or complex ideas. Ambiguity is also used to avoid conveying or creating undesirable emotions. For example, one recent study reported that people rely on more ambiguous language when communicating with people who have different values and beliefs. In this case, ambiguity minimizes the risk of conflict.

INFORMATION OVERLOAD

According to a recent Canadian survey, employees receive an average of 54 email messages every day. Add in voice mail, cell phone text messages, Web site scanning, PDF file downloads, hard copy documents, and other sources of incoming information, and you have a perfect recipe for **information overload**.[27] Information overload occurs when the volume of information received exceeds the person's capacity to get through it. Employees have a certain *information processing capacity*—the amount of information that they are able to process in a fixed unit of time. At the same time, jobs have a varying *information load*—the amount of information to be processed per unit of time.[28] As Exhibit 11.3 illustrates, information overload occurs whenever the job's information load exceeds the individual's information processing capacity.

information overload

A condition in which the volume of information received exceeds the person's capacity to process it.

■ **EXHIBIT 11.3**

Dynamics of information overload

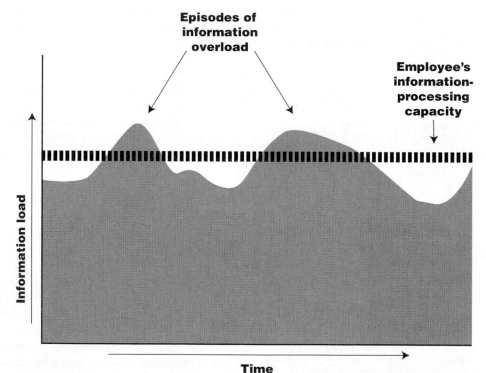

Episodes of information overload

Employee's information-processing capacity

Information load

Time

Information overload creates noise in the communication system because information gets overlooked or misinterpreted when people can't process it fast enough. It has also become a common cause of workplace stress. These problems can be minimized by increasing our information processing capacity, reducing the job's information load, or through a combination of both. Information processing capacity increases when we learn to read faster, scan through documents more efficiently, and remove distractions that slow information processing speed. Time management also increases information processing capacity. When information overload is temporary, information processing capacity can increase by working longer hours.

Microsoft chairman Bill Gates gets only about 30 to 40 email messages each day because he applies three strategies to reduce information load: buffering, omitting, and summarizing.[29] First, Gates receives approximately 300 emails each day from Microsoft addresses that are outside a core group of people; these emails are buffered— routed to an assistant who reads each and sends Gates only those considered essential reading. Second, Gates applies the omitting strategy by using software rules to redirect emails from distribution lists, nonessential sources, and junk mail (spam). These emails are dumped into pre-assigned folders to be read later, if ever. Third, Gates likely relies on the summarizing strategy by reading the executive summaries rather than the entire reports.

Perceptions, filtering, language, and information overload are not the only sources of noise in the communication process, but they are probably the most common. Noise also occurs when we communicate across cultures or genders, both of which are discussed next.

■ CROSS-CULTURAL AND GENDER COMMUNICATION

In a world of increasing globalization and cultural diversity, organizations face new opportunities as well as communication challenges.[30] Language is the most obvious cross-cultural communications challenge. Words are easily misunderstood in verbal communication, either because the receiver has a limited vocabulary or the sender's accent distorts the usual sound of some words. The problem discussed earlier of ambiguous language becomes amplified across cultures. For example, a French executive might call an event a "catastrophe" as a casual exaggeration, whereas someone in Germany usually interprets this statement literally as an earth-shaking event. Similarly, one study of government reports concluded that First Nations people and the Canadian government representatives were often talking about different things even though they used the same words.[31]

Mastering the same language improves one dimension of cross-cultural communication, but problems may still occur when interpreting voice intonation. Middle Easterners tend to speak loudly to show sincerity and interest in the discussion, whereas Japanese people tend to speak softly to communicate politeness or humility. These different cultural norms regarding voice loudness may cause one person to misinterpret the other.

NONVERBAL DIFFERENCES

Nonverbal communication is more important in some cultures than in others. For example, people in Japan interpret more of a message's meaning from nonverbal cues. To avoid offending or embarrassing the receiver (particularly outsiders),

Japanese people will often say what the other person wants to hear (called *tatemae*) but send more subtle nonverbal cues indicating the sender's true feelings (called *honne*).[32] A Japanese colleague might politely reject your business proposal by saying "I will think about that" while sending nonverbal signals that he or she is not really interested. This difference explains why Japanese employees may prefer direct conversation to email and other media that lack nonverbal cues.

Many unconscious or involuntary nonverbal cues (such as smiling) have the same meaning around the world, but deliberate gestures often have different interpretations across cultures. For example, most of us shake our head from side to side to say "No," but a variation of head shaking means "I understand" to many people in India. Filipinos raise their eyebrows to give an affirmative answer, yet Arabs interpret this expression (along with clicking one's tongue) as a negative response. Most Canadians are taught to maintain eye contact with the speaker to show interest and respect, yet people in some First Nations groups, Australian Aborigines, among others learn at an early age to show respect by looking down when an older or more senior person is talking to them.[33]

Even the common handshake communicates different meaning across cultures. Westerners tend to appreciate a firm handshake as a sign of strength and warmth in a friendship or business relationship. In contrast, many Asians and Middle Easterners favour a loose grip and regard a firm clench as aggressive. Germans prefer one good handshake stroke, whereas anything less than five or six strokes may symbolize a lack of trust in Spain. If this isn't confusing enough, people from some cultures view any touching in public—including handshakes—as a sign of rudeness.

Silence and conversational overlaps   Communication includes silence, but its use and meaning varies from one culture to another.[34] A recent study estimated that silence and pauses represented 30 percent of conversation time between Japanese doctors and patients, compared to only 8 percent of the time between American doctors and patients. Why is there more silence in Japanese conversations? In Japan, silence symbolizes respect and indicates that the listener is thoughtfully contemplating what has just been said.[35] Empathy is also important in Japan, and this shared understanding is demonstrated without using words. In contrast, most people in Canada view silence as a *lack* of communication and often interpret long breaks as a sign of disagreement.

Conversational overlaps also send different messages in different cultures. Japanese people usually stop talking when they are interrupted, whereas talking over the other person's speech is more common in Brazil and some other countries. The difference in communication

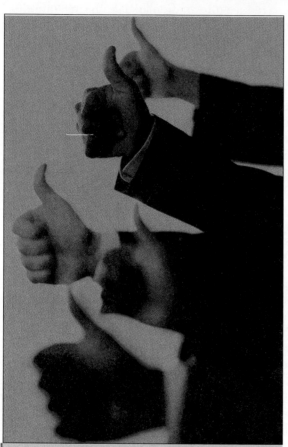

Thumbs-up for Cross-Cultural Communication
Patricia Oliveiri made several cultural adjustments when she moved from Brazil to Australia. One of the more humorous incidents occurred in the Melbourne office where she works. A co-worker would stick his thumbs up when asked about something, signalling that everything was OK. But the gesture had a totally different meaning to Oliveiri and other people from Brazil. "He asked me why I was laughing and I had to explain that in Brazil, that sign means something not very nice," recalls Oliveiri. "After that, everyone started doing it to the boss. It was really funny."[36] *M. M. Lawrence/Corbis*

behaviour is, again, due to interpretations. Talking while someone is speaking to you is considered quite rude in Japan, whereas Brazilians are more likely to interpret this as the person's interest and involvement in the conversation.

GENDER DIFFERENCES IN COMMUNICATION

After reading popular-press books on how men and women communicate, you might come to the conclusion that they are completely different life forms.[37] In reality, men and women have similar communication practices, but there are subtle distinctions that can occasionally lead to misunderstanding and conflict. One distinction is that men are more likely than women to view conversations as negotiations of relative status and power. They assert their power by directly giving advice to others (e.g., "You should do the following") and using combative language. There is also evidence that men dominate the talk time in conversations with women, as well as interrupt more and adjust their speaking style less than do women.[38]

Men tend to exert their status in conversation and engage in "report talk," in which the primary function of the conversation is impersonal and efficient information exchange. Women also engage in report talk, particularly when conversing with men, but conversations among women tend to have a higher incidence of relationship building through "rapport talk." Rather than asserting status, women use indirect requests such as "Have you considered . . . ?" Similarly, women apologize more often and seek advice from others more quickly than do men. Finally, research fairly consistently indicates that women are more sensitive than men to nonverbal cues in face-to-face meetings.[39]

Both men and women usually understand each other, but these subtle differences are occasional irritants. For instance, female scientists have complained that adversarial interaction among male scientists makes it difficult for women to participate in meaningful dialogue.[40] Another irritant occurs when women seek empathy but receive male dominance in response. Specifically, women sometimes discuss their personal experiences and problems to develop closeness with the receiver. But when men hear problems, they quickly suggest solutions because this asserts their control over the situation. As well as frustrating a woman's need for common understanding, the advice actually says: "You and I are different; you have the problem and I have the answer." Meanwhile, men become frustrated because they can't understand why women don't appreciate their advice.

■ IMPROVING INTERPERSONAL COMMUNICATION

Effective interpersonal communication depends on the sender's ability to get the message across and the receiver's performance as an active listener. In this section, we outline these two essential features of effective interpersonal communication.

GETTING YOUR MESSAGE ACROSS

This chapter began with the statement that effective communication occurs when the other person receives and understands the message. To accomplish this difficult task, the sender must learn to empathize with the receiver, repeat the message, choose an appropriate time for the conversation, and be descriptive rather than evaluative.

- ■ *Empathize*—Recall from earlier chapters that empathy is a person's ability to understand and be sensitive to the feelings, thoughts, and situation of others. In conversations, this involves putting yourself in the receiver's shoes when encoding the message. For instance, be sensitive to words that may be ambiguous or trigger the wrong emotional response.
- ■ *Repeat the message*—Rephrase the key points a couple of times. The saying "Tell them what you're going to tell them; tell them; then tell them what you've told them" reflects this need for redundancy.
- ■ *Use timing effectively*—Your message competes with other messages and noise, so find a time when the receiver is less likely to be distracted by these other matters.
- ■ *Be descriptive*—Focus on the problem, not the person, if you have negative information to convey. People stop listening when the information attacks their self-esteem. Also, suggest things the listener can do to improve, rather than point to him or her as a problem.

ACTIVE LISTENING

"Nature gave people two ears but only one tongue, which is a gentle hint that they should listen more than they talk."[41] Listening is a process of actively sensing the sender's signals, evaluating them accurately, and responding appropriately. These three components of listening—sensing, evaluating, and responding—reflect the listener's side of the communication model described at the beginning of this chapter. Listeners receive the sender's signals, decode them as intended, and provide appropriate and timely feedback to the sender (see Exhibit 11.4). Active listeners constantly cycle through sensing, evaluating, and responding during the conversation and engage in various activities to improve these processes.[42]

Sensing   Sensing is the process of receiving signals from the sender and paying attention to them. These signals include the words spoken, the nature of the sounds (speed of speech, tone of voice, etc.), and nonverbal cues. Active listeners improve sensing by postponing evaluation, avoiding interruptions, and maintaining interest.

■ **EXHIBIT 11.4**

Active listening process and strategies

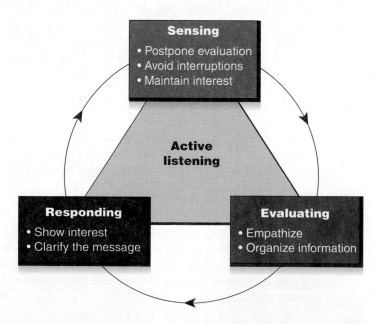

■ *Postpone evaluation*—Many listeners become victims of first impressions. They quickly form an opinion of the speaker's message and subsequently screen out important information. Active listeners, on the other hand, try to stay as open-minded as possible by delaying evaluation of the message until the speaker has finished.

■ *Avoid interruptions*—Interrupting the speaker's conversation has two negative effects on the sensing process. First, it disrupts the speaker's idea, so the listener does not receive the entire message. Second, interruptions tend to second-guess what the speaker is trying to say, which contributes to the problem of evaluating the speaker's ideas too early.

■ *Maintain interest*—As with any behaviour, active listening requires motivation. Too often, we close our minds soon after a conversation begins because the subject is boring. Instead, active listeners maintain interest by taking the view—probably an accurate one—that there is always something of value in a conversation; it's just a matter of actively looking for it.

Evaluating This component of listening includes understanding the message meaning, evaluating the message, and remembering the message. To improve their evaluation of the conversation, active listeners empathize with the speaker and organize information received during the conversation.

■ *Empathize*—Active listeners try to understand and be sensitive to the speaker's feelings, thoughts, and situation. Empathy is a critical skill in active listening because the verbal and nonverbal cues from the conversation are accurately interpreted from the other person's point of view.

■ *Organize information*—Listeners process information three times faster than the average rate of speech (450 words per minute versus 125 words per minute), so they are easily distracted. Active listeners use this spare time to organize the information into key points. In fact, it's a good idea to imagine that you must summarize what people have said after they are finished speaking.

Responding Responding, the third component of listening, is feedback to the sender, which motivates and directs the speaker's communication. Active listeners do this by showing interest and clarifying the message.

■ *Show interest*—Active listeners show interest by maintaining sufficient eye contact and sending back channel signals such as "Oh, really!" and "I see" during appropriate breaks in the conversation.

■ *Clarify the message*—Active listeners provide feedback by rephrasing the speaker's ideas at appropriate breaks ("So you're saying that . . . ?"). This further demonstrates interest in the conversation and helps the speaker determine whether you understand the message.

■ COMMUNICATING IN ORGANIZATIONAL HIERARCHIES

So far, we have focused on "micro-level" issues in the communication process, namely, the dynamics of sending and receiving information between two people in various situations. But in this era where knowledge is competitive advantage, corporate leaders also need to maintain an open flow of communication up, down,

Pixar Building Shapes Communication

Communication was a top priority when Pixar Animation
Studios designed its new campus in Emeryville, CA, a
few years ago. The animation company that created *The
Incredibles, Finding Nemo,* and other blockbuster films
created work area pods that isolate each team enough
that members have ongoing informal communication.
At the same time, the campus is designed such that
employees share knowledge through happenstance
interactions with people on other teams. Pixar executives call this the "bathroom effect," because team members must leave their isolated pods to fetch their mail,
have lunch, or visit the restroom. The building also invites
staff to mingle in the central airy atrium. "It promotes
that chance encounter," says Pixar creative director John
Lasseter. "You run into people constantly. It worked
from the minute we arrived. We just blossomed here."[46]
© Mike Kepka/The San Francisco Chronicle
www.pixar.com

and across the organization. In this section, we discuss
four organization-wide communication strategies: work
space design, e-zines/blogs/wikis, employee surveys,
and direct communication with top management.

WORKSPACE DESIGN

There's nothing like a wall to prevent employees from
talking to each other. "So often in offices, people are
stuck in little rabbit holes and you feel like you could be
the only one in the building," explains Peter Lanyon,
chairman of advertising firm Lanyon Phillips in Vancouver, B.C. To encourage more communication,
Lanyon's offices have adopted an open-space design. "In
this space, you can see from one end to the other. You
get the sense of being connected with other people."[43]
Do open-space offices actually improve communication?
Anecdotal evidence suggests that people do communicate more often with fewer walls between them.
However, research also suggests that open office
design potentially increases employee stress due to
the loss of privacy and personal space. According to an
analysis of 13,000 employee surveys in 40 major
organizations, the most important function of workspace is to provide a place to concentrate on work
without distraction. The second most important function is to support informal communication with co-
workers.[44] In other words, workspace needs to balance
privacy with opportunities for social interaction.

E-ZINES, BLOGS, AND WIKIS

For decades, employees have received official company
news through hard copy newsletters and magazines.
Many firms still use these communication devices, but
most have supplemented or replaced them completely
with Web-based information sources. Web-based elec-
tronic newsletters, called *e-zines*, are inexpensive and allow companies to post new
information quickly. However, information from e-zines tends to be brief because
many employees have difficulty reading long articles on a computer screen.[45]

The opening story to this chapter described how blogs are entering the corporate
world as another communication vehicle. Blogs written by senior executives potentially
replace e-zine information because they represent a more direct source to company
leaders and, if written casually, have a personal touch that makes them more credible
to employees. Executive blogs also allow employees to submit their comments, which
isn't possible in e-zines or newsletters. In addition to executive blogs, Matsushita
and a few other firms are turning to employee blogs in which people in a work unit
post updates of events in their area. *Wikis* are a collaborative variation of blogs in
which anyone in a group can write, edit, or remove material from the Web site.
Wikipedia, the popular online encyclopedia is a massive example of a wiki.

Although still rare in organizations, wikis might eventually generate a treasure trove of corporate knowledge that attracts employee attention for its collective wisdom and high involvement.[47]

EMPLOYEE SURVEYS

Most of Canada's "best" companies to work for conduct regular employee opinion surveys. Most of them survey employees to monitor worker morale, particularly as part of broader measures of corporate performance. For example, Bell Canada surveys its 60,000 employees each year using 84 questions on several themes, including career mobility, job challenge, information sharing, and trust in the company's leadership. Canada's largest telephone company also has quarterly "pulse surveys" that measure attitudes about specific policies, such as early retirement. These employee surveys have resulted in numerous corporate changes, such as switching from company-driven to flexible benefits.[48]

DIRECT COMMUNICATION WITH TOP MANAGEMENT

"The best fertilizer in any field is that of the farmer's footsteps!" This old Chinese saying means that farms are most successful when the farmers spend time in the fields directly observing the crop's development. In an organizational context, this means that senior executives need to get out of the executive suite and meet directly with employees at all levels and on their turf to fully understand the issues. Nearly 40 years ago, people at Hewlett-Packard coined a phrase for this communication strategy: **management by walking around (MBWA)**.[49] Greg Aasen, chief operating officer and co-founder of PMC-Sierra in Vancouver, does his MBWA by running with employees during lunch. "Even the senior guys I've worked with for 10 years, they tell you a lot more running out on the trails than they would in your office. It's less intimidating, I guess," says Aasen.[50]

Along with MBWA, executives are getting more direct communication with employees through "town hall meetings," where large groups of employees hear about a merger or other special news directly from the key decision makers. Others attend employee roundtable forums to hear opinions from a small representation of staff about various issues. All of these direct communication strategies potentially minimize filtering because executives listen directly to employees. They also help executives acquire a deeper meaning and quicker understanding of internal organizational problems. A third benefit of direct communication is that employees might have more empathy for decisions made further up the corporate hierarchy.

MBWA at Hiram Walker & Sons

Hiram Walker & Sons Ltd has a stately headquarters in Walkerville, Ontario, but CEO Ian Gourlay prefers to spend much of his time out and about. Chances are, you'll see Gourlay walking through the distillery, addressing a community reception, or attending meetings around the organization. Having the boss stop by the distillery is something of a novelty for its 400 staff. "They find that unusual, I don't," says Gourlay, who adds that employees are becoming accustomed to seeing him and learning about him. Hiram Walker employees are also discovering the benefits of a CEO who wanders around the workplace. "He sees what we're up against and what we're trying to do," says Gary Lajoie, plant superintendent of finished goods."[51] *Windsor Star*

■ COMMUNICATING THROUGH THE GRAPEVINE

No matter how much corporate leaders try to communicate through e-zines, blogs, MBWA, and other means, employees will still rely on the oldest communication channel: the corporate **grapevine**. The grapevine is an unstructured and informal network founded on social relationships rather than organizational charts or job descriptions. What do employees think about the grapevine? Surveys of employees in two U.S. firms—one in Florida, the other in California—provide the same answers. Both surveys found that almost all employees use the grapevine, but very few of these employees prefer this source of information. The California survey also reported that only one-third of employees believe grapevine information is credible. In other words, employees turn to the grapevine when they have few other options.[52]

GRAPEVINE CHARACTERISTICS

Research conducted several decades ago reported that the grapevine transmits information very rapidly in all directions throughout the organization. The typical pattern is a cluster chain, whereby a few people actively transmit rumours to many others. The grapevine works through informal social networks, so it is more active where employees have similar backgrounds and are able to communicate easily. Many rumours seem to have at least a kernel of truth, possibly because they are transmitted through media-rich communication channels (e.g., face to face) and employees are motivated to communicate effectively. Nevertheless, the grapevine distorts information by deleting fine details and exaggerating key points of the story.[53]

Some of these grapevine characteristics might still be true, but other features would have changed due to the dramatic effects of information technologies in the workplace. Email, instant messages, and now blogs have replaced the traditional water cooler as sources of gossip. Social networks have expanded as employees communicate with each other around the globe, not just around the next cubicle. Public blogs and Web forums have extended gossip to anyone, not just employees connected to social networks.

GRAPEVINE BENEFITS AND LIMITATIONS

Should the grapevine be encouraged, tolerated, or quashed? The difficulty in answering this question is that the grapevine has both benefits and limitations.[54] One benefit, as was mentioned earlier, is that employees rely on the grapevine when information is not available through formal channels. It is also the main conduit through which organizational stories and other symbols of the organization's culture are communicated. A third benefit of the grapevine is that this social interaction relieves anxiety. This explains why rumour mills are most active during times of uncertainty.[55] Finally, the grapevine is associated with the drive to bond. Being a recipient of gossip is a sign of inclusion, according to evolutionary psychologists. Trying to quash the grapevine is, in some respects, an attempt to undermine the natural human drive for social interaction.[56]

While the grapevine offers these benefits, it is not the preferred communication medium. Grapevine information is sometimes so distorted that it escalates rather than reduces employee anxiety. Furthermore, employees develop more negative attitudes toward the organization when management is slower than the grapevine in communicating information. What should corporate leaders do with the grapevine?

The best advice seems to be to listen to the grapevine as a signal of employee anxiety, then correct the cause of this anxiety. Some companies also listen to the grapevine and step in to correct blatant errors and fabrications. Most important, corporate leaders need to view the grapevine as a competitor, and eventually win the challenge to inform employees before they receive the news through the grapevine.

CHAPTER SUMMARY

Communication refers to the process by which information is transmitted and understood between two or more people. Communication supports work coordination, employee well-being, knowledge management, and decision making. The communication process involves forming, encoding, and transmitting the intended message to a receiver, who then decodes the message and provides feedback to the sender. Effective communication occurs when the sender's thoughts are transmitted to and understood by the intended receiver.

Electronic mail (email) is an increasingly popular way to communicate, and it has changed communication patterns in organizational settings. However, email is an ineffective channel for communicating emotions, tends to reduce politeness and respect, is an inefficient medium for communicating in ambiguous, complex, and novel situations, and contributes to information overload. Instant messaging, blogs, and podcasts are also gaining popularity in organizations.

Nonverbal communication includes facial gestures, voice intonation, physical distance, and even silence. Unlike verbal communication, nonverbal communication is less rule-bound and is mostly automatic and unconscious. Emotional contagion refers to the automatic and unconscious tendency to mimic and synchronize our nonverbal behaviours with other people. The most appropriate communication medium depends on its data-carrying capacity (media richness) and its symbolic meaning to the receiver. Nonroutine and ambiguous situations require rich media.

Several barriers create noise in the communication process. People misinterpret messages because of perceptual biases. Some information is filtered out as it gets passed up the hierarchy. Jargon and ambiguous language are barriers when the sender and receiver have different interpretations of the words and symbols used. People also screen out or misinterpret messages due to information overload.

Globalization and workforce diversity have brought new communication challenges. Words are easily misunderstood in verbal communication, either because the receiver has a limited vocabulary or the sender's accent distorts the usual sound of some words. Voice intonation, silence, and nonverbal cues have different meaning and importance in other cultures. There are also some communication differences between men and women, such as the tendency for men to exert status and engage in report talk in conversations, whereas women use more rapport talk and are more sensitive than are men to nonverbal cues.

To get a message across, the sender must learn to empathize with the receiver, repeat the message, choose an appropriate time for the conversation, and be descriptive rather than evaluative. Listening includes sensing, evaluating, and responding. Active listeners support these processes by postponing evaluation, avoiding interruptions, maintaining interest, empathizing, organizing information, showing interest, and clarifying the message.

Some companies try to encourage informal communication through workspace design, although open offices run the risk of increasing stress and reducing the ability to concentrate on work. Many larger organizations also rely on e-zines to communicate corporate news. Employee surveys are widely used to measure employee attitudes or involve employees in corporate decisions. Some executives also meet directly with employees, either through management by walking around or other arrangements, to facilitate communication across the organization.

In any organization, employees rely on the grapevine, particularly during times of uncertainty. The grapevine is an unstructured and informal network founded on social relationships rather than organizational charts or job descriptions. Although early research identified several unique features of the grapevine, some of these features may be changing as the Internet plays an increasing role in grapevine communication.

KEY TERMS

communication, p. 298
emotional contagion, p. 303
flaming, p. 300

grapevine, p. 316
information overload, p. 308
jargon, p. 307

management by walking around
  (MBWA), p. 315
media richness, p. 305

DISCUSSION QUESTIONS

1. A company in a country that is just entering the information age intends to introduce electronic mail for office staff at its three buildings located throughout the city. Describe two benefits as well as two potential problems that employees will likely experience with this medium.

2. Corporate and employee blogs might become increasingly popular over the next few years. What are the advantages and disadvantages of this communication medium?

3. Marshall McLuhan coined the popular phrase: "The medium is the message." What does this phrase mean, and why should we be aware of it when communicating in organizations?

4. Why is emotional contagion important in organizations and what effect does the increasing reliance of email have on this phenomenon?

5. Under what conditions, if any, do you think it is appropriate to use email to notify an employee that he or she has been laid off or fired? Why is email usually considered an inappropriate channel to convey this information?

6. Explain why men and women are sometimes frustrated with each other's communication behaviours.

7. In your opinion, has the introduction of email and other information technologies increased or decreased the amount of information flowing through the corporate grapevine? Explain your answer.

8. Wikis are collaborative Web sites where anyone in the group can post, edit, or delete any information. Where might this communication technology be most useful in organizations?

CASE STUDY 11.1

BRIDGING THE TWO WORLDS—THE ORGANIZATIONAL DILEMMA

By William Todorovic, Purdue University.

I had been hired by Aluminum Elements Corp. (AEC), and it was my first day of work. I was 26 years old, and I was now the manager of AEC's customer service group which looked after customers, logistics, and some of the raw material purchasing. My superior, George, was the vice-president of the company. AEC manufactured most of its products, a majority of which was destined for the construction industry, from aluminum.

As I walked around the shop floor, the employees appeared to be concentrating on their jobs, barely noticing me. Management held daily meetings, in which various production issues were discussed. No one from the shop floor was invited to these meetings, unless there was a specific problem. Later, I also learned that management had separate wash-rooms, separate lunchrooms as well as other perks that floor employees did not have. Most of the floor employees felt that management, although polite on the surface, did not really feel they had anything to learn from the floor employees.

John, who worked on the aluminum slitter, a crucial operation required before any other operations could commence, had a number of unpleasant encounters with George. As a result, George usually sent written memos to the floor in order to avoid a direct confrontation with John. Because the directions in the memos were complex, these memos were often more than two pages in length.

One morning, as I was walking around, I noticed that John was very upset. Feeling that perhaps there was something I could do, I approached

John and asked him if I could help. He indicated that everything was just fine. From the looks of the situation, and John's body language, I felt that he was willing to talk, but John knew that this was not the way things were done at AEC. Tony, who worked at the machine next to John's, then cursed and said that the office guys only cared about schedules, not about the people down on the floor. I just looked at him, and then said that I only began working here last week, and thought that I could address some of their issues. Tony gave me a strange look, shook his head, and went back to his machine. I could hear him still swearing as I left. Later I realized that most of the office staff were also offended by Tony's language.

On the way back to my office, Lesley, a recently hired engineer from Russia, approached me and pointed out that the employees were not accustomed to management talking to them. Management only issued orders, and made demands. As we discussed the different perceptions between office and floor staff, we were interrupted by a very loud lunch bell, which startled me. I was happy to join Lesley for lunch, but she asked me why I was not eating in the office lunch room. I replied that if I was going to understand how AEC worked, I had to get to know all the people better. In addition, I realized that this was not how things were done, and wondered about the nature of this apparent division between the management and the floor. In the lunchroom, the other workers were amazed to see me there, commenting that I was just new and had not learned the ropes yet.

After lunch, when I asked George, my supervisor, about his recent confrontation with John, George was surprised that John got upset, and exclaimed, "I just wanted John to know that he did a great job, and as a result, we will be able to ship on time one large order to the West Coast. In fact, I thought I was complimenting him."

Earlier, Lesley had indicated that certain behaviour was expected from management, and therefore from me. I reasoned that I do not think that this behaviour works, and besides it is not what I believe or how I care to behave. For the next couple of months, I simply walked around the floor and took every opportunity to talk to the shop floor employees. Often when the employees related specific information about their workplaces, I felt that it went over my head. Frequently I had to write down the information and re-

visit it later. I made a point of listening to them, identifying where they were coming from, and trying to understand them. I needed to keep my mind open to new ideas. Because the shop employees expected me to make requests and demands, I made a point of not doing any of that. Soon enough, the employees became friendly, and started to accept me as one of their own, or at least as a different type of a management person.

During my third month of work, the employees showed me how to improve the scheduling of jobs, especially those on the aluminum slitter. In fact, the greatest contribution was made by John who demonstrated better ways to combine the most common slitting sizes, and reduce waste by retaining some of the "common-sized" material for new orders. Seeing the opportunity, I programmed a spreadsheet to calculate and track inventory. This, in addition to better planning and forecasting allowed us to reduce our new order turnarounds from four to five weeks to in by 10 a.m. out by 5 p.m. on the same day.

By the time I was employed for four months, I realized that members from other departments came to me and asked me to relay messages to the shop employees. When I asked why they were delegating this task to me, they stated that I spoke the same language as the shop employees. Increasingly, I became the messenger for the office to floor shop communication.

One morning, George called me into his office and complimented me on the levels of customer service, and the improvements that have been achieved. As we talked, I mentioned that we could not have done it without John's help. "He really knows his stuff, and he is good," I said. I suggested that we consider him for some type of a promotion. Also, I hoped that this would be a positive gesture that would improve the communication between the office and shop floor.

George turned and pulled a flyer out of his desk; "Here is a management skills seminar. Do you think we should send John to it?"

"That is a great idea," I exclaimed, "Perhaps it would be good if he were to receive the news from you directly, George." George agreed, and after discussing some other issues, we departed company.

That afternoon, John came into my office, upset and ready to quit. "After all my effort and work, you guys are sending me for training seminars. So, am I not good enough for you?"

Discussion Questions

1. What barriers to effective communication existed in AEC Limited? How did the writer deal with these? What would you do differently?

2. Identify and discuss why John was upset at the end of the case. What do you recommend the writer should do at this time?

CASE STUDY 11.2

THE TROUBLE WITH ARTHUR

By Beth Gilbert, University of New Brunswick, St. John.

Arthur is a talented, smart, and energetic student in the co-op program of a Business faculty. He is involved in a variety of organizations, both on and off campus, and in many ways the co-op staff is proud to have him as one of their students. However, Arthur is constantly missing commitments, such as attendance at professional development seminars, classes, and networking sessions. In addition, although he is positive and outgoing, he is somewhat aggressive and expects accommodations to be made for him and other students. However, even some students are starting to become irritated with him. The proverbial "last straw" occurs when Arthur misses a job interview, which annoys the employer. Missing a job interview reflects badly on Arthur and on the entire program.

Numerous efforts at influencing Arthur's behaviour using traditional approaches, such as discussion, reasoning, positive reinforcement, coercion, and threats, have not been successful. Although the director is furious with Arthur (as she has been so many times in the past), she forces herself to sit down, reflect on the situation, and develop a plan. The director has been conducting research and teaching in the areas of emotional intelligence and effective communications for several years, and she considers herself to be reasonably skilled in these areas. However, after reflecting on her difficulties with Arthur, she realizes that she has not been applying the principles of these concepts to this sit-uation. Because Arthur contributes in many positive ways, the program does not want to lose him; but his missing commitments cannot be tolerated any longer. The director of the co-op program asks Arthur to come to her office to discuss the situation. Arthur arrives at the director's office and in "true Arthur style" pounds aggressively on the door. The director decides that she had better apply the concepts she had been researching. Clearly, the more traditional approaches have not been effective.

Discussion Questions

1. What are some possible reasons that the director of the co-op program has not used the principles of active listening and emotional intelligence, even though she had been doing research in the field and teaching it to students and managers?

2. Why do you think that the more traditional approaches have not been working? Why do you think that Arthur has been behaving as he has?

3. Why doesn't the director simply expel Arthur from the program?

4. How might the situation be improved if active listening and emotional intelligence are applied appropriately? Specifically, what might the director do? Discuss fully. Do you think that the director is likely to change Arthur's behaviour? What are the risks?

TEAM EXERCISE 11.3

ANALYZING THE BLOGOSPHERE

Purpose   This exercise is designed to help you understand the dynamics of corporate blogs as a way to communicate around organizations.

Instructions   This activity is usually conducted in between classes as a homework assignment. The instructor will divide the class into teams (although this can also be conducted as individuals). Each team will identify a corporate blog (written by a company or government executive and aimed for customers, employees, or the wider community). The team will

analyze content on the selected blog and answer the following questions for class (preferably with brief samples where applicable).

1. Who is the main intended audience of the selected blog?

2. To what extent do you think this blog attracts the interest of its intended audience? Explain.

3. What are the main topics in recent postings about this organization? Are they mostly good or bad news? Why?

TEAM EXERCISE 11.4

ACTIVE LISTENING EXERCISE

Mary Gander, Winona State University.

Purpose   This exercise is designed to help you understand the dynamics of active listening in conversations and to develop active listening skills.

Instructions   For each of the four vignettes presented below, student teams (or students working individually) will compose three statements that demonstrate active listening. Specifically, one statement will indicate that you show empathy for the situation; the second asks for clarification and detail in a nonjudgmental way; the third statement will provide nonevaluative feedback to the speaker. Here are details about each of these three types of responses:

■ *Showing empathy—acknowledge feelings.* Sometimes it sounds like the speaker wants you to agree with him/her but, in reality, they mainly want you to understand how they feel. "Acknowledging feelings" involves taking in their statements, but looking at the "whole message" including body language, tone of voice, and level of arousal, and trying to determine what emotion they are conveying. Then you let them know that you realize they are feeling that emotion by just acknowledging it in a sentence.

■ *Asking for clarification and detail while withholding your judgment and own opinions.* This conveys that you are making a good effort to understand and are not just trying to push your opinions onto them. To formulate a relevant question in asking for more clarification, you will have to listen carefully to what they say. Frame your question as someone trying to understand in more detail, often asking for a specific example is useful. This also helps the speaker evaluate their own opinions and perspective.

■ *Providing non-evaluative feedback—feeding back the message you heard.* This will allow the speaker to determine if he/she really got the message across to you and help prevent troublesome miscommunication. It will also help the speaker become more aware of how he/she is coming across to another person (self-evaluation). Just think about what the speaker is conveying and paraphrase it in your own words, and say it back to the speaker (without judging the correctness or merit of what they said), asking him/her if that is what they meant.

After teams (or individual students) have prepared the three statements for each vignette, the instructor will ask them to present their statements and explain how these statements satisfy the active listening criteria.

Vignette #1

A colleague stops by your desk and says, "I am tired of the lack of leadership around here. The boss is so wishy washy, he can't get tough with some of the slackers around here. They just keep milking the company, living off the rest of us. Why doesn't management do something about these guys? And YOU are always so supportive of the boss; he's not as good as you make him out to be."

Develop three statements that respond to the speaker in this vignette by: (a) showing empathy, (b) seeking clarification, and (c) providing non-evaluative feedback.

Vignette #2

Your co-worker stops by your cubicle, her voice and body language show stress, frustration, and even some fear. You know she has been working hard and has a strong need to get her work done on time and done well. You are trying to concentrate on some work and have had a number of interruptions already. She just abruptly interrupts you and says, "This project is turning out to be a mess, why can't the other three people on my team quit fighting each other?"

Develop three statements that respond to the speaker in this vignette by: (a) showing empathy, (b) seeking clarification, and (c) providing non-evaluative feedback.

Vignette #3

One of your subordinates is working on an important project. He is an engineer who has good technical skills and knowledge and was selected for the project team because of that. He stops by your office and appears to be quite agitated; his voice is loud and strained, and his face has a look of bewilderment. He says, "I'm supposed to be working with four other people from four other departments on this new project, but they never listen to my ideas and seem to hardly know I'm at the meeting!"

Develop three statements that respond to the speaker in this vignette by: (a) showing empathy, (b) seeking clarification, and (c) providing non-evaluative feedback.

Vignette #4

Your subordinate comes into your office in a state of agitation, and asks if she can talk to you. She is polite and sits down. She seems calm and does not have an angry look on her face. However, she says, "It seems like you consistently make up lousy schedules. You are unfair and unrealistic in the kinds of assignments you give certain people, me included. Everyone else is so intimidated they don't complain but I think you need to know that this isn't right and it's got to change."

Develop three statements that respond to the speaker in this vignette by: (a) showing empathy, (b) seeking clarification, and (c) providing non-evaluative feedback.

TEAM EXERCISE 11.5

CROSS-CULTURAL COMMUNICATION GAME

Purpose   This exercise is designed to develop and test your knowledge of cross-cultural differences in communication and etiquette.

Materials   The instructor will provide one set of question/answer cards to each pair of teams.

Instructions

- *Step 1:* The class is divided into an even number of teams. Ideally, each team would have three students. (Teams may have more or less than three students if matched with an equal-sized team.) Each team is then paired with another team and the paired teams (Team "A" and Team "B") are assigned a private space away from other matched teams.

- *Step 2:* The instructor will hand each pair of teams a stack of cards with the multiple choice questions face down. These cards have questions and answers about cross-cultural differences in communication and etiquette. No books or other aids are allowed.

- *Step 3:* The exercise begins with a member of Team A picking up one card from the top of the pile and asking the question on that card to the students on Team B. The information given to

Team B includes the question and all alternatives listed on the card. Team B has 30 seconds after the question and alternatives have been read to give an answer. Team B earns one point if the correct answer is given. If Team B's answer is incorrect, however, Team A earns that point. Correct answers to each question are indicated on the card and, of course, should not be revealed until the question is correctly answered or time is up. Whether or not Team B answers correctly, it picks up the next card on the pile and asks it to members of Team A. In other words, cards are read alternatively to each team. This procedure is repeated until all of the cards have been read or no time remains. The team receiving the most points wins.

Important note: The textbook provides very little information pertaining to the questions in this exercise. Rather, you must rely on past learning, logic, and luck to win.

Copyright © 2001 Steven L. McShane.

SELF-ASSESSMENT EXERCISE 11.6

ACTIVE LISTENING SKILLS INVENTORY

Purpose   This self-assessment is designed to help you estimate your strengths and weaknesses on various dimensions of active listening

Instructions   Think back to face-to-face conversations you have had with a co-worker or client in the office, hallway, factory floor, or other setting. Indicate the extent that each item below describes your behaviour during those conversations. Answer

each item as truthfully as possible so that you get an accurate estimate of where your active listening skills need improvement. Then use the scoring key in Appendix B to calculate your results for each scale. This exercise is completed alone so students assess themselves honestly without concerns of social comparison. However, class discussion will focus on the important elements of active listening.

ACTIVE LISTENING SKILLS INVENTORY

Circle the best response to the right that indicates the extent to which each statement describes you when listening to others.   **Score**

1. I keep an open mind about the speaker's point of view until he/she has finished talking	Not at all	A little	Somewhat	Very much	_____
2. While listening, I mentally sort out the speaker's ideas in a way that makes sense to me.	Not at all	A little	Somewhat	Very much	_____
3. I stop the speaker and give my opinion when I disagree with something he/she has said.	Not at all	A little	Somewhat	Very much	_____
4. People can often tell when I'm not concentrating on what they are saying.	Not at all	A little	Somewhat	Very much	_____
5. I don't evaluate what a person is saying until he/she has finished talking.	Not at all	A little	Somewhat	Very much	_____
6. When someone takes a long time to present a simple idea, I let my mind wander to other things.	Not at all	A little	Somewhat	Very much	_____
7. I jump into conversations to present my views rather than wait and risk forgetting what I wanted to say.	Not at all	A little	Somewhat	Very much	_____
8. I nod my head and make other gestures to show I'm interested in the conversation.	Not at all	A little	Somewhat	Very much	_____
9. I can usually keep focused on what people are saying to me even when they don't sound interesting.	Not at all	A little	Somewhat	Very much	_____
10. Rather than organizing the speaker's ideas, I usually expect the person to summarize them for me.	Not at all	A little	Somewhat	Very much	_____
11. I always say things like "I see" or "uh-huh" so people know that I'm really listening to them.	Not at all	A little	Somewhat	Very much	_____
12. While listening, I concentrate on what is being said and regularly organize the information.	Not at all	A little	Somewhat	Very much	_____
13. While the speaker is talking, I quickly determine whether I like or dislike his/her ideas.	Not at all	A little	Somewhat	Very much	_____
14. I pay close attention to what people are saying even when they are explaining something I already know.	Not at all	A little	Somewhat	Very much	_____
15. I don't give my opinion until I'm sure the other person has finished talking.	Not at all	A little	Somewhat	Very much	_____

After studying the preceding material, be sure to check out our Online Learning Centre at

www.mcgrawhill.ca/college/mcshane

for more in-depth information and interactivities that correspond to this chapter.

·12·

POWER AND INFLUENCE IN THE WORKPLACE

LEARNING OBJECTIVES

AFTER READING THIS CHAPTER, YOU SHOULD BE ABLE TO:

■ Define the meaning of power and counterpower.

■ Describe the five bases of power in organizations.

■ Explain how information relates to power in organizations.

■ Discuss the four contingencies of power.

■ Summarize the eight types of influence tactics.

■ Discuss three contingencies to consider when deciding which influence tactic to use.

■ Distinguish influence from organizational politics.

■ Describe the organizational conditions and personal characteristics that support organizational politics.

■ Identify ways to minimize organizational politics.

Edmonton-born Bernie Ebbers built WorldCom, Inc. (now MCI, Inc.) into one of the world's largest telecommunications firms. Yet he and chief financial officer (CFO) Scott Sullivan have become better known for creating a massive corporate accounting fraud that led to the largest bankruptcy in U.S. history. Two investigative reports and subsequent court cases concluded that WorldCom executives were responsible for billions in fraudulent or unsupported accounting entries. How did this mammoth accounting scandal occur without anyone raising the alarm? Evidence suggests that Ebbers and Sullivan held considerable power and influence that prevented accounting staff from complaining, or even knowing, about the fraud.

Ebbers's inner circle held tight control over the flow of all financial information. The geographically dispersed accounting groups were discouraged from sharing information. Ebbers's group also restricted distribution of company-level financial reports and prevented sensitive reports from being prepared at all. Accountants didn't even have access to the computer files where some of the largest fraudulent entries were made. As a result, employees had to rely on Ebbers's executive team to justify the accounting entries that were requested.

Another reason why employees complied with questionable accounting practices was that CFO Scott Sullivan wielded immense personal power. He was considered a "whiz kid" with impeccable integrity who had won the prestigious "CFO Excellence Award." Thus, when Sullivan's office asked staff to make questionable entries, some accountants assumed Sullivan had found an innovative—

Through excessive power and influence, former WorldCom CEO Bernard Ebbers (centre), Scott Sullivan (right), and other executives perpetrated one of the largest cases of accounting fraud in history. *AP Photo/Kenneth Lambert*

and legal—accounting loophole. If Sullivan's expert power didn't work, other executives took a more coercive approach. Employees cited incidents where they were publicly berated for questioning headquarters' decisions and intimidated if they asked for more information. When one employee at a branch refused to alter an accounting entry, WorldCom's controller threatened to fly in from WorldCom's Mississippi headquarters to make the change himself. The employee changed the entry.

Ebbers had similar influence over WorldCom's board of directors. Sources indicate that his personal charisma and intolerance of dissension produced a passive board that rubber-stamped most of his recommendations. As one report concluded: "The Board of Directors appears to have embraced suggestions by Mr. Ebbers without question or dissent, even under circumstances where its members now readily acknowledge they had significant misgivings regarding his recommended course of action."[1] ■

The WorldCom saga illustrates how power and influence can have profound consequences for employee behaviour and the organization's success. Although this story has an unhappy ending, power and influence can equally influence ethical conduct and improve corporate performance. The reality is that no one escapes from organizational power and influence. They exist in every business and, according to some writers, in every decision and action.

This chapter unfolds as follows: First, we define power and present a basic model depicting the dynamics of power in organizational settings. The chapter then discusses the five bases of power, as well as information as a power base. Next, we look at the contingencies necessary to translate those sources into meaningful power. The latter part of this chapter examines the various types of influence in organizational settings as well as the contingencies of effective influence strategies. The final section of this chapter looks at situations in which influence becomes organizational politics, as well as ways of minimizing dysfunctional politics.

■ THE MEANING OF POWER

power
The capacity of a person, team, or organization to influence others.

Power is the capacity of a person, team, or organization to influence others.[2] Power is not the act of changing others' attitudes or behaviour; it is only the potential to do so. People frequently have power they do not use; they might not even know they have power.

The most basic prerequisite of power is that one person or group believes it is dependent on another person or group for something of value.[3] This relationship is shown in Exhibit 12.1, where Person A has power over Person B by controlling something that Person B needs to achieve his or her goals. You might have power over others by controlling a desired job assignment, useful information, important resources, or even the privilege of being associated with you! To make matters more complex, power is ultimately a perception, so people might gain power simply by convincing others that they have something of value. Thus, power exists when others believe that you control resources that they want.[4]

counterpower
The capacity of a person, team, or organization to keep a more powerful person or group in the exchange relationship.

Although power requires dependence, it is really more accurate to say that the parties are interdependent. One party may be more dependent than the other, but the relationship exists only when each party has something of value to the other. Exhibit 12.1 shows a dashed line to illustrate the weaker party's (Person B's) power over the dominant participant (Person A). This **counterpower**, as it is known, is strong enough to maintain Person A's participation in the exchange relationship.

■ EXHIBIT 12.1

Dependence in the power relationship

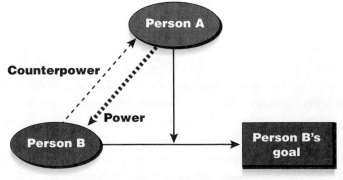

Courtesy of Rapid Phase Group, www.madameve.co.sa

For example, executives have power over subordinates by controlling their job security and promotional opportunities. At the same time, employees have counterpower by controlling the ability to work productively and thereby creating a positive impression of the supervisor to his or her boss. Counterpower usually motivates executives to apply their power judiciously, so that the relationship is not broken.

A MODEL OF POWER IN ORGANIZATIONS

Power involves more than just dependence. As we see in Exhibit 12.2, the model of power includes both power sources and contingencies. It indicates that power is derived from five sources: legitimate, reward, coercive, expert, and referent. The model also indicates that these sources yield power only under certain conditions. The four contingencies of power include the employee's or department's substitutability, centrality, discretion, and visibility. Finally, as we will discuss later, the type of power applied affects the type of influence the powerholder has over the other person or work unit.

■ SOURCES OF POWER IN ORGANIZATIONS

More than 40 years ago, social scientists John French and Bertrand Raven listed five sources of power within organizations: legitimate, reward, coercive, expert, and referent. Many researchers have studied these five power bases and searched for others. For the most part, French and Raven's list remains intact.[5] The first three power bases are derived from the powerholder's position; that is, the person receives these power bases because of the specific authority or roles he or she is assigned in the organization. The latter two sources of power originate from the powerholder's own characteristics. In other words, people bring these power bases to the organization.

legitimate power
The capacity to influence others through formal authority.

LEGITIMATE POWER

Legitimate power is an agreement among organizational members that people in certain roles can request certain behaviours of others. This perceived right partly comes from formal job descriptions as well as informal rules of conduct. Executives

It is largely a function of the person's interpersonal skills and usually develops slowly. Referent power is usually associated with charismatic leadership. *Charisma* is often defined as a form of interpersonal attraction whereby followers develop a respect for and trust in the charismatic individual.[11]

INFORMATION AND POWER

Information is power.[12] This phrase is increasingly relevant in a knowledge-based economy. Information power derives from either the legitimate or expert sources of power described above and exists in two forms: (1) control over the flow and interpretation of information given to others and (2) the perceived ability to cope with organizational uncertainties.

Control over information flow Not long ago, SAP, the German business-software company, introduced innovative ways for employees to receive the latest company news through their car radios, email newsletters, and intranet Web sites. SAP employees appreciated this direct communication, but the company's middle managers objected because it undermined their power as the gatekeepers of company information.[13] Previously, SAP's middle managers were communication "traffic cops." Their job was to distribute, regulate, and filter out information throughout the organizational hierarchy. This right to control information flow is a form of legitimate power and is most common in highly bureaucratic firms. The wheel formation in Exhibit 12.3 depicts this highly centralized control over information flow. In this communication structure, employees are dependent on the information gatekeeper in the middle of this configuration—such as the middle managers at SAP—to provide the information they require.

■ **EXHIBIT 12.3**

Power through the control of information

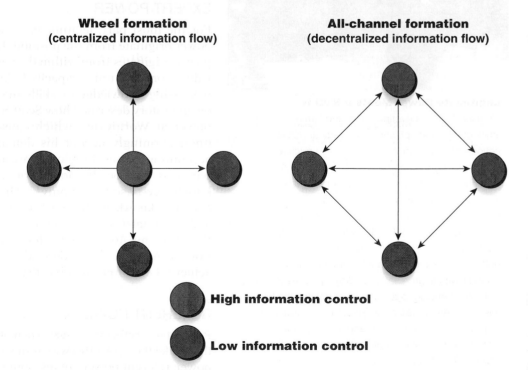

Wheel formation
(centralized information flow)

All-channel formation
(decentralized information flow)

High information control

Low information control

The problem facing these information gatekeepers is that this centralized information control structure is incompatible with knowledge management and high-performance work teams. Consequently, SAP and other organizations are encouraging more knowledge sharing by moving toward the all-channels communication structure (see Exhibit 12.3) in which all employees have relatively equal access to information. This allows employees and self-directed work teams to make better decisions. In its purest form, the all-channels network may seem chaotic, so large organizations with bureaucratic cultures tend to slip back into the wheel pattern. The wheel pattern also re-emerges because, as we saw at SAP, it confers more power on those who distribute the information.[14]

Coping with uncertainty   Organizations operate in changing environments, so they depend on information to reduce the uncertainty of future events. The more firms can cope with the uncertainty of future events, the more easily they can achieve their goals. Individuals and work units acquire power by helping the organization to cope with uncertainty. Coping includes any activity that effectively deals with environmental uncertainties affecting the organization. A groundbreaking study of Canadian breweries and container companies identified three general strategies to help organizations cope with uncertainty. These coping strategies are arranged in a hierarchy of importance, with the first being the most powerful:[15]

- *Prevention*—The most effective strategy is to prevent environmental changes from occurring. For example, financial experts acquire power by preventing the organization from experiencing a cash shortage or defaulting on loans.
- *Forecasting*—The next best strategy is to predict environmental changes or variations. In this respect, marketing specialists gain power by predicting changes in consumer preferences.
- *Absorption*—People and work units also gain power by absorbing or neutralizing the impact of environmental shifts as they occur. An example is the ability of maintenance crews to come to the rescue when machines break down and the production process stops.

CONTINGENCIES OF POWER

Let's say that you have expert power by virtue of your ability to forecast and possibly even prevent dramatic changes in the organization's environment. Does this expertise mean that you are influential? Not necessarily. As we saw earlier in Exhibit 12.2, power bases generate power only under certain conditions. The four conditions—called the contingencies of power—include substitutability, centrality, discretion, and visibility.[16] These are not sources of power; rather, they determine the extent to which people can leverage their power bases. You may have lots of expert power, but you won't be able to influence others with this power base if the contingency factors are not in place.

SUBSTITUTABILITY

substitutability
The extent to which people dependent on a resource have alternatives.

Substitutability refers to the availability of alternatives. Power is strongest when someone has a monopoly over a valued resource. Conversely, power decreases as the number of alternative sources of the critical resource increases. If only you have expertise across the organization on an important issue, you would be more powerful than if several people in your company possess this valued knowledge.

Substitutability refers not only to other sources that offer the resource, but also to substitutions of the resource itself. For instance, labour unions are weakened when companies introduce technologies that replace the need for their union members. At one time, a strike by telephone employees would have shut down operations, but computerized systems and other technological innovations now ensure that telephone operations continue during labour strikes and reduce the need for telephone operators during normal operations. Technology is a substitute for employees and, consequently, reduces union power.

How do people and work units increase their power through nonsubstitutability? There are several ways, although not all of them are ethical. We describe some of them here for your information—not necessarily for you to practice.

- *Controlling tasks*—Governments pass laws that give certain professions an exclusive right to perform particular tasks. As an example, most countries require publicly traded corporations to have their financial statements audited by a specific accounting group (certified public accountants, chartered accountants, etc.). The simmering conflict between medical doctors and nurse practitioners is also based around the exclusive rights of doctors to perform specific medical procedures that nurse practitioners want within their mandate.

- *Controlling knowledge*—Professions control access to the knowledge of their work domain, such as through restricted enrolment in educational programs. Knowledge is also restricted on the job. Several years ago, maintenance workers in a French tobacco processing plant had become very powerful because they controlled the knowledge required to repair the tobacco machines.[17] The maintenance manuals had mysteriously disappeared and the machines had been redesigned enough that only the maintenance staff knew how to fix them if they broke down (which they often did). Knowing the power of nonsubstitutability, maintenance staff carefully avoided documenting the repair procedures and didn't talk to production employees about their trade knowledge.

- *Controlling labour*—Aside from their knowledge resource, people gain power by controlling the availability of their labour. Labour unions attempt to organize as many people as possible within a particular trade or industry so that employers have no other source of labour supply. Unions have an easier time increasing wages when their members produce almost all of a particular product or service in the industry. The union's power during a strike is significantly weakened when the employer can continue production through outside contractors or other non-union facilities.

- *Differentiation*—Differentiation occurs when an individual or work unit claims to have a unique resource—such as raw materials or knowledge—that the organization would want. By definition, the uniqueness of this resource means that no one else has it. The tactic here isn't so much the non-substitutability of the resource, but making organizational leaders believe that the resource is unique. Some people claim that consultants use this tactic. They take skills and knowledge that many consulting firms can provide and wrap them into a package (with the latest buzz words, of course) so it looks like a service that no one else can offer.

CENTRALITY

centrality
The degree and nature of interdependence between the powerholder and others.

Centrality refers to the degree and nature of interdependence between the powerholder and others.[18] Airline pilots have high centrality because their actions affect many people and because their actions quickly affect other people. Think about your own centrality for a moment: If you decided not to show up for work or school tomorrow, how many people would be affected, and how much time would pass before they are affected? If you have high centrality, most people in the organization would be adversely affected by your absence, and they would be affected quickly.

DISCRETION

The freedom to exercise judgment—to make decisions without referring to a specific rule or receiving permission from someone else—is another important contingency of power in organizations. Consider the plight of first-line supervisors. It may seem that they have legitimate and reward power over employees, but this power is often curtailed by specific rules. This lack of discretion makes supervisors largely powerless even though they may have access to some of the power bases described earlier in this chapter. "Middle managers are very much 'piggy-in-the-middle,'" complains a middle manager at Britain's National Health System. "They have little power, only what senior managers are allowed to give them."[19]

The Scent of Centrality

Employees in the City of Toronto have a high degree of centrality, particularly in summer. This was quickly apparent a few summers ago when they decided to leverage their power by going on strike. Tourism and the recreation of city residents were immediately affected by closed public swimming pools and cancelled Toronto Islands ferry services. A planned visit by the Pope in mid-summer also put pressure on government officials to end the strike quickly. But the biggest factor was undoubtedly the stench of garbage that permeated throughout the city. Without garbage collection, illegal dumps sprung up, and the heat of summer made living in Toronto a nightmare to many residents. "I can smell this through two doors, air conditioning, cologne, and my own gym socks," quipped one resident, referring to the built up garbage on his street. "I thought there was nothing stinkier than my gym socks. I was really wrong."[22] *CP/Kevin Frayer*
www.toronto.ca

VISIBILITY

Several years ago as a junior copywriter at advertising agency Chiat/Day, Mimi Cook submitted an idea for a potential client to her boss, who then presented it to co-founder Jay Chiat. Chiat was thrilled with the concept, but Cook's boss "never mentioned the idea came from me," recalls Cook. Cook confronted her boss, who claimed the oversight was unintentional. But when a similar incident occurred a few months later, Cook left the agency for another firm.[20]

Mimi Cook, who has since progressed to associate creative director at another ad agency, knows that power does not flow to unknown people in the organization. Those who control valued resources or knowledge will yield power only when others are aware of these power bases, in other words, when it is visible. One way to increase visibility is to take people-oriented jobs and work on projects that require frequent interaction with senior executives. "You can take visibility in steps," advises a pharmaceutical executive. "You can start by making yourself visible in a small group, such as a staff meeting. Then when you're comfortable with that, seek out larger arenas."[21]

Employees also gain visibility by being, quite literally, visible. Some people strategically move into offices or cubicles where co-workers pass most often (such as closest to the elevator or office lunch room). Many professionals display their educational diplomas and awards on office walls to remind visitors of their expertise. Others spend more time at work and show that they are working productively. One engineer working on a colour laser printer project made a habit of going to the office once each week at 2 A.M., after her boss once saw her working at that hour. "After the reaction I got from my manager I decided it was important to do that early morning work in the office," explains the engineer. "It is better to be seen here if you are going to work in the middle of the night."[23]

mentoring
The process of learning the ropes of organizational life from a senior person within the company.

Another way to increase visibility is through **mentoring**—the process of learning the ropes of organizational life from a senior person within the company. Mentors give protégés more visible and meaningful work opportunities and open doors for them to meet more senior people in the organization. Mentors also teach these newcomers influence tactics supported by the organization's senior decision makers.[24]

NETWORKING AND POWER

"It's not what you know, but who you know that counts!" This often-heard statement reflects the reality that employees get ahead not just by developing their competencies, but by **networking**—cultivating social relationships with others to accomplish one's goals. Networking increases a person's power in three ways. First, networks represent a critical component of **social capital**—the knowledge and other resources available to people or social units (teams, organizations) due to a durable network that connects them to others. Networks consist of people who trust each other, which increases the flow of knowledge among those within the network. The more you network, the more likely you will receive valuable information that increases your expert power in the organization.[25]

networking
Cultivating social relationships with others to accomplish one's goals.

Second, people tend to identify more with partners within their own networks, which increases referent power among people within each network. This network-based referent power may lead to more favourable decisions by others in the network. Finally, effective networkers are better known by others in the organization, so their talents are more readily recognized. This power increases when networkers place themselves in strategic positions in the network, thereby gaining centrality.[26] For example, these people might play a central role in distributing information to others in the network.

social capital
The knowledge and other resources available to people or social units due to a durable network that connects them to others.

Networking is a natural part of the informal organization, yet it can create a formidable barrier to those who are not actively connected to it.[27] Women are often excluded from powerful networks because they do not participate in golf games and other male-dominated social events. That's what Deloitte and Touche executives discovered when they investigated why so many junior female employees left the accounting and consulting firm before reaching partnership level. Deloitte and Touche now relies on mentoring, formal women's network groups, and measurement of career progress to ensure that female staff members have the same career development opportunities as their male colleagues.[28] Meanwhile, as Connections 12.1 describes, an increasing number of people in the business world are taking up golfing as a way to increase their power through networking.

influence
Any behaviour that attempts to alter another person's attitudes or behaviour.

■ INFLUENCING OTHERS

Thus far, we have focused on the sources and contingencies of power. But power is only the *capacity* to influence others. It represents the potential to change someone's attitudes and behaviour. **Influence**, on the other hand, refers to any behav-

Networking on the Green

As a corporate road warrior, Jane Buckley knows that she needs to take more than her suitcase and computer on important business trips. The corporate director of strategic solutions for Compass Group, the Vancouver-based food services management provider, also carries one of the most important business tools: her golf clubs. "Our company cares who it does business with and likes to establish long-term relationships with clients," explains Buckley. "Golf is one way of establishing those personal connections."

Canadians play over 64 millions rounds of golf each year, and many of those sessions result in valuable business connections and deals. Men have traditionally done most of this networking, but women are now developing their golfing skills to assist their power and influence in organizations. "Women should be aware of where the networking is happening, and if they do feel that a lot of connections and networking with people are happening on the links, then by all means get involved with that," advises Sharon Crozier, director of the University of Calgary's Counselling & Student Development Centre.

Judith MacBride, director of human resources management research for the Conference Board of Canada, agrees. "We've heard so many times that a lot of business, a lot of networking and deal-making, gets done on the golf course," she says. The Conference Board of Canada's research indicates that many women feel their career success has been restricted because they are not on the golf course with their male colleagues. This is consistent with a U.S. survey reporting that almost 50 percent of women in senior executive positions say that exclusion from informal networks was a major barrier to the career advancement of women. More startling was

Jayne Buckley, an executive with Compass Group in Vancouver, travels with her golf clubs to support the power of networking with colleagues and clients. *C. Price, Vancouver Province*

that only 15 percent of male CEOs saw this as a problem. In other words, CEOs fail to see that networking is one of the main reasons why women are held back in their careers.

Sources: G. Teel, "The Ultimate Power Play for Sealing Deals," *Calgary Herald*, June 29, 2002; I. Bailey, "Golf 101: Put Down that Club, We're Making Deals over Here," *National Post*, September 27, 2001; T. Wanless, "Business and Golfing—Par for the Course," *Vancouver Province*, June 10, 2001; S.J. Wells, "Smoothing the Way," *HRMagazine* 46 (June 2001), pp. 52–58. **www.conferenceboard.ca**

iour that actually attempts to alter someone's attitudes or behaviour.[29] Influence is power in motion. It applies one or more power bases to get people to alter their beliefs, feelings, and activities. Consequently, our interest in the remainder of this chapter is on how people use power to influence others.

Influence tactics are woven throughout the social fabric of all organizations. This is because influence is an essential process through which people coordinate their effort and act in concert to achieve organizational objectives. Indeed, influence is central to the definition of leadership. Influence operates down, across, and up the corporate hierarchy. Executives ensure that subordinates complete required tasks. Employees influence co-workers to help them with their job requirements. Subordinates engage in upward influence tactics so corporate leaders make decisions compatible with subordinates' needs and expectations.

TYPES OF INFLUENCE TACTICS

Organizational behaviour researchers have devoted considerable attention to the various types of influence tactics found in organizational settings. Unfortunately, they do not agree on a definitive list of influence tactics. A groundbreaking study 25 years ago identified several influence strategies, but recent evidence suggests that some of them overlap.[30] The original list also seems to have a Western bias that ignores influence tactics used in non-Western cultures.[31] With these caveats in mind, let's look at the following influence tactics identified in the most recent literature (see Exhibit 12.4): silent authority, assertiveness, exchange, coalition formation, upward appeal, ingratiation and impression management, persuasion, and information control.

Silent authority   The silent application of authority occurs where someone complies with a request because of the requester's legitimate power as well as the target person's role expectations. We often refer to this condition as deference to authority.[32] This deference occurs when you comply with your boss's request to complete a particular task. If the task is within your job scope and your boss has the right to make this request, then this influence strategy operates without negotiation, threats, persuasion, or other tactics.

Silent authority is often overlooked as an influence strategy, but it is the most common form of influence in high power distance cultures. Employees comply with supervisor requests without question because they respect the supervisor's higher authority in the organization. Silent authority also occurs when leaders influence subordinates through role modelling. One study reported that Japanese managers typically influence subordinates by engaging in the behaviours that they want employees to mimic.[33]

■ **EXHIBIT 12.4**   Types of influence tactics in organizations

Influence Tactic	Description
Silent authority	Influencing behaviour through legitimate power without explicitly referring to that power base
Assertiveness	Actively applying legitimate and coercive power through pressure or threats
Exchange	Promising benefits or resources in exchange for the target person's compliance
Coalition formation	Forming a group that attempts to influence others by pooling the resources and power of its members
Upward appeal	Gaining support from one or more people with higher authority or expertise
Ingratiation/impression management	Attempting to increase liking by, or perceived similarity to, some targeted person
Persuasion	Using logical arguments, factual evidence, and emotional appeals to convince people of the value of a request
Information control	Explicitly manipulating someone else's access to information for the purpose of changing their attitudes and/or behaviour

Assertiveness   In contrast to silent authority, assertiveness might be called "vocal authority" because it involves actively applying legitimate and coercive power to influence others. Assertiveness includes persistently reminding the target of his or her obligations, frequently checking the target's work, confronting the target, and using threats of sanctions to force compliance. Assertiveness typically applies or threatens to apply punishment if the target does not comply. Explicit or implicit threats range from job loss to losing face by letting down the team. Extreme forms of assertiveness include blackmailing colleagues, such as by threatening to reveal the other person's previously unknown failures unless he or she complies with your request.

Exchange   Exchange activities involve the promise of benefits or resources in exchange for the target person's compliance with your request. This tactic also includes reminding the target of past benefits or favours with the expectation that the target will now make up for that debt. The norm of reciprocity is a central and explicit theme in exchange strategies. According to the norm of reciprocity, individuals are expected to help those who have helped them.[34] Negotiation, which we discuss more fully in Chapter 13, is also an integral part of exchange influence activities. For instance, you might negotiate your boss for a day off in return for working a less desirable shift at a future date. Networking is another form of exchange as an influence strategy. Active networkers build up "exchange credits" by helping colleagues in the short-term for reciprocal benefits in the long term.

   Networking as an influence strategy is a deeply ingrained practice in several cultures. The Chinese term *guanxi* refers to special relationships and active interpersonal connectedness. It is based on traditional Confucian values of helping others without expecting future repayment. However, modern guanxi seems to implicitly include long-term reciprocity, which can slip into cronyism. As a result, some Asian governments are discouraging guanxi-based decisions, preferring more arm's-length transactions in business and government decisions.[35] *Blat* is a Russian word that also refers to special relationships or connections. Unlike guanxi, however, blat was originally associated with survival during times of scarcity and continues to have a connotation of self-interest and possible illegality.[36]

coalition
A group that attempts to influence people outside the group by pooling the resources and power of its members.

Coalition formation   When people lack sufficient power alone to influence others in the organization, they might form a **coalition** of people who support the proposed change. A coalition is influential in three ways.[37] First, it pools the power and resources of many people, so the coalition potentially has more influence than any number of people operating alone. Second, the coalition's mere existence can be a source of power by symbolizing the legitimacy of the issue. In other words, a coalition creates a sense that the issue deserves attention because it has broad support. Third, coalitions tap into the power of the social identity process introduced in Chapter 3. A coalition is essentially an informal group that advocates a new set of norms and behaviours. If the coalition has a broad-based membership (i.e., its members come from various parts of the organization), then other employees are more likely to identify with that group and, consequently, accept the ideas the coalition is proposing.

upward appeal
A type of coalition in which one or more members is someone with higher authority or expertise.

Upward appeal   Have you ever had a disagreement with a colleague in which one of you eventually says "I'm sure the boss (or teacher) will agree with me on this. Let's find out!" This tactic—called **upward appeal**—is a form of coalition in which one or more members is someone with higher authority or expertise. Upward appeal ranges from a formal alliance to the perception of informal support from someone with higher authority or expertise. Upward appeal also includes relying on the authority of the firm as an entity without approaching anyone further up the hierarchy. For instance, one study reported that Japanese managers remind employees of their obligation to support the organization's objectives.[38] By reminding the target that your request is consistent with the organization's overarching goals, you are implying support from senior executives without formally involving anyone with higher authority in the situation.

Ingratiation and impression management   Upward appeals, assertiveness, and coalitions are somewhat (or very!) forceful ways to influence other people. At the opposite extreme is a "soft" influence tactic called **ingratiation**. Ingratiation includes any attempt to increase liking by, or perceived similarity to, some targeted person.[39] Flattering your boss in front of others, helping co-workers with their work, exhibiting similar attitudes (e.g., agreeing with your boss's proposal to change company policies), and seeking the other person's counsel (e.g., asking for his or her "expert" advice) are all examples of ingratiation. Collectively, ingratiation behaviours are better than most other forms of influence at predicting career success (performance appraisal feedback, salaries, and promotions).[40]

Ingratiation is potentially influential because it increases the perceived similarity of the source of ingratiation to the target person, which causes the target person to form more favourable opinions of the ingratiator. However, people who are obvious in their ingratiation risk losing any influence because their behaviours are considered insincere and self-serving. The terms "apple polishing" and "brown-nosing" are applied to those who ingratiate to excess or in ways that suggest selfish motives for the ingratiation. Sure enough, research indicates that people who engage in high levels of ingratiation are less (not more) influential and less likely to get promoted.[41]

Ingratiation is part of a larger influence tactic known as impression management. **Impression management** is the practice of actively shaping our public images.[42] These public images might be crafted as being important, vulnerable, threatening, or pleasant. For the most part, employees routinely engage in pleasant impression management behaviours to satisfy the basic norms of social behaviour, such as the way they dress and how they behave toward colleagues and customers. Impression management is a common strategy for people trying to get ahead in the workplace. For instance, almost all job applicants in a recent study relied on one or more types of impression management. An extreme example of impression management occurs when people pad their résumé. One study of 1.86 million background checks by a reference-checking firm revealed that about 25 percent of applicants falsify information about work experience and education. As with ingratiation, employees who use too much impression management tend to be less influential because their behaviours are viewed as insincere.[43]

Persuasion   Along with ingratiation, **persuasion** is one of the most effective influence strategies for career success. The ability to present facts, logical arguments, and emotional appeals to change another person's attitudes and behaviour is not just an acceptable way to influence others; in many societies, it is a noble art and a quality of effective leaders. The literature on influence strategies has typically described persuasion as the use of reason through factual evidence and logical arguments. However, recent studies have begun to adopt a "dual process" perspective in which

ingratiation
Any attempt to increase the extent to which a target person likes us or perceives that he or she is similar to us.

impression management
The practice of actively shaping our public image.

persuasion
Using logical arguments, facts, and emotional appeals to encourage people to accept a request or message.

persuasion is influenced by both the individual's emotional reaction and rational interpretation of incoming information.[44] Thus, persuasion is an attempt to convince people by using emotional appeals as well as factual evidence and logical arguments.

The effectiveness of persuasion as an influence tactic depends on characteristics of the persuader, message content, communication medium, and the audience being persuaded.[45] What makes one person more persuasive than another? One factor is the person's perceived expertise. Persuasion attempts are more successful when listeners believe the speaker is knowledgeable about the topic. People are also more persuasive when they demonstrate credibility, such as when the persuader does not seem to profit from the persuasion attempt and states a few points against the position.[46]

Message content is more important than the messenger when the issue is important to the audience. Persuasive message content acknowledges several points of view so the audience does not feel cornered by the speaker. The message should also be limited to a few strong arguments, which are repeated a few times, but not too frequently. The message content should use emotional appeals (such as graphically showing the unfortunate consequences of a bad decision), but only in combination with logical arguments so the audience doesn't feel manipulated. Also, emotional appeals should always be accompanied with specific recommendations to overcome the threat. Finally, message content is more persuasive when the audience is warned about opposing arguments. This **inoculation effect** causes listeners to generate counterarguments to the anticipated persuasion attempts, which makes the opponent's subsequent persuasion attempts less effective.[47]

Two other considerations when persuading people are the medium of communication and characteristics of the audience. Generally, persuasion works best in face-to-face conversations and through other media-rich communication channels. The personal nature of face-to-face communication increases the persuader's credibility, and the richness of this channel provides faster feedback that the influence strategy is working. With respect to audience characteristics, it is more difficult to persuade people who have high self-esteem and intelligence, as well as those whose targeted attitudes are strongly connected to their self-identity.[48]

Information control   Persuasion may involve selectively presenting information, whereas information control involves explicitly manipulating others' access to information for the purpose of changing their attitudes and/or behaviour. As described in the opening vignette for this chapter, this tactic was used by WorldCom's executive team to ensure that employees made illegal accounting entries. With limited access to vital information, accounting staff often did not realize

inoculation effect
A persuasive communication strategy of warning listeners that others will try to influence them in the future and that they should be wary about the opponent's arguments.

Steve Jobs' Reality Distortion Field
Wearing his trademark black turtleneck and faded blue jeans, Apple Computer co-founder and CEO Steve Jobs is famous for stirring up crowds with evangelical fervour as he draws them into his "reality distortion field." A reality distortion field occurs when people are caught in Steve Jobs' visionary headlights. Apple Computer manager Bud Tribble borrowed the phrase from the TV series *Star Trek* to describe Jobs' overwhelming persuasiveness. "In his presence, reality is malleable," Tribble explained to newly hired Andy Hertzfeld in 1981. "He [Steve Jobs] can convince anyone of practically anything. It wears off when he's not around, but it makes it hard to have realistic schedules." As one journalist wrote: "Drift too close to Jobs in the grip of one of his manias and you can get sucked in, like a wayward asteroid straying into Jupiter's gravitational zone."[49] *J. G. Mabanglo/Corbis*
www.apple.com

that the entries violated accounting rules. Even employees who were suspicious had to trust explanations from headquarters that any irregularities were corrected elsewhere in the organization.

The WorldCom story is an extreme example of information control, but this influence tactic is quite common. Almost half of employees in one major survey believe people keep their colleagues in the dark about work issues if it helps their own cause. Employees also influence executive decisions by screening out (filtering) information flowing up the hierarchy. Indeed, one recent study found that CEOs also influence their boards of directors by selectively feeding information to board members.[50]

CONSEQUENCES AND CONTINGENCIES OF INFLUENCE TACTICS

Now that we've covered the main strategies used to influence people, you are probably asking: Which influence tactics are best? The best way to answer this question is to identify the three ways that people react when others try to influence them: resistance, compliance, or commitment.[51] *Resistance* occurs when people or work units oppose the behaviour desired by the influencer and, consequently refuse, argue, or delay engaging in the behaviour. *Compliance* occurs when people are motivated to implement the influencer's request at a minimal level of effort and for purely instrumental reasons. Without external sources to prompt the desired behaviour, it would not occur. *Commitment* is the strongest form of influence, whereby people identify with the influencer's request and are highly motivated to implement it even when extrinsic sources of motivation are no longer present.

Research has found that people generally react more favourably to "soft" tactics such as friendly persuasion and subtle ingratiation than to "hard" tactics such as upward appeal and assertiveness (see Exhibit 12.5). Soft tactics rely on personal power bases (expert and referent power), which tend to build commitment to the influencer's request. For example, co-workers tend to "buy in" to your ideas when you apply moderate levels of ingratiation and impression management tactics or use persuasion based on expertise. In contrast, hard influence tactics rely on position power (legitimate, reward, and coercion), so they tend to produce compliance or, worse, resistance. Hard tactics also tend to undermine trust, which can hurt future relationships. For example, coalitions are often successful, but their effect may be limited when the group's forcefulness is threatening.[52]

Upward, downward, or lateral influence   Aside from the general preference for soft rather than hard tactics, the most appropriate influence strategy depends on a few contingencies. One consideration is whether the person being influenced is higher, lower, or at the same level in the organization. Employees have some legitimate power over their boss, but they may face adverse career consequences by being too assertive with this power. Similarly, it may be more acceptable for supervisors to control information access than for employees to control what information they distribute to co-workers and people at higher levels in the organization.

Influencer's power base   A second contingency is the influencer's power base. Those with expertise tend to be more successful using persuasion, whereas those with a strong legitimate power base are usually more successful applying silent authority.[53]

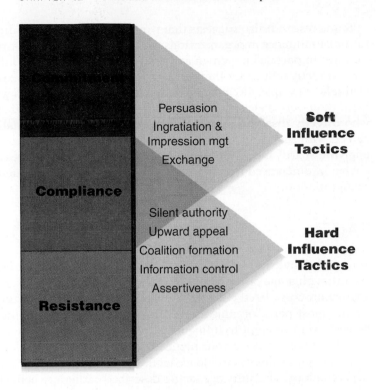

■ EXHIBIT 12.5

Consequences
of hard and soft
influence tactics

Compliance

Compliance

Resistance

Persuasion
Ingratiation &
Impression mgt
Exchange

**Soft
Influence
Tactics**

Silent authority
Upward appeal
Coalition formation
Information control
Assertiveness

**Hard
Influence
Tactics**

Personal and cultural values   Studies indicate that personal values guide our preference for some influence methods more than others.[54] The general trend in North America and elsewhere is toward softer influence tactics because younger employees tend to have more egalitarian values compared with those near retirement. As such, silent authority and assertiveness are tolerated less than they were a few decades ago. Acceptance of influence tactics also varies across cultures. Canadian and American managers and subordinates alike often rely on ingratiation because it minimizes conflict and supports a trusting relationship. In contrast, managers in Hong Kong and other high power distance cultures rely less on ingratiation, possibly because this tactic disrupts the more distant roles that managers and employees expect in these cultures. Instead, as we noted earlier, influence through exchange tends to be more common and accepted in Asian cultures than in Canada because of the importance of interpersonal relationships (guanxi).

GENDER DIFFERENCES IN INFLUENCE TACTICS

Men and women seem to differ in their use of influence tactics. Some writers say that men are more likely than women to rely on direct impression management tactics. Specifically, men tend to advertise their achievements and take personal credit for successes of others reporting to them, whereas women are more reluctant to force the spotlight on themselves, preferring instead to share the credit with others. At the same time, women are more likely to apologize—personally take blame—even for problems not caused by them. Men are more likely to assign blame and less likely to assume it.[55]

Some research also suggests that women generally have difficulty exerting some forms of influence in organizations, and this has limited their promotional opportunities. In particular, women are viewed as less (not more) influential when they try to directly influence others by exerting their authority or expertise. In job interviews, for example, direct and assertive female job applicants were less likely to be hired than were male applicants using the same influence tactics. Similarly, women who directly disagreed in conversations were less influential than women who agreed with the speaker.[56] These findings suggest that women may face problems applying "hard" influence tactics such as assertiveness. Instead, until stereotypes change, women need to rely on softer and more indirect influence strategies, such as ingratiation.

■ INFLUENCE TACTICS AND ORGANIZATIONAL POLITICS

You might have noticed that organizational politics has not been mentioned yet, even though some of the practices or examples described over the past few pages are usually considered political tactics. The phrase was carefully avoided because, for the most part, "organizational politics" is in the eye of the beholder. I might perceive your attempt to influence our boss as normal behaviour, whereas someone else might perceive your tactic as brazen organizational politics. This is why scholars mainly discuss influence tactics as behaviours and organizational politics as perceptions. The influence tactics described earlier are behaviours that might be considered organizational politics, or they might be considered normal behaviour. It all depends on the observer's perception of the situation.[57]

When are influence tactics perceived as **organizational politics**? Increasingly, OB researchers say that influence tactics are organizational politics when observers view the tactics are self-serving behaviours at the expense of others and sometimes contrary to the interests of the entire organization or work unit. Organizational politics is usually undesirable and, not surprisingly, has a number of negative effects on employees. People who believe their organization is steeped in organizational politics have lower job satisfaction, organizational commitment, and organizational citizenship, as well as high levels of work-related stress. Organizational politics also increases the incidence of "neglect" behaviours, such as reducing work effort, paying less attention to quality, and increasing absenteeism and lateness.[58]

organizational politics
Behaviours that others perceive as self-serving tactics for personal gain at the expense of other people and possibly the organization.

CONDITIONS SUPPORTING ORGANIZATIONAL POLITICS

Organizational politics flourishes under the right conditions.[59] One of those conditions is scarce resources. When budgets are slashed, people rely on political tactics to safeguard their resources and maintain the status quo. Office politics also flourishes when resource allocation decisions are ambiguous, complex, or lack formal rules. This occurs because decision makers are given more discretion over resource allocation, so potential recipients of those resources use political tactics to influence the factors that should be considered in the decision. Organizational change encourages political behaviours for this reason. Change creates uncertainty and ambiguity as the company moves from an old set of rules and practices to a new set. During these times, employees apply political strategies to protect their valued resources, position, and self-image.[60]

Organizational politics also becomes commonplace when it is tolerated and transparently supported by the organization.[61] Companies sometimes promote people who are the best politicians, not necessarily the best talent to run the company. If left unchecked, organizational politics can paralyze an organization as people focus more on protecting themselves than fulfilling their roles. Political activity becomes self-reinforcing unless the conditions supporting political behaviour are altered.

Personal characteristics   Several personal characteristics affect a person's motivation to engage in organizational politics.[62] Some people have a strong need for personal as opposed to socialized power. They seek power for its own sake and use political tactics to acquire more power. People with an internal locus of control are more likely than those with an external locus of control to engage in political behaviours. This does not mean that internals are naturally political; rather, they are more likely to use influence tactics when political conditions are present because, unlike externals, they feel very much in charge of their own destiny.

Some individuals have strong **Machiavellian values**. Machiavellianism is named after Niccolò Machiavelli, the sixteenth-century Italian philosopher who wrote *The Prince*, a famous treatise about political behaviour. People with high Machiavellian values are comfortable with getting more than they deserve, and they believe that deceit is a natural and acceptable way to achieve this goal. They seldom trust co-workers and tend to use cruder influence tactics, such as bypassing one's boss or being assertive, to get their own way.[63] GLOBAL Connections 12.2 describes how the rogue trader who operated National Australia Bank's foreign currency options desk in Melbourne, Australia, displayed Machiavellian characteristics, including rough assertiveness and controlling information.

Machiavellian values
The belief that deceit is a natural and acceptable way to influence others.

Minimizing organizational politics and its consequences   The conditions that fuel organizational politics also give us some clues about how to control dysfunctional political activities.[64] One strategy to keep organizational politics in check is to introduce clear rules and regulations to specify the use of scarce resources. Corporate leaders also need to actively support the all-channels communication structure described earlier in this chapter so that political employees do not misuse power through information control. As mentioned, organizational politics can become a problem during times of organizational change. Effective organizational change practices—particularly training and involvement—can minimize uncertainty and, consequently, politics during the change process.

Organizational politics is either supported or punished, depending on team norms and the organization's culture. Thus, leaders need to actively manage group norms to curtail self-serving influence activities. They also need to support organizational values that oppose political tactics, such as altruism and customer-focus. One of the most important strategies is for leaders to become role models of organizational citizenship rather than examples of successful organizational politicians.

Along with minimizing organizational politics, companies can limit the adverse effects of political perceptions by giving employees more control over their work and keeping them informed of organizational events. Research has found that employees who are kept informed of what is going on in the organization and who are involved in organizational decisions are less likely to experience stress, job dissatisfaction, and absenteeism as a result of organizational politics.

National Australia Bank's Rogue Trader's Machiavellian Tactics

For three long days, junior trader Dennis Gentilin received the cold shoulder from his boss, Luke Duffy. Duffy, who ran National Australia Bank's (NAB) foreign currency options desk in Melbourne, had discovered that Gentilin complained to Duffy's boss, Gary Dillon, that Duffy was altering transaction records to "smooth" his group's profits. Smoothing (which includes carrying forward trading losses) was apparently common at one time, but traders had recently been warned to stop the practice.

On the fourth day, Duffy called Gentilin into a private meeting and, according to Gentilin, launched into a tirade: "I felt like...killing someone the other day," Duffy said pointedly to Gentilin. "If you want to stay in the team, I demand loyalty and don't want you going to Dillon about what's happening in the team."

Duffy was apparently accustomed to getting his way. Gentilin explained that Duffy, Dillon, and a few other senior traders were "untouchables" who were given free rein at NAB due to their expertise. "They just created this power base where they were laws unto themselves," claims Gentilin.

Anyone who interfered with Duffy's plans was apparently mocked into submission. For example, Duffy taunted a co-worker in London who he thought was too skeptical and conservative. Duffy called him "the London stench boy" because he "was always making a stink about things whether they were going on both good and bad, and you could smell the stink coming from London," Duffy admitted in court.

Soon after his private meeting with Duffy, Gentilin was transferred to NAB's London office, still working in the foreign exchange group. Duffy's unit in Melbourne continued to fudge the numbers so upper management wouldn't notice any problems with the trading results. But when the group bet the wrong way against a rising Australian dollar, the cover-ups escalated, including creation of fictitious trades to offset the losses. The idea was that they could recover the losses and receive their cherished bonuses by year end.

Fatefully, Gentilin got wind of the problems from London, so he asked Vanessa McCallum, a junior NAB trader in Melbourne, to have other people look into Duffy's

National Australia Bank rogue trader Luke Duffy and his colleagues created losses of Cdn$330 million, thanks in part to Duffy's Machiavellian influence tactics.
© Craig Abraham/Fairfax Photos

transactions. McCallum later acknowledged that she was terrified about asking for the audit. "My greatest fear was, if nothing is wrong I'm going to have to leave the desk because you had to be loyal to Luke [Duffy]," explained McCallum, who no longer works at the bank.

What senior NAB executives discovered shook the Australian bank to its core. Duffy and other senior traders had become a rogue team that amassed Cdn$330 million in losses in one year. Their unrestrained power and influence kept everyone (except Gentilin and McCallum) in line, resulting in countless transaction record irregularities and over 800 breaches of the bank's trading limits. Duffy and a few other traders were jailed for securities violations. Several executives, including both NAB's chief executive and chairman, lost their jobs.

Sources: E. Johnston, "'Anything goes,' Ex-Trader Says," *Australian Financial Review,* August 2, 2005, p. 3; R. Gluyas, "Fear and Loathing in NABs Forex Fiasco," *The Australian,* August 6, 2005, p. 35; E. Johnston, "Expletives and Stench in Hothouse of NAB Dealers," *Australian Financial Review,* August 6, 2005, p. 3.
www.nabgroup.com

CHAPTER SUMMARY

Power is the capacity to influence others. It exists when one party perceives that he or she is dependent on the other for something of value. However, the dependent person must also have counterpower—some power over the dominant party—to maintain the relationship.

There are five power bases. Legitimate power is an agreement among organizational members that people in certain roles can request certain behaviours of others. Reward power is derived from the ability to control the allocation of rewards valued by others and to remove negative sanctions. Coercive power is the ability to apply punishment. Expert power is the capacity to influence others by possessing knowledge or skills that they value. People have referent power when others identify with them, like them, or otherwise respect them.

Information plays an important role in organizational power. Employees gain power by controlling the flow of information that others need and by being able to cope with uncertainties related to important organizational goals.

Four contingencies determine whether these power bases translate into real power. Individuals and work units are more powerful when they are non-substitutable, that is, there is a lack of alternatives. Employees, work units, and organizations reduce substitutability by controlling tasks, knowledge, and labour, and by differentiating themselves from competitors. A second contingency is centrality. People have more power when they have high centrality, that is, the number of people affected is large and people are quickly affected by their actions. Discretion, the third contingency of power, refers to the freedom to exercise judgment. Power increases when people have freedom to use their power. The fourth contingency, visibility, refers to the idea that power increases to the extent that a person's or work unit's competencies are known to others.

Networking involves cultivating social relationships with others to accomplish one's goals. This activity increases an individual's expert and referent power as well as visibility and possibly centrality. However, networking can limit opportunities for people outside the network, as many women in senior management positions have discovered.

Influence refers to any behaviour that attempts to alter someone's attitudes or behaviour. Influence operates down, across, and up the corporate hierarchy, applies one or more power bases, and is an essential process through which people achieve organizational objectives. The most widely studied influence tactics are silent authority (influence through passive application of legitimate power), assertiveness (actively applying legitimate and coercive power), exchange (promising benefits or resources in exchange for compliance), coalition formation (a group formed to support a particular change), upward appeal (a coalition in which one or more members is someone with higher authority or expertise), ingratiation (any attempt to increase liking by, or perceived similarity to, some targeted person) and impression management (actively shaping our public images), persuasion (using logical arguments, factual evidence, and emotional appeals to convince people), and information control (explicitly manipulating access to information).

"Soft" influence tactics such as friendly persuasion and subtle ingratiation are more acceptable than "hard" tactics such as upward appeal and assertiveness. However, the most appropriate influence tactic also depends on the influencer's power base; whether the person being influenced is higher, lower, or at the same level in the organization; and personal and cultural values regarding influence behaviour.

Organizational politics refers to influence tactics that others perceive to be self-serving behaviours at the expense of others and sometimes contrary to the interests of the entire organization or work unit. Organizational politics is more prevalent when scarce resources are allocated using complex and ambiguous decisions and when the organization tolerates or rewards political behaviour. Individuals with a high need for personal power, an internal locus of control, and strong Machiavellian values have a higher propensity to use political tactics.

Organizational politics can be minimized by providing clear rules for resource allocation, establishing a free flow of information, using education and involvement during organizational change, supporting team norms and a corporate culture that discourage dysfunctional politics, and having leaders who role model organizational citizenship rather than political savvy.

KEY TERMS

centrality, p. 334

coalition, p. 339

counterpower, p. 328

impression management, p. 340

influence, p. 336

ingratiation, p. 340

inoculation effect, p. 341

legitimate power, p. 329

Machiavellian values, p. 345

mentoring, p. 336

networking, p. 336

organizational politics, p. 344

persuasion, p. 340

power, p. 328

referent power, p. 331

social capital, p. 336

substitutability, p. 333

upward appeal, p. 339

DISCUSSION QUESTIONS

1. What role does counterpower play in the power relationship? Give an example of your own encounter with counterpower at school or work.

2. Several years ago, the major league baseball players association went on strike in September, just before the World Series started. The players' contract expired in the springtime, but they held off the strike until September when they would lose only one-sixth of their salaries. In contrast, a September strike would hurt the owners financially because they earn a larger portion of their revenue during the playoffs. As one player explained: "If we strike next spring, there's nothing stopping [the club owners] from letting us go until next June or July because they don't have that much at stake." Use your knowledge of the sources and contingencies of power to explain why the baseball players association had more power in negotiations by walking out in September rather than March.

3. You have just been hired as a brand manager of toothpaste for a large consumer products company. Your job mainly involves encouraging the advertising and production groups to promote and manufacture your product more effectively. These departments aren't under your direct authority, although company procedures indicate that they must complete certain tasks requested by brand managers. Describe the sources of power you can use to ensure that the advertising and production departments will help you make and sell toothpaste more effectively.

4. How does networking increase a person's power? What networking strategies could you initiate now to potentially enhance your future career success?

5. List the eight influence tactics described in this chapter in terms of how they are used by students to influence university or college instructors. Which influence tactic is applied most often? Which is applied least often, in your opinion? To what extent is each influence tactic considered legitimate behaviour or organizational politics?

6. How do cultural differences affect the following influence factors: (a) silent authority and (b) upward appeal?

7. A few years ago, the CEO of Apple Computer invited Steve Jobs (who was not associated with the company at the time) to serve as a special adviser and raise morale among Apple employees and customers. While doing this, Jobs spent more time advising the CEO on how to cut costs, redraw the organization chart, and hire new people. Before long, most of the top people at Apple were Jobs's colleagues, who began to systematically evaluate and weed out teams of Apple employees. While publicly supporting Apple's CEO, Jobs privately criticized him and, in a show of nonconfidence, sold 1.5 million shares of Apple stock he had received. This action caught the attention of Apple's board of directors, who soon after decided to replace the CEO with Steve Jobs. The CEO claimed Jobs was a conniving backstabber who used political tactics to get his way. Others suggest that Apple would be out of business today if Jobs hadn't taken over the company. In your opinion, were Steve Jobs's actions examples of organizational politics? Justify your answer.

8. This book frequently emphasizes that successful companies engage in knowledge management. How do political tactics interfere with knowledge management objectives?

CASE STUDY 12.1

RHONDA CLARK: TAKING CHARGE AT THE SMITH FOUNDATION

By Joseph C. Santora, Essex County College & TST, Inc.

Dr. Rhonda Clark was ecstatic as she hung up the telephone. Bennett Mitchell, chairperson of KLS Executive Search firm, had just informed her that she landed the coveted position of chief executive officer (CEO) at the Smith Foundation, a nonprofit organization whose mission was to fund public awareness campaigns and research programs about eye care. Clark knew that she had just pulled off a major coup. Her appointment to this new, challenging position would indeed be the high point in a long arduous climb to the executive suite. As an organizational outsider—one with no work experience within the hiring organization—she assumed that her appointment as CEO signalled a strong desire by the board to shake up the organizational status quo. However, she heard from a very reliable inside source that the very board that hired her and charged her with the responsibility of transforming the foundation was extremely fragmented. The often rambunctious board had forced the last five CEOs to resign after very short tenures. Clark's feeling of exhilaration was rapidly being replaced by cautious optimism. As a new CEO, she pondered the rather thorny question: how could she take charge of the board of directors to ensure the mission of the organization would be accomplished?

Background

Charlie Smith, an industrialist and philanthropist, founded the Smith Foundation 40 years ago with a multimillion-dollar endowment. Despite this generous financial startup capital and additional income derived from several financial investments and major corporate donations, in recent years, the foundation's endowment has been slowly dwindling as a result of rather significant funding awards to academics, community organizations, and smaller, less well-funded foundations. Board members have held some preliminary discussions about developing new innovative strategies to strengthen the balance sheet of the organization. Currently, the foundation operates on an annual budget of slightly less than US$1.5 million.

In the last five years, some foundation board members have begun to abandon many of their fiduciary responsibilities. Over the past few months, several board meetings have been cancelled because the meetings lacked a quorum. In general, this 13-member board seemed to drift aimlessly in one direction or another. The board has been operating at only 70 percent capacity for the past two years with nine active board members—five men and four women.

Challenges

Dr. Rhonda Clark believed she was the one who could lead the Smith Foundation. She had great academic credentials and management experience that would help her tackle her new position as the foundation head. In the last 30 years, the 54-year-old Clark, who holds a Ph.D. in political science and policy analysis from a major U.S. west coast university, has gained an enviable amount of managerial experience in the non-profit and public sectors. Past professional experiences included a graduate school professorship; a director of research for a major statewide political office holder, the director of planning in a large metropolitan hospital, and the director of programs at a small foundation.

Immediately upon taking office, Clark was astounded to learn that a small, but active and influential faction on the board, had withdrawn its initial verbal promise to assist her in working closely with the corporate community. Essentially, she was informed that she was solely responsible for all external corporate relations. Clark thought to herself, "I wonder if they hired me because they thought they would get a 'do-nothing' female leader. These folks want me to either sink or swim on my own. Perhaps they set me up for failure by giving me a one-year appointment." She lamented: "I won't let this happen. I really need to learn about the key decision makers and stakeholders on the board and in the larger community, and fast."

At the last board meeting Clark detailed the major elements of her latest proposal. Yet, several board members seemed totally unfazed by it. Soon she began to encounter stiff resistance from some male board members. Jim Jackson, in particular, told Clark: "We are disappointed that you failed to win a city contract to conduct a feasibility study to determine if we can erect a facility in another section of town. We're not certain if you have the right stuff to run this foundation, and we certainly won't help you to gain financial support for the foundation by using our personal, corporate, or political contacts." Jackson thought to himself: "We've removed CEOs before, we can remove Clark, too."

After hearing Jackson's comments Clark decided to take another tack. She began to focus her attention on making external and internal inroads that she believed could result in some modest gains for the foundation. For example, she identified and developed a close relationship with a few well-connected city agency executives, persuaded some supporters to nominate her for membership on two very influential boards, and forged a relationship with two key foundation decision makers and political power brokers. She reconfigured the internal structure of the foundation to increase maximum productivity from the staff, and she tightened budgetary controls by changing some fiscal policies and procedures.

Clark also sought the support of Susan Frost, a board member who likely had been instrumental in Clark's appointment as CEO. Clark said to herself, "If I can develop a strong symbiotic relationship with some female board members, like Sue, to support my plan, then maybe I can get some traction." To do this, Clark held a number of late evening meetings with Sue and another female board member. They indicated their willingness to help her, but only if she would consider implementing a few of their ideas for the foundation as well as recommending their close friend for a current staff vacancy. Clark knew they were trying to exercise their political influence; yet, she believed that everyone could benefit from this quid quo pro relationship. She said to herself "I guess it's a matter of you scratch my back, and I scratch yours." She eagerly agreed to move their agenda along. In a matter of a few weeks, as promised, they began working on a couple of relatively "sympathetic" board members. One day Clark got a very terse, but critical telephone call from Sue. "Several of us support you. Proceed!"

Once she heard this, Clark began to move at lightening speed. She formed a 15-member coalition of community, educational, and quasi-governmental agencies that would apply for a collaborative federal grant to create a public awareness eye campaign for children. Through the dissemination of various media, coalition members would help to inform the community-at-large about various eye diseases that afflict young school age children. Shortly afterwards, Clark received notification from a federal agency that this multi-agency project would be awarded a million-dollar grant. Clark would serve as the administrative and fiscal agent of the grant, and as a result, she would be able to earmark a considerable amount of the administrative oversight dollars for the foundation's budget. For her efforts at coordinating this project, Clark received high marks from coalition and community members alike.

Yet, despite this important initial accomplishment, Clark had the unpleasant task of notifying the full board that, due to some unforeseen problems and their lack of support on certain key initiatives, the foundation would still experience a financial deficit. She heard several rumours that her next employment contract would not be renewed by the executive committee of the board. At this point she thought about directly confronting the obstructionists on the board by telling them that they were unreasonable and in fact that they were the cause the foundation had not recovered during the past year ... but she hesitated: she had signed on to do a job, and she was unsure if it was the wisest course of action to take at this time.

Despite this latest conflict between herself and certain board members, she paused to reflect on what she believed to have been a tumultuous year as CEO.

Discussion Questions

1. Does Clark have any sources of power and any contingencies of power? If so, list and discuss them.

2. To what degree were Clark's methods of influencing board members the most effective possible under the circumstances presented in the case?

3. Do you think her methods to get things done at the foundation were ethical? Why or why not?

NB. The names and some managerial actions in this case have been altered to preserve the integrity and anonymity of the organization. This case is intended to be used as a basis for class discussion rather than to illustrate either effective or ineffective handling of a management situation.

Source: © Joseph C. Santora. Joseph C. Santora, Essex County College & TST, Inc.

TEAM EXERCISE 12.2

BUDGET DELIBERATIONS

By Sharon Card.

Purpose This exercise is designed to help you understand some of the power dynamics and influence tactics that occur across hierarchical levels in organizations.

Materials This activity works best where one small room leads to a larger room, which leads to a larger area.

Instructions These exercise instructions are based on a class size of about 30 students. The instructor may adjust the size of the first two groups slightly for larger classes. The instructor will organize students as follows: A few (three to four) students are assigned the position of executives. They are preferably located in a secluded office or corner of a large classroom. Another six to eight students are assigned positions as middle managers. These people will ideally be located in an adjoining room or space, allowing privacy for the executives. The remaining students represent the non-management employees in the organization. They are located in an open area outside the executive and management rooms.

Rules Members of the executive group are free to enter the space of either the middle management or non-management groups and to communicate whatever they wish, whenever they wish. Members of the middle management group may enter the space of the non-management group whenever they wish, but must request permission to enter the executive group's space. The executive group can refuse the middle management group's request.

Members of the non-management group are not allowed to disturb the top group in any way unless specifically invited by members of the executive group. The non-management group does have the right to request permission to communicate with the middle management group. The middle management group can refuse the lower group's request.

Task Your organization is in the process of preparing a budget. The challenge is to balance needs with the financial resources. Of course, the needs are greater than the resources. The instructor will distribute a budget sheet showing a list of budget requests and their costs. Each group has control over a portion of the budget and must decide how to spend the money over which they have control. Non-management has discretion over a relatively small portion and the executive group has discretion over the greatest portion. The exercise is finished when the organization has negotiated a satisfactory budget, or until the instructor calls time out. The class will then debrief with the following questions and others the instructor might ask.

Discussion Questions

1. What can we learn from this exercise about power in organizational hierarchies?

2. How is this exercise similar to relations in real organizations?

3. How did students in each group feel about the amount of power they held?

4. How did they exercise their power in relations with the other groups?

UPWARD INFLUENCE SCALE

Purpose This exercise is designed to help you understand several ways of influencing people up the organizational hierarchy as well as estimate your preferred upward influence tactics.

Instructions Read each of the statements below and circle the response that you believe best indicates how often you engaged in that behaviour over the past six months. Then use the scoring key in Appendix B to calculate your results. This exercise is completed alone so students assess themselves honestly without concerns of social comparison. However, class discussion will focus on the types of influence in organizations and the conditions under which particular influence tactics are most and least appropriate.

UPWARD INFLUENCE SCALE

How often in the past six months have you engaged in the behaviours?	Never ▼	Seldom ▼	Occasionally ▼	Frequently ▼	Almost Always ▼
1. I obtain the support of my co-workers in persuading my manager to act on my request.	1	2	3	4	5
2. I offer an exchange in which I will do something that my manager wants if he or she will do what I want.	1	2	3	4	5
3. I act very humble and polite while making my request.	1	2	3	4	5
4. I appeal to higher management to put pressure on my manager.	1	2	3	4	5
5. I remind my manager of how I have helped him or her in the past and imply that now I expect compliance with my request.	1	2	3	4	5
6. I go out of my way to make my manager feel good about me, before asking him or her to do what I want.	1	2	3	4	5
7. I use logical arguments in order to convince my manager.	1	2	3	4	5
8. I have a face-to-face confrontation with my manager in which I forcefully state what I want.	1	2	3	4	5
9. I act in a friendly manner toward my manager before making my request.	1	2	3	4	5
10. I present facts, figures, and other information to my manager in support of my position.	1	2	3	4	5

(continued)

UPWARD INFLUENCE SCALE (continued)					
How often in the past six months have you engaged in the behaviours?	Never ▼	Seldom ▼	Occasionally ▼	Frequently ▼	Almost Always ▼
11. I obtain the support and cooperation of my subordinates to back up my request.	1	2	3	4	5
12. I obtain the informal support of higher management to back me.	1	2	3	4	5
13. I offer to make a personal sacrifice such as giving up my free time if my manager will do what I want.	1	2	3	4	5
14. I very carefully explain to my manager the reasons for my request.	1	2	3	4	5
15. I verbally express my anger to my manager in order to get what I want.	1	2	3	4	5
16. I use a forceful manner. I try such things as making demands, setting deadlines, and expressing strong emotion.	1	2	3	4	5
17. I rely on the chain of command—on people higher up in the organization who have power over my supervisor.	1	2	3	4	5
18. I mobilize other people in the organization to help me in influencing my supervisor.	1	2	3	4	5

Source: C. Schriesheim and T. Hinkin, "Influence Tactics Used by Subordinates: A Theoretical and Empirical Analysis and Refinement of the Kipnis, Schmidt, and Wilkinson subscales," *Journal of Applied Psychology*, 75 (1990), pp. 246–57

S E L F - A S S E S S M E N T   E X E R C I S E   **12.4**

GUANXI ORIENTATION SCALE

Go to the Online Learning Centre to complete this interactive self-assessment.

Guanxi, which is translated as *interpersonal connections*, is an important element of doing business in China and some other Asian countries with strong Confucian cultural values. Guanxi is based on traditional Confucian values of helping others without expecting future repayment. This instrument estimates your guanxi orientation; that is, the extent to which you accept and apply guanxi values. This self-assessment is completed alone so that students rate themselves honestly without concerns of social comparison. However, class discussion will focus on the meaning of guanxi and its relevance for organizational power and influence.

SELF-ASSESSMENT EXERCISE   12.5

MACHIAVELLIANISM SCALE

Go to the Online Learning Centre to complete this interactive self-assessment.

Machiavellianism is named after Niccolò Machiavelli, the sixteenth-century Italian philosopher who wrote *The Prince*, a famous treatise about political behaviour. Out of Machiavelli's work emerged this instrument that estimates the degree to which you have a Machiavellian personality. Indicate the extent to which you agree or disagree that each statement in this instrument describes you. Complete each item honestly to get the best estimate of your level of Machiavellianism.

SELF-ASSESSMENT EXERCISE   12.6

PERCEPTIONS OF POLITICS SCALE (POPS)

Go to the Online Learning Centre to complete this interactive self-assessment.

Organizations have been called "political arenas"—environments where political tactics are common because decisions are ambiguous and resources are scarce. This instrument estimates the degree to which you believe the school where you attend classes has a politicized culture. This scale consists of several statements that might or might not describe the school where you are attending classes. These statements refer to the administration of the school, not the classroom. Please indicate the extent to which you agree or disagree with each statement.

Online LearningCentre with POWERWEB

After studying the preceding material, be sure to check out our Online Learning Centre at

www.mcgrawhill.ca/college/mcshane

for more in-depth information and interactivities that correspond to this chapter.

·13·

CONFLICT AND NEGOTIATION IN THE WORKPLACE

LEARNING OBJECTIVES

AFTER READING THIS CHAPTER, YOU SHOULD BE ABLE TO:

■ Outline the conflict process.

■ Distinguish constructive from socioemotional conflict.

■ Discuss the advantages and disadvantages of conflict in organizations.

■ Identify six sources of organizational conflict.

■ Outline the five interpersonal styles of conflict management.

■ Summarize six structural approaches to managing conflict.

■ Outline four situational influences on negotiations.

■ Compare and contrast the three types of third-party dispute resolution.

Its advertisements say "the future is friendly," but TELUS management and union leaders have been feuding ever since TELUS (formerly Alberta-based AGT) merged with B.C. Telecom nearly five years ago to become Canada's second largest telecommunications company. After more than 200 negotiation meetings, TELUS management imposed its final contract offer, which triggered a series of strikes and lockouts across both provinces.

The union says the dispute is about protecting jobs. "This company wants to be able to contract out any job they want," warns Bruce Bell, president of the Telecommunications Workers Union (TWU) that represents 13,000 TELUS employees. TELUS management claims that it will not outsource core jobs, but neither does it want to sign a contract that makes it less competitive in the deregulated telecom environment. "What the union wants is a contract based in the 1950s, when B.C. Tel was a monopoly," argues TELUS vice-president Bruce Okabe.

Managers and staff who crossed the picket line Tuesday show support for TELUS.
Calgary Herald/Jenelle Schneider

The strong rhetoric is one obvious sign of the deep divide and strong emotional conflict between the two sides. Even with coaching from one of Canada's top public relations firms, TELUS management hurled a few stinging barbs. "The union has done one thing very well, and that's cast fear, doubt and uncertainty," claims TELUS corporate affairs vice-president Drew McArthur.

TELUS management has infuriated union leaders by luring employees back to work with financial incentives and free iPod digital music players (allegedly to drown out the jeers from striking co-workers when employees cross the picket line each day). The company also blocked a union Web site that criticized employees who crossed the picket line. The TWU also escalated the conflict by launching a radio ad campaign urging customers to drop TELUS services or switch to rival providers.

Along with the management-union battle, the dispute reveals a deep division between employees in B.C. and Alberta who previously worked at AGT (later renamed TELUS). A few weeks after the strike began, almost all B.C. staff remained off the job, whereas up to 50 percent of them in Alberta had crossed the picket lines. In fact, a rally of striking workers at the company's Calgary offices was overwhelmed when 500 TELUS employees and managers came out of those offices wearing TELUS jerseys and waving signs supporting the company's contract offer.

The conflict residual effect after the strike ends is yet another major concern. "It's going to be poisonous for a while," warns Rob King, a TELUS Web designer in Edmonton. "It's going to be very difficult for those who have crossed and those who stayed out."[1] ∎
www.telus.ca

conflict

The process in which one party perceives that its interests are being opposed or negatively affected by another party.

The TELUS dispute may be somewhat unusual in that it is based on drawn-out negotiations over nearly five years, but it illustrates several dimensions of conflict that we will learn about in this chapter. **Conflict** is a process in which one party perceives that its interests are being opposed or negatively affected by another party.[2] TELUS management believes that the union leaders threaten the company's survival, whereas the union leaders consider management's actions a serious threat to its members and, ultimately, its own survival as an organization. This chapter looks at the dynamics of conflict in organizational settings. We begin by describing the conflict process and discussing the consequences and sources of conflict in organizational settings. Five conflict management styles are then described, followed by a discussion of the structural approaches to conflict management. The last two sections of this chapter introduce two procedures for resolving conflict: negotiation and third-party resolution.

■ THE CONFLICT PROCESS

When describing an incident involving conflict, we are usually referring to the observable part of conflict—the angry words, shouting matches, and actions that symbolize opposition. But this manifest conflict is only a small part of the conflict process. As Exhibit 13.1 illustrates, the conflict process begins with the sources of conflict.[3] Incompatible goals, different values, and other conditions lead one or both parties to perceive that conflict exists. We will look closely at these sources of conflict later in this chapter because understanding and changing them is the key to effective conflict management.

CONFLICT PERCEPTIONS AND EMOTIONS

At some point, the sources of conflict lead one or both parties to perceive that conflict exists. They become aware that one party's statements and actions are incompatible with their own goals. These perceptions usually interact with emotions experienced about the conflict. The TELUS dispute is riddled with emotions, such as when angry strikers jeer at iPod-wearing co-workers who cross the picket line, and TELUS management complain that strikers have deliberately disrupted service and threatened the safety of employees who returned to work.

■ **EXHIBIT 13.1**   The conflict process

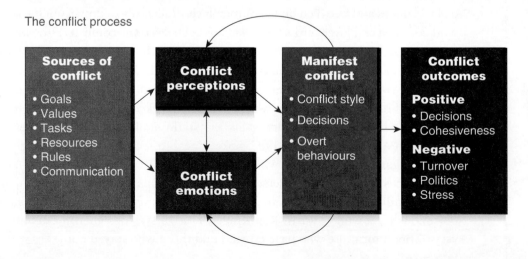

MANIFEST CONFLICT

Conflict perceptions and emotions usually manifest themselves in the decisions and overt behaviours of one party toward the other. These conflict episodes may range from subtle nonverbal behaviours to warlike aggression. Particularly when people experience high levels of conflict emotions, they have difficulty finding the words and expressions that communicate effectively without further irritating the relationship.[4] Conflict is also manifested by the style each side uses to resolve the conflict. Some people tend to avoid the conflict whereas others try to defeat those with opposing views. Conflict management styles will be described later in this chapter. At this point, you should know that these styles influence the other party's perceptions and actions regarding the conflict, which then either diffuses or further escalates the conflict.

Conflict escalation cycle The conflict process in Exhibit 13.1 shows arrows looping back from manifest conflict to conflict perceptions and emotions. These loops represent the fact that the conflict process is really a series of episodes that potentially link in an escalation cycle or spiral.[5] It doesn't take much to start this conflict cycle—just an inappropriate comment, a misunderstanding, or action that lacks diplomacy. These behaviours communicate to the other party in a way that creates a perception of conflict. If the first party did not intend to demonstrate conflict, then the second party's response may create that perception.

If the conflict remains focused on perceptions, both parties can often resolve the conflict through logical analysis. However, the communication process has enough ambiguity that a wrong look or word may trigger strong emotions and set the stage for further conflict escalation. These distorted beliefs and emotions reduce each side's motivation to communicate, making it more difficult for them to discover common ground and ultimately resolve the conflict. The parties then rely more on stereotypes and emotions to reinforce their perceptions of the other party. Some structural conditions increase the likelihood of conflict escalation. Employees who are more confrontational and less diplomatic also tend to escalate conflict.[6]

CONFLICT OUTCOMES

Recent events at TELUS illustrates some of the dysfunctional consequences of conflict: verbal barbs from both parties, management actions that have questionable benefits for stakeholders, and possibly sabotage of equipment and customer relations by a few wayward strikers. Even in nonstrike situations, employees are distracted from their work by internal feuds and engage in dysfunctional behaviours such as withholding valuable knowledge and other resources. Ongoing conflict also increases stress and turnover, while reducing organizational commitment and job satisfaction. At the intergroup level, conflict with people outside the team may cause the team to become more insular—increasing their cohesiveness while distancing themselves from outsiders who are critical of the team's past decisions.[7]

Given these problems, it's not surprising that people normally associate **conflict management** with reducing or removing conflict. However, conflict management refers to interventions that alter the level and form of conflict in ways that maximize its benefits and minimize its dysfunctional consequences. This sometimes means increasing the level of **constructive conflict** (also known as *task-related conflict*).[8] Recall from Chapter 10 that constructive conflict occurs when team members debate their different perceptions about an issue in a way that keeps the conflict focused on the task rather than people. This form of conflict tests the logic

conflict management

Interventions that alter the level and form of conflict in ways that maximize its benefits and minimize its dysfunctional consequences.

constructive conflict

Any situation where people debate their different opinions about an issue in a way that keeps the conflict focused on the task rather than on people.

of arguments and encourages participants to re-examine their basic assumptions about the problem and its possible solution.

The challenge is to engage in constructive conflict without having it escalate into **socioemotional conflict** (also known as *relationship conflict*). When socioemotional conflict dominates, differences are viewed as personal attacks rather than attempts to resolve an issue. The parties become defensive and competitive toward each other, which motivates them to reduce communication and information sharing. Once again, the model nicely reflects events at TELUS.

socioemotional conflict
Any situation where people view their differences as personal attacks rather than attempts to resolve an issue.

Minimizing socioemotional conflict   The solution here seems obvious: encourage constructive conflict for better decision making and minimize socioemotional conflict in order to avoid dysfunctional emotions and behaviours. Sounds good in theory, but recent evidence suggests that separating these two types of conflict isn't easy. Most of us experience some degree of socioemotional conflict during or after any constructive debate.[9] In other words, it is difficult to suppress defensive emotions when trying to resolve conflicts calmly and rationally. Fortunately, conflict management experts have identified three strategies that might reduce the level of socioemotional conflict during constructive conflict episodes.[10]

- *Emotional intelligence.* Socioemotional conflict is less likely to occur, or is less likely to escalate, when team members have high levels of emotional intelligence. Emotionally intelligent employees are better able to regulate their emotions during debate, which reduces the risk of escalating perceptions of interpersonal hostility. People with high emotional intelligence are also more likely to view a co-worker's emotional reaction as valuable information about that person's needs and expectations, rather than as a personal attack.

- *Cohesive team.* Socioemotional conflict is suppressed when the conflict occurs within a highly cohesive team. The longer people work together, get to know each other, and develop mutual trust with each other, the more latitude they give to each other to show emotions without being personally offended. Strong cohesion also allows each person to know about and anticipate the behaviours and emotions of their teammates. Another benefit is that cohesion produces a stronger social identity with the group, so team members are motivated to avoid escalating socioemotional conflict that might damage team relations.

- *Supportive team norms.* Various team norms can hold socioemotional conflict at bay during constructive debate. When team norms encourage openness, for instance, team members learn to appreciate honest dialogue without personally reacting to any emotional display during the disagreements. Other norms might discourage team members from displaying negative emotions toward co-workers. Team norms also encourage tactics that diffuse socioemotional conflict when it first appears. For instance, research has found that teams with low socioemotional conflict use humour to maintain positive group emotions, which offsets negative feelings team members might develop toward some co-workers during debate.

■ SOURCES OF CONFLICT IN ORGANIZATIONS

Manifest conflict is really the tip of the proverbial iceberg. What we really need to understand are the sources of this conflict, which lie under the surface. The six main conditions that cause conflict in organizational settings are shown in Exhibit 13.2.

■ **EXHIBIT 13.2**

Sources of conflict
in organizations

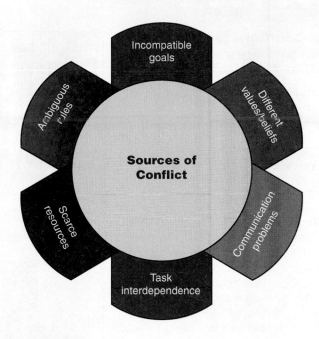

INCOMPATIBLE GOALS

A common source of conflict is goal incompatibility.[11] Goal incompatibility occurs when personal or work goals seem to interfere with another person's or department's goals. This source of conflict is apparent in the opening story. Union leaders representing TELUS employees fear that management plans to undermine their goals of maintaining job security for members as well as union dues levels for the union's financial survival. These fears were reinforced when TELUS management acquired a call centre in the Philippines and imposed a contract that did not explicitly promise job security. At the same time, TELUS management believes the union's actions will undermine its goals of making the company more competitive against low-cost rivals entering the market. Management's fears were reinforced when the union paid for radio advertisements for customers to abandon TELUS, and when Bell Canada started a marketing campaign in Western Canada to attract customers soon after the TELUS strike began.

Incompatible goals is also the main source of conflict between the original Air Canada pilots and the pilots who previously worked at Canadian Airlines (which Air Canada acquired a few years ago). As Connections 13.1 describes, pilots in each group want to receive the highest possible seniority to improve their career and job status. But if the former Canadian Airlines pilots get their wish to have seniority levels comparable to their previous jobs, then many Air Canada pilots will have relatively lower seniority, resulting in lower salaries and less desirable duties. The preference of Air Canada pilots is to deny any seniority to the former Canadian Airlines pilots. This battle has produced considerable manifest conflict, including fistfights on the buses taking pilots to work! The point here is that people with divergent goals are more likely to experience conflict.

DIFFERENTIATION

Not long ago, a British automotive company proposed a friendly buyout of an Italian firm. Executives at both companies were excited about the opportunities for

Midair Conflicts for Air Canada and Former Canadian Airlines Pilots

For the first two years after Air Canada acquired its arch rival Canadian Airlines International (CAI), a solid wall divided pilots from the two airlines. One door at Toronto's Pearson International Airport led to the large crew room where the 2,400 Air Canada pilots prepare for their flights. Another door further up the hallway led to a much smaller room for the 1,200 former CAI pilots.

The physical wall dividing the two rooms was probably knocked down when Air Canada scheduled the two pilot groups to work in the same cockpits, but the psychological wall of conflict is as strong as ever. "There will always be a wall there in our eyes," admits Robert Cohen, a former CAI first officer with 13 years of experience. "We will not mingle with those people and the feeling is mutual. They [Air Canada pilots] don't even want us in their system. It's evident."

The conflict between the two pilot groups isn't due to their past rivalries; it's due to a much more important feud over seniority rights. Many Air Canada pilots believe the CAI pilots should be placed at the bottom of the seniority list because they would have had no seniority if Air Canada hadn't rescued CAI from bankruptcy. CAI pilots, on the other hand, believe they are entitled to the same rights and seniority because the two airlines merged. The outcome is critical because seniority determines what aircraft and routes pilots fly as well as their days off, vacation, pay, and pensions. "For a pilot, seniority is everything," says Peter Foster, spokesman for the Air Canada Pilots Association.

The two pilot groups tried to negotiate a single seniority list, but the effort failed after one day. A subsequent arbitration decision discounted the seniority of CAI pilots by an average of more than nine years, which outraged the CAI pilots. A federal labour board later agreed with CAI pilots and a subsequent arbitration decision favoured the former CAI pilots. The reverse decision angered the Air Canada pilots, many of whom have formed a grouped called the "Original Air Canada" pilots.

The pilots' battle over seniority is so severe that it scuttled Air Canada's recent $7-billion deal to purchase several dozen next-generation aircraft from Boeing. Original Air Canada pilots campaigned to reject the deal so Air Canada would agree to change the seniority list again. "[The vote] was our last chance to get our voice heard, to have fairness brought to this," explained Glen Phillips, who represents the Original Air Canada pilots. The disgruntled pilots succeeded in rejecting the proposal, effectively cancelling the competitively priced Boeing contract. A few days later, they sent out emails

Conflict between Air Canada pilots and former Canadian Airlines pilots has created tension and ill feelings as they battle over seniority rights. *CP/Ryan Remiorz*

encouraging co-workers to delay flights as a further protest against the seniority list.

Former CAI pilots were quick to condemn these tactics. "The vote, in our opinion, was hijacked by a vocal minority of Original Air Canada pilots who were not satisfied with the pilot seniority list," announced Capt. Rob McInnis, who has served as leader for the former CAI pilots. "The hijackers' behaviour reflects badly on the maturity and professional image of all Air Canada pilots."

Sources: S. Pigg, "Air Canada: An Airline Divided, *Toronto Star*, June 2, 2001, p. E1; A. Swift, "Pilots for Air Canada, Canadian Airlines Begin Campaign for One Union," *Canadian Press*, January 6, 2001; S. Pigg, "Panel to Review Pilots' Seniority," *Toronto Star*, June 27, 2003, p. E1; B. Jang, "Air Canada Pilots Strafe Each Other Over Seniority," *The Globe & Mail*, June 24, 2005, p. B4; S. Erwin, "Disgruntled Air Canada Pilots to Meet with Feds over Seniority Concerns," *Canadian Press*, June 24, 2005; "Some Air Canada Pilots Threatening Flight Delays: Letter," CBC News, June 27, 2005.
www.acpa.ca

sharing distribution channels and manufacturing technologies. But the grand vision of a merged company turned to a nightmare as executives began meeting over the details. Their backgrounds and experiences were so different that they were endlessly confused and constantly apologizing to the other side for oversights and misunderstandings. At one meeting—the last as it turned out—the president of the Italian firm stood up and, smiling sadly, said, "I believe we all know what is the problem here . . . it seems your forward is our reverse; your down, our up; your right, our wrong. Let us finish now, before war is declared."[12]

These automobile executives discovered that conflict is often caused by different values and beliefs due to unique backgrounds, experiences, or training. Mergers often produce conflict because they bring together people with divergent corporate cultures. Employees fight over the "right way" to do things because of their unique experiences in the separate companies. The British and Italian automobile executives probably also experienced conflict due to their different national cultures. Cultural diversity makes it difficult to understand or accept the beliefs and values that other people hold toward organizational decisions and events.

Along with conflict generated from cultural diversity, many companies are experiencing the rising incidence of cross-generational conflict.[13] Younger and older employees have different needs, different expectations, and somewhat different values, which sometimes produces conflicting preferences and actions. Generational gaps have always existed, but this source of conflict is more common today because employees across age groups work together more than ever before. Virtual teams represent a third area where conflict is amplified due to differentiation. Recent investigations indicate that virtual teams have a high incidence of conflict because, in addition to increased cultural diversity, they have more difficulty than face-to-face (co-located) teams at establishing common mental models, norms, and temporal rhythms.[14]

TASK INTERDEPENDENCE

Conflict tends to increase with the level of task interdependence. Task interdependence exists when team members must share common inputs to their individual tasks, need to interact in the process of executing their work, or receive outcomes (such as rewards) that are partly determined by the performance of others. The higher the level of task interdependence, the greater the risk of conflict, because there is a greater chance that each side will disrupt or interfere with the other side's goals.[15]

Other than complete independence, employees tend to have the lowest risk of conflict when working with others in a pooled interdependence relationship. Pooled interdependence occurs where individuals operate independently except for reliance on a common resource or authority (see Chapter 9). The potential for conflict is higher in sequential interdependence work relationships, such as an assembly line. The highest risk of conflict tends to occur in reciprocal interdependence situations. With reciprocal interdependence, employees are highly dependent on each other and, consequently, have a higher probability of interfering with each other's work and personal goals.

SCARCE RESOURCES

Resource scarcity generates conflict because higher scarcity reduces the ability of each person to fulfill his or her goals without undermining others. TELUS management does not believe it can guarantee job security sufficiently to write that promise in the collective agreement, yet failing to do so interferes with the union's needs to ensure security to its members. If the competitive environment gave the company a plentiful supply of customers for the future, this dispute would have been far less likely to occur.

AMBIGUOUS RULES

Ambiguous rules—or the complete lack of rules—breed conflict. This occurs because uncertainty increases the risk that one party intends to interfere with the other party's goals. Ambiguity also encourages political tactics and, in some cases, employees enter a free-for-all battle to win decisions in their favour. This explains why conflict is more common during mergers and acquisitions. Employees from both companies have conflicting practices and values, and few rules have developed to minimize the manoeuvring for power and resources.[16] When clear rules exist, on the other hand, employees know what to expect from each other and have agreed to abide by those rules. GLOBAL Connections 13.2 illustrates how ambiguity bred conflict at Arthur Andersen. The now defunct accounting and consulting firm lacked clear guidelines to determine who would be the engagement partner (the person who gets financial credit for soliciting a customer), so partners and associates battled and postured over who would get this coveted position.

COMMUNICATION PROBLEMS

Conflict often occurs due to the lack of opportunity, ability, or motivation to communicate effectively. Let's look at each of these causes. First, when two parties lack the opportunity to communicate, they tend to use stereotypes to explain past behaviours and anticipate future actions. Unfortunately, stereotypes are sufficiently subjective that emotions can negatively distort the meaning of an opponent's actions, thereby escalating perceptions of conflict. Furthermore, without direct interaction, the two sides have less psychological empathy for each other. Second, some people lack the necessary skills to communicate in a diplomatic, nonconfrontational manner. When one party communicates its disagreement in an arrogant way, opponents are more likely to heighten their perception of the conflict. Arrogant behaviour also sends a message that one side intends to be competitive rather than cooperative. This may lead the other party to reciprocate with a similar conflict management style.[17] Consequently, as we explained earlier, ineffective communication often leads to an escalation in the conflict cycle.

Ineffective communication can also lead to a third problem: less motivation to communicate in the future. Socioemotional conflict is uncomfortable, so people avoid interacting with others in a conflicting relationship. Unfortunately, less communication can further escalate the conflict because there is less opportunity to empathize with the opponent's situation and opponents are more likely to rely on distorted stereotypes of the other party. In fact, conflict tends to further distort these stereotypes through the process of social identity (see Chapter 3). We begin to see competitors less favourably so that our self-image remains strong during these uncertain times.[18]

The lack of motivation to communicate also explains (along with different values and beliefs, described earlier) why conflict is more common in cross-cultural relationships. People tend to feel uncomfortable or awkward interacting with co-workers from different cultures, so they are less motivated to engage in dialogue

Ambiguous Fee Structure Creates Fractious Divisions at Arthur Andersen

To outsiders, Arthur Andersen's "One Firm" policy was solid. The Chicago-based accounting firm provided the same quality of work anywhere in the world by the same type of people trained the same way. But when Barbara Toffler joined Andersen as an ethics consultant in 1996, she discovered plenty of infighting. Arthur Andersen is now gone, the result of accounting fraud at its client Enron, but internal conflict may have contributed to the accounting firm's demise as well.

Much of the dysfunctional conflict was caused by Arthur Andersen's fee structure, which generously rewarded one engagement partner (the person in charge of the overall project) at the expense of other partners who provided services to the client. To maximize fees, executives fought over who should be the project's engagement partner and played games that would minimize the fees going to other groups. "While I was at Arthur Andersen, the fight for fees defined my existence," recalls Toffler.

In one incident, a partner demanded that he should be the engagement partner because he had made the initial connection with a client, even though the project relied mainly on expertise from Barbara Toffler's ethical practices group. The two argued all the way to the airport and in several subsequent "violent" phone arguments. In another client proposal, Toffler flew to Japan, only to spend two days of her time there negotiating through a translator with Andersen's Japanese engagement partner over how to split fees.

In a third incident, several Arthur Andersen partners met with a potential client supposedly to discuss their

While Arthur Andersen employees put up a united front during the firm's dying days (as this photo shows), its ambiguous fee structure generated internal conflict that undermined the accounting firm's performance.
© AP Photo/David Phillip

services. Instead, the partners openly criticized each other during the pitch so the client would spend more money on their particular specialization. A couple of partners also extended the length of their presentations so other partners would have less time to convince the client of their particular value in the project. "Eventually, I learned to screw someone else before they screwed me," says Toffler. "The struggle to win fees for your office and your group—and not someone else's—came to define the Firm."

Source: Based on information in B. L. Toffler, *Final Accounting: Ambition, Greed, and the Fall of Arthur Andersen* (New York: Broadway Books, 2003).

---

with them. With limited communication, people from divergent cultures rely more on stereotypes to fill in missing information. They also tend to misunderstand each other's verbal and nonverbal signals, further escalating the conflict.[19]

■ INTERPERSONAL CONFLICT MANAGEMENT STYLES

win–win orientation

The belief that the parties will find a mutually beneficial solution to their disagreement.

The six structural conditions described above set the stage for conflict. The conflict process identified earlier in Exhibit 13.1 illustrated that these sources of conflict lead to perceptions and emotions. Some people enter a conflict with a **win–win orientation**. This is the perception that the parties will find a mutually beneficial solution to their disagreement. They believe that the resources at stake are expandable rather than fixed if the parties work together to find a creative solution. Other people enter a conflict with a win–lose orientation. They adopt the belief that the parties are drawing from a fixed pie, so the more one party receives, the less the other party will receive.

Conflict tends to escalate when the parties develop a **win–lose orientation** because they rely on power and politics to gain advantage. A win–lose orientation may occasionally be appropriate when the conflict really is over a fixed resource, but few organizational conflicts are due to perfectly opposing interests with fixed resources. Some degree of win–win orientation is usually advantageous, that is, believing that each side's goals are not perfectly opposing. One possibility is that each party needs different parts of the resource. Another possibility is that various parts of the shared resource have different levels of value to each side.

Consider the example of a supplier and customer resolving a disagreement over the price of a product. Initially, this seems like a clear win–lose situation—the supplier wants to receive more money for the product, whereas the customer wants to pay less money for it. Yet, further discussion may reveal that the customer would be willing to pay more if the product could be provided earlier than originally arranged. The vendor may actually value that earlier delivery because it reduces inventory costs. By looking at the bigger picture, both parties can often discover common ground.[20]

Adopting a win–win or win–lose orientation influences our conflict management style, that is, how we act toward the other person. The five conflict resolution styles described below can be placed in a two-dimensional grid reflecting the person's degree of concern for his or her own interests and concern for the other party's interests (see Exhibit 13.3). Problem solving is the only style that represents a purely win–win orientation. The other four styles represent variations of the win–lose approach.

NHLPA Shifts from Forcing to Problem Solving

Bob Goodenow was called the Darth Vader of hockey. The National Hockey League Players' Association (NHLPA) boss whose forceful style catapulted NHL player salaries from an average of $276,000 in the early 1990s to $1.8 million today. But while Goodenow's uncompromising approach rewarded players handsomely, critics say it also helped sink the public's image of NHL players, priced professional hockey out of most Canadian markets, and contributed to the cancellation of the entire 2004–2005 season. Goodenow stepped down when players agreed to the NHL owners' request to cap team salaries. Taking his place is Montreal lawyer Ted Saskin (shown in photo), whose diplomatic problem-solving conflict resolution style couldn't be more different from Goodenow's. "We've got to be able to work more co-operatively [with the NHL] in the future," Saskin announced on the day he took over. NHL board of governors chairman Harley Hotchkiss thinks Saskin's approach to resolving differences is good for the sport's future. "I will say nothing bad about Bob Goodenow," insists Hotchkiss. "I just think that in any business you need a spirit of co-operation to move forward, and I think Ted Saskin will handle that well."[22] *CP/Adrian Wyld*
www.nhlpa.com

- *Problem solving*—Problem solving tries to find a mutually beneficial solution for both parties. Information sharing is an important feature of this style because both parties collaborate to identify common ground and potential solutions that satisfy both (or all) of them.

- *Avoiding*—Avoiding tries to smooth over or avoid conflict situations altogether. It represents a low concern for both self and the other party; in other words, avoiders try to suppress thinking about the conflict. For example, some employees will rearrange their work area or tasks to minimize interaction with certain co-workers.[21]

- *Forcing*—Forcing tries to win the conflict at the other's expense. This style, which has the strongest win–lose orientation, relies on some of the "hard" influence tactics described in Chapter 12, particularly assertiveness, to get one's own way.

■ **EXHIBIT 13.3**   Interpersonal conflict management styles

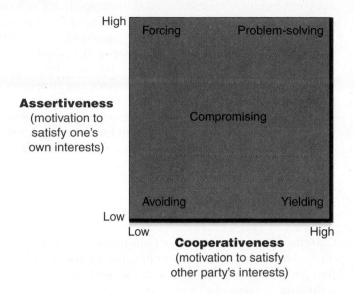

Source: C. K. W. de Dreu, A. Evers, B. Beersma, E. S. Kluwer, and A. Nauta, "A Theory-based Measure of Conflict Management Strategies in the Workplace," *Journal of Organizational Behavior*, 22 (2001), pp. 645–68. For earlier variations of this model, see: T. L. Ruble and K. Thomas, "Support For a Two-Dimensional Model of Conflict Behavior," *Organizational Behavior and Human Performance*, 16 (1976), p. 145.

■ *Yielding*—Yielding involves giving in completely to the other side's wishes, or at least cooperating with little or no attention to your own interests. This style involves making unilateral concessions and unconditional promises, as well as offering help with no expectation of reciprocal help.

■ *Compromising*—Compromising involves looking for a position in which your losses are offset by equally valued gains. It involves matching the other party's concessions, making conditional promises or threats, and actively searching for a middle ground between the interests of the two parties.[23]

CHOOSING THE BEST CONFLICT MANAGEMENT STYLE

Most of us have a preferred conflict management style, but the best style varies with the situation.[24] The problem-solving style is the preferred approach to resolving conflict in many situations because it is the only one that actively tries to optimize the value for both parties. However, this style only works well when the parties do not have perfectly opposing interests and when they have enough trust and openness to share information.

You might think that avoiding is an ineffective conflict management strategy, but it is actually the best approach where conflict has become socioemotional or where negotiating has a higher cost than the benefits of conflict resolution.[25] At the same time, conflict avoidance should not be a long-term solution where the conflict persists because it increases the other party's frustration. The forcing style of conflict resolution is usually inappropriate because organizational relationships rarely involve complete opposition. However, forcing may be necessary where you know you are correct and the dispute requires a quick solution. For example, a forcing style may be necessary when the other party engages in unethical conduct because any degree of unethical behaviour is unacceptable. The forcing style may also be necessary where the other party would take advantage of more cooperative strategies.

The yielding style may be appropriate when the other party has substantially more power or the issue is not as important to you as to the other party. On the other hand, yielding behaviours may give the other side unrealistically high expectations, thereby motivating them to seek more from you in the future. In the long run, yielding may produce more conflict rather than resolve it. The compromising style may be best when there is little hope for mutual gain through problem solving, both parties have equal power, and both are under time pressure to settle their differences. However, compromise is rarely a final solution and may cause the parties to overlook options for mutual gain.

CULTURAL AND GENDER DIFFERENCES IN CONFLICT MANAGEMENT STYLES

Cultural differences are more than just a source of conflict. Cultural background also affects the preferred conflict management style.[26] Some research suggests that people from collectivist cultures—where group goals are valued more than individual goals—are motivated to maintain harmonious relations and, consequently, are more likely than those from low collectivism cultures to manage disagreements through avoidance or problem solving. However, this view may be somewhat simplistic because people in some collectivist cultures are also more likely to publicly shame those whose actions conflict with expectations.[27]

Some writers suggest that men and women also tend to rely on different conflict management styles.[28] Generally speaking, women pay more attention than do men to the relationship between the parties. Consequently, they tend to adopt a problem-solving style in business settings and are more willing to compromise to protect the relationship. Men tend to be more competitive and take a short-term orientation to the relationship. Of course, we must be cautious about these observations because gender has a weak influence on conflict management style.

■ STRUCTURAL APPROACHES TO CONFLICT MANAGEMENT

Conflict management styles refer to how we approach the other party in a conflict situation. But conflict management also involves altering the underlying structural causes of potential conflict. The main structural approaches are identified in Exhibit 13.4. Although this section discusses ways to reduce conflict, we should keep in mind that conflict management sometimes calls for increasing conflict. This occurs mainly by reversing the strategies described over the next few pages.[29]

EMPHASIZING SUPERORDINATE GOALS

superordinate goal
A common objective held by conflicting parties that is more important than their conflicting departmental or individual goals.

Superordinate goals are common objectives held by conflicting parties that are more important than the departmental or individual goals on which the conflict is based. By increasing commitment to corporate-wide goals, employees place less emphasis and therefore feel less conflict with co-workers regarding competing individual or departmental-level goals. They also potentially reduce the problem of dif-

■ **EXHIBIT 13.4**

Structural approaches
to conflict management

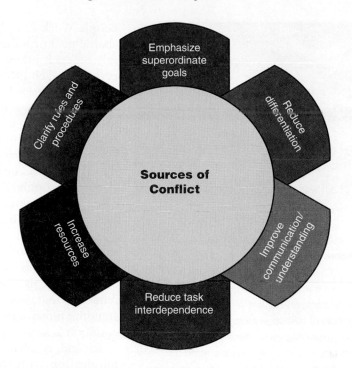

ferentiation by establishing a common frame of reference. For example, research
indicates that the most effective executive teams frame their decisions as superordinate goals that rise above each executive's departmental or divisional goals.[30]

REDUCING DIFFERENTIATION

Another way to minimize dysfunctional conflict is to reduce the differences that
produce the conflict in the first place. The more employees think they have common backgrounds or experiences with co-workers, the more motivated they are to
coordinate their activities and resolve conflict through constructive discussion
with those co-workers.[31] One way to increase this commonality is by creating
common experiences. The Manila Diamond Hotel in the Philippines accomplishes
this by rotating staff across different departments. Hibernia Management and
Development Company, which operates a large oil platform off the coast of Newfoundland, removed the "destructive differences" between hourly and salaried
personnel by putting employees on salary rather than hourly wages. Multinational
peacekeeping forces reduce differentiation among troops from the representative
nations by providing opportunities for them to socialize and engage in common
activities, including eating together.[32]

IMPROVING COMMUNICATION AND UNDERSTANDING

A third way to resolve dysfunctional conflict is to give the conflicting parties more
opportunities to communicate and understand each other. This recommendation
relates back to the contact hypothesis described in Chapter 3. Specifically, the
more meaningful interaction we have with someone, the less we rely on stereotypes to understand that person.[33] This positive effect is more pronounced when

Toyota Drums Out Differences

With increasing diversity and geographic dispersion, employees require a vehicle to reduce their differentiation. For some companies, that vehicle is a drum circle, an ensemble of far-flung employees with little or no percussion experience who literally learn to develop a common beat using a variety of drums. "Companies, like music, are made up of a variety of different rhythms," explains Danny Aaron, president of Vancouver-based Drum Cafe Canada, shown in this photo with musician and master facilitator Mbuyiselp Ncapayi. "You can have sales, marketing, accounting. You can have Vancouver, Calgary, and Toronto. But as long as those different rhythms can play to that same beat—the foundation—and can listen to each other— the communication—then as an organization they can make music." Drum circles have been so effective in some firms that Toyota USA and McDonnell Douglas send a random group of employees through their internal drum circle sessions each week. "Drumming cuts across language and cultural barriers," says Paul Houle, a Toronto-based professional percussionist who had facilitated drum circles for Black & Decker Canada, TD Bank, and many other firms. "It has a primal energy that brings everyone together—without PowerPoint presentations."[37] *Lyle Stafford*

www.drumcafe.ca

people work closely and frequently together on a shared goal or a meaningful task where they need to rely on each other (i.e., cooperate rather than compete with each other). Another important ingredient is that the parties have equal status in that context.

There are two important caveats regarding the communication–understanding strategy. First, this strategy should be applied only *after* differentiation between the two sides has been reduced. If perceived differentiation remains high, attempts to manage conflict through dialogue might have the opposite effect because defence mechanisms are more likely to kick into action. These self-preservation forces increase stereotyping and tend to distort incoming sensory information. In other words, when forced to interact with people who we believe are quite different and in conflict with us, we tend to select information that reinforces that view.[34] Thus, communication and understanding interventions are effective only when differentiation is sufficiently low.

Second, resolving differences through direct communication with the opposing party is a distinctly Western strategy that is not as comfortably applied in most parts of Asia and in other collectivist cultures.[35] As noted earlier, people in high collectivism cultures prefer an avoidance conflict management style because it is the most consistent with harmony and face saving. Direct communication is a high-risk strategy because it easily threatens the need to save face and maintain harmony.

Talking circles　Where avoidance is ineffective in the long run, some collectivist groups engage in structured forms of dialogue that enable communication with less risk of upsetting harmony. One such practice in First Nations and Native American culture is the talking circle.[36] A talking circle is an ancient group process used to educate, make decisions, and repair group harmony due to conflict. Participants sit in a circle and often begin with song, prayer, shaking hands with the next person, or some other communal activity. Then they share their experiences, information, and stories relating to the issue. A talking stick or other natural object (rock, feather) is held by the person speaking, which minimizes interruptions and dysfunctional verbal reactions by others. Talking circles are not aimed at solving problems through negotiated discussion. In fact, talking circle norms usually discourage participants from responding to someone else's statements. Rather, the emphasis is on healing relationships and restoring harmony, typically through the circle's communal experience and improved understanding of each person's views.

REDUCING TASK INTERDEPENDENCE

Conflict increases with the level of interdependence so minimizing dysfunctional conflict might involve reducing the level of interdependence between the parties. If cost effective, this might occur by dividing the shared resource so that each party has exclusive use of part of it. Sequentially or reciprocally interdependent jobs might be combined so that they form a pooled interdependence. For example, rather than having one employee serve customers and another operate the cash register, each employee could handle both customer activities alone. Buffers also help to reduce task interdependence between people. Buffers include resources, such as adding more inventory between people who perform sequential tasks.

Organizations also use human buffers—people who serve as intermediaries between interdependent people or work units who do not get along through direct interaction. For instance, one Canadian business school dean who held little affection for faculty (but worked effectively with corporate leaders) hired an associate dean who fulfilled the internal leadership role. The associate dean became an intermediary who minimized the amount of time that the dean and faculty needed to directly interact with each other.

INCREASING RESOURCES

An obvious way to reduce conflict due to resource scarcity is to increase the amount of resources available. Corporate decision makers might quickly dismiss this solution because of the costs involved. However, they need to carefully compare these costs with the costs of dysfunctional conflict arising out of resource scarcity.

CLARIFYING RULES AND PROCEDURES

Conflicts that arise from ambiguous rules can be minimized by establishing rules and procedures. Armstrong World Industries, Inc. applied this strategy when consultants and information systems employees clashed while working together on development of a client–server network. Information systems employees at the flooring and building materials company thought they should be in charge, whereas consultants believed they had the senior role. Also, the consultants wanted to work long hours and take Friday off to fly home, whereas Armstrong employees wanted to work regular hours. The company reduced these conflicts by having both parties agree on specific responsibilities and roles. The agreement also assigned two senior executives at the companies to establish rules if future disagreements arose.[38]

Rules establish changes to the terms of interdependence, such as an employee's hours of work or a supplier's fulfillment of an order. In most cases, the parties affected by these rules are involved in the process of deciding these terms of interdependence. By redefining the terms of interdependence, the strategy of clarifying rules is part of the larger process of negotiation.

■ RESOLVING CONFLICT THROUGH NEGOTIATION

Think back through yesterday's events. Maybe you had to work out an agreement with other students about what tasks to complete for a team project. Chances are that you shared transportation with someone, so you had to clarify the timing of the ride. Then perhaps there was the question of who made dinner. Each of these daily events created potential conflict, and they were resolved through negotiation. **Negotiation** occurs whenever two or more conflicting parties attempt to resolve their divergent goals by redefining the terms of their interdependence. In other words, people negotiate when they think that discussion can produce a more satisfactory arrangement (at least for them) in their exchange of goods or services.

As you can see, negotiation is not an obscure practice reserved for labour and management bosses when hammering out a workplace agreement. Everyone negotiates—every day. Most of the time, you don't even realize that you are in negotiations. Negotiation is particularly evident in the workplace because employees work interdependently with each other. They negotiate with their supervisors over next month's work assignments, with customers over the sale and delivery schedules of their product, and with co-workers over when to have lunch. And yes, they occasionally negotiate with each other in labour disputes and workplace agreements.

Some writers suggest that negotiations are more successful when the parties adopt a problem-solving style, whereas others caution that this conflict management style is sometimes costly.[39] We know that any win–lose style (forcing, yielding, etc.) is unlikely to produce the optimal solution, because the parties have not shared information necessary to discover a mutually satisfactory solution. On the other hand, we must be careful about adopting an openly problem-solving style until mutual trust has been established.

The concern with the problem-solving style is that information is power, so information sharing gives the other party more power to leverage a better deal if the opportunity occurs. Skilled negotiators often adopt a cautious problem-solving style at the outset by sharing information slowly and determining whether the other side will reciprocate. In this respect, they try to establish trust with the other party.[40] They switch to one of the win–lose styles only when it becomes apparent that a win–win solution is not possible or the other party is unwilling to share information with a cooperative orientation.

BARGAINING ZONE MODEL OF NEGOTIATIONS

The negotiation process moves each party along a continuum with an area of potential overlap called the *bargaining zone*.[41] Exhibit 13.5 displays one possible bargaining zone situation. This linear diagram illustrates a purely win–lose situation—one side's gain will be the other's loss. However, the bargaining zone model can also be applied to situations in which both sides potentially gain from the negotiations. As this model illustrates, the parties typically establish three main negotiating points. The *initial offer* point is the team's opening offer to the other party. This may be its best expectation or a pie-in-the-sky starting point. The *target point* is the team's realistic goal or expectation for a final agreement. The *resistance point* is the point beyond which the team will make no further concessions.

The parties begin negotiations by describing their initial offer point for each item on the agenda. In most cases, the participants know that this is only a starting point that will change as both sides offer concessions. In win–lose situations, neither the target nor the resistance point is revealed to the other party. However, people try to discover the other side's resistance point because this knowledge helps them determine how much they can gain without breaking off negotiations. When the parties have a win–win orientation, on the other hand, the objective is to find a

■ **EXHIBIT 13.5**   Bargaining zone model of negotiations

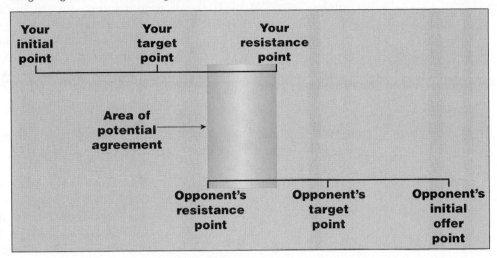

creative solution that keeps everyone close to their initial offer points. They hope to find an arrangement by which each side loses relatively little value on some issues and gains significantly more on other issues.

SITUATIONAL INFLUENCES ON NEGOTIATIONS

The effectiveness of negotiating depends on both the situation and the behaviours of the negotiators. Four of the most important situational factors are location, physical setting, time, and audience.

Location   It is easier to negotiate on your own turf because you are familiar with the negotiating environment and are able to maintain comfortable routines.[42] Also, there is no need to cope with travel-related stress or depend on others for resources during the negotiation. Of course, you can't walk out of negotiations as easily when on your own turf, but this is usually a minor issue. Considering these strategic benefits of home turf, many negotiators agree to neutral territory. Telephones, videoconferences, and other forms of information technology potentially avoid territorial issues, but skilled negotiators usually prefer the media richness of face-to-face meetings.[43]

Physical setting   The physical distance between the parties and formality of the setting can influence their orientation toward each other and the disputed issues. So can the seating arrangements. People who sit face to face are more likely to develop a win–lose orientation toward the conflict situation. In contrast, some negotiation groups deliberately intersperse participants around the table to convey a win–win orientation. Others arrange the seating so that both parties face a white board, reflecting the notion that both parties face the same problem or issue.

Time passage and deadlines   The more time people invest in negotiations, the stronger is their commitment to reaching an agreement. This increases the motivation to resolve the conflict, but it also fuels the escalation of commitment problems described in Chapter 8. For example, the more time put into negotiations, the stronger the tendency to make unwarranted concessions so that the negotiations do not fail.

Time deadlines may be useful to the extent that they motivate the parties to complete negotiations. However, time pressures are usually a liability in negotiations.[44] One problem is that time pressure inhibits a problem-solving conflict management style, because the parties have less time to exchange information or present flexible offers. Negotiators under time pressure also process information less effectively, so they have less creative ability to discover a win–win solution to the conflict. There is also anecdotal evidence that negotiators make excessive concessions and soften their demands more rapidly as the deadline approaches.

Audience characteristics   Most negotiators have audiences—anyone with a vested interest in the negotiation outcomes, such as executives, other team members, or the general public. Negotiators tend to act differently when their audience observes the negotiation or has detailed information about the process, compared to situations in which the audience sees only the end results.[45] When the audience has direct surveillance over the proceedings, negotiators tend to be more competitive, less willing to make concessions, and more likely to engage in political tactics against the other party. This "hardline" behaviour shows the audience that the negotiator is working for their interests. With their audience watching, negotiators also have more interest in saving face.

NEGOTIATOR BEHAVIOURS

Negotiator behaviours play an important role in resolving conflict. Four of the most important behaviours are setting goals, gathering information, communicating effectively, and making concessions.

Preparation Improves Negotiation

Paul Tellier (left in photo) is a master negotiator who has worked through numerous contracts and disputes as former CEO of two of Canada's largest transportation companies, Bombardier and CN. Now, as Canada's chief negotiator in the difficult softwood lumber dispute with the United States, Tellier is likely applying the one recommendation for negotiation that he places above all others: preparation. "You have to be prepared every which way about the people, the subject, and your fallback position," advises Tellier. Part of the preparation process is to anticipate and practise unexpected issues that may arise. "Before walking into the room for the actual negotiation, I ask my colleagues to throw some curve balls at me," he says.[49]
CP/Francois Roy
www.for.gov.bc.ca/HET

- *Preparation and goal setting*—Research has consistently reported that people have more favourable negotiation results when they prepare for the negotiation and set goals.[46] In particular, negotiators should carefully think through their initial offer, target, and resistance points. They need to consider alternative strategies in case the negotiation fails. Negotiators also need to check their underlying assumptions, as well as goals and values. Equally important is the need to research what the other party wants from the negotiation.
- *Gathering information*—"Seek to understand before you seek to be understood." This popular philosophy from management guru Stephen Covey applies to effective negotiations. It means that we should spend more time listening closely to the other party and asking for details.[47] One way to improve the information-gathering process is to have a team of people participate in negotiations. Asian companies tend to have large negotiation teams for this purpose.[48] With more information about the opponent's interests and needs, negotiators are better able to discover low-cost concessions or proposals that will satisfy the other side.

- *Communicating effectively*—Effective negotiators communicate in a way that maintains effective relationships between the parties. Specifically, they minimize socioemotional conflict by focusing on issues rather than people. Effective negotiators also avoid irritating statements such as "I think you'll agree that this is a generous offer." Third, effective negotiators are masters of persuasion. They structure the content of their message so it is accepted by others, not merely understood.[50]
- *Making concessions*—Concessions are important because they (1) enable the parties to move toward the area of potential agreement, (2) symbolize each party's motivation to bargain in good faith, and (3) tell the other party of the relative importance of the negotiating items.[51] How many concessions should you make? This varies with the other party's expectations and the level of trust between you. For instance, many Chinese negotiators are wary of people who change their position during the early stages of negotiations. Similarly, some writers warn that Russian negotiators tend to view concessions as a sign of weakness, rather than a sign of trust.[52] Generally, the best strategy is to be moderately tough and give just enough concessions to communicate sincerity and motivation to resolve the conflict.[53] Being too tough can undermine relations between the parties; giving too many concessions implies weakness and encourages the other party to use power and resistance.

■ THIRD-PARTY CONFLICT RESOLUTION

third-party conflict resolution
Any attempt by a relatively neutral person to help the parties resolve their differences.

Most of this chapter has focused on people directly involved in a conflict, yet many disputes in organizational settings are resolved with the assistance of a third party. **Third-party conflict resolution** is any attempt by a relatively neutral person to help the parties resolve their differences. There are generally three types of third-party dispute resolution activities: arbitration, inquisition, and mediation. These activities can be classified by their level of control over the process and control over the decision (see Exhibit 13.6).[54]

- *Arbitration*—Arbitrators have high control over the final decision, but low control over the process. Executives engage in this strategy by following previously agreed rules of due process, listening to arguments from the disputing employees, and making a binding decision. Arbitration is applied as the final stage of grievances by unionized employees, but it is also becoming more common in nonunion conflicts.
- *Inquisition*—Inquisitors control all discussion about the conflict. Like arbitrators, they have high decision control because they choose the form of conflict resolution. However, they also have high process control because they choose which information to examine and how to examine it, and they generally decide how the conflict resolution process will be handled.
- *Mediation*—Mediators have high control over the intervention process. In fact, their main purpose is to manage the process and context of interaction between the disputing parties. However, the parties make the final decision about how to resolve their differences. Thus, mediators have little or no control over the conflict resolution decision.

CHOOSING THE BEST THIRD-PARTY INTERVENTION STRATEGY

Team leaders, executives, and co-workers regularly intervene in disputes between employees and departments. Sometimes they adopt a mediator role; other times they serve as arbitrators. However, research suggests that people in positions of

■ **EXHIBIT 13.6**   Types of third-party intervention

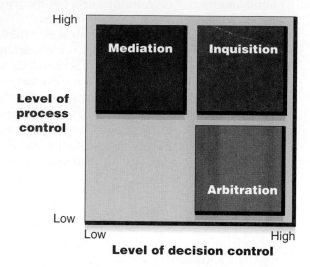

authority (e.g., managers) usually adopt an inquisitional approach whereby they dominate the intervention process as well as make a binding decision.[55] Managers like the inquisition approach because it is consistent with the decision-oriented nature of managerial jobs, gives them control over the conflict process and outcome, and tends to resolve disputes efficiently.

However, the inquisitional approach to third-party conflict resolution is usually the least effective in organizational settings.[56] One problem is that leaders who take an inquisitional role tend to collect limited information about the problem using this approach, so their imposed decision may produce an ineffective solution to the conflict. Also, employees often view inquisitional procedures and outcomes as unfair because they have little control over this approach.

Which third-party intervention is most appropriate in organizations? The answer partly depends on the situation, such as the type of dispute, the relationship between the manager and employees, and cultural values such as power distance.[57] But generally speaking, for everyday disputes between two employees, the mediation approach is usually best because this gives employees more responsibility for resolving their own disputes. The third-party representative merely establishes an appropriate context for conflict resolution. Although not as efficient as other strategies, mediation potentially offers the highest level of employee satisfaction with the conflict process and outcomes.[58] When employees cannot resolve their differences, arbitration seems to work best because the predetermined rules of evidence and other processes create a higher sense of procedural fairness. Moreover, arbitration is preferred where the organization's goals should take priority over individual goals.

CHAPTER SUMMARY

Conflict is the process in which one party perceives that its interests are being opposed or negatively affected by another party. The conflict process begins with the sources of conflict. These sources lead one or both sides to perceive a conflict and to experience conflict emotions. This, in turn, produces manifest conflict, such as behaviours toward the other side. The conflict process often escalates through a series of episodes.

Conflict management maximizes the benefits and minimizes the dysfunctional consequences of conflict. Constructive conflict, a possible benefit of conflict, occurs when team members debate their different perceptions about an issue in a way that keeps the conflict focused on the task rather than people. Socioemotional conflict, a negative outcome, occurs when differences are viewed as personal attacks rather than attempts to resolve an issue. Socioemotional conflict tends to emerge in most constructive conflict episodes, but it is less likely to dominate when the parties are emotionally intelligent, have a cohesive team, and have supportive team norms. The main problems with conflict are that it may lead to job stress, dissatisfaction, and turnover.

Conflict tends to increase when people have incompatible goals, differentiation (different values and beliefs), interdependent tasks, scarce resources, ambiguous rules, and problems communicating with each other. Conflict is more common in a multicultural workforce because of greater differentiation and communication problems among employees.

People with a win–win orientation believe the parties will find a mutually beneficial solution to their dis-

agreement. Those with a win–lose orientation adopt the belief that the parties are drawing from a fixed pie. The latter tends to escalate conflict. Among the five interpersonal conflict management styles, only problem solving represents a purely win–win orientation. The four other styles—avoiding, forcing, yielding, and compromising—adopt some variation of a win–lose orientation. Women and people with high collectivism tend to use a problem-solving or avoidance style more than men and people with high individualism.

Structural approaches to conflict management include emphasizing superordinate goals, reducing differentiation, improving communication and understanding, reducing task interdependence, increasing resources, and clarifying rules and procedures. These elements can also be altered to stimulate conflict.

Negotiation occurs whenever two or more conflicting parties attempt to resolve their divergent goals by redefining the terms of their interdependence. Negotiations are influenced by several situational factors, including location, physical setting, time passage and deadlines, and audience. Important negotiator behaviours include preparation and goal setting, gathering information, communicating effectively, and making concessions.

Third-party conflict resolution is any attempt by a relatively neutral person to help the parties resolve their differences. The three main forms of third-party dispute resolution are mediation, arbitration, and inquisition. Managers tend to use an inquisition approach, although mediation and arbitration are more appropriate, depending on the situation.

KEY TERMS

conflict, p. 358

conflict management, p. 359

constructive conflict, p. 359

negotiation, p. 372

socioemotional conflict, p. 360

superordinate goal, p. 368

third-party conflict resolution, p. 375

win–lose orientation, p. 366

win–win orientation, p. 365

DISCUSSION QUESTIONS

1. Distinguish constructive conflict from socioemotional conflict and explain how to apply the former without having the latter become a problem.

2. The chief executive officer of Creative Toys Ltd. read about cooperation in Japanese companies and vowed to bring this same philosophy to the company. The goal is to avoid all conflict, so that employees

would work cooperatively and be happier at Creative Toys. Discuss the merits and limitations of the CEO's policy.

3. Conflict among managers emerged soon after a French company acquired a Swedish firm. The Swedes perceived the French management as hierarchical and arrogant, whereas the French thought

the Swedes were naive, cautious, and lacking an achievement orientation. Describe ways to reduce dysfunctional conflict in this situation.

4. This chapter describes three levels of task interdependence that exist in interpersonal and intergroup relationships. Identify examples of these three levels in your work or school activities. How do these three levels affect potential conflict for you?

5. Jane was just appointed purchasing manager of Trois-Rivières Technologies Ltd. The previous purchasing manager, who recently retired, was known for his "winner-take-all" approach to suppliers. He continually fought for more discounts and was skeptical about any special deals proposed by suppliers. A few suppliers refused to do business with Trois-Rivières Technologies, but senior management was confident that the former purchasing manager's approach minimized the company's costs. Jane wants to try a more problem-solving approach to working with suppliers. Will her approach work? How should she adopt a more problem-solving approach in future negotiations with suppliers?

6. You are a special assistant to the commander-in-chief of a peacekeeping mission to a war-torn part of the world. The unit consists of a few thousand peacekeeping troops from Canada, France, India, and four other countries. The troops will work together for approximately one year. What strategies would you recommend to improve mutual understanding and minimize conflict among these troops?

7. Suppose that you head one of five divisions in a multinational organization and are about to begin this year's budget deliberations at headquarters. What are the characteristics of your audience in these negotiations and what effect might they have on your negotiation behaviour?

8. Managers tend to use an inquisitional approach to resolving disputes between employees and departments. Describe the inquisitional approach and discuss its appropriateness in organizational settings.

C A S E   S T U D Y   13.1

NORTHWEST CANADIAN FOREST PRODUCTS LIMITED

By Peter Seidl, British Columbia Institute of Technology.

Northwest Canadian Forest Products Limited owns and operates five sawmills in British Columbia and Alberta. These mills produce high-quality lumber for use in the manufacture of window frames, doors, and mouldings for markets in the United States and Japan in addition to lower-quality, commodity-type lumber used in the Canadian construction industry. Currently, the president of the company is thinking about the long-term prospects of each of the mills and is paying particular attention to the Jackson Sawmill located in the small town of Jackson, B.C.

This mill was originally built in 1950 and was last upgraded in 1986. The president knows she will soon (in 2007) have to decide whether or not to invest substantial sums of money ($50 million) in new plant and equipment at the Jackson Sawmill. New investment is required in order to keep the mill up-to-date and competitive with similar mills throughout North America. However, the mill has consistently been the poorest performer (in terms of productivity and

product quality) in the company since 1986 even though its equipment is of similar age, type, and quality as that found in the other mills.

The president would like to invest the money needed because the alternative to re-investing in Jackson would be to downsize the Jackson Sawmill by reducing production capacity and permanently laying off over half the 200-person workforce. The remaining part of the mill would serve the domestic market only. A new mill would then be built in Alberta in order to serve the more demanding, quality-conscious export markets. A new mill in Alberta would cost more than the $50-million investment required at the Jackson Sawmill. However, the president is willing to seriously consider implementing this alternative because she thinks that the labour relations climate in Alberta is much better than the one found at Jackson.

In fact, she attributes most, if not all, of the problems at Jackson to its poor labour-management relations. During the last round of collective bargaining, there was a strike at all four of the company's B.C. mills. The strike was, however, much more bitter at Jackson than elsewhere. Company buildings suffered minor damage during the strike at the hands of some striking employees. Since then, there were two separate occasions when the entire workforce walked off the job for a day to protest the firings of two employees who were dismissed for insubordination.

The Jackson Sawmill has the worst safety record of all the company's mills. There is a joint labour-management safety committee (as required by law) but it is viewed as a waste of time by both sides. One management member of the safety committee, Des, the production manager and the second highest manager at the mill, has said: "The union guys start each safety committee meeting by complaining about safety but they just can't wait to complain about everything else they can possibly think of. Their whining and complaining is so predictable that I go to every safety meeting ready for a fight on workload and production issues as well as for a fight on safety. Of course, safety is everyone's responsibility but production issues are none of their business. Production is a management responsibility. Plans, budgets, and other management concerns are very definitely not part of the committee's job. Most of what's said at these meetings isn't worth listening to."

The union is also dissatisfied with the functioning of the safety committee. Ivan, the chief union steward who also serves on the committee, observes: "If the safety committee wasn't mandatory by law, management wouldn't even pretend to listen to us. We put forward our safety concerns but management says that we are mixing safety in with workload and production issues. They only want to talk about what they think are safety issues—like serious accidents. Thankfully, we don't have too many of those! But safety is more than just avoiding major accidents. We get far too many 'little accidents' and 'near-accidents' here. At least that's what management calls them. They just want us to work faster and faster. We complain and complain at the meetings but they just say 'that's a production issue and this is a safety committee.' They accuse us of trying to run the company when we ask for better equipment. They say we don't understand things like costs and limited budgets. We don't care about their

budgets, we've got work issues to talk about and we'll keep speaking out for the crew no matter what. That's what the union is for."

Big Bad John, one of the mill's toughest and most experienced supervisors, describes his job as follows: "The job of supervisor is to keep a close watch on every move the crew makes. If I look away for a second, some guy is going to be doing something wrong—either with the equipment or with the logs. They're always making mistakes. Lots of mistakes! Some of these guys are just plain dumb. And lazy, too! Any chance they can get to steal some company time, they take. They start work late, they take long lunch breaks, they talk too much during their shifts. A minute here, a minute there—it all adds up. The younger guys are the worst. They always want to talk back to me, they can't follow my orders like most of the older guys can. Lousy attitude, that's what they've got."

Vic, the youngest union steward, gives his view of labour-management relations: "The supervisors and the managers, they know it all. They think they're so smart. They treat the guys on the crew like children. Almost everyone on the crew has a high school education. Some even have college backgrounds. Most are raising families. We're not stupid! Sure, some guys come in late and miss a day of work now and then. Who can blame them? The pace of work is exhausting. How can you do a good job when you're tired and rushing all the time?" He adds: "Of course, we're not perfect. We make mistakes just like everyone else does. But nobody ever explains anything to the crew members. The supervisors just watch everyone like hawks and jump all over them, criticize them, and make them feel stupid when they use a piece of equipment the wrong way. We're always so rushed and busy here that the senior crew members don't have much time to explain things to the newer workers—the younger guys. Also, the equipment could be in better shape, that would help."

The production manager, Des, observes that "the union just doesn't understand—or even care about—the connection between the poor work ethic, the poor attitude on the part of the crew members here, and the mill's mediocre productivity and product quality. The union and the crew only take their very narrow 'employee-view' of how things are done around here. They don't understand the bigger picture. Well, it's very competitive out there. They don't understand what tight budgets, increasing costs, declining quality, missed production targets, and complaining customers mean to a business. They just sit back and complain about our management style. What they don't realize is that their attitude makes our management style necessary. Complaining is easy, no responsibility is needed. Managing, on the other hand, is challenging. And it's especially tough to control and manage this particular crew. We've currently got 30 unresolved grievances— that's a lot of formal complaints for a mill of our size. Some of the union stewards actually go out among the crew and look for grievances just because they're mad they can't run the mill the way they want to. Sometimes I think the stewards want to create grievances where no real problems exist. They want to give us in management headaches."

The president of the company has recently informed Digby, the mill's new general manager (he started at Jackson last month after a career in eastern Canada), of the decision she will soon have to make regarding the mill's future. She told Digby that significant improvements in mill productivity and product quality are required if the mill is to receive the $50-million investment in new plant and equipment. Without such improvements, the mill would be downsized and over half of the workforce would be permanently laid off. Half the supervisory and managerial personnel would also lose their jobs.

Digby has just telephoned Moe (the president of the local union who does not work at the mill but who is very familiar with developments at the mill) to tell him about the message from the company president. Upon hearing of the potential job losses, Moe was troubled and asked to meet with Digby to discuss the situation. However, Moe was also somewhat skeptical because the previous general manager once told him that some permanent layoffs would occur unless productivity was improved. No layoffs subsequently occurred. Therefore, Moe is uncertain if the company is serious about these potential future layoffs or merely bluffing in order to get the employees to work harder.

Discussion Questions

1. Apply the conflict process model (Exhibit 13.1) to this case. That is, explain the facts of this case using the concepts in the model.

2. From the perspective of management, what is the problem(s) in this case? From the union/employee perspective, what is the problem(s) in this case? Are these problems connected to one another? Why (or why not)? Explain.

3. How could the parties in this case work together to ensure that the mill will receive the investment of funds needed to avoid any layoffs?

T E A M   E X E R C I S E   13.2

UGLI ORANGE ROLE PLAY

Purpose This exercise is designed to help you understand the dynamics of interpersonal and intergroup conflict as well as the effectiveness of negotiation strategies under specific conditions.

Materials The instructor will distribute roles for Dr. Roland, Dr. Jones, and a few observers. Ideally, each negotiation should occur in a private area away from other negotiations.

Instructions

- *Step 1:* The instructor will divide the class into an even number of teams of three people each, with one participant left over for each team formed (e.g., six observers if there are six teams). One-half

of the teams will take the role of Dr. Roland and the other half will be Dr. Jones. The instructor will distribute roles after these teams have been formed.

- *Step 2:* Members within each team are given 10 minutes (or other time limit stated by the instructor) to learn their roles and decide negotiating strategy.

- *Step 3:* After reading their roles and discussing strategy, each Dr. Jones team is matched with a Dr. Roland team to conduct negotiations. Observers will receive observation forms from the instructor, and two observers will be assigned to watch the paired teams during prenegotiations and subsequent negotiations.

- *Step 4:* As soon as Roland and Jones reach agreement or at the end of the time allotted for the negotiation (which ever comes first), the Roland and Jones teams report to the Instructor for further instruction.

- *Step 5:* At the end of the exercise, the class will congregate to discuss the negotiations. Observers, negotiators, and instructors will then discuss their observations and experiences and the implications for conflict management and negotiation.

NOTE: This exercise was developed by Robert J House, Wharton Business School, University of Pennsylvania. A similar incident is also attributed to earlier writing by R. R. Blake and J. S. Mouton.

S E L F - A S S E S S M E N T   E X E R C I S E   13.3

THE DUTCH TEST FOR CONFLICT HANDLING

Purpose   This self-assessment is designed to help you identify your preferred conflict management style.

Instructions   Read each of the statements below and circle the response that you believe best reflects your position regarding each statement. Then use the scoring key in Appendix B to calculate your results for each conflict management style. This exercise is completed alone so students assess themselves honestly without concerns of social comparison. However, class discussion will focus on the different conflict management styles and the situations in which each is most appropriate.

DUTCH TEST FOR CONFLICT HANDLING					
When I have a conflict at work, I do the following:	**Not at All** ▼	▼	▼	▼	**Very Much** ▼
1. I give in to the wishes of the other party.	1	2	3	4	5
2. I try to realize a middle-of-the-road solution.	1	2	3	4	5
3. I push my own point of view.	1	2	3	4	5
4. I examine issues until I find a solution that really satisfies me and the other party.	1	2	3	4	5
5. I avoid confrontation about our differences.	1	2	3	4	5
6. I concur with the other party.	1	2	3	4	5
7. I emphasize that we have to find a compromise solution.	1	2	3	4	5
8. I search for gains.	1	2	3	4	5
9. I stand for my own and other's goals and interests.	1	2	3	4	5
10. I avoid differences of opinion as much as possible.	1	2	3	4	5
11. I try to accommodate the other party.	1	2	3	4	5
12. I insist we both give in a little.	1	2	3	4	5
13. I fight for a good outcome for myself.	1	2	3	4	5
14. I examine ideas from both sides to find a mutually optimal solution.	1	2	3	4	5
15. I try to make differences loom less severe.	1	2	3	4	5
16. I adapt to the parties' goals and interests.	1	2	3	4	5
17. I strive whenever possible towards a fifty-fifty compromise.	1	2	3	4	5
18. I do everything to win.	1	2	3	4	5
19. I work out a solution that serves my own as well as other's interests as good as possible.	1	2	3	4	5
20. I try to avoid a confrontation with the other.	1	2	3	4	5

Source: C. K. W. de Dreu, A. Evers, B. Beersma, E. S. Kluwer, and A. Nauta, "A Theory-based Measure of Conflict Management Strategies in the Workplace," *Journal of Organizational Behavior*, 22 (2001), pp. 645–68.

·14·

LEADERSHIP IN ORGANIZATIONAL SETTINGS

LEARNING OBJECTIVES

AFTER READING THIS CHAPTER, YOU SHOULD BE ABLE TO:

- Define leadership.

- List seven competencies of effective leaders.

- Describe the people-oriented and task-oriented leadership styles.

- Outline the path–goal theory of leadership.

- Contrast transactional with transformational leadership.

- Describe the four elements of transformational leadership.

- Explain how perceptions of followers influence leadership.

- Discuss the influence of culture on perceptions of effective leaders.

- Discuss similarities and differences in the leadership styles of women and men.

W hen Teresa Cascioli was recruited to lead Lakeport Beverage Corp. a few years ago, the Hamilton, Ontario-based brewer was in bankruptcy protection with $18 million in debt from lenders who were ready to shut the doors. Lakeport had been devastated by fierce marketing and pricing wars and its manufacturing couldn't compete more efficiently. "Some of the equipment here was being held together with chicken wire and duct tape," Cascioli recalls.

In spite of the grim situation, Cascioli and her investment partners had a vision that Lakeport could be a successful company. "Buying the company was based on a gut feeling," she admits, adding that "when a company is in distress, you don't have time to do a lot of due diligence."

Cascioli immediately shut the plant for nearly eight weeks to complete a massive $1.5-million overhaul. She cut costs by removing several middle management positions and introducing a just-in-time system for packaging materials. New equipment was later purchased to provide more flexible and efficient service to co-pack partners (beverage marketers for whom Lakeport manufactures alcoholic mix beverages). Cascioli and her new management team also generated competitive optimism that resonated with employees. "We brought a sense of urgency to this place that was never here before," she says.

Within one year, Lakeport's fortunes started to rebound. The brewer attracted new co-pack clients and plant efficiency soared. But plant capacity was still below its potential, so Cascioli and her top management team took another bold step that some observers now call the "Lakeport Effect." At a time when a case of 24 beers was priced at about $35, Lakeport introduced the "$24 for 24" strategy—selling a case of beer for less than a loonie per bottle.

Teresa Cascioli's leadership has transformed Hamilton-based Lakeport Beverage Corp. into a major competitor in Ontario's take-home beer market. *Courtesy of Lakeport Beverages Corp.*

That bold action, in which Lakeport's market share surged while national and regional brewers stumbled slowly in response, was an important leadership lesson. "I understand better now what our core competencies are, and that is to be flexible, be quick to market, and be driven to win," Cascioli explains. "I now have a better sense of confidence in those strengths versus when I first did this."

Today, with 200 employees and more than 5 percent of the Ontario take-home beer market, Lakeport is on solid financial footing and poised to take on larger opportunities. Cascioli has received several accolades, including Turnaround Entrepreneur of the Year and one of Canada's top 10 women entrepreneurs. "I like being the boss," she says. "I make decisions very quickly, and I think that's something employees value."[1]

www.lakeportbrewing.ca

By any measure, Teresa Cascioli has demonstrated superior leadership in the transformation of Lakeport Beverage Corp. But what is leadership? A few years ago, 54 leadership experts from 38 countries reached a consensus that **leadership** is about influencing, motivating, and enabling others to contribute toward the effectiveness and success of the organizations of which they are members.[2] Leaders apply various forms of influence—from subtle persuasion to direct application of power—to ensure that followers have the motivation and role clarity to achieve specified goals. Leaders also arrange the work environment—such as allocating resources and altering communication patterns—so that employees can achieve corporate objectives more easily.

Leadership isn't restricted to the executive suite. Anyone in the organization may be a leader in various ways and at various times.[3] This view is variously known as shared leadership or the leaderful organization. Effective self-directed work teams, for example, consist of members who share leadership responsibilities or otherwise allocate this role to a responsible coordinator. For example, W. L. Gore & Associates is organized around self-directed work teams and, consequently, has few formal leaders. Yet, when asked in the company's annual survey "Are you a leader?" more than 50 percent of Gore employees answer "Yes."[4]

The notion that leadership exists beyond formal roles was also dramatically illustrated in the recent revival of St. Magloire, a small village in Quebec near the Maine border that had suffered population decline as children grew up and moved to larger centres. When the Quebec government threatened to close the only school, Julie Bercier and a handful of other citizens rallied to attract new residents. At first, people were skeptical, suggesting that Bercier and her friends were dreaming to think that anyone could reverse the rural exodus. But persistence paid off as people eventually got involved in marketing and developing St. Magloire as a better lifestyle for city folks.

Newspaper campaigns, a new resident welcoming program, and government support attracted 54 people within a year. The school remained open as enough children enrolled the following year. Although the village mayor and school leaders played important roles, Bercier and others became leaders by providing the passion and vision of what the small community could become with enough ingenuity and effort.[5]

Shared Leadership at Newfoundland Power

Newfoundland Power Inc. depends on leadership in each of its employees. "When there is a truck on the side of the road, there are two guys who are working without supervision. We trust them," explains Philip Hughes, former Newfoundland Power CEO and currently CEO of sister company FortisAlberta. "Both of these guys have to have leadership qualities or nothing will happen." The power utility has dramatically improved customer service by recognizing that leadership is not restricted to the executive suite. "If there is a storm, there is no handbook or manual," Hughes explains. "The employees have to be part construction worker, part electrician, and part journey person. This takes teamwork and leadership."[7]

Photo courtesy The Telegram

www.nfpower.nf.ca

■ PERSPECTIVES OF LEADERSHIP

Leadership has been contemplated since the days of Greek philosophers and it is one of the most popular research topics among organizational behaviour scholars. This has resulted in an enormous volume of leadership literature, most of which can be organized into the five perspectives shown in Exhibit 14.1.[6] Although some of these perspectives are currently more popular than others, each helps us to more fully understand this complex issue.

■ **EXHIBIT 14.1**

Perspectives
of leadership

Some research examines leadership competencies, whereas others examine leadership behaviours. Recent studies have looked at leadership from a contingency approach by considering the appropriate leader behaviours in different settings. Currently, the most popular perspective is that leaders transform organizations through their vision, communication, and ability to build commitment. Finally, an emerging perspective suggests that leadership is mainly a perceptual bias. We rely on leader prototypes and attribute events to leaders because we feel more comfortable believing that a competent individual is at the organization's helm. This chapter explores each of these five perspectives of leadership. In the final section, we also consider cross-cultural and gender issues in organizational leadership.

■ COMPETENCY (TRAIT) PERSPECTIVE OF LEADERSHIP

Kathleen Taylor, head of worldwide operations at Four Seasons Hotels and Resorts, is highly regarded for her leadership characteristics. "There's a combination of being very intelligent with a practical sense of common sense," says her boss, Isadore Sharp, who is founder and CEO of the Toronto-based hotel chain. "She's very self-confident with great humility," Sharp said. "She has a great sense of fairness and sensitivity while being very direct with a high measure of integrity."[8]

Self-confidence, humility, fairness, sensitivity, and integrity. Isadore Sharp's description of Kathleen Taylor reflects the notion that effective leaders possess specific personal characteristics. Since the beginning of recorded civilization, people have been interested in the traits that distinguish great leaders from the rest of us. A major review in the late 1940s concluded that no consistent list of traits could be distilled from the hundreds of studies conducted up to that time. A subsequent review suggested that a few traits are consistently associated with effective leaders, but most are unrelated to effective leadership.[9] These conclusions caused many scholars to give up their search for personal characteristics that distinguish effective leaders.

Over the past decade, leadership researchers and consultants have returned to the notion that leadership requires specific personal characteristics. One recent study established that inherited personality characteristics significantly influence leadership emergence—the perception that someone is a leader—in a leaderless situation.[10] More striking, however, is the resurgence in interest in discovering leadership *competencies* that enable companies to select future leaders and to provide leadership development programs.[11] Competencies encompass a broad range of personal characteristics, including knowledge, skills, abilities, and values. The recent leadership literature identifies seven competencies that are characteristic of effective leaders (see Exhibit 14.2).[12]

- *Emotional intelligence*—Kathleen Taylor's sensitivity illustrates that she and other effective leaders have a high level of emotional intelligence.[13] They have the ability to perceive and express emotion, assimilate emotion in thought, understand and reason with emotion, and regulate emotion in themselves and others (see Chapter 4). They possess the ability to empathize with others and possess the social skills necessary to build rapport as well as network with others. Emotional intelligence requires a strong self-monitoring personality, which means that leaders have a high level of sensitivity to the expressive behaviour of others and the ability to adapt appropriately to these situational cues (see Chapter 2).[14] High self-monitors sense the situation and adjust their own behaviour to suit that situation. Moreover, the contingency leadership perspective described later in this chapter assumes that effective leaders have high emotional intelligence so they can adjust their behaviour to match the situation.

- *Integrity*—This refers to the leader's truthfulness and tendency to translate words into deeds. This characteristic is sometimes called "authentic leadership" because the individual acts with sincerity. He or she has a higher moral capacity to judge dilemmas based on sound values and to act accordingly. Several large-scale studies have reported that integrity or honesty is the most important leadership characteristic. Employees want honest leaders whom they can trust.[15] The problem is that most employees don't' trust their leaders and don't think they have integrity. Only about half of employees in one survey said they have trust and confidence in senior management. In another poll, 73 percent said chief executives of large corporations could not be trusted.[16]

- *Drive*—Leaders have a high need for achievement (see Chapter 5). You can see this in Teresa Cascioli, described at the beginning of this chapter. The CEO of Lakeport Beverage Corp. has a strong motivation to compete in the marketplace and to take the company into uncharted waters. This drive represents the inner motivation that leaders possess to pursue their goals and encourage others to move forward with theirs. Drive inspires an inquisitiveness and need to learn.

- *Leadership motivation*—The opening vignette to this chapter also described how Teresa Cascioli was motivated to serve as leader of Lakeport Beverage Corp. In fact, when investors approached the company where she was working to assist in the takeover, she put herself forward as a candidate for the CEO role. This leadership motivation involves a strong need for socialized power whereby leaders use their power to benefit the organization and society rather than themselves alone.[17]

- *Self-confidence*—Kathleen Taylor at Toronto's Four Seasons Hotels and Resorts and other leaders believe in their leadership skills and ability to achieve objec-

■ **EXHIBIT 14.2**   Seven competencies of effective leaders

Leadership trait	Description
Emotional intelligence	The leader's ability to monitor his or her own and others' emotions, discriminate among them, and use the information to guide his or her thoughts and actions.
Integrity	The leader's truthfulness and tendency to translate words into deeds.
Drive	The leader's inner motivation to pursue goals.
Leadership motivation	The leader's need for socialized power to accomplish team or organizational goals.
Self-confidence	The leader's belief in his/her own leadership skills and ability to achieve objectives.
Intelligence	The leader's above average cognitive ability to process enormous amounts of information.
Knowledge of the business	The leader's understanding of the company's environment to make more intuitive decisions.

Sources: Most elements of this list were derived from S. A. Kirkpatrick and E. A. Locke, "Leadership: Do Traits Matter?" *Academy of Management Executive*, 5 (May 1991), pp. 48–60. Several of these ideas are also discussed in: H. B. Gregersen, A. J. Morrison, and J. S. Black, "Developing Leaders for the Global Frontier," *Sloan Management Review*, 40 (Fall 1998), pp. 21–32; R. J. House and R. N. Aditya, "The Social Scientific Study of Leadership: Quo Vadis?" *Journal of Management*, 23 (1997), pp. 409–73.

tives. Effective leaders are typically extroverted—outgoing, sociable, talkative, and assertive—but they also manage to curb their assertiveness enough to remain humble.

■ *Intelligence*—Leaders have above-average cognitive ability to process enormous amounts of information. Leaders aren't necessarily geniuses; rather, they have superior ability to analyze a variety of complex alternatives and opportunities.

■ *Knowledge of the business*—Effective leaders know the business environment in which they operate. This assists the leader's intuition to recognize opportunities and understand the organization's capacity to capture those opportunities.

COMPETENCY (TRAIT) PERSPECTIVE LIMITATIONS AND PRACTICAL IMPLICATIONS

Although the competency perspective is gaining popularity (again), it assumes that all leaders have the same personal characteristics and that all of these qualities are equally important in all situations. This is probably a false assumption; leadership is far too complex to have a universal list of traits that apply to every condition. Some competencies might not be important all the time. Another limitation is that alternative combinations of competencies may be equally successful. In other words, people with two different sets of competencies might be equally good leaders.[18]

As we will learn later in this chapter, several leadership researchers have also warned that some personal characteristics might only influence our perception that someone is a leader, not whether the individual really makes a difference to the organization's success. People who exhibit self-confidence, extroversion, and other traits are called leaders because they fit our stereotype of an effective leader. Or we might see a successful person, call that person a leader, and then attribute unobservable traits that we consider essential for great leaders.

Aside from these limitations, the competency perspective recognizes that some people possess personal characteristics that offer them a higher potential to be great leaders. The most obvious implication of this is that organizations are turn-ing to competency-based methods to hire people with strong leadership potential. The competency perspective of leadership does not necessarily imply that leader-ship is something you are either born with or must live without. On the contrary, competencies only indicate leadership potential, not leadership performance. Peo-ple with these characteristics become effective leaders only after they have devel-oped and mastered the necessary leadership behaviours. People with somewhat lower leadership competencies may become very effective leaders because they have leveraged their potential more fully. In fact, as Connections 14.1 describes, executives in several Canadian organizations now believe that competency-based leadership development is an important source of their firm's future success.

■ BEHAVIOURAL PERSPECTIVE OF LEADERSHIP

In the 1940s and 1950s, leadership experts at several universities launched an inten-sive research investigation to answer the question: What behaviours make leaders effective? Questionnaires were administered to subordinates, asking them to rate their supervisors on a large number of behaviours. These studies distilled two clusters of leadership behaviours from literally thousands of leadership behaviour items.[19]

One cluster represented people-oriented behaviours. This included showing mutual trust and respect for subordinates, demonstrating a genuine concern for their needs, and having a desire to look out for their welfare. Leaders with a strong people-oriented style listen to employee suggestions, do personal favours for employees, support their interests when required, and treat employees as equals.

The other cluster represented a task-oriented leadership style and included behav-iours that define and structure work roles. Task-oriented leaders assign employees to specific tasks, clarify their work duties and procedures, ensure that they follow company rules, and push them to reach their performance capacity. They establish stretch goals and challenge employees to push beyond those high standards.

CHOOSING TASK- VERSUS PEOPLE-ORIENTED LEADERSHIP

Should leaders be task-oriented or people-oriented? This is a difficult question to answer because each style has its advantages and disadvantages. Recent evidence suggests that both styles are positively associated with leader effectiveness, but differences are often apparent only in very high or very low levels of each style. Generally, absenteeism, grievances, turnover, and job dissatisfaction are higher among employees who work with supervisors with very low levels of people-oriented leadership. Job performance is lower among employees who work for supervisors with low levels of task-oriented leadership.[20] Research suggests that Canadian university students value task-oriented instructors because they want clear objectives and well-prepared lectures that abide by the unit's objectives.[21]

One problem with the behavioural leadership perspective is that the two cate-gories are broad generalizations that mask specific behaviours within each cate-gory. For instance, task-oriented leadership includes planning work activities, clarifying roles, and monitoring operations and performance. Each of these clusters of activities are fairly distinct and likely have different effects on employee well-being and performance. A second concern is that the behavioural approach assumes high levels of both styles are best in all situations. In reality, the best leadership

Canadian Firms Learn to Grow Their Own Leaders

"How much energy do we really put into being and creating leaders? Hardly any." That blunt assessment from Glen Leblanc, vice president of finance and controller at Aliant Inc. reflects the opinions of many Canadian executives who believe that companies are not doing enough to develop the necessary leadership capabilities for the future. Fortunately, some firms have taken the initiative by adopting a leadership competencies framework and applying relevant selection and training strategies.

Dofasco is one of the forward thinking firms in leadership development. The Hamilton-based steelmaker begins its leadership competencies search at campus interviews with prospective employees. "We are looking for leadership qualities right from day one," says Dofasco human resources manager Dave Santi. "It is not just the highest marks that get you into the company."

A large number of Dofasco managers will be retiring over the next few years, so the Hamilton, Ontario, steelmaker is looking for ways to speed up the leadership development process. "It takes about 15 years to develop a good manager," Santi explains. "We just have to figure out a way to do it in seven or eight." In some cases, Dofasco is searching three or four levels below the manager to identify people with future leadership potential. "We are trying to find out as much as we can about an individual's qualities as early as possible," says Santi.

Along with the standard reviews and career talks with their immediate boss, the top 500 managers at Torstar (which owns *Toronto Star* and Harlequin) engage in several simulations to develop and help them reflect on their leadership skills and potential. One activity called Press Time teaches managers to work together internally to compete externally. In another simulation, managers work in teams to roll out new products for a global business. These activities, which take place every few months at Torstar's Toronto headquarters as well as at other sites around the world, are supplemented with self-assessments and 360-degree feedback reports.

Sources: D. Brown, "Success Starts in the Middle," *Canadian HR Reporter*, June 2, 2003, p. 1; K. Whitney, "Torstar Corp.: Risk-Free Employee Development," *Chief Learning Officer* (Special Report: Simulations), October 2004, pp. 24–26; R. Colman, "Creating the Go-To Team," *CMA Management*, June/July 2005, pp. 42–45. **www.aliant.ca**

style depends on the situation.[22] On a positive note, the behavioural perspective lays the foundation for two of the main leadership styles—people-oriented and task-oriented—found in many contemporary leadership theories. These contemporary theories adopt a contingency perspective, which are described next.

■ CONTINGENCY PERSPECTIVE OF LEADERSHIP

The contingency perspective of leadership is based on the idea that the most appropriate leadership style depends on the situation. Most (although not all) contingency leadership theories assume that effective leaders must be both insightful and flexible.[23] They must be able to adapt their behaviours and styles to the immediate situation. This isn't easy to do, however. Leaders typically have a preferred style. It takes considerable effort for leaders to learn when and how to alter their styles to match the situation. As we noted earlier, leaders must have high emotional intelligence, so they can diagnose the circumstances and match their behaviours accordingly.

path–goal leadership theory
A contingency theory of leadership based on expectancy theory of motivation that relates several leadership styles to specific employee and situational contingencies.

PATH–GOAL THEORY OF LEADERSHIP

Several contingency theories have been proposed over the years, but **path–goal leadership theory** has withstood scientific critique better than the others. The theory has its roots in the expectancy theory of motivation (see Chapter 5).[24] Early research incorporated expectancy theory into the study of how leader behaviours influence employee perceptions of expectancies (paths) between employee effort and performance (goals). Out of this early work was born path–goal theory as a contingency leadership model.

Using the language of expectancy theory (Chapter 5), path–goal theory states that effective leaders strengthen the performance-to-outcome expectancy and valences of those outcomes by ensuring that employees who perform their jobs well have a higher degree of need fulfillment than employees who perform poorly. Effective leaders also strengthen the effort-to-performance expectancy by providing the information, support, and other resources necessary to help employees complete their tasks.[25] In other words, path–goal theory advocates **servant leadership**.[26] Servant leaders do not view leadership as a position of power; rather, they are coaches, stewards, and facilitators. Leadership is an obligation to understand employee needs and to facilitate their work performance. Servant leaders ask, "How can I help you?" rather than expect employees to serve them.

Leadership styles   Exhibit 14.3 presents the path–goal theory of leadership. This model specifically highlights four leadership styles and several contingency factors leading to three indicators of leader effectiveness. The four leadership styles are:[27]

- *Directive*—These are clarifying behaviours that provide a psychological structure for subordinates. The leader clarifies performance goals, the means to reach those goals, and the standards against which performance will be judged. It also includes judicious use of rewards and disciplinary actions. Directive leadership is the same as task-oriented leadership described earlier and echoes our discussion in Chapter 2 on the importance of clear role perceptions in employee performance.

- *Supportive*—These behaviours provide psychological support for subordinates. The leader is friendly and approachable; makes the work more pleasant; treats employees with equal respect; and shows concern for the status, needs, and well-being of employees. Supportive leadership is the same as people-oriented leadership described earlier and reflects the benefits of social support to help employees cope with stressful situations.

- *Participative*—These behaviours encourage and facilitate subordinate involvement in decisions beyond their normal work activities. The leader consults with employees, asks for their suggestions, and takes these ideas into serious consideration before making a decision. Participative leadership relates to involving employees in decisions (see Chapter 8).

servant leadership
The belief that leaders serve followers by understanding their needs and facilitating their work performance.

■ **EXHIBIT 14.3**

Path–goal leadership theory

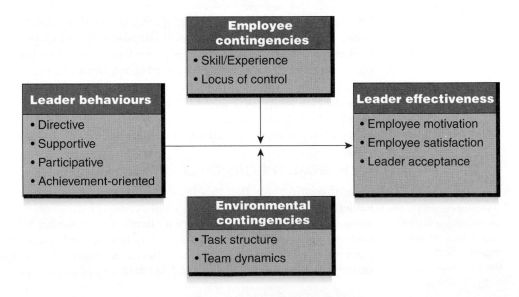

LaSorda Leads with Direction

Raised in a family of union leaders in Windsor, Ontario, Tom LaSorda (shown here with Chrysler employees in Mexico) understands the needs of employees in the auto industry. But as incoming CEO of Chrysler Group, LaSorda's leadership style is also focused on improving efficiency and performance. In fact, he has become well known for setting tough goals and pointing out wasted time when employees move from one station to the next. "With every second, you've lost productivity," explains LaSorda, who developed his penchant for lean manufacturing at the General Motors–Suzuki CAMI manufacturing plant in Ingersoll, Ontario. "That's kind of how my mind works." A few years before joining Chrysler, LaSorda was a General Motors executive put in charge of a troubled plant in Eisenbach, Germany. His lean manufacturing focus and combination of directive and achievement-oriented leadership helped the Eisenbach plant become one of GM's most efficient operations. Still, some observers believe that as Chrysler CEO, LaSorda needs to shift from these transactional leadership styles to something more transformational. "Tom LaSorda, who's more of a nuts-and-bolts type of guy, needs to take it to the next level and set Chrysler up for the next decade," suggests auto consultant Michael Robinet.[28] *AP/World Wide Photos*

www.daimlerchrysler.ca

- *Achievement-oriented*—These behaviours encourage employees to reach their peak performance. The leader sets challenging goals, expects employees to perform at their highest level, continuously seeks improvement in employee performance, and shows a high degree of confidence that employees will assume responsibility and accomplish challenging goals. Achievement-oriented leadership applies goal-setting theory (Chapter 5) as well as positive expectations in self-fulfilling prophecy (Chapter 3).

The path–goal model contends that effective leaders are capable of selecting the most appropriate behavioural style (or styles) for that situation. Leaders might simultaneously use two or more styles. For example, they might be both supportive and participative in a specific situation.

CONTINGENCIES OF PATH–GOAL THEORY

As a contingency theory, path–goal theory states that each of these four leadership styles will be effective in some situations but not in others. The path–goal leadership model specifies two sets of situational variables that moderate the relationship between a leader's style and effectiveness: (1) employee characteristics and (2) characteristics of the employee's work environment. Several contingencies have already been studied within the path–goal framework, and the model is open for more variables in the future.[29] However, only four contingencies are reviewed here (see Exhibit 14.4).

Skill and experience A combination of directive and supportive leadership is best for employees who are (or perceive themselves to be) inexperienced and unskilled. Directive leadership gives subordinates information about how to accomplish the

■ **EXHIBIT 14.4**   Selected contingencies of path–goal theory

	Directive	Supportive	Participative	Achievement-oriented
Employee contingencies				
Skill/Experience	Low	Low	High	High
Locus of control	External	External	Internal	Internal
Environmental contingencies				
Task structure	Nonroutine	Routine	Nonroutine	???
Team dynamics	Negative norms	Low cohesion	Positive norms	???

task, whereas supportive leadership helps them cope with the uncertainties of unfamiliar work situations. Directive leadership is detrimental when employees are skilled and experienced because it introduces too much supervisory control.

Locus of control   Recall from Chapter 2 that people with an internal locus of control believe that they have control over their work environment. Consequently, these employees prefer participative and achievement-oriented leadership styles and may become frustrated with a directive style. In contrast, people with an external locus of control believe that their performance is due more to luck and fate, so they tend to be more satisfied with directive and supportive leadership.

Task structure   Leaders should adopt the directive style when the task is non-routine, because this style minimizes role ambiguity that tends to occur in these complex work situations (particularly for inexperienced employees).[30] The directive style is ineffective when employees have routine and simple tasks because the manager's guidance serves no purpose and may be viewed as unnecessarily close control. Employees in highly routine and simple jobs may require supportive leadership to help them cope with the tedious nature of the work and lack of control over the pace of work. Participative leadership is preferred for employees performing nonroutine tasks because the lack of rules and procedures gives them more discretion to achieve challenging goals. The participative style is ineffective for employees in routine tasks because they lack discretion over their work.

Team dynamics   Cohesive teams with performance-oriented norms act as a substitute for most leader interventions. High team cohesiveness substitutes for supportive leadership, whereas performance-oriented team norms substitute for directive and possibly achievement-oriented leadership. Thus, when team cohesiveness is low, leaders should use the supportive style. Leaders should apply a directive style to counteract team norms that oppose the team's formal objectives. For example, the team leader may need to use legitimate power if team members have developed a norm to "take it easy" rather than get a project completed on time.

PRACTICAL IMPLICATIONS AND LIMITATIONS OF PATH–GOAL THEORY

Path–goal theory has received considerable research support, certainly more than other contingency leadership models. However, one or two contingencies (i.e., task structure) have found limited research support. Other contingencies and leadership styles in the path–goal leadership model haven't received research investigation at all.[31] For example, some cells in Exhibit 14.4 have question marks because we do not yet know how those leadership styles apply to those contingencies. The path–goal model was expanded a few years ago to include more leadership styles and contingencies, but they have not yet been tested. Until further study comes along, it is unclear whether particular conditions need to be considered when choosing the best leadership style.

Another concern is that as path–goal theory expands, the model may become too complex for practical use. Although the expanded model provides a closer representation of the complexity of leadership, it may become too cumbersome for training people in leadership styles. Few people would be able to remember all the contingencies and appropriate leadership styles for those contingencies. In spite of these limitations, path–goal theory remains a relatively robust contingency leadership theory.

OTHER CONTINGENCY THEORIES

At the beginning of this chapter we noted that numerous leadership theories have developed over the years. Most of them are found in the contingency perspective of leadership. Some overlap with the path–goal model in terms of leadership styles, but most use simpler and more abstract contingencies. We will very briefly mention only two here because of their popularity and historical significance to the field.

situational leadership theory
Developed by Hersey and Blanchard, suggests that effective leaders vary their style with the "readiness" of followers.

Situational leadership theory   One of the most popular contingency theories among practitioners is the **situational leadership theory (SLT)** also called life-cycle theory of leadership, developed by Paul Hersey and Ken Blanchard.[32] SLT actually derived from the 3-D managerial effectiveness model that the late University of New Brunswick professor Bill Reddin introduced in the mid-1960s. SLT suggests that effective leaders vary their style with the "readiness" of followers. (An earlier version of the model called this "maturity.") Readiness refers to the employee's or work team's ability and willingness to accomplish a specific task. Ability refers to the extent that the follower has the skills and knowledge to perform the task without the leader's guidance. Willingness refers to the follower's self-motivation and commitment to perform the assigned task. The model compresses these distinct concepts into a single situational condition.

The situational leadership model also identifies four leadership styles—telling, selling, participating, and delegating—that Hersey and Blanchard distinguish in terms of the amount of directive and supportive behaviour provided. For example, "telling" has high task behaviour and low supportive behaviour. The situational leadership model has four quadrants with each quadrant showing the leadership style that is most appropriate under different circumstances.

In spite of its popularity, several studies and at least three reviews have concluded that the situational leadership model lacks empirical support.[33] Only one part of the model apparently works; namely that leaders should use "telling" (i.e., directive style) when employees lack motivation and ability. (Recall that this is also documented in path–goal theory.) The model's elegant simplicity is attractive and entertaining, but most parts don't represent reality very well.

Fiedler's contingency model
Developed by Fred Fiedler, suggests that leader effectiveness depends on whether the person's natural leadership style is appropriately matched to the situation.

Fiedler's contingency model   The earliest contingency theory of leadership, called **Fiedler's contingency model**, was developed by Fred Fiedler and his associates.[34] According to this model, leader effectiveness depends on whether the person's natural leadership style is appropriately matched to the situation. The theory examines two leadership styles that essentially correspond to the previously described people-oriented and task-oriented styles. Unfortunately, Fiedler's model relies on a questionnaire that does not measure either leadership style very well.

Fiedler's model suggests that the best leadership style depends on the level of *situational control*; that is, the degree of power and influence that the leader possesses in a particular situation. Situational control is affected by three factors in the following order of importance: leader–member relations, task structure, and position power.[35] Leader–member relations is the degree to which employees trust and respect the leader and are willing to follow his or her guidance. Task structure refers to the clarity or ambiguity of operating procedures. Position power is the extent to which the leader possesses legitimate, reward, and coercive power over subordinates. These three contingencies form the eight possible combinations of *situation favourableness* from the leader's viewpoint. Good leader–member relations, high task structure, and strong position power create the most favourable situation for the leader because he or she has the most power and influence under these conditions.

Fiedler has gained considerable respect for pioneering the first contingency theory of leadership. However, his theory has fared less well. As mentioned, the leadership style scale used by Fiedler has been widely criticized. There is also no scientific justification for placing the three situational control factors in a hierarchy. Moreover, it seems that leader–member relations is actually an indicator of leader effectiveness (as in path–goal theory) rather than as a situational factor. Finally, the theory considers only two leadership styles whereas other models present a more complex and realistic array of behaviour options. These concerns explain why the theory has limited empirical support.[36]

Changing the situation to match the leader's natural style   Fiedler's contingency model may have become a historical footnote, but it does make an important and lasting contribution by suggesting that leadership style is related to the individual's personality and, consequently, is relatively stable over time. Leaders might be able to alter their style temporarily, but they tend to use a preferred style in the long term. More recent scholars have also proposed that leadership styles are "hard-wired" more than most contingency leadership theories assume.[37]

If leadership style is influenced by a person's personality, then organizations should engineer the situation to fit the leader's dominant style, rather than expect leaders to change their style with the situation. A directive leader might be assigned inexperienced employees who need direction rather than seasoned people who work less effectively under a directive style. Alternatively, companies might transfer supervisors to workplaces where their dominant style fits best. For instance, directive leaders might be parachuted into work teams with counterproductive norms, whereas leaders who prefer a supportive style should be sent to departments in which employees face work pressures and other stressors.

LEADERSHIP SUBSTITUTES

leadership substitutes

A theory that identifies contingencies that either limit the leader's ability to influence subordinates or make that particular leadership style unnecessary.

So far, we have looked at theories that recommend using different leadership styles in various situations. But one theory, called **leadership substitutes**, identifies conditions that either limit the leader's ability to influence subordinates or make that particular leadership style unnecessary. The literature identifies several conditions that possibly substitute for task-oriented or people-oriented leadership. For example, performance-based reward systems keep employees directed toward organizational goals, so they might replace or reduce the need for task-oriented leadership. Task-oriented leadership is also less important when employees are skilled and experienced. Notice how these propositions are similar to path–goal leadership theory, namely that directive leadership is unnecessary—and may be detrimental—when employees are skilled or experienced.[38]

Some research suggests that effective leaders help team members learn to lead themselves through leadership substitutes, which makes co-workers substitute for leadership in high involvement team structures.[39] Co-workers instruct new employees, thereby providing directive leadership. They also provide social support, which reduces stress among fellow employees. Teams with norms that support organizational goals may substitute for achievement-oriented leadership, because employees encourage (or pressure) co-workers to stretch their performance levels.[40]

Self-leadership—the process of influencing oneself to establish the self-direction and self-motivation needed to perform a task (see Chapter 6)—is another possible leadership substitute.[41] Employees with high self-leadership set their own goals, reinforce their own behaviour, maintain positive thought processes, and monitor their own performance, thereby managing both personal motivation and abilities. As employees become more proficient in self-leadership, they presumably require less supervision to keep them focused and energized toward organizational objectives.

The leadership substitutes model has intuitive appeal, but the evidence so far is mixed. Some studies show that a few substitutes do replace the need for task or people-oriented leadership, but others do not. The messiness of statistically testing for leadership substitutes may account for some problems, but a few writers contend that the limited support is evidence that leadership plays a critical role regardless of the situation.[42] At this point, we can conclude that a few conditions such as self-directed work teams, self-leadership, and reward systems might reduce the importance of task or people-oriented leadership, but probably won't completely replace leaders in these roles.

▪ TRANSFORMATIONAL PERSPECTIVE OF LEADERSHIP

transformational leadership
A leadership perspective that explains how leaders change teams or organizations by creating, communicating, and modelling a vision for the organization or work unit and inspiring employees to strive for that vision.

When Rick George became CEO of Calgary-based Suncor Energy Inc. in 1991, he soon discovered that he was put in charge of "the unluckiest oil company in Canada." It experienced a devastating fire and crippling labour dispute at a time when it was one of the world's highest-cost oil producers. At a time when Suncor managers were ready to jump ship, George began communicating to employees a vague but promising future. He gave subordinates power to improve productivity and, as the company's financial position stabilized, to expand production. Then George did something that still shocks some in Canada's oil patch; he urged employees and the industry to become environmentally friendly. Today, just about every Suncor employee can proudly repeat "Rick's mantra," which is to increase production, reduce costs, and reduce the environmental footprint.[43]

By any measure, Rick George is a transformational leader. Through his vision, communication, and actions, he has transformed Suncor into a more effective organization. **Transformational leaders** such as Rick George, Wayne Sales (Canadian Tire), Teresa Cascioli (Lakeport Beverages), Terry Matthews (Mitel and Newbridge Networks), and Isadore Sharp (Four Seasons Hotels and Resorts) dot the Canadian landscape. These leaders are agents of change. They develop a vision for the organization or work unit, inspire and collectively bond employees to that vision, and give them a "can do" attitude that makes the vision achievable.[44]

TRANSFORMATIONAL VERSUS TRANSACTIONAL LEADERSHIP

transactional leadership

Leadership that helps organizations achieve their current objectives more efficiently, such as linking job performance to valued rewards and ensuring that employees have the resources needed to get the job done.

Transformational leadership differs from **transactional leadership**.[45] Transactional leadership is "managing"—helping organizations achieve their current objectives more efficiently, such as by linking job performance to valued rewards and ensuring that employees have the resources needed to get the job done. The contingency and behavioural theories described earlier adopt the transactional perspective because they focus on leader behaviours that improve employee performance and satisfaction. In contrast, transformational leadership is about "leading"—changing the organization's strategies and culture so that they have a better fit with the surrounding environment.[46] Transformational leaders are change agents who energize and direct employees to a new set of corporate values and behaviours.

Organizations require both transactional and transformational leadership.[47] Transactional leadership improves organizational efficiency, whereas transformational leadership steers companies onto a better course of action. Transformational leadership is particularly important in organizations that require significant alignment with the external environment. Canadian research suggests that organizations that drive societal change—such as environmental organizations—are highly receptive contexts for transformational leadership.[48] Unfortunately, too many leaders get trapped in the daily managerial activities that represent transactional leadership.[49] They lose touch with the transformational aspect of effective leadership. Without transformational leaders, organizations stagnate and eventually become seriously misaligned with their environments.

TRANSFORMATIONAL VERSUS CHARISMATIC LEADERSHIP

One topic that has generated some confusion and controversy is the distinction between transformational and charismatic leadership.[50] Many researchers either use the words interchangeably, as if they have the same meaning, or view charismatic leadership as an essential ingredient of transformational leadership. Others take this view further by suggesting that charismatic leadership is the highest degree of transformational leadership.

However, the emerging view, which this book adopts, comes from a third group of experts who contend that charisma is distinct from transformational leadership. These academics point out that charisma is a personal trait that provides referent power over followers, whereas transformational leadership is a set of behaviours that people use to lead the change process.[51] Charismatic leaders might be transformational leaders; indeed, their personal power through charisma is a tool to change the behaviour of followers. However, some research points out that charismatic or "heroic" leaders easily build allegiance in followers, but do not necessarily change the organization. Other research suggests that charismatic leaders produce dependent followers, whereas transformational leaders have the opposite effect—they support follower empowerment, which tends to reduce dependence on the leader.[52]

The main point here is that transformational leaders are not necessarily charismatic. Alan G. Lafley, the CEO of Proctor & Gamble, is not known for being charismatic, but has transformed the household goods company like no leader in recent memory. Similarly, IBM CEO Sam Palmisano speaks with humility, yet continues to drive IBM's success. "I don't have much curb appeal," Palmisano says of his minimal charisma, adding that with over 300,000 brilliant people he isn't driving the organization. "I just try to lead them and get them to come together around a common point of view," he explains.[53] In other words, Palmisano and Lafley lead by applying transformational leadership behaviours.

Transformational Leadership without Charisma

Charisma is not a word that comes to mind when seeing Alan George Lafley in action as a leader. Various sources say that the Procter & Gamble (P&G) CEO is distinctly "unassuming" with "a humble demeanour that belies his status." Lafley is so soft-spoken that colleagues have to bend forward to hear him. One industry observer declared that "if there were 15 people sitting around the conference table, it wouldn't be obvious that he was the CEO." Lafley may lack the charismatic leadership style for which the previous P&G CEO was well known, but he nevertheless transformed the household products company, which his charismatic predecessor failed to do (leading him to be ousted after just 18 months). Lafley's calm self-assurance, consistent vision, and symbolic and strategic actions towards a more customer-friendly and innovative organization have provided the direction and clarity that P&G lacked. Importantly, Lafley also walks the talk; for 10–15 days each year, he personally interviews and observes customers using P&G products in their homes from Germany to Venezuela. The result: P&G has become the industry's hotspot for innovation, its market share and profitability have experienced sustained growth, and its stock price has soared.[54] *AP/World Wide Photos*

www.pg.com

ELEMENTS OF TRANSFORMATIONAL LEADERSHIP

There are several descriptions of transformational leadership, but most include the four elements illustrated in Exhibit 14.5. These elements include creating a strategic vision, communicating the vision, modelling the vision, and building commitment toward the vision.

Creating a strategic vision   Transformational leaders shape a strategic vision of a realistic and attractive future that bonds employees together and focuses their energy toward a superordinate organizational goal. Strategic vision represents the substance of transformational leadership. It reflects a future for the company or work unit that is ultimately accepted and valued by organizational members. Strategic vision creates a "higher purpose" or superordinate goal that energizes and unifies employees.[55] A strategic vision might originate with the leader, but it is just as likely to emerge from employees, clients, suppliers, or other constituents. A shared strategic vision plays an important role in organizational effectiveness.[56] Visions offer the motivational benefits of goal setting, but are compelling future states that bond employees and motivate them to strive for those objectives. Visions are typically described in a way that distinguishes them from the current situation, yet makes the goal both appealing and achievable.

Communicating the vision   If vision is the substance of transformational leadership, then communicating that vision is the process. Canadian CEOs say that the most important leadership qualities are being able to build and share their vision for the organization. "Part of a leader's role is to set the vision for the company and to communicate that vision to staff to get their buy-in,"

■ **EXHIBIT 14.5**

Elements of
transformational
leadership

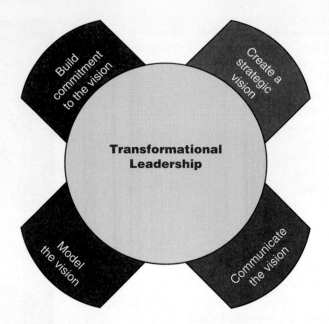

explains Dave Anderson, president of the Workers' Compensation Board of
British Columbia.[57] Transformational leaders communicate meaning and ele-
vate the importance of the visionary goal to employees. They frame messages
around a grand purpose with emotional appeal that captivates employees and
other corporate stakeholders. Framing helps transformational leaders establish
a common mental model so that the group or organization will act collectively
toward the desirable goal.[58]

Transformational leaders bring their visions to life through symbols, metaphors,
stories, and other vehicles that transcend plain language. Metaphors borrow
images of other experiences, thereby creating richer meaning of the vision that has
not yet been experienced. When George Cohen, the ebullient CEO of McDonald's
Canada, faced the difficult challenge of opening restaurants in Moscow, he frequently reminded his team members that they were establishing "hamburger
diplomacy." And in the mid-1800s, when ocean transportation was treacherous,
Samuel Cunard emphasized that he was creating an "ocean railway." Railroads
provided one of the safest forms of transportation, so Cunard's metaphor reinforced the notion to employees and passengers alike that Cunard Steamship Lines,
which at the time was based in Halifax, Nova Scotia, would provide equally safe
transportation across the Atlantic Ocean."[59]

Modelling the vision   Transformational leaders not only talk about a vision;
they enact it. They "walk the talk" by stepping outside the executive suite and
doing things that symbolize the vision.[60] They are also reliable and persistent in
their actions, thereby legitimizing the vision and providing further evidence that
they can be trusted. Leaders walk the talk through significant events, but they also
alter mundane activities—meeting agendas, office locations, executive schedules—so they are consistent with the vision and its underlying values. "The example you set at the top is probably the most important thing a CEO does in terms of
what you ask people to do," says Calgary-based Suncor CEO Rick George. "You
have got to walk that same line yourself."[61]

Canadian Executive's Visionary Leadership
Ray G. Young is quickly gaining recognition as a
transformational leader as president of General
Motors Brazil. The Canadian-born executive joined
GM Canada in finance, but moved into line management after serving as vice-president and chief financial officer of GM North America. Now in one of the
world's toughest automobile markets, Young is determined that GM will regain market leadership. He
makes sure that everyone is involved by distributing
monthly updates to employees on the company's performance. He has also rebuilt employee morale by
holding celebrations to thank employees publicly for
their accomplishments. "He has brought a sense of
purpose to General Motors that they didn't seem to
have before," said Ricardo Durazzo, a vice-president
at the consulting firm A. T. Kearney in São Paulo.[62]
Paul Fridman for The New York Times
www.gm.com/company

Modelling the vision is important because employees and other stakeholders are executive watchers who
look for behaviours that symbolize values and expectations. The greater the consistency between the
leader's words and actions, the more employees will
believe and follow the leader. Walking the talk also
builds employee trust because it is partly determined
by the consistency of the person's actions.

Building commitment toward the vision   Transforming a vision into reality requires employee commitment. Transformational leaders build this commitment
in several ways. Their words, symbols, and stories build
a contagious enthusiasm that energizes people to
adopt the vision as their own. Leaders demonstrate a
"can do" attitude by enacting their vision and staying
on course. Their persistence and consistency reflect
an image of honesty, trust, and integrity. Finally, leaders build commitment by involving employees in the
process of shaping the organization's vision.

EVALUATING THE TRANSFORMATIONAL LEADERSHIP PERSPECTIVE

Transformational leaders do make a difference. Subordinates are more satisfied and have higher affective
organizational commitment under transformational
leaders. They also perform their jobs better, engage in
more organizational citizenship behaviours, and make
better or more creative decisions. One study of Canadian bank branches also reported that organizational
commitment and financial performance increased
where the branch manager completed a transformational leadership training program.[63]

Transformational leadership is currently the most
popular leadership perspective, but it faces a number
of challenges. One problem is that some writers
engage in circular logic by defining transformational
leadership in terms of the leader's success.[64] They suggest that leaders are transformational when they successfully bring about change, rather than whether they
engage in certain behaviours we call transformational. Another concern is that
the transformational leadership model seems to be universal rather than contingency-oriented. Only very recently have writers begun to explore the idea that
transformational leadership is more appropriate in some situations than others.[65]
For instance, transformational leadership is probably more appropriate when
organizations need to adapt than when environmental conditions are stable. Preliminary evidence suggests that the transformational leadership perspective is relevant across cultures. However, there may be specific elements of transformational
leadership, such as the way visions are formed and communicated, which are
more appropriate in North America than other cultures.

■ IMPLICIT LEADERSHIP PERSPECTIVE

The competency, behaviour, contingency, and transformational leadership perspectives make the basic assumption that leaders "make a difference." Certainly, there is evidence that senior executives do influence organizational performance. However, leaders might have less influence than most of us would like to believe. Some leadership experts suggest that people inflate the importance of leadership in explaining organizational events. These processes, including stereotyping, attribution errors, and the need for situational control, are collectively called **implicit leadership theory**.[66]

implicit leadership theory
A theory stating that people rely on preconceived traits to evaluate others as leaders, and that they tend to inflate the influence of leadership on organizational events.

STEREOTYPING LEADERSHIP

Implicit leadership theory states that everyone has preconceived notions about the features and behaviours of an effective leader. These perceptions are stereotypes or prototypes of idealized leadership that develop through socialization within the family and society.[67] Mental images of an ideal leader shape our expectations and acceptance of people as leaders which, in turn, affect their ability to influence us as followers. We rely on leadership stereotypes partly because a leader's success might not be known for months or possibly years. Consequently, employees depend on immediate information to decide whether the leader is effective. If the leader fits the mold, then employees are more confident that the leader is effective.[68]

ATTRIBUTING LEADERSHIP

Implicit leadership is also influenced by attribution errors. Research has found that (at least in Western cultures) people tend to attribute organizational events to the leader, even when those events are largely caused by factors beyond the leader's control. This attribution is partly caused by fundamental attribution error (see Chapter 3) in which leaders are given credit or blame for the company's success or failure because employees do not readily see the external forces that also influence these events. Leaders reinforce this belief by taking credit for organizational successes.[69]

NEED FOR SITUATIONAL CONTROL

A third perceptual distortion of leadership suggests that people want to believe leaders make a difference. There are two basic reasons for this belief.[70] First, leadership is a useful way for us to simplify life events. It is easier to explain organizational successes and failures in terms of the leader's ability than by analyzing a complex array of other forces. For example, there are usually many reasons why a company fails to change quickly enough in the marketplace, yet we tend to simplify this explanation down to the notion that the company president or some other corporate leader was ineffective.

Second, there is a strong tendency in Canada and similar cultures to believe that life events are generated more from people than from uncontrollable

"A year ago, I was a skinny, green-haired, skate boarding CEO of a dot-com company. But that didn't work out."

natural forces.[71] This illusion of control is satisfied by believing that events result from the rational actions of leaders. In short, employees feel better believing that leaders make a difference, so they actively look for evidence that this is so.

The implicit leadership perspective questions the importance of leadership, but it also provides valuable advice to improve leadership acceptance. This approach highlights the fact that leadership is a perception of followers as much as the actual behaviours and characteristics of people calling themselves leaders. Potential leaders must be sensitive to this fact, understand what followers expect, and act accordingly. Individuals who do not make an effort to fit leadership prototypes will have more difficulty bringing about necessary organizational change.

■ CROSS-CULTURAL AND GENDER ISSUES IN LEADERSHIP

Along with the five perspectives of leadership presented throughout this chapter, we need to keep in mind that societal cultural values and practices affect what leaders do. Culture shapes the leader's values and norms, which influence his or her decisions and actions. These cultural values also shape the expectations that followers have of their leaders. This is apparent in GLOBAL Connections 14.2, which looks into the "ubuntu" values that shape the preferred leadership behaviours and style in Africa.

An executive who acts inconsistently with cultural expectations is more likely to be perceived as an ineffective leader. Moreover, leaders who deviate from those values may experience various forms of influence to get them to conform to the leadership norms and expectations of that society. In other words, implicit leadership theory described in the previous section of this chapter explains differences in leadership practices across cultures.

Over the past few years, 150 researchers from dozens of countries have worked together on Project GLOBE (Global Leadership and Organizational Behaviour Effectiveness) to identify the effects of cultural values on leadership.[72] The project organized countries into 10 regional clusters, of which Canada is grouped into the "Anglo" cluster with Great Britain, Australia, New Zealand, and the United States. The results of this massive investigation are just beginning to appear, but preliminary work suggests that some features of leadership are universal and some differ across cultures.

Specifically, the GLOBE Project reports that "charismatic visionary" is a universally recognized concept, and that middle managers around the world believe that it is characteristic of effective leaders. Charismatic visionary represents a cluster of concepts including visionary, inspirational, performance-orientation, integrity, and decisiveness.[73] In contrast, participative leadership is perceived as characteristic of effective leadership in low power distance cultures but less so in high power distance cultures. For instance, one study reported that Mexican employees expect managers to make decisions affecting their work. Mexico is a high power distance culture, so followers expect leaders to apply their authority rather than delegate their power most of the time.[74] In summary, there are similarities and differences in the concept and preferred practice of leadership across cultures.

GENDER DIFFERENCES IN LEADERSHIP

Do women lead differently than men? Most Canadian CEOs think so. A Conference Board of Canada survey reported that 76 percent of male and female chief executives believe the leadership and management skills of women differ

Leading Through Ubuntu Values

Woven into the fabric of African society is the concept of "ubuntu." Ubuntu represents a collection of values, including harmony, compassion, respect, human dignity, and collective unity. It is "that profound African sense that each of us is human through the humanity of other human beings," explains former South African president Nelson Mandela. Ubuntu is often described through the Zulu maxim: "umuntu ngumuntu ngabantu." Archbishop Desmond Tutu offers this translation: "We believe that a person is a person through other persons; that my humanity is caught up, bound up and inextricably in yours."

The ubuntu value system provides a framework for how people should lead others in Africa, whether in politics or organizations. First, ubuntu is about connectedness, so leaders must be comfortable with the highly participative process of making decisions through consensus. Everyone must have a chance to speak without imposed tight time restrictions. The process itself will determine the time required. This consensus process does not call for leadership abdication; rather, it requires leaders to coach, facilitate, and possibly mediate as the group moves toward mutual agreement.

Along with building consensus, ubuntu values a collective respect for everyone in the system. It places the good of the community above self-interest; to help others as an inherent part of your own well-being. For leaders, this condition requires the ability to provide support to followers, to mediate differences, and to serve followers rather than have followers serve leaders. The heroic leader who steps in front—and typically looks down from a higher plateau—is not consistent with ubuntu. Instead, leaders are respected for their wisdom and ability, so ubuntu selects leaders for their age and experience.

Ubuntu is "that profound African sense that each of us is human through the humanity of other human beings," explains Nelson Mandela.
© EPA Photo/EPA/Kim Ludbrook/Corbis

Sources: L. van der Colff, "Leadership Lessons from the African Tree," *Management Decision*, 41 (2003), pp. 257–61; L. van der Colff, "Ubuntu, Isivivane and Uhluhlasa: The Meaning of Leadership and Management in South Africa," *Equity-Skills News & Views*, 1 (December 2002/January 2003); L. D. Krause and R. Powell, "Preparing School Leaders in Post-Apartheid South Africa: A Survey of Leadership Preferences of Principals in Western Cape," *Journal of Leadership Studies*, 8 (January 2002), pp. 63ff; M. P. Mangaliso, "Building Competitive Advantage from Ubuntu: Management Lessons from South Africa," *Academy of Management Executive*, 15 (August 2001), pp. 23–43; Speech by President Nelson Mandela at his 80th Birthday Party, Kruger National Park, July 16, 1998.
www.ubuntu.org

markedly from those of their male counterparts, with women generally seen as consensus builders better able to "nurture strong interpersonal relationships."[75]

These perceptions are consistent with the views of several writers who suggest that women have an interactive style that includes more people-oriented and participative leadership.[76] They suggest that women are more relationship-oriented, cooperative, nurturing, and emotional in their leadership roles. They further assert that these qualities make women particularly well suited to leadership roles at a time when companies are adopting a stronger emphasis on teams and employee involvement. These arguments are consistent with sex role stereotypes, namely that men tend to be more task oriented whereas women are more people oriented.

Are these stereotypes true? Do women adopt more people-oriented and participative leadership styles? The answer is no and yes, respectively. Leadership studies outside university labs (i.e., in real work settings) have generally found that male and female leaders do not differ in their levels of task-oriented or people-oriented leadership. The main explanation is that real-world jobs require similar behaviour from male and female job incumbents.[77]

However, women do adopt a participative leadership style more readily than their male counterparts. One possible reason is that, compared to boys, girls are often raised to be more egalitarian and less status oriented, which is consistent with being participative. There is also some evidence that women have somewhat better interpersonal skills than men, and this translates into their relatively greater use of the participative leadership style. A third explanation is that subordinates expect female leaders to be more participative, based on their own sex stereotypes, so female leaders comply with follower expectations to some extent.

Several recent surveys report that women are rated higher than men on the emerging leadership qualities of coaching, teamwork, and empowering employees.[78] Yet, research also suggests that women are evaluated negatively when they try to apply the full range of leadership styles, particularly more directive and autocratic approaches. Thus, ironically, women may be well suited to contemporary leadership roles, yet they often continue to face limitations of leadership through the gender stereotypes and prototypes of leaders held by followers.[79] Overall, both male and female leaders must be sensitive to the fact that followers have expectations about how leaders should act, and negative evaluations may go to leaders who deviate from those expectations.

CHAPTER SUMMARY

Leadership is a complex concept that is defined as the ability to influence, motivate, and enable others to contribute toward the effectiveness and success of the organizations of which they are members. Leaders use influence to motivate followers, and arrange the work environment so that they do the job more effectively. Leaders exist throughout the organization, not just in the executive suite.

The competency perspective tries to identify the characteristics of effective leaders. Recent writing suggests that leaders have emotional intelligence, integrity, drive, leadership motivation, self-confidence, above-average intelligence, and knowledge of the business. The behavioural perspective of leadership identified two clusters of leader behaviour, people-oriented and task-oriented. People-oriented behaviours include showing mutual trust and respect for subordinates, demonstrating a genuine concern for their needs, and having a desire to look out for their welfare. Task-oriented behaviours include assigning employees to specific tasks, clarifying their work duties and procedures, ensuring that they follow company rules, and pushing them to reach their performance capacity.

The contingency perspective of leadership takes the view that effective leaders diagnose the situation and adapt their style to fit that situation. The path–goal model is the prominent contingency theory that identifies four leadership styles—directive, supportive, participative, and achievement-oriented—and several contingencies relating to the characteristics of the employee and of the situation.

Two other contingency leadership theories include the situational leadership theory and Fiedler's contingency theory. Research support is quite weak for both theories. However, a lasting element of Fiedler's theory is the idea that leaders have natural styles and, consequently, companies need to change the leader's environment to suit his/her style. Leadership substitutes identify contingencies that either limit the leader's ability to influence subordinates or make that particular leadership style unnecessary.

Transformational leaders create a strategic vision, communicate that vision through framing and use of metaphors, model the vision by "walking the talk" and acting consistently, and build commitment toward the vision. This contrasts with transactional leadership, which involves linking job performance to valued rewards and ensuring that employees have the resources needed to get the job done. The contingency and behavioural perspectives adopt the transactional view of leadership.

According to the implicit leadership perspective, people inflate the importance of leadership through attribution, stereotyping, and fundamental needs for human control. Implicit leadership theory is evident across cultures because cultural values shape the behaviours that followers expect of their leaders.

Cultural values also influence the leader's personal values that, in turn, influence his or her leadership practices. The GLOBE Project data reveal that there are similarities and differences in the concept and preferred practice of leadership across cultures. Women generally do not differ from men in the degree of people-oriented or task-oriented leadership. However, female leaders more often adopt a participative style. Research also suggests that people evaluate female leaders based on gender stereotypes, which may result in higher or lower ratings.

KEY TERMS

Fiedler's contingency model, p. 393
implicit leadership theory, p. 400
leadership, p. 384

leadership substitutes, p. 394
path–goal leadership theory, p. 389
servant leadership, p. 390

situational leadership theory, p. 393
transactional leadership, p. 396
transformational leadership, p. 395

DISCUSSION QUESTIONS

1. Why is it important for top executives to value and support leadership demonstrated at all levels of the organization?

2. Find two newspaper ads for management or executive positions. What leadership competencies are mentioned in these ads? If you were on the selection panel, what methods would you use to identify these competencies in job applicants?

3. Consider your favourite teacher. What people-oriented and task-oriented leadership behaviours did he or she use effectively? In general, do you think students prefer an instructor who is more people-oriented or task-oriented? Explain your preference.

4. Your employees are skilled and experienced customer service representatives who perform nonroutine tasks, such as solving unique customer problems or special needs with the company's equipment. Use path–goal theory to identify the most appropriate leadership style(s) you should use in this situation. Be sure to fully explain your answer and discuss why other styles are inappropriate.

5. Transformational leadership is currently the most popular perspective of leadership. However, it is far from perfect. Discuss the limitations of transformational leadership.

6. This chapter emphasized that charismatic leadership is not the same as transformational leadership. Still, charisma is often mentioned in the discussions about leadership. In your opinion, how does charisma relate to leadership?

7. Identify a current world political leader (e.g., prime minister, premier, mayor) and his or her recent accomplishments. Now, using the implicit leadership perspective, think of ways that these accomplishments of the leader may be overstated. In other words, explain why they may be due to factors other than the leader.

8. You hear two people debating the merits of women as leaders. One person claims that women make better leaders than do men because women are more sensitive to their employees' needs and involve them in organizational decisions. The other person counters that although these leadership styles may be increasingly important, most women have trouble gaining acceptance as leaders when they face tough situations in which a more autocratic style is required. Discuss the accuracy of the comments made in this discussion.

CASE STUDY 14.1

THE STAFF SERGEANT'S LEADERSHIP DILEMMA

By James Buchkowsky, Saskatchewan Institute of Science and Technology.

Donna Lindsay, staff sergeant and commander of a Canadian regional police force detachment, just learned that she was not getting a replacement for a constable who had recently retired. Lindsay's superintendent said, "Hiring freezes are in effect until the next budget year, so you'll have to figure out a way for the other constables to pick up the work." Donna spent the rest of the day deciding how to divide the work among the other officers in her detachment.

The next morning at the daily briefing session, Donna announced the hiring freeze and that the constable position would not be replaced. She explained how she had divided the job into seven categories so that one constable would be responsible for each. Donna then informed the officers of the additional work that would be added to their duties. During the rest of the session, Donna couldn't help notice that many weren't reacting favourably to the announced assignments.

The next day, one constable, Earl, was waiting for her at her office door. "Why did you assign me to deal with the media?" he asked. "I hate being in front a camera. Can't you tell someone else they have to do this?"

Before long another staff member, Joe, was at Donna's door. "Can't you reassign the travelling presentations to someone else? I have a wife and young children. This detachment covers a large area with small communities, and asking me to travel all over is really unfair to my family."

By the end of the day, the seven constables had produced seven complaints. Donna re-examined the tasks and duties, attempted to juggle and switch assignments, and considered everyone's concerns but it nearly drove her crazy. She concluded there was nothing she could do to make everyone happy.

She called another staff meeting and said, "I've tried to accommodate you, but it can't be done. Take the assignments I've given you and do your best."

The officers didn't take to this decision very well and started taking matters into their own hands. Earl said to Joe, "I know you hate the travelling presentations, so I'll do them if you'll take my assignment." Roz told Linda, "I'll give you my research work if you'll do the evidence cataloguing." When other staff heard about the trading, they joined right in also. With more people making more offers, this wheeling and dealing kept getting louder and louder. Donna came out of her office to see what all the noise was about.

When Donna learned the staff were trading assignments without her consent, she was upset. A few days later, while discussing other matters on the telephone with her immediate supervisor in the regional office, Donna mentioned the events. "Some officers seem happy with their trades, but the ones who didn't get the trade they wanted are unhappy and directing the blame at me. What did I do wrong? How should I have handled this? What am I going to do now?"

Discussion Questions

1. What leadership style did Donna use? Was it appropriate for the situation?

2. Analyze the environmental and employee factors in this case to determine which style she should have adopted.

3. Since her approach did not work, what style should Donna use now?

TEAM EXERCISE 14.2

LEADERSHIP DIAGNOSTIC ANALYSIS

Purpose   To help students learn about the different path–goal leadership styles and when to apply each style.

Instructions

■ *Step 1:* Students individually write down two incidents in which someone had been an effective manager or leader over them. The leader and situation might be from work, a sports team, a student work group, or any other setting where leadership might emerge. For example, students might describe how their supervisor in a summer job pushed them to reach higher performance goals than they would have done otherwise. Each incident should state the actual behaviours that the leader used, not just general statements (e.g., "My boss sat down with me and we agreed on specific targets and deadlines, then he said several times over the next few weeks that I was capable of reaching those goals"). Each incident only requires two or three sentences.

■ *Step 2:* After everyone has written their two incidents, the instructor will form small groups (typically between four or five students). Each team will answer the following questions for each incident presented in that team:

1. Which path–goal theory leadership style(s)—directive, supportive, participative, or achievement-oriented—did the leader apply in this incident?

2. Ask the person who wrote the incident about the conditions that made this leadership style (or these styles, if more than one was used) appropriate in this situation? The team should list these contingency factors clearly and, where possible, connect them to the contingencies described in path–goal theory. (Note: the team might identify path–goal leadership contingencies that are not described in the book. These, too, should be noted and discussed.)

■ *Step 3:* After the teams have diagnosed the incidents, each team will describe to the entire class the most interesting incidents as well as its diagnosis of that incident. Other teams will critique the diagnosis. Any leadership contingencies not mentioned in the textbook should also be presented and discussed.

LEADERSHIP DIMENSIONS INSTRUMENT

Purpose   This assessment is designed to help you understand two important dimensions of leadership and identify which of these dimensions is more prominent in your supervisor, team leader, coach, or other person to whom you are accountable.

Instructions   Read each of the statements below and circle the response that you believe best describes

your supervisor. You may substitute "supervisor" with anyone else to whom you are accountable, such as a team leader, CEO, course instructor, or sports coach. Then use the scoring key in Appendix B to calculate the results for each leadership dimensions. After completing this assessment, be prepared to discuss in class the distinctions between these leadership dimensions

LEADERSHIP DIMENSIONS INSTRUMENT					
My supervisor ...	**Strongly Agree** ▼	**Agree** ▼	**Neutral** ▼	**Disagree** ▼	**Strongly Disagree** ▼
1. Focuses attention on irregularities, mistakes, exceptions and deviations from what is expected of me.	5	4	3	2	1
2. Engages in words and deeds that enhance his/her image of competence.	5	4	3	2	1
3. Monitors performance for errors needing correction.	5	4	3	2	1
4. Serves as a role model for me.	5	4	3	2	1
5. Points out what I will receive if I do what is required.	5	4	3	2	1
6. Instills pride in being associated with him/her.	5	4	3	2	1
7. Keeps careful track of mistakes.	5	4	3	2	1
8. Can be trusted to help me overcome any obstacle.	5	4	3	2	1
9. Tells me what to do to be rewarded for my efforts.	5	4	3	2	1
10. Makes me aware of strongly held values, ideals, and aspirations which are shared in common.	5	4	3	2	1
11. Is alert for failure to meet standards.	5	4	3	2	1
12. Mobilizes a collective sense of mission.	5	4	3	2	1
13. Works out agreements with me on what I will receive if I do what needs to be done.	5	4	3	2	1
14. Articulates a vision of future opportunities.	5	4	3	2	1
15. Talks about special rewards for good work.	5	4	3	2	1
16. Talks optimistically about the future.	5	4	3	2	1

Source: Items and dimensions are adapted from D. N. Den Hartog, J. J. Van Muijen, and P. L. Koopman, "Transactional Versus Transformational Leadership: An Analysis of the MLQ," *Journal of Occupational & Organizational Psychology* 70 (March 1997), pp. 19–34. Den Hartog et al. label transactional leadership as "rational-objective leadership" and label transformational leadership as "inspirational leadership." Many of their items may have originated from B. M. Bass and B. J. Avolio, *Manual for the Multifactor Leadership Questionnaire*. (Palo Alto, CA: Consulting Psychologists Press, 1989).

Case 1   FORECASTING IN BUSINESS

High up in a Calgary office tower, half a dozen people are helping the Royal Bank of Canada (RBC) plan for extraordinary events that might never happen. Over in Vancouver, Finning International is working through a similar exercise. For two years now, the industrial equipment distributor has been paying their consultant to "scare" them with scenarios such as: what if the equipment manufacturers began copying each other's machines and a price war broke out? Both companies are engaging in scenario planning—imagining the worst things that might happen and how the company can prevent or respond to those conditions. This CBC video program provides a brief overview of scenario planning, including the reasons why RBC, Finning, and other Canadian companies are making decisions long before problems or opportunities arise.

Discussion Questions

1. Based on the human problems with decision making described in the textbook, how does scenario planning improve the decision-making process?

2. Scenario planning occurs in teams rather than with the top executive alone. What are the benefits of team rather than individual decision making in scenario planning?

Case 2   BOOM (DRUM ROOM TEAMBUILDING)

Over the years, employees have been put through many different forms of team building, from board games to outdoor experiences. Now, some Canadian companies are putting a little more beat into team building by having their employees participate in drum circles and similar percussion activities. This CBC video takes the viewer to some of these events, from large assembly percussion orchestras to smaller group drum gatherings. In this program, you'll also hear what employees and executives who participated in these sessions think about them.

Discussion Questions

1. In your opinion, how would these drum circle and percussion sessions improve team dynamics? Under what conditions might they not work effectively?

2. What other organizational behaviour topics seem to be related to the effects of drum circles?

Case 3 CELEBRITY CEO CHARISMA

Does the cult of CEO charisma really make a difference to company profits? This NBC program takes a brief look at chief executives who acted like superheroes but failed to deliver, as well as a few low-key executives who really made a difference. The program hears from Harvard business school professor Rakesh Khurana, author of *Searching for a Corporate Savior*, a book warning that charismatic leaders are not necessarily effective leaders.

Discussion Questions

1. Why do company boards tend to hire charismatic CEOs?

2. What can corporate boards do to minimize the charisma effect when filling chief executive officer and other senior executive positions?

·15·

ORGANIZATIONAL STRUCTURE

LEARNING OBJECTIVES

AFTER READING THIS CHAPTER, YOU SHOULD BE ABLE TO:

- Describe three types of coordination in organizational structures.

- Explain why firms can have flatter structures than previously believed.

- Discuss the dynamics of centralization and formalization as organizations get larger and older.

- Contrast functional structures with divisional structures.

- Explain why geographic divisional structures are becoming less common than other divisional structures.

- Outline the features and advantages of the matrix structure.

- Describe the features of team-based organizational structures.

- Evaluate the advantages and disadvantages of the network structure.

- Summarize the contingencies of organizational design.

- Explain how organizational strategy relates to organizational structure.

Ray Muzyka and Greg Zeschuk faced an organizational dilemma not long after they (along with a third partner) formed BioWare Corp. The Edmonton-based electronic games company had been organized around one team to create their first product, *Shattered Steel*. But during that game's development, Muzyka and Zeschuk started a second game project, called *Baldur's Gate*. This led to a dilemma: what organizational structure would best support a multi-project company?

BioWare could simply have two teams working independently on the two games. However, a multi-team structure would duplicate resources, possibly undermine information sharing among people with the same expertise across teams, and weaken employee loyalty to the overall company. Alternatively, employees could be assigned to various specializations, including art, programming, audio, quality assurance, and design. This would improve the depth of expertise as people share information within their specialization. However, employees would not have the same level teamwork or commitment to the final product as they would in a team-based project structure.

To gain the benefits of both teams and departments, BioWare created a matrix structure in which employees belonged to departments but were assigned to specific teams based on needs. This encouraged employees to think in terms of the final product, yet kept them organized around their expertise to encourage knowledge sharing. "The matrix structure also supports our overall company culture where BioWare is the team, and everyone is always willing to help each other whether they are on the same project or not," explains Muzyka and Zeschuk.

The matrix structure proved effective, particularly as BioWare has now grown to 250 employees in as many as seven game projects. Still, an effective matrix structure requires careful coordination, so the co-CEOs host several "synchronization meetings" each year involving all department directors (art, design, audio, etc.), producers (i.e., game project leaders), and the human resources manager. "These meetings are essential in making sure that the people needed to do the job are working on the most appropriate projects," advises BioWare's co-CEOs.

The matrix structure seems to fit Bioware's needs for a more creative and adaptive organization. The company produces some of the world's most popular electronic games and has become one of Canada's best places to work. "They've been amazingly successful," the editor of one electronic games magazine recently applauded. "Anything that comes out of [BioWare] is on everyone's radar."[1] ■

www.bioware.com

Bioware cofounders Ray Muzyka (left) and Greg Zeschuk (right) designed an organizational structure for their Edmonton-based electronic games company that balances various needs for teamwork and information sharing.
Ed Kaiser/Edmonton Journal

organizational structure

The division of labour and the patterns of coordination, communication, work flow, and formal power that direct organizational activities.

T here is something of a revolution occurring in how organizations are structured. BioWare and other companies are constantly rethinking their organizational charts and trying out new designs that they hope will achieve organizational objectives more effectively. **Organizational structure** refers to the division of labour as well as the patterns of coordination, communication, workflow, and formal power that direct organizational activities. An organizational structure reflects the organization's culture and power relationships.[2]

Organizational structures are frequently used as tools for change because they establish new communication patterns and align employee behaviour with the corporate vision.[3] For example, to steer Charles Schwab Co. out of its financial trouble, the board of directors at the discount brokerage firm recently fired the CEO and brought back in Charles Schwab, the company's retired founder. One of Schwab's first tasks was to hold a two-day marathon session in which the company's top executives were asked to redraw the organization chart in a way that would make the company simpler, more decentralized, and refocused on the customer. Every executive in the room, including those whose jobs would be erased from the new structure, were asked for their input. "You had to answer," recalls Schwab's executive vice-president of human resources.[4]

We begin this chapter by considering the two fundamental processes in organizational structure: division of labour and coordination. This is followed by a detailed investigation of the four main elements of organizational structure: span of control, centralization, formalization, and departmentalization. The latter part of this chapter examines the contingencies of organizational design, including organizational size, technology, external environment, and strategy.

▪ DIVISION OF LABOUR AND COORDINATION

All organizational structures include two fundamental requirements: the division of labour into distinct tasks and the coordination of that labour so that employees are able to accomplish common goals.[5] Organizations are groups of people who work interdependently toward some purpose. To efficiently accomplish their goals, these groups typically divide the work into manageable chunks, particularly when there are many different tasks to perform. They also introduce various coordinating mechanisms to ensure that everyone is working effectively toward the same objectives.

DIVISION OF LABOUR

Division of labour refers to the subdivision of work into separate jobs assigned to different people. Subdivided work leads to job specialization, because each job now includes a narrow subset of the tasks necessary to complete the product or service. For example, designing and manufacturing an aircraft at Montreal-based Bombardier requires thousands of specific tasks that are divided among thousands of people. Tasks are also divided vertically, such as having supervisors coordinate work while employees perform the work.

Work is divided into specialized jobs because it potentially increases work efficiency.[6] Job incumbents can master their tasks quickly because work cycles are very short. Less time is wasted changing from one task to another. Training costs are reduced because employees require fewer physical and mental skills to accomplish the assigned work. Finally, job specialization makes it easier to match people with specific aptitudes or skills to the jobs for which they are best suited.

■ **EXHIBIT 15.1**   Coordinating mechanisms in organizations

Form of coordination	Description	Sub-types
Informal communication	Sharing information on mutual tasks; forming common mental models to synchronize work activities	• Direct communication • Liaison roles • Integrator roles
Formal hierarchy	Assigning legitimate power to individuals, who then use this power to direct work processes and allocate resources	• Direct supervision • Corporate structure
Standardization	Creating routine patterns of behaviour or output	• Standardized skills • Standardized processes • Standardized output

Source: Based on information in D. A. Nadler and M. L. Tushman, *Competing by Design: The Power of Organizational Architecture* (New York: Oxford University Press, 1997), Chapter 6; H. Mintzberg, *The Structuring of Organizations* (Englewood Cliffs, N.J.: Prentice Hall, 1979), Chapter 1; J. Galbraith, *Designing Complex Organizations* (Reading, MA: Addison-Wesley, 1973), pp. 8–19.

COORDINATING WORK ACTIVITIES

As soon as people divide work among themselves, coordinating mechanisms are needed to ensure that everyone works in concert. Every organization—from the two-person corner convenience store to the largest corporate entity—uses one or more of the following coordinating mechanisms:[7] informal communication, formal hierarchy, and standardization (see Exhibit 15.1).

Coordination through informal communication   Informal communication is a coordinating mechanism in all organizations. This includes sharing information on mutual tasks as well as forming common mental models so that employees synchronize work activities using the same mental road map.[8] Informal communication is vital in nonroutine and ambiguous situations because employees can exchange a large volume of information through face-to-face communication and other media-rich channels.

Coordination through informal communication is easiest in small firms, although information technologies have further leveraged this coordinating mechanism in large organizations. Larger organizations such as Canadian automobile parts maker Magna International also support informal communication by keeping each workplace small (around 200 employees). Toyota and other automakers further support this coordinating mechanism by occasionally moving dozens of employees responsible for developing a new product into one large room.[9]

Larger organizations also encourage coordination through informal communication by creating *integrator roles*. These people are responsible for coordinating a work process by encouraging employees in each work unit to share information and informally coordinate work activities. For example, brand managers at Procter & Gamble serve as integrators by coordinating marketing, production, and design groups. Integrators do not have authority over the people involved in that process, so they must rely on persuasion and similar influence tactics.[10]

Coordination through formal hierarchy   Informal communication is the most flexible form of coordination, but it can be time-consuming. Consequently, as organizations grow, they develop a second coordinating mechanism: formal hierarchy.

Hierarchy assigns legitimate power to individuals, who then use this power to direct work processes and allocate resources. In other words, work is coordinated through direct supervision. Any organization with a formal structure coordinates work to some extent through the formal hierarchy. For instance, team leaders at BioWare, described in the opening story to this chapter, coordinate work by ensuring that employees in their group remain on schedule and that their respective tasks are compatible with tasks completed by others in the group.

The formal hierarchy also coordinates work among executives through the division of organizational activities. If the organization is divided into geographic areas, the structure gives those regional group leaders legitimate power over executives responsible for production, customer service, and other activities in those areas. If the organization is divided into product groups, then the heads of those groups have the right to coordinate work across regions.

The formal hierarchy has traditionally been applauded as the optimal coordinating mechanism for large organizations. A century ago, administrative scholars argued that organizations are most effective where managers exercise their authority and employees receive orders from only one supervisor. Coordination should occur through the chain of command; that is, up the hierarchy and across to the other work unit.[11] Coordination through formal hierarchy may have been popular with classic organizational theorists, but it is often a very inefficient coordinating mechanism. Without relying on other coordinating mechanisms, managers can supervise only a limited number of employees. As the business grows, the number of supervisors and layers of management must also increase, resulting in a costly bureaucracy. Second, communicating through the chain of command is rarely as fast or accurate as direct communication between employees. Third, today's workforce is less tolerant of rigid structures. For instance, BioWare (described in the opening story) is one of Canada's best places to work in part because it minimizes formal hierarchy as a coordinating mechanism.

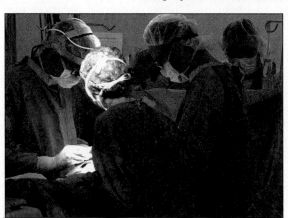

Medical Team Coordinates through Expertise

Led by Dr. Tirone David, this open-heart surgery team at Toronto General Hospital is divided into specialized jobs so that each person has the required competencies for each position. To some extent, surgical work is coordinated through informal communication. However, much of the work activity can occur without discussion because team members also coordinate through standardization of skills. Through extensive training, each medical professional has learned precise role behaviours so that his or her task activities are coordinated with others on the surgical team. *CP/Don Denton*

www.uhn.ca/tgh

Coordination through standardization Standardization, the third means of coordination, involves creating routine patterns of behaviour or output. This coordinating mechanism takes three distinct forms:

- *Standardized processes*—Quality and consistency of a product or service can often be improved by standardizing work activities through job descriptions and procedures.[12] This coordinating mechanism is feasible when the work is routine (such as mass production) or simple (such as making pizzas), but is less effective in nonroutine and complex work such as product design.

- *Standardized outputs*—This form of standardization involves ensuring that individuals and work units have clearly defined goals and output measures (e.g., customer satisfaction, production efficiency). For instance, to coordinate the work of salespeople, companies assign sales targets rather than specific behaviours.

■ *Standardized skills*—When work activities are too complex to standardize through processes or goals, companies often coordinate work effort by extensively training employees or hiring people who have learned precise role behaviours from educational programs. This form of coordination is used in hospital operating rooms. Surgeons, nurses, and other operating room professionals coordinate their work more through training than goals or company rules.

Division of labour and coordination of work represent the two fundamental ingredients of all organizational structures. How work is divided, who makes decisions, which coordinating mechanisms are emphasized, and other issues are related to the four elements of organizational structure.

■ ELEMENTS OF ORGANIZATIONAL STRUCTURE

Every company is configured in terms of four basic elements of organizational structure. This section introduces three of them: span of control, centralization, and formalization. The fourth element—departmentalization—is presented in the next section.

SPAN OF CONTROL

span of control
The number of people directly reporting to the next level in the organizational hierarchy.

Span of control refers to the number of people directly reporting to the next level in the hierarchy. Almost 100 years ago, French engineer and administrative theorist Henri Fayol strongly recommended the formal hierarchy as the primary coordinating mechanism. Consequently, he prescribed a relatively narrow span of control, typically no more than 20 employees per supervisor and six supervisors per manager. These prescriptions were based on the assumption that managers simply cannot monitor and control any more subordinates closely enough. Today, we know better. The best performing manufacturing facilities currently have an average of 31 employees per supervisor. Most expect to increase this span of control in the future to more than 70 employees per supervisor.[13]

What's the secret here? Did Fayol and others miscalculate the optimal span of control? The answer is that Fayol and many other scholars sympathetic to hierarchical control believed that employees should "do" the work, whereas supervisors and other management personnel should monitor employee behaviour and make most of the decisions. In contrast, the best performing manufacturing operations today rely on self-directed work teams, so direct supervision (formal hierarchy) is just a back-up coordinating mechanism.

In extreme cases, there is almost no supervision at all. Pratt & Whitney's turbine blade plant near Halifax, Nova Scotia, illustrates this point. The facility has no middle managers, no supervisors, no executive washrooms, no executive parking spaces, and no fancy job titles. Instead, a team of six executives sets overall plant objectives for manufacturing turbine blades and related aircraft engine parts. The operation's 450 employees belong to self-directed work teams that are almost completely responsible for meeting those objectives.[14] In effect, employees manage themselves, thereby releasing supervisors from the time-consuming tasks of monitoring behaviour and making everyone else's decisions.

The underlying principle here is that the optimal span of control depends on the presence of other coordinating mechanisms. Self-directed work teams supplement direct supervision with informal communication and specialized knowledge. This also explains why dozens of surgeons and other medical professionals may report to just one head surgeon in a major hospital. The head surgeon doesn't engage in much direct supervision because the standardized skills of medical staff coordinate the unit's work.[15]

Tall and flat structures   BASF's European Seal Sands plant recently organized employees into self-directed work teams and dramatically restructured the work process. These actions did much more than increase efficiency and lower costs at the bulk chemical plant. They also chopped out several layers of hierarchy. "Seven levels of management have been cut basically to two," says a BASF executive.[16]

BASF's European Seal Sands plant joins a long list of companies that are moving toward flatter organizational structures. This trend toward delayering—moving from a tall to flat structure—is partly in response to the recommendations of management gurus. Nearly 20 years ago, for example, management guru Tom Peters challenged corporate leaders to cut the number of layers to three within a facility and to five within the entire organization.[17]

The main reasons why BASF and other companies are moving toward flatter organizational structures is that it potentially cuts overhead costs and puts decision makers closer to front-line staff and information about customer needs. With fewer managers, employees might also experience more empowerment due to the greater autonomy over their work roles. "I think by having that flattened structure there is more job enrichment," says Cheryl Barber, Ducks Unlimited Canada's human resources administrator. "People feel that they are in control of what they are doing and that also helps to retain the employees."[18]

However, some organizational experts warn that corporate leaders may be cutting out too much hierarchy. They argue that the much-maligned "middle managers" serve a valuable function by controlling work activities and managing corporate growth. Moreover, companies will always need hierarchy because someone has to make quick decisions and represent a source of appeal over conflicts.[19] The conclusion here is that there is an optimal level of delayering in most organizations. Flatter structures offer several benefits, but cutting out too much management can offset these benefits.

One last point before leaving this topic: The size of an organization's hierarchy depends on both the average span of control and the number of people employed by the organization. Exhibit 15.2 illustrates this principle. A tall structure has many hierarchical levels, each with a relatively narrow span of control, whereas a flat structure has few levels, each with a wide span of control. Larger organizations that depend on hierarchy for coordination necessarily develop taller structures. For instance, Microsoft is considered a high-involvement organization, yet it has at least seven levels of corporate hierarchy to coordinate its tens of thousands of employees.[20]

CENTRALIZATION AND DECENTRALIZATION

centralization
The degree to which formal decision authority is held by a small group of people, typically those at the top of the organizational hierarchy.

Centralization and decentralization represents a second element of organizational design. **Centralization** means that formal decision-making authority is held by a small group of people, typically those at the top of the organizational hierarchy. Most organizations begin with centralized structures, as the founder makes most of the decisions and tries to direct the business toward his or her vision. But as organizations grow, they diversify and their environments become more complex. Senior executives aren't able to process all the decisions that significantly influence the business. Consequently, larger organizations tend to *decentralize*, that is, they disperse decision authority and power throughout the organization.

■ EXHIBIT 15.2   Span of control and tall/flat structures

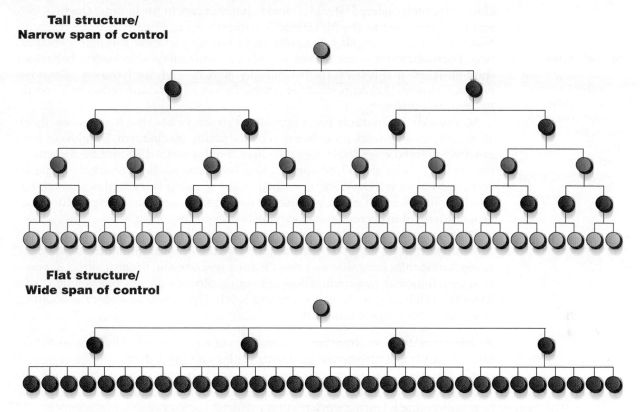

**Tall structure/
Narrow span of control**

**Flat structure/
Wide span of control**

Greg Wilkins, CEO of Toronto-based Barrick Gold Corp., recognized that large firms can't remain centralized forever. "Barrick had always been run on this command-and-control model, a centrist approach that saw all the decision making made in Toronto," Wilkins said recently after his promotion to chief executive. "That worked while the company was small and operating only in North America. But all of a sudden we are in four continents and seven countries and it becomes pretty clear that you just can't do it any more." The company has since decentralized its operations around three regions of the world.[21]

The optimal level of centralization or decentralization depends on several contingencies that we will examine later in this chapter. However, we also need to keep in mind that different degrees of decentralization can occur simultaneously in different parts of the organization. Nestlé has decentralized marketing decisions to remain responsive to local markets. At the same time, the Swiss-based food company has centralized production, logistics, and supply chain management activities to improve cost efficiencies and avoid having too much complexity across the organization. "If you are too decentralized, you can become too complicated— you get too much complexity in your production system," explains Nestlé CEO Peter Brabeck.[22] Firms also tend to rapidly centralize during times of turbulence and organizational crisis. When the problems are over, the company should decentralize decisions again, although this reversal tends to occur slowly because leaders are reluctant to give up decision-making power.

FORMALIZATION

formalization
The degree to which organizations standardize behaviour through rules, procedures, formal training, and related mechanisms.

Have you ever wondered why McDonald's hamburgers in St. Jerome, Quebec, look and taste the same as the MacDonald's hamburgers in Singapore? The reason is that the fast-food company has engineered out all variation through formalization. **Formalization** is the degree to which organizations standardize behaviour through rules, procedures, formal training, and related mechanisms.[23] In other words, formalization represents the establishment of standardization as a coordinating mechanism.

McDonald's Restaurants has a formalized structure because it relies heavily on standardization of work processes as a coordinating mechanism. Employees have precisely-defined roles, right down to how much mustard should be dispensed, how many pickles should be applied, and how long each hamburger should be cooked. In contrast, BioWare, described in the opening story to this chapter, has relatively little formalization because job descriptions and output expectations are broadly defined to accommodate varying tasks and responsibilities.

Older companies tend to become more formalized because work activities become routinized, making them easier to document into standardized practices. Larger companies formalize as a coordinating mechanism, because direct supervision and informal communication among employees do not operate as easily. External influences, such as government safety legislation and strict accounting rules, also encourage formalization.

Problems with formalization   Formalization may increase efficiency and compliance, but it can also create problems. Rules and procedures reduce organizational flexibility, so employees follow prescribed behaviours even when the situation clearly calls for a customized response. Thus, high levels of formalization undermine a learning orientation required for knowledge management and creativity. Some work rules become so convoluted that organizational efficiency would decline if they were actually followed as prescribed. Labour unions sometimes invoke work-to-rule strikes, in which their members closely follow the formalized rules and procedures established by an organization. This tactic is effective because the company's productivity actually falls when employees follow the rules that are supposed to guide their behaviour.

Formalized structures are fine for employees who value a stable workplace, but many employees today feel disempowered—they lack feelings of self-determination, meaning, competence, and impact of their organizational role—when working in highly formalized organizations. Finally, rules and procedures have been known to take on a life of their own in some organizations. They become the focus of attention rather than the organization's ultimate objectives of producing a product or service and serving its dominant stakeholders.

MECHANISTIC VERSUS ORGANIC STRUCTURES

mechanistic structure
An organizational structure with a narrow span of control and high degrees of formalization and centralization.

We have discussed span of control, centralization, and formalization together because they usually cluster into two forms: mechanistic and organic structures.[24] A **mechanistic structure** is characterized by a narrow span of control and high degrees of formalization and centralization. Mechanistic structures have many rules and procedures, limited decision making at lower levels, tall hierarchies of people in specialized roles, and vertical rather than horizontal communication flows. Tasks are rigidly defined, and are altered only when sanctioned by higher authorities.

Harbinger's Organic Structure Excludes Managers

Harbinger Partners is a "manager-free zone." That's because the business intelligence and creative services company has no bosses. All 20 employees (actually, they're partners) own a piece of the company and are involved in making company decisions. Harbinger doesn't even have a formal headquarters, just a post office box number in St. Paul, Minnesota. The company's partners work either from their homes or in clients' offices. This arrangement might give some executives sleepless nights, but not Scott Grausnick (centre in photo), who founded Harbinger in 1999. Instead, he deliberately created this highly organic structure so staff could cater more effectively to customer needs while satisfying their entrepreneurial spirit. The structure seems to work; Harbinger Partners weathered the downturn that affected other firms, and receives very high satisfaction ratings from customers and staff alike.[25]

The Minnesota Business Journal. Used with permission by Harbinger Partners Inc.

www.harbinger-partners.com

organic structure
An organizational structure with a wide span of control, little formalization, and decentralized decision making.

Companies with an **organic structure** have the opposite characteristics. BioWare, the Edmonton-based electronic games developer, is a clear example of an organic structure because it has a wide span of control, decentralized decision making, and little formalization. Tasks are fluid, adjusting to new situations and organizational needs. The organic structure values knowledge and takes the view that information may be located anywhere in the organization rather than among senior executives. Thus, communication flows in all directions with little concern for the formal hierarchy.

Mechanistic structures operate best in stable environments because they rely on efficiency and routine behaviours. However, as we have emphasized throughout this book, most organizations operate in a world of dramatic change. Information technology, globalization, a changing workforce, and other factors have strengthened the need for more organic structures that are flexible and responsive to these changes. Organic structures are also more compatible with knowledge and quality management because they emphasize information sharing rather than hierarchy and status.[26]

■ FORMS OF DEPARTMENTALIZATION

Span of control, centralization, and formalization are important elements of organizational structure, but most people think about organizational charts when the discussion of organizational structure arises. The organizational chart represents the fourth element in the structuring of organizations, called departmentalization. Departmentalization specifies how employees and their activities are grouped

Montreal Firm Outgrows Its Simple Structure

Servomax had a classic simple organizational structure when Arie Koifman first offered coffee services to Montreal business clients in the late 1990s. In fact, he was initially the only employee, taking orders and making deliveries. "I was sitting on boxes with my head out the sunroof," recalls Koifman, shown in this photo lifting a box of coffee with a few staff watching. As sales increased, Koifman hired employees with broadly defined roles to assist with deliveries and manage accounts. Today, Servomax has more than 1,000 regular business clients, a fleet of 11 delivery trucks, and estimated sales of $4 million, making it one of the largest providers of coffee services around Montreal. This means that Servomax will be replacing its simple structure to accommodate the company's increased complexity.[27] *R. Arless Jr. The Gazette/(Montreal)*
www.servomax.com

together. It is a fundamental strategy for coordinating organizational activities because it influences organizational behaviour in the following ways.[28]

■ Departmentalization establishes the chain of command, that is, the system of common supervision among positions and units within the organization. It frames the membership of formal work teams and typically determines which positions and units must share resources. Thus, departmentalization establishes interdependencies among employees and subunits.

■ Departmentalization focuses people around common mental models or ways of thinking, such as serving clients, developing products, or supporting a particular skill set. This focus is typically anchored around the common budgets and measures of performance assigned to employees within each departmental unit.

■ Departmentalization encourages coordination through informal communication among people and subunits. With common supervision and resources, members within each configuration typically work near each other, so they can use frequent and informal interaction to get the work done.

There are almost as many organizational charts as there are businesses, but we can identify six pure types of departmentalization: simple, functional, divisional, matrix, team-based, and network.

SIMPLE STRUCTURE

Most companies begin with a *simple structure*.[29] They employ only a few people and typically offer only one distinct product or service. There is minimal hierarchy—usually just employees reporting to the owner(s). Employees are grouped into broadly defined roles because there are insufficient economies of scale to assign them to specialized roles. Simple structures are flexible, yet they usually depend on the owner's direct supervision to coordinate work activities. Consequently, this structure is very difficult to operate as the company grows and becomes more complex.

FUNCTIONAL STRUCTURE

functional structure
An organizational structure that organizes employees around specific knowledge or other resources.

As firms grow, they adopt functional structures at some level of the hierarchy or at some time in their history. A **functional structure** organizes employees around specific knowledge or other resources. Employees with marketing expertise are grouped into a marketing unit, those with production skills are located in manufacturing, engineers are found in product development, and so on. Organizations with functional structures are typically centralized to coordinate their activities effectively. Standardization of work processes is the most common form of coordination used in a functional structure. Most organizations use functional structures at some level or at some time in their development.

Evaluating the functional structure   The functional structure encourages specialization and increases employees' identity with their profession. It permits greater specialization so that the organization has expertise in each area. Direct supervision is easier, because managers have backgrounds in that functional area and employees approach them with common problems and issues. Finally, the functional structure creates common pools of talent that typically serve everyone in the organization. This provides more economies of scale than if functional specialists are spread over different parts of the organization.[30]

The functional structure also has limitations.[31] Grouping employees around their skills tends to focus attention on those skills and related professional needs rather than on the company's product/service or client needs. Unless people are transferred from one function to the next, they might not develop a broader understanding of the business. Compared with other structures, the functional structure usually produces higher dysfunctional conflict and poorer coordination in serving clients or developing products. These problems occur because employees need to work with co-workers in other departments to complete organizational tasks, yet they have different subgoals and mental models of ideal work. Together, these problems require substantial formal controls and coordination when people are organized around functions.

DIVISIONAL STRUCTURE

divisional structure

An organizational structure that groups employees around geographic areas, clients, or outputs.

The **divisional structure** groups employees around geographic areas, outputs (products/services), or clients. This type of structure creates mini-businesses that may operate as subsidiaries rather than departments (sometimes called *strategic business units*); they are far more autonomous than functional departments. Exhibit 15.3 illustrates the three pure forms of divisional structure. The *geographic structure* organizes employees around distinct regions of the country or globe. Exhibit 15.3 *(a)* illustrates a geographic divisionalized structure recently adopted by Toronto-based Barrick Gold Corp. The *product/service structure* organizes work around distinct outputs. Exhibit 15.3 *(b)* illustrates this type of structure at Philips. The Dutch electronics company divides its workforce mainly into five product divisions, ranging from consumer electronics to semiconductors. The *client structure* represents the third form of divisional structure, in which employees are organized around specific customer groups. Exhibit 15.3 *(c)* illustrates the customer-focused structure similar to one adopted by Bell Canada.[32]

Which form of divisionalization should large organizations adopt? The answer depends mainly on the primary source of environmental diversity or uncertainty.[33] Suppose an organization has one type of product sold to people across the country. If customer needs vary across regions, or if provincial governments impose different regulations on the product, then a geographic structure would be best to be more vigilant of this diversity. On the other hand, if the company sells several types of products across the country and customer preferences and government regulations are similar everywhere, then a product structure would likely work best.

Coca-Cola, Nestlé, and many other food and beverage companies are organized mainly around geographic regions because consumer tastes and preferred marketing strategies vary considerably around the world. Even though McDonald's makes the same Big Mac around the planet, it has more fish products in Hong Kong and more vegetarian products in India in line with traditional diets in those countries. Philips,

■ **EXHIBIT 15.3** Three types of divisional structure

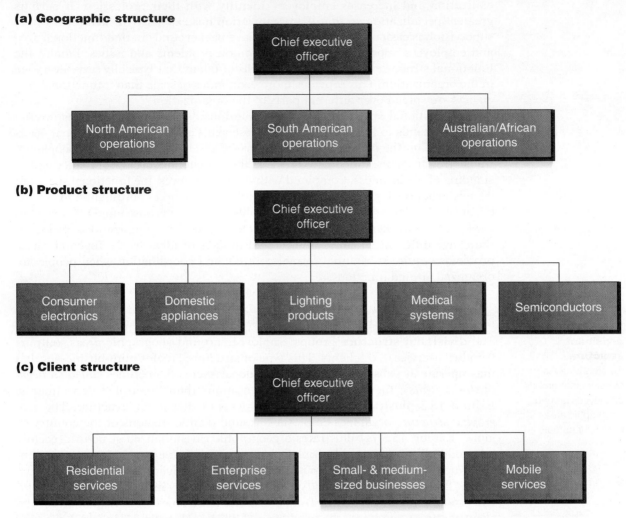

(a) Geographic structure

(b) Product structure

(c) Client structure

Note: Diagram (a) is similar to the global divisional structure of Toronto-based Barrick Gold Corp.; diagram (b) is similar to the product divisions at Philips; diagram (c) is similar to the customer-focused structure at Bell Canada.

on the other hand, is organized around products because consumer preferences are similar within each group. Hospitals from Geneva, Switzerland to Santiago, Chile, purchase similar medical equipment from Philips, whereas manufacturing and sales of these products are quite different from Philips' semiconductor business.

Many divisionalized companies are moving away from geographical structures.[34] Since clients can purchase online and communicate with businesses from almost anywhere in the world, local representation is less critical. Reduced geographic variation is another reason for the shift away from geographical structures; freer trade has reduced government intervention for many products, and consumer preferences for many products and services are becoming more similar (converging) around the world. The third reason is that large companies increasingly have global business customers who demand one global point of purchase, not one in every country or region.

Evaluating the divisionalized structure   The divisional form is a building block structure, because it accommodates growth relatively easily. Related products or clients can be added to existing divisions with little need for additional learning. Different products, services, or clients can be accommodated by sprouting a new division. Because coordinating functional units becomes too unwieldy with increasing diversity, organizations typically reorganize around divisional structures as they expand into distinct products, services, and domains of operation.[35]

These advantages are offset by a number of limitations. First, the divisionalized structure tends to duplicate resources, such as production equipment and engineering or information technology expertise. Also, unless the division is quite large, resources are not used as efficiently as in functional structures where resources are pooled across the entire organization. The divisionalized structure also creates silos of knowledge. Expertise is spread throughout the various business units, which reduces the ability and perhaps motivation of these people to share their knowledge with counterparts in other divisions. In contrast, a functional structure groups experts together, which supports knowledge sharing.

Finally, as was explained earlier, the preferred divisionalized structure depends on the company's primary source of environmental diversity or uncertainty. This principle seems to be applied easily enough at Coca-Cola, McDonalds, and Philips. But the decision is really quite difficult because global organizations experience diversity and uncertainties in many ways. The decision also affects political dynamics in the organization. If corporate leaders switch from a geographic to product structure, people who led the geographical fiefdoms suddenly get demoted under the product chiefs. The dilemma of which divisionalized structure to apply is illustrated in Connections 15.1, which describes the evolving restructure of Nortel, the high technology company headquartered in Brampton, Ontario.

MATRIX STRUCTURE

Ralph Szygenda faced a dilemma when he became General Motors' first corporate chief information officer.[36] His group serves the company's regional divisions, and each region's information technology needs differ to some extent. At the same time, GM has five diverse IT services, such as product development and supply chain management. Each of these services requires deep expertise, so staff providing one service would have quite different knowledge than staff providing one of the other IT services. The dilemma was whether to organize GM's hundreds of IT employees around a geographic or process structure.

matrix structure
A type of departmentalization that overlays two organizational forms in order to leverage the benefits of both.

Szygenda's solution was to do both by adopting a **matrix structure**. A matrix structure overlays two organizational forms in order to leverage the benefits that each has to offer. GM's IT group is organized around both geography and processes, as Exhibit 15.4 illustrates. The processes dimension is led by five process information officers (PIOs), each of whom is responsible for specific IT processes around the world. These PIOs report only to Szygenda. The geographic dimension is led by five regional chief information officers (CIOs) who are responsible for IT functions in each of General Motors' five regions around the world. These CIOs report to Szygenda as well as to the heads of their respective geographic business division. For example, the North American CIO reports to Szygenda and to the President of GM North America. Because they work closely with GM's regional executives and understand their priorities, the regional CIOs control the region's IT budget. This means that GM's PIOs compete with each other for financial resources towards IT projects in their specialization.

The Evolving Organizational Structure of Nortel

Nortel Networks keeps evolving its organizational structure in line with the diversity of its external environment. In the early 1980s, the Brampton, Ontario-based firm (then called Northern Telecom) was mainly a telecommunications equipment provider for telephone companies, most of which were either owned or highly regulated by governments. Thus, Nortel organized geographically because it had to cater to different regulations and needs across regions. The executives heading each geographical area were responsible for marketing, manufacturing, and most product development for their region.

In 1991, Nortel introduced a hybrid divisionalized structure consisting of three product groups responsible for global product development and four geographically based subsidiaries responsible for marketing and manufacturing in their territories. All seven leaders reported to Nortel's CEO. The new structure was created because of decreasing geographic diversity and increasing product diversity. The telephone industry was deregulating, which meant that telephone companies in most countries were developing increasingly similar needs and standards. Meanwhile, Nortel was developing more diverse telecom technologies used by businesses rather than just telecom firms.

Unfortunately, this seven-division hybrid arrangement was too unwieldy and generated too much infighting between the geographic and product leaders. Two years later, Nortel re-organized again, this time around two geographical groups—North America and World Trade. What happened to the product divisions? They now reported to the head of the company's North American operations.

But returning to a geographic structure didn't work for long either, because geography was no longer a key source of diversity. So, a few years later, Nortel effectively demoted the geographic leaders and made prod-
uct leaders in charge of key divisions. This purely product-based divisionalized structure allowed Nortel to pay more attention to developing and marketing these diverse products. Nortel made some changes over the next few years to its product-based divisions as products developed and merged. By 2004, for example, Nortel had four product divisions: carrier packet networks, enterprise networks, and two types of wireless units.

Recently, Nortel executives felt it was time to restructure the Canadian company again. Nortel is currently organizing into just two divisions: (1) enterprise solutions and packet networks and (2) mobility and converged core networks. Why the most recent changes? Nortel watchers aren't sure, but CEO Bill Owens, Nortel's current CEO, offers an explanation that fits classic organizational structure theory: "Convergence is here and now, and our enterprise and carrier customers are demanding partners who can deliver enterprise innovation on carrier-grade platforms."

In other words, the main source of diversity is clients, not product groups. Some products (mobility and core networks) serve telecom providers who want the same people to deliver the full range of Nortel products relevant to them. Meanwhile, business clients want one source of Nortel products relevant to them, including business telephony, Ethernet, wireline data, and packet networks.

Will the organizational structure stay with Nortel for years to come? Don't count on it!

Sources: L. Surtees, "Power Shifts at Northern Telecom," *The Globe & Mail*, February 14, 1991, pp. B1–B2; "Nortel Splits Operating Roles," *The Globe & Mail*, December 23, 1993, p. B3; "A World of Networks: Building the Foundation for the Future," *Telesis*, October 1995; Nortel Networks, *Corporate Backgrounder*, July 2000; "Nortel Streamlines Corporate Structure," *Ottawa Business Journal*, September 30, 2005; C. McLean, "Analysts Puzzled at Nortel's Latest Shuffle," *The Globe & Mail*, October 1, 2005, p. B8.

The matrix structure that organizes hundreds of IT professionals at General Motors is just one of many possible matrix structure combinations. Most global firms with a matrix structure have geography on one dimension, but the other dimension might be products/services (such as GM's IT processes) or client groups. Instead of combining two divisional forms, the matrix structure applied at BioWare (see opening story to this chapter) overlays a functional structure with project teams.[37] Employees are assigned to a cross-functional team responsible for a specific game project, yet they also belong to a permanent functional unit (design, audio, programming, etc.) from which they are redistributed when their work is completed on a particular project.

■ **EXHIBIT 15.4**
Simplified General
Motors' IT division
matrix structure

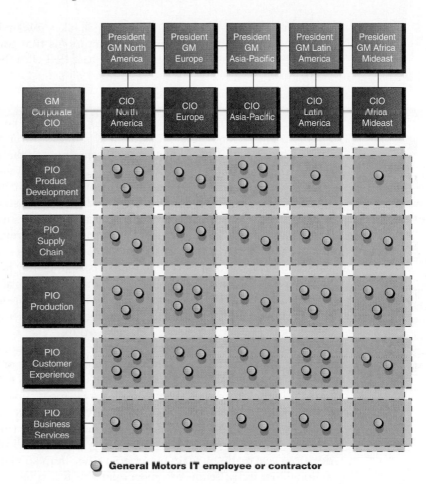

◯ **General Motors IT employee or contractor**

Evaluating the matrix structure   The matrix structure usually optimizes the use of resources and expertise, making it ideal for project-based organizations with fluctuating workloads. When properly managed, it improves communication efficiency, project flexibility, and innovation compared to purely functional or divisional designs. It focuses employees on serving clients or creating products, yet keeps expertise organized around their specialization so knowledge sharing improves and resources are used more efficiently. The matrix structure is also a logical choice when, as in the case of GM's IT group, two different dimensions are equally important. Structures determine executive power and what is important; the matrix structure works when two different dimensions deserve equal attention.

In spite of these advantages, the matrix structure has several well-known problems.[38] One concern is that it increases goal conflict and ambiguity. Employees working at the matrix level have two bosses and, consequently, two sets of priorities which aren't always aligned with each other. At BioWare, project leaders might squabble over specific employees who are assigned to other projects. They may also disagree with employee decisions, but the employee's functional leader has more say than the project leader as to the individual's technical competence.

Another challenge is that the existence of two bosses can dilute accountability. In a functional or divisionalized structure, one manager is responsible for everything, even the most unexpected issues. But in a matrix structure, the unusual problems don't get resolved because neither manager takes ownership for them.[39] The result of conflict and ambiguity in matrix structures is that some employees experience more stress, and some managers are less satisfied with their work arrangements.

TEAM-BASED STRUCTURE

About a dozen ago, The Criterion Group adopted a team-based organization to improve quality and efficiency. The New Zealand manufacturer of ready-to-assemble furniture organizes its 140 production employees into self-directed work teams with their own performance indicators and activity-based costing systems. Criterion now has just one layer of eight managers between the managing director and production staff.[40]

The Criterion Group has adopted a **team-based structure** in its production operations. The team-based structure has a few distinguishing features from other organizational forms. First, it is built around self-directed work teams (SDWTs) rather than traditional teams or departments. SDWTs complete an entire piece of work requiring several interdependent tasks, and they have substantial autonomy over the execution of their tasks. The teams operating at Criterion plan, organize, and control their own work activities without traditional supervision. Second, these teams are typically organized around work processes, such as making a specific product or serving a specific client group.

A third distinguishing feature of the team-based organizational structure is that it has a very flat hierarchy, usually with no more than two or three management levels. This flatter structure is possible because self-directed teams do not rely on direct supervision to coordinate their work. Because most supervisory activities have been delegated to the team, The Criterion Group has just one layer of management between production employees and the chief executive (managing director).

Finally, the team-based structure has very little formalization. Almost all day-to-day decisions are made by team members rather than someone further up the organizational hierarchy. Teams are given relatively few rules about how to organize their work. Instead, the executive team typically assigns output goals to the team, such as the volume and quality of product or service, or productivity improvement targets for the work process. Teams are then encouraged to use available resources and their own initiative to achieve those objectives.

Team-based structures are usually found within the manufacturing operations of larger divisionalized structures. For example, Pratt & Whitney's turbine blade plant near Halifax, Nova Scotia, has a team-based structure, but this exists within the company's divisionalized structure. However, a small number of firms apply the team-based structure from top to bottom. Perhaps the most famous example of this extreme level of team-based structure is W. L. Gore & Associates, which is described in GLOBAL Connections 15.2.

Evaluating the team-based structure   The team-based organization represents an increasingly popular structure because it is usually more responsive and flexible than the traditional functional or divisionalized structures.[41] It tends to reduce costs because teams have less reliance on formal hierarchy (direct supervision). A cross-functional team structure improves communication and cooperation across traditional boundaries. With greater autonomy, this structure also allows quicker and more informed decision making.[42] For this reason, some Canadian hospitals have shifted from functional departments to cross-functional teams. Teams composed of nurses, radiologists, anesthetists, a pharmacology representa-

---

team-based structure

A type of departmentalization with a flat hierarchy and relatively little formalization, consisting of self-directed work teams responsible for various work processes.

The Extreme Team Structure of W. L. Gore & Associates

Diane Davidson admits that her first few months at W. L. Gore & Associates Inc. were a bit frustrating. "When I arrived at Gore, I didn't know who did what," recalls the apparel industry sales executive hired to market Gore-Tex fabrics to brand name designers. "I wondered how anything got done here. It was driving me crazy." Davidson kept asking her "starting sponsor" who her boss was, but the sponsor firmly replied: "Stop using the B-word." Gore must have managers, she thought, but they probably downplay their status. But there really aren't any bosses, not in the traditional sense. "Your team is your boss, because you don't want to let them down," Davidson eventually learned. "Everyone's your boss, and no one's your boss."

From its beginnings in 1958, the Newark, Delaware-based manufacturer of fabrics (Gore-Tex), electronics, industrial, and medical products has adopted an organizational chart where most employees are organized around self-directed teams. The company has an incredibly flat hierarchy with a high degree of decentralized authority. Employees make day-to-day decisions within their expertise without approval from anyone higher up. Bigger issues, such as hiring and compensating staff, are decided by teams. "We make our own decisions and everything is discussed as well," explains Phyllis Tait, a medical business support leader at Gore's U.K. business unit.

The company has a divisional structure at the top, organized around products and clients, such as Fabrics, Medical, Electronics, and Industrial. But most of Gore's 6,000 employees work at 45 self-sufficient manufacturing and sales offices around the world. Each facility is deliberately kept to about 200 people so they can coordinate more effectively through informal communication. Within those units, new projects are started through individual initiative and support from others. "There is no positional power," explains Mike Cox, technical director of the industrial products division. "You are only a leader if teams decide to respect and follow you."

W. L. Gore & Associates Inc. has an extreme team-based organizational structure that eliminates the traditional hierarchy. "There's no fear of any person going over another's head," says Gore sales veteran Tom Erickson, shown here (left) with co-worker John Cusick in Gore's testing room. © Bill Kramer/Contact: Bill Kramer Photography Inc.

As Diane Davidson discovered, Gore operates without job descriptions or a formal chain of command. This ambiguous structure was established so employees can be creative and responsive by coordinating directly with people in other areas of the organization. "You go to whomever you need to get things done," says Gore sales veteran Tom Erickson. "If I want to talk to a person on the manufacturing line about a particular job, I just go out and talk to him. That's one thing that sets us apart. There's no fear of any person going over another's head."

Sources: "The Firm That Lets Staff Breathe," *Sunday Times (London)*, March 24, 2002; A. Brown, "Satisfaction All in a Day's Work for Top 3," *Evening News* (Edinburgh, Scotland), March 23, 2002, p. 13; M. Weinreb, "Power to the People," *Sales & Marketing Management*, April 2003, pp. 30–35; L. D. Maloney, "Smiles in the Workplace," *Test & Measurement World*, March 2004, p. 5; A. Deutschman, "The Fabric of Creativity," *Fast Company*, December 2004, p. 54.
www.gore.com

tive, possibly social workers, a rehabilitation therapist, and other specialists communicate and coordinate more efficiently, therefore reducing delays and errors.[43]

Against these benefits, the team-based structure can be difficult to maintain due to the need for ongoing interpersonal skills training. Teamwork potentially takes more time to coordinate than formal hierarchy during the early stages of team development. Employees may experience more stress due to increased ambiguity in their roles. Team leaders also experience more stress due to increased conflict, loss of functional power, and unclear career progression ladders.[44]

NETWORK STRUCTURE

A decade ago, Irwin Toy was a venerable Canadian toy company with more than 1,800 products and a few hundred employees. Family infighting, management problems, and globalization sent Irwin spiralling into receivership, but George Irwin, whose family once owned Irwin, bought up pieces of the company, including rights to the table hockey game that the former company invented in the 1930s. His new firm, iToys Inc., markets the highly popular electronic spinning top called i-Top and has many more contemporary products in the pipeline.

But while Irwin Toy employed hundreds of people, iToys counts only a dozen staff in Toronto and 30 more in Hong Kong. One reason for the small employment numbers is that iToys is the marketing hub of a network structure that spans the globe. "The i-Top was invented in Israel," Irwin explains. "The guy who sold it to us is in New York. We're in Toronto. It's manufactured in China. The package was designed in Boston. The design of the top itself was done in San Francisco. And the software developer was in Springfield, Massachusetts."[45]

network structure
An alliance of several organizations for the purpose of creating a product or serving a client.

iToys is a **network structure** because it is an alliance of several organizations for the purpose of creating a product or serving a client.[46] Exhibit 15.5 illustrates how this collaborative structure typically consists of several satellite organizations bee-hived around a "hub" or "core" firm. The core firm "orchestrates" the network process and provides one or two other core competencies, such as marketing or product development. In our example, iToys is the hub that provides marketing and management whereas other firms perform most other functions.

The core firm might be the main contact with customers, but most of the product or service delivery and support activities are farmed out to satellite organizations located anywhere in the world. Extranets (Web-based networks with partners) and

■ **EXHIBIT 15.5**

A network structure

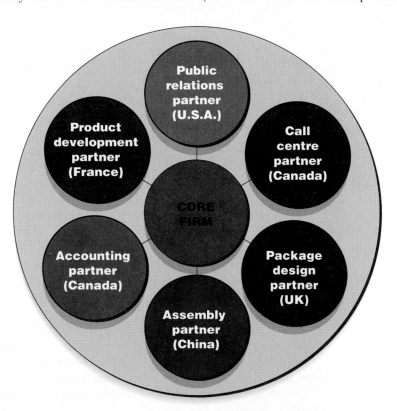

other technologies ensure that information flows easily and openly between the core firm and its array of satellites. "The traditional idea of the unit of business has always been the company," explains an executive at the Alliance of Manufacturers and Exporters Canada. "Now, it's the network, going beyond one company and encompassing all its suppliers and many of its customers."[47]

One of the main forces pushing toward a network structure is the recognition that an organization has only a few *core competencies*. A core competency is a knowledge base that resides throughout the organization and provides a strategic advantage. As companies discover their core competency, they "unbundle" non-critical tasks to other organizations that have a core competency at performing those tasks. For instance, Mitel Networks decided that its core competency is designing Internet protocol-based communications equipment, not manufacturing that equipment. Consequently, the Ottawa-based high technology firm outsourced its manufacturing and repair business to BreconRidge Manufacturing Solutions, which has a contract to manufacture Mitel products.[48]

Companies are also more likely to form network structures when technology is changing quickly and production processes are complex or varied.[49] Many firms cannot keep up with the hyperfast changes in information technology, so they have outsourced their entire information systems departments to IBM, EDS, and other firms that specialize in information systems services. Similarly, many high-technology firms form networks with Toronto-based Celestica Inc. because Celestica has expertise in diverse production processes.

Virtual corporations   The network structures that exist at iToys, Mitel Networks, Dell Computer, and other firms generally perform a patterned set of tasks for all clients. In contrast, some network structures—known as **virtual corporations**—represent several independent companies that form unique partnership teams to provide customized products or services, usually to specific clients, for a limited time.[50] The British advertising firm, host universal (which spells its name all lower case), is a good example of this. It has no employees or clients. Instead, it serves a specific project by forming a unique team of partners, who then disband when the project is finished. "At host we have no clients or employees, which enables us to pull the most effective teams together from our network without foisting redundant skills, fees and hierarchy onto clients," explains one of host's founding partners.[51]

Virtual corporations exist temporarily and reshape themselves quickly to fit immediate needs. When an opportunity emerges, a unique combination of partners in the alliance form a virtual corporation that works on the assignment until it is completed. Virtual corporations are self-organizing, meaning that they rearrange their own communication patterns and roles to fit the situation. The relationship among the partners is mutually determined rather than imposed by a core firm.

Evaluating the network structure   For several years, organizational behaviour theorists have argued that organizational leaders must develop a metaphor of organizations as plasma-like organisms rather than rigid machines.[52] Network structures come close to the organism metaphor because they offer the flexibility to realign their structure with changing environmental requirements. If customers demand a new product or service, the core firm forms new alliances with other firms offering the appropriate resources. For example, by finding partners with available plant facilities, Toronto-based iToys was able to launch i-Top soon after the company was formed, whereas product launch would take much longer

virtual corporations
Network structures representing several independent companies that form unique partnership teams to provide customized products or services, usually to specific clients, for a limited time.

if it had to build its own production facilities. When iToys needs a different type of manufacturing (such as metal rather than plastic fabrication), it isn't saddled with nonessential facilities and resources. Network structures also offer efficiencies because the core firm becomes globally competitive as it shops worldwide for subcontractors with the best people and the best technology at the best price. Indeed, the pressures of global competition have made network structures more vital, and computer-based information technology have made them possible.[53]

A potential disadvantage of network structures is that they expose the core firm to market forces. Other companies may bid up the price for subcontractors, whereas the short-term cost would be lower if the company hired its own employees to provide this function. Another problem is that although information technology makes worldwide communication much easier, it will never replace the degree of control organizations have when manufacturing, marketing, and other functions are in house. The core firm can use arm's-length incentives and contract provisions to maintain the subcontractor's quality, but these actions are relatively crude compared to those used to maintain performance of in-house employees.

■ CONTINGENCIES OF ORGANIZATIONAL DESIGN

Most organizational behaviour theories and concepts have contingencies—ideas that work well in one situation might not work as well in another situation. This contingency approach is certainly relevant when choosing the most appropriate organizational structure.[54] In this section, we introduce four contingencies of organizational design: external environment, size, technology, and strategy.

EXTERNAL ENVIRONMENT

The best structure for an organization depends on its external environment. The external environment refers to anything outside the organization, including most stakeholders (e.g., clients, suppliers, government), resources (e.g., raw materials, human resources, information, finances), and competitors. Four characteristics of external environments influence the type of organizational structure best suited to a particular situation: dynamism, complexity, diversity, and hostility.[55]

■ *Dynamic versus stable environments*—Dynamic environments have a high rate of change, leading to novel situations and a lack of identifiable patterns. Organic structures, including the matrix structure with teams at BioWare, are better suited to this type of environment so that the organization can adapt more quickly to changes.[56] In contrast, stable environments are characterized by regular cycles of activity and steady changes in supply and demand for inputs and outputs. Events are more predictable, enabling the firm to apply rules and procedures. Mechanistic structures tend to work best under these conditions because they are more efficient when the environment is predictable.

■ *Complex versus simple environments*—Complex environments have many elements whereas simple environments have few things to monitor. As an example, a major university library operates in a more complex environment than a small town public library. The university library's clients require several types of services—book borrowing, online full-text databases, research centres, course reserve collections, and so on. A small town public library has fewer of these demands placed on it. The more complex the environment, the more decentralized the

7-Eleven's Centralized–Decentralized Structure
7-Eleven tries to leverage the buying power and efficiencies of its 25,000 stores in 19 countries by centralizing decisions about information technology and supplier purchasing. At the same time, the convenience store chain's customers have diverse preferences from Japan to North America. This diversity exists even within countries. For example, weather and special events across Canada can dramatically vary product demand at each store. To thrive in this diverse and complex environment, 7-Eleven has what it calls a "centrally-decentralized" structure in which store managers make local inventory decisions using a centralized inventory management system. Along with ongoing product training and guidance from regional consultants, store managers have the best information about their customers and can respond quickly to local market needs. "We could never predict a busload of football players on a Friday night, but the store manager can," explains 7-Eleven president and CEO Jim Keyes, shown in this photo with a 7-Eleven employee.[57] *Courtesy of 7-Eleven, Inc.*
www.7-eleven.com

organization should become. Decentralization is a logical response to complexity because decisions are pushed down to people and subunits with the expertise needed to make informed choices.

- *Diverse versus integrated environments*—Organizations located in diverse environments have a greater variety of products or services, clients, and regions. In contrast, an integrated environment has only one client, product, and geographic area. The more diversified the environment, the more the firm needs to use a divisionalized form aligned with that diversity. If it sells a single product around the world, a geographic divisionalized structure would align best with the firm's geographic diversity, for example.

- *Hostile versus munificent environments*—Firms located in a hostile environment face resource scarcity and more competition in the marketplace. Hostile environments are typically dynamic ones because they reduce the predictability of access to resources and demand for outputs. Organic structures tend to be best in hostile environments. However, when the environment is extremely hostile—such as a severe shortage of supplies or lower market share—organizations tend to temporarily centralize so that decisions can be made more quickly and executives feel more comfortable being in control.[58] Ironically, centralization may result in lower-quality decisions during organizational crises, because top management has less information, particularly when the environment is complex.

ORGANIZATIONAL SIZE

Larger organizations should have different structures from smaller organizations.[59] As the number of employees increases, job specialization increases due to a greater division of labour. This greater division of labour requires more elaborate coordinating mechanisms. Thus, larger firms make greater use of standardization (particularly work processes and outcomes) to coordinate work activities. These coordinating mechanisms create an administrative hierarchy and greater formalization. Historically, larger organizations make less use of informal communication as a coordinating mechanism. However, emerging information technologies and increased emphasis on empowerment have caused informal communication to regain its importance in large firms.[60]

Larger organizations also tend to be more decentralized. Executives have neither sufficient time nor expertise to process all the decisions that significantly influence the business as it grows. Therefore, decision-making authority is pushed down to lower levels, where incumbents are able to cope with the narrower range of issues under their control.

TECHNOLOGY

Technology is another factor to consider when designing the best organizational structure for the situation.[61] Technology refers to the mechanisms or processes by which an organization turns out its product or service. One technological contingency is its *variability*—the number of exceptions to standard procedure that tend to occur. In work processes with low variability, jobs are routine and follow standard operating procedures. Another contingency is *analyzability*—the predictability or difficulty of the required work. The less analyzable the work, the more it requires experts with sufficient discretion to address the work challenges.

Assembly line technology has low variability and high analyzability; the jobs are routine and highly predictable. This type of technology works best with a structure consisting of high formalization and centralization. When employees perform tasks with high variety and low analyzability, they apply their skills to unique situations with little opportunity for repetition. Research project teams operate under these conditions. These situations call for an organic structure, one with low formalization, highly decentralized decision-making authority, and coordination mainly through informal communication among team members.

High variety and high analyzability tasks have many exceptions to routines, but these exceptions can usually be resolved through standard procedures. Maintenance groups and engineering design teams experience these conditions. Work units that fall into this category should use an organic structure, but it is possible to have somewhat greater formalization and centralization due to the analyzability of problems. Skilled trades people tend to work in situations with low variety and low analyzability. Their tasks involve few exceptions but the problems that arise are difficult to resolve. This situation allows more centralization and formalization than in a purely organic structure, but coordination must include informal communication among the skilled employees so that unique problems can be resolved.

ORGANIZATIONAL STRATEGY

organizational strategy

The way an organization positions itself in its setting in relation to its stakeholders, given the organization's resources, capabilities, and mission.

Organizational strategy refers to the way the organization positions itself in its setting in relation to its stakeholders, given the organization's resources, capabilities, and mission.[62] In other words, strategy represents the decisions and actions applied to achieve the organization's goals. Although size, technology, and environment influence the optimal organizational structure, these contingencies do not necessarily determine structure. Instead, corporate leaders formulate and implement strategies that shape both the characteristics of these contingencies as well as the organization's resulting structure.

This concept is summed up with the simple phrase: structure follows strategy.[63] Organizational leaders decide how large to grow and which technologies to use. They take steps to define and manipulate their environments, rather than let the organization's fate be entirely determined by external influences. Furthermore, organizational structures don't evolve as a natural response to these contingencies. Instead, they result from organizational decisions. Thus, organizational strategy influences both the contingencies of structure and the structure itself.

The structure follows strategy thesis has become the dominant perspective of business policy and strategic management. An important aspect of this view is that organizations can choose the environments in which they want to operate. Some businesses adopt a *differentiation strategy* by bringing unique products to the market or attracting clients who want customized goods and services. They try to distinguish their outputs from those provided by other firms through marketing, providing special services, and innovation. Others adopt a *cost leadership strategy*, in which they maximize productivity and are, thereby, able to offer popular products or services at a competitive price.[64]

The type of organizational strategy selected leads to the best organizational structure to adopt.[65] Organizations with a cost leadership strategy should adopt a mechanistic, functional structure with high levels of job specialization and standardized work processes. This is similar to the routine technology category described earlier because they maximize production and service efficiency. A differentiation strategy, on the other hand, requires more customized relations with clients. A matrix or team-based structure with less centralization and formalization is most appropriate here so that technical specialists are able to coordinate their work activities more closely with the client's needs. Overall, it is now apparent that organizational structure is influenced by size, technology, and environment, but the organization's strategy may reshape these elements and loosen their connection to organizational structure.

CHAPTER SUMMARY

Organizational structure refers to the division of labour as well as the patterns of coordination, communication, workflow, and formal power that direct organizational activities. All organizational structures divide labour into distinct tasks and coordinate that labour to accomplish common goals. The primary means of coordination are informal communication, formal hierarchy, and standardization.

The four basic elements of organizational structure include span of control, centralization, formalization, and departmentalization. At one time, scholars suggested that firms should have a tall hierarchy with a narrow span of control. Today, most organizations have a flatter hierarchy because they rely on informal communication and standardization, rather than mainly direct supervision, to coordinate work processes.

Centralization occurs when formal decision authority is held by a small group of people, typically senior executives. Many companies decentralize as they become larger and more complex because senior executives lack the necessary time and expertise to process all the decisions that significantly influence the business. Formalization is the degree to which organizations standardize behaviour through rules, procedures,

formal training, and related mechanisms Companies become more formalized as they get older and larger.

Span of control, centralization, and formalization cluster into mechanistic and organic structures. Mechanistic structures are characterized by a narrow span of control and high degree of formalization and centralization. Companies with an organic structure have the opposite characteristics.

Departmentalization specifies how employees and their activities are grouped together. It establishes the chain of command, focuses people around common mental models, and encourages coordination through informal communication among people and subunits. A functional structure organizes employees around specific knowledge or other resources. This fosters greater specialization and improves direct supervision, but increases conflict in serving clients or developing products. It also focuses employee attention on functional skills rather than on the company's product/service or client needs.

A divisional structure groups employees around geographic areas, clients, or outputs. This structure accommodates growth and focuses employee attention on products or customers rather than tasks. However, this structure creates silos of knowledge and duplication of resources. The matrix structure combines two structures to leverage the benefits of both of them. However, this approach requires more coordination than functional or pure divisional structures, may dilute accountability, and increases conflict.

Team-based structures are very flat with low formalization that organize self-directed teams around work processes rather than functional specialties. A network structure is an alliance of several organizations for the purpose of creating a product or serving a client. Virtual corporations are network structures that can quickly reorganize themselves to suit the client's requirements.

The best organizational structure depends on the firm's external environment, size, technology, and strategy. The optimal structure depends on whether the environment is dynamic or stable, complex or simple, diverse or integrated, and hostile or munificent. As organizations increase in size, they become more decentralized and more formalized, with greater job specialization and elaborate coordinating mechanisms. The work unit's technology—including variety of work and analyzability of problems—influences whether to adopt an organic or mechanistic structure. These contingencies influence but do not necessarily determine structure. Instead, corporate leaders formulate and implement strategies that shape both the characteristics of these contingencies as well as the organization's resulting structure.

KEY TERMS

centralization, p. 416

divisional structure, p. 421

formalization, p. 418

functional structure, p. 420

matrix structure, p. 423

mechanistic structure, p. 418

network structure, p. 428

organic structure, p. 419

organizational strategy, p. 432

organizational structure, p. 412

span of control, p. 415

team-based structure, p. 426

virtual corporations, p. 429

DISCUSSION QUESTIONS

1. W. L. Gore & Associates has a team-based structure throughout most levels of the organization. What coordinating mechanism dominates in this type of organizational structure? To what extent and in what ways would the other two types of coordination exist at Gore?

2. Think about the business school or other organizational unit whose classes you are currently attending. What is the dominant coordinating mechanism used to guide or control the instructor? Why is this coordinating mechanism used the most here?

3. Administrative theorists concluded many decades ago that the most effective organizations have a narrow span of control. Yet, today's top-performing manufacturing firms have a wide span of control. Why is this possible? Under what circumstances, if any, should manufacturing firms have a narrow span of control?

4. If one could identify "trends" in organizational structure, one of them would be decentralization. Why is decentralization becoming more common in contemporary organizations? What should companies consider when determining the degree of decentralization?

5. Diversified Technologies Ltd. (DTL) makes four types of products, each type to be sold to different types of clients. For example, one product is sold exclusively to automobile repair shops, whereas another is used mainly in hospitals. Customer expectations and needs are surprisingly similar throughout the world. However, the company has separate marketing, product design, and manufacturing facilities in North America, Europe, Asia, and South America because, until recently, each jurisdiction had unique regulations governing the production and sales of these products. However, several governments have begun the process of deregulating the products that DTL designs and manufactures, and trade agreements have opened several markets to foreign-made products. Which form of departmentalization might be best for DTL if deregulation and trade agreements occur?

6. Why are many organizations moving away from the geographic divisional structures?

7. From an employee perspective, what are the advantages and disadvantages of working in a matrix structure?

8. Suppose that you have been hired as a consultant to diagnose the environmental characteristics of your college or university. How would you describe the school's external environment? Is the school's existing structure appropriate for this environment?

CASE STUDY 15.1

FTCA—REGIONAL AND HEADQUARTERS RELATIONS

By Swee C. Goh, University of Ottawa.

The FTCA is a government organization that provides services to the Canadian public but also serves an enforcement role. It employs over 20,000 people, who are located at headquarters in Ottawa and in a large number of regional offices across Canada. Most staff are involved with direct counter-type services for both individuals and businesses. This includes collections, inquiries, payments, and audits. The agency also has large centres in various parts of Canada to process forms and payments submitted by individuals and businesses.

FTCA is a typical federal government department; many employees are unionized and have experienced numerous changes over the years. Because of the increasing complexity of regulations and the need to be more cost effective in the delivery of services, FTCA has evolved into an organization that uses technology a great deal. The agency's leaders increasingly emphasize the need for easier and faster service and turnaround in dealing with clients. They also expect staff to depend more on electronic means of communication for interaction with the public.

As the Canadian population grew over the years, the regional offices of this government organization expanded. An Assistant Deputy Minister (ADM) heads each regional office; each ADM has a budget and an increasing number of staff for the various functional activities related to the region, such as a manager for information systems. Every region also has offices located in the major cities. The directors of these city centre offices report directly to the regional ADM. The regional ADMs report directly to the Deputy Minister (DM), who is the overall head of the department.

FTCA has a strong emphasis on centralized control, particularly in the functional units. This emphasis occurs because of legislative requirements as well as the fact that the agency has extensive direct interaction with the public. For example one functional unit at headquarters (HQ) is responsible for collections and enforcement. If a regional manager has the same functional activity, FTCA executives believe that that person should be accountable to the HQ functional ADM. However, as mentioned earlier, the regional manager also reports directly

to the regional ADM and the budget for the department comes from the regional budget allocations and not from the HQ functional group.

This arrangement produces a dual-reporting relationship for regional functional managers. Regional managers complain that this situation is very awkward because they don't know who their real boss is: the regional ADM or the functional HQ ADM. Also, who should be responsible for evaluating the work performance of these dual-reporting regional managers? And if a regional manager makes a serious error, which of the two supervisors of that manager is ultimately accountable?

The potential for confusion about responsibility and accountability has made the roles and reporting relationships of the senior managers very vague. This also increased the occurrences of conflict between regional managers and HQ managers.

In order to deal with this growing problem, a consultant was brought in to do an independent evaluation of the current organization structure of FTCA. The consultant asked for an organization chart of FTCA, which is shown on page 436. The consultant became aware of the concerns described above by conducting interviews with various staff members throughout the agency. Other information such as budgets and financial allocations, some earlier organizational studies, and the mandate of the department were also provided to the consultant.

The discussions with staff members were very interesting. Some viewed this issue as a people problem and not a structural one. That is, if regional and HQ managers learned how to cooperate, took a shared responsibility approach, and work together with one another, this would not be an issue at all. But the view of the HQ functional groups was very different: They argued that FTCA is a functional organization so these functional unit leaders should have authority and power over regional managers performing the same function. In effect, these regional managers should report to the functional unit ADMs or at least be accountable to HQ policies and objectives.

To compound the problem, the regional managers saw this problem completely differently again! They

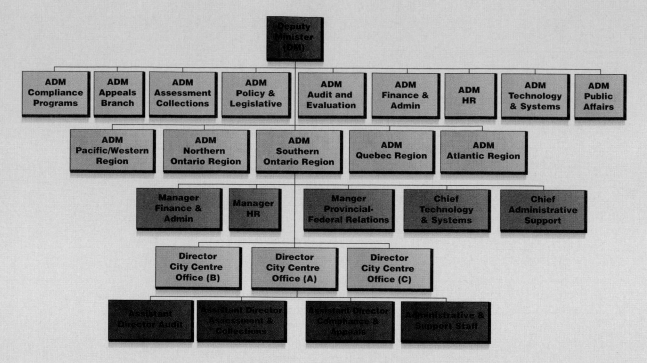

argued that the functional HQ managers should have a policy development function. On an annual basis they should develop broad objectives and targets in consultation with regional managers. Once approved, it should be the responsibility of the regional managers to carry them out in light of the environment and constraints they face. The functional unit ADMs oppose the regional managers' position, pointing out that if the regional managers do not achieve their objectives, the functional ADMs suffer the consequences.

After hearing these views, the consultant formed the opinion that this was an intractable and complex problem that could be related to both people and structure. The consultant also noted that the regional budgets were huge, sometimes larger than the budgets for functional groups at HQ. Regional ADMs also met infrequently—only once a month—with the deputy minister and functional ADMs at HQ in Ottawa. Mostly, the regions seemed to operate fairly autonomously, whereas the deputy minister seemed to have ongoing involvement with the functional ADMs.

An HQ staff member in Ottawa observed that, over time, the regional offices seemed to be getting bigger and bigger with the result that they have become fairly autonomous with functional staff complements that mirror the staff functions at HQ. The implication is that the regional staff will soon view the functional units in Ottawa as a distant group that only sets policy that the regions can interpret or ignore as they please.

A functional ADM with several years of seniority at FTCA warned that the functional units must have some control audit and other functional activities in the region. The ADM explained that without clear roles, reporting relationships, and accountability between the region and HQ, FTCA will not be able to provide Canadians with transparent and fair treatment to the services under their mandate.

The regional ADMs, however, saw their responsibilities as facilitating horizontal coordination within the region to ensure that actions and decisions are consistent and reflect the legislative responsibility of the department.

After a month of study and discussions with staff at FTCA, the consultant realized that this was not going to be an easy problem to resolve. There were also rumblings as the project progressed that some regional ADMs did not like the idea of restructuring FTCA to deal with this issue. These regional ADMs seemed to have considerable authority and power in the organization as a group and were resistant to any change to the status quo.

As the consultant sat down to write the report, a number of critical questions became apparent when deliberating on a solution to the problem at hand. Some of these include: Is FTCA a purely functional organization? Can the accountability issues be resolved through an acceptable organizational process and people training without the need for restructuring? What about power, politics, and conflict in this situation? Finally, will resistance to change become a problem as well?

Discussion Questions

1. Describe the current organization structure of FTCA? What is it? What are the strengths and weaknesses of such a structure?

2. Can FTCA operate effectively as a pure functional structure?

3. In what way does power and politics play in the current situation?

4. What kind of conflict is FTCA experiencing between HQ and regional managers?

5. Suggest a practical and workable solution to the problem at FTCA. If a restructuring is part of your solution, describe what the structure would look like and justify from your knowledge of organization theory and design why it would work, i.e., improve the working relationship between headquarters and regional staff.

Source: Materials in this case are based on factual and non-factual information of a Canadian federal government department. This case is written for classroom discussion and not to demonstrate effective or ineffective management of an organization.

Copyright © 2005 Swee C. Goh.

TEAM EXERCISE 15.2

ORGANIZATIONAL STRUCTURE AND DESIGN: THE CLUB ED EXERCISE

By Cheryl Harvey and Kim Morouney, Wilfrid Laurier University.

Purpose This exercise is designed to help you understand the issues to consider when designing organizations at various stages of growth.

Materials Each student team should have enough overhead transparencies or flip chart sheets to display several organizational charts.

Instructions Each team discusses the scenario presented. The first scenario is presented below. The instructor will facilitate discussion and notify teams when to begin the next step. The exercise and debriefing require approximately 90 minutes, although fewer scenarios can reduce the time somewhat.

■ *Step 1:* Students are placed in teams (typically four or five people).

■ Step 2: After reading Scenario #1 presented below, each team will design an organizational chart (departmentalization) that is most appropriate for this situation. Students should be able to describe the type of structure drawn and explain why it is appropriate. The structure should be drawn on an overhead transparency or flip chart for others to see during later class discussion. The instructor will set a fixed time (e.g., 15 minutes) to complete this task.

Scenario #1 Determined never to shovel snow again, you are establishing a new resort business on a small Caribbean island. The resort is under construction and is scheduled to open one year from now. You decide it is time to draw up an organizational chart for this new venture, called Club Ed.

■ *Step 3:* At the end of the time allowed, the instructor will present Scenario #2 and each team will be asked to draw another organizational chart to suit that situation. Again, students should be able to describe the type of structure drawn and explain why it is appropriate.

■ *Step 4:* At the end of the time allowed, the instructor will present Scenario #3 and each team will be asked to draw another organizational chart to suit that situation.

■ *Step 5:* Depending on the time available, the instructor might present a fourth scenario. The class will gather to present their designs for each scenario. During each presentation, teams should describe the type of structure drawn and explain why it is appropriate.

Source: Adapted from C. Harvey and K. Morouney, *Journal of Management Education* 22 (June 1998), pp. 425–29. Used with permission of the authors.

IDENTIFYING YOUR PREFERRED ORGANIZATIONAL STRUCTURE

Purpose This exercise is designed to help you understand how an organization's structure influences the personal needs and values of people working in that structure.

Instructions Personal values influence how comfortable you are working in different organizational structures. You might prefer an organization with clearly defined rules or no rules at all. You might prefer a firm where almost any employee can make important decisions, or where important decisions are screened by senior executives. Read the statements below and indicate the extent to which you would like to work in an organization with that characteristic. When finished, use the scoring key in Appendix B to calculate your results. This self-assessment is completed alone so students will complete this self-assessment honestly without concerns of social comparison. However, class discussion will focus on the elements of organizational design and their relationship to personal needs and values.

ORGANIZATIONAL STRUCTURE PREFERENCE SCALE

I would like to work in an organization where. . .					Score
1. A person's career ladder has several steps toward higher status and responsibility.	Not at all	A little	Somewhat	Very much	_____
2. Employees perform their work with few rules to limit their discretion.	Not at all	A little	Somewhat	Very much	_____
3. Responsibility is pushed down to employees who perform the work.	Not at all	A little	Somewhat	Very much	_____
4. Supervisors have few employees, so they work closely with each person.	Not at all	A little	Somewhat	Very much	_____
5. Senior executives make most decisions to ensure that the company is consistent in its actions.	Not at all	A little	Somewhat	Very much	_____
6. Jobs are clearly defined so there is no confusion over who is responsible for various tasks.	Not at all	A little	Somewhat	Very much	_____
7. Employees have their say on issues, but senior executives make most of the decisions.	Not at all	A little	Somewhat	Very much	_____
8. Job descriptions are broadly stated or nonexistent.	Not at all	A little	Somewhat	Very much	_____
9. Everyone's work is tightly synchronized around top management operating plans.	Not at all	A little	Somewhat	Very much	_____
10. Most work is performed in teams without close supervision.	Not at all	A little	Somewhat	Very much	_____
11. Work gets done through informal discussion with co-workers rather than through formal rules.	Not at all	A little	Somewhat	Very much	_____
12. Supervisors have so many employees that they can't watch anyone very closely.	Not at all	A little	Somewhat	Very much	_____
13. Everyone has clearly understood goals, expectations, and job duties.	Not at all	A little	Somewhat	Very much	_____
14. Senior executives assign overall goals, but leave daily decisions to front line teams.	Not at all	A little	Somewhat	Very much	_____
15. Even in a large company, the CEO is only three or four levels above the lowest position.	Not at all	A little	Somewhat	Very much	_____

·16·

ORGANIZATIONAL CULTURE

LEARNING OBJECTIVES

AFTER READING THIS CHAPTER, YOU SHOULD BE ABLE TO:

- Describe the elements of organizational culture.

- Discuss the importance of organizational subcultures.

- List four categories of artifacts through which corporate culture is deciphered.

- Identify three functions of organizational culture.

- Discuss the conditions under which cultural strength improves corporate performance.

- Compare and contrast four strategies for merging organizational cultures.

- Identify five strategies to strengthen an organization's culture.

- Describe the stages of organizational socialization.

- Explain how realistic job previews assist the socialization process.

C irque du Soleil, the Montreal-based troupe that combines circus with theatre, thrives on a culture of risk and creativity. In 1980, Gilles Ste-Croix, now Cirque du Soleil's vice-president of creation, asked the Quebec government for funding to start up a street theatre group in Baie-Saint-Paul, northwest of Quebec City. When the government rejected the application, Ste-Croix walked 90 kilometres from Baie-Saint-Paul to Quebec City...on stilts! The gruelling 22-hour trip got the government's attention and financial support.

Ste-Criox's band of 15 performers included Guy Laliberté who founded Cirque du Soleil in 1984. In 1987, Cirque du Soleil was invited to perform in a Los Angeles arts festival, but without upfront money to pay for travel. With barely enough funds to transport the performers and equipment to California, Laliberté agreed to cover the costs if the festival would give them the opening act and additional publicity. The gamble paid off. "I bet everything on that one night," Laliberté recalls. "If we failed, there was no cash for gas to come home."

The risk-taking and creative culture that Laliberté and Ste-Croix brought to Cirque du Soleil eventually led to an agreement with casino magnate Steve Wynn to open a new show, *Mystère*, at Wynn's new hotel in Las Vegas. Wynn threatened to pull out of the deal when he discovered that *Mystère's* storyline would be dark and moody, a sharp contrast to the upbeat style of Las Vegas entertainment. But Laliberté held Wynn to his word and *Mystère* had sell-out crowds soon after its opening night.

"(We stop growing) if we start being afraid of taking risks and if we start diminishing our creative pertinence," says Laliberté. Cirque du Soleil currently has four Las Vegas shows (with a fifth in development), drawing more than 5 percent of the city's visitors every night. Its most recent production, *Ka*, is a $150-million extravaganza repre-

Through its strong culture of risk-taking and creativity, Montreal-based Cirque du Soleil has become a leader in the entertainment industry.
CP/Paul Chiasson

senting the largest entertainment gamble ever made in Las Vegas. Cirque du Soleil also has a permanent show at Disney World in Florida and five travelling events around the world.

With more than 3,000 employees worldwide, Cirque du Soleil continues to thrive on creativity and risk-taking. It plows 40 percent of its profits back into research and development, including production development, costume design, and technology to aid the performers' mesmerizing on-stage antics. To put this into perspective, the troupe spends more than the average large Canadian or U.S. corporation on developing new products. "I believe in nurturing creativity and offering a haven for creators, enabling them to develop their ideas to the fullest," Laliberté explains.[1] ■
www.cirquedusoleil.com

irque du Soleil's phenomenal global success is a testament to the power of organizational culture. **Organizational culture** is the basic pattern of shared assumptions, values, and beliefs considered to be the correct way of thinking about and acting on problems and opportunities facing the organization. It defines what is important and unimportant in the company. You might think of it as the organization's DNA—invisible to the naked eye, yet a powerful template that shapes what happens in the workplace.[2]

This chapter begins by examining the elements of organizational culture and how culture is deciphered through artifacts. This is followed by a discussion of the relationship between organizational culture and corporate performance, including the effects of cultural strength, fit, and adaptability. Then we turn to the issue of mergers and corporate culture, followed by specific strategies for maintaining a strong organizational culture. The last section of this chapter zooms in on employee socialization, which is identified as one of the more important ways to strengthen organizational culture.

▪ ELEMENTS OF ORGANIZATIONAL CULTURE

As Exhibit 16.1 illustrates, the assumptions, values, and beliefs that represent organizational culture operate beneath the surface of behaviour. *Assumptions* are the shared mental models that people rely on to guide their perceptions and behaviours. They represent the deepest part of organizational culture because they are unconscious and taken for granted. At Cirque du Soleil, for example, risk-taking and creativity aren't just valued; they are assumed to be the best way to develop performances and ensure the company's success. *Beliefs* represent the individual's perceptions of reality. *Values* are more stable, evaluative beliefs that guide our preferences for outcomes or courses of action in a variety of situations.[3] They help us define what is right or wrong, or good or bad, in the world.

▪ **EXHIBIT 16.1**
Elements of organizational culture

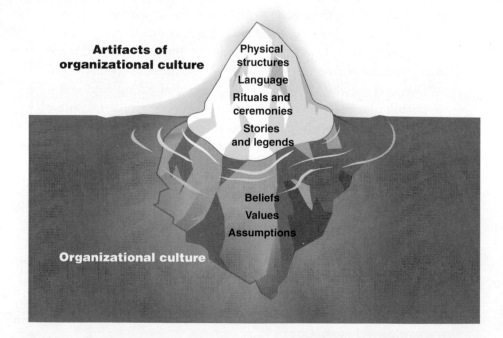

Artifacts of organizational culture

- Physical structures
- Language
- Rituals and ceremonies
- Stories and legends

- Beliefs
- Values
- Assumptions

Organizational culture

CONTENT OF ORGANIZATIONAL CULTURE

Organizations differ in their cultural content; that is, the relative ordering of beliefs, values, and assumptions. Consider the following companies and their apparent dominant cultures:

■ *Toronto Star*—One of the first things that rookie journalists at the *Toronto Star* learn about are the "Atkinson Principles." These principles reflect the newspaper's values of Canadian independence, social justice, and civic duties that Joseph Atkinson established a century ago as the founding publisher. The Atkinson principles are so deeply embedded in the newspaper's culture that staff today continue to debate whether editorial and news items live up to Atkinson's values.[4]

■ *ICICI Bank*—India's second largest bank exudes a performance-oriented culture. Its organizational practices place a premium on training, career development, goal setting, and pay-for-performance, all with the intent of maximizing employee performance and customer service. "We believe in defining clear performance for employees and empowering them to achieve their goals," says ICICI Bank executive director Kalpana Morparia. "This has helped to create a culture of high performance across the organization."[5]

■ *PCL Construction Group*—PCL is Canada's largest contractor (with $3.6 billion in annual revenue) and one of the best places to work in Canada, yet you rarely hear about the employee-owned company because it doesn't like to boast its successes. It is also a highly egalitarian company that operates out of a utilitarian one-story building on Edmonton's industrial southside. The CEO does get a corner office, but with a window facing busy traffic. And in spite of Edmonton's limited airline service, PCL executives don't have a corporate jet and "never will because it doesn't fit with the culture," explains PCL's chief executive.[6]

Socially responsible. Performance-oriented. Humble and egalitarian. How many corporate cultural values are there? No one knows for certain. There are dozens of individual and cross-cultural values, so there are likely as many organizational values. Some writers and consultants have attempted to classify organizational cultures into a few categories with catchy labels such as "mercenaries" and "communes." Although these typologies might reflect the values of a few organizations, they oversimplify the diversity of cultural values in organizations. Worse, they tend to distort rather than clarify our attempts to diagnose corporate culture.

RIM Culture

Research in Motion (RIM) has a fast-paced, entrepreneurial, yet supportive, culture. Employees at the Waterloo, Ontario, company that created the wireless digital assistant are in a constant race to beat competitors at the latest technology. At the same time, RIM's culture emphasizes having fun, including barbecues, Popsicle days, and special events. For example, RIM recently rented several movie theatres to treat its 3,000 employees around the world to a special screening of the latest *Star Wars* flick. For its 20th anniversary, RIM executives surprised employees with a rock concert featuring Barenaked Ladies and Aerosmith at the Kitchener Memorial Auditorium. Staff from Ottawa were bussed in for the event. "This is a fun, creative, intense and inclusive corporate culture," explains RIM co-CEO Jim Balsillie (right). "It's a collegial culture," adds Mike Lazaridis, RIM's other co-CEO (left).[7]

CP/Kitchener–Waterloo Record

www.rim.com

ORGANIZATIONAL SUBCULTURES

When discussing organizational culture, we are actually referring to the *dominant culture*, that is, the themes shared most widely by the organization's members. However, organizations are also comprised of *subcultures* located throughout its various divisions, geographic regions, and occupational groups.[8] Some subcultures enhance the dominant culture by espousing parallel assumptions, values, and beliefs; others are called *countercultures* because they directly oppose the organization's core values.

Subcultures, particularly countercultures, potentially create conflict and dissension among employees, but they also serve two important functions.[9] First, they maintain the organization's standards of performance and ethical behaviour. Employees who hold countercultural values are an important source of surveillance and critique over the dominant order. They encourage constructive conflict and more creative thinking about how the organization should interact with its environment. Subcultures prevent employees from blindly following one set of values and thereby help the organization to abide by society's ethical values.

The second function of subcultures is that they are the spawning grounds for emerging values that keep the firm aligned with the needs of customers, suppliers, society, and other stakeholders. Companies eventually need to replace their dominant values with ones that are more appropriate for the changing environment. If subcultures are suppressed, the organization may take longer to discover and adopt values aligned with the emerging environment.

artifacts
The observable symbols and signs of an organization's culture.

■ DECIPHERING ORGANIZATIONAL CULTURE THROUGH ARTIFACTS

We can't directly see an organization's cultural assumptions, values, and beliefs. Instead, as Exhibit 16.1 illustrated earlier, organizational culture is deciphered indirectly through **artifacts**. Artifacts are the observable symbols and signs of an organization's culture, such as the way visitors are greeted, the physical layout, and how employees are rewarded.[10] Understanding a company's culture requires more than surveying employees. It requires painstaking assessment of many artifacts because they are subtle and often ambiguous.[11]

Thus, discovering an organization's culture is very much like an anthropological investigation of a new society. It involves observing workplace behaviour, listening for unique language in everyday conversations, studying written documents, and interviewing staff about corporate stories. The four broad categories of artifacts are organizational stories and legends, rituals and ceremonies, language, and physical structures and symbols.

ORGANIZATIONAL STORIES AND LEGENDS

In the late 1980s, so the story goes, executives at Maritime Life Assurance Co. (now a subsidiary of Manulife Financial) were poring over the plans for a new head

Mayo Clinic's Cultural Expedition
The Mayo Clinic has a well-established culture at its original clinic in Rochester, Minn., but maintaining that culture at its expanding operations in Jacksonville, Fla., and Scottsdale, Ariz., has been challenging. "We were struggling with growing pains [and] we didn't want to lose the culture, [so] we were looking at how to keep the heritage alive," explains Matt McElrath, Mayo Clinic human resources director in Scottsdale. The Mayo Clinic retained anthropologist Linda Catlin to decipher Mayo's culture and identify ways to reinforce it at the two newer sites. Catlin shadowed employees and posed as a patient to observe what happens in waiting rooms. "She did countless interviews, joined physicians on patient visits, and even spent time in the operating room," says McElrath. At the end of her six-week cultural expedition, Catlin submitted a report outlining Mayo's culture and how its satellite operations varied from that culture. The Mayo Clinic adopted all of Catlin's 11 recommendations, such as requiring all new physicians at the three sites to attend an orientation in Rochester where they learn about Mayo's history and values.[12] *Courtesy of Mayo Clinic*
www.mayoclinic.com

office in Halifax. The crowning glory of the architectural design was a spectacular ocean view from the ninth-floor offices. Naturally, the architects designed the space for the executive suite. But Maritime's CEO believed that this would be inconsistent with the company's culture. Instead, the plum location went to the employees in the form of an elegant, wood-panelled cafeteria. The executives had to park their offices elsewhere.[13]

This story illustrates one of Maritime Life's core values—that employee well-being and satisfaction come before executive status. Stories and legends about past corporate incidents serve as powerful social prescriptions of the way things should (or should not) be done. They provide human realism to corporate expectations, individual performance standards, and assumptions about the way things should work around the organization. For instance, the opening vignette to this chapter described Gilles Ste-Croix's gruelling stilt walk to Quebec City and Guy Laliberté's gamble on the Los Angeles festival. Both of these incidents reveal Cirque du Soleil's risk-taking and creative culture.

Stories are important artifacts because they personalize the culture and generate emotions that help people to remember lessons within these stories. Stories have the greatest effect at communicating corporate culture when they describe real people, are assumed to be true, and are known by employees throughout the organization. Stories are also prescriptive—they advise people what to do or not to do.[14]

RITUALS AND CEREMONIES

rituals
The programmed routines of daily organizational life that dramatize the organization's culture.

Rituals are the programmed routines of daily organizational life that dramatize the organization's culture. They include how visitors are greeted, how often senior executives visit subordinates, how people communicate with each other, how much time employees take for lunch, and so on. Ceremonies are more formal artifacts than rituals. **Ceremonies** are planned activities conducted specifically for the benefit of an audience. This would include publicly rewarding (or punishing) employees, or celebrating the launch of a new product or newly won contract.

ceremonies
Planned and usually dramatic displays of organizational culture, conducted specifically for the benefit of an audience.

ORGANIZATIONAL LANGUAGE

The language of the workplace speaks volumes about the company's culture. How employees address co-workers, describe customers, express anger, and greet stakeholders are all verbal symbols of cultural values. Employees at The Container Store, an American retail store that sells containers, compliment each other about "being Gumby," meaning that they are being as flexible as the once-popular green toy—going outside their regular job to help a customer or another employee. (A human-sized Gumby is displayed at the retailer's headquarters.)[15] Language also highlights values held by organizational subcultures. For instance, consultants working at Whirlpool kept hearing employees talk about the appliance company's "PowerPoint culture." This phrase, which names Microsoft's presentation software, is a critique of Whirlpool's hierarchical culture in which communication is one-way (from executives to employees).[16]

PHYSICAL STRUCTURES AND SYMBOLS

Winston Churchill once said: "We shape our buildings; thereafter, they shape us."[17] The former British Prime Minister was reminding us that buildings both reflect and influence an organization's culture. The size, shape, location, and age of buildings

MEC's Built-in Enviro-Culture

Mountain Equipment Co-op's (MEC) retail outlet in Toronto (as well as most other cities where MEC has outlets) reveals a company whose culture is eco-conscious. Three large pine slabs near the entrance say "Tread Lightly. Leave No Trace. Take Only Memories." Concrete floors and beams are made from recycled slag (a by-product of coal-fired generating stations that usually ends up in landfill). Wood beams are recycled from demolished buildings. The roof holds a 930-square-metre (10,000-square-foot) garden with 100-mm (4-inch) thick soil that insulates the building while reducing urban temperatures and adding greenery and oxygen to Toronto's downtown. "Every aspect of the building was questioned," explains an executive at the Toronto architectural firm that designed the building. "It's a very unusual retail store—it's like an experiment in environmental solutions."[23]

Courtesy Mountain Equipment Co-op

www.mec.ca

might suggest the company's emphasis on teamwork, environmental friendliness, flexibility, or any other set of values. Even if the building doesn't make much of a statement, there is a treasure trove of physical artifacts inside. Desks, chairs, office space, and wall hangings (or lack of them) are just a few of the items that might convey cultural meaning. Stroll through Wal-Mart's headquarters in Bentonville, Arkansas, and you will find a workplace that almost screams out frugality and efficiency. The world's largest retailer has a spartan waiting room for suppliers, rather like government office waiting areas. Visitors pay for their own soft drinks and coffee. In each of the building's inexpensive cubicles, employees sit at inexpensive desks finding ways to squeeze more efficiencies and lower costs out of suppliers as well as their own work processes.[18]

■ ORGANIZATIONAL CULTURE AND PERFORMANCE

Does organizational culture affect corporate performance? Several writers think so, claiming that companies with strong cultures are more likely to be successful.[19] A *strong* organizational culture exists when most employees across all subunits hold the dominant values. The company's values are also institutionalized through well-established artifacts, thereby making it difficult for those values to change. Furthermore, strong cultures tend to be long-lasting; some can be traced back to the beliefs and values established by the company's founder. In contrast, companies have weak cultures when the dominant values are short lived and held mainly by a few people at the top of the organization.

A strong corporate culture is potentially good for business because it serves three important functions:

1. *Control system*. Organizational culture is a deeply embedded form of social control that influences employee decisions and behaviour.[20] Culture is pervasive and operates unconsciously. It is the company's automatic pilot, directing employees in ways that are consistent with organizational expectations.

2. *Social glue*. Organizational culture is the "social glue" that bonds people together and makes them feel part of the organizational experience.[21] Employees are motivated to internalize the organization's dominant culture because it fulfills their need for social identity. This social glue is increasingly important as a way to attract new staff and retain top performers.

3. *Sense-making*. Organizational culture assists the sense-making process.[22] It helps employees understand what goes on and why things happen in the com-

pany. Corporate culture also makes it easier for them to understand what is expected of them and to interact with other employees who know the culture and believe in it.

ORGANIZATIONAL CULTURE STRENGTH AND FIT

Strong cultures are *potentially* good for business, as was just explained, but this isn't always true. On the contrary, studies have found only a modestly positive relationship between culture strength and success.[24] One reason for the weak relationship is that a strong culture increases organizational performance only when the cultural content is appropriate for the organization's environment (see Exhibit 16.2). When a firm's strong culture is misaligned with its environment, it is unable to effectively serve customers and other dominant stakeholders. As GLOBAL Connections 16.1 describes, Judith Mair developed a strong "back to work" culture at her German advertising and Web design firm because she believed the typical "cool" cultures at other firms contributed to their downfall.

A second reason why companies with strong cultures aren't necessarily more effective is that strong cultures lock decision makers into mental models that blind them to new opportunities and unique problems. Thus, strong cultures might cause decision makers to overlook or incorrectly define subtle misalignments between the organization's activities and the changing environment. Several bankrupt steel manufacturers in the United States and Canada apparently suffered from this problem. "It was 100 years of integrated culture," recalls Mittal Steel vice-president John Mang, III, who worked at one of the now-bankrupt firms for three decades. "People in the organization are inbreds, including myself. You grew up in the culture; you didn't see anything else. You didn't typically see people at even very high levels in the steel organization coming in from the outside— even financial, executive, management. It is a culture from within so you have these rose-coloured glasses that everything's fine."[25]

A third consideration is that very strong cultures tend to suppress dissenting subcultural values. As we noted earlier, subcultures encourage constructive conflict, which improves creative thinking and offers some level of ethical vigilance over the dominant culture. In the long run, the subculture's nascent values could become important dominant values as the environment changes. Strong cultures suppress subcultures, thereby undermining these benefits.

■ **EXHIBIT 16.2**

Organizational culture and performance

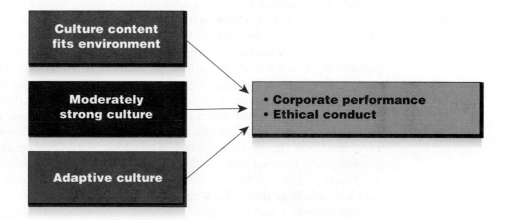

German Advertising Firm Embraces a "Back to Work" Culture

It's time to get back to work! No more office foosball or pool tables. No more flexible hours. No more casual dress. No Christmas party this year...or any year. In a rebellion against new economy work practices, a small advertising and Web design firm in Cologne, Germany, is returning to a no-nonsense, disciplined corporate culture. "The office is not an amusement park," advises Judith Mair, the 30-year-old entrepreneur who started Mair & Company a few years ago with three colleagues. "Work is just work, and that's exactly what it needs to become again."

Mair & Company's business-like culture is apparent as soon as you enter its offices. Mair and her co-workers wear company uniforms—smart blue suits when visiting clients and blue-grey tracksuits at the office. Everyone addresses each other formally by their family name. Smiling is not required; it's not even encouraged. Non-work topics are discussed only during official five-minute breaks. The offices are spartan: no pictures on the white walls and no personal items that would distract employees from their duties. New age gibberish from America such as "team spirit," "workflow," and "brainstorming" is strictly verboten.

The corporate culture also advocates strict working hours from 9:00 a.m. to 5:30 p.m. and minimal socializing afterwards. Weekend work is forbidden and no one is allowed to take work home. "It's dangerous if work and free time are being mixed up," Mair warns, suggesting that employees experience more stress when their company tries to take over their life beyond normal working hours.

These cultural artifacts are not dictums from the CEO. Mair & Company shifted away from the typical dot-com culture after seeing many other German Internet companies fail. They also found it more stressful to act like a "cool" young firm by dressing in the latest fashions and having company drinks in hip bars. "Yeah, it's strict, but it's OK," says co-worker Vanessa Plotkin, who helped to develop the disciplined culture. "It works."

Many Germans also think Mair & Company's culture "works" in today's tough economy. Mair's recently published book about her company's culture, called *Schluss mit Lustig* (meaning "End the Fun") has been snapped up by German business leaders looking for ways to survive in Germany's current economic slump.

Sources: R. Boyes, "Germans Told: Work is Not Fun," *The Times* (London), December 6, 2002, p. 20; T. Paterson, "German Woman Boss Puts Back Clock to Outlaw Fun," *The Telegraph* (London), December 8, 2002; K. James, "Germany Concern Looks at Making the Workplace Stricter and Less Friendly," *Marketplace: Minnesota Public Radio*, January 9, 2003; K. Gehmlich, "'Work is Just Work'," *The Globe & Mail*, July 11, 2003, p. C7; B. Bloch, "Controls Freaks Work Wonders on Shop Floor," *Daily Telegraph* (London), October 6, 2005, p. 6.

ADAPTIVE CULTURES

So far, we have learned that strong cultures are more effective when the cultural values are aligned with the organization's environment. Also, no corporate culture should be so strong that it blinds employees to alternative viewpoints or completely suppresses dissenting subcultures. One last point to add to this discussion is that organizations are more likely to succeed when they have an adaptive culture.[26] An **adaptive culture** exists when employees focus on the changing needs of customers and other stakeholders, and support initiatives to keep pace with these changes. Adaptive cultures have an external focus and employees assume responsibility for the organization's performance. As a result, they are proactive and quick. Employees seek out opportunities, rather than wait for them to arrive.

Organizational culture experts are starting to piece together the elements of adaptive cultures.[27] First and foremost, adaptive cultures have an external focus. Employees hold a common mental model that the organization's success depends on continuous change to support stakeholders. Nortel Networks has shifted from telephones to Internet gear. Nokia has moved from toilet paper and rubber boots to cellphones. Both of these firms have maintained an adaptive culture because employees believe that to keep pace with a changing external environment change is both necessary and inevitable.

adaptive culture
An organizational culture in which employees focus on the changing needs of customers and other stakeholders, and support initiatives to keep pace with these changes.

Citibank's Culture Pushes Ethical Boundaries

Citibank Japan director Koichiro Kitade thrived in Citigroup's bottom-line culture. Each year, his group handily exceeded the ever-increasing targets set by Citigroup's top executives in New York. Over six years, Citibank Japan outscored all other private banks in the company's huge network by increasing its clientele tenfold and delivering record profits. Unfortunately, the Japanese government's financial watchdog recently concluded that Citibank's culture also encouraged Kitade to push aside ethical and financial compliance rules. Japan's regulator accused Citibank of constructing "a law-evading sales system," citing infractions ranging from grossly overcharging clients to helping them to falsify profit and manipulate stock. With 83 infractions, Citigroup was told to close some of its Japanese operations. "It's our fault, because all we talk about is delivering the numbers. We've done this forever," admits Citigroup chief executive Charles Prince. This photo shows Prince (right) with a colleague at a Tokyo news conference bowing in apology for the violations. Prince fired several top executives in Tokyo and New York and is now on a mission to change Citibank's culture. He has a major challenge ahead of him. The Japan affair occurred after Citibank paid dearly for its involvement in the Enron accounting disaster. Dow Jones news service reports that Citibank has an "established reputation for pushing the limits of acceptable banking behaviour."[28] *Yuriko Nakao/Reuters*
www.citibank.com

Second, employees in adaptive cultures pay as much attention to organizational processes as they do to organizational goals. They engage in continuous improvement of internal processes (production, customer service, etc.) to serve external stakeholders. Third, employees in adaptive cultures have a strong sense of ownership. They assume responsibility for the organization's performance. In other words, they believe in "it's our job" rather than "it's not my job." Fourth, adaptive cultures are proactive and quick. Employees seek out opportunities, rather than wait for them to arrive. They act quickly to learn through discovery rather than engage in "paralysis by analysis."

ORGANIZATIONAL CULTURE AND BUSINESS ETHICS

Along with other forms of performance, an organization's culture can potentially influence ethical conduct. In fact, Canadian executives identify organizational culture as one of the three main influences on ethical conduct at work. (The other two were executive leadership and personal commitment to ethical principles.)[29] This makes sense because, as we learned in Chapter 2, good behaviour is driven by ethical values. An organization can guide the conduct of its employees by embedding ethical values in its dominant culture.

The relationship between ethics and organizational culture can be found in companies accused of serious discrimination or sexual harassment. These firms typically have a "gendered culture" that support discriminatory organizational rules and maintain assumptions that limit the career potential of women.[30] In extreme cases, the corporate culture reinforces perceptions of female staff as sexual objects, which increases the frequency of harassment. Thus, companies require more than policies and practices to repair sex discrimination and harassment problems; they must change the underlying culture into one that views men and women as equal partners in the enterprise.

Organizational culture is also potentially a source of ethical problems when it applies excessive control over employees. All organizations require some values congruence. As explained in Chapter 2, this congruence ensures employees make decisions that are compatible with organizational objectives. Congruence also improves employee satisfaction, loyalty, and longevity (i.e., low turnover). But a few organizations imprint their cultural values so strongly on employees that they risk becoming corporate cults. They take over employee lives and rob their individualism.

This cult-like phenomenon was apparently one of the factors that led to the downfall of Arthur Andersen. The accounting firm's uniting principle, called "One Firm," emphasized consistent service throughout the world by developing Andersen employees the same way. Andersen carefully selected university graduates with compatible values, then subjected these "green beans" to a powerful indoctrination process to further imprint Andersen's culture. This production of Andersen think-alikes, called "Androids," improved service consistency, but it also undermined the ethics of individualism.[31] Thus, an organization's culture should be consistent with society's ethical values and the culture should not be so strong that it undermines individual freedom.

■ MERGING ORGANIZATIONAL CULTURES

4C Corporate Culture Clash and Chemistry is a company with an unusual name and mandate. The Dutch consulting firm helps clients to determine whether their culture is aligned ("chemistry") or incompatible with ("clash") a potential acquisition or merger partner. The firm also compares the company's culture with its strategy. There should be plenty of demand for 4C's expertise. One study of more than 100 Canadian mergers and acquisitions discovered that 60 percent of these corporate marriages reduced rather than increased shareholder value. Others report that 77 percent of all mergers fail to return a positive investment. In many cases, corporate leaders are so focused on the financial or marketing logistics of a merger that they fail to conduct due-diligence audits on their respective corporate cultures.[32]

The corporate world is littered with mergers that failed or had a difficult gestation because of clashing organizational cultures.[33] Montreal-based Quebecor felt the side effects of imposing its "tight ship" culture on SunMedia. Morale apparently plummeted and turnover increased because staff at Toronto Sun and other SunMedia newspapers had difficulty adjusting to Quebecor's harsh values. The marriage of AOL Time Warner is another culture clash casualty. AOL's culture valued youthful, high-flying, quick deal-making, whereas Time Warner had a button-down, hierarchical, and systematic culture. A third example is Charles Schwab & Co.'s acquisition of U.S. Trust. Connections 16.2 describes how the diametrically opposing cultures of the discount brokerage firm and the "old money" firm undermined job performance, increased dysfunctional conflict, and resulted in lost talent.

Schwab Suffers the Perils of Clashing Cultures

During the peak of the dot-com boom, Charles Schwab & Co. executives were convinced that as investors got wealthier they would migrate to full-service firms that offered more personalized service than the San Francisco-based discount broker. So, Schwab paid top dollar to acquire U.S. Trust, a high-brow New York-based private bank that only served clients with at least $10 million to invest. Schwab customers that got wealthy would be shunted over to U.S. Trust for more personalized service.

The strategy backfired, partly because Schwab's customers still wanted cheap trades as they got wealthier, and partly because Schwab ignored the acquisition's cultural dynamics. Schwab values rapid change, cost-cutting frugality, process efficiency, and egalitarianism. Schwab employees see themselves as nimble noncon-formists who empowered millions of people through low-cost Internet-based stock trading. In contrast, U.S. Trust was an exclusive club that preferred to admit clients who were referred by existing clients. It was slow to adopt Internet technology. Instead, clients were pampered by "wealth advisors" who earned huge bonuses and worked in an environment that reeked of luxury.

While negotiating the takeover, U.S. Trust executives expressed concern about these cultural differences, so Schwab agreed to leave the firm as a separate entity. This separation strategy didn't work for very long. Schwab cut U.S. Trust's lucrative bonuses and tied their annual rewards to Schwab's financial performance. U.S. Trust executives were pushed to cut costs and set more aggressive goals. Schwab even tried to acculturate several hundred U.S. Trust employees with a board game that used a giant mat showing hills, streams, and a mountain with founder Charles Schwab's face carved into the side. U.S. Trust staff complained that the game was demeaning, particularly wearing smocks as they played the role of investors.

In meetings immediately following the acquisition, U.S. Trust executives winced when Schwab executives fre-quently used the term "customers." Schwab's staff were reminded that U.S. Trust has "clients," which implies much more of a long-term relationship. They also resis-ted Schwab's referrals of newly minted millionaires in blue jeans. "We were flabbergasted," said one Schwab board member of the cultural clash. "Some of the U.S. Trust officers simply refused to accept our referrals."

When the depth of cultural intransigence became apparent, U.S. Trust's CEO was replaced with with Schwab executive Alan Weber. Weber later insisted that "there is no culture clash," because Schwab "never tried to change the nature of the organization." Meanwhile, sources say that more than 300 U.S. Trust wealth advisors have defected to competitors since the acquisition, taking many valued clients with them. Schwab's CEO was fired, in part because the U.S. Trust acquisition stumbled. The acquisition is now worth less than half of its original purchase price.

"Here are two first-class companies, but structural and cultural problems keep the combination from the kind of success they expected," explains a financial advisor in Florida.

Sources: F. Vogelstein and E. Florian, "Can Schwab Get Its Mojo Back?" *Fortune*, September 17, 2001, p. 93; B. Morris, "When Bad Things Happen to Good Companies," *Fortune*, Decem-ber 8, 2003, p. 78; S. Craig and K. Brown, "Schwab Ousts Pot-truck as CEO," *Wall Street Journal*, July 21, 2004, p. A1; R. Frank, "U.S. Trust Feels Effects of Switch," *Wall Street Journal*, July 21, 2004, p. A8; R. Frank and S. Craig, "White-Shoe Shuffle," *Wall Street Journal*, September 15, 2004, p. A1; C. Harrington, "Made in Heaven? Watching the Watchovia-Tanager Union," *Accounting Today*, December 20, 2004, p. 18; J. Kador, "Cul-tures in Conflict," *Registered Rep.*, October 2004, p. 43.
www.schwab.com

BICULTURAL AUDIT

bicultural audit

Diagnoses cultural relations between companies prior to a merger and deter-mines the extent to which cultural clashes will likely occur.

Organizational leaders can minimize these cultural collisions and fulfill their duty of due diligence by conducting a bicultural audit. A **bicultural audit** diagnoses cultural relations between the companies and determines the extent to which cultural clashes will likely occur. The bicultural audit process begins by identifying cultural dif-ferences between the merging companies. Next, the bicultural audit data are ana-lyzed to determine which differences between the two firms will result in conflict and which cultural values provide common ground on which to build a cultural foundation in the merged organization. The final stage involves identifying strate-gies and preparing action plans to bridge the two organizations' cultures.

A few years ago, Toronto-based pulp and paper conglomerate Abitibi-Price applied a bicultural audit before it agreed to merge with its Montreal rival, Stone Consolidated. Specifically, Abitibi developed the Merging Cultures Evaluation Index (MCEI), an evaluation system that helped Abitibi executives compare its culture with other companies in the industry. The MCEI analyzed several dimensions of corporate culture, such as concentration of power versus diffusion of power, innovation versus tradition, wide versus narrow flow of information, and consensus versus authoritative decision making. Abitibi and Stone executives completed the questionnaire to assess their own culture, then compared the results. The MCEI results, along with financial and infrastructural information, served as the basis for Abitibi-Price to merge with Stone Consolidated to become Montreal-based Abitibi-Consolidated, the world's largest pulp-and-paper firm.[34]

STRATEGIES TO MERGE DIFFERENT ORGANIZATIONAL CULTURES

In some cases, the bicultural audit results in a decision to end merger talks because the two cultures are too different to merge effectively. However, even with substantially different cultures, two companies may form a workable union if they apply the appropriate merger strategy. The four main strategies for merging different corporate cultures are assimilation, deculturation, integration, and separation (see Exhibit 16.3).[35]

Assimilation   Assimilation occurs when employees at the acquired company willingly embrace the cultural values of the acquiring organization. Typically, this strategy works best when the acquired company has a weak dysfunctional culture, whereas the acquiring company's culture is strong and aligned with the external environment. Culture clash is rare with assimilation because the acquired firm's culture is weak and employees are looking for better cultural alternatives. Research in Motion (RIM), the Waterloo, Ontario, company that makes Blackberry wireless devices, applies the assimilation strategy by deliberately acquiring only small start-up firms. "Small companies…don't have cultural issues," says RIM co-CEO Jim Balsillie, adding that they are typically absorbed into RIM's culture with little fuss or attention.[36]

■ **EXHIBIT 16.3**

Strategies for merging different organizational cultures

Merger strategy	Description	Works best when:
Assimilation	Acquired company embraces acquiring firm's culture.	Acquired firm has a weak culture.
Deculturation	Acquiring firm imposes its culture on unwilling acquired firm.	Rarely works—may be necessary only when acquired firm's culture doesn't work but employees don't realize it.
Integration	Combining the two or more cultures into a new composite culture.	Existing cultures can be improved.
Separation	Merging companies remain distinct entities with minimal exchange of culture or organizational practices.	Firms operate successfully in different businesses requiring different cultures.

Sources: Based on ideas in K.W. Smith, "A Brand-New Culture for the Merged Firm," *Mergers and Acquisitions*, 35 (June 2000), pp. 45–50; A. R. Maleazedeh and A. Nahavandi, "Making Mergers Work by Managing Cultures," *Journal of Business Strategy,* May/June 1990, pp. 55–57.

Deculturation Assimilation is rare. Employees usually resist organizational change, particularly when they are asked to throw away personal and cultural values. Under these conditions, some acquiring companies apply a *deculturation* strategy by imposing their culture and business practices on the acquired organization. The acquiring firm strips away artifacts and reward systems that support the old culture. People who cannot adopt the acquiring company's culture are often terminated. Deculturation may be necessary when the acquired firm has a dysfunctional culture, yet its employees continue to embrace that culture. However, this strategy is difficult to apply effectively because the acquired firm's employees resist the cultural intrusions from the buying firm, thereby delaying or undermining the merger process.

Integration A third strategy is to combine the two or more cultures into a new composite culture that preserves the best features of the previous cultures. Integration is slow and potentially risky, because there are many forces preserving the existing cultures. Still, this strategy should be considered when the companies have relatively weak cultures, or when their cultures include several overlapping values. Integration also works best when people realize that their existing cultures are ineffective and are, therefore, motivated to adopt a new set of dominant values.

Separation A separation strategy occurs where the merging companies agree to remain distinct entities with minimal exchange of culture or organizational practices. This strategy is most appropriate when the two merging companies are in unrelated industries or operate in different countries, because the most appropriate cultural values tend to differ by industry and national culture. Discount brokerage firm Charles Schwab & Co. tried to apply a separation strategy when it first acquired U.S. Trust. However, as was described earlier in Connections 16.2, this separation strategy didn't last long. In fact, this is one of many examples where executives in the acquiring firm have difficulty keeping their hands off the acquired firm. According to one survey, only 15 percent of acquiring firms leave the acquired organization as a stand-alone unit.[37]

▪ CHANGING AND STRENGTHENING ORGANIZATIONAL CULTURE

Whether merging two cultures or reshaping the firm's existing values, most Canadian corporate leaders—72 percent of them according to a recent survey—say their organization's culture is not what they want for the future.[38] Although cultural change is often a necessary part of effective organizational change, altering an organization's culture can be tremendously difficult. It requires the change management toolkit that we will learn about in the next chapter. Corporate leaders need to make employees aware of the urgency for change. Then they need to "unfreeze" the existing culture by removing artifacts that represent that culture and "refreeze" the new culture by introducing artifacts that communicate and reinforce the new values.

STRENGTHENING ORGANIZATIONAL CULTURE

Artifacts communicate and reinforce the new corporate culture, but we also need to consider ways to further strengthen that culture. Five approaches that are commonly cited in the literature are the actions of founders and leaders, introducing culturally consistent rewards, maintaining a stable work force, managing the cultural network, and selecting and socializing new employees (see Exhibit 16.4).

■ EXHIBIT 16.4

Strategies for strengthening
organizational culture

Actions of founders and leaders   Founders establish an organization's culture.[39] You can see this at Cirque du Soleil, which was described at the beginning of this chapter. The risk-taking and creative values that Gilles Ste-Croix and Guy Laliberté instilled in the organization during the early years has remained today. Founders develop the systems and structures that support their personal values. They are also typically the visionaries whose energetic style provides a powerful role model for others to follow. In spite of the founder's effect, subsequent leaders can break the organization away from the founder's values if they apply the transformational leadership concepts that were described in Chapter 14. Transformational leaders alter and strengthen organizational culture by communicating and enacting their vision of the future.[40]

Introducing culturally consistent rewards   Reward systems strengthen corporate culture when they are consistent with cultural values.[41] For example, Husky Injection Molding Systems has an unusual stock incentive program that supports its environmentalist culture. Employees at the Bolton, Ontario-based plastics equipment manufacturer earn 1/20th of a company share for each seedling they plant, one share for each month of car pooling, and so on. The idea is to align rewards to the cultural values the company wants to reinforce.

Maintaining a stable work force   An organization's culture is embedded in the minds of its employees. Organizational stories are rarely written down; rituals and ceremonies do not usually exist in procedure manuals; organizational metaphors are not found in corporate directories. Thus, organizations depend on a stable work force to communicate and reinforce the dominant beliefs and values. The organization's culture can literally disintegrate during periods of high turnover and precipitous downsizing because the corporate memory leaves with these employees.[42] Conversely, corporate leaders who want to change the corporate culture have accelerated the turnover of senior executives and older employees who held the cultural values in place.

Managing the cultural network Organizational culture is learned through informal communication, so an effective network of cultural transmission is necessary to strengthen the company's underlying assumptions, values, and beliefs. According to Max De Pree, former CEO of furniture manufacturer Herman Miller Inc., every organization needs "tribal storytellers" to keep the organization's history and culture alive.[43] The cultural network exists through the organizational grapevine. It is also supported through frequent opportunities for interaction so employees can share stories and re-enact rituals.

Company magazines and other media can also strengthen organizational culture by communicating cultural values and beliefs more efficiently. The cultural network also encourages opportunities for senior executives to directly discuss and share the company's values with employees. Executives at Vancouver City Savings Credit Union apply this idea by meeting staff in all departments and branches twice yearly to discuss the company's cultural values. VanCity's values also figure into the decision-making process. "Even on the formal business plan, notations are made where actions demonstrate the commitment to corporate values, and rewards are being given out for behaviours supporting the values," explains a VanCity executive.[44]

Selecting and socializing employees Organizational culture is strengthened by hiring people who already embrace the cultural values. A good person-organization fit reinforces the culture; it also improves job satisfaction and organizational loyalty because new hires with values compatible to the corporate culture adjust more quickly to the organization.[45] Job applicants also pay attention to corporate culture during the hiring process. They look at corporate culture artifacts to determine whether the company's values are compatible to their own.

organizational socialization
The process by which individuals learn the values, expected behaviours, and social knowledge necessary to assume their roles in the organization.

Along with selecting people with compatible values, companies maintain strong cultures through the process of organizational socialization. **Organizational socialization** refers to the process by which individuals learn the values, expected behaviours, and social knowledge necessary to assume their roles in the organization.[46] By communicating the company's dominant values, job candidates and new hires tend to more quickly and deeply internalize these values. Socialization is an important process for absorbing corporate culture as well as helping newcomers to adjust to co-workers, work procedures, and other corporate realities. Thus, the final section of this chapter looks more closely at the organizational socialization process.

■ ORGANIZATIONAL SOCIALIZATION

Nadia Ramos had plenty of job opportunities after the Montrealer graduated from business school, but Bank of Nova Scotia won the contest hands down. Ramos was impressed by the opportunity for overseas field assignments and the panel interview with senior managers in commercial banking. But it was the little things that really won Ramos over to ScotiaBank. Rather than seeing only the company boardroom and company recruiters, Ramos toured the offices where she would actually work and met with fellow international banking associates who immediately welcomed her to the team and offered advice for apartment hunting in Toronto. ScotiaBank also assigned a buddy to help Ramos adjust to the workplace over the first two years. "We have to make sure, once they are in the door, that they start having a great experience as an employee—and that we haven't overpromised," says Sylvia Chrominska, ScotiaBank's executive vice-president of human resources.[47]

ScotiaBank successfully brings employees into the organization by going beyond selecting applicants with the right competencies. It relies on several organizational socialization practices to help newcomers learn about and adjust to the company's culture, physical layout, procedures, and so on. Research indicates that when employees are effectively socialized into the organization, they tend to perform better and have higher job satisfaction.[48]

Organizational socialization is a process of both learning and adjustment. It is a learning process because newcomers try to make sense of the company's physical workplace, social dynamics, and strategic/cultural environment. They learn about the organization's performance expectations, power dynamics, corporate culture, company history, and jargon. Organizational socialization is also a process of adjustment, because individuals need to adapt to their new work environment. They develop new work roles that reconfigure their social identity, adopt new team norms, and practise new behaviours. Research reports that the adjustment process is fairly rapid for many people, usually within a few months. However, newcomers with diverse work experience seem to adjust better than those with limited previous experience, possibly because the former has a larger toolkit of knowledge and skills to make the adjustment possible.[49]

Newcomers absorb the organization's dominant culture to varying degrees. Some people deeply internalize the company's culture; a few others rebel against these attempts to change their mental models and values. Ideally, newcomers adopt a level of "creative individualism" in which they accept the essential elements of the organization's culture and team norms, yet also hold other values that add to the company's diversity.

STAGES OF SOCIALIZATION

Socialization is a continuous process, beginning long before the first day of employment and continuing throughout one's career within the company. However, it is most intense when people move across organizational boundaries, such as when they first join a company, or get transferred to an international assignment. Each of these transitions is a process that can be divided into three stages. Our focus here is on the socialization of new employees, so the three stages are called pre-employment socialization, encounter, and role management (see Exhibit 16.5). These stages parallel the individual's transition from outsider, to newcomer, and then to insider.[50]

■ **EXHIBIT 16.5**   Stages of organizational socialization

Pre-employment socialization (outsider)	Encounter (newcomer)	Role management (insider)	Socialization outcomes
• Learn about the organization and the job • Form employment relationship expectations	• Test expectations against perceived realities	• Strengthen work relationships • Practise new role behaviours • Resolve work–nonwork conflicts	• Higher motivation • Higher loyalty • Higher satisfaction • Lower stress • Lower turnover

Stage 1: Pre-employment socialization   Think back to the months and weeks before you began working in a new job (or attending a new school). You actively searched for information about the company, formed expectations about working there, and felt some anticipation about fitting into that environment. The pre-employment socialization stage encompasses all of the learning and adjustment that occurs prior to the first day of work in a new position. In fact, a large part of the socialization adjustment process occurs prior to the first day of work.[51]

The main problem with pre-employment socialization is that individuals are outsiders, so they must rely on friends, employment interviews, recruiting literature, and other indirect information to form expectations about what it is like to work in the organization. Furthermore, the information exchange between applicants and employers is usually less than perfectly honest.[52] Job applicants might distort their résumés, while employers hide their blemishes by presenting overly positive images of organizational life. Job applicants avoid asking sensitive questions—such as pay increases and faster promotions—in order to present a good image to recruiters.

To make matters worse, job applicants tend to engage in postdecisional justification during pre-employment socialization. Before the first day of work, they tend to increase the importance of favourable elements of the job and justify or completely forget about some negative elements. At the same time, they reduce the perceived quality of job offers that they turned down. Employers often distort their expectations of new hires in the same way. The result is that both parties develop higher expectations of each other than they will actually experience during the encounter stage.

Stage 2: Encounter   The first day on the job typically marks the beginning of the encounter stage of organizational socialization. This is the stage in which newcomers test their prior expectations with the perceived realities. Many jobs fail the test, resulting in varying degrees of **reality shock**. Reality shock occurs when newcomers perceive discrepancies between their pre-employment expectations and on-the-job reality.[53] The larger the gap, the stronger the reality shock. Reality shock doesn't necessarily occur on the first day; it might develop over several weeks or even months as newcomers form a better understanding of their new work environment. Along with experiencing unmet expectations, reality shock occurs when newcomers are overwhelmed by the experience of sudden entry into a new work environment. They experience the stress of information overload and have difficulty adjusting quickly to their new role.

reality shock
Occurs when newcomers perceive discrepancies between their pre-employment expectations and on-the-job reality.

Reality Shock in India Call Centres
Rajit Gangadharan thought his dream had come true when offered a job at a call centre in Bangalore, India. The recent business school graduate looked forward to the fun office environment, decent salary, free entertainment passes, and working with customers half a world away. But it didn't take long for Gangadharan to discover the downside of the job, including long night shifts, irregular eating habits, and few opportunities to meet his old friends. "Social life is nil in such a job," complains Gangadharan, who no longer works in a call centre. A survey by NFO WorldGroup reports that Gangadharan is typical of call centre employees in India. They are well educated and highly qualified, yet their high job expectations result in reality shock and turnover rates of 30 to 50 percent.[54] *Gideon Mendel/Corbis*

Stage 3: Role management   During the role management stage in the social-ization process, employees settle in as they make the transition from newcomers to insiders. They strengthen relationships with co-workers and supervisors, practise new role behaviours, and adopt attitudes and values consistent with their new position and organization. Role management also involves resolving the conflicts between work and nonwork activities. In particular, employees must redistribute their time and energy between work and family, reschedule recreational activities, and deal with changing perceptions and values in the context of other life roles. They must address any discrepancies between their existing values and those emphasized by the organizational culture. New social identities are formed that are more compatible with the work environment.

IMPROVING THE SOCIALIZATION PROCESS

Before hiring people for its new computer assembly plant in North Carolina, Dell, Inc., invited applicants to understand the company and the jobs better. "We will discuss the soul of Dell, give them a realistic job preview, and give them the oppor-tunity to complete a job application," explains Ann Artzer, Dell's human resource manager for the plant. "It will be a chance to determine the mutual interest between the candidates and Dell." Kal Tire, one of Canada's largest retail distrib-utors of automobile tires and batteries, takes this process one step further by allowing job candidates to spend a day at one of the company's stores before accepting a job. "By aligning the candidate's expectations with ours, we have reduced the number of people who leave early on because they decide the career is not for them," explains Paula Olmstead, human resources manager at the Ver-non, British Columbia firm.[55]

Kal Tire and Dell have tried to improve the socialization process by providing a **realistic job preview (RJP)**—a balance of positive and negative information about the job and work context.[56] Companies often exaggerate positive features of the job and neglect to mention the undesirable elements in the hope that the best applicants will get "stuck" on the organization. In contrast, an RJP helps job appli-cants to decide for themselves whether their skills, needs, and values are compati-ble with the job and organization.

Although RJPs scare away some applicants, they tend to reduce turnover and increase job performance.[57] This occurs because RJPs help applicants develop more accurate pre-employment expectations that, in turn, minimize reality shock. RJPs represent a type of vaccination by preparing employees for the more chal-lenging and troublesome aspects of work life. There is also some evidence that RJPs increase organizational loyalty. A possible explanation for this is that compa-nies providing candid information are easier to trust. They also show respect for the psychological contract and concern for employee welfare.[58]

Socialization agents   Nadia Ramos received plenty of support to help her adjust to a career at ScotiaBank. As was mentioned at the beginning of this section on organizational socialization, Ramos' future co-workers welcomed her to the team and offered advice on finding an apartment. ScotiaBank also assigned an experienced employee (a buddy) to offer Ramos special assistance and guidance. Clearly, ScotiaBank leaders seem to be aware that a lot of organizational socializa-tion occurs informally through socialization agents, including co-workers, bosses, and friends who work for the company.

realistic job preview (RJP)
Giving job applicants a balance of positive and negative infor-mation about the job and work context.

Supervisors tend to provide technical information, performance feedback, and information about job duties. They also improve the socialization process by giving newcomers reasonably challenging first assignments, buffering them from excessive demands, and helping them form social ties with co-workers.[59] Co-workers are particularly important socialization agents because they are easily accessible, can answer questions when problems arise, and serve as role models for appropriate behaviour. New employees tend to receive this information and support when co-workers integrate them into the work team. Co-workers also aid the socialization process by being flexible and tolerant in their interactions with these new hires. Newcomers who quickly form social relations with co-workers tend to have a less traumatic socialization experience and are less likely to quit their jobs within the first year of employment.[60]

The challenge is for organizations to ensure that co-workers offer the necessary support. ScotiaBank and other Canadian businesses set up a buddy system whereby newcomers are assigned to co-workers for sources of information and social support. ExtendMedia, the Toronto-based company that develops digital media software, also has a formal buddy system, but equally valuable is the box of doughnuts put on every newcomer's desk on the first day of work. "The [doughnuts] are there to break the ice so that other people come and talk to them. We are introducing people through their stomachs," explains an ExtendMedia executive.[61]

CHAPTER SUMMARY

Organizational culture is the basic pattern of shared assumptions, values, and beliefs that govern behaviour within a particular organization. Assumptions are the shared mental models or theories-in-use that people rely on to guide their perceptions and behaviours. Beliefs represent the individual's perceptions of reality. Values are more stable, long-lasting beliefs about what is important. They help us define what is right or wrong, or good or bad, in the world. Culture content refers to the relative ordering of beliefs, values, and assumptions.

Organizations have subcultures as well as the dominant culture. Subcultures maintain the organization's standards of performance and ethical behaviour. They are also the source of emerging values that replace aging core values.

Artifacts are the observable symbols and signs of an organization's culture. Four broad categories of artifacts include organizational stories and legends, rituals and ceremonies, language, physical structures and symbols. Understanding an organization's culture requires assessment of many artifacts because they are subtle and often ambiguous.

Organizational culture has three main functions. It is a deeply embedded form of social control. It is also the "social glue" that bonds people together and makes them feel part of the organizational experience. Third, corporate culture helps employees make sense of the workplace.

Companies with strong cultures generally perform better than those with weak cultures, but only when the cultural content is appropriate for the organization's environment. Also, the culture should not be so strong that it drives out dissenting values, which may form emerging values for the future. Organizations should have adaptive cultures so that employees focus on the need for change and support initiatives and leadership that keeps pace with these changes.

Organizational culture relates to business ethics in two ways. First, corporate cultures can support ethical values of society, thereby reinforcing ethical conduct. Second, some cultures are so strong that they rob a person's individualism and discourage constructive conflict.

Mergers should include a bicultural audit to diagnose the compatibility of the organizational cultures. The four main strategies for merging different corporate cultures are integration, deculturation, assimilation, and separation.

Organizational culture may be strengthened through the actions of founders and leaders, introducing culturally consistent rewards, maintaining a stable work force, managing the cultural network, and selecting and socializing employees.

Organizational socialization is the process by which individuals learn the values, expected behaviours, and social knowledge necessary to assume their roles in the organization. It is a process of both learning about the work context and adjusting to new work roles, team norms, and behaviours. Employees typically pass through three socialization stages: pre-employ-ment, encounter, and role management. To improve the socialization process, organizations should introduce realistic job previews (RJPs) and recognize the value of socialization agents in the process.

KEY TERMS

adaptive culture, p. 448

artifacts, p. 444

bicultural audit, p. 451

ceremonies, p. 445

organizational culture, p. 442

organizational socialization p. 455

realistic job preview (RJP), p. 458

reality shock, p. 457

rituals, p. 445

DISCUSSION QUESTIONS

1. Superb Consultants have submitted a proposal to analyze the cultural values of your organization. The proposal states that Superb has developed a revolutionary new survey to tap the company's true culture. The survey takes just 10 minutes to complete and the consultants say results can be based on a small sample of employees. Discuss the merits and limitations of this proposal.

2. Some people suggest that the most effective organizations have the strongest cultures. What do we mean by the "strength" of organizational culture, and what possible problems are there with a strong organizational culture?

3. The CEO of a manufacturing firm wants everyone to support the organization's dominant culture of lean efficiency and hard work. The CEO has introduced a new reward system to reinforce this culture and personally interviews all professional and managerial applicants to ensure that they bring similar values to the organization. Some employees who criticized these values had their careers sidelined until they left. Two mid-level managers were fired for supporting contrary values, such as work/life balance. Based on your knowledge of organizational subcultures, what potential problems is the CEO creating?

4. Identify at least two artifacts you have observed in your department where you work or are a student from each of the four broad categories: a) Organizational stories and legends, b) Rituals and ceremonies, c) Language, d) Physical structures and symbols.

5. "Organizations are more likely to succeed when they have an adaptive culture." What can an organization do to foster an adaptive culture?

6. Acme Ltd. is planning to acquire Beta Ltd., which operates in a different industry. Acme's culture is entrepreneurial and fast paced, whereas Beta employees value slow, deliberate decision making by consensus. Which merger strategy would you recommend to minimize culture shock when Acme acquires Beta? Explain your answer.

7. Suppose you are asked by senior officers of a city government to identify ways to reinforce a new culture of teamwork and collaboration. The senior executive group clearly supports these values, but it wants everyone in the organization to embrace them. Identify four types of activities that would strengthen these cultural values.

8. ScotiaBank, ExtendMedia, and other organizations rely on current employees to socialize new recruits. What are the advantages of relying on this type of socialization agent? What problems can you foresee (or you have personally experienced) with co-worker socialization practices?

CASE STUDY 16.1

ASSETONE BANK

AssetOne Bank is one of Asia's largest financial institutions, but it had difficulty entering the personal investment business where several other companies dominate the market. To gain entry to this market, AssetOne decided to acquire TaurusBank, a much smaller financial institution that had aggressively developed investment funds (unit trusts) and online banking in the region. Taurus was owned by a European conglomerate that wanted to exit the financial sector, so the company was quietly put up for sale. The opportunity to acquire Taurus seemed like a perfect fit to AssetOne's executives, who saw the purchase as an opportunity to finally gain a competitive position in the personal investment market. In particular, the acquisition would give AssetOne valuable talent in online banking and investment fund businesses.

Negotiations between AssetOne and TaurusBank occurred secretly, except for communication with government regulatory agencies, and took several months as AssetOne's executive team deliberated over the purchase. When AssetOne finally decided in favour of the acquisition, employees of both companies were notified only a few minutes before the merger was announced publicly. During the public statement, AssetOne's CEO boldly announced that TaurusBank would become a "seamless extension of AssetOne." He explained that, like AssetOne, Taurus employees would learn the value of detailed analysis and cautious decision making.

The comments by AssetOne's CEO shocked many employees at Taurus, which was an aggressive and entrepreneurial competitor in online banking and personal investments. Taurus was well known for its edgy marketing, innovative products, and tendency to involve employees to generate creative ideas. The company didn't hesitate to hire people from other industries who would bring different ideas to the investment and online banking business. AssetOne, on the other hand, almost completely promoted its executives from within the ranks. Every one of the senior executive team had started at AssetOne. The company also emphasized decision making at the top to maintain better control and consistency.

Frustration was apparent within a few months after the merger. Several Taurus executives quit after repeated failure of AssetOne's executive team to decide quickly on critical online banking initiatives. For example, at the time of the acquisition, Taurus was in the process of forming affinity alliances with several companies. Yet, six months later, AssetOne's executive team still had not decided whether to proceed with these partnerships.

The biggest concerns occurred in the investment fund business where 20 of TaurusBank's 60 fund managers were lured away by competitors within the first year. Some left for better opportunities. Six fund managers left with the Taurus executive in charge of the investment fund business, who joined an investment firm that specializes in investment funds. Several employees left Taurus after AssetOne executives insisted that all new investment funds must be approved by AssetOne's executive group. Previously, Taurus had given the investment fund division enough freedom to launch new products without approval of the entire executive team.

Two years later, AssetOne's CEO admitted that the acquisition of TaurusBank did not gain the opportunities that they had originally hoped. AssetOne had more business in this area, but many of the more talented people in investment funds and online banking had left the firm. Overall, the merged company had not kept pace with other innovative financial institutions in the market.

Discussion Questions

1. Based on your understanding of mergers and organizational culture, discuss the problems that occurred in this case.

2. What strategies would you recommend to AssetOne's executives to avoid these corporate culture clashes in future mergers and acquisitions?

WEB EXERCISE 16.2

DIAGNOSING CORPORATE CULTURE PROCLAMATIONS

Purpose To understand the importance and contents in which corporate culture is identified and discussed in organizations.

Instructions This exercise is a take-home activity, although it can be completed in classes with computers and Internet connections. The instructor will divide the class into small teams (typically four to five people per team). Each team is assigned a specific industry—such as energy, biotechnology, or computer hardware.

The team's task is to search Web sites of several companies in the selected industry for company statements about their corporate culture. Use the company Web site search engine (if it exists) to find documents with key phrases such as "corporate culture" or "company values."

In the next class, or at the end of the time allotted in the current class, students will report on their observations by answering the following three discussion questions:

Discussion Questions

1. What values seem to dominate the corporate culture of the companies you searched? Are these values similar or diverse across companies in the industry?

2. What was the broader content of the Web pages where these companies described or mentioned its corporate culture?

3. Do companies in this industry refer to their corporate culture on the Web sites more or less than companies in other industries searched by the team in this class?

TEAM EXERCISE 16.3

TRUTH IN ADVERTISING

Purpose This team activity is designed to help you diagnose the degree to which recruitment advertisements and brochures provide realistic previews of the job and/or organization.

Materials The instructor will bring to class either recruiting brochures or newspaper advertisements.

Instructions The instructor will place students into teams and give them copies of recruiting brochures and/or advertisements. The instructor might assign one lengthy brochure; alternatively several newspaper advertisements may be assigned. All teams should receive the same materials so that everyone is familiar with the items and results can be compared. Teams will evaluate the recruiting material(s) and answer the following questions for each item.

Discussion Questions

1. What information in the text of this brochure/advertisement identifies conditions or activities in this organization or job that some applicants may not like?

2. If there are photographs or images of people at work, do they show only positive conditions, or do any show conditions or events that some applicants may not like?

3. After reading this item, would you say that it provides a realistic preview of the job and/or organization?

CORPORATE CULTURE PREFERENCE SCALE

Purpose This self-assessment is designed to help you identify a corporate culture that fits most closely with your personal values and assumptions.

Instructions Read each pair of statements in the Corporate Culture Preference Scale and circle the statement that describes the organization you would prefer to work in. Then use the scoring key in Appendix B to calculate your results for each sub-scale. The scale does not attempt to measure your preference for every corporate culture, just a few of the more common varieties. Also, keep in mind none of these corporate cultures is inherently good or bad. The focus here is on how well you fit within each of them. This exercise is completed alone so students assess themselves honestly without concerns of social comparison. However, class discussion will focus on the importance of matching job applicants to the organization's dominant values.

CORPORATE CULTURE PREFERENCE SCALE

I would prefer to work in an organization:

1a. Where employees work well together in teams.	OR	1b. That produces highly respected products or services.
2a. Where top management maintains a sense of order in the workplace.	OR	2b. Where the organization listens to customers and responds quickly to their needs.
3a. Where employees are treated fairly.	OR	3b. Where employees continuously search for ways to work more efficiently.
4a. Where employees adapt quickly to new work requirements.	OR	4b. Where corporate leaders work hard to keep employees happy.
5a. Where senior executives receive special benefits not available to other employees.	OR	5b. Where employees are proud when the organization achieves its performance goals.
6a. Where employees who perform the best get paid the most.	OR	6b. Where senior executives are respected.
7a. Where everyone gets their jobs done like clockwork.	OR	7b. That is on top of new innovations in the industry.
8a. Where employees receive assistance to overcome any personal problems.	OR	8b. Where employees abide by company rules.
9a. That is always experimenting with new ideas in the marketplace.	OR	9b. That expects everyone to put in 110 percent for peak performance.
10a. That quickly benefits from market opportunities.	OR	10b. Where employees are always kept informed of what's happening in the organization.
11a. That can quickly respond to competitive threats.	OR	11b. Where most decisions are made by the top executives.
12a. Where management keeps everything under control.	OR	12b. Where employees care for each other.

·17·

ORGANIZATIONAL CHANGE

LEARNING OBJECTIVES

AFTER READING THIS CHAPTER, YOU SHOULD BE ABLE TO:

■ Describe the elements of Lewin's force field analysis model.

■ Outline six reasons why people resist organizational change.

■ Discuss six strategies to minimize resistance to change.

■ Outline the conditions for effectively diffusing change from a pilot project.

■ Describe the action research approach to organizational change.

■ Outline the "Four-D" model of appreciative inquiry and explain how this approach differs from action research.

■ Explain how parallel learning structures assist the change process.

■ Discuss four ethical issues in organizational change.

Printing is a highly competitive business in which the survivors must continuously adapt to new technology, changing customer needs, and foreign competition. Friesens Corporation, which employs about 550 people in the small town of Altona, Manitoba, isn't just a survivor in this tough business; it is a frequently awarded role model that recently became the first Canadian printer to enter the industry's hall of fame for its superior business leadership. Friesens's products touch most Canadians, such as the latest Harry Potter bestseller, school yearbooks, boxes containing popular board games, and fancy stationery.

What makes Friesens an industry leader? To begin with, the company keeps pace with breathtaking technological change. "We're always adding equipment," says CEO David Friesen, who is a descendant of the founder. "Instead of replacing presses every 10 years, we're replacing them every five."

Rapid technological change is challenge enough for most printers, but ensuring that employees embrace, rather than resist, this continuous change is what sets Friesens apart. "It's important that the company invest in technology and equipment, but our success is because of our staff who are also our shareholders," Friesen advises.

Friesens Corporation has become one of North America's best managed printing firms through an adaptive culture that supports continuous change.
Courtesy of Friesens

Friesens is one of North America's largest employee-owned companies. And as owners of the business, employees are willing to trade in their stable work routines to make the company successful. "They're motivated by their share ownership," Friesen explains. "They take the same kind of interest as I do in ensuring this company is profitable. The staff are not only shareholders but they think and act like owners."

Friesens president and chief operating officer Curwin Friesen (one of 30 Friesens employees who is *not* related to the founder) holds monthly "coffee with Curwin" meetings in which employees are updated on the firm's financial information, strategies, and competition. The result is that employees, not just top managers, personally experience the pressures and opportunities that drive the urgency for change.

Curwin Friesen also believes that Friesens is driving change by hiring new talent. "When I first started here, most of the senior management was in their 50s," he recalls. "But in order for the company to succeed into the future, there has been a transition so that now there are management people" across the age spectrum. Curwin Friesen also points out that Friesens Corporation has been in business for 100 years. "We want to be around for another 100 years as well," he says.[1] ■
www.friesens.com

Friesens Corporation is a role model in the printing industry because it has mastered the challenges of managing change. Ongoing communication generates an urgency for change, while employee ownership, training, and other practices minimize resistance to change. The transformational leadership of David Friesen, Curwin Friesen, and others also plays a decisive role. This chapter examines ways to bring about meaningful change in organizations. We begin by introducing Lewin's model of change and its component parts. This includes sources of resistance to change, ways to minimize this resistance, and stabilizing desired behaviours. Next, this chapter examines three approaches to organizational change—action research, appreciative inquiry, and parallel learning structures. The last section of this chapter considers both cross-cultural and ethical issues in organizational change.

■ LEWIN'S FORCE FIELD ANALYSIS MODEL

force field analysis
Lewin's model of systemwide change that helps change agents diagnose the forces that drive and restrain proposed organizational change.

Social psychologist Kurt Lewin developed the **force field analysis** model to help us understand how the change process works (see Exhibit 17.1).[2] Although developed more than 50 years ago, Lewin's force field analysis model remains the prominent way of viewing this process.

One side of the force field model represents the *driving forces* that push organizations toward a new state of affairs. Chapter 1 described some of the driving forces in the external environment, including globalization, virtual work, and a changing workforce. Emerging technology, increased competition, and changing consumer needs are among the forces that drive continuous change at Friesens Corporation, for instance. Along with these external forces, corporate leaders create driving forces within the organization so the organization anticipates the external forces. These internally originating forces are difficult to apply because they lack external justifications, so effective transformational leadership as well as structural change mechanisms are necessary to legitimate and support internal driving forces.

The other side of Lewin's model represents the *restraining forces* that maintain the status quo. These restraining forces are commonly called "resistance to change" because they appear as employee behaviours that block the change process. Stability occurs when the driving and restraining forces are roughly in equilibrium, that is, they are of approximately equal strength in opposite directions.

■ **EXHIBIT 17.1**
Lewin's force field analysis model

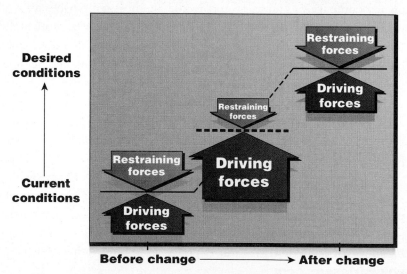

unfreezing
The first part of the change process whereby the change agent produces disequilibrium between the driving and restraining forces.

Lewin's force field model emphasizes that effective change occurs by **unfreezing** the current situation, moving to a desired condition, and then **refreezing** the system so that it remains in this desired state. Unfreezing involves producing disequilibrium between the driving and restraining forces. As we will describe later, this may occur by increasing the driving forces, reducing the restraining forces, or having a combination of both. Refreezing occurs when the organization's systems and structures are aligned with the desired behaviours. They must support and reinforce the new role patterns and prevent the organization from slipping back into the old way of doing things. Over the next few pages, we use Lewin's model to understand why change is blocked and how the process can evolve more smoothly.

refreezing
The latter part of the change process in which systems and conditions are introduced that reinforce and maintain the desired behaviours.

RESTRAINING FORCES

A few years ago, Darren Entwistle was hired as chief executive of Telus Corp. to turn the former bureaucratic monopoly into a nimble telecommunications competitor. Telus is trying to build a "high-performance culture that is changing the company down to its very roots," says Entwistle. That objective sounds good, but it has been painfully difficult to put into action. Staff members say they feel burnt out by Entwistle's attempts to change the company. Management and the union representing most Telus employees held more than 200 meetings over the past five years to thrash out these proposed changes, but their differences ultimately produced a bitter strike and lockout. "It's a workforce that's been low in productivity and has consistently resisted any change over the years," suggests telecommunications consultant Eamon Hoey.[3]

FBI Meets Its Own Resistance

In 1993, following the first terrorist attacks on the World Trade Center, the U.S. Federal Bureau of Investigation (FBI) promised to refocus from a reactive law-enforcement agency (solving crimes) to a proactive domestic intelligence agency (preventing terrorism). Yet, two government reports recently concluded that resistance from FBI staff has hampered this change process. One report even stated that both the FBI (as well as CIA) "seem to be working harder and harder just to maintain a status quo that is increasingly irrelevant to the new challenges." The reports claim that FBI employees and managers are unable or unwilling to change because solving crimes (rather than intelligence gathering) is burned into their mindset, routines, career paths, and decentralized structure. Most FBI field managers were trained in law enforcement, so they continue to give preferential treatment and resources to enforcement than terrorist prevention initiatives. An information access barrier called "the wall" further isolates FBI intelligence officers from the mainstream criminal investigation staff. Historical turf wars with the CIA have also undermined FBI respect for the bureau's intelligence gathering initiative. "One of the most difficult things one has to do is to bring an entity through the development of a change of business practices," FBI director Robert Mueller recently admitted.[4]
AP/Wide World Photos

According to various surveys, more than 40 percent of executives identify employee resistance as the most important barrier to corporate restructuring or improved performance.[5] This resistance takes many forms, including passive noncompliance, complaints, absenteeism, turnover, and collective action (e.g., strikes, walkouts). In extreme cases of resistance, the chief change agent eventually leaves or is pushed out.

Employee resistance is a symptom of deeper problems in the change process, so change agents need to investigate and remove the causes of resistance.[6] So, rather than directly correcting incidences of passive noncompliance, leaders need to understand why employees are not changing their behaviour in the desired ways. In some situations, employees may be worried about the consequences of change, such as how the new conditions will take away their power and status. In other situations, employees show resistance because of concerns about the process of change itself, such as the effort required to break old habits and learn new skills. The main reasons why people resist change are shown in Exhibit 17.2 and described below:[7]

- *Direct costs*—People tend to block actions that result in higher direct costs or lower benefits than the existing situation. For instance, some Telus employees likely resisted Entwistle's plans because they threatened job security and long-held perks of the position.
- *Saving face*—Some people resist change as a political strategy to "prove" that the decision is wrong or that the person encouraging change is incompetent. This occurred when senior executives in a manufacturing firm bought a computer other than the system recommended by the information systems department. Soon after the system was in place, several information systems employees let minor implementation problems escalate to demonstrate that senior management had made a poor decision.
- *Fear of the unknown*—People resist change because they are worried that they cannot adjust to the new work requirements. This fear of the unknown increases the risk of personal loss. For example, one company owner wanted sales staff to telephone rather than personally visit prospective customers. With no experience in telephone sales, they complained about the changes. Some even avoided the training program that taught them how to make telephone sales.[8]

■ **EXHIBIT 17.2**   Forces resisting organizational change

■ *Breaking routines*—Chapter 1 described how organizations need to unlearn, not just learn. This means that employees need to abandon the behavioural routines that are no longer appropriate. Unfortunately, people are creatures of habit. They like to stay within the comfort zones by continuing routine role patterns that make life predictable. Consequently, many people resist organizational changes that force employees out of their comfort zones and require investing time and energy learning new role patterns.

■ *Incongruent systems*—Rewards, selection, training, and other control systems ensure that employees maintain desired role patterns. Yet the organizational systems that maintain stability also discourage employees from adopting new ways. The implication, of course, is that organizational systems must be altered to fit the desired change. Unfortunately, control systems can be difficult to change, particularly when they have supported role patterns that worked well in the past.[9]

■ *Incongruent team dynamics*—Teams develop and enforce conformity to a set of norms that guide behaviour. However, conformity to existing team norms may discourage employees from accepting organizational change. Team norms that conflict with the desired changes need to be altered.

■ UNFREEZING, CHANGING, AND REFREEZING

According to Lewin's force field analysis model, effective change occurs by unfreezing the current situation, moving to a desired condition, and then refreezing the system so that it remains in this desired state. Unfreezing occurs when the driving forces are stronger than the restraining forces. This happens by making the driving forces stronger, weakening or removing the restraining forces, or a combination of both.

With respect to the first option, driving forces must increase enough to motivate change. Change rarely occurs by increasing driving forces alone, however, because the restraining forces often adjust to counterbalance the driving forces. It is rather like the coils of a mattress. The harder corporate leaders push for change, the stronger the restraining forces push back. This antagonism threatens the change effort by producing tension and conflict within the organization. The preferred option is to both increase the driving forces and reduce or remove the restraining forces. Increasing the driving forces creates an urgency for change, whereas reducing the restraining forces minimizes resistance to change.

CREATING AN URGENCY FOR CHANGE

It is almost cliché to say that organizations today operate in more dynamic fast-paced environments than they did a few decades ago. These environmental pressures represent the driving forces that push employees out of their comfort zones. They energize people to face the risks that change creates. In many organizations, however, external driving forces are hardly felt by anyone below the top executive level. The problem is that corporate leaders tend to buffer employees from the external environment, yet are surprised when change does not occur. Thus, the change process must begin by informing employees about competitors, changing consumer trends, impending government regulations, and other driving forces.[10]

Customer-driven change   Shell Europe has a well-known brand name, excellent assets, and highly qualified staff, but a few years ago these three ingredients weren't achieving either Shell's financial goals or customer needs. To make matters worse, many Shell executives believed that Shell Europe's performance was quite satisfactory. So, to create an urgency for change, the European executives were loaded onto buses and taken out to talk with customers and employees who work with customers every day. "We called these 'bus rides.' The idea was to encourage people to think back from the customer's perspective rather than from the head office," explains Shell Europe's vice-president of retailing. "The bus rides were difficult for a lot of people who, in their work history, had hardly ever had to talk to a customer and find out what was good and not so good about Shell from the customer's standpoint."[11]

Shell Europe is one of many organizations that have fuelled the urgency for change by putting employees in direct contact with customers. Dissatisfied customers represent a compelling driving force for change because of the adverse consequences for the organization's survival and success. Customers also provide a human element that further energizes employees to change current behaviour patterns.[12]

Urging change without external forces   Exposing employees to external forces can strengthen the urgency for change, but leaders often need to begin the change process before the problems come knocking at the company's door. "You want to create a burning platform for change even when there isn't a need for one," says Steve Bennett, CEO of financial software company Intuit.[13] Creating an urgency for change when the organization is riding high requires a lot of persuasive influence that helps employees visualize future competitive threats and environmental shifts.

For instance, Apple Computer's iPod dominates the digital music market, but Steve Jobs wants the company to be its own toughest competitor. Just when sales of the iPod Mini were soaring, Jobs challenged a gathering of 100 top executives and engineers to develop a better product to replace it. "Playing it safe is the most dangerous thing we can do," Jobs warned. Nine months later, the company launched the iPod Nano, which replaced the still-popular iPod Mini before competitors could offer a better alternative.[14]

REDUCING THE RESTRAINING FORCES

Effective change requires more than making employees aware of the driving forces. It also involves reducing or removing the restraining forces. Exhibit 17.3 summarizes six ways to overcome employee resistance. Communication, learning, employee involvement, and stress management try to reduce the restraining

Sizzling with Change in Moose Jaw
Some residents of Moose Jaw, Saskatchewan say that not much changes in the city of 35,000 people. But within Moose Jaw's tranquil environment is General Cable Corp.'s underground cable manufacturing plant, a world-beating production unit that sizzles with an urgency for change. Plant manager Ray Funke doesn't hold back good or bad news about the company's performance. Instead, employees receive weekly reports on scrap rates, defects, and expenses. Every month, 25 percent of them attend a plant operations review session, and every three months all employees attend a meeting at which Funke frankly discusses the plant's performance. Exposed to these workplace and competitive realities, employees feel a strong need for change, which translates into their drive for continuous improvement. The result: *Industry Week* recently identified General Cable's Moose Jaw facility as one of the four top manufacturing plants in North America, making it one of the few Canadian operations to ever receive this distinction.[15] *Courtesy of General Cable*
www.generalcable.com

■ **EXHIBIT 17.3**   Methods for dealing with resistance to change

Strategy	Example	When Used	Problem
Communication	Customer complaint letters shown to employees.	When employees don't feel an urgency for change, or don't know how the change will affect them.	Time-consuming and potentially costly.
Learning	Employees learn how to work in teams as company adopts team-based structure.	When employees need to break old routines and adopt new role patterns.	Time-consuming and potentially costly.
Employee involvement	Company forms task force to recommend new customer service practices.	When the change effort needs more employee commitment, some employees need to save face, and/or employee ideas would improve decisions about the change strategy.	Very time-consuming. Might also lead to conflict and poor decisions if employees' interests are incompatible with organizational needs.
Stress management	Employees attend sessions to discuss their worries about the change.	When communication, training, and involvement do not sufficiently ease employee worries.	Time-consuming and potentially expensive. Some methods may not reduce stress for all employees.
Negotiation	Employees agree to replace strict job categories with multi-skilling in return for increased job security.	When employees will clearly lose something of value from the change and would not otherwise support the new conditions. Also neccessary when the company must change quickly.	May be expensive, particularly if other employees want to negotiate their support. Also tends to produce compliance but not commitment to the change.
Coercion	Company president tells managers to "get on board" the change or leave.	When other strategies are ineffective and the company needs to change quickly.	Can lead to more subtle forms of resistance as well as long-term antagonism with the change agent.

Sources: Adapted from J. P. Kotter and L. A. Schlesinger, "Choosing Strategies for Change," *Harvard Business Review* 57 (1979), pp. 106–14; P. R. Lawrence, "How to Deal with Resistance to Change," *Harvard Business Review* (May–June 1954), pp. 49–57.

forces and, if feasible, should be attempted first.[16] However, negotiation and coercion are necessary for people who will clearly lose something from the change and when the speed of change is critical.

Communication Honest and frequent communication is the highest priority and first strategy required for any organizational change.[17] Communication improves the change process in at least two ways. First, it is the conduit through which employees typically learn about the driving forces for change. Whether through town hall meetings with senior management or by directly meeting with disgruntled customers, employees become energized to change. Second, communication can potentially reduce fear of the unknown. The more corporate leaders communicate their images of the future, the more easily employees can visualize their own role in that future. This effort may also begin the process of adjusting team norms to be more consistent with the new reality.

Scotiabank relied on a three-pronged communication strategy to move employees toward a more customer-focused financial institution.[18] Employees at the Canadian financial institution participated in learning map sessions, which present a visual representation of the company's desired future. Scotiabank's corporate newsletter provided further details from the learning maps and the need for a more customer-focused company. Finally, the bank opened a toll-free telephone line so employees could receive more information and provide feedback about their experiences. As a result of this communication process, every Scotiabank branch across Canada implemented the bank's new sales delivery model on or ahead of schedule with strong employee buy-in.

Learning   Learning is an important process in most change initiatives because employees require new knowledge and skills to fit the organization's evolving requirements. Friesens Corporation, described in the opening story to this chapter, is constantly buying new equipment and introducing technological change in the workplace. Yet the Manitoba printing firm is able to minimize resistance to this ongoing change by extensively training its employees so they have the knowledge and skills to adapt.

Action learning, which was described in Chapter 3, is another potentially powerful learning process for organizational change because it develops management skills while discovering ways to improve the organization.[19] Coaching is yet another form of learning that provides more personalized feedback and direction during the learning process. Coaching and other forms of learning are time consuming, but they help employees break routines by learning new role patterns.

Employee involvement   The opening vignette to this chapter described how employees at Friesens Corporation embrace change because they own the company. While the financial impact of the company's success is a key factor, so is involvement in making decisions that influence the company's and their immediate work unit's direction. Rather than viewing themselves as agents of someone else's decision, Friesens employees feel personally responsible for the success of the change effort.

Employee involvement can be time consuming and might result in poor decisions if employees' interests are incompatible with the organization's needs. However, this strategy is often valuable because it creates employee ownership and empowerment in the change process, thereby minimizing problems of saving face and fear of the unknown.[20] Employees usually have more detailed information about what needs to be changed, so involvement brings out this information. These benefits played a vital role in the transformation of Nissan Motor Co., described in GLOBAL Connections 17.1. Soon after Carlos Ghosn became CEO of the Japanese automaker, he formed a dozen cross-functional management teams and gave them three months to identify ways to save the company from possible bankruptcy.

Minimizing resistance to change through employee involvement is also possible in large organizations through **future search** events. Future search conferences "put the entire system in the room," meaning that they try to involve as many employees and other stakeholders as possible associated with the organizational system. These multi-day events ask participants to identify trends or issues and establish strategic solutions for those conditions.

Every five years, Whole Foods Market gathers together several hundred employees, shoppers, and shareholders for a future search meeting to help identify new directions for the food retailer. The state of Tasmania, Australia, held an unprecedented future

future search
Systemwide group sessions, usually lasting a few days, in which participants identify trends and identify ways to adapt to these changes.

Carlos Ghosn Relies on High Involvement to Transform Nissan

Nissan Motor Company was on the brink of bankruptcy when French automaker Renault purchased a controlling interest and installed Carlos Ghosn as the effective head of the Japanese automaker. Along with Nissan's known problems of high debt and plummeting market share, Ghosn (pronounced "gone") saw that Nissan managers had no apparent sense of urgency to change. "Even though the evidence is against them, they sit down and they watch the problem a little bit longer," says Ghosn.

Ghosn's challenge was to act quickly, yet minimize the inevitable resistance that arises when an outsider tries to change traditional Japanese business practices. "I was non-Nissan, non-Japanese," he says. "I knew that if I tried to dictate changes from above, the effort would backfire, undermining morale and productivity. But if I was too passive, the company would simply continue its downward spiral."

To resolve this dilemma, Ghosn formed nine cross-functional teams of 10 middle managers each, and gave them the mandate to identify innovative proposals for a specific area (marketing, manufacturing, etc.) within three months. Each team could form subteams with additional people to analyze issues in more detail. In all, over 500 middle managers and other employees were involved in the so-called "Nissan Revival Plan."

After a slow start—Nissan managers weren't accustomed to such authority or working with colleagues across functions or cultures—ideas began to flow as Ghosn stuck to his deadline, reminded team members of the automaker's desperate situation, and encouraged teams to break traditions. Three months later, the nine teams submitted a bold plan to close three assembly plants, eliminate thousands of jobs, cut the number of suppliers by half, reduce purchasing costs by 20 percent, return to profitability, cut the company's debt by half, and introduce 22 new models within the next two years.

Although risky, Ghosn accepted all of the proposals. Moreover, when revealing the plan publicly on the eve of the annual Tokyo Motor Show, Ghosn added his own

Carlos Ghosn launched a turnaround at Nissan Motor Company that saved the Japanese automaker and relied on change management practices rarely seen in Japan.
Copyright © Eriko Sugita/Reuters/Corbis

commitment to the plan: "If you ask people to go through a difficult period of time, they have to trust that you're sharing it with them," Ghosn explains. "So I said that if we did not fulfill our commitments, I would resign."

Ghosn's strategy for organizational change and the Nissan Revival Plan worked. Within 12 months, the automaker had increased sales and market share, and posted its first profit in seven years. The company has introduced innovative models and expanded operations. Ghosn has received high praise throughout Japan and abroad, and has since become head of Renault.

Sources: C. Lebner, "Nissan Motor Co.," *Fast Company*, July 2002, p. 80; C. Dawson, "On Your Marks," *Business Week*, March 17, 2003, p. 52; D. Magee, *Turn Around: How Carlos Ghosn Rescued Nissan* (New York: HarperCollins, 2003); C. Ghosn and P. Riès, *Shift: Inside Nissan's Historic Revival* (New York: Currency Doubleday, 2005).
www.nissan-global.com

search conference, called Tasmania Together, involving 14,000 individuals and organizations in 60 formal community discussions. Every word uttered and submitted was entered into a database, then sorted into common topics.[21] In Canada, the Toronto School Board, Richmond Savings Credit Union, and the Canadian Nature Federation have held future search gatherings to assist the change process.[22]

Future search meetings potentially minimize resistance to change and assist the quality of the change process, but they also have limitations.[23] One problem is that involving so many people invariably limits the opportunity to contribute and increases the risk that a few people will dominate the process. Another concern is that these events generate high expectations about an ideal future state that is difficult to satisfy in practice. Furthermore, some executives forget that future search conferences and other forms of employee involvement require follow-up action. If employees do not see meaningful decisions and actions resulting from these meetings, they begin to question the credibility of the process and are more cynical of similar subsequent change management activities.

Stress management   Organizational change is a stressful experience for many people because it threatens self-esteem and creates uncertainty about the future. Communication, learning, and employee involvement can reduce some of these stressors. However, research indicates that companies also need to introduce stress management practices to help employees cope with the changes.[24] In particular, stress management minimizes resistance by removing some of the direct costs and fear of the unknown of the change process. Stress also saps energy, so minimizing stress potentially increases employee motivation to support the change process.

Negotiation   As long as people resist change, organizational change strategies will require some influence tactics. Negotiation is a form of influence that involves the promise of benefits or resources in exchange for the target person's compliance with the influencer's request. This strategy potentially activates those who would otherwise lose out from the change. However, it merely gains compliance rather than commitment to the change effort, so might not be effective in the long term.

Coercion   If all else fails, leaders rely on coercion to change organizations. Coercion can include persistently reminding people of their obligations, frequently monitoring behaviour to ensure compliance, confronting people who do not change, and using threats of sanctions to force compliance. Replacing people who will not support the change is an extreme step, but it is neither rare nor, in some cases, inappropriate.

For example, Baycrest Centre for Geriatric Care in Toronto recently began a major transformation to a more values-based caring and respectful (rather than just technically competent) workplace. Unfortunately, as with many deep change efforts, some people were unable or unwilling to support the change process. "We're turning over the rocks and a lot of worms are crawling out," says Joy Richards, Baycrest's vice-president of nursing and ambulatory and outreach services. "Some staff were not performing up to standard. Some of the clinical leadership was not interested in engag-

Change the Principal, Change the School

A few years ago, test results at Sun Valley Middle School were so low that the San Fernando Valley, California, school was put on a U.S. federal government watch list for closer scrutiny. The Los Angeles unified school district tried to help the principal and staff to improve, but to no avail. When a state audit reported that the school suffered from poor management, unsanitary conditions, and uneven classroom instruction, the school district applied a more radical change strategy: it replaced Sun Valley's principal and four assistant principals with new leaders. Sun Valley's new principal, Jeff Davis (shown with students in this photo), introduced extra English language instruction, re-organized class locations, and launched team teaching to foster a more collegial atmosphere among staff. Sun Valley still has a long way to go, but student test scores in math and English have tripled over the past three years. "That school is absolutely headed in the right direction," says Sue Shannon, superintendent of schools in the eastern San Fernando Valley.[25]
© Brian Vander Brug, Los Angeles Times.
Reprinted with permission, 2004

ing with the nurses…Half of my leadership group has turned over in the last year," admits Richards. "It's not easy and it's not fun. Things get ugly before they get better," she says of the change process.[26]

Replacing staff is a radical form of organizational "unlearning" (see Chapter 1) because replacing executives removes knowledge of the organization's past routines. This potentially opens up opportunities for new practices to take hold.[27] At the same time, coercion is a risky strategy because survivors (employees who are not fired) may have less trust in corporate leaders and engage in more political tactics to protect their own job security.

REFREEZING THE DESIRED CONDITIONS

Unfreezing and changing behaviour patterns won't result in lasting change. People are creatures of habit, so they easily slip back into past patterns. Therefore, leaders need to refreeze the new behaviours by realigning organizational systems and team dynamics with the desired changes.[28] One of the most popular refreezing strategies is to realign the reward system around desired behaviour and outcomes.[29] Feedback, information systems, organizational structures, and physical layout of buildings are among the other tools used to refreeze desired behaviours.

■ STRATEGIC VISIONS, CHANGE AGENTS, AND DIFFUSING CHANGE

Kurt Lewin's force field analysis model provides a rich understanding of the dynamics of organizational change. But it overlooks three other ingredients in effective change processes: strategic visions, change agents, and diffusing change. Every successful change requires a well-articulated and appealing vision of the desired future state.[30] This vision provides a sense of direction and establishes the critical success factors against which the real changes are evaluated. It also minimizes employee fear of the unknown and provides a better understanding about what behaviours employees must learn for the future state.

CHANGE AGENTS

change agent
Anyone who possesses enough knowledge and power to guide and facilitate the organizational change effort.

Every organizational change, whether large or small, requires one or more change agents. A **change agent** is anyone who possesses enough knowledge and power to guide and facilitate the change effort. Change agents come in different forms, and more than one person is often required to serve these different roles. Transformational leaders are the primary agents of change because they form a vision of the desired future state, communicate that vision in ways that are meaningful to others, behave in ways that are consistent with the vision, and build commitment to the vision.[31] Transformational leaders are the architects who shape the overall direction for the change effort and motivate employees to achieve that objective.

Organizational change also requires transactional leaders who implement the change by aligning the behaviour of individual employees on a day-to-day basis with the organization's new goals.[32] If a company wants to provide better customer service, then supervisors and other transactional leaders need to arrange rewards, resources, feedback, and other conditions that support better customer service behaviours in employees. Consultants from either inside or outside the organization represent a third change agent role. Consultants typically bring unique expertise to the change process through a toolkit of change processes, some of which we introduce later in this chapter. Finally, just as employees are encouraged to become leaders anytime and anywhere, they also assist the change process as role models for others to follow.

DIFFUSION OF CHANGE

Change agents often test the transformation process with a pilot project, and then diffuse what has been learned from this experience to other parts of the organization. Unlike centralized, system-wide changes, pilot projects are more flexible and less risky.[33] The pilot project approach also makes it easier to select organizational groups that are most ready for change, which increases the pilot project's success.

But how do we ensure that the change process started in the pilot project is adopted by other segments of the organization? The MARS model introduced in Chapter 2 offers a useful template to organize the answer to this question. First, employees are more likely to adopt the practices of a pilot project when they are motivated to do so.[34] This occurs when they see that the pilot project is successful and people in the pilot project receive recognition and rewards for changing their previous work practices. Diffusion also requires supervisor support and reinforcement of the desired behaviours. More generally, change agents need to minimize the sources of resistance to change that we discussed earlier in this chapter.

Second, employees must have the ability—the required skills and knowledge—to adopt the practices introduced in the pilot project. According to innovation diffusion studies, people adopt ideas more readily when they have an opportunity to interact and learn from others who have already applied the new practices.[35] Thus, pilot projects get diffused when employees in the original pilot are dispersed to other work units as role models and knowledge sources.

Third, pilot projects get diffused when employees have clear role perceptions; that is, they understand how the practices in a pilot project apply to them even though in a completely different functional area. For instance, accounting department employees won't easily recognize how they can adopt quality improvement practices developed by employees in the production department. The challenge here is for change agents to provide guidance that is neither too specific, because it might not seem relevant to other areas of the organization, nor too abstract, because this makes the instructions too vague. Finally, employees require supportive situational factors, including the resources and time necessary to adopt the practices demonstrated in the pilot project.

■ THREE APPROACHES TO ORGANIZATIONAL CHANGE

action research
A data-based, problem-oriented process that diagnoses the need for change, introduces the intervention, and then evaluates and stabilizes the desired changes.

So far, we have looked at the dynamics of change that occur every day in organizations. However, organizational change agents and consultants also apply various approaches to organizational change. This section introduces three of the leading approaches to organizational change: action research, appreciative inquiry, and parallel learning structures.

ACTION RESEARCH APPROACH

Along with introducing the force field model, Kurt Lewin recommended an **action research** approach to the change process. Action research takes the view that meaningful change is a combination of action-orientation (changing attitudes and behaviour) and research orientation (testing theory).[36] On the one hand, the change process needs to be action-oriented because the ultimate goal is to bring about change. An action orientation involves diagnosing current problems and applying interventions that resolve those problems. On the other hand, the change process is a research study because change agents apply a conceptual framework (such as team dynamics or organizational culture) to a real situation. As with any good research, the change process involves collecting data to diagnose problems more effectively and to evaluate systematically how well the theory works in practice. In other words, action research embraces the notion of organizational learning and knowledge management (see Chapter 1).[37]

Within this dual framework of action and research, the action research approach adopts an open systems view. It recognizes that organizations have many interdependent parts, so change agents need to anticipate both the intended and unintended consequences of their interventions. Action research is also a highly participative process because open systems change requires both the knowledge and commitment of members within that system. Indeed, employees are essentially co-researchers as well as participants in the intervention. Overall, action research is a data-based, problem-oriented process that diagnoses the need for change, introduces the intervention, and then evaluates and stabilizes the desired changes (see Exhibit 17.4).[38]

1. *Form client–consultant relationship*—Action research usually assumes that the change agent originates outside the system (such as a consultant), so the process begins by forming the client–consultant relationship. Consultants need to determine the client's readiness for change, including whether people are motivated to participate in the process, are open to meaningful change, and possess the abilities to complete the process.

2. *Diagnose the need for change*—Action research is a problem-oriented activity that carefully diagnoses the problem through systematic analysis of the situation. Organizational diagnosis identifies the appropriate direction for the change effort by gathering and analyzing data about an ongoing system, such as through interviews and surveys of employees and other stakeholders. Organizational diagnosis also includes employee involvement in agreeing on the appropriate change method, the schedule for these actions, and the expected standards of successful change.

3. *Introduce intervention*—This stage in the action research model applies one or more actions to correct the problem. It may include any of the prescriptions mentioned in this textbook, such as building more effective teams, managing conflict, building a better organizational structure, or changing the corporate culture. An important issue is how quickly the changes should occur.[39] Some experts recommend incremental change in which the organization fine-tunes the system and takes small steps toward a desired state. Others claim that quantum change is often required, in which the system is overhauled decisively and quickly. Quantum

■ **EXHIBIT 17.4**   The action research process

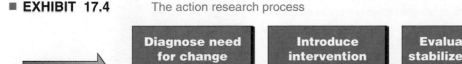
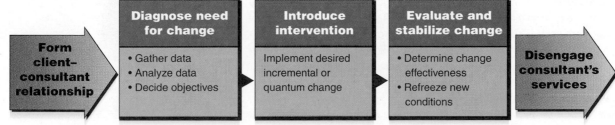

change is usually traumatic to employees and offers little opportunity for correction. But incremental change is also risky when the organization is seriously misaligned with its environment, thereby threatening its survival.

4. *Evaluate and stabilize change*—Action research recommends evaluating the effectiveness of the intervention against the standards established in the diagnostic stage. Unfortunately, even when these standards are clearly stated, the effectiveness of an intervention might not be apparent for several years, or might be difficult to separate from other factors. If the activity has the desired effect, then the change agent and participants need to stabilize the new conditions. This is the refreezing process that we described earlier. Rewards, information systems, team norms, and other conditions are redesigned so that they support the new values and behaviours.

The action research approach has dominated organizational change thinking ever since it was introduced in the 1940s. However, some experts complain that the problem-oriented nature of action research—in which something is wrong that must be fixed—focuses on the negative dynamics of the group or system rather than its positive opportunities and potential. This concern with action research has led to the development of a more positive approach to organizational change, called appreciative inquiry.[40]

APPRECIATIVE INQUIRY APPROACH

appreciative inquiry

An organizational change process that directs attention away from the group's own problems and focuses participants on the group's potential and positive elements.

Appreciative inquiry tries to break out of the problem-solving mentality of traditional change management practices by reframing relationships around the positive and the possible. It searches for organizational (or team) strengths and capabilities, then adapts or applies that knowledge for further success and well-being. Appreciative inquiry is therefore deeply grounded in the emerging philosophy of *positive organizational behaviour*, which suggests that focusing on the positive rather than negative aspects of life will improve organizational success and individual well-being.[41]

Canadian Tire's Appreciative Journey

After effectively battling the American juggernauts Wal-Mart and Home Depot over the past decade, Canadian Tire CEO Wayne Sales and his executive team wanted to hear from employees and storeowners about what makes Canadian Tire so successful, then rebuild its core values around those positive experiences. Appreciative inquiry played an important role in this re-visioning process. Internal consultants conducted detailed interviews with 377 staff across the organization, asking each to describe occasions where they felt Canadian Tire was working at its best and what they value most about the company. Some people described the excitement of holiday season where products are flying out the door. Others recalled the teamwork of employees volunteering to work late to clean up a store after a major delivery. These appreciative incidents were organized around six team values (owners, driven, accountable, etc.), which the executive team discussed and affirmed. Canadian Tire then held a one-day conference in which middle and senior management developed a common understanding of these values. Next, store managers discussed the six team values with their staff and participated in an appreciative exercise in which employees visualized a good news story about Canadian Tire's success.[42] *CP/Toronto Star—Andrew Stawicki*
www2.canadiantire.ca

Appreciative inquiry typically directs its inquiry toward successful events and successful organizations or work units. This external focus becomes a form of behavioural modelling, but it also increases open dialogue by redirecting the group's attention away from its own problems. Appreciative inquiry is especially useful when participants are aware of their "problems" or already suffer from enough negativity in their relationships. The positive orientation of appreciative inquiry enables groups to overcome these negative tensions and build a more hopeful perspective of their future by focusing on what is possible.[43]

The "Four-D" model of appreciative inquiry shown in Exhibit 17.5 begins with *discovery*—identifying the positive elements of the observed events or organization.[44] This might involve documenting positive customer experiences elsewhere in the organization. Or it might include interviewing members of another organization to discover its fundamental strengths. As participants discuss their findings, they shift into the *dreaming* stage by envisioning what might be possible in an ideal organization. By directing their attention to a theoretically ideal organization or situation, participants feel safer revealing their hopes and aspirations than if they were discussing their own organization or predicament.

As participants make their private thoughts public to the group, the process shifts into the third stage, called *designing*. Designing involves the process of dialogue, in which participants listen with selfless receptivity to each other's models and assumptions and eventually form a collective model for thinking within the team. In effect, they create a common image of what should be. As this model takes shape, group members shift the focus back to their own situation. In the final stage of appreciative inquiry, called *delivering*, participants establish specific objectives and direction for their own organization based on their model of what will be.

Appreciative inquiry is a relatively new approach to organization change, but has already generated success stories at AVON Mexico, American Express, Green Mountain Coffee Roasters, and Hunter Douglas, among others. At the same time, this approach has not always been successful and experts warn that it is not always the best approach to changing teams or organizations.[45] It requires a particular mindset among participants where they are willing to let go of the problem-oriented approach, and where leaders are willing to accept appreciative inquiry's less structured process. Another concern is that research has not yet examined the contingencies of this approach.[46] Specifically, we don't yet know the conditions in which appreciate inquiry is the best approach to organizational change, and under what conditions it is less effective. Overall, appreciative inquiry has much to offer the organizational change process, but we are just beginning to understand its potential and limitations.

■ **EXHIBIT 17.5**
The appreciative inquiry process

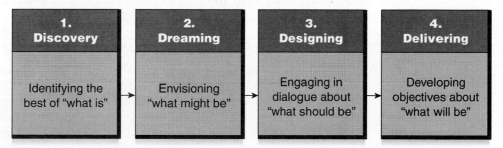

Sources: Based on F. J. Barrett and D. L. Cooperrider, "Generative Metaphor Intervention: A New Approach for Working with Systems Divided by Conflict and Caught in Defensive Perception," *Journal of Applied Behavioral Science*, 26 (1990), p. 229; D. Whitney and C. Schau, "Appreciative Inquiry: An Innovative Process for Organization Change," *Employment Relations Today*, 25 (Spring 1998), pp. 11–21; J. M. Watkins and B. J. Mohr, *Appreciative Inquiry: Change at the Speed of Imagination* (San Francisco: Jossey-Bass, 2001), pp. 25, 42–45.

PARALLEL LEARNING STRUCTURE APPROACH

parallel learning structures

Highly participative groups constructed alongside (i.e., parallel to) the formal organization with the purpose of increasing the organization's learning and producing meaningful organizational change.

Parallel learning structures are highly participative arrangements, composed of people from most levels of the organization who follow the action research model to produce meaningful organizational change. They are social structures developed alongside the formal hierarchy with the purpose of increasing the organization's learning.[47] Ideally, participants in parallel learning structures are sufficiently free from the constraints of the larger organization so they can more effectively solve organizational issues.

Royal Dutch/Shell relied on a parallel learning structure to introduce a more customer-focused organization.[48] Rather than try to change the entire organization at once, executives held week-long "retail boot camps" with six country teams of front-line people (e.g., gas station managers, truck drivers, marketing professionals). Participants learned about competitive trends in their regions and were taught powerful marketing tools to identify new opportunities. The teams then returned home to study their market and develop proposals for improvement.

Four months later, boot camp teams returned for a second workshop where each proposal was critiqued by Royal/Dutch Shell executives. Each team had 60 days to put its ideas into action, then return for a third workshop to analyze what worked and what didn't. This parallel learning process did much more than introduce new marketing ideas. It created enthusiasm in participants that spread contagiously to their co-workers, including managers above them, when they returned to their home countries.

■ CROSS-CULTURAL AND ETHICAL ISSUES IN ORGANIZATIONAL CHANGE

One significant concern with organizational change interventions or philosophies originating from North America is that they potentially conflict with cultural values in some other countries.[49] A few experts point out that the North American perspective of change is linear, such as in Lewin's force field model shown earlier. Change management in this part of the world also assumes that the change process is punctuated by tension and overt conflict. Indeed, some organizational change practices encourage the open display of conflict.

But change as a linear and conflict-ridden process is incompatible with cultures that view change as a natural cyclical process with harmony and equilibrium as the objectives.[50] For instance, people in many Asian countries try to minimize conflict in order to respect others and save face.[51] These concerns do not mean that Western-style change interventions are necessarily ineffective elsewhere. Rather, it suggests that we need to develop a more contingency-oriented perspective with respect to the cultural values of its participants.

ETHICAL CONCERNS WITH ORGANIZATIONAL CHANGE

Some organizational change practices also face ethical issues.[52] One ethical concern is threats to the privacy rights of individuals. The action research model is built on the idea of collecting information from organizational members, yet this requires employees to provide personal information and emotions that they may not want to divulge.[53] A second ethical concern is that some change activities potentially increase management's power by inducing compliance and conformity in organizational members. This power shift occurs because change creates uncertainty and may re-establish management's position in directing the organization.

For instance, action research is a system-wide activity that requires employee participation rather than allowing individuals to get involved voluntarily.

A third concern is that some organizational change interventions undermine the individual's self-esteem. The unfreezing process requires participants to disconfirm their existing beliefs, sometimes including their own competence at certain tasks or interpersonal relations. Some specific change practices involve direct exposure to personal critique by co-workers as well as public disclosure of one's personal limitations and faults.

One extreme example of this threat to self-esteem occurred a decade ago when SaskTel hired consultants to improve team dynamics. The 20 SaskTel employees involved in the project claim the consultants isolated them in an office suite with paper taped over its glass walls so that no one could see inside. They were also quarantined in small cubicles and prevented from talking to each other. The employees eventually united and forced SaskTel to get rid of the consulting firm. "Team members regularly received insults in front of the group," recalls one SaskTel manager. "The isolation, long hours, and purposeless activity left me feeling abandoned, betrayed, and frightened." Several other SaskTel employees took sick leave when they abandoned the project.[54]

A fourth ethical concern is the change management consultant's role in the change process. Ideally, consultants should occupy "marginal" positions with the clients they are serving. This means that they must be sufficiently detached from the organization to maintain objectivity and avoid having the client become too dependent on them. However, some consultants tend to increase rather than decrease clients' dependence for financial gain. Others have difficulty maintaining neutrality because they often come to the situation with their own biases and agendas.

Organizational change is a complex process with a variety of approaches and issues. Many corporate leaders have promised more change than they were able to deliver because they underestimated the time and challenges involved with this process. Yet, the dilemma is that most organizations operate in hyper-fast environments that demand continuous and rapid adaptation. Successful organizations, such as Friesens Corporation described in the opening vignette to this chapter, have mastered the complex dynamics of moving people through the continuous process of change.

■ PERSONAL CHANGE FOR THE ROAD AHEAD

In this last section of *Canadian Organizational Behaviour*, we thought it would be a good idea to shift attention from organizational change to a few practical ideas on personal change and development in organizations. Whether you are just starting your career or are already well along the trail, the following principles should help you improve both your prospects and long-term career satisfaction. These points do not cover everything you need to remember about developing your career. Instead, they highlight some of the key strategies that will help you along the road ahead.

UNDERSTAND YOUR NEEDS AND VALUES

Randy VanDerStarren planned to be an architect, but he soon realized that he wasn't excited about designing suburban homes for the next few decades. Instead, he studied graphic arts in college and soon discovered his passion for advertising—the creativity, strategic thinking, and never-ending churn of ideas. Armed with a college and university education, VanDerStarren joined a major Toronto ad agency. His love of advertising and a knack at strategy led to jobs at other ad agencies over the next decade. VanDerStarren is now senior vice-president of marketing with Canadian mutual fund firm AGF Management Ltd., a position that continues to fulfill his personal needs. "AGF has allowed me...to do what I love," says VanDer-Starren. "It's a pretty amazing ride for me right now."[55]

Randy VanDerStarren is following the first piece of advice regarding personal growth and development: understand your needs and values. "Find something you love, that you would do for free and then try to make a living at it," advises Toronto comedian and former talk show host Mike Bullard.[56] How do you know what path is most fulfilling for you? This involves doing self-assessments of your vocational interests and recounting experiences that you enjoyed. Holland's occupational choice model presented in Chapter 2 helps to align your personality and interests with the work environment. It may also be useful to get feedback from others regarding activities that they notice you like or dislike. This applies the Johari Window model described in Chapter 3, whereby you learn more about yourself through information presented by close associates.

UNDERSTAND YOUR COMPETENCIES

Knowing yourself also involves knowing what you are capable of doing.[57] Although we might visualize our future as an engineering wizard or prime minister of Canada, we need to take our potential abilities into account. The more the work we perform is aligned with our personal competencies, the more we develop a "can-do" attitude that fuels our feelings of empowerment. Self-assessments, performance results, and constructive feedback from friends can help us to identify our capabilities. Also, keep in mind that competencies extend beyond technical skills; employers are also looking for generic competencies, such as communication, problem solving, and emotional intelligence.

SET CAREER GOALS

Goal setting is a powerful way to motivate and achieve results, and this applies as much to careers as to any other activity. Career goals are benchmarks against which we evaluate our progress and identify strategies to develop our competencies. Toronto-based career consultant Barbara Moses emphasizes that career goal setting is a fundamental element in becoming a "career activist." It involves writing your own script rather than waiting for someone to write it for you, being vigilant by identifying and preparing for opportunities, and becoming an independent agent by separating your self-identity from your job title, your organization, or what other people think you should be.[58]

MAINTAIN NETWORKS

Networking makes a difference in personal career growth. This observation is supported by several research studies and from evidence in executive placement firms. One large placement firm reported that 64 percent of the 7,435 clients in its executive career transition program found new employment through networking. As one successful Canadian job hunter advises: "Be prepared, know your story, and network, network, network."[59] Some networks are more effective than others, however. Specifically, job seekers tend to be more successful with large nonredundant networks. Networks that extend beyond your current sphere of work are also critical. The reason is that careers change much more today than in the past, so you need to establish connections to other fields where you may someday find yourself.[60]

GET A MENTOR

Thus far, our discussion has emphasized self-leadership in personal development. We need to set our own goals, motivate ourselves for career advancement, and visualize where we want to go. But personal development in organizational settings also benefits from the help of others. Mentoring is the process of learning the ropes of organizational life from a senior person within the company. Mentors give protégés more visible and meaningful work opportunities, and they also provide ongoing career guidance. You might think of them as a career coach because they provide ongoing advice and feedback.[61]

■ ORGANIZATIONAL BEHAVIOUR: THE JOURNEY CONTINUES

Nearly 100 years ago, industrialist Andrew Carnegie said: "Take away my people, but leave my factories, and soon grass will grow on the factory floors. Take away my factories, but leave my people, and soon we will have a new and better factory." Carnegie's statement reflects the message woven throughout this textbook that organizations are not buildings, or machinery or financial assets. Rather, they are the people in them. Organizations are human entities—full of life, sometimes fragile, always exciting.

CHAPTER SUMMARY

Lewin's force field analysis model states that all systems have driving and restraining forces. Change occurs through the process of unfreezing, changing, and refreezing. Unfreezing produces disequilibrium between the driving and restraining forces. Refreezing realigns the organization's systems and structures with the desired behaviours.

Restraining forces are manifested as employee resistance to change. The main reasons why people resist change are direct costs, saving face, fear of the unknown, breaking routines, incongruent organizational systems, and incongruent team dynamics. Resistance to change may be minimized by keeping employees informed about what to expect from the change effort (communicating); teach employees valuable skills for the desired future (learning); involve them in the change process; help employees cope with the stress of change; negotiate trade-offs with those who will clearly lose from the change effort; and use coercion (sparingly and as a last resort).

Organizational change also requires driving forces. This means that employees need to have an urgency for change by becoming aware of the environmental conditions that demand change in the organization. The change process also requires refreezing the new behaviours by realigning organizational systems and team dynamics with the desired changes.

Every successful change requires a clear, well-articulated vision of the desired future state. Change agents rely on transformational leadership to develop a vision, communicate that vision, and build commitment to the vision of a desirable future state. The change process also often applies a diffusion process in which change begins as a pilot project and eventually spreads to other areas of the organization.

Action research is a highly participative, open-systems approach to change management that combines an action-orientation (changing attitudes and behaviour) with research orientation (testing theory). It is a data-based, problem-oriented process that diagnoses the need for change, introduces the intervention, and then evaluates and stabilizes the desired changes.

Appreciative inquiry embraces the positive organizational behaviour philosophy by focusing participants on the positive and possible. It tries to break out of the problem-solving mentality that dominates organizational change through the action research model. The four stages of appreciative inquiry include discovery, dreaming, designing, and delivering. A third approach, called *parallel learning structures*, relies on social structures developed alongside the formal hierarchy with the purpose of increasing the organization's learning. They are highly participative arrangements, composed of people from most levels of the organization who follow the action research model to produce meaningful organizational change.

One significant concern with organizational change originating from North America is that they potentially conflict with cultural values in some other countries. Also, organizational change practices can raise one or more ethical concerns, including increasing management's power over employees, threatening individual privacy rights, undermining individual self-esteem, and making clients dependent on the change consultant.

Five strategies that assist personal development in organizational settings are: understand your needs and values, understand your competencies, set career goals, maintain networks, and get a mentor.

KEY TERMS

action research, p. 476
appreciative inquiry, p. 478
change agent, p. 475

force field analysis, p. 466
future search, p. 472
parallel learning structures, p. 480

refreezing, p. 467
unfreezing, p. 467

DISCUSSION QUESTIONS

1. Chances are that the school you are attending is currently undergoing some sort of change to adapt more closely with its environment. Discuss the external forces that are driving these changes. What internal drivers for change also exist?

2. Use Lewin's force field analysis to describe the dynamics of organizational change at Nissan Motor Company (see GLOBAL Connections 17.1 on page 473).

3. Employee resistance is a symptom, not a problem, in the change process. What are some of the real problems that may underlie employee resistance?

4. Senior management of a large multinational corporation is planning to restructure the organization. Currently, the organization is decentralized around geographical areas so that the executive responsible for each area has considerable autonomy over manufacturing and sales. The new structure will transfer power to the executives responsible for different product groups; the executives responsible for each geographic area will no longer be responsible for manufacturing in their area but will retain control over sales activities. Describe two types of resistance senior management might encounter from this organizational change.

5. Web Circuits Ltd. is an Ottawa-based custom manufacturer for high-technology companies. Senior management wants to introduce lean management practices to reduce production costs and remain competitive. A consultant has recommended that the company start with a pilot project in one

department and, when successful, diffuse these practices to other areas of the organization. Discuss the advantages of this recommendation and identify three ways (other than the pilot project's success) to make diffusion of the change effort more successful.

6. Suppose that you are vice-president of branch services at the Bank of Lethbridge. You notice that several branches have consistently low customer service ratings even though there are no apparent differences in resources or staff characteristics. Describe an appreciative inquiry process in one of these branches that might help to overcome these problems.

7. This chapter suggests that some organizational change activities face ethical concerns. Yet, several consultants actively use these processes because they believe they benefit the organization and do less damage to employees than it seems on the surface. For example, some activities try to open up the employee's hidden area (see Johari Window in Chapter 3) so that there is better mutual understanding with co-workers. Discuss this argument and identify where you think organizational change interventions should limit this process.

8. Career activism is a concept that is gaining interest because it emphasizes managing your own development in organizations. What concepts introduced throughout this book are compatible with the career activist concept? In what ways might a person be a career activist?

CASE STUDY 17.1

THE EXCELLENT EMPLOYEE

By Mary Gander, Winona State University.

Emily, who has the reputation of being an excellent worker, is a machine operator in a furniture manufacturing plant that has been growing at a rate of between 15 percent and 20 percent each year for the past decade. New additions have been built onto the plant, new plants opened in the region, workers hired, new product lines developed, lots of expansion, but with no significant change in overall approach to operations, plant layout, ways of managing workers, or in the design processes. Plant operations as well as organizational culture are rooted in traditional Western management practices and logic, based largely on the notion of mass production and economies of scale. Over the past four years, the company has been growing in number and variety of products produced and in market penetration, however, profitability has been flattening and showing signs of decline. As a result, management is beginning to focus on production operations (internal focus) rather than mainly focusing on new market strategies, new products, and new market segments (external focus), in developing their strategic plans. They hope to get manufacturing costs down, improve consistency of quality and ability to meet delivery times better, while decreasing inventory and increasing flexibility.

One of several new programs initiated by management in this effort to improve flexibility and lower costs, was to get workers cross-trained. However, when a representative from human resources explained this program to Emily's supervisor, Jim, he reluctantly agreed to cross-train most of his workers, but NOT Emily.

Jim explained to the human resources person that Emily works on a machine that is very complex and not easy to effectively operate. She has to "babysit" it much of the time. He has tried many workers on it, tried to train them, but Emily is the only one who can consistently get product through the machine that is within specification and still meet production schedules. When anyone else tries to operate the machine, which performs a key function in the manufacturing process, it either ends up being a big bottle neck or producing excessive waste, which creates a lot of trouble for Jim.

Jim goes on to explain that Emily knows this sophisticated and complicated machine inside and out, she has been running it for five years. She likes the challenge, she says it makes the day go by faster, too. She is meticulous in her work, a very skilled employee who really cares about the quality of her work. Jim told the HR person that he wished all of his workers were like Emily. In spite of the difficulty of running this machine, Emily can run it so well that product piles up at the next work station downstream in the production process, they can't keep up with her!

Jim was adamant about keeping Emily on this machine and not cross-training her. The HR person was frustrated. He could see Jim's point but he had to follow executive orders: "Get these people cross-trained."

Around the same period of time, a university student was doing a field study in the section of the plant where Emily worked and Emily was one of the workers he interviewed. Emily told the student that, in spite of the fact that the plant had some problems with employee morale and excessive employee turnover, she really liked working there. She liked the piece-rate pay system very much and hoped that she did not have to participate in the recent "Program of the Month" that was having operators learn each other's jobs. She told the student that it would just create more waste if they tried to have other employees run her machine. She told him that other employees had tried to learn how to operate her machine but couldn't do it as well as she could.

Emily seemed to take a special liking for the student and began to open up to him. She told him that her machine really didn't need to be so difficult and touchy to operate, with a couple of rather minor design changes in the machine and better maintenance, virtually anyone could run it. She had tried to explain this to her supervisor a couple of years ago but he just told her to "do her work and leave operations to the manufacturing engineers." She also said that, if workers up stream in the process would spend a little more time and care to keep the raw material in slightly tighter specifications, it would go through her machine much more easily and trouble-free, but that they were too focused on going fast and making more piece-rate pay. She expressed a lack of respect for the managers who couldn't see this and even joked about how "managers didn't know anything."

Discussion Questions

1. Identify the sources of resistance to change in this short case.

2. Discuss whether this resistance is justified or could be overcome.

3. Recommend ways to minimize resistance to change in this incident or in future incidents.

T E A M   E X E R C I S E   **17.2**

STRATEGIC CHANGE INCIDENTS

Purpose   This exercise is designed to help you identify strategies to facilitate organizational change in various situations.

Instructions

■ *Step 1:* The instructor will place students into teams, and each team will be assigned one of the scenarios presented below.

■ *Step 2:* Each team will diagnose its assigned scenario to determine the most appropriate set of change management practices. Where appropriate, these practices should (a) create an urgency to change, (b) minimize resistance to change, and (c) refreeze the situation to support the change initiative. Each of these scenarios is based on real events.

■ *Step 3:* Each team will present and defend its change management strategy. Class discussion regarding the appropriateness and feasibility of each strategy will occur after all teams assigned the same scenario have presented. The instructor will then describe what the organizations actually did in these situations.

Scenario 1: Greener Telco   The board of directors at a large telephone company wants its executives to make the organization more environmentally friendly by encouraging employees to reduce waste in the workplace. There are also expectations by government and other stakeholders for the company to take this action

and be publicly successful. Consequently, the managing director wants to significantly reduce the use of paper, refuse, and other waste throughout the company's many widespread offices. Unfortunately, a survey indicates that employees do not value environmental objectives and do not know how to "reduce, reuse, recycle." As the executive responsible for this change, you have been asked to develop a strategy that might bring about meaningful behavioural change toward these environmental goals. What would you do?

Scenario 2:   Go Forward Airline   A major airline had experienced a decade of rough turbulence, including two bouts of bankruptcy protection, 10 managing directors, and morale so low that employees had ripped off company logos from their uniforms out of embarrassment. Service was terrible and the airplanes rarely arrived or left the terminal on time. This was costing the airline significant amounts of money in passenger layovers. Managers were paralyzed by anxiety and many had been with the firm so long that they didn't know how to set strategic goals that worked. One-fifth of all flights were losing money and the company overall was near financial collapse (just three months to defaulting on payroll obligations). You and the newly-hired managing director must get employees to quickly improve operational efficiency and customer service. What actions would you take to bring about these changes in time?

TOLERANCE OF CHANGE SCALE

Purpose This exercise is designed to help you understand how people differ in their tolerance of change.

Instructions Read each of the statements below and circle the response that best fits your personal belief. Then use the scoring key in Appendix B of this book to calculate your results. This self-assessment is completed alone so students rate themselves honestly without concerns of social comparison. However, class discussion will focus on the meaning of the concept measured by this scale and its implications for managing change in organizational settings.

TOLERANCE OF CHANGE SCALE

To what extent does each statement describe you? Indicate your level of agreement by marking the appropriate response on the right.	Strongly Agree ▼	Moderately Agree ▼	Slightly Agree ▼	Neutral ▼	Slightly Disagree ▼	Moderately Disagree ▼	Strongly Disagree ▼
1. An expert who doesn't come up with a definite answer probably doesn't know too much.	☐	☐	☐	☐	☐	☐	☐
2. I would like to live in a foreign country for a while.	☐	☐	☐	☐	☐	☐	☐
3. There is really no such thing as a problem that can't be solved	☐	☐	☐	☐	☐	☐	☐
4. People who fit their lives into a schedule probably miss most of the joy of living.	☐	☐	☐	☐	☐	☐	☐
5. A good job is one where it is always clear what is to be done and how it is to be done.	☐	☐	☐	☐	☐	☐	☐
6. It is more fun to tackle a complicated problem than to solve a simple one.	☐	☐	☐	☐	☐	☐	☐
7. In the long run, it is possible to get more done by tackling small, simple problems rather than large, complicated ones.	☐	☐	☐	☐	☐	☐	☐
8. Often the most interesting and stimulating people are those who don't mind being different and original.	☐	☐	☐	☐	☐	☐	☐
9. What we are used to is always preferable to what is unfamiliar.	☐	☐	☐	☐	☐	☐	☐
10. People who insist on a yes or no answer just don't know how complicated things really are.	☐	☐	☐	☐	☐	☐	☐
11. A person who leads an even, regular life in which few surprises or unexpected happenings arise really has a lot to be grateful for.	☐	☐	☐	☐	☐	☐	☐

TOLERANCE OF CHANGE SCALE (continued)						
To what extent does each statement describe you? Indicate your level of agreement by marking the appropriate response on the right.	Strongly Agree ▼	Moderately Agree ▼	Slightly Agree ▼	Neutral ▼	Slightly Disagree ▼	Moderately Disagree ▼	Strongly Disagree ▼
12. Many of our most important decisions are based on insufficient information.	☐	☐	☐	☐	☐	☐	☐
13. I like parties where I know most of the people more than ones where all or most of the people are complete strangers.	☐	☐	☐	☐	☐	☐	☐
14. Teachers or supervisors who hand out vague assignments give one a chance to show initiative and originality.	☐	☐	☐	☐	☐	☐	☐
15. The sooner everyone acquires similar values and ideals, the better.	☐	☐	☐	☐	☐	☐	☐
16. A good teacher is one who makes you wonder about your way of looking at things.	☐	☐	☐	☐	☐	☐	☐

Source: Adapted from S. Budner, "Intolerance of Ambiguity as a Personality Variable," *Journal of Personality,* 30 (1962), pp. 29–50.

Case 1 | WENDY'S RESTAURANTS OF CANADA

Employees at Wendy's Restaurants of Canada are about to be swept up in a tide of extraordinary change. To boost profits, Wendy's wanted to break down the military style of management and, in its place, create a culture of vulnerability and trust. To launch this change process, Wendy's brought together 160 restaurant managers from across Canada to an Ontario resort; there, New Mexico–based Pecos River guided them to a new way of working with their employees. This classic CBC video program takes the viewer through the Pecos River program then transports us to Winnipeg, where district manager Craig Stapon is responsible for getting his managers on-board the change process. Although this program was filmed in the early 1990s, it remains one of the best video clips to illustrate the trials and tribulations of introducing change in the workplace.

Discussion Questions

1. What changes did executives at Wendy's Restaurants of Canada expect to result from the Pecos River program? Did these changes occur in the Winnipeg restaurants?

2. Was there any resistance to change among the Winnipeg restaurant managers? If so, what form of resistance did it take?

3. What change management strategies did Craig Stapon use among the Winnipeg managers? Were these strategies effective? Why or why not?

Case 2 | JETBLUE AIRWAYS

JetBlue Airways is one of America's great aviation success stories. In just a few short years after its startup, the New York–based discount airline has become both profitable and highly popular among customers. Founder David Neeleman (who also assisted in the start-up of Calgary-based WestJet) claims that the notion of a "JetBlue experience" emerged from customer feedback about their travels on JetBlue. This unique experience is based on the company's customer-focused culture and the many decisions focused on giving customers the best possible encounters.

Discussion Questions

1. Identify the activities or conditions that have developed and maintained JetBlue's customer service culture.

2. How has JetBlue's culture and explicit values influenced its decision making?

CASE 1   Arctic Mining Consultants

Tom Parker enjoyed working outdoors. At various times in the past, he worked as a ranch hand, high steel rigger, headstone installer, prospector, and geological field technician. Now 43, Parker is a geological field technician and field coordinator with Arctic Mining Consultants. He has specialized knowledge and experience in all nontechnical aspects of mineral exploration, including claim staking, line cutting and grid installation, soil sampling, prospecting, and trenching. He is responsible for hiring, training, and supervising field assistants for all of Arctic Mining Consultants' programs. Field assistants are paid a fairly low daily wage (no matter how long they work, which may be up to 12 hours or more) and are provided meals and accommodation. Many of the programs are operated by a project manager who reports to Parker.

Parker sometimes acts as a project manager, as he did on a job that involved staking 15 claims near Eagle Lake, British Columbia. He selected John Talbot, Greg Boyce, and Brian Millar, all of whom had previously worked with Parker, as the field assistants. To stake a claim, the project team marks a line with flagging tape and blazes along the perimeter of the claim, cutting a claim post every 457 metres (500 yards) (called a "length"). The 15 claims would require almost 96 kilometres (60 miles) of line in total. Parker had budgeted seven days (plus mobilization and demobilization) to complete the job. This meant that each of the four stakers (Parker, Talbot, Boyce, and Millar) would have to complete a little over seven "lengths" each day. The following is a chronology of the project.

Day 1

The Arctic Mining Consultants crew assembled in the morning and drove to Eagle Lake, from where they were flown by helicopter to the claim site. On arrival, they set up tents at the edge of the area to be staked, and agreed on a schedule for cooking duties. After supper, they pulled out the maps and discussed the job—how long it would take, the order in which the areas were to be staked, possible helicopter landing spots, and areas that might be more difficult to stake.

Parker pointed out that with only a week to complete the job, everyone would have to average seven and a half lengths per day. "I know that is a lot," he said, "but you've all staked claims before and I'm confident that each of you is capable of it. And it's only for a week. If we get the job done in time, there's a $300 bonus for each man." Two hours later, Parker and his crew members had developed what seemed to be a workable plan.

Day 2

Millar completed six lengths, Boyce six lengths, Talbot eight, and Parker eight. Parker was not pleased with Millar's or Boyce's production. However, he didn't make an issue of it, thinking that they would develop their "rhythm" quickly.

Day 3

Millar completed five and a half lengths, Boyce four, and Talbot seven. Parker, who was nearly twice as old as the other three, completed eight lengths. He also had enough time remaining to walk over and check the quality of stakes that Millar and Boyce had completed, then walk back to his own area for helicopter pickup back to the tent site.

That night Parker exploded with anger. "I thought I told you that I wanted seven and a half lengths a day!" he shouted at Boyce and Millar. Boyce said that he was slowed down by unusually thick underbrush in his assigned area. Millar said that he had done his best and would try to pick up the pace. Parker did not mention that he had inspected their work. He explained that as far as he was concerned, the field assistants were supposed to finish their assigned area for the day, no matter what.

Talbot, who was sharing a tent with Parker, talked to him later. "I think that you're being a bit hard on them, you know. I know that it has been more by luck than anything else that I've been able to do my quota. Yesterday I only had five lengths

done after the first seven hours and there was only an hour before I was supposed to be picked up. Then I hit a patch of really open bush, and was able to do three lengths in 70 minutes. Why don't I take Millar's area tomorrow and he can have mine? Maybe that will help."

"Conditions are the same in all of the areas," replied Parker, rejecting Talbot's suggestion. "Millar just has to try harder."

Day 4

Millar did seven lengths and Boyce completed six and a half. When they reported their production that evening, Parker grunted uncommunicatively. Parker and Talbot did eight lengths each.

Day 5

Millar completed six lengths, Boyce six, Talbot seven and a half, and Parker eight. Once again Parker blew up, but he concentrated his diatribe on Millar. "Why don't you do what you say you are going to do? You know that you have to do seven and a half lengths a day. We went over that when we first got here, so why don't you do it? If you aren't willing to do the job then you never should have taken it in the first place!"

Millar replied by saying that he was doing his best, that he hadn't even stopped for lunch, and that he didn't know how he could possibly do any better. Parker launched into him again: "You have got to work harder! If you put enough effort into it, you will get the area done!"

Later Millar commented to Boyce, "I hate getting dumped on all the time! I'd quit if it didn't mean that I'd have to walk 80 kilometres (50 miles) to the highway. And besides, I need the bonus money. Why doesn't he pick on you? You don't get any more done than me; in fact, you usually get less. Maybe if you did a bit more he wouldn't be so bothered about me."

"I only work as hard as I have to," Boyce replied.

Day 6

Millar raced through breakfast, was the first one to be dropped off by the helicopter, and arranged to be the last one picked up. That evening the production figures were Millar eight and a quarter lengths, Boyce seven, and Talbot and Parker eight each. Parker remained silent when the field assistants reported their performance for the day.

Day 7

Millar was again the first out and last in. That night, he collapsed in an exhausted heap at the table, too tired to eat. After a few moments, he announced in an abject tone, "Six lengths. I worked like a dog all day and I only got a lousy six lengths!" Boyce completed five lengths, Talbot seven, and Parker seven and a quarter.

Parker was furious. "That means we have to do a total of 34 lengths tomorrow if we are to finish this job on time!" With his eyes directed at Millar, he added: "Why is it that you never finish the job? Don't you realize that you are part of a team, and that you are letting the rest of the team down? I've been checking your lines and you're doing too much blazing and wasting too much time making picture-perfect claim posts! If you worked smarter, you'd get a lot more done!"

Day 8

Parker cooked breakfast in the dark. The helicopter dropoffs began as soon as morning light appeared on the horizon. Parker instructed each assistant to complete 8 lengths and, if they finished early, to help the others. Parker said that he would finish the other 10 lengths. Helicopter pickups were arranged for one hour before dark.

By noon, after working as hard as he could, Millar had only completed three lengths. "Why bother," he thought to himself, "I'll never be able to do another five lengths before the helicopter comes, and I'll catch the same amount of abuse from Parker for doing six lengths as for seven and a half." So he sat down and had lunch and a rest. "Boyce won't finish his eight lengths either, so even if I did finish mine, I still wouldn't get the bonus. At least I'll get one more day's pay this way."

That night, Parker was livid when Millar reported that he had completed five and a half lengths. Parker had done ten and a quarter lengths, and Talbot had completed eight. Boyce proudly announced that he finished seven and a half lengths, but sheepishly added that Talbot had helped him with some of it. All that remained were the two and a half lengths that Millar had not completed.

The job was finished the next morning and the crew demobilized. Millar has never worked for Arctic Mining Consultants again, despite being offered work several times by Parker. Boyce sometimes does staking for Arctic, and Talbot works full time with the company.

CASE 2   A Window on Life

For Gilles LaCroix, there is nothing quite as beautiful as a handcrafted wood-framed window. LaCroix's passion for windows goes back to his youth in St. Jean, Quebec, where he was taught how to make residential windows by an elderly carpenter. He learned about the characteristics of good wood, the best tools to use, and how to choose the best glass from local suppliers. LaCroix apprenticed with the carpenter in his small workshop and, when the carpenter retired, was given the opportunity to operate the business himself.

LaCroix hired his own apprentice as he built up business in the local area. His small operation soon expanded as the quality of windows built by LaCroix Industries Ltd. became better known. Within eight years, the company employed nearly 25 people and the business had moved to larger facilities to accommodate the increased demand from southern Quebec. In these early years, LaCroix spent most of his time in the production shop, teaching new apprentices the unique skills that he had mastered and applauding the journeymen for their accomplishments. He would constantly repeat the point that LaCroix products had to be of the highest quality because they gave families a "window on life."

After 15 years, LaCroix Industries employed over 200 people. A profit-sharing program was introduced to give employees a financial reward for their contribution to the organization's success. Due to the company's expansion, headquarters had to be moved to another area of town, but the founder never lost touch with the work force. Although new apprentices were now taught entirely by the master carpenters and other craftspeople, LaCroix would still chat with plant and office employees several times each week.

When a second work shift was added, LaCroix would show up during the evening break with coffee and boxes of doughnuts and discuss how the business was doing and how it became so successful through quality workmanship. Production employees enjoyed the times when he would gather them together to announce new contracts with developers from Montreal and Toronto. After each announcement, LaCroix would thank everyone for making the business a success. They knew that LaCroix quality had become a standard of excellence in window manufacturing across Canada.

It seemed that almost every time he visited, LaCroix would repeat the now well-known phrase that LaCroix products had to be of the highest quality because they provided a window on life to so many families. Employees never grew tired of hearing this from the company founder. However, it gained extra meaning when LaCroix began posting photos of families looking through LaCroix windows. At first, LaCroix would personally visit developers and homeowners with a camera in hand. Later, as the "window on life" photos became known by developers and customers, people would send in photos of their own families looking through elegant front windows made by LaCroix Industries. The company's marketing staff began using this idea, as well as LaCroix's famous phrase, in their advertising. After one such marketing campaign, hundreds of photos were sent in by satisfied customers. Production and office employees took time after work to write personal letters of thanks to those who had submitted photos.

As the company reached the quarter-century mark, LaCroix, now in his mid-fifties, realized that the organization's success and survival depended on expansion into the United States. After consulting with employees, LaCroix made the difficult decision to sell a majority share to Build-All Products, Inc., a conglomerate with international marketing expertise in building products. As part of the agreement, Build-All brought in a vice-president to oversee production operations while LaCroix spent more time meeting with developers around North America. LaCroix would return to the plant and office at every opportunity, but often this would be only once a month.

Rather than visiting the production plant, Jan Vlodoski, the new production vice-president, would rarely leave his office in the company's downtown headquarters. Instead, production orders were sent to supervisors by memorandum. Although product quality had been a priority throughout the company's history, less attention had been paid to inventory controls. Vlodoski introduced strict inventory guidelines and outlined procedures on using supplies for each shift. Goals were established for supervisors to meet specific inventory targets. Whereas employees previously could have tossed out several pieces of warped wood, they would now have to justify this action, usually in writing.

Vlodoski also announced new procedures for purchasing production supplies. LaCroix Industries had highly trained purchasing staff who worked closely with senior craftspeople when selecting suppliers, but Vlodoski wanted to bring in Build-All's procedures. The new purchasing methods removed production leaders from the decision process and, in some cases, resulted in trade-offs that LaCroix's employees would not have made earlier. A few employees quit during this time, saying that they did not feel comfortable about producing a window that would not stand the test of time. However, unemployment was high in St. Jean, so most staff members remained with the company.

After one year, inventory expenses decreased by approximately 10 percent, but the number of defective windows returned by developers and wholesalers had increased markedly. Plant employees knew that the number of defective windows would increase as they used somewhat lower-quality materials to reduce inventory costs. However, they heard almost no news about the seriousness of the problem until Vlodoski sent a memo to all production staff saying that quality must be maintained. During the latter part of the first year under Vlodoski, a few employees had the opportunity to personally ask LaCroix about the changes and express their concerns. LaCroix apologized, saying due to his travels to new regions, he had not heard about the problems, and that he would look into the matter.

Exactly 18 months after Build-All had become majority shareholder of LaCroix Industries, LaCroix called together five of the original staff in the plant. The company founder looked pale and shaken as he said that Build-All's actions were inconsistent with his vision of the company and, for the first time in his career, he did not know what to do. Build-All was not pleased with the arrangement either. Although LaCroix windows still enjoyed a healthy market share and were competitive for the value, the company did not quite provide the minimum 18 percent return on equity that the conglomerate expected. LaCroix asked his long-time companions for advice.

CASE 3   Big Screen's Big Failure

By Fiona A. E. McQuarrie, University College of the Fraser Valley.

Bill Brosnan stared at the financial statements in front of him and shook his head. The losses from *Conquistadors*, the movie that was supposed to establish Big Screen Studios as a major Hollywood power, were worse than anyone had predicted. In fact, the losses were so huge that Brosnan's predecessor, Buck Knox, had been fired as a result of this colossal failure. Brosnan had wanted to be the head of a big movie production company for as long as he could remember, and was thrilled to have been chosen by the board of directors to be the new president. But he had never expected that the first task in his dream job would be to deal with the fallout from one of the most unsuccessful movies ever.

The driving force behind *Conquistadors* was its director, Mark Frazier. Frazier had made several profitable movies for other studios and had a reputation as being a maverick with a "vision." He was a director with clearly formulated ideas of what his movies should look like, and he also had no hesitations about being forceful with producers, studios, actors, and technical staff to ensure that his idea came to life as he had envisioned it. For several years, while Frazier had been busy on other projects, he had also been working on a script about two Spanish aristocrats in the 16th century who set out for America to find riches and gold, and encountered many amazing adventures on their travels. Frazier was something of an amateur historian, which led to his interest in the real-life stories of the Spanish conquistadors and bringing those stories to life for a 21st century audience. But he also felt that creating an epic tale like this would establish him as a serious writer and filmmaker in the eyes of Hollywood, some of whose major powers had dismissed his past work as unimaginative or clichéd.

At the time Big Screen Studios approached Frazier to see if he would be interested in working for them, the company was going through something of a rough spot. Through several years of hard work and mostly successful productions, Buck Knox, the president of Big Screen, had established Big Screen as a studio that produced cost-efficient and profitable films. The studio also had a good reputation for being supportive of the creative side of filmmaking; actors, writers, directors, and producers generally felt that Big Screen trusted them enough to give them autonomy in making decisions appropriate for their productions. (Other studios had reputations for keeping an overly tight rein on production budgets and for dictating choices based on cost rather than artistic considerations.) However, in the last two years Big Screen had invested in several major productions—a musical, a horror film, and the sequel to a wildly successful film adaptation of a comic book—that for various reasons had all performed well below expectations. Knox had also heard through the grapevine that several of the studio's board members were prepared to join together to force him out of the presidency if Big Screen did not come up with a hit soon.

Knox knew that Frazier was being wooed by several other studios for his next project, and decided to contact Frazier to see if he was interested in directing any of the productions Big Screen was considering in the next year or so. After hearing Knox's descriptions of the upcoming productions, Frazier said, "What I'd really be interested in doing is directing this script I've been writing." He described the plot of *Conquistadors* to Knox, and Knox was enchanted by the possibilities—two strong male lead characters, a beautiful woman the men encountered in South America whose affections they fought over, battles, sea journeys, and challenging journeys over mountains and through jungles. However, Knox could also see that this movie might be extremely expensive to produce. He expressed this concern to Frazier, and Frazier replied, "Yes, but it will be an investment that will pay off. I know this movie will work. And I've mentioned it to two other studios and they are interested in it. I would prefer to make it with Big Screen, but if I have to, I will go somewhere else to get it made. That is how strongly I believe in it. However, any studio I work with has to trust me. I won't make the film without adequate financial commitment from the studio, I want final approval over casting, and I won't make the film if I don't get final cut." ("Final cut" means the director, not the studio, edits the version of the movie that is released to theatres, and that the studio cannot release a version of the movie that the director does not approve.)

Knox told Frazier that he would get back to him later that week, and asked Frazier not to commit to any other project until then. He spent several days mulling over the possibilities. Like Frazier, he believed that *Conquistadors* could be a huge success. It certainly sounded like it had more potential than anything else Big Screen had in development. However, Knox was still concerned about the potential cost, and the amount of control over the project that Frazier was demanding. Frazier's reputation as a maverick meant that he likely would not compromise on his demands. Knox was also concerned about his own vulnerability if the movie failed. But on the other hand, Big Screen needed a big hit, and it needed one soon. Big Screen would look very bad if it turned down *Conquistadors* and the movie became a gigantic hit for some other studio. Frazier had a

respectable track record of producing moneymakers, so even if he might be difficult to work with, the end product usually was successful. At the end of the week, Knox phoned Frazier and told him that Big Screen was willing to produce *Conquistadors*. Frazier thanked Knox, and added, "This film is going to redeem me, and it's going to redeem Big Screen as well."

Pre-production on the film started almost immediately, after Frazier and the studio negotiated a budget of $50 million. This was slightly higher than Knox had anticipated, but he believed this was not an excessive amount to permit Frazier to realize the grand vision he had described. Knox further reassured himself by assigning John Connor, one of his trusted vice-presidents, to act as the studio's liaison with Frazier and to be executive producer on the film. Connor was a veteran of many years in the movie production industry and was experienced in working with directors and budgets. Knox trusted Connor to be able to make Frazier contain the costs of the production within the agreed-upon limits.

The first major problem the film encountered involved casting. The studio gave Frazier final approval over casting as he had requested. Frazier's first signing was Cole Rogan, a famous action star, to be one of the male leads. The studio did not object to this choice; in fact, Knox and Connor felt that Rogan was an asset because he had a reputation as a star that could "open" a film (in other words, audiences would come to a movie just because he was in it). However, Frazier then decided to cast Frank Monaco as the other male lead. Monaco had made only a few films to date, and those were fluffy romantic comedies. Frazier said that Monaco would bring important qualities of vulnerability and innocence to the role, which would be a strong contrast to Rogan's rugged machismo. However, Connor told Knox, he saw two major problems with Monaco's casting: Monaco had never proven himself in an epic adventure role, and he was an accomplished enough actor that he would make the rather wooden Rogan look bad. Knox told Connor to suggest to Frazier that Rogan's role be recast. Unfortunately, it turned out that Frazier had signed Rogan to a "pay or play" deal, meaning that if the studio released Rogan from the project, the studio would have to pay him a considerable sum of money. Knox was somewhat bothered that Frazier had made this deal with Rogan without consulting either him or Connor, but he told Connor to instruct Frazier to release Rogan and recast the role, and the studio would just accept the payment to Rogan as part of the production costs. Although Frazier complained, he did as the studio asked and chose as a replacement Marty Jones, an actor who had had some success in films but mostly in supporting roles. However, Jones was thrilled to be cast in a major role, and Connor felt that he would be capable of convincingly playing the part.

A few weeks after casting was completed, Connor called Knox and asked to see him immediately. "Buck," he told him once he arrived at Knox's office, "we have a really big problem." Connor said that Frazier was insisting the majority of the production be filmed in the jungles of South America, where most of the action took place, rather than on a studio soundstage or in a more accessible location that resembled the South American locale. Not only that, but Frazier was also insisting that he needed to bring along most of the crew that had worked on his previous films, rather than staffing the production locally. "Why does he want that? That's going to cost a hell of a lot," Knox said. "I know," Connor said, "but he says it's the only way that the film is going to work. He says it just won't be the same if the actors are in a studio or in some swamp in the southern U.S. According to him, the actors and the crew need to be in the real location to truly understand what the conquistadors went through, and audiences won't believe it's a real South American jungle if the film isn't made in one."

Knox told Connor that Frazier had to provide an amended budget to reflect the increased costs before he would approve the location filming. Connor took the request to Frazier, who complained that the studio was weakening on its promise to support the film adequately, and added that he might be tempted to take the film to another studio if he was not allowed to film on location in South America. After a few weeks, he produced an amended budget of $75 million. Knox was horrified that the budget for *Conquistadors* had doubled by half in a few weeks. He told Connor that he would only accept the amended budget under two conditions: one, that Connor would go on the location shoot to ensure that costs stayed within the amended budget, and

two, that if the costs exceeded Frazier's estimates, he would have to pay any excess himself. Frazier again complained that the studio was attempting to compromise his vision, but grudgingly accepted the modified terms.

Frazier, Connor, and the cast and crew then headed off to the South American jungles for a scheduled two-month shoot. Immediately it became apparent that there was more trouble. Connor, who reported daily to Knox, told him after two weeks had passed that Frazier was shooting scenes several times over—not because the actors or the crew were making mistakes, or because there was something wrong with the scene, but because the output just didn't meet his artistic standards. This attention to detail meant that the filming schedule was nearly a week behind after only the first week's work. Also, because the filming locations were so remote, the cast and crew were spending nearly four hours of a scheduled seven-hour work day travelling to and from location, leaving only three hours in which they could work at regular pay rates. Work beyond those hours meant they had to be paid overtime, and as Frazier's demanding vision required shooting 10 or 12 hours each day, the production was incurring huge overtime costs. As if that wasn't bad enough, the "rushes" (the finished film produced each day) showed that Monaco and Jones didn't have any chemistry as a pair, and Gia Norman, the European actress Frazier had cast as the love interest, had such a heavy accent that most of her lines couldn't be understood.

Knox told Connor that he was coming to the location right away to meet with Frazier. After several days of very arduous travel, Knox, Connor, and Frazier met in the canvas tent that served as the director's "office" in the middle of the jungle. Knox didn't waste any time with pleasantries. "Mark," he told Frazier, "there is no way you can bring this film in for the budget you have promised or within the deadline you agreed to. John has told me how this production is being managed, and it's just not acceptable. I've done some calculations, and at the rate you are going, this picture is going to cost $85 million and have a running time of four and a half hours. Big Screen is not prepared to support that. We need a film that's a commercially viable length, and we need it at a reasonable cost."

"It needs to be as long as it is," replied Frazier, "because the story has to be told. And if it has to cost this much, it has to cost this much. Otherwise it will look like crap and no one will buy a ticket to see it."

"Mark," replied Knox, "we are prepared to put $5 million more into this picture, and that is it. You have the choice of proceeding under those terms, and keeping John fully appraised of the costs so that he can help you stay within the budget. If you don't agree to that, you can leave the production, and we will hire another director and sue you for breach of contract."

Frazier looked as though he was ready to walk into the jungle and head back to California that very minute, but the thought of losing his dream project was too much for him. He muttered, "OK, I'll finish it."

Knox returned to California, nursing several nasty mosquito bites, and Connor stayed in the jungle and reported to him regularly. Unfortunately, it didn't seem like Frazier was paying much attention to the studio's demands. Connor estimated that the shoot would run three months rather than two, and that the total cost of the shoot would be $70 million. This only left $10 million of the budget for post-production, distribution, and marketing, which was almost nothing for an epic adventure. To add to Knox's problems, he got a phone call from Richard Garrison, the chairman of Big Screen's board of directors. Garrison had heard gossip about what was going on with *Conquistadors* in the jungles of South America, and wanted to know what Knox was going to do to curb Frazier's excesses. Knox told Garrison that Frazier was operating under clearly understood requirements, and that Connor was on the set to monitor the costs. Unfortunately, Knox thought, Connor was doing a good job of reporting, but he didn't seem to be doing much to correct the problems he was observing.

Frazier eventually came back to California after three and a half months of shooting, and started editing the several hundred hours of film he had produced. Knox requested that Frazier permit Connor or himself to participate in the editing, but Frazier retorted that permitting that would infringe on his right to "final cut," and refused to allow anyone associated with the studio to be in the editing room. Knox scheduled a release date for the film in six months' time, and asked the stu-

dio's publicity department to start working on an ad campaign for the film, but not much could be done on either of these tasks without at least a rough cut of the finished product.

Three weeks into the editing, Connor called Knox. "I heard from Mark today," he said. "He wants to do some reshoots." "Is that a problem?" Knox asked. "No," said Connor, "most of it is interior stuff that we can do here. But he wants to add a prologue. He says that the story doesn't make sense without more development of how the two lead characters sailed from Spain to South America. He wants to hire a ship."

"He wants to WHAT?" exclaimed Knox.

"He wants to hire a sailing ship, like the conquistadors travelled on. There's a couple of tall ships that would do, but the one he wants is in drydock in Mexico, and would cost at least a million to make seaworthy and sail up to southern California. And that's on top of the cost of bringing the actors and crew back for a minimum of a week. I suggested to him that we try some special effects or a computerized animation for the scenes of the ship on the ocean, and shoot the shipboard scenes in the studio, but he says that won't be the same and it needs to be authentic."

At this point, Knox was ready to drive over to the editing studios and take care of Frazier himself. Instead, he called Garrison and explained the situation. "I won't commit any more money to this without the board's approval. But we've already invested $80 million into this already, so is a few more million that much of a deal if it gets the damn thing finished and gets Frazier out of our hair? If we tell him no, we'll have to basically start all over again, or just dump the whole thing and kiss $80 million goodbye." At the other end of the line, Garrison sighed, and said, "Do whatever you have to do to get it done."

Knox told Connor to authorize the reshoots, with a schedule of two months and the expectation that Frazier would have a rough cut of the film ready for the studio executives to view in three months. However, because of the time Frazier had already spent in editing, Knox had to change the release date, which meant changing the publicity campaign as well—and releasing the film at the same time that one of Big Screen's major competitors was releasing another epic adventure that was considered a surefire hit. However, Knox felt he had no choice. If he didn't enforce some deadline, Frazier might sit in the editing room and tinker with his dream forever.

Connor supervised the reshoots, and reported that they went as well as could be expected. The major problem was that Gia Norman had had plastic surgery on her nose after the first shoot was completed, and looked considerably different than she had in the jungles of South America. However, creative lighting, makeup and costuming managed to minimize the change in her appearance. By all accounts, the (very expensive) sailing ship looked spectacular in the rushes, and Frazier was satisfied that his vision had been sufficiently dramatized.

Amazingly, Frazier delivered the rough cut of the film at the agreed-upon time. Knox, Connor, Garrison, and the rest of the studio's executives crowded into the screening room to view the realization of Frazier's dream. Five and a half hours later, they were in shock. No one could deny that the movie looked fantastic, and that it was an epic on a grand scale, but there was no way the studio could release a five-and-a-half-hour long film commercially, plus Frazier had agreed to produce a movie that was at most two and a half hours long. Knox was at his wits' end. He cornered Garrison in the hallway outside the screening room. "Will you talk to Mark? He won't listen to me, he won't listen to John. But we can't release this. It won't work." Garrison agreed, and contacted Frazier the next day. He reported back to Knox that Frazier, amazingly, had agreed to cut the film to two hours and 15 minutes. Knox, heartened by this news, proceeded with the previously set release date, which by now was a month away, and got the publicity campaign going.

Two days before the scheduled release date, Frazier provided an advance copy of his shortened version of *Conquistadors* for a studio screening. Knox had asked him to provide a copy sooner, but Frazier said that he could not produce anything that quickly. As a consequence, the version of the film that the studio executives were seeing for the first time was the version that had already had thousands of copies duplicated for distribution to movie theatres all across North America. In fact, those copies were on their way by courier to the theatres as the screening started.

At the end of the screening, the studio executives were stunned. Yes, the movie was shorter, but now it made no sense. Characters appeared and disappeared randomly, the plot was impossible to follow, and the dialogue did not make sense at several key points in the small parts of plot that were discernible. The film was a disaster. Several of the executives present voiced the suspicion that Frazier had deliberately edited the movie this way to get revenge on the studio for not "respecting" his vision and forcing him to reduce the film's length. Others suggested that Frazier was simply a lunatic who never should have been given so much autonomy in the first place.

Knox, Garrison, and Connor held a hastily called meeting the next morning. What could the studio do? Recall the film and force Frazier to produce a more coherent shorter version? Recall the film and release the five-and-a-half hour version? Or let the shorter version be released as scheduled and hope that it wouldn't be too badly received? Knox argued that the film should be recalled and Frazier should be forced to produce the product he agreed to produce. Connor said that he thought Frazier had been doing his best to do what the studio wanted, based on what Connor saw on the set, and that making Frazier cut the movie so short compromised the vision that Frazier wanted to achieve. He said the studio should release the long version and present it as a "special cinematic event." Garrison, as chairman of the board, listened to both sides, and after figuring out the costs of recalling and/or reediting the film—not to mention the less tangible costs of further worsening the film's reputation—said, "Gentlemen, we really don't have any choice. *Conquistadors* will be released tomorrow."

Knox immediately cancelled the critics' screenings of *Conquistadors* scheduled for that afternoon, so that bad reviews would not appear on the day of the film's release. Despite that pre-emptive step and an extensive advertising campaign, *Conquistadors* was a complete and utter flop. On a total outlay of $90 million, the studio recouped less than $9 million. The reviews of the film were terrible, and audiences stayed away in droves. The only place *Conquistadors* was even close to successful was in some parts of Europe, where film critics called the edited version an example of American studios' crass obsession with making money by compromising the work of a genius. The studio attempted to capitalize on this note of hope by releasing the five-and-a-half hour version of *Conquistadors* for screening at some overseas film festivals and cinema appreciation societies, but the revenues from these screenings were so small that they made no difference to the overall financial results.

Three months after *Conquistadors* was released, Garrison called Knox in and told him he was fired. Garrison told Knox the board appreciated what a difficult production *Conquistadors* had been to manage, but that the costs of the production had been unchecked to a degree that the board no longer had confidence in Knox's ability to operate Big Screen Studios efficiently. Connor was offered a very generous early retirement package, and accepted it. The board then hired Bill Brosnan, a vice-president at another studio, as Knox's replacement.

After reviewing *Conquistadors'* financial records and the notes that Knox had kept throughout the production, Brosnan was determined that a disaster like this would not undermine his career as it had Knox's. But what could he do to ensure this would not happen?

CASE 4 The Case of Lightco

By Jean Helms Mills, St. Mary's University.

The Culture Change

It was a beautiful late summer day and David White was seated at his desk, enjoying the view from his 18th floor office, and contemplating what to do next. White had just received the results of an employee attitude survey, which confirmed what he already suspected. His company, Lightco, was facing a serious morale problem among its employees and White knew he had to do something about it quickly.

Since being appointed as president of the publicly owned utility, White had travelled extensively throughout the region in order to meet all of the 2,600 employees. It was during these visits that he started to notice the employee discontent. As the largest employer of engineers in the province, it was true that Lightco was often referred to as a construction company, rather than an electric utility. White could see that the employees, in addition to those who were located in head office's 18 storey office tower, were spread over six thermal plants, a couple of hydro plants, and four zone (regional) offices. As such, the divisions seemed to operate as a number of separate companies, with little interaction.

White was also aware that traditionally the management positions were held mainly by engineers, whose style of management was autocratic at worst and paternalistic at best. It seemed to White, who had only been in the position a short time, that task accomplishment was Lightco's primary goal and that inanimate resources were being given more consideration than human resources. For White, who had been both a politician and college president prior to this current appointment, morale problems were disturbing because as well as affecting the efficiency of the Crown corporation, they were contradicting his basic values and beliefs. White asked his human resources director to conduct an employee attitude survey to see if he could get to the bottom of this problem so he could look for some solutions. Eight months later, the results were in and they confirmed what White already knew. Employees were dissatisfied with the way they were being treated and managers were unhappy with the lack of communication and support from head office. It was time to take action.

Implementing the Culture Change

A few days later, White called a meeting of the executive and presented them with an idea that he had been thinking about for a while. Recently he had read that Florida Power and Light had faced similar problems and had turned to culture change as a way of both increasing efficiency and boosting morale. Also, he knew that the local telephone company was introducing corporate values in an effort to change its culture. He suggested to the executive that maybe a planned culture change would work for Lightco. Within short order, tenders were sent out and a local consulting firm was hired to help Lightco establish its values and lead them into the change process.

The human resource department, working closely with the consultants, began the day to day process of operationalizing the change. It was decided, after a series of meetings with the executive, to focus on four values:

- The Province
- The Environment
- The Customer
- The Employee

The human resource manager and the consultants then decided to invite all the senior managers to a four-day session that would educate them about the culture change and give them the skills they would need to become facilitators for the one-day sessions that would be offered to the remaining employees to explain the values and the change. Meanwhile, in order to reinforce the importance of the program, employees were given coffee mugs printed with "we value the environment," pens and fridge magnets that highlighted the four values, and "values" posters were prominently displayed. Although employees certainly could identify the values, few knew how to recognize them in action, and fewer still were unable to understand how and when the culture change would become obvious. Most employees were focused on the value of "Employee" and waited to see how their contribution to Lightco would be rewarded.

Six Months Later...

Phil Roberts, an engineer in the thermal division, who was a 10-year veteran of the company, had seen the company introduce a number of different changes, but he hadn't paid much attention to them. The various techniques that the company had tried had little direct effect on him or how he carried out his day-to-day activities. But, recently he had attended a mandatory four-day training session for managers on changing the culture through the living of four values. This seemed very different from the change techniques that Lightco normally used because instead of focusing on how to get the job done, the company finally seemed to want to recognize the input of its employees and the importance of its customers. Maybe this new president was going to be okay after all. If anyone or anything could turn around the morale in this company, this could only benefit the company.

At the end of the four-day session, when volunteers were being solicited to act as facilitators for the one-day sessions for non managerial employees, Phil decided to sign up. He was convinced that incorporating the values into everyday work activities would help to bring the different company divisions together and improve morale throughout.

It was late Friday afternoon and Carol Isenor was anxious to get home. It had been a rough week. As a customer service clerk in the district office, Isenor had borne the brunt of disgruntled customers' anger and frustration because of the latest hike in electricity rates. The last thing she had wanted to do was to end her week by attending this one-day 'facilitation" meeting about the culture change program Lightco had recently embarked on. Like many of the others in the room, Carol felt that if Lightco really did value her as an employee, they would have given her a four-day training session, led by a consultant, like all the managers had received, not this one-day meeting with some engineer from the thermal division acting as a facilitator. What did he know about her job and why was this program any different from the others that Lightco had tried? Since starting with the company eight years earlier, Carol had seen the company introduce a variety of changes. While this latest "flavour of the month" seemed to be talking about corporate values as a way to build employee commitment, Carol found it difficult to see how this could have any direct affect on her. And, it already seemed that the abbreviated training session contradicted the value of "employee" that the facilitator was talking about. Carol looked at her watch again. Only 15 more minutes and she could catch the 5 p.m. bus home.

One Year Later...

Carol was in the lunchroom waiting for the kettle to boil. Looking around the room, she was reminded how much a part of their lives the Lightco values had become in such a short period of time. Not only were there tangible reminders of the values, but people were starting to act differently too. Early on, the values had been reinforced through a number of symbols, slogans, and practices. For example, four posters, depicting the four values, were on the wall behind Carol, and the styrofoam coffee cups on the shelf had been replaced by ceramic mugs that said "At Lightco, we value the environment." Now employees throughout the company had made values an issue. At one extreme were those who viewed them in a negative way... saying that everything had become a values issue, while others embraced them in an evangelical way and used values as a template for day to day behaviour.

Most, like Carol, saw the culture change as a positive step in the direction of making Lightco a better place to work. Although she and others had initially been skeptical about how long the company's commitment to the culture change would last, she had to admit that they certainly seemed to be trying to make it work. In fact, in the most recent annual report, the President's Report promised a commitment to employment equity and stated that "visible minorities and more women in management" would be a bigger part of the company. An Equity Advisory Committee had just been set up and women were being encouraged to go into previously male dominated trades. But, it was the recently announced job sharing program that was of greatest interest to Carol. For the first time since joining the company, she could apply to a program that would allow her to share her work duties with another co-worker, in order to give her more time and flexibility to spend with her family.

Phil was in his office studying the results of the latest employee attitude survey. Since becoming a facilitator, Phil had done a number of the one-day training sessions throughout the province. Initially, there had been a great deal of suspicion about the company's motives for change. But over time, and with the help of some of the union members who had also become facilitators, even the most skeptical employees had begun to believe that the company was serious about changing its ways and living the values. For example, the recent decision to do away with the different coloured hard hats, which distinguished management from non-management employees, had done a lot to blur the boundaries between management and staff in the Transmission and Distribution Division. Now, instead of management wearing a white hat and the trade employees wearing yellow, everyone would wear yellow. As well, in Phil's plant, the manager had decided to let employees finish their shift 15 minutes early so that they could shower and leave the plant on time and clean.

Although these were only little things, together they were changing the perception of Lightco as large, bureaucratic, and uncaring. Despite the usual complainers, most employees seemed to regard the changes that had been made in the past year as positive. The only real problem that Phil could identify was that probably people were far too happy with the values and saw them as a way to justify reasons for getting what they wanted. Still things could be worse and it certainly was good to see that morale had improved and employees were less suspicious of management's motives. Phil had to give a lot of credit to David White, as a president, he certainly was one of the people and employees liked and trusted him.

Privatization

Since taking over the reins of Lightco in 1983, David White had known that the Crown corporation would one day have to stand on its own two feet. By 1991, several key developments were beginning to impact decision-making within the company and causing a major change in thinking. Canada had entered into a North American Free Trade Agreement (NAFTA) with the U.S. that promised (or threatened) to open up a number of areas new to competition, including telecommunications and electricity supply. In order to meet the demands of remaining effective in a highly competitive environment, he knew that the company needed to take action and needed a strategy to achieve this. It came as no surprise to White when the premier of the province announced that Lightco would be privatized in June 1992. Although he was still committed to the culture change, White now had other issues to think about, the most important being to find ways to make the company more efficient and competitive. These factors dominated his thinking, as White looked for ways to achieve these new challenges while still remaining committed to the culture change.

Re-engineering

David White had just met with Lightco's auditors in order to finalize their statement for the 1992 Annual Report. Following privatization, he had been trying to reconcile various methods that would allow for the increase of the efficiency and effectiveness of the company, while still maintaining the integrity of the corporate culture and its values. When Lightco's auditors mentioned that their firm had a consulting arm with an established reputation of developing and implementing Business Process Improvement (BPI), he was interested. And when he found out that their consultants had successfully re-engineered a number of major electrical companies in Canada, White began to think that maybe they could do the same for Lightco. After discussing it a bit further, a meeting was arranged between the consulting division and White for later in the week.

After laying out a proposal, the consultants had little trouble convincing White and Lightco's senior executives that their re-engineering strategy would provide them with the key to creating an effective organization that would meet the demands of competition and globalization that were now facing the newly privatized company. Quickly, an agreement was signed and several consultants were assigned to work full time with Lightco's internal change agent, the director of Internal Auditing. Early on, a series of 'Effectiveness" bulletins were circulated among employees to explain the latest strategy. Employees who had previously worked as facilitators were encouraged to "volunteer" to be members of the re-engineering project assessment teams. Although the commitment to the values and the "new" corporate culture was not forgotten, it became the consultants' job to take Lightco into the second stage of the culture change, called "organizational effectiveness." Soon it became clear that this change program was going to be quite different from the culture change program and its concern for the employee. For one thing, the director of Employee Development was not directly involved with the planning and implementation of the re-engineering initiatives, and for another, the focus was on the value of the job, rather than the value of the employee.

In conjunction with the newly created "corporate effectiveness" department, composed of a project manager, an external consultant, a human resources specialist, and six communications support staff, the consultants formed the initial assessment team. Early on, it had become evident to the re-engineering leadership that Lightco was overstaffed and had a great deal of duplication of services. So these "business process improvement teams" interviewed and observed employees in the units being re-engineered, in order to decide how to streamline jobs and cut down on unnecessary costs. This process, which had taken 16 weeks and included an analysis of the current method of carrying out the task of "creating a vision and detailed concept of the future state of the process" and developing an implementation plan, was now concluding. With advice from the consultants, the process teams had identified jobs that didn't offer 'value' to the accomplishment of organizational goals and had offered employees in these positions the chance to take early retirement or to apply for jobs that were considered as having "added value." In this way, over 300 positions had already been eliminated, mostly through attrition, before the two pilot projects were initiated.

When Carol first heard that Customer Service was one of the departments that had been selected to be part of the re-engineering pilot projects, she was excited. This restructuring, combined with the earlier mandate of the culture change to promote women into positions of management through the value of employee, meant that she might finally have a chance at promotion. Although Carol had been with the company long enough to be considered for promotion and everyone said she knew the job better than anyone else, she had been overlooked the last few times a supervisory position had opened up in favour of her male colleagues. This time might be different. The company had certainly changed since this emphasis on values and culture had started and it really did seem to value its employees and to be committed to making the workplace more equitable.

Six Months Later...

Following the announcement that the company was going to implement two pilot projects, employees in the Customer Service division had been advised that one of the projects was going to involve the centralization and consolidation of all customer service related activities to one large call centre. This meant that employees would be trained to carry out a number of different tasks that would not only serve the customer better but give customer service representatives, like Carol, more autonomy and variety in doing their jobs.

It was only when Lightco called a meeting and announced that the closure of the satellite offices meant that 150 dislocated employees would now have to compete for about 70 new positions that would be created in the new call centre that the enormity of the project set in. As well, in addition to the competition from employees in the soon-to-be-closed locations, "linesmen" (sic) from the recently cancelled apprenticeship program, would also be competing for the same 70 positions. Rumour had it that those who weren't successful would be let go with a severance package.

Suddenly Carol wasn't worried about promotion, as job security became a primary focus. While the latest annual report had described re-engineering as "revolutionizing the way we work," nothing had prepared her for this. Not only was she overworked because the company had drastically underestimated the staff it would need for this new centre, but it was a joke to hear her manager describe the external consultant as a "visionary." But then he had been on the team that had thought up this whole scheme. Yesterday she had heard one co-worker refer to the consultant as "undertakers" and "hatchet men." Even her supervisor called them "gunslingers" when he thought no one was listening. What had happened to valuing the employee, Carol wondered? Things were certainly a mess. Many of her co-workers, fed up and stressed by the constant understaffing, were calling in sick. Others were resentful that their former co-workers had lost their jobs and many like Carol were wondering what would happen next. Although the company had just announced that they had retained the services of a psychological counselling firm to deal with employees' problems, the rumour that more lay-offs were about to occur was even more urgent.

Following the announcement that volunteers were been sought to serve on the Business Process team, Phil Roberts was encouraged to volunteer. Since his experience as a facilitator of the culture change had been so positive, Phil looked forward to again meeting with employees in other divisions and serving as an ambassador for Lightco. He was assigned to the team that was assessing the feasibility of consolidating the regional call centres. Initially, the team met two to three times a week for a few hours and Phil was able to return to the project he was completing in his own division. As the project got well underway, Phil was assigned full time to the team and was seconded to the Internal Audit division.

It was late Tuesday and Phil had just returned from another meeting that had gone on far longer than he anticipated. If he had known that employees were going to blame him personally for the problems created by the re-engineering processes, he would never have agreed to take on this task. Today had been particularly upsetting. An employee, who had just been given two weeks notice, had come to him crying and begging him to do something to help her get her job back. After all this, Phil was anxious to get home but first he had to return a call to his boss that was marked urgent. When he hung up, Phil was speechless. It seemed that the company had decided to outsource the work that Phil's department had been doing. Phil was waiting for security to arrive and escort him off the premises. After all the work he had done for Lightco, he was being given 20 minutes to clear out his desk.

At the same time, David White had just come from a meeting with the senior managers. Things were not good. Following the latest round of lay-offs, morale among the remaining employees was at an all-time low. The managers were reporting that employees were angry, unhappy, and stressed by the amount of work they were having to do and did not feel that their efforts were been acknowledged. White was hearing reports that employees felt that the changes that were occurring were not being explained in a timely manner, and rumours surrounding the changes were causing panic at all levels. More importantly, employees felt that Lightco was not holding true to the values and that the culture change was a thing of the past.

While re-engineering had seemed the ideal solution, White now wondered how he had failed to recognize that re-engineering would be a fairly rigid process that focused on getting tasks done in the most efficient and cost effective manner, while de-emphasizing the importance of creating a happy workforce and employee well-being. It seemed that his plans for creating a humanistic workplace and promoting employment equity had been derailed by factors that were out of his control. The culture had changed, but not in the way that he had hoped. Had he made a mistake? Should he have stuck with the original plan and not been talked into changing the company's strategy? Was it too late to gain back the trust of his employees?

CASE 5   From Lippert-Johanson Incorporated to Fenway Waste Management

By Lisa V. Williams, Jeewon Cho, and Alicia Boisnier, SUNY at Buffalo.

Part One

Catherine O'Neill was very excited to finally graduate from Flagship University at the end of the semester. She had always been interested in accounting, following from her father's lifelong occupation, and she very much enjoyed the challenging major. She was involved in many highly regarded student clubs in the business school and worked diligently to earn good grades. Now her commitment to the profession would pay off, she hoped, as she turned her attention to her job search. In late fall, she had on-campus interviews with several firms, but her interview with the prestigious Lippert-Johanson Incorporated (LJI) stood out in her mind as the most attractive opportunity. That's why Catherine was thrilled to learn she made it to the next level of interviews, to be held at the firm's main office later that month.

When Catherine entered the elegant lobby of LJI's Toronto offices, she was immediately impressed by all there was to take in. Catherine had always been one to pay attention to detail, and her acute observations of her environment had always been an asset. She was able to see how social and environmental cues told her what was expected of her, and she always set out to meet and exceed those expectations. On a tour of the office, she had already begun to size up her prospective workplace. She appreciated the quiet, focused work atmosphere. She liked how everyone was dressed: most wore suits and their conservative apparel supported the professional attitudes that seemed to be omnipresent. People spoke to her in a formal, but friendly manner, and seemed enthusiastic. Some of them even took the time to greet her as she was guided to the conference room for her individual interview. "I like the way this place feels and I would love to come to work here every day," Catherine thought. "I hope I do well in my interview!"

Before she knew it, Catherine was sitting in a nicely appointed office with one of the eight managers in the firm. Sandra Jacobs was the picture of a professional woman, and Catherine naturally took her cue from Sandra about how to conduct herself in the interview. It seemed to go very quickly, although the interview lasted an hour. As soon as Catherine left the office, she could not wait to phone her father about the interview. "I loved it there and I just know I'm a good fit!" she told her proud father. "Like them, I believe it is important to have the highest ethical standards and quality of work. Ms. Jacobs really emphasized the mission of the firm, as well as its policies. She did say that all the candidates have an excellent skill set and are well qualified for the job, so mostly, they are going to base their hiring decision on how well they think each of us will fit into the firm. Reputation is everything to an accounting firm. I learned that from you, Dad!"

After six weeks of apprehensive waiting, Catherine's efforts were rewarded when LJI and another firm contacted her with job offers. Catherine knew she would accept the offer from LJI. She saw the firm as very ethical, with the highest standards for work quality, and an excellent reputation. Catherine was grateful to have been selected from such a competitive hiring process. "There couldn't be a better choice for me! I'm so proud to become a member of this company!"

Catherine's first few days at LJI were a whirlwind of a newcomer's experiences. She had meetings with her supervisor to discuss the firm mission statement, her role in the firm, and what was expected of her. She was also told to spend some time looking at the employee handbook that covers many important policies of the firm, such as dress code, sick time, grievances, the chain of command, job descriptions, and professional ethics. Everyone relied on the handbook to provide clear guidance about what is expected of each employee. Also, Catherine was informed that she would soon begin participating in continuing professional education, which would allow her to update her skills and knowledge in her field. "This is great," thought Catherine, "I'm so glad to know the firm doesn't just talk about its high standards, it actually follows through with action."

What Catherine enjoyed most about her new job were her warm and welcoming colleagues who invited her to their group lunches, beginning her first day. They talked about work and home; they seemed close, both professionally and personally. She could see that everyone had a similar attitude about work: they cared about their work and the firm, they took responsibility for their own tasks, but they also helped one another out. Catherine also got involved in LJI activities outside of work, like their baseball and soccer teams, happy hours, picnics and parties, and enjoyed the chance to mingle with her co-workers. In what seemed like no time at all, Catherine started to really see herself as a fully integrated member of LJI.

Before tax season started, Catherine attended some meetings of the Canadian Institute of Chartered Accountants (CICA) and other professional accounting societies. There, she met many accountants from other firms who all seemed very impressed when she told them where she worked. Catherine's pride and appreciation for being a member of LJI grew as she realized how highly regarded the firm is among others in the accounting industry.

Part Two

Over the past seven years, Catherine's career in Toronto had flourished. Her reputation as one of the top tax accountants in her company was well established, and was recognized by colleagues outside the firm as well. However, Catherine entered a new chapter of her life when she married Ted Lewis, an oncology intern, who could not turn down an offer of residency at a top cancer centre in Montreal. Wanting to support Ted's once-in-a-lifetime career opportunity, Catherine decided it was time to follow the path of many of her colleagues and leave public accounting for a position that would be more conducive to starting a family.

Still, her heart was in the profession, so she took an available position as a controller of a small recycling company located a few miles from Catherine and Ted's new Montreal home. She knew that with this position she could both have children and maintain her career.

Fenway Waste Management is small—about 35 employees. There are about 25 people who work in the warehouse, three administrative assistants, two supervisors, and five people in management. Catherine had trouble adjusting to her new position and surroundings. Often she was asked to perform work that formally belonged to someone else; because it is a smaller company managers seem to "wear many hats." This was quite different from what she had experienced at LJI. In addition, the warehouse crew often has to work with greasy materials, and sometimes tracks the grease into the offices. Catherine half-laughed and half-worried when she saw a piece of paper pinned to the wall that said, "Clean Up After Yourself!" She supposed that the nature of the business was why the offices are functional, but furnished with old pieces. She couldn't imagine having a business meeting there! Also, for most of the employees, the casual dress matches the casual attitudes. But, Catherine continues to wear a dressed-down version of her formal LJI attire, even though her new co-workers consider her overdressed.

With all the changes Catherine has experienced, she has maintained one familiar piece of her past. Although it is not required for her new position, Catherine still attends CICA meetings and makes a point to continue updating her knowledge of current tax laws. At this year's conference, she told a former colleague, "Being here, I feel so much more like myself—I am so much more connected to these people and this environment than to those at my new job. It's too bad I don't feel this way at Fenway. I guess I'm just more comfortable with professionals who are similar to me."

CASE 6   Keeping Suzanne Chalmers

Thomas Chan hung up the telephone and sighed. The vice-president of software engineering at Advanced Photonics Ltd. (APL) had just spoken to Suzanne Chalmers, who called to arrange a meeting with Chan later that day. She didn't say what the meeting was about, but Chan almost instinctively knew that Suzanne was going to quit after working at APL for the past four years. Chalmers is a software engineer in Internet Protocol (IP), the software that directs fibre-optic light through APL's routers. It was very specialized work, and Suzanne was one of APL's top talents in that area.

Thomas Chan had been through this before. A valued employee would arrange a private meeting. The meeting would begin with a few pleasantries, then the employee announces that he or she wants to quit. Some employees say they are leaving because of the long hours and stressful deadlines. They say they need to decompress, get to know the kids again, or whatever. But that's not usually the real reason. Almost every organization in this industry is scrambling to keep up with technological advances and the competition. They would just leave one stressful job for another one.

Also, many of the people who leave APL join a start-up company a few months later. These start-up firms can be pressure cookers where everyone works 16 hours each day and has to perform a variety of tasks. For example, engineers in these small firms might have to meet customers or work on venture capital proposals rather than focus on specialized tasks related to their knowledge. APL has over 1,000 employees, so it is easier to assign people to work that matches their technical competencies.

No, the problem isn't the stress or long hours, Chan thought. The problem is money—too much money. Most of the people who leave are millionaires. Suzanne Chalmers is one of them. Thanks to generous share options that have skyrocketed on the Toronto and NASDAQ stock markets, many employees at APL have more money than they can use. Most are under 40 years old, so are too early to retire. But their financial independence gives them less reason to remain with APL.

The Meeting

The meeting with Suzanne Chalmers took place a few hours after the telephone call. It began like the others, with the initial pleasantries and brief discussion about progress on the latest fibre-optic router project. Then, Suzanne made her well-rehearsed statement: "Thomas, I've really enjoyed working here, but I'm going to leave Advanced Photonics." Suzanne took a breath, then looked at Chan. When he didn't reply after a few seconds, she continued: "I need to take time off. You know, get away to recharge my batteries. The project's nearly done and the team can complete it without me. Well, anyway, I'm thinking of leaving."

Chan spoke in a calm voice. He suggested that Suzanne should take an unpaid leave for two or maybe three months, complete with paid benefits, then return refreshed. Suzanne politely rejected that offer, saying that she needs to get away from work for a while. Thomas then asked Suzanne whether she was unhappy with her work environment—whether she was getting the latest computer technology to do her work and whether there were problems with co-workers. The workplace was fine, Susanne replied. The job was getting a bit routine at times, but she had a comfortable workplace with excellent co-workers.

Chan then apologized for the cramped workspace, due mainly to the rapid increase in the number of people hired over the past year. He suggested that if Suzanne took a couple of months off, APL would have a larger workspace with a better view of the park behind the campus-like building when she returned. She politely thanked Chan for that offer, but it wasn't what she needed. Besides, it wouldn't be fair to have a large workspace when other team members work in smaller quarters.

Chan was running out of tactics, so he tried his last hope: money. He asked whether Suzanne had higher offers. Suzanne replied that she regularly received calls from other companies, and some of them offered more money. Most were start-up firms that offered a lower salary but higher potential gains in share options. Chan knew from market surveys that Suzanne was already paid well in the industry. He also knew that APL couldn't compete on share option potential. Employees working in start-up firms sometimes saw their shares increase by five or 10 times their initial value, whereas shares at APL and other large firms increased more slowly. However, Chan promised Suzanne that he would recommend that she receive a significant raise—maybe 25 percent more—and more share options. Chan added that Chalmers was one of

APL's most valuable employees and that the company would suffer if she left the firm.

The meeting ended with Chalmers promising to consider Chan's offer of higher pay and share options. Two days later, Chan received her resignation in writing. Five months later, Chan learned that after a few months travelling with her husband, Chalmers joined a start-up software firm in the area.

CASE 7   South West Ontario Health Region (SWOHR)

By Cathy Fitzgerald, Okanagan College.

Kyle Fitzgerald was the Internal Organizational Development Consultant with the South West Ontario Health Region (SWOHR) responsible for the creation and articulation of SWOHR's People Vision with the ultimate objective that SWOHR would become an "organization of choice." In January 2005, he received results from the SWOHR organization of choice employee opinion survey. His review gave him an overall understanding of the employees' concerns and was consistent with the massive changes SWOHR had undergone in merging 23 smaller organizations over the past year. Kyle and the senior healthcare management team had to decide how to present the organization of choice employee opinion survey results to the health service areas leadership teams, ensuring that follow-up action plans were established.

An Integrated Model Of Healthcare

In September 2004, 23 diverse health service organizations and agencies throughout the southwest region of Ontario were brought together to form the newly created SWOHR. With a corporate office in London, Ontario, and four geographically located health service areas throughout the southwest region, SWOHR served a population of over 700,000 residents, administered a budget of $1.1 billion, provided a range of public and mental health services, and employed more than 12,000 health professionals and support staff. In addition SWOHR utilized over 600 volunteers and had

more than 1,200 physicians working within the region. This merger saved the region $4.3 million. An important theme in the merger was that SWOHR would move towards a more integrated system of hospital and community-based care.

SWOHR was represented by a nine-member board of directors and maintained its corporate office in London, Ontario. For administrative purposes, SWOHR was divided into four health service areas with leadership teams. SWHOR was working towards breaking down the hierarchical organizational structure traditionally found in the health sector with the aim to create a team-based organizational structure. One of the senior healthcare managers stated that "we see everyone as leaders responsible and accountable for what they are doing in their healthcare areas." Kyle Fitzgerald was located in the corporate office but worked closely with the senior healthcare management team and the four health service areas leadership teams.

The People Vision and Organization of Choice

The SWOHR vision was to create a restructured healthcare system that would be sustainable, accountable, and focused on the patient needs through good fiscal management and well-coordinated care. Kyle felt that this vision could be achieved through their employee's assets. "It is the people that will help us reform healthcare" and "It's about how we value our employees." He was particularly concerned about conversations with team leaders suggesting that SWOHR did not care about its employees and did not have a culture customized around its healthcare people. There were also constant conflicting department views and concerns that were emerging from the continued restructuring. Comments heard from employees in the four health services areas ranged from "management does not consider the impact of their decisions on us" to "the way management is managing change is less than impressive."

One of Kyle's responsibilities was to create and articulate a People Vision with the objective that SWOHR would become an "organization of choice" —an organization that would attract, optimize and retain talent. An "organization of choice" was about the way SWOHR did business—about setting a People Vision and leading towards it. It meant that employees would choose to work for SWOHR when presented with other employment opportunities. The senior healthcare management team and the board of directors supported the People Vision as an important corporate direction. They were interested in knowing what they are doing well at, what they could improve on, and whether or not they were living up to the organizations' values. Some of the senior healthcare management team felt that they should wait to present the survey results until after the restructuring was complete. They also expressed concern that some of the team leaders may not be receptive to employee feedback.

The majority of senior healthcare management team felt the move towards an "organization of choice" would help align SWOHR's people resources with the strategic direction of the organization. One senior manager stated "when is the right time to treat employees right?" Another senior manager questioned whether they could get the continued long-term commitment of all the diverse major stakeholders that ranged from unions and line mangers to physicians and corporate business partners.

Shortages of healthcare professionals was a well-documented global issue that was occurring in countries with aging populations. As a result, organizations such as SWOHR had to compete for skilled employees. Employees were moving across borders to healthcare providers who were aggressively recruiting, providing new hires with extrinsic and intrinsic incentives and rewards. SWOHR was currently experiencing staff shortages in nursing, physical and occupational therapy, pharmacy, and other healthcare professionals. Patient waiting times to see physician specialists has increased by 500 percent. Sixty percent of the SWOHR employees will be eligible for retirement in 2014. From a recruitment and retention perspective, fostering a culture that incorporated the elements of an organization of choice was crucial to having the best employees involved in Ontario healthcare.

Healthcare Sustainability

An increasing number of healthcare support services such as maintenance and food services began to be contracted out to the private sector. Union strikes continued to rotate between the various healthcare professionals. Negative employee reactions to the changes ranged from low morale and productivity to a growing distrust in their team leadership and senior management. Communicating in newly formed teams was creating higher levels of stress. The continued layoffs were resulting in increased employee workloads and stress leave requests. Many of the healthcare administrators felt that the current system was not sustainable. SWOHR felt that they would need to continue to make changes in order to sustain an effective and efficient healthcare system for future generations. To this end, SWOHR continued to review and reallocate healthcare resources and services and continued downsizing with the closure of several healthcare sites. SWOHR had to provide appropriate health services within a fixed budget, as well as balance these parameters with the dimensions of quality outlined by the Canadian Council on Health Services Accreditation. They were facing budget deficits and were required to balance their budgets within three years. They also had to reduce their expenditures by $137 million in order to balance the budget by March 31, 2007. Adding to the complexity, the demographics of the region were projected to grow. Kyle wondered how it would be possible to build an "organization of choice" environment in times of such significant change.

An Organization of Choice Survey

Kyle contracted Watson Wyatt Worldwide and Ontario Magazine to administer a formalized sur-

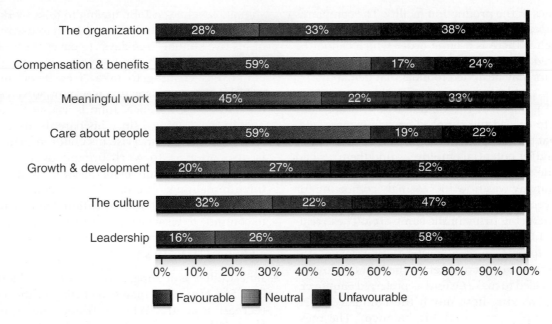

Source: Adapted from Roger E. Herman and Joyce L. Gioia, *How to Become an Employer of Choice*, Oakhill Press: Virginia, 2000.

vey entitled The Best Companies to Work For in Ontario. Watson Wyatt Worldwide was a global consulting firm specializing in people and financial management. It was through The Best Companies to Work For employee opinion survey process that organizations were awarded the designation of Organization of Choice. He wanted to see how the employees viewed their organization and if the organization was living up to its values and vision. The survey measured the satisfaction and commitment of 1,200 employees. Watson Wyatt Worldwide compiled the survey and provided SWOHR with data benchmarking the survey results against organizations across Ontario. The top 10 companies in Ontario scored in the high 80–95 percent satisfaction and commitment range on all the elements. The results served as a baseline to help SWOHR understand their strengths and weaknesses so that they could become an "organization of choice" (see Exhibit 1).

Kyle believed that an organization of choice is the only way to attract and retain their number 1 asset. He planned to use the survey results to establish baseline data, and to initiate processes that would ensure that follow-up action plans were established.

CASE 8   Introducing Work/Life Balance at Oxford Manufacturing

By Fiona A. E. McQuarrie, University College of the Fraser Valley.

Oxford Manufacturing is a company with 350 employees located in central Canada. It specializes in producing custom plastic products, although it also manufactures a range of small plastic items (e.g., storage boxes, water bottles) which it sells to wholesale distributors. Because of the variety of products the firm produces, there is a wide range of skill levels and qualifications among its workers, from engineers with university degrees working on design and production specifications for customized products, to assembly line workers, some of whom did not finish high school, operating machines in the production facility. The company's plant operates 12 hours a day, seven days a week, although if there is a large order which cannot be produced during regular hours, additional operating hours may be added to meet that demand.

Over the last few years, in the area where Oxford is located, the demand for workers has begun to exceed the supply. Oxford's owners realized that the company could no longer afford to sit back and let potential employees find them, as had been the case in the past. They also realized that the company was now increasingly competing for employees, especially skilled ones, with other manufacturing firms in the same area. These realities led Oxford's owners to decide that Oxford needed to be seen as a "preferred employer" if it was going to attract and retain the best employees. They decided to make Oxford a "preferred employer" by emphasizing how much the company cared about employees' "work/life balance." The message communicated to potential and current employees was that Oxford wanted to help them achieve a lifestyle where work and non-work commitments were equally important. The company adopted a policy that gave employees five "free days" off per year to use for whatever purpose the employee desired, in addition to generous vacation and sick leave benefits. The company also encouraged department managers to schedule workers' shifts to accommodate the workers' outside commitments as much as possible. The company felt that offering these sorts of benefits would not only attract good workers to Oxford but also help retain the ones already working for them.

Peter Macnee is a manager of one of the production areas. He has received requests from two of his employees to make accommodations in their work schedules because of their non-work commitments.

- John Mason is an engineer whose marriage has recently ended. He is now a single parent to a daughter, age 9, and a son, age 6. His parents are helping him with child care, but they are not always available to take care of the children during the day when John is at work. In addition, John's daughter was badly affected by her parents' divorce; occasionally she has temper tantrums and refuses to go to school or stay with her grandparents, insisting that only her father can take care of her. These situations have occa-

sionally resulted in John having to miss work on short notice. Peter has allowed John to use three of his five annual "free days" to cover these situations, even though company policy states that employees wishing to take "free days" must notify their supervisor two weeks in advance of the date of the absence. John is asking to work only in the evenings, since his parents are regularly available to supervise his children then. He is also offering to work unpaid overtime in exchange for formally being allowed to take his three remaining "free days" as needed without the required period of notification. He is willing to continue to be available for unpaid overtime if the company gives him a yearly allocation of five additional "free days."

- Jane Collier is a supervisor on the production line. She also participates in curling at the local recreation centre. When a friend encouraged her to take up curling for fun a few years ago, she was having problems with her health, and was also somewhat shy. Since she has been curling regularly, her fitness level has increased, and her health problems are no longer affecting her attendance at work. In addition, because success in curling requires working effectively as part of a team, her social and supervisory skills at work have noticeably improved. Jane's curling team has an opportunity to join a new curling league which is more competitive than the one they currently belong to, but which will also allow them to compete at regional, national, and possibly even international levels. Jane's team has decided not only to join this league but also to start working with a coach to improve their technique. Jane is asking to be scheduled for day shifts only because of the time demands of this new level of participation and because most of her curling-related activities will take place in the evenings. She is also asking for two week-long unpaid leaves per year to attend curling bonspiels (competitions) out of town.

Peter was not sure what to do with these requests. He knew that the company encouraged employee work/life balance and expected its managers to support employees trying to manage both work and non-work activities. He realized that John and Jane would not have made their requests unless they felt the requested accommodations were the only way they could successfully balance their work lives with their non-work commitments. However, there was no way he could grant both requests, because the products John helped design were manufactured by the production line Jane supervised, and both of them needed to be at work at the same time at least twice a week to share information about the products they were working on. He was also aware that John and Jane were talented and experienced employees, and if he turned down either one's request, they would have no trouble finding comparable jobs with any of Oxford's competitors.

As Peter was considering this dilemma, he shuffled through the pile of mail that had arrived on his desk that morning. An interoffice memo caught his eye, and he pulled it out of the pile and opened it. The memo was from the three office administrators in his area. The administrators complained that they were becoming increasingly upset with their co-workers, most of who were married and had families, "dumping" work on them because of family crises. The memo described several recent incidents where co-workers had received phone calls about family problems and then left for the rest of the day, asking the office administrators to cover for them and complete their work. After dealing with their co-workers' unfinished tasks, the administrators often had to stay beyond the end of their scheduled shifts to finish their own work. The last paragraph of the memo stated, "We don't mind helping out once in a while, but not having kids or elderly parents to take care of doesn't mean we don't have anything to do besides work. If we have to stay late on short notice, we often have to cancel activities that are important to us. This is unfair, and if other people can't manage their family responsibilities, they should be the ones making the adjustments, not us. We want you to address this problem immediately, as it is occurring more and more frequently."

A

Theory Building and Systematic Research Methods

People need to make sense of their world, so they form theories about the way the world operates. A **theory** is a general set of propositions that describes interrelationships among several concepts. We form theories for the purpose of predicting and explaining the world around us.[1] What does a good theory look like? First, it should be stated clearly and simply as possible so that the concepts can be measured and there is no ambiguity regarding the theory's propositions. Second, the elements of the theory must be logically consistent with each other, because we cannot test anything that doesn't make sense. Finally, a good theory provides value to society; it helps people understand their world better than without the theory.[2]

Theory building is a continuous process that typically includes the inductive and deductive stages shown in Exhibit A.1.[3] The inductive stage draws on personal experience to form a preliminary theory, whereas the deductive stage uses the scientific method to test the theory.

The inductive stage of theory building involves observing the world around us, identifying a pattern of relationships, and then forming a theory from these personal observations. For example, you might casually notice that new employees want their supervisor to give direction, whereas this leadership style irritates long-service employees. From these observations, you form a theory about the effectiveness of directive leadership. (See Chapter 14 for a discussion of this leadership style.)

Positivism Versus Interpretivism

Research requires an interpretation of reality, and researchers tend to perceive reality in one of two ways. A common view, called **positivism**, is that reality exists independent of people. It is "out there" to be discovered and tested. Positivism is the foundation for most quantitative research (statistical analysis). It assumes that we can measure variables and those variables have fixed relationships with other variables. For example, the positivist perspective says that we could study whether a supportive style of leadership reduces stress. If we find evidence of this, then someone

■ **EXHIBIT A.1**

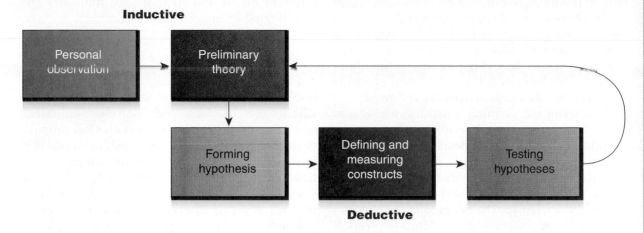

else studying leadership and stress would "discover" the same relationship.

Interpretivism takes a different view of reality. It suggests that reality comes from shared meaning among people in that environment. For example, supportive leadership is a personal interpretation of reality, not something that can be measured across time and people. Interpretivists rely mainly on qualitative data, such as observation and nondirective interviews. They particularly listen to the language people use to understand the common meaning that people have toward various events or phenomena. For example, they might argue that you need to experience and observe supportive leadership to effectively study it. Moreover, you can't really predict relationships because the specific situation shapes reality.[4]

Most OB scholars identify themselves somewhere between the extreme views of positivism and interpretivism. Many believe that inductive research should begin with an interpretivist angle. We should enter a new topic with an open mind and search for shared meaning of people in that situation. In other words, researchers should let the participants define reality rather than let the researcher's preconceived notions shape that reality. This process involves gathering qualitative information and letting this information shape their theory.[5] After the theory emerges, researchers shift to positivist perspective by quantitatively testing relationships in that theory.

Theory Testing: The Deductive Process

Once a theory has been formed, we shift into the deductive stage of theory building. This process includes forming hypotheses, defining and measuring constructs, and testing hypotheses (see Exhibit A.1). **Hypotheses** make empirically testable declarations that certain variables and their corresponding measures are related in a specific way proposed by the theory. For instance, to find support for the directive leadership theory described earlier, we need to form and then test a specific hypothesis from that theory. One such hypothesis might be: "New employees are more satisfied with supervisors who exhibit a directive rather than nondirective leadership style." Because they provide the vital link between the theory and empirical verification, hypotheses are indispensable tools of scientific research.

Defining and measuring constructs   Hypotheses are testable only if we can define and then form measurable indicators of the concepts stated in those hypotheses. Consider the hypothesis in the previous paragraph about new employees and directive leadership. To test this hypothesis, we first need to define the concepts, such as "new employees," "directive leadership," and "supervisor." These are known as **constructs**, because they are abstract ideas constructed by the researcher that can be linked to observable information. Organizational behaviour researchers developed the construct called *directive leadership* to help them understand the different effects that leaders have over followers. We can't directly see, taste, or smell directive leadership; instead, we rely on indirect indicators that it exists, such as observing someone giving directions, maintaining clear performance standards, and ensuring that procedures and practices are followed.

As you can see, defining constructs well is very important, because these definitions become the foundation for finding or developing acceptable measures of those constructs. We can't measure directive leadership if we only have a vague idea about what this concept means. The better the construct is defined, the better our chances are of applying a measure that adequately represents that construct. However, even with a good definition, constructs can be difficult to measure, because the empirical representation must capture several elements in the definition. A measure of directive leadership must be able to identify not only people who give directions, but also those who maintain performance standards and ensure that procedures are followed.

Testing hypotheses   The third step in the deductive process is to collect data for the empirical measures of the variables. Following our directive leadership example, we might conduct a formal survey in which new employees indicate the behaviour of their supervisors and their attitudes toward their supervisor. Alternatively, we might design an experiment in which people work with someone who applies either a directive or nondirective leadership style. When the data have been collected, we can use various procedures to statistically test our hypotheses.

A major concern in theory building is that some researchers might inadvertently find support for their theory simply because they use the same information used to form the theory during the inductive stage. Consequently, the deductive stage must collect new data that are completely independent of the data used during the inductive stage. For instance, you might decide to test your theory of directive leadership by studying employees in another organization. Moreover, the inductive process may have relied mainly on personal observation, whereas the deductive process might use survey question-naires. By studying different samples and using different measurement tools, we minimize the risk of conducting circular research.

Using the Scientific Method

Earlier, we said that the deductive stage of theory building follows the scientific method. The **scientific method** is systematic, controlled, empirical, and critical investigation of hypothetical propositions about the presumed relationships among natural phenomena.[6] There are several elements to this definition, so let's look at each one. First, because researchers want to rule out all but one explanation for a set of interrelated events, scientific research is systematic and controlled. To rule out alternative explanations, we need to control them in some way, such as by keeping them constant or removing them entirely from the environment.

Second, we say that scientific research is empirical because researchers need to use objective reality—or as close as we can get to it—to test theory. They measure observable elements of the environment, such as what a person says or does, rather than rely on their own subjective opinion to draw conclusions. Moreover, scientific research analyzes these data using acceptable principles of mathematics and logic.

Finally, scientific research involves critical investigation. This means that the study's hypotheses, data, methods, and results are openly described so that other experts in the field can properly evaluate this research. It also means that scholars are encouraged to critique and build on previous research. The scientific method encourages the refinement and eventually the replacement of a particular theory with one that better suits our understanding of the world.

Grounded Theory: An Alternative Approach

The scientific method dominates the quantitative approach to systematic research, but another approach, called **grounded theory**, dominates research using qualitative methods.[7] Grounded theory is a process of developing knowledge through the constant interplay of data collection, analysis, and theory development. It relies mainly on qualitative methods to form categories and variables, analyze relationships among these concepts, and form a model based on the observations and analysis. Grounded theory combines the inductive stages of theory development by cycling back and forth between data collection and analysis to converge on a robust explanatory model. This ongoing reciprocal process results in theory that is grounded in the data (thus, the name grounded theory).

Like the scientific method, grounded theory is a systematic and rigorous process of data collection and analysis. It requires specific steps and documentation, and adopts a positivist view by assuming that the results are generalizable to other settings. However, grounded theory also takes an interpretivist view by building categories and variables from the perceived realities of the subjects rather than from an assumed universal truth.[8] It also recognizes that personal biases are not easily removed from the research process.

Selected Issues in Organizational Behaviour Research

There are many issues to consider in theory building, particularly when we use the deductive process to test hypotheses. Some of the more important issues are sampling, causation, and ethical practices in organizational research.

Sampling in Organizational Research   When finding out why things happen in organizations, we typically gather information from a few sources and then draw conclusions about the larger population. If we survey several employees and determine that older employees are more loyal to their company, then we would like to generalize this statement to all older employees in our population, not just those whom we surveyed. Scientific inquiry generally requires researchers to engage in **representative sampling**—that is, sampling a population in such a way that we can extrapolate the results of that sample to the larger population.

One factor that influences representativeness is whether the sample is selected in an unbiased way from the larger population. Let's suppose that you want to study organizational commitment among employees in your organization. A casual procedure might result in sampling too few employees from the head office and too many located elsewhere in the country. If head office employees actually have higher loyalty than employees located elsewhere, then the biased sampling would cause the results to underestimate the true level of loyalty among employees in the company. If you repeat the process again next year but somehow overweight employees from the head office, the results might wrongly suggest that employees have increased their organizational commitment over the past year. In reality, the only change may be the direction of sampling bias.

How do we minimize sampling bias? The answer is to randomly select the sample. A randomly drawn sample gives each member of the population an equal probability of being chosen, so there is less likelihood that a subgroup within that population dominates the study's results.

The same principle applies to random assignment of subjects to groups in experimental designs. If we want to test the effects of a team development training program, we need to randomly place some employees in the training group and randomly place others in a group that does not receive training. Without this random selection, each group might have different types of employees, so we wouldn't know whether the training explains the differences between the two groups. Moreover, if employees respond differently to the training program, we couldn't be sure that the training program results are representative of the larger population. Of course, random sampling does not necessarily produce a perfectly representative sample, but we do know that this is the best approach to ensure unbiased selection.

The other factor that influences representativeness is sample size. Whenever we select a portion of the population, there will be some error in our estimate of the population values. The larger the sample, the less error will occur in our estimate. Let's suppose that you want to find out how employees in a 500-person firm feel about smoking in the workplace. If you asked 400 of those employees, the information would provide a very good estimate of how the entire work force in that organization feels. If you survey only 100 employees, the estimate might deviate more from the true population. If you ask only 10 people, the estimate could be quite different from what all 500 employees feel.

Notice that sample size goes hand in hand with random selection. You must have a sufficiently large sample size for the principle of randomization to work effectively. In our example of attitudes toward smoking, we would do a poor job of random selection if our sample consisted of only 10 employees from the 500-person organization. The reason is that these 10 people probably wouldn't capture the diversity of employees throughout the organization. In fact, to provide adequate representation through random selection, the more diverse the population, the larger the sample size should be.

Causation in Organizational Research Theories present notions about relationships among constructs. Often, these propositions suggest a causal relationship, namely, that one variable has an effect on another variable. When discussing causation, we refer to variables as being independent or dependent. Independent variables are the presumed causes of dependent variables, which are the presumed effects. In our earlier example of directive leadership, the main independent variable (there might be others) would be the supervisor's directive or nondirective leadership style, because we presume that it causes the dependent variable (satisfaction with supervision).

In laboratory experiments (described later), the independent variable is always manipulated by the experimenter. In our research on directive leadership, we might have subjects (new employees) work with supervisors who exhibit directive or nondirective leadership behaviours. If subjects are more satisfied under the directive leaders, then we would be able to infer an association between the independent and dependent variables.

Researchers must satisfy three conditions to provide sufficient evidence of causality between two variables.[9] The first condition of causality is that the variables are empirically associated with each other. An association exists whenever one measure of a variable changes systematically with a measure of another variable. This condition of causality is the easiest to satisfy, because there are several well-known statistical measures of association. A research study might find, for instance, that heterogeneous groups (in which members come from diverse backgrounds) produce more creative solutions to problems. This might be apparent because the measure of creativity (such as number of creative solutions produced within a fixed time) is higher for teams that have a high score on the measure of group heterogeneity. They are statistically associated or correlated with each other.

The second condition of causality is that the independent variable precedes the dependent variable in time. Sometimes, this condition is satisfied through simple logic. In our group heterogeneity example, it doesn't make sense to say that the number of creative solutions caused the group's heterogeneity, because the group's heterogeneity existed before it produced the creative solutions. In other situations, however, the temporal relationship among variables is less clear. One example is the ongoing debate about job satisfaction and organizational commitment. Do companies develop more loyal employees by increasing their job satisfaction, or do changes in organizational loyalty cause changes in job satisfaction? Simple logic does not answer these questions; instead, researchers must use sophisticated longitudinal studies to build up evidence of a temporal relationship between these two variables.

The third requirement for evidence of a causal relationship is that the statistical association between two variables cannot be explained by a third variable. There are many associations that we quickly dismiss as being causally related. For example, there is a statistical association between the number of storks in an area and the birth rate in that area. We know that storks don't bring babies, so something else must cause the association between these two variables. The real explanation is that both storks and birth rates have a higher incidence in rural areas.

In other studies, the third variable effect is less apparent. Many years ago, before polio vaccines were available, a study in the United States reported a surprisingly strong association between consumption of a certain soft drink and the incidence of polio. Was polio caused by drinking this pop, or did people with polio have a unusual craving for this beverage? Neither. Both polio and consumption of the pop drink were caused by a third variable: climate. There was a higher incidence of polio in the summer months and in warmer climates, and people drink more liquids in these climates.[10] As you can see from this example, researchers have a difficult time supporting causal inferences, because third variable effects are sometimes difficult to detect.

Ethics in Organizational Research   Organizational behaviour researchers need to abide by the ethical standards of the society in which the research is conducted. One of the most important ethical considerations is the individual subject's freedom to participate in the study. For example, it is inappropriate to force employees to fill out a questionnaire or attend an experimental intervention for research purposes only. Moreover, researchers have an obligation to tell potential subjects about any potential risks inherent in the study so that participants can make an informed choice about whether or not to be involved.

Finally, researchers must be careful to protect the privacy of those who participate in the study. This usually includes letting people know when they are being studied as well as guaranteeing that their individual information will remain confidential (unless publication of identities is otherwise granted). Researchers maintain anonymity through careful security of data. The research results usually aggregate data in numbers large enough that they do not reveal the opinions or characteristics of any specific individual. For example, we would report the average absenteeism of employees in a department rather than state the absence rates of each person. When sharing data with other researchers, it is usually necessary to specially code each case so that individual identities are not known.

Research Design Strategies

So far, we have described how to build a theory, including the specific elements of empirically testing that theory within the standards of scientific inquiry. But what are the different ways to design a research study so that we get the data necessary to achieve our research objectives? There are many strategies, but they mainly fall under three headings: laboratory experiments, field surveys, and observational research.

Laboratory Experiments

A **laboratory experiment** is any research study in which independent variables and variables outside the researcher's main focus of inquiry can be controlled to some extent. Laboratory experiments are usually located outside the everyday work environment, such as a classroom, simulation lab, or any other artificial setting in which the researcher can manipulate the environment. Organizational behaviour researchers sometimes conduct experiments in the workplace (called *field experiments*) in which the independent variable is manipulated. However, the researcher has less control over the effects of extraneous factors in field experiments than in laboratory situations.

Advantages of laboratory experiments   There are many advantages of laboratory experiments. By definition, this research method offers a high degree of control over extraneous variables that would otherwise confound the relationships being studied. Suppose we wanted to test the effects of directive leadership on the satisfaction of new employees. One concern might be that employees are influenced by how much leadership is provided, not just the type of leadership style. An experimental design would allow us to control how often the supervisor exhibited this style so that this extraneous variable does not confound the results.

A second advantage of lab studies is that the independent and dependent variables can be developed more precisely than in a field setting. For example, the researcher can ensure that supervisors in a lab study apply specific directive or nondirective behaviours, whereas real-life supervisors would use a more complex mixture of leadership behaviours. By using more precise measures, we are more certain that we are measuring the intended construct. Thus, if new employees are more satisfied with supervisors in the directive leadership condition, we are more confident that the independent variable was directive leadership rather than some other leadership style.

A third benefit of laboratory experiments is that the independent variable can be distributed more evenly among participants. In our directive leadership study, we can ensure that approximately half of the subjects have a directive supervisor, whereas the other half have a nondirective supervisor. In natural settings, we might have trouble finding people who have worked with a nondirective leader and, consequently, we couldn't determine the effects of this condition.

Disadvantages of laboratory experiments   With these powerful advantages, you might wonder why laboratory experiments are the least appreciated form of organizational behaviour research.[11] One obvious limitation of this research method is that it lacks realism and, consequently, the results might be different in the real world. One argument is that laboratory experiment subjects are less involved than their counterparts in an actual work situation. This is sometimes true, although many lab studies have highly motivated participants. Another criticism is that the extraneous variables controlled in the lab setting might produce a different effect of the independent variable on the dependent variables. This might also be true, but remember that the experimental design controls variables in accordance with the theory and its hypotheses. Consequently, this concern is really a critique of the theory, not the lab study.

Finally, there is the well-known problem that if participants are aware they are being studied they will act differently than they normally would. Some participants try to figure out how the researcher wants them to behave and then deliberately try to act that way. Other participants try to upset the experiment by doing just the opposite of what they believe the researcher expects. Still others might act unnaturally simply because they know they are being observed. Fortunately, experimenters are well aware of these potential problems and are usually (although not always) successful at disguising the study's true intent.

Field Surveys

Field surveys collect and analyze information in a natural environment—an office, factory, or other existing location. The researcher takes a snapshot of reality and tries to determine whether elements of that situation (including the attitudes and behaviours of people in that situation) are associated with each other as hypothesized. Everyone

does some sort of field research. You might think that people from some provinces are better drivers than others, so you "test" your theory by looking at the way people with out-of-province licence plates drive. Although your methods of data collection might not satisfy scientific standards, this is a form of field research because it takes information from a naturally occurring situation.

Advantages and disadvantages of field surveys One advantage of field surveys is that the variables often have a more powerful effect than they would in a laboratory experiment. Consider the effect of peer pressure on the behaviour of members within the team. In a natural environment, team members would form very strong cohesive bonds over time, whereas a researcher would have difficulty replicating this level of cohesiveness and corresponding peer pressure in a lab setting.

Another advantage of field surveys is that the researcher can study many variables simultaneously, thereby permitting a fuller test of more complex theories. Ironically, this is also a disadvantage of field surveys, because it is difficult for the researcher to contain his or her scientific inquiry. There is a tendency to shift from deductive hypothesis testing to more inductive exploratory browsing through the data. If these two activities become mixed together, the researcher can lose sight of the strict covenants of scientific inquiry.

The main weakness with field surveys is that it is very difficult to satisfy the conditions for causal conclusions. One reason is that the data are usually collected at one point in time, so the researcher must rely on logic to decide whether the independent variable really preceded the dependent variable. Contrast this with the lab study in which the researcher can usually be confident that the independent variable was applied before the dependent variable occurred. Increasingly, organizational behaviour studies use longitudinal research to provide a better indicator of temporal relations among variables, but this is still not as precise as the lab setting. Another reason why causal analysis is difficult in field surveys is that extraneous variables are not controlled as they are in lab studies. Without this control, there is a higher chance that a third variable might explain the relationship between the hypothesized independent and dependent variables.

Observational Research

In their study of brainstorming and creativity, Robert Sutton and Andrew Hargadon observed 24 brainstorming sessions at IDEO, a product design firm in Palo Alto, California. They also attended a dozen "Monday morning meetings," conducted 60 semi-structured interviews with IDEO executives and designers, held hundreds of informal discussions with these people, and read through several dozen magazine articles about the company.[12]

Sutton and Hargadon's use of observational research and other qualitative methods was quite appropriate for their research objectives, which were to re-examine the effectiveness of brainstorming beyond the number of ideas generated. Observational research generates a wealth of descriptive accounts about the drama of human existence in organizations. It is a useful vehicle for learning about the complex dynamics of people and their activities, such as brainstorming. (The results of Sutton and Hargadon's study are discussed in Chapter 8.)

Participant observation takes the observation method one step further by having the observer take part in the organization's activities. This experience gives the researcher a fuller understanding of the activities compared to just watching others participate in those activities.

In spite of its intuitive appeal, observational research has a number of weaknesses. The main problem is that the observer is subject to the perceptual screening and organizing biases that we discuss in Chapter 3 of this textbook. There is a tendency to overlook the routine aspects of organizational life, even though they may prove to be the most important data for research purposes. Instead, observers tend to focus on unusual information, such as activities that deviate from what the observer expects. Because observational research usually records only what the observer notices, valuable information is often lost.

Another concern with the observation method is that the researcher's presence and involvement may influence the people whom he or she is studying. This can be a problem in short-term observations, but in the long term people tend to return to their usual behaviour patterns. With ongoing observations, such as Sutton and Hargadon's study of brainstorming sessions at IDEO, employees eventually forget that they are being studied.

Finally, observation is usually a qualitative process, so it is more difficult to empirically test hypotheses with the data. Instead, observational research provides rich information for the inductive stages of theory building. It helps us to form ideas about the way things work in organizations. We begin to see relationships that lay the foundation for new perspectives and theory. We must not confuse this inductive process of theory building with the deductive process of theory testing.

B

Scoring Keys for Self-Assessment Exercises

The following pages provide scoring keys for self-assessments that are fully presented in this textbook. Most (although not all) of these self-assessments, as well as the self-assessments that are summarized in this book, are scored on the Online Learning Centre.

CHAPTER 2
Scoring Key for Self-Monitoring Scale

Scoring Instructions: Use the table below to assign numbers to each box you checked. Insert the number for each statement on the appropriate line below the table. For example, if you checked "Somewhat false" for statement #1 ("In social situations, I have the ability..."), you would write a "2" on the line with "(1)" underneath it. After assigning numbers for all 13 statements, add up your scores to estimate your self-monitoring personality.

For statement items 1, 2, 3, 4, 5, 6, 7, 8, 10, 11, 13:	For statement items 9, 12:
Very true = 6	Very true = 1
Somewhat true = 5	Somewhat true = 2
Slightly more true than false = 4	Slightly more true than false = 3
Slightly more false than true = 3	Slightly more false than true = 4
Somewhat false = 2	Somewhat false = 5
Very false = 1	Very false = 6

Sensitive to Expressive Behaviour of Others

___ + ___ + ___ + ___ + ___ + ___ = ___
(2)   (4)   (5)   (6)   (8)   (11)   (A)

Ability to Modify Self-Presentation

___ + ___ + ___ + ___ + ___ + ___ + ___ = ___
(1)   (3)   (7)   (9)   (10)   (12)   (13)   (B)

Self-Monitoring Total Score

___ + ___ = ___
(A)   (B)   Total

Interpreting Your Score: Self-monitoring consists of two dimensions: (a) sensitivity to expressive behaviour of others and (b) ability to modify self-presentation. These two dimensions as well as the total score are defined in the following table, along with the range of scores for high, medium, and low levels of each scale.

Self-Monitoring Dimension and Definition	Score Interpretation
Sensitive to Expressive Behaviour of Others: This scale indicates the extent that you are aware of the feelings and perceptions of others, as expressed by their facial expressions, subtle statements, and other behaviours.	High: 25 to 36 Medium: 18 to 24 Low: Below 18

Self-Monitoring Dimension and Definition	Score Interpretation
Ability to Modify Self-Presentation: This scale indicates the extent to which you are adept at modifying your behaviour in a way that is most appropriate for the situation or social relationship.	High: 30 to 42 Medium: 21 to 29 Low: Below 21
Self-Monitoring Total: Self-monitoring refers to an individual's level of sensitivity to the expressive behaviour of others and the ability to adapt appropriately to these situational cues.	High: 55 to 78 Medium: 39 to 54 Low: Below 39

nurses reported a mean PNS score of 34 whereas a study of 236 male and 303 female undergraduate psychology students in the United States had a mean score of 42. The norms in the following table are based on scores from these undergraduate students.

Personal Need for Structure Scale	
Score	**Interpretation**
58 to 72	High need for personal structure
47 to 57	Above average need for personal structure
38 to 46	Average need for personal structure
27 to 37	Below average need for personal structure
12 to 26	Low need for personal structure

CHAPTER 3
Scoring Key for Assessing Your Personal Need for Structure

Scoring Instructions: Use the table below to assign numbers to each box you checked. Insert the number for each statement on the appropriate line below the table. For example, if you checked "Moderately Disagree" for statement #3 ("I enjoy being spontaneous."), you would assign a "5" to that statement. After assigning numbers for all 12 statements, add up your scores to estimate your personal need for structure.

For statement items 1, 5, 6, 7, 8, 9, 10, 12:	For statement items 2, 3, 4, 11:
Strongly Agree = 6	Strongly Agree = 1
Moderately Agree = 5	Moderately Agree = 2
Slightly Agree = 4	Slightly Agree = 3
Slightly Disagree = 3	Slightly Disagree = 4
Moderately Disagree = 2	Moderately Disagree = 5
Strongly Disagree = 1	Strongly Disagree = 6

Interpreting Your Score: Some people need to "make sense" of things around them more quickly or completely than do other people. This personal need for perceptual structure relates to selective attention as well as perceptual organization and interpretation. For instance, people with a strong personal need for closure might form first impressions, fill in missing pieces, and rely on stereotyping more quickly than people who don't mind incomplete perceptual situations.

This personal need for structure (PNS) scale assesses the degree to which people are motivated to structure their world in a simple and unambiguous way. Scores range from 12 to 72 with higher scores indicating a high personal need for structure. PNS norms vary from one group to the next. For instance, a study of Finnish

CHAPTER 4
Scoring Key for School Commitment Scale

Scoring Instructions: Use the table below to assign numbers to each box you checked. Insert the number for each statement on the appropriate line below the table. For example, if you checked "Moderately Disagree" for statement #1 ("I would be very happy..."), you would write a "2" on the line with "(1)" underneath it. After assigning numbers for all 12 statements, add up your scores to estimate your affective and continuance school commitment.

For statement items 1, 2, 3, 4, 6, 8, 10, 11, 12:	For statement items 5, 7, 9:
Strongly Agree = 7	Strongly Agree = 1
Moderately Agree = 6	Moderately Agree = 2
Slightly Agree = 5	Slightly Agree = 3
Neutral = 4	Neutral = 4
Slightly Disagree = 3	Slightly Disagree = 5
Moderately Disagree = 2	Moderately Disagree = 6
Strongly Disagree = 1	Strongly Disagree = 7

Affective Commitment   ___ + ___ + ___ + ___ + ___ + ___ = _____
        (1)   (3)   (5)   (7)   (9) (11)

Continuance Commitment   ___ + ___ + ___ + ___ + ___ + ___ = _____
        (2)   (4)   (6)   (8) (10) (12)

Interpreting Your Affective Commitment Score: This scale measures both affective commitment and continuance commitment. Affective commitment refers to a person's emotional attachment to, identification with, and involvement in a particular organization. In this scale, the organization is the school where you are attending as a student. How high or low is your affective commitment? The ideal would be to compare your score with

Creative Disposition	
Score	Interpretation
Above +9	You have a high creative personality
+1 to +9	You have an average creative personality.
Below +1	You have a low creative personality.

CHAPTER 9
Scoring Key for the Team Roles Preferences Scale

Scoring Instructions: Write the scores circled for each item on the appropriate line below (statement numbers are in brackets), and add up each scale.

Encourager ____ + ____ + ____ = _____
            (6)   (9)   (11)

Gatekeeper ____ + ____ + ____ = _____
          (4)   (10)   (13)

Harmonizer ____ + ____ + ____ = _____
          (3)   (8)   (12)

Initiator ____ + ____ + ____ = _____
       (1)   (5)   (14)

Summarizer ____ + ____ + ____ = _____
          (2)   (7)   (15)

Interpreting Your Score: The five team roles measured here are different from Belbin's roles described in the textbook. However, these roles are also based on academic writing. These five roles are defined as follows, along with the range of scores for high, medium, and low levels of each role. These norms are based on results from a sample of MBA students.

Team Role and Definition	Interpretation
Encourager: People who score high on this dimension have a strong tendency to praise and support the ideas of other team members, thereby showing warmth and solidarity to the group.	High: 12 and above Medium: 9 to 11 Low: 8 and below
Gatekeeper: People who score high on this dimension have a strong tendency to encourage all team members to participate in the discussion.	High: 12 and above Medium: 9 to 11 Low: 8 and below
Harmonizer: People who score high on this dimension have a strong tendency to mediate intragroup conflicts and reduce tension.	High: 11 and above Medium: 9 to 10 Low: 8 and below

Team Role and Definition	Interpretation
Initiator: People who score high on this dimension have a strong tendency to identify goals for the meeting, including ways to work on those goals.	High: 12 and above Medium: 9 to 11 Low: 8 and below
Summarizer: People who score high on this dimension have a strong tendency to keep track of what was said in the meeting (i.e., act as the team's memory).	High: 10 and above Medium: 8 to 9 Low: 7 and below

CHAPTER 10
Scoring Key for the Team Player Inventory

Scoring Instructions: To calculate your score on the Team Player Inventory, use the table below to assign numbers to each box that you checked. Then add up the numbers to determine your total score.

For statement items 1, 3, 6, 8, 10:	For statement items 2, 4, 5, 7, 9:
Completely agree = 5	Completely agree = 1
Agree somewhat = 4	Agree somewhat = 2
Neither agree nor disagree = 3	Neither agree nor disagree = 3
Disagree somewhat = 2	Disagree somewhat = 4
Completely disagree = 1	Completely disagree = 5

Interpreting Your Score: The Team Player Inventory estimates the extent to which you are positively predisposed to working on teams. The higher your score, the more you enjoy working in teams and believe that teamwork is beneficial. The following table allows you to compare your Team Player Inventory score against the norms for this scale. These norms are derived from undergraduate psychology students.

Team Player Inventory	
Score	Interpretation
40 to 50	You have a strong predisposition or preference for working in teams
21 to 39	You are generally ambivalent about working in teams.
10 to 20	You have a low predisposition or preference for working in teams

CHAPTER 11

Scoring Key for the Active Listening Skills Inventory

Scoring Instructions: Use the table below to score the response you circled for each statement. Write the score for each item on the appropriate line below the table (statement numbers are in brackets), and add up each subscale. For example, if you checked "A little" for statement #1 ("I keep an open mind..."), you would write a "1" on the line with "(1)" underneath it. Then calculate the overall Active Listening Inventory score by summing all subscales.

For statement items 3, 4, 6, 7, 10, 13:	For statement items 1, 2, 5, 8, 9, 11, 12, 14, 15:
Not at all = 3	Not at all = 0
A little = 2	A little = 1
Somewhat = 1	Somewhat = 2
Very much = 0	Very much = 3

Avoiding
Interruption (AI)   ____ + ____ + ____ = ____
               (3)   (7)   (15)

Maintaining
Interest (MI)   ____ + ____ + ____ = ____
            (6)   (9)   (14)

Postponing
Evaluation (PE)   ____ + ____ + ____ = ____
            (1)   (5)   (13)

Organizing
Information (OI)   ____ + ____ + ____ = ____
            (2)   (10) (12)

Showing
Interest (SI)   ____ + ____ + ____ = ____
            (4)   (8)   (11)

Active Listening (total score):   ____

Interpreting Your Score: The five active listening dimensions and the overall active listening scale measured here are defined below, along with the range of scores for high, medium, and low levels of each dimension based on a sample of MBA students:

Active Listening Dimension and Definition	Score Interpretation
Avoiding Interruption: People with high scores on this dimension have a strong tendency to let the speaker finish his or her statements before responding.	High: 8 to 9 Medium: 5 to 7 Low: Below 5
Maintaining Interest: People with high scores on this dimension have a strong tendency to remain focused and concentrate on what the speaker is saying even when the conversation is boring or the information is well known.	High: 6 to 9 Medium: 3 to 5 Low: Below 3
Postponing Evaluation: People with high scores on this dimension have a strong tendency to keep an open mind and avoid evaluating what the speaker is saying until the speaker has finished.	High: 7 to 9 Medium: 4 to 6 Low: Below 4
Organizing Information: People with high scores on this dimension have a strong tendency to actively organize the speaker's ideas into meaningful categories.	High: 8 to 9 Medium: 5 to 7 Low: Below 5
Showing Interest: People with high scores on this dimension have a strong tendency to use nonverbal gestures or brief verbal acknowledgements to demonstrate that they are paying attention to the speaker.	High: 7 to 9 Medium: 5 to 6 Low: Below 5
Active Listening (total): People with high scores on this total active listening scale have a strong tendency to actively sense the sender's signals, evaluate them accurately, and respond appropriately.	High: Above 31 Medium: 26 to 31 Low: Below 26

Note: The Active Listening Inventory does not explicitly measure two other dimensions of active listening, namely, empathizing and providing feedback. Empathizing is difficult to measure with behaviours; providing feedback involves similar behaviours as showing interest.

CHAPTER 12

Scoring Key for the Upward Influence Scale

Scoring Instructions: To calculate your scores on the Upward Influence Scale, write the number circled for each statement on the appropriate line below (statement numbers are in brackets), and add up each scale.

Assertiveness   ____ + ____ + ____ = ____
           (8)   (15) (16)

Exchange   ____ + ____ + ____ = ____
           (2)   (5)   (13)

Coalition Formation   ____ + ____ + ____ = ____
           (1)   (11) (18)

Upward Appeal   ___ + ___ + ___ = ___
                 (4)   (12) (17)

Ingratiation   ___ + ___ + ___ = ___
                (3)   (6)   (9)

Persuasion   ___ + ___ + ___ = ___
              (7)   (10) (14)

Interpreting Your Score: Influence refers to any behaviour that attempts to alter someone's attitudes or behaviour. There are several types of influence, including the following six measured by this instrument: assertiveness, exchange, coalition formation, upward appeal, ingratiation, and persuasion. This instrument assesses your preference for using each type of influence on your boss or other people at higher levels in the organization. Each scale has a potential score ranging from 3 to 15 points. Higher scores indicate that the person has a higher preference for that particular tactic. The six upward influence dimensions measured here are defined below, along with the range of scores for high, medium, and low levels of each tactic.

Influence Tactic and Definition	Score Interpretation
Assertiveness: Assertiveness involves actively applying legitimate and coercive power to influence others. This tactic includes persistently reminding others of their obligations, frequently checking their work, confronting them, and using threats of sanctions to force compliance.	High: 8 to 15 Medium: 5 to 7 Low: 3 to 4
Exchange: Exchange involves the promise of benefits or resources in exchange for the target person's compliance with your request. This tactic also includes reminding the target of past benefits or favours with the expectation that the target will now make up for that debt. Negotiation is also part of the exchange strategy.	High: 10 to 15 Medium: 6 to 9 Low: 3 to 5
Coalition Formation: Coalition formation occurs when a group of people with common interests band together to influence others. This tactic pools the power and resources of many people, so the coalition potentially has more influence than if each person operated alone.	High: 11 to 15 Medium: 7 to 10 Low: 3 to 6
Upward Appeal: Upward appeal occurs when you rely on support from a higher-level person to influence others. In effect, this is a form of coalition in which one or more members are someone with higher authority or expertise.	High: 9 to 15 Medium: 6 to 8 Low: 3 to 5

Influence Tactic and Definition	Score Interpretation
Ingratiation: Flattering your boss in front of others, helping your boss with his or her work, agreeing with your boss's ideas, and asking for your boss's advice are all examples of ingratiation. This tactic increases the perceived similarity of the source of ingratiation to the target person.	High: 13 to 15 Medium: 9 to 12 Low: 3 to 8
Persuasion: Persuasion refers to using logical and emotional appeals to change others' attitudes. According to several studies, it is also the most common upward influence strategy.	High: 13 to 15 Medium: 9 to 12 Low: 3 to 8

CHAPTER 13

Scoring Key for the Dutch Test for Conflict Handling

Scoring Instructions: Write the number circled for each item on the appropriate line below (statement number is under the line), and add up each subscale.

Conflict Handling				
Dimension	**Calculation**			**Your Score**
Yielding	___ + ___ + ___ + ___ = ___ Item 1 Item 6 Item 11 Item 16			
Compromising	___ + ___ + ___ + ___ = ___ Item 2 Item 7 Item 12 Item 17			
Forcing	___ + ___ + ___ + ___ = ___ Item 3 Item 8 Item 13 Item 18			
Problem Solving	___ + ___ + ___ + ___ = ___ Item 4 Item 9 Item 14 Item 19			
Avoiding	___ + ___ + ___ + ___ = ___ Item 5 Item 10 Item 15 Item 20			

Interpreting Your Score: The five conflict handling dimensions are defined below, along with the range of scores for high, medium, and low levels of each dimension:

Conflict Handling Dimension and Definition	Score Interpretation
Yielding: Yielding involves giving in completely to the other side's wishes, or at least cooperating with little or no attention to your own interests. This style involves making unilateral concessions, unconditional promises, and offering help with no expectation of reciprocal help.	High: 14 to 20 Medium: 9 to 13 Low: 4 to 8

Conflict Handling Dimension and Definition	Score Interpretation
Compromising: Compromising involves looking for a position in which your losses are offset by equally valued gains. It involves matching the other party's concessions, making conditional promises or threats, and actively searching for a middle ground between the interests of the two parties	High: 17 to 20 Medium: 11 to 16 Low: 4 to 10
Forcing: Forcing involves trying to win the conflict at the other's expense. It includes "hard" influence tactics, particularly assertiveness, to get one's own way.	High: 15 to 20 Medium: 9 to 14 Low: 4 to 8
Problem Solving: Problem solving tries to find a mutually beneficial solution for both parties. Information sharing is an important feature of this style because both parties need to identify common ground and potential solutions that satisfy both (or all) of them.	High: 17 to 20 Medium: 11 to 16 Low: 4 to 10
Avoiding: Avoiding tries to smooth over or avoid conflict situations altogether. It represents a low concern for both self and the other party. In other words, avoiders try to suppress thinking about the conflict.	High: 13 to 20 Medium: 8 to 12 Low: 4 to 7

CHAPTER 14
Scoring Key for Leadership Dimensions Instrument

Transactional Leadership

Scoring Instructions: Add up scores for the odd numbered items (i.e., 1, 3, 5, 7, 9, 11, 13, 15). Maximum score is 40.

Interpreting Your Score: Transactional leadership is "managing"—helping organizations to achieve their current objectives more efficiently, such as by linking job performance to valued rewards and ensuring that employees have the resources needed to get the job done. The following table shows the range of scores for high, medium, and low levels of transactional leadership.

Transactional Leadership	
Score	**Interpretation**
32 to 40	The person you evaluated seems to be a highly transactional leader.
25 to 31	The person you evaluated seems to be a moderately transactional leader.
Below 25	The person you evaluated seems to display few characteristics of a transactional leader.

Transformational Leadership

Scoring Instructions: Add up scores for the even numbered items (i.e., 2, 4, 6, 8, 10, 12, 14, 16). Maximum score is 40. Higher scores indicate that your supervisor has a strong inclination toward transformational leadership.

Interpreting Your Score: Transformational leadership involves changing teams or organizations by creating, communicating, and modelling a vision for the organization or work unit, and inspiring employees to strive for that vision. The following table shows the range of scores for high, medium, and low levels of transformational leadership.

Transformational Leadership	
Score	**Interpretation**
32 to 40	The person you evaluated seems to be a highly transformational leader.
25 to 31	The person you evaluated seems to be a moderately transformational leader.
Below 25	The person you evaluated seems to display few characteristics of a transformational leader.

CHAPTER 15
Scoring Key for the Organizational Structure Preference Scale

Scoring Instructions: Use the table below to assign numbers to each response you circled. Insert the number for each statement on the appropriate line below the table. For example, if you checked "Not at all" for item #1 ("A person's career ladder..."), you would write a "0" on the line with "(1)" underneath it. After assigning numbers for all 15 statements, add up the scores to estimate your degree of preference for a tall hierarchy, formalization, and centralization. Then calculate the overall score by summing all scales.

For statement items 2, 3, 8, 10, 11, 12, 14, 15:	For statement items 1, 4, 5, 6, 7, 9, 13:
Not at all = 3	Not at all = 0
A little = 2	A little = 1
Somewhat = 1	Somewhat = 2
Very much = 0	Very much = 3

Tall Hierarchy (H)   ___ + ___ + ___ + ___ + ___ = ___
                     (1)   (4)   (10) (12) (15)   (H)

Formalization (F)   ___ + ___ + ___ + ___ + ___ = ___
                     (2)   (6)   (8)   (11) (13)   (F)

Centralization (C)   ___ + ___ + ___ + ___ + ___ = ___
                     (3)   (5)   (7)   (9)   (14)   (C)

Total Score (Mechanistic)   ___ + ___ + ___ = ___
                            (H)   (F)   (C)   Total

Interpreting Your Score: The three organizational structure dimensions and the overall score are defined below, along with the range of scores for high, medium, and low levels of each dimension based on a sample of MBA students:

Organizational Structure Dimension and Definition	Interpretation
Tall Hierarchy: People with high scores on this dimension prefer to work in organizations with several levels of hierarchy and a narrow span of control (few employees per supervisor).	High: 11 to 15 Medium: 6 to 10 Low: Below 6
Formalization: People with high scores on this dimension prefer to work in organizations where jobs are clearly defined with limited discretion.	High: 12 to 15 Medium: 9 to 11 Low: Below 9
Centralization: People with high scores on this dimension prefer to work in organizations where decision making occurs mainly among top management rather than spread out to lower level staff.	High: 10 to 15 Medium: 7 to 9 Low: Below 7
Total Score (Mechanistic): People with high scores on this dimension prefer to work in mechanistic organizations, whereas those with low scores prefer to work in organic organizational structures. Mechanistic structures are characterized by a narrow span of control and high degree of formalization and centralization. Organic structures have a wide span of control, little formalization, and decentralized decision making.	High: 30 to 45 Medium: 22 to 29 Low: Below 22

CHAPTER 16
Scoring Key for the Corporate Culture Preference Scale

Scoring Instructions: In each space below, write in a "1" if you circled the statement and "0" if you did not. Then add up the scores for each subscale.

Control Culture	___ (2a)	+ ___ (5a)	+ ___ (6b)	+ ___ (8b)	+ ___ (11b)	+ ___ (12a)	= ___
Performance Culture	___ (1b)	+ ___ (3b)	+ ___ (5b)	+ ___ (6a)	+ ___ (7a)	+ ___ (9b)	= ___
Relationship Culture	___ (1a)	+ ___ (3a)	+ ___ (4b)	+ ___ (8a)	+ ___ (10b)	+ ___ (12b)	= ___
Responsive Culture	___ (2b)	+ ___ (4a)	+ ___ (7b)	+ ___ (9a)	+ ___ (10a)	+ ___ (11a)	= ___

Interpreting Your Score: These corporate cultures may be found in many organizations, but they represent only four of many possible organizational cultures. Also, keep in mind none of these subscales is inherently good or bad. Each is effective in different situations. The four corporate cultures are defined below, along with the range of scores for high, medium, and low levels of each dimension based on a sample of MBA students:

Corporate Culture Dimension and Definition	Score Interpretation
Control Culture: This culture values the role of senior executives to lead the organization. Its goal is to keep everyone aligned and under control.	High: 3 to 6 Medium: 1 to 2 Low: 0
Performance Culture: This culture values individual and organizational performance and strives for effectiveness and efficiency.	High: 5 to 6 Medium: 3 to 4 Low: 0 to 2
Relationship Culture: This culture values nurturing and well-being. It considers open communication, fairness, teamwork, and sharing a vital part of organizational life.	High: 6 Medium: 4 to 5 Low: 0 to 3
Responsive Culture: This culture values its ability to keep in tune with the external environment, including being competitive and realizing new opportunities.	High: 6 Medium: 4 to 5 Low: 0 to 3

CHAPTER 17
Scoring Key for the Tolerance of Change Scale

Scoring Instructions: Use the table below to assign numbers to each box you checked. For example, if you checked "Moderately disagree" for statement #1 ("An expert who doesn't come up …"), you would write a "2" beside that statement. After assigning numbers for all 16 statements, add up your scores to estimate your tolerance for change.

For statement items 2, 4, 6, 8, 10, 12, 14, 16:	For statement items 1, 3, 5, 7, 9, 11, 13, 15:
Strongly Agree = 7	Strongly Agree = 1
Moderately Agree = 6	Moderately Agree = 2
Slightly Agree = 5	Slightly Agree = 3
Neutral = 4	Neutral = 4
Slightly Disagree = 3	Slightly Disagree = 5
Moderately Disagree = 2	Moderately Disagree = 6
Strongly Disagree = 1	Strongly Disagree = 7

Interpreting Your Score: This measurement instrument is formally known as the "tolerance of ambiguity" scale. Although it was developed 40 years ago, the instrument is still used in research today. People with a high tolerance of ambiguity are comfortable with uncertainty, sudden change, and new situations. These are characteristics of the hyperfast changes occurring in many organizations today. The exhibit below indicates the range of scores for high, medium, and low tolerance for change. These norms are based on results for MBA students:

Tolerance of Change	
Score	**Interpretation**
81 to 112	You seem to have a high tolerance for change.
63 to 80	You seem to have a moderate level of tolerance for change.
Below 63	You seem to have a low degree of tolerance for change. Instead, you prefer stable work environments.

The number following each definition indicates the chapter in which the term receives the fullest description.

A

ability Both the natural aptitudes and learned capabilities required to successfully complete a task. (2)

absorptive capacity The ability to recognize the value of new information, assimilate it, and apply it to commercial ends. (1)

achievement-nurturing orientation A competitive versus cooperative view of relations with other people. (2)

action learning Occurs when employees, usually in teams, investigate and apply solutions to a situation that is both real and complex, with immediate relevance to the company. (3)

action research A data-based, problem-oriented process that diagnoses the need for change, introduces the intervention, and then evaluates and stabilizes the desired changes. (17)

adaptive culture An organizational culture in which employees focus on the changing needs of customers and other stakeholders, and support initiatives to keep pace with these changes. (16)

appreciative inquiry An organizational change process that directs attention away from the group's own problems and focuses participants on the group's potential and positive elements. (17)

artifacts The observable symbols and signs of an organization's culture. (16)

attitudes The cluster of beliefs, assessed feelings, and behavioural intentions toward an object. (4)

attribution process The perceptual process of deciding whether an observed behaviour or event is caused largely by internal or by external factors. (3)

autonomy The degree to which a job gives employees the freedom, independence, and discretion to schedule their work and determine the procedures used in completing it. (6)

B

balanced scorecard A reward system that pays bonuses to executives for improved measurements on a composite of financial, customer, internal process, and employee factors. (6)

behaviour modification A theory that explains learning in terms of the antecedents and consequences of behaviour. (3)

bicultural audit Diagnoses cultural relations between companies prior to a merger and determines the extent to which cultural clashes will likely occur. (16)

"Big Five" personality dimensions The five abstract dimensions representing most personality traits: conscientiousness, agreeableness, neuroticism, openness to experience, and extroversion (CANOE). (2)

bounded rationality Processing limited and imperfect information and satisficing rather than maximizing when choosing among alternatives. (8)

brainstorming A freewheeling, face-to-face meeting where team members generate as many ideas as possible, piggyback on the ideas of others, and avoid evaluating anyone's ideas during the idea-generation stage. (10)

C

categorical thinking The mostly unconscious process of organizing people and objects into preconceived categories that are stored in our long-term memory. (3)

centrality The degree and nature of interdependence between the power-holder and others. (12)

centralization The degree to which formal decision authority is held by a small group of people, typically those at the top of the organizational hierarchy. (15)

ceremonies Planned and usually dramatic displays of organizational culture, conducted specifically for the benefit of an audience. (16)

change agent Anyone who possesses enough knowledge and power to guide and facilitate the organizational change effort. (17)

coalition A group that attempts to influence people outside the group by pooling the resources and power of its members. (12)

cognitive dissonance Occurs when people perceive an inconsistency between their beliefs, feelings, and behaviour. (4)

collectivism The extent to which people value duty to groups to which they belong as well as group harmony. (2)

communication The process by which information is transmitted and understood between two or more people. (11)

communities of practice Informal groups bound together by shared expertise and passion for a particular activity or interest. (1)

competencies The abilities, values, personality traits, and other characteristics of people that lead to superior performance. (2)

conflict The process in which one party perceives that its interests are being opposed or negatively affected by another party. (13)

conflict management Interventions that alter the level and form of conflict in ways that maximize its benefits and minimize its dysfunctional consequences. (13)

constructive conflict Any situation where people debate their different opinions about an issue in a way that keeps the conflict focused on the task rather than on people. (10, 13)

constructs Abstract ideas constructed by researchers that can be linked to observable information. (Appendix A)

contact hypothesis The theory that as individuals interact with one another they rely less on stereotypes about each other. (3)

contingency approach The idea that a particular action may have different consequences in different situations. (1)

contingent work Any job in which the individual does not have an explicit or implicit contract for long-term employment, or one in which the minimum hours of work can vary in a nonsystematic way. (1)

continuance commitment A bond felt by an employee that motivates him or her to stay only because leaving would be costly. (4)

corporate social responsibility (CSR) An organization's moral obligation toward its stakeholders. (1)

counterpower The capacity of a person, team, or organization to keep a more powerful person or group in the exchange relationship. (12)

counterproductive work behaviours (CWBs) Voluntary behaviours that have the potential to directly or indirectly harm the organization. (2)

creativity The development of original ideas that make a socially recognized contribution. (8)

D

decision making A conscious process of making choices among one or more alternatives with the intention of moving toward some desired state of affairs. (8)

Delphi method A structured team decision-making process of systematically pooling the collective knowledge of experts on a particular subject to make decisions, predict the future, or identify opposing views. (10)

dialogue A process of conversation among team members in which they learn about each other's mental models and assumptions, and eventually form a common model for thinking within the team. (10, 13)

distributive justice The perceived fairness in outcomes we receive relative to our contributions and the outcomes and contributions of others. (5)

distributive justice principle The moral principle stating that people who are similar should be rewarded similarly and those dissimilar should be rewarded differently. (2)

divergent thinking Involves reframing a problem in a unique way and generating different approaches to the issue. (8)

divisional structure An organizational structure that groups employees around geographic areas, clients, or outputs. (15)

drives Instinctive or innate tendencies to seek certain goals or maintain internal stability. (5)

E

electronic brainstorming Using special computer software, participants share ideas while minimizing the team dynamics problems inherent in traditional brainstorming sessions. (10)

emotional contagion The automatic and unconscious tendency to mimic and synchronize one's own nonverbal behaviours with those of other people. (11)

emotional dissonance The conflict between required and true emotions. (4)

emotional intelligence (EI) The ability to perceive and express emotion, assimilate emotion and thought, understand and reason with emotion, and regulate emotion in oneself and others. (4)

emotional labour The effort, planning, and control needed to express organizationally desired emotions during interpersonal transactions. (4)

emotions Psychological and physiological episodes experienced toward an object, person, or event that create a state of readiness. (4)

empathy A person's ability to understand and be sensitive to the feelings, thoughts, and situations of others. (3)

employability An employment relationship in which people are expected to continually develop their skills to remain employed. (1)

employee assistance programs (EAPs) Counselling services that help employees overcome personal or organizational stressors and adopt more effective coping mechanisms. (7)

employee engagement How much employees identify with and are emotionally committed to their work, are cognitively focused on that work, and possess the ability and resources to do so. (2)

employee involvement The degree to which employees influence how their work is organized and carried out. (8)

employee stock ownership plans (ESOPs) A reward system that encourages employees to buy shares of the company. (6)

empowerment A psychological concept in which people experience more self-determination, meaning, competence, and impact regarding their role in the organization. (6)

enacted values Values we rely on to guide our decisions and actions. (2)

equity sensitivity A person's outcome/input preferences and reaction to various outcome/input ratios. (5)

equity theory Theory that explains how people develop perceptions of fairness in the distribution and exchange of resources. (5)

ERG theory A motivation theory of three needs arranged in a hierarchy, in which people progress to the next higher need when a lower one is fulfilled, and regress to a lower need if unable to fulfill a higher one. (5)

escalation of commitment   The tendency to repeat an apparently bad decision or allocate more resources to a failing course of action. (8)

espoused values   Values that we say we use and think we use. (2)

ethical sensitivity   A personal characteristic that enables people to recognize the presence and determine the relative importance of an ethical issue. (2)

ethics   The study of moral principles or values that determine whether actions are right or wrong and outcomes are good or bad. (1, 2)

evaluation apprehension   When individuals are reluctant to mention ideas that seem silly because they believe (often correctly) that other team members are silently evaluating them. (10)

executive coaching   A helping relationship using behavioural methods to assist clients in identifying and achieving goals for their professional performance and personal satisfaction. (5)

exit-voice-loyalty-neglect   (EVLN) model   The four ways, as indicated in the name, employees respond to job dissatisfaction. (4)

expectancy theory   A motivation theory based on the idea that work effort is directed toward behaviours that people believe will lead to desired outcomes. (5)

extinction   Occurs when the target behaviour decreases because no consequence follows it. (3)

extroversion   A "Big Five" personality dimension that characterizes people who are outgoing, talkative, sociable, and assertive. (2)

F

feedback   Any information that people receive about the consequences of their behaviour. (5)

Fiedler's contingency model   Developed by Fred Fiedler, suggests that leader effectiveness depends on whether the person's natural leadership style is appropriately matched to the situation. (14)

field surveys   A research design strategy that involves collecting and analyzing information in a natural environment, an office, a factory, or other existing location. (Appendix A)

flaming   The act of sending an emotionally charged electronic mail message to others. (11)

force field analysis   Lewin's model of systemwide change that helps change agents diagnose the forces that drive and restrain proposed organizational change. (17)

formalization   The degree to which organizations standardize behaviour through rules, procedures, formal training, and related mechanisms. (15)

four-drive theory   A motivation theory based on the innate drives to acquire, bond, learn, and defend that incorporates both emotions and rationality. (5)

functional structure   An organizational structure that organizes employees around specific knowledge or other resources. (15)

fundamental attribution error   The tendency to attribute the behaviour of other people more to internal than to external factors. (3)

future search   Systemwide group sessions, usually lasting a few days, in which participants identify trends and identify ways to adapt to these changes. (17)

G

gainsharing plan   A reward system that rewards team members for reducing costs and increasing labour efficiency in their work process. (6)

general adaptation syndrome   A model of the stress experience, consisting of three stages: alarm reaction, resistance, and exhaustion. (7)

globalization   Economic, social, and cultural connectivity (and interdependence) with people in other parts of the world. (1)

goal setting   The process of motivating employees and clarifying their role perceptions by establishing performance objectives. (5)

grapevine   An unstructured and informal communication network founded on social relationships rather than organizational charts or job descriptions. (11)

grounded theory   A process adopted in most qualitative research of developing knowledge through the constant interplay of data collection, analysis, and theory development. (1, Appendix A)

group polarization   The tendency of teams to make more extreme decisions than individuals working alone. (10)

groups   Two or more people with a unifying relationship. (9)

groupthink   The tendency of highly cohesive groups to value consensus at the price of decision quality. (10)

H

halo effect   A perceptual error whereby our general impression of a person, usually based on one prominent characteristic, colours the perception of other characteristics of that person. (3)

heterogeneous teams   Teams that include members with diverse personal characteristics and backgrounds. (9)

homogeneous teams   Teams that include members with common technical expertise, demographics (age, gender), ethnicity, experiences, or values. (9)

hypotheses   Statements making empirically testable declarations that certain variables and their corresponding measures are related in a specific way proposed by theory. (Appendix A)

I

implicit favourite   The decision maker's preferred alternative against which all other choices are judged. (8)

implicit leadership theory   A theory stating that people rely on preconceived traits to evaluate others as leaders, and that they tend to inflate the influence of leadership on organizational events. (14)

impression management The practice of actively shaping our public image. (12)

individualism The extent to which a person values independence and personal uniqueness. (2)

individual rights principle The moral principle stating that every person is entitled to legal and human rights. (2)

influence Any behaviour that attempts to alter another person's attitudes or behaviour. (12)

information overload A condition in which the volume of information received exceeds the person's capacity to process it. (11)

ingratiation Any attempt to increase the extent to which a target person likes us or perceives that he or she is similar to us. (12)

inoculation effect A persuasive communication strategy of warning listeners that others will try to influence them in the future and that they should be wary about the opponent's arguments. (12)

intellectual capital The sum of an organization's human capital, structural capital, and relationship capital. (1)

interpretivism The view held in many qualitative studies that reality comes from shared meaning among people in that environment. (Appendix A)

introversion A "Big Five" personality dimension that characterizes people who are territorial and solitary. (2)

intuition The ability to know when a problem or opportunity exists and select the best course of action without conscious reasoning. (8)

J

jargon The technical language and acronyms as well as recognized words with specialized meanings in specific organizations or groups. (11)

job burnout The process of emotional exhaustion, depersonalization, and reduced personal accomplishment resulting from prolonged exposure to stress. (7)

job characteristics model A job design model that relates the motivational properties of jobs to specific personal and organizational consequences of those properties. (6)

job design The process of assigning tasks to a job, including the interdependency of those tasks with other jobs. (6)

job enlargement Increasing the number of tasks employees perform within their job. (6)

job enrichment Employees are given more responsibility for scheduling, coordinating, and planning their own work. (6)

job evaluation Systematically evaluating the worth of jobs within an organization by measuring their required skill, effort, responsibility, and working conditions. Job evaluation results create a hierarchy of job worth. (6)

job rotation The practice of moving employees from one job to another. (6)

job satisfaction A person's evaluation of his or her job and work context. (2, 4)

job specialization The result of division of labour in which each job includes a subset of the tasks required to complete the product or service. (6)

Johari Window The model of personal and interpersonal understanding that encourages disclosure and feedback to increase the open area and reduce the blind, hidden, and unknown areas of oneself. (3)

joint optimization The balance that is struck between social and technical systems to maximize an operation's effectiveness. (10)

K

knowledge management Any structured activity that improves an organization's capacity to acquire, share, and use knowledge in ways that improve its survival and success. (1)

L

laboratory experiment Any research study in which independent variables and variables outside the researcher's main focus of inquiry can be controlled to some extent. (Appendix A)

leadership Influencing, motivating, and enabling others to contribute toward the effectiveness and success of the organizations of which they are members. (14)

leadership substitutes A theory that identifies contingencies that either limit the leader's ability to influence subordinates or make that particular leadership style unnecessary. (14)

learning A relatively permanent change in behaviour that occurs as a result of a person's interaction with the environment. (3)

learning orientation The extent to which an organization or individual supports knowledge management, particularly opportunities to acquire knowledge through experience and experimentation. (3)

legitimate power The capacity to influence others through formal authority. (12)

locus of control A personality trait referring to the extent to which people believe events are within their control. (2)

M

Machiavellian values The belief that deceit is a natural and acceptable way to influence others. (12)

management by walking around (MBWA) A communication practice in which executives get out of their offices and learn from others in the organization through face-to-face dialogue. (11)

Maslow's needs hierarchy theory A motivation theory of needs arranged in a hierarchy, whereby people are motivated to fulfill a higher need as a lower one becomes gratified. (5)

matrix structure   A type of departmentalization that overlays two organizational forms in order to leverage the benefits of both. (15)

mechanistic structure   An organizational structure with a narrow span of control and high degrees of formalization and centralization. (15)

media richness   The data-carrying capacity of a communication medium, including the volume and variety of information it can transmit. (11)

mental imagery   Mentally practising a task and visualizing its successful completion. (6)

mental models   The broad worldviews or "theories in-use" that people rely on to guide their perceptions and behaviours. (3)

mentoring   The process of learning the ropes of organizational life from a senior person within the company. (12)

moral intensity   The degree to which an issue demands the application of ethical principles. (2)

motivation   The forces within a person that affect his or her direction, intensity, and persistence of voluntary behaviour. (2, 5)

motivator–hygiene theory   Herzberg's theory stating that employees are primarily motivated by growth and esteem needs, not by lower-level needs. (6)

multisource (360-degree) feedback   Performance feedback received from a full circle of people around an employee. (5)

Myers-Briggs Type Indicator (MBTI)   A personality test that measures each of the traits in Jung's model. (2)

N

need for achievement (nAch)   A learned need in which people want to accomplish reasonably challenging goals through their own efforts, like being successful in competitive situations, and desire unambiguous feedback regarding their success. (5)

need for affiliation (nAff)   A learned need in which people seek approval from others, conform to their wishes and expectations, and avoid conflict and confrontation. (5)

need for power (nPow)   A learned need in which people want to control their environment, including people and material resources, to benefit either themselves (personalized power) or others (socialized power). (5)

needs   Deficiencies that energize or trigger behaviours to satisfy those needs. (5)

negative reinforcement   Occurs when the removal or avoidance of a consequence increases or maintains the frequency or future probability of a behaviour. (3)

negotiation   Occurs whenever two or more conflicting parties attempt to resolve their divergent goals by redefining the terms of their interdependence. (13)

network structure   An alliance of several organizations for the purpose of creating a product or serving a client. (15)

networking   Cultivating social relationships with others to accomplish one's goals. (12)

nominal group technique   A structured team decision-making process whereby team members independently write down ideas, describe and clarify them to the group, and then independently rank or vote on them. (10)

norms   The informal rules and expectations that groups establish to regulate the behaviour of their members. (9)

O

open systems   Organizations that take their sustenance from the environment and, in turn, affect that environment through their output. (1)

organic structure   An organizational structure with a wide span of control, little formalization, and decentralized decision making. (15)

organizational behaviour (OB)   The study of what people think, feel, and do in and around organizations. (1)

organizational citizenship   Behaviours that extend beyond the employee's normal job duties. (2)

organizational (affective) commitment   The employee's emotional attachment to, identification with, and involvement in a particular organization. (4)

organizational culture   The basic pattern of shared assumptions, values, and beliefs considered to be the correct way of thinking about and acting on problems and opportunities facing the organization. (16)

organizational memory   The storage and preservation of intellectual capital. (1)

organizational politics   Behaviours that others perceive as self-serving tactics for personal gain at the expense of other people and possibly the organization. (12)

organizational socialization   The process by which individuals learn the values, expected behaviours, and social knowledge necessary to assume their roles in the organization. (16)

organizational strategy   The way an organization positions itself in its setting in relation to its stakeholders, given the organization's resources, capabilities, and mission. (15)

organizational structure   The division of labour and the patterns of coordination, communication, work flow, and formal power that direct organizational activities. (15)

organizations   Groups of people who work interdependently toward some purpose. (1)

P

parallel learning structures   Highly participative groups constructed alongside (i.e., parallel to) the formal organization with the purpose of increasing the organization's learning and producing meaningful organizational change. (17)

path–goal leadership theory   A contingency theory of leadership based on expectancy theory of motivation that relates several leadership styles to specific employee and situational contingencies. (14)

perception The process of selecting, organizing, and interpreting information in order to make sense of the world around us. (3)

personality The relatively stable pattern of behaviours and consistent internal states that explain a person's behavioural tendencies. (2)

persuasion Using logical arguments, facts, and emotional appeals to encourage people to accept a request or message. (12)

positive reinforcement Occurs when the introduction of a consequence increases or maintains the frequency or future probability of a behaviour. (3)

positivism A view held in quantitative research in which reality exists independent of the perceptions and interpretations of people. (Appendix A)

postdecisional justification Justifying choices by unconsciously inflating the quality of the selected option and deflating the quality of the discarded options. (8)

power The capacity of a person, team, or organization to influence others. (12)

power distance The extent to which people accept unequal distribution of power in a society. (2)

prejudice The unfounded negative emotions and attitudes toward people belonging to a particular stereotyped group. (3)

primacy effect A perceptual error in which we quickly form an opinion of people based on the first information we receive about them. (3)

procedural justice The fairness of the procedures used to decide the distributions of resources. (5)

process losses Resources (including time and energy) expended toward team development and maintenance rather than the task. (9)

production blocking A time constraint in team decision making due to the procedural requirement that only one person may speak at a time. (10)

profit-sharing plans A reward system that pays bonuses to employees based on the previous year's level of corporate profits. (6)

projection bias A perceptual error in which an individual believes that other people have the same beliefs and behaviours that he/she does. (3)

prospect theory An effect in which losing a particular amount is more disliked than gaining the same amount. (8)

psychological contract The individual's beliefs about the terms and conditions of a reciprocal exchange agreement between that person and another party. (4)

psychological harassment Repeated and hostile or unwanted conduct, verbal comments, actions or gestures, which affect an employee's dignity or integrity and result in a harmful work environment for the employee. (7)

punishment Occurs when a consequence decreases the frequency or future probability of a behaviour. (3)

R

realistic job preview (RJP) Giving job applicants a balance of positive and negative information about the job and work context. (16)

reality shock Occurs when newcomers perceive discrepancies between their pre-employment expectations and on-the-job reality. (16)

recency effect A perceptual error in which the most recent information dominates one's perception of others. (3)

referent power The capacity to influence others based on the identification and respect they have for the power holder. (12)

refreezing The latter part of the change process in which systems and conditions are introduced that reinforce and maintain the desired behaviours. (17)

representative sampling The process of sampling a population in such a way that one can extrapolate the results of that sample to the larger population. (Appendix A)

resilience The capability of individuals to cope successfully in the face of significant change, adversity, or risk. (7)

rituals The programmed routines of daily organizational life that dramatize the organization's culture. (16)

role A set of behaviours that people are expected to perform because they hold certain positions in a team and organization. (9)

role ambiguity Uncertainty about job duties, performance expectations, level of authority, and other job conditions. (7)

role conflict Conflict that occurs when people face competing demands. (7)

S

satisficing Selecting a solution that is satisfactory, or "good enough" rather than optimal or "the best." (8)

scenario planning A systematic process of thinking about alternative futures, and what the organization should do to anticipate and react to those environments. (8)

scientific management Involves systematically partitioning work into its smallest elements and standardizing tasks to achieve maximum efficiency. (6)

scientific method A set of principles and procedures that help researchers to systematically understand previously unexplained events and conditions. (1, Appendix A)

selective attention The process of filtering information received by our senses. (3)

self-actualization The need for self-fulfillment in reaching one's potential. (5)

self-directed work teams (SDWTs) Cross-functional work groups organized around work processes that complete an entire piece of work requiring several interdependent tasks, and that have substantial autonomy over the execution of those tasks. (10)

self-fulfilling prophecy Occurs when our expectations about another person cause that person to act in a way that is consistent with those expectations. (3)

self-leadership The process of influencing oneself to establish the self-direction and self-motivation needed to perform a task. (6)

self-monitoring A personality trait referring to an individual's level of sensitivity and ability to adapt to situational cues. (2)

self-reinforcement Occurs whenever an employee has control over a reinforcer but delays it until completing a self-set goal. (3)

self-serving bias A perceptual error whereby people tend to attribute their favourable outcomes to internal factors and their failures to external factors. (3)

self-talk Talking to ourselves about our own thoughts or actions for the purpose of increasing our self-confidence and navigating through decisions in a future event. (6)

servant leadership The belief that leaders serve followers by understanding their needs and facilitating their work performance. (14)

sexual harassment Unwelcome conduct of a sexual nature that detrimentally affects the work environment or leads to adverse job-related consequences for its victims. (7)

situational leadership theory Developed by Hersey and Blanchard, suggests that effective leaders vary their style with the "readiness" of followers. (14)

skill variety The extent to which employees must use different skills and talents to perform tasks within their job. (6)

social capital The knowledge and other resources available to people or social units due to a durable network that connects them to others. (12)

social identity theory States that self-perception and social perception are shaped by a person's unique characteristics (personal identity) and membership in various groups (social identity). (3)

social learning theory A theory stating that much learning occurs by observing others and then modelling the behaviours that lead to favourable outcomes and avoiding the behaviours that lead to punishing consequences. (3)

social loafing A situation in which people exert less effort (and usually perform at a lower level) when working in groups than when working alone. (9)

socioemotional conflict Any situation where people view their differences as personal attacks rather than attempts to resolve an issue. (13)

sociotechnical systems (STS) theory A theory stating that effective work sites have joint optimization of their social and technological systems, and that teams should have sufficient autonomy to control key variances in the work process. (10)

span of control The number of people directly reporting to the next level in the organizational hierarchy. (15)

stakeholders Shareholders, customers, suppliers, governments, and any other groups with a vested interest in the organization. (1)

stereotyping The process of assigning traits to people based on their membership in a social category. (3)

stock options A reward system that gives employees the right to purchase company shares at a future date at a predetermined price. (6)

stress An individual's adaptive response to a situation that is perceived as challenging or threatening to the person's well-being. (7)

stressors The causes of stress, including any environmental conditions that place a physical or emotional demand on the person. (7)

substitutability The extent to which people dependent on a resource have alternatives. (12)

superordinate goal A common objective held by conflicting parties that is more important than their conflicting departmental or individual goals. (13)

T

tacit knowledge Knowledge embedded in our actions and ways of thinking, and transmitted only through observation and experience. (3)

task identity The degree to which a job requires completion of a whole or an identifiable piece of work. (6)

task interdependence The degree to which a task requires employees to share common inputs or outcomes, or to interact in the process of executing their work. (9)

task performance Goal-directed activities that are under that individual's control. (2)

task significance The degree to which the job has a substantial impact on the organization and/or larger society. (6)

team-based structure A type of departmentalization with a flat hierarchy and relatively little formalization, consisting of self-directed work teams responsible for various work processes. (15)

team building Any formal activity intended to improve the development and functioning of a team. (10)

team cohesiveness The degree of attraction people feel toward the team and their motivation to remain members. (9)

team effectiveness The extent to which a team achieves its objectives, achieves the needs and objectives of its members, and sustains itself over time. (9)

teams Groups of two or more people who interact and influence each other, are mutually accountable for achieving common objectives, and perceive themselves as a social entity within an organization. (9)

theory A general set of propositions that describes interrelationships among several concepts. (Appendix A)

third-party conflict resolution Any attempt by a relatively neutral person to help the parties resolve their differences. (13)

transactional leadership Leadership that helps organizations achieve their current objectives more efficiently, such as linking job performance to valued rewards and ensuring that employees have the resources needed to get the job done. (14)

transformational leadership A leadership perspective that explains how leaders change teams or organizations by creating, communicating, and modelling a vision for the organization or work unit and inspiring employees to strive for that vision. (14)

trust A psychological state comprising the intention to accept vulnerability based upon positive expectations of the intent or behaviour of another person. (4, 10)

Type A behaviour pattern A behaviour pattern associated with people having premature heart disease; Type A people tend to be impatient, lose their tempers easily, talk rapidly, and interrupt others. (7)

U

uncertainty avoidance The degree to which people tolerate ambiguity or feel threatened by ambiguity and uncertainty. (2)

unfreezing The first part of the change process whereby the change agent produces disequilibrium between the driving and restraining forces. (17)

upward appeal A type of coalition in which one or more members is someone with higher authority or expertise. (12)

utilitarianism The moral principle stating that decision makers should seek the greatest good for the greatest number of people when choosing among alternatives. (2)

V

valence The anticipated satisfaction or dissatisfaction that an individual feels toward an outcome. (5)

values Stable, long-lasting beliefs about what is important in a variety of situations. (1, 2)

values congruence A situation wherein two or more entities have similar value systems. (2)

virtual corporations Network structures representing several independent companies that form unique partnership teams to provide customized products or services, usually to specific clients for a limited time. (15)

virtual teams Teams whose members operate across space, time, and organizational boundaries and are linked through information technologies to achieve organizational tasks. (1, 10)

virtual work Employees use information technology to perform their jobs away from the traditional physical workplace. (1)

W

win–lose orientation The belief that the conflicting parties are drawing from a fixed pie, so the more one party receives, the less the other party will receive. (13)

win–win orientation The belief that the parties will find a mutually beneficial solution to their disagreement. (13)

workaholic A person who is highly involved in work, feels compelled to work, and has a low enjoyment of work. (7)

work/life balance The minimization of conflict between work and nonwork demands. (1)

NOTES

CHAPTER ONE

1. J. Terret, "Dofasco Engages Workforce to Profit in Tough Steel Market," *Plant*, 6 May 2002, 15; B. Dunn, "John Mayberry's Mark Lands Dofasco on a Firm Footing," *American Metal Market*, 16 June 2003, 22A–23A; R. Raizel, "Taking Care of Business," *Canadian Business*, 24 Nov-7 Dec 2003; M. Rola, "Dofasco Retools to Create 'Communities of Practice'," *Computing Canada*, 11 April 2003, 6; S. Brunt, "Heavy Mettle," *Report on Business Magazine*, May 2004, 58ff; J. Murray, "Our Product Is Steel, Our Strength Is People," *Quality Congress (ASQ's Annual Quality Congress Proceedings)* 58 (2004): 163–180; T. Perkins and J. De Almeida, "As Strong as Steel," *Hamilton Spectator*, 5 October 2004, G05.

2. M. Warner, "Organizational Behavior Revisited," *Human Relations* 47 (October 1994): 1151–1166; R. Westwood and S. Clegg, "The Discourse of Organization Studies: Dissensus, Politics, and Peradigms," in *Debating Organization: Point-Counterpoint in Organization Studies*, ed. R. Westwood and S. Clegg (Malden, MA: Blackwood, 2003), 1–42. Some of the historical bases of OB mentioned in this paragraph are described in: J. A. Conger, "Max Weber's Conceptualization of Charismatic Authority: Its Influence on Organizational Research," *The Leadership Quarterly* 4, no. 3–4 (1993): 277–288; R. Kanigel, *The One Best Way: Frederick Winslow Taylor and the Enigma of Efficiency* (New York: Viking, 1997); J. H. Smith, "The Enduring Legacy of Elton Mayo," *Human Relations* 51, no. 3 (1998): 221–249; T. Takala, "Plato on Leadership," *Journal of Business Ethics* 17 (May 1998): 785–798; J. A. Fernandez, "The Gentleman's Code of Confucius: Leadership by Values," *Organizational Dynamics* 33, no. 1 (February 2004): 21–31.

3. J. Micklethwait and A. Wooldridge, *The Company: A Short History of a Revolutionary Idea* (New York: Random House, 2003).

4. B. Schlender, "The Three Faces of Steve," *Fortune*, 9 November 1998, 96–101.

5. D. K. Katz, R. L., *The Social Psychology of Organizations* (New York: Wiley, 1966), Chap. 2; R. N. Stern and S. R. Barley, "Organizations as Social Systems: Organization Theory's Neglected Mandate," *Administrative Science Quarterly* 41 (1996): 146–162.

6. J. Pfeffer, *New Directions for Organization Theory* (New York: Oxford University Press, 1997), pp. 7–9.

7. P. R. Lawrence and N. Nohria, *Driven: How Human Nature Shapes Our Choices* (San Francisco: Jossey-Bass, 2002), Chap. 6.

8. P. R. Lawrence, "Historical Development of Organizational Behavior," in *Handbook of Organizational Behavior*, ed. L. W. Lorsch (Englewood Cliffs, N. J.: Prentice Hall, 1987), 1–9; S. A. Mohrman, C. B. Gibson, and A. M. Mohrman Jr., "Doing Research That Is Useful to Practice: A Model and Empirical Exploration," *Academy of Management Journal* 44 (April 2001): 357–375. For a contrary view, see: A. P. Brief and J. M. Dukerich, "Theory in Organizational Behavior: Can It Be Useful?" *Research in Organizational Behavior* 13 (1991): 327–352.

9. M. S. Myers, *Every Employee a Manager* (New York: McGraw Hill, 1970).

10. D. Yankelovich, "Got to Give to Get," *Mother Jones* 22 (July 1997): 60–63; D. MacDonald, "Good Managers Key to Buffett's Acquisitions," *Montreal Gazette*, 16 November 2001. The two studies on OB and financial performance are: B. N. Pfau and I. T. Kay, *The Human Capital Edge* (New York: McGraw-Hill, 2002); I. S. Fulmer, B. Gerhart, and K. S. Scott, "Are the 100 Best Better? An Empirical Investigation of the Relationship between Being a 'Great Place to Work' and Firm Performance," *Personnel Psychology* 56, no. 4 (Winter 2003): 965–993.

11. M. Franner, "A Lesson in Success," *Commerce & Industry (Special Supplement)* 50, no. 5 (January 1999): S1–S19; D. McCutcheon, "Inner Strength," *Advanced Manufacturing* 6, no. 1 (Jan/Feb 2004): 23ff; R. Deruyter, "Shop Floor Home to ATS Founder," *Kitchener-Waterloo Record*, 8 February 2005, A5.

12. S. Fischer, "Globalization and Its Challenges," *American Economic Review* (May 2003): 1–29. For discussion of the diverse meanings of "globalization," see: M. F. Guillén, "Is Globalization Civilizing, Destructive or Feeble? A Critique of Five Key Debates in the Social Science Literature," *Annual Review of Sociology* 27 (2001): 235–260.

13. The ongoing debate regarding the advantages and disadvantages of globalization are discussed in: Guillén, "Is Globalization Civilizing, Destructive or Feeble?"; D. Doane, "Can Globalization Be Fixed?" *Business Strategy Review* 13, no. 2 (2002): 51–58; J. Bhagwati, *In Defense of Globalization* (New York: Oxford University Press, 2004); M. Wolf, *Why Globalization Works* (New Haven, CT: Yale University Press, 2004).

14. C. L. Cooper and R. J. Burke, *The New World of Work: Challenges and Opportunities* (Oxford: Blackwell, 2002); C. Higgins and L. Duxbury, *The 2001 National Work–Life Conflict Study: Report One, Final Report* (Ottawa: Health Canada, March 2002)

15. K. Ohmae, *The Next Global Stage* (Philadelphia: Wharton School Publishing, 2005).

16. R. Hallowell, D. Bowen, and C.-I. Knoop, "Four Seasons Goes to Paris," *Academy of Management Executive* 16, no. 4 (November 2002): 7–24; Four Seasons Hotels and Resorts, *2004 Annual Report* (Toronto: Four Seasons Hotels and Resorts, March 2005).

17. C. Cobb, "Canadians Want Diverse Society: Poll," *Ottawa Citizen*, 18 February 2002, A5. The HSBC Bank Canada quotation is found in: A. Wahl, "Opening Doors," *Canadian Business*, 29 March 2004, 45.

18. K. Kelly, *Visible Minorities: A Diverse Group*, Canadian Social Trends

(Ottawa: Statistics Canada, 6 February 2004); A. Bélanger and E. C. Malenfant, *Population Projections of Visible Minority Groups, Canada, Provinces, and Regions: 2001–2017* (Ottawa: Statistics Canada, March 2005).

19. I. A. Dhalla *et al.*, "Characteristics of First-Year Students in Canadian Medical Schools," *Canadian Medical Association Journal* 166, no. 8 (16 April 2002): 1029–1035.

20. R. Zemke, C. Raines, and B. Filipczak, *Generations at Work: Managing the Clash of Veterans, Boomers, Xers, and Nexters in Your Workplace* (New York: Amacom, 2000); C. Loughlin and J. Barling, "Young Workers' Work Values, Attitudes, and Behaviours," *Journal of Occupational and Organizational Psychology* 74 (November 2001): 543–558; C. A. Martin and B. Tulgan, *Managing Generation Y* (Amherst, MA: HRD Press, 2001); M. R. Muetzel, *They're Not Aloof, Just Generation X* (Shreveport, LA: Steel Bay, 2003); S. H. Applebaum, M. Serena, and B. T. Shapiro, "Generation X and the Boomers: Organizational Myths and Literary Realities," *Management Research News* 27, no. 11/12 (2004): 1–28.

21. O. C. Richard, "Racial Diversity, Business Strategy, and Firm Performance: A Resource-Based View," *Academy of Management Journal* 43 (2000): 164–177; D. D. Frink *et al.*, "Gender Demography and Organization Performance: A Two-Study Investigation with Convergence," *Group & Organization Management* 28 (March 2003): 127–147; T. Kochan *et al.*, "The Effects of Diversity on Business Performance: Report of the Diversity Research Network," *Human Resource Management* 42 (2003): 3–21.

22. R. J. Ely and D. A. Thomas, "Cultural Diversity at Work: The Effects of Diversity Perspectives on Work Group Processes and Outcomes," *Administrative Science Quarterly* 46 (June 2001): 229–273; D. van Knippenberg and S. A. Haslam, "Realizing the Diversity Dividend: Exploring the Subtle Interplay between Identity, Ideology and Reality," in *Social Identity at Work: Developing Theory for Organizational Practice*, ed. S. A. Haslam *et al.* (New York: Taylor and Francis, 2003), 61–80.

23. Ipsos-Reid, "What Are Canadians' Top Indicators of Career Success?" News release, (Toronto: 7 May 2003);

Towers Perrin, "Workplace Stress Costs Canadian Economy Billions," News release, (Calgary: 21 April 2005).

24. W. G. Bennis and R. J. Thomas, *Geeks and Geezers* (Boston: Harvard Business School Press, 2002), 74–79; E. D. Y. Greenblatt, "Work/Life Balance: Wisdom or Whining," *Organizational Dynamics* 31, no. 2 (2002): 177–193.

25. P. Kennedy, "Game Firms Get Creative to Lure Talent," *Globe & Mail*, 11 February 2004, B2; W. Frey, "Radical Career Choice," *Metro Vancouver*, 25 April 2005, 11.

26. M. V. Roehling *et al.*, "The Nature of the New Employment Relationship(S): A Content Analysis of the Practitioner and Academic Literatures," *Human Resource Management* 39 (2000): 305–320; W. R. Boswell *et al.*, "Responsibilities in the 'New Employment Relationship': An Empirical Test of an Assumed Phenomenon," *Journal of Managerial Issues* 13 (Fall 2001): 307–327; M. Fugate, A. J. Kinicki, and B. E. Ashforth, "Employability: A Psycho-Social Construct, Its Dimensions, and Applications," *Journal of Vocational Behavior* 65, no. 1 (2004): 14–38.

27. M. Jenkins, "Your for the Taking," *Boeing Frontiers*, June 2004, http://www.boeing.com/news/frontiers/index.html.

28. A. E. Polivka, "Contingent and Alternative Work Arrangements, Defined," *Monthly Labor Review* 119 (October 1996): 3–10; D. H. Pink, *Free Agent Nation* (New York: Time Warner, 2002); C. E. Connelly and D. G. Gallagher, "Emerging Trends in Contingent Work Research," *Journal of Management* 30, no. 6 (2004): 959–983.

29. S. Canada, "Employment Indexes, by Job Permanency," (Ottawa: Statistics Canada, 17 November 2004), http://www.statcan.ca/english/freepub/71-222-XIE/2004000/chart-i49.htm (accessed 9 June 2005); R. Morisette and A. Johnson, *Are Good Jobs Disappearing in Canada?* Analytical Studies Branch research paper series (Ottawa: Statistics Canada, January 2005).

30. B. A. Lautsch, "Uncovering and Explaining Variance in the Features and Outcomes of Contingent Work," *Industrial & Labor Relations Review* 56 (October 2002): 23–43; S. Ang, L. Van Dyne, and T. M. Begley, "The Employment Relationships of Foreign Workers

Versus Local Employees: A Field Study of Organizational Justice, Job Satisfaction, Performance, and OCB," *Journal of Organizational Behavior* 24 (2003): 561–583; A. L. Kalleberg, "Flexible Firms and Labor Market Segmentation," *Work and Occupations* 30, no. 2 (May 2003): 154–175; B. A. Lautsch, "The Influence of Regular Work Systems on Compensation for Contingent Workers," *Industrial Relations* 42, no. 4 (October 2003): 565–588; Connelly and Gallagher, "Emerging Trends in Contingent Work Research,"

31. J. Gannon, "The Perfect Commute," *Post-Gazette (Pittsburgh, PA)*, 24 April 2003, E1.

32. G. Marr, "Home Is Not Where the Office Is," *National Post*, 6 August 2004, FP10; D. Bricker and J. Wright, *What Canadians Think About Almost Everything* (Toronto: Doubleday Canada, 2005); J. Cummings, "Masters of a Virtual World," *Network world*, 25 April 2005, 76–77. These estimates exclude employees who bring work home from the office because this practice isn't usually considered virtual work.

33. Ipsos-Reid, *Canadian Families and the Internet* (Report to The Royal Bank of Canada, January 2002); D.-G. Tremblay, "Telework: Work Organization and Satisfaction of Teleworkers" in *Annual Conference of the Administrative Sciences Association of Canada, Human Resource Management Division*, ed. J. Carrière, (25–28 May, 2002), 73–83; M. Bennet, "Law to Encourage Teleworking," *IT Week*, 11 April 2003; S. Raghuram and B. Wiesenfeld, "Work-Nonwork Conflict and Job Stress among Virtual Workers," *Human Resource Management* 43, no. 2/3 (Summer/Fall 2004): 259–277. The advantages and disadvantages, and contingencies of telecommute are nicely detailed in: L. Duxbury and C. Higgins, "Telecommute: A Primer for the Millennium Introduction," in *The New World of Work: Challenges and Opportunities*, ed. C. L. Cooper and R. J. Burke (Oxford: Blackwell, 2002), 157–199; V. Illegems and A. Verbeke, "Telework: What Does It Mean for Management?" *Long Range Planning* 37 (2004): 319–334.

34. D. E. Bailey and N. B. Kurland, "A Review of Telework Research: Findings, New Directions, and Lessons for

the Study of Modern Work," *Journal of Organizational Behavior* 23 (2002): 383–400; D. W. McCloskey and M. Igbaria, "Does 'out of Sight' Mean 'out of Mind'? An Empirical Investigation of the Career Advancement Prospects of Telecommuters," *Information Resources Management Journal* 16 (April-June 2003): 19–34.

35. D. Bruser, "Working at Home: Mistrust Still Rules," *Toronto Star*, 18 May 2005, C01.

36. J. Lipnack and J. Stamps, *Virtual Teams: People Working across Boundaries with Technology* (New York: John Wiley & Sons, 2001); L. L. Martins, L. L. Gilson, and M. T. Maynard, "Virtual Teams: What Do We Know and Where Do We Go from Here?" *Journal of Management* 30, no. 6 (2004): 805–835; G. Hertel, S. Geister, and U. Konradt, "Managing Virtual Teams: A Review of Current Empirical Research," *Human Resource Management Review* 15, no. 1 (2005): 69–95.

37. K. Kernaghan, "Integrating Values into Public Service: The Values Statement as Centrepiece," *Public Administration Review* 63, no. 6 (November/December 2003): 711–719.

38. B. M. Meglino and E. C. Ravlin, "Individual Values in Organizations: Concepts, Controversies, and Research," *Journal of Management* 24, no. 3 (1998): 351–389; B. R. Agle and C. B. Caldwell, "Understanding Research on Values in Business," *Business and Society* 38, no. 3 (September 1999): 326–387; S. Hitlin and J. A. Pilavin, "Values: Reviving a Dormant Concept," *Annual Review of Sociology* 30 (2004): 359–393.

39. Middle East Company News, "Accountability, Teamwork, and Continuous Improvement Define Core Operating Values at DED," News release, (Dubai: 4 January 2005).

40. The role of values as a control system is discussed in: M. S. Fenwick, H. L. DeCieri, and D. E. Welch, "Cultural and Bureaucratic Control in MNEs: The Role of Expatriate Performance Management," *Management International Review* 39, no. Special Issue 3 (1999): 107–124; T. M. Begley and D. P. Boyd, "Articulating Corporate Values through Human Resource Policies," *Business Horizons* 43, no. 4 (July 2000): 8–12; M. G. Murphy and K. M.

Davey, "Ambiguity, Ambivalence and Indifference in Organisational Values," *Human Resource Management Journal* 12 (2002): 17–32.

41. S. R. Chatterjee and C. A. L. Pearson, "Indian Managers in Transition: Orientations, Work Goals, Values and Ethics," *Management International Review* 40 (January 2000): 81–95.

42. This cynicism of executive ethics is beautifully captured in: D. Olive, "How Celebrity CEOs Failed to Deliver," *Toronto Star*, 24 August 2002, A1.

43. Vector Research, "Analysis of the Public Opinion Poll Conducted for the Canadian Democracy and Corporate Accountability Commission", 2001, Toronto. The quotation by Friedman is cited in: S. Zadek, *The Civil Corporation: The New Economy of Corporate Citizenship* (London: Earthscan, 2001), pp. 50–51.

44. Canadian Democracy And Corporate Accountability Commission, *The New Balance Sheet: Corporate Profits and Responsibility in the 21st Century, Final Report* (Toronto: January 2002); M. van Marrewijk, "Concepts and Definitions of Csr and Corporate Sustainability: Between Agency and Communion," *Journal of Business Ethics* 44 (May 2003): 95–105.

45. Zadek, *The Civil Corporation: The New Economy of Corporate Citizenship*, Chap. 9; S. Zambon and A. Del Bello, "Towards a Stakeholder Responsible Approach: The Constructive Role of Reporting," *Corporate Governance* 5, no. 2 (2005): 130–142.

46. D. Keeler, "Spread the Love and Make It Pay," *Global Finance* 16, no. 5 (May 2001): 20–25.

47. D. Mowat, "The VanCity Difference—a Case for the Triple Bottom Line Approach to Business," *Corporate Environmental Strategy* 9 (February 2002): 24–29; M. Lynch, "Why Every Credit Union Should 'Audit' Its Values," *Credit Union Journal* 8, no. 48 (29 November 2004): 6.

48. M. N. Zald, "More Fragmentation? Unfinished Business in Linking the Social Sciences and the Humanities," *Administrative Science Quarterly* 41 (1996): 251–261. Concerns about the "trade deficit" in OB are raised in: C. Heath and S. B. Sitkin, "Big-B Versus Big-O: What Is Organizational About

Organizational Behavior?" *Journal of Organizational Behavior* 22 (2001): 43–58.

49. N. Nicholson, "Evolutionary Psychology: Toward a New View of Human Nature and Organizational Society," *Human Relations* 50 (September 1997): 1053–1078; B. D. Pierce and R. White, "The Evolution of Social Structure: Why Biology Matters," *Academy of Management Review* 24 (October 1999): 843–853; Lawrence and Nohria, *Driven: How Human Nature Shapes Our Choices*.

50. CCNMatthews (Canada), "Bridges Team Wins Kelowna's Corporate Spirit Award," News release, (Kelowna, B.C.: 4 October 2004); S. MacNaull, "Earth Day a Natural," *Kelowna Daily Courier*, 23 April 2005, A4.

51. A. C. Strauss, J., *Grounded Theory in Practice* (London: Sage Publications, 1997). For an overview of the importance of qualitative methods in organizational behaviour, see: R. P. Gephart Jr, "Qualitative Research and the *Academy of Management Journal*," *Academy of Management Journal* 47 (2004): 454–462.

52. C. M. Christensen and M. E. Raynor, "Why Hard-Nosed Executives Should Care About Management Theory," *Harvard Business Review* (September 2003): 66–74. For excellent critique of the "one best way" approach in early management scholarship, see: P. F. Drucker, "Management's New Paradigms," *Forbes* (October 5 1998): 152–177.

53. H. L. Tosi and J. W. Slocum Jr., "Contingency Theory: Some Suggested Directions," *Journal of Management* 10 (1984): 9–26.

54. D. M. H. Rousseau, R. J., "Meso Organizational Behavior: Avoiding Three Fundamental Biases," in *Trends in Organizational Behavior*, ed. C. L. Cooper and D. M. Rousseau (Chichester, UK: John Wiley & Sons, 1994), 13–30.

55. H. Trinca, "Her Way," *Boss Magazine*, 9 October 2000, 16.

56. F. E. Kast and J. E. Rosenweig, "General Systems Theory: Applications for Organization and Management," *Academy of Management Journal* (1972): 447–465; P. M. Senge, *The Fifth Discipline: The Art and Practice of the Learning Organization* (New York: Doubleday Currency, 1990); A. De Geus, *The Living Company* (Boston: Harvard Business School Press, 1997); R. T. Pascale, M.

Millemann, and L. Gioja, *Surfing on the Edge of Chaos* (London: Texere, 2000)

57. R. Mitchell, "Feeding the Flames," *Business 2.0* (May 1 2001).

58. V. P. Rindova and S. Kotha, "Continuous 'Morphing': Competing through Dynamic Capabilities, Form, and Function," *Academy of Management Journal* 44 (2001): 1263–1280; J. McCann, "Organizational Effectiveness: Changing Concepts for Changing Environments," *Human Resource Planning* 27, no. 1 (2004): 42–50.

59. R. Martin, "The Virtue Matrix: Calculating the Return on Corporate Responsibility," *Harvard Business Review* 80 (March 2002): 68–85.

60. M. L. Tushman, M. B. Nadler, and D. A. Nadler, *Competing by Design: The Power of Organizational Architecture* (New York: Oxford University Press, 1997).

61. G. Huber, "Organizational Learning: The Contributing Processes and Literature," *Organizational Science* 2 (1991): 88–115; E. C. Nevis, A. J. DiBella, and J. M. Gould, "Understanding Organizations as Learning Systems," *Sloan Management Review* 36 (1995): 73–85; G. Miles *et al.*, "Some Conceptual and Research Barriers to the Utilization of Knowledge," *California Management Review* 40 (Spring 1998): 281–288.

62. T. A. Stewart, *Intellectual Capital: The New Wealth of Organizations* (New York: Currency/Doubleday, 1997); H. Saint-Onge and D. Wallace, *Leveraging Communities of Practice for Strategic Advantage* (Boston: Butterworth-Heinemann, 2003), pp. 9–10; J.-A. Johannessen, B. Olsen, and J. Olaisen, "Intellectual Capital as a Holistic Management Philosophy: A Theoretical Perspective," *International Journal of Information Management* 25, no. 2 (2005): 151–171.

63. N. Bontis, "Assessing Knowledge Assets: A Review of the Models Used to Measure Intellectual Capital," *International Journal of Management Reviews* 3 (2001): 41–60; P. N. Bukh, H. T. Larsen, and J. Mouritsen, "Constructing Intellectual Capital Statements," *Scandinavian Journal of Management* 17 (March 2001): 87–108.

64. There is no complete agreement on the meaning of organizational learning (or learning organization), and the relationship between organizational learning and knowledge management is still somewhat ambiguous. For example, see: S. C. Goh, "The Learning Organization: An Empirical Test of a Normative Perspective," *International Journal of Organization Theory & Behavior* 4, no. 3/4 (August 2001): 329–355; B. R. McElyea, "Knowledge Management, Intellectual Capital, and Learning Organizations: A Triad of Future Management Integration," *Futurics* 26 (2002): 59–65.

65. C. W. Wick and L. S. Leon, "From Ideas to Actions: Creating a Learning Organization," *Human Resource Management* 34 (Summer 1995): 299–311; L. Falkenberg *et al.*, "Knowledge Acquisition Processes for Technology Decisions" in *Proceedings of the Academy of Management 2002 Annual Conference*, (2002), J1–J6.

66. W. Cohen and D. Levinthal, "Absorptive Capacity: A New Perspective on Learning and Innovation," *Administrative Science Quarterly* 35 (1990): 128–152; J. L. Johnson, R. S. Sohi, and R. Grewal, "The Role of Relational Knowledge Stores in Interfirm Partnering," *Journal of Marketing* 68 (July 2004): 21–36; M. Rogers, "Absorptive Capacity and Economic Growth: How Do Countries Catch Up?" *Cambridge Journal of Economics* 28, no. 4 (July 2004): 577–596.

67. G. S. Richards and S. C. Goh, "Implementing Organizational Learning: Toward a Systematic Approach," *The Journal of Public Sector Management* (Autumn 1995): 25–31; C. O'Dell and C. J. Grayson, "If Only We Knew What We Know: Identification and Transfer of Internal Best Practices," *California Management Review* 40 (Spring 1998): 154–174; R. Ruggles, "The State of the Notion: Knowledge Management in Practice," *California Management Review* 40 (Spring 1998): 80–89.

68. R. Garud and A. Kumaraswamy, "Vicious and Virtuous Circles in the Management of Knowledge: The Case of Infosys Technologies," *MIS Quarterly* 29, no. 1 (March 2005): 9–33.

69. E. C. Wenger and W. M. Snyder, "Communities of Practice: The Organizational Frontier," *Harvard Business Review* 78 (January-February 2002): 139–145; Saint-Onge and Wallace, *Leveraging Communities of Practice for Strategic Advantage*.

70. Saint-Onge and Wallace, *Leveraging Communities of Practice for Strategic Advantage*, Chap. 5.

71. D. Cline, "On a Roll," *Augusta Chronicle*, 2 February 2003, D1.

72. H. Beazley, J. Boenisch, and D. Harden, "Knowledge Continuity: The New Management Function," *Journal of Organizational Excellence* 22 (2003): 65–81.

73. P. Withers, "Few Rules Rule," *BC Business*, 1 January 2002, 24.

74. M. E. McGill and J. W. Slocum Jr., "Unlearn the Organization," *Organizational Dynamics* 22, no. 2 (1993): 67–79; D. Lei, J. W. Slocum, and R. A. Pitts, "Designing Organizations for Competitive Advantage: The Power of Unlearning and Learning," *Organizational Dynamics* 27 (Winter 1999): 24–38.

75. A. Wahl and L. Bogomolny, "Leaders Wanted," *Canadian Business*, 1–14 March 2004, 31–36.

CHAPTER TWO

1. N. P. Rothbard, "Enriching or Depleting? The Dynamics of Engagement in Work and Family Roles," *Administrative Science Quarterly* 46, no. 4 (December 2001): 655–684; J. Harter, F. L. Schmidt, and T. L. Hayes, "Business-Unit-Level Relationship between Employee Satisfaction, Employee Engagement, and Business Outcomes: A Meta-Analysis," *Journal of Applied Psychology* 87, no. 2 (2002): 268–279; D. Brown, "Most Canadian Workers Only Moderately Engaged," *Canadian HR Reporter*, 14 July 2003, 1; Towers Perrin, *Working Today: Understanding What Drives Employee Engagement* (Stamford, CT, 2003); R. Baumruk, "The Missing Link: The Role of Employee Engagement in Business Success," *Workspan* 47, no. 11 (November 2004): 48–52; Canada Newswire, "Pfizer Canada Consistently Chosen among the Best Companies to Work for in Canada," *Canada Newswire*, 31 December, 2004; M. Hoekstra, "Fraser Health Authority Unveils Logo," *Delta Optimist* (Delta, B.C.), 26 April 2004; A. Thomas and A. MacDiarmid, "Encouraging Employee Engagement," *CMA Management*, June 2004, 14–15; Auditor General of British Columbia, *Building a Strong Public Service: Reassessing the Quality of the Work Environment in British Columbia's Public Service* (Victoria: Auditor General of British Columbia, February, 2005).

2. Thanks to senior officers in the Singapore Armed Forces for discovering the handy "MARS" acronym. Thanks also to Chris Perryer at the University of Western Australia for pointing out that the full model should be called the "MARS BAR" because the outcomes are "behaviour and results"! The MARS model is a variation of earlier models and writing by several sources, including: E. E. Lawler III and L. W. Porter, "Antecedent Attitudes of Effective Managerial Performance," *Organizational Behavior and Human Performance* 2, no. 2 (1967): 122–142; K. F. Kane, "Special Issue: Situational Constraints and Work Performance," *Human Resource Management Review* 3 (Summer 1993): 83–175.

3. T. A. Judge and R. Illies, "Relationship of Personality to Performance Motivation: A Meta-Analytic Review," *Journal of Applied Psychology* 87, no. 4 (2002): 797–807; S. Roccas *et al.*, "The Big Five Personality Factors and Personal Values," *Personality and Social Psychology* 28 (June 2002): 789–801.

4. C. C. Pinder, *Work Motivation in Organizational Behavior* (Upper Saddle River, N. J.: Prentice-Hall, 1998); G. P. Latham and C. C. Pinder, "Work Motivation Theory and Research at the Dawn of the Twenty-First Century," *Annual Review of Psychology* 56 (2005): 485–516.

5. T. Hellstrom, "Knowledge and Competence Management at Ericsson: Decentralization and Organizational Fit," *Journal of Knowledge Management* 4 (2000); J. A. Conger and D. A. Ready, "Rethinking Leadership Competencies," *Leader to Leader* (Spring 2004): 41–47. For a detailed discussion of competencies, see: L. M. Spencer and S. M. Spencer, *Competence at Work: Models for Superior Performance* (New York: Wiley, 1993).

6. R. Jacobs, "Using Human Resource Functions to Enhance Emotional Intelligence," in *The Emotionally Intelligent Workplace*, ed. C. Cherniss and D. Goleman (San Francisco: Jossey-Bass, 2001), 159–181.

7. S. Brady, "Deep in the Heart of AT&T Dallas," *Cable World*, 7 October 2002, 37.

8. Canada Newswire, "Canadian Organizations Must Work Harder to Productively Engage Employees," *Canada Newswire*, 25 January, 2005.

9. B. Power, "Hanging around Truly Mandatory in Course," *Chronicle-Herald* (Halifax), 25 January 2002.

10. Kane, "Special Issue: Situational Constraints and Work Performance"; S. B. Bacharach and P. Bamberger, "Beyond Situational Constraints: Job Resources Inadequacy and Individual Performance at Work," *Human Resource Management Review* 5, no. 2 (1995): 79–102; G. Johns, "Commentary: In Praise of Context," *Journal of Organizational Behavior* 22 (2001): 31–42.

11. J. P. Campbell, "The Definition and Measurement of Performance in the New Age," in *The Changing Nature of Performance: Implications for Staffing, Motivation, and Development*, ed. D. R. Ilgen and E. D. Pulakos (San Francisco: Jossey-Bass, 1999), 399–429; R. D. Hackett, "Understanding and Predicting Work Performance in the Canadian Military," *Canadian Journal of Behavioural Science* 34, no. 2 (2002): 131–140.

12. D. W. Organ, "Organizational Citizenship Behavior: It's Construct Cleanup Time," *Human Performance* 10 (1997): 85–97; J. A. LePine, A. Erez, and D. E. Johnson, "The Nature and Dimensionality of Organizational Citizenship Behavior: A Critical Review and Meta-Analysis," *Journal of Applied Psychology* 87 (February 2002): 52–65; B. Erickson, "Nature Times Nurture: How Organizations Can Optimize Their People's Contributions," *Journal of Organizational Excellence* 24, no. 1 (Winter 2004): 21–30; M. A. Vey and J. P. Campbell, "In-Role or Extra-Role Organizational Citizenship Behavior: Which Are We Measuring?" *Human Performance* 17, no. 1 (2004): 119–135.

13. M. Rotundo and P. Sackett, "The Relative Importance of Task, Citizenship, and Counterproductive Performance to Global Ratings of Job Performance: A Policy-Capturing Approach," *Journal of Applied Psychology* 87 (February 2002): 66–80 P. D. Dunlop and K. Lee, "Workplace Deviance, Organizational Citizenship Behaviour, and Business Unit Performance: The Bad Apples Do Spoil the Whole Barrel," *Journal of Organizational Behavior* 25 (2004): 67–80.

14. R. Athey, *It's 2008: Do You Know Where Your Talent Is?* (Deloitte & Touche USA, November, 2004); T. Hirsch, *Toward a Bright Future* (Calgary: Canada West Foundation, January, 2005).

15. S. M. Jacoby, "Most Workers Find a Sense of Security in Corporate Life," *Los Angeles Times* (7 September 1998): B5; W. Wyatt, *WorkCanada 2004/2005 —Pursuing Productive Engagement* (Toronto: Watson Wyatt, January, 2005).

16. T. R. Mitchell, B. C. Holtom, and T. W. Lee, "How to Keep Your Best Employees: Developing an Effective Retention Policy," *Academy of Management Executive* 15 (November 2001): 96–108.

17. "Work Absences: Recent Trends— 1997 to 2003," *Perspectives on Labour and Income* 16, no. 2 (Summer 2004): 59–68. For data comparing absenteeism in Canada and other OECD countries, see: R. M. Leontaridi and M. E. Ward, "Dying to Work? An Investigation into Work-Related Stress, Quitting Intentions, and Absenteeism" (paper presented at the Royal Economic Society, University of Warwick, Coventry, UK, March, 2002).

18. I. Ng, "The Effect of Vacation and Sick Leave Policies on Absenteeism," *Canadian Journal of Administrative Sciences* 6 (December 1989): 18–27; D. F. Coleman and N. V. Schaefer, "Weather and Absenteeism," *Canadian Journal of Administrative Sciences* 7, no. 4 (1990): 35–42; D. A. Harrison and J. J. Martocchio, "Time for Absenteeism: A 20-Year Review of Origins, Offshoots, and Outcomes," *Journal of Management* 24 (Spring 1998): 305–350; A. Vaananen *et al.*, "Job Characteristics, Physical and Psychological Symptoms, and Social Support as Antecedents of Sickness Absence among Men and Women in the Private Industrial Sector," *Social Science & Medicine* 57, no. 5 (2003): 807–824.

19. I. Greenberg, "Creating Values in a Competitive Media Industry" (paper presented at the Empire Club of Canada, Toronto, 4 March, 2004).

20. Some of the more popular books that encourage executives to develop values statements include: J. C. Collins and J. I. Porras, *Built to Last: Successful Habits of Visionary Companies* (London: Century, 1995); C. A. O'Reilly III and J. Pfeffer, *Hidden Value* (Cambridge, MA: Harvard Business School Press, 2000); J. M. Kouzes and B. Z. Posner, *The Leadership Challenge*, 3rd ed. (San Francisco: Jossey-Bass, 2002).

21. B. M. Meglino and E. C. Ravlin, "Individual Values in Organizations: Concepts, Controversies, and Research,"

Journal of Management 24, no. 3 (1998): 351–389; B. R. Agle and C. B. Caldwell, "Understanding Research on Values in Business," *Business and Society* 38, no. 3 (September 1999): 326–387; S. Hitlin and J. A. Pilavin, "Values: Reviving a Dormant Concept," *Annual Review of Sociology* 30 (2004): 359–393.

22. D. Lubinski, D. B. Schmidt, and C. P. Benbow, "A 20-Year Stability Analysis of the Study of Values for Intellectually Gifted Individuals from Adolescence to Adulthood," *Journal of Applied Psychology* 81 (1996): 443–451.

23. B. Kabanoff and J. Daly, "Espoused Values in Organisations," *Australian Journal of Management* 27, no. Special issue (2002): 89–104.

24. S. H. Schwartz, "Universals in the Content and Structure of Values: Theoretical Advances and Empirical Tests in 20 Countries," *Advances in Experimental Social Psychology* 25 (1992): 1–65; S. H. Schwartz, "Are There Universal Aspects in the Structure and Contents of Human Values?" *Journal of Social Issues* 50 (1994): 19–45; M. Schwartz, "The Nature of the Relationship between Corporate Codes of Ethics and Behaviour," *Journal of Business Ethics* 32, no. 3 (2001): 247; D. Spini, "Measurement Equivalence of 10 Value Types from the Schwartz Value Survey across 21 Countries," *Journal of Cross-Cultural Psychology* 34, no. 1 (January 2003): 3–23; S. H. Schwartz and K. Boehnke, "Evaluating the Structure of Human Values with Confirmatory Factor Analysis," *Journal of Research in Personality* 38, no. 3 (2004): 230–255.

25. G. R. Maio and J. M. Olson, "Values as Truisms: Evidence and Implications," *Journal of Personality and Social Psychology* 74, no. 2 (1998): 294–311; G. R. Maio *et al.*, "Addressing Discrepancies between Values and Behavior: The Motivating Effect of Reasons," *Journal of Experimental Social Psychology* 37, no. 2 (2001): 104–117; B. Verplanken and R. W. Holland, "Motivated Decision Making: Effects of Activation and Self-Centrality of Values on Choices and Behavior," *Journal of Personality and Social Psychology* 82, no. 3 (2002): 434–447; A. Bardi and S. H. Schwartz, "Values and Behavior: Strength and Structure of Relations," *Personality and Social Psychology Bulletin* 29, no. 10 (October 2003): 1207–1220; M. M.

Bernard and G. R. Maio, "Effects of Introspection About Reasons for Values: Extending Research on Values-as-Truisms," *Social Cognition* 21, no. 1 (2003): 1–25.

26. P. Pruzan, "The Question of Organizational Consciousness: Can Organizations Have Values, Virtues and Visions?" *Journal of Business Ethics* 29 (February 2001): 271–284.

27. K. F. Alam, "Business Ethics in New Zealand Organizations: Views from the Middle and Lower Level Managers," *Journal of Business Ethics* 22 (November 1999): 145–153; Aspen Institute, "Scandals, Economy Alter Attitudes of Next Generation Business Leaders, Mba Student Survey Shows," *Business Wire*, 20 May, 2003.

28. S. Whittaker, "Bringing Your Own Values to Work," *Ottawa Citizen*, 7 April 2001, J1. For research on person-organization values congruence, see: A. L. Kristof, "Person-Organization Fit: An Integrative Review of Its Conceptualizations, Measurement, and Implications," *Personnel Psychology* 49, no. 1 (Spring 1996): 1–49; M. L. Verquer, T. A. Beehr, and S. H. Wagner, "A Meta-Analysis of Relations between Person-Organization Fit and Work Attitudes," *Journal of Vocational Behavior* 63 (2003): 473–489; J. W. Westerman and L. A. Cyr, "An Integrative Analysis of Person-Organization Fit Theories," *International Journal of Selection and Assessment* 12, no. 3 (September 2004): 252–261.

29. K. M. Eisenhardt, J. L. Kahwajy, and L. J. Bourgeois III, "Conflict and Strategic Choice: How Top Management Teams Disagree," *California Management Review* 39 (Winter 1997): 42–62 D. Arnott, *Corporate Cults* (New York: AMACOM, 1999).

30. T. Simons, "Behavioral Integrity: The Perceived Alignment between Managers' Words and Deeds as a Research Focus," *Organization Science* 13, no. 1 (Jan-Feb 2002): 18–35.

31. T. A. Joiner, "The Influence of National Culture and Organizational Culture Alignment on Job Stress and Performance: Evidence from Greece," *Journal of Managerial Psychology* 16 (2001): 229–242 Z. Aycan, R. N. Kanungo, and J. B. P. Sinha, "Organizational Culture and Human Resource Management Practices: The Model of

Culture Fit," *Journal Of Cross-Cultural Psychology* 30 (July 1999): 501–526.

32. C. Fox, "Firms Go Warm and Fuzzy to Lure Staff," *Australian Financial Review*, 15 May 2001, 58.

33. D. Oyserman, H. M. Coon, and M. Kemmelmeier, "Rethinking Individualism and Collectivism: Evaluation of Theoretical Assumptions and Meta-Analyses," *Psychological Bulletin* 128 (2002): 3–72; C. P. Earley and C. B. Gibson, "Taking Stock in Our Progress on Individualism-Collectivism: 100 Years of Solidarity and Community," *Journal of Management* 24 (May 1998): 265–304; F. S. Niles, "Individualism-Collectivism Revisited," *Cross-Cultural Research* 32 (November 1998): 315–341.

34. Oyserman, Coon, and Kemmelmeier, "Rethinking Individualism and Collectivism: Evaluation of Theoretical Assumptions and Meta-Analyses," The relationship between individualism and collectivism is still being debated. Some researchers suggest that there are different types of individualism and collectivism, and some of these types may be opposites. Others say the lack of association is due to the way we measure these concepts. See: E. G. T. Green, J.-C. Deschamps, and D. Paez, "Variation of Individualism and Collectivism within and between 20 Countries," *Journal of Cross-Cultural Psychology* 36, no. 3 (May 2005): 321–339; S. Oishi *et al.*, "The Measurement of Values across Cultures: A Pairwise Comparison Approach," *Journal of Research in Personality* 39, no. 2 (2005): 299–305.

35. M. H. Bond, "Reclaiming the Individual from Hofstede's Ecological Analysis – a 20-Year Odyssey," *Psychological Bulletin* 128 (2002): 73–77; M. Voronov and J. A. Singer, "The Myth of Individualism-Collectivism: A Critical Review," *Journal of Social Psychology* 142 (August 2002): 461–480.

36. G. Hofstede, *Culture's Consequences: Comparing Values, Behaviors, Institutions, and Organizations across Nations*, 2nd ed. (Thousand Oaks, CA: Sage, 2001)

37. G. Hofstede, *Cultures and Organizations: Software of the Mind* (New York: McGraw-Hill, 1991). Hofstede used the terms "masculinity" and "femininity" for achievement and nurturing orientation, respectively. We have adopted the latter to minimize the sexist perspective of these concepts.

38. J. S. Osland *et al.*, "Beyond Sophisticated Stereotyping: Cultural Sensemaking in Context," *Academy of Management Executive* 14 (February 2000): 65–79; Voronov and Singer, "The Myth of Individualism-Collectivism: A Critical Review."

39. P. Brent, "Store Wars," *National Post*, 16 October 2001, FP10; B. Simon, "Canada Warms to Wal-Mart," *New York Times*, 1 September 2001, 1; C. Daniels *et al.*, "Wal-Mart Wars," *Time Canada*, 28 February 2005, 26–28; A. Freeman and M. Strauss, "Wal-Mart— What's to Hate?" *Globe & Mail*, 19 February 2005, F1.

40. M. Adams, *Fire and Ice: The United States, Canada, and the Myth of Converging Values* (Toronto: Penguin Canada, 2004), p. 142.

41. J. Laxer, *The Border: Canada, the U.S. And Dispatches from the 49th Parallel* (Toronto: Anchor Canada, 2004).

42. Adams, Fire and Ice. For earlier research, see: M. Adams, *Sex in the Snow* (Toronto: Penguin Canada, 1998); M. Adams, *Better Happy Than Rich?* (Toronto: Viking, 2001); M. Adams, "What Makes Us Different," *Globe & Mail*, 4 July 2001, A11.

43. C. Cobb, "Canadians Want a Diverse Society: Poll," *Ottawa Citizen*, 18 February 2002, A5; K. May, "Canadian Nationalism Growing: Study," *Ottawa Citizen*, 5 June 2002, A8 C. Boucher, "Canada-US Values: Distinct, Inevitably Carbon Copy, or Narcissism of Small Differences?" *Horizons: Policy Research Initiative* 7, no. 1 (June 2004): 42–49.

44. D. Baer, E. Grabb, and W. Johnston, "National Character, Regional Culture, and the Values of Canadians and Americans," *Canadian Review of Sociology and Anthropology* 30, no. 1 (1993): 13–36; E. Grabb and J. Curtis, *The Four Societies of Canada and the United States* (New York: Oxford University Press, 2005). Evidence of small differences in Canadian-American culture are also reported in: Boucher, "Canada-US Values."

45. Z. Wu and D. Baer, "Attitudes toward Family and Gender Roles: A Comparison of English and French Canadian Women," *Journal of Comparative Family Studies* 27 (Autumn 1996): 437–452. The reference to "two solitudes" comes from: H. McLennan, *Two Solitudes* (Toronto: MacMillan of Canada, 1945).

46. M. Major *et al.*, "Meanings of Work and Personal Values of Canadian Anglophone and Francophone Middle Managers," *Canadian Journal of Administrative Sciences* 11 (September 1994): 251–263; M. Laroche *et al.*, "The Influence of Culture on Pro-Environmental Knowledge, Attitudes, and Behavior: A Canadian Perspective," *Advances In Consumer Research* 23 (1996): 196–202.

47. I. Chapman, D. McCaskill, and D. Newhouse, "Management in Contemporary Aboriginal Organizations," *Canadian Journal of Native Studies* 11, no. 2 (1991): 333–349; L. Redpath and M. O. Nielsen, "A Comparison of Native Culture, Non-Native Culture and New Management Ideology," *Canadian Journal of Administrative Sciences* 14, no. 3 (September 1997): 327–339.

48. R. B. Anderson, "Nunavut Politics: When Caribou Culture Meets Westminster," *Christian Science Monitor*, 28 April 2000, 1.

49. M. Adams, "New Canadians, Old Values?" *Globe & Mail*, 2 March 2005, A17.

50. Business Council of British Columbia, *2004 Biennial Skills and Attributes Survey Report* (Vancouver: Business Council of British Columbia, October, 2004).

51. B. Jang, "Police Nab Fugitive Ex-CEO in Czech Republic," *Globe & Mail*, 10 June 2004, B5; D. Olive, "Westjet CEO's Halo Tarnished," *Toronto Star*, 15 July 2004, D1; D. Olive, "CIBC's an Argument for Bank Mergers," *Toronto Star*, 11 February 2004, E12; S. Pearlstein, "Hollinger Paid for Lord Black's Costly Hubris," *Washington Post*, 3 September 2004, E1; P. Vieira, "Airlines Damaging Reputation, Expert Says: Westjet V. Air Canada," *National Post*, 2 July 2004, FP1; B. A. Masters, "Worldcom's Ebbers Convicted," *Washington Post*, 16 March 2005, A1; C. McLean, "Five Leave Nortel Board," *Globe & Mail*, 11 January 2005; R. Westhead, "Livent Preliminary Hearing Begins," *Toronto Star*, 11 January 2005, D1.

52. P. L. Schumann, "A Moral Principles Framework for Human Resource Management Ethics," *Human Resource Management Review* 11 (Spring-Summer 2001): 93–111; J. Boss, *Analyzing Moral Issues*, 3rd ed. (New York: McGraw-Hill, 2005), Chap. 1; M. G. Velasquez, *Business Ethics: Concepts and Cases*, 6th ed. (Upper Saddle River, NJ: Prentice-Hall, 2006), Chap. 2.

53. T. J. Jones, "Ethical Decision Making by Individuals in Organizations: An Issue Contingent Model," *Academy of Management Review* 16 (1991): 366–395; B. H. Frey, "The Impact of Moral Intensity on Decision Making in a Business Context," *Journal of Business Ethics* 26 (August 2000): 181–195; D. R. May and K. P. Pauli, "The Role of Moral Intensity in Ethical Decision Making," *Business and Society* 41 (March 2002): 84–117.

54. J. R. Sparks and S. D. Hunt, "Marketing Researcher Ethical Sensitivity: Conceptualization, Measurement, and Exploratory Investigation," *Journal of Marketing* 62 (April 1998): 92–109.

55. Alam, "Business Ethics in New Zealand Organizations: Views from the Middle and Lower Level Managers"; K. Blotnicky, "Is Business in Moral Decay?" *Chronicle-Herald* (Halifax), 11 June 2000; B. Stoneman and K. K. Holliday, "Pressure Cooker," *Banking Strategies*, January-February 2001, 13.

56. M. S. Schwartz, "A Code of Ethics for Corporate Code of Ethics," *Journal of Business Ethics* 41 (2002): 27–43; M. S. Schwartz, "Effective Corporate Codes of Ethics: Perceptions of Code Users," *Journal of Business Ethics* 55 (2004): 323–343.

57. "CIBC Plans Ethics Tuneup," *Winnipeg Free Press*, 24 February 2004, C10; P. O'Neil, "Public Works Gets a Course in Ethics," *Ottawa Citizen*, 6 August 2004, A3.

58. E. Aronson, "Integrating Leadership Styles and Ethical Perspectives," *Canadian Journal of Administrative Sciences* 18 (December 2001): 266–276; D. R. May *et al.*, "Developing the Moral Component of Authentic Leadership," *Organizational Dynamics* 32 (2003): 247–260.

59. Roccas *et al.*, "The Big Five Personality Factors and Personal Values."

60. H. C. Triandis and E. M. Suh, "Cultural Influences on Personality," *Annual Review of Psychology* 53 (2002): 133–160.

61. B. Reynolds and K. Karraker, "A Big Five Model of Disposition and Situation Interaction: Why a 'Helpful' Person May Not Always Behave Helpfully," *New Ideas in Psychology* 21 (April 2003): 1–13; W. Mischel, "Toward an Integrative Science of the Person," *Annual Review of Psychology* 55 (2004): 1–22.

62. W. Immen, "Prospective Hires Put to the Test," *Globe & Mail*, 26 January 2005, C1.

63. R. M. Guion and R. F. Gottier, "Validity of Personnel Measures in Personnel Selection," *Personnel Psychology* 18 (1965): 135–164; N. Schmitt *et al.*, "Meta-Analyses of Validity Studies Published between 1964 and 1982 and the Investigation of Study Characteristics," *Personnel Psychology* 37 (1984): 407–422.

64. P. G. Irving, "On the Use of Personality Measures in Personnel Selection," *Canadian Psychology* 34 (April 1993): 208–214.

65. K. M. DeNeve and H. Cooper, "The Happy Personality: A Meta-Analysis of 137 Personality Traits and Subjective Well-Being," *Psychological Bulletin* 124 (September 1998): 197–229; T. A. Judge *et al.*, "Personality and Leadership: A Qualitative and Quantitative Review," *Journal of Applied Psychology* 87, no. 4 (2002): 765–780; R. Ilies, M. W. Gerhardt, and H. Le, "Individual Differences in Leadership Emergence: Integrating Meta-Analytic Findings and Behavioral Genetics Estimates," *International Journal of Selection and Assessment* 12, no. 3 (September 2004): 207–219.

66. This historical review, and the trait descriptions in this section are discussed in: J. M. Digman, "Personality Structure: Emergence of the Five-Factor Model," *Annual Review of Psychology* 41 (1990): 417–440; M. K. Mount and M. R. Barrick, "The Big Five Personality Dimensions: Implications for Research and Practice in Human Resources Management," *Research in Personnel and Human Resources Management* 13 (1995): 153–200; R. J. Schneider and L. M. Hough, "Personality and Industrial/Organizational Psychology," *International Review of Industrial and Organizational Psychology* 10 (1995): 75–129.

67. T. A. Judge and R. Ilies, "Relationship of Personality to Performance Motivation: A Meta-Analytic Review," *Journal of Applied Psychology* 87, no. 4 (2002): 797–807; A. Witt, L. A. Burke, and M. R. Barrick, "The Interactive Effects of Conscientiousness and Agreeableness on Job Performance," *Journal of Applied Psychology* 87 (February 2002): 164–169.

68. C. G. Jung, *Psychological Types*, trans. H. G. Baynes (Princeton, NJ: Princeton University Press, 1971); I. B. Myers, *The Myers-Briggs Type Indicator* (Palo Alto, CA: Consulting Psychologists Press, 1987).

69. M. Gladwell, "Personality Plus," *New Yorker*, 20 September 2004, 42–48; R. B. Kennedy and D. A. Kennedy, "Using the Myers-Briggs Type Indicator in Career Counseling," *Journal of Employment Counseling* 41, no. 1 (March 2004): 38–44.

70. W. L. Johnson and e. al., "A Higher Order Analysis of the Factor Structure of the Myers-Briggs Type Indicator," *Measurement and Evaluation in Counseling and Development* 34 (July 2001): 96–108; R. M. Capraro and M. M. Capraro, "Myers-Briggs Type Indicator Score Reliability across Studies: A Meta-Analytic Reliability Generalization Study," *Educational and Psychological Measurement* 62 (August 2002): 590–602; J. Michael, "Using the Myers -Briggs Type Indicator as a Tool for Leadership Development? Apply with Caution," *Journal of Leadership & Organizational Studies* 10 (Summer 2003): 68–81.

71. P. E. Spector, "Behavior in Organizations as a Function of Employee's Locus of Control," *Psychological Bulletin* 91 (1982): 482–497; J. M. Howell and B. J. Avolio, "Transformational Leadership, Transactional Leadership, Locus of Control, and Support for Innovation: Key Predictors of Consolidated-Business-Unit Performance," *Journal of Applied Psychology* 78 (1993): 891–902; P. E. Spector *et al.*, "Do National Levels of Individualism and Internal Locus of Control Relate to Well-Being: An Ecological Level International Study," *Journal of Organizational Behavior* 22 (2001): 815–832.

72. M. Snyder, *Public Appearances/Private Realities: The Psychology of Self-Monitoring* (New York: W. H. Freeman, 1987).

73. R. J. Ellis and S. E. Cronshaw, "Self-Monitoring and Leader Emergence: A Test of Moderator Effects," *Small Group Research* 23 (1992): 113–129; M. Kilduff and D. V. Day, "Do Chameleons Get Ahead? The Effects of Self-Monitoring on Managerial Careers," *Academy of Management Journal* 37 (1994): 1047–1060; M. A. Warech *et al.*, "Self-Monitoring and 360-Degree Ratings," *Leadership Quarterly* 9 (Winter 1998): 449–473; A. Mehra, M. Kilduff, and D. J. Brass, "The Social Networks of High and Low Self-Monitors: Implications for Workplace Performance," *Administrative Science Quarterly* 46 (March 2001): 121–146.

74. J. L. Holland, *Making Vocational Choices: A Theory of Careers* (Englewood Cliffs, N. J.: Prentice Hall, 1973).

75. G. D. Gottfredson and J. L. Holland, "A Longitudinal Test of the Influence of Congruence: Job Satisfaction, Competency Utilization, and Counterproductive Behavior," *Journal of Counseling Psychology* 37 (1990): 389–398; A. Furnham, "Vocational Preference and P-O Fit: Reflections on Holland's Theory of Vocational Choice," *Applied Psychology: An International Review* 50 (2001): 5–29.

76. J. Tupponce, "Listening to Those Inner Voices," *Richmond Times-Dispatch*, 11 May 2003, S3.

77. Furnham, "Vocational Preference and P-O Fit: Reflections on Holland's Theory of Vocational Choice,"; R. P. Tett and D. D. Burnett, "A Personality Trait-Based Interactionist Model of Job Performance," *Journal of Applied Psychology* 88, no. 3 (2003): 500–517; W. Yang, G. S. Stokes, and C. H. Hui, "Cross-Cultural Validation of Holland's Interest Structure in Chinese Population," *Journal of Vocational Behavior* (2005): In Press.

78. G. D. Gottfredson, "John L. Holland's Contributions to Vocational Psychology: A Review and Evaluation," *Journal of Vocational Behavior* 55, no. 1 (1999): 15–40.

CHAPTER THREE

1. B. Oswald, "Venture Series Lets Bosses Walk in Their Workers' Shoes," *Winnipeg Free Press*, 11 October 2003, C5; E. Pope, "Domino's Puts Execs on the Line," *Detroit News*, 1 August 2003; W. Frey, "Rubbish Boy Doing Well as Junk Man," *Metro-Vancouver*, 25 April 2005, 11; A. Swift, "Along for the Ride," *Chronicle-Herald* (Halifax), 18 April 2005.

2. Plato, *The Republic*, trans. D. Lee (Harmondsworth, England: Penguin, 1955).

3. R. H. Fazio, D. R. Roskos-Ewoldsen, and M. C. Powell, "Attitudes, Perception, and Attention," in *The Heart's Eye: Emotional Influences in Perception and Attention*, ed. P. M. Niedenthal and S. Kitayama (San Diego,CA: Academic Press, 1994), 197–216.

4. The effect of the target in selective attention is known as "bottom-up selection"; the effect of the perceiver's psychodynamics on this process is known as "top-down selection". C. E. Connor, H. E. Egeth, and S. Yantis, "Visual Attention: Bottom-up Versus Top-Down," *Current Biology* 14, no. 19 (2004): R850–R852.

5. A. Mack *et al.*, "Perceptual Organization and Attention," *Cognitive Psychology* 24, no. 4 (1992): 475–501; A. R. Damasio, *Descartes' Error: Emotion, Reason, and the Human Brain* (New York: Putnam Sons, 1994).

6. C. N. Macrae *et al.*, "Tales of the Unexpected: Executive Function and Person Perception," *Journal of Personality and Social Psychology* 76 (1999): 200–213; C. Frith, "A Framework for Studying the Neural Basis of Attention," *Neuropsychologia* 39, no. 12 (2001): 1367–1371; N. Lavie, "Distracted and Confused? Selective Attention under Load," *Trends in Cognitive Sciences* 9, no. 2 (2005): 75–82.

7. C. N. Macrae and G. V. Bodenhausen, "Social Cognition: Thinking Categorically About Others," *Annual Review of Psychology* 51 (2000): 93–120. For literature on the automaticity of the perceptual organization and interpretation process, see: J. A. Bargh, "The Cognitive Monster: The Case against the Controllability of Automatic Stereotype Effects," in *Dual Process Theories in Social Psychology*, ed. S. Chaiken and Y. Trope (New York: Guilford, 1999), 361–382; J. A. Bargh and M. J. Ferguson, "Beyond Behaviorism: On the Automaticity of Higher Mental Processes," *Psychological Bulletin* 126, no. 6 (2000): 925–945; M. Gladwell, *Blink: The Power of Thinking without Thinking* (New York: Little, Brown, 2005).

8. E. M. Altmann and B. D. Burns, "Streak Biases in Decision Making: Data and a Memory Model," *Cognitive Systems Research* 6, no. 1 (2005): 5–16. For discussion of cognitive closure and perception, see: A. W. Kruglanski and D. M. Webster, "Motivated Closing of the Mind: "Seizing" and "Freezing"," *Psychological Review* 103, no. 2 (1996): 263–283.

9. N. Ambady and R. Rosenthal, "Half a Minute: Predicting Teacher Evaluations from Thin Slices of Nonverbal Behavior and Physical Attractiveness," *Journal of Personality and Social Psychology* 64, no. 3 (March 1993): 431–441. For other research on thin slices, see: N. Ambady and R. Rosenthal, "Thin Slices of Expressive Behavior as Predictors of Interpersonal Consequences: A Meta-Analysis," *Psychological Bulletin* 111, no. 2 (1992): 256–274; N. Ambady *et al.*, "Surgeons' Tone of Voice: A Clue to Malpractice History," *Surgery* 132, no. 1 (July 2002): 5–9.

10. P. M. Senge, *The Fifth Discipline: The Art and Practice of the Learning Organization* (New York: Doubleday Currency, 1990), Chap. 10; P. N. Johnson-Laird, "Mental Models and Deduction," *Trends in Cognitive Sciences* 5, no. 10 (2001): 434–442; A. B. Markman and D. Gentner, "Thinking," *Annual Review of Psychology* 52 (2001): 223–247; T. J. Chermack, "Mental Models in Decision Making and Implications for Human Resource Development," *Advances in Developing Human Resources* 5, no. 4 (2003): 408–422.

11. J. M. Beyer and e. al., "The Selective Perception of Managers Revisited," *Academy of Management Journal* 40 (June 1997): 716–737; J. Rupert, "We Haven't Forgotten About Her," *Ottawa Citizen*, December 6 1999; "Abduction of Toronto Girl Not Random Act: Police," *CBC News Online*, 23 October 2003.

12. H. Tajfel, *Social Identity and Intergroup Relations* (Cambridge: Cambridge University Press, 1982); B. E. Ashforth and F. Mael, "Social Identity Theory and the Organization," *Academy of Management Review* 14 (1989): 20–39; M. A. Hogg and D. J. Terry, "Social Identity and Self-Categorization Processes in Organizational Contexts," *Academy of Management Review* 25 (January 2000): 121–140; S. A. Haslam, R. A. Eggins, and K. J. Reynolds, "The Aspire Model: Actualizing Social and Personal Identity Resources to Enhance Organizational Outcomes," *Journal of Occupational and Organizational Psychology* 76 (2003): 83–113. Although this topic is labelled "social identity theory," it also incorporates an extension of social identity theory, called self-categorization theory.

13. J. E. Dutton, J. M. Dukerich, and C. V. Harquail, "Organizational Images and Member Identification," *Administrative Science Quarterly* 39 (June 1994): 239–263; B. Simon and C. Hastedt, "Self-Aspects as Social Categories: The Role of Personal Importance and Valence," *European Journal of Social Psychology* 29 (1999): 479–487.

14. M. A. Hogg *et al.*, "The Social Identity Perspective: Intergroup Relations, Self-Conception, and Small Groups," *Small Group Research* 35, no. 3 (June 2004): 246–276; J. Jetten, R. Spears, and T. Postmes, "Intergroup Distinctiveness and Differentiation: A Meta-Analytic Integration," *Journal of Personality and Social Psychology* 86, no. 6 (2004): 862–879.

15. J. W. Jackson and E. R. Smith, "Conceptualizing Social Identity: A New Framework and Evidence for the Impact of Different Dimensions," *Personality & Social Psychology Bulletin* 25 (January 1999): 120–135.

16. L. Falkenberg, "Improving the Accuracy of Stereotypes within the Workplace," *Journal of Management* 16 (1990): 107–118; S. T. Fiske, "Stereotyping, Prejudice, and Discrimination," in *Handbook of Social Psychology*, ed. D. T. Gilbert, S. T. Fiske, and G. Lindzey, Fourth ed. (New York: McGraw-Hill, 1998), 357–411; Macrae and Bodenhausen, "Social Cognition: Thinking Categorically About Others."

17. C. N. Macrae, A. B. Milne, and G. V. Bodenhausen, "Stereotypes as Energy-Saving Devices: A Peek inside the Cognitive Toolbox," *Journal of Personality and Social Psychology* 66 (1994): 37–47; J. W. Sherman *et al.*, "Stereotype Efficiency Reconsidered: Encoding Flexibility under Cognitive Load," *Journal of Personality and Social Psychology* 75 (1998): 589–606; Macrae and Bodenhausen, "Social Cognition: Thinking Categorically About Others."

18. L. Sinclair and Z. Kunda, "Motivated Stereotyping of Women: She's Fine If She Praised Me but Incompetent If She Criticized Me," *Personality and Social Psychology Bulletin* 26 (November 2000): 1329–1342; J. C. Turner and S. A. Haslam, "Social Identity, Organizations, and Leadership," in *Groups at Work: Theory and Research*, ed. M. E. Turner (Mahwah, NJ: Lawrence Erlbaum Associates, 2001), 25–65.

19. Y. Lee, L. J. Jussim, and C. R. McCauley, *Stereotype Accuracy: Toward Appreciating Group Differences*, vol.

American Psychological Association (Washington, DC: 1996); S. Madon and e. al., "The Accuracy and Power of Sex, Social Class, and Ethnic Stereotypes: A Naturalistic Study in Person Perception," *Personality & Social Psychology Bulletin* 24 (December 1998): 1304–1318; F. T. McAndrew, "A Multicultural Study of Stereotyping in English-Speaking Countries," *Journal of Social Psychology* (August 2000): 487–502.

20. A. L. Friedman and S. R. Lyne, "The Beancounter Stereotype: Towards a General Model of Stereotype Generation," *Critical Perspectives on Accounting* 12, no. 4 (2001): 423–451.

21. S. Hayward, "Discrimination Troubles," *Metro-Toronto*, 21 March 2005.

22. S. O. Gaines and E. S. Reed, "Prejudice: From Allport to Dubois," *American Psychologist* 50 (February 1995): 96–103; Fiske, "Stereotyping, Prejudice, and Discrimination"; M. Billig, "Henri Tajfel's 'Cognitive Aspects of Prejudice' and the Psychology of Bigotry," *British Journal of Social Psychology* 41 (2002): 171–188; M. Hewstone, M. Rubin, and H. Willis, "Intergroup Bias," *Annual Review of Psychology* 53 (2002): 575–604.

23. M. G. Reed, "Marginality and Gender at Work in Forestry Communities of British Columbia, Canada," *Journal of Rural Studies* 19, no. 3 (2003): 373–389; M. Patriquin, "Quebec Farm Segregated Black Workers," *Globe & Mail*, 30 April 2005, A1.

24. J. A. Bargh and T. L. Chartrand, "The Unbearable Automaticity of Being," *American Psychologist* 54, no. 7 (July 1999): 462–479; S. T. Fiske, "What We Know Now About Bias and Intergroup Conflict, the Problem of the Century," *Current Directions in Psychological Science* 11, no. 4 (August 2002): 123–128. For recent evidence that shows that intensive training can minimize stereotype activation, see: K. Kawakami *et al.*, "Just Say No (to Stereotyping): Effects of Training in the Negation of Stereotypic Associations on Stereotype Activation," *Journal of Personality and Social Psychology* 78, no. 5 (2000): 871–888; E. A. Plant, B. M. Peruche, and D. A. Butz, "Eliminating Automatic Racial Bias: Making Race Non-Diagnostic for Responses to Criminal Suspects," *Journal of Experimental Social Psychology* 41, no. 2 (2005): 141–156.

25. M. Bendick, M. L. Egan, and S. M. Lofhjelm, "Workforce Diversity Training: From Anti-Discrimination Compliance to Organizational Development HR," *Human Resource Planning* 24 (2001): 10–25; L. Roberson, C. T. Kulik, and M. B. Pepper, "Using Needs Assessment to Resolve Controversies in Diversity Training Design," *Group & Organization Management* 28, no. 1 (March 2003): 148–174; D. E. Hogan and M. Mallott, "Changing Racial Prejudice through Diversity Education," *Journal of College Student Development* 46, no. 2 (March/April 2005): 115–125.

26. T. F. Pettigrew, "Intergroup Contact Theory," *Annual Review of Psychology* 49 (1998): 65–85; S. Brickson, "The Impact of Identity Orientation on Individual and Organizational Outcomes in Demographically Diverse Settings," *Academy of Management Review* 25 (January 2000): 82–101; J. Dixon and K. Durrheim, "Contact and the Ecology of Racial Division: Some Varieties of Informal Segregation," *British Journal of Social Psychology* 42 (March 2003): 1–23.

27. B. F. Reskin, "The Proximate Causes of Employment Discrimination," *Contemporary Sociology* 29 (March 2000): 319–328.

28. H. H. Kelley, *Attribution in Social Interaction* (Morristown, N.J.: General Learning Press, 1971).

29. J. M. Feldman, "Beyond Attribution Theory: Cognitive Processes in Performance Appraisal," *Journal of Applied Psychology* 66 (1981): 127–148.

30. J. M. Crant and T. S. Bateman, "Assignment of Credit and Blame for Performance Outcomes," *Academy of Management Journal* 36 (1993): 7–27; B. Weiner, "Intrapersonal and Interpersonal Theories of Motivation from an Attributional Perspective," *Educational Psychology Review* 12 (2000): 1–14; N. Bacon and P. Blyton, "Worker Responses to Teamworking: Exploring Employee Attributions of Managerial Motives," *International Journal of Human Resource Management* 16, no. 2 (February 2005): 238–255.

31. Fundamental attribution error is part of a larger phenomenon known as correspondence bias. See: D. T. Gilbert and P. S. Malone, "The Correspondence Bias," *Psychological Bulletin* 117, no. 1 (1995): 21–38.

32. I. Choi, R. E. Nisbett, and A. Norenzayan, "Causal Attribution across Cultures: Variation and Universality," *Psychological Bulletin* 125, no. 1 (1999): 47–63; D. S. Krull *et al.*, "The Fundamental Fundamental Attribution Error: Correspondence Bias in Individualist and Collectivist Cultures," *Personality and Social Psychology Bulletin* 25, no. 10 (October 1999): 1208–1219; R. E. Nisbett, *The Geography of Thought: How Asians and Westerners Think Differently—and Why* (New York: Free Press, 2003), Chap. 5.

33. P. Rosenthal and D. Guest, "Gender Difference in Managers' Causal Explanations for Their Work Performance: A Study in Two Organizations," *Journal of Occupational & Organizational Psychology* 69 (1996): 145–151. The performance ratings study is reported in: P. J. Taylor and J. L. Pierce, "Effects of Introducing a Performance Management System on Employees' Subsequent Attitudes and Effort," *Public Personnel Management* 28 (Fall 1999): 423–452.

34. F. Lee and L. Z. Tiedens, "Who's Being Served? "Self-Serving" Attributions in Social Hierarchies," *Organizational Behavior and Human Decision Processes* 84, no. 2 (2001): 254–287; E. W. K. Tsang, "Self-Serving Attributions in Corporate Annual Reports: A Replicated Study," *Journal of Management Studies* 39, no. 1 (January 2002): 51–65.

35. A. R. Remo, "Nurture the Good to Create an Asset," *Philippine Daily Inquirer*, 6 December 2004.

36. Similar models are presented in D. Eden, "Self-Fulfilling Prophecy as a Management Tool: Harnessing Pygmalion," *Academy of Management Review* 9 (1984): 64–73; R. H. G. Field and D. A. Van Seters, "Management by Expectations (MBE): The Power of Positive Prophecy," *Journal of General Management* 14 (Winter 1988): 19–33; D. O. Trouilloud *et al.*, "The Influence of Teacher Expectations on Student Achievement in Physical Education Classes: Pygmalion Revisited," *European Journal of Social Psychology* 32 (2002): 591–607.

37. D. Eden, "Interpersonal Expectations in Organizations," in *Interpersonal Expectations: Theory, Research, and*

Applications (Cambridge, UK: Cambridge University Press, 1993), 154–178.

38. D. Eden, "Pygmalion Goes to Boot Camp: Expectancy, Leadership, and Trainee Performance," *Journal of Applied Psychology* 67 (1982): 194–199; R. P. Brown and E. C. Pinel, "Stigma on My Mind: Individual Differences in the Experience of Stereotype Threat," *Journal of Experimental Social Psychology* 39, no. 6 (2003): 626–633.

39. S. Madon *et al.*, "Self-Fulfilling Prophecies: The Synergistic Accumulative Effect of Parents' Beliefs on Children's Drinking Behavior," *Psychological Science* 15, no. 12 (2005): 837–845 A. E. Smith, L. Jussim, and J. Eccles, "Do Self-Fulfilling Prophecies Accumulate, Dissipate, or Remain Stable over Time?" *Journal of Personality and Social Psychology* 77, no. 3 (1999): 548–565.

40. S. Madon, L. Jussim, and J. Eccles, "In Search of the Powerful Self-Fulfilling Prophecy," *Journal of Personality and Social Psychology* 72, no. 4 (April 1997): 791–809.

41. D. Eden *et al.*, "Implanting Pygmalion Leadership Style through Workshop Training: Seven Field Experiments," *Leadership Quarterly* 11 (2000): 171–210; S. S. White and E. A. Locke, "Problems with the Pygmalion Effect and Some Proposed Solutions," *Leadership Quarterly* 11 (Autumn 2000): 389–415; H. A. Wilkinson, "Hope, False Hope, and Self-Fulfilling Prophecy," *Surgical Neurology* 63, no. 1 (2005): 84–86. For literature on positive organizational behaviour, see: K. Cameron, J. E. Dutton, and R. E. Quinn, *Positive Organizational Scholarship: Foundations of a New Discipline* (San Francisco: Berrett Koehler, 2003).

42. C. L. Kleinke, *First Impressions: The Psychology of Encountering Others* (Englewood Cliffs, N.J.: Prentice Hall, 1975); E. A. Lind, L. Kray, and L. Thompson, "Primacy Effects in Justice Judgments: Testing Predictions from Fairness Heuristic Theory," *Organizational Behavior and Human Decision Processes* 85 (July 2001): 189–210; O. Ybarra, "When First Impressions Don't Last: The Role of Isolation and Adaptation Processes in the Revision of Evaluative Impressions," *Social Cognition* 19 (October 2001): 491–520.

43. D. D. Steiner and J. S. Rain, "Immediate and Delayed Primacy and Recency Effects in Performance Evaluation," *Journal of Applied Psychology* 74 (1989): 136–142; K. T. Trotman, "Order Effects and Recency: Where Do We Go from Here?" *Accounting & Finance* 40 (2000): 169–182; W. Green, "Impact of the Timing of an Inherited Explanation on Auditors' Analytical Procedures Judgements," *Accounting and Finance* 44 (2004): 369–392.

44. W. H. Cooper, "Ubiquitous Halo," *Psychological Bulletin* 90 (1981): 218–244; K. R. Murphy, R. A. Jako, and R. L. Anhalt, "Nature and Consequences of Halo Error: A Critical Analysis," *Journal of Applied Psychology* 78 (1993): 218–225; T. H. Feeley, "Comment on Halo Effects in Rating and Evaluation Research," *Human Communication Research* 28, no. 4 (October 2002): 578–586.

45. G. G. Sherwood, "Self-Serving Biases in Person Perception: A Re-Examination of Projection as a Mechanism of Defense," *Psychological Bulletin* 90 (1981): 445–459; R. L. Gross and S. E. Brodt, "How Assumptions of Consensus Undermine Decision Making," *Sloan Management Review* (January 2001): 86–94.

46. C. Duan and C. E. Hill, "The Current State of Empathy Research," *Journal of Counseling Psychology* 43 (1996): 261–274; W. G. Stephen and K. A. Finlay, "The Role of Empathy in Improving Intergroup Relations," *Journal of Social Issues* 55 (Winter 1999): 729–743; S. K. Parker and C. M. Axtell, "Seeing Another Viewpoint: Antecedents and Outcomes of Employee Perspective Taking," *Academy of Management Journal* 44 (December 2001): 1085–1100; G. J. Vreeke and I. L. van der Mark, "Empathy, an Integrative Model," *New Ideas in Psychology* 21, no. 3 (2003): 177–207.

47. F. Shalom, "Catching the Next Wave at Pratt," *Montreal Gazette*, 27 July 2002, C3. For details about coaching and empathy, see: D. Goleman, R. Boyatzis, and A. McKee, *The New Leaders* (London: Little, Brown, 2002).

48. T. W. Costello and S. S. Zalkind, *Psychology in Administration: A Research Orientation* (Englewood Cliffs, N.J.: Prentice Hall, 1963), pp. 45–46; J. M. Kouzes and B. Z. Posner, *The Leadership Challenge*, 3rd ed. (San Francisco: Jossey-Bass, 2002), Chap. 3.

49. J. Luft, *Group Processes* (Palo Alto, Calif: Mayfield Publishing, 1984). For a variation of this model, see: J. Hall, "Communication Revisited," *California Management Review* 15 (Spring 1973): 56–67.

50. L. C. Miller and D. A. Kenny, "Reciprocity of Self-Disclosure at the Individual and Dyadic Levels: A Social Relations Analysis," *Journal of Personality and Social Psychology* 50 (1986): 713–719.

51. G. Condon, "Walking in Another's Shoes," *Hartford Courant* (Connecticut), July 11 2003, B1.

52. "Wipro: Leadership in the Midst of Rapid Growth," *Knowledge@Wharton*, February 2005.

53. I. Nonaka and H. Takeuchi, *The Knowledge-Creating Company* (New York: Oxford University Press, 1995); E. N. Brockmann and W. P. Anthony, "Tacit Knowledge and Strategic Decision Making," *Group & Organization Management* 27 (December 2002): 436–455; P. Duguid, "'The Art of Knowing': Social and Tacit Dimensions of Knowledge and the Limits of the Community of Practice," *The Information Society* 21 (2005): 109–118.

54. B. F. Skinner, *About Behaviorism* (New York: Alfred A. Knopf, 1974); J. Komaki, T. Coombs, and S. Schepman, "Motivational Implications of Reinforcement Theory," in *Motivation and Leadership at Work*, ed. R. M. Steers, L. W. Porter, and G. A. Bigley (New York: McGraw-Hill, 1996), 34–52; R. G. Miltenberger, *Behavior Modification: Principles and Procedures* (Pacific Grove, CA: Brooks/Cole, 1997).

55. T. K. Connellan, *How to Improve Human Performance* (New York: Harper & Row, 1978), pp. 48–57; F. Luthans and R. Kreitner, *Organizational Behavior Modification and Beyond* (Glenview, Ill.: Scott, Foresman, 1985), pp. 85–88.

56. Miltenberger, *Behavior Modification: Principles and Procedures*, Chap. 4–6.

57. Punishment can also include removing a pleasant consequence, such as when employees must switch from business to economy class flying when their sales fall below the threshold for top tier sales "stars".

58. T. R. Hinkin and C. A. Schriesheim, "If You Don't Hear from Me You Know You Are Doing Fine"," *Cornell Hotel & Restaurant Administration Quarterly* 45, no. 4 (November 2004): 362–372.

59. L. K. Trevino, "The Social Effects of Punishment in Organizations: A Justice Perspective," *Academy of Management Review* 17 (1992): 647–676; L. E. Atwater *et al.*, "Recipient and Observer Reactions to Discipline: Are Managers Experiencing Wishful Thinking?" *Journal of Organizational Behavior* 22, no. 3 (May 2001): 249–270.

60. G. P. Latham and V. L. Huber, "Schedules of Reinforcement: Lessons from the Past and Issues for the Future," *Journal of Organizational Behavior Management* 13 (1992): 125–149; B. A. Williams, "Challenges to Timing-Based Theories of Operant Behavior," *Behavioural Processes* 62 (April 2003): 115–123.

61. T. C. Mawhinney, "Philosophical and Ethical Aspects of Organizational Behavior Management: Some Evaluative Feedback," *Journal of Organizational Behavior Management* 6 (Spring 1984): 5–13; G. A. Merwin, J. A. Thomason, and E. E. Sandford, "A Methodological and Content Review of Organizational Behavior Management in the Private Sector: 1978–1986," *Journal of Organizational Behavior Management* 10 (1989): 39–57; "New Warnings on the Fine Points of Safety Incentives," *Pay for Performance Report*, September 2002.

62. Bargh and Ferguson, "Beyond Behaviorism: On the Automaticity of Higher Mental Processes." Some writers argue that behaviourists long ago accepted the relevance of cognitive processes in behaviour modification. See: I. Kirsch *et al.*, "The Role of Cognition in Classical and Operant Conditioning," *Journal of Clinical Psychology* 60, no. 4 (April 2004): 369–392.

63. A. Bandura, *Social Foundations of Thought and Action: A Social Cognitive Theory* (Englewood Cliffs, N.J: Prentice Hall, 1986).

64. A. Pescuric and W. C. Byham, "The New Look of Behavior Modeling," *Training & Development* 50 (July 1996): 24–30.

65. M. E. Schnake, "Vicarious Punishment in a Work Setting," *Journal of Applied Psychology* 71 (1986): 343–345; Trevino, "The Social Effects of Punishment in Organizations: A Justice Perspective"; J. B. DeConinck, "The Effect of Punishment on Sales Managers' Outcome Expectancies and Responses to Unethical Sales Force Behavior," *American Business Review* 21, no. 2 (June 2003): 135–140.

66. A. Bandura, "Self-Reinforcement: Theoretical and Methodological Considerations," Behaviorism 4 (1976): 135–155; C. A. Frayne and J. M. Geringer, "Self-Management Training for Improving Job Performance: A Field Experiment Involving Salespeople," *Journal of Applied Psychology* 85, no. 3 (June 2000): 361–372; J. B. Vancouver and D. V. Day, "Industrial and Organisation Research on Self-Regulation: From Constructs to Applications," *Applied Psychology* 54, no. 2 (April 2005): 155–185.

67. D. Woodruff, "Putting Talent to the Test," *Wall Street Journal Europe*, November 14 2000, 25. The simulation events described here were experienced by the author of this article, but we reasonably assume that Mandy Chooi, who also completed the simulation, experienced similar scenarios.

68. D. A. Kolb, *Experiential Learning* (Englewood Cliffs, NJ: Prentice-Hall, 1984); S. Gherardi, D. Nicolini, and F. Odella, "Toward a Social Understanding of How People Learn in Organizations," *Management Learning* 29 (September 1998): 273–297; D. A. Kolb, R. E. Boyatzis, and C. Mainemelis, "Experiential Learning Theory: Previous Research and New Directions," in *Perspectives on Thinking, Learning, and Cognitive Styles*, ed. R. J. Sternberg and L. F. Zhang (Mahwah, NJ: Lawrence Erlbaum, 2001), 227–248.

69. I. Teotonio, "Rescuers Pull 'Victims' from Rubble," *Toronto Star*, April 8, 2005, B01, B03.

70. J. Jusko, "Always Lessons to Learn," *Industry Week* (February 15 1999): 23; R. Farson and R. Keyes, "The Failure-Tolerant Leader," *Harvard Business Review* 80 (August 2002): 64–71.

71. R. W. Revans, *The Origin and Growth of Action Learning* (London: Chartwell Bratt, 1982), pp. 626–627; M. J. Marquardt, *Optimizing the Power of Action Learning: Solving Problems and Building Leaders in Real Time* (Palo Alto, CA: Davies-Black, 2004).

72. J. A. Conger and K. Xin, "Executive Education in the 21st Century," *Journal of Management Education* (February 2000): 73–101; R. M. Fulmer, P. Gibbs, and M. Goldsmith, "Developing Leaders: How Winning Companies Keep on Winning," *Sloan Management Review*

(October 2000): 49–59. Action learning at TB Bank is described in: D. Brown, "Action Learning Popular in Europe, Not yet Caught on in Canada," *Canadian HR Reporter*, 25 April 2005, 1–2.

73. M. J. Marquardt, "Harnessing the Power of Action Learning," *T+D*, June 2004, 26–32.

CHAPTER FOUR

1. K. Macklem, "Vancity Confidential," *Maclean's*, 11–18 October 2004, 22; B. Morton, "Positive Work Environment Keeps Them Happy, Staffers Say," *Vancouver Sun*, 5 October 2004, D1; Y. Zacharias, "Laughing Is Good for Business," *Vancouver Sun*, 1 April 2004, F1.

2. The centrality of emotions in marketing, economics, and sociology is discussed in: G. Loewenstein, "Emotions in Economic Theory and Eonomic Behavior," *American Economic Review* 90, no. 2 (May 2000): 426–432; D. S. Massey, "A Brief History of Human Society: The Origin and Role of Emotion in Social Life," *American Sociological Review* 67 (February 2002): 1–29; J. O'Shaughnessy and N. J. OShaughnessy, *The Marketing Power of Emotion* (New York: Oxford University Press, 2003).

3. The definition presented here is constructed from information in the following sources: N. M. Ashkanasy, W. J. Zerbe, and C. E. J. Hartel, "Introduction: Managing Emotions in a Changing Workplace," in *Managing Emotions in the Workplace*, ed. N. M. Ashkanasy, W. J. Zerbe, and C. E. J. Hartel (Armonk, N. Y.: M. E. Sharpe, 2002), 3–18; H. M. Weiss, "Conceptual and Empirical Foundations for the Study of Affect at Work," in *Emotions in the Workplace*, ed. R. G. Lord, R. J. Klimoski, and R. Kanfer (San Francisco: Jossey-Bass, 2002), 20–63. However, the meaning of emotions is still being debated. See, for example: M. Cabanac, "What Is Emotion?" *Behavioural Processes* 60 (2002): 69–83.

4. R. Kanfer and R. J. Klimoski, "Affect and Work: Looking Back to the Future," in *Emotions in the Workplace*, ed. R. G. Lord, R. J. Klimoski, and R. Kanfer (San Francisco: Jossey-Bass, 2002), 473–490; J. A. Russell, "Core Affect and the Psychological Construction of Emotion," *Psychological Review* 110, no. 1 (2003): 145–172.

5. R. B. Zajonc, "Emotions," in *Handbook of Social Psychology*, ed. D. T.

Gilbert, S. T. Fiske, and L. Gardner (New York: Oxford University press, 1998), 591–634.

6. N. A. Remington, L. R. Fabrigar, and P. S. Visser, "Reexamining the Circumplex Model of Affect," *Journal of Personality and Social Psychology* 79, no. 2 (2000): 286–300; R. J. Larson, E. Diener, and R. E. Lucas, "Emotion: Models, Measures, and Differences," in *Emotions in the Workplace*, ed. R. G. Lord, R. J. Klimoski, and R. Kanfer (San Francisco: Jossey-Bass, 2002), 64–113.

7. A. H. Eagly and S. Chaiken, The *Psychology of Attitudes* (Orlando, FL: Harcourt Brace Jovanovich, 1993); A. P. Brief, *Attitudes in and around Organizations* (Thousand Oaks, CA: Sage, 1998). There is ongoing debate about whether attitudes represent only feelings or all three components described here. However, those who adopt the single factor perspective still refer to beliefs as the cognitive *component* of attitudes. For example, see: I. Ajzen, "Nature and Operation of Attitudes," *Annual Review of Psychology* 52 (2001): 27–58.

8. S. D. Farley and M. F. Stasson, "Relative Influences of Affect and Cognition on Behavior: Are Feelings or Beliefs More Related to Blood Donation Intentions?" *Experimental Psychology* 50, no. 1 (2003): 55–62.

9. C. D. Fisher, "Mood and Emotions While Working: Missing Pieces of Job Satisfaction?" *Journal of Organizational Behavior* 21 (2000): 185–202; M. Pergini and R. P. Bagozzi, "The Role of Desires and Anticipated Emotions in Goal-Directed Behaviors: Broadening and Deepening the Theory of Planned Behavior," *British Journal of Social Psychology* 40 (March 2001): 79–; J. D. Morris *et al.*, "The Power of Affect: Predicting Intention," *Journal of Advertising Research* 42 (May–June 2002): 7–17. For a review of the predictability of the traditional attitude model, see: C. J. Armitage and M. Conner, "Efficacy of the Theory of Planned Behavior: A Meta-Analytic Review," *British Journal of Social Psychology* 40 (2001): 471–499.

10. This explanation refers to a singular "cognitive (logical reasoning) centre" and "emotional centre." While many scholars do refer to a single location for most emotional transactions, an emerging view is that both the emotional and rational "centres" are dis-tributed throughout the brain. J. Schulkin, B. L. Thompson, and J. B. Rosen, "Demythologizing the Emotions: Adaptation, Cognition, and Visceral Representations of Emotion in the Nervous System," *Brain and Cognition (Affective Neuroscience)* 52 (June 2003): 15–23.

11. J. A. Bargh and M. J. Ferguson, "Beyond Behaviorism: On the Automaticity of Higher Mental Processes," *Psychological Bulletin* 126, no. 6 (2000): 925–945; R. H. Fazio, "On the Automatic Activation of Associated Evaluations: An Overview," *Cognition and Emotion* 15, no. 2 (2001): 115–141; M. Gladwell, *Blink: The Power of Thinking without Thinking* (New York: Little, Brown, 2005).

12. A. R. *Damasio, Descartes' Error: Emotion, Reason, and the Human Brain* (New York: Putnam Sons, 1994); A. Damasio, *The Feeling of What Happens* (New York: Harcourt Brace and Co., 1999); P. Ekman, "Basic Emotions," in *Handbook of Cognition and Emotion*, ed. T. Dalgleish and M. Power (San Francisco: Jossey-Bass, 1999), 45–60; J. E. LeDoux, "Emotion Circuits in the Brain," *Annual Review of Neuroscience* 23 (2000): 155–184; R. J. Dolan, "Emotion, Cognition, and Behavior," *Science* 298, no. 5596 (8 November 2002): 1191–1194.

13. H. M. Weiss and R. Cropanzano, "Affective Events Theory: A Theoretical Discussion of the Structure, Causes, and Consequences of Affective Experiences at Work," *Research in Organizational Behavior* 18 (1996): 1–74.

14. N. Schwarz, "Emotion, Cognition, and Decision Making," *Cognition and Emotion* 14, no. 4 (2000): 433–440; M. T. Pham, "The Logic of Feeling," *Journal of Consumer Psychology* 14, no. 4 (2004): 360–369.

15. G. R. Maio, V. M. Esses, and D. W. Bell, "Examining Conflict between Components of Attitudes: Ambivalence and Inconsistency Are Distinct Constructs," *Canadian Journal of Behavioural Science* 32, no. 2 (2000): 71–83.

16. P. C. Nutt, *Why Decisions Fail* (San Francisco, CA: Berrett-Koehler, 2002); S. Finkelstein, *Why Smart Executives Fail* (New York: Viking, 2003); P. C. Nutt, "Search During Decision Making," *European Journal of Operational Research* 160 (2005): 851–876.

17. Weiss and Cropanzano, "Affective Events Theory."

18. L. Festinger, *A Theory of Cognitive Dissonance* (Evanston, Ill.: Row, Peterson, 1957); G. R. Salancik, "Commitment and the Control of Organizational Behavior and Belief," in *New Directions in Organizational Behavior*, ed. B. M. Staw and G. R. Salancik (Chicago: St. Clair, 1977), 1–54; A. D. Galinsky, J. Stone, and J. Cooper, "The Reinstatement of Dissonance and Psychological Discomfort Following Failed Affirmation," *European Journal of Social Psychology* 30, no. 1 (2000): 123–147.

19. T. A. Judge, E. A. Locke, and C. C. Durham, "The Dispositional Causes of Job Satisfaction: A Core Evaluations Approach," *Research in Organizational Behavior* 19 (1997): 151–188; A. P. Brief and H. M. Weiss, "Organizational Behavior: Affect in the Workplace," *Annual Review of Psychology* 53 (2002): 279–307.

20. C. M. Brotheridge and A. A. Grandey, "Emotional Labor and Burnout: Comparing Two Perspectives of 'People Work," *Journal of Vocational Behavior* 60 (2002): 17–39; P. G. Irving, D. F. Coleman, and D. R. Bobocel, "The Moderating Effect of Negative Affectivity in the Procedural Justice-Job Satisfaction Relation," *Canadian Journal of Behavioural Science* 37, no. 1 (January 2005): 20–32.

21. J. Schaubroeck, D. C. Ganster, and B. Kemmerer, "Does Trait Affect Promote Job Attitude Stability?" *Journal of Organizational Behavior* 17 (1996): 191–196; C. Dormann and D. Zapf, "Job Satisfaction: A Meta-Analysis of Stabilities," *Journal of Organizational Behavior* 22 (2001): 483–504.

22. R. Corelli, "Dishing out Rudeness," *Maclean's*, 11 January 1999, 44–47; D. Matheson, "A Vancouver Cafe Where Rudeness Is Welcomed," *Canada AM, CTV Television* (January 11 2000).

23. B. E. Ashforth and R. H. Humphrey, "Emotional Labor in Service Roles: The Influence of Identity," *Academy of Management Review* 18 (1993): 88–115. For a recent review of the emotional labour concept, see: T. M. Glomb and M. J. Tews, "Emotional Labor: A Conceptualization and Scale Development," *Journal of Vocational Behavior* 64, no. 1 (2004): 1–23.

24. G. Van Moorsel, "Call Centres Deserve Ringing Endorsement," *Lon-*

don Free Press, 27 October 2001; K. McArthur, "Air Canada Tells Employees to Crack a Smile More Often," Globe & Mail, 14 March 2002, B1.

25. R. Hallowell, D. Bowen, and C.-I. Knoop, "Four Seasons Goes to Paris," Academy of Management Executive 16, no. 4 (November 2002): 7–24.

26. J. Strasburg, "The Making of a Grand Hotel," San Francisco Chronicle, March 25 2001, B1. The antecedents of emotional labour are discussed in: J. A. Morris and D. C. Feldman, "The Dimensions, Antecedents, and Consequences of Emotional Labor," Academy of Management Review 21 (1996): 986–1010; D. Zapf, "Emotion Work and Psychological Well-Being: A Review of the Literature and Some Conceptual Considerations," Human Resource Management Review 12 (2002): 237–268.

27. E. Forman, "'Diversity Concerns Grow as Companies Head Overseas,' Consultant Says," Sun-Sentinel (Fort Lauderdale, FL), 26 June 1995. Cultural differences in emotional expression are discussed in: F. Trompenaars, "Resolving International Conflict: Culture and Business Strategy," Business Strategy Review 7, no. 3 (Autumn 1996): 51–68; F. Trompenaars and C. Hampden-Turner, Riding the Waves of Culture, 2nd ed. (New York: McGraw-Hill, 1998), Chap. 6.

28. This relates to the automaticity of emotion, which is summarized in: P. Winkielman and K. C. Berridge, "Unconscious Emotion," Current Directions in Psychological Science 13, no. 3 (2004): 120–123; K. N. Ochsner and J. J. Gross, "The Cognitive Control of Emotions," TRENDS in Cognitive Sciences 9, no. 5 (May 2005): 242–249.

29. W. J. Zerbe, "Emotional Dissonance and Employee Well-Being," in Managing Emotions in the Workplace, ed. N. M. Ashkanasy, W. J. Zerbe, and C. E. J. Hartel (Armonk, N.Y.: M. E. Sharpe, 2002), 189–214; R. Cropanzano, H. M. Weiss, and S. M. Elias, "The Impact of Display Rules and Emotional Labor on Psychological Well-Being at Work," Research in Occupational Stress and Well Being 3 (2003): 45–89.

30. Brotheridge and Grandey, "Emotional Labor and Burnout: Comparing Two Perspectives of 'People Work'"; Zapf, "Emotion Work and Psychological Well-Being"; J. M. Diefendorff, M. H. Croyle,

and R. H. Gosserand, "The Dimensionality and Antecedents of Emotional Labor Strategies," Journal of Vocational Behavior 66, no. 2 (2005): 339–357.

31. A. Schwitzerlette, "Cici's Pizza Coming to Beckley," Register-Herald (Beckley, WV), 24 August 2003.

32. J. Stuller, "Unconventional Smarts," Across the Board 35 (January 1998): 22–23; T. Schwartz, "'How Do You Feel?" Fast Company, June 2000, 296.

33. J. D. Mayer, P. Salovey, and D. R. Caruso, "Models of Emotional Intelligence," in Handbook of Human Intelligence, ed. R. J. Sternberg, 2nd ed. (New York: Cambridge University Press, 2000), 396–420. This definition is also recognized in: C. Cherniss, "Emotional Intelligence and Organizational Effectiveness," in The Emotionally Intelligent Workplace, ed. C. Cherniss and D. Goleman (San Francisco: Jossey-Bass, 2001), 3–12.

34. These four dimensions of emotional intelligence are discussed in detail in: D. Goleman, R. Boyatzis, and A. McKee, Primal Leadership, (Boston: Harvard Business School Press, 2002), Chap. 3. Slight variations of this model are presented in: R. Boyatzis, D. Goleman, and K. S. Rhee, "Clustering Competence in Emotional Intelligence," in The Handbook of Emotional Intelligence, ed. R. Bar-On and J. D. A. Parker (San Francisco: Jossey-Bass, 2000), 343–362; D. Goleman, "An Ei-Based Theory of Performance," in The Emotionally Intelligent Workplace, ed. C. Cherniss and D. Goleman (San Francisco: Jossey-Bass, 2001), 27–44.

35. H. A. Elfenbein and N. Ambady, "Predicting Workplace Outcomes from the Ability to Eavesdrop on Feelings," Journal of Applied Psychology 87, no. 5 (2002): 963–971.

36. The hierarchical nature of the four EI dimensions is discussed by Goleman, but is more explicit in the Salovey and Mayer model. See: D. R. Caruso and P. Salovey, The Emotionally Intelligent Manager (San Francisco: Jossey-Bass, 2004).

37. P. J. Jordan et al., "Workgroup Emotional Intelligence: Scale Development and Relationship to Team Process Effectiveness and Goal Focus," Human Resource Management Review 12 (2002): 195–214; H. Nel, W. S. De Villiers, and A. S. Engelbrecht, "The Influence of Emotional Intelligence on Perfor-

mance in a Call Centre Environment" in First International Conference on Contemporary Management, ed. A. Travaglione et al., (Adelaide, Australia, 1-2 September, 2003), 81–90; P. N. Lopes et al., "Emotional Intelligence and Social Interaction," Personality and Social Psychology Bulletin 30, no. 8 (August 2004): 1018–1034; C. S. Daus and N. M. Ashkanasy, "The Case for the Ability-Based Model of Emotional Intelligence in Organizational Behavior," Journal of Organizational Behavior 26 (2005): 453–466. Not all studies have found that EI predicts job performance. See: S. Newsome, A. L. Day, and V. M. Catano, "Assessing the Predictive Validity of Emotional Intelligence," Personality and Individual Differences, no. 29 (December 2000): 1005–1016; A. L. Day and S. A. Carroll, "Using an Ability-Based Measure of Emotional Intelligence to Predict Individual Performance, Group Performance, and Group Citizenship Behaviours," Personality and Individual Differences 36 (2004): 1443–1458.

38. R. J. Grossman, "Emotions at Work," Health Forum Journal, no. 43 (Sept–Oct 2000): 18–22; J. Brown, "School Board, Employment Centers Test Emotional Intelligence," Technology in Government, no. 8 (April 2001): 9; S. C. Clark, R. Callister, and R. Wallace, "Undergraduate Management Skills Courses and Students' Emotional Intelligence," Journal of Management Education 27, no. 1 (February 2003): 3–23.

39. For recent critiques of emotional intelligence, see: F. J. Landy, "Some Historical and Scientific Issues Related to Research on Emotional Intelligence," Journal of Organizational Behavior 26 (2005): 411–424; E. A. Locke, "Why Emotional Intelligence Is an Invalid Concept," Journal of Organizational Behavior 26 (2005): 425–431.

40. E. A. Locke, "The Nature and Causes of Job Satisfaction," in Handbook of Industrial and Organizational Psychology, ed. M. Dunnette (Chicago: Rand McNally, 1976), 1297–1350; H. M. Weiss, "Deconstructing Job Satisfaction: Separating Evaluations, Beliefs and Affective Experiences," Human Resource Management Review, no. 12 (2002): 173–194. Some definitions still include emotion as an element of job satisfaction, whereas the definition

presented in this book views emotion as a cause of job satisfaction. Also, this definition views job satisfaction as a "collection of attitudes," not several "facets" of job satisfaction.

41. For recent Canadian job satisfaction polls, see: Ipsos-Reid, "So Who Hates Their Boss?" News release, (Toronto: 12 March 2003); "Many Workers Want a New Job," *Toronto Star*, 10 July 2004, D12. For global comparisons of job satisfaction, see: Ipsos-Reid, "Ipsos-Reid Global Poll Finds Major Differences in Employee Satisfaction around the World," News release, (Toronto: 8 January 2001); International Survey Research, *Employee Satisfaction in the World's 10 Largest Economies: Globalization or Diversity?* (Chicago: International Survey Research, 2002); R. Brisbois, *How Canada Stacks Up: The Quality of Work—an International Perspective* (Ottawa: Canadian Policy Research Networks, December 2003).

42. K. Keis, "HR Needs Happy Staff to Show Its Success," *Canadian HR Reporter*, 14 February 2005, 14.

43. The problems with measuring attitudes and values across cultures is discussed in: G. Law, "If You're Happy & You Know It, Tick the Box," *Management-Auckland*, no. 45 (March 1998): 34–37; P. E. Spector and e. al., "Do National Levels of Individualism and Internal Locus of Control Relate to Well-Being: An Ecological Level International Study," *Journal of Organizational Behavior*, no. 22 (2001): 815–832; L. Saari and T. A. Judge, "Employee Attitudes and Job Satisfaction," *Human Resource Management* 43, no. 4 (Winter 2004): 395–407.

44. ANZ Banking Group, *The Journey* (Melbourne: ANZ Banking Group, November 2002); L. Cossar, "IQ? But How Does Your EQ Rate?" *Business Review Weekly* (22 August 2002): 68; C. Nader, "EQ Begins to Edge out IQ as Desirable Quality in the Boss," *Sunday Age (Melbourne)*, 18 May 2003, 10; C. Fox and A. Cornell, "The Anz Experience," *Australian Financial Review*, 12 March 2004, 30.

45. M. Troy, "Motivating Your Workforce: A Home Depot Case Study," *DSN Retailing Today*, 10 June 2002, 29.

46. M. J. Withey and W. H. Cooper, "Predicting Exit, Voice, Loyalty, and Neglect," *Administrative Science Quarterly*, no. 34 (1989): 521–539; W. H. Turnley and D. C. Feldman, "The Impact of Psychological Contract Violations on Exit, Voice, Loyalty, and Neglect," *Human Relations*, no. 52 (July 1999): 895–922.

47. T. R. Mitchell, B. C. Holtom, and T. W. Lee, "How to Keep Your Best Employees: Developing an Effective Retention Policy," *Academy of Management Executive* 15 (November 2001): 96–108; C. P. Maertz and M. A. Campion, "Profiles of Quitting: Integrating Process and Content Turnover Theory," *Academy of Management Journal* 47, no. 4 (2004): 566–582.

48. A. A. Luchak, "What Kind of Voice Do Loyal Employees Use?" *British Journal of Industrial Relations* 41 (March 2003): 115–134.

49. J. D. Hibbard, N. Kumar, and L. W. Stern, "Examining the Impact of Destructive Acts in Marketing Channel Relationships," *Journal of Marketing Research* 38 (February 2001): 45–61; J. Zhou and J. M. George, "When Job Dissatisfaction Leads to Creativity: Encouraging the Expression of Voice," *Academy of Management Journal* 44 (August 2001): 682–696.

50. M. J. Withey and I. R. Gellatly, "Situational and Dispositional Determinants of Exit, Voice, Loyalty and Neglect," *Proceedings of the Administrative Sciences Association of Canada, Organizational Behaviour Division* (June 1998); M. J. Withey and I. R. Gellatly, "Exit, Voice, Loyalty and Neglect: Assessing the Influence of Prior Effectiveness and Personality," *Proceedings of the Administrative Sciences Association of Canada, Organizational Behaviour Division* 20 (1999): 110–119.

51. D. P. Schwab and L. L. Cummings, "Theories of Performance and Satisfaction: A Review," *Industrial Relations* 9 (1970): 408–430; M. T. Iaffaldano and P. M. Muchinsky, "Job Satisfaction and Job Performance: A Meta-Analysis," *Psychological Bulletin* 97 (1985): 251–273.

52. T. A. Judge *et al.*, "The Job Satisfaction-Job Performance Relationship: A Qualitative and Quantitative Review," *Psychological Bulletin* 127 (2001): 376–407; Saari and Judge, "Employee Attitudes and Job Satisfaction,"

53. Judge *et al.*, "The Job Satisfaction-Job Performance Relationship: A Qualitative and Quantitative Review."

54. S. OndraSek, "Four Seasons Makes Local Debut," *Prague Post*, 7 February 2001; "The Greatest Briton in Management and Leadership," *Personnel Today* (18 February 2003): 20.

55. J. I. Heskett, W. E. Sasser, and L. A. Schlesinger, *The Service Profit Chain* (New York: Free Press, 1997); D. J. Koys, "The Effects of Employee Satisfaction, Organizational Citizenship Behavior, and Turnover on Organizational Effectiveness: A Unit-Level, Longitudinal Study," *Personnel Psychology* 54 (April 2001): 101–114; W.-C. Tsai and Y.-M. Huang, "Mechanisms Linking Employee Affective Delivery and Customer Behavioral Intentions," *Journal of Applied Psychology* 87, no. 5 (2002): 1001–1008; T. DeCotiis *et al.*, "How Outback Steakhouse Created a Great Place to Work, Have Fun, and Make Money," *Journal of Organizational Excellence* 23, no. 4 (Autumn 2004): 23–33; G. A. Gelade and S. Young, "Test of a Service Profit Chain Model in the Retail Banking Sector," *Journal of Occupational & Organizational Psychology* 78 (2005): 1–22. However, some studies have found only a weak relationship between employee attitudes and sales outcomes.

56. P. Guenzi and O. Pelloni, "The Impact of Interpersonal Realtionships on Customer Satisfaction and Loyalty to the Service Provider," *International Journal of Service Industry Management* 15, no. 3–4 (2004): 365–384; S. J. Bell, S. Auh, and K. Smalley, "Customer Relationship Dynamics: Service Quality and Customer Loyalty in the Context of Varying Levels of Customer Expertise and Switching Costs," *Journal of the Academy of Marketing Science* 33, no. 2 (Spring 2005): 169–183.

57. S. Franklin, *The Heroes: A Saga of Canadian Inspiration* (Toronto: McClelland & Stewart, 1967), pp. 53–59.

58. R. T. Mowday, L. W. Porter, and R. M. Steers, *Employee Organization Linkages: The Psychology of Commitment, Absenteeism, and Turnover* (New York: Academic Press, 1982).

59. J. P. Meyer, "Organizational Commitment," *International Review of Industrial and Organizational Psychology* 12

(1997): 175–228. Along with affective and continuance commitment, Meyer identifies "normative commitment," which refers to employee feelings of obligation to remain with the organization. This commitment has been excluded so that students focus on the two most common perspectives of commitment.

60. R. D. Hackett, P. Bycio, and P. A. Hausdorf, "Further Assessments of Meyer and Allen's (1991) Three-Component Model of Organizational Commitment," *Journal of Applied Psychology* 79 (1994): 15–23.

61. F. F. Reichheld, *The Loyalty Effect* (Boston: Harvard Business School Press, 1996), Chap. 4; J. P. Meyer *et al.*, "Affective, Continuance, and Normative Commitment to the Organization: A Meta-Analysis of Antecedents, Correlates, and Consequences," *Journal of Vocational Behavior* 61 (2002): 20–52; M. Riketta, "Attitudinal Organizational Commitment and Job Performance: A Meta-Analysis," *Journal of Organizational Behavior* 23 (2002): 257–266.

62. B. L. Toffler, *Final Accounting: Ambition, Greed, and the Fall of Arthur Andersen* (New York: Broadway Books, 2003).

63. J. Dean, "Wal-Mart High on Best Employers List," *Mississauga News* (Mississauga, ON), 9 January 2005.

64. P. Arab, "CIBC Takeover of Merrill Lynch Brokerage Makes Bank Biggest Brokerage," *Canadian Press*, 22 November 2001.

65. J. P. Meyer *et al.*, "Organizational Commitment and Job Performance: It's the Nature of the Commitment That Counts," *Journal of Applied Psychology* 74 (1989): 152–156; A. A. Luchak and I. R. Gellatly, "What Kind of Commitment Does a Final-Earnings Pension Plan Elicit?" *Relations Industrielles* 56 (Spring 2001): 394–417; Z. X. Chen and A. M. Francesco, "The Relationship between the Three Components of Commitment and Employee Performance in China," *Journal of Vocational Behavior* 62, no. 3 (2003): 490–510; D. M. Powell and J. P. Meyer, "Side-Bet Theory and the Three-Component Model of Organizational Commitment," *Journal of Vocational Behavior* 65, no. 1 (2004): 157–177.

66. E. W. Morrison and S. L. Robinson, "When Employees Feel Betrayed: A Model of How Psychological Con-

tract Violation Develops," *Academy of Management Review* 22 (1997): 226–256; J. E. Finegan, "The Impact of Person and Organizational Values on Organizational Commitment," *Journal of Occupational and Organizational Psychology* 73 (June 2000): 149–169.

67. D. M. Cable and T. A. Judge, "Person-Organization Fit, Job Choice Decisions, and Organizational Entry," *Organizational Behavior and Human Decision Processes* 67, no. 3 (1996): 294–311; T. J. Kalliath, A. C. Bluedorn, and M. J. Strube, "A Test of Value Congruence Effects," *Journal of Organizational Behavior* 20, no. 7 (1999): 1175–1198; J. W. Westerman and L. A. Cyr, "An Integrative Analysis of Person-Organization Fit Theories," *International Journal of Selection and Assessment* 12, no. 3 (September 2004): 252–261.

68. D. M. Rousseau *et al.*, "Not So Different after All: A Cross-Disicipline View of Trust," *Academy of Management Review* 23 (1998): 393–404.

69. S. Ashford, C. Lee, and P. Bobko, "Content, Causes, and Consequences of Job Insecurity: A Theory-Based Measure and Substantive Test," *Academy of Management Journal* 32 (1989): 803–829; C. Hendry, Chris, and R. Jenkins, "Psychological Contracts and New Deals," *Human Resource Management Journal* 7 (1997): 38–44.

70. T. S. Heffner and J. R. Rentsch, "Organizational Commitment and Social Interaction: A Multiple Constituencies Approach," *Journal of Vocational Behavior* 59 (2001): 471–490.

71. A. Dastmalchain and M. Javidan, "High-Commitment Leadership: A Study of Iranian Executives," *Journal of Comparative International Management* 1 (1998): 23–37; J. Godard, "High Performance and the Transformation of Work? The Implications of Alternative Work Practices for the Experience and Outcomes of Work," *Industrial and Labor Relations Review* 54, no. 4 (July 2001): 776–805.

72. R. Simone, "Dispute Shuts Down Toyota Production," *Kitchener-Waterloo Record*, 24 October 2003, C14; R. Simone, "Toyota Drops Overtime Battle," *Kitchener-Waterloo Record*, 6 March 2003.

73. P. Kruger, "Betrayed by Work," *Fast Company*, November 1999, 182.

74. S. L. Robinson, M. S. Kraatz, and D. M. Rousseau, "Changing Obligations and the Psychological Contract: A Longitudinal Study," *Academy of Management Journal* 37 (1994): 137–152; Morrison and Robinson, "When Employees Feel Betrayed: A Model of How Psychological Contract Violation Develops."

75. D. M. Rousseau, *Psychological Contracts in Organizations* (Thousand Oaks, CA: Sage, 1995); M. Janssens, L. Sels, and I. Van den Brande, "Multiple Types of Psychological Contracts: A Six-Cluster Solution," *Human Relations* 56, no. 11 (2003): 1349–1378.

76. P. R. Sparrow, "Reappraising Psychological Contracting: Lessons for the Field of Human-Resource Development from Cross-Cultural and Occupational Psychology Research," *International Studies of Management & Organization* 28 (March 1998): 30–63; D. C. Thomas, K. Au, and E. C. Ravlin, "Cultural Variation and the Psychological Contract," *Journal of Organizational Behavior* 24 (2003): 451–471.

CHAPTER FIVE

1. British Columbia Government, "Recognition Best Practices, www.bcpublicservice.ca/awards/best_practices/best_practices_index.htm (accessed April 10, 2005); M. McMaster, "Grassroots Recognition," *Potentials* 36, no. 1 (January 2003): 48; S. McGovern, "Feedback Rated Tops for Boosting Morale," *Calgary Herald* (Calgary), 29 June 2004, C4.

2. C. C. Pinder, *Work Motivation in Organizational Behavior* (Upper Saddle River, NJ: Prentice-Hall, 1998); R. M. Steers, R. T. Mowday, and D. L. Shapiro, "The Future of Work Motivation Theory," *Academy of Management Review* 29 (2004): 379–387.

3. "Towers Perrin Study Finds, Despite Layoffs and Slow Economy, a New, More Complex Power Game Is Emerging between Employers and Employees," *Business Wire*, 30 August, 2001; D. Brown, "Most Canadian Workers Only Moderately Engaged," *Canadian HR Reporter*, 14 July 2003, 1; K. V. Rondeau and T. H. Wagar, "Downsizing and Organizational Restructuring: What Is the Impact on Hospital Performance?" *International Journal of Public Administration* 26 (2003): 1647–1668.

4. C. Lachnit, "The Young and the Dispirited," *Workforce 81* (August 2002): 18; S. H. Applebaum, M. Serena, and B. T. Shapiro, "Generation X and the Boomers: Organizational Myths and Literary Realities," *Management Research News* 27, no. 11/12 (2004): 1–28. Motivation and needs across generations is also discussed in: R. Zemke and B. Filipczak, *Generations at Work: Managing the Clash of Veterans, Boomers, Xers, and Nexters in Your Workplace* (N. Y.: AMACOM, 2000).

5. T. V. Sewards and M. A. Sewards, "Fear and Power-Dominance Drive Motivation: Neural Representations and Pathways Mediating Sensory and Mnemonic Inputs, and Outputs to Premotor Structures," *Neuroscience and Biobehavioral Reviews* 26 (2002): 553–579; K. C. Berridge, "Motivation Concepts in Behavioral Neuroscience," *Physiology & Behavior* 81, no. 2 (2004): 179–209.

6. A. H. Maslow, "A Preface to Motivation Theory," *Psychsomatic Medicine* 5 (1943): 85–92.

7. A. H. Maslow, "A Theory of Human Motivation," *Psychological Review* 50 (1943): 370–396; A. H. Maslow, *Motivation and Personality* (New York: Harper & Row, 1954).

8. D. T. Hall and K. E. Nougaim, "An Examination of Maslow's Need Hierarchy in an *Organizational Setting*," *Organizational Behavior and Human Performance* 3, no. 1 (1968): 12; M. A. Wahba and L. G. Bridwell, "Maslow Reconsidered: A Review of Research on the Need Hierarchy Theory," *Organizational Behavior and Human Performance* 15 (1976): 212–240; E. L. Betz, "Two Tests of Maslow's Theory of Need Fulfilllment," *Journal of Vocational Behavior* 24, no. 2 (1984): 204–220; P. A. Corning, "Biological Adaptation in Human Societies: A 'Basic Needs' Approach," *Journal of Bioeconomics* 2, no. 1 (2000): 41–86.

9. K. Dye, A. J. Mills, and T. G. Weatherbee, "Maslow: Man Interrupted—Reading Management Theory in Context", February 2005, Wolfville, N.S.

10. A. H. Maslow, *Maslow on Management* (New York: John Wiley & sons, 1998).

11. C. P. Alderfer, *Existence, Relatedness, and Growth* (New York: Free Press, 1972).

12. J. Rauschenberger, N. Schmitt, and J. E. Hunter, "A Test of the Need Hierarchy Concept by a Markov Model of Change in Need Strength," *Administrative Science Quarterly* 25, no. 4 (December 1980): 654–670; J. P. Wanous and A. A. Zwany, "A Cross-Sectional Test of Need Hierarchy Theory," *Organizational Behavior and Human Performance* 18 (1977): 78–97.

13. S. A. Haslam, C. Powell, and J. Turner, "Social Identity, Self-Categorization, and Work Motivation: Rethinking the Contribution of the Group to Positive and Sustainable Organisational Outcomes," *Applied Psychology: An International Review* 49 (July 2000): 319–339; E. A. Locke, "Motivation, Cognition, and Action: An Analysis of Studies of Task Goals and Knowledge," *Applied Psychology: An International Review* 49 (2000): 408–429.

14. B. A. Agle and C. B. Caldwell, "Understanding Research on Values in Business," *Business and Society* 38 (September 1999): 326–387; B. Verplanken and R. W. Holland, "Motivated Decision Making: Effects of Activation and Self-Centrality of Values on Choices and Behavior," *Journal of Personality and Social Psychology* 82, no. 3 (2002): 434–447; S. Hitlin and J. A. Pilavin, "Values: Reviving a Dormant Concept," *Annual Review of Sociology* 30 (2004): 359–393.

15. P. R. Lawrence and N. Nohria, *Driven: How Human Nature Shapes Our Choices* (San Francisco: Jossey-Bass, 2002).

16. R. E. Baumeister and M. R. Leary, "The Need to Belong: Desire for Interpersonal Attachments as a Fundamental Human Motivation," *Psychological Bulletin* 117 (1995): 497–529.

17. W. H. Bexton, W. Heron, and T. H. Scott, "Effects of Decreased Variation in the Sensory Environment," *Canadian Journal of Psychology* 8 (1954): 70–76; G. Loewenstein, "The Psychology of Curiosity: A Review and Reinterpretation," *Psychological Bulletin* 116, no. 1 (1994): 75–98.

18. This explanation refers to a singular "rational centre" and "emotional centre." While many scholars do refer to a single location for most emotional transactions, an emerging view is that both the emotional and rational "centres" are distributed throughout the brain. See: J. Schulkin, B. L. Thompson, and J. B. Rosen, "Demythologizing the Emotions: Adaptation, Cognition, and Visceral Representations of Emotion in the Nervous System," *Brain and Cognition* 52, no. 1 (2003): 15–23.

19. A. R. Damasio, *Descartes' Error: Emotion, Reason, and the Human Brain* (New York: Putnam Sons, 1994); J. E. LeDoux, "Emotion Circuits in the Brain," *Annual Review of Neuroscience* 23 (2000): 155–184; P. Winkielman and K. C. Berridge, "Unconscious Emotion," *Current Directions in Psychological Science* 13, no. 3 (2004): 120–123.

20. Lawrence and Nohria, *Driven: How Human Nature Shapes Our Choices*, pp. 145–147.

21. D. McMurdy, "Office Bash Is Good Therapy," *The Gazette* (Montreal), 20 November 2003, B4; S. Brunt, "Heavy Mettle," *Report on Business Magazine*, May 2004, 58; C. Phillips, "Dofasco Party Is a Kid's Thing," *Hamilton Spectator* (Hamilton, ON), 20 December 2004, A03.

22. D. C. McClelland, *The Achieving Society* (New York: Van Nostrand Reinhold, 1961).

23. S. Shane, E. A. Locke, and C. J. Collins, "Entrepreneurial Motivation," *Human Resource Management Review* 13, no. 2 (2003): 257–279.

24. D. C. McClelland and D. H. Burnham, "Power Is the Great Motivator," *Harvard Business Review* 73 (January-February 1995): 126–139; J. L. Thomas, M. W. Dickson, and P. D. Bliese, "Values Predicting Leader Performance in the U.S. Army Reserve Officer Training Corps Assessment Center: Evidence for a Personality-Mediated Model," *The Leadership Quarterly* 12, no. 2 (2001): 181–196.

25. D. Vredenburgh and Y. Brender, "The Hierarchical Abuse of Power in Work Organizations," *Journal of Business Ethics* 17 (September 1998): 1337–1347.

26. D. Miron and D. C. McClelland, "The Impact of Achievement Motivation Training on Small Business," *California Management Review* 21 (1979): 13–28.

27. Lawrence and Nohria, *Driven: How Human Nature Shapes Our Choices*, Chap. 11.

28. Human Resources and Skill Development Canada, "Organizational Profiles: Pancanadian Petroleum," (July 2001),

http://www.hrsdc.gc.ca/en/lp/spila/wlb/ell/12pancanadian_petroleum.shtml, Accessed on 13 April, 2005.

29. Expectancy theory of motivation in work settings originated in V. H. Vroom, *Work and Motivation* (New York: Wiley, 1964). The version of expectancy theory presented here was developed by Edward Lawler. Lawler's model provides a clearer presentation of the model's three components. P-to-O expectancy is similar to "instrumentality" in Vroom's original expectancy theory model. The difference is that instrumentality is a correlation whereas P-to-O expectancy is a probability. See: J. P. Campbell *et al.*, *Managerial Behavior, Performance, and Effectiveness* (New York: McGraw-Hill, 1970); E. E. Lawler III, *Motivation in Work Organizations* (Monterey, CA: Brooks-Cole, 1973); D. A. Nadler and E. E. Lawler, "Motivation: A Diagnostic Approach," in *Perspectives on Behavior in Organizations*, ed. J. R. Hackman, E. E. Lawler III, and L. W. Porter, second ed. (New York: McGraw-Hill, 1983), 67–78.

30. M. Zeelenberg *et al.*, "Emotional Reactions to the Outcomes of Decisions: The Role of Counterfactual Thought in the Experience of Regret and Disappointment," *Organizational Behavior and Human Decision Processes* 75, no. 2 (1998): 117–141; B. A. Mellers, "Choice and the Relative Pleasure of Consequences," *Psychological Bulletin* 126, no. 6 (November 2000): 910–924; R. P. Bagozzi, U. M. Dholakia, and S. Basuroy, "How Effortful Decisions Get Enacted: The Motivating Role of Decision Processes, Desires, and Anticipated Emotions," *Journal of Behavioral Decision Making* 16, no. 4 (October 2003): 273–295.

31. Nadler and Lawler, "Motivation: A Diagnostic Approach,"

32. T. Janz, "Manipulating Subjective Expectancy through Feedback: A Laboratory Study of the Expectancy-Performance Relationship," *Journal of Applied Psychology* 67 (1982): 480–485; K. A. Karl, A. M. O' Leary-Kelly, and J. J. Martoccio, "The Impact of Feedback and Self-Efficacy on Performance in Training," *Journal of Organizational Behavior* 14 (1993): 379–394; R. G. Lord, P. J. Hanges, and E. G. Godfrey, "Integrating Neural Networks into Decision-Making and Motivational

Theory: Rethinking VIE Theory," *Canadian Psychology* 44, no. 1 (2003): 21–38.

33. P. W. Mulvey *et al.*, *The Knowledge of Pay Study: E-Mails from the Frontline* (Scottsdale, Arizona: WorldatWork, 2002).

34. M. L. Ambrose and C. T. Kulik, "Old Friends, New Faces: Motivation Research in the 1990s," *Journal of Management* 25 (May 1999): 231–292; C. L. Haworth and P. E. Levy, "The Importance of Instrumentality Beliefs in the Prediction of Organizational Citizenship Behaviors," *Journal of Vocational Behavior* 59 (August 2001): 64–75; Y. Chen, A. Gupta, and L. Hoshower, "Marketing Students' Perceptions of Teaching Evaluations: An Application of Expectancy Theory," *Marketing Education Review* 14, no. 2 (Summer 2004): 23–36.

35. T. Matsui and I. Terai, "A Cross-Cultural Study of the Validity of the Expectancy Theory of Motivation," *Journal of Applied Psychology* 60 (1979): 263–265; D. H. B. Welsh, F. Luthans, and S. M. Sommer, "Managing Russion Factory Workers: The Impact of U.S.-Based Behavioral and Participative Techniques," *Academy of Management Journal* 36 (1993): 58–79.

36. G. Beckstrand, "Without Controls Peer Recognition Collapses into a Free-for-All," *Canadian Human Resources Reporter*, 10 March 2003, 7–8.

37. Canadian Marketing Association, *Call Centre Call Recording Study Report* (Canadian Marketing Association, December, 2004).

38. K. H. Doerr and T. R. Mitchell, "Impact of Material Flow Policies and Goals on Job Outcomes," *Journal of Applied Psychology* 81 (1996): 142–152; L. A. Wilk and W. K. Redmon, "The Effects of Feedback and Goal Setting on the Productivity and Satisfaction of University Admissions Staff," *Journal of Organizational Behavior Management* 18 (1998): 45–68.

39. G. P. Latham, "Goal Setting: A Five-Step Approach to Behavior Change," *Organizational Dynamics* 32, no. 3 (2003): 309–318; E. A. Locke and G. P. Latham, *A Theory of Goal Setting and Task Performance* (Englewood Cliffs, N.J: Prentice Hall, 1990). Some practitioners rely on the acronym "SMART" goals, referring to goals that are specific, measurable, acceptable, relevant,

and timely. However, this list overlaps key elements (e.g., specific goals are measurable and timely) and overlooks the key elements of challenging and feedback-related.

40. K. Tasa, T. Brown, and G. H. Seijts, "The Effects of Proximal, Outcome and Learning Goals on Information Seeking and Complex Task Performance," *Proceedings of the Annual Conference of the Administrative Sciences Association of Canada, Organizational Behavior Division* 23, no. 5 (2002): 11–20.

41. K. R. Thompson, W. A. Hochwarter, and N. J. Mathys, "Stretch Targets: What Makes Them Effective?" *Academy of Management Executive* 11 (August 1997): 48–60; S. Kerr and S. Landauer, "Using Stretch Goals to Promote Organizational Effectiveness and Personal Growth: General Electric and Goldman Sachs," *Academy of Management Executive* 18, no. 4 (2004): 134–138.

42. A. Li and A. B. Butler, "The Effects of Participation in Goal Setting and Goal Rationales on Goal Commitment: An Exploration of Justice Mediators," *Journal of Business and Psychology* 19, no. 1 (Fall 2004): 37–51.

43. Locke and Latham, *A Theory of Goal Setting and Task Performance*, Chap. 6 and 7; J. Wegge, "Participation in Group Goal Setting: Some Novel Findings and a Comprehensive Model as a New Ending to an Old Story," *Applied Psychology: An International Review* 49 (2000): 498–516.

44. M. London, E. M. Mone, and J. C. Scott, "Performance Management and Assessment: Methods for Improved Rater Accuracy and Employee Goal Setting," *Human Resource Management* 43, no. 4 (Winter 2004): 319–336; G. P. Latham and C. C. Pinder, "Work Motivation Theory and Research at the Dawn of the Twenty-First Century," *Annual Review of Psychology* 56 (2005): 485–516.

45. A. Ross and A. MacMillan, "Frontline Planning and Scheduling at Inco's Copper Cliff Smelter Complex," *JOM: Minerals, Metals, and Materials Society Journal* 56, no. 12 (December 2004): 28; K. Lacey, "Collective Approach to Scheduling Work at Inco," *Northern Life*, 27 February 2005.

46. S. P. Brown, S. Ganesan, and G. Challagalla, "Self-Efficacy as a Moderator of Information-Seeking Effective-

ness," *Journal of Applied Psychology* 86, no. 5 (2001): 1043–1051; P. A. Heslin and G. P. Latham, "The Effect of Upward Feedback on Managerial Behaviour," *Applied Psychology: An International Review* 53, no. 1 (2004): 23–37; D. Van-Dijk and A. N. Kluger, "Feedback Sign Effect on Motivation: Is It Moderated by Regulatory Focus?" *Applied Psychology: An International Review* 53, no. 1 (2004): 113–135; J. E. Bono and A. E. Colbert, "Understanding Responses to Multi-Source Feedback: The Role of Core Self-Evaluations," *Personnel Psychology* 58, no. 1 (Spring 2005): 171–203.

47. L. Hollman, "Seeing the Writing on the Wall," *Call Center* (August 2002): 37.

48. S. Brutus and M. Derayeh, "Multisource Assessment Programs in Organizations: An Insider's Perspective," *Human Resource Development Quarterly* 13 (July 2002): 187–202.

49. W. W. Tornow and M. London, *Maximizing the Value of 360-Degree Feedback: A Process for Successful Individual and Organizational Development* (San Francisco: Jossey-Bass, 1998); L. E. Atwater, D. A. Waldman, and J. F. Brett, "Understanding and Optimizing Multisource Feedback," *Human Resource Management Journal* 41 (Summer 2002): 193–208; J. W. Smither, M. London, and R. R. Reilly, "Does Performance Improve Following Multisource Feedback? A Theoretical Model, Meta-Analysis, and Review of Empirical Findings," *Personnel Psychology* 58, no. 1 (2005): 33–66.

50. A. S. DeNisi and A. N. Kluger, "Feedback Effectiveness: Can 360-Degree Appraisals Be Improved?" *Academy of Management Executive* 14 (February 2000): 129–139; M. A. Peiperl, "Getting 360 Degree Feedback Right," *Harvard Business Review* 79 (January 2001): 142–147; "Perils & Payoffs of Multi-Rater Feedback Programs," *Pay for Performance Report* (May 2003): 1; M.-G. Seo, L. F. Barrett, and J. M. Bartunek, "The Role of Affective Experience in Work Motivation," *Academy of Management Review* 29 (2004): 423–449.

51. P. Withers, "Bigger and Better," *BC Business* 29 (April 2001): 50–51; J. W. Smither *et al.*, "Can Working with an Executive Coach Improve Multisource Feedback Ratings over Time? A Quasi-Experimental Field Study," *Personnel Psychology* 56 (Spring 2003): 23–44.

52. S. J. Ashford and G. B. Northcraft, "Conveying More (or Less) Than We Realize: The Role of Impression Management in Feedback Seeking," *Organizational Behavior and Human Decision Processes* 53 (1992): 310–334; M. London, "Giving Feedback: Source-Centered Antecedents and Consequences of Constructive and Destructive Feedback," *Human Resource Management Review* 5 (1995): 159–188; J. R. Williams *et al.*, "Increasing Feedback Seeking in Public Contexts: It Takes Two (or More) to Tango," *Journal of Applied Psychology* 84 (December 1999): 969–976.

53. J. B. Miner, "The Rated Importance, Scientific Validity, and Practical Usefulness of Organizational Behavior Theories: A Quantitative Review," *Academy of Management Learning and Education* 2, no. 3 (2003): 250–268. Also see: C. C. Pinder, *Work Motivation in Organizational Behavior* (Upper Saddle River, NJ: Prentice-Hall, 1997), p. 384.

54. P. M. Wright, "Goal Setting and Monetary Incentives: Motivational Tools That Can Work Too Well," *Compensation and Benefits Review* 26 (May-June 1994): 41–49; E. A. Locke and G. P. Latham, "Building a Practically Useful Theory of Goal Setting and Task Motivation: A 35-Year Odyssey," *American Psychologist* 57, no. 9 (2002): 705–717.

55. A. Lue, "Women Seethe over Gender Gap in Salaries," *Taipei Times*, 6 March 2003.

56. J. Greenberg and E. A. Lind, "The Pursuit of Organizational Justice: From Conceptualization to Implication to Application," in *Industrial and Organizational Psychology: Linking Theory with Practice*, ed. C. L. Cooper and E. A. Locke (London: Blackwell, 2000), 72–108; R. Cropanzano and M. Schminke, "Using Social Justice to Build Effective Work Groups," in *Groups at Work: Theory and Research*, ed. M. E. Turner (Mahwah, N.J.: Lawrence Erlbaum Associates, 2001), 143–171; D. T. Miller, "Disrespect and the Experience of Injustice," *Annual Review of Psychology* 52 (2001): 527–553.

57. J. S. Adams, "Toward an Understanding of Inequity," *Journal of Abnormal and Social Psychology* 67 (1963): 422–436; R. T. Mowday, "Equity Theory Predictions of Behavior in Organizations," in *Motivation and Work Behavior*, ed. L. W. Porter and R. M. Steers,

5th ed. (New York: McGraw-Hill, 1991), 111–131; R. G. Cropanzano, J., "Progress in Organizational Justice: Tunneling through the Maze," in *International Review of Industrial and Organizational Psychology*, ed. C. L. Cooper and I. T. Robertson (New York: Wiley, 1997), 317–372; L. A. Powell, "Justice Judgments as Complex Psychocultural Constructions: An Equity-Based Heuristic for Mapping Two- and Three-Dimensional Fairness Representations in Perceptual Space," *Journal of Cross-Cultural Psychology* 36, no. 1 (January 2005): 48–73.

58. C. T. Kulik and M. L. Ambrose, "Personal and Situational Determinants of Referent Choice," *Academy of Management Review* 17 (1992): 212–237; G. Blau, "Testing the Effect of Level and Importance of Pay Referents on Pay Level Satisfaction," *Human Relations* 47 (1994): 1251–1268.

59. T. P. Summers and A. S. DeNisi, "In Search of Adams' Other: Reexamination of Referents Used in the Evaluation of Pay," *Human Relations* 43 (1990): 497–511.

60. Y. Cohen-Charash and P. E. Spector, "The Role of Justice in Organizations: A Meta-Analysis," *Organizational Behavior and Human Decision Processes* 86 (November 2001): 278–321.

61. Canadian Press, "Pierre Berton, Canadian Cultural Icon, Enjoyed Long and Colourful Career," *Times Colonist* (Victoria, B.C.), 30 November 2004.

62. K. S. Sauleya and A. G. Bedeian, "Equity Sensitivity: Construction of a Measure and Examination of Its Psychometric Properties," *Journal of Management* 26 (September 2000): 885–910.

63. The meaning of these three groups has evolved over the years. These definitions are based on W. C. King Jr. and E. W. Miles, "The Measurement of Equity Sensitivity," *Journal of Occupational and Organizational Psychology* 67 (1994): 133–142.

64. M. Ezzamel and R. Watson, "Pay Comparability across and within Uk Boards: An Empirical Analysis of the Cash Pay Awards to Ceos and Other Board Members," *Journal of Management Studies* 39, no. 2 (March 2002): 207–232; J. Fizel, A. C. Krautman, and L. Hadley, "Equity and Arbitration in Major League Baseball," *Managerial and Decision Economics* 23, no. 7 (Oct-Nov 2002): 427–435.

65. Miner, "The Rated Importance, Scientific Validity, and Practical Usefulness of Organizational Behavior Theories: A Quantitative Review."

66. Cohen-Charash and Spector, "The Role of Justice in Organizations: A Meta-Analysis"; J. A. Colquitt et al., "Justice at the Millennium: A Meta-Analytic Review of 25 Years of Organizational Justice Research," Journal of Applied Psychology 86 (2001): 425–445.

67. Several types of justice have been identified and there is some debate whether they represent forms of procedural justice or are distinct from procedural and distributive justice. The discussion here adopts the former view which seems to dominate the literature. C. Viswesvaran and D. S. Ones, "Examining the Construct of Organizational Justice: A Meta-Analytic Evaluation of Relations with Work Attitudes and Behaviors," Journal of Business Ethics 38 (July 2002): 193.

68. Greenberg and Lind, "The Pursuit of Organizational Justice: From Conceptualization to Implication to Application." For a recent study of voice and injustice, see: J. B. Olson-Buchanan and W. R. Boswell, "The Role of Employee Loyalty and Formality in Voicing Discontent," Journal of Applied Psychology 87, no. 6 (2002): 1167–1174.

69. R. Folger and J. Greenberg, "Procedural Justice: An Interpretive Analysis of Personnel Systems," Research in Personnel and Human Resources Management 3 (1985): 141–183; L. B. Bingham, "Mediating Employment Disputes: Perceptions of Redress at the United States Postal Service," Review of Public Personnel Administration 17 (Spring 1997): 20–30.

70. R. Hagey et al., "Immigrant Nurses' Experience of Racism," Journal of Nursing Scholarship 33 (Fourth Quarter 2001): 389–395; K. Roberts and K. S. Markel, "Claiming in the Name of Fairness: Organizational Justice and the Decision to File for Workplace Injury Compensation," Journal of Occupational Health Psychology 6 (October 2001): 332–347; D. A. Jones and D. P. Skarlicki, "The Effects of Overhearing Peers Discuss an Authority's Fairness Reputation on Reactions to Subsequent Treatment," Journal of Applied Psychology 90, no. 2 (2005): 363–372.

71. Miller, "Disrespect and the Experience of Injustice."

72. S. Fox, P. E. Spector, and E. W. Miles, "Counterproductive Work Behavior (Cwb) in Response to Job Stressors and Organizational Justice: Some Mediator and Moderator Tests for Autonomy and Emotions," Journal of Vocational Behavior 59 (2001): 291–309; I. M. Jawahar, "A Model of Organizational Justice and Workplace Aggression," Journal of Management 28, no. 6 (2002): 811–834; M. M. LeBlanc and J. Barling, "Workplace Aggression," Current Directions in Psychological Science 13, no. 1 (2004): 9–12.

73. M. L. Ambrose, M. A. Seabright, and M. Schminke, "Sabotage in the Workplace: The Role of Organizational Injustice," Organizational Behavior and Human Decision Processes 89, no. 1 (2002): 947–965.

74. N. D. Cole and G. P. Latham, "Effects of Training in Procedural Justice on Perceptions of Disciplinary Fairness by Unionized Employees and Disciplinary Subject Matter Experts," Journal of Applied Psychology 82 (1997): 699–705 D. P. Skarlicki and G. P. Latham, "Increasing Citizenship Behavior within a Labor Union: A Test of Organizational Justice Theory," Journal of Applied Psychology 81 (1996): 161–169.

CHAPTER SIX

1. T. Hogue, "The Little Airline That Could," Hamilton Spectator (29 December 2001): M2; A. A. Davis, "Sky High," Profit, March 2004, 20–23; P. Grescoe, Flight Path (Toronto: John Wiley & Sons Canada, 2004), pp. 85, 141–143, 171, 193, 234; J. Ott, "Trauma in the Down Cycle," Aviation Week & Space Technology, 28 February 2005, 46; WestJet, Annual Information Form, 2004, (Calgary: WestJet, 30 March 2005).

2. H. Das, "The Four Faces of Pay: An Investigation into How Canadian Managers View Pay," International Journal of Commerce & Management 12 (2002): 18–40. For recent ratings of the importance of pay and benefits, see: P. Babcock, "Find What Workers Want," HRMagazine, April 2005, 50–56.

3. R. Lynn, The Secret of the Miracle Economy (London: SAE, 1991), cited in A. Furnham and R. Okamura, "Your Money or Your Life: Behavioral and Emotional Predictors of Money Pathology," Human Relations 52 (September 1999): 1157–1177. The opinion polls are summarized in: J. O'Rourke, "Show Boys the Money and Tell Girls You Care," Sun-Herald (Sydney, Australia), 10 December 2000, 43; M. Steen, "Study Looks at What Good Employees Want from a Company," San Jose Mercury (19 December 2000).

4. A. Furnham, B. D. Kirkcaldy, and R. Lynn, "National Attitudes to Competitiveness, Money, and Work among Young People: First, Second, and Third World Differences," Human Relations 47 (January 1994): 119–132; V. K. G. Lim, "Money Matters: An Empirical Investigation of Money, Face and Confucian Work Ethic," Personality and Individual Differences 35 (2003): 953–970; T. L.-P. Tang, A. Furnham, and g. M.-T. Davis, "A Cross-Cultural Comparison of the Money Ethic, the Protestant Work Ethic, and Job Satisfaction: Taiwan, the USA, and the UK," International Journal of Organization Theory and Behavior 6, no. 2 (Summer 2003): 175–194.

5. K. Martens, "Nygård Hands out 1007 $10,000 Bonus Cheques," Winnipeg Sun, 10 May 2003.

6. R. J. Long, "Job Evaluation in Canada: Has Its Demise Been Greatly Exaggerated?" in Annual Conference of the Administrative Sciences Association of Canada, Human Resource Management Division, ed. J. Carrière, (Winnipeg, May, 2002), 61–72; R. J. Long, Strategic Compensation in Canada, 2nd ed. (Toronto: Thomson Nelson, 2002), Chap. 9.

7. E. E. Lawler III, Rewarding Excellence: Pay Strategies for the New Economy (San Francisco: Jossey-Bass, 2000), pp. 30–35, 109–119; R. McNabb and K. Whitfield, "Job Evaluation and High Performance Work Practices: Compatible or Conflictual?" Journal of Management Studies 38 (March 2001): 293–312.

8. "Syracuse's Restructured Flexible Pay Plan Makes Managing Employees Easier," HR On Campus (5 December 2002).

9. E. E. Lawler III, "From Job-Based to Competency-Based Organizations," Journal of Organizational Behavior 15 (1994): 3–15; R. L. Heneman, G. E. Ledford Jr., and M. T. Gresham, "The Changing Nature of Work and Its Effects on Compensation Design and

Delivery," in *Compensation in Organizations: Current Research and Practice*, ed. S. Rynes and B. Gerhart (San Francisco: Jossey-Bass, 2000), 195–240; B. Murray and B. Gerhart, "Skill-Based Pay and Skill Seeking," *Human Resource Management Review* 10 (August 2000): 271–287; R. J. Long, "Paying for Knowledge: Does It Pay?" *Canadian HR Reporter*, 28 March 2005, 12–13; J. D. Shaw *et al.*, "Success and Survival of Skill-Based Pay Plans," *Journal of Management* 31, no. 1 (February 2005): 28–49.

10. E. B. Peach and D. A. Wren, "Pay for Performance from Antiquity to the 1950s," *Journal of Organizational Behavior Management* (1992): 5–26.

11. T. Chapelle, "Facts and Fictions About Teams," *On Wall Street* (January 2003); A. Daniels and C. Leonard, "Retailer Gives out Annual Bonuses Wal-Mart Began Tradition in 1962," *Arkansas Democrat-Gazette*, 14 March 2003, 33. For discussion of team-based rewards, see: J. S. DeMatteo, L. T. Eby, and E. Sundstrom, "Team-Based Rewards: Current Empirical Evidence and Directions for Future Research," *Research in Organizational Behavior* 20 (1998): 141–183; Lawler III, *Rewarding Excellence*, Chap. 9.

12. "Canadian Companies Encourage Employees with Innovative Bonus Plans," *Coal International* (March/April 2002): 68; J. M. Welch, "Gainsharing Returns: Hospitals and Physicians Join to Reduce Costs," *Journals of Health Care Compliance* 7, no. 3 (May/June 2005): 39–42. For evaluations of gainsharing programs, see: L. R. Gomez-Mejia, T. M. Welbourne, and R. M. Wiseman, "The Role of Risk Sharing and Risk Taking under Gainsharing," *Academy of Management Review* 25 (July 2000): 492–507; K. M. Bartol and A. Srivastava, "Encouraging Knowledge Sharing: The Role of Organizational Reward System," *Journal of Leadership & Organizational Studies* 9 (Summer 2002): 64–76.

13. A. J. Maggs, "Enron, Esops, and Fiduciary Duty," *Benefits Law Journal* 16, no. 3 (Autumn 2003): 42–52; C. Brodzinski, "Esop's Fables Can Make Coverage Risky," *National Underwriter. P & C*, 13 June 2005, 16–17. The popularity of ESOPs and profit sharing in fast-growth Canadian firms is described in: J. Myers, "Dream Teams," *Profit*, June 2003, 24.

14. G. Bellett, "Worker-Friendly Policies Connect with Telus Staff: Stock Options, Education Raise Employees' Worth," *Edmonton Journal*, 20 February 2002, F6.

15. Nova Scotia Power's balanced scorecard is described in: R. S. Kaplan and D. P. Norton, *The Strategy-Focused Organization* (Cambridge, MA: Harvard Business School Press, 2001), pp. 121–123; P. R. Niven, *Balanced Scorecard Step-by-Step* (New York: John Wiley & Sons, 2002).

16. J. Chelius and R. S. Smith, "Profit Sharing and Employment Stability," *Industrial and Labor Relations Review* 43 (1990): 256s–273s; S. H. Wagner, C. P. Parkers, and N. D. Christiansen, "Employees That Think and Act Like Owners: Effects of Ownership Beliefs and Behaviors on Organizational Effectiveness," *Personnel Psychology* 56, no. 4 (Winter 2003): 847–871; G. Ledford, M. Lucy, and P. Leblanc, "The Effects of Stock Ownership on Employee Attitudes and Behavior: Evidence from the Rewards at Work Studies," *Perspectives (Sibson)*, January 2004.

17. B. Hill, "It's Been a Long Six Years," *Ottawa Citizen*, 28 April 2005, D1.

18. J. Pfeffer, *The Human Equation* (Boston: Harvard Business School Press, 1998); B. N. Pfau and I. T. Kay, *The Human Capital Edge* (New York: McGraw-Hill, 2002). The problems with performance-based pay are discussed in: W. C. Hammer, "How to Ruin Motivation with Pay," *Compensation Review* 7, no. 3 (1975): 17–27; A. Kohn, *Punished by Rewards* (Boston: Houghton Mifflin, 1993); M. O'Donnell and J. O' Brian, "Performance-Based Pay in the Australian Public Service," *Review of Public Personnel Administration* 20 (Spring 2000): 20–34; M. Beer and M. D. Cannon, "Promise and Peril of Implementing Pay-for-Performance," *Human Resource Management* 43, no. 1 (Spring 2004): 3–48.

19. M. Buckingham and D. O. Clifton, *Now, Discover Your Strengths* (New York: Free Press, 2001); M. Rotundo and P. Sackett, "The Relative Importance of Task, Citizenship, and Counterproductive Performance to Global Ratings of Job Performance: A Policy-Capturing Approach," *Journal of Applied Psychology* 87 (February 2002): 66–80; Watson Wyatt, *Workcanada 2004/2005—Pursuing Productive Engagement*, (Toronto: Watson Wyatt, January 2005).

20. S. Kerr, "Organization Rewards: Practical, Cost-Neutral Alternatives That You May Know, but Don't Practice," *Organizational Dynamics* 28 (Summer 1999): 61–70.

21. DeMatteo, Eby, and Sundstrom, "Team-Based Rewards," ; S. Rynes, B. Gerhart, and L. Parks, "Personnel Psychology: Performance Evaluation and Pay for Performance," *Annual Review of Psychology* 56 (2005): 571–600.

22. "Dream Teams," *Human Resources Professional* (November 1994): 17–19.

23. D. R. Spitzer, "Power Rewards: Rewards That Really Motivate," *Management Review* (May 1996): 45–50. For a classic discussion on the unintended consequences of pay, see: S. Kerr, "On the Folly of Rewarding a, While Hoping for B," *Academy of Management Journal* 18 (1975): 769–783.

24. D. MacDonald, "Good Managers Key to Buffett's Acquisitions," *The Gazette (Montreal)*, 16 November 2001.

25. J. R. Edwards, J. A. Scully, and M. D. Brtek, "The Nature and Outcomes of Work: A Replication and Extension of Interdisciplinary Work-Design Research," *Journal of Applied Psychology* 85, no. 6 (2000): 860–868; F. P. Morgeson and M. A. Campion, "Minimizing Tradeoffs When Redesigning Work: Evidence from a Longitudinal Quasi-Experiment," *Personnel Psychology* 55, no. 3 (Autumn 2002): 589–612.

26. D. Whitford, "A Human Place to Work," *Fortune*, 8 January 2001, 108–119.

27. Accel-Team, "Scientific Management: Lessons from Ancient History through the Industrial Revolution," www.accel-team.com, ; A. Smith, *The Wealth of Nations* (London: Dent, 1910).

28. H. Fayol, *General and Industrial Management*, trans. C. Storrs (London: Pitman, 1949); E. E. Lawler III, *Motivation in Work Organizations* (Monterey, Calif.: Brooks/Cole, 1973), Chap. 7; M. A. Campion, "Ability Requirement Implications of Job Design: An Interdisciplinary Perspective," *Personnel Psychology* 42 (1989): 1–24.

29. F. W. Taylor, *The Principles of Scientific Management* (New York: Harper & Row, 1911); R. Kanigel, *The One Best Way: Frederick Winslow Taylor and the Enigma of Efficiency* (NY: Viking, 1997).

30. C. R. Walker and R. H. Guest, *The Man on the Assembly Line* (Cambridge, MA: Harvard University Press, 1952); W. F. Dowling, "Job Redesign on the Assembly Line: Farewell to Blue-Collar Blues?" *Organizational Dynamics* (Autumn 1973): 51–67; E. E. Lawler III, *High-Involvement Management* (San Francisco: Jossey-Bass, 1986).

31. M. Keller, *Rude Awakening* (New York: Harper Perennial, 1989), p. 128.

32. F. Herzberg, B. Mausner, and B. B. Snyderman, *The Motivation to Work* (New York: Wiley, 1959).

33. S. K. Parker, T. D. Wall, and J. L. Cordery, "Future Work Design Research and Practice: Towards an Elaborated Model of Work Design," *Journal of Occupational and Organizational Psychology* 74 (November 2001): 413–440. For a decisive critique of motivator-hygiene theory, see: N. King, "Clarification and Evaluation of the Two Factor Theory of Job Satisfaction," *Psychological Bulletin* 74 (1970): 18–31.

34. J. R. Hackman and G. Oldham, *Work Redesign* (Reading, MA: Addison-Wesley, 1980).

35. Whitford, "A Human Place to Work."

36. J. E. Champoux, "A Multivariate Test of the Job Characteristics Theory of Work Motivation," *Journal of Organizational Behavior* 12, no. 5 (September 1991): 431–446; R. B. Tiegs, L. E. Tetrick, and Y. Fried, "Growth Need Strength and Context Satisfactions as Moderators of the Relations of the Job Characteristics Model," *Journal of Management* 18, no. 3 (September 1992): 575–593.

37. J. Stauffer, "The Changing Face of Construction," *Business Times (Kitchener-Waterloo)*, 18 December 2004.

38. M. Ouellette, "Rotate Workers to Reduce Repetitive Strain Injuries," *Plant*, 22 September 2003, 17.

39. M. Grotticelli, "CNN Moves to Small-Format Eng," *Broadcasting & Cable* (14 May 2001): 46.

40. M. A. Campion and C. L. McClelland, "Follow-up and Extension of the Interdisciplinary Costs and Benefits of Enlarged Jobs," *Journal of Applied Psychology* 78 (1993): 339–351; N. G. Dodd and D. C. Ganster, "The Interactive Effects of Variety, Autonomy, and Feedback on Attitudes and Performance," *Journal of Organizational Behavior* 17 (1996): 329–347.

41. J. R. Hackman *et al.*, "A New Strategy for Job Enrichment," *California Management Review* 17, no. 4 (1975): 57–71; R. W. Griffin, *Task Design: An Integrative Approach* (Glenview, IL: Scott Foresman, 1982).

42. P. E. Spector and S. M. Jex, "Relations of Job Characteristics from Multiple Data Sources with Employee Affect, Absence, Turnover Intentions, and Health," *Journal of Applied Psychology* 76 (1991): 46–53; P. Osterman, "How Common Is Workplace Transformation and Who Adopts It?" *Industrial and Labor Relations Review* 47 (1994): 173–188; R. Saavedra and S. K. Kwun, "Affective States in Job Characteristics Theory," *Journal of Organizational Behavior* 21 (2000): 131–146.

43. Hackman and Oldham, *Work Redesign*, pp. 137–138.

44. A. Hertting *et al.*, "Personnel Reductions and Structural Changes in Health Care: Work-Life Experiences of Medical Secretaries," *Journal of Psychosomatic Research* 54 (February 2003): 161–170.

45. B. Lewis, "Westjet — a Crazy Idea That Took Off," *Vancouver Province*, 21 October 2001.

46. This definition is based mostly on G. M. Spreitzer and R. E. Quinn, "*A Company of Leaders: Five Disiplines for Unleashing the Power in Your Workforce*," (2001). However, most elements of this definition appear in other discussions of empowerment. See, for example: R. Forrester, "Empowerment: Rejuvenating a Potent Idea," *Academy of Management Executive* 14 (August 2000): 67–80; W. A. Randolph, "Re-Thinking Empowerment: Why Is It So Hard to Achieve?" *Organizational Dynamics* 29 (November 2000): 94–107; S. T. Menon, "Employee Empowerment: An Integrative Psychological Approach," *Applied Psychology: An International Review* 50 (2001): 153–180.

47. The positive relationship between these structural empowerment conditions and psychological empowerment is reported in: H. K. S. Laschinger *et al.*, "A Longitudinal Analysis of the Impact of Workplace Empowerment on Work Satisfaction," *Journal of Organizational Behavior* 25, no. 4 (June 2004): 527–545.

48. C. S. Koberg *et al.*, "Antecedents and Outcomes of Empowerment," *Group and Organization Management* 24 (1999): 71–91; Y. Melhem, "The Antecedents of Customer-Contact Employees' Empowerment," *Employee Relations* 26, no. 1/2 (2004): 72–93.

49. B. J. Niehoff *et al.*, "The Influence of Empowerment and Job Enrichment on Employee Loyalty in a Downsizing Environment," *Group and Organization Management* 26 (March 2001): 93–113; J. Yoon, "The Role of Structure and Motivation for Workplace Empowerment: The Case of Korean Employees," *Social Psychology Quarterly* 64 (June 2001): 195–206; T. D. Wall, J. L. Cordery, and C. W. Clegg, "Empowerment, Performance, and Operational Uncertainty: A Theoretical Integration," *Applied Psychology: An International Review* 51 (2002): 146–169.

50. R. Semler, *The Seven-Day Weekend* (London: Century, 2003), p. 61. The organizational factors affecting empowerment are discussed in: G. M. Spreitzer, "Social Structural Characteristics of Psychological Empowerment," *Academy of Management Journal* 39 (April 1996): 483–504; J. Godard, "High Performance and the Transformation of Work? The Implications of Alternative Work Practices for the Experience and Outcomes of Work," *Industrial & Labor Relations Review* 54 (July 2001): 776–805; P. A. Miller, P. Goddard, and H. K. Spence Laschinger, "Evaluating Physical Therapists' Perception of Empowerment Using Kanter's Theory of Structural Power in Organizations," *Physical Therapy* 81 (December 2001): 1880–1888.

51. J.-C. Chebat and P. Kollias, "The Impact of Empowerment on Customer Contact Employees' Role in Service Organizations," *Journal of Service Research* 3 (August 2000): 66–81; H. K. S. Laschinger, J. Finegan, and J. Shamian, "The Impact of Workplace Empowerment, Organizational Trust on Staff Nurses' Work Satisfaction and Organizational Commitment," *Health Care Management Review* 26 (Summer 2001): 7–23.

52. P. Verberg, "Prepare for Takeoff," *Canadian Business* (25 December 2000): 94–99.

53. C. P. Neck and C. C. Manz, "Thought Self-Leadership: The Impact of Mental Strategies Training on Employee Cognition, Behavior, and Affect," *Journal of Organizational Behavior* 17 (1996): 445–467.

54. C. C. Manz, "Self-Leadership: Toward an Expanded Theory of Self-Influence Processes in Organizations," *Academy of Management Review* 11 (1986): 585–600; C. C. Manz and C. Neck, *Mastering Self-Leadership*, 3rd ed. (Upper Saddle River, NJ: Prentice Hall, 2004).

55. O. J. Strickland and M. Galimba, "Managing Time: The Effects of Personal Goal Setting on Resource Allocation Strategy and Task Performance," *Journal of Psychology* 135 (July 2001): 357–367.

56. R. M. Duncan and J. A. Cheyne, "Incidence and Functions of Self-Reported Private Speech in Young Adults: A Self-Verbalization Questionnaire," *Canadian Journal of Behavioral Science* 31 (April 1999): 133–136.

57. J. E. Driscoll, C. Copper, and A. Moran, "Does Mental Practice Enhance Performance?" *Journal of Applied Psychology* 79 (1994): 481–492; C. P. Neck, G. L. Stewart, and C. C. Manz, "Thought Self-Leadership as a Framework for Enhancing the Performance of Performance Appraisers," *Journal of Applied Behavioral Science* 31 (September 1995): 278–302. Some research separates mental imagery from mental practice, whereas most studies combine both into one concept.

58. A. Wrzesniewski and J. E. Dutton, "Crafting a Job: Revisioning Employees as Active Crafters of Their Work," *Academy of Management Review* 26 (April 2001): 179–201.

59. M. I. Bopp, S. J. Glynn, and R. A. Henning, *Self-Management of Performance Feedback During Computer-Based Work by Individuals and Two-Person Work Teams*, Paper presented at the APA-NIOSH conference (March 1999).

60. A. W. Logue, *Self-Control: Waiting until Tomorrow for What You Want Today* (Englewood Cliffs, NJ: Prentice-Hall, 1995).

61. Neck and Manz, "Thought Self-Leadership: The Impact of Mental Strategies Training on Employee Cognition, Behavior, and Affect"; A. M. Saks and B. E. Ashforth, "Proactive Socialization and Behavioral Self-Management," *Journal of Vocational Behavior* 48 (1996): 301–323; L. Morin and G. Latham, "The Effect of Mental Practice and Goal Setting as a Transfer of Training Intervention on Supervisors' Self-Efficacy and Communication Skills: An Exploratory Study," *Applied Psychology: An International Review* 49 (July 2000): 566–578; J. S. Hickman and E. S. Geller, "A Safety Self-Management Intervention for Mining Operations," *Journal of Safety Research* 34 (2003): 299–308.

62. S. Ming and G. L. Martin, "Single-Subject Evaluation of a Self-Talk Package for Improving Figure Skating Performance," *Sport Psychologist* 10 (1996): 227–238; D. Landin and E. P. Hebert, "The Influence of Self-Talk on the Performance of Skilled Female Tennis Players," *Journal of Applied Sport Psychology* 11 (September 1999): 263–282; K. E. Thiese and S. Huddleston, "The Use of Psychological Skills by Female Collegiate Swimmers," *Journal of Sport Behavior* (December 1999): 602–610; J. Bauman, "The Gold Medal Mind," *Psychology Today* 33 (May 2000): 62–69; A. Papaioannou *et al.*, "Combined Effect of Goal Setting and Self-Talk in Performance of a Soccer-Shooting Task," *Perceptual and Motor Skills* 98, no. 1 (February 2004): 89–99.

63. J. Houghton, D. *et al.*, "The Relationship between Self-Leadership and Personality: A Comparison of Hierarchical Factor Structures," *Journal of Managerial Psychology* 19, no. 4 (2004): 427–441. For discussion of constructive thought patterns in the context of organizations, see: J. Godwin, C. P. Neck, and J. Houghton, "The Impact of Thought Self-Leadership on Individual Goal Performance: A Cognitive Perspective," *Journal of Management Development* 18 (1999): 153–169.

64. F. Piccolo, "freeTHINK Tank," *Atlantic Business Magazine*, Oct-Nov 2004.

CHAPTER SEVEN

1. R. Brisbois, *How Canada Stacks Up: The Quality of Work—an International Perspective*, (Ottawa: Canadian Policy Research Networks, December 2003); "Employee Wellness," *Canadian HR Reporter*, 23 February 2004, 9–12; V. Galt, "Heavy Workloads Hit Health Care: Study," *Globe & Mail*, 10 November 2004, B1; J. Gerstel, "Take Off and Turn It Off," *Toronto Star*, 16 July 2004, D01; Canada NewsWire, *Canadians Need More 'Joie De Vivre', Global Vacation Deprivation Survey Reveals*, (Toronto: Expedia.ca, 19 May 2005); T. Lai, "Vacation: Why Aren't You Taking Yours?" *Globe & Mail*, 6 July 2005, C1; T. Taylor, "Hard-Working Canadians Find It Tough to Disconnect," *Calgary Herald*, 18 May 2005, A10; S. Wintrob, "Take Time Off, Eh!" *National Post*, 6 July 2005, FP9.

2. J. MacBride-King and K. Bachmann, *Is Work-Life Balance Still an Issue for Canadians and Their Employers? You Bet It Is*, (Ottawa: Conference Board of Canada, 1999); Canadian Mental Health Association, *The 2001 Canadian Mental Health Survey*, (Toronto: Canadian Mental Health Association, 2001); "Canadian Workers among the Most Stressed," *Worklife* 14, no. 2 (2002): 8–9; A. Derfel, "Boy, Are We Stressed Out," *Montreal Gazette*, 29 May 2003, A1.

3. T. Haratani, "Job Stress Trends in Japan" in *Job Stress Trends in East Asia (Proceedings of the First East-Asia Job Stress Meeting)*, ed. A. Tsutsumi, (Waseda University, Tokyo, 8 January, 2000), 4–10; "New Survey: Americans Stressed More Than Ever," *PR Newswire*, 26 June 2003; "India's Call Centers Suffer High Quit Rate," *CNET Asia*, 8 August 2003; S. James, "Work Stress Taking Larger Financial Toll," *Reuters* (9 August 2003); Mind, *Stress and Mental Health in the Workplace*, (London: Mind, May 2005).

4. J. C. Quick *et al.*, *Preventive Stress Management in Organizations* (Washington, D.C.: American Psychological Association, 1997), pp. 3–4; R. S. DeFrank and J. M. Ivancevich, "Stress on the Job: An Executive Update," *Academy of Management Executive* 12 (August 1998): 55–66.

5. Quick *et al.*, *Preventive Stress Management in Organizations*, pp. 5–6; B. L. Simmons and D. L. Nelson, "Eustress at Work: The Relationship between Hope and Health in Hospital Nurses," *Health Care Management Review* 26, no. 4 (October 2001): 7ff.

6. H. Selye, *Stress without Distress* (Philadelphia: J. B. Lippincott, 1974).

7. S. E. Taylor, R. L. Repetti, and T. Seeman, "Health Psychology: What Is an Unhealthy Environment and How Does It Get under the Skin?" *Annual Review of Psychology* 48 (1997): 411–447.

8. K. Danna and R. W. Griffin, "Health and Well-Being in the Workplace: A Review and Synthesis of the Literature," *Journal of Management* (Spring 1999): 357–384.

9. N. Wager, G. Fieldman, and T. Hussey, "The Effect on Ambulatory Blood Pressure of Working under Favourably and Unfavourably Perceived Supervisors," *Occupational and Environmental Medicine* 60, no. 7 (1 July 2003): 468–474. For further details on the stressful effects of bad bosses, see: E. K. Kelloway *et al.*, "Poor Leadership," in *Handbook of Workplace Stress*, ed. J. Barling, E. K. Kelloway, and M. Frone (Thousand Oaks, CA: Sage, 2005), 89–112.

10. J. D. Leck, "Violence in the Workplace: A New Challenge," *Optimum* 31 (November 2001); V. Di Martino, *Workplace Violence in the Health Sector: Country Case Studies* (Geneva: International Labour Organisation, 2002); A. Upson, *Violence at Work: Findings from the 2002/2003 British Crime Survey*, (London: Home Office, United Kingdom, 2004).

11. Children's Aid Society of Cape Breton-Victoria V. Workers' Compensation Board (N.S.), 2005 NSCA 38 (CanLII) (14 February).

12. This is a slight variation of the definition in the Quebec anti-harassment legislation. See www.cnt.gouv.qc.ca. For related definitions and discussion of workplace incivility, see: H. Cowiea and e. al., "Measuring Workplace Bullying," *Aggression and Violent Behavior* 7 (2002): 33–51; C. M. Pearson and C. L. Porath, "On the Nature, Consequences and Remedies of Workplace Incivility: No Time for 'Nice'? Think Again," *Academy of Management Executive* 19, no. 1 (February 2005): 7–18.

13. T. Goldenberg, "Thousands of Workers Intimidated on Job: Study," *Montreal Gazette*, 11 June 2005, A9; A. Marchand, A. Demers, and P. Durand, "Does Work Really Cause Stress? The Contribution of Occupational Structure and Work Organization to the Experience of Psychological Distress," *Social Science & Medicine* 61 (2005): 1–14.

14. V. Schultz, "Reconceptualizing Sexual Harassment," *Yale Law Journal* 107 (April 1998): 1683–1805; M. Rotundo, D.-H. Nguyen, and P. R. Sackett, "A Meta-Analytic Review of Gender Differences in Perceptions of Sexual Harassment," *Journal of Applied Psychology* 86 (October 2001): 914–922.

15. S. B. Hood, "Workplace Bullying," *Canadian Business*, 13–26 September 2004, 87–89.

16. E. K. Kelloway and J. Barling, "Job Characteristics, Role Stress and Mental Health," *Journal of Occupational Psychology* 64 (1991): 291–304; M. Siegall and L. L. Cummings, "Stress and Organizational Role Conflict," *Genetic, Social, and General Psychology Monographs* 12 (1995): 65–95; J. Lait and J. E. Wallace, "Stress at Work: A Study of Organizational-Professional Conflict and Unmet Expectations," *Relations Industrielles* 57, no. 3 (Summer 2002): 463–487; E. Grunfeld *et al.*, "Job Stress and Job Satisfaction of Cancer Care Workers," *Psycho-Oncology* 14, no. 1 (May 2005): 61–69.

17. A. M. Saks and B. E. Ashforth, "Proactive Socialization and Behavioral Self-Management," *Journal of Vocational Behavior* 48 (1996): 301–323; A. Nygaard and R. Dahlstrom, "Role Stress and Effectiveness in Horizontal Alliances," *Journal of Marketing* 66 (April 2002): 61–82.

18. Ipsos-Reid/Workopolis, "Workin' Past 9 to 5—New Study Finds Many Canadian White-Collar Workers Tied to Job around the Clock," News release, (Toronto: 27 March 2001); C. Higgins and L. Duxbury, *The 2001 National Work–Life Conflict Study: Report One, Final Report*, (Ottawa: Health Canada, March 2002); J. MacBride-King, *Wrestling with Workload: Organizational Strategies for Success*, (Ottawa: Conference Board of Canada, 2005). Past predictions of future work hours are described in: B. K. Hunnicutt, *Kellogg's Six-Hour Day* (Philadelphia: Temple University Press, 1996).

19. J. Ryall, "Japan Wakes up to Fatal Work Ethic," *Scotland on Sunday*, 15 June 2003, 22; C. B. Meek, "The Dark Side of Japanese Management in the 1990s: Karoshi and Ijime in the Japanese Workplace," *Journal of Managerial Psychology* 19, no. 3 (2004): 312–331.

20. L. Wahyudi S., "'Traffic Congestion Makes Me Crazy," *Jakarta Post*, 18 March 2003. Traffic congestion is linked to stress in: G. W. Evans, R. E. Wener, and D. Phillips, "The Morning Rush Hour: Predictability and Commuter Stress," *Environment and Behavior* 34 (July 2002): 521–530.

21. P. Fayerman, "Job Stress Linked to Control, Says Statistics Canada," *Vancouver Sun*, 18 January 1999, B1, B3; F. Kittell and e. al., "Job Conditions and Fibrinogen in 14,226 Belgian Workers: The Belstress Study," *European Heart Journal* 23 (2002): 1841–1848; s. K. Parker, "Longitudinal Effects of Lean Production on Employee Outcomes and the Mediating Role of Work Characteristics," *Journal of Applied Psychology* 88, no. 4 (2003): 620–634.

22. R. J. Burke and C. L. Cooper, *The Organization in Crisis: Downsizing, Restructuring, and Privatization* (Oxford, UK: Blackwell, 2000); M. Kivimaki *et al.*, "Factors Underlying the Effect of Organizational Downsizing on Health of Employees: Longitudinal Cohort Study," *British Medical Journal* 320 (8 April 2000): 971–975; M. Sverke, J. Hellgren, and K. Näswall, "No Security: A Meta-Analysis and Review of Job Insecurity and Its Consequences," *Journal of Occupational Health Psychology* 7 (July 2002): 242–264; R. J. Burke, "Correlates of Nursing Staff Survivor Responses to Hospital Restructuring and Downsizing," *Health Care Manager* 24, no. 2 (2005): 141–149.

23. L. T. Eby *et al.*, "Work and Family Research in IO/OB: Content Analysis and Review of the Literature (1980–2002)," *Journal of Vocational Behavior* 66, no. 1 (2005): 124–197.

24. Higgins and Duxbury, *The 2001 National Work–Life Conflict Study: Report One, Final Report*; M. Shields, "Shift Work and Health," *Health Reports (Statistics Canada)* 13 (Spring 2002): 11–34.

25. W. Stewart and J. Barling, "Fathers' Work Experiences Effect on Children's Behaviors Via Job-Related Affect and Parenting Behaviors," *Journal of Organizational Behavior* 17 (1996): 221–232; E. K. Kelloway, B. H. Gottlieb, and L. Barham, "The Source, Nature, and Direction of Work and Family Conflict: A Longitudinal Investigation," *Journal of Occupational Health Psychology* 4 (October 1999): 337–346.

26. A. S. Wharton and R. J. Erickson, "Managing Emotions on the Job and at

Home: Understanding the Consequences of Multiple Emotional Roles," *Academy of Management Review* (1993): 457–486.

27. B. Keil, "The 10 Most Stressful Jobs in NYC," *New York Post*, 6 April 1999, 50; A. Smith *et al.*, *The Scale of Occupational Stress: A Further Analysis of the Impact of Demographicc Factors and Type of Job*, (Sudbury, Suffolk: United Kingdom, Health & Safety Executive, 2000).

28. S. J. Havlovic and J. P. Keenen, "Coping with Work Stress: The Influence of Individual Differences; Handbook on Job Stress [Special Issue]," *Journal of Social Behavior and Personality* 6 (1991): 199–212.

29. S. C. Segerstrom *et al.*, "Optimism Is Associated with Mood, Coping, and Immune Change in Response to Stress," *Journal of Personality & Social Psychology* 74 (June 1998): 1646–1655; S. M. Jex *et al.*, "The Impact of Self-Efficacy on Stressor–Strain Relations: Coping Style as an Explanatory Mechanism," *Journal of Applied Psychology* 86 (2001): 401–409.

30. S. S. Luthar, D. Cicchetti, and B. Becker, "The Construct of Resilience: A Critical Evaluation and Guidelines for Future Work," *Child Development* 71, no. 3 (May-June 2000): 543–562; F. Luthans, "The Need for and Meaning of Positive Organizational Behavior," *Journal of Organizational Behavior* 23 (2002): 695–706; G. A. Bonanno, "Loss, Trauma, and Human Resilience: Have We Underestimated the Human Capacity to Thrive after Extremely Aversive Events?" *American Psychologist* 59, no. 1 (2004): 20–28.

31. K. M. Connor and J. R. T. Davidson, "Development of a New Resilience Scale: The Connor-Davidson Resilience Scale (CD-RISC)," *Depression and Anxiety* 18, no. 2 (2003): 76–82; M. M. Tugade, B. L. Fredrickson, and L. Feldman Barrett, "Psychological Resilience and Positive Emotional Granularity: Examining the Benefits of Positive Emotions on Coping and Health," *Journal of Personality* 72, no. 6 (2004): 1161–1190; L. Campbell-Sills, S. L. Cohan, and M. B. Stein, "Relationship of Resilience to Personality, Coping, and Psychiatric Symptoms in Young Adults," *Behaviour Research and Therapy* In Press (2006).

32. M. Beasley, T. Thompson, and J. Davidson, "Resilience in Response to Life Stress: The Effects of Coping Style and Cognitive Hardiness," *Personality and Individual Differences* 34, no. 1 (2003): 77–95; I. Tsaousis and I. Nikolaou, "Exploring the Relationship of Emotional Intelligence with Physical and Psychological Health Functioning," *Stress and Health* 21, no. 2 (2005): 77–86.

33. Y. Kim and L. Seidlitz, "Spirituality Moderates the Effect of Stress on Emotional and Physical Adjustment," *Personality and Individual Differences* 32, no. 8 (June 2002): 1377–1390; G. E. Richardson, "The Metatheory of Resilience and Resiliency," *Journal of Clinical Psychology* 58, no. 3 (2002): 307–321.

34. J. L. Hernandez, "What's the Buzz in Schuyler? Just Ask Beekeeper Finster," *Observer-Dispatch (Utica, NY)*, 23 June 2003.

35. J. T. Spence, A. S., and Robbins, "Workaholism: Definition, Measurement and Preliminary Results," *Journal of Personality Assessment* 58 (1992): 160–178; R. J. Burke, "Workaholism in Organizations: Psychological and Physical Well-Being Consequences," *Stress Medicine* 16, no. 1 (2000): 11–16; I. Harpaz and R. Snir, "Workaholism: Its Definition and Nature," *Human Relations* 56 (2003): 291–319; R. J. Burke, A. M. Richardson, and M. Martinussen, "Workaholism among Norwegian Senior Managers: New Research Directions," *International Journal of Management* 21, no. 4 (December 2004): 415–426.

36. R. J. Burke, "Workaholism and Extra-Work Satisfactions," *International Journal of Organizational Analysis* 7 (1999): 352–364; A. Kemeny, "Driven to Excel: A Portrait of Canada's Workaholics," *Canadian Social Trends* (Spring 2002): 2–7.

37. R. J. Burke and G. MacDermid, "Are Workaholics Job Satisfied and Successful in Their Careers?" *Career Development International* 4 (1999): 277–282; R. J. Burke and S. Matthiesen, "Short Communication: Workaholism among Norwegian Journalists: Antecedents and Consequences," *Stress and Health* 20, no. 5 (2004): 301–308.

38. D. Ganster, M. Fox, and D. Dwyer, "Explaining Employees' Health Care Costs: A Prospective Examination of Stressful Job Demands, Personal Control, and Physiological Reactivity," *Journal of Applied Psychology* 86 (May 2001): 954–964.

39. M. Kivimaki *et al.*, "Work Stress and Risk of Cardiovascular Mortality: Prospective Cohort Study of Industrial Employees," *British Medical Journal* 325 (19 October 2002): 857–860; A. Rosengren *et al.*, "Association of Psychosocial Risk Factors with Risk of Acute Myocardial Infarction in 11 119 Cases and 13 648 Controls from 52 Countries (the Interheart Study): Case-Control Study," *The Lancet* 364, no. 9438 (11 September 2004): 953–962; S. Yusuf *et al.*, "Effect of Potentially Modifiable Risk Factors Associated with Myocardial Infarction in 52 Countries (the Interheart Study): Case-Control Study," *The Lancet* 364, no. 9438 (11 September 2004): 937–952.

40. R. C. Kessler, "The Effects of Stressful Life Events on Depression," *Annual Review of Psychology* 48 (1997): 191–214; M. Jamal and V. V. Baba, "Job Stress and Burnout among Canadian Managers and Nurses: An Empirical Examination," *Canadian Journal of Public Health* 91, no. 6 (Nov-Dec 2000): 454–458.

41. C. Maslach, W. B. Schaufeli, and M. P. Leiter, "Job Burnout," *Annual Review of Psychology* 52 (2001): 397–422; J. R. B. Halbesleben and M. R. Buckley, "Burnout in Organizational Life," *Journal of Management* 30, no. 6 (2004): 859–879.

42. M. Jamal, "Job Stress and Job Performance Controversy: An Empirical Assessment," *Organizational Behavior and Human Performance* 33 (1984): 1–21; G. Keinan, "Decision Making under Stress: Scanning of Alternatives under Controllable and Uncontrollable Threats," *Journal of Personality and Social Psychology* 52 (1987): 638–644. The positive effects of moderate stress are reported in: L. Van Dyne, K. A. Jehn, and A. Cummings, "Differential Effects of Strain on Two Forms of Work Performance: Individual Employee Sales and Creativity," *Journal of Organizational Behavior* 23, no. 1 (2002): 57–74; E. Chajut and D. Algom, "Selective Attention Improves under Stress: Implications for Theories of Social Cognition," *Journal of Personality and Social Psychology* 85, no. 2 (2003): 231–248.

43. R. D. Hackett and P. Bycio, "An Evaluation of Employee Absenteeism as a Coping Mechanism among Hospital Nurses," *Journal of Occupational & Organizational Psychology* 69 (December 1996): 327–338; A. Vaananen *et al.*, "Job Characteristics, Physical and Psychological Symptoms, and Social Support as Antecedents of Sickness Absence among Men and Women in the Private Industrial Sector," *Social Science & Medicine* 57, no. 5 (September 2003): 807–824; L. Tourigny, V. V. Baba, and T. R. Lituchy, "Job Burnout among Airline Employees in Japan: A Study of the Buffering Effects of Absence and Supervisory Support," *International Journal of Cross Cultural Management* 5, no. 1 (April 2005): 67–85.

44. L. Greenburg and J. Barling, "Predicting Employee Aggression against Coworkers, Subordinates and Supervisors: The Roles of Person Behaviors and Perceived Workplace Factors," *Journal of Organizational Behavior* 20 (1999): 897–913; H. Steensma, "Violence in the Workplace: The Explanatory Strength of Social (in) Justice Theories," in *The Justice Motive in Everyday Life*, ed. M. Ross and D. T. Miller (New York: Cambridge University Press, 2002), 149–167; J. D. Leck, "Violence in the Canadian Workplace," *Journal of the American Academy of Business* 7, no. 2 (September 2005): 308–315.

45. H. Levitt, "Healthy Workplace Is up to Employers," *National Post*, 12 July 2004, FP11; J. F. Kirk, "Maybe the Courts Will Force Change," *Toronto Star*, 4 June 2005, D11.

46. Siegall and Cummings, "Stress and Organizational Role Conflict."

47. "Employee Wellness."

48. J. L. Howard, "Workplace Violence in Organizations: An Exploratory Study of Organizational Prevention Techniques," *Employee Responsibilities and Rights Journal* 13 (June 2001): 57–75.

49. W. Immen, "Part-Time Work: The New Career Track," *Globe & Mail*, 17 March 2005.

50. C. R. Cunningham and S. S. Murray, "Two Executives, One Career," *Harvard Business Review* 83, no. 2 (February 2005): 125–131.

51. S. R. Madsen, "The Effects of Home-Based Teleworking on Work-Family Conflict," *Human Resource Development Quarterly* 14, no. 1 (2003): 35–58.

52. R. W. Yerema, *Canada's Top 100 Employers*, 2004 ed. (Toronto: Mediacorp Canada, 2004); K. Vermond, "2004 Workplace Winners," *Today's Parent*, December/January 2005. Childcare at Riverdale Hospital is described in: Bureau of Municipal Research, *Work-Related Day Care—Helping to Close the Gap*, (Toronto: BMR, 1981).

53. M. Blair-Loy and A. S. Wharton, "Employees' Use of Work-Family Policies and the Workplace Social Context," *Social Forces* 80 (March 2002): 813–845; M. Jackson, "Managers Measured by Charges' Work-Life Accountability Programs Let Firms Calculate Progress," *Boston Globe*, 2 February 2003, G1.

54. S. Moreland, "Strike up Creativity," *Crain's Cleveland Business* (14 April 2003): 3.

55. F. Piccolo, "Brownie Points," *Atlantic Business*, Oct/Nov 2004, 22; L. Carter, "Teletech Is Wired Up," *Simcoe Business Magazine*, Spring 2005.

56. P. Kuitenbrouwer, "Given Time, What Would You Do?" *National Post*, 19 February 2005, FW3. The Western Canadian leisure study is reported in: Y. Iwasaki *et al.*, "A Short-Term Longitudinal Analysis of Leisure Coping Used by Police and Emergency Response Service Workers," *Journal of Leisure Research* 34 (July 2002): 311–339. On the value of sabbaticals, see: A. E. Carr and T. L.-P. Tang, "Sabbaticals and Empoyee Motivation: Benefits, Concerns, and Implications," *Journal of Education for Business* 80, no. 3 (Jan/Feb 2005): 160–164.

57. M. Waung, "The Effects of Self-Regulatory Coping Orientation on Newcomer Adjustment and Job Survival," *Personnel Psychology* 48 (1995): 633–650; Saks and Ashforth, "Proactive Socialization and Behavioral Self-Management,"

58. W. M. Ensel and N. Lin, "Physical Fitness and the Stress Process," *Journal of Community Psychology* 32, no. 1 (January 2004): 81–101.

59. S. Armour, "Rising Job Stress Could Affect Bottom Line," *USA Today*, 29 July 2003; V. A. Barnes, F. A. Treiber, and M. H. Johnson, "Impact of Transcendental Meditation on Ambulatory Blood Pressure in African-American Adolescents," *American Journal of Hypertension* 17, no. 4 (2004): 366–369; M. S. Lee *et al.*, "Effects of Qi-Training on Anxiety and Plasma Concentrations of Cortisol, Acth, and Aldosterone: A Randomized Placebo-Controlled Pilot Study," *Stress and Health* 20, no. 5 (2004): 243–248; P. Manikonda *et al.*, "Influence of Non-Pharmacological Treatment (Contemplative Meditation and Breathing Technique) on Stress Induced Hypertension—a Randomized Controlled Study," *American Journal of Hypertension* 18, no. 5, Supplement 1 (2005): A89–A90.

60. Danna and Griffin, "Health and Well-Being in the Workplace: A Review and Synthesis of the Literature"; "Town of Richmond Hill Receives First Well Workplace Award," *Benefits Canada*, February 2002.

61. T. Rotarius, A. Liberman, and J. S. Liberman, "Employee Assistance Programs: A Prevention and Treatment Prescription for Problems in Health Care Organizations," *Health Care Manager* 19 (September 2000): 24–31; J. J. L. van der Klink *et al.*, "The Benefits of Interventions for Work-Related Stress," *American Journal of Public Health* 91 (February 2001): 270–276.

62. S. E. Taylor *et al.*, "Biobehavioral Responses to Stress in Females: Tend-and-Befriend, Not Fight-or-Flight," *Psychological Review* 107, no. 3 (July 2000): 411–429; R. Eisler and D. S. Levine, "Nurture, Nature, and Caring: We Are Not Prisoners of Our Genes," *Brain and Mind* 3 (2002): 9–52.

63. J. S. House, *Work Stress and Social Support* (Reading, Mass: Addison-Wesley, 1981).

64. S. Schachter, *The Psychology of Affiliation, Stanford, Calif* (Stanford University Press: 1959).

CHAPTER EIGHT

1. P. Withers, "Few Rules Rule," *B. C. Business*, January 2002, 24; G. Huston, I. Wilkinson, and D. Kellogg, "Dare to Be Great," *B.C. Business*, May 2004, 28–29; P. Withers and L. Kloet, "The Best Companies to Work for in B.C.," *B.C. Business*, December 2004, 37–53; M. Andrews, "How to Make Robot Bees, and Other Sound Secrets," *National Post*, 5 March 2005, TO32; P. Wilson, "Radical Entertainment to Hire Staff, Expand Studio," *Vancouver Sun*, 6 May 2005, C3.

2. F. A. Shull Jr., A. L. Delbecq, and L. L. Cummings, *Organizational Decision Making* (New York: McGraw-Hill, 1970), p. 31.

3. R. E. Nisbett, *The Geography of Thought: How Asians and Westerners Think Differently—and Why* (New York: Free Press, 2003); D. Baltzly, "Stoicism," (Stanford Encyclopedia of Philosophy, 2004), http://plato.stanford.edu/entries/stoicism/, (accessed March 8 2005); R. Hanna, "Kant's Theory of Judgment," (Stanford Encyclopedia of Philosophy, 2004), http://plato. stanford.edu/entries/kant-judgment/, (accessed March 12 2005).

4. This model is adapted from several sources, including: H. A. Simon, *The New Science of Management Decision* (New York: Harper & Row, 1960); H. Mintzberg, D. Raisinghani, and A. Théorét, "The Structure of 'Unstructured' Decision Processes," *Administrative Science Quarterly* 21 (1976): 246–275; W. C. Wedley and R. H. G. Field, "A Predecision Support System," *Academy of Management Review* 9 (1984): 696–703.

5. P. F. Drucker, *The Practice of Management* (New York: Harper & Brothers, 1954), 353–357; B. M. Bass, *Organizational Decision Making* (Homewood, Ill: Irwin, 1983), Chap. 3.

6. L. R. Beach and T. R. Mitchell, "A Contingency Model for the Selection of Decision Strategies," *Academy of Management Review* 3 (1978): 439–449; I. L. Janis, *Crucial Decisions* (New York: The Free Press, 1989), pp. 35–37; W. Zhongtuo, "Meta-Decision Making: Concepts and Paradigm," *Systematic Practice and Action Research* 13, no. 1 (February 2000): 111–115.

7. J. G. March and H. A. Simon, *Organizations* (New York: John Wiley & Sons, 1958).

8. N. Schwarz, "Social Judgment and Attitudes: Warmer, More Social, and Less Conscious," *European Journal of Social Psychology* 30 (2000): 149–176; N. M. Ashkanasy and C. E. J. Hartel, "Managing Emotions in Decision-Making," in *Managing Emotions in the Workplace*, ed. N. M. Ashkanasy, W. J. Zerbe, and C. E. J. Hartel (Armonk, N.Y: M. E. Sharpe, 2002); S. Maitlis and H. Ozcelik, "Toxic Decision Processes: A Study of Emotion and Organizational Decision Making," *Organization Science* 15, no. 4 (July-August 2004): 375–393.

9. A. Howard, "Opinion," *Computing* (8 July 1999): 18.

10. A. R. Damasio, *Descartes' Error: Emotion, Reason, and the Human Brain* (New York: Putnam Sons, 1994); P. Winkielman and K. C. Berridge, "Unconscious Emotion," *Current Directions in Psychological Science* 13, no. 3 (2004): 120–123; A. Bechara and A. R. Damasio, "The Somatic Marker Hypothesis: A Neural Theory of Economic Decision," *Games and Economic Behavior* 52, no. 2 (2005): 336–372.

11. T. K. Das and B. S. Teng, "Cognitive Biases and Strategic Decision Processes: An Integrative Perspective," *Journal Of Management Studies* 36, no. 6 (Nov 1999): 757–778; P. Bijttebier, H. Vertommen, and G. V. Steene, "Assessment of Cognitive Coping Styles: A Closer Look at Situation-Response Inventories," *Clinical Psychology Review* 21, no. 1 (2001): 85–104; P. C. Nutt, "Expanding the Search for Alternatives During Strategic Decision-Making," *Academy of Management Executive* 18, no. 4 (November 2004): 13–28.

12. P. C. Nutt, *Why Decisions Fail* (San Francisco, CA: Berrett-Koehler, 2002); S. Finkelstein, *Why Smart Executives Fail* (New York: Viking, 2003).

13. E. Witte, "Field Research on Complex Decision-Making Processes—the Phase Theorum," *International Studies of Management and Organization* (1972): 156–182; J. A. Bargh and T. L. Chartrand, "The Unbearable Automaticity of Being," *American Psychologist* 54, no. 7 (July 1999): 462–479.

14. H. A. Simon, *Administrative Behavior*, Second ed. (New York: The Free Press, 1957); H. A. Simon, "Rational Decision Making in Business Organizations," *American Economic Review* 69, no. 4 (September 1979): 493–513.

15. D. Sandahl and C. Hewes, "Decision Making at Digital Speed," *Pharmaceutical Executive* 21 (August 2001): 62.

16. Simon, *Administrative Behavior*, pp. xxv, 80–84.

17. A. L. Brownstein, "Biased Predecision Processing," *Psychological Bulletin* 129, no. 4 (2003): 545–568.

18. F. Phillips, "The Distortion of Criteria after Decision-Making," *Organizational Behavior and Human Decision Processes* 88 (2002): 769–784.

19. H. A. Simon, "Rational Choice and the Structure of Environments," *Psychological Review* 63 (1956): 129–138; H. Schwartz, "Herbert Simon and Behavioral Economics," *Journal of Socio-Economics* 31 (2002): 181–189.

20. P. C. Nutt, "Search During Decision Making," *European Journal of Operational Research* 160 (2005 2005): 851–876.

21. J. S. Lerner and D. Keltner, "Beyond Valence: Toward a Model of Emotion-Specific Influences on Judgement and Choice," *Cognition and Emotion* 14, no. 4 (2000): 473–493; J. P. Forgas and J. M. George, "Affective Influences on Judgments and Behavior in Organizations: An Information Processing Perspective," *Organizational Behavior and Human Decision Processes* 86 (September 2001): 3–34; G. Loewenstein and J. S. Lerner, "The Role of Affect in Decision Making," in *Handbook of Affective Sciences*, ed. R. J. Davidson, K. R. Scherer, and H. H. Goldsmith (New York: Oxford University Press, 2003), 619–642; J. S. Lerner, D. A. Small, and G. Loewenstein, "Heart Strings and Purse Strings: Carryover Effects of Emotions on Economic Decisions," *Psychological Science* 15, no. 5 (2004): 337–341.

22. M. T. Pham, "The Logic of Feeling," *Journal of Consumer Psychology* 14 (September 2004): 360–369; N. Schwarz, "Metacognitive Experiences in Consumer Judgment and Decision Making," *Journal of Consumer Psychology* 14 (September 2004): 332–349.

23. L. Sjöberg, "Intuitive vs. Analytical Decision Making: Which Is Preferred?" *Scandinavian Journal of Management* 19 (2003): 17–29.

24. M. Lyons, "Cave-in Too Close for Comfort, Miner Says," *Saskatoon Star-Phoenix*, 6 May 2002.

25. W. H. Agor, "The Logic of Intuition," *Organizational Dynamics* (Winter 1986): 5–18; H. A. Simon, "Making Management Decisions: The Role of Intuition and Emotion," *Academy of Management Executive* (February 1987): 57–64; O. Behling and N. L. Eckel, "Making Sense out of Intuition," *Academy of Management Executive* 5 (February 1991): 46–54.

26. M. D. Lieberman, "Intuition: A Social Cognitive Neuroscience Approach," *Psychological Bulletin* 126 (2000):

109–137; G. Klein, *Intuition at Work* (New York: Currency/Doubleday, 2003); E. Dane and M. G. Pratt, "Intuition: It's Boundaries and Role in Organizational Decision-Making" in *Academy of Management Best Papers Proceedings*, (New Orleans, 2004), A1–A6.

27. Klein, *Intuition at Work*, pp. 12–13, 16–17.

28. Y. Ganzach, A. H. Kluger, and N. Klayman, "Making Decisions from an Interview: Expert Measurement and Mechanical Combination," *Personnel Psychology* 53 (Spring 2000): 1–20; A. M. Hayashi, "When to Trust Your Gut," *Harvard Business Review* 79 (February 2001): 59–65. Evidence of high failure rates from quick decisions is reported in: Nutt, *Why Decisions Fail*; Nutt, "Search During Decision Making."

29. P. Goodwin and G. Wright, "Enhancing Strategy Evaluation in Scenario Planning: A Role for Decision Analysis," *Journal of Management Studies* 38 (January 2001): 1–16; R. Bradfield *et al.*, "The Origins and Evolution of Scenario Techniques in Long Range Business Planning," *Futures* 37, no. 8 (2005): 795–812.

30. R. N. Taylor, *Behavioral Decision Making* (Glenview, Ill.: Scott, Foresman, 1984), pp. 163–166.

31. G. Whyte, "Escalating Commitment to a Course of Action: A Reinterpretation," *Academy of Management Review* 11 (1986): 311–321; J. Brockner, "The Escalation of Commitment to a Failing Course of Action: Toward Theoretical Progress," *Academy of Management Review* 17, no. 1 (January 1992): 39–61.

32. J. Lorinc, "Power Failure," *Canadian Business*, November 1992, 50–58; P. Ayton and H. Arkes, "Call It Quits," *New Scientist* (20 June 1998); M. Fackler, "Tokyo's Newest Subway Line a Saga of Hubris, Humiliation," *Associated Press Newswires* (20 July 1999); P. Gallagher, "New Bid to Rein in Rising Costs of Scots Parliament," *Aberdeen Press and Journal (Scotland)*, 11 June 2003, 1; I. Swanson, "Holyrood Firms Face Grilling over Costs," *Evening News (Edinburgh)*, 6 June 2003, 2.

33. F. D. Schoorman and P. J. Holahan, "Psychological Antecedents of Escalation Behavior: Effects of Choice, Responsibility, and Decision Consequences," *Journal of Applied Psychology* 81 (1996): 786–793.

34. G. Whyte, "Escalating Commitment in Individual and Group Decision Making: A Prospect Theory Approach," *Organizational Behavior and Human Decision Processes* 54 (1993): 430–455; D. J. Sharp and S. B. Salter, "Project Escalation and Sunk Costs: A Test of the International Generalizability of Agency and Prospect Theories," *Journal of International Business Studies* 28, no. 1 (1997): 101–121.

35. S. McKay, "When Good People Make Bad Decisions," *Canadian Business*, February 1994, 52–55.

36. R. Matas, "Spiralling Costs Torpedoed Fast Ferries," *Globe & Mail*, 13 June 2000, A2; C. McInnes, "Victoria Sinks Fast Ferries," *Vancouver Sun*, 14 March 2000; A. Redekop, "Ferry-Tale Alarms," *Vancouver Province*, 14 June 2000; M. Hume, "B.C. Rolls Dice on Ferries," *National Post*, 10 January 2003, A08; "Fast Ferries May Be Sold for Use as Floating Casinos after Refits," *Canadian Press*, 1 March 2004.

37. J. D. Bragger *et al.*, "When Success Breeds Failure: History, Hysteresis, and Delayed Exit Decisions," *Journal of Applied Psychology* 88, no. 1 (2003): 6–14. A second logical reason for escalation, called the martingale strategy, is described in: J. A. Aloysius, "Rational Escalation of Costs by Playing a Sequence of Unfavorable Gambles: The Martingale," *Journal of Economic Behavior & Organization* 51 (2003): 111–129.

38. I. Simonson and B. M. Staw, "De-Escalation Strategies: A Comparison of Techniques for Reducing Commitment to Losing Courses of Action," *Journal of Applied Psychology*, no. 77 (1992): 419–426; W. Boulding, R. Morgan, and R. Staelin, "Pulling the Plug to Stop the New Product Drain," *Journal of Marketing Research*, no. 34 (1997): 164–176; B. M. Staw, K. W. Koput, and S. G. Barsade, "Escalation at the Credit Window: A Longitudinal Study of Bank Executives' Recognition and Write-Off of Problem Loans," *Journal of Applied Psychology*, no. 82 (1997): 130–142; M. Keil and D. Robey, "Turning around Troubled Software Projects: An Exploratory Study of the Deescalation of Commitment to Failing Courses of Action," *Journal of Management Information Systems*, no. 15 (Spring 1999): 63–87.

39. M. Fenton-O'Creevy, "Employee Involvement and the Middle Manager:

Saboteur or Scapegoat?" *Human Resource Management Journal*, no. 11 (2001): 24–40. Also see: V. H. Vroom and A. G. Jago, *The New Leadership: Managing Participation in Organizations* (Englewood Cliffs, N.J.: Prentice Hill, 1988).

40. P. Delean, "These Caps Are Tops," *Montreal Gazette*, 27 September 1999; T. Heaps and P. Fengler, "Aqua Purus," *Corporate Knights* 1, no. 2 (Fall 2002): 23; P. Grescoe, *Flight Path* (Toronto: John Wiley & Sons Canada, 2004), pp. 132–133.

41. Some of the early OB writing on employee involvement includes: C. Argyris, *Personality and Organization* (New York: Harper & Row, 1957); D. McGregor, *The Human Side of Enterprise* (New York: McGraw-Hill, 1960); R. Likert, *New Patterns of Management* (New York: McGraw-Hill, 1961).

42. A. G. Robinson and D. M. Schroeder, *Ideas Are Free* (San Francisco: Berrett-Koehler, 2004).

43. A. Kleingeld, H. Van Tuijl, and J. A. Algera, "Participation in the Design of Performance Management Systems: A Quasi-Experimental Field Study," *Journal of Organizational Behavior* 25, no. 7 (2004): 831–851.

44. K. T. Dirks, L. L. Cummings, and J. L. Pierce, "Psychological Ownership in Organizations: Conditions under Which Individuals Promote and Resist Change," *Research in Organizational Change and Development*, no. 9 (1996): 1–23; J. P. Walsh and S.-F. Tseng, "The Effects of Job Characteristics on Active Effort at Work," *Work & Occupations*, no. 25 (February 1998): 74–96. The quotation is from: E. E. Lawler III, *Rewarding Excellence: Pay Strategies for the New Economy* (San Francisco: Jossey-Bass, 2000), pp. 23–24.

45. G. P. Latham, D. C. Winters, and E. A. Locke, "Cognitive and Motivational Effects of Participation: A Mediator Study," *Journal of Organizational Behavior*, no. 15 (1994): 49–63; J. A. Wagner III *et al.*, "Cognitive and Motivational Frameworks in U.S. Research on Participation: A Meta-Analysis of Primary Effects," *Journal of Organizational Behavior*, no. 18 (1997): 49–65.

46. Y. Utsunomiya, "Yamato Continues to Deliver New Ideas," *Japan Times*, 8 July 2003.

47. J. Zhou and C. E. Shalley, "Research on Employee Creativity: A Critical Review

and Directions for Future Research," *Research in Personnel and Human Resources Management* 22 (2003): 165–217; M. A. Runco, "Creativity," *Annual Review of Psychology* 55 (2004): 657–687.

48. B. Kabanoff and J. R. Rossiter, "Recent Developments in Applied Creativity," *International Review of Industrial and Organizational Psychology*, no. 9 (1994): 283–324.

49. R. S. Nickerson, "Enhancing Creativity," in *Handbook of Creativity*, ed. R. J. Sternberg (New York: Cambridge University Press, 1999), 392–430.

50. R. I. Sutton, *Weird Ideas That Work* (New York: Free Press, 2002), p. 26.

51. For a thorough discussion of insight, see: R. J. Sternberg and J. E. Davidson, *The Nature of Insight* (Cambridge, MA: MIT Press, 1995).

52. R. J. Sternberg and L. A. O' Hara, "Creativity and Intelligence," in *Handbook of Creativity*, ed. R. J. Sternberg (New York: Cambridge University Press, 1999), 251–272; S. Taggar, "Individual Creativity and Group Ability to Utilize Individual Creative Resources: A Multilevel Model," *Academy of Management Journal*, no. 45 (April 2002): 315–330.

53. G. J. Feist, "The Influence of Personality on Artistic and Scientific Creativity," in *Handbook of Creativity*, ed. R. J. Sternberg (New York: Cambridge University Press, 1999), 273–296; Sutton, *Weird Ideas That Work*, pp. 8–9, Chap. 10.

54. R. W. Weisberg, "Creativity and Knowledge: A Challenge to Theories," in *Handbook of Creativity*, ed. R. J. Sternberg (New York: Cambridge University Press, 1999), 226–250.

55. B. Breen, "Rapid Motion," *Fast Company*, August 2001, 49; L. Pratt, "Persistence in Motion," *Profit Magazine*, May 2001, 18–22.

56. Sutton, *Weird Ideas That Work*, pp. 121, 153–154; C. Andriopoulos, "Six Paradoxes in Managing Creativity: An Embracing Act," *Long Range Planning* 36 (2003): 375–388.

57. T. Koppell, *Powering the Future* (New York: Wiley, 1999), p. 15.

58. D. K. Simonton, "Creativity: Cognitive, Personal, Developmental, and Social Aspects," *American Psychologist* 55 (January 2000): 151–158.

59. M. D. Mumford, "Managing Creative People: Strategies and Tactics for Innovation," *Human Resource Management Review* 10 (Autumn 2000): 313–351; T. M. Amabile *et al.*, "Leader Behaviors and the Work Environment for Creativity: Perceived Leader Support," *The Leadership Quarterly* 15, no. 1 (2004): 5–32; C. E. Shalley, J. Zhou, and G. R. Oldham, "The Effects of Personal and Contextual Characteristics on Creativity: Where Should We Go from Here?" *Journal of Management* 30, no. 6 (2004): 933–958.

60. "Five up-and-Comers," *Atlantic Business Magazine*, January/February 2005.

61. T. M. Amabile, "Motivating Creativity in Organizations: On Doing What You Love and Loving What You Do," *California Management Review* 40 (Fall 1997): 39–58; A. Cummings and G. R. Oldham, "Enhancing Creativity: Managing Work Contexts for the High Potential Employee," *California Management Review*, no. 40 (Fall 1997): 22–38.

62. T. M. Amabile, "Changes in the Work Environment for Creativity During Downsizing," *Academy of Management Journal* 42 (December 1999): 630–640.

63. J. M. Howell and K. Boies, "Champions of Technological Innovation: The Influence of Contextual Knowledge, Role Orientation, Idea Generation, and Idea Promotion on Champion Emergence," *The Leadership Quarterly* 15, no. 1 (2004): 123–143; Shalley, Zhou, and Oldham, "The Effects of Personal and Contextual Characteristics on Creativity."

64. A. Hiam, "Obstacles to Creativity and How You Can Remove Them," *Futurist* 32 (October 1998): 30–34.

65. M. A. West, *Developing Creativity in Organizations* (Leicester, UK: BPS Books, 1997), pp. 33–35.

66. P. Brown, "Across the Table into the Bedroom," *Times of London*, 1 March 2001, D4; P. Luke, "Business World's a Stage," *Vancouver Province*, 2 September 2001.

67. J. Neff, "At Eureka Ranch, Execs Doff Wing Tips, Fire up Ideas," 9 March 1998, 28–29.

68. A. Hargadon and R. I. Sutton, "Building an Innovation Factory," *Harvard Business Review* 78 (May-June 2000): 157–166; T. Kelley, *The Art of Innovation* (New York: Currency Doubleday, 2001), pp. 158–162.

69. K. S. Brown, "The Apple of Jonathan Ive's Eye," *Investor's Business Daily* (19 September 2003).

CHAPTER NINE

1. S. Agrell, "What Went Wrong?" *National Post*, 4 August 2005, A1; T. Blackwell and S. Agrell, "Weather, Pilots' Judgment under Scrutiny," *Ottawa Citizen*, 4 August 2005, A1; S. Frank, "What Went Right," *Time (Canada)*, 15 August 2005; H. Kennedy, "Perfect Evacuation," *New York Daily News*, 4 August 2005, 30; William Osler Health Centre, "Emergency Response Procedures Worked According to Plan after Air France Plane Crash," CNW News release, (Brampton, ON: 5 August 2005).

2. E. Hart, "Manager of the Year: John Mang," *Iron & Steelmaker* (June 2003): 5–7; P. Haw, "Learning from Lean Principles," *Business Day* (7 July 2003): 7.

3. This definition and very similar variations are found in: M. E. Shaw, *Group Dynamics*, 3 ed. (New York: McGraw-Hill, 1981), 8; S. A. Mohrman, S. G. Cohen, and A. M. Mohrman Jr., *Designing Team-Based Organizations: New Forms for Knowledge Work* (San Francisco: Jossey-Bass, 1995), 39–40; M. A. West, "Preface: Introducing Work Group Psychology," in *Handbook of Work Group Psychology*, ed. M. A. West (Chichester, UK: Wiley, 1996), xxvi; S. G. Cohen and D. E. Bailey, "What Makes Teams Work: Group Effectiveness Research from the Shop Floor to the Executive Suite," *Journal of Management* 23 (May 1997): 239–290; E. Sundstrom, "The Challenges of Supporting Work Team Effectiveness," in *Supporting Work Team Effectiveness*, ed. E. Sundstrom and Associates (San Francisco, CA: Jossey-Bass, 1999), 6–9.

4. Several sources affirm that the term "teams" has largely replaced "groups" in organizational behaviour, except for "informal groups." See R. A. Guzzo and M. W. Dickson, "Teams in Organizations: Recent Research on Performance and Effectiveness," *Annual Review of Psychology* 47 (1996): 307–338; D. A. Nadler, "From Ritual to Real Work: The Board as a Team," *Directors and Boards* 22 (Summer 1998): 28–31; L. R. Offerman and R. K. Spiros, "The Science and Practice of Team Development: Improving the Link," *Academy of Management Journal* 44 (April 2001): 376–392.

5. B. D. Pierce and R. White, "The Evolution of Social Structure: Why Biology Matters," *Academy of Management*

Review 24 (October 1999): 843–853; P. R. Lawrence and N. Nohria, *Driven: How Human Nature Shapes Our Choices* (San Francisco: Jossey-Bass, 2002); J. R. Spoor and J. R. Kelly, "The Evolutionary Significance of Affect in Groups: Communication and Group Bonding," *Group Processes & Intergroup Relations* 7, no. 4 (2004): 398–412.

6. M. A. Hogg *et al.*, "The Social Identity Perspective: Intergroup Relations, Self-Conception, and Small Groups," *Small Group Research* 35, no. 3 (June 2004): 246–276; N. Michinov, E. Michinov, and M.-C. Toczek-Capelle, "Social Identity, Group Orocesses, and Performance in Synchronous Computer-Mediated Communication," *Group Dynamics: Theory, Research, and Practice* 8, no. 1 (2004): 27–39; M. Van Vugt and C. M. Hart, "Social Identity as Social Glue: The Origins of Group Loyalty," *Journal of Personality and Social Psychology* 86, no. 4 (2004): 585–598.

7. S. Schacter, *The Psychology of Affiliation* (Stanford, CA: Stanford University Press, 1959), 12–19; R. Eisler and D. S. Levine, "Nurture, Nature, and Caring: We Are Not Prisoners of Our Genes," *Brain and Mind* 3 (2002): 9–52; A. C. DeVries, E. R. Glasper, and C. E. Detillion, "Social Modulation of Stress Responses," *Physiology & Behavior* 79, no. 3 (August 2003): 399–407.

8. M. Moldaschl and W. Weber, "The 'Three Waves' of Industrial Group Work: Historical Reflections on Current Research on Group Work," *Human Relations* 51 (March 1998): 347–388. The survey quotation is found in: "What Makes Teams Work?" *Hrfocus* (April 2002): 17. Several popular books in the 1980s encouraged team work, based on the Japanese economic miracle. These books included: W. Ouchi, *Theory Z: How American Management Can Meet the Japanese Challenge* (Reading, Mass.: Addison-Wesley, 1981); R. T. Pascale and A. G. Athos, *Art of Japanese Management* (New York: Simon and Schuster, 1982).

9. C. R. Emery and L. D. Fredenhall, "The Effect of Teams on Firm Profitability and Customer Satisfaction," *Journal of Service Research* 4 (February 2002): 217–229; G. S. Van der Vegt and O. Janssen, "Joint Impact of Interdependence and Group Diversity on Innovation," *Journal of Management* 29 (2003): 729–751.

10. J. Godard, "High Performance and the Transformation of Work? The Implications of Alternative Work Practices for the Experience and Outcomes of Work," *Industrial & Labor Relations Review* 54 (July 2001): 776–805.

11. M. A. West, C. S. Borrill, and K. L. Unsworth, "Team EffectIveness In Organizations," *International Review of Industrial and Organizational Psychology* 13 (1998): 1–48; R. Forrester and A. B. Drexler, "A Model for Team-Based Organization Performance," *Academy of Management Executive* 13 (August 1999): 36–49; J. E. McGrath, H. Arrow, and J. L. Berdahl, "The Study of Groups: Past, Present, and Future," *Personality & Social Psychology Review* 4, no. 1 (2000): 95–105; M. A. Marks, J. E. Mathieu, and S. J. Zaccaro, "A Temporally Based Framework and Taxonomy of Team Processes," *Academy of Management Review* 26, no. 3 (July 2001): 356–376.

12. G. P. Shea and R. A. Guzzo, "Group Effectiveness: What Really Matters?" *Sloan Management Review* 27 (1987): 33–46; J. R. Hackman *et al.*, "Team Effectiveness in Theory and in Practice," in *Industrial and Organizational Psychology: Linking Theory with Practice*, ed. C. L. Cooper and E. A. Locke (Oxford, UK: Blackwell, 2000), 109–129.

13. J. N. Choi, "External Activities and Team Effectiveness: Review and Theoretical Development," *Small Group Research* 33 (April 2002): 181–208; T. L. Doolen, M. E. Hacker, and E. M. Van Aken, "The Impact of Organizational Context on Work Team Effectiveness: A Study of Production Team," *IEEE Transactions on Engineering Management* 50, no. 3 (August 2003): 285–296.

14. J. S. DeMatteo, L. T. Eby, and E. Sundstrom, "Team-Based Rewards: Current Empirical Evidence and Directions for Future Research," *Research in Organizational Behavior* 20 (1998): 141–183; E. E. Lawler III, *Rewarding Excellence: Pay Strategies for the New Economy* (San Francisco: Jossey-Bass, 2000), 207–214; G. Hertel, S. Geister, and U. Konradt, "Managing Virtual Teams: A Review of Current Empirical Research," *Human Resource Management Review* 15 (2005): 69–95.

15. D. McCutcheon, "Chipping Away: Celestica's Toronto Plant Cuts Waste Blitz by Blitz," *Advanced Manufacturing* 6, no. 6 (Nov/Dec 2004): 23.

16. R. Wageman, "Case Study: Critical Success Factors for Creating Superb Self-Managing Teams at Xerox," *Compensation and Benefits Review* 29 (September-October 1997): 31–41; G. Gard, K. Lindström, and M. Dallner, "Towards a Learning Organization: The Introduction of a Client-Centered Team-Based Organization in Administrative Surveying Work," *Applied Ergonomics* 34 (2003): 97–105.

17. A. Niimi, "The Slow and Steady Climb toward True North," Toyota Motor Manufacturing North America News release, (7 August 2003); B. Andrews, "Room with Many Views," *Business Review Weekly*, 15 January 2004, 68.

18. S. D. Dionne *et al.*, "Transformational Leadership and Team Performance," *Journal Of Organizational Change Management* 17, no. 2 (2004): 177–193.

19. A. S. Sohal, M. Terziovski, and A. Zutshi, "Team-Based Strategy at Varian Australia: A Case Study," *Technovation* 23 (2003): 349–357.

20. M. A. Campion, E. M. Papper, and G. J. Medsker, "Relations between Work Team Characteristics and Effectiveness: A Replication and Extension," *Personnel Psychology* 49 (1996): 429–452; D. C. Man and S. S. K. Lam, "The Effects of Job Complexity and Autonomy on Cohesiveness in Collectivistic and Individualistic Work Groups: A Cross-Cultural Analysis," *Journal of Organizational Behavior* 24 (2003): 979–1001.

21. R. Wageman, "The Meaning of Interdependence," in *Groups at Work: Theory and Research*, ed. M. E. Turner (Mahwah, N. J.: Lawrence Erlbaum Associates, 2001), 197–217.

22. R. Wageman, "Interdependence and Group Effectiveness," *Administrative Science Quarterly* 40 (1995): 145–180; G. S. Van der Vegt, J. M. Emans, and E. Van de Vliert, "Patterns of Interdependence in Work Teams: A Two-Level Investigation of the Relations with Job and Team Satisfaction," *Personnel Psychology* 54 (Spring 2001): 51–69; S. M. Gully *et al.*, "A Meta-Analysis of Team-Efficacy, Potency, and Performance: Interdependence and Level of Analysis as Moderators of Observed Relationships," *Journal Of Applied Psychology* 87, no. 5 (Oct 2002): 819–832.

23. J. D. Thompson, *Organizations in Action* (New York: McGraw-Hill, 1967), 54–56. One concern with Thompson's

typology is that it isn't clear how much more interdependence is created by each of these three forms. See: G. Van der Vegt and E. Van de Vliert, "Intragroup Interdependence and Effectiveness: Review and Proposed Directions for Theory and Practice," *Journal of Managerial Psychology* 17, no. 1/2 (2002): 50–67.

24. R. Semler, *The Seven-Day Weekend* (London: Century, 2003), 183.

25. G. Stasser, "Pooling of Unshared Information During Group Discussion," in *Group Process and Productivity*, ed. S. Worchel, W. Wood, and J. A. Simpson (Newbury Park, California: Sage, 1992); J. R. Katzenbach and D. K. Smith, *The Wisdom of Teams: Creating the High-Performance Organization* (Boston: Harvard University Press, 1993), 45–47.

26. S. E. Nedleman, "Recruiters Reveal Their Top Interview Questions," *Financial News Online*, 16 February 2005.

27. P. C. Earley, "East Meets West Meets Mideast: Further Explorations of Collectivistic and Individualistic Work Groups," *Academy of Management Journal* 36 (1993): 319–348; L. T. Eby and G. H. Dobbins, "Collectivist Orientation in Teams: An Individual and Group-Level Analysis," *Journal of Organizational Behavior* 18 (1997): 275–295; S. B. Alavi and J. McCormick, "Theoretical and Measurement Issues for Studies of Collective Orientation in Team Contexts," *Small Group Research* 35, no. 2 (April 2004): 111–127.

28. M. R. Barrick *et al.*, "Relating Member Ability and Personality to Work-Team Processes and Team Effectiveness," *Journal of Applied Psychology* 83 (1998): 377–391; S. Sonnentag, "Excellent Performance: The Role of Communication and Cooperation Processes," *Applied Psychology: An International Review* 49 (2000): 483–497.

29. S. E. Jackson and A. Joshi, "Diversity in Social Context: A Multi-Attribute, Multilevel Analysis of Team Diversity and Sales Performance," *Journal of Organizational Behavior* 25 (2004): 675–702; D. van Knippenberg, C. K. W. De Dreu, and A. C. Homan, "Work Group Diversity and Group Performance: An Integrative Model and Research Agenda," *Journal of Applied Psychology* 89, no. 6 (2004): 1008–1022.

30. R. Muzyka and G. Zeschuk, "Managing Multiple Projects," *Game Developer*, March 2003, 34–39; J. Myers, "Dream Teams," *Profit*, June 2003, 24.

31. D. A. Harrison *et al.*, "Time, Teams, and Task Performance: Changing Effects of Surface- and Deep-Level Diversity on Group Functioning," *Academy of Management Journal* 45 (October 2002): 1029–1045.

32. K. Y. O. R. Williams, C.A., "Demography and Diversity in Organizations: A Review of 40 Years of Research," in *Research in Organizational Behavior*, ed. B. M. Staw and L. L. Cummings (Greenwich, CT: JAI, 1998), 77–140; C. M. Riodan, "Relational Demography within Groups: Past Developments, Contradictions, and New Directions," in *Research in Personnel and Human Resources Management*, ed. G. R. Ferris (Greenwich, CT: JAI, 2000), 131–173.

33. D. C. Lau and J. K. Murnighan, "Interactions within Groups and Subgroups: The Effects of Demographic Faultlines," *Academy of Management Journal* 48, no. 4 (August 2005): 645–659.

34. The NTSB and NASA studies are summarized in: J. R. Hackman, "New Rules for Team Building," *Optimize* (July 2002): 50–62.

35. R. Deruyter, "Budd Workers Reject Shift Change," *Kitchener-Waterloo Record* (1 June 2002).

36. B. W. Tuckman and M. A. C. Jensen, "Stages of Small-Group Development Revisited," *Group and Organization Studies* 2 (1977): 419–442.

37. J. E. Mathieu and G. F. Goodwin, "The Influence of Shared Mental Models on Team Process and Performance," *Journal of Applied Psychology* 85 (April 2000): 273–284.

38. A. Edmondson, "Psychological Safety and Learning Behavior in Work Teams," *Administrative Science Quarterly* 44 (1999): 350–383.

39. D. L. Miller, "The Stages of Group Development: A Retrospective Study of Dynamic Team Processes," *Canadian Journal of Administrative Sciences* 20, no. 2 (2003): 121–134. For other models of team development, see: J. G. Gersick, "Time and Transition in Work Teams: Toward a New Model of Group Development," *Academy of Management Journal* 31 (March 1988): 9–41; J. E. Jones and W. L. Bearley, "Facilitating Team Development: A View from the Field," *Group Facilitation* 3 (Spring 2001): 56–65; H. Arrow *et al.*, "Time, Change, and Development: The Temporal Perspective on Groups," *Small Group Research* 35, no. 1 (February 2004): 73–105.

40. D. C. Feldman, "The Development and Enforcement of Group Norms," *Academy of Management Review* 9 (1984): 47–53; E. Fehr and U. Fischbacher, "Social Norms and Human Cooperation," *Trends in Cognitive Sciences* 8, no. 4 (2004): 185–190.

41. G. Johns, "Absenteeism Estimates by Employees and Managers: Divergent Perspectives and Self-Serving Perceptions," *Journal of Applied Psychology* 79 (1994): 229–239; I. R. Gellatly, "Individual and Group Determinants of Employee Absenteeism: Test of a Causal Model," *Journal of Organizational Behavior* 16 (1995): 469–485.

42. "Employees Terrorized by Peer Pressure in the Workplace," *Morgan & Banks news release*, September 2000. For further discussion on sanctions applied to people who outperform others in the group, see: J. J. Exline and M. Lobel, "The Perils of Outperformance: Sensitivity About Being the Target of a Threatening Upward Comparison," *Psychological Bulletin* 125, no. 3 (1999): 307–337.

43. N. Ellemers and F. Rink, "Identity in Work Groups: The Beneficial and Detrimental Consequences of Multiple Identities and Group Norms for Collaboration and Group Performance," *Advances in Group Processes* 22 (2005): 1–41.

44. C. R. Graham, "A Model of Norm Development for Computer-Mediated Teamwork," *Small Group Research* 34, no. 3 (June 2003): 322–352.

45. J. J. Dose and R. J. Klimoski, "The Diversity of Diversity: Work Values Effects on Formative Team Processes," *Human Resource Management Review* 9, no. 1 (Spring 1999): 83–108.

46. R. Hallowell, D. Bowen, and C.-I. Knoop, "Four Seasons Goes to Paris," *Academy of Management Executive* 16, no. 4 (November 2002): 7–24.

47. L. Y. Chan and B. E. Lynn, "Operating in Turbulent Times: How Ontario's Hospitals Are Meeting the Current Funding Crisis," *Health Care Management Review* 23, no. 3 (1998): 7–18.

48. L. Coch and J. French, J.R. P., "Overcoming Resistance to Change," *Human Relations* 1 (1948): 512–532.

49. A. P. Hare, "Types of Roles in Small Groups: A Bit of History and a Current Perspective," *Small Group Research* 25 (1994): 443–448.

50. S. H. N. Leung, J. W. K. Chan, and W. B. Lee, "The Dynamic Team Role Behavior: The Approaches of Investigation," *Team Performance Management* 9 (2003): 84–90.

51. R. M. Belbin, *Team Roles at Work* (Oxford, UK: Butterworth-Heinemann, 1993).

52. W. G. Broucek and G. Randell, "An Assessment of the Construct Validity of the Belbin Self-Perception Inventory and Observer's Assessment from the Perspective of the Five-Factor Model," *Journal of Occupational and Organizational Psychology* 69 (December 1996): 389–340; S. G. Fisher, T. A. Hunter, and W. D. K. Macrosson, "The Structure of Belbin's Team Roles," *Journal of Occupational and Organizational Psychology* 71 (September 1998): 283–288; J. S. Prichard and N. A. Stanton, "Testing Belbin's Team Role Theory of Effective Groups," *Journal of Management Development* 18 (1999): 652–665; G. Fisher, T. A. Hunter, and W. D. K. Macrosson, "Belbin's Team Role Theory: For Non-Managers Also?" *Journal of Managerial Psychology* 17 (2002): 14–20.

53. C. R. Evans and K. L. Dion, "Group Cohesion and Performance: A Meta-Analysis," *Small Group Research* 22 (1991): 175–186; B. Mullen and C. Copper, "The Relation between Group Cohesiveness and Performance: An Integration," *Psychological Bulletin* 115 (1994): 210–227; A. V. Carron *et al.*, "Cohesion and Performance in Sport: A Meta-Analysis," *Journal of Sport and Exercise Psychology* 24 (2002): 168–188; D. J. Beal *et al.*, "Cohesion and Performance in Groups: A Meta-Analytic Clarification of Construct Relations," *Journal of Applied Psychology* 88, no. 6 (2003): 989–1004.

54. N. Ellemers, R. Spears, and B. Doosie, "Self and Social Identity," *Annual Review of Psychology* 53 (2002): 161–186; K. M. Sheldon and B. A. Bettencourt, "Psychological Need-Satisfaction and Subjective Well-Being within Social Groups," *British Journal of Social Psychology* 41 (2002): 25–38.

55. K. A. Jehn, G. B. Northcraft, and M. A. Neale, "Why Differences Make a Difference: A Field Study of Diversity, Conflict, and Performance in Workgroups," *Administrative Science Quarterly* 44, no. 4 (1999): 741–763; van Knippenberg, De Dreu, and Homan, "Work Group Diversity and Group Performance: An Integrative Model and Research Agenda." For evidence that diversity/similarity does not always influence cohesion, see: S. S. Webber and L. M. Donahue, "Impact of Highly and Less Job-Related Diversity on Work Group Cohesion and Performance: A Meta-Analysis," *Journal of Management* 27, no. 2 (2001): 141–162.

56. E. Aronson and J. Mills, "The Effects of Severity of Initiation on Liking for a Group," *Journal of Abnormal and Social Psychology* 59 (1959): 177–181; J. E. Hautaluoma and R. S. Enge, "Early Socialization into a Work Group: Severity of Initiations Revisited," *Journal of Social Behavior & Personality* 6 (1991): 725–748.

57. Mullen and Copper, "The Relation between Group Cohesiveness and Performance: An Integration."

58. M. Rempel and R. J. Fisher, "Perceived Threat, Cohesion, and Group Problem Solving in Intergroup Conflict," *International Journal of Conflict Management* 8 (1997): 216–234; M. E. Turner and T. Horvitz, "The Dilemma of Threat: Group Effectiveness and Ineffectiveness under Adversity," in *Groups at Work: Theory and Research*, ed. M. E. Turner (Mahwah, N. J.: Lawrence Erlbaum Associates, 2001), 445–470.

59. F. Piccolo, "Brownie Points," *Atlantic Business*, Oct/Nov 2004, 22.

60. W. Piper *et al.*, "Cohesion as a Basic Bond in Groups," *Human Relations* 36 (1983): 93–108; C. A. O'Reilly, D. E. Caldwell, and W. P. Barnett, "Work Group Demography, Social Integration, and Turnover," *Administrative Science Quarterly* 34 (1989): 21–37.

61. P. Sullivan, J. and D. L. Feltz, "The Relationship between Intrateam Conflict and Cohesion within Hockey Teams," *Small Group Research* 32 (June 2001): 34–55.

62. C. Langfred, "Is Group Cohesiveness a Double-Edged Sword? An Investigation of the Effects of Cohesiveness on Performance," *Small Group Research* 29 (1998): 124–143; K. L. Gammage, A. V. Carron, and P. A. Estabrooks, "Team Cohesion and Individual Productivity: The Influence of the Norm for Productivity and the Identifiablity of Individual Effort," *Small Group Research* 32 (February 2001): 3–18.

63. "The Trouble with Teams," *Economist* (14 January 1995): 6; H. Robbins and M. Finley, *Why Teams Don't Work* (Princeton, NJ: Peterson's/Pacesetters, 1995), Chap. 20; E. A. Locke et al, "The Importance of the Individual in an Age of Groupism," in *Groups at Work: Theory and Research*, ed. M. E. Turner (Mahwah, N. J.: Lawrence Erbaum Associates, 2001), 501–528; N. J. Allen and T. D. Hecht, "The 'Romance of Teams': Toward an Understanding of Its Psychological Underpinnings and Implications," *Journal of Occupational and Organizational Psychology* 77 (2004): 439–461.

64. P. Panchak, "The Future Manufacturing," *Industry Week* 247 (September 21 1998): 96–105.

65. I. D. Steiner, *Group Process and Productivity* (New York: Academic Press, 1972); N. L. Kerr and S. R. Tindale, "Group Performance and Decision Making," *Annual Review of Psychology* 55 (2004): 623–655.

66. D. Dunphy and B. Bryant, "Teams: Panaceas or Prescriptions for Improved Performance?" *Human Relations* 49 (1996): 677–699. For discussion of Brooke's Law, see: F. P. Brooks, ed., *The Mythical Man-Month: Essays on Software Engineering*, Second ed. (Reading, Mass.: Addison-Wesley, 1995).

67. R. Cross, "Looking before You Leap: Assessing the Jump to Teams in Knowledge-Based Work," *Business Horizons* (September 2000); Q. R. Skrabec Jr., "The Myth of Teams," *Industrial Management* (September-October 2002): 25–27.

68. S. J. Karau and K. D. Williams, "Social Loafing: A Meta-Analytic Review and Theoretical Integration," *Journal of Personality and Social Psychology* 65 (1993): 681–706; R. C. Liden *et al.*, "Social Loafing: A Field Investigation," *Journal of Management* 30 (2004): 285–304.

69. M. Erez and A. Somech, "Is Group Productivity Loss the Rule or the Exception? Effects of Culture and Group-Based Motivation," *Academy of Management Journal* 39 (1996): 1513–1537; Kerr and Tindale, "Group Performance and Decision Making."

70. E. Kidwell and N. Bennett, "Employee Propensity to Withhold Effort: A Con-

ceptual Model to Intersect Three Avenues of Research," *Academy of Management Review* 19 (1993): 429–456; J. M. George, "Asymmetrical Effects of Rewards and Punishments: The Case of Social Loafing," *Journal of Occupational and Organizational Psychology* 68 (1995): 327–338; T. A. Judge and T. D. Chandler, "Individual-Level Determinants of Employee Shirking," *Relations Industrielles* 51 (1996): 468–486.

CHAPTER TEN

1. R. Dyck and N. Halpern, "Team-Based Organizations Redesign at Celestica," *Journal for Quality & Participation* 22 (September-October 1999): 36–40; B. Jorgensen, "Look before You Leap," *Electronic Business* 30, no. 12 (2004): 35–36; D. McCutcheon, "Chipping Away: Celestica's Toronto Plant Cuts Waste Blitz by Blitz," *Advanced Manufacturing* 6, no. 6 (Nov/Dec 2004): 23.

2. C. Eberting, "The Harley Mystique Comes to Kansas City," *Kansas City Star*, 6 January 1998, A1; D. Fields, "Harley Teams Shoot for Better Bike," *Akron Beacon Journal*, 15 June 1998; J. Singer and S. Duvall, "High-Performance Partnering by Self-Managed Teams in Manufacturing," *Engineering Management Journal* 12 (December 2000): 9–15; P. A. Chansler, P. M. Swamidass, and C. Cammann, "Self-Managing Work Teams: An Empirical Study of Group Cohesiveness in 'Natural Work Groups' at a Harley-Davidson Motor Company Plant," *Small Group Research* 34 (February 2003): 101–120.

3. Statistics Canada, *Workplace and Employee Survey Compendium*, (Ottawa: Statistics Canada, October 2004). For U.S. estimates, see: S. G. Cohen, J. Ledford, G. E., and G. M. Spreitzer, "A Predictive Model of Self-Managing Work Team Effectiveness," *Human Relations* 49 (1996): 643–676; E. E. Lawler, *Organizing for High Performance* (San Francisco: Jossey-Bass, 2001).

4. S. A. Mohrman, S. G. Cohen, and J. Mohrman, A. M., *Designing Team-Based Organizations: New Forms for Knowledge Work* (San Francisco: Jossey-Bass, 1995); B. L. Kirkman and D. L. Shapiro, "The Impact of Cultural Values on Employee Resistance to Teams: Toward a Model of Globalized Self-Managing Work Team Effectiveness,"

Academy of Management Review 22 (July 1997): 730–757; D. E. Yeatts and C. Hyten, *High-Performing Self-Managed Work Teams: A Comparison of Theory and Practice* (Thousand Oaks, CA: Sage, 1998).

5. Lean manufacturing and self-directed work teams seem to be loosely rather than tightly connected, because research indicates that team autonomy decreases rather than increases in some organizations that introduce lean practices. For example, see: S. K. Parker, "Longitudinal Effects of Lean Production on Employee Outcomes and the Mediating Role of Work Characteristics," *Journal of Applied Psychology* 88, no. 4 (2003): 620–634.

6. P. S. Goodman, R. Devadas, and T. L. G. Hughson, "Groups and Productivity: Analyzing the Effectiveness of Self-Managing Teams," in *Productivity in Organizations*, ed. J. P. Campbell, R. J. Campbell, and a. Associates (San Francisco: Jossey-Bass, 1988), 295–327.

7. D. Tjosvold, *Teamwork for Customers* (San Francisco: Jossey-Bass, 1993); J. Childs, "Five Years and Counting: The Path to Self-Directed Work Teams," *Hospital Materiel Management Quarterly* 18 (May 1997): 34–43; A. de Jong and K. de Ruyter, "Adaptive Versus Proactive Behavior in Service Recovery: The Role of Self-Managing Teams," *Decision Sciences* 35, no. 3 (2004): 457–491.

8. E. L. Trist *et al.*, *Organizational Choice* (London: Tavistock, 1963); N. Adler and P. Docherty, "Bringing Business into Sociotechnical Theory and Practice," *Human Relations* 51, no. 3 (1998): 319–345; R. J. Torraco, "Work Design Theory: A Review and Critique with Implications for Human Resource Development," *Human Resource Development Quarterly* 16, no. 1 (Spring 2005): 85–109.

9. The main components of sociotechnical systems are discussed in: M. Moldaschl and W. G. Weber, "The 'Three Waves' of Industrial Group Work: Historical Reflections on Current Research on Group Work," *Human Relations* 51 (March 1998): 259–287; W. Niepce and E. Molleman, "Work Design Issues in Lean Production from Sociotechnical System Perspective: Neo-Taylorism or the Next Step in Sociotechnical Design?" *Human Relations* 51, no. 3 (March 1998): 259–287.

10. E. Ulich and W. G. Weber, "Dimensions, Criteria, and Evaluation of Work Group Autonomy," in *Handbook of Work Group Psychology*, ed. M. A. West (Chichester, UK: John Wiley and Sons, 1996), 247–282.

11. K. P. Carson and G. L. Stewart, "Job Analysis and the Sociotechnical Approach to Quality: A Critical Examination," *Journal of Quality Management* 1 (1996): 49–65; C. C. Manz and G. L. Stewart, "Attaining Flexible Stability by Integrating Total Quality Management and Socio-Technical Systems Theory," *Organization Science* 8 (1997): 59–70.

12. Dyck and Halpern, "Team-Based Organizations Redesign at Celestica."

13. C. R. Emery and L. D. Fredendall, "The Effect of Teams on Firm Profitability and Customer Satisfaction," *Journal of Service Research* 4 (February 2002): 217–229; I. M. Kunii, "He Put the Flash Back in Canon," *Business Week* (16 September 2002): 40; A. Krause and H. Dunckel, "Work Design and Customer Satisfaction: Effects of the Implementation of Semi-Autonomous Group Work on Customer Satisfaction Considering Employee Satisfaction and Group Performance (Translated Abstract)," *Zeitschrift fur Arbeits-und Organisationspsychologie* 47, no. 4 (2003): 182–193.

14. J. P. Womack, D. T. Jones, and D. Roos, *The Machine That Changed the World* (New York: MacMIllan, 1990); P. S. Adler and R. E. Cole, "Designed for Learning: A Tale of Two Auto Plants," *Sloan Management Review* 34 (Spring 1993): 85–94; C. Berggren, "Volvo Uddevalla: A Dead Horse or a Car Dealer's Dream?" in *Actes du GERPISA*, (May, 1993), 129–143; J. A. Granath, "Torslanda to Uddevalla Via Kalmar: A Journey in Production Practice in Volvo," Paper presented at Seminário Internacional Reestruturação Produtiva, Flexibilidade do Trabalho e Novas Competências Profissionais COPPE/UFRJ, Rio de Janeiro, Brasil, 24–25 August 1998; "High-Class Products for Exclusive Vehicles," *Business Life in Uddevalla*, August 2002, 4–5; J. Boudreau *et al.*, "On the Interface between Operations and Human Resources Management," *Manufacturing & Service Operations Management* 5, no. 3 (Summer 2003): 179–202.

15. C. E. Nicholls, H. W. Lane, and M. B. Brechu, "Taking Self-Managed Teams to Mexico," *Academy of Management Executive* 13 (August 1999): 15–25; B. L. Kirkman and D. L. Shapiro, "The Impact of Cultural Values on Job Satisfaction and Organizational Commitment in Self-Managing Work Teams: The Mediating Role of Employee Resistance," *Academy of Management Journal* 44 (June 2001): 557–569.

16. C. Pavett and T. Morris, "Management Styles within a Multinational Corporation: A Five Country Comparative Study," *Human Relations* 48 (1995): 1171–1191; Kirkman and Shapiro, "The Impact of Cultural Values on Employee Resistance to Teams: Toward a Model of Globalized Self-Managing Work Team Effectiveness"; C. Robert and T. M. Probst, "Empowerment and Continuous Improvement in the United States, Mexico, Poland, and India," *Journal of Applied Psychology* 85 (October 2000): 643–658.

17. C. C. Manz, D. E. Keating, and A. Donnellon, "Preparing for an Organizational Change to Employee Self-Management: The Managerial Transition," *Organizational Dynamics* 19 (Autumn 1990): 15–26; J. D. Orsburn and L. Moran, *The New Self-Directed Work Teams: Mastering the Challenge* (New York: McGraw-Hill, 2000), Chap. 11. The Robert Frost quotation is found at: www.quoteland.com.

18. M. Fenton-O'Creevy, "Employee Involvement and the Middle Manager: Saboteur or Scapegoat?" *Human Resource Management Journal* 11 (2001): 24–40; R. Wageman, "How Leaders Foster Self-Managing Team Effectiveness," *Organization Science* 12, no. 5 (Sept-Oct 2001): 559–577; C. Douglas and W. L. Gardner, "Transition to Self-Directed Work Teams: Implications of Transition Time and Self-Monitoring for Managers' Use of Influence Tactics," *Journal of Organizational Behavior* 25 (2004): 47–65. The TRW quotation is found in: J. Jusko, "Always Lessons to Learn," *Industry Week* (February 15 1999): 23–30.

19. G. Garda, K. Lindstrom, and M. Dallnera, "Towards a Learning Organization: The Introduction of a Client-Centered Team-Based Organization in Administrative Surveying Work," *Applied Ergonomics* 34 (2003): 97–105.

20. R. Hodson, "Dignity in the Workplace under Participative Management: Alienation and Freedom Revisited," *American Sociological Review* 61 (1996): 719–738; R. Yonatan and H. Lam, "Union Responses to Quality Improvement Initiatives: Factors Shaping Support and Resistance," *Journal of Labor Research* 20 (Winter 1999): 111–131.

21. K. Marron, "Close Encounters of the Faceless Kind," *Globe & Mail*, 9 February 2005, C1.

22. J. Lipnack and J. Stamps, *Virtual Teams: People Working across Boundaries with Technology* (New York: John Wiley and Sons, 2001); B. S. Bell and W. J. Kozlowski, "A Typology of Virtual Teams: Implications for Effective Leadership," *Group & Organization Management* 27 (March 2002): 14–49; G. Hertel, S. Geister, and U. Konradt, "Managing Virtual Teams: A Review of Current Empirical Research," *Human Resource Management Review* 15 (2005): 69–95.

23. D. Stafford, "Sharing the Driver's Seat," *Kansas City Star*, 11 June 2002, D1.

24. G. Gilder, *Telecosm: How Infinite Bandwidth Will Revolutionize Our World* (New York: Free Press, 2001); L. L. Martins, L. L. Gilson, and M. T. Maynard, "Virtual Teams: What Do We Know and Where Do We Go Form Here?" *Journal of Management* 30, no. 6 (2004): 805–835. The Novartis quotation is from: S. Murray, "Pros and Cons of Technology: The Corporate Agenda: Managing Virtual Teams," *Financial Times (London)*, 27 May 2002, 6.

25. L. Vaas, "Shipshape Design," *PCWeek Online*, 23 August 1999.

26. J. S. Lureya and M. S. Raisinghani, "An Empirical Study of Best Practices in Virtual Teams," *Information & Management* 38 (2001): 523–544; Y. L. Doz, J. F. P. Santos, and P. J. Williamson, "The Metanational Advantage," *Optimize* (May 2002): 45ff.

27. Martins, Gilson, and Maynard, "Virtual Teams," The quotation is found in: S. Gasper, "Virtual Teams, Real Benefits," *Network World*, 24 September 2001, 45.

28. D. Robey, H. M. Khoo, and C. Powers, "Situated Learning in Cross-Functional Virtual Teams," *Technical Communication* (February 2000): 51–66.

29. Lureya and Raisinghani, "An Empirical Study of Best Practices in Virtual Teams."

30. S. Alexander, "Virtual Teams Going Global," *InfoWorld* (13 November 2000): 55–56.

31. S. Prashad, "Building Trust Tricky for 'Virtual' Teams," *Toronto Star*, 23 October 2003, K06.

32. S. Van Ryssen and S. H. Godar, "Going International without Going International: Multinational Virtual Teams," *Journal of International Management* 6 (2000): 49–60.

33. B. J. Alge, C. Wiethoff, and H. J. Klein, "When Does the Medium Matter? Knowledge-Building Experiences and Opportunities in Decision-Making Teams," *Organizational Behavior and Human Decision Processes* 91, no. 1 (2003): 26–37; D. Robey, K. S. Schwaig, and L. Jin, "Intertwining Material and Virtual Work," *Information & Organization* 13 (2003): 111–129; U. Bernard, R. Gfrörer, and B. Staffelbach, "Der Einfluss Von Telearbeit Auf Das Team: Empirisch Analysiert Am Beispiel Eines Versicherungsunternehmens (Translated Abstract)," *Zeitschrift für Personalforschung* 19, no. 2 (2005): 120–138.

34. S. L. Robinson, "Trust and Breach of the Psychological Contract," *Administrative Science Quarterly* 41 (1996): 574–599; D. M. Rousseau *et al.*, "Not So Different after All: A Cross-Discipline View of Trust," *Academy of Management Review* 23 (1998): 393–404; D. L. Duarte and N. T. Snyder, *Mastering Virtual Teams: Strategies, Tools, and Techniques That Succeed*, 2nd ed. (San Francisco, CA: Jossey-Bass, 2000), 139–155.

35. D. J. McAllister, "Affect- and Cognition-Based Trust as Foundations for Interpersonal Cooperation in Organizations," *Academy of Management Journal* 38, no. 1 (February 1995): 24–59; M. Williams, "In Whom We Trust: Group Membership as an Affective Context for Trust Development," *Academy of Management Review* 26, no. 3 (July 2001): 377–396.

36. O. E. Williamson, "Calculativeness, Trust, and Economic Organization," *Journal of Law and Economics* 36, no. 1 (1993): 453–486.

37. E. M. Whitener *et al.*, "Managers as Initiators of Trust: An Exchange Relationship Framework for Understand-

ing Managerial Trustworthy Behavior," *Academy of Management Review* 23 (July 1998): 513–530; J. M. Kouzes and B. Z. Posner, *The Leadership Challenge*, 3rd ed. (San Francisco: Jossey-Bass, 2002), Chap. 2; T. Simons, "Behavioral Integrity: The Perceived Alignment between Managers' Words and Deeds as a Research Focus," *Organization Science* 13, no. 1 (Jan-Feb 2002): 18–35.

38. M. A. Hogg *et al.*, "The Social Identity Perspective: Intergroup Relations, Self-Conception, and Small Groups," *Small Group Research* 35, no. 3 (June 2004): 246–276.

39. J. R. Dunn and M. E. Schweitzer, "Feeling and Believing: The Influence of Emotion on Trust," *Journal of Personality and Social Psychology* 88, no. 5 (May 2005): 736–748; H. Gill *et al.*, "Antecedents of Trust: Establishing a Boundary Condition for the Relation between Propensity to Trust and Intention to Trust," *Journal of Business and Psychology* 19, no. 3 (Spring 2005): 287–302.

40. T. K. Das and B. Teng, "Between Trust and Control: Developing Confidence in Partner Cooperation in Alliances," *Academy of Management Review* 23 (1998): 491–512; S. L. Jarvenpaa and D. E. Leidner, "Communication and Trust in Global Virtual Teams," *Organization Science* 10 (1999): 791–815; J. K. Murnighan, J. M. Oesch, and M. Pillutla, "Player Types and Self-Impression Management in Dictatorship Games: Two Experiments," *Games and Economic Behavior* 37, no. 2 (2001): 388–414; M. M. Pillutla, D. Malhotra, and J. Keith Murnighan, "Attributions of Trust and the Calculus of Reciprocity," *Journal of Experimental Social Psychology* 39, no. 5 (2003): 448–455.

41. K. T. Dirks and D. L. Ferrin, "The Role of Trust in Organizations," *Organization Science* 12, no. 4 (July-August 2004): 450–467.

42. V. H. Vroom and A. G. Jago, *The New Leadership* (Englewood Cliffs, NJ: Prentice-Hall, 1988), 28–29.

43. M. Diehl and W. Stroebe, "Productivity Loss in Idea-Generating Groups: Tracking Down the Blocking Effects," *Journal of Personality and Social Psychology* 61 (1991): 392–403; R. B. Gallupe *et al.*, "Blocking Electronic Brainstorms," *Journal of Applied Psy-*

chology 79 (1994): 77–86; B. A. Nijstad, W. Stroebe, and H. F. M. Lodewijkx, "Production Blocking and Idea Generation: Does Blocking Interfere with Cognitive Processes?" *Journal of Experimental Social Psychology* 39, no. 6 (November 2003): 531–548.

44. B. E. Irmer, P. Bordia, and D. Abusah, "Evaluation Apprehension and Perceived Benefits in Interpersonal and Database Knowledge Sharing," *Academy of Management Proceedings* (2002): B1–B6.

45. I. L. Janis, *Groupthink: Psychological Studies of Policy Decisions and Fiascoes*, Second ed. (Boston: Houghton Mifflin, 1982); J. K. Esser, "Alive and Well after 25 Years: A Review of Groupthink Research," *Organizational Behavior and Human Decision Processes* 73, no. 2–3 (1998): 116–141.

46. J. N. Choi and M. U. Kim, "The Organizational Application of Groupthink and Its Limitations in Organizations," *Journal of Applied Psychology* 84, no. 2 (April 1999): 297–306; N. L. Kerr and S. R. Tindale, "Group Performance and Decision Making," *Annual Review of Psychology* 55 (2004): 623–655.

47. D. Miller, *The Icarus Paradox: How Exceptional Companies Bring About Their Own Downfall* (New York: HarperBusiness, 1990); S. Finkelstein, *Why Smart Executives Fail* (New York: Viking, 2003); K. Tasa and G. Whyte, "Collective Efficacy and Vigilant Problem Solving in Group Decision Making: A Non-Linear Model," *Organizational Behavior and Human Decision Processes* 96, no. 2 (March 2005): 119–129.

48. D. Isenberg, "Group Polarization: A Critical Review and Meta-Analysis," *Journal of Personality and Social Psychology* 50 (1986): 1141–1151; C. McGarty *et al.*, "Group Polarization as Conformity to the Prototypical Group Member," *British Journal of Social Psychology* 31 (1992): 1–20; C. R. Sunstein, "Deliberative Trouble? Why Groups Go to Extremes," *Yale Law Journal* 110, no. 1 (Oct 2000): 71–119.

49. D. Friedman, "Monty Hall's Three Doors: Construction and Deconstruction of a Choice Anomaly," *American Economic Review* 88 (September 1998): 933–946; D. Kahneman, "Maps of Bounded Rationality: Psychology for Behavioral Economics," *American Eco-*

nomic Review 93, no. 5 (December 2003): 1449–1475.

50. K. M. Eisenhardt, J. L. Kahwajy, and L. J. Bourgeois III, "Conflict and Strategic Choice: How Top Management Teams Disagree," *California Management Review* 39 (1997): 42–62; R. Sutton, *Weird Ideas That Work* (New York: Free Press, 2002); C. J. Nemeth *et al.*, "The Liberating Role of Conflict in Group Creativity: A Study in Two Countries," *European Journal of Social Psychology* 34, no. 4 (2004): 365–374. For discussion on how all conflict is potentially detrimental to teams, see: C. K. W. De Dreu and L. R. Weingart, "Task Versus Relationship Conflict, Team Performance, and Team Member Satisfaction: A Meta-Analysis," *Journal of Applied Psychology* 88 (August 2003): 587–604; P. Hinds and D. E. Bailey, "Out of Sight, out of Sync: Understanding Conflict in Distributed Teams," *Organization Science* 14, no. 6 (2003): 615–632.

51. A. F. Osborn, *Applied Imagination* (New York: Scribner, 1957).

52. B. Mullen, C. Johnson, and E. Salas, "Productivity Loss in Brainstorming Groups: A Meta-Analytic Integration," *Basic and Applied Psychology* 12 (1991): 2–23. For recent evidence that group brainstorming is beneficial, see: V. R. Brown and P. B. Paulus, "Making Group Brainstorming More Effective: Recommendations from an Associative Memory Perspective," *Current Directions in Psychological Science* 11, no. 6 (2002): 208–212; K. Leggett Dugosh and P. B. Paulus, "Cognitive and Social Comparison Processes in Brainstorming," *Journal of Experimental Social Psychology* 41, no. 3 (2005): 313–320.

53. R. I. Sutton and A. Hargadon, "Brainstorming Groups in Context: Effectiveness in a Product Design Firm," *Administrative Science Quarterly* 41 (1996): 685–718; T. Kelley, *The Art of Innovation* (New York: Currency Doubleday, 2001), Chap. 4.

54. K. Darce, "Ground Control: NASA Attempts a Cultural Shift," *Seattle Times*, 24 April 2005, A3; R. Shelton, "NASA Attempts to Change Mindset in Wake of Columbia Tragedy," *Macon Telegraph (Macon, GA)*, 7 July 2005.

55. R. B. Gallupe, L. M. Bastianutti, and W. H. Cooper, "Unblocking Brainstorms," *Journal of Applied Psychology*

76 (1991): 137–142; W. H. Cooper *et al.*, "Some Liberating Effects of Anonymous Electronic Brainstorming," *Small Group Research* 29, no. 2 (April 1998): 147–178; A. R. Dennis, B. H. Wixom, and R. J. Vandenberg, "Understanding Fit and Appropriation Effects in Group Support Systems Via Meta-Analysis," *MIS Quarterly* 25, no. 2 (June 2001): 167–193; D. S. Kerr and U. S. Murthy, "Divergent and Convergent Idea Generation in Teams: A Comparison of Computer-Mediated and Face-to-Face Communication," *Group Decision and Negotiation* 13, no. 4 (July 2004): 381–399.

56. P. Bordia, "Face-to-Face Versus Computer-Mediated Communication: A Synthesis of the Experimental Literature," *Journal of Business Communication* 34 (1997): 99–120; P. B. Paulus and H.-C. Yang, "Idea Generation in Groups: A Basis for Creativity in Organizations," *Organizational Behavior and Human Decision Processes* 82, no. 1 (2000): 76–87.

57. G. Crone, "Electrifying Brainstorms," *National Post*, 3 July 1999, D11.

58. B. Kabanoff and J. R. Rossiter, "Recent Developments in Applied Creativity," *International Review of Industrial and Organizational Psychology* 9 (1994): 283–324; A. Pinsoneault *et al.*, "Electronic Brainstorming: The Illusion of Productivity," *Information Systems Research* 10 (1999): 110–133.

59. H. A. Linstone and M. Turoff, *The Delphi Method: Techniques and Applications* (Reading, MA: Addison-Wesley, 1975); P. M. Mullen, "Delphi: Myths and Reality," *Journal of Health Organization and Management* 17, no. 1 (2003): 37–51.

60. A. L. Delbecq, A. H. Van de Ven, and D. H. Gustafson, *Group Techniques for Program Planning: A Guide to Nominal Group and Delphi Processes* (Middleton, Wis: Green Briar Press, 1986).

61. S. Frankel, "NGT + MDS: An Adaptation of the Nominal Group Technique for Ill-Structured Problems," *Journal of Applied Behavioral Science* 23 (1987): 543–551; H. Barki and A. Pinsonneault, "Small Group Brainstorming and Idea Quality: Is Electronic Brainstorming the Most Effective Approach?" *Small Group Research* 32, no. 2 (April 2001): 158–205.

62. A. G. Dawson, "Administrators Settle into New Digs," *Delaware Coast Press* (16 July 2003).

63. W. G. Dyer, *Team Building: Current Issues and New Alternatives*, 3rd ed. (Reading, MA: Addison-Wesley, 1995); C. A. Beatty and B. A. Barker, *Building Smart Teams: Roadmap to High Performance* (Thousand Oaks, CA: Sage Publications, 2004).

64. M. Beer, *Organizational Change and Development: A Systems View* (Santa Monica, CA: Goodyear, 1980), 143–146; E. Sundstrom, K. P. De Meuse, and D. Futrell, "Work Teams: Applications and Effectiveness," *American Psychologist* 45 (1990): 120–133.

65. J. Langan-Fox and J. Anglim, "Mental Models, Team Mental Models, and Performance: Process, Development, and Future Directions," *Human Factors and Ergonomics in Manufacturing* 14, no. 4 (2004): 331–352; J. E. Mathieu *et al.*, "Scaling the Quality of Teammates' Mental Models: Equifinality and Normative Comparisons," *Journal of Organizational Behavior* 26 (2005): 37–56.

66. R. Beckhard, "The Confrontation Meeting," *Harvard Business Review* 45, no. 4 (1967): 159–165; H. D. Glover, "Organizational Change and Development: The Consequences of Misuse," *Leadership & Organization Development Journal* 13, no. 1 (1992): 9–16. For recent discussion about problems with confrontation in teams, see: M. A. Von Glinow, D. L. Shapiro, and J. M. Brett, "Can *We Talk*, and Should We? Managing Emotional Conflict in Multinational Teams," *Academy of Management Review* 29, no. 4 (2004): 578–592.

67. N. Devine, "Sick Kids Team Heads for the Hills," *Toronto Star*, 3 June 2004, G12; T. Taylor, "Volunteers Build Houses for Low-Income Families," *Calgary Herald*, 5 August 2005, B11.

68. "German Businesswoman Demands End to Fun at Work," *Reuters* (9 July 2003).

69. R. W. Woodman and J. J. Sherwood, "The Role of Team Development in Organizational Effectiveness: A Critical Review," *Psychological Bulletin* 88 (1980): 166–186.

70. L. Mealiea and R. Baltazar, "A Strategic Guide for Building Effective Teams," *Personnel Management* 34, no. 2 (Summer 2005): 141–160.

71. G. E. Huszczo, "Training for Team Building," *Training and Development Journal* 44 (February 1990): 37–43; P. McGraw, "Back from the Mountain: Outdoor Management Development Programs and How to Ensure the Transfer of Skills to the Workplace," *Asia Pacific Journal of Human Resources* 31 (Spring 1993): 52–61.

CHAPTER ELEVEN

1. P. Brieger and S. O'Shea, "Private Blog Wasn't," *National Post*, 3 September 2004, A1; G. Smith, "Bloggers Learn Lesson," *Globe & Mail*, 22 September 2004, A1; S. Burling, "Blogs Can Help or Hurt Careers," *Knight Ridder Tribune Business News (Washington, DC)*, 21 August 2005, 1; J. Chow, "Blogger Beware," *National Post Business Magazine*, April 2005, 40; E. Cone, "Rise of the Blog," *CIO Insight*, April 2005, 54; V. Galt, "Top-Down Communication with an Interactive Twist," *Globe & Mail*, 20 August 2005, B10; G. Suhanic, "Blogging Comes to the Corner Office," *National Post*, 25 June 2005, FW5.

2. I. Nonaka and H. Takeuchi, *The Knowledge-Creating Company* (New York: Oxford University Press, 1995); R. T. Barker and M. R. Camarata, "The Role of Communication in Creating and Maintaining a Learning Organization: Preconditions, Indicators, and Disciplines," *Journal of Business Communication* 35 (October 1998): 443–467; D. Te'eni, "A Cognitive-Affective Model of Organizational Communication for Designing It," *MIS Quarterly* 25 (June 2001): 251–312.

3. T. Wanless, "Let's Hear It for Workers!" *Vancouver Province*, June 13 2002; "What Are the Bottom Line Results of Communicating?" *Pay for Performance Report* (June 2003): 1; R. Maitland, "Bad Drivers," *People Management* (May 29 2003): 49.

4. C. E. Shannon and W. Weaver, *The Mathematical Theory of Communication* (Urbana, Il: University of Illinois Press, 1949); K. J. Krone, F. M. Jablin, and L. L. Putnam, "Communication Theory and Organizational Communication: Multiple Perspectives," in *Handbook of Organizational Communication: An Interdisciplinary Perspective*, ed. F. M. Jablin *et al.* (Newbury Park, California: Sage, 1987), 18–40.

5. W. Lucas, "Effects of E-Mail on the Organization," *European Management Journal* 16, no. 1 (February 1998): 18–30; D. A. Owens, M. A. Neale, and R. I. Sutton, "Technologies of Status Management Status Dynamics in E-Mail Communications," *Research on Managing Groups and Teams* 3 (2000): 205–230; N. Ducheneaut and L. A. Watts, "In Search of Coherence: A Review of E-Mail Research," *Human-Computer Interaction* 20, no. 1–2 (2005): 11–48.

6. S. Prashad, "Building Trust Tricky for 'Virtual' Teams," *Toronto Star*, 23 October 2003, K06.

7. J. Gordon, "Do Your Virtual Teams Deliver Only Virtual Performance?" *Training*, June 2005, 20–24. On communicating emotions in computer-mediated media, see: J. B. Walther, "Language and Communication Technology: Introduction to the Special Issue," *Journal of Language and Social Psychology* 23, no. 4 (December 2004): 384–396; J. B. Walther, T. Loh, and L. Granka, "Let Me Count the Ways: The Interchange of Verbal and Nonverbal Cues in Computer-Mediated and Face-to-Face Affinity," *Journal of Language and Social Psychology* 24, no. 1 (March 2005): 36–65.

8. G. Hertel, S. Geister, and U. Konradt, "Managing Virtual Teams: A Review of Current Empirical Research," *Human Resource Management Review* 15 (2005): 69–95; H. Lee, "Behavioral Strategies for Dealing with Flaming in an Online Forum," *The Sociological Quarterly* 46, no. 2 (2005): 385–403.

9. K. Cox, "Irving Oil Fuels Its Leaders," *Globe & Mail*, 21 April 2004, C1.

10. C. Meyer and S. Davis, *Blur: The Speed of Change in the Connected Economy* (Reading, MA: Addison-Wesley, 1998); S. Stellin, "The Intranet Is Changing Many Firms from Within," *New York Times*, January 30 2001.

11. D. Robb, "Ready or Not...Instant Messaging Has Arrived as a Financial Planning Tool," *Journal of Financial Planning* (July 2001): 12–14; J. Black, "Why Offices Are Now Open Secrets," *Business Week* (17 September 2003); A. F. Cameron and J. Webster, "Unintended Consequences of Emerging Communication Technologies: Instant Messaging in the Workplace," *Computers in Human Behavior* 21, no. 1 (2005): 85–103.

12. K. Restivo, "Coming to an iPod near You," *National Post*, 16 July 2005, FP4.

13. L. Z. Tiedens and A. R. Fragale, "Power Moves: Complementarity in Dominant and Submissive Nonverbal Behavior," *Journal of Personality and Social Psychology* 84, no. 3 (2003): 558–568. Nonverbal communication at Maple Leaf is described in: M. Macleod, "Hog Plant in Brandon: Modern and Efficient," *Hamilton Spectator*, 8 August 2005, A1.

14. P. Ekman and E. Rosenberg, *What the Face Reveals: Basic and Applied Studies of Spontaneous Expression Using the Facial Action Coding System* (Oxford, England: Oxford University Press, 1997); P. Winkielman and K. C. Berridge, "Unconscious Emotion," *Current Directions in Psychological Science* 13, no. 3 (2004): 120–123.

15. E. Hatfield, J. T. Cacioppo, and R. L. Rapson, *Emotional Contagion* (Cambridge, UK: Cambridge University Press, 1993); S. G. Barsade, "The Ripple Effect: Emotional Contagion and Its Influence on Group Behavior," *Administrative Science Quarterly* 47 (December 2002): 644–675; M. Sonnby-Borgstrom, P. Jonsson, and O. Svensson, "Emotional Empathy as Related to Mimicry Reactions at Different Levels of Information Processing," *Journal of Nonverbal Behavior* 27 (Spring 2003): 3–23.

16. J. R. Kelly and S. G. Barsade, "Mood and Emotions in Small Groups and Work Teams," *Organizational Behavior and Human Decision Processes* 86 (September 2001): 99–130.

17. I. Lamont, "Do Your Far-Flung Users Want to Communicate as If They Share an Office?" *Network World*, 13 November 2000.

18. R. L. Daft and R. H. Lengel, "Information Richness: A New Approach to Managerial Behavior and Organization Design," *Research in Organizational Behavior* 6 (1984): 191–233; R. H. Lengel and R. L. Daft, "The Selection of Communication Media as an Executive Skill," *Academy of Management Executive* 2 (1988): 225–232.

19. R. E. Rice, "Task Analyzability, Use of New Media, and Effectiveness: A Multi-Site Exploration of Media Richness," *Organization Science* 3 (1992): 475–500.

20. J. R. Carlson and R. W. Zmud, "Channel Expansion Theory and the Experiential Nature of Media Richness Perceptions," *Academy of Management Journal* 42 (April 1999): 153–170; N. Kock, "- Media Richness or Media Naturalness? The Evolution of Our Biological Communication Apparatus and Its Influence on Our Behavior toward E-Communication Tools," *IEEE Transactions on Professional Communication* 48, no. 2 (June 2005): 117–130.

21. M. McLuhan, *Understanding Media: The Extensions of Man* (New York: McGraw-Hill, 1964).

22. K. Griffiths, "KPMG Sacks 670 Employees by E-Mail," *The Independent (London)*, 5 November 2002, 19; P. Nelson, "Work Practices," *Personnel Today*, 12 November 2002, 2.

23. D. Goleman, R. Boyatzis, and A. McKee, *Primal Leaders* (Boston: Harvard Business School Press, 2002), pp. 92–95.

24. L. Larwood, "Don't Struggle to Scope Those Metaphors Yet," *Group and Organization Management* 17 (1992): 249–254. The jargon statement can be loosely translated as: "Our company has gone through major changes, which will enable employees to make better use of the company's strengths and, in the future, grab the easiest business opportunities."

25. K. M. Jackson, "Buzzword Backlash Looks to Purge Jibba-Jabba from Corporate-Speak," *Boston Globe*, 17 April 2005, G1.

26. L. L. Putnam, N. Phillips, and P. Chapman, "Metaphors of Communication and Organization," in *Handbook of Organization Studies*, ed. S. R. Clegg, C. Hardy, and W. R. Nord (London: Sage, 1996), 373–408; G. Morgan, *Images of Organization*, Second ed. (Thousand Oaks, CA: Sage, 1997); M. Rubini and H. Sigall, "Taking the Edge Off of Disagreement: Linguistic Abstractness and Self-Presentation to a Heterogeneous Audience," *European Journal of Social Psychology* 32 (2002): 343–351.

27. T. Koski, "Reflections on Information Glut and Other Issues in Knowledge Productivity," *Futures* 33 (August 2001): 483–495; D. D. Dawley and W. P. Anthony, "User Perceptions of E-Mail at Work," *Journal of Business and Technical Communication* 17, no. 2 (April

2003): 170–200; "Email Brings Costs and Fatigue," *Western News (University of Western Ontario) (London, Ontario)*, 9 July 2004.

28. A. G. Schick, L. A. Gordon, and S. Haka, "Information Overload: A Temporal Approach," *Accounting, Organizations & Society* 15 (1990): 199–220; A. Edmunds and A. Morris, "The Problem of Information Overload in Business Organisations: A Review of the Literature," *International Journal of Information Management* 20 (2000): 17–28.

29. D. Kirkpatrick, "Gates and Ozzie: How to Escape E-Mail Hell," *Fortune*, 27 June 2005, 169–171.

30. D. C. Thomas and K. Inkson, *Cultural Intelligence: People Skills for Global Business* (San Francisco: Berrett-Koehler, 2004), Chap. 6.

31. G. Erasmus, "Why Can't We Talk?" *Globe & Mail*, 9 March 2002, F6. The catastrophe example is found in: D. Woodruff, "Crossing Culture Divide Early Clears Merger Paths," *Asian Wall Street Journal* (May 28 2001): 9.

32. H. Yamada, *American and Japanese Business Discourse: A Comparison of Interaction Styles* (Norwood, NJ: Ablex, 1992), p. 34; R. M. March, *Reading the Japanese Mind* (Tokyo: Kodansha International, 1996), Chap. 1.

33. P. Harris and R. Moran, *Managing Cultural Differences* (Houston: Gulf, 1987); H. Blagg, "A Just Measure of Shame?" *British Journal of Criminology* 37 (Autumn 1997): 481–501; R. E. Axtell, *Gestures: The Do's and Taboos of Body Language around the World*, Revised ed. (New York: Wiley, 1998).

34. S. Ohtaki, T. Ohtaki, and M. D. Fetters, "Doctor-Patient Communication: A Comparison of the USA and Japan," *Family Practice* 20 (June 2003): 276–282; M. Fujio, "Silence During Intercultural Communication: A Case Study," *Corporate Communications* 9, no. 4 (2004): 331–339.

35. D. C. Barnlund, *Communication Styles of Japanese and Americans: Images and Realities* (Belmont, Calif.: Wadsworth, 1988); Yamada, *American and Japanese Business Discourse: A Comparison of Interaction Styles*, Chap. 2; H. Yamada, *Different Games, Different Rules* (New York: Oxford University Press, 1997), pp. 76–79.

36. M. Griffin, "The Office, Australian Style," *Sunday Age* (June 22 2003): 6.

37. This stereotypic notion is prevalent throughout J. Gray, *Men Are from Mars, Women Are from Venus* (New York: Harper Collins, 1992). For a critique of this view see: J. T. Wood, "A Critical Response to John Gray's Mars and Venus Portrayals of Men and Women," *Southern Communication Journal* 67 (Winter 2002): 201–210.

38. D. Tannen, *You Just Don't Understand: Men and Women in Conversation* (New York: Ballentine Books, 1990); D. Tannen, *Talking from 9 to 5* (New York: Avon, 1994); M. Crawford, *Talking Difference: On Gender and Language* (Thousand Oaks, CA: Sage, 1995), pp. 41–44; L. L. Namy, L. C. Nygaard, and D. Sauerteig, "Gender Differences in Vocal Accommodation: The Role of Perception," *Journal of Language and Social Psychology* 21, no. 4 (December 2002): 422–432.

39. A. Mulac and *et al.*, "Uh-Huh. What's That All About?' Differing Interpretations of Conversational Backchannels and Questions as Sources of Miscommunication across Gender Boundaries," *Communication Research* 25 (December 1998): 641–668; N. M. Sussman and D. H. Tyson, "Sex and Power: Gender Differences in Computer-Mediated Interactions," *Computers in Human Behavior* 16 (2000): 381–394; D. R. Caruso and P. Salovey, *The Emotionally Intelligent Manager* (San Francisco: Jossey-Bass, 2004), p. 23.

40. P. Tripp-Knowles, "A Review of the Literature on Barriers Encountered by Women in Science Academia," *Resources for Feminist Research* 24 (Spring/Summer 1995): 28–34.

41. Cited in: K. Davis and J. W. Newstrom, *Human Behavior at Work: Organizational Behavior*, Seventh ed. (New York: McGraw-Hill, 1985), p. 438.

42. The three components of listening discussed here are based on several recent studies in the field of marketing, including: S. B. Castleberry, C. D. Shepherd, and R. Ridnour, "Effective Interpersonal Listening in the Personal Selling Environment: Conceptualization, Measurement, and Nomological Validity," *Journal of Marketing Theory and Practice* 7 (Winter 1999): 30–38; L. B. Comer and T. Drollinger, "Active Empathetic Listening and Selling Success: A Conceptual Framework," *Journal of Personal Selling & Sales*

Management 19 (Winter 1999): 15–29; K. de Ruyter and M. G. M. Wetzels, "The Impact of Perceived Listening Behavior in Voice-to-Voice Service Encounters," *Journal of Service Research* 2 (February 2000): 276–284.

43. H. Ditmars, "The Cold, Hard World of Advertising," *Report on Business Magazine*, 28 September 2001.

44. G. Evans and D. Johnson, "Stress and Open-Office Noise," *Journal of Applied Psychology* 85 (2000): 779–783; F. Russo, "My Kingdom for a Door," *Time Magazine*, 23 October 2000, B1.

45. B. Sosnin, "Digital Newsletters 'E-Volutionize' Employee Communications," *HRMagazine*, May 2001, 99–107.

46. S. P. Means, "Playing at Pixar," *Salt Lake Tribune (Utah)*, 30 May 2003, D1; G. Whipp, "Swimming against the Tide," *Daily News of Los Angeles*, 30 May 2003, U6.

47. K. Swisher, "Boomtown: 'Wiki' May Alter How Employees Work Together," *Wall Street Journal*, 29 July 2004, B1; M. Delio, "The Enterprise Blogosphere," *InfoWorld*, 28 March 2005, 42–47.

48. S. Greengard, "Employee Surveys: Ask the Right Questions, Probe the Answers for Insight," *Workforce Management*, December 2004, 76.

49. The original term is "management by wandering around", but this has been replaced with "walking" over the years. See: W. Ouchi, *Theory Z* (New York: Avon Books, 1981), pp. 176–177; T. Peters and R. Waterman, *In Search of Excellence* (New York: Harper and Row, 1982), p. 122.

50. D. Penner, "Putting the Boss out Front," *Vancouver Sun*, 7 June 2002.

51. T. Whipp, "Walking in the President's Shoe," *Windsor Star*, 3 December 2001.

52. R. Rousos, "Trust in Leaders Lacking at Utility," *The Ledger (Lakeland, Fl)*, 29 July 2003, B1; B. Whitworth and B. Riccomini, "Management Communication: Unlocking Higher Employee Performance," *Communication World*, Mar-Apr 2005, 18–21.

53. K. Davis, "Management Communication and the Grapevine," *Harvard Business Review* 31 (September-October 1953): 43–49; W. L. Davis and J. R. O'Connor, "Serial Transmission of Information: A Study of the Grapevine," *Journal of Applied Communication Research* 5 (1977): 61–72.

54. H. Mintzberg, *The Structuring of Organizations* (Englewood Cliffs, N.J.: Prentice Hall, 1979), pp. 46–53; D. Krackhardt and J. R. Hanson, "Informal Networks: The Company Behind the Chart," *Harvard Business Review* 71 (July-August 1993): 104–111.

55. C. J. Walker and C. A. Beckerle, "The Effect of State Anxiety on Rumor Transmission," *Journal of Social Behaviour & Personality* 2 (August 1987): 353–360; R. L. Rosnow, "Inside Rumor: A Personal Journey," *American Psychologist* 46 (May 1991): 484–496; M. Noon and R. Delbridge, "News from Behind My Hand: Gossip in Organizations," *Organization Studies* 14 (1993): 23–36.

56. N. Nicholson, "Evolutionary Psychology: Toward a New View of Human Nature and Organizational Society," *Human Relations* 50 (September 1997): 1053–1078.

CHAPTER TWELVE

1. United States Bankruptcy Court, Southern District Of New York. In Re: WorldCom, Inc., *et al.*, Debtors. Chapter 11 Case No. 02-15533 (Ajg) Jointly Administered Second Interim Report Of Dick Thornburgh, Bankruptcy Court Examiner, June 9, 2003; Report Of Investigation by the Special Investigative Committee of the Board Of Directors Of Worldcom, Inc. Dennis R. Beresford, Nicholas Deb. Katzenbach, C.B. Rogers, Jr., Counsel, Wilmer, Cutler & Pickering, Accounting Advisors, Pricewaterhousecoopers Llp, March 31, 2003. Also see: T. Catan *et al.*, "Before the Fall," *Financial Times (London)*, 19 December 2002, 17; J. O'Donnell and A. Backover, "Ebbers' High-Risk Act Came Crashing Down on Him," *USA Today*, 12 December 2002, B1; C. Stern, "Ebbers Dominated Board, Report Says," *Washington Post*, 5 November 2002, E1; D. S. Hilzenrath, "How a Distinguished Roster of Board Members Failed to Detect Company's Problems," *Washington Post*, 16 June 2003, E1; S. Pulliam and A. Latour, "Lost Connection," *Wall Street Journal*, 12 January 2005, A1; S. Rosenbush, "Five Lessons of the Worldcom Debackle," *Business Week Online*, 16 March 2005.

2. For a discussion of the definition of power, see: H. Mintzberg, *Power in and around Organizations* (Englewood Cliffs, NJ: Prentice Hall, 1983), Chap.

1; J. Pfeffer, Managing with Power (Boston: Harvard Business University Press, 1992), pp. 17, 30; J. Pfeffer, *New Directions in Organizational Theory* (New York: Oxford University Press, 1997), Chap. 6; J. M. Whitmeyer, "Power through Appointment," *Social Science Research* 29 (2000): 535–555.

3. R. A. Dahl, "The Concept of Power," *Behavioral Science* 2 (1957): 201–218; R. M. Emerson, "Power-Dependence Relations," *American Sociological Review* 27 (1962): 31–41; A. M. Pettigrew, *The Politics of Organizational Decision-Making* (London: Tavistock, 1973).

4. K. M. Bartol and D. C. Martin, "When Politics Pays: Factors Influencing Managerial Compensation Decisions," *Personnel Psychology* 43 (1990): 599–614; D. J. Brass and M. E. Burkhardt, "Potential Power and Power Use: An Investigation of Structure and Behavior," *Academy of Management Journal* 36 (1993): 441–470.

5. J. R. P. French and B. Raven, "The Bases of Social Power," in Studies in Social Power, ed. D. Cartwright (Ann Arbor, Mich: University of Michigan Press, 1959), 150–167; P. Podsakoff and C. Schreisheim, "Field Studies of French and Raven's Bases of Power: Critique, Analysis, and Suggestions for Future Research," *Psychological Bulletin* 97 (1985): 387–411; S. Finkelstein, "Power in Top Management Teams: Dimensions. Measurement, and Validation," *Academy of Management Journal* 35 (1992): 505–538; P. P. Carson and K. D. Carson, "Social Power Bases: A Meta-Analytic Examination of Interrelationships and Outcomes," *Journal of Applied Social Psychology* 23 (1993): 1150–1169.

6. B. H. Raven, "The Bases of Power: Origins and Recent Developments," *Journal of Social Issues* 49 (1993): 227–251; G. A. Yukl, *Leadership in Organizations*, 3rd ed. (Englewood Cliffs, N.J.: Prentice Hall, 1994), p. 13.

7. C. Barnard, *The Function of the Executive* (Cambridge, MA: Harvard University Press, 1938); C. Hardy and S. R. Clegg, "Some Dare Call It Power," in *Handbook of Organization Studies*, ed. S. R. Clegg, C. Hardy, and W. R. Nord (London: Sage, 1996), 622–641.

8. L. A. Conger, *Winning 'Em Over: A New Model for Managing in the Age of Persuasion* (New York: Simon & Schuster, 1998), Appendix A.

9. C. Mabin, "Steeling Themselves: Workers Burned by a Dwindling Industry," *Journal Gazette* (Fort Wayne, Ind.), 3 July 2005, 1H.

10. P. F. Drucker, "The New Workforce," *The Economist* (3 November 2001): 8–12.

11. J. D. Kudisch and M. L. Poteet, "Expert Power, Referent Power, and Charisma: Toward the Resolution of a Theoretical Debate," *Journal of Business & Psychology* 10 (Winter 1995): 177–195; H. L. Tosi *et al.*, "CEO Charisma, Compensation, and Firm Performance," *Leadership Quarterly* 15, no. 3 (2004): 405–420.

12. Information was identified as a form of influence, but not power, in the original French and Raven writing. Information was added as a sixth source of power in subsequent writing by Raven, but this book takes the view that information power is derived from the original five sources. See: G. Yukl and C. M. Falbe, "Importance of Different Power Sources in Downward and Lateral Relations," *Journal of Applied Psychology* 76 (1991): 416–423; B. H. Raven, "Kurt Lewin Address: Influence, Power, Religion, and the Mechanisms of Social Control," *Journal of Social Issues* 55 (Spring 1999): 161–186.

13. "Corporate Culture Instilled Online," *The Economist*, 11 November 2000.

14. P. L. Dawes, D. Y. Lee, and G. R. Dowling, "Information Control and Influence in Emergent Buying Centers," *Journal of Marketing* 62, no. 3 (July 1998): 55–68; D. J. Brass *et al.*, "Taking Stock of Networks and Organizations: A Multilevel Perspective," *Academy of Management Journal* 47, no. 6 (December 2004): 795–817.

15. C. R. Hinings *et al.*, "Structural Conditions of Intraorganizational Power," *Administrative Science Quarterly* 19 (1974): 22–44. Also see: C. S. Saunders, "The Strategic Contingency Theory of Power: Multiple Perspectives," *The Journal of Management Studies* 27 (1990): 1–21.

16. D. J. Hickson *et al.*, "A Strategic Contingencies' Theory of Intraorganizational Power," *Administrative Science Quarterly* 16 (1971): 216–227; Hinings *et al.*, "Structural Conditions of Intraorganizational Power,"; R. M. Kanter, "Power Failure in Management Cir-

cuits," *Harvard Business Review* (July-August 1979): 65–75.

17. M. Crozier, *The Bureaucratic Phenomenon* (London: Tavistock, 1964).

18. Hickson *et al.*, "A Strategic Contingencies' Theory of Intraorganizational Power"; J. D. Hackman, "Power and Centrality in the Allocation of Resources in Colleges and Universities," *Administrative Science Quarterly* 30 (1985): 61–77; Brass and Burkhardt, "Potential Power and Power Use: An Investigation of Structure and Behavior."

19. Kanter, "Power Failure in Management Circuits,"; B. E. Ashforth, "The Experience of Powerlessness in Organizations," *Organizational Behavior and Human Decision Processes* 43 (1989): 207–242; L. Holden, "European Managers: HRM and an Evolving Role," *European Business Review* 12 (2000).

20. J. Voight, "When Credit Is Not Due," *Adweek*, 1 March 2004, 24.

21. R. Madell, "Ground Floor," *Pharmaceutical Executive (Women in Pharma Supplement)*, June 2000, 24–31.

22. "Medical Officer of Health Orders Garbage Cleanup," *CBC News*, 5 July 2002; "Toronto Tourism Industry Worried Strike Will Damage Reputation," *CBC News*, 5 July 2002; "Toronto Strike Keeps Growing," *CBC News*, 4 July 2002; D. Wanagas, "Still Possible to Save Some Face," *National Post*, 6 July 2002.

23. L. A. Perlow, "The Time Famine: Toward a Sociology of Work Time," *Administrative Science Quarterly* 44 (March 1999): 5–31.

24. B. R. Ragins, "Diversified Mentoring Relationships in Organizations: A Power Perspective," *Academy of Management Review* 22 (1997): 482–521; M. C. Higgins and K. E. Kram, "Reconceptualizing Mentoring at Work: A Developmental Network Perspective," *Academy of Management Review* 26 (April 2001): 264–288.

25. D. Krackhardt and J. R. Hanson, "Informal Networks: The Company Behind the Chart," *Harvard Business Review* 71 (July-August 1993): 104–111; P. S. Adler and S.-W. Kwon, "Social Capital: Prospects for a New Concept," *Academy of Management Review* 27, no. 1 (2002): 17–40.

26. A. Mehra, M. Kilduff, and D. J. Brass, "The Social Networks of High and Low Self-Monitors: Implications

for Workplace Performance," *Administrative Science Quarterly* 46 (March 2001): 121–146.

27. B. R. Ragins and E. Sundstrom, "Gender and Power in Organizations: A Longitudinal Perspective," *Psychological Bulletin* 105 (1989): 51–88; M. Linehan, "Barriers to Women's Participation in International Management," *European Business Review* 13 (2001).

28. D. M. McCracken, "Winning the Talent War for Women: Sometimes It Takes a Revolution," *Harvard Business Review* (November-December 2000): 159–167; D. L. Nelson and R. J. Burke, "Women Executives: Health, Stress, and Success," *Academy of Management Executive* 14 (May 2000): 107–121.

29. K. Atuahene-Gima and H. Li, "Marketing's Influence Tactics in New Product Development: A Study of High Technology Firms in China," *Journal of Product Innovation Management* 17 (2000): 451–470; A. Somech and A. Drach-Zahavy, "Relative Power and Influence Strategy: The Effects of Agent/Target Organizational Power on Superiors' Choices of Influence Strategies," *Journal of Organizational Behavior* 23 (2002): 167–179.

30. D. Kipnis, S. M. Schmidt, and I. Wilkinson, "Intraorganizational Influence Tactics: Explorations in Getting One's Way," *Journal of Applied Psychology* 65 (1980): 440–452. Also see: C. Schriesheim and T. Hinkin, "Influence Tactics Used by Subordinates: A Theoretical and Empirical Analysis and Refinement of the Kipnis, Schmidt, and Wilkinson Subscales," *Journal of Applied Psychology* 75 (1990): 246–257; W. A. Hochwarter *et al.*, "A Reexamination of Schriesheim and Hinkin's (1990) Measure of Upward Influence," *Educational and Psychological Measurement* 60 (October 2000): 755–771.

31. Some of the more thorough lists of influence tactics are presented in: A. Rao and K. Hashimoto, "Universal and Culturally Specific Aspects of Managerial Influence: A Study of Japanese Managers," *Leadership Quarterly* 8 (1997): 295–312; L. A. McFarland, A. M. Ryan, and S. D. Kriska, "Field Study Investigation of Applicant Use of Influence Tactics in a Selection Interview," *Journal of Psychology* 136 (July 2002): 383–398.

32. R. B. Cialdini and N. J. Goldstein, "Social Influence: Compliance and

Conformity," *Annual Review of Psychology* 55 (2004): 591–621.

33. Rao and Hashimoto, "Universal and Culturally Specific Aspects of Managerial Influence," Silent authority as an influence tactic in non-Western cultures is also discussed in: S. F. Pasa, "Leadership Influence in a High Power Distance and Collectivist Culture," *Leadership & Organization Development Journal* 21 (2000): 414–426.

34. A. W. Gouldner, "The Norm of Reciprocity: A Preliminary Statement," *American Sociological Review* 25 (1960): 161–178.

35. Y. Fan, "Questioning Guanxi: Definition, Classification, and Implications," *International Business Review* 11 (2002): 543–561; D. Tan and R. S. Snell, "The Third Eye: Exploring Guanxi and Relational Morality in the Workplace," *Journal of Business Ethics* 41 (December 2002): 361–384; W. R. Vanhonacker, "When Good Guanxi Turns Bad," *Harvard Business Review* 82, no. 4 (April 2004): 18–19.

36. A. Ledeneva, *Russia's Economy of Favors: Blat, Networking and Informal Exchange* (New York: Cambridge University Press, 1998); S. Michailova and V. Worm, "Personal Networking in Russia and China: Blat and Guanxi," *European Management Journal* 21 (2003): 509–519.

37. A. T. Cobb, "Toward the Study of Organizational Coalitions: Participant Concerns and Activities in a Simulated Organizational Setting," *Human Relations* 44 (1991): 1057–1079; E. A. Mannix, "Organizations as Resource Dilemmas: The Effects of Power Balance on Coalition Formation in Small Groups," *Organizational Behavior and Human Decision Processes* 55 (1993): 1–22; D. J. Terry, M. A. Hogg, and K. M. White, "The Theory of Planned Behavior: Self-Identity, Social Identity and Group Norms," *British Journal of Social Psychology* 38 (September 1999): 225–244.

38. Rao and Hashimoto, "Universal and Culturally Specific Aspects of Managerial Influence."

39. D. Strutton and L. E. Pelton, "Effects of Ingratiation on Lateral Relationship Quality within Sales Team Settings," *Journal of Business Research* 43 (1998): 1–12; R. Vonk, "Self-Serving Interpretations of Flattery: Why Ingratiation

Works," Journal of *Personality and Social Psychology* 82 (2002): 515–526.

40. C. A. Higgins, T. A. Judge, and G. R. Ferris, "Influence Tactics and Work Outcomes: A Meta-Analysis," *Journal of Organizational Behavior* 24 (2003): 90–106.

41. D. Strutton, L. E. Pelton, and J. Tanner, J. F., "Shall We Gather in the Garden: The Effect of Ingratiatory Behaviors on Buyer Trust in Salespeople," *Industrial Marketing Management* 25 (1996): 151–162; J. O'Neil, "An Investigation of the Sources of Influence of Corporate Public Relations Practitioners," *Public Relations Review* 29 (June 2003): 159–169.

42. A. Rao and S. M. Schmidt, "Upward Impression Management: Goals, Influence Strategies, and Consequences," *Human Relations* 48 (1995): 147–167.

43. A. P. J. Ellis *et al.*, "The Use of Impression Management Tactics in Structured Interviews: A Function of Question Type?" *Journal of Applied Psychology* 87 (December 2002): 1200–1208; M. C. Bolino and W. H. Tunley, "More Than One Way to Make an Impression: Exploring Profiles of Impression Management," *Journal of Management* 29 (2003): 141–160.

44. J. Dillard and E. Peck, "Persuasion and the Structure of Affect: Dual Systems and Discrete Emotions as Complementary Models," *Human Communication Research* 27 (2000): 38–68; S. Fox and Y. Amichai-Hamburger, "The Power of Emotional Appeals in Promoting Organizational Change Programs," *Academy of Management Executive* 15 (November 2001): 84–94; E. H. H. J. Das, J. B. F. de Wit, and W. Stroebe, "Fear Appeals Motivate Acceptance of Action Recommendations: Evidence for a Positive Bias in the Processing of Persuasive Messages," *Personality and Social Psychology Bulletin* 29 (May 2003): 650–664; R. Buck *et al.*, "Emotion and Reason in Persuasion: Applying the Ari Model and the Casc Scale," *Journal of Business Research* 57, no. 6 (2004): 647–656.

45. A. P. Brief, *Attitudes in and around Organizations* (Thousand Oaks, CA: Sage, 1998), pp. 69–84; D. J. O'Keefe, *Persuasion: Theory and Research* (Thousand Oaks, CA: Sage Publications, 2002).

46. Conger, *Winning 'Em Over: A New Model for Managing in the Age of Persuasion*; J. J. Jiang, G. Klein, and R. G. Vedder, "Persuasive Expert Systems:

The Influence of Confidence and Discrepancy," *Computers in Human Behavior* 16 (March 2000): 99–109.

47. These and other features of message content in persuasion are detailed in: R. Petty and J. Cacioppo, *Attitudes and Persuasion: Classic and Contemporary Approaches* (Dubuque, Iowa: W. C. Brown, 1981); D. G. Linz and S. Penrod, "Increasing Attorney Persuasiveness in the Courtroom," *Law and Psychology Review* 8 (1984): 1–47; M. Pfau, E. A. Szabo, and J. Anderson, "The Role and Impact of Affect in the Process of Resistance to Persuasion," *Human Communication Research* 27 (April 2001): 216–252; O'Keefe, Persuasion: Theory and Research, Chap. 9.

48. N. Rhodes and W. Wood, "Self-Esteem and Intelligence Affect Influenceability: The Mediating Role of Message Reception," *Psychological Bulletin* 111, no. 1 (1992): 156–171.

49. S. Gilmor, "Ahead of the Curve," *Infoworld* (13 January 2003): 58; M. Hiltzik, "Apple CEO's Visions Don't Guarantee Sustained Gains," *Los Angeles Times* (14 April 2003): C1. The origin of "reality distortion field" is described at www.folklore.org.

50. "Be Part of the Team If You Want to Catch the Eye," *Birmingham Post* (UK), 31 August 2000, 14; S. Maitlis, "Taking It from the Top: How CEOs Influence (and Fail to Influence) Their Boards," *Organization Studies* 25, no. 8 (2004): 1275–1311.

51. C. M. Falbe and G. Yukl, "Consequences for Managers of Using Single Influence Tactics and Combinations of Tactics," *Academy of Management Journal* 35 (1992): 638–652.

52. Falbe and Yukl, "Consequences for Managers of Using Single Influence Tactics and Combinations of Tactics"; Atuahene-Gima and Li, "Mmarketing's Influence Tactics in New Product Development."

53. R. C. Ringer and R. W. Boss, "Hospital Professionals' Use of Upward Influence Tactics," *Journal of Managerial Issues* 12 (2000): 92–108.

54. G. Blickle, "Do Work Values Predict the Use of Intraorganizational Influence Strategies?" *Journal Of Applied Social Psychology* 30, no. 1 (January 2000): 196–205; P. P. Fu *et al.*, "The Impact of Societal Cultural Values and

Individual Social Beliefs on the Perceived Effectiveness of Managerial Influence Strategies: A Meso Approach," *Journal of International Business Studies* 35, no. 4 (July 2004): 284–305.

55. D. Tannen, *Talking from 9 to 5* (New York: Avon, 1994), Chap. 2; M. Crawford, *Talking Difference: On Gender and Language* (Thousand Oaks, CA: Sage, 1995), pp. 41–44.

56. S. Mann, "Politics and Power in Organizations: Why Women Lose Out," *Leadership & Organization Development Journal* 16 (1995): 9–15; E. H. Buttner and M. McEnally, "The Interactive Effect of Influence Tactic, Applicant Gender, and Type of Job on Hiring Recommendations," *Sex Roles* 34 (1996): 581–591; L. L. Carli, "Gender, Interpersonal Power, and Social Influence," *Journal of Social Issues* 55 (Spring 1999): 81–99.

57. This definition of organizational politics has become the dominant perspective over the past 15 years. See: G. R. Ferris and K. M. Kacmar, "Perceptions of Organizational Politics," *Journal of Management* 18 (1992): 93–116; R. Cropanzano *et al.*, "The Relationship of Organizational Politics and Support to Work Behaviors, Attitudes, and Stress," *Journal of Organizational Behavior* 18 (1997): 159–180; E. Vigoda and A. Cohen, "Influence Tactics and Perceptions of Organizational Politics: A Longitudinal Study," *Journal of Business Research* 55 (2002): 311–324. However, organizational politics was previously viewed as influence tactics outside the formal role that could be either selfish or altruistic. This older definition is less common today, possibly because it is incongruent with popular views of politics and because it overlaps too much with the concept of influence. For the older perspective of organizational politics, see: J. Pfeffer, *Power in Organizations* (Boston: Pitman, 1981); Mintzberg, *Power in and around Organizations*.

58. K. M. Kacmar and R. A. Baron, "Organizational Politics: The State of the Field, Links to Related Processes, and an Agenda for Future Research," in *Research in Personnel and Human Resources Management*, ed. G. R. Ferris (Greenwich, CT: JAI Press, 1999), 1–39; L. A. Witt, T. F. Hilton, and W. A. Hochwarter, "Addressing Politics in Matrix

Teams," *Group & Organization Management* 26 (June 2001): 230–247; E. Vigoda, "Stress-Related Aftermaths to Workplace Politics: The Relationships among Politics, Job Distress, and Aggressive Behavior in Organizations," *Journal of Organizational Behavior* 23 (2002): 571–591.

59. C. Hardy, *Strategies for Retrenchment and Turnaround: The Politics of Survival* (Berlin: Walter de Gruyter, 1990), Chap. 14; M. C. Andrews and K. M. Kacmar, "Discriminating among Organizational Politics, Justice, and Support," *Journal of Organizational Behavior* 22 (2001): 347–366.

60. S. Blazejewski and W. Dorow, "Managing Organizational Politics for Radical Change: The Case of Beiersdorf-Lechia S.A., Poznan," *Journal of World Business* 38 (August 2003): 204–223.

61. H. Mitzberg, "The Organization as Political Arena," *Journal of Management Studies* 22 (1985): 133–154; G. R. Ferris, G. S. Russ, and P. M. Fandt, "Politics in Organizations," in *Impression Management in the Organization*, ed. R. A. Giacalone and P. Rosenfeld (Hillsdale, NJ: Erlbaum, 1989), 143–170.

62. L. W. Porter, R. W. Allen, and H. L. Angle, "The Politics of Upward Influence in Organizations," *Research in Organizational Behavior* 3 (1981): 120–122; R. J. House, "Power and Personality in Complex Organizations," *Research in Organizational Behavior* 10 (1988): 305–357.

63. R. Christie and F. Geis, *Studies in Machiavellianism* (New York: Academic Press, 1970); S. M. Farmer *et al.*, "Putting Upward Influence Strategies in Context," *Journal of Organizational Behavior* 18 (1997): 17–42; K. S. Sauleya and A. G. Bedeian, "Equity Sensitivity: Construction of a Measure and Examination of Its Psychometric Properties," *Journal of Management* 26 (September 2000): 885–910.

64. G. R. Ferris and e. al., "Perceptions of Organizational Politics: Prediction, Stress-Related Implications, and Outcomes," *Human Relations* 49 (1996): 233–263.

CHAPTER THIRTEEN

1. B. Badelt, "Things Are Getting Ugly," *Vancouver Sun*, 25 July 2005, A1; B. Constantineau, "Telus Eyes East for Help," *Vancouver Sun*, 6 August 2005;

T. Gignac, "Telus Workers Picket Strikers," *Calgary Herald*, 27 July 2005, A1; T. Gignac, "Telus at War: The Great Divide," *Calgary Herald*, 7 August 2005, E1; D. Gutstein, "The Sun's Unfair Slant on the Telus Dispute," *The Tyee*, 31 August 2005; M. Hume, "Telus Union Ordered to Stop Intimidation," *Globe & Mail*, 12 September 2005, B1; P. Marck, "A House Divided," *Edmonton Journal*, 27 August 2005, F1; C. McLean, "Free MP3s? For Some at Telus, It's the Sound of Crossing the Picket Line," *Globe & Mail*, 25 August 2005, B1.

2. J. A. Wall and R. R. Callister, "Conflict and Its Management," *Journal of Management*, 21 (1995): 515–558; M. A. Rahim, "Toward a Theory of Managing Organizational Conflict," *International Journal of Conflict Management* 13, no. 3 (2002): 206–235.

3. L. Pondy, "Organizational Conflict: Concepts and Models," *Administrative Science Quarterly* 2 (1967): 296–320; K. W. Thomas, "Conflict and Negotiation Processes in Organizations," in *Handbook of Industrial and Organizational Psychology*, ed. M. D. Dunnette and L. M. Hough, Second ed. (Palo Alto, CA: Consulting Psychologists Press, 1992), 651–718.

4. M. A. Von Glinow, D. L. Shapiro, and J. M. Brett, "Can We Talk, and Should We? Managing Emotional Conflict in Multicultural Teams," *Academy of Management Review* 29, no. 4 (2004): 578–592.

5. G. E. Martin and T. J. Bergman, "The Dynamics of Behavioral Response to Conflict in the Workplace," *Journal of Occupational & Organizational Psychology* 69 (December 1996): 377–387; J. M. Brett, D. L. Shapiro, and A. L. Lytle, "Breaking the Bonds of Reciprocity in Negotiations," *Academy of Management Journal* 41 (August 1998): 410–424.

6. H. Witteman, "Analyzing Interpersonal Conflict: Nature of Awareness, Type of Initiating Event, Situational Perceptions, and Management Styles," *Western Journal of Communications* 56 (1992): 248–280; Wall and Callister, "Conflict and Its Management."

7. M. Rempel and R. J. Fisher, "Perceived Threat, Cohesion, and Group Problem Solving in Intergroup Conflict," *International Journal of Conflict Management* 8 (1997): 216–234.

8. D. Tjosvold, *The Conflict-Positive Organization* (Reading, MA: Addison-

Wesley, 1991); K. M. Eisenhardt, J. L. Kahwajy, and L. J. Bourgeois III, "Conflict and Strategic Choice: How Top Management Teams Disagree," *California Management Review* 39 (Winter 1997): 42–62; L. H. Pelled, K. M. Eisenhardt, and K. R. Xin, "Exploring the Black Box: An Analysis of Work Group Diversity, Conflict, and Performance," *Administrative Science Quarterly* 44 (March 1999): 1–28; S. Schulz-Hardt, M. Jochims, and D. Frey, "Productive Conflict in Group Decision Making: Genuine and Contrived Dissent as Strategies to Counteract Biased Information Seeking," *Organizational Behavior and Human Decision Processes* 88 (2002): 563–586.

9. C. K. W. De Dreu and L. R. Weingart, "Task Versus Relationship Conflict, Team Performance, and Team Member Satisfaction: A Meta-Analysis," *Journal of Applied Psychology* 88 (August 2003): 587–604.

10. J. Yang and K. W. Mossholder, "Decoupling Task and Relationship Conflict: The Role of Intergroup Emotional Processing," *Journal of Organizational Behavior* 25 (2004): 589–605.

11. R. E. Walton and J. M. Dutton, "The Management of Conflict: A Model and Review," *Administrative Science Quarterly* 14 (1969): 73–84.

12. D. M. Brock, D. Barry, and D. C. Thomas, "Your Forward Is Our Reverse, Your Right, Our Wrong': Rethinking Multinational Planning Processes in Light of National Culture," *International Business Review* 9 (2000): 687–701.

13. R. Zemke and B. Filipczak, *Generations at Work: Managing the Clash of Veterans, Boomers, Xers, and Nexters in Your Workplace* (New York: Amacom, 1999); P. Harris, "Boomers vs. Echo Boomer: The Work War," *T+D* (May 2005): 44–49.

14. P. Hinds and D. E. Bailey, "Out of Sight, out of Sync: Understanding Conflict in Distributed Teams," *Organization Science* 14, no. 6 (2003): 615–632; P. Hinds and M. Mortensen, "Understanding Conflict in Geographically Distributed Teams: The Moderating Effects of Shared Identity, Shared Context, and Spontaneous Communication," *Organization Science* 16, no. 3 (May-June 2005): 290–307.

15. P. C. Earley and G. B. Northcraft, "Goal Setting, Resource Interdepen-

dence, and Conflict Management," in *Managing Conflict: An Interdisciplinary Approach*, ed. M. A. Rahim (New York: Praeger, 1989), 161–170; K. Jelin, "A Multimethod Examination of the Benefits and Detriments of Intragroup Conflict," *Administrative Science Quarterly* 40 (1995): 245–282.

16. A. Risberg, "Employee Experiences of Acquisition Processes," *Journal of World Business* 36 (March 2001): 58–84.

17. K. A. Jehn and C. Bendersky, "Intragroup Conflict in Organizations: A Contingency Perspective on the Conflict-Outcome Relationship," *Research In Organizational Behavior* 25 (2003): 187–242.

18. J. Jetten, R. Spears, and T. Postmes, "Intergroup Distinctiveness and Differentiation: A Meta-Analytic Integration," *Journal of Personality and Social Psychology* 86, no. 6 (2004): 862–879.

19. Von Glinow, Shapiro, and Brett, "Can We Talk, and Should We?"

20. J. M. Brett, *Negotiating Globally: How to Negotiate Deals, Resolve Disputes, and Make Decisions across Cultural Boundaries* (San Francisco: Jossey-Bass, 2001); R. J. Lewicki *et al.*, Negotiation, 4th ed. (Burr Ridge, Ill.: McGraw-Hill/Irwin, 2003), Chap. 4.

21. Jelin, "A Multimethod Examination of the Benefits and Detriments of Intragroup Conflict."

22. D. Cox, "Goodenow's Downfall," *Toronto Star*, 29 July 2005, A1; A. Maki, "NHLPA's New Leader Is a Peacemaker, Not Warrior," *Globe & Mail*, 29 July 2005, S1; M. Spector, "Players: He Is Your Father," *National Post*, 29 July 2005, B8.

23. C. K. W. De Dreu *et al.*, "A Theory-Based Measure of Conflict Management Strategies in the Workplace," *Journal of Organizational Behavior* 22 (2001): 645–668.

24. D. W. Johnson *et al.*, "Effects of Cooperative, Competitive, and Individualistic Goal Structures on Achievement: A Meta-Analysis," *Psychological Bulletin* 89 (1981): 47–62; D. Tjosvold, *Working Together to Get Things Done* (Lexington, Mass.: Lexington, 1986); C. K. W. De Dreu, E. Giebels, and E. Van de Vliert, "Social Motives and Trust in Integrative Negotiation: The Disruptive Effects of Punitive Capability," *Journal of Applied Psychology* 83, no. 3 (June 1998): 408–422.

25. C. K. W. De Dreu and A. E. M. Van Vianen, "Managing Relationship Conflict and the Effectiveness of Organizational Teams," *Journal of Organizational Behavior* 22 (2001): 309–328; Lewicki *et al.*, *Negotiation*, pp. 35–36.

26. M. W. Morris and H.-Y. Fu, "How Does Culture Influence Conflict Resolution? Dynamic Constructivist Analysis," *Social Cognition* 19 (June 2001): 324–349; S. Ting-Toomey, J. G. Oetzel, and K. Yee-Jung, "Self-Construal Types and Conflict Management Styles," *Communication Reports* 14 (Summer 2001): 87–104; C. H. Tinsley, "How Negotiators Get to Yes: Predicting the Constellation of Strategies Used across Cultures to Negotiate Conflict," *Journal of Applied Psychology* 86, no. 4 (2001): 583–593.

27. C. H. Tinsley and E. Weldon, "Responses to a Normative Conflict among American and Chinese Managers," *International Journal of Conflict Management* 3, no. 2 (2003): 183–194. Also see: D. A. Cai and E. L. Fink, "Conflict Style Differences between Individualists and Collectivists," *Communication Monographs* 69 (March 2002): 67–87.

28. N. Brewer, P. Mitchell, and N. Weber, "Gender Role, Organizational Status, and Conflict Management Styles," *International Journal of Conflict Management* 13 (2002): 78–95; N. B. Florea *et al.*, "Negotiating from Mars to Venus: Gender in Simulated International Negotiations," *Simulation & Gaming* 34 (June 2003): 226–248.

29. E. Van de Vliert, "Escalative Intervention in Small Group Conflicts," *Journal of Applied Behavioral Science* 21 (Winter 1985): 19–36.

30. M. Sherif, "Superordinate Goals in the Reduction of Intergroup Conflict," *American Journal of Sociology* 68 (1958): 349–358; K. M. Eisenhardt, J. L. Kahwajy, and L. J. Bourgeois III, "How Management Teams Can Have a Good Fight," *Harvard Business Review* (July-August 1997): 77–85; X. M. Song, J. Xile, and B. Dyer, "Antecedents and Consequences of Marketing Managers' Conflict-Handling Behaviors," *Journal of Marketing* 64 (January 2000): 50–66.

31. H. C. Triandis, "The Future of Workforce Diversity in International Organisations: A Commentary," *Applied Psychology: An International Journal* 52, no. 3 (2003): 486–495.

32. E. Elron, B. Shamir, and E. Bem-Ari, "Why Don't They Fight Each Other? Cultural Diversity and Operational Unity in Multinational Forces," *Armed Forces & Society* 26 (October 1999): 73–97; "How Hibernia Helped Its Hourly Employees Make a Leap to PFP," *Pay for Performance Report*, January 2000, 2; "Teamwork Polishes This Diamond," *Philippine Daily Inquirer*, 4 October 2000, 10.

33. T. F. Pettigrew, "Intergroup Contact Theory," *Annual Review of Psychology* 49 (1998): 65–85; S. Brickson, "The Impact of Identity Orientation on Individual and Organizational Outcomes in Demographically Diverse Settings," *Academy of Management Review* 25 (January 2000): 82–101; J. Dixon and K. Durrheim, "Contact and the Ecology of Racial Division: Some Varieties of Informal Segregation," *British Journal of Social Psychology* 42 (March 2003): 1–23.

34. Triandis, "The Future of Workforce Diversity in International Organisations."

35. Von Glinow, Shapiro, and Brett, "Can We Talk, and Should We?"

36. P. O. Walker, "Decolonizing Conflict Resolution: Addressing the Ontological Violence of Westernization," *American Indian Quarterly* 28, no. 3/4 (July 2004): 527–549; Native Dispute Resolution Network, "Glossary of Terms," (Tucson, Ariz., 2005), http://nativenetwork.ecr.gov, (accessed 15 September 2005).

37. K. R. Lewis, "(Drum) Beatings Build Corporate Spirit," *Star Tribune (Minneapolis, Minn.)*, 3 June 2003, 3E; D. McMurdy, "Marching to a Different Drummer," *Vancouver Sun*, 26 April 2004, D4; S. Wintrob, "Drum Circles Encourage Rhythm in Companies," *National Post*, 30 July 2005, FW3.

38. E. Horwitt, "Knowledge, Knowledge, Who's Got the Knowledge," *Computerworld* (April 8 1996): 80, 81, 84.

39. For a critical view of the problem solving style in negotiation, see: J. M. Brett, "Managing Organizational Conflict," *Professional Psychology: Research and Practice* 15 (1984): 664–678.

40. R. E. Fells, "Developing Trust in Negotiation," *Employee Relations* 15 (1993): 33–45; R. E. Fells, "Overcoming the Dilemmas in Walton and Mckersie's Mixed Bargaining Strategy," *Industrial Relations (Laval)* 53 (March 1998): 300–325.

41. R. Stagner and H. Rosen, *Psychology of Union—Management Relations* (Belmont, Calif.: Wadsworth, 1965), pp. 95–96, 108–110; R. E. Walton and R. B. McKersie, *A Behavioral Theory of Labor Negotiations: An Analysis of a Social Interaction System* (New York: McGraw-Hill, 1965), pp. 41–46; L. Thompson, *The Mind and Heart of the Negotiator* (Upper Saddle River, NJ: Prentice-Hall, 1998), Chap. 2.

42. J. W. Salacuse and J. Z. Rubin, "Your Place or Mine? Site Location and Negotiation," *Negotiation Journal* 6 (January 1990): 5–10; J. Mayfield *et al.*, "How Location Impacts International Business Negotiations," *Review of Business* 19 (December 1998): 21–24.

43. For a full discussion of the advantages and disadvantages of face-to-face and alternative negotiations situations, see: M. H. Bazerman *et al.*, "Negotiation," *Annual Review of Psychology* 51 (2000): 279–314.

44. A. F. Stuhlmacher, T. L. Gillespie, and M. V. Champagne, "The Impact of Time Pressure in Negotiation: A Meta-Analysis," *International Journal of Conflict Management* 9, no. 2 (April 1998): 97–116; C. K. W. De Dreu, "Time Pressure and Closing of the Mind in Negotiation," *Organizational Behavior and Human Decision Processes* 91 (July 2003): 280–295. However, one recent study reported that speeding up these concessions leads to better negotiated outcomes. See: D. A. Moore, "Myopic Prediction, Self-Destructive Secrecy, and the Unexpected Benefits of Revealing Final Deadlines in Negotiation," *Organizational Behavior and Human Decision Processes* 94, no. 2 (2004): 125–139.

45. Lewicki *et al.*, *Negotiation*, pp. 298–322.

46. S. Doctoroff, "Reengineering Negotiations," *Sloan Management Review* 39 (March 1998): 63–71; D. C. Zetik and A. F. Stuhlmacher, "Goal Setting and Negotiation Performance: A Meta-Analysis," *Group Processes & Intergroup Relations* 5 (January 2002): 35–52.

47. L. L. Thompson, "Information Exchange in Negotiation," *Journal of Experimental Social Psychology* 27 (1991): 161–179.

48. L. Thompson, E. Peterson, and S. E. Brodt, "Team Negotiation: An Examinaton of Integrative and Distributive Bargaining," *Journal of Personality and Social Psychology* 70 (1996): 66–78; Y. Paik and R. L. Tung, "Negotiating with East Asians: How to Attain "Win-Win" Outcomes," *Management International Review* 39 (1999): 103–122.

49. B. McRae, *The Seven Strategies of Master Negotiators* (Toronto: McGraw-Hill Ryerson, 2002), pp. 7–11.

50. D. J. O'Keefe, *Persuasion: Theory and Research* (Thousand Oaks, CA: Sage Publications, 2002).

51. Lewicki *et al.*, *Negotiation*, pp. 90–96; S. Kwon and L. R. Weingart, "Unilateral Concessions from the Other Party: Concession Behavior, Attributions, and Negotiation Judgments," *Journal of Applied Psychology* 89, no. 2 (2004): 263–278.

52. J. J. Zhao, "The Chinese Approach to International Business Negotiation," *Journal of Business Communication* (July 2000): 209–237; N. Crundwell, "U.S.-Russian Negotiating Strategies," *BISNIS Bulletin*, October 2003, 5–6.

53. J. Z. Rubin and B. R. Brown, *The Social Psychology of Bargaining and Negotiation* (New York: Academic Press, 1976), Chap. 9.

54. L. L. Putnam, "Beyond Third Party Role: Disputes and Managerial Intervention," *Employee Responsibilities and Rights Journal* 7 (1994): 23–36; A. R. Elangovan, "The Manager as the Third Party: Deciding How to Intervene in Employee Disputes," in *Negotiation: Readings, Exercises, and Cases*, ed. R. J. Lewicki, J. A. Litterer, and D. Saunders, Third ed. (New York: McGraw-Hill, 1999), 458–469. For a somewhat different taxonomy of managerial conflict intervention, see: P. G. Irving and J. P. Meyer, "A Multidimensional Scaling Analysis of Managerial Third-Party Conflict Intervention Strategies," *Canadian Journal Of Behavioural Science* 29, no. 1 (January 1997): 7–18.

55. B. H. Sheppard, "Managers as Inquisitors: Lessons from the Law," in *Bargaining inside Organizations*, ed. M. H. Bazerman and R. J. Lewicki (Beverly Hills, CA: Sage, 1983); N. H. Kim, D. W. Sohn, and J. A. Wall, "Korean Leaders' (and Subordinates') Conflict Management," *International Journal Of Conflict Management* 10, no. 2 (April 1999): 130–153.

56. R. Karambayya and J. M. Brett, "Managers Handling Disputes: Third Party Roles and Perceptions of Fairness," *Academy of Management Journal* 32 (1989): 687–704; R. Cropanzano *et al.*, "Disputant Reactions to Managerial Conflict Resolution Tactics," *Group & Organization Management* 24 (June 1999): 124–153.

57. A. R. Elangovan, "Managerial Intervention in Organizational Disputes: Testing a Prescriptive Model of Strategy Selection," *International Journal of Conflict Management* 4 (1998): 301–335; P. S. Nugent, "Managing Conflict: Third-Party Interventions for Managers," *Academy Of Management Executive* 16, no. 1 (February 2002): 139–154.

58. J. P. Meyer, J. M. Gemmell, and P. G. Irving, "Evaluating the Management of Interpersonal Conflict in Organizations: A Factor-Analytic Study of Outcome Criteria," *Canadian Journal of Administrative Sciences* 14 (1997): 1–13.

CHAPTER FOURTEEN

1. D. Menzies, "From Beer to Eternity," *Profit*, October 2000, 58; "CEO Buys Control of Hamilton's Lakeport Brewing," *Kitchener-Waterloo Record*, 7 January 2005, A10; E. Kobayashi, "Brewing up Business," *National Post*, 1 April 2005, 78; S. Nagy, "Teresa Cascioli," *Globe & Mail*, 21 September 2005.

2. R. House, M. Javidan, and P. Dorfman, "Project Globe: An Introduction," *Applied Psychology: An International Review* 50 (2001): 489–505; R. House *et al.*, "Understanding Cultures and Implicit Leadership Theories across the Globe: An Introduction to Project Globe," *Journal of World Business* 37 (2002): 3–10.

3. R. G. Issac, W. J. Zerbe, and D. C. Pitt, "Leadership and Motivation: The Effective Application of Expectancy Theory," *Journal of Managerial Issues* 13 (Summer 2001): 212–226; C. L. Pearce and J. A. Conger, eds., *Shared Leadership: Reframing the Hows and Whys of Leadership* (Thousand Oaks, Calif: Sage, 2003); J. S. Nielson, *The Myth of Leadership* (Palo Alto, Calif.: Davies-Black, 2004).

4. J. Raelin, "Preparing for Leaderful Practice," *T&D*, March 2004, 64.

5. L. Gyulai, "It Takes Children to Raise a Village," *Montreal Gazette*, 30 July 2005, A14.

6. Many of these perspectives are summarized in R. N. Kanungo, "Leader-

ship in Organizations: Looking Ahead to the 21st Century," *Canadian Psychology* 39 (Spring 1998): 71–82; G. A. Yukl, *Leadership in Organizations*, 6th ed. (Upper Saddle River, NJ: Pearson Education, 2006).

7. M. Callahan, "Key to Success Is Happy Employees, Says Utility's CEO," *Western Star (Cornerbrook, Nfld)*, May 18 2002.

8. J. Higley, "Head of the Class," *Hotel & Motel Management*, November 2001, 92ff.

9. R. M. Stogdill, *Handbook of Leadership* (New York: The Free Press, 1974), Chap. 5.

10. R. Ilies, M. W. Gerhardt, and H. Le, "Individual Differences in Leadership Emergence: Integrating Meta-Analytic Findings and Behavioural Genetics Estimates," *International Journal of Selection and Assessment* 12, no. 3 (September 2004): 207–219.

11. M. D. Mumford *et al.*, "Leadership Skills for a Changing World: Solving Complex Social Problems," *The Leadership Quarterly* 11, no. 1 (2000): 11–35; J. A. Conger and D. A. Ready, "Rethinking Leadership Competencies," *Leader to Leader* (Spring 2004): 41–47; S. J. Zaccaro, C. Kemp, and P. Bader, "Leader Traits and Attributes," in *The Nature of Leadership*, ed. J. Antonakis, A. T. Cianciolo, and R. J. Sternberg (Thousand Oaks, CA: Sage, 2004), 101–124.

12. This list is based on: S. A. Kirkpatrick and E. A. Locke, "Leadership: Do Traits Matter?" *Academy of Management Executive* 5 (May 1991): 48–60; R. M. Aditya, R. J. House, and S. Kerr, "Theory and Practice of Leadership: Into the New Millennium," in *Industrial and Organizational Psychology: Linking Theory with Practice*, ed. C. L. Cooper and E. A. Locke (Oxford, UK: Blackwell, 2000), 130–165; D. Goleman, R. Boyatzis, and A. McKee, *Primal Leaders* (Boston: Harvard Business School Press, 2002); T. A. Judge *et al.*, "Personality and Leadership: A Qualitative and Quantitative Review," *Journal Of Applied Psychology* 87, no. 4 (August 2002): 765–780; T. A. Judge, A. E. Colbert, and R. Ilies, "Intelligence and Leadership: A Quantitative Review and Test of Theoretical Propositions," *Journal Of Applied Psychology* 89, no. 3 (June 2004): 542–552.

13. J. George, "Emotions and Leadership: The Role of Emotional Intelligence," *Human Relations* 53 (August 2000): 1027–1055; Goleman, Boyatzis, and McKee, *Primal Leaders*; R. G. Lord and R. J. Hall, "Identity, Deep Structure and the Development of Leadership Skill," *Leadership Quarterly* 16, no. 4 (August 2005): 591–615.

14. S. E. Cronshaw and R. J. Ellis, "A Process Investigation of Self-Monitoring and Leader Emergence," *Small Group Research* 22 (1991): 403–420; J. A. Kolb, "The Relationship between Self-Monitoring and Leadership in Student Project Groups," *Journal of Business Communication* 35 (April 1998): 264–282; J. J. Sosik, D. Potosky, and D. I. Jung, "Adaptive Self-Regulation: Meeting Others' Expectations of Leadership and Performance," *Journal of Social Psychology* 142 (April 2002): 211–232.

15. D. R. May *et al.*, "The Moral Component of Authentic Leadership," *Organizational Dynamics* 32 (August 2003): 247–260 The large-scale studies are reported in: C. Savoye, "Workers Say Honesty Is Best Company Policy," *Christian Science Monitor*, June 15 2000; J. M. Kouzes and B. Z. Posner, *The Leadership Challenge*, 3rd ed. (San Francisco: Jossey-Bass, 2002), Chap. 2; J. Schettler, "Leadership in Corporate America," *Training & Development*, September 2002, 66–73.

16. J. Norman, "Ethical Fallout," *Orange County Register (Calif.)*, 5 August 2002, 1; K. Melymuka, "Layoff Survivors," *Computerworld*, 9 June 2003, 26; A. Sidimé, "Company Ethics on Mend," *Express-News (San Antonio, Texas)*, 1 September 2003; Watson Wyatt, "Workers' Attitudes toward Leaders Rebounded Strongly between 2002 and 2004, Watson Wyatt Survey Finds," Watson Wyatt News release, (Washington, D.C.: 14 December 2004).

17. R. J. House and R. N. Aditya, "The Social Scientific Study of Leadership: Quo Vadis?" *Journal of Management* 23 (1997): 409–473.

18. R. Jacobs, "Using Human Resource Functions to Enhance Emotional Intelligence," in *The Emotionally Intelligent Workplace*, ed. C. Cherniss and D. Goleman (San Francisco: Jossey-Bass, 2001), 161–163; Conger and Ready, "Rethinking Leadership Competencies."

19. P. G. Northouse, *Leadership: Theory and Practice*, 3rd ed. (Thousand Oaks,

CA: Sage, 2004), Chap. 4; Yukl, *Leadership in Organizations*, Chap. 3.

20. A. K. Korman, "Consideration, Initiating Structure, and Organizational Criteria—a Review," *Personnel Psychology* 19 (1966): 349–362; E. A. Fleishman, "Twenty Years of Consideration and Structure," in *Current Developments in the Study of Leadership*, ed. E. A. Fleishman and J. C. Hunt (Carbondale, Ill.: Southern Illinois University Press, 1973), 1–40; T. A. Judge, R. F. Piccolo, and R. Ilies, "The Forgotten Ones? The Validity of Consideration and Initiating Structure in Leadership Research," *Journal of Applied Psychology* 89, no. 1 (2004): 36–51; Yukl, *Leadership in Organizations*, pp. 62–75.

21. V. V. Baba, "Serendipity in Leadership: Initiating Structure and Consideration in the Classroom," *Human Relations* 42 (1989): 509–525.

22. S. Kerr *et al.*, "Towards a Contingency Theory of Leadership Based Upon the Consideration and Initiating Structure Literature," *Organizational Behaviour and Human Performance* 12 (1974): 62–82; L. L. Larson, J. G. Hunt, and R. N. Osborn, "The Great Hi—Hi Leader Behaviour Myth: A Lesson from Occam's Razor," *Academy of Management Journal* 19 (1976): 628–641.

23. R. Tannenbaum and W. H. Schmidt, "How to Choose a Leadership Pattern," *Harvard Business Review* (May-June 1973): 162–180.

24. For a thorough study of how expectancy theory of motivation relates to leadership, see: R. G. Isaac, W. J. Zerbe, and D. C. Pitt, "Leadership and Motivation: The Effective Application of Expectancy Theory," *Journal of Managerial Issues* 13 (Summer 2001): 212–226.

25. R. J. House, "A Path-Goal Theory of Leader Effectiveness," *Administrative Science Quarterly* 16 (1971): 321–338; M. G. Evans, "Extensions of a Path-Goal Theory of Motivation," *Journal of Applied Psychology* 59 (1974): 172–178; R. J. House and T. R. Mitchell, "Path-Goal Theory of Leadership," *Journal of Contemporary Business* (Autumn 1974): 81–97; M. G. Evans, "Path Goal Theory of Leadership," in *Leadership*, ed. L. L. Neider and C. A. Schriesheim (Greenwich, CT: Information Age Publishing, 2002), 115–138.

26. Various thoughts on servant leadership are presented in: L. C. Spears and M. Lawrence, eds., *Focus on Leadership: Servant-Leadership* (New York: John Wiley & Sons, 2002).

27. R. J. House, "Path-Goal Theory of Leadership: Lessons, Legacy, and a Reformulated Theory," *Leadership Quarterly* 7 (1996): 323–352.

28. D.-A. Durbin, "Canadian in Driver's Seat at Chrysler," *Calgary Herald*, 15 August 2005, F5.

29. J. Indvik, "Path-Goal Theory of Leadership: A Meta-Analysis," *Academy of Management Proceedings* (1986): 189–192; J. C. Wofford and L. Z. Liska, "Path-Goal Theories of Leadership: A Meta-Analysis," *Journal of Management* 19 (1993): 857–876.

30. R. T. Keller, "A Test of the Path-Goal Theory of Leadership with Need for Clarity as a Moderator in Research and Development Organizations," *Journal of Applied Psychology* 74 (1989): 208–212.

31. C. A. Schriesheim and L. L. Neider, "Path-Goal Leadership Theory: The Long and Winding Road," *Leadership Quarterly* 7 (1996): 317–321.

32. P. Hersey and K. H. Blanchard, *Management of Organizational Behaviour: Utilizing Human Resources*, 5th ed. (Englewood Cliffs, N.J.: Prentice Hall, 1988).

33. R. P. Vecchio, "Situational Leadership Theory: An Examination of a Prescriptive Theory," *Journal of Applied Psychology* 72 (1987): 444–451; W. Blank, J. R. Weitzel, and S. G. Green, "A Test of the Situational Leadership Theory," *Personnel Psychology* 43 (1990): 579–597; C. L. Graeff, "Evolution of Situational Leadership Theory: A Critical Review," *Leadership Quarterly* 8 (1997): 153–170.

34. F. E. Fiedler, *A Theory of Leadership Effectiveness* (New York: McGraw-Hill, 1967); F. E. Fiedler and M. M. Chemers, *Leadership and Effective Management* (Glenview, Ill.: Scott, Foresman, 1974).

35. F. E. Fiedler, "Engineer the Job to Fit the Manager," *Harvard Business Review* 43, no. 5 (1965): 115–122.

36. For a summary of criticisms, see: Yukl, *Leadership in Organizations*, pp. 217–218.

37. N. Nicholson, *Executive Instinct* (New York: Crown, 2000).

38. This observation has also been made by C. A. Schriesheim, "Substitutes-for-Leadership Theory: Development and Basic Concepts," *Leadership Quarterly* 8 (1997): 103–108.

39. D. F. Elloy and A. Randolph, "The Effect of Superleader Behaviour on Autonomous Work Groups in a Government Operated Railway Service," *Public Personnel Management* 26 (Summer 1997): 257–272; C. C. Manz and H. Sims Jr., *The New SuperLeadership: Leading Others to Lead Themselves* (San Francisco: Berrett-Koehler, 2001).

40. M. L. Loughry, "Coworkers Are Watching: Performance Implications of Peer Monitoring," *Academy of Management Proceedings* (2002): 01–06.

41. C. C. Manz and C. Neck, *Mastering Self-Leadership*, 3rd ed. (Upper Saddle River, NJ: Prentice Hall, 2004).

42. P. M. Podsakoff and S. B. MacKenzie, "Kerr and Jermier's Substitutes for Leadership Model: Background, Empirical Assessment, and Suggestions for Future Research," *Leadership Quarterly* 8 (1997): 117–132; S. D. Dionne *et al.*, "Neutralizing Substitutes for Leadership Theory: Leadership Effects and Common-Source Bias," *Journal Of Applied Psychology* 87, no. 3 (June 2002): 454–464; J. R. Villa *et al.*, "Problems with Detecting Moderators in Leadership Research Using Moderated Multiple Regression," *Leadership Quarterly* 14, no. 1 (February 2003): 3–23; S. D. Dionne *et al.*, "Substitutes for Leadership, or Not," *The Leadership Quarterly* 16, no. 1 (2005): 169–193.

43. A. Cattaneo, "The Man Who Saved Suncor," *National Post*, 11 September 1999, D1; A. Nikiforuk, "Saint or Sinner?" *Canadian Business*, 13 May 2002, 54–59.

44. J. M. Burns, *Leadership* (New York: Harper & Row, 1978); B. M. Bass, *Transformational Leadership: Industrial, Military, and Educational Impact* (Hillsdale, NJ: Erlbaum, 1998); B. J. Avolio and F. J. Yammarino, eds., *Transformational and Charismatic Leadership: The Road Ahead* (Greenwich, CT: JAI Press, 2002).

45. V. L. Goodwin, J. C. Wofford, and J. L. Whittington "A Theoretical and Empirical Extension to the Transformational Leadership Construct," *Journal of Organizational Behaviour*, 22 (November 2001), pp. 759–774.

46. A. Zaleznik, "Managers and Leaders: Are They Different?" *Harvard Business Review* 55, no. 5 (1977): 67–78; W. Bennis and B. Nanus, *Leaders: The Strategies for Taking Charge* (New York: Harper & Row, 1985); R. H. G. Field, "Leadership Defined: Web Images Reveal the Differences between Leadership and Management" in *Annual Conference of the Administrative Sciences Association of Canada, Organizational Behaviour Division*, ed. P. Mudrack, (Winnipeg, Manitoba, 25–28 May, 2002), 93.

47. Both transformational and transactional leadership improve work unit performance. See: B. M. Bass *et al.*, "Predicting Unit Performance by Assessing Transformational and Transactional Leadership," *Journal of Applied Psychology* 88 (April 2003): 207–218.

48. C.P. Egri and S. Herman, "Leadership in the North American Environmental Sector: Values, Leadership Styles, and Contexts of Environmental Leaders and Their Organizations," *Academy of Management Journal*, 43 (August 2000), pp. 571–604.

49. For discussion on the tendency to slide from transformational to transactional leadership, see: W. Bennis, *An Invented Life: Reflections on Leadership and Change* (Reading, MA: Addison-Wesley, 1993).

50. R. J. House, "A 1976 Theory of Charismatic Leadership," in *Leadership: The Cutting Edge*, ed. J. G. Hunt and L. L. Larson (Carbondale, IL.: Southern Illinois University Press, 1977), 189–207; J. A. Conger, "Charismatic and Transformational Leadership in Organizations: An Insider's Perspective on These Developing Streams of Research," *Leadership Quarterly* 10 (Summer 1999): 145–179.

51. J. Barbuto, J. E., "Taking the Charisma out of Transformational Leadership," *Journal of Social Behaviour & Personality* 12 (September 1997): 689–697; Y. A. Nur, "Charisma and Managerial Leadership: The Gift That Never Was," *Business Horizons* 41 (July 1998): 19–26; M. D. Mumford and J. R. Van Doorn, "The Leadership of Pragmatism—Reconsidering Franklin in the Age of Charisma," *Leadership Quarterly* 12, no. 3 (Fall 2001): 279–309.

52. R. E. De Vries, R. A. Roe, and T. C. B. Taillieu, "On Charisma and Need for Leadership," *European Journal of Work and Organizational Psychology* 8 (1999):

109–133; R. Khurana, *Searching for a Corporate Savior: The Irrational Quest for Charismatic CEOs* (Princeton, NJ: Princeton University Press, 2002).

53. D. Olive, "The 7 Deadly Chief Executive Sins," *Toronto Star*, 17 February 2004, D01.

54. K. Brooker and J. Schlosser, "The Un-CEO," *Fortune*, 16 September 2002, 88–93; B. Nussbaum, "The Power of Design," *BusinessWeek*, 17 May 2004, 86; N. Buckley, "The Calm Reinventor," *Financial Times (London)*, 29 January 2005, 11; S. Ellison, "Women's Touch Guides P&G Chief's Firm Hand in Company Turnaround," *Wall Street Journal Europe*, 1 June 2005, A1; S. Hill Jr., "P&G's Turnaround Proves Listening to Customer Pays," *Manufacturing Business Technology*, July 2005, 64; J. Tylee, "Procter's Creative Gamble," *Campaign*, 18 March 2005, 24–26.

55. Bennis and Nanus, Leaders, pp. 27–33, 89; I. M. Levin, "Vision Revisited," *Journal of Applied Behavioural Science* 36 (March 2000): 91–107; J. R. Sparks and J. A. Schenk, "Explaining the Effects of Transformational Leadership: An Investigation of the Effects of Higher-Order Motives in Multilevel Marketing Organizations," *Journal of Organizational Behaviour* 22 (2001): 849–869; D. Christenson and D. H. T. Walker, "Understanding the Role of 'Vision' in Project Success," *Project Management Journal* 35, no. 3 (September 2004): 39–52; R. E. Quinn, *Building the Bridge as You Walk on It: A Guide for Leading Change* (San Francisco: Jossey-Bass, 2004), Chap. 11.

56. J. R. Baum, E. A. Locke, and S. A. Kirkpatrick, "A Longitudinal Study of the Relation of Vision and Vision Communication to Venture Growth in Entrepreneurial Firms," *Journal of Applied Psychology* 83 (1998): 43–54; S. L. Hoe and S. L. McShane, "Leadership Antecedents of Informal Knowledge Acquisition and Dissemination," *International Journal of Organisational Behaviour* 5 (2002): 282–291.

57. L. Manfield, "Creating a Safety Culture from Top to Bottom," *WorkSafe Magazine*, February 2005, 8–9. The Canadian CEO survey is reported in: "Canadian CEOs Give Themselves Top Marks for Leadership!" *Canada NewsWire*, 9 September 1999.

58. J. A. Conger, "Inspiring Others: The Language of Leadership," *Academy of Management Executive* 5 (February 1991): 31–45; G. T. Fairhurst and R. A. Sarr, *The Art of Framing: Managing the Language of Leadership* (San Francisco, CA: Jossey-Bass, 1996); A. E. Rafferty and M. A. Griffin, "Dimensions of Transformational Leadership: Conceptual and Empirical Extensions," *Leadership Quarterly* 15, no. 3 (2004): 329–354.

59. S. Franklin, *The Heroes: A Saga of Canadian Inspiration* (Toronto: McClelland and Stewart, 1967); L. Black, "Hamburger Diplomacy," *Report on Business Magazine*, August 1988, 30–36.

60. D. E. Berlew, "Leadership and Organizational Excitement," *California Management Review* 17, no. 2 (Winter 1974): 21–30; Bennis and Nanus, *Leaders*, pp. 43–55; T. Simons, "Behavioural Integrity: The Perceived Alignment between Managers' Words and Deeds as a Research Focus," *Organization Science* 13, no. 1 (Jan-Feb 2002): 18–35.

61. S. Ewart, "Unique Suncor Boasts Unique CEO," *Calgary Herald*, 11 September 1999, 1.

62. T. Benson, "Teaching Some New Samba Steps to G.M. Brazil," *New York Times*, 11 March 2005, 2.

63. J. Barling, T. Weber, and E. K. Kelloway, "Effects of Transformational Leadership Training on Attitudinal and Financial Outcomes: A Field Experiment," *Journal of Applied Psychology* 81 (1996): 827–832.

64. A. Bryman, "Leadership in Organizations," in *Handbook of Organization Studies*, ed. S. R. Clegg, C. Hardy, and W. R. Nord (Thousand Oaks, CA: Sage, 1996), 276–292.

65. B. S. Pawar and K. K. Eastman, "The Nature and Implications of Contextual Influences on Transformational Leadership: A Conceptual Examination," *Academy of Management Review* 22 (1997): 80–109; C. P. Egri and S. Herman, "Leadership in the North American Environmental Sector: Values, Leadership Styles, and Contexts of Environmental Leaders and Their Organizations," *Academy of Management Journal* 43, no. 4 (2000): 571–604.

66. J. R. Meindl, "On Leadership: An Alternative to the Conventional Wisdom," *Research in Organizational Behaviour* 12 (1990): 159–203; L. R. Offermann, J. J. K. Kennedy, and P. W. Wirtz, "Implicit Leadership Theories: Content, Structure, and Generalizability," *Leadership Quarterly* 5, no. 1 (1994): 43–58; R. J. Hall and R. G. Lord, "Multi-Level Information Processing Explanations of Followers' Leadership Perceptions," *Leadership Quarterly* 6 (1995): 265–287; O. Epitropaki and R. Martin, "Implicit Leadership Theories in Applied Settings: Factor Structure, Generalizability, and Stability over Time," *Journal of Applied Psychology* 89, no. 2 (2004): 293–310.

67. L. M. A. Chong and D. C. Thomas, "Leadership Perceptions in Cross-Cultural Context: Pakeha and Pacific Islanders in New Zealand," *Leadership Quarterly* 8 (1997): 275–293; R. G. Lord *et al.*, "Contextual Constraints on Prototype Generation and Their Multilevel Consequences for Leadership Perceptions," *The Leadership Quarterly* 12, no. 3 (2001): 311–338; T. Keller, "Parental Images as a Guide to Leadership Sensemaking: An Attachment Perspective on Implicit Leadership Theories," *Leadership Quarterly* 14 (2003): 141–160.

68. S. F. Cronshaw and R. G. Lord, "Effects of Categorization, Attribution, and Encoding Processes on Leadership Perceptions," *Journal of Applied Psychology* 72 (1987): 97–106; J. L. Nye and D. R. Forsyth, "The Effects of Prototype-Based Biases on Leadership Appraisals: A Test of Leadership Categorization Theory," *Small Group Research* 22 (1991): 360–379.

69. R. Weber *et al.*, "The Illusion of Leadership: Misattribution of Cause in Coordination Games," *Organization Science* 12, no. 5 (2001): 582–598; N. Ensari and S. E. Murphy, "Cross-Cultural Variations in Leadership Perceptions and Attribution of Charisma to the Leader," *Organizational Behaviour and Human Decision Processes* 92 (2003): 52–66; M. L. A. Hayward, V. P. Rindova, and T. G. Pollock, "Believing One's Own Press: The Causes and Consequences of CEO Celebrity," *Strategic Management Journal* 25, no. 7 (July 2004): 637–653.

70. Meindl, "On Leadership: An Alternative to the Conventional Wisdom," p. 163.

71. J. Pfeffer, "The Ambiguity of Leadership," *Academy of Management Review* 2 (1977): 102–112.

72. Six of the Project GLOBE clusters are described in a special issue of the *Journal of World Business*, 37 (2000). For an overview of Project GLOBE, see: House, Javidan, and Dorfman, "Project Globe: An Introduction,"; House *et al.*, "Understanding Cultures and Implicit Leadership Theories across the Globe: An Introduction to Project Globe,"

73. J. C. Jesiuno, "Latin Europe Cluster: From South to North," *Journal of World Business* 37 (2002): 88. Another GLOBE study of Iranian managers also reported that charismatic visionary stands out as a primary leadership dimension. See: A. Dastmalchian, M. Javidan, and K. Alam, "Effective Leadership and Culture in Iran: An Empirical Study," *Applied Psychology: An International Review* 50 (2001): 532–558.

74. D. N. Den Hartog *et al.*, "Culture Specific and Cross-Cultural Generalizable Implicit Leadership Theories: Are Attributes of Charismatic/Transformational Leadership Universally Endorsed?" *Leadership Quarterly* 10 (1999): 219–256; F. C. Brodbeck and *et al.*, "Cultural Variation of Leadership Prototypes across 22 European Countries," *Journal of Occupational and Organizational Psychology* 73 (2000): 1–29; E. Szabo and *et al.*, "The Europe Cluster: Where Employees Have a Voice," *Journal of World Business* 37 (2002): 55–68. The Mexican study is reported in: C. E. Nicholls, H. W. Lane, and M. B. Brechu, "Taking Self-Managed Teams to Mexico," *Academy of Management Executive* 13 (August 1999): 15–25.

75. The Conference Board of Canada survey is summarized in: L. Elliott, "Women Switch Jobs to Climb the Power Ladder," *Toronto Star*, 15 June 2000, NE1.

76. J. B. Rosener, "Ways Women Lead," *Harvard Business Review* 68 (November-December 1990): 119–125; S. H. Appelbaum and B. T. Shaprio, "Why Can't Men Lead Like Women?" *Leadership and Organization Development Journal* 14 (1993): 28–34; N. Wood, "Venus Rules," *Incentive* 172 (February 1998): 22–27.

77. G. N. Powell, "One More Time: Do Female and Male Managers Differ?" *Academy of Management Executive* 4 (1990): 68–75; M. L. van Engen and T. M. Willemsen, "Sex and Leadership Styles: A Meta-Analysis of Research

Published in the 1990s," *Psychological Reports* 94, no. 1 (February 2004): 3–18.

78. R. Sharpe, "As Leaders, Women Rule," *BusinessWeek*, 20 November 2000, 74; M. Sappenfield, "Women, It Seems, Are Better Bosses," *Christian Science Monitor*, 16 January 2001; A. H. Eagly and L. L. Carli, "The Female Leadership Advantage: An Evaluation of the Evidence," *The Leadership Quarterly* 14, no. 6 (December 2003): 807–834; A. H. Eagly, M. C. Johannesen-Schmidt, and M. L. van Engen, "Transformational, Transactional, and Laissez-Faire Leadership Styles: A Meta-Analysis Comparing Women and Men," *Psychological Bulletin* 129 (July 2003): 569–591.

79. A. H. Eagly, S. J. Karau, and M. G. Makhijani, "Gender and the Effectiveness of Leaders: A Meta-Analysis," *Psychological Bulletin* 117 (1995): 125–145; J. G. Oakley, "Gender-Based Barriers to Senior Management Positions: Understanding the Scarcity of Female CEOs," *Journal of Business Ethics* 27 (2000): 821–334; N. Z. Stelter, "Gender Differences in Leadership: Current Social Issues and Future Organizational Implications," *Journal of Leadership Studies* 8 (2002): 88–99; M. E. Heilman *et al.*, "Penalties for Success: Reactions to Women Who Succeed at Male Gender-Typed Tasks," *Journal of Applied Psychology* 89, no. 3 (2004): 416–427; A. H. Eagly, "Achieving Relational Authenticity in Leadership: Does Gender Matter?" *The Leadership Quarterly* 16, no. 3 (June 2005): 459–474.

CHAPTER FIFTEEN

1. R. Muzyka and G. Zeschuk, "Managing Multiple Projects," *Game Developer*, March 2003, 34–42; M. Saltzman, "The Ex-Doctors Are In," *National Post*, 24 March 2004, AL4; R. McConnell, "For Edmonton's Bioware, Today's the Big Day," *Edmonton Journal*, 14 April 2005, C1.

2. S. Ranson, R. Hinings, and R. Greenwood, "The Structuring of Organizational Structure," *Administrative Science Quarterly* 25 (1980): 1–14.

3. J.-E. Johanson, "Intraorganizational Influence," *Management Communication Quarterly* 13 (February 2000): 393–435.

4. B. Morris, "Charles Schwab's big Challenge," *Fortune*, 30 May 2005, 88.

5. H. Mintzberg, *The Structuring of Organizations* (Englewood Cliffs, N.J.: Prentice Hall, 1979), 2–3.

6. E. E. Lawler III, *Motivation in Work Organizations* (Monterey, Calif.: Brooks/Cole, 1973); M. A. Campion, "Ability Requirement Implications of Job Design: An Interdisciplinary Perspective," *Personnel Psychology* 42 (1989): 1–24.

7. Mintzberg, *The Structuring of Organizations*, 2–8; D. A. Nadler and M. L. Tushman, *Competing by Design: The Power of Organizational Architecture* (N. Y.: Oxford University Press, 1997), Chap. 6.

8. C. Downs, P. Clampitt, and A. L. Pfeiffer, "Communication and Organizational Outcomes," in *Handbook of Organizational Communication*, ed. G. Goldhaber and G. Barnett (Norwood, N.J.: Ablex, 1988), 171–211; I. Nonaka and H. Takeuchi, *The Knowledge-Creating Company* (New York: Oxford University Press, 1995).

9. A. L. Patti, J. P. Gilbert, and S. Hartman, "Physical Co-Location and the Success of New Product Development Projects," *Engineering Management Journal* 9 (September 1997): 31–37; M. Hoque, M. Akter, and Y. Monden, "Concurrent Engineering: A Compromise Approach to Develop a Feasible and Customer-Pleasing Product," *International Journal of Production Research* 43, no. 8 (15 April 2005): 1607–1624.

10. For a discussion of the role of brand manager at Procter & Gamble, see C. Peale, "Branded for Success," *Cincinnati Enquirer* (May 20 2001): A1. Details about how to design integrator roles in organizational structures are presented in: J. R. Galbraith, *Designing Organizations* (San Francisco: Jossey-Bass, 2002), 66–72.

11. Fayol's work is summarized in J. B. Miner, *Theories of Organizational Structure and Process* (Chicago: Dryden, 1982), pp. 358–66.

12. Y.-M. Hsieh and A. Tien-Hsieh, "Enhancement of Service Quality with Job Standardisation," *Service Industries Journal* 21 (July 2001): 147–166.

13. J. H. Sheridan, "Lessons from the Best," *Industry Week*, February 20 1995, 13–22.

14. K. Dorrell, "The Right Stuff," *Plant*, December 16, 1996, pp. 18–19; D. Jones, "Robo-Shop," *Report on Business Magazine*, March 1994, pp. 54–62;

L. Gutri, "Pratt & Whitney Employees Don't Want to Be Managed: Teams Demand Leadership," *Canadian HR Reporter*, May 2, 1988, p. 8; J. Todd, "Firm Fashions Workplace for High-Tech Era," *Montreal Gazette*, December 12, 1987, p. B4.

15. D. D. Van Fleet and B. A. G., "A History of the Span of Management," *Academy of Management Review* 2 (1977): 356–372; Mintzberg, *The Structuring of Organizations*, Chap. 8.

16. "BASF Culling Saves (Gbp) 4m," *Personnel Today* (19 February 2002): 3.

17. T. Peters, *Thriving on Chaos* (New York: Knopf, 1987), 359.

18. "Taking Care of the People," *Canadian Healthcare Manager* 6 (April-May 1999), pp. 5–9.

19. Q. N. Huy, "In Praise of Middle Managers," *Harvard Business Review* 79 (September 2001): 72–79; H. J. Leavitt, *Top Down: Why Hierarchies Are Here to Stay and How to Manage Them More Effectively* (Cambridge: Harvard Business School Press, 2005).

20. The number of layers at Microsoft is inferred from F. Jebb, "Don't Call Me Sir," *Management Today* (August 1998): 44–47.

21. W. Stueck, "Revamped Barrick Keeps Eyes on the Hunt for the Golden Prize," *Globe & Mail*, 17 September 2005, B4.

22. P. Brabeck, "The Business Case against Revolution: An Interview with Nestle's Peter Brabeck," *Harvard Business Review* 79 (February 2001): 112; H. A. Richardson *et al.*, "Does Decentralization Make a Difference for the Organization? An Examination of the Boundary Conditions Circumscribing Decentralized Decision-Making and Organizational Financial Performance," *Journal of Management* 28, no. 2 (2002): 217–244; G. Masado, "To Centralize or Decentralize?" *Optimize*, May 2005, 58.

23. Mintzberg, *The Structuring of Organizations*, Chap. 5.

24. T. Burns and G. Stalker, *The Management of Innovation* (London Tavistock: 1961).

25. D. Youngblood, "Computer Consultants Win Business with Creative Strategies," *Star Tribune (Minneapolis, MN)*, 15 July 2001; S. Brouillard, "Right at Home," *Minneapolis-St. Paul Business Journal*, 23 August 2002; J. Fure, "Staying Connected," *Minneapolis-St. Paul Business Journal*, 20 August 2004.

26. J. Tata, S. Prasad, and R. Thom, "The Influence of Organizational Structure on the Effectiveness of TQM Programs," *Journal of Managerial Issues* 11, no. 4 (Winter 1999): 440–453; A. Lam, "Tacit Knowledge, Organizational Learning and Societal Institutions: An Integrated Framework," *Organization Studies* 21 (May 2000): 487–513.

27. M. King, "Perking up the Bottom Line," *The Gazette (Montreal)*, 18 August 2005.

28. Mintzberg, *The Structuring of Organizations*, 106.

29. Mintzberg, *The Structuring of Organizations*, Chap. 17.

30. Galbraith, *Designing Organizations*, 23–25.

31. E. E. Lawler III, *Rewarding Excellence: Pay Strategies for the New Economy* (San Francisco: Jossey-Bass, 2000), 31–34.

32. These structures were identified from corporate Web sites and annual reports. These companies include a mixture of other structures, so the charts shown are adapted for learning purposes.

33. M. Goold and A. Campbell, "Do You Have a Well-Designed Organization," *Harvard Business Review* 80 (March 2002): 117–124.

34. J. R. Galbraith, "Structuring Global Organizations," in *Tomorrow's Organization*, ed. S. A. Mohrman *et al.* (San Francisco: Jossey-Bass, 1998), 103–129; C. Homburg, J. P. Workman Jr., and O. Jensen, "Fundamental Changes in Marketing Organization: The Movement toward a Corganizational Structure," *Academy of Marketing Science. Journal* 28 (Fall 2000): 459–478; T. H. Davenport, J. G. Harris, and A. K. Kohli, "How Do They Know Their Customers So Well?" *Sloan Management Review* 42 (Winter 2001): 63–73; J. R. Galbraith, "Organizing to Deliver Solutions," *Organizational Dynamics* 31 (2002): 194–207.

35. D. Robey, *Designing Organizations*, Third ed. (Homewood, Ill.: Irwin, 1991), 191–97.

36. J. Teresko, "Transforming GM," *Industry Week*, Dec/Jan 2002, 34–38; E. Prewitt, "GM's Matrix Reloads," *CIO Magazine*, 1 September 2003.

37. R. C. Ford and W. A. Randolph, "Cross-Functional Structures: A Review and Integration of Matrix Organization and Project Management," *Journal of Management* 18 (1992): 267–294.

38. G. Calabrese, "Communication and Co-Operation in Product Development: A Case Study of a European Car Producer," *R & D Management* 27 (July 1997): 239–252; T. Sy and L. S. D'Annunzio, "Challenges and Strategies of Matrix Organizations: Top-Level and Mid-Level Managers' Perspectives," *Human Resource Planning* 28, no. 1 (2005): 39–48.

39. Nadler and Tushman, *Competing by Design*, Chap. 6; M. Goold and A. Campbell, "Structured Networks: Towards the Well-Designed Matrix," *Long Range Planning* 36, no. 5 (October 2003): 427–439.

40. C. Campbell-Hunt and *et al.*, *World Famous in New Zealand* (Auckland: University of Auckland Press, 2001), 89.

41. J. R. Galbraith, E. E. Lawler III, and Associates, *Organizing for the Future: The New Logic for Managing Complex Organizations* (San Francisco, CA: Jossey-Bass, 1993); R. Bettis and M. Hitt, "The New Competitive Landscape," *Strategic Management Journal* 16 (1995): 7–19.

42. P. C. Ensign, "Interdependence, Coordination, and Structure in Complex Organizations: Implications for Organization Design," *Mid-Atlantic Journal of Business* 34 (March 1998): 5–22.

43. M. M. Fanning, "A Circular Organization Chart Promotes a Hospital-Wide Focus on Teams," *Hospital & Health Services Administration* 42 (June 1997): 243–254; L. Y. Chan and B. E. Lynn, "Operating in Turbulent Times: How Ontario's Hospitals Are Meeting the Current Funding Crisis," *Health Care Management Review* 23 (June 1998): 7–18.

44. R. Cross, "Looking before You Leap: Assessing the Jump to Teams in Knowledge-Based Work," *Business Horizons* (September 2000); M. Fenton-O'Creevy, "Employee Involvement and the Middle Manager: Saboteur or Scapegoat?" *Human Resource Management Journal* 11 (2001): 24–40; G. Garda, K. Lindstrom, and M. Dallnera, "Towards a Learning Organization: The Introduc-

tion of a Client-Centered Team-Based Organization in Administrative Surveying Work," *Applied Ergonomics* 34 (2003): 97–105; C. Douglas and W. L. Gardner, "Transition to Self-Directed Work Teams: Implications of Transition Time and Self-Monitoring for Managers' Use of Influence Tactics," *Journal of Organizational Behavior* 25 (2004): 47–65.

45. C. Nuttall-Smith, "How to Make Mega Bucks," *Globe & Mail*, 24 March 2005, 56.

46. R. F. Miles and C. C. Snow, "The New Network Firm: A Spherical Structure Built on a Human Investment Philosophy," *Organizational Dynamics* 23, no. 4 (1995): 5–18; C. Baldwin and K. Clark, "Managing in an Age of Modularity," *Harvard Business Review* 75 (September-October 1997): 84–93.

47. G. Ip, "Outsourcing Becoming a Way of Life for Firms," *Globe & Mail*, 2 October 1996, B8; J. Hagel III and M. Singer, "Unbundling the Corporation," *Harvard Business Review* 77 (March-April 1999): 133–141; R. Hacki and J. Lighton, "The Future of the Networked Company," *McKinsey Quarterly* 3 (2001): 26–39.

48. J. Vardy, "Mitel Outsources Manufacturing to New Company," *National Post* (September 6 2001).

49. M. A. Schilling and H. K. Steensma, "The Use of Modular Organizational Forms: An Industry-Level Analysis," *Academy of Management Journal* 44 (December 2001): 1149–1168.

50. W. H. Davidow and T. W. Malone, *The Virtual Corporation* (New York: Harper Business, 1992); L. Fried, *Managing Information Technology in Turbulent Times* (New York: John Wiley and Sons, 1995).

51. C. Taylor, "Agency Teams Balancing. In an Ever-Changing Media World," *Media Week* (June 1 2001): 20.

52. G. Morgan, *Images of Organization*, Second ed. (Newbury Park: Sage, 1996); G. Morgan, *Imagin-I-Zation: New Mindsets for Seeing, Organizing and Managing* (Thousand Oaks, CA: Sage, 1997).

53. H. Chesbrough and D. J. Teece, "When Is Virtual Virtuous? Organizing for Innovation," *Harvard Business Review* (January-February 1996): 65–73; P. M. J. Christie and R. Levary, "Virtual Corporations: Recipe for Success," *Industrial Management* 40 (July 1998): 7–11.

54. L. Donaldson, *The Contingency Theory of Organizations* (Thousand Oaks, CA: Sage, 2001); J. Birkenshaw, R. Nobel, and J. Ridderstrâle, "Knowledge as a Contingency Variable: Do the Characteristics of Knowledge Predict Organizational Structure?" *Organization Science* 13, no. 3 (May-June 2002): 274–289.

55. P. R. Lawrence and J. W. Lorsch, *Organization and Environment* (Homewood, Ill.: Irwin, 1967); Mintzberg, *The Structuring of Organizations*, Chap. 15.

56. Burns and Stalker, *The Management of Innovation;* Lawrence and Lorsch, *Organization and Environment.*

57. J. G. Kelley, "Slurpees and Sausages: 7-Eleven Holds School," *Richmond (Va.) Times-Dispatch*, 12 March 2004, C1; S. Marling, "The 24-Hour Supply Chain," *InformationWeek*, 26 January 2004, 43.

58. Mintzberg, *The Structuring of Organizations*, p. 282.

59. D. S. Pugh and C. R. Hinings, *Organizational Structure: Extensions and Replications* (Farnborough, England: Lexington Books, 1976); Mintzberg, *The Structuring of Organizations*, Chap. 13.

60. G. Hertel, S. Geister, and U. Konradt, "Managing Virtual Teams: A Review of Current Empirical Research," *Human Resource Management Review* 15 (2005): 69–95.

61. C. Perrow, "A Framework for the Comparative Analysis of Organizations," *American Sociological Review* 32 (1967): 194–208; D. Gerwin, "The Comparative Analysis of Structure and Technology: A Critical Appraisal," *Academy of Management Review* 4, no. 1 (1979): 41–51; C. C. Miller *et al.*, "Understanding Technology-Structure Relationships: Theory Development and Meta-Analytic Theory Testing," *Academy of Management Journal* 34, no. 2 (1991): 370–399.

62. R. H. Kilmann, *Beyond the Quick Fix* (San Francisco: Jossey-Bass, 1984), p. 38.

63. A. D. Chandler, *Strategy and Structure* (Cambridge, Mass.: MIT Press, 1962).

64. A. M. Porter, *Competitive Strategy* (New York: The Free Press, 1980).

65. D. Miller, "Configurations of Strategy and Structure," *Strategic Management Journal* 7 (1986): 233–249.

CHAPTER SIXTEEN

1. M. Miller, "The Acrobat," *Forbes*, 15 March 2004, 100–103; R. Ouzounian, "Cirque's Dream Factory," *Toronto Star*, 1 August 2004; "Cirque Du Soleil's Creator Goes from a Busker to a Billionaire," *Knight Ridder Tribune Business News*, 9 January 2005, 1; P. Donnelly, "Grandiose at the Grand," *The Gazette (Montreal)*, 29 January 2005, D1; L. Tischler, "Join the Circus," *Fast Company*, July 2005, 52–58.

2. A. Williams, P. Dobson, and M. Walters, *Changing Culture: New Organizational Approaches* (London: Institute of Personnel Management, 1989); E. H. Schein, "What Is Culture?" in *Reframing Organizational Culture*, ed. P. J. Frost *et al.* (Beverly Hills, CA: Sage, 1991), 243–253.

3. B. M. Meglino and E. C. Ravlin, "Individual Values in Organizations: Concepts, Controversies, and Research," *Journal of Management* 24, no. 3 (1998): 351–389; B. R. Agle and C. B. Caldwell, "Understanding Research on Values in Business," *Business and Society* 38, no. 3 (September 1999): 326–387; S. Hitlin and J. A. Pilavin, "Values: Reviving a Dormant Concept," *Annual Review of Sociology* 30 (2004): 359–393.

4. J. Allemang, "The Tightrope Walker," *Globe & Mail*, 16 October 2004, M3; D. Hayes, "Star Crossed," *Toronto Life*, October 2004, 70–80.

5. "New-Age Banks Bet on Variable Pay Plan," *Business Line (India)*, 22 September 2003; "Golden Handshake, the Icici Bank Way," *Financial Express (India)*, 6 July 2003.

6. D. Yedlin, "PCL Builds on Its Own Formula for Success," *Globe & Mail*, 9 July 2004, B2.

7. S. Chilton, "High-Flying RIM Reaches for the Stars," *Kitchener-Waterloo Record*, 22 May 1999, E1; S. Scott, "Shock of the New," *National Post Business Magazine*, August 2002, 44; L. Elliott and K. Crowley, "RIM Rocks the Aud," *Kitchener-Waterloo Record*, 19 April 2004, A1; "RIM Workers See New Star Wars," *Kitchener-Waterloo Record*, 19 May 2005, C14.

8. J. S. Ott, *The Organizational Culture Perspective* (Pacific Grove, CA: Brooks/ Cole, 1989), pp. 45–47; S. Sackmann, "Culture and Subcultures: An Analysis of Organizational Knowledge," *Admin-*

istrative Science Quarterly 37 (1992): 140–161.

9. A. Sinclair, "Approaches to Organizational Culture and Ethics," *Journal of Business Ethics* 12 (1993); A. Boisnier and J. Chatman, "The Role of Subcultures in Agile Organizations," in *Leading and Managing People in Dynamic Organizations*, ed. R. Petersen and E. Mannix (Mahwah, NJ: Lawrence Erlbaum Associates, 2003), 87–112.

10. Ott, *The Organizational Culture Perspective*, Chap. 2; J. S. Pederson and J. S. Sorensen, *Organizational Cultures in Theory and Practice* (Aldershot, England: Gower, 1989), pp. 27–29; M. O. Jones, *Studying Organizational Symbolism: What, How, Why?* (Thousand Oaks, CA: Sage, 1996).

11. E. H. Schein, "Organizational Culture," *American Psychologist* (February 1990): 109–119; A. Furnham and B. Gunter, "Corporate Culture: Definition, Diagnosis, and Change," *International Review of Industrial and Organizational Psychology* 8 (1993): 233–261; E. H. Schein, *The Corporate Culture Survival Guide* (San Francisco: Jossey-Bass, 1999), Chap. 4.

12. M. Doehrman, "Anthropologists—Deep in the Corporate Bush," *Daily Record (Kansas City, MO)*, 19 July 2005, 1.

13. A. Gordon, "Perks and Stock Options are Great, But it's Attitude that Makes the Difference," *Globe & Mail*, 28 January 2000.

14. A. L. Wilkins, "Organizational Stories as Symbols Which Control the Organization," in *Organizational Symbolism*, ed. L. R. Pondy *et al.* (Greenwich, CT: JAI Press, 1984), 81–92; R. Zemke, "Storytelling: Back to a Basic," *Training* 27 (March 1990): 44–50; J. C. Meyer, "Tell Me a Story: Eliciting Organizational Values from Narratives," *Communication Quarterly* 43 (1995): 210–224; W. Swap *et al.*, "Using Mentoring and Storytelling to Transfer Knowledge in the Workplace," *Journal of Management Information Systems* 18 (Summer 2001): 95–114.

15. D. Roth, "My Job at the Container Store," *Fortune*, 10 January 2000, 74–78.

16. R. E. Quinn and N. T. Snyder, "Advance Change Theory: Culture Change at Whirlpool Corporation," in *The Leader's Change Handbook*, ed. J. A. Conger, G. M. Spreitzer, and E. E. Lawler III (San Francisco: Jossey-Bass, 1999), 162–193.

17. Churchill apparently made this statement on October 28, 1943 in the British House of Commons, when London, damaged by bombings in World War II, was about to be rebuilt.

18. A. D'Innocenzio, "Wal-Mart's Town Becomes New Address for Corporate America," *Associated Press*, September 19 2003; J. Useem, "One Nation under Wal-Mart," *Fortune*, 3 March 2003, 65–78.

19. T. E. Deal and A. A. Kennedy, *Corporate Cultures* (Reading, Mass.: Addison-Wesley, 1982); J. B. Barney, "Organizational Culture: Can It Be a Source of Sustained Competitive Advantage?" *Academy of Management Review* 11 (1986): 656–665; C. Siehl and J. Martin, "Organizational Culture: A Key to Financial Performance?" in *Organizational Climate and Culture*, ed. B. Schneider (San Francisco, CA: Jossey-Bass, 1990), 241–281.

20. C. A. O'Reilly and J. A. Chatman, "Culture as Social Control: Corporations, Cults, and Commitment," *Research in Organizational Behavior* 18 (1996): 157–200; J. C. Helms Mills and A. J. Mills, "Rules, Sensemaking, Formative Contexts, and Discourse in the Gendering of Organizational Culture," in *International Handbook of Organizational Climate and Culture*, ed. N. Ashkanasy, C. Wilderom, and M. Peterson (Thousand Oaks, CA: Sage, 2000), 55–70; J. A. Chatman and S. E. Cha, "Leading by Leveraging Culture," *California Management Review* 45 (Summer 2003): 20–34.

21. B. Ashforth and F. Mael, "Social Identity Theory and the Organization," *Academy of Management Review* 14 (1989): 20–39.

22. M. R. Louis, "Surprise and Sensemaking: What Newcomers Experience in Entering Unfamiliar Organizational Settings," *Administrative Science Quarterly* 25 (1980): 226–251; S. G. Harris, "Organizational Culture and Individual Sensemaking: A Schema-Based Perspective," *Organization Science* 5 (1994): 309–321.

23. "Design Scales New Heights on Eco Values," *Toronto Star*, 8 April 2002; G. Bonnell, "Green Roofs on Businesses Help Cut City Smog, Runoff," *Toronto Star*, 18 September 2004, M07.

24. D. R. Denison, *Corporate Culture and Organizational Effectiveness* (New York: Wiley, 1990); G. G. Gordon and N. DiTomasco, "Predicting Corporate Performance from Organizational Culture," *Journal of Management Studies* 29 (1992): 783–798; J. P. Kotter and J. L. Heskett, *Corporate Culture and Performance* (New York: Free Press, 1992).

25. A. Holeck, "Griffith, Ind., Native Takes over as Steel Plant Manager," *The Times (Munster, Ind.)*, 24 May 2003.

26. Kotter and Heskett, *Corporate Culture and Performance*; J. P. Kotter, "Cultures and Coalitions," *Executive Excellence* 15 (March 1998): 14–15.

27. The features of adaptive cultures are described in W. F. Joyce, *MegaChange: How Today's Leading Companies Have Transformed Their Workforces* (N.Y.: Free Press, 1999), pp. 44–47.

28. "Japanese Officials Order Citibank to Halt Some Operations," *Dow Jones Business News*, 17 September 2004; "Citigroup CEO Prince Holds Press Conference in Japan," *Business Wire (Tokyo)*, 25 October 2004; A. Morse, "Citigroup Extends Apology to Japan," *Wall Street Journal*, 26 October 2004, A3; M. Pacelle, M. Fackler, and A. Morse, "Mission Control," *Wall Street Journal*, 22 December 2004, A1.

29. M. Acharya, "A Matter of Business Ethics," *Kitchener-Waterloo Record*, 23 March 1999, C2.

30. Helms Mills and Mills, "Rules, Sensemaking, Formative Contexts, and Discourse in the Gendering of Organizational Culture"; I. Aaltio-Marjosola and A. J. Mills, eds., *Gender, Identity and the Culture of Organizations* (London: Routledge, 2002). Also see: Aaltio-Marjosola, I., Mills, A. J., and Helms Mills, J. [Eds.] Special Issue on "Exploring Gendered Organizational Cultures" in *Culture and Organization* 8 (2) (2002).

31. D. Griesing, "'Boot Camp' Failed to Teach All They Could Be," *Chicago Tribune*, 21 April 2002, C1; B. L. Toffler, *Final Accounting: Ambition, Greed, and the Fall of Arthur Andersen* (New York: Broadway Books, 2003).

32. Schein, *The Corporate Culture Survival Guide*, Chap. 8; M. L. Marks, "Mixed Signals," *Across the Board* (May 2000): 21–26; J. P. Daly, R. W. Pouder, and B. Kabanoff, "The Effects of Initial Differences in Firms' Espoused Values

on Their Postmerger Performance," *Journal of Applied Behavioral Science* 40, no. 3 (September 2004): 323–343. The Canadian and international merger failure rates are cited in: G. Costa, "More to Mergers Than Just Doing the Deal," *Sydney Morning Herald*, 8 January 2004; J. Kirby, "The Trouble with Mergers," *Canadian Business*, 16–29 February 2004, 64.

33. "The Newspaper Wars," *Canoe (Online)*, 2 March 1999; M. Lamey, "Sun Sets for Godfrey," *The Gazette (Montreal)*, 15 June 2000; A. Klein, "A Merger Taken AO-Ill," *Washington Post*, 21 October 2002, E1; A. Klein, *Stealing Time: Steve Case, Jerry Levin, and the Collapse of AOL Time Warner* (New York: Simon & Shuster, 2003).

34. S. Greengard, "Due Diligence: The Devil in the Details," *Workforce* (October 1999): 68; M. L. Marks, "Adding Cultural Fit to Your Diligence Checklist," *Mergers & Acquisitions* 34, no. 3 (Nov-Dec 1999): 14–20.

35. A. R. Malekazedeh and A. Nahavandi, "Making Mergers Work by Managing Cultures," *Journal of Business Strategy* (May-June 1990): 55–57; K. W. Smith, "A Brand-New Culture for the Merged Firm," *Mergers and Acquisitions* 35 (June 2000): 45–50.

36. T. Hamilton, "RIM on a Roll," *Toronto Star*, 22 February 2004, C01.

37. Hewitt Associates, "Mergers and Acquisitions May Be Driven by Business Strategy—but Often Stumble over People and Culture Issues," PR Newswire News release, (Lincolnshire, IL: 3 August 1998).

38. Waterstone Human Capital Ltd., "WestJet, Tim Hortons and RBC Financial Group—Canada's Most Admired Corporate Cultures of 2005," CNW News release, (Toronto: 13 October 2005).

39. E. H. Schein, "The Role of the Founder in Creating Organizational Culture," *Organizational Dynamics* 12, no. 1 (Summer 1983): 13–28; R. House, M. Javidan, and P. Dorfman, "Project Globe: An Introduction," *Applied Psychology: An International Review* 50 (2001): 489–505; R. House *et al.*, "Understanding Cultures and Implicit Leadership Theories across the Globe: An Introduction to Project Globe," *Journal of World Business* 37 (2002): 3–10.

40. T. J. Peters, "Symbols, Patterns, and Settings: An Optimistic Case for Getting Things Done," *Organizational Dynamics* 7, no. 2 (Autumn 1978): 2–23; E. H. Schein, *Organizational Culture and Leadership* (San Francisco, CA: Jossey-Bass, 1985), Chap. 10.

41. J. Kerr and J. W. Slocum Jr., "Managing Corporate Culture through Reward Systems," *Academy of Management Executive* 1 (May 1987): 99–107; K. R. Thompson and F. Luthans, "Organizational Culture: A Behavioral Perspective," in *Organizational Climate and Culture*, ed. B. Schneider (San Francisco: Jossey-Bass, 1990), 319–344.

42. K. McNeil and J. D. Thompson, "The Regeneration of Social Organizations," *American Sociological Review* 36 (1971): 624–637; W. G. Ouchi and A. M. Jaeger, "Type Z Organization: Stability in the Midst of Mobility," *Academy of Management Review* 3 (1978): 305–314.

43. M. De Pree, *Leadership Is an Art* (East Lansing, MI: Michigan State University Press, 1987).

44. D. Grigg and J. Newman, "Corporate Values Can Help Leaders, Workers," *Vancouver Sun*, 24 November 2001, E2; D. Brown, "Good Ideas Going Wrong," *Canadian HR Reporter*, 6 May 2002, 2.

45. D. M. Cable and T. A. Judge, "Person-Organization Fit, Job Choice Decisions, and Organizational Entry," *Organizational Behavior and Human Decision Processes* 67, no. 3 (1996): 294; A. E. M. Van Vianen, "Person-Organization Fit: The Match between Newcomers' and Recruiters' Preferences for Organizational Cultures," *Personnel Psychology* 53 (Spring 2000): 113–149; K. J. Lauver and A. Kristof-Brown, "Distinguishing between Employees' Perceptions of Person-Job and Person-Organization Fit," *Journal of Vocational Behavior* 59, no. 3 (December 2001): 454–470; J. W. Westerman and L. A. Cyr, "An Integrative Analysis of Person-Organization Fit Theories," *International Journal of Selection and Assessment* 12, no. 3 (September 2004): 252–261.

46. J. Van Maanen, "Breaking In: Socialization to Work," in *Handbook of Work, Organization, and Society*, ed. R. Dubin (Chicago: Rand McNally, 1976).

47. V. Galt, "Kid-Glove Approach Woos New Grads," *Globe & Mail*, 9 March 2005, C1.

48. C. L. Adkins, "Previous Work Experience and Organizational Socialization: A Longitudinal Examination," *Academy of Management Journal* 38 (1995): 839–862; j. D. Kammeyer-Mueller and C. R. Wanberg, "Unwrapping the Organizational Entry Process: Disentangling Multiple Antecedents and Their Pathways to Adjustment," *Journal of Applied Psychology* 88, no. 5 (2003): 779–794.

49. J. M. Beyer and D. R. Hannah, "Building on the Past: Enacting Established Personal Identities in a New Work Setting," *Organization Science* 13 (November/December 2002): 636–652; H. D. C. Thomas and N. Anderson, "Newcomer Adjustment: The Relationship between Organizational Socialization Tactics, Information Acquisition and Attitudes," *Journal of Occupational and Organizational Psychology* 75 (December 2002): 423–437.

50. L. W. Porter, E. E. Lawler III, and J. R. Hackman, *Behavior in Organizations* (New York: McGraw-Hill, 1975), pp. 163–167; Van Maanen, "Breaking In: Socialization to Work"; D. C. Feldman, "The Multiple Socialization of Organization Members," *Academy of Management Review* 6 (1981): 309–318.

51. B. E. Ashforth and A. M. Saks, "Socialization Tactics: Longitudinal Effects on Newcomer Adjustment," *Academy of Management Journal* 39 (1996): 149–178; Kammeyer-Mueller and Wanberg, "Unwrapping the Organizational Entry Process."

52. Porter, Lawler III, and Hackman, *Behavior in Organizations*, Chap. 5.

53. Louis, "Surprise and Sensemaking: What Newcomers Experience in Entering Unfamiliar Organizational Settings."

54. S. Barancik, "Different World, Same Old Stress," *St. Petersburg Times (Florida)*, 3 September 2003; A. Daga, "Dial C for Crisis at India's Call Centres," *The Age (Melbourne, Australia)*, 12 July 2003.

55. M. Gravelle, "The Five Most Common Hiring Mistakes and How to Avoid Them," *Canadian Manager*, October 2004, 11; R. Craver, "Dell Thinning out List of Job Candidates," *Winston-Salem Journal*, 23 April 2005.

56. J. A. Breaugh, *Recruitment: Science and Practice* (Boston: PWS-Kent, 1992); J. P. Wanous, *Organizational Entry* (Reading, Mass.: Addison-Wesley, 1992).

57. J. M. Phillips, "Effects of Realistic Job Previews on Multiple Organizational Outcomes: A Meta-Analysis," *Academy of Management Journal* 41 (December 1998): 673–690.

58. Y. Ganzach *et al.*, "Social Exchange and Organizational Commitment: Decision-Making Training for Job Choice as an Alternative to the Realistic Job Preview," *Personnel Psychology* 55 (Autumn 2002): 613–637.

59. C. Ostroff and S. W. J. Koslowski, "Organizational Socialization as a Learning Process: The Role of Information Acquisition," *Personnel Psychology* 45 (1992): 849–874; E. W. Morrison, "Newcomer Information Seeking: Exploring Types, Modes, Sources, and Outcomes," *Academy of Management Journal* 36 (1993): 557–589; U. Anakwe and J. H. Greenhaus, "Effective Socialization of Employees: Socialization Content Perspective," *Journal of Managerial Issues* 11, no. 3 (Fall 1999): 315–329.

60. S. L. McShane, *Effect of Socialization Agents on the Organizational Adjustment of New Employees*, (Big Sky, Montana: Annual Conference of the Western Academy of Management, March 1988).

61. D. Francis, "Work Is a Warm Puppy," *National Post*, 27 May 2000, W20.

CHAPTER SEVENTEEN

1. G. Kirbyson, "Pride in Ownership Fuels Firm," *Winnipeg Free Press*, 17 August 2002, B3; M. Cash, "Friesens President in Top 40 under 40," *Winnipeg Free Press*, 11 May 2005, D9; C. Cleaveland, "They Came, They Managed, They Conquered," *American Printer*, August 2005, 60; D. Rinehart, "Curwin Friesen, 35," *Globe & Mail*, 3 May 2005, T10.

2. K. Lewin, *Field Theory in Social Science* (New York: Harper & Row, 1951).

3. "Efficiency Top Priority for Telus, Says CEO," *Times Colonist (Victoria, B.C.)*, 11 July 2002; P. Arab, "Telus Union Criticized," *Hamilton Spectator*, 6 July 2002, B3; H. Enchin, "Onerous Provisions in B.C. Contract with Union," *Vancouver Sun*, 31 October 2002, C8; M. Evans, "Telus Highlights Great Divide among Employees," *National Post*, 5 August 2005, FP1; D. Penner, "Ottawa Should Step into Telus Labour Dispute, B.C. MP Says," *Vancouver Sun*, 7 September 2005, D5.

4. "The Wrong People Doing the Right Job: Reforming the FBI," *The Economist*, 17 April 2004, 371; National Commission on Terrorist Attacks Upon the United States, *The 9/11 Commission Report*, (Washington, D.C.: U.S. Government Printing Office, July 2004); D. Eggen, "FBI Fails to Transform Itself, Panel Says," *Washington Post*, 7 June 2005, A04; C. Ragavan and C. S. Hook, "Fixing the FBI," *U.S. News & World Report*, 28 March 2005, 18–24, 26, 29–30; The Commission on the Intelligence Capabilities of the United States Regarding Weapons of Mass Destruction, *Report to the President of the United States*, (Washington, D.C.: 31 March 2005).

5. C. O. Longenecker, D. J. Dwyer, and T. C. Stansfield, "Barriers and Gateways to Workforce Productivity," *Industrial Management*, March-April 1998, 21–28; J. Seifman, "Middle Managers—the Meat in the Corporate Sandwich," *China Staff*, June 2002, 7.

6. E. B. Dent and S. G. Goldberg, "Challenging 'Resistance to Change'," *Journal of Applied Behavioral Science* 35 (March 1999): 25–41.

7. D. A. Nadler, "The Effective Management of Organizational Change," in *Handbook of Organizational Behavior*, ed. J. W. Lorsch (Englewood Cliffs, N.J.: Prentice Hall, 1987), 358–369; R. Maurer, *Beyond the Wall of Resistance: Unconventional Strategies to Build Support for Change* (Austin, TX: Bard Books, 1996); P. Strebel, "Why Do Employees Resist Change?" *Harvard Business Review* (May-June 1996): 86–92; D. A. Nadler, *Champions of Change* (San Francisco, CA: Jossey-Bass, 1998).

8. "Making Change Work for You—Not against You," *Agency Sales Magazine* 28 (June 1998): 24–27.

9. D. Miller, "What Happens after Success: The Perils of Excellence," *Journal of Management Studies* 31 (1994): 325–358.

10. T. G. Cummings, "The Role and Limits of Change Leadership," in *The Leader's Change Handbook*, ed. J. A. Conger, G. M. Spreitzer, and E. E. Lawler III (San Francisco: Jossey-Bass, 1999), 301–320; J. P. Kotter and D. S. Cohen, *The Heart of Change* (Boston: Harvard Business School Press, 2002), pp. 15–36.

11. I. J. Bozon and P. N. Child, "Refining Shell's Position in Europe," *McKinsey Quarterly*, no. 2 (2003): 42–51.

12. L. D. Goodstein and H. R. Butz, "Customer Value: The Linchpin of Organizational Change," *Organizational Dynamics* 27 (June 1998): 21–35.

13. D. Darlin, "Growing Tomorrow," *Business 2.0*, May 2005, 126.

14. L. Grossman and S. Song, "Stevie's Little Wonder," *Time*, 19 September 2005, 63; S. Levy, "Honey, I Shrunk the iPod. A Lot," *Newsweek*, 19 September 2005, 58.

15. J. S. McClenahen, "Prairie Home Champion," *Industry Week*, October 2005, 45–47.

16. J. P. Kotter and L. A. Schlesinger, "Choosing Strategies for Change," *Harvard Business Review* (March–April 1979): 106–114.

17. B. Nanus and S. M. Dobbs, *Leaders Who Make a Difference* (San Francisco: Jossey-Bass, 1999); Kotter and Cohen, *The Heart of Change*, pp. 83–98.

18. T. White, "Supporting Change: How Communicators at Scotiabank Turned Ideas into Action," *Communication World*, April 2002, 22–24.

19. M. J. Marquardt, *Optimizing the Power of Action Learning: Solving Problems and Building Leaders in Real Time* (Palo Alto, CA: Davies-Black, 2004).

20. K. T. Dirks, L. L. Cummings, and J. L. Pierce, "Psychological Ownership in Organizations: Conditions under Which Individuals Promote and Resist Change," *Research in Organizational Change and Development* 9 (1996): 1–23.

21. B. B. Bunker and B. T. Alban, *Large Group Interventions: Engaging the Whole System for Rapid Change* (San Francisco, CA: Jossey-Bass, 1996); M. Weisbord and S. Janoff, *Future Search: An Action Guide to Finding Common Ground in Organizations and Communities* (San Francisco: Berrett-Koehler, 2000); P. Botsman, "Government by the People," *Courier Mail (Brisbane, Australia)*, 23 July 2002, 11; Darlin, "Growing Tomorrow."

22. T. McCallum, "Vision 2001: Staying Ahead of the Competition," *Human Resource Professional*, November 1996, 25–26; R. E. Purser and S. Cabana, *The Self-Managing Organization* (New York: Free Press, 1998); J. Pratt, "Naturalists Deserve More Credit," *St. John's Telegram*, 22 June 2002, B3.

23. For criticism of a recent search conference for lacking innovative or

realistic ideas, see: A. Oels, "Investigating the Emotional Roller-Coaster Ride: A Case Study-Based Assessment of the Future Search Conference Design," *Systems Research and Behavioral Science* 19 (July-August 2002): 347–355; M. F. D. Polanyi, "Communicative Action in Practice: Future Search and the Pursuit of an Open, Critical and Non-Coercive Large-Group Process," *Systems Research and Behavioral Science* 19 (July 2002): 357–366.

24. M. McHugh, "The Stress Factor: Another Item for the Change Management Agenda?" *Journal of Organizational Change Management* 10 (1997): 345–362; D. Buchanan, T. Claydon, and M. Doyle, "Organisation Development and Change: The Legacy of the Nineties," *Human Resource Management Journal* 9 (1999): 20–37.

25. D. Helfand, "School Is Down but Looking Up," *Los Angeles Times*, 14 October 2004, B1; "Mrs. Bush Remarks on Helping America's Youth in Sun Valley, California," The White House News release, (Sun Valley, Calif.: 27 April 2005), http://www.whitehouse.gov/news/releases/2005/04/20050427-5.html.

26. J. Mawhinney, "Baycrest: Brave New World," *Toronto Star*, 19 November 2004, G05.

27. D. Nicolini and M. B. Meznar, "The Social Construction of Organizational Learning: Conceptual and Practical Issues in the Field," *Human Relations* 48 (1995): 727–746.

28. Kotter and Cohen, *The Heart of Change*, pp. 161–177.

29. R. H. Miles, "Leading Corporate Transformation: Are You up to the Task?" in *The Leader's Change Handbook*, ed. J. A. Conger, G. M. Spreitzer, and E. E. Lawler III (San Francisco: Jossey-Bass, 1999), 221–267; E. E. Lawler III, "Pay Can Be a Change Agent," *Compensation & Benefits Management* 16 (Summer 2000): 23–26.

30. R. E. Quinn, *Building the Bridge as You Walk on It: A Guide for Leading Change* (San Francisco: Jossey-Bass, 2004), Chap. 11.

31. J. P. Kotter, "Leading Change: Why Transformation Efforts Fail," *Harvard Business Review* (March-April 1995): 59–67; J. P. Kotter, "Leading Change: The Eight Steps to Transformation," in *The Leader's Change Handbook*, ed. J. A.

Conger, G. M. Spreitzer, and E. E. Lawler III (San Francisco: Jossey-Bass, 1999), 221–267.

32. R. Caldwell, "Models of Change Agency: A Fourfold Classification," *British Journal of Management* 14 (June 2003): 131–142.

33. M. Beer, R. A. Eisenstat, and B. Spector, *The Critical Path to Corporate Renewal* (Boston, Mass.: Harvard Business School Press, 1990).

34. R. E. Walton, "Successful Strategies for Diffusing Work Innovations," *Journal of Contemporary Business* (Spring 1977): 1–22; R. E. Walton, *Innovating to Compete: Lessons for Diffusing and Managing Change in the Workplace* (San francisco: Jossey-Bass, 1987); Beer, Eisenstat, and Spector, *The Critical Path to Corporate Renewal*, Chap. 5.

35. E. M. Rogers, *Diffusion of Innovations*, Fourth ed. (New York: Free Pree, 1995).

36. P. Reason and H. Bradbury, *Handbook of Action Research, London* (Sage: 2001); D. Coghlan and T. Brannick, "Kurt Lewin: The "Practical Theorist" for the 21st Century," *Irish journal of Management* 24, no. 2 (2003): 31–37; C. Huxham and S. Vangen, "Researching Organizational Practice through Action Research: Case Studies and Design Choices," *Organizational Research Methods* 6 (July 2003): 383–403.

37. V. J. Marsick and M. A. Gephart, "Action Research: Building the Capacity for Learning and Change," *Human Resource Planning* 26 (2003): 14–18.

38. L. Dickens and K. Watkins, "Action Research: Rethinking Lewin," *Management Learning* 30 (June 1999): 127–140; J. Heron and P. Reason, "The Practice of Co-Operative Inquiry: Research 'with' Rather Than 'on' People," in *Handbook of Action Research*, ed. P. Reason and H. Bradbury (Thousand Oaks, CA: Sage, 2001), 179–188.

39. D. A. Nadler, "Organizational Frame Bending: Types of Change in the Complex Organization," in *Corporate Transformation: Revitalizing Organizations for a Competitive World*, ed. R. H. Kilmann, T. J. Covin, and a. Associates (San Francisco: Jossey-Bass, 1988), 66–83; K. E. Weick and R. E. Quinn, "Organizational Change and Development," *Annual Review of Psychology* (1999): 361–386.

40. T. M. Egan and C. M. Lancaster, "Comparing Appreciative Inquiry to Action Research: OD Practitioner Perspectives," *Organization Development Journal* 23, no. 2 (Summer 2005): 29–49.

41. F. Luthans, "The Need for and Meaning of Positive Organizational Behavior," *Journal of Organizational Behavior* 23 (2002): 695–706; N. Turner, J. Barling, and A. Zacharatos, "Positive Psychology at Work," in *Handbook of Positive Psychology*, ed. C. R. Snyder and S. Lopez (Oxford, UK: Oxford University Press, 2002), 715–730; K. Cameron, J. E. Dutton, and R. E. Quinn, eds., *Positive Organizational Scholarship: Foundation of a New Discipline* (San Francisco: Berrett Koehler Publishers, 2003); J. I. Krueger and D. C. Funder, "Towards a Balanced Social Psychology: Causes, Consequences, and Cures for the Problem-Seeking Approach to Social Behavior and Cognition," *Behavioral and Brain Sciences* 27, no. 3 (June 2004): 313–327.

42. Canadian Tire, *Team Values Development Process (Powerpoint File)*, (Toronto: Canadian Tire, 24 September 2001); Canadian Tire, *Leadership Guide*, (Toronto: Canadian Tire, 2002).

43. D. Whitney and D. L. Cooperrider, "The Appreciative Inquiry Summit: Overview and Applications," *Employment Relations Today* 25 (Summer 1998): 17–28; J. M. Watkins and B. J. Mohr, *Appreciative Inquiry: Change at the Speed of Imagination* (San Francisco: Jossey-Bass, 2001).

44. F. J. Barrett and D. L. Cooperrider, "Generative Metaphor Intervention: A New Approach for Working with Systems Divided by Conflict and Caught in Defensive Perception," *Journal of Applied Behavioral Science* 26 (1990): 219–239; Whitney and Cooperrider, "The Appreciative Inquiry Summit: Overview and Applications"; Watkins and Mohr, *Appreciative Inquiry: Change at the Speed of Imagination*, pp. 15–21.

45. T. F. Yaeger, P. F. Sorensen, and U. Bengtsson, "Assessment of the State of Appreciative Inquiry: Past, Present, and Future," *Research in Organizational Change and Development* 15 (2004): 297–319; G. R. Bushe and A. F. Kassam, "When Is Appreciative Inquiry Transformational? A Meta-Case Analysis," *Journal of Applied Behavioral Science* 41, no. 2 (June 2005): 161–181.

46. G. R. Bushe, "Five Theories of Change Embedded in Appreciative Inquiry" in *18th Annual World Congress of Organization Development*, (Dublin, Ireland, July 14-18, 1998).

47. G. R. Bushe and A. B. Shani, *Parallel Learning Structures* (Reading, Mass.: Addison-Wesley, 1991); E. M. Van Aken, D. J. Monetta, and S. D. S., "Affinity Groups: The Missing Link in Employee Involvement," *Organization Dynamics* 22 (Spring 1994): 38–54.

48. D. J. Knight, "Strategy in Practice: Making It Happen," *Strategy & Leadership* 26 (July-August 1998): 29–33; R. T. Pascale, "Grassroots Leadership—Royal Dutch/Shell," *Fast Company*, no. 14 (April-May 1998): 110–120; R. T. Pascale, "Leading from a Different Place," in *The Leader's Change Handbook*, ed. J. A. Conger, G. M. Spreitzer, and E. E. Lawler III (San Francisco: Jossey-Bass, 1999), 301–320; R. Pascale, M. Millemann, and L. Gioja, *Surfing on the Edge of Chaos* (London: Texere, 2000).

49. C.-M. Lau, "A Culture-Based Perspective of Organization Development Implementation," *Research in Organizational Change and Development* 9 (1996): 49–79.

50. T. C. Head and P. F. Sorenson, "Cultural Values and Organizational Development: A Seven-Country Study," *Leadership and Organization Development Journal* 14 (1993): 3–7; R. J. Marshak, "Lewin Meets Confucius: A Review of the OD Model of Change," *Journal of Applied Behavioral Science* 29 (1993): 395–415; C. M. Lau and H. Y. Ngo, "Organization Development and Firm Performance: A Comparison of Multinational and Local Firms," *Journal Of International Business Studies* 32, no. 1 (2001): 95–114.

51. For an excellent discussion of conflict management and Asian values, see several articles in K. Leung and D. Tjosvold, eds., *Conflict Management in the Asia Pacific: Assumptions and Approaches in Diverse Cultures* (Singapore: John Wiley & Sons, 1998).

52. M. McKendall, "The Tyranny of Change: Organizational Development Revisited," *Journal of Business Ethics* 12 (February 1993): 93–104; C. M. D. Deaner, "A Model of Organization Development Ethics," *Public Administration Quarterly* 17 (1994): 435–446.

53. G. A. Walter, "Organization Development and Individual Rights," *Journal of Applied Behavioral Science* 20 (1984): 423–439.

54. "Perils of Public Sector Work: A Case Study," *Consultants News*, April 1996, 5; S. Parker Jr., "Sasktel Dials the Wrong Number," *Western Report*, 26 February 1996, 14–17.

55. P. Allossery, "AGF 'Light Years Ahead' of Most Fund Firms in Branding," *National Post*, 15 May 2000.

56. P. Chisholm, "What the Boss Needs to Know," *Maclean's*, 29 May 2000, 18.

57. B. Moses, "Give People Belief in the Future," *Workforce* (June 2000): 134–141.

58. B. Moses, "Career Activists Take Command," *Globe & Mail* (March 20 2000): B6.

59. Drake Beam Morin, *1999 DBM Career Transition Study*, (Drake Beam Morin, November 2000); F. T. McCarthy, "Career Evolution," *The Economist* (29 January 2000).

60. B. Moses, *The Good News About Careers: How You'll Be Working in the Next Decade* (San Francisco: Jossey-Bass, 1999); S. E. Sullivan, "The Changing Nature of Careers: A Review and Research Agenda," *Journal of Management* 25 (May 1999): 457–484.

61. S.-C. Van Collie, "Moving up through Mentoring," *Workforce*, March 1998, 36–40; N. Beech and A. Brockbank, "Power/Knowledge and Psychosocial Dynamics in Mentoring," *Management Learning* 30 (March 1999): 7–24.

APPENDIX A

1. Kerlinger, *Foundations of Behavioral Research* (New York: Holt, Rinehart, & Winston, 1964), p. 11.

2. J. B. Miner, *Theories of Organizational Behavior* (Hinsdale, Ill.: Dryden, 1980), pp. 7–9.

3. Ibid. pp. 6–7.

4. J. Mason, *Qualitative Researching* (London: Sage, 1996).

5. A. Strauss and J. Corbin (Eds.), *Grounded Theory in Practice* (London: Sage Publications, 1997); B. G. Glaser and A. Strauss, *The Discovery of Grounded Theory: Strategies for Qualitative Research* (Chicago, IL: Aldine Publishing Co, 1967).

6. Kerlinger, *Foundations of Behavioral Research*, p. 13.

7. A. Strauss and J. Corbin (Eds.), *Grounded Theory in Practice* (London: Sage Publications, 1997); B. G. Glaser and A. Strauss, *The Discovery of Grounded Theory: Strategies for Qualitative Research* (Chicago, IL: Aldine Publishing Co, 1967).

8. W. A. Hall and P. Callery, "Enhancing the Rigor of Grounded Theory: Incorporating Reflexivity and Relationality," *Qualitative Health Research*, 11 (March 2001), pp. 257–72.

9. P. Lazarsfeld, *Survey Design and Analysis* (New York: The Free Press, 1955).

10. This example is cited in D. W. Organ and T. S. Bateman, *Organizational Behavior*, 4th ed. (Homewood, Ill.: Irwin, 1991), p. 42.

11. Ibid. p. 45

12. R. I. Sutton and A. Hargadon, "Brainstorming Groups in Context: Effectiveness in a Product Design Firm," *Administrative Science Quarterly*, 41 (1996), pp. 685–718.

ORGANIZATION INDEX